AT DAWN WE SLEPT

The Untold Story of Pearl Harbor

GORDON W. PRANGE

IN COLLABORATION WITH DONALD M. GOLDSTEIN AND KATHERINE V. DILLON

MICHAEL JOSEPH · LONDON

First published in Great Britain by Michael Joseph Ltd
44 Bedford Square, London WC1
1982
ISBN 0 7181 20906

CONTENTS

v

Part II: ACTION

Part III: AFTERMATH

APPENDIX

INTRODUCTION

This work is the culmination of thirty-seven years of study and research by Gordon W. Prange, whose untimely death occurred in May 1980. In accordance with his wishes, two of his former students, Dr. Donald M. Goldstein and CWO Katherine V. Dillon, USAF (Ret.), continued the massive job of editing a multivolume manuscript totaling more than 3,500 pages into the present work. The editors have striven, however, to retain the essence of Professor Prange's monumental research to present the story of Pearl Harbor as seen from both the Japanese and American points of view in the context of the time.

The editors believe that Gordon Prange approached this study with as nearly an open mind as any American could bring to the subject of Pearl Harbor. (Of course, we might be prejudiced!) He was not a Far Eastern expert; his field was European history. During his tour of duty in Japan in Headquarters, Far East Command, when he made the acquaintance of a number of Japanese connected with Operation Hawaii, he became interested in Pearl Harbor. As he often said, he began this project with "no ax to grind, no preconceived thesis to prove, no one to attack, no one to defend." He tried at all times to be as objective as humanly possible.

The interweaving of action and thinking between the Japanese and American sides of the story fascinated Prange. In *At Dawn We Slept* he attempted to weave the narrative together so as to bring this to the reader's consciousness. In his opinion, few events in history so demonstrated the importance of the human element as Pearl Harbor; hence he wanted to provide a look into the minds and personalities of the American and Japanese leaders.

Prange believed that there were no deliberate villains in the Pearl Harbor story. He considered those involved on both sides to be honest, hardworking, dedicated, and for the most part intelligent. But as human beings some were brilliant and some mediocre, some broad-minded and some of narrow vision, some strong and some weak—and every single one fallible, capable of mistakes of omission and commission.

In the text of this work we have related the fate of certain American participants. However, the reader may be interested in knowing what happened to some of the key Japanese. Many of these men lost their lives as a result of the war they helped unleash. American airmen shot down Yamamoto over Bougainville on April 18, 1943; Nagumo perished on Saipan; Yamaguchi went down with his carrier at Midway; Ugaki flew in a *kamikaze* attack on the last day of the war and never returned.

Of those who led elements of the Pearl Harbor attack, first to go was Takahashi, leader of the dive bombers in the first wave. He met death on May 8, 1942, at the Battle of the Coral Sea. Murata, who headed the torpedomen, fell at Santa Cruz. Egusa, the dive-bombing leader of the second wave, crashed over Saipan. Fighter Leader Itaya died as he had lived, a little apart from his fellow fliers—Japanese Army pilots shot him down by mistake over the Kuriles. Shimazaki, who spearheaded the second wave, plunged into the sea between Formosa and the Philippines on January 9, 1945.

But many lived to see the amazing changes in Asia since that historic day in December 1941. The tactical planner, Minoru Genda, served as Chief of Staff of Japan's Self-Defense Air Force with the rank of lieutenant general and later became a member of the upper house of the Diet, equivalent to the United States Senate. After enough adventures for ten men, Flight Leader Fuchida watched the surrender ceremonies aboard *Missouri* in Tokyo Bay. Thus he whose "*Tora! Tora! Tora!*" initiated the Pacific war witnessed its ending. Later he became a convert to Christianity. Until his recent death he served the Prince of Peace as a nondenominational evangelist, frequently testifying in the United States.

The Japanese put very little about the Pearl Harbor plan on paper, and what was available aboard four of the carriers of Nagumo's force (including his flagship, *Akagi*) went down at Midway in June 1942. The only possible way to secure the Japanese side of the story was to interview as many as possible of the surviving planners and participants, then to compare and evaluate their stories. This Prange did with great diligence. His field of inquiry ranged from the imperial household to airmen who participated in the attack. He considered himself extremely fortunate in being able to conduct these interviews close enough in time to the event so that memories were still fresh. (See list of interviews in bibliography.)

Prange originally intended to confine his study to the Japanese side of the operation; hence he did not interview Americans concerned until later. However, his countrymen proved no less cooperative and helpful than the Japanese, giving him generously of their time, memories, counsel, documents, and pictures. In many cases they suggested further contacts and passed him from one to another in a sort of intraservice shuttle.

This work provides a classic example of the old truism that no author produces a book alone, for without the kind cooperation and generous assistance of scores of people on the United States mainland, in Hawaii, and in Japan, this saga never would have been possible. To all these good people Gordon Prange owes a deep and eternal debt of gratitude. Space and the lack of firm information about sources do not permit acknowledging every individual on both sides of the Pacific who helped bring this study to fruition. To the best of our knowledge, all have been included in the list of interviews in the bibliography. Anyone whose name has been omitted inadvertently may be assured that Gordon Prange was just as grateful to those whose names do not appear as to those that do.

However, he would want to mention particularly Lieutenant General Minoru Genda, who as a commander in the Imperial Japanese Navy was the tactical genius behind Operation Hawaii; Captain Mitsuo Fuchida, who led the air attack; RADM Baron Sadatoshi Tomioka, who in 1941 headed the Operations Section of the Naval General Staff, which was responsible for naval war plans; and Masataka Chihaya, former commander, IJN, who for many years was Prange's representative in Japan and whose services as go-between, adviser, interpreter, and, above all, honored friend were invaluable.

Among the Americans, Prange would wish to give special thanks to VADM William Ward "Poco" Smith, who not only gave him interviews packed full of information but put him in touch with many key members of the Pacific Fleet staff of 1941. It was Admiral Smith who persuaded RADM Husband E. Kimmel, former Commander in Chief of the Pacific Fleet, to receive Prange. Admiral Kimmel in turn granted him four full days of his time and provided a mine of documentation.

Nevertheless, the primary source of the American side of the problem was and probably always will remain the forty volumes comprising the report and testimony of the joint congressional committee which investigated the disaster. These volumes include the committee's own record plus those of all the preceding investigations, as well as a host of supporting documents. This compilation has never been indexed, so the serious researcher almost has no alternative but to read every word of the testimony. These pages are loaded with interesting facts and insights, but the reader must proceed with caution, for frequently witnesses disagree with each other and even themselves. In such cases the historian must exercise his right and prerogative to evaluate on the basis of the bulk of testimony and the dictates of common sense.

Like all extensive works, this book contains some limitations and idiosyncrasies which the reader should understand at the outset. We list these not necessarily in order of importance:

1. Space did not allow treatment of the revisionist thesis that President Roosevelt wanted and either permitted the attack or deliberately engineered it to bring the United States into World War II by "the back door." For the record, Prange dealt with this exhaustively in his original manuscript and reached the conclusion that neither the evidence nor common sense justified this view of the matter.

Revisionists came in a wide range. Some believed that Roosevelt's foreign policy was unsound because the United States had no real stake in the war. Prange believed that this was eternally arguable and never provable. Another brand of revisionism believed that Roosevelt was not just mistaken but deliberately dragged the United States into the war. The proponents of this theory stop short of claiming that the President schemed to have the Japanese attack Pearl Harbor. From this position a step led to the ultimate in revisionism—the thesis that Roosevelt had planned the whole thing deliberately, knew about the attack in advance and wanted it to happen.

Prange emphasized that the Japanese were not puppets for Roosevelt to manipulate at will. The suggestion that the President dragged them into World War II kicking and screaming is predicated upon profound misunderstanding of Japanese character and Japanese records. Tokyo, not Washington, established Japan's foreign policy; the individual responsible for the Pearl Harbor attack was Isoroku Yamamoto, not Franklin Delano Roosevelt.

Thus in his unpublished Volume IV, Prange deals with the concept that in the context of the time, war between Japan and the United States was virtually inevitable, Pearl Harbor or no Pearl Harbor. Japan was on the march toward what she honestly believed to be her manifest destiny. If the United States would stand aside to let her pass, well and good. If not, the United States must take the consequences. Obviously Washington had very little practical option. If it allowed Japan to proceed without protest, Tokyo would have been so contemptuous that she would go ahead until eventually the United States would have to fight. On the other hand, if the United States took drastic action, Japan would be enraged and defiantly continue her march to empire. It was "heads I win, tails you lose." (See Revisionists Revisited, in Appendix.)

From the perspective of a burnt-out bunker in Berlin and the deck of *Missouri* it was easy for the revisionists to claim that the United States had no direct reason to fear Japan. But to Prange the view was different during those years when predator nations were on the rampage.

2. Because of the same editorial constraints, many Pearl Harbor "buffs" will miss reference to their favorite episode or their pet theory, and they will regret the lack of in-depth treatment accorded such subjects as basing the Fleet in Pearl Harbor in 1940 and the transfer of ships to the Atlantic in 1941.

3. Times are given in the military twenty-four-hour clock. This is for two reasons: First, in most cases the original military documents use the twenty-four-hour system; secondly, it helps avoid confusion between A.M. and P.M. when we deal with the interweaving of times between Japan and the United States. All times given are local unless otherwise indicated in the text.

4. In the discussion of Japanese training for the attack, the voyage to Hawaii, and the attack itself, distances are given in meters and nautical miles.

5. In accordance with naval usage of the period, the article "the" is omitted before the names of ships (e.g., *Arizona*, not "the *Arizona*") and the word "Fleet" is capitalized when referring to the U.S. Fleet or the U.S. Pacific Fleet.

6. In most instances the editors have attempted to be precise in footnoting;

however, in some cases in which reconstruction of an incident came from many different interviews and specific footnoting would only confuse the reader, the sources have been combined in a single note.

7. To list every book, article, or newspaper which Gordon Prange read in the course of thirty-seven years of research would be manifestly impossible; hence the bibliography is a selected one. A more comprehensive version is available in the author's files for study by historians.

8. The charts and pictures in this book represent a choice among many available with the view to those of most potential use or interest to the reader.

Gordon Prange hoped and planned to publish his study of Pearl Harbor in the form of four volumes, and if the fates are kind, this project may yet come to pass. However, instead of four volumes, this work now consists of this single book, which is divided into three major parts:

Part I, "Prelude," covers the planning period from January 1941 to mid-October 1941, when the Naval General Staff accepted Yamamoto's Pearl Harbor project as an authorized part of the Japanese naval war plan.

"Action," Part II, contains events from acceptance of the plan through the attack, ending with the decision of the Japanese not to make a second major attack on Pearl Harbor.

Part III, "Aftermath," describes the action on Oahu and in Washington following the attack. It takes the task force back to Japan, deals with the various investigations of the tragedy which took place in the United States, and offers some conclusions.

Even in the context of a multivolume study, Prange never nourished the illusion that his would be the last word on the subject. Much ground remains to be plowed, and there is ample room for the historians of the future. As consolidators and editors the undersigned accept responsibility for any errors in the present volume.

If Gordon W. Prange were writing this introduction, he would stress that this work calls not for judgment, but for reflection, as a good book should. We hope that it also brings the reader enjoyment, as a good book should. If the story as we tell it raises more questions than it provides answers, then we feel it has succeeded, for such reaction is inevitable. In the poignant words of one of Admiral Kimmel's counsels, "Pearl Harbor never dies, and no living person has seen the end of it."

DONALD M. GOLDSTEIN, Ph.D.
Associate Professor of
Public and International
Affairs
University of Pittsburgh
Pittsburgh, Pennsylvania

KATHERINE V. DILLON
CWO, USAF (Ret.)
Arlington, Virginia

PREFACE

Pearl Harbor was more than one of the most daring and brilliant naval operations of all time; it was one of the turning points in history. The event provides a milestone at which to pause and take historical inventory. But in so doing, one should not credit to the event an entire generation of the world's developments. The temptation to do this is very real because those who lived through that period tend to divide their lives into two periods—before Pearl Harbor and after Pearl Harbor. It is also one of the greatest of all war stories. It combined so much, so suddenly, so unexpectedly, so spectacularly, in such brief and tragic compass. It embraced so much which in the perspective of the years still seems inexplicable and mysterious.

But Pearl Harbor did not unfold with all the inevitability of a Greek tragedy. The operation was not an "act of God." Admiral Isoroku Yamamoto, Commander in Chief of Japan's Combined Fleet and the initiator of the plan, might well have abandoned it if training in shallow-water torpedo bombing had failed, if high-level bombing had proved unsuccessful, or if the United States had closed the Japanese consulate in Honolulu, thus cutting off his primary source of intelligence on the U.S. Pacific Fleet. Then, too, the Naval General Staff strongly opposed his dangerous enterprise and could have refused to sanction it. What is more, the Japanese government could have decided against war with the United States. The options on both sides of the Pacific were in human hands, not in the laps of the gods.

Pearl Harbor resulted from a vast combination of interrelated, complicated, and strange historical factors: on the one hand, bountiful human errors of great variety, false assumptions, fallacious views, a vast store of intelligence badly handled; on the other, precise planning, tireless training, fanatical dedication, iron determination, technical know-how, tactical excellence, clever deception measures, intelligence well gathered and effectively disseminated, plain guts—and uncommon luck.

One cannot point a finger at any one of these factors and say, "Ah, that did it!" any more than one can look at a building and say, "See that brick; it is the whole structure." The story of Pearl Harbor has suffered altogether too long from oversimplification, from interpretation in terms of black and white, from failure to understand that it embodies all the colors of the spectrum in a wide variety of mixtures and gradations.

The question of why Japan caught the United States napping on Oahu is exceedingly complicated and controversial. One must constantly keep in mind that nothing takes place in a vacuum. Events flow out of one another in an unending stream. History often hinges upon such elements as that fickle and cruel dictator the weather; the quirks of personality; an upset stomach; a prejudice; an accident or other unforeseen whim of fate. Therefore, it cannot be reduced to a scientific formula or factored like a mathematical problem.

Countless silent, unseen forces are incessantly at work in history's "majestic sweep," "innumerable waves," "slow rhythms," "surging forces"—call them what you will—those small yet numerous incidents which are often little more than scratches on history's slate, those elusive intangibles that alter men's thinking and actions; all in their way so illogical, yet so relative and relevant, and virtually impossible to deal with adequately. How does one accurately separate cause from effect, fact from fiction, moment from momentum, or determine the influence of time, place, and circumstance on any given event? It is impossible for the historian to read the whole record of the past, which invariably is incomplete. And to write that record? Ah, that is where, to paraphrase Voltaire, history plays tricks on the dead. By his nature the historian must be selective, choosing this or that fact, event, circumstance, example, or quotation which he considers relevant to his subject.

Thus, Gordon Prange laid no claim to omniscience. Nor did he wish to create the impression of finality. Indeed, it is extremely doubtful whether a completely satisfactory answer ever will be forthcoming. Anyone who claims to know and to present to his readers "The Final Secret of Pearl Harbor" is either a charlatan or a self-deluder.

If Gordon Prange were alive, he would want to dedicate this book to his wife, Anne, his son, Winfred, his daughters, Polly and Nancy, and his grandson Robbie, all of whom bore long and patiently with his "magnificent obsession"; to all those Americans and Japanese who helped and encouraged him in so many ways and without whom this work would have been impossible; to all his students over the years, to whom he devoted so much of himself and who in return gave him their affectionate admiration; and to the dead and the survivors of Pearl Harbor in the hope that they did not suffer and die in vain.

PART I

PRELUDE

CHAPTER 1

"CANCER

OF THE

PACIFIC"

Long before sunrise on New Year's Day, 1941, Emperor Hirohito rose to begin the religious service at the court marking the 2,601st anniversary of the founding of the Japanese Empire.[1] No doubt he prayed for his nation and for harmony in the world. For this mild, peaceable man himself had chosen the word *Showa*—"enlightened peace"—to characterize his reign.

But in statements greeting the new year, Japanese leaders prophesied strife and turmoil. Veteran journalist Soho Tokutomi warned of storms ahead: "There is no denying that the seas are high in the Pacific. . . . The time has come for the Japanese to make up their minds to reject any who stand in the way of their country. . . ."[2]

What true son of Nippon could doubt who stood in the way? Relations between the United States and Japan left tremendous room for improvement. Japan surged ahead under full sail on a voyage of expansion that dated back to 1895. Riding the winds of conquest, Japan invaded North China in 1937. Though it tried desperately to "solve" what it euphemistically termed the China Incident, it remained caught in a whirlpool that sucked down thousands upon thousands of its young men, tons upon tons of military equipment, and millions of yen. Still, nothing could stop its compulsive drive deeper and deeper into the heart of that tormented land. Thus, the unresolved China problem became the curse of Japan's foreign policy.

Japan turned southward in 1939. On February 10 it took over Hainan Island off the southern coast of China. In March of the same year Japan laid claim to the Spratlys—coral islands offering potential havens for planes and small naval craft, located on a beautiful navigational fix between Saigon and North Borneo, Manila, and Singapore.

With the fall of France in 1940 Japan stationed troops in northern French Indochina, its key stepping-stone to further advancement southward. And dazzled by Hitler's military exploits, it joined forces with Germany and Italy, signing the Tripartite Pact on September 27, 1940. By this treaty the three partners agreed to "assist one another with all political, economic and military means when one of the three Contracting Parties is attacked by a power at present not involved in the European War or in the Sino-Japanese conflict."[3] Inasmuch as no major nation remained uninvolved except the United States and the Soviet Union—and Germany had a nonaggression pact with the latter—the target of this treaty stood out with blinding clarity.

By 1941, that fateful Year of the Snake,* Japan poised for further expansionist adventures into Southeast Asia—Malaya, the Philippines, and the Netherlands East Indies. The Japanese convinced themselves that necessity and self-protection demanded they take over the vast resources of these promised lands to break through real or imagined encirclement and beat off the challenge of any one or a combination of their international rivals—the United States, Great Britain, and Soviet Russia.

Throughout the early years of Japan's emergence, the United States cheered on the Japanese, whom they regarded in a measure as their protégés. But in time it became apparent that the "plucky Little Japs" were not only brave and clever but dangerous and a bit on the devious side. By New Year's Day of 1941 knowledgeable people in both countries already believed that an open clash would be only a matter of time. Even Ambassador Joseph C. Grew, a friend of Japan, could find no silver lining. "It seems to me increasingly clear that we are bound to have a showdown some day, and the principal question at issue is whether it is to our advantage to have that showdown sooner or have it later," he lamented in a "Dear Frank" letter to President Franklin D. Roosevelt on December 14, 1940.[4]

Events in Europe inevitably colored the American attitude toward the Japanese, who labored under the self-imposed handicap of their alliance with Adolf Hitler, regarded by most Americans as little less than the Father of Evil. Japan's strong-arm methods of persuading Vichy to permit Japanese troops to enter northern Indochina smacked of Benito Mussolini's famous "dagger in the back" treatment of France. Now all signs pointed to the Netherlands East Indies as next on the list. The United States had to consider Japan in the context of its Axis alliance, for aid and concessions to Tokyo in effect meant aid and concessions to Berlin and Rome.

In essence China was the touchstone of Japanese-American relations, yet China was only part of the so-called Greater East Asia Co-Prosperity Sphere, a concept the very fluidity of which made the democracies uneasy. The Japanese never tired of expounding the principle in the loftiest phrases but fought shy of actually stating in geographical terms just what "Greater East Asia" covered. Presumably it would expand as Japan moved outward to include all that the traffic would bear.

---

*In the Buddhist fortune calendar cycle of twelve years, 1941 was the Year of the Snake.

To the Japanese the fulfillment of this dream was imperative. "I am convinced that the firm establishment of a Mutual Prosperity Sphere in Greater East Asia is absolutely necessary to the continued existence of this country," declared Japan's premier, Prince Fumimaro Konoye, on January 24.[5]

Japan had a long list of grievances against the United States, the foremost being the recognition of the Chiang Kai-shek regime and the nonrecognition of Manchukuo. The very presence in Asia of the United States, along with the European powers, was a constant irritation to Japanese pride. The press lost no occasion to assure such intruders that Japan would slam the Open Door in their faces. "Japan must remove all elements in East Asia which will interfere with its plans," asserted the influential *Yomiuri*. "Britain, the United States, France and the Netherlands must be forced out of the Far East. Asia is the territory of the Asiatics. . . ."[6]

On a number of scores the Japanese objected vociferously to American aid to Great Britain and to Anglo-American cooperation. In the first place, Britain was at war with Japan's allies, Germany and Italy, so what helped the British hindered the Axis. In the second, Japan considered that Washington's bolstering of London perpetuated the remnants of British colonialism and hence the obnoxious presence of European flags on Asian soil.

Japanese anger also focused on the embargoes which the United States had slapped on American exports to Japan. By the end of 1940 Washington had cut it off from all vital war materials except petroleum. As far back as 1938 the United States had placed Japan under the so-called moral embargo. The termination on January 26, 1940, of the Treaty of Commerce and Navigation of 1911 removed the legal obstacle to actual restrictions. Beginning in July 1940, Washington placed all exports of aviation fuel and high-grade scrap iron and steel under federal license and control. In September 1940, after Japanese forces moved into northern Indochina, Roosevelt finally announced an embargo on scrap iron and steel to Japan. Thus, by the end of that year Japan had begun to experience a real pinch and a shadow of genuine fear mingled with its resentment of these discriminatory measures.

Tokyo also had an old bone to pick with Washington—the immigration policy which excluded Japanese from American shores and refused United States citizenship to those Japanese residents not actually born there.

Above all, Japan considered America's huge naval expansion program aimed directly at it. Since the stationing of a large segment of the Fleet at Pearl Harbor in the spring of 1940, the United States Navy had stood athwart Japan's path—a navy which Japanese admirals thought capable of menacing their nation's very existence.

Since Commodore Matthew Perry had opened Japan to the modern world, the two nations had enjoyed a unique history of friendship and mutually profitable trade. Yet now they stood face-to-face like two duelists at the salute. The Japanese had a name for this ugly situation: *Taiheiyo-no-gan* ("Cancer of the Pacific").

But the Japanese would try the hand of diplomacy before they unsheathed the sword. If they could keep the United States immobilized in the Pacific by peaceful means, they would prefer to do so. To negotiate their differences with Washington, in November 1940 Tokyo selected as ambassador Admiral Kichisaburo Nomura. Called out of retirement at sixty-four, Nomura had filled numerous important positions in his long, illustrious career in the Navy. During a tour as naval attaché in Washington he became friendly with the then Assistant Secretary of the Navy Franklin D. Roosevelt. More important, Nomura felt at home in the United States and cherished his American friends. Seldom have two nations at official loggerheads been represented by two such men of mutual goodwill as Grew and Nomura—two physicians who would make every effort to help cure the "Cancer of the Pacific."

At six feet, Nomura loomed over most of his countrymen. On April 29, 1932, when he was attending a celebration in Shanghai, a Chinese terrorist had thrown a bomb into a group of Japanese dignitaries. The explosion robbed Nomura of his right eye and also crippled him, so that he walked with a limp for the rest of his life. In repose thoughtful, even a little anxious, his broad, good-natured face frequently beamed with jovial friendliness. All Japan knew him to be a man of sincerity, moderation, and liberality of thought, a sturdy opponent of the jingoists. He advocated peace and friendship with the United States; in American naval circles, consequently, he was both liked and respected.

Until the last moment Japan's fire-eating expansionists, along with the Germans in Tokyo, tried to block Nomura's appointment. Indeed, he himself had not sought the post. Throughout the late summer and early fall of 1940 the admiral consistently refused the offer, despite the persistent pleas of Foreign Minister Yosuke Matsuoka. Only when his moderate naval colleagues implored him to accept and help reach an agreement with the United States did he reluctantly consent. Not that he considered the prospects entirely hopeless, but he had to admit that conditions were "very bad," and he feared that "the situation would probably get worse."[7]

During numerous talks with Prime Minister Konoye, War Minister Hideki Tojo, and others, Nomura cautioned them not to expect miracles of him; the question of war or peace was beyond his powers as a single representative of the Japanese government. In the postwar years, when Nomura tried to explain how he felt during those tense days in Washington in 1941, he quoted a Japanese proverb: "When a big house falls, one pillar cannot stop it."[8]

Little wonder that on January 1, 1941, the official *Japan Times and Advertiser* admitted that although Nomura's appointment was widely approved, "the role he is to play at Washington is no enviable one. When it is certain that Japanese diplomacy will be governed first and foremost by Axis motives, relations with the United States are pregnant with no end of potential issues."

On January 20, 1941, just three days before sailing, Nomura spent about half an hour with Grew. The American ambassador certainly did not expect Nomura to reverse the tide. As he said in his diary, "The only potential usefulness I can see in Admiral Nomura's appointment lies in the hope that he will honestly report to his Government what the American government and people are thinking, writing and saying."[9]

Grew kept a sharp, uneasy eye on the developments in Tokyo. Tall, dignified, with impeccable manners, he appeared to be the perfect senior career diplomat. A smooth thatch of snowy hair topped an intelligent, attractive face. Beneath heavy black brows the candid dark eyes opened to all possible contingencies yet looked out on mankind with good humor and common sense.

After almost nine years on the job he ranked as doyen of Tokyo's diplomatic colony. Limited in part by deafness, Grew never mastered the Japanese language, but his wife spoke it excellently. Alice Grew had a special link with Japan, being the granddaughter of Commodore Perry. Blessed with a sharp mind and mature judgment, Grew became a shrewd observer of the Japanese scene and called the shots exactly as he saw them, both in his reports to Washington and in his conferences with Japanese leaders.

"With all our desire to keep America out of war and at peace with all nations, especially with Japan, it would be the height of folly to allow ourselves to be lulled into a feeling of false security," Grew wrote on January 1, 1941, in his diary—that invaluable manuscript in which he not only recorded in detail the major diplomatic and political events of the day but also blew off steam when the pressure grew too great. Nevertheless, even when the Japanese most irritated him, his language was that of an affectionate father toward a beloved but exasperating son. "Japan, not we, is on the warpath . . . " he continued. "If those Americans who counsel appeasement could read even a few of the articles by leading Japanese in the current Japanese magazines wherein their real desires and intentions are given expression, our peace-minded fellow country-men would realize the utter hopelessness of a policy of appeasement." Grew added a grim note: "In the meantime let us keep our powder dry and be ready—for anything."[10]

Nomura was prepared to look on the bright side when he sailed from Yokohama on January 23, 1941, to take up his new post. But his departure did not strike much optimism from the Japanese press. The next day commentator Teiichi Muto wrote: "The new ambassador to the United States, in fact, may be likened to a sailor who ventures to cross an ocean of angry waves in a tiny boat."[11] And about two weeks later the strongly nationalist *Kokumin* added this gloomy touch: "We offer our respect and gratitude to Ambassador Nomura with the same attitude as to soldiers going to the front with the determination to die."[12]

Nomura had been at sea only four days when Matsuoka sounded off ominously in a speech in Tokyo:

> The Co-Prosperity Sphere in the Far East is based on the spirit of Hakko Ichiu, or the Eight Corners of the Universe under One Roof. . . . We must control the western Pacific. . . . We must request United States reconsideration, not only for the sake of Japan but for the world's sake. And if this request is not heard, there is no hope for Japanese-American relations.[13]

When Admiral Koshiro Oikawa became navy minister on September 4, 1940, he acknowledged, "Heavy are the responsibilities of the Navy which must be fully prepared to meet any emergency arising from the current trend of world events."[14] Oikawa had been a full admiral since 1939 and was one of Japan's most able and distinguished naval officers. A large, dignified man of robust health, he had a broadly pleasant but unreadable face flanked by enormous ears. A man of few words, he expressed opinions rather than convictions.

When Admiral Koshiro Oikawa became navy minister on September 4, 1940, he acknowledged, "Heavy are the responsibilities of the Navy which must be fully prepared to meet any emergency arising from the current trend of world events."[14] Oikawa had been a full admiral since 1939 and was one of Japan's most able and distinguished naval officers. A large, dignified man of robust health, he had a broadly pleasant but unreadable face flanked by enormous ears. A man of few words, he expressed opinions rather than convictions.

He believed firmly in Japanese destiny and strongly supported the doctrine of southern expansion. He spoke of the war in China as a "sacred campaign." He thought Japan might be "running some risk of picking Germany's chestnuts out of the fire" because of the Tripartite Pact, but he believed that "America was so unlikely to go to war that the situation was fairly safe."[15] Even so, he preferred steady diplomatic and naval pressure to military action. Yet before the end of January 1941 Oikawa assured his countrymen that "the navy is prepared fully for the worst and . . . measures are being taken to cope with the United States naval expansion."[16]

By that time his head bulged with the weightiest of secrets. He knew a lot more than he was prepared to tell. Nor did he dare tell all he knew.

CHAPTER 2

"ON A

MOONLIGHT

NIGHT

OR AT

DAWN"

An intensely serious man sat at his desk in his cabin aboard the 32,000-ton battleship *Nagato* as she swung at anchor at Hashirajima in Hiroshima Bay on January 7, 1941. [1] One can picture this man as he placed a piece of paper before him, grasped his brush, and marshaled his thoughts. Then, when the spirit moved him, he wrote in quick, bold strokes one of the most historically revealing letters in the annals of the Imperial Japanese Navy.

A photograph taken at the height of his powers portrays a man short even by Japanese standards (five feet three inches), with broad shoulders accentuated by massive epaulets and a thick chest crowded with orders and medals. But a strong, commanding face dominates and subdues the trappings. The angular jaw slants sharply to an emphatic chin. The lips are full, clean-cut, under a straight, prominent nose; the large, well-spaced eyes, their expression at once direct and veiled, harbor potential amusement or the quick threat of thunder. Short, pointed eyebrows lend an inquisitive look to the nettled brow. Gray hair in an uncompromising crew cut surmounts the whole. It is the face of a man of action and a visionary, reflecting willpower and drive as well as sensitivity.

This man was Isoroku Yamamoto,* Commander in Chief of Japan's Combined Fleet.

On this particular morning of January 7, 1941, presumably Yamamoto

---

*Yamamoto's real father, Teikichi Takano, was fifty-six years old when his wife presented him with his sixth and last male offspring. To mark the proud product of his full maturity, he chose the name Isoroku, spelled with the ideographs of the number 56 (*i*—5; *so*—10; *roku*—6). Born in Nagaoka, Honshu, on April 4, 1884, Isoroku Takano was adopted into the Yamamoto family in 1916. Such adoptions were a common practice in Japan, particularly in a family with no male heir, to keep the line from dying out.

showed none of his usual good nature and zest for living. If an evil spirit had set about bestowing on him the task he most dreaded, it would have come up with exactly the one he had imposed upon himself—that of initiating war against the United States by a surprise attack upon its Pacific Fleet.

There is no more ironic fact in a situation loaded with ironies than this: Probably no man in Japan more earnestly wanted to avoid war with the United States than the one who planned the Pearl Harbor attack. Yamamoto clearly understood that Japan had no hope of ultimate victory over the United States. He knew that America vastly outstripped Japan in science, technology, and especially natural resources. Not only was the United States Fleet larger than the Japanese Navy, but America's mass production system could replace battle losses much faster than Japan's inferior economy. He had seen the industrial might of the United States firsthand when he studied at Harvard University and later, in the mid-twenties, when he served as naval attaché in Washington.

Since his appointment as Commander in Chief in August 1939, Yamamoto had assiduously prepared Hirohito's Navy for every possible contingency while still nourishing the hope that Japan and the United States would not come to blows. Yet by early autumn of 1940 he saw dangers ahead. The unhappy prospect of a German-Italian-Japanese alliance distressed him considerably, for he had long mistrusted the "machinations of Ribbentrop and Hitler," as witness his letter to his naval academy classmate Vice Admiral Shigetaro Shimada on September 4, 1939. "I shudder as I think of the problem of Japan's relations with Germany and Italy in the face of the tremendous changes now taking place in Europe."[2]

But the tide of pro-Axis feeling in Japan could not be stemmed. In late September 1940 he conferred with Konoye in Tokyo. According to the premier's memoirs, Yamamoto informed him, "If I am told to fight regardless of the consequences, I shall run wild for the first six months or a year, but I have utterly no confidence for the second or third year. The Tripartite Pact has been concluded, and we cannot help it. Now that the situation has come to this pass, I hope you will endeavor to avoid a Japanese-American war."[3]

But Yamamoto did not have much faith in Japan's political leaders. Writing with the utmost frankness to Shimada on December 10, 1940, he observed bitterly:

> . . . the present Government appears to be in complete confusion. Its action in showing surprise now at America's economic pressure and fuming and complaining against it reminds me of the aimless action of a schoolboy which has no more consistent motive than the immediate need or whim of the moment. . . . It would be extremely dangerous for the Navy to make any move in the belief that such men as Prince Konoye and Foreign Minister Matsuoka can be relied upon. . . .

Yamamoto also doubted whether Japanese-American difficulties could be negotiated. "Nomura has no confidence that he will succeed in his mission," he continued, "and besides, it is expecting too much to adjust our relations with America through diplomacy at this late stage. . . ."[4]

In spite of Yamamoto's pessimistic outlook, his heavy correspondence during 1941 reveals that he still wished to avoid war with the United States if at all possible. Certainly he never uttered the widely reported statement which was to distort his true image both at home and abroad. What actually happened is this: On January 26, 1941, fearful of the drift toward war and disgusted by the jingoists in full cry, Yamamoto wrote a letter to Ryoichi Sasakawa, an ultranationalist, in which he stated:

> Should hostilities break out between Japan and the United States, it would not be enough that we take Guam and the Philippines, nor even Hawaii and San Francisco. To make victory certain, we would have to march into Washington and dictate the terms of peace in the White House. I wonder if our politicians, among whom armchair arguments about war are being glibly bandied about in the name of state politics, have confidence as to the final outcome and are prepared to make the necessary sacrifices.[5]

As originally written, and in its entirety, this paragraph has all the biting sarcasm of which Yamamoto was so thoroughly capable. He was warning the far right bluntly that the United States was not, as certain wishful thinkers believed, a hollow giant to fall and smash to pieces at the first blow. For Japan to conquer the Americans, it must land its forces on the Pacific coast, push across mountains, deserts and vast plains, fighting every inch of the way, and occupy Washington itself. But Japan's nationalists deliberately distorted Yamamoto's meaning. They published an altered version of the statement, with the last sentence deleted, thereby creating the impression that Yamamoto promised to dictate peace in the White House. Unfortunately, by the time this distortion reached the public Japan had already taken the plunge, so Yamamoto could not create dissension by contradicting it publicly.

How then could a man who so clearly foresaw its consequences have engineered the stroke that precipitated the very war he wished to avoid? Alas, Japan had already committed itself to a course that left Yamamoto little alternative. Its mountainous terrain and volcanic soil barely supported a population which increased by leaps and bounds each year. Nor could its land supply all the raw materials necessary for its efficient, ambitious industries. Consequently, a compulsive drive toward expansion engulfed the Japanese. By 1941 Japan was looking southward to Malaya, the Philippines, and the Netherlands East Indies, areas bursting with the rich resources it craved. Such a move would have serious consequences. In his letter of December 10, 1940, Yamamoto told Shimada:

> The probability is great that the launching of our operation against the Netherlands Indies will lead to an early commencement of war with America, and since Britain and Holland will side with America, our operations against the Netherlands Indies are almost certain to develop into a war with America, Britain and Holland before those operations are half over. Consequently we should not launch out on the southern operation unless we are at least prepared to face such an eventuality and are, moreover, adequately equipped. . . .

He added a sentence which must have struck ice into Shimada's soul: "If . . . it is felt that war cannot be avoided, it would be best to decide on war with America from the beginning and to begin by taking the Philippines, thereby reducing the line of operations and assuring the sound execution of operations. . . ." He added, "The southern operations, unlike the operations in China, will determine the nation's rise or fall, for they will lead to a war in which the nation's very fate will be at stake. . . ."[6]

Make no mistake about one thing: Yamamoto was a robust nationalist and Japanese to the marrow of his bones. He loved his Emperor and homeland, and his fighting heart followed the samurai tradition. Like many Japanese at the time, he believed his people to be a chosen race, selected by a far-seeing Providence to fulfill an ineluctable destiny. So, quite logically, Japan should play the dominant role in the Asian community of nations.

But he was trapped between two fires. On the one hand lay the bleak prospect of a resources-poor Japan fighting not only the United States but China, the British Empire, the Netherlands Indies, and perhaps Soviet Russia as well; on the other pressed the hard necessity of doing his duty as Commander in Chief of the Combined Fleet. The Southern Operation would depend largely on the Navy's ability to transport the troops, hold the Allied warships at bay, and keep Japan's sea-lanes open. For success to crown the campaign, the U.S. Pacific Fleet must be barred from southern waters, at least during the first critical months. How could this be done?

Not, in Yamamoto's opinion, by following the strictly defensive doctrine of the Great All-Out Battle in the western Pacific (*Kantai Kessen*) which he inherited. When he took over the Combined Fleet in August 1939, Japanese strategy went something like this: Let the enemy come to us; fight him on our own terms near the home islands, where the inner lines of communication and close supply give us a tremendous tactical and strategic advantage; use both land- and carrier-based planes to blast him from the skies; at the right moment lure him into the trap and annihilate him.

Japanese admirals envisaged events proceeding along these lines: A powerful U.S. Fleet steamed confidently westward. According to the principles of Operation Attrition (*Zengen Sakusen*), Japanese submarines trailing the huge armada would whittle it down to size as the distance from its base widened with each advancing mile. Then, when the U.S. Fleet finally reached a position strategically favorable to Japan, the Armageddon of the seas would begin. Both sides would deploy their ships across the vast ocean in battle formation and slug it out to the last shell. Once the smoke and fire had cleared, a Japanese victory would emerge. One U.S. steel monster after another would limp forlornly homeward or, thrusting its bow upward as if in a dying salute to the sea, disappear forever.

But in Yamamoto's thinking, this concept did not fit the needs of Japan's all-out thrust southward against numerous widely separated objectives several thousand miles from the homeland. He had to find a valid answer to the problem of clearing the Japanese flank of the U.S. Fleet and at the same time committing his major forces to the Southern Operation.

Yamamoto's training and experience conditioned his approach to the task confronting him. Though not a pilot, he had been closely associated with naval aviation for years and realized its immense potential as a new weapon of sea power. In December 1924 Yamamoto had been appointed executive officer of the Navy's flight school at Kasumigaura (Japan's Pensacola), some sixty miles northeast of Tokyo. Although he had never flown a plane in his life, under the spur of his dynamic drive, Kasumigaura became a base transformed, with a higher level of discipline, a stronger sense of mission, better physical fitness, more rigorous flight rules, and a genuine esprit de corps.

When Yamamoto became commander of the First Carrier Division in the early thirties, he seized the opportunity to make the fleet air arm an efficient part of the Navy. He inspired trust and confidence, but he was a severe taskmaster and once more bore down on training with a passion.

On December 2, 1936, Yamamoto was appointed director of the Aeronautical Department of the Navy Ministry. In that capacity he gave the naval air arm a long-needed thrust toward the future and established a momentum which carried it far into World War II.

Yamamoto's temperament also had much to do with the strategy he eventually conceived. Some of the maxims he loved to employ for self-guidance or to score a point reveal his turn of mind: "An efficient hawk hides his claws"; "A cornered rat will bite a cat"; "If you want the tiger's cubs, you must go into the tiger's lair." A bold, original thinker and an inveterate gambler, he enjoyed nothing more than a competitive round of chess (*shogi*), poker, or bridge. Often Yamamoto would challenge anyone on hand to play poker all night with the specific understanding that whoever quit first would lose the hand. He had a genuine passion for testing men—their wits, nerves, endurance, and patience —because at the same time he tested himself. "In all games Yamamoto loved to take chances just as he did in naval strategy," explained Captain Yasuji Watanabe, Yamamoto's prime favorite among his staff officers. "He had a gambler's heart."[7]

He fought valiantly for the improvement of the Imperial Navy. "The number of ships in the Combined Fleet should be doubled," he told his friend Baron Kumao Harada, private secretary to the revered elder statesman, Prince Saionji, on November 24, 1940. He went on typically:

> The number of planes must be doubled also. If such a large fleet is organized, I will not be content to withdraw to the Inland Sea and such places and wait for an opportunity to strike out. This is even in the event that war should break out and Tokyo should be in flames by the action of the United States Air Forces. If huge fires break out in Tokyo and Tokyo is completely destroyed by fire three or four times; and if I must witness it while waiting for a strategically opportune time, I cannot remain still.[8]

The program Yamamoto instituted when he took over the Combined Fleet boiled down to two essential points: a heavy emphasis on air warfare and the advancement of the line for the Great All-Out Battle eastward from the Bonins and Marianas to the Carolines and Marshalls. The movement of the U.S. Fleet to Hawaii in 1940 was also a serious consideration for Yamamoto. Thus, he and his staff reached the conclusion that Japan could best achieve an early decisive engagement with the U.S. Navy by moving the scene of action to waters near the Hawaiian Islands. This would force the enemy out to do battle in the only way that a Japanese fleet of inferior strength could overcome its formidable opponent. Moreover, if war must come, Yamamoto had better force the issue before the rapid expansion of the U.S. Navy made any direct confrontation impossible.[9]

As a small judo expert may toss a much larger opponent by catching him off-balance, so Japan had to seize the initiative. By knocking out the U.S. Fleet in one bold stroke, Yamamoto hoped to shift the strategic balance in the Pacific in Japan's favor and protect its all-important southern flank in Southeast Asia. If Japan could move fast enough and hard enough in the breathing spell thus gained, it might conquer those vast regions, thus securing the resources it so urgently needed to carry on a protracted war. It might also consolidate its position to the point where a negotiated peace acknowledging the status quo might be possible.

We do not know exactly when Yamamoto first thought of attacking Pearl Harbor. But reliable evidence on this point comes from Vice Admiral Shigeru Fukudome, a highly intelligent, level-headed officer who served as Yamamoto's chief of staff from November 15, 1939, to April 10, 1941. Yamamoto often discussed naval strategy with Fukudome, whom he liked personally and considered a very able officer. To the best of Fukudome's recollection, Yamamoto first spoke to him about his daring plan in either March or April 1940.[10]

Fukudome was a man of medium height and build, with a sturdy chest and solid shoulders. His mouth was firm, with finely modeled lips, and his chin edged confidently forward. He usually wore a serious look, and his infrequent smiles were enigmatic. Ideas did not explode in his brain as they did in Yamamoto's. They matured slowly, like the growth of a plant. Not one to launch out first or to hold back and be last, Fukudome was a solid in-betweener. A fervid nationalist, he maintained a strong link with Japanese naval tradition and supported the doctrine of expansion southward. But he did not have the mentality, personality, or training to harbor the avant-garde perceptions of Yamamoto, and he did not set too much stock in the Pearl Harbor concept when the latter initially broached the subject.

By the first half of 1940 Japan's fleet air warfare training had achieved such progress that Yamamoto and Fukudome were convinced that "aerial torpedoing would play a predominant role in a decisive battle." One day the two admirals were congratulating themselves over this when Yamamoto murmured to Fukudome as if to himself, "I wonder if an aerial attack can't be made on Pearl Harbor?" Fukudome believed this idea to be no more than a passing notion which had strayed into his chief's receptive mind. To Fukudome such an operation seemed impracticable. But it was no novelty to him, because the Naval General Staff had considered the notion of attacking Pearl Harbor over a period of years during its annual planning meetings and war games. Each time the suggestion came up, however, the staff members dropped it, deciding "it was impossible." Fukudome believed that only submarines could strike at such a remote location from Japanese waters. His answer was: "It's better to have a decisive battle once and for all with our entire fleet at sea near Hawaii; then we can launch an air attack there."[11]

In the late autumn of 1940 the Combined Fleet completed its annual maneuvers, which included some remarkably effective carrier-mounted air attacks. Toward the end of the year the annual reorganization and personnel reshuffle took place. At that time Yamamoto decided to continue the training program into the new year, with much more emphasis on aerial warfare tactics. When he chatted with Fukudome about this arrangement, he told him, "I want to have [Rear Admiral Takijiro] Onishi study a Pearl Harbor attack plan as a tentative step. After studying the result of his report, the problem may be included in the fleet training program, and I want to keep it top secret until that time." Having had some months to become accustomed to the idea, Fukudome replied briefly, "I think that's good."[12]

Although the plan never proceeded beyond the conceptual stage during 1940, Yamamoto had already envisioned a task force made up primarily of aircraft carriers, cruisers, and destroyers, to deliver an annihilating aerial strike against the U.S. Fleet in Pearl Harbor. But to carry the war to the very threshold of the enemy's power, he must catch his foe unawares. Secrecy and surprise therefore formed the keystones of the entire plan. Yet Yamamoto still did not plan on attacking Pearl Harbor as such. He wanted to knock out Uncle Sam's ships. And if the enemy fleet did not lie in the great Hawaiian anchorage when zero hour came, Yamamoto planned to seek it out and attack it "wherever it might be found in the Pacific."[13]

We have his own words for the approximate date when he finally decided on his bold venture. "The plan of launching a surprise attack against Pearl Harbor at the outset of war to give a fatal blow to the enemy fleet was decided in December of last year, when the fleet strategy was revised," he wrote to his friend Admiral Sankichi Takahashi on December 19, 1941. The same day he repeated the identical message in a letter to Baron Harada.[14] So the evidence seems conclusive.

We might ask: Since when have field commanders promulgated their nation's war plans? Indeed, Japanese naval planning lay supposedly in the hands of the Operations Section of the Naval General Staff, a gingery collection of up-and-coming, surprisingly young officers. And their designs were ruled on by the top brass—not by the Combined Fleet. The latter carried out the missions planned and approved in Tokyo. The Combined Fleet was not empowered to make a single operational move without official approval from the Naval General Staff.

This arrangement held true unless the Combined Fleet's Commander in Chief happened to be Isoroku Yamamoto. He felt about the ordinary guidelines as a confirmed bachelor feels about a wife—an excellent idea for other people. And such was the force of his personality and prestige that no one challenged him successfully. So it was that we find him outlining an operational concept to the navy minister instead of to the Chief of the Naval General Staff. He did so because he himself wished to command the Pearl Harbor striking force, and as navy minister Admiral Koshiro Oikawa controlled personnel appointments.

Yamamoto also violated security by committing his explosive ideas to paper in personal letters. But he did not pursue his priceless correspondence for the benefit of posterity or for the official files. It was strictly between his friends and him. He never dictated these letters; he brushed out both drafts and final versions with his own hand. Even his chief of staff never saw them. He could pack a lot of meaning into a few words, writing in a style which virtually amounted to a code, with any number of shortcuts and historical allusions. Fortunately his correspondents were a small group of men with similar interests who knew exactly what he meant.[15]

So, bearing in mind that this man was a law unto himself, let us return to that cold winter's day of January 7, 1941. In his cabin Yamamoto sat composing a long letter to Oikawa.[16] As he wrote, an observer might note that his left hand lacked the fore and middle fingers—lost in the Battle of Tsushima against the Russians in May 1905.

The brush splashed forcefully across the paper. In view of the bleak international situation, wrote Yamamoto, the time had come for the Navy "to devote itself seriously to war preparations" because "a conflict with the United States and Great Britain is inevitable." Yamamoto emphasized that the Japanese Navy should "fiercely attack and destroy the U.S. main fleet at the outset of the war, so that the morale of the U.S. Navy and her people" would "sink to the extent that it could not be recovered." Strange that Yamamoto, who so surely judged America's physical strength, should have so completely misunderstood its spirit!

Gathering momentum, he insisted that "we should do our very best at the outset of the war with the United States . . . to decide the fate of the war on the very first day." Next, Yamamoto outlined his two-part "operational plan": "1. In case the majority of the enemy's main force is at Pearl Harbor, attack it vigorously with our air force, and blockade the harbor. 2. If the enemy remains outside the harbor, apply the same method as above."

He also informed Oikawa what forces he had in mind and their assignments: the First and Second Carrier divisions, or the latter alone at a pinch, in order "to launch a forced or surprise attack with all their air strength, risking themselves on a moonlight night or at dawn"; one destroyer squadron "to rescue survivors of carriers sunk by enemy counterattack"; one submarine squadron "to attack the enemy fleeing in confusion after closing in on Pearl Harbor (or other anchorages) and, if possible, to attack them at the entrance of Pearl Harbor so that the entrance may be blocked by sunken ships." And last: "several tankers . . . for refueling at sea.

"In case the enemy main force comes out from Hawaii before our attack and keeps coming at us," he continued, the Japanese attack group must "encounter it with all our decisive force to destroy it with one stroke."

Yamamoto acknowledged that success would not be easy, but he thought that the Japanese could be "favored by God's blessing" if all those taking part were "firmly determined to devote themselves to their task even at the sacrifice of their lives."

Nor did Yamamoto lose sight of Japan's principal objective. A "forestalling and surprise attack on enemy air forces in the Philippines and Singapore should definitely be made almost at the same time as the attacks against Hawaii." If the U.S. main force at Pearl Harbor were destroyed, the enemy's "untrained forces deploying in the southern regions would lose morale to such an extent that they could scarcely be of any use."

If the Japanese Navy feared that "such an operation against Hawaii is too risky" and remained in home waters awaiting the Americans, "we cannot rule out the possibility that the enemy would dare to launch an attack upon our homeland to burn down our capital and other cities.

"If such a thing happens," he continued, "our Navy will be subject to fierce attack by the public, even if we should be successful in the southern operation. . . ." In this case, Japanese national morale would be lost beyond recovery.

Then Yamamoto made his personal appeal: "I sincerely desire to be appointed Commander in Chief of the air fleet to attack Pearl Harbor so that I may personally command that attack force." Obviously he understood the dangers involved, for he urged Oikawa to "pass a favorable judgment on my request . . . so that I may be able to devote myself exclusively to my last duty to our country. . . ."

CHAPTER 3

"DIFFICULT

BUT NOT

IMPOSSIBLE"

Erect as a lance, wiry as a steel spring, Rear Admiral Takijiro Onishi, chief of staff of the Eleventh Air Fleet, was blessed with undaunted confidence, a forceful personality, and a husky physique. He never bluffed, and he walked tall—"the central figure in any environment."[1] He had a special genius for working out the details of tactical plans. Once he turned to a problem, he concentrated so intensely that he saw nothing except the task at hand.[2] He drove himself harder than he did his officers and men. But he loved to play, too, and when in his cups—no rare event—"he was almost rude to Yamamoto."[3]

Yet within about a week of his communication to Oikawa, in January 1941, Yamamoto wrote a second missive on the subject of Pearl Harbor—a three-page letter to his close friend Onishi. As he brushed it out, Yamamoto took his aggressive idea from the amorphous to the concrete. He reviewed the major points of his communication to Oikawa. Japan must keep the U.S. Navy out of the western Pacific at least until the first stage of operations had been completed, a period of approximately six months. Yamamoto added that he wished to command the task force to Hawaii. Then he asked Onishi to begin a study of the proposal and to prepare a reply for him as soon as possible. Naturally the project must be kept top secret.[4]

Yamamoto had selected an excellent officer to test his idea. Besides enjoying his trust and confidence, Onishi rated as one of Japan's few genuine air admirals. Though primarily concerned at the time with land-based aviation, and a tactician rather than a strategist, he vigorously expounded carrier warfare. Ambassador Nomura, under whom Onishi once served in China, stated that Onishi was "one of the officers who consistently advocated expansion and improvement of the Japanese naval air arm."[5]

Onishi was no intellectual. In fact, he had flunked his entrance examination to the Naval Staff College and never attended that school for future admirals. Nor was he original or imaginative. But what he lacked of those qualities he made up in diligent application and sheer driving power. "Onishi was a very ardent person, the type who believed that nothing was impossible if one went forward with great spiritual determination," said Rear Admiral Sadatoshi Tomioka, who in 1941 was chief of the Operations Section of the Naval General Staff.[6] Just a few months under fifty when he entered the Pearl Harbor picture, Onishi had enough hard practical experience to deepen his knowledge, ripen his judgment, and give him a sound approach to aviation problems.

Yamamoto followed up his letter to Onishi by discussing his concept with him in person. The two admirals most probably held their initial meeting on the afternoon of either January 26 or 27 in Yamamoto's flag cabin in *Nagato*, by then anchored in Ariake Bay in southern Kyushu.[7] No source can tell us exactly what they said during their conference. But to judge from the discussions these two officers subsequently held with a restricted group of colleagues, they devoted their attention to the technical aspects and to the feasibility of the Pearl Harbor attack, which Yamamoto later described as "so difficult and so dangerous that we must be prepared to risk complete annihilation."[8]

After this conference with Yamamoto, Onishi returned to his headquarters in Kanoya, inland on the eastern side of Kagoshima Bay in southern Kyushu, and went to work that same night. He was standing beside a table in his office, peering intently at a map of Pearl Harbor, when the door swung open to admit his senior staff officer, Commander Kosei Maeda, whom Onishi had summoned.

Now in his early forties, Maeda well deserved his reputation as an expert on aerial torpedo warfare—the exact area in which Onishi needed advice. As Maeda approached his chief, the latter, his eyes still riveted on the map, remained deep in concentration. Then he looked up abruptly and fired: "If the warships of the U.S. Navy were moored around Ford Island, could a successful torpedo attack be launched against them?"

The question caught Maeda completely off guard. A torpedo attack against Pearl Harbor! He knew that Onishi, a man of intense likes and dislikes, often lacked the breadth of mind to listen to an opposing point of view. Not knowing Onishi's stand on the problem, he thought the question through carefully. Then, proceeding from the doubtful assumption that a Japanese task force could sail all that distance to Hawaii without interception, Maeda replied, "A torpedo attack against U.S. warships at Pearl Harbor, from the technical standpoint alone, would be virtually impossible. The water of the base is too shallow."

Onishi's strong face hardened slightly, and his catlike eyes rebuked Maeda, for he did not like to hear the word "impossible." But Maeda stuck by his convictions. "Unless a technical miracle can be achieved in torpedo bombing," he declared firmly, "this type of attack would be altogether impractical." Then he added, "Such a difficult operation might conceivably be possible if parachutes could be fastened to the torpedoes to keep them from sinking too deeply into the water and lodging in the soft mud below, or if they could be launched from a very low level."

But whoever heard of an aerial torpedo wafting to the attack by parachute? And the attempts of the Japanese Navy thus far to launch torpedoes at low altitudes had left much to be desired. How, too, could the torpedomen fire their missiles into the sides of closely moored ships in Pearl Harbor's restricted air-maneuvering space?

So the conversation turned to other types of bombing. Maeda stressed the advantages of high-altitude attack aimed at piercing the thick deck armor of U.S. vessels. Onishi, however, thought dive bombing would assure a greater degree of accuracy and thus produce more effective results. Both officers agreed that an aerial strike against ships in Pearl Harbor posed grave risks. As far as Maeda knew, these questions were purely hypothetical. Onishi did not tell him that Yamamoto had such a scheme in mind, and Maeda did not learn about the actual plan until later in the year.[9]

After his colleague had left, Onishi continued to work on the problem. One thing was certain—for a surprise attack on Pearl Harbor to be even remotely possible, it must ride the wings of Japan's naval air arm. To evaluate the basic idea, then breathe life into it, Onishi needed an honest and precise worker, a true flier with a sure grasp of air power's capabilities, and, above all, a daring thinker whose originality bordered on genius. A tall order in anyone's navy, but Onishi knew exactly where to fill it.

Early in February 1941 he dispatched a message to the staff officer for air aboard the carrier *Kaga*, then in Ariake Bay. This note requested Commander Minoru Genda to "come to Kanoya at once about an urgent matter." Thus, Onishi took a dynamic step which was to have a profound and lasting influence on Yamamoto's project.

Genda needed no second invitation, for Onishi was his hero and model as man, airman, and patriot. No one had influenced his thoughts on strategy and his outlook on life more strongly. Curiosity consumed Genda as he hastened to the headquarters of the Eleventh Air Fleet, where admiral and commander met in the office of the chief of staff. Close personal and professional bonds linked the two men, dating as far back as 1935.[10] Despite Genda's relatively junior rank (he had made commander only the previous November), Onishi knew that he had picked the right man for the job.

In an atmosphere of the utmost secrecy, Onishi unfolded Yamamoto's design, while Genda listened intently. Then he handed Genda Yamamoto's letter and sat back to wait while his friend digested its contents. He watched the mobile, sensitive face kindle as Genda read carefully, thoughtfully, admiring, as he did so, "Yamamoto's daring plan and brave spirit." This time Onishi could expect no hesitancy in the reply, no fear lest the answer not please the hearer. For Genda called the shots as he saw them and was indifferent to audience reaction. When he finished the letter, he met Onishi's challenging regard and said calmly, "The plan is difficult but not impossible."[11]

Onishi grunted his satisfaction. Then the two men got down to cases.

"Yamamoto not only intends to cripple the U.S. Pacific Fleet severely at the beginning of hostilities; he counts heavily on smashing the morale of the American people by sinking as many battleships as possible," Onishi explained. Most Americans—like most Japanese—still believed battleships to be the mightiest weapons of war. The sinking of one or, better yet, a number of these giant vessels would be considered a most appalling thing, akin to a disaster of nature. Such destruction, Yamamoto reasoned, would paralyze the vaunted Yankee spirit.[12]

Moreover, fantastic as it may sound, Yamamoto toyed with the idea of not recovering the planes aboard their carriers. Originally he had in mind a one-way strike delivered only by torpedo bombers. In fact, according to Onishi, if this method of assault did not prove feasible, Yamamoto thought that Japan should fly off their carrier decks 500 to 600 miles from Oahu—a distance well beyond their radius of action.[13] The idea was in keeping with the concept of a one-way attack (*katamichi kogeki*), then under discussion among airmen of the Combined Fleet, and seemed to offer certain advantages: It would increase the striking range of the planes, move the carriers quickly out of the danger zone, and get them well on their way back home soon after launching the attack.[14] In the meantime, the pilots would fly to the target, release their deadly cargo, turn back to sea in the direction of their carriers, and land in the water, where destroyers or submarines could fish them out.[15]

Yamamoto also presumed, with rare naïveté, that in the face of this type of attack the American people might think the Japanese such a unique and fearless race that it would be useless to fight them. That Yamamoto—Harvard student, former attaché at Washington, associate of American naval officers—should have seriously entertained such an idea is a sharp indication of the mutual underestimation between Japanese and Americans at this time, even between those who should have known better.

Genda torpedoed these notions on the spot. A one-way attack represented a defeatism utterly alien to his nature, and he had little of the usual Japanese preoccupation with death. When the ancestral spirits called, he would meet them gallantly, but he had no intention of bursting in on them uninvited or asking his men to do so. "To obtain the best results, all carriers must approach as close to Pearl Harbor as possible," he emphasized. "Denuding them of planes and departing the scene of action minus their scoring punch would invite disaster in case the Americans launched a counterattack." And Genda noted that Yamamoto's plan would in no way allow for repeated attacks to make the action decisive. "To secure complete success, we must stay within effective bomber and fighter range of the target until we accomplish our mission," he pointed out.[16]

Yamamoto's original design also struck Genda as too narrow. It lacked diversity because it called for only one type of attack. This entailed a severe tactical risk, for it put all the Japanese hopes on torpedo bombing—the most difficult type in naval air warfare. If the weather were bad, visibility poor, or the enemy alerted, the operation might well fail.

"A one-way attack would have a bad psychological effect on the airmen if they knew their only means of survival would be the slim chance of being picked up at sea," he added. "Ditching in enemy territory would be a needless waste of planes and highly trained airmen."[17] Genda scored his last point vigorously: "Our prime target should be U.S. carriers."[18]

After the two officers had conferred for the better part of two hours, Onishi made a few concluding remarks. "I think this is a good plan and should be carried out," he told Genda. But "secrecy is the keynote and surprise the all-important factor," he stressed. "Japan should employ every carrier capable of making the voyage to Hawaii." Alert to the formidable challenge inherent in Yamamoto's project, Genda agreed completely. At the end of their long discussion Onishi asked Genda to prepare a preliminary draft and report to him in about a week or ten days.[19] He urged him to make the study in the utmost secrecy, "with special attention to the feasibility of the operation, method of execution, and the forces to be used."[20]

A photograph of Genda in his commander's uniform reveals a symmetrical face with regular, aristocratic features. Thick, level eyebrows, a straight nose, and a firm chin are dominated by piercing eyes, almost frightening in their intensity of expression. No one who ever looked into those eyes could forget them. At thirty-six Genda was impatient with mediocrity, at ease only with perfection. Behind his keen dark eyes lay a razor-sharp mind that cut straight to the heart of any problem. He radiated the poise and *savoir-faire* of a man who knows and loves his job. His slim figure sometimes suggested frailty, but in fact, his body was as tough as whalebone. A man of controlled discipline and unyielding honesty, he combined dashing adventurousness with mental probity, trigger thinking with cool restraint. Virtually every Japanese naval officer consulted for this study readily agreed that in 1941 Genda was the most brilliant airman in the Imperial Navy. "Genda stood head and shoulders above the majority of his colleagues in the field of naval aviation," Tomioka confirmed. "He was without doubt ten years ahead of his time."[21]

Born to an ancient family in 1904, Genda seemed earmarked by fate as a part of his nation's story. In November 1929 he won his wings, graduating at the head of his class. For the next six years he moved rapidly from one operational and staff air assignment to the other. Soon he became the ace fighter pilot and fighter pilot instructor of the Japanese Navy. Almost everyone in the fleet knew him. And almost everyone in Japan knew "Genda's Flying Circus," a group of daredevils who amazed audiences all across the country with their death-defying stunts.

"Genda was sometimes too willing, too risky in his judgment when he should have been more careful," said Captain Mitsuo Fuchida, who led the air attack against Pearl Harbor. "Genda was like a daring quarterback who would risk the game on one turn of pitch and toss. He was a man of brilliant ideas. Sometimes, however, his ideas were too flashy and needed a practical hand for their realization."[22]

When Genda was appointed to serve aboard the carrier *Ryujo* in 1933, Yamamoto was the division commander, and they became acquainted. During many shipboard discussions on air power Yamamoto's would be one of the few voices raised in support of Genda. And those discussions could wax hot indeed. Standard naval air doctrine of the time cast the fighter plane in a purely defensive role, with the offensive thrust confined to the bomber. Genda challenged this theory vigorously. "What can a bomber accomplish unless it reaches its target?" He insisted that fighters should escort the bombers all the way to the objective, thus guarding them in flight and securing command of the air above the enemy's ships and bases—not just remain behind, hovering over the carrier as a protective umbrella. When some of his colleagues scoffed, Yamamoto spoke up: "The idea of using aircraft for defensive purposes is wrong in itself. As Mr. Genda says, naturally they should be used for the offensive."[23]

In November 1934 Genda reported as an instructor to the Yokosuka Air Corps. There he expanded his ideas on the use of fighters and carriers in combat—theories which were to become known as Gendaism. At this time he asserted that a fighter must have two outstanding qualities for superior battle performance—maneuverability and speed, as later exemplified by the famous Japanese Zero.[24]

At Yokosuka Genda met Onishi, then a captain and executive officer of the base. Their ideas in common, their admiration for Yamamoto, and their mutually attracting personalities soon made them warm friends.[25] Significantly enough, during this tour of duty Genda first thought of attacking Pearl Harbor with carrier-based aircraft and discussed the possibility with Onishi.[26] The fact that this venture leaped into Genda's mind more than six years before the attack provides another index to his thinking. Such was Genda's love of flying that he brushed aside any suggestion that he should enter the Naval Staff College, that needle's eye for the camel of ambition. It was Onishi who changed his mind for him: ". . . if a man sticks only to riding in fighter planes as you insist on doing, he can never lead or direct aviation policy. I expect you to construct a highly efficient military system. To do that, even if it may seem silly, you must enter the Naval Staff College and build the background which will later place you in a position to do so."[27]

Some six months after Genda went to the Staff College, he began to entertain grave doubts about Japan's naval establishment. He wrote a report advocating the complete reorganization of the Imperial Navy. War preparations should place major stress on the aerial forces and on bases, carriers, and submarines. A minimum of destroyers and cruisers should serve as auxiliary vessels. All battleships then being built should be converted to carriers, and the rest turned into scrap iron. What is more, all shore installations and factories should be reorganized to make these reforms possible.

A Japanese Billy Mitchell, Genda was intolerant of those who did not share his ideas. In the highly competitive Naval Staff College some thought him mad.[28] Despite his classmates' opinion, he could not have been far out of his mind because he was graduated second in his class. From Tokyo he moved on to the Second Combined Air Corps in China, where he gained valuable combat experience.

In November 1938 Genda went to London as assistant naval attaché. He remained at the post long enough to see World War II explode over Europe, France sink in ignominious defeat, and England battered by the first blows of Göring's Luftwaffe. As the Germans blasted England's cities and countryside but scarcely dented the armor plate of the Home Fleet, Genda began to worry about reaction in Japan. Would not the battleship school of thought gain confidence in its conservative theories by the failure of the Luftwaffe to sweep the seas of England's ships? Later he wrote a report stating that failure to follow through after Dunkirk had cost Hitler the Battle of Britain. Needless to say, following on the heels of the Tripartite Pact, Genda's report did not match the mood of the hour. "Mr. Genda's story makes it sound like Britain is going to win"—which was unthinkable.[29]

In November Genda joined the staff of the First Carrier Division and also received his promotion to commander. During the next several months he preoccupied himself with the use of carriers and their formation in battle—the second aspect of Gendaism. In maneuvers since 1935 the Navy had dispersed its carriers, using them primarily to provide defensive air cover for the other fleet units which delivered the main offensive thrust. The Navy also theorized that scattering the carriers would deny the enemy a mass target. But this meant that the Japanese would have considerable difficulty in gathering and organizing their planes for a simultaneous attack in great force on a given objective.[30]

One evening Genda took time off to go to a movie. There on the screen he saw the U.S. Fleet at sea with four carriers sailing majestically in single column. Probably it was for a demonstration, thought Genda. But the seed had taken root in his subconscious. Several days later, as he jumped off a streetcar, the lightning struck. "Why should we have trouble in gathering planes in the air if we concentrate our carriers?"

Having broken the mental deadlock, Genda sped to the next stage in his thinking: If the Japanese Navy massed "six or more carriers," they could send up their aircraft in "two big attack waves," each having "about 80 bombers and approximately 30 fighter planes for protection." They could also pool their fighter strength, thus providing enough aircraft to protect the carriers and at the same time escort the bombers to their objective and control the air over the target. Genda further believed that the flattops could best defend themselves from block formation.[31] Thus, in Gendaism we see the forerunner of the carrier task force.

Genda despised the defensive psychology implicit in the standard doctrine of the Great All-Out Battle. He considered the pre-1941 naval maneuvers based on that blueprint "exercises in masturbation." He contended that the Japanese Navy should go out to meet the enemy, strike first, and keep on striking until it destroyed him. To this end the Navy should build carriers, destroyers, and submarines—the tools of the offensive—not outdated mountains of steel like the 63,700-ton *Yamato* and *Musashi,* with their 18.2-inch guns, then under construction. "Such ships," he said contemptuously at the time, "are the Chinese Wall of the Japanese Navy."[32] He insisted that for total victory Japan must have air superiority over every enemy base in the Pacific—and that would include Hawaii.[33]

The day following his discussion with Onishi, Genda returned to *Kaga*, his mind bursting with ideas. In his off-duty time he began to develop them and to prepare a draft. The whole design with all its daring, risk, and challenge appealed to his creative imagination and excited him both intellectually and emotionally. Not once through all the problems and trials that lay ahead would Genda lose his enthusiasm for the plan. Although too realistic to minimize the difficulties inherent in such an attack, Genda backed the operation to the hilt and later fought for it with the same tenacity as Yamamoto himself. In one nostalgic postwar discussion Genda said, "The attack against Pearl Harbor was the summit of my career as a Navy officer."[34] Indeed, his work on the Hawaiian venture alone will seal his name in the history of the Imperial Navy. For about two weeks he labored in secret aboard *Kaga*. Then in late February he returned to Kanoya for a second conference with Onishi. The basic elements of Genda's draft were:[35]

1. *The attack must catch the enemy completely by surprise.* This point followed the traditions of Japanese military history. If surprise could not be achieved, Genda thought they might as well drop the whole idea. For if the Americans expected the attack, the task force could sail into a well-laid trap. At best bombing would be ineffective, casualties among the attacking planes and crews exorbitantly high, and the danger of fatal damage to the carrier fleet prohibitive.

2. *The main objective of the attack should be U.S. carriers.* In contrast with Yamamoto's original idea, Genda visualized the primary target as the long-range striking arm of the U.S. Pacific Fleet. If Japan could sink America's carriers and escape with the majority of its flattops undamaged, it would have a double advantage. With U.S. naval air power badly shattered and its own still capable of powerful offensive action, in time Japan could destroy other major units of the enemy fleet. Eventually the Imperial Navy could roam the Pacific with impunity. Of course, Genda wished to sink battleships, too, but carriers held first priority.

3. *Another priority target should be U.S. land-based planes on Oahu.* Destruction of as many enemy aircraft as possible—preferably on the ground at the outset of the strike—would secure control of the air over the target. It would also preclude the enemy's following the Japanese aircraft back to the carriers and bombing the task force.

4. *Every available carrier should participate in the operation.* Instead of Yamamoto's tentative suggestion of one or at the most two carrier divisions, Genda, like Onishi, wanted the greatest application of power—the military principle of mass. He wished to inflict maximum damage to the U.S. Fleet. The stronger the carrier force, the better chance the Japanese would have of a successful attack and the better they would be prepared to face unexpected developments at the scene of action.

5. *The attack should utilize all types of bombing—torpedo, dive, and*

high-level. Genda placed priority on torpedo bombing; like most Japanese airmen, he considered the aerial torpedo their highest-yield weapon. But he doubted that a successful torpedo attack could be launched in the shallow waters of Pearl Harbor. In fact, he considered it "practically out of the question."[36] Genda's draft also reminded Onishi that there might be "antitorpedo obstructions" around U.S. warships. Should hard training and enemy countermeasures prove that torpedo bombing was not feasible, the Japanese should rely on dive bombing. This was his second preference because high-level bombing had not proved entirely satisfactory in China.[37]

6. *Fighter planes should play an active part in the attack.* A strong fighter escort should protect the bombers en route to and from Pearl Harbor. Once over the target, they would sweep the skies clear of enemy planes. During the attack other fighters should hover over the carrier fleet to ward off enemy counterstrokes.

7. *The attack should be made in daylight, preferably in the early morning.* Neither the Imperial Navy nor the Army had precise instruments to assist in air strikes under cover of darkness. So Genda suggested that the air armada should take off from the carriers long before sunrise, timed to reach Pearl Harbor at dawn.

8. *Refueling at sea would be necessary.* Most Japanese warships had a limited radius of action. Therefore, tankers had to accompany the task force. Inasmuch as refueling would constitute one of the most knotty problems of the entire operation, it must be studied thoroughly.

9. *All planning must be done in strict secrecy.* Tight security was imperative to prevent the enemy from even guessing that the Japanese were preparing such a dangerous enterprise. Then, too, as Genda stressed, "The success of this attack depends on the outcome of the initial strike." All the more reason why the operation must be a complete surprise.[38]

Onishi took Genda's draft without comment, and the two officers proceeded to discuss Yamamoto's brainchild for about two hours. "I do not think battleships are necessary for the task force," said Genda. "They would make it too large and increase the risk of discovery. I do not believe we will miss them in case of surface action. We can depend on our superiority in carriers. Besides, the addition of battleships will magnify the fuel problem."[39]

From the moment Genda began preparing his draft, he favored a full-scale execution of the enterprise. "We should follow up this attack on Hawaii with a landing," he said. "If Hawaii is occupied, America will lose her largest and best advance base and, furthermore, our command of future operations will be very good." Such a measure would make the attack decisive; America's fighting forces on Hawaii would have to retire to the West Coast, and Japan would dominate the central Pacific. With the assumption that the aerial blow was successful, 10,000 to 15,000 well-equipped troops should suffice for the job.

Although he was an aggressive officer, Onishi turned down Genda's suggestion: "With our present strength, we are not able to take the offensive in both the eastern and southern areas. First, we must destroy the larger part of the American Fleet."[40] Further, an attack on Hawaii was incompatible with Yamamoto's original project.

But Genda never changed his opinion that Japan's best move would have been destruction of the U.S. Pacific Fleet and its mid-ocean bastion. The Americans commanded the central Pacific and could launch striking forces against Japanese bases or fleet units because they held Oahu with its excellent naval base and its ring of Navy and Army installations. Without taking and holding Oahu, Japan could not hope to win the war. And Genda believed it should do so at the outset of the conflict while surprise and initiative still worked in its favor.

If Genda had had the last word, therefore, the Pearl Harbor attack would have been Japan's major military objective. Whereas Yamamoto conceived the potential strike as a knockdown blow—damage and temporary containment—Genda saw it as a knockout punch—annihilation of the enemy's forces at one decisive stroke. Yamamoto espoused a limited strategy; Genda, the all-out.

When Genda left, Onishi retained his draft. Using it as a basis, he prepared a more extensive report for presentation to Yamamoto. According to Genda, who studied this report carefully several times later in the year, Onishi's document ran about ten pages in length and contained most of the points in Genda's original draft plus certain additions and modifications.

The admiral agreed that carriers should be the number one target, but he added cruisers as a close second, to unbalance the U.S. Pacific Fleet. Onishi originally was inclined to emphasize torpedo bombing, as did Genda, but the adverse reaction of his torpedo expert, Maeda, probably chilled his ardor considerably. He also feared that this technique, requiring a very close run into the targets, would cost Japan heavily in pilots and planes. In contrast with the opinion he expressed to Maeda, Onishi now had second thoughts about dive bombing. The pilots would have to plunge down to a very low level, probably straight into withering antiaircraft and machine-gun fire. He knew that this type of bomb did not carry the momentum to penetrate the deck armor of capital ships. Thus, by the process of elimination, Onishi placed his priority on horizontal bombing. This would permit aircraft to remain at a safer altitude and still inflict severe damage with the velocity a high-level release would give a heavier missile.

Onishi suggested that two merchant ships should precede the task force, one at an angle to port, the other to starboard. These vessels would serve as the eyes of the fleet and act as decoys. He preferred merchantmen to destroyers or submarines because if the enemy sighted the latter anywhere near Hawaii, he would undoubtedly investigate closely and thus discover the attack fleet. To increase security further, the route to Hawaii should be the one providing the best chance for surprise.[41]

An analysis of Yamamoto's letter, Genda's draft, and Onishi's additions establishes one cardinal point: The Japanese were after the U.S. Pacific Fleet and Oahu's air power—not the military installations, the tank farms, the dry docks, the machine shops, or the submarine base. A clear recognition of this fact is essential to understanding the Pearl Harbor story.

To the best of our knowledge, Onishi boarded *Nagato* on about March 10 to hand Yamamoto the expanded draft which represented a compromise between the air admiral's ideas and those of the Navy's most original thinker on air power. As the project matured, many of Onishi's amendments fell by the wayside. The Pearl Harbor blueprint finally adopted and executed bore Genda's hallmark so unmistakably that some of his colleagues referred to it as Genda's plan.

Contrary to legend, the Hawaiian venture was not a supersecret known only to Yamamoto and a few high-ranking admirals. The Japanese nurtured this myth during the war crimes trials in Tokyo. It is true, of course, that the Pearl Harbor plan was highly classified, closely guarded, and one of the outstanding secrets of World War II. But a considerable number of people—not only in the Japanese Navy but in the Army and, to a limited degree, in the government— knew about it before the task force left Japan. The planning of the air strike against Hawaii did not take place in a little watertight compartment within the Imperial Navy. It required the closest coordination of the Navy's main branches—the Naval General Staff, the Navy Ministry, and the Combined Fleet. The Pearl Harbor venture was also closely coordinated with the vast Southern Operation, thus implicating many other officers.

The task force which attacked Pearl Harbor could not have been assembled, outfitted, fueled, manned, and trained without many people's knowing what was going on. The true miracle is that with so many involved, the Japanese kept the secret so well, enabling the attackers to reap the full, if temporary, benefits of two cardinal principles of war—offensive and surprise.

Of course, a secret shared is no longer a secret. Yamamoto had tossed a pebble into the pool of history, and nothing could stop the ever-widening circles from spreading. While Genda worked over his draft, Yamamoto talked with one of Japan's ablest and most experienced sea dogs—Vice Admiral Jisaburo Ozawa, commander of the Third Battleship Division. In his early fifties, Ozawa had spent most of his career at sea, where the brassy sun and invigorating air had kept him healthy, active, and alert. The clear mahogany skin pulled taut over high cheekbones, the deep-set eyes, and tall, dignified presence reminded one of a proud Apache chieftain. So, too, did his massive imperturbability. While not an air admiral in the strict sense of the term, Ozawa had commanded the First Carrier Division in 1940 and remained well versed in the theories of naval aviation.

Ozawa boarded *Nagato* from time to time to chat with his good friend Yamamoto, as he did one day in February 1941. As so often happens between two gifted men in the same line of work, they started to talk shop.

Yamamoto spoke seriously.. "The lesson which impressed me most deeply when I studied the Russo-Japanese War was the fact that our Navy launched a night assault against Port Arthur at the very beginning," he told Ozawa. "I believe this was the most excellent strategical initiative ever envisaged during the war. But," he added a trifle grimly, "it is regrettable that we were not thoroughgoing in carrying out the attack, with the result that we failed to achieve a satisfactory result."

Ozawa was a sophisticated officer, accustomed to catching ideas on the wing. And he knew Yamamoto would not dwell on the past unless it had some application to the present. "In view of the gradually increasing tension between America and Japan, this statement of Admiral Yamamoto's was enough to make me understand what he meant," Ozawa wrote later. "I thought his idea was to attack Pearl Harbor at the beginning of war when it came." If he had any doubts, they were dissolved in April 1941, when Yamamoto actually consulted Ozawa about his Pearl Harbor project.[42]

Yet Japan's overall plan of war kept Yamamoto much too busy to give Pearl Harbor his undivided attention. Operations did not fall within Oikawa's province as navy minister, a post which he left in mid-October 1941. Even Onishi moved from the central focus of the Pearl Harbor picture after April 1941 to help prepare the land-based Eleventh Air Fleet for its attack on the Philippines. Thus, of the early group privy to the operation, only Yamamoto, Fukudome, and Genda worked on it to its final execution. And of this trio, Fukudome never endorsed the scheme. Later he and Onishi ranged themselves with those opposed to the risky undertaking. This left only Yamamoto and Genda of the original group who backed the plan to the limit. Of the two, Genda possessed by far the greater technical knowledge, whereas Yamamoto carried the rank, position, enormous prestige, and driving force.

But his enthusiastic endorsement of this bold design did not necessarily guarantee its adoption. In the first place, the idea had originated with the Combined Fleet, not in the Naval General Staff, the supreme source of planning and strategy in the Japanese Navy. The high brass in Tokyo had its own theories on how a naval war against the United States should be fought, and these did not include an attack on Pearl Harbor. Thus, in early 1941 Yamamoto's project was merely an operational concept of the Commander in Chief of the Combined Fleet, not an accepted war plan. In the second place, in February and March 1941 it was not certain that the United States and Japan would fight. The Japanese government, with the knowledge and consent of the Emperor, would have to make the final decision after long deliberation.

Even if war became inevitable, and the Navy decided to accept the Pearl Harbor project, numerous problems pressed urgently for solution: pilot training, torpedo bombing, refueling at sea, organization of the task force, selection of personnel, types and number of ships, the route of approach, securing intelligence on the enemy, determination of strike day, deception tactics, coordination with the Southern Operation, and a host of others. So a realistic question demanded a realistic answer: In case of war, was Yamamoto's plan feasible?

CHAPTER 4

"NO

CREDENCE

IN THESE

RUMORS"

How secret is secret in a country where years of censorship have trained an inquisitive, alert population in the discreet whisper and the fine art of putting two and two together? And how secret is secret when one's ideas are no longer exclusively one's own? There is a strong possibility that several members of the Operations Section of the Naval General Staff knew about Yamamoto's Pearl Harbor project in January 1941.

Take, for example, Commander Shigeshi Uchida, whose assignment in that section included operations against the United States. Uchida was a most intelligent and level-headed officer, an academy classmate of Genda's who knew him well and held him in high esteem. With his thin face and air of modest self-assurance, he was friendly and approachable. He had spent two years as a language student in the United States, spoke English well, and was thoroughly acquainted with the customs and routines of the U.S. Fleet. Uchida joined the Operations Section in November 1940, worked closely with all its members, and kept a brief diary which buttressed his memory.

"Already at the end of January and the beginning of February [1941] I was writing up my own plans of naval warfare against the United States—plans which included my own ideas concerning the operation against Pearl Harbor," wrote Uchida. And he further testified that several other members of the Operations Section knew about Yamamoto's design at this early date.[1]

Of course, Uchida's planning in the Naval General Staff need not necessarily have been connected with Yamamoto's consultations with Oikawa and Onishi early in the new year. The idea of an attack on Pearl Harbor occasionally came up for discussion, and keeping it up to date would naturally have been part of Uchida's duties as head of the American desk.

In any case, somewhere along the line, the hint of a possible attack on Pearl Harbor came out. This rumor may have had nothing to do with either Yamamoto's scheme or Uchida's work. It may have been merely a coincidental upsurge of a swashbuckling notion which had intrigued Japanese fiction writers for years.

Whatever the source, sometime near the end of January a rumor reached Ricardo Rivera-Schreiber, Peru's veteran minister to Tokyo, one disturbing enough for him to go immediately to his friend Edward S. Crocker, first secretary of the United States Embassy. Rivera-Schreiber said that "he considered it a fantastic rumor, at the same time that it was sufficiently important to justify his passing it on. . . ." Crocker straightway relayed it to Ambassador Grew, whose credulity it strained to the utmost. Nevertheless, he had "full confidence" in Rivera-Schreiber. "I knew him very well, I had known him for years, and I was quite certain that he would not mislead me in anything that he might pass on to me," Grew testified.[2]

So, a mere twenty days after Yamamoto wrote his historic letter to Oikawa, on the advice of his naval attaché Grew composed a dispatch, one of the most remarkable ever to flash between an American ambassador and the State Department. He handed it over to his encoding staff, and at 1800* on January 27 they sent it off:

> My Peruvian Colleague told a member of my staff that he had heard from many sources including a Japanese source that the Japanese military forces planned, in the event of trouble with the United States, to attempt a surprise mass attack on Pearl Harbor using all of their military facilities. He added that although the project seemed fantastic the fact that he had heard it from many sources prompted him to pass on the information.[3]

But what steps did Grew or other American officials in Japan take to track the rumor to its "many sources" and try to determine whether the Japanese actually had such a plan under way? On the basis of information currently available, the answer appears to be "None." Grew did not recall having asked Rivera-Schreiber the sources of the story. "After all," he explained, "sometimes when an official, diplomatic official, received information of that kind or even a rumor report of that kind, it may put him in a rather difficult position to ask him to reveal the source."[4]

The rumor seems to have flared up and died down as suddenly as a lighted match. "I wouldn't say the talk was widespread, but it came from various sources," Grew testified. "I could not now recollect from what sources, because they were not important, but this telegram which I sent on January 27 was based practically entirely on the report which had been brought to me by my Peruvian colleague." He remembered no more talk along these lines after that time.[5] Very likely he believed that the best thing he could do was send the

---

*All times quoted are local on the twenty-four-hour clock system, which is in general military use and which risks no confusion between A.M. and P.M.

incredible item to Washington, where experts in the field could evaluate it in the context of other information available to them. Grew had no effective Intelligence setup for doing his own sleuthing.

Japan kept close tabs on Lieutenant Colonel Harry I. T. Creswell and Lieutenant Commander Henri H. Smith-Hutton, respectively Grew's military and naval attachés. Creswell, though neither brilliant nor imaginative, was an intelligent, hardworking officer. He had been a language student in Japan and liked the country and its people. But Creswell was a marked man.

So was Smith-Hutton, a gifted, dedicated officer with an analytical brain. Like Creswell, he had been a language officer in Japan and developed a fluent command of Japanese. Those who knew him agree that he had an unrivaled knowledge of the Japanese Navy and its officers. [6]

The Japanese Navy not only kept close watch on the two attachés but guarded their installations like a tigress her cubs, in striking contrast with the ease with which their agents found access to information about the American Navy during the same period in both the mainland United States and Hawaii.

The United States made use of agents located in various ports in Japan and on the Asian continent, as well as the consular authorities. [7] Nevertheless, Washington lacked a special spy ring in Japan working independently of its official representatives to provide a steady flow of military information and to ferret out startling rumors like the one of a possible attack on Pearl Harbor. Certainly that story indicates exceptionally quick work even for Dame Rumor, a lady who seldom tarries on the way. For the ink had barely dried on Yamamoto's letter to Oikawa and Yamamoto had scarcely discussed his bold scheme with Onishi aboard *Nagato* when Grew sent the news of this astounding venture straight to the United States government.

In Washington the ambassador's communication wound through the State Department, then over to the Navy Department. In neither did the message stir much interest beyond a mild astonishment that an ambassador of Grew's caliber could have taken such nonsense seriously. However, the Chief of Naval Operations' daily staff conference decided to send it to the Commander in Chief of the U.S. Pacific Fleet in Hawaii. Captain Jules James, acting director of Naval Intelligence, received this assignment and passed it on to Commander Arthur H. McCollum, chief of the Far Eastern Section. [8]

Born in 1898 in Nagasaki, Japan, of Southern Baptist missionary parents, McCollum was another expert on Japanese affairs. From 1928 to 1930 he was assistant naval attaché in Tokyo. He came to know Emperor Hirohito when the latter was prince regent, as well as his brother Prince Takamatsu and Admirals Nomura and Yamamoto and other naval officers.

The early and mid-thirties found McCollum in Washington, where he headed the Far Eastern Section of the Office of Naval Intelligence (ONI) from 1933 to 1935. Then followed special intelligence duties on the West Coast and a tour as fleet intelligence officer (1936–1938). In October 1939 McCollum returned to Washington once more as head of the Far Eastern Section of ONI. Bright, confident, and dynamic, he inspired the respect and trust of his colleagues and superiors. He had two officers under him—specialists in Japanese and Chinese affairs respectively—and also four civilians versed in the Oriental field.[9]

Grew's message did not alarm McCollum because the idea of a Japanese attack on Pearl Harbor was nothing new to him.[10] For almost a decade the defense of Hawaii had been virtually a cliché of American naval war games. In particular the record of the joint Army-Navy maneuvers of January 1933 reads like a prophecy, except that the objective of the attacking force was to destroy the naval base and its supporting installations, not the Fleet, which was not yet stationed at Pearl Harbor. And the exercise was based upon foreknowledge of the enemy's approach, hence provided no answer to how the defenders would react if the Japanese took them by surprise.[11]

What is more, McCollum knew that for years Japanese writers of fact and fiction had intrigued their readers with stories of just such an assault. He had read his first such paperback in 1924.[12] How could he imagine that Yamamoto had plucked the concept from the stony field of popular fiction and transplanted it into the fertile soil of fact, where he could nurture it to full fruition?

On the basis in part of his personal background and knowledge of Japan, together with the most recent information available to him in ONI, McCollum prepared a message on January 31 for his chief's signature. Captain James signed it "by direction"—meaning with the approval of the Chief of Naval Operations (CNO). On February 1 this went to Admiral Husband E. Kimmel, the newly assigned Commander in Chief of the U.S. Fleet. The message paraphrased Grew's telegram, then drew its teeth by adding a second paragraph: "The Division of Naval Intelligence places no credence in these rumors. Furthermore, based on known data regarding the present disposition and employment of Japanese naval and army forces, no move against Pearl Harbor appears imminent or planned for in the forseeable [*sic*] future."[13]

By that term McCollum meant a projection of no more than a month. Within those limits his evaluation was correct. For Yamamoto's plan would require almost nine months before the Naval General Staff accepted it as an integral part of Japan's overall war strategy. Another reason why McCollum placed a low evaluation on the tip-off was that Grew's message did not indicate any time limit within which the rumored attack might take place.[14] But this was asking too much of any ambassador; it would have been a major coup for the best of undercover agents.

ONI did not stand alone. Brigadier General Sherman Miles, assistant chief of staff for Intelligence (G-2), testified that the rumor received no more credence in the Army than it did in the Navy. In 1941 Miles was fifty-four years old, a tall, fine-looking man of wide military experience. None of it, however, had been in the Far East. He had served as G-3 of the Hawaiian Department from April 1929 to May 1932, during which time he supervised war plans and defense projects, prepared maneuvers and exercises of all kinds. He also served four years as head of the Plans and Projects Section of the War Plans Division in Washington, where he performed the same type of work for the three overseas departments—the Philippines, Panama, and Hawaii.[15] Thus, Miles had an excellent overall view of the scope of military thinking in both Washington and Oahu.

Asked why his office had discounted Grew's warning, Miles replied at some length:

> One, because it was inconceivable that any source in the know would have communicated that to the Latin-American Ambassador, I believe the Peruvian; and, second, for a great many years we had known that a Japanese surprise attack on Pearl Harbor was always possible. It was inherent as a possibility in any war in which we became involved with Japan.
>
> . . . the great fortress of Oahu . . . was built solely for one purpose, the defense of that naval base against one sole enemy, Japan, the only enemy in the world that could put on a real attack against that naval base. . . .

Further asked why he had brushed aside Grew's message when it seemed to tie in with Pearl Harbor as "a likely point of attack and that the Japanese were likely to use surprise," Miles answered, "I discounted that report . . . as being a bona fide piece of information that he got from a responsible Japanese source. I did not at any time discount the possibility of a Japanese surprise attack on Hawaii."[16]

Moreover, Captain Roscoe E. "Pinky" Schuirmann, one of whose duties was liaison with the State Department, testified that so far as he knew, the Navy did not discuss the matter with State because "the report was given a low evaluation . . . and appeared to be hearsay information which was not substantiated. . . ."[17]

But however incredible the Navy thought Grew's message, McCollum's division did some detective work and about a month later determined that Rivera-Schreiber's scoop had originated with his Japanese cook on about December 18, 1940—very near the time that Yamamoto himself established as the date he firmed up his decision. Postwar information indicated the source may have been the minister's Japanese translator-secretary.[18]

Whatever the origin of the rumor, this incident leaves a number of questions hanging fire. Miles testified that by far the most important source of information on the Japanese was the American Embassy in Tokyo.* "We had a very excellent Ambassador who had been there a number of years with a staff that had been there a good deal longer than that."[19] Yet, according to McCollum, Washington simply wondered why so experienced an ambassador should fall for such a tale.

Most disturbing of all is the fact that active probing into the incident seems to have stopped when Rivera-Schreiber's cook came into view as the primary source. Such menials, moving unnoticed through a great city, their ears open to

---

*Actually Magic—the U.S. system of breaking the Japanese diplomatic code, which we will discuss later—was the prime source of information about Japan. At the time Miles testified, Magic was still top secret, and he could not refer to it.

the voice of the people, can be excellent intelligence sources, and the investigator ignores them at his peril.

No doubt some American naval officers had too high an opinion of the good sense of their Japanese opposites to credit them with attempting such a gamble. "I did not think that such an attack would be made," Commander Vincent Murphy, Kimmel's assistant war plans officer, testified.

> I thought it would be utterly stupid for the Japanese to attack the United States at Pearl Harbor. . . . We could not have materially affected their control of the waters they wanted to control, whether or not the battleships were sunk at Pearl Harbor. In other words, I did not believe we could move the United States Fleet to the Western Pacific . . . until such time as the Pacific Fleet was materially reinforced.[20]

The Army took much the same attitude. Miles outlined it clearly:

> In estimating the situation . . . there are two principles that should be followed: One is never to lose sight of or ignore anything that the enemy may do which is within its capabilities whether you think it wise for him to do that or not.
>
> The second is to concede to your enemy the highest form of good sense and good judgment.
>
> . . . We did grant the Japanese the best of good sense. We did very much question whether they would attack Hawaii, because such an attack must result from two separate decisions on the part of the Japanese, one to make war against the United States, which we thought at that time in the long run would be suicidal . . . and, two, to attack a great fortress and fleet, risking certain ships that he could not replace, and knowing that the success in that attack must rest very largely on that surprise being successful; in other words, finding that fortress and that fleet unprepared to meet the attack.[21]

Actually, Miles gave a very fair outline of the arguments Yamamoto's opponents put forth against the scheme. But the U.S. Army and Navy overlooked Yamamoto's will, which, like a mountain torrent, tumbled everything out of its way. They also—with a few exceptions—failed to consider the possibility of an attack aimed solely at the U.S. Pacific Fleet.

A further very significant link in the Pearl Harbor chain is the general underestimation of Japan by the United States in the years before World War II. Americans assured one another that Japan was virtually bankrupt, short of raw materials, and hopelessly bogged down in China. It lagged a hundred years behind the times, and in case of a major conflict, its wheel-barrow economy would shatter like a teacup hurled against a brick wall.

What is more, Americans held the average Japanese in utter contempt. Behold him as seen through myopic American eyes in that age of innocence—a funny little creature with buck teeth, strutting arrogantly over the map of Asia, a silly grin on his inscrutable face, with horn-rimmed glasses covering slanted slits of eyes. He bows so deeply his chin almost touches his knees. "So solly, please!" This comic figure was a slow-brained, inefficient, literate but unthinking slave to routine, an unimaginative copycat who could never adjust to new situations. We took insidious delight in poking fun at the Japanese and their country in cartoons, magazines, and newspapers.

"The Japanese are not going to risk a fight with a first-class nation. They are unprepared to do so and no one knows that better than they do," declared Congressman Charles I. Faddis of Pennsylvania on February 19, 1941. ". . . They will not dare to get into a position where they must face the American Navy in open battle. Their Navy is not strong enough and their homeland is too vulnerable."[22]

Such was the general atmosphere in the United States when Grew's message arrived in Washington—an atmosphere that was to exist throughout 1941, even though a certain awareness of danger simultaneously permeated the highest civilian and military echelons in the U.S. government. Yet another of the strange ironies in the Pearl Harbor story is that during this period Yamamoto was indeed thinking of attacking the U.S. Pacific Fleet at Hawaii. In fact, he may well have talked with Onishi aboard *Nagato* on the very day that Grew dispatched his message to Washington. The intriguing interplay between the Japanese and American military scenes in early 1941 is more than enough to make one believe in telepathy.

CHAPTER 5

"YOU HURT

THE PRESIDENT'S

FEELINGS"

Hawaii greeted the new year, 1941, with a song in its heart and a prayer for peace on its lips. No doubt Admiral James O. Richardson, Commander in Chief of the United States Fleet, was pleased to see 1940 disappear into history. In many ways it had been a frustrating, unsatisfactory year for him. He had assumed command of the Fleet on January 6, 1940. In the early spring Navy Headquarters had dispatched him to Hawaii for maneuvers. His ships stood into Lahaina Roads off Maui on April 10. Before that, a small unit at Pearl Harbor composed of a carrier, heavy cruisers, and destroyers, called the Hawaiian Detachment, had been the only force of consequence in the area.

The exercises over, Richardson expected to take his armada (minus the Hawaiian Detachment) back to its permanent base at San Pedro, California, on May 9. Instead, the Navy Department kept him and his fleet in Hawaiian waters because, in the words of Chief of Naval Operations Harold R. Stark, "of the deterrent effect which it is thought your presence may have on the Japs going into the East Indies." If the Japanese did invade that territory, what would the United States do about it? "My answer to that is, I don't know, and I think there is nobody on God's green earth who can tell you," Stark admitted.[1]

Shortly after the Fleet, as Richardson said, "gradually drifted into staying" in Hawaii,[2] the War Department reached the rather peculiar conclusion that the "recent Japanese-Russian agreement to compose their differences . . . was arrived at and so timed as to permit Japan" to attack Oahu, "following the departure of the U.S. Fleet from Hawaii." So Washington sent to Major General Charles D. Herron, commanding general of the Hawaiian Department, a message reading in part, "Immediately alert complete defensive organization to deal with possible trans-Pacific raid. . . . Maintain alert until further orders. . . ."[3]

37

Herron, who was to become a lieutenant general on July 31, 1940, believed in only one kind of alert—total. This he established at once and "within the hour"[4] conferred with his opposite number, Rear Admiral Claude C. Bloch, commandant of the Fourteenth Naval District, and Vice Admiral Adolphus Andrews, commander of the Hawaiian Detachment. Andrews was the senior naval officer at Pearl Harbor, Richardson being located at Lahaina. As a result of their conference, they decided that the Navy would provide "morning and dusk reconnaissance patrols. . . ."[5]

Richardson knew little about this exercise. The CNO had not alerted his officers in Hawaii because he was "not impressed . . . with any particular gravity at that time" and looked upon the alert "largely as an Army affair."[6]

Herron kept his forces on their toes throughout the summer; then the flap faded out as vaguely as it had begun.[7] But it left its ghost behind to haunt the future. No ambiguity had clouded the War Department order, and Herron immediately took military action suited to the directive. The alert revealed a healthy state of cooperation between the Hawaiian Department and the Fourteenth Naval District. Nonetheless, in ordering this alert, the War Department erroneously assumed that the target for attack would be the shore installations and the islands themselves—not the ships of the Fleet. For this reason some Army and Navy planners believed that the Japanese would not move against Hawaii unless the Fleet were at sea. Yamamoto was far too clever to try anything of the kind. Why break the scabbard unless the sword lay sheathed within it?

Since becoming CinCUS, Richardson had studiously avoided any fleet exercises which might be interpreted as offensive action against Japan. A strong believer in air patrols, he had kept his eagles soaring, but he never ordered a single simulated carrier attack on Pearl Harbor. "Although I felt there was absolutely no danger at that time of an attack by the Japanese fleet," he later testified, "I feared that there was, at any time, a possibility that some fanatical, ill-advised officer in command of a submarine or a ship might attack."[8]

So Richardson did not object to retaining the Fleet in Hawaii because he feared the Japanese would come swooping in on him. He had other reasons, almost entirely logistical. Because of such facts, and because he believed that his ships "could be better prepared for war on a normal basis on the west coast," Richardson earnestly desired to pull them back to the mainland.[9]

So in July 1940 he traveled to Washington, among other reasons to urge the return of the Fleet to the West Coast. On July 8 he conferred with the President. He also talked with Dr. Stanley D. Hornbeck, adviser on political relations to the secretary of state. As their talk progressed, the admiral became convinced that "Dr. Hornbeck was exercising a greater influence over the disposition of the fleet than I was." And he reflected: ". . . he is the strong man on the Far East and the cause of our staying in Hawaii where he will hold us as long as he can."[10]

Richardson took home with him a very definite idea that the Fleet was being "retained in the Hawaiian area solely to support diplomatic representations and as a deterrent to Japanese aggressive action," but at the same time the United States had "no intention of embarking on actual hostilities against Japan."[11] He also left the capital "with the distinct impression that there was an opinion in Washington that Japan could be bluffed."[12]

But Japan could not be bluffed. It considered the colonial territories of France, Britain, and the Netherlands its legitimate area of expansion. If Japan could seize and hold this vast resource area in Southeast Asia, the political and strategic weights and balances in the Orient would shift in its favor. The whole El Dorado of the South might well fall into Japan's lap like a ripe plum except for that black-hat villain Uncle Sam, hanging over the orchard gate with a shotgun—his powerful fleet at Hawaii. Regardless of how strong Richardson's position was, nothing and no one could make Japan change the plotted course of its national policy by one degree.

In Richardson's opinion his command was not yet ready for war, and he believed that the Japanese knew too much about the Fleet to regard it as a deterrent. This view he expressed at a conference with Roosevelt in the White House on October 8, 1940. But the President answered in effect, "Despite what you believe, I know that the presence of the fleet in the Hawaiian area, has had, and is now having, a restraining influence on the actions of Japan." The admiral persisted doggedly: "Mr. Roosevelt, I still do not believe it, and I know that our fleet is disadvantageously disposed for preparing for or initiating war operations."[13]

Direct contradiction of the President would have been controversial enough, but Richardson "very deliberately" dropped this bombshell on his Commander in Chief: "Mr. President, I feel that I must tell you that the senior officers of the Navy do not have the trust and confidence in the civilian leadership of this country that is essential for a successful prosecution of a war in the Pacific." Although obviously shocked, Roosevelt answered mildly enough.[14] Nevertheless, the admiral had pushed his luck far. As long as he confined himself strictly to naval factors, he stood on firm ground. But in debating the statesmanship involved, he invaded presidential territory and came perilously near to violating one of the most rigid of American taboos—interference in national policy making on the part of an officer of the armed forces.

On October 10 Richardson met with Secretary of the Navy Frank Knox, Stark, and other officers. Knox told them that Roosevelt, worried over possible Japanese reaction when Britain reopened the Burma Road on October 17, was thinking about cutting off Japanese trade with the Americas. To this end he suggested establishment of "a patrol of light ships in two lines extending from Hawaii westward to the Philippines, and from Samoa toward the Dutch East Indies." Amazed at the proposal, Richardson protested vigorously that the Fleet was not prepared "to put such a plan into effect, nor for the war which would certainly result from such a course of action, and that we would certainly lose many of the ships."

After further discussion Knox, apparently "displeased at the general reaction" and that of Richardson in particular, said somewhat testily, "I am not a strategist; if you don't like the President's plan, draw up one of your own to accomplish the purpose." Stark and Richardson with their respective war plans officers promptly did so. But Stark, with a weather eye on the Atlantic, decided to hold off the final word until he could talk it over with Roosevelt.[15]

At Bremerton, Washington, on October 22, Richardson wrote an official memorandum to Stark in which he ruthlessly demolished the current war plans against Japan: O-1 Plan (Orange), WPUSF 44, and WPUSF 45 (War Plans United States Fleet). He added that he found himself in what might "suddenly become a critical situation, without an applicable directive. . . ." Unequivocally he announced, "The Commander-in-Chief must be better informed than he is now as to the Department's plans and intentions if he is to perform his full duty."[16] This matter of keeping the CinCUS informed would become even more crucial in the critical year 1941.

Richardson still expressed no concern over the Fleet's safety while in Pearl Harbor, but others were not so sure. The British naval air attack on the Italian fleet at Taranto in southern Italy on November 12 had demonstrated the vulnerability of ships in an exposed anchorage. In less than an hour the British rendered half the Italian battle fleet *hors de combat* for about six months and shifted the balance of naval power in the Mediterranean.[17]

This incident conjured up disturbing pictures in Stark's mind. Even before the spectacular raid, he had shown increasing uneasiness over Pearl Harbor.[18] Now he turned over his notes on "a better defense of the fleet at Hawaii" to his new chief of war plans, Captain Richmond Kelly Turner, a brilliant but corrosive man of enormous ego and ambition who was to become one of Stark's chief advisers. In January 1941 the President was to give Turner a spot promotion to rear admiral so that he might carry sufficient clout in the American-British-Canadian (ABC) planning conversations.[19]

From Turner's labors emerged a letter for Stark's signature which the CNO dispatched on November 22. "By far the most profitable object of a sudden attack in Hawaiian waters would be the Fleet units based in that area," he wrote. And he inquired if it might not be desirable "to place torpedo nets within the harbor itself. . . ."[20]

But Richardson brushed aside these well-founded fears. He thought torpedo nets within the harbor "neither necessary nor practicable. The area is too restricted and ships, at present, are not moored within torpedo range of the entrance."[21] Obviously Richardson thought of torpedoes as being launched from ships or submarines, not from aircraft. His postwar testimony confirms this: "I had not considered that it was likely that the fleet would be attacked by a carrier raid. . . ."[22]

In the meantime, Stark had been at work upon a project of even greater scope and importance. This culminated in a memorandum for Knox, later famous as Plan Dog, which was to reorient U.S. planning and set the course of strategy in World War II. His main thesis was this: ". . . if Britain wins decisively against Germany we could win everywhere; but if she loses *everywhere*, we might possibly not *win anywhere* [Stark's italics]." The CNO faced the sensitive question of direct American participation in the war:

(D) Shall we direct our effort toward eventual strong offensive in the Atlantic as an ally of the British, and a defensive in the Pacific? Any strength that we might send to the Far East would, by just so much, reduce the force of our blows against Germany and Italy. About the least that we would do for an ally would be to send strong naval light forces and aircraft to Great Britain and the Mediterranean. Probably we could not stop with a purely naval effort. . . . [23]

Plan Dog was probably Stark's most significant contribution as CNO and the high-water mark of a long career. By 1940, his fifty-ninth year, Stark's hair had turned almost white, but his light blue eyes behind rimless glasses remained steady and clear, his skin flushed with health. He answered to the improbable nickname of Betty, which dated from plebe days at Annapolis when upper classmen would waylay the future CNO and make him declaim the words of Revolutionary hero John Stark: "We win today or Betty Stark will be a widow."[24]* Stark lacked the ruthlessness of decision required of a hell-for-leather combat commander and tended to hedge too much, yet he had outstanding qualities as a staff officer. He was a precise, thorough thinker who sometimes worked until two or three in the morning—Sundays and holidays included.

His career presents almost a textbook example of a naval officer on his way to the top: duty with destroyers, cruisers, battleships, and chief of the powerful Bureau of Ordnance. Stark was heading the Cruiser Division of the Battle Force when Roosevelt selected him as CNO over the heads of more than fifty of his seniors. He took office on August 1, 1939.

A close professional associate of many years sized him up like this: "Stark was the right man in the right place at the right time to get a lot of things done that needed doing."[25] But a Cabinet member who worked closely with Stark thought the admiral "a timid and ineffective man to be in the post he holds" and "the weakest one of all" the President's advisers.[26]

Thus, from his vantage point atop the naval hierarchy Stark could figuratively see both oceans at once and had to consider the problems of the Pacific in a global context. He, too, could ring out the old year on no note of good cheer. On December 30, 1940, Bloch submitted a memorandum to the CNO through Richardson on the vital subject "Situation Concerning the Security of the Fleet and the Present Ability of the Local Defense Forces to Meet Surprise Attacks." On the scores of thorough research and clear presentation, Stark had no cause for complaint about Bloch's effort, but the contents could well give rise to uneasy speculation.

Aircraft attacking the base at Pearl Harbor will undoubtedly be brought by carriers. Therefore, there are two ways of repelling attack. First, by locating and destroying the carrier prior to launching planes. Second, by driving off attacking bombers with anti-aircraft guns and fighters. The Navy component of the local defense forces has no planes for distant reconnaissance with which to locate enemy carriers and the only planes belonging to the local defense

---

*Some history books call Mrs. Stark Molly.

forces to attack carriers when located would be the Army bombers. The Army
has in the Hawaiian area fifty-nine B-18 bombers . . . neither numbers nor
types are satisfactory for the purpose intended. . . . For distant reconnaissance, requisition would have to be made on the forces afloat for such as could
be spared by the Fleet.

Bloch then turned to his second alternative: "To drive off bombing planes after
they have been launched will require both fighting planes and anti-aircraft
guns. The Army has in the Hawaiian area thirty-six pursuit planes, all of which
are classified as obsolete. . . ."[27]

What is more, Bloch did not anticipate any improvement in the future:
"The Army is charged with the protection of the Pearl Harbor base by
anti-aircraft guns. There are in Hawaii twenty-six 3-inch guns and forty-four
mobile 3-in. guns. There are projected twenty-four more, to be delivered in
1941. . . . The Army plans to place the greater part of the 3-inch guns around
Pearl Harbor. . . ."

Bloch pointed out that in addition, "the Army has planned an aircraft
warning service which will consist of eight Radar stations. Three of these
stations are fixed and five are mobile. When completed at an indefinite time in
the future, this warning net should be adequate."[28] But they would be no help if
the Japanese swarmed down on Oahu within the next few months.

Bloch dealt next with the naval situation. "The ideal defense against
submarines would be conducted by patrol vessels and aircraft working in
conjunction. The district has no aircraft for this purpose. . . ." He cited three
destroyers equipped with listening gear recently assigned to him, and he went
on: "A large number of patrol vessels will be required for anti-submarine work
in the vicinity of Oahu and the other islands. At present, the district has
none. . . . No anti-submarine nets are planned, nor are any considered
desirable. Anti-torpedo nets are projected for the entrances of Honolulu and
Pearl Harbor. They will probably be delivered about 1 March 1941. . . ."

After a few comments about antimine defense, Bloch moved to the
ever-present subject of sabotage. He evaluated the two oil-tank farms on Oahu
as "reasonably secure" and "fairly secure" respectively.[29] Secure against
sabotage, yes, but a most inviting target for air attacks.

Bloch went into great detail about the base pass system and related
measures which the Fourteenth Naval District had instituted to protect Pearl
Harbor from unauthorized people. He concluded by suggesting that the CNO
consult the War Department to find out the Army's plans. However, he himself
did not want to become involved. "It is considered highly undesirable from my
point of view that the War Department should in any way come to believe that
there is a lack of agreement between the Army authorities and Navy authorities
here, or that the officials of the Fourteenth Naval District are pressing the Navy
Department to do something in regard to Army matters."[30] This paragraph
contains ominous overtones. Where true friendship and cooperation existed,
such overreaction would have been unnecessary.

Richardson endorsed this memorandum to Stark on January 7. In general, he concurred with Bloch; indeed, the basic memorandum had been the result of a meeting between the two admirals and Herron. But Richardson's endorsement softened the impact of Bloch's alarming report, which had revealed that Oahu was in no position to defend either itself or the Fleet.

As usual, "J.O." thought in terms of here and now and of what effect the current situation would have on his ships and men. "As neither the increased antiaircraft batteries nor the augmented pursuit squadrons will be available for an extended period the defense of Fleet units within Pearl Harbor will have to be augmented by that portion of the Fleet which may be in Pearl Harbor in the event of attack by hostile aircraft. . . ." In short, the Fleet would have to protect itself. Richardson continued: "The improbability of such an attack under present conditions does not, in the opinion of the Commander-in-Chief, warrant interrupting entirely the training required by Fleet Air Units which would have to be largely curtailed if constant readiness of a fighter squadron were required."[31] He could not bring himself to accept the idea of Japanese bombers and fighters actually attacking his ships or their base. He still had no particular use for antitorpedo measures:

> There does not appear to be any practicable way of placing torpedo baffles or nets within the harbor to protect the ships moored therein against torpedo plane attack without greatly limiting the activities within the harbor. . . . Inasmuch as Pearl Harbor is the only operating base available to the Fleet in this area any passive defense measures that will further restrict the use of the base as such should be avoided. Considering this and the improbability of such an attack under present conditions and the unlikelihood of an enemy being able to advance carriers sufficiently near in wartime in the face of active Fleet operations, it is not considered necessary to lay such nets.[32]

A number of preconceived notions clung like barnacles to "J.O.'s" mind. He forgot that a bit of inconvenience and restriction in Pearl Harbor would be a cheap price to pay when the alternative might be total inability to use the base. He did not consider torpedo baffles around his ships necessary. Yet, as we shall see, during their planning of the attack the Japanese fretted incessantly over the probable presence of nets and made special efforts to find out whether the U.S. Navy would install them. They could not conceive that the Americans should have neglected this obvious precaution—one that could have saved the United States considerable damage to capital ships, not to mention casualties.

Richardson was indulging in the exceedingly tricky game of trying to outguess the Japanese. He asked himself, in effect, Will they attack? rather than, Can they attack? And he continued to assume, despite the evidence of recent history, that in the unlikely event that the Japanese tried to strike Hawaii, they would do so after a declaration of war, which would give him time to deploy his ships.

Nevertheless, Richardson urgently recommended that Washington beef up the Fourteenth Naval District to provide local defense forces "sufficient for full protection" and "independent of the presence or absence of ships of the U.S. Fleet."[33] Thus, despite the sharpness of Stark and his advisors in spotting after Taranto that the prime objective in Hawaii would be the ships, Richardson seemed less preoccupied with protecting them than with protecting Hawaii, as evidenced by his concern for adequate local forces independent of the Fleet.

It is somewhat surprising that Richardson did not seize upon this sudden anxiety in Washington over the safety of his ships in Pearl Harbor and use it as another reason to return to San Pedro. He may have disdained to make use of an argument in which he did not believe, or he may have recognized that the subject was no longer open to discussion.

By all normal procedures Richardson should have remained as CinCUS for at least another full year. In fact, before he left Washington in October, Stark and Rear Admiral Chester W. Nimitz, chief of the Bureau of Navigation (BuNav), which at the time handled personnel matters, informed him that they believed he would remain in command until he had completed two years' service in that post.[34] Consequently, "J.O." and some of his officers were rocked back on their heels when at 1130 on Sunday, January 5, he received orders relieving him of command. "What happened?" asked Captain William Ward "Poco" Smith, skipper of the cruiser *Brooklyn.* "I don't know," replied Richardson flatly.[35] Yet some of Richardson's staff were not too surprised. Dundas P. Tucker, his radio officer, had noted that the admiral appeared worried and frustrated after his return from Washington and obviously had differed seriously with Roosevelt. "We all felt at the time that Richardson was not long for the job," he recalled.[36]

"J.O.'s" flag secretary, George C. Dyer, personally handed the admiral the dispatch ordering his relief and saw that it both surprised and shocked Richardson.[37] Yet he must have known that he could scarcely expect to cross swords with the President without some resulting sparks, and the tone of Stark's correspondence had cooled appreciably since that eventful October visit to the White House. It was in the cards that the Navy Department should have been shopping for a new Commander in Chief.

The same Sunday found Rear Admiral Husband E. Kimmel, commander of Cruisers, Battle Force, tramping around the local golf course with his chief of staff, Captain Walter DeLany. When the two officers returned to the dock, a member of Kimmel's staff told him that he was to report to the Fleet flagship; a communication which he should read immediately had just come in. Kimmel and DeLany hurried to the officers' landing at the navy yard and scrambled into the small boat which plied between the flagship and the dock. Aboard *Pennsylvania,* Kimmel read the dispatch which informed him that he would become Commander in Chief of the United States Fleet, effective on or about February 1. He was too realistic not to know that his superiors thought well of him; still the action "came as a complete surprise. . . ." In fact, he looked so stricken that for a moment DeLany thought his chief was going to faint.[38]

Kimmel was exceedingly sensitive and easily hurt, and his first thought was for his old friend. "Hell, there was nothing wrong with Richardson," he said later. "He was an excellent officer, absolutely topflight."[39] In agitation

Kimmel hastened to Richardson's quarters to assure the CinCUS that he saw no justification for his relief, that he knew nothing about it and had made no effort whatsoever to take over his job.[40]

Back in Washington Turner was thoroughly digesting the Bloch memorandum with Richardson's endorsement. On the basis of material in the Navy and War departments, as well as some of his own, he drafted a letter to Secretary of War Henry L. Stimson for Knox's signature "because it was an official communication of the greatest importance to the War Department. . . ." Stark approved the document and forwarded it to Knox, who signed and dispatched it dated January 24. Copies to CinCPAC and the Fourteenth Naval District reached Pearl Harbor on February 5.[41] The letter proved to be one of the most historic Knox ever signed. It read in part:

> The security of the U.S. Pacific Fleet while in Pearl Harbor, and of the Pearl Harbor Naval Base itself, has been under renewed study by the Navy Department and forces afloat for the past several weeks. This reexamination has been, in part, prompted by the increased gravity of the situation with respect to Japan, and by reports from abroad of successful bombing and torpedo plane attacks on ships while in bases. If war eventuates with Japan, it is believed easily possible that hostilities would be initiated by a surprise attack upon the Fleet or the Naval Base at Pearl Harbor.
>
> In my opinion, the inherent possibilities of a major disaster to the fleet or naval base warrant taking every step, as rapidly as can be done, that will increase the joint readiness of the Army and Navy to withstand a raid of the character mentioned above.

It listed the dangers "in their order of importance and probability," of which "Air bombing attack" and "Air torpedo plane attack" ranked first and second respectively. The letter added, "Both types of air attack are possible. They may be carried out successively, simultaneously, or in combination with any of the other operations enumerated."[42]

Knox then listed proposed countermeasures, the first of which was "Location and engagement of enemy carriers and supporting vessels before air attack can be launched." He pointed out that these measures were "largely functions of the Fleet but, quite possibly, might not be carried out in case of an air attack initiated without warning prior to a declaration of war."[43]

It is fascinating to note the gradual buildup of the eventual design. First, and for a long time, American thinking and maneuvers were predicated entirely in terms of a possible Japanese strike on Hawaii. Second, after the object lesson of Taranto, came the awareness in Washington that the prime target of such an attack would be the ships in harbor. Thirdly, Richardson's endorsement of January 7 conceded the possibility—albeit unlikely—of an aerial strike at Pearl Harbor if Japan and the United States went to war. Now, as the fourth step, Knox's prophetic letter pinpointed a carrier-borne bombing and/or torpedo force ripping into the Fleet "without warning prior to a declaration of war." Turner and his War Plans Division certainly did a magnificent job of forecasting.

Knox had two suggestions to make for Stimson's consideration, in addition to those Bloch had outlined: barrage balloons and smoke screens. Then he summed up his proposals:

(1) That the Army assign the highest priority to the increase of pursuit aircraft and anti-aircraft artillery, and the establishment of an air warning net in Hawaii.

(2) That the Army gives [sic] consideration to the question of balloon barrages, the employment of smoke, and other special devices for improving the defense of Pearl Harbor.

(3) That local joint plans be drawn for the effective coordination of naval and military aircraft operations, and ship and shore anti-aircraft gun fire, against surprise aircraft raids.

(4) That the Army and Navy forces in Oahu agree on appropriate degrees of joint readiness for immediate action in defense against surprise aircraft raids against Pearl Harbor.

(5) That joint exercises, designed to prepare Army and Navy forces in Oahu for defense against surprise aircraft raids, be held at least once weekly so long as the present uncertainty continues to exist.

He ended by assuring Stimson, "Your concurrence in these proposals and the rapid implementing of the measures to be taken by the Army, which are of the highest importance to the security of the Fleet, will be met with the closest cooperation on the part of the Navy Department."[44]

The next day, obviously with no knowledge of Knox's letter to Stimson of the twenty-fourth, Richardson and Kimmel collaborated on a memorandum for Richardson to send to Stark in connection with Plan Dog, which had emphasized that the United States' major offensive effort would be in the Atlantic. Washington had made its choice not because the government downgraded the Pacific or because of defense-mindedness, but out of hard necessity. The United States could not give the same priority, the same effort, to both seas at once. Roosevelt's two-ocean navy was still in the blueprint stage.

Richardson outlined the Fleet's assumptions of the situation for Plan Dog:

(a) The United States is at war with Germany and Italy.

(b) War with Japan is imminent.

(c) Units of the Pacific Fleet may be detached to the Atlantic on short notice. . . .

(e) Japan may attack without warning, and these attacks may take any form—even to attacks by Japanese ships flying German or Italian flags or by submarines. . . .

(f) Japanese attacks may be expected against shipping, outlying possessions or naval units. Surprise raids on Pearl Harbor, or attempts to block the channel, are possible.

(g) Local sabotage is possible.

Under these assumptions, the Fleet would take on certain tasks, among them "full security measures for the protection of Fleet units, at sea or in port."[45] It would also assist in local defense of the naval district until suitable vessels became available to Bloch. The two admirals pointed out:

> Ideally, a Fleet Base should afford refuge and rest for personnel as well as opportunity for maintenance and upkeep of material installation. When Fleet planes, Fleet guns and Fleet personnel are required to be constantly ready for defense of its own base, the wear and tear on both men and material cannot but result in impaired readiness for active operations at sea.[46]

They recommended immediate correction of existing deficiencies, to "take priority over the needs of continental districts, the training program, and material aid to Great Britain."[47]

Such was the basic thinking in American naval circles concerning a possible Japanese attack against Pearl Harbor at the very time when Yamamoto was beginning to develop his adventurous project. How closely interwoven were the American and Japanese threads of the Pearl Harbor fabric! On January 7, Japanese time—a day or so before Richardson endorsed Bloch's estimate —Yamamoto confided his daring plan in writing to Navy Minister Oikawa. Knox's letter of January 24 probably followed closely Yamamoto's letter about Pearl Harbor to Onishi. The Knox document preceded Yamamoto's secret conference with Onishi aboard *Nagato* by approximately three days. Furthermore, it antedated Grew's classic warning to the State Department by about the same period.

Yet a strange ambivalence was at work. Stark's concern over the Fleet as a result of the Taranto raid had initiated a chain of awareness which on January 24 culminated in Knox's letter to Stimson. But eight days later the CNO dispatch went off to Kimmel quoting Grew's famous warning, placing "no credence in these rumors," and declaring that "no move against Pearl Harbor appears imminent or planned for in the forseeable [*sic*] future."

The memorandum which Richardson prepared with Kimmel represented his last major effort in Hawaii. In public he took his relief as CinCUS like the officer and gentleman he was.[48] Nevertheless, it rankled. His self-respect demanded that he know what lay behind his summary dismissal. When he reported to Knox in Washington on March 24, he asked respectfully but firmly for an explanation. "In my experience in the Navy," he said in effect, "I have never known of a flag officer being detached from command of the United States Fleet in the same manner that I was, and I feel that I owe it to myself to inquire why I was detached." Knox told Richardson that the President would send for him and talk the matter over. (Incidentally, Roosevelt never did summon Richardson for the promised interview.) Knox then gave Richardson a hint: "The last time you were here you hurt the President's feelings."[49]

Would the Pearl Harbor story have differed had Richardson remained at the helm? We have no evidence to indicate that such a change of cast would have affected the plot in any way. Richardson's skepticism about a possible attack does not promise that he would have proved any more security-conscious than Kimmel. His rejection of torpedo nets proved a major error in judgment.

But his decision rested on the technical opinion of ordnance experts that torpedoes could not be used effectively in Pearl Harbor. In Japan Onishi received the same evaluation from Maeda, and even the aggressive and imaginative Genda was most doubtful on this point.

"J.O." had served his country well and deserved a more courteous dismissal. But looking at the results, we must reflect that the admiral had an unusually alert guardian angel. Thanks to Roosevelt's wounded sensibilities, Richardson slipped quietly out of the hot seat at Pearl Harbor into his role in the Navy's tradition as beloved "J.O.," standing forever in the sunlight of unshadowed memory.

CHAPTER 6

"THAT

MUST

HENCEFORTH

BEAR

RESPONSIBILITY"

Stand in imagination on the quarterdeck of the battleship *Pennsylvania* in Pearl Harbor on a golden Saturday morning, February 1, 1941. Always spanking clean as befits a flagship, her brasswork flashed blindingly in the sun. Her crewmen lined up on the main deck, their dress uniforms dazzlingly white under the turquoise blue sky. A soft breeze occasionally ruffled a white collar here, a black tie there.

The bosun's pipe shrilled with clocklike regularity as one party of gold braid after another came up the accommodation ladder. No fewer than sixteen flag officers faced forward in a row. Captains of the numerous ships in Pearl Harbor and many staff officers crowded the remaining deck space.

At last the band struck up "The Admiral's March." Then promptly, from the port companionway leading below, the chief dignitaries emerged. Richardson stood tall and straight "beneath the 14 inch guns of the after main turret," his good-natured face solemn and intent. Kimmel, the new CinCUS, stiffly erect, gave this occasion equal respect, for he loved the Navy, its rituals and its daily tasks. And this morning, thirty-seven years after his graduation from Annapolis in 1904, marked the proudest hour of his life. He stood at the very pinnacle of his career—a full admiral and Commander in Chief of the United States Fleet.

The ceremonies started at precisely 1005. "Officers and men of the fleet!" Richardson began in a deep, steady voice. "My regret in leaving you is tempered by the fact that I turn over this command to Admiral Kimmel, a friend of long standing, a forthright man, an officer of marked ability and a successor of whom I am proud. . . ."

Now it was Kimmel's turn. He slipped on a pair of horn-rimmed spectacles, rattled a sheet of paper, and read from it in clear, businesslike tones. He paid his respects to Richardson, then, in a voice conveying a strong whiff of bluegrass, promised his men and his nation: "I can say only this, that it shall be my personal motto—or guiding principle—to maintain the fleet at the highest level of efficiency and preparedness, and that whatever expansion is ordered, I will attempt to carry out to the best of my ability."

Mark Matthews of the Honolulu *Advertiser,* who watched the ceremony, wrote with sensitive perception in the next morning's issue: "The crisp, blue-eyed Kentuckian had become now the sole, solitary, infinitely lonely figure that must henceforth bear responsibility for a million tons of fighting steel, the world's greatest aggregation of warships—the security of his nation."[1]

A handsome man in his late fifties, Kimmel carried himself proudly. He stood five feet ten inches and weighed some 180 pounds of solid bone and muscle. This man of dark destiny had a fine head that tilted slightly over sturdy shoulders. His hair, still full and dark blond, was flecked with gray. Beneath a broad, level brow his clear, direct eyes reflected wisdom and experience. A well-shaped nose and strongly set mouth and chin completed a rather stern Germanic countenance. Virile, with a clean look that carried the tang of the sea, Kimmel seemed the living embodiment of "NAVY."

Husband Edward Kimmel was born on February 26, 1882, in Henderson, a small town in northwestern Kentucky not far from the Indiana border. True to family tradition, he had attempted to secure an appointment to West Point. Only when this fell through did he try for the U.S. Naval Academy, and this time he succeeded.

He plunged into life at Annapolis as if to prove to the Military Academy that it had missed a good man, as indeed it had. His records as a midshipman show that he excelled in navigation, seamanship, ordnance, and languages. He rated the number two spot in efficiency, an indication of things to come. Throughout his naval career Kimmel's insistence on order, routine, and efficiency reached almost frightening proportions. He managed to escape Annapolis without his unfortunate midshipman nickname of Hubby catching on. He was Kim to most of his friends. Stark called him Mustapha—a pun on Kemal Pasha.[2]

Kimmel graduated thirteenth in his class of sixty-two, but nothing in the career upon which he embarked hinted that bad luck lurked in wait for him.[3] On the contrary, every break seemed to come his way. On January 31, 1912, he married Dorothy Kinkaid, the daughter of an admiral. Her brother, Thomas C. Kinkaid, of the Annapolis class of 1918, also was destined for flag rank. The union was to produce three fine sons. When their father became Commander in Chief, the two eldest, Manning and Thomas, were both serving aboard the submarine *S-38* in Philippines waters, and the third, Edward, was a junior at Princeton.

After a well-balanced, highly successful career at sea and ashore, in 1933 Kimmel realized the dream of every "black-shoe" officer: the command of a battleship. As skipper of *New York* Kimmel was an exacting taskmaster. After a year aboard her, Kimmel joined the Battle Force as chief of staff to the commander, Battleships. Three things stand out in these formative years before Kimmel attained his flag: an excellent record in gunnery, important staff assignments, and a solid background with battleships.

In due course Washington assigned Kimmel as the Navy Department's budget officer. The position involved numerous contacts with Capitol Hill, where Kimmel's combination of self-evident honesty and straightforward courtesy, softened with the charm he could exercise when he chose, stood him in good stead. He became known as an administration man in a mild way. In this connection we might note in passing that among the usual scattering of special details which fall to any presentable junior officer, Kimmel had briefly been aide to the then Assistant Secretary of the Navy Franklin D. Roosevelt during a Panama Canal celebration. While budget officer, Kimmel became a rear admiral—November 1937—and in July of the next year he went back to sea as commander of Cruiser Division Seven.

One year later, in 1939, he stepped aboard *Honolulu* as commander, Cruisers, Battle Force. As such he demanded taut ships. Anchor chains rattled on the split second, speeds and courses at sea were exact, signals came across clearly and forcefully, drills went off briskly with precise formations and resolute maneuvers, or Kimmel knew the reason why. On the debit side of the ledger, his solid knowledge of naval history, tactics, and strategy was unfired by the spark of creative imagination. While an incongruous situation or good joke could bring forth his hearty laugh, he lacked a genuine sense of humor.

He may have been an easier man to admire than to love, yet the atmosphere in his staff was tonic with unspoken loyalty. As he ate with his officers at mess, conversation circulated freely and generally centered on shop. When the evening shadows settled over his cruisers, Kimmel might play a hand or two of cards, but more often than not he retired to his cabin to study war plans or to lose himself in a book.

By this time Kimmel's file of fitness reports bulged with high ratings and predictions of great things to come, all expressing the pride and satisfaction of his superiors. Yet when Washington summoned him as Commander in Chief, Navy-wide reaction, from the admiral himself down the line, was one of surprise. Kimmel was relatively junior and not too well known.

To a direct question from a member of the Roberts Commission*—one of several bodies appointed to investigate the Pearl Harbor disaster—on whether he had "made any efforts to get command of the fleet or used any influence" to do so, Kimmel replied firmly, "None whatever, sir . . . the only influence I used to become commander of the fleet was to do my job the best I could. . . ."[4] Quite so! Despite all the postattack probings into why Kimmel had received the appointment over a goodly list of more senior admirals, it appears extremely probable that the Navy Department selected him for the simple reason that it considered him the best man for the job.

Thus, command of the United States Fleet passed into the hands of one

*See Chapter 70.

who had many points in common with his remarkable adversary, Yamamoto. Both were small-town boys. Each had graduated from his country's naval academy in 1904—the year of the Japanese surprise attack on Port Arthur. Each was a bundle of driving energy; each had a strong will and fierce devotion to his profession. Each made his presence keenly felt wherever he went, and when either wanted his way, he could lean hard. Each gathered to himself a staff of exceptional capability, taking these men into his complete confidence and treating them like a family. Each encouraged individual initiative in his officers, disliked yes-men, and was always ready to hear both sides of a question. Each gave his staff intense loyalty and in return gained a devotion which withstood every pressure and bridged the years with a span of steel. Above all, each was a patriot and a sailor's sailor down to the last drop of his blood.

And each admiral had a summer-lightning temper. Yamamoto could, and did, stamp until his cabin shook, while Kimmel had been known to hurl the nearest book at the bulkhead.[5] When he really got his dander up, he flung his hat on the deck and jumped on it. This happened so often at sea that one of the messboys kept an old sea cap or hat handy so that when Kimmel went into his act, he could stomp on an old hat instead of a new one. On such occasions their respective staffs would batten down the hatches until the storm blew over, as it did in a matter of minutes. These men thought none the worse of their admirals because they did not suffer fools gladly.[6]

Kimmel realized the magnitude of his task, and he faced it soberly but fearlessly. Had he not studied, labored, and trained for just such responsibilities? Nevertheless, the naval setup which went into effect concurrently with his appointment was not calculated to reassure him. This reorganization divided the Navy into three fleets—Atlantic, Pacific, and Asiatic—a situation which had not existed since 1922. But times had changed, and the Atlantic and Pacific fleets no longer engaged in joint maneuvers, so the proud title of Commander in Chief U.S. Fleet had become largely honorary. Kimmel's orders designated him concurrently as Commander in Chief, U.S. Pacific Fleet (CinCPAC), and he understood very well that this was his real job.

On Tuesday, February 4, only a few days after Kimmel took over his new command, twenty-four bombers of the Eighteenth Bombardment Wing at Hickam Field thundered over the liner *Matsonia* near Diamond Head as she edged toward Honolulu Harbor. This aloha review was a special gesture of welcome to the new commander of the Hawaiian Department, Major General Walter C. Short, aboard the vessel. His predecessor, General Herron, stood on dock to greet the veteran infantry officer.[7]

On the stroke of 0900 on February 7 Short's car drove up to the sun-splashed parade ground of Fort Shafter. After brief ceremonies Herron formally tendered his colors and flag to Short. That noon, in another impressive ceremony at Fort Shafter, this time at Hawaiian Department Headquarters, Short received his promotion to lieutenant general. Smiling and happy at the general's side, Mrs. Short pinned the insignia of his new rank on his shoulders;[8] it was a question who was the more proud.

Born in Fillmore, Illinois, on March 30, 1880, Short had graduated from the University of Illinois in 1902. In March of that year he received a direct commission effective February 2, 1902.[9] For almost forty years he provided a case history of a typical regular infantry officer of his generation. He spent his early career in Texas, at the Presidio in San Francisco, in the Philippines, in Nebraska and Alaska. From February 1912 to March 1916 he was secretary, School of Musketry at Fort Sill, Oklahoma; then he accompanied the Sixteenth Infantry Regiment to Mexico with the punitive expedition under Pershing.

During World War I he racked up a respectable record. As a captain he sailed for France in June 1917 and was "in the first group of officers sent to the British and French fronts" and helped organize the First Corps' automatic weapons school. He soon joined the General Staff training section, directing instruction of machine-gun units. After the Armistice he was one of the hard-core group that remained overseas until July 1919. During that time he served as assistant chief of staff in charge of the Third Army's training in Germany.

He emerged from the war a colonel but, like other officers, reverted to his permanent rank. Promoted to major in 1920, he graduated from the School of the Line (later Command and General Staff School) at Fort Leavenworth, Kansas, that same year. Beginning in July 1921, he served a three-year hitch in Washington with the War Department General Staff, then entered the Army War College, which he graduated from in 1925. He spent the next three years in Puerto Rico, then returned to Leavenworth to serve as a staff member until September 1930. Next came four more years in Washington in the Bureau of Insular Affairs. Then he returned to the field for a number of command positions. By 1937 he wore the single star of a brigadier general. With the outbreak of war in Europe he received further command assignments, first at Fort Hamilton, then at Columbia, South Carolina. Finally, as the climax of his career, the Army called him to Hawaii.

No such speculation arose over Short's selection as over Kimmel's. Herron was due for retirement, and not an eyebrow lifted when Short took over. In fact, he was not enthusiastic about going to Honolulu. When the Chief of Staff, General George C. Marshall, broke the news to him, Short advised him that if this were the usual routine assignment, he would prefer a stateside job because of his father-in-law's poor health. But Marshall informed Short that the appointment was important and that he must go to Hawaii.[10]

Kimmel and Short immediately set up an excellent personal relationship. Soon they established a biweekly golf date for Sunday mornings. The two men must have been an intriguing sight as they sat together in their offices or strolled around the turf. If not technically professional opposites, they were certainly so in the civilian sense of the word. Whereas physically Kimmel's appearance fairly shouted "Admiral, USN," one doubts if a *What's My Line?* panel would have labeled Short "Lieutenant General, USA." His thin, sensitive face with its delicate-boned, spare, and nervy look of the thoroughbred could have peered out from beneath a powdered peruke with no incongruity. His slim, wiry figure of five feet ten inches, clad in neat, practical khakis, gave the impression that time had slipped a cog. Unusually large, deep-set, and luminous eyes watched from beneath lifted brows and a high, smooth forehead. The slightly bulbous nose was high-bridged; the ears were close-set. The slender, cleanly defined upper lip slanted a trifle downward at the corners past the rather full, almost sullen lower lip. He held his head high, and his whole appearance radiated the consciousness of authority and alert self-confidence.

From Short's own testimony and that of others the picture emerges of a capable and conscientious officer, neither brilliant nor overly aggressive, but polished, competent, honest, and determined to do a good job. His career had been top-heavy with training assignments. Such a background always implies the danger that the individual may come to mistake the shadow for the substance and regard training as an end in itself. Certainly Short was acutely alive to the necessity for training from the moment he set foot on Hawaiian soil.

Yet the task of licking rookies into shape was not a mission. It was essentially a problem of command—one which Short shared with every other commander in 1941, when the small cadre of the regular military establishment was trying to absorb and make good use of the raw material funneled to it from the draft boards. When Short took over the Hawaiian Department, its basic mission was twofold: protection of the Pacific Fleet as it lay at its moorings in Pearl Harbor and coastal defense of the Hawaiian Islands. Later in the year the task of shuttling aircraft between the Philippines and the mainland would be added. Any one of these responsibilities could have taken all the limited forces at Short's disposal. To have accomplished all three would have required enough men and matériel to sink the Islands.

For all the reams of testimony, Short remains one of the most elusive of the major characters in the Pearl Harbor story. He wrote no book, as did Kimmel and several of the key Japanese participants. To the best of our knowledge he left no treasure trove of letters like Yamamoto's; he kept no voluminous diary, as did Stimson and a number of Japanese. Nor did he let down his guard in personal, well-remembered conversations. He stands before the inquisitive historian in taut watchfulness, courteous, painstaking, and inscrutable, forever holding the citadel of his own personality.

CHAPTER 7

"OUR FIRST

CONCERN

IS TO

PROTECT

THE FLEET"

The seventh of February, 1941, is one of the dates on which the separate threads of fate mingled briefly. While Mrs. Short was pinning on her husband's third star at Fort Shafter, Kimmel flourished a vigorous pen in his shipshape office aboard *Pennsylvania*. In Washington, Stimson and Marshall were at their respective desks, signing significant letters on the subject of the U.S. Pacific Fleet in Pearl Harbor.

Henry L. Stimson joined Roosevelt's Cabinet in June 1940, when the President decided that his official family needed an infusion of Republican blood. One can easily see why he turned to Stimson. They came from identical backgrounds and understood each other's fundamentally aristocratic tempera- ments. Stimson had no political ax to grind, and his international views at this time coincided with Roosevelt's in all essentials. Long an advocate of British-American friendship, he favored all possible aid to Britain and resistance to aggression on every front.

A lawyer by profession, he had served in some capacity under no fewer than five Presidents. He had been Taft's secretary of war, Coolidge's high commissioner of the Philippines, and Hoover's secretary of state. Naturally Stimson had his detractors. Some termed him high-hat, hard to get along with, possessed of a one-track mind, short-fuse temper, and open-mesh memory. All that was true to a degree. Yet even his worst enemies conceded Stimson's moral and physical courage and devotion to duty.

At seventy-three the oldest member of the Cabinet, Stimson remained physically fit and proud of it. Thoughtful and thought-provoking, he worked best behind the scenes. Equally free of personal ambition or dependence upon party patronage, Stimson responded again and again to his country's summons. Yet he was basically a home and nature lover, relaxed and happy only at his own hearthside or out of doors. He adored his New York home, Highhold, and it was a real sacrifice for him to come to "this infernal hole they call Washington."[1]

The letter under Stimson's hand that February 7 was addressed to his colleague Frank Knox, who had joined the Cabinet as secretary of the navy at the same time Stimson came on board. Knox, too, voted Republican and had been a Teddy Roosevelt man, but there the resemblance ended. Whereas Stimson had been born to wealth and position, Knox had earned his way up delivering newspapers and working his way through college by waiting on tables and doing other chores. He responded promptly to the call for volunteers in the Spanish-American War and went to Cuba as one of the Rough Riders. Later he enthusiastically followed Teddy into the Bull Moose party. In this he differed from Stimson, who, despite his affection for TR, remained loyal to Taft.

Although overage, Knox volunteered as a private in World War I, saw action with the Seventy-eighth Division, and emerged wearing a major's gold leaves. For some mysterious reason he was known thenceforth as Colonel. After the Armistice he returned to the newspaper field. In 1930 he took over the Chicago *Daily News*, and by 1936 he had attained sufficient national stature to rate the Republican Vice-Presidential nomination.

Less intellectually endowed than Stimson, Knox had much more going for him as a personality. He shared TR's outgoing delight in the business of living and throve on public contacts. What he knew about the Navy would not have taxed a slender notebook, but he realized his limitations and was eager to fill the gaps. Not that he had any illusions about who really ran the Navy, but he accepted the situation with complete good nature.

Stimson's missive replied to Knox's memorandum of January 24. Under the subject "Air Defense of Pearl Harbor, Hawaii," Stimson expressed "complete concurrence as to the importance of this matter and the urgency of our making every possible preparation to meet such a hostile effort." He declared definitely, "The Hawaiian Department is the best equipped of all our overseas departments, and continues to hold a high priority for the completion of its projected defenses because of the importance of giving full protection to the Fleet."

When it came down to details, however, the picture he painted was not too bright. He could promise "thirty-one P-37 pursuit planes assembled at San Diego for shipment to Hawaii within the next ten days" and informed Knox that the total Hawaiian antiaircraft project called for "ninety-eight 3-inch AA guns, one hundred and twenty 37 mm AA guns, and three hundred and eight caliber .50 AA machine guns." But he gave no indication of just when all this matériel would come Short's way.

He further advised Knox that aircraft warning service equipment had been ordered and would be delivered to Hawaii in June. By that time arrangements for installation would have been made. Stimson then promised that he would direct Short to look into the barrage balloon and smoke screen situation; about neither did he offer encouragement, however. Barrage balloons would not be available before summer, and according to "qualified opinion," the "atmosphere and geographic conditions in Oahu render the employment of smoke impracticable for large scale screening operations."[2]

A copy of this letter went to Short as well as to Kimmel and Bloch. It would be interesting to know Short's immediate reaction to the statement that his was "the best equipped of all our overseas departments. . . ." Nor did Short need Stimson's instructions to cooperate with the Navy; he had no intention of doing anything else. And he had at hand another letter dated February 7, 1941—this one from Marshall—stressing that very subject.

General George C. Marshall became Chief of Staff of the U.S. Army at the age of fifty-nine only a few hours after Hitler's legions slammed into Poland on September 1, 1939. This quiet, rangy six-footer with blue eyes and graying hair had a rugged face which bespoke a forceful character. Like all men of powerful personality, especially those in top positions, Marshall aroused strong feelings. He inspired either steadfast devotion or sharp aversion. Although he could be somewhat unapproachable, he was always open to reason, but once he made up his mind, the staff officer who continued to oppose him did so at his own risk.

Marshall had met with Stark on February 6, and the Chief of Staff gave Short the benefit of their discussion. Marshall began with a brief character sketch of Kimmel as given him by Stark:

> He said Kimmel was very direct, even brusque and undiplomatic in his approach to problems; that he was at heart a very kindly man, though he appeared rather rough in his methods of doing business. I gather that he is entirely responsive to plain speaking on the part of the other fellow if there is frankness and logic in the presentation. Stark went so far as to say that he had, in the past, personally objected to Kimmel's manner in dealing with officers, but that Kimmel was outstanding in his qualifications of command, and that this was the opinion of the entire Navy.

Stark had also told Marshall of Kimmel's complaints about "deficiencies of Army matériel for the protection of Pearl Harbor." Marshall admitted to Short that, in general, the facts were as the admiral indicated. He added, however, "What Kimmel does not realize is that we are tragically lacking in this matériel throughout the Army, and that Hawaii is on a far better basis than any other command in the Army."[3]

Marshall then emphasized a most vital point: "The fullest protection for the Fleet is *the* rather than *a* [Marshall's italics] major consideration for us . . . but the Navy itself makes demands on us for commands other than Hawaii, which makes it difficult for us to meet the requirements of Hawaii. . . ."[4]

For all "the pressures on the Department," Marshall emphasized that "we are keeping clearly in mind that our first concern is to protect the Fleet." He continued: "My impression of the Hawaiian problem has been that if no serious harm is done us during the first six hours of known hostilities, thereafter the existing defenses would discourage an enemy against the hazard of an attack. . . ." How could Marshall foresee that the first six minutes of war would break the back of the Pacific Fleet? "The risk of sabotage and the risk involved in a surprise raid by Air and by submarine constitutes [*sic*] the real perils of the situation. Frankly, I do not see any landing threat in the Hawaiian Islands so long as we have air superiority."[5]

This fixation with sabotage both in Washington and in Hawaii was understandable. The Islands' population included some 160,000 Japanese, about 37,500 of whom were foreign-born.[6] The United States had seen to what good use Hitler had put the discontents and aspirations of minorities. Below the surface the Japanese on Hawaii presented an entirely different picture from the native European minorities, but Marshall and Short were soldiers, not sociologists. Once more Marshall iterated:

> Please keep clearly in mind in all of your negotiations that our mission is to protect the base and the Naval concentrations, and that purpose should be made clearly apparent to Admiral Kimmel. I accentuate this because I found . . . that old Army and Navy feuds, engendered from fights over appropriations . . . still persist in confusing issues of national defense. . . . Fortunately, and happily I might say, Stark and I are on the most intimate personal basis, and that relationship has enabled us to avoid many serious difficulties.[7]

Short hastened to reply on the nineteenth, assuring Marshall that he had found both Kimmel and Bloch—his opposite number—"most approachable and cooperative in every way" and that "our relations should be extremely cordial." He listed the conditions he believed of great importance and the steps he wished to take to effect the necessary changes. Of these, "Cooperation with the Navy" ranked as number one, and he advised Marshall that to bring this about, joint committees of Army and Navy officers would meet and report on March 1.[8]

Short also wrote that same day to The Adjutant General* concerning the dispersal and protection of fighters and bombers. "The concentration of these airplanes at Wheeler Field and at Hickam Field presents a very serious problem in their protection against hostile aviation," he stressed. And he asked for bunker protection for "142 single engine pursuit ships and 121 double engine pursuit ships and for 25 two engine bombers and 70 four engine bombers" at a total cost of $1,565,600—reasonable enough considering the value of the aircraft.[9] Nothing concrete came of these pleas. Of course, the War Department neither ignored Short nor put him in an impossible position deliberately. It had precisely the same problem as he on a larger scale—how to build a fortress with what was available, and quickly. Hawaii got what Washington could send, which was not enough.

Short's official correspondence and his testimony reveal a thorough awareness of the danger to Hawaii; they also display a sound understanding of

---

*Most upper Army echelons had an adjutant general. "The Adjutant General"—like "The Judge Advocate General"—designated the official at War Department level.

the day-to-day aspects of his command. In fact, one cannot escape the impression that he was surer of himself in the precise field of detailed operations than in the larger area of mission. He took hold efficiently and made good use of what he had available. Yet he was strictly a soldier, and although his primary mission had been spelled out for him in the plainest possible terms, he never really understood the nature of his responsibility to the Pacific Fleet. In exceedingly revealing testimony, Short observed, speaking of a potential attack on Pearl Harbor: "If the fleet had been ordered away from the Hawaiian waters I would have been extremely apprehensive. . . . I definitely would have expected it if the fleet had not been there."[10] In his heart, Short regarded the presence of the Pacific Fleet as a protection for his Hawaiian Department, rather than vice versa. Nor did he realize that any Japanese attack would be aimed at the very ships he was charged with protecting.

Short's basic aim—to do his duty as best he could in the sphere to which God and the War Department had called him—paralleled Kimmel's, but Short had very different ideas about how it should be accomplished. A firm believer in contacts, he set out to make himself agreeable. As Bloch, who knew Short well and liked him, reminisced, "Short was not too hard a worker. He was definitely not a busy beaver. He was the type who considered it his duty to know everyone in the area, to be good to them, and to swap lies with them from time to time."[11]

Indeed, Short's *savoir-faire* may well have been an important factor in his appointment. The Hawaiian Department's commander absolutely had to get along with the civilian authorities if he was to obtain the cooperation necessary for smooth coordination. A certain gap had always existed between civilian and military Hawaii, and Short made it his business to bridge it. This he did with excellent results.

It is evident that defense of the Islands was the part of his mission which he understood best and in which he was most successful—at least to the degree to which he was called upon. We cannot know whether he could have held the archipelago against an all-out Japanese assault. It is a military axiom that any position can be taken by an attacking force which hits quickly enough, hits hard enough, and stays long enough. Geographically isolated, yet dependent on the mainland for food and fuel, Hawaii presented almost a classic case of vulnerability, and well Short knew it.

The general did not immediately gather around him a cohesive staff. His officers went through so many changes throughout the year that not until about a month before the Pearl Harbor attack did they settle down to fairly permanent status. Herron had left behind a first-rate chief of staff, Colonel Philip Hayes. But Hayes was due for rotation, and his successor lacked his background, presence, and grasp of the job. "In December 1940, after a very successful series of maneuvers in the first division" Short requested the assignment of Lieutenant Colonel Walter C. Phillips, the First Division's operations officer, to Hawaii as chief of staff.[12]

With Marshall's personal blessing, Phillips arrived in Hawaii on March 1.

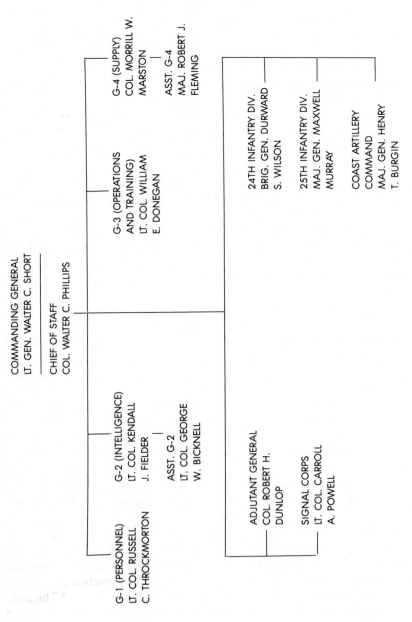

SIMPLIFIED CHART OF HAWAIIAN DEPARTMENT
AS OF DECEMBER 7, 1941

COMMANDING GENERAL
LT. GEN. WALTER C. SHORT

CHIEF OF STAFF
COL. WALTER C. PHILLIPS

G-1 (PERSONNEL)
LT. COL. RUSSELL
C. THROCKMORTON

G-2 (INTELLIGENCE)
LT. COL. KENDALL
J. FIELDER

ASST. G-2
LT. COL. GEORGE
W. BICKNELL

G-3 (OPERATIONS
AND TRAINING)
LT. COL. WILLIAM
E. DONEGAN

G-4 (SUPPLY)
COL. MORRILL W.
MARSTON

ASST. G-4
MAJ. ROBERT J.
FLEMING

ADJUTANT GENERAL
COL. ROBERT H.
DUNLOP

SIGNAL CORPS
LT. COL. CARROLL
A. POWELL

24TH INFANTRY DIV.
BRIG. GEN. DURWARD
S. WILSON

25TH INFANTRY DIV.
MAJ. GEN. MAXWELL
MURRAY

COAST ARTILLERY
COMMAND
MAJ. GEN. HENRY
T. BURGIN

Phillips was well intentioned and exceedingly loyal to Short, but from all reports his raucous voice and blustering manner could rub people the wrong way. After training in various staff sections throughout the spring and summer, Phillips took over as chief of staff on November 1 and five days later became a full colonel. The Army Pearl Harbor Board remarked of his work: "Phillips was recognized by the staff as without force and far too weak for a position of such importance. Short's selection of Phillips appears to have been a mistake. . . ." Mistake or not, Short stuck by his man, as his postwar testimony indicates: "Colonel Hayes was an excellent administrative man. He had had dealings with the Navy over considerable periods of time. Colonel Phillips was a far more competent man on field work and training."[13]

Lieutenant Colonel Russell C. Throckmorton served Short successively as G-3 (Operations) and G-1 (Personnel). He was a good officer, obliging and cooperative, a fine person, and a holdover from Herron, whom he admired greatly. Although not close to Short, he got along with the general and respected him.

Lieutenant Colonel Kendall J. "Wooch" Fielder was intelligent and shrewd. Although he had never served under Short, they were good friends, and in July 1941 Fielder became his intelligence officer (G-2), replacing Lieutenant Colonel Morrill W. Marston. Although Fielder had no previous Intelligence background, he worked hard at his job and served the general faithfully.

Major William E. Donegan was first Herron's, then Short's deputy assistant chief of staff, Operations (G-3). In July he was placed on the General Staff and he received his promotion to lieutenant colonel on September 15, 1941. On November 5, when Throckmorton became G-1, Donegan moved to the top slot in G-3, one of the most important posts on the staff. He was a man of honest opinions, loyal to his superiors and fellow officers.

Lieutenant Colonel Marston, who had originally served under Herron and Short as G-2, became assistant G-4 (Supply) on July 21, 1941, when Fielder took over Intelligence. His colleagues knew this quiet, unassuming officer as one of the most conscientious and dutiful men on Oahu. Marston moved up the ladder to assistant chief of staff, G-4 on October 19, 1941.[14]

While Short shook down his staff, the War Department continued to give considerable thought to defense of the Pacific Fleet. At a meeting of key brass held on the morning of February 25 Marshall raised the main issue. "In view of the Japanese situation the Navy is concerned with the security of the fleet in Hawaii. . . . They are in the situation where they must guard against a surprise or trick attack. It is necessary for the fleet to be in anchorage part of the time and they are particularly vulnerable at that time. I do not feel," he added, "that it is a possibility or even a probability but they must guard against everything."[15]

Here again that old serpent dichotomy raised its snaky head. Marshall was aware of the danger to Hawaii and would do everything he could to provide protection to the outpost, yet deep down he did not believe the Japanese would attack. Then, on the very day (or exceedingly close to it) on which Genda submitted his draft plan to Onishi, Marshall continued: "We also have information regarding the possible use of torpedo planes. There is the possible sudden introduction of Japanese carrier-based planes of the Messerschmidt type. . . . The Navy viewpoint is that the whole fleet is involved and that the sea power of the United States might be jeopardized. . . ." With this conference fresh in his mind, on March 5 Marshall urged Short to send him an early review of "the situation in the Hawaiian Department with regard to defense from air attack" and stressed that the "establishment of a satisfactory system of coordinating all means available to this end is a matter of first priority."[16]

Before receiving the Chief of Staff's letter, Short had dispatched a missive on the sixth which reveals him as a clear-thinking, courageous man who no more hesitated to speak his mind than did Richardson or Kimmel, although he walked with a lighter tread: "One of the first projects which I investigated in the Department was the Aircraft Warning Service which I believe is vital to the defense of these islands." He asked that permission be obtained "from the Secretary of the Interior to construct the Haleakala* installation without the necessity of submitting detailed plans for consideration by the National Park Service." And he ended flatly: "Defense of these Islands and adequate warning for the United States Fleet is so depending upon the early completion of this Aircraft Warning Service that I believe all quibbling over details should be stopped at once. . . ."[17]

From the vantage of hindsight, the War Department's reply, dated March 15, gives one the sensation of having wandered into the Mad Hatter's tea party:

> . . . The National Park Service officials are willing to give us the temporary use of their lands when other lands are not suitable for the purpose, but they will not waive the requirements as to the submission of preliminary building plans showing the architecture and general appearance. They are also very definitely opposed to permitting structures of any type to be erected at such places as will be open to view and materially alter the natural appearance of the reservation. . . .[18]

It was just as well for Short's blood pressure that he did not wait to receive this letter before he responded to Marshall's of March 5 on the air defense situation. In fact, Short replied to that letter on the fifteenth also. He began uncompromisingly: "The most serious situation with reference to an air attack is the vulnerability of both Army and Navy air fields to the attack." This shows excellent perception because the Japanese planners knew that for maximum success they had to pin American air power to the ground before and during the strike on the ships. After spelling out his numerous shortages, the general emphasized:

---

*This mountain, located on Maui, is one of the highest points in the Hawaiian Islands.

The coordination of Antiaircraft defense presents quite a different picture at Hawaii from that existing in most places on the mainland. The island is so small there there would not be the same degree of warning that would exist on the mainland. After the installation of our new detectors we shall have some warning from the different islands and almost continuous service in the most dangerous direction for approximately 75 miles. The pursuit aviation, however, will have to be prepared to take the air in the minimum amount of time. . . . [19]

One cannot help sympathizing with Short. On the one hand, he was constantly occupied with correspondence in the most serious tone to and from Washington concerning the air defense of Hawaii and the Fleet. On the other, he was being told, in official language, that all things considered, the view from the top of a mountain was much more important than the establishment of an efficient radar screen for the detection of an approaching enemy.

This attitude was all the more disquieting because Pearl Harbor was the only place within thousands of miles where the U.S. Pacific Fleet could refuel, refit, and revictual. Shaped roughly like a shamrock, with its petals respectively the West, Middle, and East lochs, it was accessible only by the slender stem, a long channel so narrow that capital ships had to use it one at a time. No wonder Richardson called Pearl Harbor a "God-damn mousetrap."[20]

Kimmel knew of the disadvantages to the Fleet at Pearl Harbor as well as did Richardson, but he wasted no time flogging a dead horse. He shared the fighting man's traditional belief that any decision was better than none, and he itched to get on with the job of preparing his forces. On that busy February 7 he wrote to Stark one of the first of a series of long, persistent but fruitless letters begging for personnel.[21]

Nimitz received it for reply. His answer to Kimmel's request for increased complements, contained in a lengthy missive of March 3, gives an interesting hint of the curious factors involved in naval decisions. Roosevelt had received from the families of sailors a number of complaints that the men were packed into their ships like sardines. For this reason, "The President now feels so strongly that we will make our ships unhappy by overcrowding that Stark and I will need every bit of assistance and assurance that you can give in order to obtain his consent to carrying more than the present 100% complement on board. . . ."[22] Perhaps it is just as well that Kimmel's immediate reaction to this did not go on record.

Stark was having his own troubles with the President, who wished to send a naval detachment to the Philippines via the Phoenix, Gilbert, or Fiji islands as a warning gesture to Japan. Wanting no part of a two-front war, on February 11 Stark sent Roosevelt a memorandum in an attempt to squelch such presidential exuberance. "There is a chance that further moves against Japan will precipitate hostilities rather than prevent them. We want to give Japan no excuse for coming in in case we are forced into hostilities with Germany who we all consider our major problem."[23]

Here, in brief, was the bedrock of American naval policy at this time. Stark had no illusions about the Japanese tiger, but he was not about to poke it into action while Hitler's killer sharks infested the Atlantic. Keep Great Britain above water—that was the prime objective.

Without waiting for a reply to his request for personnel, on February 15 Kimmel issued to his command Pacific Fleet Confidential Letter 2 CL 41, concerned with possible attack on the Fleet. It outlined every conceivable contingency, with provisions to cover each insofar as his resources permitted.

The second paragraph postulated that "no responsible foreign power will provoke war, under present existing conditions, by attack on the Fleet or Base, but that irresponsible and misguided nationals of such powers" might try it.[24] The letter further assumed that "a declaration of war might be preceded by:

> (1) a surprise attack on ships in Pearl Harbor.
> (2) a surprise submarine attack on ships in operating area.
> (3) a combination of these two."[25]

Thus, Kimmel shared the general belief that Japan would never deliberately initiate war with the United States. The idea was almost laughable—a mouse kicking a cat! But individuals were less predictable. And he knew from Japanese history that they might hit first and go through the formalities later.

His orders on "defense against air attack" were clear and comprehensive. The Army, with Marine assistance, would man the antiaircraft shore guns. Furthermore, "any part of the Fleet in Pearl Harbor, plus all Fleet aviation shore-based on Oahu, will augment the local air defense."[26] Kimmel designated the commandant of the Fourteenth Naval District (Bloch) as naval base defense officer and spelled out his responsibilities, which included this caution: "It must be remembered too that a single submarine attack may indicate the presence of a considerable surface force probably composed of fast ships accompanied by a carrier. . . ."[27] On the contrary, the Japanese plan would call for "fast ships" to accompany the carriers. Later, Japanese airmen would worry lest one of their own submarines should tip off the Americans to the forthcoming air attack.

Kimmel's Fleet Letter makes no mention of long-distance reconnaissance, the magic key to the protection of Oahu. This was an Army function at the time, although the Navy would soon take over the responsibility.

On February 15 Stark dispatched to Kimmel a letter which could only have reinforced his belief that the principal danger to his ships when in port came from beneath the sea. Stark's letter opened:

> 1. Consideration has been given to the installation of A/T baffles within Pearl Harbor for protection against torpedo plane attacks. It is considered that the relatively shallow depth of water limits the need for anti-torpedo nets in Pearl Harbor. In addition the congestion and the necessity for maneuvering room limit the practicability of the present style of baffles. . . .
>   (a) A minimum depth of water of seventy-five feet may be assumed necessary to successfully drop torpedoes from planes. One hundred and fifty feet of water is desired. The maximum height planes at present

experimentally drop torpedoes is 250 feet. Launching speeds are between 120 and 150 knots. Desirable height for dropping is sixty feet or less. About two hundred yards of torpedo run is necessary before the exploding device is armed, but this may be altered. . . . [28]

Such assumptions could have drastic consequences. Sparked by the indefatigable Genda, the Japanese took nothing for granted. With a dynamic faith that what had to be accomplished could be, they planned, tested, and trained until they made hay of Stark's figures.

On the eighteenth Kimmel reemphasized his own concern over his ships' safety, stressing to Stark, "I feel that a surprise attack (submarine, air, or combined) on Pearl Harbor is a possibility. We are taking immediate practical steps to minimize the damage inflicted and to ensure that the attacking force will pay. We need antisubmarine forces—DDs and patrol craft. . . ."[29]

Kimmel did not write of preventing such an attack, only of making the attackers pay for it. But like Short and others, he thought that an attack would be more likely if his ships were not in Pearl Harbor. "I felt, as the situation developed, the Fleet might move away from Pearl Harbor, and in such a contingency the possibility of a quick raid on the installations at Pearl Harbor might be attempted," he later testified.[30]

Actually Kimmel had no direct responsibility for protection of his vessels when they moored in Pearl Harbor. He was "responsible" only insofar as the armed forces consider the commander answerable for everything under his jurisdiction. As the Navy Court of Inquiry* stated after its investigation of the Pearl Harbor attack, "The defense of a permanent naval base is the direct responsibility of the Army. The Navy is expected to assist with the means provided the naval district within whose limits the permanent naval base is located."[31]

The Pacific Fleet considered itself geared for the offensive. Once war had been declared, Kimmel's vessels would race to the Mandates and range through the western Pacific to make Japan rue the day it had decided to try conclusions with the United States Navy. Once the war started, the Fleet's own offensive operations would be the best possible defense of Pearl Harbor.

Kimmel added a significant postscript to his letter of February 18:

> I have recently been told by an officer fresh from Washington that ONI [Office of Naval Intelligence] considers it is the function of Operations to furnish the Commander-in-Chief with information of a secret nature. I have heard also that Operations considers the responsibility for furnishing the same type of information to be that of ONI. I do not know that we have missed anything, but if there is any doubt as to whose responsibility it is to keep the Commander-in-Chief fully informed with pertinent reports on subjects that should be of interest to the Fleet, will you kindly fix that responsibility so that there will be no misunderstanding?[32]

Stark's absence from Washington delayed his reply, but he answered on March

---

*See Chapter 73.

22 that "ONI is fully aware of its responsibility in keeping you adequately informed concerning foreign nations, activities of those nations and disloyal elements within the United States. . . ."[33]

Richardson's operating schedule had called for half the Fleet to be at sea and the other half in port in an alternating pattern. After about a month on the job Kimmel revised the scheme to allow for three task forces. He kept at least one at sea at all times, sometimes two, so that any one ship spent 40 percent of its time at sea and 60 percent in port. Although acutely aware that the unit plowing the waters might run into hostile submarines, he took this chance. As he later testified, "We had to accept it, because if you keep a fleet in port you might just as well disband them, quit: they are no good to you."[34]

Task Force One came under the command of Vice Admiral William Satterlee Pye, second in rank to Kimmel and thus expected to act as CinCPAC in Kimmel's absence. Pye had the reputation of being a brilliant strategist; during a tour in the War Plans Division he had drafted the Navy's basic war plan for the Pacific.

Task Force Two fell to the redoubtable Vice Admiral William F. Halsey. Swashbuckling, crinkle-faced Bill Halsey had been an Annapolis classmate of Kimmel's; by 1934, at the age of fifty-one, when already a captain and a grandfather, he had won his wings at Pensacola. He loved and understood naval aviation as few men of his age could do. Kimmel set great store by him.

Task Force Three received as its commander Vice Admiral Wilson Brown, the "officer fresh from Washington" whom Kimmel had mentioned to Stark. Brown's distinguished career included command of the New London submarine base and the battleship *California*. He had also been superintendent of the Naval Academy.

This setup was operational. Pye's official title was Commander, Battle Force, while Brown was Commander, Scouting Force. Halsey answered to Commander, Aircraft, Battle Force. Under them were a number of type commanders—rear admirals in charge of every major type of vessel.[35]

Kimmel would have preferred to keep two task forces at sea at all times, but the critical fuel shortage prohibited this. The Pacific Fleet had only eleven tankers, a mere four of which were capable of fueling other ships at sea. Keeping in mind that a single destroyer steaming at full power would use up its entire fuel supply in thirty to forty hours, one gets some idea of the staggering needs of an entire fleet.[36] Yet Hawaii produced no oil. Every teaspoonful had to be transported over 2,000 miles from the mainland. The entire oil supply had to be stored in plain sight aboveground, and one of the Fleet's recurring nightmares was the possibility of the vast tank farm's catching fire, either accidentally or by enemy action.

Kimmel's reorganization gave Bloch a second post: commander, Task Force Four. In this capacity he was base defense officer, responsible for the Hawaiian Sea Frontier, including the outlying islands of Johnston, Midway, Wake, and Palmyra. Technically Bloch had two bosses. As commandant, Fourteenth Naval District, he was under Stark; as a task force commander he

SIMPLIFIED CHART OF U.S. PACIFIC FLEET
AS OF DECEMBER 7, 1941

COMMANDER IN CHIEF
ADMIRAL HUSBAND E. KIMMEL

CHIEF OF STAFF
CAPT. WILLIAM W. SMITH

OPERATIONS OFFICER	WAR PLANS OFFICER	GUNNERY OFFICER	COMMUNICATIONS OFFICER	AVIATION OFFICER	INTELLIGENCE OFFICER
CAPT. W. S. DELANY	CAPT. C. E. McMORRIS	CMDR. W. A. KITTS III	CMDR. M. E. CURTS	CMDR. A. C. DAVIS	LT. CMDR. E. T. LAYTON
1ST ASST. OPS. OFFICER	ASSISTANT		ASSISTANT		
CMDR. R. F. GOOD	CMDR. V. R. MURPHY		LT. (j.g.) W. J. EAST, JR.		

COMMANDER BATTLE FORCE
(TASK FORCE 1)
VADM. W. S. PYE

COMMANDER AIRCRAFT, BATTLE FORCE (TASK FR. 2)
VADM. W. F. HALSEY

COMMANDER SCOUTING FORCE
(TASK FORCE) 3
VADM. WILSON BROWN

COMMANDER TASK FORCE 4
RADM. C. C. BLOCH

COMMANDER SUBMARINES SCOUTING FORCE
(TASK FORCE 7)
RADM. T. WITHERS

COMMANDER TASK FORCE 9
RADM. P. N. L. BELLINGER

COMMANDER BASE FORCE
(TASK FORCE 15)
RADM. W. L. CALHOUN

came under Kimmel. Actually the channels did not cross because Bloch answered to Stark for administrative matters and to Kimmel in the operational field.[37]

To assist him in carrying out his multitudinous duties, Kimmel handpicked a staff of unusually clever officers, many of whom he had known for years. For his chief of staff he took popular Captain William Ward "Poco" Smith from *Brooklyn*'s bridge. Smith stood slightly under six feet and kept in condition by playing golf like a pro. An unusually retentive memory reinforced his mental agility, and an irrepressible sense of humor leavened the whole. As a chief of staff he was a natural, fielding everything belted his way with dispatch. Sometimes he formed judgments quickly, shooting from the hip.

In many ways the closest to Kimmel of all his official family was his assistant chief of staff and operations officer, Captain Walter S. DeLany. Down-to-earth and intelligent, DeLany had much in common with Kimmel, including a passion for hard work and professional integrity of a very high order. He did not hesitate to disagree with Kimmel when he thought the occasion demanded it.

For war plans officer, Kimmel tapped Captain Charles E. "Soc" McMorris, whose angular, pockmarked features resembled a medieval woodcut. He was a delightful person who could put across his ideas without table thumping. For many Navy officers, Soc's initials on a plan of action sufficed to guarantee it; others believed that at times he let his imagination and enthusiasm carry him out to sea.

Kimmel kept several members of Richardson's staff, including McMorris's assistant, Commander Vincent Murphy, whom Richardson considered "the finest officer in the United States Navy."[38] Another holdover was sharp-minded Commander Arthur C. Davis, the Fleet aviation officer, a pilot and the only member of Kimmel's official family who knew naval aviation from the deck up. Kimmel also retained Richardson's intelligence officer, Lieutenant Commander Edwin T. Layton. Confident and alert, Layton had been assistant naval attaché in Japan from April 1937 to March 1939 and thus had firsthand knowledge of the Japanese scene and particularly the Imperial Navy. He also spoke the language fluently.

With Richardson's relief from duty, Commander Maurice "Germany" Curts hoped he could leave his job in Communications and return to the sea he loved. When Kimmel summoned him to the flagship and asked him, "Young man, would you like to be on my staff?" Curts countered this flattering query with a firm "Hell, no!" The prompt negative took Kimmel by surprise, and the blood surged up into the admiral's face. "You've got to," he answered quickly. "There's no getting out of it." Curts then muttered, "Oh, hell!" in tones of such disgusted resignation that everyone present, including Kimmel, burst out laughing. Thus, he drew Curts into the charmed circle.[39]

These then were some of the representative officers on Kimmel's staff, embodying a remarkable combination of mental power, professional knowledge, ability, and personality. They enjoyed excellent relationships among themselves, complemented one another, and shared a deep loyalty to their chief and to each other.

No man can assume supreme command and remain exactly as before, but the changes his officers noted in Kimmel were of degree rather than kind. Always a hard worker, he now became almost obsessed with devotion to duty to a point which at least touched, if it did not cross, the boundary between dedication and fanaticism. He spent much time on details and exhibited undue concern over appearances.

Kimmel left his wife on the mainland when he came to Hawaii. In answer to a question from Poco Smith as to why he had not brought her out, Kimmel replied, "Well, to tell you the truth, Smith, I feel that I could not do my job with my family present."[40] This lack of confidence in his ability to function in the normal double harness of home and work is difficult to understand because Mrs. Kimmel had spent her entire life in the Navy and well appreciated the claims of her husband's position.

Kimmel's preoccupation with his work did not escape the notice of the Fleet medical officer, who suggested to several members of the CinCUS's staff that they induce him to play as much golf as possible. Accordingly, DeLany and others lured Kimmel out on the green whenever they could. But he obviously begrudged the time away from his desk.[41]

The admiral demanded much from his men and more from himself. He expected his people to produce and did not acknowledge good intentions as an acceptable substitute for concrete results. But no more conscientious, hard-working, patriotic, and honest man ever wore the Navy blue, and he well merited the loyalty which his officers gave him in abundance to the end of his life and beyond.

CHAPTER 8

"THE

HOTBED

OF

ESPIONAGE"

"It was a matter of common knowledge that the Japanese Consulate in Honolulu was the hotbed of espionage in Oahu," said Herron. "The Consul General himself was always under suspicion no matter who his errand boys were."[1] In 1941 this consulate was one of the busiest in Japan's diplomatic service. It also formed a key link in the long chain of Japanese Naval Intelligence.

Japanese agents had long been active in Hawaii, and when Roosevelt based the Fleet in those waters in May 1940, the Japanese Foreign Office requested Consul General Kiichi Gunji to send regular reports on the size, disposition, and activities of the U.S. Navy in Hawaii. This request originated in the Naval General Staff, which, like its Army counterpart, enjoyed the closest possible relations with the Foreign Office and used its representatives abroad for espionage and other intelligence purposes. In turn, Gunji relied heavily on the Honolulu newspapers for his information on the U.S. Fleet. At that time the press consistently reported on the size, numbers, and movements of Richardson's warships, conveniently citing exact names and times of arrival and departure.

Gunji returned to Japan on September 11, 1940, and his deputy, Otojiro Okuda, took over as acting consul general. Alert, suave, and knowledgeable, Okuda was a seasoned careerist. Medium-sized, with strong features reflecting business and duty, he exuded a certain air of Oriental mystery.

There is no direct evidence that Japan dispatched Okuda to Honolulu specifically to run its intelligence net in Hawaii. He had never served in the United States or any of its possessions. Nor had he any special background in naval lore.[2] Nevertheless, evidence available to American Intelligence circles indicated that in the Japanese consulate at Honolulu the vice consul was *ex officio* in charge of espionage.[3] Certainly, Gunji lost no time in giving Okuda the word. He explained that he had received instructions from the Navy through the Foreign Office to report on U.S. Fleet movements and ship locations. This information did not exactly amaze Okuda. But he did not like it; the responsibility imposed a risk, and it did not accord with normal consular duties and functions. Gunji assured Okuda that he would not find reporting on the U.S. Fleet difficult because the press covered all its movements.

Okuda swung into his espionage quickly and efficiently. For a time, as Gunji had predicted, checking on Fleet movements presented no special problems. The local press reported them faithfully, and Okuda extracted the germane items, coded them, and sent them to Tokyo by commercial telegraph. What was public information in Hawaii became classified as soon as it reached the Foreign Ministry, which immediately relayed it to the Naval General Staff. There it all became grist for the intelligence mill.

But Okuda was too thorough to depend only on newspapers. He sent his agents to check on the Fleet in Pearl Harbor and to verify press stories. Toward the end of 1940 he thought he noted a tapering off of such accounts.[4] Perhaps he did, because the news leaks at Hawaii had caused reverberations as far as Manila. On December 15, 1940, Admiral Thomas C. Hart, Commander in Chief of the Asiatic Fleet, wrote to Bloch "in the interest of stopping undesirable publicity about the movements of naval ships and forces." He was considering asking the Navy Department for "a certain amount of general shutting down . . ." but stated frankly "that the news source that has been worrying me most is somewhere right around where you are."[5] In any case, Okuda decided that he had to turn to other means of information gathering. He hesitated to attempt recruitment of dependable agents from among the Japanese nationals living on Oahu, so he inventoried his staff.

The only individual present with any qualifications for the task proved to by Kohichi Seki, the consulate's treasurer, a frail, rather sickly looking man of thirty-nine. He had attended the Naval Academy at Eta Jima but had been honorably discharged because his health did not meet Navy standards. The Foreign Office secured for Seki's use a copy of *Jane's Fighting Ships.* After about two months of practice in learning the types of American vessels, Seki set forth to scout the U.S. Pacific Fleet.[6]

He required no more than an hour to check on Pearl Harbor, which lay within seven miles of the consulate. So long as he stayed off the military reservation and avoided restricted areas, Seki broke no law. He made a practice of taking a taxi to the harbor area, watching directly from the taxi windows, then returning to the consulate to draft a report. Okuda reviewed these messages and passed them along to Sainon Tsukikawa, the secretary in charge of the code room. Like many men engaged in coding, Tsukikawa was completely wrapped up in his work; if he ever took the slightest interest in any other subject, his colleagues did not notice it.

Throughout January 1941 messages raced off to Tokyo periodically. Sometime in that month Seki received help in his espionage activities when

Okuda asked one Richard Masayuki Kotoshirodo to drive Seki to Pearl City and Aiea, overlooking Pearl Harbor from the north and east respectively.[7] An engaging, sturdy young Nisei* of about twenty-five, Kotoshirodo had joined the consulate in 1935. Just as his name was part Japanese and part American, so he himself was a somewhat ambivalent individual. Like many of his background in Hawaii, he was a Japanese citizen by Japanese law and an American citizen by American law. Kotoshirodo's wide teak-colored face, intelligent eyes, crew cut, and easy, companionable ways were a familiar part of the consular scene. Being a native of Hawaii, he could and did give valuable service to Seki as combined chauffeur and guide. Moreover, he was a clever young man, blessed with almost total recall and remarkable powers of observation.

Tokyo took increasing interest in American military activities and buildup, as evidenced by a message dispatched to Washington on February 15, paragraphs one and two of which especially applied to Honolulu:

> The information we particularly desire with regard to intelligence involving U.S. and Canada are [sic] the following:
>
> 1. Strengthening or supplementing of military preparations on the Pacific Coast and the Hawaii area; amount and type of stores and supplies; alterations to air ports (also carefully note the clipper traffic).
>
> 2. Ship and plane movements (particularly of the large bombers and sea planes). . . .[8]

Okuda required no prompting. By this time his reports had become regular and detailed, and Seki's scouting had improved considerably. But the United States was quite security-conscious by now. On February 10 Knox pleaded for protection of military secrets. And he begged American citizens "not to disclose the movements of fleet personnel." He could have saved his breath. The very day Short arrived in Hawaii—February 5, 1941—the new department commander had to take a back seat to a large headline splashed across the Honolulu *Star-Bulletin*: MAIN BODY OF FLEET TO SEA. What reasonable spy could ask for more? Evidently that thought occurred to Bloch, for on March 4 he protested to the *Star-Bulletin* about a similar story because "such information as published by your paper, if true, would furnish any real or potential enemy a valuable basis on which to predicate their operations."[9]

Seki did not rely solely on newspaper accounts. With typical Japanese thoroughness he kept on checking with his own eyes. On the twenty-seventh Okuda could tell his superiors, "Apparently the Fleet goes to sea for a week of training and stays in Pearl Harbor one week. Every Wednesday, those at sea and those in the harbor change places. This movement was noted on last Wednesday, the 26th. . . ."[10]

Here began what would persist throughout the year—report after report accurately identifying the schedules and routines of the U.S. Pacific Fleet. Schedules and routines! How beguiling they are, so easy to follow! What a comforting sense they give of security and predictability! For this reason, over

---

*Second-generation Japanese born on American soil.

many generations the men aware of the value of such intelligence have handed down a mighty commandment: Thou Shalt Not Establish a Habit Pattern. But by early December 1941 the American commanders had neglected this cardinal rule. The Japanese planners had to know where to put their finger on target ships; reliable U.S. patterns plus excellent reporting from the consulate enabled them to do just that.

Honolulu's new Japanese consul general, Nagao Kita, disembarked from *Tatuta Maru* on March 14; after being duly wined and dined, he paid courtesy calls on local dignitaries, including Short. Kita's broad face, thick hair, bushy brows, and flat pug nose above a short, chubby body gave him the look of a prizefighter. He dressed well, played an enthusiastic, if average, game of golf, and was something of a social lion. His years on the Asian mainland had given him the Chinese gentleman's gift of infinite leisure. He was flexible and adjusted to the needs and circumstances of the moment, always calm, detached, and alert. A widower whose only son attended school in Japan, he could devote his abundant energies exclusively to his job in Honolulu.[11]

To assist him, his superiors sent him a young man whose name appeared as "Tadashi Morimura" on the passenger list of the liner *Nitta Maru* as she nosed into Pier 8 in Honolulu Harbor on March 27, 1941. Actually he was Takeo Yoshikawa, a trained intelligence agent. When Okuda draped a welcoming lei around Yoshikawa's neck and shepherded his charge through customs, the Japanese Navy had slipped ashore its top secret spy as unobtrusively as any tourist. Okuda immediately took him to the consulate and ushered him into Kita's office. Yoshikawa presented the consul general with a letter from Captain Bunjiro Yamaguchi of the Intelligence Section of the Naval General Staff. The letter enclosed six $100 bills for use in Yoshikawa's mission.[12]

Kita saw before him a slender man of medium height who looked much younger than his twenty-nine years. His rather long black hair waved back from a smooth forehead. Large startled-fawn eyes looked out from beneath mobile brows. The first joint of his left index finger was missing—just the sort of disfigurement that would make identification easy. Altogether he looked wildly unlike the popular conception of a spy. Moreover, he had no previous experience as a field agent.

After a flurry of bows and assorted pleasantries Okuda escorted Yoshikawa from Kita's office to meet the rest of the staff. These people would know him only as Tadashi Morimura. At first Kita, like Okuda, wondered whether this man could make a good spy.[13] But Tokyo had not been mistaken. Yoshikawa was a walking encyclopedia of the United States Navy. A graduate of Eta Jima, he had appeared well on the way to advancement in his chosen career when a serious stomach ailment forced his retirement. He was moping unhappily when a Navy personnel officer told him that the service still held a place for him. However, he must forgo all hope of future advancement. This seemed to Yoshikawa a small price to pay for a return to his beloved Navy.[14]

In the Intelligence Division of the Naval General Staff, Yoshikawa received simple but comprehensive instructions: He must improve his English and become an expert on the U.S. Pacific Fleet and the American bases at Guam,

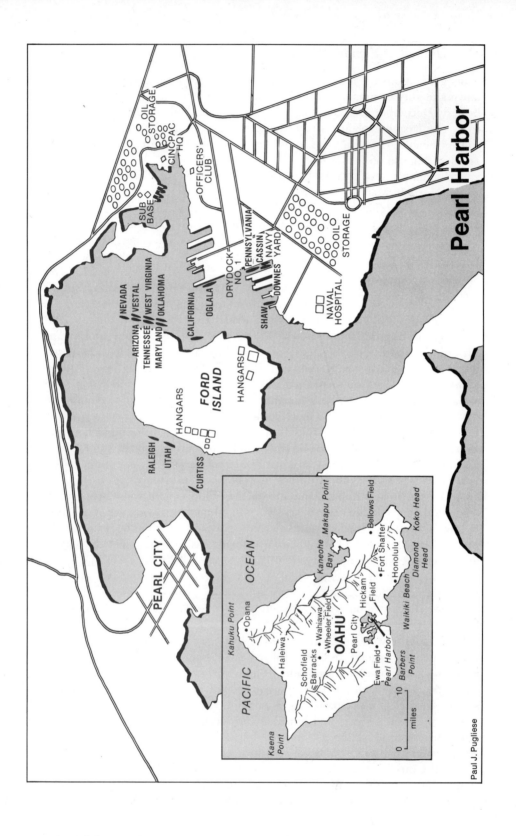

Pearl Harbor

OIL STORAGE
CINCPAC HQ
OFFICERS' CLUB
SUB BASE
OGLALA
DRYDOCK NO. 1
PENNSYLVANIA
CASSIN
DOWNES
NAVY YARD
SHAW
OIL STORAGE
NAVAL HOSPITAL

NEVADA
VESTAL
ARIZONA
TENNESSEE
WEST VIRGINIA
MARYLAND
OKLAHOMA
CALIFORNIA

HANGARS
FORD ISLAND
HANGARS

RALEIGH
UTAH
CURTISS

PEARL CITY

OAHU

PACIFIC OCEAN

Kahuku Point
Opana
Haleiwa
Kaena Point
Schofield Barracks
Wahiawa
Wheeler Field
Pearl City
Ewa Field
Pearl Harbor
Barbers Point
Kaneohe Bay
Makapu Point
Bellows Field
Hickam Field
Fort Shafter
Honolulu
Waikiki Beach
Diamond Head
Koko Head

0   10
miles

Paul J. Pugliese

Manila, and Pearl Harbor. After four years of intensive study he took the Foreign Ministry's English-language examinations, and a few weeks later he became a junior diplomat. Now he had the necessary cover for his true mission. In August 1940 his chief, Captain Masao Nishida, informed him that he was going to Honolulu as a diplomat and would report by diplomatic code on the daily status of the U.S. Fleet and its bases. Captain Bunjiro Yamaguchi gave him his final instructions just before he sailed, directing him to place major emphasis on Oahu. [15]

For security reasons, Kita assigned Yoshikawa one of the cottages in the compound. Here he could work in seclusion and privacy. Shortly after he settled in, Kita briefed him thoroughly. He gave his agent a broad view of the situation on Oahu, then got down to particulars, stressing the need for caution. [16]

Yoshikawa was given a desk in Okuda's office adjoining Kita's inner sanctum. Ostensibly his job involved processing dual-nationality Japanese. Yoshikawa's co-workers—consular secretary Kyonosuke Yuge and his clerk, Takaichi Sakai—were swamped in papers and looked forward to more help. But Sakai soon noted that "Morimura" appeared to know nothing about this sort of work and for the first three or four weeks confined his efforts to aiding in routine matters. Thereafter he abandoned all pretense of helping, and the burden fell back on Yuge and Sakai. [17]

Soon after his arrival Yoshikawa took several sight-seeing trips around Oahu, observing the terrain and keeping a sharp eye out for military installations and airfields. [18] On his initial expedition and for many other drives around Pearl Harbor, Yoshikawa hired a taxi driver, John Yoshige Mikami. This man was in his sixties and looked it. Although poorly educated, he made a hobby of naval affairs and had acquired a broad, if somewhat superficial, knowledge of the subject. By 1941 he had made himself so useful as an errand boy that he was practically a member of the consular family. Yoshikawa soon came to rely upon Mikami and to use his taxi frequently. [19] But Mikami had a low opinion of Yoshikawa. When the consular clerks speculated about their elusive co-worker, Mikami insisted that Yoshikawa "lacked the sharp eye and the smart gait of a Japanese military or naval officer." [20]

Yoshikawa also had at his frequent disposal Kotoshirodo's 1937 Ford along with its owner, who became Yoshikawa's trusted and valuable assistant. Within a week of his arrival the agent had visited the Pearl Harbor area. [21] In these early days Okuda occasionally went along. But as the spy became more surefooted, Okuda eased out. This was probably all right with Yoshikawa because he never warmed to Okuda, who was not so "open-hearted" as Kita. [22] When Yoshikawa first arrived, Seki went with him to observe ships in Pearl Harbor, and Kotoshirodo sometimes accompanied them. Yoshikawa coached Kotoshirodo to the point where, in addition to the trips the two men made together, Kotoshirodo could scout the Fleet by himself or with Mikami at Yoshikawa's direction. [23]

Kita gave Yoshikawa the title Chancellor in the consulate as a cover for his real activities. In due course the consul general introduced him to a Japanese-style teahouse called the Shuncho-ro. The place charmed Yoshikawa, for the proprietress came from his native prefecture in Japan and the geishas reminded him of home. More important, the teahouse, located in Alewa Heights, contained a second-floor room which commanded a view of Pearl Harbor and Hickam Field. Although too far removed for precise checking with the naked eye, the Shuncho-ro had a telescope which Yoshikawa used to advantage.[24]

By the end of April 1941 Yoshikawa had acquired a number of espionage locations. From a point on Aiea Heights he had an excellent view of Pearl Harbor, while the best look at the submarine base called for a stop on Kamehameha Highway between Aiea and Makalapa. Occasionally he would take a jitney to Honolulu bound for any point beyond Pearl Harbor, get off at Aiea, and prowl about. The cane fields at Aiea gave the best view of all. Yoshikawa would dress in laborer's garb and hide amid the cane. After using this site ten times, he broke off the habit, deciding that he had pushed his luck far enough or else had seen all he could see.[25]

Mikami and Kotoshirodo often drove Yoshikawa to Pearl City, northwest of the naval base. On a pier at the end of the peninsula there Yoshikawa could clearly see Pearl Harbor and Ford Island and its airstrips. He observed that the battleships moored in pairs, so that the inshore ship was practically impervious to torpedo attack. Despite its value, Yoshikawa dared not risk visiting the pier more than twice or three times a week, and each time he did so, he wore a change of clothes.[26]

In general, the western part of Pearl Harbor held little interest for Yoshikawa. However, he wanted to see the channel which Hickam Field blocked from view on the eastern side; he tried to reach the channel mouth by going west of Waipahu and then swinging south. This area near the West Loch was closely guarded, and Yoshikawa feared to risk moving close enough for a good view. Neither he nor the other consulate members knew for sure whether or not submarine nets guarded the entrance, but they went on that assumption. Spying on the submarines was difficult for Yoshikawa, and he never developed satisfactory notes on them.[27]

With true Japanese meticulousness, Yoshikawa charted every bit of information he secured. In time a pattern emerged. As the year progressed, he observed that a large number of ships always were in port on Saturdays and Sundays. To check air patrols, he left the consulate very early and went to some vantage point. There he observed the number of planes, their general direction of flight, and times of departure and return. He knew this to be a primitive method, but it was the only one he could use. He dared not risk field glasses, which would have drawn attention to him. He recorded patrol flights carefully, but once the planes took off, they flew rapidly out of sight, so he could never be sure exactly where they went or if they changed direction. But one thing he soon discovered—north of Oahu the Americans conducted scarcely any patrols at all.[28]

To anyone whose ideas of espionage derive from Hollywood and the works of Ian Fleming, Yoshikawa would seem a peculiar sort of spy. But neither Kita nor Okuda had the faintest intention of trying any spectacular coups which could backfire on them. So for the most part Yoshikawa's duties were tame enough, if one discounts the ever-present fear of discovery: study—scout—evaluate—report—study—scout—evaluate—report—day after day.

Yoshikawa assures us that he always worked alone, but the evidence does not support this. Obviously a highly efficient central team carried out the consulate's espionage mission, ranging from Kita, the polished career diplomat, down to Mikami, the taxi driver. Yoshikawa, the star, often scouted alone, but he was ably seconded when necessary by his predecessor, Seki, and by Kotoshirodo with his detailed memory. And always in the background moved the courtly, sound, and shrewd Okuda.

CHAPTER 9

"IN

RATHER

A SPOT"

When Robert L. Shivers stepped onto Hawaiian soil on August 23, 1939, this slight, soft-spoken man had already accumulated nineteen years of service in the Federal Bureau of Investigation.[1] That very afternoon he set up his office in the Federal Building in downtown Honolulu. After a careful briefing by Herron on the Japanese situation in Hawaii, Shivers began a tour of the Islands, asking the *haoles* (Caucasians), especially businessmen, plantation owners, and managers, about the Japanese. He found the experience more baffling than enlightening. "I got just about as many different answers as the number of people that I talked to," he observed ruefully.[2]

By 1941 Shivers had a staff of about twenty-five, including clerical employees. His Honolulu field office was responsible for "all cases of subversive activity (including espionage) involving the general civilian population." In cases of Japanese subjects, the FBI shared concurrent authority and responsibility with the Navy District Intelligence Office (DIO). The DIO consisted of a main office in Honolulu, three zone offices on outlying islands, and ten Intelligence units located within naval stations on Oahu, Maui, and Midway. This organization could investigate all counterespionage affairs in which the subjects were Navy personnel and employees and naval contractors' employees, and it shared counterespionage responsibility with the FBI in cases of Japanese subjects.[3]

On March 15, 1941, Captain Irving Mayfield was assigned as head of the DIO in his capacity as intelligence officer of the Fourteenth Naval District. Mayfield was "a very capable officer, forceful, intelligent and a fighter."[4] However, he by no means matched Shivers in experience, having served for only two weeks on temporary Intelligence duty in Washington and two years as naval attaché in Chile—not exactly the ideal background for the Navy's counterintelligence officer in a spot like Hawaii. Mayfield established his office in the Alexander Young Hotel.[5] There he had charge of about a dozen individuals in the main office, plus an agent on each of the principal islands, at Kaneohe, and at the naval munitions depot at Lualualei.[6]

Mayfield doubted that Japanese espionage centered on the Japanese consulate on Oahu:

> . . . I felt that the consulate would perhaps be advised of the existence and would cooperate with the net, but that the consulate . . . itself was not the head of the net nor [sic] necessarily an important part of the net, as the consulate might expect to be closed in similar fashion to the German and Italian consulates, and that therefore they must have prepared a plan which could be carried on without any assistance from the consulate.[7]

The Japanese had indeed prepared such a plan, and they did use a few outside agents. But regardless of Mayfield's opinion, the consulate was the center of Japanese espionage in Hawaii.

Mayfield longed to lay his hands on the cablegrams which the consulate sent to Tokyo. He tried his luck with the commercial companies, but they refused to violate Section 605 of the Federal Communications Act of 1934, which explicitly prohibited wiretaps or interception of messages from and to foreign countries.[8] One of Mayfield's enlisted men, Theodore Emmanuel, did manage to tap a number of the consulate's telephone lines, recording as many as fifty or sixty calls each day over an extended period.[9] Of course, neither Kita nor anyone else in the consulate would discuss important classified matters over the telephone. The best Mayfield could hope for was some general idea about consular personnel and the names of their frequent contacts in the islands.

The chief investigative officer for the Hawaiian Department was Lieutenant Colonel George W. Bicknell, an imposing man who stood a hefty six feet four inches. He had an attractive freckled face with twinkling eyes. He usually worked in civilian clothes. A Reserve officer, able, alert, and intelligence-minded, Bicknell had come to Hawaii in October 1940 as assistant to the G-2. Herron had a very high opinion of Bicknell and in his initial briefing of Short informed the new commander that he had planned to make Bicknell his G-2. But Short did not take the hint.[10] Bicknell therefore remained as assistant G-2 and was known as the contact officer. Generally speaking, he was Mayfield's counterpart.

Bicknell's main duties were to keep the department commander thoroughly informed of the civil population's activities on the Islands. He also met and kept in touch with all visiting officials and businessmen returning from the Orient, in order "to obtain any information which they might have on the general situation in the Pacific area." Then, too, he was responsible for the internal security of the Islands and for observations of "all counter-intelligence measures necessary. . . ."[11] And he had investigative responsibility in counterespionage if the subjects were in or employed by the Army or had access to an Army reservation.[12]

Bicknell worked out of the Federal Building, which also housed Shivers and his small band of FBI people. Every Tuesday Shivers, Bicknell, and Mayfield met to exchange information, and a cordial working relationship existed among their offices.[13] Both the FBI and DIO kept a partial watch on activities at the Japanese consulate and the Nippon Yusen Kaisha (NYK) steamship line.[14] But either of them could have done little to cut off Yoshikawa, Seki, or Kotoshirodo. A host nation usually bends over backward to let accredited diplomatic and consular personnel go their ways so long as they operate within the letter of the law. And Kita and Okuda were very careful to have their people carry on "legal espionage."

To the best of our knowledge, no one from the consulate ever entered a restricted military area unless at the invitation of the American authorities. There is no record that the Japanese ever stole or photographed classified information. They violated no law in pausing to look at the imposing spectacle of men-of-war moored in Pearl Harbor. In fact, the base was an open book by its very nature. And the individual services could do nothing about this. Pearl Harbor was too big, and in too open a position, to be hidden or camouflaged from either sea or land view. The only way to cut off observation would have been to make the entire island of Oahu a restricted military reservation— something no American government could tolerate. The very law the Americans swore to uphold and protect tripped them up. This law guaranteed the privacy of the airways, and the local companies very properly refused to give the FBI, Army Intelligence, or Navy Intelligence copies of the consulate's messages—until early December 1941, when it was too little and too late.

But irony of ironies, Washington was scooping up these and other Japanese diplomatic messages by the bucketful. The basic story is as follows: The Japanese used several diplomatic codes, the most secret of which was an exceedingly complicated cipher system known as Purple. Tokyo had a childlike faith in the complete infallibility of its diplomatic codes. It never credited the Americans with the ability to crack the Purple system.

In fact, the Signal Intelligence Service (SIS) under the tireless direction of Lieutenant Colonel William F. Friedman, succeeded in doing so as early as August 1940, after eighteen to twenty months of the most intense labor.[15] Rated "the world's greatest cryptologist," Friedman, though quiet and unassuming, possessed a drive and tenacity that refused to recognize the word "impossible." The decrypting of Purple and its brother systems earned the name Magic. Friedman paid a high price for his magnificent gift to his country. In December 1940 he suffered a nervous collapse from overwork, and as 1941 opened, he was under treatment in Walter Reed General Hospital in Washington.[16] The "individual genius . . . of Harry Larry Clark, one of the younger civilian cryptanalysts," triggered the breakthrough. The Navy assisted throughout 1939 and 1940 by furnishing the intercepts and taking over all other Japanese diplomatic systems so that the Army could concentrate on Purple.

"The Army provided the solution and wiring diagram; the Navy provided the funds and manufacturing facilities."[17]

From the summer of 1940 on, therefore, U.S. Intelligence had been reading Japan's diplomatic messages. This meant that the U.S. government had full knowledge of virtually all the traffic which passed between the Foreign Office in Tokyo and its most important embassies and consulates abroad. So Washington knew Tokyo's instructions to Nomura and his reports from the embassy. U.S. cryptanalysts were also reading lower-grade Japanese diplomatic ciphers, notably the so-called J codes, the current one being J-19. These were mainly in use between the Foreign Ministry and many consulates, including Honolulu. Thus, the United States also picked up the traffic between Tokyo and Honolulu about the U.S. Pacific Fleet.

By the fall of 1941 American policy makers actually knew more than Nomura about his country's intentions, for Tokyo was by no means candid with its ambassador. The United States Army, Navy, and State departments acknowledged the enormous worth of the Magic data and leaned heavily upon them for command decisions.

But Magic was not a cure-all or an enchanted key to the mazes of all Japanese thinking. Its messages revealed only what the Foreign Office gave its own diplomats. And the Foreign Ministry itself was not omniscient. The Army and Navy dictated Japanese foreign policy, and they did not always clue in the foreign minister and his associates until matters had proceeded well along—sometimes too far. So Magic could not answer all the questions the United States wanted to ask.

For instance, in 1941 U.S. Intelligence had not yet broken through the chain of Japanese naval codes. Generally speaking, military codes are more difficult to break than diplomatic, and in addition, the Japanese Navy prudently changed some of its codes several times during 1941. Hence Washington did not know of the orders Yamamoto sent to the ships of the Combined Fleet or the messages which the Naval General Staff radioed to the Pearl Harbor task force as it sailed across the northern Pacific to Hawaii.

The main mission of the Communications Intelligence Unit of the Fourteenth Naval District at Pearl Harbor was to break down the "Japanese flag officers system." From approximately 1926 to late 1940 this code and cipher had provided most of the U.S. Navy's information about its Japanese counterpart. Unfortunately for the United States, on about December 1, 1940, the Japanese changed their flag officers' code. Despite the best efforts of both the Washington and Pearl Harbor units, they had not succeeded in cracking the new version,[18] although Commander Joseph J. Rochefort, who took over the Pearl Harbor Intelligence Unit on about May 15, 1941, was one of the highest qualified men in the business.

Eight Purple decrypting machines existed in 1941. Washington had four—two each for the Army and Navy. The switches and "intricate rat's-nest of wiring" seldom cooled off.[19] In November 1941 "the diplomatic traffic . . . averaged about 26 messages a day."[20] To avoid duplication of effort, the services divided the messages by date of origin in Tokyo, the Navy taking the odd days, the Army the even.[21]

In April 1941 a machine went to Cavite; it was transferred in August to Corregidor, where the Communications Intelligence Unit had been assigned the Purple, Red, and J codes. Stark approved sending this machine because the Philippines were "the best place to intercept Japanese traffic and receive information during that time. . . ." Any benefit to Admiral Hart "was a secondary consideration."[22] A copy of all of this unit's diplomatic translations went daily to the Army locally. In addition, all Purple and some Red and J-19 "were immediately enciphered and sent to Washington." These cryptologists also maintained liaison with their British opposites at Singapore and furnished Washington with anything of interest from that source.[23]

London received two Purple machines in January 1941. By July of that year Pearl Harbor could have had one, "but only at the expense of Washington." Then the question arose of a third for the British. The "best compromise" was to send the machine to London "and at the same time order parts of more machines." So around "September or early October" London had its third apparatus, and a requisition for stepping switches for four more machines was "bogged down in the War Production Board. . . ." Thus, Hawaii did not receive a Purple machine.[24] Whether Kimmel and Short would have derived much benefit from one is doubtful because the information of most concern to them came over the J system between Tokyo and Honolulu.

In Washington the Army's Signal Intelligence Service, headed by Lieutenant Colonel Rex W. Minckler and under the general supervision of Colonel Otis K. Sadtler, worked in the closest cooperation with the Navy's Communications Security. The latter's chief, Commander Laurence F. Safford, answered to Rear Admiral Leigh Noyes, director of Communications. One year younger than Friedman, his close co-worker, Safford, like Cassius, had a lean and hungry look. A quiet and gentle person, yet a dynamo of controlled energy, he pursued his goals with almost fanatical obstinacy. His long association with cryptology, combined with a native genius for the work, made him the Navy's recognized authority in the field.

Communications Security had a twofold mission: first, to furnish the United States with codes and ciphers; secondly, to supervise American communications security and intelligence on foreign nations, "particularly Japan—in fact, almost exclusively Japan."[25]

Magic decoding and translation lagged for a variety of reasons. Enough radio circuits and facilities did not exist to transmit all intercepts from station to the center at Washington by radio, so airmail was the usual route. If anything interfered with the normal airmail schedules, the data might go by train or ship. At this time only one air clipper a week plied between Hawaii and the mainland, and if the weather held it up, deliveries went by ship to the West Coast.[26] Once the data reached Washington, they had to take their turn in seriously undermanned offices.

Translation proved a real bottleneck. The two communications offices

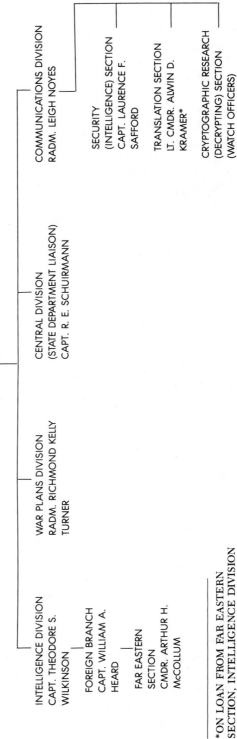

SIMPLIFIED CHART OF NAVY DEPARTMENT
AS OF DECEMBER 7, 1941

SECRETARY OF THE
NAVY
FRANK KNOX

CHIEF OF NAVAL
OPERATIONS
ADMIRAL HAROLD R.
STARK

ASST. CNO
RADM. ROYAL E.
INGERSOLL

WAR PLANS DIVISION
RADM. RICHMOND KELLY
TURNER

CENTRAL DIVISION
(STATE DEPARTMENT LIAISON)
CAPT. R. E. SCHUIRMANN

COMMUNICATIONS DIVISION
RADM. LEIGH NOYES

SECURITY
(INTELLIGENCE) SECTION
CAPT. LAURENCE F.
SAFFORD

TRANSLATION SECTION
LT. CMDR. ALWIN D.
KRAMER*

CRYPTOGRAPHIC RESEARCH
(DECRYPTING) SECTION
(WATCH OFFICERS)

INTELLIGENCE DIVISION
CAPT. THEODORE S.
WILKINSON

FOREIGN BRANCH
CAPT. WILLIAM A.
HEARD

FAR EASTERN
SECTION
CMDR. ARTHUR H.
McCOLLUM

*ON LOAN FROM FAR EASTERN
SECTION, INTELLIGENCE DIVISION

decoded but did not translate. In the Navy this function was under Commander McCollum's wing. His assistant, Lieutenant Commander Alwin D. Kramer, knew Japanese well. Younger than Safford and Friedman by almost ten years, Kramer had studied Japanese in Japan for three years beginning in 1931.[27] Able and precise-minded, he had at his disposal one officer, two yeomen, and six translators, only three of whom could be termed fully qualified.[28]

Japanese is very difficult to translate into English. To make matters worse, the messages came in as phonetic syllables. One such sound could have a variety of unrelated meanings. Even translators highly qualified in Japanese needed "considerable experience in this particular field before they could be trusted to come through with a correct interpretation. . . ." Moreover, they worked with diplomatic material, where a shade of phraseology carries a vital significance. No wonder Kramer often put in brutal hours of overtime.[29]

Much the same situation existed on the Army side. SIS received and decoded the messages. Then they were sent to Colonel Rufus S. Bratton, chief of the Far Eastern Section, a dedicated officer and West Pointer who played a vital role in Magic. He determined what to distribute for top-level considera-tion. He knew Japan, its language and its people, far better than his superiors, for he had been a language student there and attended the Imperial War College in 1932.

All during 1941 Bratton believed that Japan would expand its Asian war and that eventually the United States would be sucked into the whirlpool. His intelligence training fortified his natural ability, so that he developed almost a sixth sense for spotting developments which others might not recognize. Once he decided that a course was right, Bratton would stick with it undaunted.[30]

The Pearl Harbor inquiries did not bring out the exact number of translators available to Bratton, but it is doubtful if he had any more than Kramer. Inevitably, therefore, certain items received priority, while others piled up. The diplomatic exchanges between Washington and Tokyo received first choice. Nevertheless, Magic was usually translated the same day SIS passed it on. As Miles observed, "The astonishing thing . . . was not that these messages were delayed in the process of translation from Japanese to English, but that we were able to do it at all."[31]

Yet it is not enough for facts to be gathered and for these facts to be accurate. They must be timely, and they must be acted upon, either at the central agency or by dissemination to the most interested parties. Otherwise, their harvesting becomes a mere exercise in accumulation. Having brought off one of the most astonishing coups in the history of intelligence, the United States failed to take full advantage of it. The top brass in Washington reasoned this way: The shadow of a hint reaching Tokyo that the United States could read its diplomatic mail would trigger an immediate change in the entire chain of systems which would set American Intelligence back for months, perhaps years. Thus, as Stark testified, "anybody who was let in on that had to sign a paper never to disclose it, practically as long as he lived, or ever to talk about it."[32]

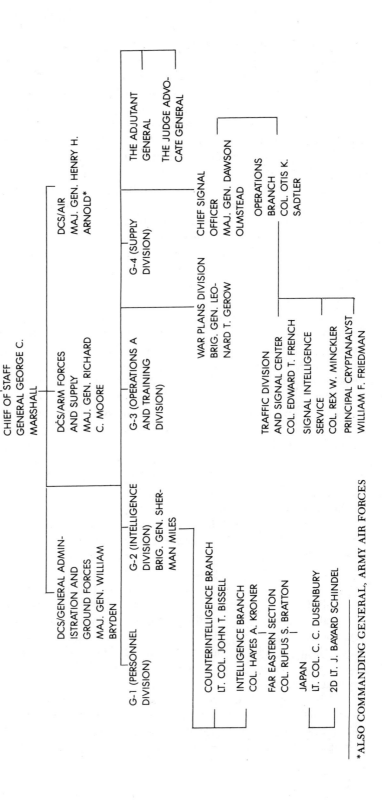

SIMPLIFIED CHART OF WAR DEPARTMENT
AS OF DECEMBER 7, 1941

SECRETARY OF WAR
HENRY L. STIMSON

CHIEF OF STAFF
GENERAL GEORGE C.
MARSHALL

DCS/GENERAL ADMIN-
ISTRATION AND
GROUND FORCES
MAJ. GEN. WILLIAM
BRYDEN

DCS/ARM FORCES
AND SUPPLY
MAJ. GEN. RICHARD
C. MOORE

DCS/AIR
MAJ. GEN. HENRY H.
ARNOLD*

THE ADJUTANT
GENERAL

THE JUDGE ADVO-
CATE GENERAL

G-1 (PERSONNEL
DIVISION)

G-2 (INTELLIGENCE
DIVISION)
BRIG. GEN. SHER-
MAN MILES

G-3 (OPERATIONS A
AND TRAINING
DIVISION)

G-4 (SUPPLY
DIVISION)

CHIEF SIGNAL
OFFICER
MAJ. GEN. DAWSON
OLMSTEAD

WAR PLANS DIVISION
BRIG. GEN. LEO-
NARD T. GEROW

OPERATIONS
BRANCH
COL. OTIS K.
SADTLER

COUNTERINTELLIGENCE BRANCH
LT. COL. JOHN T. BISSELL

INTELLIGENCE BRANCH
COL. HAYES A. KRONER

FAR EASTERN SECTION
COL. RUFUS S. BRATTON

JAPAN
LT. COL. C. C. DUSENBURY
2D LT. J. BAYARD SCHINDEL

TRAFFIC DIVISION
AND SIGNAL CENTER
COL. EDWARD T. FRENCH

SIGNAL INTELLIGENCE
SERVICE
COL. REX W. MINCKLER

PRINCIPAL CRYPTANALYST
WILLIAM F. FRIEDMAN

*ALSO COMMANDING GENERAL, ARMY AIR FORCES

Even in Washington, official distribution was so select that the GIs' cynically amused expression "Destroy Before Reading" virtually applied. By an agreement of January 23, 1941, the Army confined its list to the secretary of war; the Chief of Staff; the chief of War Plans, ACS G-2; and sometimes Major General Edwin M. "Pa" Watson, Roosevelt's military aide, who gave such dispatches to the President. The Navy permitted its equivalent dignitaries to see the messages. Of course, other War and Navy department personnel were involved *ex officio.*[33] Secretary of State Cordell Hull and his undersecretary, Sumner Welles, received Magic, and from their testimony it is evident that a few others in State were at least familiar with the subject matter of the intercepts.[34] Kramer, Bratton, and the latter's assistant, Lieutenant Colonel C. Clyde Dusenbury, and sometimes Second Lieutenant J. Bayard Schindel acted as messenger boys. The couriers transported the items in locked briefcases to which the recipient had the key. The latter signed for the day's batch, and the courier returned, either the same day or the next, to pick up the messages for immediate destruction along with the receipt.[35]

Originally Military and Naval Intelligence had prepared summaries of the information or paraphrases of the messages for distribution. In November 1941, when American-Japanese relations were mounting to a climax, the President insisted on seeing the original messages "because he was afraid when they tried to condense them, someone would change the meaning."[36] Actually Intelligence had already largely discontinued summarizing. Kramer's early screening had been intended to weed out the more important items from "material covering the whole world." By mid-1941, however, the sheer volume of traffic kept him busy checking the many references to preceding messages contained in the body of the incoming intercepts. He would dig up these citations and attach them to the current document, then place the bundle in each day's folder for distribution so that the reader had the complete picture. In the autumn the greater percentage of the traffic dealt with the Berlin–Tokyo circuit or the Japanese–American negotiations.[37]

Poco Smith later testified: "To my mind there was no danger in transmitting messages from Washington to Pearl Harbor over our system. If not safe, then it was unsafe to send our own messages back and forth between Washington and Pearl Harbor. . . ."[38] Evidently a certain amount of confusion existed at the Navy Headquarters as to just how much information Kimmel had available to him. Turner testified that he believed "at that time, and it was Admiral Stark's belief, that all of these major diplomatic messages, at least in the Pacific, were being decrypted by both Admiral Hart and by Admiral Kimmel, and I did not know that Admiral Kimmel did not hold the code for those dispatches until I was so informed at the time of the Navy court of inquiry on Pearl Harbor."[39]

Perhaps the real idea behind Washington's attitude lay in a cautious letter which McCollum sent to Layton on April 22, 1941, in reply to the latter's request for diplomatic intelligence such as he had received in February concerning Japanese designs on Vichy:

It does not seem to me to be very practical to build up an organization afloat which will merely duplicate the efforts of the Intelligence Division in the Department. I appreciate that all this leaves you in rather a spot as naturally people are interested in current developments. I believe, however, that a sharp line should be drawn and a distinction continuously emphasized between information that is of interest and information that is desirable to have on which to base action.

In other words, while you and the Fleet may be highly interested in politics, there is nothing that you can do about it. Therefore, information of political significance, except as it affects immediate action by the Fleet, is merely a matter of interest to you and not a matter of utility.[40]

This exchange between McCollum and Layton did not touch on the traffic to and from the Japanese consulate in Honolulu. This used the J system until early December 1941, when they adopted the PA-K2 code. Even to the most inexperienced eye these intercepts gave every evidence of military espionage. Again, Washington had an answer: Information of this type poured out of Japanese consulates on the West Coast, the Philippines, Panama, indeed from all over the world, and there was nothing to distinguish the Honolulu messages as being different in essence from those originating in any other city.[41] This explanation does not quite hold water. Granted, Communications and Intelligence both were inundated with items similar to those moving between Tokyo and Honolulu. But Honolulu was not just any other city. It was the home base of the U.S. Pacific Fleet, the pivot of American Asian strategy in that vast sea. Therefore, anything even remotely hinting at undue Japanese interest in that location deserved priority handling and prompt transmission to the organization concerned.

The Honolulu–Tokyo traffic, although dispatched in diplomatic code, did not deal exclusively with diplomatic matters. Often these messages contained strictly military information. The United States authorities knew very well that in Japan the military called the tune, so that the key to their probable moves would more likely rest in their military messages than in the high-level diplomatic channels.

To complicate the situation further, the all-important function of estimating enemy intentions had recently been the subject of a struggle between Naval Intelligence and War Plans. Early in 1941 Turner came to Captain James's office and requested that "ONI make no estimate of prospective enemy intentions for CNO but furnish information to War Plans who would make the required estimates." James resisted this foray into his territory, informing Turner that "existing printed organization instructions of CNO required Intelligence to make these estimates." For the time being that settled the matter.

After Captain Alan C. Kirk replaced James, Turner tried again, and this time he succeeded in carrying the discussion to Stark. Kirk maintained that ONI was responsible for interpreting possible enemy intentions after evaluating information received from whatever source. Further, he felt that ONI "was comparable to G-2 in the War Department General Staff in these respects, and should likewise prepare that section of formal Estimate known as 'Enemy Intentions.' " But "Terrible" Turner declared that his War Plans Division

> should prepare such a section of the Estimate, and should interpret and evaluate all information concerning possible hostile nations from whatever source received. Further, that the Office of Naval Intelligence was solely a collection agency and a distributing agency, and was not charged with sending out any information which would initiate any operations on the part of the fleet, or fleets, anywhere.

Whatever Stark's virtues, they did not include the backbone necessary to stand up to Turner. Predictably he took Turner's position, and Kirk accepted the decision.[42]

The net effect was to reduce Naval Intelligence to a collecting and distributing clearinghouse. Even more serious, Stark's decision placed the responsibility for evaluating Japanese intentions in the hands of officers who did not know Japan, its language, or its armed forces, as did those in ONI.

The intelligence hassle placed undue emphasis on the concept of estimating enemy intentions. Those engaged in this power struggle would have been better advised to devote that energy and time to estimating enemy capabilities. And whoever decided to withhold the Honolulu intercepts—or at least information based thereon—from Kimmel and Short must accept part of the blame for the Pearl Harbor tragedy.

CHAPTER 10

"THE MOST

LIKELY AND

DANGEROUS

FORM OF

ATTACK"

When the Army transport *Leonard Wood* arrived in Honolulu on Saturday night, November 2, 1940, a tall gentleman walked down the gangplank. He had waving gray hair and thick brows shadowing pleasant eyes. His thin face with its oblong jaw, big nose, high forehead, and large ears looked more scholarly then military.

Major General Frederick L. Martin won his wings at the age of thirty-nine, when he was already a major. He completed courses at the Air Tactical School at Langley Field, Virginia, and the Command and General Staff School at Fort Leavenworth, Kansas. Then followed a series of command assignments. Further study brought him to the Army War College. After duty at Wright Field, Ohio, he took over command of the Third Bombardment Wing at Barksdale Field, Louisiana, in the spring of 1937 with the temporary rank of brigadier general. On October 1, 1940, he became a temporary major general, and concurrently received his orders to command the Hawaiian Air Force, activated on November 1. With his two stars, he could deal with Herron and later with Short, if not on terms of equality, at least within reaching distance. When he took over his new post, he ranked as the Air Corps's senior pilot and technical observer and had logged 2,000 hours of flight time.[1]

Martin was not in the best physical condition and appeared older than his fifty-eight years. He had earlier developed a severe, chronic ulcer condition, which required surgery and undermined his health. As a result, he had not touched an alcoholic drink in years. His assignment placed him in an ambiguous position. As commander of the Hawaiian Air Force he had direct access to Major General H. H. "Hap" Arnold, chief of the Army Air Corps, but he remained under the command of Short, a foot soldier to the soles of his boots. The situation could have been delicate, and indeed, Martin had received

SIMPLIFIED CHART OF HAWAIIAN AIR FORCE
AS OF DECEMBER 7, 1941

(UNDER OVERALL COMMAND OF GENERAL SHORT)

COMMANDING GENERAL
MAJ. GENERAL FREDERICK
L. MARTIN

CHIEF OF STAFF
COL. JAMES A. MOLLISON

INTELLIGENCE
COL. EDWARD W.
RALEY

SIGNAL OFFICER
LT. COL. CLAY I.
HOPPOUGH

18TH BOMBARDMENT WING
BRIG. GEN. JACOB H.
RUDOLPH

14TH PURSUIT WING
BRIG. GEN. HOWARD
C. DAVIDSON

HICKAM FIELD
COL. WILLIAM E.
FARTHING

WHEELER FIELD
COL. WILLIAM J.
FLOOD

BELLOWS FIELD
LT. COL. LEONARD
D. WEDDINGTON

specific instructions from Arnold to end the undeclared civil war which had raged on Oahu between the Army, its Air Corps, and the Navy and for which it appears some of the blame rested with the airmen.[2]

To understand the American commanders on Oahu in 1941, one must see them in the context of the problems which bedeviled them. So Martin came to Hawaii bearing an olive branch. He took his role very seriously and at times, in the interests of harmony, would abandon a point which his fellow airmen thought he should have followed up more vigorously. His eagerness to please, combined with his rather pedantic appearance and manner, caused some individuals privately to label him a "fuddy-duddy." But the estimate did the man less than justice, for he was a hardworking, dutiful, and loyal officer, although a worrier who fretted constantly lest he not accomplish enough. With Martin's appointment, interservice relations improved steadily throughout 1941.[3]

On December 17, after about six weeks on the job, he wrote to Arnold: "These islands . . . have very few level areas suitable for the location of landing fields. Of the level areas in existence, the greater part of these are under cultivation in pineapples or sugar cane. . . . It is my purpose to provide an outlying field for each of the combat squadrons. . . ." Martin did not want his planes huddled together so that an enemy would have easy pickings if he swooped in on them. Presently he came to his major worry: "We have been satisfied in the past to supply our units in foreign possessions with obsolescent equipment until organizations in the States have been equipped with modern types. This to me is very faulty and could, in these times of uncertainty, be very detrimental to our scheme of national defense. . . ."[4]

Martin's naval counterpart was an extroverted Irishman, Rear Admiral Patrick N. L. Bellinger, who had arrived in Hawaii on October 30, 1940. He had a full thatch of dark hair parted on the left side, a rather long mouth, and direct, bright eyes. He had a most distinguished flying career with any number of Navy firsts on his record. Now at Pearl Harbor, he held no fewer than five positions and theoretically answered to five different superiors. These multiple responsibilities bothered him much less than they did a swarm of postattack investigators, and in fact, such assignments have never been rarities in the armed services.

Bellinger was not a profound thinker, but he stood obstinately by his convictions and expressed them forcibly, constantly "beefing up" the letters which his brilliant operations and plans officer, Commander Charles Coe, prepared for his signature. But he had no ounce of bluster in him, and his invincibly sunny disposition made him a general favorite.[5] Like Martin, he was running a poor man's game and had no inhibitions about sounding off loud and clear even to the highest quarters about his troubles. On January 16, 1941, he wrote a strong letter to Stark:

> 1. I arrived here in October 30, 1940, with the point of view that the International situation was critical, especially in the Pacific, and I was impressed with the need for being ready today rather than tomorrow for any even-

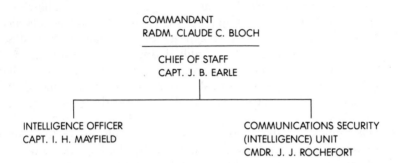

SIMPLIFIED CHART OF 14TH NAVAL DISTRICT
AS OF DECEMBER 7, 1941

COMMANDANT
RADM. CLAUDE C. BLOCH

CHIEF OF STAFF
CAPT. J. B. EARLE

INTELLIGENCE OFFICER
CAPT. I. H. MAYFIELD

COMMUNICATIONS SECURITY
(INTELLIGENCE) UNIT
CMDR. J. J. ROCHEFORT

As commandant, Fourteenth Naval District, Bloch was directly under the Navy Department. He was also commander, Hawaiian Naval Coastal Sea Frontier; commandant, Pearl Harbor Navy Yard. He was also an officer of the Fleet and under CinCPAC as commander, Naval Base Defense Forces, and commander, Task Force Four.

As commander, Naval Base Defense Forces, Bloch had administrative control over

RADM. P. N. L. BELLINGER

Bellinger held down four positions:
1. Commander, Hawaiian Based Patrol Wing and Commander, Patrol Wing Two.
2. Commander, Task Force Nine (Patrol Wings One and Two with attending surface craft).
3. Liaison with commandant, Fourteenth Naval District.
4. Commander, Naval Base Defense Air Force.
He was responsible theoretically to the following superiors:
1. Commander, Aircraft Scouting Force (type command for patrol wings), based at San Diego.
2. Commander, Scouting Force, of which Patrol Wings One and Two were a part.
3. CinCPAC when commanding Task Force Nine.
4. Commanders of Task Forces One, Two, and Three for patrol planes assigned those forces.
5. Commandant, Fourteenth Naval District in Bloch's capacity as commander, Naval Base Defense Force, when Bellinger was performing duties as commander, Naval Base Defense Air Force.

tuality that might arise. After taking over command of Patrol Wing TWO and looking over the situation, I was surprised to find that here in the Hawaiian Islands, an important naval advanced post, we were operating on a shoestring and the more I looked the thinner the shoestring appeared to be.

. . . As there are no plans to modernize the present patrol planes comprising Patrol Wing TWO, this evidently means that there is no intention to replace the present obsolescent type. .. . This, together with the many existing deficiencies, indicates to me that the Navy Department as a whole does not view the situation in the Pacific with alarm or else is not taking steps in keeping with their view. . . .

This was a heavy punch for a rear admiral to swing at the Chief of Naval Operations. Bellinger urgently recommended that "immediate steps be taken to furnish the personnel, material, facilities and equipment required. . . ." After he had laid it squarely on the line, his generous nature reasserted itself, and he added, "The tremendous and all consuming work of those in the Navy Department is fully appreciated and there is no intent to criticize or to shift responsibility." He ended with a businesslike list of specific recommendations.[6]

That Bellinger was not talking through his five hats when he spoke of the vital role of patrol planes we know from a remarkable document dated March 31, 1941. This project had its genesis when Kimmel summoned Bellinger to his office on about March 1 and directed him to report to Bloch at the Fourteenth Naval District and get together with Martin to work out a plan for joint action in the event of an attack on Oahu or fleet units in Hawaiian waters.[7]

Bloch's assignment consisted of overall responsibility for the great naval base, its vast maintenance shops, the precious, potentially dangerous farm of fuel tanks, harbor defenses, and security. It included innumerable housekeeping functions, such as housing, feeding, and clothing the men of the Fleet as well as of the shore installations. Bloch was also responsible for whatever naval elements could be made available for the defense of Pearl Harbor. He therefore had a very direct interest in the air protection of the installation and the ships.

Of course, Martin and Bellinger did not sit down at a double desk, roll up their sleeves, and proceed to write their report alone. Some of their bright staff members did the spadework, but the two flag officers worked closely with them and accepted and signed the report. So they can claim a full measure of credit.

In its final form this historic work became famous to all students of the Pacific war as the Martin-Bellinger Report. It speaks for itself clearly and crisply. Its "Summary of the Situation" observed, among other things:

> (c) A successful, sudden raid against our ships and Naval installations on Oahu might prevent effective offensive action by our forces in the Western Pacific for a long period. . . .

> (e) It appears possible that Orange submarines and/or an Orange fast raiding force might arrive in Hawaiian waters with no prior warning from our intelligence service.

The document then considered the capability of Japan in terms of actual strength: "(a) Orange might send into this area one or more submarines and/or one or more fast raiding forces composed of carriers supported by fast cruisers."[8] One notes a striking difference from Kimmel's Pacific Fleet letter of February 15. The two airmen, Martin and Bellinger, estimated that enemy carriers would be "supported by fast cruisers," instead of vice versa. These experienced exponents of aerial warfare were thinking along the same lines as Genda. The report continued: "The aircraft at present available in Hawaii are inadequate to maintain, for any extended period, from bases on Oahu, a patrol extensive enough to insure that an air attack from an Orange carrier cannot arrive over Oahu as a complete surprise. . . ." Here in a nutshell was the dilemma of Oahu's defenders—the need for a 360-degree arc of patrol without the planes necessary to accomplish such a mission.

In the area of "Possible Enemy Action," the authors virtually foretold the future:

(a) A declaration of war might be preceded by:

1. A surprise submarine attack on ships in the operating area.

2. A surprise attack on Oahu including ships and installations in Pearl Harbor.

3. A combination of these two.

(b) It appears that the most likely and dangerous form of attack on Oahu would be an air attack. It is believed that at present such an attack would most likely be launched from one or more carriers which would probably approach inside of three hundred miles.

(c) A single attack might or might not indicate the presence of more submarines or more planes awaiting to attack after defending aircraft have been drawn away by the original thrust.

(d) Any single submarine attack might indicate the presence of a considerable undiscovered surface force probably composed of fast ships accompanied by a carrier.[9]

Someone let a discrepancy slip by with this observation or else did not appreciate the vital difference between "carriers supported by fast cruisers" and "fast ships accompanied by a carrier." In fact, these estimates of enemy action somewhat echo the existing Pacific Fleet letter.

(e) In a dawn air attack there is a high probability that it could be delivered as a complete surprise in spite of any patrols we might be using and that it might find us in a condition of readiness under which pursuit would be slow to start, also it might be successful as a diversion to draw attention away from a second attacking force. . . . Submarine attacks could be coordinated with any air attack. . . . [10]

The possibility of such undersea craft prowling into the Hawaiian area was a nasty one. Actually Martin and Bellinger went somewhat ahead of Onishi and Genda's original plan for a Pearl Harbor attack, which did not envisage the use of submarines.

What then could Kimmel, Bloch, and Short do about a potential Japanese attack? Martin and Bellinger had this answer:

> (a) Run daily patrols as far as possible to seaward through 360 degrees to reduce the probabilities of surface or air surprise. This would be desirable but can only be effectively maintained with present personnel and material for a very short period and as a practicable measure cannot, therefore, be undertaken unless other intelligence indicates that a surface raid is probable within rather narrow time limits.[11]

Thus, into two short sentences Martin and Bellinger unknowingly compressed an awesome American tragedy.

The two planners next went into thorough detail concerning "Action open to us," but pointed out the painful fact that no actions could "be initiated by our forces until an attack is known to be imminent or has occurred. On the other hand, when an attack develops time will probably be vital and our actions must start with a minimum of delay."[12]

Martin and Bellinger could not have done a much better job of mind reading had they actually looked over the shoulders of Yamamoto, Onishi, Genda—and others. For in Japan the Pearl Harbor circle was widening even as Oahu's planners labored over their report. The final document bore the date of March 31, 1941, approximately the same time that Yamamoto put his Combined Fleet staff to work on his design.

Washington was pleased with the Martin-Bellinger Report. "We agreed thoroughly with it, approved it," said Turner, "and it was very comforting and gratifying to see that officers in important commands out there had the same view of the situation as was held in the War and Navy Departments."[13]

The Martin-Bellinger Report stands as a workmanlike, almost inspired example of defensive planning, but along with the Joint Coastal Frontier Defense Plan of which it was an annex, it had a basic flaw. The findings of the Navy Court of Inquiry into the Pearl Harbor disaster summarized this clearly:

> The effectiveness of these plans depended entirely upon advance knowledge that an attack was to be expected within narrow limits of time and the plans were drawn with this as a premise. It was not possible for the Commander-in-Chief of the Fleet to make Fleet planes permanently available to the Naval Base Defense Officer, because of his own lack of planes, pilots, and crews and because of the demands of the Fleet in connection with Fleet operations at sea.[14]

Under paragraph 18 (1) of the basic plan Short transferred responsibility for long-range aerial reconnaissance to Bloch's Fourteenth Naval District, retaining only scouting some twenty miles offshore.[15] The wisdom of this switch is questionable because the Hawaiian Department was charged with the protec-

tion of the Fleet in harbor as well as with defense of the Islands, and long-range
air scouting was a fundamental tool of this mission. But cold facts dictated the
decision, for Short and Martin never had at any time more than a handful of the
planes necessary for the required wide swing around Hawaii. Under the
Short-Bloch agreement, when the latter's aircraft were insufficient for the
mission, the Hawaiian Air Force would make planes available "under the
tactical control of the Naval commander directing the search operations."[16]

When Bloch accepted this solemn responsibility, he "had no patrol planes
permanently assigned to his command. . . . The only Naval patrol planes in the
Hawaiian area were the 69 planes of Patrol Wing Two and these were
handicapped by shortage of relief pilots and crews." Unfortunately, the aircraft
of Patrol Wing Two never came to a total large enough for a meaningful search
arc. More important, "The task assigned the Commander-in-Chief . . . was to
prepare his Fleet for war. . . . The Fleet planes were being constantly
employed in patrolling the operating area in which the Fleet's preparations for
war were being carried on."[17]

On April 1, exactly one day after the dating of the Martin-Bellinger
Report, Naval Intelligence in Washington alerted the commandants of all naval
districts—including the Fourteenth at Hawaii—as follows:

> Personnel of your Naval Intelligence Service should be advised that because
> of the fact that from past experience shows [sic] the Axis Powers often begin
> activities in a particular field on Saturdays and Sundays or on national holidays
> of the country concerned they should take steps on such days to see that
> proper watches and precautions are in effect.[18]

Another link in the chain of prediction! If Japan took the plunge, the defenders
could expect it to be on a Saturday, Sunday, or national holiday.

While military leaders on Oahu were busy developing plans to meet a
possible Japanese attack, many Americans conceived of Hawaii as an impregnable fortress. A vast protective belt of water shielded Oahu on all sides. Some
military experts considered the great area of "vacant sea" to the north the best
and most likely avenue of approach for the enemy, but by the same token it
provided an open highway of exposure and detection. The undeniable argument that Japan had a vast ocean in which to approach Oahu could be
countered by the simple fact that Hawaii commanded all seaways in the central
Pacific. Moreover, a screen of outlying bases into which the United States was
pouring millions of defense dollars flanked Oahu. Midway lay 1,300 miles to the
northwest; Wake about another 1,000 miles west and somewhat southward.
Johnston Island, a white spear of land, barely crested the waves 700 miles to the
southwest, with Palmyra 1,000 miles due south. Still other American and
British possessions stretched beyond this defensive rim. Up in the Aleutians a
new naval and air base at Dutch Harbor guarded the northern Pacific and
flanked Japan's shortest line of approach to the West Coast.

U.S. naval strength was concentrated heavily at Pearl Harbor. Here, at any
time the Fleet moved out in stately maneuver, one could see fighting craft of all

descriptions—six to eight battleships; two or three aircraft carriers; numerous heavy and light cruisers; dozens of destroyers, submarines, minesweepers, and auxiliary craft. Oil storage tanks, dry docks, workshops, and many other shore installations made Pearl Harbor virtually an independent maintenance base. Here, in the "Navy behind the Navy," the entire Fleet could dock, fuel, supply, and undergo repairs. From this great mid-Pacific pivotal point it could swing into action at a moment's notice and strike hard at the enemy in any direction. Hawaii was proud of its guardian of the seas. "If there were ever men and a fleet ready for any emergency," bragged the Honolulu *Advertiser* on February 1, 1941, "it's Uncle Sam's fighting ships."

The Army, too, bent every effort to make good the boast that Pearl Harbor was "the best defended naval base in the world." In 1941 Oahu had a strong garrison of about 25,000 troops. Armed with all the tools of modern warfare, kept rugged and alert by constant field exercises, these soldiers were expertly trained in the defense of the island. And if the Japanese sideslipped the American outer defense posts or succeeded in fighting through the Pacific Fleet, the Hawaiian Air Force stood ready to help smash any attack. Bombers stationed at Hickam Field gave the Air Force potent scoring punch, and the latest fighter planes organized in effective squadrons at Wheeler Field assured mastery of the skies over Oahu. In case the enemy got too close or tried to land there, field guns stood ready. Well could Short say on April 7: "Here in Hawaii we all live in a citadel or gigantically fortified island."[19]

Little wonder that so many Americans extolled their mid-ocean bastion with glowing confidence and no doubt would have regarded the Martin-Bellinger Report, could they have seen it, as a worthy but academic school exercise having no relationship to the realities of geography or logistics.

CHAPTER 11

"HOW CAN

AIR POWER

BE USED

MOST

EFFECTIVELY?"

In early April 1941 Yamamoto sat closeted in his cabin aboard *Mutsu*—*Nagato* was undergoing overhaul—with two of his key officers, Captain Kameto Kuroshima and Commander Yasuji Watanabe. Several weeks had gone by since Onishi first submitted his and Genda's draft to Yamamoto, and Kuroshima and Watanabe already knew the general trends of Yamamoto's thinking. Kuroshima, in particular, was no stranger to his ideas. Several times during 1940 Yamamoto had discussed with him the strategy Japan should follow in case of conflict with the United States. As the weaker nation Japan could not fight a defensive war; its only chance would be to seize the initiative and strike first.[1]

Yamamoto had put his staff to studying the Pearl Harbor plan no later than January. About the middle of that month Kuroshima directed Commander Akira Sasaki, Yamamoto's air officer, to examine three possible alternatives. The first assumed that the Americans would be strictly on guard. In that case the Japanese would approach within approximately 350 miles of the target and bomb only American carriers, with fighters guiding the bombers. The second called for penetration to some 200 miles and use of all the Japanese aircraft in the attack. The third was a one-way attack employing only bombers, with submarines hovering nearby to rescue the crews.[2]

Sasaki realized, of course, that the plan would be risky and dangerous, but he believed if the worse came to the worst, it might be Japan's only way out. An Eta Jima and Kasumigaura graduate, Sasaki had spent about two years in the United States as an assistant naval attaché, beginning in 1931. Before coming to *Nagato*, he had been staff officer for air of the China Area Fleet located at Shanghai.[3]

Sometime in late March Fukudome had shown Kuroshima the Onishi-Genda draft, and Watanabe saw it a few moments later. Fukudome and Kuroshima agreed that if war with the United States seemed likely, they should submit the project to the Naval General Staff. But for the time being they should study it carefully aboard *Nagato*. Sasaki also saw the draft at that time. It was then that the document's assessment of the difficulties in carrying out a torpedo strike apparently discouraged Yamamoto. He is reported to have remarked, "Since we cannot use a torpedo attack because of the shallowness of the water, we cannot expect to obtain the results we desire. Therefore, we probably have no choice but to give up the air attack operation." But Yamamoto was not the type to abandon any venture until he had thoroughly explored all avenues. Thus, on this April day once more he broached the subject to Kuroshima and Watanabe.[4]

Kuroshima had been with Yamamoto since the autumn of 1939. Primarily a gunnery officer, he had spent much time at sea, had graduated from the Naval Staff College, and had also taught there. Now he served as Yamamoto's senior staff officer. Kuroshima's actual duties consisted mainly of overall planning, and his position was somewhat like that of Kimmel's Soc McMorris. However, the ranking member of a Japanese naval staff was called the senior staff officer. Kuroshima's taut cheekbones and pale prophet's face gave him such an ascetic appearance that his colleagues called him Ganji—the Japanese form of Gandhi.

Although the Japan of his day set a premium on conformity, Kuroshima was eccentric to the point of weirdness. Even his name was unusual. *Kameto* means "tortoise man." It suited Kuroshima well enough, for he liked to retreat into his shell when working on a problem. He would lock himself in his cabin, draw the shades, and sit in the dark with his head buried in his hands. When an idea struck him, he would turn on the light and begin to scribble frantically, shedding papers all over the floor and smoking heavily. He even ate his meals in his cabin, letting dirty dishes and glasses full of cigarette butts accumulate until his colleagues would protest and order the cabin cleaned up.[5]

When Kuroshima emerged from these solitary sessions, he had the problem thought through to the smallest detail, at least to his own satisfaction, and could dictate a staff study word for word without consulting notes. Nevertheless, he sometimes lost his grip on reality and produced some far-out ideas. Yamamoto knew exactly how to sift a Kuroshima plan and toss out the chaff. When someone asked him why he kept such a strange officer on his staff, he replied, "Who else but me could use Kuroshima?" No man on the Combined Fleet staff would work harder on the Pearl Harbor plan or support it more enthusiastically than Kuroshima. In fact, Genda thought that the senior staff officer very likely knew of the plan even before he did. Sasaki, too, believed that in view of Yamamoto's full confidence in his staff "it was almost inconceivable that he would consult anyone on the outside concerning such an important operation without first considering it with such members of his staff as Fukudome, chief of staff; Kuroshima, senior staff officer; and myself, staff officer for air."[6]

If Kuroshima had a crony, it was Watanabe. This solidly built man, almost six feet tall, exuded an atmosphere of expansive maleness and simple, earthly virtues. Indianlike cheekbones lent force to his oblong face with its expressive dark eyes and wide mouth full of large white teeth. His sunny optimism freshened Kuroshima's dark melancholy. A head crammed with ideas, the strength to cut his way swiftly through a pile of work, and the discipline to follow up on his assignments made Watanabe the ideal staff officer.

Yamamoto had a soft spot for Watanabe and treated him like a son. The two often played chess (*shogi*) or cards together. Indeed, Yamamoto considered their chess sessions almost in the line of duty, believing that the game cleared his head and kept him alert.[7] Watanabe repaid his chief's kindness with a full measure of devotion. Indeed, Yamamoto's entire staff resembled that of Kimmel in its prickly allegiance, its exclusive, excluding pride.

In entrusting Kuroshima and Watanabe with detailed work on the Pearl Harbor plan, Yamamoto embarked on his own initiative. In wartime the Commander in Chief of the Combined Fleet had the responsibility and authority to draft an operational plan within the framework of any mission assigned to him from the High Command. In peacetime, however, he was not supposed to work on such a plan because of the security risk involved and also because the Naval General Staff preferred that he concentrate all his efforts on training. The Naval General Staff drafted the annual plan. In case of emergency, one of its officers brought the plan to Combined Fleet Headquarters.[8]

But in view of the immense importance of the timing of the Pearl Harbor attack—it must start the war, not follow a declaration—Yamamoto could not wait for the mills of the naval gods to grind in Tokyo. Once war had been declared, he would have lost the imperative of surprise, the one basic element upon which his air strike depended.

So within a few days Kuroshima divided Yamamoto's staff into four preliminary study groups: (1) Operations and Supply; (2) Communications and Information; (3) Navigation and Meteorological Conditions; and (4) Air and Submarine Attack.[9] Thus, the ring of knowledge expanded to include Lieutenant Commander Yushiro Wada, communications officer, and Commander Shigeru Nagata, navigation officer.

Commander Takayasa Arima also joined the inner circle. Although one of the youngest members of Yamamoto's official family, he carried weight by virtue of his assignment as submarine officer. The Japanese Navy took great pride in its submarines and expected much of them, having concentrated heavily in this area of sea warfare as a result of the posttreaty limitation on surface vessels. Arima had little submarine experience, being a torpedoman by training, but he was ready, willing, and able to learn. He had studied for two years in the United States—one at Johns Hopkins and another at Yale.

When Kuroshima first spoke to Arima about Yamamoto's plan, Arima felt clouds of pessimism drift across his mind. An air attack on Pearl Harbor? Impossible! he thought. But the idea grew on him. Soon he accepted the plan as "the only way to defend and secure the extended line of the Greater East Asia Co-Prosperity Sphere."[10] In the months to come Arima would work tirelessly, maintaining close liaison with the Sixth Fleet (Submarines) and with the Naval General Staff.

The plan's element of the unexpected had appealed to Sasaki from the first. During the development of the project Sasaki cooperated closely with Genda and became more or less the Combined Fleet's liaison with the First Air Fleet, soon to be activated. This suited his personality as well as his training because his assured and pleasing manner permitted him to establish an easy rapport. At the same time he could keep his own counsel.

Sasaki assures us that by early April 1941 most of the operations officers of the Combined Fleet staff knew about the Pearl Harbor attack plan. This included his own assistant for air, Lieutenant Commander Kaneo Inoguchi. Sasaki always suspected that Kuroshima might have originally suggested the idea to Yamamoto; however, Kuroshima consistently denied this.[11]

During this early planning period an intriguing question arose between Yamamoto and "three or four staff members": the possibility of occupying Hawaii in connection with the air attack. Someone suggested that because about half the U.S. Navy was in Hawaii, if they could take these men prisoner, the recovery of American naval strength would be difficult because of the time needed to train officers. This idea never progressed beyond informal chitchat, although the notion of running up the Rising Sun over Hawaii intrigued Watanabe for months.[12]

Thus, by mid-April Yamamoto had moved the Pearl Harbor project into command channels and established it as an authorized subject of staff study. What followed seemed only logical.

On April 10 the Navy took a momentous step which signaled a revolution in its strategic thinking. On that day it organized the First Air Fleet, bringing together in one operational unit the First Carrier Division (*Akagi* and *Kaga*), the Second Carrier Division (*Soryu* and *Hiryu*), and the Fourth Carrier Division (*Ryujo*). In addition, the First and Second Carrier divisions each had four destroyers assigned, and *Ryujo* two. *Ryujo* transferred elsewhere in the summer of 1941 and played no part in the Pearl Harbor drama; her small size and comparatively slow speed made it impractical to use her as an integral part of the First Air Fleet especially because all her fighters were the old Type 96, not Zeros. The organization included her only to assist in coordinated training.

With this move the Japanese Navy formed the nucleus of a potential aerial striking force capable of massing well over 200 planes against a given target. For at least five years Genda had advocated such an air fleet, the carriers concentrated as a unit to achieve maximum offensive power, with other vessels acting as defensive escorts.[13]

Despite his personal sympathy with naval aviation, Yamamoto had hesitated to approve the formation of the First Air Fleet for some time. It was an advanced concept, involving the sort of physical, mental, and even spiritual shake-up to which a commander cannot subject his organization without careful thought. Ozawa brought the issue to a head early in 1940, when he commanded the First Carrier Division. Four months of service with Japan's two biggest carriers convinced Ozawa that it would be possible to launch powerful air strikes only if the flattops were organized under one command. According to Captain Sadamu Sanagi, air officer on Yamamoto's staff before Sasaki, one of the burning questions among airmen in the Combined Fleet was: "How can air power be used most effectively?" And he remarked, "Ozawa had spent most of his naval life at sea and was by all odds the most vigorous exponent of uniting the carriers as a striking force."

But Ozawa ran into opposition. One of the top brass who resisted his scheme was Vice Admiral Mineichi Koga, Commander in Chief of the Second Fleet, where *Soryu* and *Hiryu* had their home. Koga believed in the battleship as devotedly as he did in the case of Japan. He feared that with the transfer of the flattops from their respective fleets, the latter would lose their protective air cover.

Twice Ozawa discussed his idea with Yamamoto, and twice his chief turned it down, sensing that the time was not yet ripe. But Ozawa was certain that in his concept lay the key to Japanese naval supremacy. Being as stubbornly audacious as his superior, he formally submitted his plan to Yamamoto in April 1940. At the same time he went a step further and presented his recommendation to the Naval General Staff and the Navy Ministry. Yamamoto blew up when he learned that Ozawa had bypassed him. Of course, Ozawa knew that Yamamoto's anger arose from the breach of protocol and had nothing to do with the carrier control plan, which his chief favored at heart, and the two officers remained good friends.

The Navy discussed Ozawa's plan during the summer and autumn of 1940. At last, in December, Yamamoto agreed, and soon everyone else fell into line. Yamamoto came around finally because he saw that such an organization was the only way to achieve maximum striking power from Japan's carriers.[14] With the swift improvement in aircraft capabilities, it had become increasingly possible that a decisive air battle would precede any final naval engagement such as the Great All-Out Battle. Then, too, the concentration of carriers offered advantages for training.[15]

Even before the official organization of the First Air Fleet, the Japanese had practiced with a mass concentration of carriers. In accordance with Genda's theory, they had combined *Kaga, Soryu,* and *Hiryu* into a unit temporarily for training in early 1941. (*Akagi* was under repairs at the time.) This method proved very effective operationally, but some "bugs" soon appeared in the organization, for it became obvious that merely combining the existing carrier divisions created command difficulties. A temporary commander had to be selected, the airmen had to become familiar with his tactics, and the training methods of both carrier divisions had to be aligned.

This experimental concentration drove home forcefully the need for a permanent unified carrier command. Moreover, Yamamoto was becoming more and more intent upon launching his carrier strike at Pearl Harbor. The

Commander in Chief signaled "Go!" Barely four months later the First Air Fleet became a reality. Genda understood very well that he could not credit himself or his devoted band of naval aviation champions with bringing about "this revolutionary change" in the Japanese fleet organization, which "marked an epoch-making progress in the field of naval strategy and tactics. . . . "He generously gave full credit to Yamamoto's farsighted belief in air power.[16]

Other shake-ups occurred at high level in the Japanese Navy on the same day that the First Air Fleet came into being. Admiral Osami Nagano became chief of the Naval General Staff. A full admiral since March 1, 1934, he had held many important posts, including vice chief of the General Staff, navy minister, and Commander in Chief of the Combined Fleet. Thus he knew all three major sections of the Navy by personal experience at the highest level. Like Yamamoto, he had studied English at Harvard and served as naval attaché in Washington. All told, he had spent five years in the United States and considered New York City his second home.

At sixty-two Nagano was the oldest officer on the Navy's active list. He had lost much of the strength and drive of youth. "He was not a forceful character or the type to lead his nation at war," one of his section chiefs summed up.[17] In reading reports of Nagano's remarks in various high-level conferences, one has the impression that he increased in belligerence as 1941 progressed, either falling under Army influence or growing in self-confidence. But his thorough, slow-moving mind was no match for the quick, sharp intelligence of Yamamoto. Such then was the admiral who as chief of the Naval General Staff wielded the power of life or death over any operational plan.

Also on April 10 Yamamoto gave up his trusty chief of staff, Fukudome, to Nagano's headquarters as chief of the First Bureau. In that capacity Fukudome headed the nerve center of the Naval General Staff and to a certain extent of the entire Navy. Its personnel originated, discussed, studied, perfected, and constantly reviewed operational plans. In exchange for Fukudome, Yamamoto received Rear Admiral Seiichi Ito, an officer with an excellent background, including language study in the United States, but of a conservative bent of mind. A good public relations type, Ito got on well with both superiors and subordinates. Naturally he learned about the Pearl Harbor scheme shortly after boarding *Nagato*. From all reports he did not exactly applaud the notion, but as always he accepted the command decision passively and did nothing to thwart his chief.

Fukudome took with him to the Naval General Staff his personal knowledge of exactly what Yamamoto had in mind. Then, about a week or so after Fukudome had settled in Tokyo, Onishi called on him and presented him with a copy of his draft. He informed the new chief of the First Bureau that he had already briefed Yamamoto, who had instructed him to give the draft copy to Fukudome for safekeeping. He then explained the outline, and the two men discussed the project briefly. When Fukudome read the draft, he believed that the idea had made considerable progress since he first talked it over with

Yamamoto in 1940 but that many serious problems remained to be solved. When Onishi left, Fukudome hastily put the document in his safe.[18]

Yamamoto had too much integrity to attempt to use Fukudome as his stooge in the Naval General Staff. So, late in April, he dispatched Kuroshima to Tokyo to discuss the possibilities of his plan with the Operations Section of Fukudome's First Bureau. This was the fountainhead of all naval planning and should have initiated any scheme to attack the U.S. Pacific Fleet or for that matter any other war plan. This key organization was loaded with smart, up-and-coming young hopefuls carefully chosen for background, brains, originality, and vision to keep the Navy on its toes.

A highly gifted officer headed this section. Captain (Baron) Sadatoshi Tomioka's record reveals a solid background of schooling and sea duty, and he had seen much of Europe. His cultivated, fastidious, and practical nature flourished particularly well in the intellectual and social climate of France, where he had studied. The complete aristocrat, Tomioka exuded the confidence and security of one who knows exactly what to do and say under any circumstances. A man of brains and common sense, he knew his job exceedingly well.

His naval training had sharpened his innate sense of responsibility until his feeling of unity with the ships had become supersensitive. But he knew the Navy's limitations as well as its capabilities, and he therefore objected to overextension. Let Japan keep its eye on the goal: Southeast Asia. If anyone went gallivanting across the Pacific, let it be the United States. The view from Tomioka's desk encompassed a broader scene than that from *Nagato*'s bridge. "The Combined Fleet could study the Pearl Harbor plan from the purely tactical and strategic point of view," he explained, "but the Naval General Staff had to include its relations with the Army, the Cabinet, the Foreign Office, and Japan's entire international situations."[19]

According to Tomioka, Kuroshima's visit of late April was the first he and certain of his officers learned about Pearl Harbor. To anyone accustomed to the methods of the American armed forces, it appears incredible that the chief of a section should be unaware of a plan on which one of his subordinates—Uchida —claimed to have been working. But the situation was not unheard of in the Japanese services, in which junior officers sometimes enjoyed a surprising amount of freedom.

In any case, Tomioka took this opportunity to discuss with Kuroshima the Naval General Staff's overall war plan, which had as its main objective the seizure of Southeast Asia and its rich resources. Absolutely nothing should interfere with the success of the prime mission. The Naval General Staff blueprint also featured a modified version of the Great All-Out Battle which would ensue when the U.S. Pacific Fleet sailed westward to block Japan's southern advance. This included the dispatch of a sizable submarine force to Hawaiian waters to begin reducing the American Fleet as it crossed the Pacific.

Neither Tomioka nor Kuroshima was at all impressed with the other's ideas. Nevertheless, Kuroshima requested that the Pearl Harbor design be included in the Naval General Staff's planning. But Tomioka believed that Yamamoto's scheme presented an inadmissible risk and that Japan could not spare from the Southern Operation the ships which an attack on the U.S. Pacific Fleet in Pearl Harbor would require. Furthermore, he thought it operationally impossible because of the limited radius of action of Japan's warships. He added decisively that none of the Japanese carriers had any experience in refueling on the high seas.

Tomioka could have informed Nagano of Yamamoto's plan after Kuroshima had returned to the Combined Fleet. In fact, Kuroshima assumed Tomioka would do so. He also thought that "even from the common sense point of view Nagano should have been informed at the time."[20] But Tomioka was not the type to go rushing to Nagano with it at that stage. Nevertheless, after Onishi's and Kuroshima's visits to Tokyo, Yamamoto's plan had been officially introduced to the Naval General Staff, whether the high brass liked it or not. In short, Yamamoto's camel had its nose in Nagano's tent.

Commander Tatsukichi Miyo, one of Tomioka's two air experts, agreed with his chief. A man of keen, down-to-earth intelligence, Miyo was a graduate of Kasumigaura. He understood and strongly backed carrier-borne aviation, but he considered Yamamoto's scheme "entirely out of the question." He estimated that the Army's air force was too weak to accomplish the mission in Southeast Asia without strong support from the Navy's carrier-based strength. Then, too, much planning and thought remained to be done on the Southern Operation. All energies should be concentrated on the primary objective, rather than on planning attacks which seemed impossible to execute.[21]

Whatever opinion Miyo may have expressed to Tomioka, he had been working on at least one phase of a Pearl Harbor operation for some months, according to a reliable source. Early in January he visited the Navy Ministry and called upon an Eta Jima classmate, Commander Fumio Aiko, an authority on torpedoes. Miyo presented Aiko with a tall order—100 percent perfection in aerial torpedo results in shallow water.

Aiko blinked at his classmate from behind his thick glasses. Japan already had 70 percent efficiency. A reasonable man, Aiko considered a perfect score impossible and flatly said so. But Miyo continued to urge the point. Finally, Aiko asked, "Why do you press for a hundred percent?"

Miyo shot a quick glance around him and lowered his voice. "I will tell you a secret," he confided. "We need this special shallow-water torpedo because the Navy has a plan to attack the U.S. Fleet in Pearl Harbor. This is an absolute secret," he stressed.

Aiko was not in the least surprised because he more or less took it for granted that eventually Japan and the United States would fight. He had been working for some time on shallow-water torpedoes. At the fleet maneuvers held in 1939 in Saeki Bay, which featured a simulated torpedo attack, Aiko became convinced that if real missiles had been used in such a low depth of water, they would have stuck in the mud.

With this thought in mind he had done some research on his own initiative into the depths of such harbors as Manila, Singapore, Vladivostok, and Pearl Harbor. He discovered that the average was from about seventeen to twenty-five feet. Obviously, to be effective in such circumstances, the torpedo could sink no lower than twelve feet. Aiko then combined his research and his previous experience of torpedo-sinking curves into a formal report for the Aeronautical Bureau of the Navy Ministry. As a result, he was assigned to the Combined Fleet, where he remained as an instructor until December 1940, when he transferred to the Aeronautical Bureau. There he was hard at work when Miyo called upon him in January 1941.

Miyo's insistence upon secrecy put Aiko in a difficult position because his associates would have to work in the dark. But the torpedo expert never told anyone about the Pearl Harbor mission. As a result of their conference, he wrote to the commanding officer of the Naval Air Corps at Yokosuka, directing him in the name of the navy minister to improve torpedo efficiency to 100 percent. However, because Aiko would give no reason for the order, the Yokosuka Air Corps assigned the project a low priority.[22]

With all three branches of the Imperial Navy involved in the Pearl Harbor venture in varying degrees, one inevitably asks: Did Yamamoto organize the First Air Fleet for the express purpose of attacking the U.S. Pacific Fleet at Pearl Harbor? The answer must be both yes and no. No because in December 1940, when he set the ball rolling, no one knew that Japan and the United States would not settle their differences by diplomacy. Nor had the cause become hopeless by April 10, 1941; Yamamoto had no intention whatsoever of starting a Japanese-American war unless he absolutely had to. Yes because, if events forced him to lead the Combined Fleet into battle with Kimmel's ships, Yamamoto determined that he must strike that first blow, and he could not do so without the nucleus of a carrier task force in being.

Although strength is not necessarily identical with numbers, with the formation of the First Air Fleet the Japanese Navy took on greater strategic potential than the U.S. Pacific Fleet. Without the First Air Fleet, which ultimately evolved into a powerful task force, Japan could not have delivered its mass air attack on December 7, 1941.

CHAPTER 12

"THE REAL

POWER AND

POTENTIALITIES"

The First Air Fleet was a revolutionary and potentially formidable instrument of sea power. Thus, its command was no ordinary post. One would expect the Navy Ministry to appoint a genuine air admiral or at least someone who understood naval aviation. But seniority and protocol dictated that the position fall to one Vice Admiral Chuichi Nagumo, who throughout a long and honorable career had had no connection whatever with air power.

Born in Yamagato Prefecture in northern Honshu on March 25, 1887, Nagumo graduated from Eta Jima in the top ten of his class. From the beginning he embarked upon a varied service aboard battleships, cruisers, and destroyers. In the mid-1920s he traveled in Europe and the United States. Returning to Japan, he went to sea once more, then taught at the Naval Staff College, where he made the coveted promotion to captain. Then he was back at sea as commander first of the light cruiser *Naka*, next of the Eleventh Destroyer Division. After that the Naval General Staff claimed him for two years. But although he appreciated the experience and the tribute to his ability, Nagumo was never really at ease except at sea. His old associates recall that after shore duty Nagumo always returned with joy and relief to the element he loved.

On November 15, 1934, he boarded the battleship *Yamashiro* as her skipper. Exactly one year later Nagumo became a rear admiral at the age of forty-eight—just about par for the course in the Japanese Navy. Steady progress upward marked the next few years. He kept a diary, but it is maddeningly sparse. He was not introspective, and he preferred action to words. Yet brief, revealing flashes come through. "I will continue to ask difficult things of them," he wrote on May 3, 1936, of his officers and men, "and be firmly resolved to accept any responsibility at any time." There speaks the perfectionist who expected much of himself and his subordinates. And his orders to Shanghai as commander of the Eighth Cruiser Division roused him to a fine glow of militant patriotism on July 15, 1937: "I solemnly swear here and now to participate in the war against China at the risk of my life. . . . I will give the Chinese some real shot and shell. My only regret is that I am not going off to battle at sea. . . ."[1]

The outbreak of World War II in Europe found Nagumo afloat as commander of the Third Battleship Division, and on November 15, 1939, he attained the high rank of vice admiral. A year later he had to come ashore again as president of the Naval Staff College in Tokyo. He was serving there when the call came to command the First Air Fleet.

A picture taken at the height of his career shows Nagumo resplendent in his blue uniform, sitting confident and composed, his left hand gripping his sword. His round cannonball of a head is bald in front, with the rest of his hair cropped in cadet style. A thoughtful forehead broken by two furrows blends into well-marked brows shadowing big, diagnostic eyes. Two sharp clefts in the skin between them as well as the deep lines running from his large nose to firmly set mouth tell a story of ready smiles and equally ready frowns of concentration. High cheekbones, solid jaws, and a rocklike chin complete the strong yet sensitive face of a man who seems to have accepted the irreversibleness of history.

A man of husky physique, Nagumo outwardly "gave the impression of being a Japanese Bull Halsey."[2] He wore his hat at a jaunty angle, paid little attention to his clothes, thrust out his chest arrogantly, and swaggered perceptibly when he walked. He was generous and outgoing, the sort to greet a friend with a shout of welcome and a stunning clap on the shoulder. He had one of the kindest hearts imaginable and took an absorbed interest in his officers and men.[3]

He accepted his new command with a heavy strike against him. "Nagumo was an old-line officer, a specialist in torpedo attack and large-scale maneuvers," explained his longtime friend Admiral Nishizo Tsukahara, Commander in Chief of the Eleventh Air Fleet. "He was wholly unfitted by background, training, experience, and interest for a major role in Japan's naval air arm. He had no conception of the real power and potentialities of the air arm when he became Commander in Chief of the First Air Fleet."[4]

In retrospect, it is all too easy to overplay the points against Nagumo. True, he was a stranger to naval aviation, but the world's navies in the 1940s did not expect every admiral to be a specialist. The very fact that a man had reached such eminence indicated that he must be a highly capable officer of varied experience.

The seniority system which put Nagumo in command had its virtues. It gave the officer corps a sense of security and stability, the knowledge that a man's career was not entirely at the mercy of politics, favoritism, or caprice in high places. It also obviated the necessity for the service to make an arbitrary choice among many admirals of almost equal worth when it selected a high-level commander—always a delicate business fraught with pitfalls. Of course, the system had its drawbacks and often hammered a square peg into a round hole or rewarded mediocrity over brilliance.

Ironically, while Nagumo's selection by seniority has cropped up against him, no investigating committee ever let the U.S. Navy forget that it tossed seniority overboard to appoint Kimmel Commander in Chief. As the cynical proverb says, nothing succeeds like success. On this basis the Japanese should have no complaints against Nagumo. In the six months Yamamoto had promised Premier Konoye, Nagumo did indeed "run wild." Throughout the course of World War II no other Japanese admiral matched his record.

To reinforce the chinks in Nagumo's professional armor, the Navy Ministry gave him as chief of staff Rear Admiral Ryunosuke Kusaka, a truly excellent choice. Although not a pilot, Kusaka came to his task with a good record of assignments in the air arm, including command of the small carrier *Hosho* and the big flattop *Akagi*. Kusaka's sturdy, slightly bowed legs carried a short, pyknic, well-shouldered frame. When he smiled, he beamed warmly and indulgently. His mind, like his body, moved slowly, with measured deliberation, focusing solidly on facts and disdaining illusion.

Kusaka possessed both purpose and courage. To the author's knowledge, he was the only man in the Japanese Navy who stood up to Yamamoto and told him what he honestly thought about the Pearl Harbor plan.* The son of a wealthy family, Kusaka had the unassuming self-assurance that only a sunny, carefree childhood can give. A devoted student and practitioner of Zen Buddhism, he had a calm confidence and inner security such as few men ever attain. Nothing short of a major upheaval of nature ever disturbed Kusaka.

Not only did his carrier know-how balance Nagumo's lack of experience in that area, but Kusaka's placidity also helped ease the many worries that would plague Nagumo in the months to come. The commander often saw the dark side of any proposition, less out of pessimism than realism. Sea warfare deals in absolutes, and the admiral carried on his shoulders the lives of thousands of men and the force of his nation's aerial striking power. Naturally his responsibilities weighed upon him. He turned gratefully to Kusaka's steadfast, sober optimism, and Kusaka became his good right arm.

Nagumo drew Commander Tamotsu Oishi as his senior staff officer to ride herd over the other staff members and see that they carried out all orders and work assignments efficiently. A good organizer, punctual as clockwork, Oishi had been on the staff of the First Carrier Division since October 1940. In later days Genda said of him, "Oishi was originally a navigator. He was half-conservative and half-progressive. He had no special characteristics. He was not a pilot and knew little about air power and its uses. But he was not obstinate and would listen to reason. Oishi did his best to understand air operations; however, his entire background operated against him."[5] Like many outstanding

---

*See Chapter 32.

people, Genda regarded his own brilliance as the norm and was impatient of those who could not follow his swift mental forays. So his judgments of his colleagues never erred on the side of charity. But Oishi's strong, serious face reflected his sense of duty, and he plunged with zeal into his new assignment.

Genda rejoiced to be the air officer of the newly hatched organization with a tough job ahead of him and no weight of tradition to cramp his style. As Nagumo's engineering officer, Lieutenant Commander Goro Sakagami, pointed out, "A heavy burden fell on Genda because he was actually the only one of us who understood air power."[6] Nagumo, Kusaka, and Oishi had brains enough to realize their limitations in that field and relied on Genda for expert advice and counsel. As time went on, they placed increasing trust in him and his judgments. Yamamoto's plan soon became virtually Genda's entire life.

Sakagami was a man of average size, soft-spoken and very gentle, "almost like a Japanese woman."[7] But he had a good, practical brain and an excellent record in naval engineering. He described himself as "somewhat of an outsider in the planning of the actual air attack,"[8] but his work on the vital refueling problem would more than earn him his due. He came to the First Air Fleet the day it was organized.

Two others completed the inner circle of Nagumo's staff: Lieutenant Commander Kenjiro Ono, the communications officer, who went about his work with quiet competence, displaying no distinguishing qualities, and Lieutenant Commander Otojiro Sasebe, the navigation officer, who had a good grip on meteorology but little to say in staff conferences.

Take two seasoned, competent flag officers, their rather colorless assistant, three experienced, if somewhat pedestrian, specialists, and one scintillating mind. Add them together, and you get the brain and nerve center of the task force destined to attack Pearl Harbor—no sinister band of geniuses, and certainly kindly, worrisome Nagumo was no Fu Manchu. It was just another staff typical of the Japanese Navy of its day—and perhaps of any armed force.

In addition to running the First Air Fleet, Nagumo and his staff headed its First Carrier Division, consisting of the flagship *Akagi* and her sister, *Kaga*. These two fine ships of about 26,900 tons each carried a complement of 2,000 men. The smaller flattops *Soryu* and *Hiryu*, around 20,000 tons, constituted the Second Carrier Division, which steamed under the flag of the unforgettable Rear Admiral Tamon Yamaguchi.[9] He came to the naval air arm in January 1940 as commander of the First Combined Air Corps in China and transferred to the Second Carrier Division in November of that year. So, in all, he had little naval air experience when he joined Nagumo's command.

Over a medium-sized, well-stuffed body Yamaguchi's oval face wore a deceptively sorrowful expression. Unlike Nagumo, he was neat, precise, and always well groomed. An impulsive, devil-may-care type, he loved a good fight, and if careful consideration ever tempered his fire, nobody noticed it. Although he was a keen advocate of Spartan training who demanded much, his airmen thought him the greatest invention since the airplane and considered him one of them. He brought to his new assignment an unusually broad, varied background of experience at sea and ashore. He knew the United States well, having served three tours of duty there, the last as naval attaché in Washington from June 1934 to August 1936. The Ivy League was well represented in the Japanese Navy in 1941. Not only had Nagano and Yamamoto attended Harvard, and Arima Yale, but Yamaguchi was a Princeton man. ·

He was close to Yamamoto, who "had great confidence in him and respected his knowledge, experience, and judgment."[10] They spent long hours together aboard *Nagato* swapping yarns and ideas. The Commander in Chief showed his regard for Yamaguchi so clearly that the cognoscenti began to speak of him as Yamamoto's heir apparent.

Commander Kyozo Ohashi, who had been with the Second Carrier Division since October 15, 1940, served as Yamaguchi's senior staff officer until late August, when he joined the Fifth Carrier Division in the same capacity. Ohashi's replacement on Yamaguchi's staff at that time was Commander Seiroku Ito. Although capable enough, Ohashi knew little about aviation, having specialized in gunnery. He had been to Hawaii in 1929 and 1934. During the latter visit he procured pictures of U.S. vessels in Pearl Harbor as well as information on the Fleet, which he submitted as a report to the Naval General Staff upon his return to Japan.[11]

Like Nagumo, Yamaguchi had a top-notch air officer, Lieutenant Commander Eijiro Suzuki. An Eta Jima classmate of Genda's, Suzuki had long been one of his disciples in the cult of naval aviation and had more than 2,000 hours of flying time to his credit. He was somewhat the same type as Genda—thin, wiry, aggressive, with a bright, intelligent face, ready tongue, and quick mind. No one from Yamamoto on down could issue any order, however hazardous, even rattlebrained, that Yamaguchi and Suzuki would not jump to carry out with positive joy.

Lieutenant Commander Susumu Ishiguro, an officer with a fine record in his field, had filled the post of communications officer aboard *Soryu* since October 1940.[12] Lieutenant Commander Takeo Kyuma, the engineering officer, completed Yamaguchi's staff.

Toward the end of April Kusaka visited Fukudome in the general headquarters in Tokyo. During their talk Fukudome tossed over his desk a booklet entitled "Pearl Harbor Attack Plan." However, its contents consisted mostly of intelligence concerning U.S. installations on Oahu. Kusaka looked at the material, then said to Fukudome, "This is very precise information on the enemy situation, but we cannot launch an operation on this basis alone because it is not an operational plan." Thereupon Fukudome replied, "That is what I want you to develop."[13]

Fukudome also showed Kusaka the Onishi-Genda draft. He explained that Yamamoto's proposal was still in the idea stage and that the Combined Fleet Staff was working on it. Although Fukudome displayed little enthusiasm, he asked Kusaka to study the project. Kusaka wondered whether Yamamoto had not received the idea from Onishi, a notion he entertained even in the postwar years. Kusaka thought from the outset that the plan presented serious difficulties. He believed that it would have to be studied thoroughly, and a training program established for the First Air Fleet, which naturally would carry out such a mission. He also realized that as chief of staff of the First Air Fleet he would shoulder a heavy load of personal responsibility for its success.

Upon returning to *Akagi*, Kusaka briefed Nagumo on Yamamoto's explosive design. From the moment Nagumo heard that his primary mission might be an attack on the U.S. Pacific Fleet in Pearl Harbor, he "had a negative attitude."[14] At first he could not believe that Yamamoto would actually go through with such a zany undertaking. All other conditions aside—and he could enumerate plenty of them—Nagumo thought that the mere feat of sailing to Hawaii undetected, refueling en route, and arriving at the target according to a pinpoint schedule posed insuperable obstacles. Moreover, he would have to execute this attack with an instrument unfamiliar to him—naval air power. Nagumo consistently opposed the scheme until the last moment, even after Yamamoto made his irrevocable decision.[15]

The more Kusaka thought of Yamamoto's design, the more he shared Nagumo's doubts. He also added a few of his own. He wondered if the refueling problem could ever be solved. He considered the whole notion an unnecessary elaboration of Japan's grandiose but fundamentally clear-cut naval strategy and a flagrant violation of the military principles of simplicity, mass, and objective. "The Japanese fleet should be like a lion in a fight," Kusaka argued. "It should concentrate on the most important and immediate objective"—conquest of Southeast Asia—and not go dashing off like an Oriental Atalanta after elusive golden apples.

If anyone plunged off into the distance, let Kimmel be the one to lead his ships deeper and deeper into hostile waters! By the time he reached the combat area his crewmen, who had never fired a shot in anger and who trained only in the most pleasant of waters, would be jaded, exhausted. And Japanese submarines would have whittled the American Fleet down to size long since. That was the time to strike the enemy—in his hour of weakness, on Japan's terms, in Japan's naval hunting ground. To Kusaka it made no sense to bait the U.S. Pacific Fleet in its own stronghold, its own waters, far from Japan's lines of communications and supply.

After putting Nagumo in the picture, Kusaka set Oishi and Genda to work on the project. So, through devious channels, the Pearl Harbor operational plan wound up right where it started—in the capable hands of Minoru Genda.[16]

Oishi also had little liking for the idea, which technically and psychologically was far out of his league. He did not bring Sakagami into the plan until around the end of May or early June, when he pledged him to strict secrecy. Oishi explained that if the attack should be carried out, refueling would be one of the knottiest problems. "Would it be possible to replenish the ships of the First Air Fleet in the northern Pacific?" he asked anxiously. But Sakagami could not answer at a moment's notice a question so fraught with difficulties, and that nagging problem remained open.

Oishi likewise wanted to know about the fuel capacity and fuel consumption of the ships. With a long cruise to Hawaii and back of about 7,000 miles, these factors were absolute fundamentals upon which they must work. Sakagami's job was to calculate fuel capacity and consumption down to the last decimal point.[17] This would not be easy because it would depend on the speed of the task force and the condition of the sea.

Sometime in April Sasaki, Yamamoto's staff officer for air, confided to his good friend Suzuki, his opposite number on Yamaguchi's staff, that the Combined Fleet was considering the Hawaiian venture. Suzuki immediately grasped both the difficulties and the daring of the plan. Therein, he thought, lay its possibilities. He believed it might succeed because of the surprise factor and because it soared far beyond the conception of the ordinary strategist. Nevertheless, he counted the cost to Japan—probably three carriers, possibly four. It would come down, he thought, to a duel between the United States' land-based planes and the Japanese carrier-based aircraft. He figured that if the enemy sent up 100 bombers, the task force's fighters and antiaircraft could take care of about 40; that meant 60 could get through to wreak their will on the lightly armored carriers.[18] This estimate appears to be a frightful price to pay, but the Japanese originally calculated that the Pearl Harbor operation would cost them about one-third of their task force.[19]

Suzuki immediately informed his admiral. Whether this was the first time Yamaguchi heard of the scheme one cannot say, because Yamamoto may well have told him in person.[20] The Commander in Chief liked to thrash out ideas with Yamaguchi, and this one was after his own heart. Its flamboyance, its challenge to the fighting spirit, its flirtation with death—all these Yamaguchi took to himself. His senior staff officer, Ohashi, recalled that all sorts of rumors were flying around the First Air Fleet at the time of its founding in April 1941. Quite soon Ohashi suspected what was afloat, although he claims he did not get the word officially until September.[21]

Suzuki also passed his information along to Ishiguro shortly after he spoke with Yamaguchi.[22] No one who has ever served aboard a Navy ship or on a military post can doubt that Yamamoto's supersecret was by now fairly well known within the official family.

Many striking ironies raise the Pearl Harbor saga above the story of a unique naval operation to the level of a great human drama. None of them is more incongruous than these: Of the three admirals thus far assigned to the First Air Fleet, not one was an airman in the true sense of the term. And the most outspoken, ingrained opposition in the entire Combined Fleet to Yamamoto's grand design would come from within the First Air Fleet itself, especially from the two admirals upon whom, whether he liked it or not, Yamamoto must depend to carry it through.

CHAPTER 13

"WITH

GUARDED

APPROVAL"

On February 12, 1941, Nomura presented his credentials to Secretary of State Cordell Hull. As the two shook hands, Nomura looked into a handsome face with deep-set eyes over which dark tufts of eyebrows hung like eaves. Hull had a high forehead under thinning silver-white hair, a straight nose, thin lips, and a short cleft chin. His whole attitude breathed an honesty and rectitude bone-deep and unconscious.

Two days later Hull accompanied Nomura to submit the credentials to Roosevelt. The President greeted Nomura cordially and announced that he would call him Admiral rather than Ambassador. Here was the kind of delicate touch at which Roosevelt excelled. It subtly established a bond between the two men, fellowship in the ancient brotherhood of the sea. He added that they could "talk candidly as friends."

But he stressed that Japan's southward move had "given this country *very* serious concern," as had Japan's signing the Tripartite Pact. He reminded Nomura that "it would be extremely easy for some incident" to arouse American anger. He suggested that Nomura get together with Hull to review Japanese-American relations over the past several years to ascertain just where their paths diverged and why, emphasizing that there was "plenty of room in the Pacific for everybody." In conclusion he remarked that "it would not do this country any good nor Japan any good, but both of them harm, to get into a war." Nomura punctuated Roosevelt's words with nods of his massive head, but he admitted that his "chief difficulty and chief obstacle" would be the "chauvinistic" military group controlling Japan.[1]

After "Bloody Sunday," there arose the suggestion that Nomura had known about Japan's dark naval secret, but this was not the case. In the postwar

114

years Nomura swore his ignorance of Yamamoto's design, and there is every reason to believe him.[2] He had no "need to know," to use the military phrase. The Japanese Navy had nothing to gain by informing him of a plan which was still in the conceptual stage when he sailed from Yokohama. Then, too, Nomura's own character and personality would give the Navy pause. It is exceedingly doubtful that he would have accepted the appointment to Washington (which he did not want in the first place) if he had known he would have to participate in duplicity. And if his patriotism had overcome his scruples, the knowledge would have hung over him like a thundercloud, darkening his conversations with Hull and others. If Nomura knew that such a plan simmered in Japan, he might inadvertently make a slip. Furthermore, knowledge of Pearl Harbor would have placed him at a psychological disadvantage. He could not represent Japan convincingly unless he believed in his mission. And lastly, the best advantage Tokyo had going for it in Washington was Nomura's transparent honesty and sincerity. His own ignorance made him the perfect smoke screen.

Hull and Nomura had their first real talk on March 8 at Hull's apartment. This meeting established a routine to be followed throughout their relationship. Usually, to avoid undue publicity, Nomura visited Hull in the evenings at his apartment. They talked openly, even bluntly, but the two respected each other and never raised their voices.[3]

On the whole, Nomura made a favorable impression on Hull, although the secretary of state retained something of his mountaineer's traditional suspicion of "furriners." The settlers of his native Tennessee hills imbued their sons with a fierce love of country and practiced a rock-bound fundamentalist religion. From his birth on October 22, 1871, Hull grew up believing that black was black and white was white and no gray nonsense about it.

During the Spanish-American War Hull served as a volunteer captain in Cuba. In 1903 he became a backwoods circuit judge. Four years later, at the age of thirty-five, he went to Congress. From that moment, as congressman and later as senator, he literally grew gray in his country's service. He became secretary of state in 1933, coming in with Roosevelt's first administration.[4] But by 1941 he did not have a firm hold on his department. Undersecretary Sumner Welles, Hull's second-in-command, a sharp, ambitious, and somewhat impulsive man, enjoyed direct access to the President, a situation which annoyed Hull exceedingly. A portion of the blame lay with Roosevelt, who skipped merrily out of channels whenever the notion struck him, a habit which occasionally left his secretaries high and dry.

Hull spoke in a high, grating voice with a slight lisp and had few literary turns of speech, although he underlined his points with gestures of his beautiful, expressive hands. Anyone who antagonized him usually lived to regret it, for this backwoodsman turned statesman neither forgot nor forgave.

The secretary entertained no illusions about Japan and its Greater East Asia Co-Prosperity Sphere. So on March 8 he informed Nomura—in suitably diplomatic language—that the American people were fed up with the efforts of Germany and Japan to rule the seas and the continents along with them and that this attitude would prevail as long as those two countries kept up their policy of expansion by conquest. When Nomura indicated that if American embargoes continued, Japan might be forced to military action, Hull countered that the responsibility would rest on Japan.[5] Throughout the ensuing months the details of the Hull-Nomura conversations would vary widely. But the first meeting set the pattern for those to follow. Wearily, patiently, the irresistible force kept on colliding with the immovable object.

On March 12, Admiral Turner visited Nomura at the embassy, at the ambassador's invitation. Nomura plunged into naval matters. In contrast with Japanese press opinion, he thought that the presence of the United States Fleet in Hawaii, "particularly in combination with the British, forms a stabilizing influence for affairs in the Pacific. This fleet would be less potent if many of the American destroyers and other light forces should move to the Atlantic to help the British." Turner believed the ambassador to be "fully sincere" and thought that he would use his influence "against further aggressive moves by the military forces of Japan."[6]

Several wholly different actors in the international drama conferred in Berlin between March 27 and April 4. Matsuoka had several talks with Hitler and Joachim von Ribbentrop, his foreign minister, before returning to Japan via the Soviet Union. Ribbentrop urged that the Japanese attack Singapore. In his eagerness to embroil the Japanese with the British, he did everything but show Matsuoka the draft of Operation Barbarossa—the plan to strike the Soviet Union three months hence. Although professing enthusiasm for a strike at Singapore, Matsuoka avoided a commitment.

Hitler crawled far out on a limb with this pledge to Matsuoka: ". . . if Japan got into a conflict with the United States, Germany on her part would take the necessary steps at once. It made no difference with whom the United States first came into conflict, whether it was with Germany or with Japan. . . ."[7] Thus reassured, Matsuoka sped on his way to Moscow, scattering behind him protests of his devotion to the Tripartite Pact. There, with the consent of the Emperor and Konoye, he signed a neutrality pact with the Soviet Union on April 13. Delighted with this achievement, Matsuoka thought that he had strengthened Japan's position vis-à-vis the United States and Britain.

Konoye, too, was pleased. The pact, he thought, promised peace, perhaps an eventual settlement with Chiang Kai-shek, and delivered Japan, if only temporarily, from the Russian threat.[8] Grew noted, however, that the Tokyo press regarded the pact "with guarded approval rather than with enthusiasm" and added dryly, "There are indications that the complete confidence which would impel a southward advance is not yet felt with regard to the northern neighbor."[9]

In Washington, meanwhile, some unusual events enlivened the diplomatic scene. On April 9 the State Department received a proposal through two Roman Catholic clerics, Bishop James E. Walsh, superior general of the

Maryknoll Society, and Father James M. Drought, formerly in Japan with that organization. Though skeptical of any possibility of their success, Matsuoka authorized them to report to Roosevelt his desires for an understanding with the United States. They worked with one Tadeo Ikawa, a Japanese businessman married to an American.

Upon arrival in the United States these two priests enlisted the support of Postmaster General Frank C. Walker, a prominent Catholic layman, who introduced them and their mission to the President. Although the story the two missionaries told was "in drastic contrast to what Matsuoka and many official leaders of Japan were proclaiming to the world," Roosevelt and Hull agreed that they "could not afford to neglect any chance to avoid a war in the Pacific."[10]

At their meeting on March 8 Hull had informed Nomura that although he appreciated the efforts of "responsible, fine and capable citizens" seeking "to make their respective contributions to better understanding," he could only deal with and through him, "the duly authorized Ambassador of Japan. . . ."[11]

This was wise of Hull because the lengthy and somewhat obscure proposal which Walsh and Drought worked out with their Japanese associates was a weird document for serious American consideration. When the secretary of state and his Far Eastern experts studied this amazing program, they were acutely disappointed. As Hull explained later, "It was much less accommodating than we had been led to believe it would be, and most of its provisions were all that the ardent Japanese imperialists could want."[12]

In fact, the original Drought memorandum was so exceedingly favorable to Japan that no doubt it gave the Japanese a highly distorted notion of how far the United States was prepared to go in meeting their terms. A second memorandum which Bishop Walsh prepared on January 23 was somewhat more reasonable by American standards. This document in turn received a thorough revision from Colonel Takeo Iwakuro, who arrived in Washington in late March to work with this group and also to assist Nomura as an expert on China affairs. Throughout the year this venture in amateur diplomacy clouded the issues. It seems obvious that at the outset the Japanese did not understand that the two clerics were operating on their own; they assumed that Washington was at least indirectly involved.

On April 16 Hull presented Nomura with his real "basis for negotiations." He requested assurance that Japan would abandon its policy of forcible conquest and adopt four principles—soon to become famous or notorious, depending on which side of the Pacific you occupied, under that title of the Four Principles:

> (1) Respect for the territorial integrity and sovereignty of each and all nations;
>
> (2) Support of the principle of noninterference in the internal affairs of other countries;
>
> (3) Support of the principle of equality, including equality of commercial opportunity;

(4) Nondisturbance of the *status quo* in the Pacific except as the *status quo* may be altered by peaceful means.

Hull then assured Nomura that the United States would consider anything the Japanese proposed within this framework. Hull never penetrated Japanese psychology and remained skeptical of their intentions. But he thought that if the Japanese government "should make up its mind to abandon its present policies of force and invasion and adopt a peaceful course with worthwhile international relationships, it could find no objection to these four points reasonably applied. . . ."[13]

Nomura passed the Walsh-Drought draft proposal to his government but unfortunately did not clarify the fact that Hull had merely suggested forwarding it so that Tokyo, if so wishing, might authorize Nomura to present it as a basis for starting conversations. For some reason, he did not submit the Four Principles until May 8. Possibly Nomura did not fully understand Hull. The discussion of April 16 had been long and complicated, and no translator was present to make sure Nomura caught all the nuances. It is also possible that Nomura thought that Tokyo understood the background, the Walsh-Drought mission having originated in Japan. Whatever the reason, Nomura did not spell out the facts clearly. This was perhaps his most serious error as ambassador. As a result of this misunderstanding, Tokyo continued for some months to place undue emphasis upon the draft proposal and failed to appreciate the importance of the Four Principles.[14]

In view of these complex discussions and the explosiveness of the entire world scene, one can readily appreciate that a meteor could scarcely have struck the American Magic code breakers a more stunning blow than the message which the Foreign Ministry cabled Nomura on May 5: "According to a fairly reliable source of information it appears almost certain that the United States Government is reading your code messages. Please let me know whether you have any suspicion of the above." The "fairly reliable source" was Ambassador Hiroshi Oshima in Berlin. He advised Matsuoka that the previous evening Heinrich Stahmer, who had negotiated the Tripartite Pact in Tokyo, had dropped in to pass along this information from German agents. The Japanese took the tip seriously because they knew the Germans had been reading Japan's coded messages.[15]

It is intriguing to speculate where this thunderbolt struck with greater impact—in Nomura's embassy or in the United States Army and Navy Intelligence. The double implication that his office had sprung a leak and that he himself might have had suspicions which he did not convey to Tokyo must have hit Nomura squarely in the solar plexus. As a former chief of the Intelligence Bureau, Naval General Staff, he knew better than most diplomats just how and why he should protect his nation's secrets. Furthermore, the thought could scarcely have escaped him that Matsuoka, annoyed because the Hull-Nomura conversations did not operate on lines he himself specifically laid down, would not be averse to catching the ambassador bending. Nomura promptly replied that his office took "the most stringent precautions" to protect "codes and ciphers, as well as other documents." He also requested that Tokyo wire back "any concrete instance or details which may turn up."[16]

One can picture the eagerness with which U.S. Intelligence experts snatched up Japan's dispatches on this subject. To keep from Japan the knowledge that the American code breakers were reading over the shoulders of its diplomats had obsessed them almost to the point of absurdity. To protect this source, they had seriously sideswiped the need-to-know principle. And now it might all blow sky-high. Unlocking Purple had been a fearsomely difficult undertaking. They did not relish the prospect of going through the whole process again, especially because the extremely delicate international situation demanded almost hourly information.

In these circumstances U.S. Intelligence went to almost farcical lengths to plug every conceivable loophole. G-2 even removed the President from those authorized to receive Purple messages in the original! Several factors went into this decision: first, a memorandum lost by the State Department in March; secondly, the German tip-off to Tokyo and "the resulting clampdown on security"; thirdly, "G-2 lack of confidence in Gen. Watson's ideas of security . . . because of the fact that earlier in the spring one Memo to the White House was found by Col. Bratton in Gen. Watson's wastebasket"; and fourthly, "the feeling of G-2 that almost without exception the subject of the memos and traffic was State business anyway and the matters should therefore be properly taken up with the White House by State, rather than being sent directly." The Navy was not prepared to shut off the White House, however, and continued deliveries. But, as we have seen, at this time the Navy was still summarizing Purple material and screening very tightly the intercepts deemed necessary for high-level distribution. It is doubtful that Roosevelt missed anything of real importance in the diplomatic line because Hull and others kept him thoroughly briefed. And in November G-2 again began to disseminate to the White House.[17]

What should have been the clincher for Japan came on May 20, when Nomura confirmed to Tokyo: "Though I do not know which ones I have discovered the United States is reading some of our codes.

"As for how I got the intelligence, I will inform you by courier or another safe way."[18] Nomura's preferring to reveal his sources by other means was in itself a disquieting hint that Purple might have been compromised. The slightest suggestion of such a thing should have set Japanese Intelligence to work immediately on a new system. Yet, as the days went by, the Magic interceptors discovered with incredulous, grateful amazement that the old code still remained in force.

The Japanese simply could not believe that the Americans had either the mentality or the know-how to break their supercode.[19] The fact that the Japanese did not alter their diplomatic codes in 1941 after the scare with the Germans was a terrific break for the United States. It is possible that the Foreign Ministry might have acted to revise the Purple system had the virtual confirmation of the German tip-off come from anyone but Nomura, whom Matsuoka disliked.[20] Nor was the ambassador at all happy with Matsuoka. The latter's evasive, ambiguous replies to Nomura's pleas for clear directions were a heavy cross for him to bear.[21]

In the normal course of events a personality clash between the foreign minister and an ambassador could result in only the latter's being reprimanded or even dismissed. However, Matsuoka was already living on borrowed time. To follow all the ramifications of the political moves in Japan and the diplomatic exchanges between Washington and Tokyo during this fateful year is beyond the scope of this study. Nevertheless, the Pearl Harbor attack did not take place in a vacuum, so we must pause occasionally to orient ourselves in the political landscape.

A correct translation of the long-delayed Japanese proposals in reply to the Walsh-Drought draft and Hull's Four Principles became available to the Americans on May 12. This document affirmed Japan's stand with the Axis and omitted a previous suggestion that Roosevelt and Konoye meet. Its proposals concerning the European situation left grave doubt that the United States could continue aid to Britain without this being considered an aggressive measure. It also recommended that the United States and Japan act together "speedily to restore peace in Europe." Too speedy a peace in the spring of 1941 would have left Hitler master of the continent. Once again Japan asked that the United States request Chiang Kai-shek to negotiate a settlement with Japan on the pain of loss of American aid. And it blandly offered to join the United States in a joint guarantee of Philippine independence.[22]

This document complicated the misunderstanding which already existed. The Japanese thought they were submitting a counterproposal; the Americans considered it Japan's initial offer. Using the original draft as a basis of comparison, the Japanese overestimated the willingness of the United States to make concessions and naturally considered later proposals as a stiffening of the American position.[23]

CHAPTER 14

"THE

STRONGEST

FORTRESS

IN THE

WORLD"

Having returned to the capital on April 21, 1941, after a brief trip to New England, Stimson telephoned Knox to bring himself up to date. Knox suggested that Stimson read "some rather startling cables" which had come in about the Far East. Stimson promptly sent for the papers and "was amazed to find that negotiations were apparently going on" of which he knew nothing—"associations between us and Japan."[1] The secretary of war's ignorance indicated a surprising lack of coordination at Cabinet level.

The situation was somewhat rectified the next morning, when Hull, Stimson, and Knox gathered in the State Department. Hull told his colleagues about his Japanese problem. Stimson recorded with obvious relish: "It was rather a singular position to be in—to be able to get the report of it to the home office in Tokyo and their comment on it and see how the Japanese mind had deviously and ingeniously tried to put us in a hole." After this meeting Stimson moved across to the White House for an 1100 appointment. The President launched into a discussion of the naval situation, telling Stimson "just how thin he was spread out in regard to the territory he had to cover."[2]

Quick to take the hint, Stimson got together with Marshall the next morning, April 23. When he informed the general of Roosevelt's view on the necessity of keeping the Fleet in Hawaii for the Islands' defense, Marshall "indicated his strong dissent." He countered that "with our heavy bombers and our fine new pursuit planes, the land forces could put up such a defense that the Japs wouldn't dare attack Hawaii. . . ." Stimson passed this to Roosevelt by phone that afternoon, whereupon the President asked Stimson to come to the White House at noon the next day, bringing "the papers regarding the defense of Hawaii." He further requested that Stimson ask Knox to come along and "bring the naval situation on that point."[3]

The noon conference of April 24 opened with a lengthy discussion about arrangements for patrolling the Atlantic. It soon blended into a dissertation from Roosevelt about "the difficulties that he was having in regard to the size and numbers of the present Atlantic Fleet. . . ." This was just the opening Stimson wanted. In preparing for the meeting, he said, he "had found that Marshall felt that Hawaii was impregnable whether there were any ships left there or not; that the land defense was amply sufficient, together with the air defense, to keep off the Japanese and the air defense could always be reenforced from the mainland of America." He then handed the President an *aide-mémoire* which embodied these views.[4]

This document which Stimson left with Roosevelt sheds much light on the thinking of Marshall, who signed it, and of those around him. It also helps clarify the Pearl Harbor picture because the two subjects of the discussion —depletion of the Pacific Fleet and the defense of the Islands—could not be separated. The memorandum began with a forceful statement much in keeping with popular opinion:

> *The Island of Oahu,* due to its fortification, its garrison, and its physical characteristics, is believed to be the strongest fortress in the world.
>
> To reduce Oahu the enemy must transport overseas an expeditionary force capable of executing a forced landing against a garrison of approximately 35,000 men, manning 127 fixed coast defense guns, 211 antiaircraft weapons, and more than 3,000 artillery pieces and automatic weapons available for beach defense. Without air superiority this is an impossible task.[5]

All very true. But the Japanese were not planning to occupy Oahu. Yamamoto's only current interest in the Hawaiian Islands was Kimmel's Pacific Fleet. And he would not attempt his daring strike without air superiority. Genda's planning called for immediate destruction of U.S. air power. The *aide-mémoire* continued:

> *Air Defense.* With adequate air defense, enemy carriers, naval escorts and transports will begin to come under air attack at a distance of approximately 750 miles. This attack will increase in intensity until when within 200 miles of the objective, the enemy forces will be subject to attack by all types of bombardment closely supported by our most modern pursuit.[6]

This was an ideal picture-book concept, but it bore no relation to the realities of the moment. Oahu did not have patrol planes that could fly out on a 750-mile arc, and even if it did, no one could guarantee that they would be able to locate an enemy moving in for a quick air strike. Nor did Short have sufficient bombers to bring the enemy under effective air attack at such range. Here, too, there was a tacit assumption of advance warning—early knowledge that the enemy was coming and from what direction. Marshall's document went on to amplify his thesis:

> *Hawaiian Air Defense.* Including the movement of aviation now in progress Hawaii will be defended by* 35 of our most modern flying fortresses, 35 medium range bombers, 13 light bombers, 150 pursuit of which 105 are of our most modern type. In addition Hawaii is capable of reinforcement by heavy bombers from the mainland by air. With this force available a major attack against Oahu is considered impracticable.[7]

A man of Marshall's innate honesty would not have deliberately given the President and Stimson a false impression. Yet when the first Japanese torpedo slammed into one of Kimmel's battleships, Short did not have thirty-five B-17s. He had twelve—only six of them operational.[8]

Moreover, it is difficult to imagine that in a real emergency Short would have had time to order twenty or thirty B-17s from the mainland as if they were so many crates of fresh eggs. In the highly problematical event that they would have been available on demand, they would still have had to fly the long distance to Hawaii. On landing, they would have needed a complete maintenance check, refueling, arming, and—last but decidedly not least—rested, competent crews standing by ready to take over.

The Army seems to have regarded the B-17 as a sort of magic cure-all. But although a fine aircraft, it had not been designed for action against ships at sea. Who knew how it would perform against Yamamoto's battlewagons? To a certain extent, therefore, the Army rested the defense of Hawaii on an unproved premise.

Marshall's *aide-mémoire* concluded: "In point of sequence, sabotage is first to be expected and may, within a very limited time, cause great damage. On this account, and in order to assure strong control, it would be highly desirable to set up a military control of the islands prior to the likelihood of our involvement in the Far East."[9]

The Chief of Staff accepted widespread sabotage in Hawaii as a fact beyond dispute. This in turn indicated that he expected one of two things: either a general advance warning, such as a formal declaration of war, at which signal thousands of Hawaii's Japanese would spring to action, or Tokyo's coordination of an attack with the local brethren. In fact, nothing could have been further from Yamamoto's intention, and one can scarcely picture the United States, with its traditional distaste for "military control," placing an entire territory outside the civil law just on "the likelihood of our involvement in the Far East."

At this stage Marshall concentrated on the Atlantic, and logically so. Washington had decided upon a "Europe First" policy to save England and defeat Hitler. German U-boats were sinking British ships, and soon the United States would engage in convoying. It was only natural that the War and Navy departments should pay primary attention to the present danger in the Atlantic instead of the potential one in the Pacific.

What Marshall, along with so many others, failed to see was that

---

*Here Marshall added an asterisk by hand, and he scribbled the following notation at the bottom of the page: "Due to make a mass flight from mainland to Hawaii May 20th. A number of this type of plane could be dispatched immediately if the situation grew critical."

Yamamoto was dead set on protecting the Japanese flank into Southeast Asia. To do so, he was prepared to risk an immensely dangerous attack against Kimmel's ships. Of course, no one could expect the Chief of Staff to be clairvoyant. Yet there is a refusal in his *aide-mémoire* to come to grips with the immediacy of the moment. Marshall preferred to explain to the President what the United States would do in the future rather than state how Short could defend Hawaii if the Japanese attacked that very day.

Pa Watson, the President's military aide, wrote across the top of the *aide-mémoire:* "Modern planes have completely changed the situation as to defensibility."[10] He never penned a truer word. But Genda or Martin could have told him that air power is essentially an offensive weapon, not a Maginot Line.

The role of aircraft as defensive instruments occupied a large part of Short's mind when, on May 12, in cooperation with the Navy, he launched "the greatest war drills ever staged" in the Islands.[11] This included a strong force of defending bombers which attacked "enemy" flattops several hundred miles at sea.[12] "Defending bombers swept down on the mythical carriers, assumed to be harassing the Hawaiian Islands, just as one carrier was in the act of sending a flight of planes off her decks, maneuver authorities said."[13] Here we have the idealized picture of Army bomber perfection—locating and hitting the enemy at the strategic moment of launching.

During the early stages twenty-one B-17s roared into Oahu from the mainland to augment the Hawaiian Air Force.[14] The decision to provide Short with Flying Fortresses entailed considerable discussion because heavy bombers had never flown en masse from the West Coast to Hawaii. However, the need to put real muscle into Hawaii's defense weighed against the risk involved in the flight tipped the scales in favor of the former.[15]

The exercises reached a smashing climax at the end of the second week. Early on May 24 the tide turned. "A huge pincers movement, combining the fire power of ground troops with the striking force of the army's newly arrived flying fortresses, caught and annihilated the enemy invading units."[16]

Short wrote an enthusiastic letter to Marshall on May 29 about his exercises. He described the maneuvers as divided into three phases. The first consisted of air action, during which U.S. forces "actually located and bombed airplane carriers 250 miles out at sea." So far American expectations moved in the same channel as Japanese planning. "The Navy cooperated very fully . . ." he reported, "and I believe we learned more about the coordination of Army Air Force, Navy Air Force and Antiaircraft than we had during any previous exercise."

The second phase, Short related, "consisted of the completion of our plans and the organization of the ground, including the construction of Field Fortifications. . . . The whole command dug diligently upon them day and night."

The third phase, "the maneuver proper," was headed "Repelling of a Serious Attack." Short thought that such an assault would be possible only under the following conditions: "Our fleet would be either absent or very greatly inferior. Our air force would be destroyed or very greatly inferior."[17]

Short had visions of wave after wave of tough Japanese troops hitting the beaches behind withering naval bombardment. And there the enemy would encounter Short's own men, equally tough, equally courageous. Hence his emphasis on training in the basics of soldiering, training to the point of reflex action. In combat one did not have time to consult manuals or consciously recall instructions; one had to react automatically. Once the enemy landed, Short, the ground soldier, would be in his element. And no doubt he would have given a good account of himself had the dice rolled in that direction.

He went all out to simulate a well-conceived assault on the Islands. But he had a few curious notions. "The situation was built up by the destruction of our large guns so that the Harbor Defense troops in the last phase of the exercise manned 3″ and 6″ secondary armament which are not normally manned on account of the lack of personnel. . . ." There is a cowboys-and-Indians touch about the mentality which could destroy heavy artillery in order to man the light guns. "Likewise air personnel which were available through almost complete destruction of our planes were used for anti-sabotage work and finally to take over a short sector of beach defense. . . ."[18]

Granted, Short's problem in this war game was to defend Oahu against a simulated invasion. To do this, he had to make certain assumptions, among them destruction of most of his air power, as he indicated to Marshall. Nevertheless, one has the impression that Short regarded this disaster as so much underbrush to be cleared away as rapidly as possible so that he could get down to the real business of fighting on the ground, where fighting belonged.

Of far more serious moment is the frightening demonstration that Short did not understand his basic mission on Oahu, despite all his instructions and despite his own lip service to the concept. We seek in vain in Short's war games of May 1941 for the slightest indication of a drill aimed at protecting Kimmel's ships. On the contrary, he based his maneuvers on the assumption that the Fleet would be somewhere at sea or else so hopelessly inferior that the enemy would not fear it and thus attack Oahu.

Almost equally disturbing is Short's obvious failure to understand or trust air power. He was entirely correct in assuming that if the Japanese tried to take Hawaii, they would do so only after clipping the wings of American aviation in the Islands. Nevertheless, he accepted the loss of command of the air with a certain nonchalance and set to work with "air personnel" thus made "available" for routine soldiering. One feels that he rather welcomed the addition to his ground forces, in which lay his own heart and interest—and acknowledged skill. His program for training airmen along these lines stirred up a bitter hassle during the summer which almost undid all the painstaking, delicate work of building up Army-Air Force goodwill.

Combine these two blind spots in Short's mentality, and one understands why he simply could not conceive of the type of attack the Japanese actually launched: an air strike complete in itself aimed at the destruction of the U.S.

Pacific Fleet, with no intention of planting one Japanese boot, let alone the Rising Sun banner, on Hawaiian soil. Short looked upon an initial air attack as a softening-up operation preliminary to the main attempt at seizure and occupation of the Islands, especially Oahu. And, of course, the whole would be coordinated with widespread sabotage. This again assumed either advance warning which activated Tokyo's Trojan Horse or full tactical contact between Japan and the local fifth column.

This was the German pattern—the worming from within; the aerial blitzkrieg; the ground battle; the occupation. Indeed, Hitler's blueprint had worked so well that it almost drove other concepts of warfare out of the free world's head at this point. But it was not the Japanese way. And the Japanese did not need instructions from Berlin on how to run a war—especially one initiated by naval aviation, which the Germans neither possessed nor understood.

Short had a good record, and he worked hard at his job, but he lacked creative imagination. When the Pearl Harbor attack came, it was a traumatic shock to him. The very nature of the operation knocked the props from under every military tenet on which he had based his life and work. And, as we have suggested before, Short failed to understand his true mission: that of protecting Kimmel's fleet. When the actual scene of Pearl Harbor confronts us, this tragic feature will stand out with blazing clarity in the spotlight's pitiless glare.

CHAPTER 15

"CRITICAL

IN THE

ATLANTIC"

Poco Smith stared sightlessly around the dining room of the Waialae Golf and Country Club on Sunday evening, May 18. He was dimly aware of Hilo Hattie, a favorite entertainer, putting across her comedy routine, but to Smith she "was not amusing that night." He applauded mechanically, smiled an ersatz copy of his usually cheerful grin. Occasionally he sipped a tasteless cup of coffee. He "felt like a sick clam."

Glancing covertly at his guests, Rear Admiral and Mrs. Kent Hewitt, he thought gloomily that the admiral, commander of Cruiser Division Eight, would not see his wife again for a long time. Hewitt had just shifted his flag from the light cruiser *Philadelphia* to *Savannah*, in the belief that his former flagship was leaving Honolulu "for extended overhaul at Mare Island Navy Yard." Smith knew that it was not.

Mrs. Vance D. Chapline, wife of *Philadelphia*'s skipper, remarked happily that she had rented a house at the yard, where their four daughters would join them both. Smith's kind heart smote him. And what about young John Briscoe Pye, second son of Admiral Pye—"a fine clean-cut lad of the class of '39"? His fiancée was on her way to Honolulu, and neither Smith nor any of his staff officers could tell the boy that his wedding had to be postponed. And when he found out the hard way, he could not even send regrets because to do so would break radio silence.

Smith's thoughts turned sadly to the battleship *New Mexico*. Her captain, Robert G. "Plug" Coman, was a classmate of Smith's, and his lovely wife, Mary, was slowly dying of cancer; Plug would not be able to receive word of her condition for weeks.[1]

What had happened to upset this peaceful naval community, so closely knit from seasoned admirals to youngsters with the gloss of Annapolis still on their boots?

German U-boats had grown bolder with every passing month as they sought to cut the vital lifeline between Britain and the New World. By mid-March 1941 merchant-ship sinkings extended well beyond Iceland and almost to the fortieth parallel. A dangerous gap existed between the point where Canadian convoy escorts turned back and the British took over. Roosevelt signed House Resolution 1776, the lend-lease agreement to aid embattled Britain, on March 11, but what good would lend-lease be if the German wolf packs sank every cargo ship as soon as it reached the mid-Atlantic?

Both Stimson and Knox had urged the use of the Navy to escort the convoys and thus ensure delivery of supplies. Technically Stimson had no business concerning himself with Navy matters, but he took a particular interest in the Fleet because he thought it "the one weapon that the United States had now ready which could make a telling blow. . . ."[2] Also, he felt driven to preserve Great Britain. If the German undersea fleet succeeded in starving it into submission, Stimson believed that not only would the United States stand in mortal peril, but with Britain would fall the whole moral code and rule of law in the Western world.[3]

By December 29, 1940, he had reached the firm conviction that "we cannot permanently be in a position of toolmakers for other nations to fight."[4] He took the typical and practical step of checking out any legal roadblocks and cautioned Knox that any restriction "which would forbid the President to use ships of the Navy to convoy was clearly unconstitutional."[5]

On March 24, 1941, Knox briefed Stimson about a series of conferences he had been having with the President on the Navy's "readiness and position." Both secretaries agreed "that the crisis is coming soon and that convoying is the only solution and that it must come practically at once."[6] The next day Stimson, Knox, Marshall, and Stark met with a group of English officers. All agreed that the British could not, "with their present naval forces, assume the entire escort duty. . . ."[7]

The situation set the President at war with himself—on the one hand, Roosevelt the statesman, who understood that if Britain fell, the Americas would live, if you could call that living, with a Nazi dagger at their throats; and on the other, Roosevelt the politician, who had promises to keep to the electorate and a determined bloc of isolationists waiting to pounce on any error of judgment he might make.

He solved his dilemma with typical suavity at a meeting in the White House on April 10 with his personal adviser Harry Hopkins in attendance, along with the Plus Four, as Mrs. Stimson nicknamed the quartet of Hull, Stimson, Knox, and Secretary of the Treasury Henry Morgenthau, Jr. Stimson captured the scene for posterity:

> We had the atlas out and by drawing a line midway between the westernmost bulge of Africa and the easternmost bulge of Brazil, we found that the medium line between the two continents was at about longitude line 25. By projecting that northward, it took into the western hemisphere most of

Greenland, running up the East side of Greenland until it finally struck the coast near Scorsby Sound, which is one of the most important, in fact the only landing place on the east side of Greenland, considerably north of the Arctic Circle.

[The President planned, therefore, that the United States should] patrol the high seas west of this median line, all the way down as far as we furnish the force to do it, and that the British will swing their convoys over westward to the west side of this line, so that they will be within our area. Then by the use of patrol planes and patrol vessels we can patrol and follow the convoys and notify them of any German raiders or German submarines that we may see and give them a chance to escape. Also notify the British warships so that they can get at the raider. Further than this, we shall defend Greenland—the major part of Greenland . . . if the Germans landed there we would put them out.[8]

This policy placed an immense burden on the Atlantic Fleet and posed the United States the question of how to cover two oceans with a one-ocean Navy. From January 29 to March 27 conversations had been going on in Washington between representatives of the United States Army and Navy and those of the United Kingdom's Chiefs of Staff. A report dated March 27 covering these talks outlined the strategy to be employed "should the United States be compelled to resort to war."[9] It arrived at the following far-reaching conclusions:

(a) Since Germany is the predominant member of the Axis Powers, the Atlantic and European area is considered to be the decisive theatre. The principal United States Military effort will be exerted in that theatre, and operations of United States forces in other theatres will be conducted in such a manner as to facilitate that effort.

(d) . . . If Japan does enter the war, the Military strategy in the Far East will be defensive. The United States does not intend to add to its present Military strength in the Far East but will employ the United States Pacific Fleet offensively in the manner best calculated to weaken Japanese economic power, and to support the defense of the Malay barrier by diverging Japanese strength away from Malaysia. . . . [10]

For Kimmel the catch was this: The United States planned not only to refrain from adding to its strength in the Pacific but actually to deplete it. In April Vice Admiral Ernest J. King, Commander in Chief of the Atlantic Fleet, reorganized that force and stationed it in Narragansett Bay virtually on a war footing. Where could he get enough combat ships to fulfill the Atlantic commitment if not from the Pacific?

Stark broke the news to Kimmel in an attachment to a letter dated April 4. In his covering note he hinted at a ray of light in the Pacific but painted the Atlantic scene in very somber colors: "On the surface, at least, the Japanese situation looks a trifle easier, but just what the Oriental *really* [Stark's italics] plans, none of us can be sure. I have had several long talks with Admiral

Nomura and unless I am completely fooled, he earnestly desires to avert a Japanese crisis with us. . . ."[11]

Stark told Kimmel that the memorandum about convoys, which he had drawn up for the President, concerned him directly. "The situation is obviously critical in the Atlantic," he explained. ". . . Without our giving effective aid I do not believe the British can much more than see the year through, if that. . . ."[12] The kernel of Stark's communication lay in the last page of the memorandum, in which he listed the anticipated requirements to ensure the safety of convoys in the western Atlantic. These included, among others, the battleships *Idaho, New Mexico,* and *Mississippi,* a carrier—preferably *Lexington*—and twelve destroyers. He added, "The possible effect of this transfer as regards Japan is realized, but must be accepted if we are to take an effective part in the Atlantic."[13]

Stark followed up with a secret letter on April 7. He retold part of the Atlantic story and informed Kimmel that some of his ships would be transferred.

> The movement of these units to the Atlantic must be accomplished with the utmost possible secrecy. In order to promote secrecy, it has been decided not to transfer all vessels at once but to make the transfer in several groups, with about two weeks elapsing between departures of groups. The Chief of Naval Operations will instruct you by secret dispatch as to the final dates for departure of each group from the Hawaiian area. . . .
>
> . . . You will direct that all vessels of the Atlantic detachments maintain radio silence, except in emergency, from the time of departure from Hawaii until arrival in Hampton Roads. . . . [14]

Kimmel had slightly more than a week to think over this distasteful prospect. Several events of early April gave the President and his more vigorous pro-Atlantic advisers pause. The signing on April 13 of the Soviet-Japanese Neutrality Pact might well remove any Japanese hesitation toward expanding southward. Then, too, the U.S. destroyer *Niblack,* seeking to rescue survivors of a U-boat attack, had depth-bombed a Nazi submarine, thus giving a fine beltful of ammunition to the isolationists. Accordingly, on April 15, Hemisphere Defense Plan No. 2 went into effect. It called for United States vessels to trail Axis warships and broadcast their positions, instead of using force to exclude them from Western Hemisphere waters. By this time the median line had moved from 25 to 26 degrees.[15]

On April 19 Stark advised Kimmel that his earlier proposal no longer applied. Roosevelt had decided that "he did not want, at this particular moment, to give any signs of seriously weakening the forces in the Pacific." The President therefore had pared the commitment down to one carrier and a division of destroyers.[16]

Accordingly Kimmel dispatched the initial increment on April 20 and 21—*Yorktown* with four destroyers—and another destroyer followed on April

26. Naturally the CinCPAC did not relish the depletion of his strength, but he took it like a good sailor. He confined himself officially to pointing out to Stark on April 22 that "the effect of detachment of a carrier or any light force from this command will affect the operations out of all proposition to the apparent fighting strength of the forces detached. . . ."[17]

But this was only the beginning. The President's Atlantic-oriented advisers renewed their pleas to revert to the escorting of convoys and to transfer from the Pacific the ships to do so. This school of thought had a large measure of reason on its side. The decision having been reached that the Atlantic should take priority, the Pacific must perforce accept second place. Even at full strength, the Pacific Fleet could not protect the Philippines, while Hawaii's defense was the responsibility of Short's air and land forces. Marshall, in particular, argued that the new heavy bombers such as the B-17 increased the American defensive posture and that twenty-one of the Flying Fortresses would shortly join the Hawaiian defenders.

The President asked Stimson and Knox "to sound out the British on the subject of moving the Fleet."[18] On April 25 Turner on instructions from Stark wrote to Rear Admiral V. H. Danckwerts, a member of a United Kingdom military-naval mission participating in joint staff discussions in Washington. Turner inquired, ". . . would it be advisable at this time, for the United States to transfer from the Pacific to the Atlantic three battleships, four light cruisers, and two destroyer squadrons?"[19] Under the circumstances how could the British object? So without waiting for a formal reply, Stark warned Kimmel on April 26 to be "mentally prepared that shortly a considerable detachment from your fleet will be brought to the Atlantic. . . ."[20] On April 28 Danckwerts replied to Turner's inquiry, forwarding the opinion of the British Chiefs of Staff that "the move proposed . . . would be advantageous." They were satisfied that "the consequential reduction in the strength of the . . . Pacific Fleet would not unduly encourage Japan."[21]

Matters hung fire for a few days because Hull was delaying the transfer. "Marshall, Admiral Stark, Secretary Knox and I are all united in feeling that the Fleet should be brought over at once," Stimson wrote, fuming. So he and Knox decided to have a showdown with Hull on May 5. At 1500 in Hull's office, Stimson and Knox, "in perfect accord," met "every point that Hull produced as the basis of his reasoning." The secretary of state was "still clinging to the treatments and fictions and everything else in his hope of by some means or another of preventing the Japanese from going down to Singapore and he keeps the Fleet there for that purpose. . . ." As Stimson saw it—and his view was both shrewd and reasonable—Hull's position resulted in neutralizing "the Fleet in the Pacific, where it is well known that we don't intend to use it actively against the Japanese and to keep it from its real function in the main theater of operations." After considerable arguing Hull finally "seemed to yield," but very reluctantly.[22]

By the next day the effect of Stimson and Knox's arguments apparently had worn off. At a meeting in the White House Hull stood firmly on his old position.

Furthermore, to Stimson's "utter surprise, Stark switched around and trimmed on the subject and was only for moving . . . three capital ships. Of course this was fatal," Stimson added bitterly, "as the President has been rather shy on the subject."[23]

On or about May 8 Knox delivered to Roosevelt an *aide-mémoire* of that date from Danckwerts, conveying a message from Winston Churchill's Cabinet. It advised that the Australian and New Zealand authorities agreed that "any marked advance by the U.S. Navy in or into the Atlantic would be on the whole more likely to deter Japan from going to war than the maintenance of the present very large U.S. Fleet at Hawaii."[24] This rather remarkable opinion presupposed a much greater degree of cooperation than existed between the two major Axis partners. The Japanese Navy danced to no tune of Hitler's piping, and the Japanese government was infinitely less concerned about serving German interests than the United States was about bolstering Britain.

The day of decision appears to have been May 13. Stimson began by putting in some missionary work on Hornbeck, who had been "one of the recalcitrants that are holding back from the movement of getting the Fleet over to the Atlantic. . . ." Parting from Hornbeck on cordial terms, he went to the State Department, where he met with Hull, Knox, Marshall, and Stark. Hull informed his colleagues that Roosevelt "was ready now to order the first three capital ships and their accompanying vessels through the Canal." They discussed how many ships should follow, Stimson urging that the "full naval force" should be in the Atlantic. Stark "held back and was very weak compared with the position that he had taken before." For once Knox had little to say, while Hull still believed that he had a one-to-ten chance "to win something out of the negotiations with the Japs."[25]

Stark was not as weak as Stimson made out. After all, it took a certain amount of fortitude to stand up under the torrent of arguments poured out by Stimson and to some extent Knox. And he was by no means unmindful of the Pacific.

Reading over a batch of cables and messages from G-2 on May 15, Stimson felt "rather horrified to find the terms of the negotiations which have been going on between the State Department and Japan."[26] One must admit that the Walsh-Drought proposals were enough to horrify a former secretary of state. These high-level discussions lay far beyond Kimmel's scope. He knew only that no matter what turn events took in Washington or Tokyo, the nation would expect him to keep the watch—and with a fleet greatly reduced in size. On May 19 the major movement of ships from Hawaii began, and by the end of the twenty-second it had been completed in an atmosphere of utter secrecy. One can easily imagine the anguish that tore Captain Coman as *New Mexico* steamed farther and farther away from his dying wife.

On the twenty-fourth Stark indicated to Kimmel that his troubles had ceased temporarily. "I do not contemplate *for the moment* [Stark's italics] ordering anything to the Atlantic except auxiliaries in connection with the Azores task and except possibly later four CA's [heavy cruisers] as per Rainbow 5. However, I am not the final 'Boss of this show.' "[27]

Too true! And during the summer additional forays would cost Kimmel three oilers, three transports, and a number of auxiliaries—a total of sixteen ships. All in all, Kimmel lost about one-fourth of his Pacific Fleet:[28] the battleships *Mississippi, Idaho,* and *New Mexico,* the carrier *Yorktown,* four light cruisers, seventeen destroyers, three oilers, three transports, and ten auxiliaries—more ships than the Japanese destroyed at Pearl Harbor.

What priceless irony! The most Yamamoto could possibly have expected from the execution of his plan would have been the elimination of between one-fifth and one-quarter of the U.S. Pacific Fleet. Even before his Pearl Harbor operation had emerged from its cocoon, the United States government obligingly dispatched about that percentage to the Atlantic! Inevitably the questions arise: Did Yamamoto understand the situation, and if so, why did he continue along his charted course? Indeed, in summarizing its voluminous evidence the joint congressional committee investigating the attack brought up that very point: "If the Japanese really knew the weakness of the Pacific Fleet they must also have known that it did not present a formidable deterrent to anything Japan desired to do in the Far East." The investigators therefore suggested that "the role played by espionage in the Pearl Harbor attack may have been magnified out of all proportion to the realities of the situation."[29]

Japanese Intelligence in Tokyo knew well enough what was going on. Despite the tight secrecy, the moves of the ships did not pass unnoticed. The President himself had practically informed the entire nation of the situation in his fireside chat of May 27. It was certainly no trick to deduce from the announced Atlantic buildup where the vessels would come from.

Yoshikawa had been reporting battleships present in Pearl Harbor by name. After his report of May 23, *Idaho, Mississippi,* and *New Mexico* disappeared from the rolls, while on May 26 he cited seven light cruisers instead of the ten reported on the twelfth.[30] Yes, the Japanese Navy had a very good idea of the exact strength of the U.S. Pacific Fleet; to keep track of the ships from Yoshikawa's reports involved a simple charting process which any competent yeoman could handle. Furthermore, if anything on earth is easily visible, it is a carrier or a battleship going through the Panama Canal. And Japan had a competent consular establishment in the Canal Zone reporting to Tokyo on the movements of American shipping.

Nevertheless, Yamamoto could not assume that this situation would continue. For the moment the United States had given the Atlantic priority, but in view of the very fluid world situation this could change rapidly. Roosevelt could send his ships back to the Pacific anytime the notion struck him. The Japanese had evolved a war plan so grandiose, with so much at stake, that Yamamoto was convinced he could not afford to leave his eastern flank uncovered. Therefore, it is unrealistic to believe that the day-to-day strength of the U.S. Pacific Fleet influenced his thinking much one way or the other.

This brings us to the crucial question: Was the reduced Pacific Fleet still a deterrent to Japan, or did the transfers to the Atlantic encourage the Japanese to strike? Actually in no case was the Pacific Fleet—at full strength, half strength, or quarter strength—a deterrent to Japan. It would carry out its policy of developing the Greater East Asia Co-Prosperity Sphere no matter where Roosevelt put his ships. Japan did not rely upon Washington for the formulation of its foreign policies.

Leadership in Washington proceeded from a false premise at the very outset: that the U.S. Pacific Fleet located in Hawaii could act as a brake on Japan. On the contrary, the stronger the Fleet, the more Yamamoto would have wanted to strike it a surprise blow to keep it from threatening the Japanese flank in Southeast Asia.

Of course, the Atlantic orientation was the inevitable corollary of the national policy to keep Britain's head above water and by every means short of war to contain the German menace. And Kimmel could not do a thing about it because in the United States, with a philosophy deeply rooted in the subordination of the military to the civil, naval strategy waited upon the State Department and the administration. No such handicap troubled Yamamoto or the Naval General Staff. In Tokyo the military held the reins of national policy and could drive the Japanese war-horses whither they willed.

CHAPTER 16

"THE

KISS OF

DEATH!"

Located in the Fleet Headquarters building at the submarine base opposite Ford Island, Kimmel's second-floor office reflected the man. Measuring about eighteen by fifteen feet, it was incredibly neat and spare, its furnishings few and unpretentious. A desk of average size rested a short distance from the northwest corner of the room. According to Fleet legend, one could back into Kimmel's office in total darkness and find every book, chair, or pencil exactly in its appointed place.

Even before he became CinCUS, Kimmel told Stark that he planned to move his staff ashore.[1] The very day he assumed command, he established Soc McMorris and his War Plans Office at the submarine base, where they would have room to work on their charts. But Kimmel soon found that the subsequent comings and goings between *Pennsylvania* and the shore offices, much of it pertaining to secret matters, interfered with training aboard the battleship.[2] Moreover, the heavy volume of headquarters traffic from *Pennsylvania* would jeopardize communications security.[3] Therefore, he decided that he could run the Fleet more efficiently from shore. Kimmel realized that this would be a drastic break with tradition for which he could incur considerable criticism. But after weighing all the pros and cons, some six weeks after taking over he moved bag and baggage into offices at the submarine base.[4]

In making this move, Kimmel showed himself more farsighted and realistic than Yamamoto. Although *Pennsylvania* remained his seaborne head-quarters in maneuvers, the battlewagon was now stripped of its administrative impedimenta and ready for action. In contrast, Yamamoto kept *Nagato* tethered to Japanese ports, and when the 63,700-ton *Yamato* came down the ways, he transferred his flag to her. As a result, what was potentially the greatest warship

135

ever constructed never engaged in actual combat under his command and remained in effect a floating hotel and office building.

The problem that worried Kimmel most of all was his lack of tools to do the big job expected of him. On May 26, shortly after his lost ships disappeared over the horizon, he sent off to Stark an eleven-page memorandum full of punch, soundly reasoned and well written. If by some quirk of fate every other document written by Kimmel should be destroyed, future historians could reconstruct the man's character and mentality from this one letter.

His first thrust pierced the grave question of stabilizing "Personnel." In essence the trouble was this: The Bureau of Navigation planned to utilize trained men from the existing Fleet units to man newly constructed ships at a ratio of 72 percent from the Pacific Fleet and 28 percent from the Atlantic Fleet. In other words, Washington was using the Pacific Fleet as a mine, not only of ships but of skilled manpower. Kimmel protested vigorously: "Unless a readjustment is made in these figures to correspond to the recent readjustment in the relative strengths of these Fleets, the Pacific Fleet will be seriously stripped of experienced men. . . ."[5]

"Aviation" caught the next barrage. Scarcely any aspect of it satisfied Kimmel. Neither the number of experienced pilots nor the quantity and quality of assigned aircraft, their armament, and spare parts pleased him. He followed with a broadside at "Material," of which he needed plenty. "Our ability to correct these deficiencies," he wrote pointedly, "is limited by two factors (1) aid to Great Britain, and (2) rapid expansion of the Army. . . . As the situation appears now, the Navy may be called on for active operations in contact with well equipped opposing forces, yet is prevented from obtaining vitally necessary needs by the magnitude of the needs of Britain and the Army. . . ."[6] Obviously Kimmel did not underestimate the Japanese. He opened his "Operations" section with another salvo:

> With the recent detachment of many of the most modern and effective units, the adequacy and suitability of the forces remaining to accomplish the tasks to which they may be assigned is [sic] very doubtful.
>
>   In the Pacific, our potential enemy is far away and hard to get at . . . and has a system of defense . . . that requires landing operations, supported by sea forces, against organized land positions supported by land-based air. This is the hardest kind of opposition to overcome. . . . It also requires a preponderance of light force and carrier strength, in which we are woefully deficient in the Pacific. Our present strength is in battleships—which come into play only after we have reduced the intervening organized positions. . . .[7]

Here is the voice of a man who appreciated the worth of the naval air arm and did not rely upon the battleship as the ultimate weapon. Furthermore, he had sized up Japanese thinking as practiced in the Naval General Staff: "The Japanese are not going to expose their main fleet until they are either forced to do so by our obtaining a position close enough to threaten their vital interests or it is advantageous for them to do so. . . ." He pointed out that under the current war plan the Pacific Fleet, perhaps justifiably, was "so reduced in light force and carrier strength that its capabilities for offensive operations of a decisive nature are severely crippled. . . ."[8] It is important to understand that when Kimmel and others of the American high brass spoke of an offensive war plan or of the Fleet's taking offensive action, they meant this in connection with a war already declared. No responsible member of the United States government or armed forces thought of starting a Pacific war by attacking Japan. In this context Kimmel chafed at being deprived of the tools of the offensive.

The same psychology lay behind his worry over the anchorage. "The defense of the Fleet base at Pearl Harbor is a matter of considerable concern." He urged that the Navy press the Army to increase its matériel on a priority basis. Furthermore:

> The naval forces available to the Commandant are meager to the point of non-existence. A Fleet base is a place of rest, recreation and resustenance [sic] and must afford protection of the Fleet at anchor and during entrance and egress independent of the units of the Fleet. If units of the Fleet must be employed for its own defense, in its base, its freedom of action for offensive operations is seriously curtailed. . . . [9]

Kimmel next bombarded "National Policy." Here the CinCUS concluded:

> . . . our national policies and diplomatic and military moves to implement them, are not fully coordinated. No policy, today, is any better than the force available to support it. While this is well recognized in principle, it is, apparently, lost sight of in practice. We retained the Fleet in Hawaii, last summer, as a diplomatic gesture, but almost simultaneously detached heavy cruisers to the Atlantic. . . .

He offered a solution: "The military branches of the government should be told, by the diplomatic branch, what effect it is desired to produce and their judgment as to the means available and the manner of its accomplishment should be accorded predominant weight."[10] Then Kimmel trained his sights on a painful subject—"Information":

> The Commander-in-Chief . . . is, as a rule, not informed as to the policy . . . reflected in current events and naval movements and, as a result, is unable to evaluate the possible effect upon his own situation. He is not even sure of what force will be available to him and has little voice in matters radically affecting his ability to carry out his assigned tasks. . . .
>
> It is realized that, on occasion, the rapid developments in the international picture, both diplomatic and military, and, perhaps, even the lack of knowledge of the military authorities themselves, may militate against the furnishing of timely information, but certainly the present situation is susceptible to marked improvement. . . .

Kimmel had put his finger on a crucial point: Washington could not inform him of matters of which it knew nothing. He suggested that because of the "factor of distance and time," he should be "guided by broad policy and objectives rather than by categorical instructions." This is rather ironical, for when disaster struck, he would complain bitterly because Washington had not, in fact, given him "categorical instructions."[11]

Last, Kimmel fired off a few shots at "Public Opinion." To his thinking, ". . . the current mental and moral preparation of our people, as reflected in the newspapers and magazines, is utterly wrong. To back into a war, unsupported or only half-heartedly supported by public opinion is to court losing it."[12]

In Washington the lack of just such decisive leadership as Kimmel looked and hoped for continued to prey upon Stimson's mind. He observed on May 23 that "the President shows evidence of waiting for the accidental shot of some irresponsible captain on either side to be the occasion of his going to war."[13] This waiting around for someone to take Roosevelt off the hook distressed the straitlaced secretary of war, who thought the President "ought to be considering the deep principles which underlie the issue. . . ."[14]

Morosely knocking a croquet ball around the grounds at Woodley, Stimson's Washington home, Hull seemed "quite discontented" and, "as usual, was pessimistic," so he could give Stimson little help. That evening, May 25, Knox joined the other two of the "Big Three" in reviewing the revised draft of the President's speech scheduled for the next night. This edition of Roosevelt's remarks pleased Stimson because it indicated that his chief intended to announce the removal of the Fleet to the Atlantic.[15]

In his fireside chat of May 27 Roosevelt proclaimed a state of "unlimited national emergency."[16] To the general public no doubt the President's speech sounded forceful enough. But a number of his advisers felt a sense of letdown. Stimson was disappointed that Roosevelt had softened his speech from the hard-hitting draft he, Hull, and Knox had read. "Thank God he can't stop the Fleet which is on its way," he wrote in his diary. "The last recession had been done under the behest of Hull. . . ."[17]

By now Stark had decided that enough was enough and resisted the continual urgings that Roosevelt siphon off still more strength from the Pacific to the Atlantic. To ensure that Kimmel understood the full picture and also, possibly, to add a strong voice to his own, Stark summoned the CinCUS to Washington. Kimmel was more than happy to consult "face to face with the Navy leaders there." So, taking McMorris with him, he set out for the mainland.[18] On June 13 Knox entertained Stark, Kimmel, and King at lunch, during which King discoursed at length about his Fleet's activities in the Atlantic.[19] Later Kimmel had a long, amicable discussion with the CNO. In its course he freely discussed all the difficulties confronting him, covering in essence the contents of his memorandum of May 26.[20]

Kimmel also spoke to Stark about the weaknesses of Pearl Harbor. The "congestion of ships, fuel oil storage, and repair facilities" invited "attack, particularly from the air." Then, too, the "single entrance channel," which all ships had to use, "exposed them to submarine attack" and presented the constant danger of blockage. "In case of attack by air or otherwise with the fleet in port," he emphasized, "it would take at least three hours to complete a sortie." All things considered, he believed "the only real answer was for the Fleet not to be in Pearl Harbor when the attack came."[21]

Nevertheless, he did not suggest that the Fleet move back to the West Coast. First, he accepted Roosevelt's command decision. Secondly, he thought in terms of offensive operations. If his country called on him to lead its Navy in war against Japan, Kimmel proposed to sail forth to engage Yamamoto and waste no time about it. For aggressive action against Japan, the closer he was to Tokyo, the better. His objections to Pearl Harbor were operational, whereas Richardson's had been almost entirely logistical.

The high point of Kimmel's trip was the appointment which, at Stark's suggestion, he sought and received with the President.[22] Their meeting took place at the White House on Monday, June 9, from 1425 to 1550. Their paths had crossed only briefly and infrequently; nor did the admiral now take to the President, although the meeting went smoothly enough. A plain man, Kimmel rather distrusted an overabundance of charm. Moreover, Roosevelt showered "Yeses" and "That's rights" and Kimmel disliked thoughtless agreement.

Roosevelt confided in Kimmel that Hull and others "were carrying on informal talks with certain Japanese (unidentified) and others concerned (also unnamed) looking forward to a peaceful Pacific 'for a hundred years.'" Obviously Roosevelt was referring to the Walsh-Drought discussions.* Listening carefully, Kimmel had the impression that "a considerable amount of wishful thinking was involved."

Roosevelt asked Kimmel what he thought of "further reducing the Pacific fleet by three battleships," adding that Knox had told him "six battleships could raid Japanese communications and defend Hawaii." Roosevelt continued: "Betty [Stark] thinks three battleships is enough to defend Hawaii" and he "supposed the other three would do a lot of raiding."

At this point Kimmel exploded, "That's crazy!" Roosevelt chimed in, "It sounds silly to me. I told Knox that it was silly." Kimmel asserted that "higher authority than himself" would resolve the question, but that he "was convinced that such further reduction would be an invitation for Japan to come into the war."

"That's right," Roosevelt observed.

After a little more conversation Kimmel asked for *North Carolina* and *Washington*, now that Japan had more battleships in the Pacific than the United States. He "pointed out that his capabilities for offensive operations in the Pacific had been greatly reduced by the recent detachments and that the addition of the battleships in question would aid in restoring the balance."

Kimmel "was left with the definite impression that the President had no intention of transferring any more battleships from the Pacific. . . ." This was a great relief to the admiral because he believed that "Once the fleet was placed there [at Pearl Harbor], for the assumed purpose of exerting a deterrent effect

---

*See Chapter 13.

upon Japan, it was not maintaining a consistent policy thereafter to weaken the fleet, visibly and plainly, by diversion of powerful units to the Atlantic."[23]

Although they discussed other matters, Roosevelt showed a distinct gift for sliding away from a subject. Toward the end of the discussion the admiral "brought to the President's attention a clear picture of the existing situation at Pearl Harbor, defense arrangements, oil storage, need for aviation development, lack of patrol craft, radar, etc."[24] He also discussed the weaknesses of Pearl Harbor as a fleet base with the President as he had with Stark.[25] Then, well satisfied with his day's work, Kimmel left the White House.

It is unfortunate that someone in the Navy Department did not take advantage of Kimmel's visit to Washington to brief him on Magic, especially because his belief that he was not getting enough information was one of the principal reasons for his visit to the capital. A close reading of his memorandum of May 26 should have dispelled any lingering illusions, such as Turner claimed to have entertained, that Kimmel had access to all the Magic traffic. No communications security would have been involved with Kimmel right on the spot.

Stark evidently believed that he had fulfilled his duty to Kimmel when on a virtual weekly basis he wrote him extensive letters, which included much information gleaned from Magic. But Washington was so preoccupied with the exchanges between the Foreign Ministry and Nomura that it shunted aside the traffic between the same ministry and its consulate in Honolulu wherein lay so many hints to which Kimmel, as well as Short, was entitled.

Kimmel may have turned the tide in keeping the remainder of the Fleet in the Pacific. Stimson, for one, had been under the impression that another quarter of Kimmel's ships "would come over at once." Later Roosevelt assured him that he "must have misunderstood . . . that it had never been contemplated to move another section of the battleships. . . ."[26] In this he was less than candid because he had asked for Kimmel's opinion on that point.

With all these crosscurrents in the air, it is no wonder that despite his victory in Washington, Kimmel never lost his fear that someday a hand would reach out to snatch more of his ships. The loss of *Yorktown* alone had deprived him of a third of his carrier strength, and with the cruisers and destroyers went a large measure of the Pacific Fleet's mobility. The shortage of fuel weighed on Kimmel ceaselessly and dictated the use of his task forces. Canceling out three oilers chained the Fleet even more tightly to Pearl Harbor than before. The fuel problem was so critical that Pye doubted whether the transfers actually made all that difference because the logistical situation was such that "the Fleet could not have operated more than 2,500 miles from Honolulu no matter what its strength."[27]

In attempting to please everyone and avoid criticism, the President had scattered his shots. He had not gone far enough to satisfy the Atlantic faction, and he had weakened the Pacific Fleet to the point where it would not be able to perform its offensive mission in case war should break out in Asia. Understandably some of Kimmel's staff officers could not help feeling that

Washington had written them off as expendable. When the destroyers pulled away from *Pennsylvania* bearing their secret orders to the battleships *Mississippi*, *Idaho*, and *New Mexico*, Smith looked at DeLany and said grimly, "The kiss of death!"[28]

CHAPTER 17

"JAPAN'S

FOREIGN

POLICY

WILL NOT

BE CHANGED"

I̲t was just as well for Kimmel's peace of mind that he was in San Diego when the Germans attacked the Soviet Union on June 22. This event threw the Atlantic into sharp relief once more, and Roosevelt's advisers bombarded him with appeals to seize this golden opportunity to help the British in full force. After a long conference with Marshall and "the men in the War Plans Division," on the twenty-third Stimson drew up a memorandum which he carried to Roosevelt. This expressed the belief that:

> . . . Germany will be thoroughly occupied in beating Russia for a minimum of one month and a possible maximum of three months. . . . By this final demonstration of Nazi ambition and perfidy, the door is opened wide for you to lead directly toward the winning of the battle of the North Atlantic and the protection of our hemisphere in the South Atlantic. . . ."[1]

On the twenty-fourth Stark visited Roosevelt, with Knox's approval, to urge that the President "seize the psychological opportunity" to "announce and start escorting immediately, and protecting the Western Atlantic on a large scale." Stark admitted that this action "would almost certainly involve us in the war," but he accepted this because he "considered every day of delay in our getting into the war as dangerous and that much more delay might be fatal to Britain's survival." He also believed that "only a war psychology could or would speed things up the way they should be speeded up. . . ."[2] But Roosevelt refused to be swept into this vortex of panicky belief that the Russians would go the way of the French within a maximum of three months.

Therefore, when Kimmel held a press conference at Pearl Harbor on June 26, he could say with sincerity, "I think the greater the effort we make now, the better chance there is of avoiding war and certainly the better chance of acquitting ourselves well if we get into the war."[3]

The outbreak of the Russo-German war put Japan on the spot. It was pledged to the Axis and had signed a neutrality pact with the Soviet Union. What path should it follow? The Japanese government did not know. Although the prospect of such a war came up for discussion regularly at liaison conferences,* curiously enough Konoye's Cabinet made no advance decision concerning a possible German attack on the Soviet Union.

One Japanese who had no doubt of his position was Matsuoka. Irrespective of the Japanese-Soviet Neutrality Pact, which he himself had negotiated, and without pausing to consult the Cabinet, he gained an immediate audience with the Emperor. There in the Imperial Palace he proffered his advice: ". . . now that the German-Soviet War has started Japan, too, must cooperate with Germany and attack Russia. To do this, it would be better for the time being to refrain from action in the south. Sooner or later Japan would have to fight there. Ultimately Japan would be fighting the Soviets, America and England simultaneously." Konoye tells us, "The Emperor was greatly astonished,"[4] and well he might be. The prospect of tackling the bear, the lion, and the eagle simultaneously, with side excursions into Indochina and the Netherlands East Indies, while still entwined in the dragon's tail, could not have appealed to a sensible man.

As Japan hesitated at the crossroads, on June 29 Nomura gave the Foreign Ministry an excellent summary of American attitudes as he saw them: "The U.S.A. does not wish to make double-front operations. Consequently it goes without saying that she desires peace in the Pacific, but, as you know, she is hastily making provision for the time when this may be impossible. . . ." He warned that if the United States stopped the talks, this would start a chain reaction: "*severance of economic relations, then, our advance to the south, and finally our clash with Britain and the U.S.A.* [Nomura's italics]." He urged that Tokyo think up some way to realize a Japanese-American understanding.[5] But the Foreign Office paid little attention to Nomura's wise, well-reasoned warnings. The fatal decision was already in the making.

The Emperor himself presided on July 2 over one of the most important conferences ever held in Tokyo, a major milestone on the tragic road to war. The document which issued from this conference did not rule out the possibility of eventual war with the Soviet Union, but it concentrated heavily on

---

*Liaison conferences took place frequently, sometimes almost daily, between representatives of the government and the armed forces. These included the prime minister, foreign minister, and the ministers of war and navy, with other officials called in when necessary. The chiefs and vice chiefs of staff attended, while the chiefs of the Military Affairs and Naval Affairs bureaus, along with the chief Cabinet secretary, acted as secretaries of the meeting. These conferences ensured that the government and military understood each other's thinking and coordinated their purposes. But the dice were heavily loaded in favor of the military because the army and navy ministers, while part of the Cabinet, were also officers on active duty.

the strategy of "Southward Ho!" Its essence was this: The government had resolved to dominate East Asia and to that end pledged to win the war in China, take over Southeast Asia, and, if the Germans crushed the Russians— which at the moment seemed likely—strike the Soviet Union.

Some of the explanatory notes attached to the formal decision were far more explicit than the basic document itself. For instance:

> 2. . . . The Imperial Government will continue all necessary diplomatic negotiations with reference to the Southern Regions and also carry out various other plans as may be necessary. In case the diplomatic negotiations break down, preparations for a war with England and America will also be carried forward. First of all, the plans which have been laid with reference to French Indo-China and Thai [sic] will be prosecuted, with a view to consolidating our position in the southern territories.
>
> In carrying out the plans outlined in the foregoing article, we will not be deterred by the possibility of being involved in a war with England and America.[6]

There it was, in black and white. Japan wanted the treasures of Southeast Asia so badly that it would fight any power or combination of powers to secure them. Here was an elastic program designed to fit all contingencies. It would give here, expand there, to suit the needs of the moment. It also demonstrated one of the major weaknesses which eventually led to the downfall of the Axis: an ambition so all-encompassing that Germany and Japan scattered their shots over an impossibly large area.

After the imperial conference of July 2 the Foreign Ministry sent Circular No. 1390 to its embassies in Washington, Moscow, and Berlin (the latter for transmission to Rome). This dispatch considerably toned down the language of the actual policy document. It made no specific reference, for instance, to preparations for war with the United States and Britain.[7]

Stark saw all signs pointing to a projected Japanese attack on Russia. He sent an estimate of Japan's intent to Kimmel and others in a top secret message on July 3.[8] He confirmed his dispatch to Kimmel in a letter containing this postscript: "It looks to us at the moment . . . as though the Germans had persuaded the Japs to attack Russia within the next month. It is anybody's guess and only time will tell."[9]

The War Department brought Short up to date by a message which repeated in substance what Stark had told Kimmel: Japan had determined on its future policy. This was likely to be

> one of watchful waiting involving probable aggressive action against maritime provinces of Russia if and when Siberian garrison has been materially reduced in strength and it becomes evident that Germany will win a decisive victory in European Russia period Opinion is that Jap activity in the south will be for the present confined to seizure and development of naval, army and air bases in Indo China although an advance against the British and Dutch cannot be entirely ruled out. . . . [10]

Short later testified that this was "the only message received from the War Department that made a definite estimate as to probable Japanese action."

Despite the Foreign Ministry's care to keep from Nomura exactly what was cooking in the Tokyo witches' caldron, he caught an unsavory whiff and warned Matsuoka on July 3: ". . . *if you are resolved to use force against the Southern Regions at this time, there seems to be no room at all for adjusting Japanese-American relations . . .* [Nomura's italics]."[11] This was perfectly all right with Matsuoka. With the imperial conference over, he could turn his attention to Washington's reworking of Japan's proposals of May 12, which Hull had presented to Nomura on June 21. This note restated the American basic principles on international relations, the "China Incident," the Philippines, and the political situation in the Pacific. Along with it, Hull sent an "Oral Statement" which contained some rather pompous comments.[12]

At about the time that Matsuoka was mulling over the Hull statement, he unwittingly gave Washington further cause to eye him with suspicion. On July 5 Stimson received from Marshall "a very interesting piece of news that had come along through authentic channels of something that Matsuoka in Tokyo had been telling Ribbentrop—about how well they had been fooling the Americans into keeping our Fleet in the Pacific. This was the last straw for me in proof of the futility of the final late efforts of the State Department."[13]

This idea made just enough sense to merit close scrutiny at American Cabinet level. This was especially true because, from that vantage point, it appeared that the best help Japan could give Hitler would be to tie up the United States Fleet in the Pacific, thus keeping the Atlantic sea-lanes virtually free of American interference.

The dispatch gave Stimson heaven-sent ammunition for use in his running battle to transfer the main strength of Kimmel's Fleet to the Atlantic. He had always believed the U.S. Pacific Fleet to be wasted in Hawaiian waters, acting as a deterrent which Washington did not intend to implement; now he had hard evidence that the United States was actually playing Japan's game by this policy.

So at 1100 he went to the White House to flourish his prize under Roosevelt's nose. The President agreed that this "had better signalize the end of our efforts of appeasement in the Pacific."[14] But on July 8 Knox stopped at the War Department to tell Stimson that "he had failed in his attempts to get more of the Fleet moved over here." To Stimson's disgust, Roosevelt had "gone back on us again in regard to the Fleet and the whole Pacific question. Evidently Hull has gotten at him again. . . ."[15]

In another sense of the expression, Hull had gotten to Matsuoka. Although his "Oral Statement" was strong medicine for diplomatic correspondence, the secretary of state had no intention of igniting a fuse that would end in the destruction of the second Konoye Cabinet. But Matsuoka took it very much to heart. On July 14, entirely against the wishes of both Konoye and the Cabinet, Matsuoka cabled to Nomura his rejection of the Hull statement.

The upshot was the resignation of the entire Konoye Cabinet on July 16. The imperial chamberlain, Marquis Koichi Kido, convened the Privy Council —the living ex-premiers of Japan—in Tokyo at 1330 on July 17 to select a new prime minister. After a mere hour's discussion the meeting adjourned with the unanimous recommendation that Konoye should succeed himself. That evening at precisely 1705 the Emperor commanded Konoye to organize a Cabinet.[16]

The premier made only one major change: Vice Admiral Teijiro Toyoda, his minister of commerce and industry, replaced Matsuoka as foreign minister. Thus, as Konoye tells us, "the important post of Foreign Minister was occupied by a representative of the Navy, which was most concerned with the American question, and hence had a significant voice in the matter. . . ." In later days Konoye blamed Nomura for neither understanding nor conveying to the Americans the significance of "this very obvious political change."[17] Yet the Foreign Ministry hastened to advise Berlin, Rome, and Nanking that "Japan's foreign policy will not be changed and she will remain faithful to the principles of the Tripartite Pact."[18]

Actually Matsuoka lost his place on the diplomatic scene not because he was anti-American, but because he had made himself obnoxious, had flouted Konoye's authority, had conducted unauthorized talks with the Germans, and had lost the Emperor's confidence. Moreover, his utterances in the liaison conferences gave rise to a serious doubt about his mental stability. Konoye had to replace him no matter what the relations with the United States; the Hull incident merely triggered a charge already cocked and primed. In fact, on July 17 Hull formally took back his "Oral Statement" without fuss.[19]

With his deep concern over the state of Japanese-American relations, Nomura would have been frantic had he seen a lengthy, important message from Japanese "military officials" in Canton to Tokyo dated July 14:

> 1. . . . The recent general mobilization order expressed the irrevocable resolution of Japan to put an end to Anglo-American assistance in thwarting her natural expansion and her indomitable intention to carry this out, if possible, with the backing of the Axis but, if necessary, alone. . . .
>
> 2. . . . We will endeavor to the last to occupy French Indo-China peacefully but, if resistance is offered, we will crush it by force, occupy the country and set up martial law. After the occupation of French Indo-China, next on schedule is the sending of an ultimatum to the Netherlands Indies. In the seizing of Singapore the Navy will play the principal part . . . we will once and for all crush Anglo-American military power and their ability to assist in any schemes against us.[20]

While the message did not specify an attack on any American possession, it provided clear evidence of Japan's grandiose war plans. In such dispatches between Tokyo and addresses other than Washington, the Japanese came out from behind their fans and showed the real face of aggression. And because the State Department had access to this information through Magic, while Nomura did not, the United States had a much better idea of Japan's true intentions than did its own ambassador.

Washington could not shrug off such outbursts as mere bluster. In Japan the military called the tune, and the government danced to its piping. Therefore, the State Department had to take such intercepts very seriously. It is easy to understand why, with such information at hand, Hull displayed no conciliatory attitude toward the Japanese and why Nomura felt such a frustrated sense of working at cross-purposes.

There is no doubt that Nomura genuinely wanted peace between Japan and the United States. So, probably, did the new administration in Tokyo. But the Japanese government did not understand what was so clear to Nomura: that a rapprochement with the United States was totally inconsistent with Japan's expansionist foreign policy and its adherence to the Tripartite Pact.

On July 21 Japan had signed a preliminary agreement with the Vichy government of Marshal Henri Pétain granting Japan substantial concessions in Indochina, including occupation of strategic airfields and use of Saigon and Camranh Bay as naval bases.[21] Nomura knew that the American leaders would not permit Japan's move into Indochina to remain on the international chessboard without a countermove.

CHAPTER 18

"AS IF

HE WERE

BEYOND

PENALTY"

The balmy month of May brought a new phase in Yoshikawa's spying activities: a scouting trip to Maui with Kotoshirodo. Compared to his day-to-day activities on Oahu, he gave Maui the once-over-lightly.[1] His interest centered on Lahaina, about which Tokyo constantly nagged the consulate for information. He wondered why his superiors appeared so concerned when he had assured them it no longer served as a base.[2] In this matter Yoshikawa was somewhat at cross-purposes with Naval Intelligence. Far from worrying lest Kimmel base his ships at Lahaina, Genda and his airmen of the First Air Fleet earnestly hoped that he would do so. For Lahaina offered unlimited aerial maneuverability and presented no shallow-water torpedo problem. Any ship sunk there would plunge so deep that the Americans could never salvage it, as they could at Pearl Harbor.[3]

Another fine day in May Yoshikawa and Kotoshirodo, with the faithful Mikami at the wheel, took an early-morning trip to Kaneohe on the eastern side of Oahu to observe the naval air station. As they drove slowly along, Yoshikawa commented to Kotoshirodo that all the hangars at the air station seemed to have been completed.[4] Throughout the year Yoshikawa made several trips to Kaneohe, always finding many seaplanes resting gull-like on the sparkling waters of the harbor. At Kaneohe he had to risk field glasses because he could not get near enough to see details from the car without them.[5]

But he could take a commercial boat excursion, which came close enough to give any trained observer a good picture. Accordingly one Sunday Yoshikawa invited two of the consular maids for the boat ride. Peering through the glass bottom of the boat, he checked the depth of the water with particular care. He had heard rumors that the U.S. Navy, unsatisfied with Pearl Harbor because of its narrow channel, was considering Kaneohe as a supplementary anchorage.

But he saw that the water was too shallow for large ships and also noted no naval construction which would warrant such a conclusion.[6]

By this time Yoshikawa's messages indicated a steady improvement in the quality of his activities. By May 12 he not only recognized and reported on battleships by name but also spotted *Utah* as a target ship.[7] Of course, he did not always report accurately. To expect perfection would have been too much, because almost invariably he observed Pearl Harbor with the naked eye, from a distance.

Yoshikawa's fellow office workers considered him a lazy "goof-off" because of his constant absence from his desk. They took a dim view of his disregard for the usual standards of behavior. "All agreed that he had special privileges. He was frequently drunk, often had women in his quarters overnight, came to work late or not at all, as he pleased, insulted the Consul General on occasions, and generally conducted himself as if he were beyond penalty. . . ." These watchful colleagues soon reached the conclusion that "Morimura" was not what he seemed. Some speculated that he might be a naval officer, but Seki denied this, saying he knew "how Japanese naval officers behaved, and that Morimura definitely did not conduct himself as an officer. . . ."[8] Yoshikawa rather cultivated his image as hard-drinking skirtchaser, with Kita's approval, to divert suspicion from his true task. "Bobby Make-Believe" he called it.[9]

Early that summer the consulate inaugurated an intensive program of document burning. The consulate did not normally keep material for more than ten years; therefore it destroyed a large accumulation annually. It burned telegrams from Japan as soon as received, if possible, and in any case no more than a week later. But this particular summer documents went up in smoke almost daily, and all the clerks pitched in to help, under instructions not to discuss the matter. At roughly the same time they received monthly bonuses.[10]

Certain events which occurred in the United States and on Hawaii at about this time may very well have put the Japanese on guard and triggered this intensive destruction program at the Honolulu consulate. The United States embarked on an overdue housecleaning of foreign agents. In May the FBI informed the State Department that it had uncovered "espionage activities" by one Lieutenant Commander Itaru Tachibana, and asked the State Department's "attitude toward his arrest." Hull's department agreed on May 27.[11]

Somewhat taciturn and not too easy to draw out, Tachibana was totally committed to any task he undertook. He had attended Eta Jima in the same class with Genda. He had the usual training ashore and afloat and also graduated from the Naval Staff College. After duty at sea in 1938 he went to the United States in June of the next year with the primary mission of espionage. He was to find out anything he could about the U.S. Navy, but in particular its technological improvements.

Tachibana had the instincts for clandestine operations but little training or experience. The Japanese Navy did not have Intelligence schools in the prewar years or give specific courses on that subject in its other establishments, and Japanese Naval Intelligence suffered from a serious lack of manpower and funds. He was an example of what he considered a makeshift Intelligence organization which worked successfully before the war because "the United States up to the very last operated on a peacetime basis with practically no restrictions on communications and the like."[12]

Tachibana operated smoothly for a while, making Los Angeles his main base. He was one of Japan's "outside agents" who did not work through consulate or embassy channels but who engaged in illegal espionage. In the spring of 1941 he tried to tap Kimmel's headquarters for information on the U.S. Pacific Fleet—a task the consulate in Honolulu did not dare attempt. Unfortunately for him, his contact man in Pearl Harbor made a few false moves, and U.S. Naval Intelligence in Hawaii and on the West Coast set a trap. The FBI moved in to spring it, and Tachibana was finished.[13]

Nomura interceded with Hull on his behalf, and the secretary of state looked carefully into the case. He decided to dismiss the charges against Tachibana out of his personal regard for Nomura and because "conversations with the Japanese were at a crucial stage" on condition that the spy leave the United States immediately and never return. On June 18 Minister Kaname Wakasugi and Maxwell Hamilton, chief of the State Department's Far Eastern Section, settled Tachibana's hash to everyone's satisfaction.[14] He returned to his homeland, where, in July 1941, he joined the Third Bureau (Intelligence) of the Naval General Staff.[15] He passes from our story for the present, but we shall meet him again in the autumn of 1941, when he will become directly involved in the Pearl Harbor venture.

If the bureau of which Tachibana became an ornament had decided to adopt a crest and motto, it could well have selected Kipling's mongoose with his "Go and find out." Through this organization funneled every scrap of information gleaned from every conceivable source throughout the world. At this time the Third Bureau directed most of its attention to the United States, with particular stress on the strength and disposition of the Pacific Fleet, its armament, its building program, and, above all, the status of aircraft carrier construction and anything pertaining to the naval air arm. In addition to reports from special agents and naval attachés, the normal sources included American books, magazines, newspapers, government documents and reports, and radio broadcasts.

Oddly enough, Rear Admiral Minoru Maeda, chief of the Third Bureau from October 1940 to June 1942, could not be hailed as an expert on the United States, having made only three short visits to that country. Smooth-browed, pouch-eyed, wispy-mustached, Maeda was clever, cagey, and closed-mouthed.

He had a most able assistant in Captain Kanji Ogawa, who came to the Third Bureau in the fall of 1940 directly from service as an assistant naval attaché in Washington. Of medium height, unobtrusive, wearing the suggestion of a mustache as did his chief, seemingly half-asleep, Ogawa reminded one of the dormouse in *Alice in Wonderland*. But no flies ever lit on Ogawa. He had served in the Third Bureau several times before, knew espionage through and through, and could have written an authoritative book on the United States without consulting a single reference.[16]

While the Japanese Embassy and the State Department were arranging Tachibana's future, the Germans felt the weight of American displeasure. On June 16 the State Department ordered all twenty-four German consulates, as well as certain other agencies, closed not later than July 10, for "activities of an improper and unwarranted character." As an afterthought, it also closed the Italian consulates on June 21. Then, late that month, the FBI arrested twenty-nine persons accused of spying for Germany.[17]

None of these moves seriously inconvenienced the Japanese. For various reasons the State Department preferred to keep the Japanese consulates open. According to one story, the United States had hired "a whole gang of burglary experts" to break into the consulate at New York. They would photograph Japanese material and carefully put it back exactly where they found it. This consulate provided such an excellent source of information that the Military Intelligence agencies begged State to hold off.[18] Then, too, with Magic intercepts giving a blow-by-blow account of Japanese transactions, Hirohito's consulates probably were of more value open than closed. Nor did Roosevelt and Hull want to cause trouble in the Pacific while Hitler was brewing such a storm in the Atlantic.

Undoubtedly the American housecleaning gave Kita and Okuda many anxious moments. The prospect of having the consulate in Honolulu closed was one matter Kita could not accept with his usual insouciance. Had Washington closed all Japanese consulates by the early autumn of 1941, it would have been a fearsome blow to Japan's entire intelligence system, especially to Maeda's Third Bureau, which needed up-to-date, authoritative information on the United States.

In particular, by turning the lock on the door at 1742 Nuuanu Street in Honolulu, Washington could have dried up Japan's primary source of information on the U.S. Pacific Fleet. Then the Japanese would have had to resort to other methods of gathering their intelligence on Kimmel's ships and Oahu's military installations. True, they had a sleeper spy in Hawaii who had been on ice for several years at a princely salary against just such an eventuality. But he was certainly not the Third Bureau's dream man, as we shall see.* The possibility that he would be caught or, worse, bought and made into a double agent always existed.

One can imagine what the Naval General Staff would have thought about the situation had the United States closed the consulates. Nagano's staff opposed Yamamoto's plan as too risky and to the last minute never ceased to ask whether the admiral could be sure the U.S. Pacific Fleet would be in Pearl Harbor or at least close by in Hawaiian waters on X-Day. Under such

---

*See Chapter 31.

circumstances Tokyo might well have refused to give Yamamoto the go-ahead.

Yamamoto himself might have had second thoughts. Could he have sent the cream of Japan's naval air arm several thousand miles from home bases just on the off chance of running into the U.S. Pacific Fleet or finding it in Pearl Harbor? Japan did not have the fuel to waste on aimless cruising without a firm target; the Southern Operation cried out for the prompt return of the carriers and their precious planes for use in Southeast Asia.

All things considered, with the closing of Kita's consulate the whole idea of striking the U.S. Pacific Fleet in Pearl Harbor could have passed from the realm of reality back into the shades of fantasy whence Yamamoto had recently managed to lift it.

So the consulate remained open, but it had to worry about another indirect threat. The Honolulu press was full of articles on such subjects as espionage, fifth columns, un-American activities, sabotage, and foreign agents. On May 7 the Honolulu *Star-Bulletin* told its readers that upon request of the FBI the Honolulu Police Department had "created the espionage bureau of one lieutenant and four officers effective January 1, 1941." So from New Year's Day the FBI, Navy DIO, and Army Counterintelligence had an ally in the cloak-and-dagger business—Chief of Police William A. Gabrielson and his men.

Determined to track the potential Japanese espionage and sabotage establishment in Hawaii to its source, the zealous Shivers took dead aim on the 234 consular agents "who had been appointed by the Consul General of Japan" in Honolulu. He had been prodding J. Edgar Hoover's headquarters on this matter since at least April 1940.[19] He considered these agents "definitely a source of potential danger."[20] He may have drawn a long bow. The *toritsugin-in** had long been a Hawaiian institution, first established to handle personal affairs for the many Japanese immigrants who lacked the education to fend for themselves in a strange land. Their duties were routine, and only in rare cases did they receive any pay from the consulate. Nevertheless, virtually every one "engaged in a number of pro-Japanese activities in addition to his duties as *toritsuginin*."[21]

In the early summer of 1941, after consulting with Angus Taylor, Jr., acting United States attorney in Honolulu, Shivers called a meeting with Mayfield (DIO); Marston, at that time Short's G-2; and his assistant, Bicknell, who was more closely connected with the problem than Marston. Shivers told the officers that the United States attorney had requested him to furnish all the information so far developed on the consular agents and that he was going to report to the attorney general "his opinion as to whether or not they should be prosecuted." He suggested that his colleagues consult with their respective

---

*One of the Japanese readers of this manuscript claimed that the word *toritsuginin* has no meaning in Japanese, yet the term crops up consistently in the Pearl Harbor documents in connection with the Honolulu consulate.

commands, although he anticipated no objections because the matter was "purely a criminal proceedings. . . ."

The group met the next day to compare notes. Speaking for Bloch, Mayfield stated "that the admiral was all for prosecuting these consular agents. . . ." But Marston, representing Short, protested, explaining that for various reasons the general wanted to let sleeping *toritsuginin* lie.[22]

It may seem paradoxical that Short, whose preoccupation with possible sabotage from the Japanese element almost reached the proportions of a mania, should be the one to intervene on behalf of the consular agents. But in reading the telegram he dispatched to the War Department on July 22, 1941, one can follow the thread of his thinking:

> We are at present engaged in a counter propaganda campaign whose object is to encourage loyalty of the Japanese population of Hawaii on promise of fair treatment. . . . Success of the campaign would promote unity and greatly reduce proportions of our defense problem. . . . I believe not over ten percent of the unregistered consular agents in Hawaii are aware that they have violated our laws. I believe further that prosecution at this time would unduly alarm entire population and jeopardize success of our current campaign to secure loyalty Japanese population.[23]

One point in Short's message rings out like a bell: "unduly alarm . . . population." We shall encounter the idea again in secret dispatches in late November when events moved irresistibly toward a climax.

Stimson concurred in Short's viewpoint and on July 25 so advised Taylor by letter. That officially terminated the matter for the Army. But not for the FBI. Shivers later received instructions from headquarters in Washington "to conduct very thorough, complete investigations of all the Japanese consular agents. . . ."[24] Realizing that he had to deal with "a very tight ring"[25] and believing that Short had made an "error in judgment,"[26] Shivers obeyed with alacrity. He assigned five men to conduct the investigations, which turned up quite a bit of pro-Japanese activity but nothing on which he could act.[27]

Along with the espionage threat on land, the Navy worried about the Japanese sampan fleet based at Kewalo Basin, some twelve miles from Pearl Harbor. The crews of these vessels could be engaging in active espionage as well as be a potential source of sabotage. Some of the ships were "large, seaworthy, radio-equipped and quite capable of prolonged cruising at sea"; other smaller boats engaged in offshore fishing, and still others fished the harbors and inlets, netting bait for the larger vessels. As Bicknell explained, "The operators of these boats knew every detail of these waters, the depths, nature of bottoms and, most important of all, were always present to observe any operations or maneuvers. Through 1938, 1939 and part of 1940 these small boats had access to Pearl Harbor itself. . . ."[28]

The Navy also fretted over the possibility that some overenthusiastic sampan captain might deliberately sink his ship in the Pearl Harbor channel; thus, any sampan venturing within three miles of Pearl Harbor did so at the risk of being overhauled by a destroyer, ushered into Honolulu Harbor, and having its crew arrested.[29]

To judge from a special inspection report dated July 9, 1941, the Army, too, was much concerned over Hawaii's reactions to that persistent nightmare: sabotage. One of the stated reasons for the inspection was "to determine the Department Commander's policy in respect to additional steps required by the recently declared unlimited emergency." But one seeks in vain for any reference to the island's operational readiness; on the contrary, it confined itself to one installation—Hickam Field, home of Short's bombers—and its personnel, administrative, and security shortcomings. The last caused deep distress. The inspector, Colonel H. S. Burwell, reported with obvious pain: ". . . the prevailing attitude of mind toward the immediate need for positive preparations to prevent the success of predictable acts of planned and ordered sabotage does not fully reflect the priority and the expressed policy of the responsible officers concerned and therefore must be reported as inadequate." Burwell continued severely:

> . . . a few bold, ruthless and intelligent saboteurs, consisting of inside military operators or civilian employees, could incapacitate Hickam Field or a similar large post on any predetermined night . . . it should be taken for granted that Germany has prepared a subversive plan of action for Hawaii, similar to her invariable custom, although the existence of the plan may not have been discovered. . . . [30]

It is somewhat incongruous to see Short, of all people, indicted for indifference to sabotage. At least he worried about Japanese on the spot instead of Germans two continents away! The report went on: "Thus the growing importance of Hickam Field as a vital terminal from which to reenforce the Navy quickly with B-17 type bombers from the mainland . . . and the belief that Hickam will be fully spot-lighted whenever the fleet departs, is not fully comprehended from a sabotage prevention viewpoint."[31] Here again is the misguided notion that if Kimmel's ships sailed out to sea, Oahu would be in danger.

Burwell's report continued: ". . . such a series of events obviously may force a hostile decision to burn up Hickam Field, by German agents acting alone or by Japanese agents acting jointly in support of her tri-parte [sic] pact. . . ." The inspector therefore recommended that "additional security measures required to protect" Hickam's far-flying bombers were to take priority. "This estimate is based upon the fact that hostile powers first organize an immediate state of air readiness and seek *first* [Burwell's italics], by any and all means, to destroy the opposing state of air-readiness."[32] True enough! Yet sabotage was not the only way "to destroy the opposing state of air-readiness."

Within five days of this report—on July 14—Short sent Marshall a tentative SOP (standing operating procedure) setting forth three alerts: No. 1 was all-out, "requiring occupation of field positions"; No. 2 put the command on the *qui vive* but did not call for such drastic action as the first; No. 3 covered defense against sabotage.[33] Significantly, by the time Pearl Harbor Day came around, Short had reversed these alerts. How much, if anything, Colonel Burwell's report had to do with this action is anybody's guess, but it was coincidental and unfortunate. Short's reversal of his alerts indicates once more his preoccupation with sabotage.

Yet if the idea gripped him, who can blame him? In recent years Hitler had raised it to a fine art, and now in virtually every corner of a sullen, hate-inflamed Europe it rose to plague him and his generals. The disease infected Short as soon as he set foot on Oahu. Nor was he alone. Stimson and Marshall shared this awareness of an accepted danger. Thus, Short focused much of his thinking, his plans, and his efforts on chasing an illusion.

Yoshikawa looked down on the local Japanese with lofty superiority. He and Seki had agreed that while Hawaii should be "the easiest place" to carry on espionage because of the large Japanese population, the poor education of the locals canceled out the advantage of race. Yoshikawa claimed that the *toritsuginin* "were no good for the work," and he wrote off most Japanese in Hawaii as "just trash."[34]

His own job called less for brilliance than for detailed work, meticulous recording, constant alertness, and irregular hours, all against the background of an unfamiliar culture and a continuous stream of new faces. The shadow of the FBI hovered over him unceasingly, although he hid his uneasiness from his colleagues. He especially feared lest the G-men install some recording device in the consulate—he did not know how thoroughly the phones were tapped— or in one of the restaurants he frequented.

Shivers visited the consulate on several occasions in Kita's off hours. Yoshikawa never forgot the picture of the FBI's top agent in Hawaii sitting there, chatting amiably with Kita in his modest, unassuming way, while the consul general beamed his toothiest grin, very much on his best behavior. Each understood the other's motivation perfectly, and they would trade easy banter from time to time with the smoothness of old tennis pros who respect each other while fighting it out. "Go ahead, Mr. Kita," Shivers said on one occasion half-mockingly, "cruise around the island and see what you can see."

"Oh, no," Kita replied silkily. "Then you would follow me and chase me."[35]

Oddly enough, although in later days Yoshikawa frequently spoke of his fear of the FBI, he never mentioned the Army, Navy, or Police Department Intelligence groups. Perhaps he used the abbreviation "FBI" as a sort of generic term to cover all American Intelligence and law enforcement agencies. Possibly, too, somewhere in the labyrinth of his complex mind, he equated the FBI with Japan's sinister *Tokko* ("Thought Police"), which had an unpleasant habit of arresting and "interrogating" suspects with no such details as evidence, warrants, or habeas corpus to cramp their style.

All this time Yoshikawa had no way of knowing whether his information filled a genuine need in Tokyo. He knew nothing of the projected Pearl Harbor attack, but this Navy man's thoughts moved in the general direction of combat use for his information. Once he remarked to Seki that "Hawaii would be a fine place from which to watch a Japanese-American war."[36]

Yoshikawa explained to Kotoshirodo:

> . . . it was Japan's policy to maintain two espionage systems in countries abroad—one system run by consulates, and the other separate from the consulates and entirely unknown to them. . . . [A] consulate would indulge only in such espionage activity as could be carried on without compromising diplomatic and consular relations (such as the gathering of facts from newspapers, viewing ship movements from places of vantage not in any restricted area, and observing airfields and beaches from public highways), whereas an extra-consulate organization would carry on "illegal" espionage (such as trespassing restricted areas and the buying of confidential information).[37]

Yoshikawa thought that "there must be such a system" in Hawaii working "directly on orders from Tokyo," but he did not know how it would operate.[38]

The intelligence problem on Oahu was unique, for here the great base lay almost as open as a goldfish bowl. In general, the problem of Military Intelligence is to penetrate the enemy's secrets, find out what he is doing, thinking, planning, what his best weapons are, and how ably he can use them under any and every circumstance. All this demands illegal espionage.

But the Japanese Intelligence problem on Hawaii was not like that. Basically Japan wanted to know what U.S. ships were in Pearl Harbor where and when and how they were protected. It also wanted information about naval and military installations in Hawaii, particularly the disposition and strength of American air power—obviously a more difficult task than scouting the Fleet. Nevertheless, this did not require illegal espionage. On the whole, Japanese Naval Intelligence, hampered by lack of funds, personnel, and organization, did not have a high batting average. However, the Japanese played championship baseball on Oahu because they read the opposition's pitching and other signs with ease and impunity and because the ball park—built-in geographic and political factors on Hawaii—gave them a big edge.

CHAPTER 19

"WE

WANT

HUSTLERS!"

Japan blossomed in a garden of flags. This was May 27—Navy Day, anniversary of the Battle of Tsushima. On this festive Tuesday in 1941 the Navy had something unusual to brag about: an excellent demonstration of torpedo and other bombing techniques which some sixty planes each from the First and Second Carrier divisions put on at Sukumo Bay off the coast of southwestern Shikoku.[1]

Captain Hideo Hiraide, the Navy's spokesman, never at a loss for words, outdid himself in a flight of eloquence that night over Tokyo's radio station JOAK. He asserted:

> . . . the naval air force has now some 4,000 planes which have constantly been drilling themselves for special war tactics. . . .
> Thus with a firm conviction and confidence, the Navy is now biding its time with full preparedness . . . to crush in a moment anyone who dares to challenge Japan.
> The Imperial Japanese Navy air force . . . are now working out stratagems that will deal instantaneous death to any nation.[2]

One would give much to have heard Yamamoto's comments at this point. Not only did he dislike this sort of bombast, but some of Hiraide's remarks came so uncomfortably close to the truth that they virtually constituted a breach of security.

By the end of May Nagumo's airmen had already been hard at work for the better part of a month. Nagumo had issued a lengthy document concerning training policy which, although undated, obviously came into being shortly after Kusaka briefed him on the Pearl Harbor project. This document established the beginning of July 1941 as the deadline by which the new organization

157

should achieve a standard of basic training equal to that of any other in the Imperial Navy. By the end of August the First Air Fleet should have reached its "battle capacity," ready to operate as a unit. After that time its efficiency would be further refined.

Nagumo underscored such items as surprise mass aerial attacks on enemy air bases, destruction of enemy carriers, maneuvering of the First Air Fleet's flattops in battle, and coordination with land-based and submarine forces. To implement this strategy, the First Air Fleet would concentrate on such tactics as use of various types of aircraft in coordinated strikes, night torpedo attacks, air battles involving large formations, night fighter techniques, repeated attacks employing the entire air force, improvement of antiaircraft and antisubmarine measures; and methods of evading torpedoes.[3]

Here was a program to delight Genda and offer Kusaka the challenge of his life. The latter withdrew into Buddhistic contemplation. Suddenly he remembered *Kinshicho-Oken*, a form of swordplay which he had learned in childhood. By this method one pressed in near the foe, held the sword over his head, and struck downward with one fierce stroke, then returned to one's original position. Kusaka resolved to adopt this as the model for his tactics in the First Air Fleet.[4]

In close teamwork with Kusaka, Genda handled "all the plans related to aviation" and also worked on studies and training concerned with "naval operations in general." He knew the hazards of so much responsibility. "When one works on planning," he mused, "he tends to fall into the illusion that he has become great and he is the commander of the whole thing." Such an attitude spelled "plenty of harm." On the other hand, Genda did not intend to become a mere paper shuffler, "not using his brain for suggestions." He took to heart a remark of Nagumo's—"Without the union of people working together, a Pearl Harbor attack is impossible"—and a crisp statement from one of his torpedo officers: "We want hustlers!" To Genda these "valuable principles distilled through long experience" were like the "rivet of a fan" holding the individual sticks in a workable whole.[5]

Meanwhile, in early June Genda launched the First Carrier Division on the initial aerial torpedo program aimed directly at carrying out Yamamoto's plan. He scheduled the torpedo practice as the first part of the training because he believed it would be the most difficult to perfect.

Kyushu, southernmost of the four main islands of Japan, had been chosen as the setting for training.[6] On its southeastern shore lies Ariake Bay, where ships of the Combined Fleet often anchored. Due west across a thick neck of land Kagoshima Bay merges into a beautiful harbor extending far inland. With a little effort of the imagination one can see a resemblance to Pearl Harbor. Stretch the fancy a bit further, and the city of Kagoshima on the northwest side of the bay becomes the Pearl Harbor shipyard. The imagination wails a protest at transforming Sakurajima, a dormant volcano about 4,000 feet high which juts far out into the water from the opposite side of the bay, into Ford Island. For the latter is flat as a pancake, though the location is roughly similar.

In this subtropical setting somewhat evocative of Hawaii the torpedomen of the First Carrier Division began their special training. All that summer and autumn so many planes screamed over Kagoshima that the city itself seemed to rock on the threshold of adventure.

Here we find another of those strange interweavings of threads between Japanese and American thinking in the days before Pearl Harbor. On June 13, just about the time Genda's torpedomen were coming to grips with their problems, Rear Admiral Royal E. Ingersoll, Stark's deputy, sent a memorandum to the commandants of all naval districts with copies to Kimmel and others. The document reminded its addressees that in the past a minimum depth of seventy-five feet had been assumed necessary for successful aerial torpedo strikes. Then it went on:

> . . . Recent developments have shown that United States and British torpedoes may be dropped from planes at heights of as much as three hundred feet, and in some cases make initial dives of considerably less than 75 feet, and make excellent runs. Hence . . . it can not be assumed that any capital ship or other valuable vessel is safe at anchor from this type of attack if surrounded by water at a sufficient distance to permit an attack to be developed and a sufficient run to arm the torpedo.
>
> 3. While no minimum depth of water in which naval vessels may be anchored can arbitrarily be assumed as providing safety for torpedo plane attack, it may be assumed that depth of water will be one of the factors considered by any attacking force, and an attack in relatively deep water (10 fathoms or more) is more likely.
>
> 4. As a matter of information the torpedoes launched by the British at Taranto were, in general, in thirteen to fifteen fathoms of water, although several torpedoes may have been launched in eleven or twelve fathoms.[7]

Kimmel gave this memorandum careful consideration, but he still did not believe that "aerial torpedoes could run in Pearl Harbor."[8] Its waters were too shallow—an average of about forty feet.

At this particular time Genda most reluctantly had to agree with Kimmel. But Genda never abandoned his vision of aerial torpedoes with their highly destructive capability slashing into the flanks of Kimmel's ships. The Japanese would just have to solve the many problems connected with this tactic to make the operation the success of which Genda dreamed.

Since 1933 the Japanese had been leaders in aerial torpedo techniques, launching from altitudes of slightly over 300 feet at relatively high speed. Nevertheless, torpedoes dropped under such conditions dived into the water anywhere from 100 to 300 feet, then shot up sharply, sometimes breaking surface. This resemblance to a playful porpoise instead of a deadly shark was caused by an ineffective "up" rudder. On the other hand, some torpedoes ran too deeply, a few even passing under the target vessel. To correct these defects, the Japanese tried reducing the torpedo speed, but this softened its impact. Thus, they had to minimize depth of run before the aerial torpedo could be a truly efficient weapon of naval warfare.[9]

In mid-1939 the Japanese used a large wooden fin attached to the torpedo as a stabilizer. This broke off as the missile hit the water. In experiments at Yokosuka Naval Base, an additional wooden plate affixed to the fin at a slight angle produced promising results. By February 1940 the experimenters had cut the depth of the torpedo's initial plunge to about 60 feet or less. Seventy percent of these missiles ran at approximately 40 feet when launched from a height of less than 100 feet at an airspeed below 150 knots. These experiments brought to light various defects which would require modification of the torpedo itself.[10]

When, in January 1941, Miyo of the Naval General Staff asked Aiko to settle the torpedo issue once and for all, the latter turned the project over to Yokosuka. He also arranged that the Navy Ministry should form a committee with the chief of the Aeronautical Research Department as its chairman to stimulate the study and testing.[11] But the Yokosuka experiments did not progress well because the researchers could not control the axis spin of the torpedo.[12] These experiments were under way when Genda and his airmen began to practice for a maximum torpedo sinkage of ten meters—about thirty-three feet.

None of them knew that Genda demanded this seemingly impossible feat because of Pearl Harbor's shallow waters. They attempted a test run, using only two planes armed with one torpedo each. These aircraft flew at the revolutionary altitude of only forty feet. In this tryout one of the torpedoes worked well, sinking to the desired level, but the other went much deeper.[13] Almost a success—but "almost" never satisfied Genda.

At first, experimental runs hinted that the depth of torpedo sinkage was related directly to the altitude of the plane—that is, forty feet high equaled forty feet deep. However, further tests proved that no such relationship actually existed. Another problem arose during these tests—maneuverability. Pearl Harbor would offer many obstacles, and the torpedo planes were difficult to maneuver under the best of circumstances. And the training circumstances were far from the best. The torpedomen had to practice shallow-water techniques from a dangerously low altitude immediately after swooping to the target through projecting smokestacks and buildings rimming Kagoshima Bay. Moreover, they had to learn how to attack battleships probably protected by antitorpedo nets.[14] Genda's daring fliers could not help wondering why the Navy set them practicing such complicated antics.

Horizontal bombing gave Genda almost as many headaches as torpedo tactics. The Japanese Navy's record in high-level bombing was so poor that as early as March 1941, even before the formation of the First Air Fleet, Genda almost gave up. The Navy had figured that in surface battle, twelve to sixteen direct hits from big guns could sink a ship. To secure the same results by horizontal bombing would require the total striking power of six *Akagi*-class carriers. But the same number of planes armed with aerial torpedoes could easily sink more than ten capital ships. The First Carrier Division therefore recommended that "the Attack Force of the aircraft carrier should abolish horizontal bombing, and concentrate on the training of torpedo and dive bombers." But neither the Combined Fleet nor the powers-that-be in Tokyo agreed because they had the technique under special study.[15]

Tests had developed that a minimum weight of 800 kilograms—almost a ton—would be necessary to destroy a battleship, while 500 kilograms would suffice for a carrier, if the bombs were released from an altitude of about 10,000 to 12,000 feet. But a shortage of the special steel required precluded the stocking of such bombs. Further researches revealed that the 40-centimeter (16-inch) shells used by battleships of the *Nagato* class could be modified into bombs of about 800 kilograms, and arrangements were made accordingly.

The Japanese Navy wanted to use armor plate of similar quality to that employed by the U.S. Navy for experiments. So early in 1941 it set up a twenty-square-meter plate of German steel at the Kashima bombing range southeast of Kasumigaura and turned loose skilled crews from the Yokosuka Air Corps to try out the modified shells. These tests proved that in its original shape the missile little more than dented the steel plates, but that shaving off the shoulder streamlined it enough for effective results. The tests further showed a minimum altitude of 12,000 feet to be required.

Other trials at the Kamegakubi experimental firing range at the Kure Naval Base determined such factors as the new bomb's power, penetration, and fuse time.[16] The bomb, designated Type 99-No. 80-3, was a huge missile of 796.9 kilograms with 22.8 kilograms of explosives. Everything seemed to be going fine when production hit a snag. As late as mid-September 1941 only 150 bombs had come off the assembly line.[17]

With the formation of the First Air Fleet on April 10, *Akagi* had received a new flier—a graduate of the bombing course at Yokosuka, Lieutenant Izumi Furukawa. This handsome young man "was a central figure among bombing experts."[18] A prime favorite of Genda's, Furukawa exuded energy, drive, and imagination. Though a severe taskmaster, he had the gift of imparting unsparingly the best of himself to those under him.[19] When he arrived in Kyushu, he had not the least idea where the training would lead him, although of course, he joined Nagumo's fur-helmeted fliers aboard *Akagi* "with some deep determination in mind."[20]

Furukawa took over *Akagi*'s horizontal bombers and within twenty days had wrought a virtual miracle. Near the end of April, as the flagship plowed her way toward Kyushu, his men practiced against the old battlewagon *Settsu*, long since demoted to the rank of target ship.[21] Then and for some time later, the horizontal bombers used a nine-plane formation, consisting of three planes in the lead, with two three-aircraft units in the rear, to port and starboard respectively. Because all the planes were equidistant, this produced a flight in the form of an inverted V, looking something like this:

X
XX
X   X
X X X X[22]

At its very first trial the *Akagi* unit, attacking *Settsu* from about 10,000 feet, scored four direct hits in nine tries. When Genda heard this, he thought Lady Luck had been working overtime. But a second and third session that day "resulted in three to five hits each time." What is more, a report from Yokosuka informed Genda that practice held there the same day had produced "results not inferior" to Furukawa's.

When Furukawa returned from his practice session, Genda pounced on him. "I wonder what explains this performance?" he asked.

"The biggest factor is the pilot," Furukawa explained. "In the past, bombing was handled by bombardiers, and the pilot was nothing but a driver. We can't expect good bombing with such a setup. We found that piloting is a big factor in accurate bombing."[23]

Furukawa's record not only restored the Navy's faith in horizontal bombing but held out high hopes for the future. If the difficulties in torpedo technique could not be resolved, the Japanese would have to rely on dive bombing to carry out a projected Pearl Harbor attack, but this method could not destroy capital ships. As long as horizontal bombing continued at a dismal 10 percent or less accuracy, they could not hope to achieve "the chief objective" of disabling the U.S. Pacific Fleet for six months. But the story would be very different if the high-level bombing program could produce such results as those of the *Akagi* unit.[24]

Another major reason for Japan's poor record in horizontal bombing was the lack of an instrument anywhere near as effective as the Norden bombsight possessed by the Americans.[25] The Japanese used a revised German Boyco bombsight, but its accuracy depended to a large extent on the skill of the pilot and bombardier.[26] For this reason, the Yokosuka Air Corps hoped to obtain better results by training skilled bombardiers picked from the spread of the Navy, each teamed with a pilot into a permanent unit. This duet would work together until it functioned almost as one man. The First Air Fleet quickly picked up this methodology and placed one of these specially trained teams in the lead horizontal bombing planes. Each of these teams would head a formation to inundate the target with a rain of bombs dropped simultaneously in the hope that such a heavy concentration would produce results, if only through the laws of probability.[27]

Genda credited the upsurge in accuracy not only to Furukawa's inspired leadership but to the work of one of these special teams. This consisted of two cheerful, eager chief petty officers, Akira Watanabe and Yanosuke Aso, an unusually diligent and persistent pair.[28] In later bombing contests they always carried off first prize. Watanabe, the pilot, strikingly demonstrated Furukawa's dictum that a pilot should be more than a chauffeur. He checked out his plane personally instead of leaving this task to the ground crew. He knew exactly how he wanted his instruments set, and woe betide anyone who touched them; he also studied precisely the "change in balance and stability of the aircraft resulting from consumption of fuel."[29] From such meticulous methods came the delicate adjustment to aerial conditions, almost by the minute, which enabled Watanabe and Aso to achieve early results of 33⅓ percent accuracy.[30] If that seems unimpressive, one must remember that in the very recent past 10 percent had been the best Japan's horizontal bombers could attain.

Fighters also trained hard in this early period. Communications in particular posed a problem. Before 1941 the Japanese Navy had never sent a fighter unit more than 100 miles from its home base or carrier, and the radiotelephone connection worked only for that distance. Now they planned to dispatch Zeros against a target 250 to 300 miles from the carriers, and at this space they had to use Morse code. So throughout the summer the Navy communications people had to train fighter pilots in this skill.[31]

In mid-June 1941 Onishi, Sasaki from the Combined Fleet staff, and Genda visited the Operations Section of the Naval General Staff. There they conferred among others with Miyo, Commander Sadamu Sanagi, and Commander Shigenori Kami.[32] A very bright and practical-minded officer, Kami had general charge of "war-preparation and operational plans."[33] Sanagi, sharp and shrewd, had served in the United States as assistant naval attaché and had traveled in England, France, Germany, and Italy to study aviation.

The delegation made a vigorous pitch for the adoption of the Pearl Harbor project as a part of Japan's overall strategy. In spite of their enthusiasm, Kami informed them only that the First Bureau would examine Yamamoto's proposal. However, Tomioka's section was to continue to study "simultaneous operations against several countries," and the plan on which it worked "did not incorporate the operation against Hawaii because it was considered too adventurous."[34] But the conferees indulged in some tactical discussions about the proposed Pearl Harbor attack. Sasaki and Uchida insisted that battleships should be the prime targets; Genda and Kami were just as forceful that carriers and land-based aircraft must receive top priority. After the meeting Tomioka gave Genda Onishi's report which he had worked out for Yamamoto. Genda took it back to *Akagi* and never showed it to anyone else.[35]

Early in June Genda recommended to Nagumo that all high-level bombing leaders go to Kagoshima Naval Airfield to train as Watanabe and Aso had done. Accordingly the sixteen horizontal-bombing leaders of the First Air Fleet set out for intensive training under Furukawa's direction. Genda hoped that at Kagoshima they would work up an intense competitive spirit and that intergroup rivalry would improve their marksmanship.[36]

Yamamoto knew even better than Genda that if Japan went to war, esprit de corps would be a strength no less sturdy for being intangible. He also wanted his personnel thoroughly indoctrinated in their jobs and able to work together with the ease of long practice. To this end, in the latter part of July he dispatched Kuroshima to Tokyo in an effort to prevent the kind of impending personnel shuffle that periodically upset the Combined Fleet.[37]

To a certain extent Yamamoto had brought this particular problem on himself. The two-year tour of duty had been instituted in the fall of 1939 at his own urgent request. This meant that about the beginning of August 1941 the Combined Fleet would experience the start of a mass turnover, to end some time in September. Because at least one month would be required to shake down the new personnel and during that month war preparations had to move along apace, the fleet might not be ready before the beginning of hostilities, "tentatively set for the end of October."[38]

In Tokyo Kuroshima presented to Rear Admiral Giichi Nakahara, chief of the Navy Ministry's Personnel Bureau, Yamamoto's request that no more major personnel shifts be made. With all the conviction and fervor with which he always served Yamamoto, Kuroshima stated that widespread changes in the lower ranks would disrupt the intensive training and operational studies under way and would certainly impair efficiency by breaking up well-knit battle crews. But Nakahara pooh-poohed Kuroshima's fears. "You should not expect war to break out in the near future," he said. Surprised and angered, Kuroshima replied with asperity, "We who are responsible for the maritime security of Japan cannot take refuge in your explanation!"[39]

Kuroshima was convinced that Nakahara was a typical desk obstructionist. Whatever Nakahara felt beneath his official exterior, he refused to lose his temper or become involved in fruitless argument. He had to think in terms of long-range efficiency arising from diversified experience and training. The fleet must be flexible enough to absorb combat casualties and proceed with unimpaired effectiveness. He also had to ensure that the commanders did not become so accustomed to one set of officers that they came to use their staffs as crutches. So he would go right ahead with his transfers, knowing that within a few months all concerned would have settled into place again.

Therefore, Nakahara spoke to Kuroshima soothingly. "If the worst comes to the worst, you will have plenty of time to train new crews," he pointed out. But he agreed that he would try not to move the lower ranks—junior officers, petty officers, and enlisted men—any more than absolutely necessary. "Please prepare a list of personnel who should not be transferred," he directed. Though far from satisfied, Kuroshima agreed to do so and hastened back to *Nagato*.

Yamamoto punctuated Kuroshima's report with grunts of disapproval, displeased that the Navy Ministry had not immediately honored his request. But he accepted the decision as philosophically as he could and ordered all units to compile the necessary lists.[40] Nakahara was as good as his word. His Personnel Bureau cooperated in making the minimum changes among the First Air Fleet's aircraft crews and those of the Sixth Fleet's submarines, which it now appeared might also participate in the Pearl Harbor project.[41]

CHAPTER 20

"PLENTY OF

POTENTIAL

DYNAMITE"

When Nomura and Stark met for lunch on July 23, 1941, the ambassador's face wore the worried expression becoming more and more habitual. Stark eyed his friend sympathetically. He liked Nomura, as did many American naval officers. On this occasion Nomura talked for quite a long time about "his country's need for the rice and minerals of Indo-China."[1] He asked Stark to arrange a meeting with the President.[2] Stark was glad to do so because he hoped that no open rupture would develop, but he could not wish away such a possibility or delude himself that Japanese-American relations were not deteriorating. He thought that the Japanese would be contented with their southern laurels for the time being unless the United States cut off their oil supply.[3]

The CNO had consistently opposed sanctions against Japan. He knew that the Far East was packed with "plenty of potential dynamite"[4] and that the United States was in no position to engage in a two-ocean war; besides, he begrudged distractions of any kind from the primary job of saving Britain and defeating Hitler. The Army's G-2, however, took a somewhat opposite position. In a memorandum to Marshall dated July 25, Miles wrote:

> Effective economic sanctions against Japan . . . would not, in the opinion of this Division, force Japan to take any steps in the way of aggressive action which she does not plan to take anyway, when a favorable opportunity arises, nor would they precipitate a declaration of war on us by Japan. . . . On the contrary, by adopting such a policy we will be able to conserve for Britain and for ourselves supplies which . . . are being worse than wasted when we place them in Japanese hands.[5]

Nomura left Stark after lunch on July 23 for a less pleasant engagement with Sumner Welles, who as Hull's second-in-command took over the conversations whenever the secretary was absent. Hull had been in White Sulphur Springs, West Virginia, for a month recuperating from an illness. At parting Welles said that he was sure Hull "would wish to talk again with the Ambassador" upon his return. But he also had stated that he must tell Nomura, "at the request of Secretary Hull, that the latter could not see that there was any basis now offered for the pursuit of the conversations. . . ."[6]

Roosevelt met with Nomura, Stark, and Welles at 1700 on July 24. At this session the President made a proposal which could have assured Japan access to Indochinese rice and minerals. He suggested that if Japan agreed not to occupy Indochina or, if it had already begun to do so, to withdraw, he would do everything possible to neutralize Indochina.[7] He had little hope of acceptance, but at least he made "one more effort to avoid Japanese expansion to South Pacific."[8] Nomura could taste the pill through the sugar coating and advised Tokyo: "I received the impression that some kind of an economic pressure will be enforced in the near future. . . ."[9]

Commander Sutegiro Onoda, liaison officer between the Naval General Staff, Navy Ministry, and the Army General Staff, believed that with the move into Indochina Japan crossed its Great Divide. "After that," he remarked, "there was no turning back. I still had a shred of desperate hope left, but that was only wishful thinking on my part."[10]

The move into Indochina threw a new light on the Pearl Harbor project. "Heretofore the Naval General Staff had planned to use carrier-borne aircraft for the invasion of the southern regions," explained Miyo. "This is one reason why the Naval General Staff was so cool to the Pearl Harbor operation: It demanded carriers, and we thought they were needed in the south. After the occupation of Indochina, however, and the establishment of land-based planes, the question of using carriers in the Southern operation was not so imperative."[11] But it still demanded thorough exploration.

The advance into Indochina also served as a testing ground for the Second Carrier Division, which accompanied the Army convoy. Yamaguchi seized upon the 2,000-mile voyage to practice under operational conditions. Aircraft sprayed off the trim flight decks of *Soryu* and *Hiryu* until the two carriers resembled steel fountains at play. While his planes hovered over and beyond the ponderous convoy, Yamaguchi kept his gun crews alert and his maintenance teams on the jump. The sternness of Yamaguchi's training measures sometimes disconcerted officers newly assigned to his command, but they soon appreciated their worth in terms of efficiency and morale.

Ishiguro, Yamaguchi's communications and intelligence officer, kept particularly busy. He knew very well that the convoy did not travel in secrecy. His radiomen aboard *Soryu* intercepted messages from Hong Kong to London. "The British in Hong Kong had excellent intelligence on our task force," he recalled. "They tracked our course and reported on the type of ship."

The cruise taught Ishiguro several important lessons, the first being the necessity for absolute radio silence at sea. He was confident that the British had not broken Japan's top naval code, but he knew they could trace the ship movements through plotted direction-finder bearings. Not only should future task forces silence their own radios, but other units back in the homeland should also send out false communications for the benefit of whatever foreign ears might be listening. And the Japanese Navy must improve its own technique for intercepting foreign messages.[12]

While *Soryu* and *Hiryu* sailed back to Japan, the First Carrier Division steamed south to meet Yamaguchi's ships between Kyushu and Okinawa. In this area the four flattops carried out combat maneuvers, with the Second Carrier Division sending out dive, horizontal, and torpedo bombers with fighter escort to attack *Akagi* and *Kaga,* and vice versa. One of the main purposes of these exercises was to see if the fighters could fly beyond 200 miles and still maintain Morse communication with their mother ships. They could and did.[13]

Now that Japan had advanced into Indochina, Roosevelt decided upon a concrete expression of American displeasure. At a Cabinet meeting held on July 24, the day of his late-afternoon conference with Nomura, he secured agreement to the prompt freezing of the assets of both Japan and China. Chiang Kai-shek had been requesting the latter for some time. But further than that the President was not yet ready to go.[14]

Stark and Marshall sent messages on July 25 to Kimmel and Short, among others, advising of the forthcoming freeze. They added, "CNO and COS do not anticipate immediate hostile reaction by Japan through the use of military means but you are furnished this information in order that you may take appropriate precautionary measures against possible eventualities."[15] Thus, Washington warned Hawaii of potential trouble with Japan, yet at the same time discounted the danger of military action. This established a pattern which Washington was to follow almost to the eve of the Pearl Harbor attack.

That evening at 2000 the summer White House at Hyde Park, New York, released a press statement: The President was issuing an executive order, effective the next day, freezing Japanese assets. With the announcement of Roosevelt's action, Nomura began "to have misgivings about the future." He believed that "once the economic freeze was on, the road to a full diplomatic break was not long." He thought, too, that Japan would now move into Malaya and the Netherlands East Indies. This would result in "very strained relations, perhaps even a diplomatic break, but not war at once," since "it would take some time on the part of the U.S. Congress to declare war."[16]

The President's action shook the imperial ship of state from stem to stern. "Perhaps the phase of our order which struck deepest into the sensibilities of the Japanese was that at last the United States has shown this country that it is no longer bluffing!" reported Commercial Attaché Frank S. Williams in an excellent summary. ". . . I believe that a large percentage of the thinking Japanese people realize that it would be national suicide for their country to become engaged in an allout [sic] war with the United States and Great Britain."[17]

While the official *Japan Times and Advertiser* at first remained editorially calm, its reprints from the Japanese-language press gave a good sampling of the rather panicky outburst of reaction. *Miyako* characterized the freeze as "a declaration of economic war. . . ." *Kokumin*, spokesman for the Army, went up in smoke: "We must have an all-embracing measure to tackle successfully any development that may ensue. And there is only one thing to do to realize this."[18]

No one worried about the explosive situation more than Grew. So when, on July 27, he received a telegram from Welles transmitting Roosevelt's proposal for neutralizing Indochina, he grabbed the chance eagerly. Although this was a Sunday, he requested an immediate interview with Toyoda, who met with him at 1130. To Grew's astonishment, Toyoda said that he had not yet received such a proposal from his embassy in Washington. Nomura's diary, however, reveals clearly that in fact he advised Tokyo of Roosevelt's suggestion by a message dispatched at 2000 on July 24, following up with the details on the twenty-ninth; actually, on the twenty-fourth Japan had already made its move.

That evening of the twenty-seventh, after his meeting with Toyoda, when the first flush of enthusiasm had paled, Grew became pessimistic about Japan's accepting the proffered solution. He comforted himself with this reflection: "Whether Japan accepts or not, the President's step places the United States in an unassailable position from the point of view of history. . . . If the Japanese fail to avail themselves of it, their own position in history will not be enviable."[19]

But Japan was not in the least concerned with the opinion of posterity, as witness the formation of Japanese naval planes winging over Chungking on July 30. Suddenly one of the pilots headed for the American Embassy area and aimed a bomb at the United States gunboat *Tutuila* anchored nearby. "By the grace of heaven the bomb missed the *Tutuila* by about eight yards," Grew recorded, "although the ship was damaged and another bomb again came dangerously near our Embassy. Fatalities were escaped only by a miracle." American witnesses unanimously agreed that the attack was deliberate.

The foreign minister apologized,[20] and responsible-minded officers in the Japanese Navy held their breaths. This was exactly the type of incident which they feared might plunge Japan prematurely into war with the United States.[21] And it could scarcely have come at a more awkward time—just when Roosevelt had offered to neutralize Indochina and when he still hesitated to clamp down on shipment of oil to Japan.

In Washington Welles summoned Nomura to a meeting at 1145 on July 30 at Roosevelt's order and handed him a stiff note. Nomura made a gallant effort to brush off the event as a mere annoyance. However, he promised to report the note to his government.[22] He did so that very day, dropping his impassive mask. Indeed, one gets the impression that seldom in six decades of an unusually full life had Kichisaburo Nomura been so agitated.

> Today I knew from the hard looks on their faces that they meant business and I could see that if we do not answer to suit them they are going to take some drastic steps. . . . Think of it! Popular demand for the freezing of Japanese

funds was subsiding and now this had to happen. I must tell you it certainly occurred at a most inopportune moment. . . .

Things being as they are, need I point out to you gentlemen that in my opinion it is necessary to take without one moment's hesitation some appeasement measures. . . . [23]

Much to Nomura's relief, however, the United States accepted Japan's prompt apology, and officially that ended the matter.

But to predict the next American step required no Nostradamus. The area in which Japan was most vulnerable to American sanctions was oil. The President had consistently resisted the pressure to stop the flow, lest total cutoff trigger a Japanese invasion of the Netherlands East Indies, thus extending the European war to Asia and making the defeat of Hitler that more difficult. Now, on August 1, after long, serious discussions, Roosevelt slammed an embargo on high-octane gasoline as well as crude oil. [24]

This put Japan in a tight spot, for it could not possibly meet its extensive oil needs by producing synthetics, exploiting oil in northern Sakhalin, or purchasing it from Iran or Peru. Japan estimated that its Navy would be disabled in two years, and important industries paralyzed in less than half that time. [25] Tomioka calculated that the stock on hand in July could fill only 75 percent of the requirements for two years of combat. In addition, the fleet had always estimated that it would need 500,000 tons in reserve for the Great All-Out Battle. Against these grim figures, peacetime consumption of the Japanese Navy ran to 300,000 tons every month. What is more, these estimates did not include any margin for loss through tanker sinkings or storage fires. [26]

The United States had no desire to strangle Japan. Thinking Americans realized that the many fine qualities of the Japanese people, flowing in productive channels, could be a strength and a blessing to all Asia. On the other hand, the United States had no intention of subsidizing Japanese expansion in Asia while at the same time opposing German expansion in Europe.

Japan had invited American sanctions by its move south. And it was typical of the Japanese in the context of the day that they did not consider pulling in their horns or seeking to obtain oil by peaceful means. The way to a potential understanding with the United States lay open through Roosevelt's offer to work for the neutralization of French Indochina and, shortly thereafter, of Thailand. Alas, Japan did not accept. Why?

The answer is most difficult, yet one may venture a few suggestions. Japan's entire national policy—internal economy, the China affair, the Greater East Asia Co-Prosperity Sphere, the southern strategy—was so indissolubly linked that the Japanese feared giving way on any one point would be to break the chain beyond repair. Take that touchstone of Japanese policy, the "China Incident," which was entering its fifth year in July 1941. In his admirable report Williams summarized the problem:

Army authorities, especially the Young Officer Group, long ago reached the definite decision that their future, as the dominating force of this country, depends entirely upon their ability to conquer China or at least bring the China Affair to a successful conclusion. And failing this it would be better for the Army to go down fighting a major power. . . . [27]

Thus, in a subtly Oriental way, China had avenged itself on its tormentor. It stood like a Great Wall between Japan and the democracies, between Japan and Japan's own peaceful, prosperous "manifest destiny."

Yet another thorny issue was Japan's Axis alliance. The Japanese insisted that the Axis formed the foundation stone of their foreign policy. Therefore, in dealing with Tokyo, the United States had to consider any problem in the light of the Tripartite Pact, which imposed an insuperable handicap. The American government desired nothing more than to be able to devote undistracted attention to aiding Britain and the Soviet Union in demolishing Hitler and all his works. But Hitler was Japan's ally.

Above all, Japan had lashed itself to the chariot wheels of its own expansionist policy. It was determined to secure territory and treasure in the south, if possible without a major new conflict, but with one if necessary. Tokyo wanted nothing less from the United States than full acceptance of its program for a Greater East Asia.

No one can say with certainty that had the United States not frozen Japanese assets and embargoed oil, Japan would have accepted the status quo. The evidence of history suggests that it would not. Its government-controlled press had fostered the idea of southern expansion so loudly and so long that one cannot wonder that the Japanese man in the street came to believe it was not merely feasible but Japan's right. The subject dominated the liaison conferences of 1941, and on July 2 Japan's statesmen made the momentous decision to advance in the south even though they fully realized that they risked war with the United States and Britain.

Could the United States have registered a formal diplomatic protest and let it go at that? Protest after protest had already gone forth to the Axis capitals unavailingly. Could Washington have imposed light sanctions? Roosevelt had done so in 1940 without the slightest effect on Japan's policy of expansion. By the summer of 1941 such action had no real meaning.

At the opposite end of the scale, could the United States have joined with Britain, China, Russia, and the Netherlands against Japan? Such an idea was not only abhorrent to American sensibilities but impracticable. The United States was not militarily ready to challenge Japan. As Stark and his advisers well knew, Kimmel's Pacific Fleet was substantially inferior to Yamamoto's Combined Fleet.

Furthermore, both the Army and the Navy needed every hour diplomacy could wring out of the situation. For the Philippines, long considered indefensible, suddenly seemed to hold the key to a southern defense. On July 26 the President issued the military order which would bring the Philippines' armed forces into the service of the United States. Therefore, the War Department established a new command in the islands—U.S. Armed Forces Far East (USAFFE)—and recalled former Chief of Staff Douglas MacArthur to active duty in the rank of major general to take command. He was already on the spot, having been serving as military adviser to the commonwealth government.[28] Until MacArthur had whipped his command into shape, the War and Navy departments wanted more time.

So, when the alternatives are examined, it is difficult to see what other course Roosevelt could have taken at this point. Economic sanctions were strong medicine, but they are legal, recognized moves on the international chessboard. The embargo was not a malicious attempt to bait Japan into war, but designed to make it stop, look, and listen.

The trouble was that the Japanese were not accustomed to thinking and acting in terms of pragmatic needs. They considered themselves a chosen race, destined by heaven as rulers and leaders. Exceedingly proud and sensitive, they reacted strongly to any real or imagined slight. Roosevelt's oil embargo delivered a stinging slap to the national psyche. With this action, the United States reached virtually the outer limits of alternatives. Nothing remained but a break in diplomatic relations, and following that, what weapon was left but an actual declaration of war?—a progression of events Nomura had pointed out specifically to Tokyo. Little wonder, from the Japanese point of view, that they began to think more and more that the United States meant to follow up the embargo with these two final moves if Japan did not knuckle under. Being human, the Japanese were genuinely fearful; being Japanese, they responded to the challenge not with surrender but with further belligerence.

Among other things, the embargoes caused the Naval General Staff to take another close look at the Pearl Harbor project. "After the embargo was enforced, the oil stocks became less and less. Therefore, some decision had to be made concerning the Pearl Harbor operation," recalled Tomioka. "If we had waited until 1942, we would have had little faith in the success of the operation."[29] But the possibility of full-scale victory over the United States did not enter these calculations.[30]

The Japanese did not think through the problem of war with the United States from one logical point to the next. If Washington miscalculated Japanese reaction, Tokyo reciprocated. On the one hand, the Japanese dreamed of a compromise peace with their great Pacific rival; on the other, Yamamoto was planning an operation guaranteed to rouse the United States to such cataclysmic fury that nothing short of unconditional surrender would satisfy the national temper.

CHAPTER 21

"A CUNNING

DRAGON

SEEMINGLY

ASLEEP"

Stark's words danced before Kimmel's eyes as he read the CNO's letter of July 25, 1941: "You may be called upon to send a carrier load of planes to one of the Asiatic Russian ports. I don't know that you will, but the President has told me to be prepared for it, and I want you to have the thought."[1]

This thought Kimmel could do without. After discussing the problem with his staff, he sent a brisk answer to Stark on July 30: "Whether or not planes are to be supplied to the Russians may be outside my province, but I do remain keenly aware of our own deficiencies in aircraft. It is quite an undertaking for the United States to supply planes to any quarter of the globe in which fighting against Axis Powers may occur."

The admiral's most vociferous objections arose from his conviction that any such move would anger the Japanese beyond all restraint. "I entertain no doubt that such an operation, if discovered (as is highly probable), will be tantamount to initiation of a Japanese-American War," he declared uncompromisingly. "If we are going to take the initiative in commencing such a war, I can think of more effective ways for gaining initial advantage. . . .

"In short," Kimmel continued, "it is my earnest conviction that use of a carrier to deliver aircraft to Asiatic Russian ports in the present period of strained relations is to invite war. If we have decided upon war, it would be far better to take direct offensive action." Kimmel knew that Stark had been straining every nerve to avoid war with Japan in the U.S. Navy's current state of unpreparedness, so he bore down hard on Stark's fears rather than on the danger to the Fleet. "If for reasons of political expediency, it has been determined to force Japan to fire the first shot," he went on, "let us choose a method that will be more advantageous to ourselves. Certainly an operation such as that proposed is far less likely to bluff Japan into acquiescence or inactivity than it is to disturb her to the point of hostile use of bombs, torpedoes and guns."[2]

Of course, Kimmel was indulging in irony, a hazardous thing to do on paper, as Yamamoto was later to discover. Kimmel no more thought that the United States was prepared to launch a war against Japan than Yamamoto believed he could dictate peace in the White House.*

Although the German-Soviet war had changed the entire political complexion in Asia as well as Europe, the U.S. Navy had not amended its instructions to Kimmel. So, on July 26, he had posed some pertinent queries to Stark concerning the "importance of keeping the Commander-in-Chief advised of Department policies and decisions and the changes in policies and decisions to meet changes in the international situation." He reminded Stark that the Pacific Fleet had not yet received

> official information on the U.S. attitude toward Russian participation in the war, particularly as to the degree of cooperation, if any, in the Pacific, between the U.S. and Russia if and when we become active participants. Present plans do not include Russia and do not provide for coordinated action, joint use of bases, joint communication systems and the like. The new situation opens up possibilities for us which should be fully explored and full advantage taken of any opportunities for mutual support.

Kimmel then asked whether England would declare war on Japan should that country attack the Maritime Provinces. If so, would "we actively assist, as tentatively provided in case of attack on N.E.I. [Netherlands East Indies] or Singapore?" and were "plans being prepared for joint action, mutual support, etc?" On the other hand, if England did not declare war over a Japanese invasion of Soviet territory, what would be its attitude and that of the United States? And if England declared war on Japan, but the United States did not, what would be the American position "in regard to Japanese shipping, patrol of Pacific waters, commerce raiders, etc?" Kimmel pointed out:

> . . . the Russian situation appears to offer an opportunity for strengthening of our Far Eastern defenses, particularly Guam and the Philippines. Certainly, no matter how the fighting goes, Japan's attention will be partially diverted from the China and Southern adventures by either (1) diversion of forces for attack on Russia or (2) necessity for providing for Russian attack on her. It is conceivable that the greater the German success on the Eastern front, the more Russia will be pushed toward Asia, with consequent increased danger to Japan's "New Order" for that area. . . .

He then went into lengthy technical priorities to meet such contingencies.[3]

The question of what Japan would do vis-a-vis the Soviets was so inextricably snarled with its activities in the south that no one could disentangle

*See Chapter 2.

a single clear thread. But Stark did his best. "Certainly there can be no joy in our camp over the occupation of Indo-China," he informed Kimmel on July 31. "I think it is fairly safe to say opinion here in general holds that Japan will not go into the N.E.I."[4] On the contrary, "we have felt that the Maritime Provinces [of the USSR] are now definitely Japanese objectives. Turner thinks Japan will go up there in August. He may be right. He usually is." In this case he was dead wrong, but understandably so.

Stark did not necessarily concur with his chief of War Plans: "My thought has been that while Japan would ultimately go to Siberia, she would delay going until she had the Indo-China Thailand situation more or less to her liking and until there is some clarification of the Russian-German clash. Also she may concentrate on the China 'incident.' "[5]

Nor could Stark pry a concrete policy out of Roosevelt. "To some of my very pointed questions . . . I get a smile or a 'Betty, please don't ask me that,' " Stark wrote to Captain Charles M. "Savvy" Cooke, Jr., aboard *Pennsylvania*, with a copy to Kimmel. "Policy seems to be something never fixed, always fluid and changing." And Stark burst out with uncharacteristic bitterness: "God knows I would surrender this job quickly if somebody else wants to take it up and I have offered to, more than once. . . ."[6]

Not only American tempers showed signs of fraying at the edges. Since Hitler's attack on Russia the relationship between Germany and Japan had taken on a tinge of acrimony. The alliance had always been a somewhat unnatural one in view of Hitler's rabid racism, and on July 26 the United States received an intriguing hint that the honeymoon might be on the wane. The prime minister of Thailand advised the American minister that the German military attaché had warned him against "going too far" with Japan because "you cannot trust Japan." The attaché added ominously that Germany would "settle with Japan after she has won the war in Europe."[7]

On July 31 the Foreign Ministry sent Oshima a lengthy and significant message evidently intended to pour oil on troubled waters. An information copy went to Nomura. This dispatch contained this significant passage:

> Commercial and economic relations between Japan and third countries, led by England and the United States, are gradually becoming so horribly strained that we cannot endure it much longer. Consequently, our Empire, to save its very life, must take measures to secure the raw materials of the South Seas. Our Empire must immediately take steps to break asunder this ever-strengthening chain of encirclement which is being woven under the guidance and with the participation of England and the United States, acting like a cunning dragon seemingly asleep. This is why we decided to obtain military bases in French Indo-China and to have our troops occupy that territory. . . .[8]

Here was a clear-cut assurance (picked up by Magic) that Japan intended to use French Indochina as a launching pad for further conquest, despite all official reassurances to the contrary.

"Needless to say," Toyoda's office went on in bland self-revelation, "the Russo-German war has given us an excellent opportunity to settle the northern question, and it is a fact that we are proceeding with our preparations to take advantage of this occasion. Not only will we have to prepare, however, but we must choose well our chance."[9] Thus, the Japanese attempted to placate their partners with promises of assistance against the Soviet Union in some vague by-and-by.

"I know the Germans are somewhat dissatisfied over our negotiations with the United States," this revealing message admitted, "but we wished at any cost to prevent the United States from getting into the war, and we wished to settle the Chinese incident. . . . Let him who will gainsay the fact that as a result we have indelibly impressed upon the United States the profoundness of the determination of the Empire of Japan and restrained her from plunging into the conflict against Germany."[10] One would give much for a candid camera snap of Hull's face when he read that paragraph in translation!

The message ended with a rather fulsome assurance that "all measures which our Empire shall take will be based upon a determination to bring about the success of the objectives of the Tripartite Pact. . . ."[11] Dispatches such as this, frankly expressing in a code long overdue for revision sentiments which should have remained locked in a courier's briefcase, gave the United States a clear understanding of Japan's true intentions.

So one cannot blame Roosevelt's Cabinet secretaries who had access to Magic for taking an increasingly dim view of Japan's international dealings as revealed in Tokyo's own words. The message to Berlin of July 31 became available on August 4 and probably was one of a batch which Stimson took to Hull on the eighth, when the two secretaries had their first conference since Hull's return to duty. Stimson states that on that occasion he brought along "the last magics . . . which gave a very recent example of Japan's duplicity." Discovering that the secretary of state had not yet read these dispatches, Stimson showed them to him. Small wonder that Stimson recorded: "He has made up his mind that we have reached the end of any possible appeasement with Japan and that there is nothing further that can be done with that country except by a firm policy and, he expected, force itself."[12] The Japanese themselves have a cogent proverb: "Even a rabbit will bite if it is fooled three times."

Nomura anticipated trouble and called for reinforcements. On August 4 he reported to Tokyo the strength of American popular support of the government's firm policy. Then he suggested:

As I will have no excuse to offer if I should commit mistakes at this time, and besides, as there is a limit to my humble ability, I wish that you would be good enough to arrange to send some veteran diplomat who is well informed on the state of things at home and abroad (say, Ambassador Kurusu) by the first available ship in order to cooperate with me for the present . . . [Nomura's italics].[13]

Quite a clever move on Nomura's part! By associating with himself Saburo Kurusu or someone similarly high in the government's confidence, Nomura would ensure that at least a part of the blame and hard work fell where it belonged. As ambassador to Germany Kurusu had signed the Tripartite Pact. He had married an American and spoke exact, idiomatic English, so he could not possibly misinterpret what any American said to him. Seemingly with a foot in both camps, he could lean whichever way the wind blew.

In the meantime, Konoye had a brain wave. Why not revive the idea of a personal meeting with Roosevelt, even as Hitler had met with Chamberlain? A complete aristocrat, Konoye liked the idea of settling national affairs on a gentleman-to-gentleman basis. He outlined the plan to Tojo and Oikawa on August 4. The navy minister approved, but Tojo demurred because he thought that such a meeting would displease the Germans. However, after thinking it over, he wrote Konoye that the Army would agree, provided Konoye intended to support Japan's basic principles and go to war with the United States if Roosevelt did not yield. "You shall not resign your post as a result of the meeting on the grounds that it was a failure," he concluded; "rather, you shall be prepared to assume leadership in the war against America."[14] Such phraseology reveals very clearly just who called the shots in Japan in the summer of 1941.

The next day Tokyo forwarded to Nomura a new set of proposals, so totally unacceptable that it is no wonder Hull met Nomura with a perceptible frost when the ambassador brought them to him on August 6. He remarked that "so long as Japan did not stop her conquest by force, there was no room for reaching an understanding" and that "so long as the Japanese Government termed the United States [sic] actions an 'encircling' policy, there was nothing to be expected from Japan."[15]

On August 7 the Foreign Ministry instructed Nomura about the proposed Konoye-Roosevelt meeting.[16] This message evidently crossed one of Nomura's excellent evaluations of the American attitude toward Japan, which he had written the same day. In it he warned his superiors: "There is no doubt whatsoever that the United States is prepared to take drastic action depending on the way Japan moves." That included northward because Washington had "suddenly established very close relations with the Soviet Union."[17]

As it happened, on the same day Roosevelt and a large party of advisers, including Marshall, Stark, Arnold, and Welles, arrived in Argentia, Newfoundland, to await Winston Churchill. The prime minister was crossing from England on *Prince of Wales* for a summit conference of quite a different nature from that which Konoye suggested.

Japan loomed large in the consciousness of both Roosevelt and Churchill. Welles and Permanent Undersecretary of State for Foreign Affairs Sir Alexander Cadogan discussed a "Draft of Parallel Communications to the Japanese Government" which the British had prepared. In seeking this joint declaration, nothing was further from Churchill's intentions than to provoke Japan into war.

On the contrary, he believed that such a declaration "participated in by the United States, Great Britain, the Dominions, the Netherlands and possibly the Soviet Union would definitely restrain Japan."[18]

No one ever accused Churchill of lacking imagination, yet it never appeared to dawn on him that Japan might deliberately choose war with the United States. Roosevelt, too, "felt very strongly that every effort should be made to prevent the outbreak of war with Japan." He discussed the Japanese proposals of August 6 with Churchill, who found them "particularly unacceptable."[19]

Nomura was not one of Konoye's more ardent fans. He thought the premier "weak and inexperienced, and he had made many mistakes, . . . he was grass-green in diplomacy, and . . . he was not a first-rate statesman." Still, he credited him with being "in dead earnest" about meeting Roosevelt. Nomura believed that Konoye had become "frightened of the entire situation and wanted to do something—anything to settle the problem and prevent war." Nomura set little store by the idea.[20] He clearly understood that in this matter, as in *l'affaire* Matsuoka, the issues far transcended personalities.

Scanning the Japanese proposal in the Magic translation, Stimson regarded it as "another example of Japanese duplicity." He recorded:

> They are trying now to get up a conference between . . . Konoye and President Roosevelt on a most engaging program of peace while at the same time they are carrying on negotiations with their Ambassadors throughout the world showing that on its face this is a pure blind and that they have already made up their minds to a policy of going south through Indo-China and Thailand.[21]

In the second observation Stimson was quite correct. Back in Tokyo, Uchida scribbled briefly in his journal under August 8: "Since July war conditions between Russia and Germany not so progressive. Russian resistance good. So Japan could not begin operations in Siberia against Russia in 1941." The next day the Army Division of Imperial Headquarters decided to drop the idea of operating northward in 1941 and to concentrate on the south. It agreed to keep sixteen divisions in Korea and Manchuria, to continue the China operations, and to step up preparations to fight the United States and Great Britain, with a target date as of the end of November.[22]

On August 10 a man who agreed completely with these belligerent sentiments joined the Combined Fleet headquarters as Yamamoto's fourth—and final—chief of staff. Rear Admiral Matome Ugaki was fifty-one years of age and, according to Tomioka, who knew him well, "one of Japan's best officers and a recognized authority on Japanese naval strategy."[23] With Ito scheduled for reassignment as Nagano's vice chief in the very near future, Yamamoto had requested a new assistant who was not only extremely able—that went without saying—but also thoroughly conversant with the high naval setup in Tokyo. Ugaki filled both specifications to the letter.

"Ugaki was handsome, tall for a Japanese, very brainy, slightly bald and an eloquent speaker," said Watanabe. "He was by nature forceful and aggressive with a head full of temperament and ideas. He possessed an acute memory and was a careful, exacting man. . . ."[24] In time Ugaki became one of the Pearl Harbor plan's staunchest advocates.

Hawaii, too, faced problems uniquely its own in these warm August days. Short pulled no punches when he addressed a conference on food production at the University of Hawaii on the twelfth. "As military commander of this department of the army, let me say that an attack upon these islands is not impossible and in certain situations it might not be improbable." Short's words carried weight, for he had worked closely with the local agencies and did not speak as one removed from his civilian surroundings.

"I am not an alarmist," he continued earnestly. "I am a realist, and I am interested in facts. But where all estimates of the present political and military situation point in one direction, probability must be acted upon—and let me assure you that—so far as action in preparedness to defend Hawaii is concerned, the time has come—it is here now."[25]

Yet, for a man so vitally concerned with preparedness, Short permitted an unwise degree of laxity in the installations under his command. For instance, on August 6 Wheeler invited the public to a Galaday, the only restriction being against cameras.[26] Needless to say, "Tadashi Morimura" of the Japanese consulate accepted this gracious invitation. He wandered freely over Wheeler and missed nothing worth seeing. He watched the P-40s in flight, observed that "they were very fast" and the pilots' "flight technique most skillful." He also collected such items as the number of hangars, direction of runways, their length and width, and the fact that three aircraft took off at once. Back in the consulate he wrote up his impressions but he did not tell Kita about this visit until quite some time later.[27]

In Washington on the twelfth Hull, Stimson, and Knox resumed their informal "War Council" meetings. "We are now back again on the same ground—appeasement is over—and Hull, with his analytical mind, is asking searching questions now of the Navy what they'll do next in case any of these issues that he has been handling brings [sic] up an impasse and the necessity of force," Stimson noted in his diary.[28]

Even as they debated, Kimmel was pleading with Stark for personnel stability, just as Yamamoto had done with Nakahara. He particularly asked that captains and executive officers of battleships and cruisers should remain a minimum of two years, and he told Stark that "gunnery in the Fleet is much better than we have any right to expect considering the enormous changes in personnel and the lack of permanency in the officers. We have of course stressed battle procedures above everything else."[29]

Up on Capitol Hill, Congress extended the term of the Selective Service Act to eighteen months by a slight majority. The Senate voted 45 to 30; it squeaked through the House 203 to 202. No wonder Nomura could never quite convince the Foreign Ministry that the Americans "meant business"; talk and bluster were cheap, but when it came to a hard vote to lay before their constituents, Congress felt safe in nearly scuttling the draft.

Nothing in the news gave the congressmen any indications to justify such complacency. And behind the scenes, disquieting hints began to appear that the Japanese tiger was coiling its muscles for another spring. Thus, the CNO's office advised Kimmel and other key admirals on August 14: "Japanese rapidly completing withdrawal from world shipping routes. Scheduled sailings cancelled and majority ships in other than China and Japan sea areas homeward bound."[30]

The Army General Staff was deep in war games rehearsing the Southern Operations on August 14 and 15. The Naval General Staff sent four representatives from Tomioka's section: Uchida; Miyo; Lieutenant Commander Prince Kacho; and Commander Yuji Yamamoto.[31]

Strangely enough, on August 16 G-2 presented a memorandum for Marshall which sized up the Japanese position very well:

> a. Adherence to Tripartite Pact.
>
> b. Establishment of a Greater East Asia sphere of co-prosperity (under Japanese domination and control) regardless of other developments in the world situation.
>
> c. Disposal of the China Incident.
>
> d. Expansion southward for reasons of economic and strategic security.

Nevertheless, the report estimated that in implementing this policy the Japanese would "resort to every means available to keep the United States out of the war." G-2 further observed acutely:

> The great danger in the situation lies in the fact, so often proved, that Japanese military and naval authorities are not under the complete control of their Government. We have seen for the past year an extraordinary example of discipline and selfcontrol [sic] exercised by the German military in conformity to their Government's decree of avoiding any possible armed clash with the United States. We can, unfortunately, expect no such selfdenial [sic] and restraint on the part of the Japanese military. . . . [32]

Nomura chose the same day, August 16, to send Tokyo a long message following another conference with Hull. "Japanese-American relations have today reached a stage in which anything might happen at any moment, and they are likely to grow worse suddenly as Japan makes her next move," he stated, and added this accurate judgment:

> . . . the United States has not yet attained sufficient unity of mind with regard to participation in the European war, and the President himself is hesitant. However, the people are unanimous with regard to taking a strong hand in the Far East. . . .
>
> I hear that they are beginning to think that I have been fooled by my country and that his [Roosevelt's] having conferred with me was an exceptional thing. . . . [33]

When Nomura first came to Washington, Grew had hoped that he would honestly and faithfully report the real voice of the American people.* Nomura did just that, with true insight. He made mistakes, and like so many in the Pearl Harbor story, they originated in the perpetrator's own goodwill. Nomura's errors were principally of the kind to interest historians concerned with the interplay of diplomacy; it is doubtful that they affected the ultimate result. The plain fact is, Nomura's mission was not meant to succeed on any terms short of virtual American capitulation to Japanese demands.

---

*See Chapter 1.

CHAPTER 22

"PROPHETIC

IN ITS

ACCURACY"

When in deep concentration, Kuroshima generally clasped long, lean fingers over his high, bald skull as if to keep any elusive thought from escaping. On this humid day in early August, he captured a very practical idea: The Navy should hold its annual war games in September instead of waiting for late November and early December. Above all, the games should include study of the Pearl Harbor project in a special room with access only to those directly involved.

Yamamoto took little persuading. Even before the midsummer freeze he had begun to worry lest the customary date might be too late to hold the war games.[1] If he waited until then to deal with all the problems which inevitably turned up during these sessions, winter would seize Japan and the Pacific in its icy fist, seriously hampering operations. He realized, too, that this was the logical moment to broach the Pearl Harbor plan once more to the Naval General Staff, now that the presence of land-based aircraft in Indochina somewhat lessened the need for carrier-borne planes in the Southern Operation.

It so happened that at this same time the Naval General Staff had asked the Combined Fleet to send someone to Tokyo because the Navy and Army General Staffs were preparing plans in case of war with the United States and Britain. This offered Yamamoto a double opportunity. "As the relations between the United States and Japan became worse," he said to Kuroshima thoughtfully, "it is all the more necessary to study the Pearl Harbor plan and to urge the Naval General Staff to accept it."[2]

Yamamoto considered the existing Naval General Staff plan inadequate for war against the American, British, Chinese, and Dutch (ABCD) powers, especially against the United States. A study of the southern strategy along with his Pearl Harbor operation at the annual war games would give Nagano and others in his organization a chance to reconsider the latter for inclusion in the overall planning. It would also provide the operational units of the Hawaii air strike force an opportunity to visualize their mission and the problems involved. So once more Yamamoto dispatched Kuroshima to Tokyo to exercise his powers of persuasion on the higher echelon.[3]

Kuroshima arrived at Naval General Staff Headquarters on August 7 to discuss the "Pearl Harbor air strike and operations against the Philippines and Russia"; he brought with him Arima, Yamamoto's torpedo and submarine officer.[4] Kuroshima conferred long and seriously with Tomioka and members of his Operations Section. He explained that since the embargoes Yamamoto was all the more determined to strike a sudden initial blow against the U.S. Pacific Fleet.

He asked that the Naval General Staff agree to hold the annual war games in September, thus giving Yamamoto plenty of time to study any questions which might arise. He also asked Tomioka to arrange for rooms and equipment in the Naval War College, including a special room to house the Pearl Harbor exercise. He further requested that Tomioka's office provide all the information necessary on the U.S. Pacific Fleet, the number of American planes, and anything else required for realistic war games. Tomioka agreed to move up the date for the table maneuvers. Accordingly the Naval General Staff set aside the second week in September for the purpose.

But incorporating Yamamoto's Pearl Harbor plan into Japan's grand strategy was another matter. Once more Tomioka trotted out the outline he had shown Kuroshima in early spring—the time-honored naval Armageddon following submarine attrition of American warships. Kuroshima read it carefully, but he still considered it "old-fashioned and inadequate." Then he seized the opportunity to clarify the position of the Combined Fleet.

"As the situation between the United States and Japan is getting serious, an agreement between the Army and Navy is indispensable," he acknowledged. "But the most important thing under consideration in the Combined Fleet is a plan of operations to defeat the U.S. Fleet at the outset of the war. The Combined Fleet therefore urges the Naval General Staff to study the problem of an attack on Pearl Harbor more seriously."[5]

At this point the two men settled down to examine their respective views. Tomioka ticked off the Naval General Staff's objections with the inexorable logic of a computer.

The success of the operation depended upon surprise, and he did not see how secrecy could be maintained. Such a large force moving so far across the Pacific might conceivably "meet enemy ships or aircraft or ships of neutral countries on the way." Even if the Americans did not thus uncover the plot, most likely they would do so before the actual strike because of "cautious measures like careful aerial reconnaissance." In that case Japan would lose the initiative and suffer heavy casualties. Then, too, fighting might break out elsewhere before X-Day and alert the Americans on Oahu.[6]

Most of the ships would require refueling en route, and the techniques remained to be perfected. The plan might well "collapse in the ocean because of fuel supply," Tomioka stressed. Nor did the Japanese have any guarantee of finding Kimmel's ships in port if they did reach the target area, and they would not have sufficient scouting forces to search for the enemy. In addition, the U.S. Pacific Fleet at sea might find and attack the task force in coordination with land-based aircraft. Still another imponderable was the weather, which might force Nagumo to cancel the air raid. "But even in this case," Tomioka emphasized, "it would be impossible to delay the opening of the war." And with the beginning of hostilities Oahu and the Pacific Fleet would go on an immediate war footing.[7]

Even if everything worked out perfectly up to the moment of attack, Tomioka did not expect "sufficient achievement out of the air strike itself." Once again he listed the factors militating against successful results and set them against the undoubted risks: the shallow water and lack of maneuvering space in Pearl Harbor; probable antitorpedo nets; poor accuracy of horizontal bombing; and ineffective dive bombing. Finally, since land-based air power was both too little and too short-ranged to handle the Southern Operation alone, Japan could not really spare carriers from this area.[8]

"In summary," Tomioka concluded, "this Hawaii Operation is speculative and has little chance for success. In the worse case we may even lose our forces which are like tiger cubs now. . . . And . . . we may not only stumble in the Southern Operation, but also have the advance of our task force detected while the diplomatic relationship is still tense, thus becoming a decisive factor in the negotiations." As for Yamamoto's chief argument—the need to block the U.S. Pacific Fleet from a flank attack on Japan's forces going south—Tomioka pointed out that the Americans might instead hit the Marshalls, an attack which would not be "a disadvantageous move from the long-term point of view since we can easily prepare and intercept the enemy . . . when he comes west."[9] Having thus considered every possible eventuality short of the First Air Fleet's being sunk by a meteor shower, Tomioka rested his case.

Kuroshima then gave the other side of the picture. Tomioka had presented him with no arguments that he was not prepared to refute, though perhaps with more enthusiasm than clear-cut reason. He acknowledged the overriding importance of secrecy but added, "Since there will be appropriate measures for secrecy, we should not worry about it so much." He admitted that the project involved "various unpredictable factors" and therefore was "an adventurous operation," but, he emphasized, "war always involves risk and we cannot wage war and be afraid of taking chances."

Kuroshima insisted that while the invasion of Southeast Asia might go more smoothly with carriers than without, still "it should not be too difficult to carry out the operation with land-based air forces and army air forces. . . ." He stressed that "we should consider the Southern Operation as a part of the entire war against the United States instead of as an independent operation." For this reason, the Combined Fleet must "first strike a damaging blow against the

American Pacific Fleet which controls the Hawaiian area. . . . If we allow the enemy fleet to take the Marshalls and permit them to prepare many flying boats, our recapture of these islands will be difficult and the areas of the southern Pacific will be taken one after the other."

After further arguments on both sides the match ended in a draw, each agreeing to reexamine his own plan in the light of the other's.[10] To the dispassionate eye, Tomioka appears to have had much the better of the discussion. However, Kuroshima held one potent, if unplayed, trump: *Vox Kuroshima, vox* Yamamoto, as Tomioka well knew.

Even so, on August 7, 1941, the Naval General Staff had another opportunity to abort Yamamoto's project. Kuroshima had offered the First Bureau an excellent chance to take the problem directly to Nagano and secure his absolute veto. Yet despite its opposition to Yamamoto's risky undertaking, it did not do so.

Aboard *Nagato*, Yamamoto continued to think seriously about attacking Pearl Harbor. Indeed, on August 10, while his flagship rode at anchor in Saeki Bay, he told his Eta Jima classmate Admiral Zengo Yoshida about his plan. Another of Japan's most distinguished admirals, Yoshida had been Commander in Chief of the Combined Fleet before Yamamoto and had subsequently served as navy minister in three successive Cabinets. He was now a member of the Supreme War Council, a small, select advisory group of admirals who had little, if anything, to do with operations. Yoshida had come to discuss the general political and military situation with his close friend.

"Japan must deal the U.S. Navy a fatal blow at the outset of war," Yamamoto said. "It is the only way she can fight with any reasonable prospect of success. The Pearl Harbor attack is necessary to give Japan a free hand in the Southern Operation." Then, distressed that his apprehensions about a conflict with the United States seemed to be taking concrete shape, he added unhappily, "I cannot help feeling that the authorities in Tokyo think war is unavoidable." As usual, Yamamoto emphasized the absolute secrecy of his plan.

This was the first time Yoshida had heard of the daring design. Being a cautious, practical admiral of the old school, he embodied his immediate reaction in a question: "How will it be possible to send a task force so far from Japan with the present radius of action of the Fleet?"

Yamamoto knew that Yoshida had put his finger on one of the principal difficulties. "The task force will refuel at sea," he answered. "Training in refueling is now going on. Prospects are favorable for its success."[11]

With Yoshida's inclusion in the Pearl Harbor fraternity, the circle of those in the know continued to widen and would do so increasingly.

At this point there again appears one of those curious circumstances which seem to suggest a stream of thought flowing between Washington and Tokyo, Oahu and Japan. At the very time when the Japanese Navy was improving the means and techniques for attacking Kimmel's ships, and Yamamoto was securing permission to bring forward the date of the war games in anticipation of initiating the Pearl Harbor strike, the Hawaiian Air Force was preparing a staff study aimed at preventing just such an operation.

On July 10 Colonel William E. Farthing, the six-foot Texan who command-ed the Fifth Bombardment Group at Hickam Field, had completed a survey for the Eighteenth Bombardment Wing. This document analyzed "the mission of bombardment aviation in the defense of Oahu" and was in some ways as startlingly prophetic as the Martin-Bellinger Report.[12] The ink was scarcely dry on Farthing's signature when, on July 17, the War Department asked the Hawaiian Department to prepare a study of "the air situation in Hawaii."[13] Because Farthing had already delved into the problem and was an experienced airman, Martin turned the request over to him for action.

The colonel went to work with a will. Major Elmer Rose, his A-4 (Supply), and Captain L. C. Coddington, his A-3 (Operations), assisted him.[14] They leaned heavily on Farthing's original study and gathered all the information available to them on Oahu. They labored hard and imaginatively for about a month. At the end of that period they submitted a detailed, penetrating document of almost 10,000 words.

Not until August 20 did the report, headed "Plan for the Employment of Bombardment Aviation in the Defense of Oahu," go forward to Washington. Martin sent it through Short to Arnold's headquarters as an enclosure to a letter under the subject "Study of the Air Situation in Hawaii." In the last paragraph of the covering letter Martin agreed that by strengthening the Hawaiian Air Force "a positive defense of the Hawaiian Islands can be assured without any assistance from the naval forces giving the Navy complete freedom of action."[15]

The Farthing Report, as we shall call it for the sake of brevity, opened:

> The key to this plan is found in the provision for first, a complete and thorough search of the Hawaiian area daily during daylight; secondly, an attack force available on call to hit a known objective located as a result of the search and thirdly, if the objective is a carrier, to hit it the day before it could steam to a position offshore of Oahu where it could launch its planes for an attack.[16]

These would be good tricks if Martin could bring them off.

The report reiterated the Army's mission: "To defend the Naval Base of Oahu." It further pointed out that "to perform its missions, the Fleet must have freedom of action without responsibility for the defense of its base."[17]

Three "Assumptions" carry unusual interest. "The Hawaiian Air Force is primarily concerned with the destruction of hostile carriers in this vicinity before they approach within range of Oahu where they can launch their bombardment aircraft for a raid or an attack on Oahu."[18] Here the report acknowledged a fundamental tenet of air power: Once an aerial force reached striking distance, it could do enough damage to make the effort worthwhile, provided the attackers were willing to pay the price. Therefore, the Hawaiian Air Force hoped to smash the attempt before enemy aircraft could take off.

Farthing and his officers further assumed: "An enemy will not venture an attack against the Hawaiian Islands until control of the sea lanes of communication is obtained. Then as the enemy fleet approaches these islands, raids by surface vessels, submarine and carrier-based aircraft, may be expected."[19] They slipped up here, as others had done before them. They worked on the principles that an attack would not come until after the beginning of war, that the U.S. Pacific Fleet would not be around to dispute the passage, and that the attack would aim primarily at the Islands as such.

When they got down to tactics, however, their touch grew much surer. Their third assumption began: "Our most likely enemy, Orange, can probably employ a maximum of 6 carriers against Oahu."[20] Whang in the bull's-eye! Inasmuch as the entire United States Navy could muster only six flattops, it required a bold leap of the imagination to picture Japan's dispatching a sextet of carriers on a transoceanic Hawaiian raid. In fact, the Farthing-Rose-Coddington creative strategy ran ahead of much Japanese thinking. The First Air Fleet had to fight hard for permission to use the six which actually participated.

Section IV of the report, "Discussion," dealt exhaustively with many facets of Hawaii's bombardment aircraft problems and contained a few items of considerable historical interest. For instance, under "The Search," we find this accurate and uncomfortable statement: "The only manner in which the Hawaiian area can be thoroughly searched for enemy surface craft, particularly carriers . . . is to provide a sufficient number of aircraft to conduct a daily search of the desired area during daylight hours with 100% coverage through 360°."[21] Few would quarrel with the good sense of this assertion, but one can picture Martin thoughtfully shaking his gray head over it. Where were these planes to come from? Even with enough of them, air search would be affected by the human factor, by cloud cover and visibility.

Part 2 of Section IV contained some remarkably successful efforts to second-guess the Japanese: "An enemy should be primarily interested in obtaining the maximum cover of darkness for his carrier approach. . . . *The early morning attack is, therefore, the best plan of action to the enemy* [Farthing's italics]."[22]

The report continued with some clever assessments. "The enemy will be more concerned with delivering a successful attack than he will be with escaping after the attack. He will have carefully considered the cost of the enterprise, will probably make a determined attack with maximum force and will willingly accept his losses if his attack is successful."[23] Neither Yamamoto nor Genda could have expressed the point better.

Farthing emphasized that the enemy "will not have unlimited avenues of approach for his attack" and "must avoid the shipping lanes to negate detection."[24] This factor loomed large in choosing the task force's route to Hawaii; indeed, Japanese Intelligence worked out an elaborate screen to ensure the minimum chance of detection. Farthing and his officers estimated: "It seems that his most probable avenue of approach is the hemisphere from 0° counter-clockwise to 180° around Oahu. . . ."[25] In other words, the Japanese would strike anywhere between north and south from a westerly direction.

"Based on [*sic*] the worst situation that could arise, i.e., the employment of 6 enemy carriers against Oahu simultaneously each approaching on a different course," the report concluded, "an attack force of 36 B-17D's would be required to disable or destroy the carriers."[26] No one on Nagumo's staff had any intention of dispersing the carriers to converge on Oahu from six different directions, which would have disrupted the task force, multiplied almost every problem by six, and flown in the face of Gendaism. The six carriers would approach in a body. Nevertheless, there was something to be said for Farthing's postulating a diversified approach. By keeping their flattops together, the Japanese ran the risk that discovery of one would mean the discovery of all, as occurred at Midway. But Genda and his airmen were willing to take the chance to achieve concentrated air power.

Farthing and his assistants really hit their stride in Section VI, "Recommendations." First, they asked that "the War Department give immediate consideration to the allotment of 180 B-17D type airplanes or other four-engine bombers with equal or better performance and operating range and 36 long-range torpedo-carrying medium bombers to the Hawaiian Air Force. . . ."[27] This was a stunning order for 1941.

To back this up, the report declared:

> The sole purpose of the existence of the military establishment on Oahu, ground and air, is for the defense of Oahu as an outlying naval base. The best defense is an aggressive and well-organized offense. . . . We have had clearly demonstrated to us in Europe the fallacy of depending upon passive measures of defense. . . . We must ferret out the enemy and destroy him before he can take action to destroy us.[28]

Here again the planners thought in terms of a war already declared.

> It has been said, and it is a popular belief, that Hawaii is the strongest outlying naval base in the world and could, therefore, withstand indefinitely attacks and attempted invasions. Plans based on such convictions are inherently weak and tend to create a false sense of security with the consequent unpreparedness for offensive action.

These modern Paul Reveres sounded another alarm: "With the United States living and working under a condition of unlimited National Emergency, Japan making its southward movement and the world in general in a complete state of turmoil we must be prepared for D Day at any time." They ended with an urgent plea:

> It is believed that a force of 180 four-motored aircraft with 36 long-range torpedo airplanes is a small force when compared with the importance of this outpost. This force can be provided at less cost to the Government than the cost of one modern battleship. It is further believed that this force should be made available as soon as possible even at the expense of other units on the Mainland.[29]

The Army Pearl Harbor Board called Farthing's effort "prophetic in its accuracy and uncanny in its analysis of the enemy's intention."[30]* It was both of these, and could it have been fulfilled, it would have taken from the Navy's shoulders a burden it should never have been called upon to assume. A 360-degree search might well have discovered Nagumo's task force and changed history. Unfortunately, however "prophetic," even "uncanny" the Farthing Report, it was not practical. According to Arnold, in August the entire U.S. Army had only 109 B-17s.[31] And these had been heavily committed to mainland defense, Britain, and the Philippines.

The main flaw in the Farthing Report was that which marred all the interservice agreements reached on Oahu and which looked so good on paper. It postulated that war would have begun, giving the Army and Navy time to move into high gear, before the attack would be attempted. Marshall had fallen into this same trap; so had Short in his maneuvers.

One notes the fundamental difference between the American and Japanese planning in connection with the defense and attack, respectively, of the U.S. Pacific Fleet at Pearl Harbor. In theory the American plans could scarcely have been improved. They were clear-cut, farsighted, almost inspired, and revealed a solid understanding of the tactics which the Japanese would conduct on December 7. But these studies lacked substance because they depended for their implementation upon aircraft which the United States did not have in sufficient quantity.

They also lacked the psychological impetus which only a genuine belief can impart. The fact is, however frequently the defenders of Oahu expressed in writing their acceptance of the possibility of a Japanese attack, they considered it improbable. And that included Farthing himself. "I didn't think they could do it. I didn't think they had that ability," he later testified.[32]

In contrast, the Japanese plan appeared fantastic, an inadmissible risk, almost suicidal, justifying every one of the objections which Tomioka had presented so clearly to Kuroshima. Yet the task force carried it out because such men as Yamamoto, Genda, and many others breathed life into it by their dynamic faith. They counted on aircraft and ships either in existence or soon to be, and where they lacked weapons or techniques, they created them. Theirs was a triumph of spirit over matter, yes, even over intellect.

---

*The Army board was confused between the Martin-Bellinger and Farthing reports. Although quoting the latter and citing it for praise, they referred to it as the former. A number of books have perpetuated this same mistake.

CHAPTER 23

"PRESENT

ATTITUDE

AND PLANS"

W hile Farthing and his assistants were working on their clear-sighted report, once more Short put the cart before the horse. In line with an SOP of July 14, the general instituted a six weeks' to two months' training schedule to indoctrinate Hawaiian Air Force enlisted personnel as infantrymen. He explained his reasoning to Marshall when the latter questioned the wisdom of the move later in the autumn, replying on October 14:

> At the time our tentative Standing Operating Procedure was put out the Air Corps had 7,229 men. Full Combat details and all overhead required only 3,885 men for the planes and organizations actually on hand. This left a surplus of 3,344 men with no assigned duties during Maneuvers. One of the main reasons for the assignment was to give these men something to do during the Maneuvers. Another reason was the belief that any serious threat of an enemy ground attack on Oahu could come only after destruction of our Air Forces. The fact that our planes had been destroyed would not mean that all the men had been put out of action. It is probable that several thousand men would still be left and it would not look plausible to have them sit down and do nothing while Infantrymen were detailed to protect them and their air fields. . . .

Short concluded sarcastically: "If it is not desired to train Air Corps men for their own protection and for the final defense of the air fields I would like to be so advised."[1]

This letter vividly recalls Short's maneuvers of May 1941.* If Short indeed believed that the enemy would attempt no invasion until he had broken

---

*See Chapter 14.

Hawaii's air power, the general should have utilized his ground forces to back up the initial line of defense—the Hawaiian Air Force—and not the other way around.

One gets the impression that Short and his ground staff officers believed that airmen hung by their heels, like bats, when not actually flying. It was indiscreet of Short to refer to these men as "surplus," especially because he had been fighting all year for more personnel. With the acute shortage of trained men throughout the Army Air Corps, one can only wonder why Washington did not immediately order Short to release the airmen for reassignment where the War Department could "give these men something to do." Plenty of commanders would have known how to make use of them if Short had not.

Indeed, Hap Arnold made that very point to Martin when he learned of this development. "It would appear," he said in a letter dated September 25,

> that we have overestimated the requirements for the Hawaiian Air Force. Obviously, it would be impossible for the Hawaiian Air Force to carry out the mission above noted in addition to its Air Force combat mission, unless there were a surplus of Air Corps and related troops.
>
> As we are so short of trained officers and personnel in the Air Force, it is most undesirable to employ such personnel for other than Air Corps duties, except under most unusual circumstances.[2]

Short's ill-advised program set tempers soaring in the Hawaiian Air Force. In general, Martin's officers believed that Colonel Phillips had originated the action and sold it to Short. Needless to say, the scheme did nothing to help the morale of the airmen.

In late July Martin had acquired a new chief of staff of his own selection, Lieutenant Colonel James A. "Jimmy" Mollison, an able airman and a warm, outgoing person. Although beset each day by a multitude of problems, he smiled easily and cooperated willingly with one and all. But chunky, friendly Jimmy Mollison could be firm and was a practical man. He had advanced through the ranks, loved the Air Corps, and knew it from the ground up.

On Oahu he soon learned that although interservice relations had moved steadily upward throughout 1941, some ill feeling remained. He resolved to make every possible effort to end once and for all this silly, futile waste of energy. Because Phillips would not become chief of staff until November 1, Mollison worked directly with Colonel Hayes, whom he admired wholeheartedly. He found Martin eager, nay, determined to please, and Short amiably willing to be pleased. So ground–air relations had sailed along on an even keel until the question of infantry training upset things, much to Mollison's displeasure.[3]

He realized how much Martin's airmen needed training in their own field. For instance, when fighter pilots reached Wheeler Field, they had only 200 or 300 hours of flight time. All these pilots had received good, standard aviation training, but none in gunnery. Some of them had never fired a weapon, and "they knew very little about the stuff that is necessary for combat."[4] In contrast, many of Nagumo's airmen had flight logs reaching into thousands of hours, much of it gained in combat in the China skies.

It therefore distressed Mollison to see Martin's airmen devoting precious time to guarding barracks and other ground chores. The situation also held the inescapable corollary that the upper echelon did not understand the duties and responsibilities of Air Corps personnel.

Another kind of heat, literal and figurative, shimmered over Tokyo. In the foreign minister's office on August 18, sweat poured down the intent faces of Toyoda and Grew. They had been talking and taking notes for an entire hour when Toyoda discarded formality and sent for cold drinks and wet towels. Both men then shed their coats and rolled up their shirtsleeves.[5]

Toyoda meandered in detail over the old, thorny path of Japan's pure intentions and America's misunderstandings. The upshot of this verbosity was the desirability of a face-to-face meeting between Konoye and Roosevelt, with Honolulu as a suggested site.[6] The proposal kindled Grew's ready enthusiasm. Urging the State Department to give the suggestion "very prayerful consideration," he declared hopefully, "The good that may flow from a meeting between Prince Konoye and President Roosevelt is incalculable," and he even compared the opportunity to "the recent meeting of President and Prime Minister Churchill at sea. . . ."[7]

In his eagerness to bridge the gap separating the country he served so loyally and the Japanese he liked so much, Grew failed to consider that the Atlantic Charter meeting had taken place between two heads of government whose relations could scarcely be more cordial. No basic differences existed in their global goals, although each remained, most properly, acutely conscious of his own position in relation to his nation. On the other hand, a chasm yawned between the aims of Konoye and Roosevelt. Hence, when on August 17 Nomura met with Hull and Roosevelt, the President very carefully read aloud, then gave Nomura, a statement of warning. In essence, this declared that Japan's deeds had not matched its words. Now "nothing short of the most complete candor" on the part of the United States would be of use. The document concluded:

> . . . if the Japanese Government takes any further steps in pursuance of a policy or program of military domination by force or threat of force in neighboring countries, the Government of the United States will be compelled to take immediately any and all steps which it may deem necessary toward safeguarding the legitimate rights and interests of the United States.

If Nomura thought this stiff, he should have seen the original document framed in Argentia before Hull applied the ice pack of common sense to the Roosevelt-Churchill exuberance.

After assuring Roosevelt of his country's sincerity, Nomura asked about the possibility of the President's meeting with Konoye and of resuming the conversations which had broken off when Japan invaded Indochina. Roosevelt answered the last item first, reading another document which stated that the

United States would consider resuming the conversations if Japan would agree to suspend its expansionist activities. But first, the paper asked the Japanese government "to furnish a clearer statement than has yet been furnished us as to its present attitude and plans. . . ."

Despite the tone of these two documents, Roosevelt was in excellent spirits and cordial to the ambassador. He rather liked the idea of conferring in person with Konoye and even suggested a possible date—about October 15.[8]

Back from Argentia and again at his desk in Navy Headquarters, Stark found his inbox crowded with correspondence. Settling his spectacles firmly on his nose, he began "wading into a mass of mail." In his eagerness to bring Kimmel up to date, on the twenty-second he forwarded a lengthy draft without waiting to put it in final form. "I can readily understand your wish to be kept informed as to the Department's policies and decisions," he assured Kimmel. "This, we are trying to do, and if you do not get as much information as you think you should get, the answer probably is that the particular situation which is uppermost in your mind has just not jelled sufficiently for us to give you anything authoritative." Here was the old story that plagued Kimmel throughout the year. But Stark did relieve one of the admiral's qualms: He would not have to transport aircraft to Russia; they would fly over via Iceland.[9]

When Roosevelt met with Hull and Nomura on August 28, he still had not rejected the proposal that he meet with Konoye,[10] but in this instance he and the premier were operating on separate wavelengths. Konoye was thinking like one of the European dictators. He visualized himself and Roosevelt meeting in a figurative ivory tower and deciding all the important issues, leaving only minor details for Hull and Nomura to thresh out. Granted that Roosevelt had a good opinion of his own gifts, and granted equally that he had a large segment of the American electorate securely behind him, there were limits beyond which he could not go. In meeting with any head of a foreign government, he represented much more than just himself and therefore had to work within a set framework. Konoye never quite grasped this simple fact of American political life.

At first glance the plan might look fine, but it was fraught with dire possibilities. In fact, the President could not come out of it ahead. If he gained every point with Konoye, this would not affect the situation in Tokyo. It would only bring down the Konoye government and might even result in the prince's assassination. If Roosevelt lost, at best he saddled his administration with the image of another Munich, in which case he would lose the confidence of the American people.

Beginning in mid-August, important Army-Navy discussions took place at Imperial General Staff Headquarters. Hitherto, the Army had accepted the Navy's leadership in determining policy concerning the United States, recognizing that a war with that nation would be primarily naval. Furthermore, the Army had not been able to come up with a war plan against the United States in which it had any confidence. On August 15 the Navy section of Imperial

General Headquarters surprised the Army with a plan built around the following decisions:

> 1. To finish war preparations against Britain and the United States by 15 October.
> 2. To requisition an additional 300,000 tons of ships in both August and September.
> 3. To put into effect on 20 September the Operational Agreement between the Army and the Navy.
> 4. To extract three land combat battalions.
> 5. An additional 500,000 tons of ships are scheduled to be requisitioned in the early part of September and thereafter.[11]

Of course, this was not a war plan, but a statement of intent. According to Uchida's notes, in July a "detailed operational plan against the U.S." had been completed.[12] Moreover, at the end of July Uchida thought the Japanese should expect war to break out by October 15.[13] Nevertheless, the Navy's declaration of August 15 is another Pearl Harbor milestone because here for the first time the Japanese Navy admitted outside the family that it would seriously consider fighting the United States. And in submitting this document, the Navy tacitly assumed leadership in any such war.

But Japanese debate on this schedule revealed a division of opinion. Fundamentally the Navy position was this: Let the Navy prepare for war. If it came, the Navy would be ready; if not, it had lost nothing. This outline implied that a decision for war or peace might hang fire until mid-October. Nor did it commit the Navy to fight, no matter how the negotiations ended. Fearing that the Navy might pull out at the last minute, the Army preferred an immediate decision to the effect that Japan should fight if diplomacy failed to satisfy its desires and on that basis should proceed at full throttle on both military and diplomatic tracks.

The Army had a more acute personnel and logistics problem than the Navy. Basically the latter had merely to shuffle men and ships already available; the Army had to mobilize, organize, arm, and transport men to the prospective battlefield. Obviously this cut too deeply into the life of the Japanese man in the street to be carried out without a firm national policy.[14]

For its part, the Naval General Staff moved right along. On August 19 Genda, Sasaki, and Captain Chihaya Takahashi, senior staff officer of the Eleventh Air Fleet, met in the Operations Section "to discuss over-all operations." This phase covered the southern strategy and also the Pearl Harbor attack plan. And the next day Uchida noted: "To complete the Southern Operation, the Army needs five (5) divisions. The Navy must expedite the commencement of the war."[15] Obviously Uchida meant five more divisions; five divisions alone could not carry out the vast Southern Operation.

On the twenty-third he took part in war games held at the Army General Staff. He was the only Navy representative present, and he briefed those attending on naval operations. This audience included Tojo and Major General Akira Muto, chief of the Military Affairs Bureau.[16] Muto and his Navy opposite, Rear Admiral Takuzumi Oka, who headed the Navy Ministry's Bureau of Naval Affairs, were in some respects the *éminences grises* of the armed services. Any other government agencies having business with the Army or Navy had to work through respectively Muto and Oka. Both were *ex officio* members of the highly important liaison conference and had their fingers in every Japanese diplomatic, military, or naval pie worth sampling.[17]

In an attempt to clarify their thinking about war with the United States, Army and Navy Bureau chiefs held a two-day conference on August 27 and 28. Oka spoke out forcefully against an immediate decision to fight. He advised that even if the negotiations with Washington broke down, Japan should carefully weigh the state of affairs in Europe before committing itself. An Army spokesman proposed that they change the wording of their draft on national policy from "determined to wage war" to "with a determination to wage war." Unimpressed by this exercise in hairsplitting, Oka refused, and matters carried over to the next day. Evidently mellowed by a night's sleep, Oka then agreed to accept the phraseology "under a determination not to decline a war."

Hattori tells us: "As to when, if ever, hostilities should be opened, an agreement had already been reached between the Supreme Commands of the Army and Navy that the date should be set for the beginning of November. . . ." But before launching actual combat, the Army had to concentrate heavy air forces in Indochina and gather transports in the South China sea. The Army still insisted that such massive movements could not begin without a decision for war. Obviously they could not proceed full scale while Japan negotiated for a peaceful settlement. Both services agreed that these preliminaries should begin in early October. All that remained was to persuade the government to decide on war.[18] And on the basis of past performances, few, if any, of the top brass could doubt that the Cabinet and Konoye would jump through the hoop when the military cracked the whip.

CHAPTER 24

"A VERY

STRONG

FIGHTING

SPIRIT"

"The boss is back!" The word flashed among *Akagi's* airmen almost before Lieutenant Commander Mitsuo Fuchida had time to hang up his hat at his Kagoshima billet on August 25. Within a few days he received his assignment orders. As senior flight commander he would take charge of the entire training of the First Air Fleet's airmen and command them when they flew as a group.[1]

Just how large a task he had undertaken Fuchida did not yet know. Genda's long arm had reached into the Navy Ministry to pick Fuchida as commander of the entire air strike on Pearl Harbor. The leader of such a force must be both flight commander and staff officer, able to comprehend and work with the young fliers as well as the high brass and to interpret each to the other. He must combine mastery of his craft with inspirational leadership, aggression with endless patience. Genda knew Fuchida well, their friendship dating back to their days as Eta Jima cadets together. Although two other names were on the list for the job, Genda knew that his friend was the man.[2]

Fuchida's entire thirty-nine years seemed to lead inevitably to this climactic assignment.[3] He squalled his way into life in historic Nara Prefecture on December 2, 1902. In later days he would point out smilingly that this was a Year of the Tiger, Japan's mythical symbol of good fortune, strength, and authority. According to Oriental tradition, tiger people are sensitive, courageous, thoughtful, and stubborn. And any Occidental might reflect that by their zodiac he was born under Sagittarius, the centaur archer, spirit fused to the flesh, forever aiming at the stars—clever, fiery, fearless, and outspoken.

On August 26, 1921, he entered the Naval Academy as part of a star-studded class. Fuchida and Genda became friends in their second year, when the flying bug hit them. Fuchida entered Kasumigaura in December

1927, as did Suzuki, who in 1941 would be air officer on Yamaguchi's staff. Genda followed them a year later.

Flight training sealed Fuchida's love of sky and sea into an indissoluble marriage. On November 1, 1933, he entered the Yokosuka Air Corps for specialized training in horizontal bombing, and in October 1935 he returned as an instructor in the technique. Then, on December 1, 1936, twin honors came to him—promotion to lieutenant commander and selection to the Naval Staff College. There once more he found himself Suzuki's classmate, this time one year behind Genda, and Fuchida became a leading spirit in the small group of enthusiastic airmen who espoused the potential supremacy of air power.

He joined *Akagi* in 1939 as flight commander, and while on sea exercises aboard the carrier, he met Yamamoto. The Commander in Chief's dynamic personality and his knowledgeable interest in aviation won Fuchida's ardent, lifelong devotion. The two men talked about the naval air arm, in particular Fuchida's specialty of night bombing.

Next, Fuchida moved to the small flattop *Ryujo* as air officer of the Third Carrier Division. By the time he received orders returning him to *Akagi* he had racked up about 3,000 hours of flight time, some of it under combat conditions in China. He was much more than a skilled, dedicated flier; he had a rich, complex personality. He considered himself, and was, a hardheaded man with no nonsense about him, yet he had a touch of the mystic. He clung to an idea stubbornly but knew when and where to compromise.

At this time Fuchida admired Hitler extravagantly and tried to look like him; he grew a toothbrush mustache and cultivated a piercing stare. But these adjuncts could not conceal pleasant, mischievous brown eyes or his warm grin. He had a kindly disposition, a soft spot for the underdog, and would not willingly have hurt anyone.

"Fuchida had a very strong fighting spirit—his best quality," said Genda. "He was also a gifted leader with the ability to understand any given situation and to react to it quickly. He was not only our best flight leader but a good staff man as well—cooperative, with a clear head. The success of the Pearl Harbor attack depended upon the character and ability of its flight leader, and that is why Fuchida was selected for the job."[4]

The return to Kagoshima with all his companions from his beloved *Akagi* seemed to Fuchida like a homecoming. He thrilled with pride at being a part of the revolutionary First Air Fleet. He regretted that he barely had time for a word of greeting with Genda, but for the next few weeks he kept on the jump. He had to acquaint himself with the carriers and their flight personnel, line up a sizable training program and confer with the various key men in his organization. Of these colleagues, Fuchida already knew Lieutenant Shigeharu Murata well and appreciated his mettle.

That engaging young man sailed through life with adventure at his masthead and laughter trailing in his wake. Nicknamed *Butsu-san* ("Buddha") because of his unfailing good nature, he was the perfect physical type for a pilot—short, wiry, whip-thin, and lizard-quick. By the summer of 1941 he had spilled more blood in China than now flowed in his whole body.

Early in his China period a high-level bomber pilot, Murata switched to torpedoes and was soon considered "the torpedo ace of the Japanese Navy," as Genda said. "He would fly his bomber anywhere at any time," Genda reminisced. "Murata knew no fear; he was calm and cold as a rock in zero weather, was never nervous and under the worst of circumstances always smiling."[5]

Indeed, Murata was the leader of whom every commander dreams—both spark plug and tranquilizer. Tension and discord could not exist in the same unit with his cheerful grin and impish humor. His sense of fun found the whole business of living an enjoyable joke, and the fact that he was something of a hero among the airmen of the Imperial Navy struck him as the most comical thing of all.[6]

Murata preceded Fuchida to *Akagi* by a short period to take over as leader of the torpedomen, reaching his new post from Yokosuka in late August during what appeared to be a gathering of the eagles.[7] Within a few days some of Japan's ace airmen, not only the best in their respective fields but men with the gift of leadership, began to appear in the First Air Fleet.

Among these men Fuchida was "very close" to good-looking Lieutenant Commander Takeshige Egusa, who joined the First Air Fleet the same day that Fuchida returned to *Akagi*—August 25. Originally Egusa did not show too much promise as a Navy officer, but once he grasped the control stick of a plane, the ugly duckling changed into an eagle. "Egusa excelled as an air tactician and seemed to have an intuitive grasp of precisely the right thing to do in flight under almost any set of circumstances," said Genda.[8] At thirty-two, Egusa brought to his assignment eight years of experience in the air and a firsthand knowledge of combat gained in the skies over China.

Fuchida considered Egusa superior in sheer bravery even to Murata, who could be heroic because he simply did not care, whereas Egusa went into danger with his eyes open and his mind cool. "He never knew the meaning of the word 'quit'; he never complained," recalled Fuchida. Egusa loved life and his fellowmen almost to a fault, being so openhearted and generous with others that he himself was chronically broke; Fuchida frequently had to slip him enough yen to tide him over until payday.[9] Genda selected Egusa to be one of the top-ranking instructors during the training period because "he was the number-one dive-bombing pilot in all Japan."[10]

In the first half of 1941 the Japanese dive-bombing performance had dropped slightly below the post-1935 average hit rate of 45 percent because the Navy changed from the Model 96 to the Model 99 bomber. However, as the pilots grew accustomed to the new model, the average edged up again to 50 and even 60 percent.[11] Thus, in comparison with the troublesome horizontal- and torpedo-bombing programs, Egusa had an easy time of it. His primary concern was to secure the most accurate results from the relatively light bombs.

Nevertheless, to hit a moving target, even by dive bombing, was no cinch. Therefore, Egusa and his men concentrated on unremitting practice.

So tightly did the Navy hold the security reins that Fuchida, Murata, and Egusa as yet did not know about the Pearl Harbor plan; nor would they for another month or so. Neither did Lieutenant Commander Shigeru Itaya, in charge of the First and Second Carrier divisions' fighter training at Saeki. He had come to *Akagi* on April 1, shortly before the formation of the First Air Fleet. He had been a pupil of Genda, who selected him as a fighter pilot leader because he considered him one of the best in the Navy.[12] Itaya brought with him nine years of experience in naval aviation.

He was something of a loner who preferred the company of books to that of his colleagues. He was extremely sensitive, and Fuchida weighed every word he spoke to him lest he inadvertently give offense. But Itaya was a keen studnet of world affairs who had been graduated at the top of his class at Eta Jima.[13] His men knew him as a tough, durable "slave for work," with the polish that comes from a fine mind diligently honed against every problem. Well muscled and strong-nerved, Itaya flew with precise timing and a sure, cold confidence. . . .

He and his men concentrated on bomber escort, carrier protection, and shooting at towed targets.[14] In mastering the Zero, they practiced dogfighting in formation, to increase the confidence of the less skilled pilots.[15] And they stressed teamwork. "Two planes fought three planes, then three against six, and then six against nine."[16] Day after day Itaya's fighters shattered the air above Kyushu with such routine techniques as clearing the sky of enemy interceptors, landing on and taking off from a carrier flight deck, zooming in on their targets like hornets. These men had no such problems of logistics and bombing accuracy as faced their other colleagues. The objective of day-to-day training was to fit man and plane together until each fighter pilot knew and understood his craft and could put it through its paces as a jockey manages his racehorse.

The Japanese Navy did not need to devise or test new equipment for the fighter craft. On the contrary, the deadly Zero was the pride and joy of the naval air arm. It could speed at 300 miles per hour and maneuver like a swallow. In China it flew rings around enemy planes. And with its two machine guns and two 20-mm. cannon it knocked Chinese aircraft out of the skies. Although the Zero had displayed its qualities on the mainland for about a year, the Japanese managed to keep its prowess relatively secret.

But Zero production was slow. The First Air Fleet by no means could be certain of having all the Zeros needed to protect the task force, let alone escort the attacking bombers and strafe the airfields on Oahu to pin the American fliers to the ground. Japan would be fortunate to have 150 of these deadly aircraft by October 1941—not enough to supply the First and Eleventh Air Fleets. Thus, both organizations could not receive a full wartime complement of planes and crews. This was another reason why the Naval General Staff opposed the Pearl Harbor venture: It would further split an already divided shortage. In addition, 20-mm. machine guns were even scarcer than the

LOCATION OF FLIGHT TRAINING—FIRST AIR FLEET
(FROM END OF AUGUST TO 15TH NOVEMBER 1941)

AIR BASE	COMDG. OFFICER OF THE AIR BASE	CARRIER AND LAND BASES	FLIGHT STATIONED THERE			
			TYPE OF PLANE	NUMBER OF PLANES	ATTACHED CARRIERS	SENIOR FLIGHT OFFICER
KAGOSHIMA	COMDR. SHOGO MASUDA	AKAGI	HORIZONTAL BOMBER / TORPEDO BOMBER	30 / 24 (54)	AKAGI & KAGA	COMDR. MITSUO FUCHIDA
TOMITAKA	COMDR. NAOHIRO SATA	KAGA	DIVE BOMBER	45	AKAGI & KAGA	LT. TAKEHIKO CHIHAYA
IZUMI	COMDR. TAKAHISA AMAGAI	HIRYU	HORIZONTAL BOMBER / TORPEDO BOMBER	20 / 16 (36)	SORYU & HIRYU	LT. COMDR. TADASHI KUSUMI
KASANOHARA	COMDR. IKUTO KUSUMOTO	SORYU	DIVE BOMBER	36	SORYU & HIRYU	LT. COMDR. TAKASHIGE EGUSA
SAEKI	(COMDG. OFFICER OF SAEKI AIR CORPS)	(SAEKI AIR CORPS)	FIGHTER	72	AKAGI & KAGA SORYU & HIRYU	LT. COMDR. SHIGERU ITAYA
USA	(COMDG. OFFICER OF USA AIR CORPS)	(USA AIR CORPS)	HORIZONTAL BOMBER	54	SHOKAKU & ZUIKAKU	LT. COMDR. SHIGEKAZU SHIMAZAKI
OITA	(COMDG. OFFICER OF OITA AIR CORPS)	(OITA AIR CORPS)	DIVE BOMBER	54	SHOKAKU & ZUIKAKU	LT. COMDR. KAKUICHI TAKAHASHI
OMURA	(COMDG. OFFICER OF OMURA AIR CORPS)	(OMURA AIR CORPS)	FIGHTER	36	SHOKAKU & ZUIKAKU	LT. TADASHI KANEKO

Zeros—so much so that in the early stages of training each plane mounted only one gun instead of the two originally planned.[17]

The direction of communications training fell to Ishiguro of Yamaguchi's staff. Because he had responsibility for communications with all fighter units, not merely those of the Second Carrier Division, Ishiguro worked closely with Itaya's pilots.[18] Yamaguchi drove his men so severely that when the weekend rolled around, the pilots were too tired to do anything but fall asleep. A twelve-hour workday was not unusual.[19]

As we have seen, Yamaguchi's Air Staff Officer Suzuki, Fuchida's classmate, had told Ishiguro that an attack on Pearl Harbor might be under consideration shortly after he had spoken to Yamaguchi in early spring, 1941.* Ishiguro recalled that in mid-August Suzuki advised him of the actual plan.[20] Here is another example of the odd way in which knowledge of Yamamoto's project filtered through the First Air Fleet without regard to channels. None of the flight leaders knew the object of their training, but Ishiguro, with a relatively specialized function, knew it and had known for months. Of course, Ishiguro's duties in communications security gave ample reason to bring him in on the ground floor. Besides, Yamaguchi's staff was a close-knit group, fiercely loyal to him and to one another.

More than key airmen joined the First Air Fleet around this time. The new carrier *Shokaku* had originally been scheduled for completion "by early fall," and her sister ship, *Zuikaku*, by early winter. These flattops were not merely sisters but twins. At 29,800 tons, each displaced about 4,000 tons less than *Akagi* but nosed her out by exactly one meter in length, measuring 820.20 feet. They also had the advantage of *Akagi* by some 3.2 knots in speed. But the new vessels showed their real advantage in the number of aircraft they could carry.

As tension increased in the Pacific, the Naval General Staff decided that regardless of whether or not these carriers would ever be used in a strike at Pearl Harbor, production must be stepped up. Accordingly on August 8 *Shokaku* left the Yokosuka Naval Dockyard and received her complement of aircraft. These units of twelve fighters and eighteen dive and eighteen torpedo bombers had already been formed so that they might train ashore. This ship, with her escort destroyers, became the temporary Fifth Carrier Division effective September 1, 1941. For a short time *Kasuga Maru,* a merchant ship converted to a flattop, carrying twenty-one planes, joined *Shokaku*, but when *Zuikaku* was completed on September 25, 1941, the two sister flattops and their escorts became the permanent Fifth Carrier Division.[21]

That organization received as its commander Rear Admiral Chuichi Hara from the Second China Expeditionary Fleet. With Nagumo and Yamaguchi, Hara completed the trio of carrier division commanders destined to participate

---

*See Chapter 12.

in the Pearl Harbor attack—not one of whom actually qualified as an air admiral. Like Nagumo, Hara was a torpedo expert.[22]

In contrast with the almost self-conscious swagger of his two colleagues, Hara gave the impression of being an easygoing man, albeit a determined one. His friends nicknamed him King Kong because of his wrestler's shoulders, long arms, and strangler's hands, which looked capable of pulling a man's head off his body like a cork from a bottle. Being heavy, he waddled slowly, like a duck; however, the fat stopped at his neck, and his fellow officers considered him a quick and original thinker. But Genda, who classified Japanese admirals as lions or tigers, had this to say about Hara: "He looked tough, but he did not have the tiger's heart."[23]

Hara's memory played tricks on him concerning the time he first heard about the Pearl Harbor plan. However, his senior staff officer stated that Yamamoto himself briefed them both early in September aboard *Nagato*. And Hara's senior staff officer was none other than Ohashi, who had served Yamaguchi in that capacity and who transferred to the Fifth Carrier Division on September 1. Ohashi had worked with Hara in China in 1939, one reason why the admiral selected him. Knowing nothing about naval aviation, King Kong depended upon Ohashi for most of the plans and preparations in that area.[24] Ohashi's recollection gives a reasonable date for Hara's indoctrination. It is hardly likely that Yamamoto would turn the Fifth Carrier Division over to Hara without alerting him to what was in the wind. Of course, Ohashi had known the score for some time.

Hara considered the Fifth Carrier Division something of an afterthought and himself a Johnny-come-lately to the Pearl Harbor plan. He took great pride in his command and thought *Shokaku* and *Zuikaku* the pick of the flattops. He viewed the prospect of war with the United States with considerable apprehension. But he believed that once Yamamoto had determined to start the conflict with an attack on the U.S. Pacific Fleet, the project should be carried through to its logical conclusion.[25]

Hara also received an air staff officer on September 1—Lieutenant Commander Takeshi Mieno, who had graduated from Eta Jima a year behind Genda and Fuchida. After the usual training in gunnery and torpedoes Mieno had spent about a year with submarines and then turned to naval aviation. A capable officer, he had served aboard *Hosho* and *Kaga* and had been a flight commander aboard *Soryu* and *Akagi* before joining Hara's staff. In fact, a whole spate of flying officers either joined the First Air Fleet or exchanged places within it at this time.

So by late summer new pieces of the Pearl Harbor puzzle began to fall into place. With the arrival of Flight Commander Fuchida, training would soon take on a new dimension. Some of Hirohito's "Wild Eagles of khe Sky" who gathered in Kyushu came with a sense of high expectancy. A few thought that something unusual was afoot, although they knew not what. Whatever it might be, they were content to accept the final decision: victory or death.

CHAPTER 25

"RESOLVED

TO GO

TO WAR"

Yamamoto's fine dark eyes rested thoughtfully on Vice Admiral Mitsumi Shimizu, Commander in Chief of the Sixth Fleet (Submarines). Shimizu was a handsome man of calm and dignified presence. His benevolent smile and friendly eyes revealed a spirit well disposed toward his fellowmen. The whole Navy recognized him as an officer of sterling qualities and professional competence.

"Under present conditions I think war is unavoidable," Yamamoto said somberly. Then he delivered his punch line. "If it comes, I believe there would be nothing for me to do but attack Pearl Harbor at the outset, thus tipping the balance of power in our favor."

Shimizu knew well that Yamamoto could come up with ideas of daring originality. Nevertheless, had he not heard this incredible message straight from the horse's mouth, he would not have believed it. "I know the operation is a gamble," Yamamoto went on, as if reading Shimizu's mind, "but I am absolutely convinced that it is the only method that can be used to meet the present situation. It will be the most effective way of holding the U.S. Fleet in check because this is what they will least expect." Then he showed Shimizu precisely where he would fit into the picture. "I would like you to command our submarine forces as commander of the *Senken Butai* [Advance Force]."

Such evidence of Yamamoto's faith and regard stirred Shimizu deeply. *This is a very tall order,* he thought, *especially since I am not a submarine man.* Even as the thought of his inexperience ran through Shimizu's head, his calm self-confidence took over. *All my subordinates from my chief of staff on down are veterans of submarine warfare,* he reflected, *and I have been given this honorable assignment in the face of a number of capable high-ranking submarine officers.* So he answered Yamamoto earnestly, "I will do my very best to fulfill your expectations."[1]

Thus, at this morning conference on July 29 Yamamoto had established the Big Three of the Pearl Harbor plan: himself, Commander in Chief of the Combined Fleet, who hated the idea of the war he must wage; Nagumo, a carrier task force leader who was a shipborne torpedo expert; and Shimizu, a submarine fleet commander who lacked five minutes' personal experience in that specialty.

From this point began the integration of the two forms of attack—air and underwater. The First Air Fleet's officers were apprehensive when they learned that submarines would participate. Undersea warfare added a new, difficult, and controversial dimension to the Pearl Harbor planning. Neither Genda's nor Onishi's drafts had included the use of submarines. The airmen could not imagine a circumstance in which the undersea branch could accomplish anything commensurate with the risk of ruining the entire venture by premature exposure.[2]

In the context of the time the Pacific Fleet would be much more likely to expect and prepare for a submarine strike than an airborne assault. Indeed, Kimmel thought an undersea attack would be the most feasible and probable Japanese action at the outset of war.[3] One ribbon of broken water threading astern of a periscope, and Nagumo's task force could move straight into a double trap, one that would snap shut not only on the First Air Fleet but on the entire Japanese nation.

Still, an air attack on Pearl Harbor, however brilliantly conceived and meticulously prepared, posed so many imponderables that no one could guarantee its success even if no accident alerted the enemy beforehand. "The air raid plan was a new development and risky at the outset," explained Rear Admiral Hisashi Mito, Shimizu's chief of staff. Unlike Shimizu, Mito was virtually a creature of the deep, having been a submariner since World War I. "No one knew whether it would be successful or not; speculation was rife. The submarine operation, however, had been based on planning of longer duration. It was considered sound and in some degree more certain. The hope was that if the air attack should not succeed, the submarines would deal the knockout blow in case the U.S. Fleet came out. In other words, the submarines were double insurance."[4] With the whole plan such a hideous gamble, why quibble over a little additional risk? The object of the raid was maximum damage to the enemy, not minimum risk to the Japanese. So why not shore up every potential weak spot in the offensive?

In short, now that the Pearl Harbor plan was no longer just a gleam in Yamamoto's eye but a definite possibility, the Japanese Navy could not bring itself to admit that the air arm could carry it through unaided. Indeed, on the basis of Yamamoto's post-Pearl Harbor operations, it is quite evident that he was somewhat more conventional than many of his ex-colleagues were prepared to admit.

Operation Hawaii, as Yamamoto's plan came to be called, provided the opportunity to test a secret weapon—the midget submarine. The pygmies weighed about forty-six tons, carried two torpedoes and two crewmen, and measured approximately seventy-eight by six feet. Their actual maximum speed was nineteen knots when submerged, but they could run at full throttle for only about fifty minutes; when held to four knots, they could achieve a radius of approximately 100 miles. The midget submariner had to be an excellent judge of speed and distance as well as a good navigator.[5] And the ancestral gods have mercy on him if he had a tendency toward claustrophobia, for these small craft were a tight squeeze even for two men. At first glance they seemed the epitome of the Japanese preoccupation with smallness and precision—the mechanical counterpart of a bonsai tree.

As of late August and early September, however, the Pearl Harbor package did not yet include midget submarines. The undersea participation which Yamamoto visualized at this time consisted of elements of Shimizu's Sixth Fleet engaged in important, hazardous, but essentially conventional full-scale, long-range submarine activity in line with the old plan of Operation Attrition.

The seas of the world were very much on Roosevelt's mind when he delivered a forceful Labor Day broadcast from Hyde Park on September 1. He asserted that the United States possessed "a strong Navy, a Navy gaining in strength . . ." and promised that the American people would "do everything in our power to crush Hitler and his Nazi forces."[6]

Throughout his speech Roosevelt did not so much as mention the word "Japan," but his silence seemed to bait Tokyo's metropolitan journals into an outburst of vituperation. "If the United States is going to bar Japan's advancement based on the pretence of freedom of the seas, Japan will not hesitate to break through this," shrilled *Nichi Nichi*.[7] And on September 3 the *Japan Times and Advertiser* remarked: "President Roosevelt kept silence over Japan in his last Fireside Speech, but that period of quiet was followed by the freezing order. Japan takes a position of watchful waiting to see what this new silence portends, and its own silence can be understood to mean no lack of preparedness."

All this was not lost on the United States. No doubt about it, Nomura had a rough row to hoe, and for once even the Foreign Ministry admitted to a small embarrassment in connection with the proposed Roosevelt-Konoye conference. "Since the existence of the Premier's message was inadvertently made known to the public, that gang that has been suspecting that unofficial talks were taking place, has really begun to yell and wave the Tripartite Pact banner," Tokyo advised Nomura on September 3. The government wished "to keep the matter a secret until the arrangements had been completed." His superiors asked Nomura "to make all arrangements for the meeting around the middle of September, with all possible speed, and issue a very simple statement to that effect as soon as possible. . . ."[8]

The Foreign Ministry had an excellent reason for hastening the arrangements. Konoye had called a liaison conference for September 3 to consider the "Outline Plan for the Execution of the Empire's National Policy," fruit of the

Imperial General Headquarters discussions. After considerable haggling over phraseology, the upshot of seven hours of discussion was a historic decision which the Cabinet approved on September 4. This consisted of a set of "Minimum Demands" and "Maximum Concessions."[9] After a rolling introduction, the document shot off the mark:

> I. Our Empire, for the purpose of self-defense and self-preservation, will complete preparations for war, with the last ten days of October as a tentative deadline, resolved to go to war with the United States, Great Britain and the Netherlands if necessary.
>
> II. Our Empire will concurrently take all possible diplomatic measures vis-à-vis the United States and Great Britain, and thereby endeavor to attain our objectives. . . .
>
> III. In the event that there is no prospect of our demands being met by the first ten days of October through the diplomatic negotiations mentioned above, we will immediately decide to commence hostilities against the United States, Britain and the Netherlands.
>
> Policies other than those toward the South will be based on established national policy; and we will especially try to prevent the United States and the Soviet Union from forming a united front against Japan.

The "Minimum Requirements" contained these demands: no interference with Japan's settlement of the "China Incident" and the closing of the Burma Road with no more political, economic, or military aid to the Chiang regime. In China Japan kept an ace up its sleeve:

> This does not prejudice the position that our Empire has been taking in relation to the settlement of the China Incident in the Nomura operation. We should particularly insist on stationing our troops under a new agreement between Japan and China. However, we have no objection to affirming that we are in principle prepared to withdraw our troops following the settlement of the Incident, except for those that are dispatched to carry out the purposes of the Incident. . . .

One wonders what Japanese troops were in China except those brought in for that purpose. Further "Minimum Demands" insisted that the United States and Great Britain take no action "that may threaten the defense of our Empire in the Far East" and should not "increase their military forces in the Far East beyond present strength. . . ." Japan would accept no demand "to dissolve the special relations between Japan and French Indochina. . . ." What is more, the two target nations were to "cooperate in the acquisition of goods needed by our Empire."

If these demands were met, Japan promised not to use Indochina as a base for operations against "neighboring areas other than China." Here the Japanese handsomely promised to observe their neutrality pact with the Soviet Union if the Russians did the same. Japan would withdraw its forces from French Indochina "after a just peace has been established in the Far East," and it would "guarantee the neutrality of the Philippine Islands." If the United States entered the European war, "Japan's interpretation of the Tripartite Pact and

her actions therein" would be "made by herself acting independently."
Nevertheless, Japan's leaders asserted, "The above does not alter our obligations under the Tripartite Pact."

These provisions ring an old familiar tune, being a theme and variations on
the Walsh-Drought program and an amplification of the proposals Nomura had
already presented to Hull. It is certainly difficult to believe that Japan's
diplomats and, more important, its military leaders expected any nation in the
full possession of its faculties to buy such a package deal voluntarily. This
document left no viable alternative to war. Yet neither Konoye nor Toyoda
opposed acceptance of this program, although both were trying to arrange a
summit meeting with Roosevelt, ostensibly to work out a peaceful solution to
Japanese-American problems. They may have been sincere in their own
fashion. But the cold fact remains that they sat back and watched while the
Japanese Army and Navy played Russian roulette with the destiny of Japan.

The Army did not even wait for the liaison conference's approval, let alone
that of the Cabinet or Emperor. In a brief note concerning the meeting of
September 3, Uchida observed in his private journal: "Mobilization of the
Army is expected to begin about mid-September." Nor did the Navy waste any
time. On this same date Uchida was busy taking part in tabletop maneuvers
held in the Operations Section of the Naval General Staff to review the
Southern Operation strategy. Uchida gave no details of these maneuvers,[10] but
this does not matter. What is significant is that the Naval General Staff had
already carried the Southern Operation to the war games stage within its own
headquarters.

According to a Gallup poll taken early in September, the American
people's willingness to adopt a hard-nosed attitude toward Japan had appreciably increased since July. At that time 51 percent expressed a willingness to risk
war with Japan; now 70 percent said they would "take steps to keep Japan from
becoming more powerful even if this means risking a war."[11] Of course, the poll
may well have reflected increased American anger because of the Japanese
takeover in Indochina rather than diminished respect for Japan as a possible
enemy.

Confidence in Hawaii's invulnerability and the U.S. Navy's power still
reigned supreme. "A Japanese attack on Hawaii is regarded as the most
unlikely thing in the world, with one chance in a million of being successful.
Besides having more powerful defenses than any other post under the
American flag, it is protected by distance," journalist Clarke Beach assured his
readers on September 6.

"The Japanese Fleet would have no bases from which to operate," he
continued. "It would have so far to come that American patrols would spot it
long before it arrived.

"In any case," Beach concluded, "American naval men would like nothing
better than to see the Japanese fleet outside of Pearl Harbor where they could
take it on."[12]

Perhaps somewhere one might have uncovered one or two "American naval men" spoiling for a fight with Japan because any large organization collects a few bullies and neurotics, but their names certainly would not have been either Stark or Kimmel. The CNO wanted to concentrate on the Atlantic, and Kimmel knew that his Pacific Fleet was in no condition to take on Yamamoto's full power, off Pearl Harbor or anywhere else.

CHAPTER 26

"WAVES

AND WINDS

SO

UNSETTLED"

Few people have ever seen the spectacle of a full admiral and a full general squirming like sheepish schoolboys. Add to them an angry Emperor of Japan, and you have a truly memorable scene. To complete the picture, that "shy squirrel,"[1] Konoye, stood slightly to one side, attempting, as always in a crisis, to look as though he just happened to be passing through.

The background is this: At 1630 on September 5 Konoye submitted to the Emperor a draft of the decision reached at the liaison conference on the third. He wished to discuss it informally with His Majesty before the imperial conference scheduled for the next day.[2] This gave the Emperor precious little time to study and think through such a momentous program before meeting with Japan's leaders.

Even so, Hirohito quickly absorbed the contents of the document and discovered that he did not like them. He pointed out to Konoye that the draft "placed war preparations first and diplomatic negotiations second," thus giving "precedence to war over diplomatic activities." He informed the premier that he wished to question the chiefs of the Army and Navy General Staffs at the forthcoming imperial conference—an unprecedented step. In so doing, Hirohito laid the onus squarely on the Supreme Command rather than on the ministers of war and the navy.

The suggestion upset Konoye, who suggested that the Emperor summon the chiefs for a private audience instead of questioning them at the conference; Hirohito agreed.[3]

Had Konoye been truly a peacemaker, one would expect him to seize upon this opportunity to embarrass Nagano and his opposite, General Gen Sugiyama, and rally around the Emperor whatever forces for moderation remained in his Cabinet. Beneath Konoye's sophisticated veneer lay centuries of Japanese tradition, so that he may have been genuinely horrified at the idea of the Emperor's taking an active role in an imperial conference. Whatever his motivation, Konoye moved quickly to save the military face; underlying his whole position remained the inescapable fact that in that day any prime minister of Japan held his post on sufferance of the armed forces—particularly the Army.

Nagano and Sugiyama hastened to the palace, where they met Konoye, who had been waiting for them. All three then entered the imperial presence at 1800.[4] Hirohito told the two officers that he wished diplomacy to be emphasized, instead of being pushed equally with war preparations. Sugiyama and Nagano immediately assured him that the draft of Japanese policy provided for "the utmost diplomatic endeavors for saving the situation, and that war preparations were considered only for the purpose of meeting any possible failure of such diplomatic efforts."[5]

Hirohito remained unconvinced that a program which established a definite deadline for the start of war preparations truly gave precedence to diplomacy. He turned his unfathomable dark eyes directly upon Sugiyama and proceeded to drill the general with specific questions about "the schedule for operations in the Southern Area, the degree of difficulty in landing operations, losses of ships and vessels, prospect of victory," and so on.[6]

He also asked Sugiyama how long he thought hostilities would last in case Japan and the United States went to war. The general estimated that operations in the South Pacific "could be disposed of in about three months."[7] Thereupon the blood rose in Hirohito's face, and he answered Sugiyama in an unusually loud tone: "As War Minister at the outbreak of the China Incident, you asked me to approve sending Army troops there, saying that the Incident would be settled in a short time. But has it yet been ended after more than four years? Are you trying to tell me the same thing again?"

"In trepidation," Sugiyama "went to great lengths to explain that the extensive hinterland of China prevented the consummation of operations according to the scheduled plan." This understandably exasperated the Emperor still further. Again he "raised his voice and said that if the Chinese hinterland was extensive, the Pacific was boundless." Then he asked the discomfited chief of staff, "With what confidence do you say 'three months?'" Sugiyama was "utterly at a loss' and "hung his head, unable to answer."[8]

Taking pity on his hapless colleague, Nagano stepped in. He told Hirohito that "Japan was like a patient suffering from a serious illness. . . . Should he be let alone without an operation, there was danger of a gradual decline. An operation, while it might be extremely dangerous, would still offer some hope of saving his life . . . the Army General Staff was in favor of putting hope in diplomatic negotiations to the finish, but . . . in case of failure a decisive operation would have to be performed." This morbid simile did not exhilarate Hirohito, who ignored it and went back to the principal point at issue: Were both of them in favor of "giving precedence to diplomacy"? The two chiefs answered in the affirmative.[9]

Konoye agreed completely with both officers. Japan, he said, should "seek a peaceful settlement" through diplomacy "up to the last"; the nation "should resort to arms only when this was absolutely unavoidable."[10]

The evening's experience etched itself sharply in Nagano's consciousness. "I have never seen the Emperor reprimand us in such a manner, his face turning red and raising his voice," he told Fukudome.[11]

That same day in Washington (September 4, local time), Nomura sought out Hull in his apartment at 0900 for further discussion of the proposed top-level conference. They went over the usual ground, but this time Nomura "noticed that the attitude of the other party had considerably stiffened."[12] Hull had never cared for the idea—it smelled to him of "a second Munich"—and the more the State Department thought it over, the less it liked it. Japan's insistence upon rushing into a conference of generalized aims would leave the results open to that nation's interpretation to suit itself. Hull doubted whether Konoye could accept any proposition satisfactory to the United States and, if he did, whether the Japanese military would permit its implementation.

Moreover, the meeting would have a crushing effect upon the Chinese, and the Tripartite Pact presented a formidable obstacle. The United States could not take Japan's right hand without accepting Hitler's left. Furthermore, if Konoye carried back to Tokyo an agreement with the United States, the military might well oust him and put in a premier more to its liking. Much as the State Department distrusted Konoye, he looked like an improvement over any possible successor satisfactory to the Japanese Army.[13]

On Saturday September 6 Tokyo awoke to leaden clouds hanging from a low sky; northerly winds swept over the housetops, trailing behind them ragged patches of rain.[14] That morning Hirohito convened his advisers for an imperial conference. Before this august body stood the inflexible choice: peace or war. One by one Konoye, Nagano, Sugiyama, Toyoda, and General Teiichi Suzuki, president of the Planning Board, presented their views. Their counsel was more noteworthy for its unanimity than for common sense. All paid perfunctory respects to diplomacy, but the consensus was that Japan had better prepare for war, the sooner the better. The real question was not, Shall we fight? but, When shall we fight?[15]

There is something fantastic in the picture of such men, none of them devoid of intellect, planning to go to war with the United States, Great Britain, and the Netherlands almost immediately and probably with the Soviet Union as soon as the snows melted in the spring. In the meantime, as they tacitly acknowledged, the exhausting struggle in China still drained off Japan's manpower and matériel.

At last Baron Yoshimichi Hara could present the questions he had prepared on His Majesty's behalf. As president of the Privy Council, Hara ranked high among Japan's senior statesmen, held moderate views, and shared the Emperor's anxieties on the vital issues of peace and war.

"I am happy to observe the Prime Minister's determination to meet President Roosevelt in person, and try to come to an agreement of views," he opened gracefully. Having stressed "the necessity for breaking the deadlock by strong diplomatic means," he turned to the crux of the matter. "When I scanned the proposal, I was left with the impression that war was stressed and diplomacy was given secondary consideration. However, I understand that war preparations are being made to deal with the situation resulting from diplomatic failure." Then he asked, "Am I right in believing that everything is being done diplomatically at present to save the situation and that war will be resorted to only when diplomatic means fail?"

Everyone knew that Hara spoke for the Emperor, so they could neither avoid nor skirt the issue. Sugiyama made ready to reply, but Oikawa quickly stepped in. He assured Hara that there was no contradiction; in any case a decision to go to war required formal imperial sanction.[16]

To this the chiefs of the Army and Navy General Staffs said not a word.[17] Evidently taking their silence for consent, Hara expressed his relief and concluded his remarks "by repeatedly stressing the need for saving the situation by diplomacy."[18]

In the normal course of events the imperial conference would have adjourned at this point. But obviously the Emperor did not share Hara's view that because Sugiyama and Nagano had not spoken, they necessarily agreed with Oikawa. Such an overnight conversion was too much to hope for.

So the Emperor "spoke up suddenly." Never before had Hirohito addressed an imperial conference personally. His advisers could not have been more astonished had the *Dia Butsu* [Great Buddha] at Kamakura broken his long silence. Hirohito seconded Hara's opinions and "expressed his regret that the Supreme Command had not seen fit to answer."[19]

Without waiting for a reply, he reached into his pocket and pulled out a piece of paper. With all the conferees avidly awaiting his next move, His Majesty read aloud a short poem entitled "The Four Sides of the Sea," written by his grandfather, the great emperor Meiji:

> Methinks all the people of the world are brethren, then
> Why are waves and winds so unsettled nowadays?[20]

His Majesty told his listeners that he had read this poem "over and over again." He explained that he was "striving to introduce into the present the emperor Meiji's ideal of international peace." Hirohito's advisers sat before him in uncomfortable silence. "Everyone present was struck with awe," Konoye recorded, "and there was silence throughout the hall."[21]

At length Nagano broke the taut stillness. In a tone of elaborate apology he stated that he was "filled with trepidation at the prospect of the Emperor's displeasure with the Supreme Command." He explained that he had remained silent after Oikawa spoke because "he had been under the impression that the Navy Minister was representing both the Government and the Supreme Command." But he "assured the Emperor that the chiefs of the Supreme Command most certainly concurred with the Navy Minister's answer" and added that they were also "conscious of the importance of diplomacy, and advocated a resort to arms only when there seemed no other way out."[22]

Sugiyama agreed with Nagano.[23] But it is highly doubtful that these explanations satisfied the Emperor, for the conference adjourned, as Konoye wrote, "in an atmosphere of unprecedented tenseness."[24]

As three-time premier of Japan, Konoye bore a large responsibility for many of his country's recent policies, and as he left the imperial conference, he must have felt much like the sorcerer's apprentice, who set a broom to hauling water, then forgot the spell to turn it off. He could see no way of halting the broom before it drowned him except by meeting with Roosevelt. To help speed up the arrangements, he determined to confer personally with Grew.

Knowing both himself and the ambassador to be under ceaseless surveillance, Konoye arranged that they meet at the home of a mutual friend, one Baron Ito. The prime minister brought with him his confidential secretary, Tomohiko Ushiba, while Eugene H. Dooman, counselor of the embassy, accompanied Grew.[25] Dooman spoke fluent Japanese and loved the country.

Konoye talked with Grew for about three hours.[26] He declared that he "conclusively and wholeheartedly" accepted Hull's Four Principles, offered so many months before, as a basis for rehabilitating relations between the two countries. He recognized his own responsibility for the current unhappy state of affairs and by the same token believed that only he could bring about a remedy. Nevertheless, he expressed confidence that the "divergencies in view" could be reconciled to the "mutual satisfaction" of their two countries, particularly because Japanese naval and military leaders had not only "subscribed to his proposal" but would "be represented at the suggested meeting."[27]

Konoye went on to inform Grew that the ministers of war and the navy had "given their full agreement to his proposals to the United States" and that "from the inception of the informal talks in Washington he had received the strongest concurrence from the responsible chiefs of both the Army and the Navy."[28] Of course, this does not mean that Tojo and Oikawa had agreed to go along with extensive concessions to the United States. One must keep in mind the nature of the Konoye government's proposals as submitted to the State Department many times during 1941.

Konoye named those who would accompany him—the list included at least three officers privy to the Pearl Harbor plot[29]—and promised that as soon as he came to an agreement with Roosevelt, the premier would flash the word to Tokyo and "the Emperor would immediately issue a postscript ordering the suspension forthwith of all hostile operations."[30] Grew and Dooman returned to the embassy convinced that they had been dealing with "a man of unquestioned sincerity." But, as Grew so well explained, that sincerity was "born of dire necessity" and firmly welded to Japanese interests.[31]

Not that Grew was naïve. He knew very well that Konoye was "saddled with the responsibility for some of the worst acts of banditry on the part of Japan which have been recorded in international history." But he also believed, as he testified in a wild mixture of metaphors, that the premier "saw the handwriting on the wall and realized that Japan was on the brink of an abyss and wanted, if possible, to reverse the engine."[32]

One may ask: If Konoye sincerely wanted peace and rapprochement with the United States, why did he not order a cleanup in the Army and get rid of the irresponsible elements? Unfortunately he could not have done so even had he wished. A simple device kept the Japanese government under the Army's thumb: By regulation, the minister of war had to be a general on active duty, and the premier could not choose him. A trio consisting of the inspector general for military training, the current minister of war, and the chief of the General Staff made the selection.

By refusing to name a minister of war, this trio could prevent any premier from forming a Cabinet, and they could bring down any existing government by reassigning the incumbent war minister. These generals also named their own successors, so they formed a self-perpetuating triumvirate. And if any premier grew so bold as to name the minister of war over the heads of the supreme three, they trumped his ace by removing his selectee from the active list. Thus, no one could become prime minister of Japan unless the Army at least tolerated him, and once he accepted the portfolio, he danced to the Army's tune or the Army got rid of him.[33]

By late summer Japan's hopes for a total Hitler victory in Europe had dwindled. The very fact that Japan had not jumped at the chance to attack the Soviet Union proved that it doubted the Germans could conquer the Russians in 1941. In view of this relative pessimism, apparently Konoye now had an excellent opportunity to discard the disastrous Axis tie-up. But it was not that easy. True, some farsighted Japanese officers, particularly in the Navy, deplored the Tripartite Pact; Yamamoto, for one, would have gladly buried it and danced on its grave. Yet with very few exceptions the Army ranged itself solidly behind the Axis and would never stand still for Konoye's reversing field. To do so would mean admitting that its policy had been a mistake, and this would weaken the Army's power and prestige.

Then, too, how could Konoye fulfill his guarantee to carry the Japanese people with him to and from the summit conference? For years the government-controlled press had blown the expansionist trumpet loud and long, beaten the Axis drums in thunderous roll. Three times Konoye had headed the government which spewed forth this propaganda, blueprinted this pattern of conquest. So it is very difficult to understand how he expected to bring about a productive meeting between him and Roosevelt.

In Washington Nomura had not abandoned hope. On September 15 he sent a sensible message to Toyoda, attempting to make his chief understand why the proposed meeting could not take place without preliminary agreements. He stressed that Roosevelt had told him that "if a matter could not be settled by me and Secretary Hull it would not be settled whoever conducted the conversations." He also warned that the United States would refuse to mediate between Japan and China "unless the terms were fair and just." Then he scored this important point:

In view of the national characteristics of the United States and of the President's position, it will be next to impossible to leave the interpretation of the Tripartite Pact up to the "leaders" at the conference, for them to settle from a political viewpoint. In other words, if opinions of both sides do not coincide at the preliminary conferences, then there will be no "leaders' conference."[34]

Grew understood that the opportunity afforded by such a meeting was exceedingly slim, but he was in a mood to clutch at straws. On September 22 he wrote a personal letter to Roosevelt which evidently did not reach him until mid-October. It expressed these sentiments:

The alternative to reaching a settlement now would be the greatly increased probability of war—*Facilis descensus Averno est*—and while we would undoubtedly win in the end, I question whether it is in our own interest to see an impoverished Japan reduced to the position of a third-rate Power. I therefore most earnestly hope that we can come to terms, even if we must take on trust, at least to some degree, the continued good faith and ability of the present Government fully to implement those terms.[35]

Grew knew that he was betting on a dark horse. As he testified in later years, "Nobody in the world can prove that even if Konoye had met the President and even if he had been able to give satisfactory commitments that [*sic*] he would have implemented them after he came back. That was definitely in the control of the military."[36] But the ambassador wold not tear up his pari-mutuel ticket until the results appeared on the board.

Perhaps future generations might rise up and call blessed such peacemakers as Grew and Nomura, but in the here and now the Japanese armed forces shifted their war preparations into high gear.

CHAPTER 27

"A

SERIOUS

STUDY"

Sometime in early September 1941 key staff officers of the First Air Fleet gathered in Kusaka's cabin aboard *Akagi*.[1] When the last man had taken his place, Kusaka said in his customary understated style, "In case of war with the United States, Yamamoto plans to attack the U.S. Fleet in Pearl Harbor. The First Air Fleet's mission is to carry out this operation."[2] Although everyone present gave Kusaka his close attention, the message was not new to some of them. But this marked the first occasion that Nagumo's operational staff had been informed individually and collectively of Yamamoto's adventurous project.

Kusaka briefly reviewed the general nature of the plan and emphasized the necessity for the strictest possible secrecy to ensure surprise. "You will now pool your resources," he continued, "and begin a serious study of all the problems involved—air training, communications, intelligence, navigation, weather conditions, refueling at sea, route to Hawaii and the like. You face a big task, one that will require your very best efforts."

Kusaka named Genda chief of the study group. He also assigned to Genda as his personal responsibility the air training, attack techniques, point of departure, and route to Hawaii. "You will coordinate the work of all the other staff members and report directly to me," Kusaka charged him.

Senior Staff Officer Oishi would assist Genda and maintain his usual relations with Nagumo and Kusaka, while the others devoted their energies to their respective specialties.[3] Ono tackled such communications problems as ship-to-ship signals en route, reception of messages from the homeland, radio silence, and other matters of communications security. Sasabe handled navigation and weather forecasting—distances to be covered, schedule of cruise, sea conditions, task force formation, and the like. Sakagami dealt with the difficult questions of fuel supply and refueling at sea—the fuel capacity of the various ships, amount and rate of consumption, speed of the task force, radius of action, number of tankers needed, and the actual procedure of refueling.[4]

Kusaka also turned his attention to the refueling question, vital to the mission. He did so because he had already gained experience along these lines and because this problem ranked number two on his priority list, second only to secrecy.[5]

From this meeting forward, Yamamoto's scheme left the conceptual stage and emerged as a potential war plan. From this instant, too, Nagumo's officers had a sense of direction, a realization of mission. Kusaka considered this so important that he broke with tradition and confided the secret even to the fleet paymaster and medical officer. The chief of staff believed that the First Air Fleet eventually might need their technical skills, and they would be able to prevent any possible security leaks in their respective domains.[6]

Immediately after Kusaka's briefing the study group set to work in a close race with time. Its report would form the basis for the First Air Fleet's operational plan and discussions for presentation at the war games which loomed in the near future. The group members labored so well that within a few days they had a general report ready for Kusaka.[7]

Genda devoted most of his effort to preparing a study of proposed routes from Japan to Pearl Harbor. The Japanese had to select the one which would reduce to an absolute minimum the danger of detection by American forces. Ever since they heard about the Pearl Harbor enterprise, Nagumo and Kusaka had concerned themselves deeply with this question, and Genda had mulled over the various possible approaches to Hawaii throughout the spring and summer.[8]

Long before he started his staff study for Kusaka, he had settled in his own mind what passage the task force should follow, but he had no power of decision. As a good staff officer he had to make an intensive survey of all the possibilities, setting forth exhaustively and impartially the factors for and against each one. So he developed a staff study which presented for Kusaka's evaluation and Nagumo's decision three routes: southern, central, and northern.[9]

For the southern route Genda suggested two prospective points of departure—Saeki in northern Kyushu and Hashirajima in the Inland Sea. From either of these anchorages the task force would proceed piecemeal to its rendezvous—Wotje in the Marshall Islands. Genda picked Wotje because it offered a suitable anchorage in the Mandates relatively near Pearl Harbor. Being able to refuel approximately halfway to the target, the carriers could complete the voyage without a transfusion from the tankers if necessary.[10]

Genda considered two possible routes from Wotje to Pearl Harbor. The first he called the "direct approach." Steaming out of the Marshalls in a northeasterly direction, the task force would sweep south and east of Johnston Island. Then it would angle northward until it reached the attack launch point some 200 or 250 miles south of Pearl Harbor. This approach had several

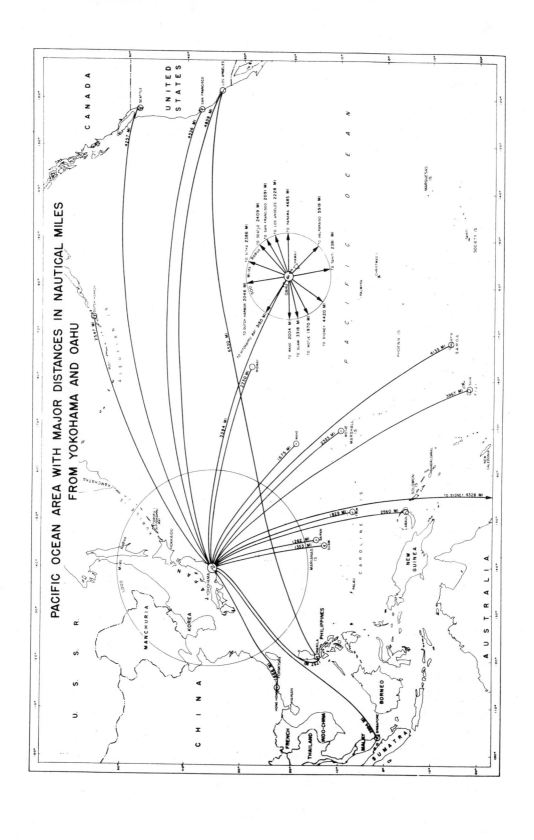

PACIFIC OCEAN AREA WITH MAJOR DISTANCES IN NAUTICAL MILES
FROM YOKOHAMA AND OAHU

advantages: a minimal fuel problem; relatively calm seas; and proximity to
Japanese bases, which would provide an important margin of safety in case of
emergencies. But Genda saw disadvantages as well. First of all, those sun-
drenched skies offered no cover for the task force. Even more dangerous,
Kimmel's fleet used this sea space southeast of Hawaii for training. Only by
fantastic good fortune could the Japanese evade both the patrols and an
American exercise.

Genda's second route from Wotje to Pearl Harbor had the task force
moving in a line between Howland, Baker, and the Phoenix islands on the
south and Kingman Reef, Palmyra, and Christmas Island on the north. Some
400 miles southeast of Christmas Island, Nagumo would swing his ships
northward. When he had reached a point about 600 miles southeast of Mauna
Loa on Hawaii, Nagumo would proceed northwest until approximately 200
miles southeast of Oahu and launch.

Genda decided that this alternate route contained all the disadvantages of
the first plus a serious refueling problem. Then, too, if the Americans spotted
the Japanese fleet, Nagumo would be trapped—Kimmel's ships cutting him off
from retreat to the Marshalls, Short's defenses in front of him, and nothing on
his starboard flank but United States-dominated ocean.

This route had only one thing to be said for it: The United States Navy
would consider a Japanese attack against Hawaii from southeast of Oahu about
as remote a possibility as hail in hell. But while Genda insisted on surprise,
there were limits![11]

Next, he turned his attention to a central route, selecting as departure
points Yokosuka and, again, Hashirajima. After due study and deliberation
Genda chose as rendezvous point Chichi-Jima, some 700 miles southeast of
Tokyo, a far from ideal spot. Its roadstead could not hold the entire task force,
and it was particularly vulnerable to U.S. submarine surveillance.[12]

Thence Genda theoretically sent Nagumo's ships northeastward to about
500 miles north of Midway. From Midway he shifted the task force to a
southerly course, which it would hold until "the extreme danger zone"—the
area about 750 miles north of Oahu. From that point Nagumo would head
directly south and, when within striking distance, launch his aircraft.

Genda discovered few advantages in this central approach. True, it steered
a happy medium between the dangerous exposure of the southern route and
the stormy seas of a more northerly one. But beyond that, troubles would
mount: the inadequate rendezvous point; the danger of American submarine,
surface, and air patrols in the Midway area; the flanking of the Hawaiian chain
to the north. He could not recommend this course, nor did anyone else when it
came up for discussion.

From the first, Genda inclined toward a northern route.[13] Any of the
Inland Sea anchorages could serve as the port of departure, although selecting
the final point of rendezvous posed a difficult problem. He had a number of
possibilities to choose from, but none fully satisfied him. After some study

Genda and Oishi agreed that not one of the places Genda had suggested was suitable from the standpoint of security.

Temporarily shelving the rendezvous problem, Genda worked on a route through the northern Pacific which provided tolerable weather conditions as well as excellent opportunities for concealment. The bulk of merchant ships shuttling between the United States or Canada and Japan or the Soviet Union sailed farther north than Genda's proposed passage. Thus, this location offered the least possibility of detection.

Again Genda offered two alternatives. The first specified departure due east from Hokkaido along 42° north latitude; once about 1,000 miles dead north of Oahu, the task force would turn sharply south for the target area. The second was rather more elaborate: Nagumo's ships would follow the first track until due north of Oahu; then they would continue southeast until they had reached a point 800 or 900 miles northeast of Pearl Harbor, where the task force would shift course southwest and approach Pearl Harbor on a straight line.

This suggestion appealed to Genda for a number of reasons. He proceeded on the premise that air and surface patrols out of Oahu would give scant attention to the northeast. A wide swing eastward would probably evade discovery from Oahu and still dodge patrols originating on the West Coast of the United States. Then, too, Nagumo's ships would lie across the path of American reinforcements from the United States.

The weakness in this route lay in the chance of discovery by commercial planes and vessels plying between the West Coast and Hawaii. Eventually Genda would discard this passage in favor of a simpler one, but at the time he believed that if the Japanese should accept his suggestion to make Operation Hawaii an all-out project complete with landing party, the task force should use the northeastern approach.

Sasabe, Nagumo's navigation officer, worked on the same aspect of the operation;[14] so did Watanabe on Yamamoto's staff. Each investigated such problems as weather, visibility, condition of the sea, and shipping routes in the northern Pacific.[15]

When Genda took this report to Kusaka, he found that the chief of staff approved a northern route. Kusaka fully realized the problems inherent in the rough seas, especially the formidable task of refueling. But in his judgment these weighed lightly against the ultimate consideration of surprise.

The inclement weather that usually lowered over the area north of Pearl Harbor in the late autumn and winter presented the Japanese with two distinct advantages: "It reduced the possibility of detection, and it made patrol activity by the American Navy more difficult." And thanks to Yoshikawa's reports from Honolulu, the Japanese Navy knew that U.S. patrols "were weakest in the area north of Pearl Harbor." Nevertheless, Kusaka expected the Americans to patrol in a full circle around Oahu; the problem therefore was "to maneuver through the patrol lines and press the sudden attack."[16]

Genda now had to embark on a very difficult task—that of selling his choice to Nagumo. The admiral and his air officer had disagreed over routes from the outset. Nagumo particularly disliked the northern course. How could his tankers possibly refuel a fleet in the pitching waters and foul weather that the northern Pacific promised in late autumn? How could the ships navigate properly, keep formation, and preserve the task force as an integrated fighting unit? He envisaged his destroyers wallowing helplessly in mountainous seas; he might even have to send them home, thus depriving himself of priceless antisubmarine protection.

But Genda continued to preach the northern route to Nagumo with evangelical zeal, trying to convince his chief that the best chance for catching the enemy unawares would be to approach from an unexpected direction. "If you think the northern route is bad," he argued, "then you must remember the American admirals will think the same."[17]

He treated the dubious Nagumo to many a pep talk, reminding him of outstanding examples in Japanese history in which resourceful commanders had surprised and defeated a foe against impressive odds. And he tried to assure Nagumo that wise planning and intensive training could overcome the disadvantages of the northern route—handicaps which Genda readily admitted.[18]

On this point a split in orientation existed between Nagumo and Genda. To the latter, surprise was the overriding factor. The Japanese must subordinate everything to the absolute necessity for catching the enemy off guard. For his part, Nagumo had virtually written off any chance of achieving complete surprise. He strongly believed that American patrols would discover the task force no matter what course it took. Therefore, Nagumo preferred to select a route which would enable the First Air Fleet to reach the target area in good condition and to function with maximum striking power. So he held tenaciously to the shorter southern route. Its calm seas and Japanese bases in the Marshall Islands, in his opinion, more than compensated for the route's dangers.[19]

While the First Air Fleet staff wrestled with these assignments, Genda received a welcome reinforcement—an assistant air officer. Sharp, flexible-minded Lieutenant Commander Chuichi Yoshioka was a distant relative of Nagumo's. He enjoyed a reputation as one of Japan's most experienced and able aviators. He was not an aggressive man, and Fuchida believed he was more at home in a staff assignment than as a warrior.[20] But when Yoshioka joined *Akagi* at the age of thirty-two, he already had several thousand hours of flight time to his credit, much of it in combat missions over China and the Burma Road. Yoshioka struck an exotic note in the Japanese Navy, being a Christian—a lifelong Methodist, whose five children attended Sunday school regularly.[21]

During the tough, exacting weeks of intensive planning and training ahead Yoshioka became Genda's alter ego because of all of Nagumo's staff, only these two officers truly understood the meaning and potentialities of naval aviation. He soon found that while Genda was "a tower of strength to both Kusaka and Nagumo," the two admirals "literally feared some of Genda's ideas" as overly radical.

Yoshioka was not particularly surprised when Genda told him about Operation Hawaii in early September, but he was shocked to learn that "Japan was really going to war with the United States." He did not immediately share Genda's enthusiasm for the Pearl Harbor scheme. "The plan might look good on paper, and make quite an impression in table maneuvers, but to carry out such an operation in the face of sharp enemy opposition was quite a different matter," he reflected after the war.[22]

A number of other changes took place in the First Air Fleet's personnel in early September. Of immediate interest to Genda and particularly to Fuchida, hard at work training for he still knew not what, Lieutenant Commander Shigekazu Shimazaki joined *Zuikaku* (which was not yet ready for action) as flight commander on September 10.

Shimazaki was one of Japan's most versatile fliers, an expert on all types of bombing—dive, horizontal, and torpedo. "A man of iron nerves, never upset or excited," said Genda. "He was the Admiral Togo type—the ideal Oriental hero variety." Although not as clever as Fuchida, he had a level head. Once he took off, his own bloodstream seemed to flow through the plane, and he was at his best under fire.[23]

Although somewhat inarticulate, this big man had a good sense of humor, a knack for leadership, and he was the solid, practical type. Fuchida liked his new assistant very much and came to depend upon him in the days to come.[24]

The September personnel shifts touched even Yamamoto's own official family. Ito, who preceded Ugaki as the Combined Fleet's chief of staff, transferred to Tokyo to take up his new duties as Nagano's vice chief. It was exceedingly rare for a rear admiral to be selected for this important post. Nagano had specifically requested him as his deputy. Fukudome characterized Ito as "a steady man, a thorough worker and deep thinker. He was considered an excellent officer with a good future. He lacked only one thing—aggressiveness and a fighting spirit."[25] Thus, as of September 1, two of Yamamoto's former chiefs of staff, both of whom knew about Pearl Harbor—Fukudome and Ito—held key positions under Nagano.

Whatever the differences—and they were many and serious—remaining between the Naval General Staff and the Combined Fleet, the torrent of events was pulling the two organizations ever closer to each other and to the maelstrom of war. On August 15 the Navy had issued orders to prepare for possible conflict with "the beginning of October as the target date for the completion of preparations." Upon receipt of these instructions, at the end of August the Combined Fleet discontinued the training and operations then under way in China and "instructed fast preparations within about a month." Then, on September 1, Yamamoto's headquarters issued orders for "complete wartime organization."[26] In addition, sometime in August or early September the Naval General Staff directed that a model of Oahu be constructed, probably at the request of the Combined Fleet.[27]

So, however much it officially disapproved of Yamamoto's plan, Nagano's branch of the service continued to cooperate with the Combined Fleet in such practical matters as moving up the war games and preparing training aids for Operation Hawaii. All these activities took place before the imperial conference of September 6 and before Konoye and Grew met that evening for their historic dinner engagement.

CHAPTER 28

"THE

WAR

GAMES"

At about 0900 on September 11 limousines and other vehicles piled up in front of the huge iron-gated entrance of the Imperial Naval Staff College.[1] Seasoned admirals and aspiring staff officers alike looked forward eagerly to this yearly visit to Tokyo. Everyone enjoyed renewing old friendships, and "there was always a certain amount of drinking and hell raising. . . ."[2] To these important exercises came most of the sharpest minds and the best staff officers of the entire Japanese Navy. A few Army officers also attended in a liaison capacity.

In the east wing, which housed Yamamoto and his Combined Fleet officers, was a secluded room, strictly off limits to all but those expressly invited to enter. We shall call this the Secret Room; here the First Air Fleet rehearsed the plan to attack Pearl Harbor.

The first day of the war games broke in the participants gradually with a "preexercise discussion" lasting only from 0900 to 1300. The next day, Friday, September 12, work began in earnest with a full schedule from 0800 to 1700 and continued through Tuesday, the sixteenth.[3] Yamamoto presided over the exercises conducted in accordance with the Combined Fleet's war plan. In simulating combat conditions, he divided his warships into task forces allocated to the numerous operations. These groups in turn split into Blue Forces representing Japan and Red Forces simulating the Americans and British. The chief of staff of each fleet usually acted as its Blue commander. Ugaki headed all the Blue Forces, while Vice Admiral Shiro Takasu, Commander in Chief of the First Fleet, ran the Red Forces.

The Blue team would carry out as faithfully as possible the operations which the Combined Fleet projected. Red Forces operated according to plans which their commanders submitted beforehand. As the games progressed, the umpires, of whom Ito was chief, determined changing operational conditions in cooperation with the Red Forces, to keep the exercises as realistic as possible and to hide Red plans from the Blue commanders. In many cases the officers chosen to represent Red had been picked because of their specialized knowledge of the countries involved.

The war games posed a massive problem: how to seize control of the Philippines, Malaya, and the Netherlands East Indies, cope with the enemy fleets stationed in those areas, and at the same time maintain control of the western Pacific. A unique feature of these games was the extension of Japan's inner defense line far eastward from the Marianas, near which traditional strategy predicated the Great All-Out Battle, to the Marshalls.[4] At the same time the Japanese had to prevent a damaging thrust into their exposed flank from American naval forces ranging out of Hawaii.

No one can understand the Pearl Harbor venture except in relation to Japan's major war plans. Having deliberated the problem all year, Tomioka and his Operations Section officers determined that if and when Japan went to war, it should snatch the southern treasure chest quickly and efficiently.[5] When he and his men took their places at the Naval Staff College, they already knew the roles which the various fleet units would play, having rehearsed these in table maneuvers in their Tokyo offices from September 3 to 5.

The war games followed much the same path as the actual Southern Operation was destined to take. Fleet commanders, size and composition of forces, points of departure, areas of rendezvous, strategic objectives, and landing beaches were virtually identical.[6] Bent with absorbed attention over broad tabletops, the admirals of the Southern Command and members of the Naval General Staff watched Vice Admiral Ibo Takahashi's Third Fleet simulate its assigned mission against the Philippines, Borneo, and Celebes.

While the Third Fleet made its move in the maneuvers, the Eleventh Air Fleet based on Formosa attacked MacArthur's air forces at Clark and Nichols fields in a series of surprise bombing raids.[7] In concert with Takahashi's and Tsukahara's operations, Vice Admiral Nobutake Kondo led his Second Fleet of battleships, cruisers, and destroyers out of Mako in the Pescadores, while from Hainan Island off the China coast sailed the Southern Expeditionary Fleet, a large, mixed flotilla under Vice Admiral Noboru Hirata. Swinging southward in a feint toward Bangkok, these two invasion units under Kondo's command headed for Malaya in a three-pronged assault against Singora, Patani, and Kota Bharu more than halfway down the peninsula. From these strategic points Japanese troops would drive down the jungle-covered land toward Singapore, key to Britain's position in the Far East. With its fall the props would be knocked from under Britain's Empire in Southeast Asia, the communications line to Australia severed, and the floodgates to the Netherlands East Indies flung wide.

As the Imperial Navy's ships plowed in imagination through the South China Sea, Rear Admiral Sadaichi Matsunaga's Twenty-second Air Flotilla, land-based in Indochina, prowled the skies in search of enemy ships and planes. Well-balanced invasion units also sortied from Camranh Bay in Indochina to land at Miri and Brunei Bay in British Borneo, more than 2,500 miles from Tokyo.

The Navy had not yet worked out detailed invasion plans for the Netherlands East Indies.[8] Nevertheless, it had defined the broad outlines of strategy. The Japanese planned to slice through the Macassar Strait, seize Tarakan and Balikpapan in eastern Borneo, take key points on Celebes, conquer Bali, and then concentrate their strength for the final push against Java.

Other Japanese forces in this monumental game of naval chess sailed to the Gilberts, Guam, and Wake.[9] Seizure of the latter two islands by Vice Admiral Shigeyoshi Inoue's Fourth Fleet would bar the United States from Japanese waters and add several more unsinkable aircraft carriers to Japan's island bases. Above all, it would put the Combined Fleet in an excellent position to fight the Great All-Out Battle if and when the United States Navy decided to gratify this desire on the part of the Japanese.

Onishi in particular stressed the necessity for more planes to carry out the Southern Operation successfully.[10] The schedule for advancing air forces to the Java line lagged heavily in the case of Zeros and to a lesser degree in that of land-based planes. Therefore, most participants expressed their opinion that all of Japan's carriers should be used in the Southern Operation, on which rested the rise or fall of the Japanese Empire.

Having seen the rehearsals for the Southern Operation well on the way to a logical conclusion, Yamamoto could devote his best energies to his Pearl Harbor scheme. He brought with him to the Secret Room Ugaki, Kuroshima, Watanabe, Sasaki, and Arima. The date was Tuesday, September 16.[11]

Some thirty-odd handpicked officers crowded toward the center of the room, intent upon a long table littered with papers. Maps of the Pacific hung from the walls, with Oahu and Pearl Harbor clearly marked as the targets. Standing over the table, Yamamoto dominated the proceedings. He had personally screened the officers to be admitted to the Secret Room, choosing only those who eventually had to pass on his Pearl Harbor project, help plan it, or execute it.[12]

Nagumo, still prey to deep misgivings, was present with most members of his First Air Fleet staff—Kusaka, Oishi, Genda, Yoshioka, and Sakagami. From the Second Carrier Division came its rambunctious Commander in Chief, Yamaguchi, with several of his staff, including Suzuki.

Here too in the Secret Room was a relative newcomer to the Hawaiian venture, Vice Admiral Gunichi Mikawa, who was to lead the Pearl Harbor Support Force, consisting of the Third Battleship Division and Eighth Cruiser Division. A man of medium height, as sturdy and strong as the capital ships he commanded, Mikawa bore his fifty-three years with easy grace. He believed in the concentration of forces; consequently, he thought that "the plan to carry out an attack against the U.S. Fleet and the Southern Operation at the same time" overloaded the capabilities of the Japanese Navy and jeopardized the success of both operations.[13]

Another newcomer, Rear Admiral Sentaro Omori, Commander in Chief of the First Destroyer Squadron, was present. He looked as subdued and appealingly shy as an elf escaped from Walt Disney's drawing board. But he was all sailor. When he learned about Pearl Harbor, Omori's biggest worry became "how to get his destroyers all the way to Oahu and back." Both Mikawa and Omori insisted that they heard about Yamamoto's plan for the first time at these war games.[14]

Present, too, were the key officers from the Sixth Fleet: Shimizu, handsome and dignified; his resourceful chief of staff, Mito; and his senior staff officer, Commander Midori Matsumura, a submariner with almost fifteen years' experience in the silent service, who had joined the Sixth Fleet on September 5.

The Naval General Staff sent as representatives Fukudome and Tomioka and his assistants, Miyo and Sanagi. The latter would serve as chief umpire for the Pearl Harbor exercise.[15] Of course, Uchida, with his special duties pertaining to operations against the United States, also attended. Likewise, Maeda, head of the Intelligence Bureau, came with his shrewd chief of American affairs, Ogawa. Nagano and Ito were conspicuous by their absence; although invited to attend, they never poked their noses inside the Secret Room.[16]

Not all these officers came to approve the Pearl Harbor venture summarily. The Naval General Staff representatives still were "highly skeptical about Yamamoto's plan." They "attended the Pearl Harbor exercises not as participants, but as spectators and observers—like businessmen who had to be sold by a salesman."[17] Yamamoto also had some high-pressure selling to do within his own Combined Fleet, notably to Nagumo, who saw big trouble awaiting his task force, and Kusaka, whose realistic mind found countless obstacles to the success of the mission in addition to his belief that it would serve no constructive purpose.

But Yamamoto had powerful supporters. "All his officers were very loyal to Yamamoto, looked up to him, and were eager to carry out his plan," Sasaki said.[18] Of course, a cynic might point out that they would have to go along with him or be transferred in short order. But in general, Yamamoto preferred to earn his staff's respect and affection rather than exact an impersonal, dutiful loyalty. Yamamoto could also count on his crony Yamaguchi and the latter's eager air officer, Suzuki. And Genda would proclaim the true faith of Yamamoto's creed with force and conviction.

Even at this time, with a tentative Pearl Harbor plan so far advanced that it could form the basis for a top-level table exercise, serious questions still urgently demanded appraisal. Of all these possible queries, the war games dealt with only two: Was the operation technically feasible, and could secrecy be achieved? Naturally the chart room exercises could not resolve these questions beyond cavil. The participants in the war games could hope to reach only an estimate of the probabilities.

One problem had to be resolved before the mock attack could start: What route should the task force choose? This provoked the first open disagreement in the Secret Room. Nagumo clung to the southern approach, but Yamaguchi, Sasaki, and Genda stoutly insisted that the northern passage would provide the shorter, more secure pathway to the target. Under this avalanche of contrary opinion Nagumo gave way reluctantly. His continual complaints against the northern approach formed an obbligato in minor key throughout the war games.[19]

Another split of opinion developed over the question of aerial reconnaissance. Yamaguchi wanted an extensive system of air patrols en route to Hawaii to scout in every direction for enemy ships, planes, or foreign merchantmen. Advance warning of possible detection could give the task force time to prepare for every conceivable emergency or even change its course.

This suggestion drew prompt protest from Genda. "It is too dangerous," he declared. "Bad weather might cause the scouts to lose contact with their mother ships. This could lead to a crackup at sea when they ran out of fuel, and the enemy could spot the wreckage. Or a panicky pilot might tip off the task force's presence by breaking radio silence. The enemy could detect patrol planes a hundred or so miles from their carriers, resulting in the same breach of security. Aerial reconnaissance will place the mission in gravest jeopardy from the outset."

Yamaguchi, who knew the value of every scrap of last-minute information, and Genda, whose tactical plan was predicated upon secrecy, sparred enthusiastically over this problem. Nagumo offered no opinion. Each argument held much merit, and each contained almost equal danger. In the end Genda converted Yamaguchi, and so it was agreed: no air patrols en route.[20]

These questions resolved, the exercises began with a proposed X-Day of November 16. First to move out were Shimizu's submarines, which left Japan theoretically on October 14, arriving at Wotje on the twentieth. They would leave Wotje between the twenty-eighth and thirtieth and by November 15 would encircle Oahu at a distance of some 300 miles.[21]

Meanwhile, Nagumo's task force moved to its rendezvous in Akkeshi Bay far up on the eastern coast of Hokkaido. This remote bight was far enough north to lessen the problem of fuel supply and could provide some protection against discovery by American submarines. "During the war games and in the period following we made a concerted effort to keep the point of rendezvous a tight secret," explained Genda. "For if this leaked out, the odds against Japan, which were already serious, would have become prohibitive."[22]

This tentative task force consisted of the First and Second Carrier Divisions, two battleships, three cruisers, plus destroyers and tankers. No submarines accompanied the armada during these war games. Nagumo set force speed at about twelve knots course easterly, gradually veering southeast as he approached the target area.[23] Refueling took place twice—on November 8 and 13. On the twelfth ships designated to watch out for fishing vessels moved into place ahead and astern, to port and starboard of the task force.

On the fourteenth Nagumo received word that the Red fleet was in Pearl

Harbor as of November 11. From this point, increasing signs of American activity came into view. On November 14 Hawaii's defenders were making aerial reconnaissance before sunrise, during the day and after sunset over a 400-mile radius. That same date the "Americans" spotted what appeared to be a submarine south of the islands.[24] On the sixteenth—X-1 Day—Red Forces noticed oil on the surface, which could have leaked from submerged submarines,[25] and expanded their search arc to 600 miles. Late that afternoon a scout plane found the task force, but the Japanese destroyed it before it completed its report.[26]

This apparently occurred shortly after Nagumo's ships began their high-speed run at twenty-four knots toward Oahu.[27] About this time Shimizu's submarines reported ten enemy cruisers heading in Nagumo's direction. Undaunted, he pressed on until he reached approximately 200 miles north of Oahu.[28] There he turned his carriers into the wind and launched his first attack wave.[29]

The Blue strike force expected heavy resistance and got it.[30] The Red team, operating from a room of its own, was under the direction of Kanji Ogawa. He had witnessed at least one American exercise during the 1930s of just such an attack against Pearl Harbor. Ably assisted by Captain Bunjiro Yamaguchi, who commanded the Red Army and Marine forces on Oahu,[31] Ogawa had set up an excellent reconnaissance screen. And the scout whom the Blue team shot down had managed, after all, to convey a warning. Although the first wave had been launched without interference, over Oahu it encountered a swarm of Ogawa's interceptors which kept it so busy fighting its way to the targets that it could not bomb effectively. At the same time ship guns and shore batteries blazed away at the attacking planes, dropping them like ducks over a hunter's blind.

While all this action went on, Nagumo's second wave droned down on Pearl Harbor an hour or so behind the initial force. But it had no better luck. Ogawa's interceptors whizzed in and out of the attack formation which buckled under a hail of steel from Yamaguchi's ground defenses. Half of Nagumo's aircraft scrambled back to their carriers, having inflicted only minor damage to the ships in Pearl Harbor and the military installations on Oahu.[32] Ogawa and Yamaguchi had given a graphic illustration of what the Japanese could expect if the Americans received a timely warning of the attack.

As the Blue remnants fled, Red bombers roared hard on their tails and rained upon the task force a shower of bombs, sinking two flattops and slightly damaging the other two as well as some of the support units. The remains of Nagumo's ships escaped to the west. Damage to the task force about equaled previous Japanese estimates—roughly one-third of the armada.

Licking their paper wounds, the Blue Forces profited by their lessons— the efficiency of the Red air patrols plus the poor timing of the task force's arrival on the scene of action.[33] In the attempt to avoid the first and correct the second, the Japanese scheduled the second dry run so that the task force would arrive at a point approximately 450 miles north of Oahu at about sunset the evening before the attack. They estimated that Red aerial reconnaissance could reach out from Hawaii no more than 600 miles in any direction, giving the attackers a margin of safety. According to their calculations, sunset would find the American reconnaissance planes well on the way home from their outer patrol limit. Thus, the task force should have several hundred miles between it and the searching eyes of United States prowlers from Oahu.[34]

Of course, they realized that it would be quite a trick to stay in the safety zone, especially during daylight hours, no matter from what direction the Blue fleet approached Pearl Harbor. The planners knew, however, thanks to Yoshikawa, that the defenders could cover effectively only a radius of 180 degrees. For the most part they covered the area south and southwest of the great base, thus leaving the vital seaways north of Oahu inadequately patrolled.[35]

With these conditions in mind, Nagumo sailed on a more northerly course on the second trial run. He proceeded eastward to approximately 450 miles directly north of Oahu and arrived near sunset.[36] The task force had now reached the position and period of greatest danger. Suppose some sharp-eyed American scout spotted it on the eve of the attack before darkness closed over it?

In their minds' eyes the planners could see the picture all too clearly in view of the abortive first attempt. Long before Nagumo's fleet had completed the high-speed run south to the launching area, the U.S. Pacific Fleet's ships and aircraft would be storming northward in superior numbers to meet the invaders head-on. In the ensuing brawl Japan could lose the greater part of its carrier strike air power within an hour and be left with its entire war plan out of gear. Hence the excruciatingly careful calculations of time and distance.

Safe at the designated point, Nagumo began his high-speed run southward. From that moment good fortune had to sail with him. The blueprint allowed no margin for mechanical breakdowns, significant course adjustments, not even a storm at sea. If the task force could reach this predawn objective without detection, the scales should dip in its favor because at this hour American air patrols would scarcely be taking off. Therefore, if Nagumo's first wave winged southward far enough before the enemy scouts started out, the attack would be a surprise. In that event chances for a successful strike would be excellent.[37]

On this second mock attack everything went smoothly. The invaders encountered no aerial or surface reconnaissance, and the Blue Forces quickly gained complete command of the air. Nagumo achieved all the surprise he could wish as his bombers swooped down on the Red fleet in harbor. Estimated damage to the enemy amounted to loss of four battleships and one severely pounded; the carriers *Lexington* and *Yorktown* sunk, with *Saratoga* seriously damaged; three cruisers sunk and three others with their fighting capability sliced in half. Red air strength on Oahu had been virtually broken, including fifty fighters shot down and eighty destroyed on the ground.[38]

The Blue Forces escaped with relatively minor damage. Red aircraft finally spotted Nagumo's ships, sank one carrier, and halved the capability of a second.[39] In exchange, Blue shot down another fifty Red planes.[40] Then "the Japanese fleet escaped to the homeland and was divinely aided by a squall just in time to permit it to leave the Pearl Harbor area without serious damage."[41]

A swift getaway, then, constituted a basic element of Nagumo's strategy. The subject of repeated attacks against Pearl Harbor did not come up for discussion in the Secret Room, although Genda and Sasaki often talked about the possibility both before and after the exercises.[42] Quite the reverse—many of the planners emphasized the idea of bringing Japan's precious carriers back quickly and safely.[43]

No serious discussion of an attempt to occupy Hawaii took place during the war games.[44] Nevertheless, the idea was intriguing. A month or so before the exercises Kuroshima had exchanged views on the subject with Yamamoto, Ugaki, and Watanabe. The prospect appealed to Watanabe, but Ugaki thought they would have enough problems in executing the aerial strike without adding an amphibious assault. Yamamoto agreed with him, readily seconding Kuroshima's recommendation that Operation Hawaii should include no plan for invasion.[45] Watanabe favored an all-out operation and did a little investigating on his own along that line during the war games, but he received no encouragement. Kuroshima flatly refused to consider it, and when Watanabe spoke to Yamamoto, the Commander in Chief cut the subject short. "The occupation of Hawaii was simply not a part of Yamamoto's strategic thinking at the time," as Watanabe put it in retrospect.[46]

Nor did the war games settle the vexing problem of how many carriers would be allocated to Nagumo's striking force. Genda believed that every available flattop and plane would be none too many to ensure the best results. But the Naval General Staff refused to denude the Southern Operations of all carrier support. Three—four at the outside limit—must suffice for a possible strike against Hawaii.

Mikawa protested against receiving a mere two battleships. He contended that *Hiei* and *Kirishima* could not wage a successful fight if they met United States surface forces during the passage to Oahu, and he demanded two more heavy warships, preferably *Kongo* and *Haruna*.[47] But eventually Takahashi insisted on these two fine vessels for his Third Fleet, and because the Southern Operation had priority, he got them.

So the war games in the Secret Room ended with the matter of carrier and battleship complements dangling in the air, along with submarine escort and reconnaissance. A number of technical questions noted earlier in this chapter remained to be solved. High among them loomed the refueling problem, held over to become the subject of a later staff study.[48]

This rehearsal of Operation Hawaii required only one day—September 16. The next morning the participants returned to the Secret Room for a postmortem on the Blue Forces' tactics and to listen to various reports. The session lasted well into the afternoon, but no one debated whether or not the Pearl Harbor attack should be carried out.[49] Instead, those present heard Oishi describe the Blue actions while Ogawa reported on the Red. Then Sanagi explained the results of the attack and his judgments as chief umpire.[50]

In the general discussion which followed, Kusaka requested "the exact air scouting radius of the enemy and location of his ships, together with the general situation within Pearl Harbor." He also asked for a destroyer squadron of sixteen ships, preferably the Fourth, Sixteenth, Seventeenth, and Eighteenth Destroyer Divisions. Then he proposed that the Sixth Fleet be placed under the commander of the task force and finally that the Zero's airspeed restriction of 280 knots be lifted.[51] After the critique of September 17 the participants gathered for a dinner which ended the exercise covering Operation Hawaii. The full war games officially adjourned at 1730 on September 20.[52]

CHAPTER 29

"TIME

WAS

RUNNING

OUT"

Nagumo was still far from happy. In fact, the success of the second mock strike in the Secret Room intensified rather than allayed his worries. The exercise had breathed a semblance of life into a hitherto-abstract concept. Now he could really visualize it and comprehend the full impact of the scheme. Nagumo could invoke much plain common sense in support of his pessimism about the Pearl Harbor project. He could have pointed out— perhaps he did—that sound strategy consists in fighting battles one at a time and in a place promising the best chance of victory. He could also urge that a commander in chief has a duty to foresee the worst in any given situation and prepare accordingly.

In particular, he resisted the adoption of the northern route. "During the war games there was no stormy sea, so we could take the northern course. But when we go to Hawaii, it will be different," he argued unanswerably. More than once during the maneuvers Nagumo tried to convey to Yamamoto the terrible hazards involved in the operation and the awful consequences should anything go wrong. On one such occasion Yamamoto put a friendly arm around Nagumo's heavy shoulders and said in effect, "Don't worry about the matter. I will take full responsibility."[1]

Nagumo was no coward, and if ordered to carry out the venture, he would give it everything he had; but he was frankly horrified by the prospect before him. It was all very well for Yamamoto to play Atlas and carry a world of responsibility on his back, but he would be aboard *Nagato* in home waters while Nagumo would be poking into the eagle's nest. Yamamoto could not raise sunken ships, reconstruct crashed aircraft, or bring dead men back to life. Nagumo's obvious gloom prompted Fukudome to remark to him cheerfully, "If you die in this operation, special shrines will be built in your memory."[2]

Doubts also beset Ogawa about the feasibility of the Pearl Harbor assault despite his long interest in the idea. He brought up a number of disquieting questions from the intelligence viewpoint. Could all the necessary data on American anchorage dispositions, defense installations, and Fleet movements be assembled, evaluated, and disseminated effectively? True, Naval Intelligence had a solid core of information on hand from Yoshikawa, but it seemed incredible to Ogawa that the Americans would not follow the stream to its source and dam it. Even if Japan's special agent continued to operate unimpeded, would the Naval General Staff have a complete G-2 picture of Pearl Harbor on attack day? Could it relay it to Nagumo somewhere in the northern Pacific in time to make it count?[3]

No one knew the answers at this time. Nor could anyone ensure that the plan would not fall into the hands of an alert enemy agent at the last minute. To catch any hint of a clue which might indicate that the United States had received a tip-off about the proposed attack, the Japanese set up a tightly meshed intelligence screen to filter all newspapers, foreign and domestic, as well as radio broadcasts from abroad. They also set a constant watch on American and British military personnel in Japan.[4] As Nagumo told Shimizu, echoing all their thoughts, "If this operation is not kept a secret, then it will fail."[5]

On the very day the exercises ended, Fukudome reported to Nagano and Ito his considered opinion of the scheme: "It is an alarming risk." He had thought so from the beginning and saw nothing in the Secret Room to change his mind. "Not only are there all the normal difficulties inherent in such a bold operation, but there are numerous unknown factors besides. If the task force should be badly damaged and several carriers sunk, the striking power of the fleet will be decidedly weakened and the Southern Operation placed in serious jeopardy. We must ask ourselves, 'Can a plan of such magnitude be kept secret?' If not, it has little chance of success, and the results very likely will prove fatal."

Then, after pausing a moment to let his hearers digest this unpleasant thought, Fukudome went on. "Our ships' limited radius of action and the necessity for refueling at sea pose still other difficulties. Nor have we any assurance that the intelligence requirements can be fulfilled. The problem there," he explained, "is to maintain a continuous, accurate flow of information on the exact whereabouts of the U.S. Fleet at all times. And the bulk of the Fleet will have to be in or near Pearl Harbor on the day of the attack, which is problematical."

His chief listened attentively to this frankly pessimistic estimate. When Fukudome had finished, Nagano remarked, "In case of war I do not favor launching operations as risky as Yamamoto's proposal. I think it is best for the Navy to limit its plans and concentrate on capturing the southern regions." Ito had little or nothing to say, although as time went on, he "took a negative view toward the Pearl Harbor operation."[6]

The Operations Section could not have agreed more heartily. "When the war games ended, my staff was strongly opposed to attacking Hawaii," said Tomioka. "In the first place, the idea cut across the grain of all our thinking and planning prior to that time. Secondly, as everyone agreed, it was a plan of tremendous complexity. Thirdly, Japan's fate so completely depended on her fleet that we could not bring ourselves to accept the staggering losses we thought inherent in such an inadmissible risk. Lastly, we considered the Southern Operation of such importance that we did not want anything else to jeopardize its success."[7]

Miyo substantially concurred with Tomioka and added some objections of his own: "We were convinced that if a good share of our air strength were allotted to the Pearl Harbor operation, there would not be enough planes left to carry out the war successfully in the south. Carrier forces simply had to be used there because simultaneous landings in Malaya and the Philippines demanded protection."[8]

If Nagumo's task force did somehow manage to reach a position to strike Hawaii, who could guarantee that results would justify the expenditure of so many men, so much time and fuel? Thus, the war games did not produce widespread reassurance throughout the Navy. To Tsukahara they seemed unrealistic and confusing. "I was in a deep fog the whole time," he confessed to a colleague.[9] Nor was the First Air Fleet staff entirely happy. Kusaka thought the war games entirely too theoretical. "The results depended too much on the various personalities of the umpires," he remarked.[10]

To Yoshioka the exercises epitomized the Japanese penchant for shortsighted, self-indulgent thinking. He saw the umpires underestimate American strength and slant their decisions in favor of the Blue team. They even equated one Zero with three enemy planes. As an experienced pilot Yoshioka felt his hackles rise at such stupidity. But when he tried to bring up these points, he received a sharp admonition for his pains.

Time and again Yoshioka saw the activities of the Red Team arbitrarily restricted when they threatened to upset Blue's planned movements as well as such acts of God permitted as the squall which miraculously blew up just in time to spare Nagumo's task force all but token damage after the successful second mock attack. Yoshioka charitably decided that in view of the serious international situation and the clear prospect of war, the umpires were trying to avoid anything which might foster misgivings or feelings of inferiority. Indeed, the tendency to underrate the enemy characterized Japanese naval war games prior to World War II, and it took the stunning defeat at Midway to bring this unrealistic practice to a halt.[11]

Nevertheless, the exercises served a vital purpose. "The war games cut through the year 1941 like the sharp edge of a dividing line," said Genda. "They clarified our problem and gave us a new sense of direction and purpose. After they were over, all elements of the Japanese Navy went to work as never before, because time was running out."[12]

If Japan planned on going to war, it must do so soon or not at all. Only enough oil remained to carry through eighteen months of fighting, and every day the stock diminished. In general, Japan's military leaders agreed that if they waited another six months, they might as well forget about it and admit defeat by default. Time and weather marched together. The First Air Fleet could not possibly be ready for war by October. It might perhaps reach combat capability in November, but not top efficiency. Yet Japan could not afford to wait beyond early December. By dead winter, northern Pacific conditions would prohibit a transoceanic strike. Weather also conditioned Japanese planning for the Southern Operation. The monsoons began in October and increased in intensity for two months. Little wonder that the Army wanted to start the ball rolling by the end of October at the latest.

Then, too, the possibility of fighting the Soviet Union motivated Japan's military planners. Because operations in Siberia would be possible after the spring thaw, the top strategists insisted that the Southern Operation be completed by the end of March 1942. Inasmuch as Japan's schedule called for conquest of the southern areas within 120 days after the outbreak of hostilities, the war had to begin not much later than December 1, 1941.[13]

Perhaps with the idea of allowing all concerned to blow off steam before they had to unite for better or worse, Fukudome and Ugaki called a highly secret conference to be held in the Operations Section of the Naval General Staff on September 24 for a frank and open discussion of the Pearl Harbor plan.[14] It was not attended by Nagano, Yamamoto, Nagumo, or any subordinate commander. Several members of the Operations Section reinforced Fuku-dome. In addition to Ugaki, Kuroshima and Sasaki represented the Combined Fleet. In their official capacities these were the logical choices, but they were also the men best calculated to support Yamamoto's project to the hilt. At this time Ugaki was not overly enthusiastic, but he had shatterproof convictions of the loyalty a chief of staff owed to his commander in chief. Sasaki conformed to the Genda pattern of a naval air power disciple and shared Yamamoto's faith in the effectiveness of audacity. Kuroshima would never dream of opposing Yamamoto, regardless of how outlandish his wishes.

Nagumo sent Kusaka, Oishi, and Genda. He could depend upon Kusaka to present all the arguments against the madcap notion and on Oishi to back him up. He could not leave Genda out of a Pearl Harbor conference, so he kept one vote solidly in the "yea" camp and two among the "nays."

This conference lasted the greater part of a day. Fukudome, who presided, opened the discussion. He took a rather neutral position, as befitted a moderator, saying nothing either for or against Yamamoto's plan.[15] Not so Kusaka. "Tactically the attack might succeed," he stated, "but strategically the chances are limited." In other words, while the strike might give Japan a temporary advantage, Kusaka doubted that it would bring about any measurable long-range advantages. He also pointed out that even a tactical victory would depend upon secrecy. The enemy might well sight and engage the task force at any point in the long voyage from Japan to Hawaii.

Kusaka further questioned whether Tokyo could take any diplomatic measure which would catch Washington off guard politically. Once more he stressed the primacy of the Southern Operation and the urgent requirement for air support of that gigantic enterprise. "I cannot agree to this risky Pearl Harbor plan," he declared. Then he added philosophically, "Of course, if ordered, the First Air Fleet will carry it out with no complaints."[16]

In complete agreement with Kusaka, Tomioka expounded on the risks inherent in the plan. He maintained his opposition to diverting attention from the vital push to the south.[17] Kami followed his chief. With his keenly analytical mind, he outlined the proposed Hawaiian strike in terms of plus and minus. On the credit side, a surprise attack might get through because it would be very difficult for the United States to maintain a twenty-four-hour air patrol in all directions. Granted that the raiders achieved surprise, the enemy would no longer be in a position to launch a massive counterattack; therefore, the task force might escape with relatively little damage.

But Kami rolled up a frightening total in the red ink column. Refueling posed formidable problems, bombing alone could not inflict maximum damage to the enemy warships, the Americans could salvage ships sunk in the shallow waters of Pearl Harbor and put them back in to operation within a reasonably short time, and the risk of detection could not be ignored.[12]

For the benefit of the nonairmen, Genda explained that horizontal and torpedo bombers were dual-purpose aircraft and could interchange their missions. By using them all as torpedo planes, he hoped to sink eight U.S. battleships. In addition, fifty-four dive bombers could concentrate on carriers, sinking three of them, while the remaining dive bombers attacked the air bases on Oahu, pinning down American air power. This all-torpedo attack against battleships would be most effective if the Japanese found the U.S. Pacific Fleet at Lahaina. Not only did Lahaina offer the raiders wide maneuvering space, but any vessel that plunged into Lahaina's depths would be gone forever. For these reasons the Japanese hoped to the very moment of attack that they would discover at least a portion of Kimmel's fleet in the Maui anchorage.

Genda's every instinct urged the all-torpedo tactic, but he knew that torpedo results so far had been disappointing and that Nagumo's pilots and bombardiers were still trying everything possible to improve their techniques. Would their best be good enough? Genda had to face the possibility that it might not. Therefore, he presented his colleagues with an alternate plan: the conversion of torpedo planes into high-level bombers and the execution of an all-horizontal-bombing attack in concert with a dive-bombing strike. He estimated maximum results from this method as about five capital ships—two or three battlewagons and three carriers.

While such losses would deal the enemy a considerable initial blow, it never occurred to Genda to settle for second best. He saw only one answer: Torpedo bombing was absolutely necessary. He realized that the difficulties were real and weighty, but he believed that intensive study and hard training could overcome them.[19]

Next, Oishi had his say. He saw eye to eye with Nagumo and Kusaka. He confined himself almost entirely to surface problems. "If enemy scouts go no further out than 300 miles, it will be easy to pick a course," he said. "But if they go 400 miles or beyond, it will be difficult." He particularly fretted over refueling, especially of the destroyers, which would require many transfusions to reach Hawaii. The larger ships could get along with only one. "Navigation and refueling in the heavy northern seas will be so complicated and difficult in themselves that the operation cannot possibly succeed," he announced gloomily.[20]

Sasaki had studied long and thoroughly the possibility of the enemy's discovering the task force en route. "If we have to take the southern course, we should abandon the operation," he said. Impatiently he snapped his conclusion: "We could talk forever about a surprise attack; we should make up our minds and be done with it."[21]

The meeting then turned its attention to the date for X-Day. By that term these officers did not mean that on a certain date the Emperor would declare war, whereupon Nagumo's task force would leave Japan headed for Pearl Harbor. X-Day would find his ships already in position some 200 miles north of Oahu, ready to launch their planes.

"It is desirable to set up X-Day around November 20," Fukudome told the group. "We have already lost our chance for a strategical surprise," he said. "An attack such as the German Army made is no longer possible. We can only try to achieve tactical surprise." So he thought it absolutely necessary to secure the southern area as soon as possible and to "prepare for eventualities with Soviet Russia."

X-Day hinged upon the operational readiness of the First Air Fleet, and Kusaka knew all the bugs still remaining in his organization. "From the viewpoint of training itself, November 20 is too early," he said point-blank.

This announcement jolted Ugaki. Shortly after the war games the Combined Fleet staff had agreed upon November 21—a Friday—as a tentative attack date. But on second thoughts Yamamoto and his officer preferred to launch the strike on a Sunday morning, when a maximum of American ships should be at anchor. X-Day thus would be neither November 16, as used in the war games, or Sunday, the twenty-third. If they had to postpone X-Day until around mid-December, reasoned Ugaki, all the more important for Japan to "make the surprise attack against Pearl Harbor at the very outbreak of the war from the point of view of overall operations."[22]

Kuroshima did not speak until the end of the conference. At last, thoroughly disgusted with the opposition, he spoke up, strongly urging the adoption of Yamamoto's plan "to assure the success of the Southern Operation."[23] Fukudome had the last official word. "From the political standpoint, the United States probably will keep its Pacific Fleet in Pearl Harbor, but there is always a possibility that it will return to the mainland for operational preparations." He ended with a brief summary of the major problems involved in the strike against Hawaii, promising, "These will undergo serious study by the General Staff so that a final decision can be made as soon as possible." As the meeting broke up amid the scraping of chairs and hum of conversation,

Kuroshima remarked sarcastically to Genda, "Talking about operations doesn't do the fighting!"[24]

When Kuroshima reported back to *Nagato* he gave his chief a blow-by-blow description. When he had finished, Yamamoto shouted in an explosive fit of temper, "Who called this foolish meeting? What's the idea behind such babbling? Does anyone think for one second that we can carry out the Southern Operation without first crippling the American Fleet? As Commander in Chief of the Combined Fleet, I will take full responsibility for my plan!"[25]

Admiral Isoroku Yamamoto, Commander-in-Chief, Combined
Fleet.

(At right) VADM Chuichi Nagumo, Commander-in-Chief, 1st Air Fleet. (Below left) VADM Mitsumi Shimizu, Commander-in-Chief, 6th Fleet (Submarines). (Below right) RADM Tamon Yamaguchi, Commander-in-Chief, 2nd Carrier Division.

(Above) RADM Chuichi "King Kong" Hara (center), Commander-in-Chief, 5th Carrier Division. (*Official U.S. Navy Photo*). (At left) Admiral Osami Nagano, Chief, Naval General Staff. (*Official U.S. Navy Photo*).

Admiral Harold R. Stark, Chief of Naval Operations. (*Official U.S. Navy Photo*).

Admiral Husband E. Kimmel (seated at right), Commander-in-Chief, U.S. Pacific Fleet; VADM Wilson Brown, Jr. (seated at left); Capt. William Ward "Poco" Smith (pointing), Chief of Staff, Pacific Fleet; Capt. Walter S. DeLany (standing), Operations Officer, Pacific Fleet.

(Left) Lt. Gen. Walter C. Short, Commanding General, Hawaiian Department. (*United Press International Photo*). (Right) Cmdr. Harold M. "Beauty" Martin, Commanding Officer, Kaneohe.

RADM Richmond Kelly Turner,
Chief, War Plans Division, Navy
Department (*Official U.S. Navy
Photo*).

Admiral C. W. Nimitz assumes command as Commander-in-
Chief, Pacific Fleet, December 31, 1941. (*Official U.S. Navy
Photo*).

Operations Section, Naval General Staff, December 11, 1941.
Front Row: Capt. Sadatoshi Tomioka, Chief of Section; Cmdr.
HIH Prince Nobuhito Takamatsu; RADM Shigeru Fukudome,
Chief, 1st Bureau; Capt. Shigenori Kami; *Back Row:* Cmdr.
Nasatomo Nakano; Cmdr. Shigeshi Uchida; Cmdr. Sadamu
Sanagi; Lt. Cmdr. Marquis Hironobu Katcho; Cmdr. Yugi
Yamamoto; Cmdr. Tatsukichi Miyo.

(Left) RADM Takijiro Onishi, Chief of Staff, 11th Fleet.
(Right) Cmdr. Minoru Genda, Air Staff Officer, 1st Air Fleet.

(At left) Lt. Cmdr. Shigekazu Shimazaki, Squadron commander, *Zuikaku*, leader of the second wave of the air attack on Pearl Harbor. (Below left) Cmdr. Mitsuo Fuchida, Leader, air attack on Pearl Harbor. (Below right) Lt. Cmdr. Shigeharu Murata, Torpedo bomber leader, 1st Air Fleet.

CHAPTER 30

"BUT

WHAT

ABOUT

THE PACIFIC?"

As Roosevelt faced the microphones of his nation's radio networks on September 11, he was furious about the German submarine attack on September 4 against the U.S. destroyer *Greer*, about 175 miles southwest of Iceland, and did not care who knew it. No one could doubt that this complex man loved his country's ships, that a blow at the United States Navy hit him where he lived. The President thundered his warning loud and clear: "From now on, if German or Italian vessels of war enter the waters the protection of which is necessary for American defense, they do so at their own peril.

"The orders which I have given as Commander-in-Chief of the United States Army and Navy are to carry out that policy—at once."[1]

Reaction to the President's historic pronouncement differed, yet few doubted that he had declared war in the Atlantic in all but name. The *Greer* affair and Roosevelt's bold address focused national attention on the showdown with Hitler. The Battle of the Atlantic, the fighting in North Africa, and the titanic struggle raging in Russia all blazed in American headlines.[2] By contrast, a few complacent articles and editorials on Japan and the Pacific peered modestly from the inner pages. Both officially and unofficially the United States played down the threat of a Far Eastern war at the very time that the Japanese Navy was conducting war games preparing to deliver devastating blows against the ABCD powers.

Of course, many in Washington realized that they had to deal with a global problem; therefore, they could not and did not neglect the Pacific. But at this time attention centered on the Philippines, not on Hawaii. As we have seen, by the late summer of 1941 certain factors had caused the Army and Navy to reexamine the long-held premise that the Philippines could not be defended. One was Hitler's monumental blunder in attacking the Soviet Union. This new phase of the war not only eased pressure in western Europe but also slipped the leash from Japan in Asia.

Then, too, in recalling MacArthur to active duty as commander of USAFFE, Washington signaled a dynamic approach to Philippine defense. MacArthur was the last man to don his uniform again only to assume passively the role of champion of a lost cause.

Above all, the rise of military aviation culminating by 1941 in an excellent, workable long-range bomber—the B-17—had added a new dimension to all military planning. A large air armada might seal off the South China Sea, and with its long-range capability the B-17 could easily overfly advance Japanese positions.

Stimson's enthusiasm for the Flying Fortress knew no bounds. He was disgusted when on September 12 he discovered that, at the urging of Ambassador Constantin Oumansky and two visiting Russian airmen of high rank, Roosevelt, "intrigued with the romance of the thing," had promised the delegation five Flying Fortresses "to fly back in a picturesque gesture over Germany. . . ."

The secretary of war bitterly lamented his loss because five bombers could make no substantial contribution to Russian victory but were vital in the Philippines. Stimson, who not only loved his B-17s but as a former high commissioner took a special interest in the Philippines, explained his thinking to the Cabinet. Roosevelt appeared contrite, "but the thing was done and it shows the results of private administration—that he should receive these people and make a promise without consulting his Air Force or the Chief of Staff," or Stimson for that matter, before going ahead.[3] Roosevelt's habit of being carried away and scattering largess without consultation probably contributed to the Cabinet's coolness to the idea of a Roosevelt-Konoye meeting.

The new, positive approach to Philippine defense constituted less a change of policy than an acknowledgment of current conditions. "Policy" implies a deliberate choice, and the United States never wrote off the Philippines from any lack of concern but rather from the logistical inability to hold them. Nevertheless, both then and later, many believed that the newly activated gestures toward protecting the commonwealth represented wishful thinking rather than realistic appraisal and that the matériel being poured into the Philippines should have gone to Hawaii.[4]

Marshall, however, believed that as of roughly the end of August, Hawaii's defenders "were reasonably prepared in meeting the requirements they had stated. . . . We had equipped, so far as we thought it possible to equip and instructed, so far as we thought it was necessary to instruct, the garrison in the Hawaiian Islands. We were now engaged in trying to do for General MacArthur that what [sic] he so urgently required."[5]

Here was a major change in orientation, once more calling for a thorough reexamination of Kimmel's mission and posture. The decision to dispatch approximately a quarter of the Pacific Fleet strength to the Atlantic in the spring had been based in part upon the availability of Flying Fortresses for the defense of Hawaii.* But now these aircraft were going to the Philippines, leaving only a token number on Oahu. Small wonder that Roosevelt's broadcast of September 11 prompted Kimmel to write to Stark the next day for clarification and to place on record a few ideas of his own:

> We all listened to the President's speech with great interest. With that and King's operation orders, of which we have copies, the situation in the Atlantic is fairly clear. But what about the Pacific? . . .
>
> This uncertainty, coupled with current rumors of U.S.–Japanese rapprochement and the absence of any specific reference to the Pacific in the President's speech, leaves me in some doubt as to just what my situation out here is. Specific questions that arise are:
>
> (a) What orders to shoot should be issued for areas other than Atlantic and Southwest Pacific sub-areas? . . .
>
> (b) Along the same lines, but more specifically related to the Japanese situation, is what to do about submarine contacts off Pearl Harbor and the vicinity. As you know, our present orders are to trail all contacts, but not to bomb unless . . . in the defensive sea area. Should we now bomb contacts, without waiting to be attacked?

Having tossed these troublesome questions into Stark's lap, Kimmel attacked his main problem: the position of his command in the world picture.

> The emphasis, in the President's speech, on the Atlantic also brings up the question of a possible further weakening of this Fleet. A strong Pacific Fleet is unquestionably a deterrent to Japan—a weaker one may be an invitation. I cannot escape the conclusion that the maintenance of the "status quo" out here is almost entirely a matter of the strength of this Fleet. It must [not] be reduced, and, in the event of actual hostilities, must be increased if we are to undertake a bold offensive.[6]

Thus, Kimmel once again made it crystal clear that he did not think of his ships as designed to protect the Hawaiian Islands or anything else, except as such protection would accrue from victory at sea. To Kimmel, the U.S. Pacific Fleet was the instrument of "a bold offensive," which he would initiate promptly once war with Japan began. He therefore requested specific, heavy reinforcements, suggesting that the movement of the battleships *North Carolina* and *Washington* "to the Pacific, now, would have a tremendous effect on Japan and would remove any impression that *all* [Kimmel's italics] our thoughts are on the Atlantic. . . ."[7]

At this point Kimmel's logic shot wide of the mark because the day for deterrents, if it ever existed, had long passed. Japan was going to invade the southern regions come hell, high water, or American battleships. In fact, the

*See Chapter 14.

presence at Pearl Harbor of two additional battlewagons would have made such enthusiastic airmen as Genda fairly smack their lips in anticipation.

The CinCUS ended his letter with one more plea to remember his area: "Until we can keep a force here strong enough to meet the Japanese Fleet we are not secure in the Pacific—and the Pacific is still very much a part of the world situation. . . ."[8]

The press showed no sign of sharing Kimmel's concern. According to Honolulu newspapers, the Japanese were "displaying marked prudence" because their "army and navy stuck out their necks to dangerously vulnerable lengths. Particularly the navy."[9] Germany's mounting troubles in Russia gave "evidence enough that the Peace of the Pacific is less likely to be violated now" than in 1940, when Hitler's successes "were at their peak."[10] The mainland, too, was optimistic. "No one doubts that the British and American naval forces now in the Far East could easily destroy the Japanese navy," claimed the Atlanta *Constitution*.[11]

Such complacent attitudes no doubt bothered Kimmel when, on Thursday, September 18, he addressed a chamber of commerce luncheon held in Honolulu's Royal Hawaiian Hotel. His audience contained such heavy guns as Governor Joseph B. Poindexter and other civilian leaders, with Short and Martin, Pye and Halsey. With the bare minimum of the usual courtesies, Kimmel launched into a hard-hitting speech over radio station KGBM.

"My job is not to formulate national policy, but to bring our fleet, particularly the Pacific Fleet, to the very highest state of efficiency." Having thus clarified his position, Kimmel emphasized: "Even more than their fellow Americans on the mainland, the people of Hawaii will be intimately concerned with any war that may come. By virtue of their geographical position they may even be exposed to the physical hazards of war."

He charged that "Hawaii has led a soft life" and was "somewhat unwilling to face the realities of the present." He gave his audience a glimpse of his naval thinking. "We of the Pacific fleet now based in this area are not here merely to aid in the defense of this American outpost. . . . If war should unfortunately be forced upon us, the duty of the fleet will be to deny vital sea areas to the enemy. . . . Sooner or later, however, the units must return to a base for fuel, provisions, repairs, essential relaxation."

The CinCUS then ran up a storm warning: "The officers and men whom I command know that I am intolerant of half measures. They know that I do not take the will for the deed. They expect me to speak bluntly. Let me be equally candid with you!" With that he proceeded to tell the Hawaiians that they had fallen short and sidestepped some of their responsibilities. They had "taken an attitude of 'mañana' about highly important matters connected with the current emergency. . . ."

It took a goodly measure of courage and conviction for a military man in 1941 to say such things to a group of distinguished leaders in beautiful, easygoing Hawaii. Kimmel switched to the subject of espionage and subversion. "Each one of you must guard against directly or indirectly aiding foreign agents"; at the same time, just and honest as always, he warned against the danger inherent in "witch hunts" and against anyone's "being unduly apprehensive or suspicious" of his neighbor.

Kimmel ended with a plea for unity and sacrifice: "The more we collectively prepare in peace the less we collectively suffer in war."[12]

A shadow hangs over Kimmel's brave, pertinent words. When the unexpected happened, it was not the civilian Hawaiians who were caught with their anchors down. To his dying day Kimmel never understood why, in his case, his fellow countrymen could not "take the will for the deed."

On September 11, the day of Roosevelt's *Greer* address, a note of genuine cheer rang through a memorandum which Miles sent to Marshall. Emperor Hirohito had assumed direct command of Army Headquarters and had publicly thanked his Cabinet. Snatching with pathetic eagerness at any sign that the United States might avoid embroilment in the Pacific, the G-2 added optimistically, "Barring a massacre of the conservatives by the militarists, an event deemed unlikely in view of the Emperor's action, it is probable that Japan will find a peaceful way out of one of the greatest crises in her history and seek a means to realign her foreign policy in an anti-Axis direction."[13]

Across the United States speculation on the meaning of the Emperor's move ran rife. Practically everyone agreed that he had done a brave thing in assuming personal control of the home armies, but what did it all mean?[14] The Honolulu *Advertiser* put little faith in this action. "The fact that Hirohito has taken control of the Japanese military . . . signifies nothing. The Japanese military will be controlled as long and as far as it deems good policy and tactics, no farther. The fiction of the Emperor's supremacy will vanish as suddenly as has the fiction of air superiority over sea power."[15]

If anyone in the Hawaiian defense establishment relaxed because of the Japanese reorganization, which occurred the very day the war games opened at the Naval Staff College in Tokyo, no evidence of it appears in the official correspondence of the time. On the tenth we find Short pleading with the War Department for bombproof aircraft repair facilities, "vital to the continued functioning of the Hawaiian Air Force during an attack on Oahu."[16]

The subject of air raids also bothered Stark's office, as witness a letter dispatched on September 16 to the chief of ordnance. The CNO asked for research toward "a lighter anti-torpedo net . . . which can be laid and removed in harbors in a short time for temporary use, and which will give good if not perfect protection for torpedoes fired from planes."[17]

On Oahu Martin still prepared U.S. forces for a potential Japanese attack. On September 20 he sent Short a timely memorandum containing a plan for joint exercises over the suggested period November 17–22, to "continue until enemy carrier-based aircraft have attacked Oahu and have theoretically destroyed the Hawaiian Air Force and Navy and Marine units present thereat. . . ." This most unpleasant prospect shows what Martin thought might happen if the Japanese launched a successful air attack on Oahu. The date span is very intriguing because Sunday, November 16, and Sunday, November 23, happened to be the days the Japanese at that very time were considering for delivery of their surprise package.

Martin had a double purpose in mind—first, to discover whether his bomber command could find and destroy the enemy far out at sea where it counted; and secondly, to see whether U.S. carriers, playing the role of Japanese, could sneak up on their objective successfully. He planned a full-scale maneuver, utilizing the new temporary aircraft warning system radar sites. Unlike the umpires at the Tokyo war games, Martin did not want to make matters easy for his team, as witness his final paragraph:

> 7. It is strongly recommended that no effort be made to "can" or to stereotype any part of this exercise. It is urged that the carriers in approaching Oahu use all tactics of concealment and evasion that they would use in actual war conditions. . . . The striking force to be used against the carriers will consist of every bombardment airplane and patrol plane that has the range to reach the objective.[18]

While Martin was planning his exercise, in Washington Stark watched the international scene bleakly. On the twenty-second he wrote at length to Hart in Manila with an information copy to Kimmel: "So far as the Atlantic is concerned, we are all but, if not actually, in it. . . ." He went on in this vein for another three paragraphs. Then he observed skeptically: "Mr. Hull has not yet given up hope of a satisfactory settlement of our differences with Japan. Chances of such a settlement are, in my judgment, very slight. Admiral Nomura is working hard on his home government and, while he appears to be making *some* [Stark's italics] progress, I am still from Missouri."[19]

But at the highest governmental level, attention centered on the Atlantic. None knew better than Roosevelt and Stimson how important that area and how thin the bulkhead between the United States and actual war with Germany were. They differed appreciably, however, in their attitudes toward the future. As an appointed rather than elected official Stimson had less concern with popular opinion than did Roosevelt, who was always sensitive to the pulse of the electorate. Stimson wanted the United States to enter the war. He was not a bloodthirsty man, but the current ambiguous situation offended his basic honesty. He preferred that his country acknowledge the realities of the moment and cease dodging behind semantics. He also believed that "getting into the frank position of war would help production very much and would help the psychology of the people. . . ."[20]

On September 23 Stark answered some of the queries Kimmel had posed on September 12:

> The existing orders, that is not to bomb suspected submarines except in the defensive sea areas, are appropriate. If conclusive, and I repeat conclusive, evidence is obtained that Japanese submarines are actually in or near United States territory, then a strong warning and a threat of hostile action against such submarines would appear to be our next step. Keep us informed.
> We have no intention of further reducing the Pacific Fleet except that

prescribed in Rainbow 5. . . . The existing force in the Pacific is all that can
be spared for the task assigned your fleet, and new construction will not make
itself felt until next year.

Stark then outlined certain British reinforcements planned for the period
from late December to early in 1942. "These . . . ought to make the task of the
Japanese in moving southward considerably more difficult. It should make
Japan think twice before taking action, if she has taken no action by that
time."[21] That last phrase contained the bitter core of the problem. British
reinforcements due in late December could not hinder Japanese forces moving
in early December.

Stark blasted Kimmel's hopes of acquiring *North Carolina* and *Washington,* neither as yet completed. The need for them was "far greater in the
Atlantic than in the Pacific." He added hopefully, "I believe that, in all
probability, the Pacific Fleet can operate successfully and effectively even
though decidedly weaker than the entire Japanese Fleet, which certainly can
be concentrated in one area only with the greatest difficulty."[22] Stark would
find out soon enough just how rapidly and capably the potential enemy could
concentrate in several areas simultaneously.

The CNO's postscripts often contain some of the most interesting thoughts
in his correspondence. He tacked one such on his letter to Kimmel:

> I have held this letter up pending a talk with Mr. Hull who has asked me to
> hold it very secret. I may sum it up by saying *that conversations with the Japs
> have practically reached an impasse* [Stark's italics]. As I see it we can get
> nowhere towards a settlement and peace in the Far East until and unless
> there is some agreement between Japan and China—and just now that seems
> remote. . . .

Stark still did not dispatch his letter. On September 29 he added a second
postscript:

> Admiral Nomura came in to see me this morning. We talked for about an
> hour. He usually comes in when he begins to feel near the end of his rope;
> there is not much to spare at the end now. . . . Conversations without results
> cannot last forever. If they fall through, and it looks like they might, the
> situation could only grow more tense. I have again talked to Mr. Hull and I
> think he will make one more try . . . if there is anything of moment I will, of
> course, hasten to let you know.[23]

The current pressures on Nomura were quite enough to drive him frantic,
let alone into his friend's company. On the twenty-sixth he received a message
from Toyoda which revealed that his chief suspected Nomura of tampering with
Tokyo's instructions: ". . . I can easily see that, concerning the negotiations,
Your Honor's views are not infrequently at variance with mine . . . this is a
very serious matter and I am proceeding cautiously and deliberately. Therefore, I wish to caution you again not to add or detract a jot or tittle on your own
without first getting in contact with me. . . ."[24]

Not content with having sent Nomura on a virtually impossible mission, the Foreign Office now wanted to clap him into a diplomatic straitjacket, almost as if fearing he might succeed in spite of its efforts. Never had flexibility been more essential than at this time when Toyoda denied it to Nomura.

The first anniversary of the Tripartite Pact loomed ominously for Konoye and Toyoda. Konoye very much wanted the best of both worlds—a return to a profitable economic relationship with the United States along with maintenance of firm ties with the Axis. Toyoda fretted over what he considered "the lack of concern" Nomura demonstrated regarding the anniversary. To this Grew expressed quite natural surprise that Toyoda "had not conveyed to the Japanese Ambassador in Washington his own concern on this point."[25] It is possible that in his distaste for the Tripartite Pact, Nomura may have underestimated pro-Axis sentiment in Japan. On August 28 he had told Hull "that with regard to Japan's relations with the Axis there should be no difficulties, as the Japanese regarded their adherence to the Axis as merely nominal and as he could not conceive of his people being prepared to go to war with the United States for the sake of Germany."[26]

The shadow of the swastika and fasces hung over Toyoda. His message to Nomura of September 28 exudes urgency. He had informed Grew, he reported, that "I wished again to emphasize that the first anniversary of the conclusion of the Tripartite Alliance is the turning point and that this occasion is all the more grave . . . for the last few days a movement to strengthen the Axis has been afoot, and the popular psychology is being adverted toward this end." He hastened to add, "This does not mean at all that the power of the present government has dwindled or that the advocates of anti-Americanism have strengthened their position."[27] If not, what did he mean? Probably not even Toyoda himself could have clarified his thinking at this stage.

On September 29 Iguchi sent a lengthy message to Taro Terasaki, chief of the Foreign Office's American Bureau, giving his views concerning progress of the discussions. Father Drought had advised him: "Japanese government circles feel that there is absolutely no reason why the United States should not accept the most recent proposals. The fact that she has not done so, must be due to interference from some Washington source, Walsh cables."

It is difficult to understand how Bishop Walsh could possibly read the Japanese proposals and wonder why Washington did not rush to accept them. Either his Japanese friends were being less than candid with him, or he was of a naïveté to make one afraid, as the French say. Iguchi, who knew his business, stated flatly that "it is exceedingly unlikely that the United States had any intention of backing down from those established stands."[28]

Even Toyoda admitted in his message to Nomura of September 28 that the presence of "one influential admiral and one general" in the proposed Konoye entourage had "made the United States suspect that a hostile military was holding the whip hand over us." But he added, "Well, the integrity of Premier Konoye and of the present government ought to be a hundred per cent reliable, and the American Ambassador must have sufficiently advised his government on the trustworthiness of Prince Konoye."[29]

Grew had done exactly that. But what with several thousand miles between them and the potent Konoye charm, and only the cold record before them, Hull and his advisers had long since formed their own idea of the premier's "trustworthiness."

CHAPTER 31

"A

SIGNIFICANT

AND OMINOUS

CHANGE"

When Uncle Sam's sturdy boot propelled Lieutenant Commander Itaru Tachibana back to Japan in the summer of 1941, he found a home in the Naval General Staff's Intelligence Section.* He came into the Pearl Harbor picture at the time of the September war games in Tokyo, when Ogawa briefed him. Both Ogawa and Tachibana realized that Naval Intelligence, which had been based on the Great All-Out Battle concept, would require an entirely new slant to meet the demands of Yamamoto's strategic about-face.

From careful study of local newspapers and information from the Honolulu consulate, a pattern had emerged: The Fleet left harbor on either Mondays or Tuesdays and returned on Saturdays or Sundays. By monitoring radio traffic of American ships and shipborne planes, the Japanese concluded that the enemy Fleet customarily practiced in an area about forty-five minutes' flight from Pearl Harbor.[1]

But for a successful attack on Kimmel's warships, the Japanese needed exact information about the ships when they were in Pearl Harbor. "It became essential," Tachibana recalled, "to foresee exactly, at least two weeks beforehand, whether or not the U.S. Fleet would be in harbor on the designated day of attack; to figure out the status of patrols around Pearl Harbor; to have the Hawaiian attack air force crews familiar with the topography of the Hawaiian district and U.S. warships; and promptly establish firm and reserve intelligence channels through which timely information could be obtained."[2]

So on September 24, at the behest of Naval Intelligence, the Foreign Ministry dispatched the most significant set of instructions thus far sent to the

---

*See Chapter 18.

Honolulu consulate. "Strictly secret" Message No. 83 clearly reflected a new orientation:

> Henceforth, we would like to have you make reports concerning vessels along the following lines insofar as possible:
> 1. The waters (of Pearl Harbor) are to be divided roughly into five sub-areas. (We have no objection to your abbreviating as much as you like.)
>   Area A. Waters between Ford Island and the Arsenal.
>   Area B. Waters adjacent to the Island south and west of Ford Island. (This area is on the opposite side of the Island from Area A.)
>   Area C. East Loch.
>   Area D. Middle Loch.
>   Area E. West Loch and the communicating water routes.
> 2. With regard to warships and aircraft carriers, we would like to have you report on those at anchor (these are not so important), tied up at wharves, buoys and in docks. (Designate types and classes briefly. If possible we would like to have you make mention of the fact when there are two or more vessels along side the same wharf.)[3]

In effect this message placed over Pearl Harbor an invisible grid whereon Yoshikawa and his assistants could plot the position of each individual ship in its specific anchorage. Heretofore Tokyo had been principally interested in U.S. Fleet movements. Now the Navy wanted precise information on the exact location of vessels in harbor as well. This dispatch became famous as the "bomb plot" message, so we shall refer to it as such for convenience.

For a number of reasons the U.S. Army did not translate this dispatch until October 9. When the document reached Col. Rufus C. Bratton in G-2, it riveted his attention, as well it might. In no other instance did the Japanese set up what amounted to a grid system for reporting the presence and position of ships in harbor.

Bratton thought that "the Japanese were showing unusual interest in the port at Honolulu,"[4] but his chief, General Miles, saw nothing to get excited about. He viewed the message as part of the normal Japanese traffic concerning American naval movements. Perhaps such information would hint to the Japanese when Kimmel intended to take his fleet to sea. Even Tokyo's desire to know when two or more vessels lay alongside the same wharf might mean that "at least the inner one could not come out as quickly or as soon . . . as the outer one. . . ." At most, Miles thought, the message might signify "the Japanese intent to execute a submarine attack on these ships."[5]

In any case, "the evaluation of those messages that primarily concerned the fleet was the primary responsibility of the ONI."[6] Bratton and his Far Eastern Section had consistently rated the probability of war with Japan higher than Miles did. "It was perfectly natural for them that they should think that their particular devil was the big devil."[7]

Bratton routed the message to Stimson, Marshall, and Brigadier General Leonard T. Gerow, chief of the War Plans Division,[8] without apparently stirring a flicker of interest at this high level. Still troubled by the dispatch's sinister import, Bratton discussed the matter several times with his colleagues in Naval Intelligence. They explained it as either "a device to reduce the volume of radio traffic" by "substituting numbers or letters for entire sentences" or "a plan for sabotage of such ships as were in Pearl Harbor"; some conceded that it might be a plan for a submarine or an air attack. But—a very big "but"—his naval friends assured Bratton "on numerous occasions" that "when the emergency arises the fleet is not going to be there, so this is a waste of time and effort on the part of the Japanese consul."[9]

Bratton had no authority to warn the Hawaiian Department, even had he considered Hawaii in immediate danger. Although convinced that war with Japan was inevitable, he did not think it logical for Japan "to go out of her way deliberately to attack an American installation."[10]

Twin handcuffs fastened Bratton's hands: a directive that G-2 would not "send any intelligence to overseas garrisons which might have tactical repercussions without the approval of the Operations Division" and a prohibition against sending out any intelligence based upon Magic because the Navy did not trust the Army networks.[11] Occasionally Bratton had tried to buck the system and paid for his zeal with a thorough chewing out.[12]

Commander Kramer of ONI sped the "bomb plot" message through Navy channels—director of Naval Intelligence, director of War Plans, Stark, Knox, and the White House. Kramer viewed the dispatch as a Japanese attempt to simplify communications and cut down on expenses.[13] He considered it worthy of one asterisk, which he bestowed upon "interesting messages," but not the double asterisk allotted to "especially important or urgent messages." He also prepared a gist of it, or flag sheet, reading succinctly: "Tokyo directs special reports on ships with [sic] Pearl Harbor which is divided into five areas for the purpose of showing exact locations." In addition, the message and its flag sheet went to Hart. Kramer was under the impression that Kimmel also received it because "everything that went to CinCAF, Asiatic Fleet, also went either as an action addressee or information addressee to Admiral Kimmel."[14] Actually he never received it.

Kramer's superiors in Naval Intelligence showed some interest, but not much. The message happened to be processed when Captain Theodore S. Wilkinson, due to become the director of ONI on September 15, was visiting his new domain. The Navy considered Wilkinson a brilliant man. But he knew little about Naval Intelligence.[15] His key subordinates did not hold this against him, however. Directors of ONI came and went with little apparent regard for logic. "In my opinion he had a magnificent mind," McCollum testified, adding ingenuously, "He accepted my recommendations almost in toto."[16]

Later Wilkinson vaguely recollected mentioning "to one or more officers that the Japs seemed quite curious as to the lay-out in Pearl Harbor and . . . that that was evidence of their nicety of intelligence." He did not recommend sending the message to the field, nor did he recall any discussion on that point.[17] He explained: ". . . we didn't recognize it pointed specifically to an attack on Hawaii, and . . . we were very jealous at that time of the security of the code and the fact that we were breaking the code. . . ." Moreover, he believed that Kimmel knew his forces were constantly being spied on. To Wilkinson, "The specific inquiry as to the division of Pearl Harbor into several areas . . . was another refinement on that intelligence."[18]

Commander McCollum, head of the Far Eastern Section of ONI, was not in Washington when the "bomb plot" message made the rounds, having returned to his desk on October 16 from a trip to Europe. He did not recall seeing the dispatch at that time. If he did, "it did not make much impression" on his mind. He believed that the Foreign Ministry was sending to Kita "explicit directions as the type of intelligence that was needed, much more in detail than any of the other key consulates on the west coast, because he did not have the benefit of the services of a Japanese Naval Intelligence officer within his consulate."[19] Obviously McCollum did not know that Kita's "Chancellor Morimura" was in reality Tadeo Yoshikawa, a Naval Intelligence Officer.

If he had seen the message, McCollum thought that like Kramer, he would have considered it an effort to cut down "the frequently voluble type of reports . . . which the Jap Navy did not like. . . ."[20] He also considered that how and where the ships anchored in Pearl Harbor "might be interpreted to indicate the facility with which the fleet was prepared to move,"[21] rather like trying to determine how rapidly the fire department can answer an alarm by charting the firemen's bunking arrangements.

The way to find out how fast a fleet can sortie is to clock it in the act, which Yoshikawa had done more than once. In this case the "devious" Oriental mind was far more direct than the Occidental. The American intelligence officers— every one a clever and dedicated man—were so busy lopping and stretching the "bomb plot" message to fit the Procrustean bed of preconception that they missed its obvious import.

Nor did the dispatch make any impression on Stark. He could not remember having seen it, and he admitted that if he had, he would have diagnosed it as "just another example of their [the Japanese's] great attention to detail." To add another ingredient to this witches' brew of misunderstandings and assumptions, Stark believed that Kimmel had "the equipment or the forces trained to decode and translate these diplomatic and military messages. . . ." He had inquired "on two or three occasions as to whether or not Kimmel could read certain dispatches when they came up" and "was told that he could."[22]

It was Turner, director of War Plans, to whom Stark posed these queries; he in turn put the question to Noyes, director of Naval Communications.[23] Turner later testified, "On every occasion I was assured that the Commander-in-Chief was getting as much as we were, and to the best of my knowledge and belief, he was getting it sooner than we were." Turner believed that this included Magic; that was why he "did not inform the Commander-in-Chief of the contents of these messages."[24]

Noyes, however, denied having told Turner that Kimmel was decrypting such dispatches. "I would never have made the statement that all ciphers could be translated in Pearl Harbor," he testified.[25]

When Turner passed his findings to Stark, the CNO "did not consider it necessary to go any further."[26] The question inevitably arises: Why did Stark not ask Noyes or Kirk, Wilkinson's predecessor? They were on the same staff level as Turner and more directly concerned with the problem. This is a good example of the dangerous misunderstandings that can arise when obtaining important information at second hand. But Stark emphasized that his belief that Kimmel had access to Magic did not influence him in what he sent or did not send to the field commanders. He admitted that it was his responsibility to keep them informed "of the main trends and of information which might be of high interest to them."[27] Certainly the "bomb plot" message fell into that category.

Later Turner claimed that he had "no recollection of having seen" the "bomb plot" message at the time and did not know why he had not seen it. He thought that it changed the picture toward Pearl Harbor sufficiently that he would have taken it up with Wilkinson or possibly Ingersoll, but he "would not have initiated any dispatch on that subject. . . ." He considered such action ONI's responsibility.[28]

Both Short and Kimmel were exceedingly bitter when they discovered long after war broke out that Washington had had this important message in hand and had not passed it to them. Short testified:

> While the War Department G-2 may not have felt bound to let me know about the routine operations of the Japanese in keeping track of our naval ships, they should certainly have let me know that the Japanese were getting reports of the exact location of the ships in Pearl Harbor . . . because such details would be useful only for sabotage, or for air or submarine attack on Hawaii. . . . This message, analyzed critically, is really a bombing plan for Pearl Harbor.[29]

Kimmel agreed with Short—and in far more forceful language. He could accept "the general pattern" of Japanese interest in American fleet movements as "conventional espionage," only to be expected. But, he stated:

> With the dispatch of September 24, 1941, and those which followed, there was a significant and ominous change in the character of the information which the Japanese Government sought and obtained. . . . It was no longer merely directed to ascertaining the general whereabouts of ships of the fleet. It was directed to the presence of particular ships of the fleet. It was directed to the presence of particular ships in particular areas. . . . These Japanese instructions and reports pointed to an attack by Japan upon the ships in Pearl Harbor. The information sought and obtained, with such painstaking detail, had no other conceivable usefulness from a military standpoint. . . . Its effective value was lost completely when the ships left their reported berthings in Pearl Harbor.
>
> . . . No one had a greater right than I to know that Japan had carved up Pearl Harbor into subareas and was seeking and receiving reports as to the precise berthings in that harbor of the ships of the fleet. . . .

He had received Grew's report of January 1941, together with the Navy's assurance that no such Japanese attack appeared "imminent or planned for in the foreseeable future." He believed that the message of September 24 indicated such a move and therefore "completely altered the information and advice previously given" him. Kimmel further declared:

> Knowledge of these intercepted Japanese dispatches would have radically changed the estimate of the situation made by me and my staff. . . . Knowledge of a probable Japanese attack on Pearl Harbor afforded an opportunity to ambush the Japanese striking force as it ventured to Hawaii. It would have suggested the wisdom of concentrating our resources at that end. . . . [30]

Miles protested that the dispatch, if "taken alone, would have been of great military significance but it was not taken alone. . . . It was one of a great number of messages being sent by the Japanese to various parts of the world in their attempt to follow the movements of our naval vessels." Miles's erroneous notion, which apparently all his colleagues who saw the message shared, reveals that Washington did not grasp the contrast between the mainstream of Japanese messages and No. 83. Taken alone or in context, the "bomb plot" message stands by itself. Later, when challenged to produce one other such dispatch, the G-2 had to admit that "if you mean similar in dividing the harbor into sections, there are no such messages that I know of." He also conceded that it was not "a ship-movement report," but "primarily a message dividing up the waters of Pearl Harbor into convenient areas for reporting the presence of ships, United States warships."[31]

Defense against an attack on Pearl Harbor had been the basis of plans, maneuvers, blackouts, and reports for years. The awareness of such danger appears throughout the correspondence of top military and civilian officials during late 1940 and early 1941. It formed the basis of the Martin-Bellinger Report of March 31 and the Farthing Report, which went to Washington in late August. The United States had poured a fortune in men and matériel into the Hawaiian Islands, especially Oahu. What was the purpose if not to be ready for war with Japan and to meet a strike by its Navy against Pearl Harbor?

By itself the "bomb plot" intercept would not prove that the Japanese intended to attack Pearl Harbor. But together with other messages which followed from Tokyo and the consulate in Honolulu, it might have provided Kimmel and Short with a clue. Information which appeared unimportant in Washington might have looked very different in Hawaii. Yet evaluation and dissemination of just such information were functions of the Army and Navy staffs in Washington. They failed to evaluate properly, and they did not disseminate to the parties of primary interest—Kimmel and Short. Still, there is no proof that a full appreciation of the "bomb plot" message in Washington would have changed the course of history, for what Kimmel and Short would have done with it must remain a matter for speculation.

Receipt of the "bomb plot" message caused quite a stir in Japan's Honolulu consulate. And it strengthened Yoshikawa's emerging conviction that his country planned some sort of attack on Pearl Harbor, possibly even a troop landing. As tension mounted through the summer and autumn, he and Kita discussed the possibility of an air strike against Pearl Harbor, although neither knew positively that this was the primary object of their intelligence gathering. Nevertheless, on the basis of the material which Tokyo requested, they assumed that such an attack would come.[32]

On September 29 Kita replied to Message No. 83 ("bomb plot") with a suggested refinement:

> The following codes will be used hereafter to designate the location of vessels:
> 1. Repair dock in Navy Yard (The repair basin referred to in my message to Washington #48): KS.
> 2. Navy dock in the Navy Yard (The Ten Ten Pier): KT.
> 3. Moorings in the vicinity of Ford Island: FV.
> 4. Alongside in Ford Island: FG (East and west sides will be differentiated by A and B respectively.)[33]

The U.S. Navy translated this message on October 10—just one day after the Army put No. 83 into clear language. Thus, Washington had a further opportunity to read more meaning into Japanese espionage activities on Oahu. But there is not even a hint in the official Pearl Harbor testimony that anyone connected the two messages.

By September Yoshikawa had gleaned all he could about the installations at Pearl Harbor, so he no longer had to waste time gathering statistical data, and the ships snuggled against their docks were old friends. Therefore, he had no difficulty in trying to fit his information into the modified "bomb plot" categories, and his past studies plus on-the-spot experience made him sensitive to any change in the military situation.[34]

He scouted numerous areas besides Pearl Harbor in trips scattered over many weeks. Mikami remembered taking him to windward Oahu five or six times, both alone and with Kotoshirodo. On these trips Yoshikawa directed Mikami to follow along the Kokokahi Road, with its excellent view of Kaneohe Naval Air Station.[35] Twice the agent and his faithful driver visited Wahiawa, which lies almost in the center of Oahu, conveniently near Schofield Barracks and Wheeler Field. On one of these jaunts Yoshikawa tried to enter Schofield Barracks, "but the sentry at the gate refused them permission . . . because Mikami's taxi did not have proper identification plates."[36]

In early autumn Yoshikawa expanded his "sight-seeing" from buses and cars into the air. He donned his brightest aloha shirt and took one of his geisha friends for a tourist flight over Oahu. During this trip he could see Wheeler Field and noted the number and direction of runways. Near the southwest coast of the island the plane swung eastward across Ewa and north of Pearl Harbor. Military security restrictions forbade sight-seeing planes to fly over Pearl Harbor, but Yoshikawa saw the anchorage and Hickam Field clearly. In his bird's-eye view of both Wheeler and Hickam, he estimated the number of planes by counting the hangars. The little aircraft then flew east of Aiea and back to Honolulu, the entire flight having taken no more than twenty or thirty minutes.

This trip gave Yoshikawa an overall picture of Oahu, firsthand experience of air conditions, a glance at Hickam, which had proved a hard nut to crack, and an aerial view, albeit restricted, of Pearl Harbor. It showed him where any destroyers or other craft might be cruising around or near Oahu. Perhaps most valuable of all, it confirmed the accuracy of his observations from ground level.[37]

The fact that the Japanese were spying on military and naval activities was no news to the Americans. But they "were helpless to stop it." Wilkinson later testified: "We could not censor the mails. We could not censor the dispatches. We could not prevent the taking of photographs. We could not arrest Japanese suspects. There was nothing we could do to stop it, and all hands knew that espionage was going on all along, and reports were going back to Japan."[38]

Several political leaders in Washington longed to do something about this deplorable situation. And it is another irony of the Pearl Harbor story that at the same time the Japanese intensified their activities on the intelligence front, Senator Guy M. Gillette of Iowa and Congressman Martin Dies of Texas planned to investigate Japanese subversion. Both men had been interested in the problem for some time; both had studied it carefully, were alarmed at what they found, and thought action should be taken without delay. What is more, both men were on the right track.

As chairman of the House Un-American Activities Committee, Dies was primarily interested in Communist machinations in the United States. But he had also been directing an investigation of Japanese propaganda and espionage. By August Dies and his committee had accumulated enough evidence to conclude that Japanese subversion represented a real threat to the United States. In order "to arouse the whole American people into a sense of impending crisis," he "made arrangements for 52 witnesses to proceed to Washington for public hearings early in September 1941."

Before taking final action, Dies wrote to the attorney general on August 27 to ascertain whether the hearings "would be satisfactory from the standpoint of the administration's plans as they related to the Japanese." On September 8 Matthew F. McGuire, acting attorney general, replied that the President, the secretary of state, and the attorney general all felt "quite strongly that hearings such as you contemplate would be inadvisable."[39]

But Dies did not accept McGuire's letter as final and continued to prod the executive branch. After conferring with Roosevelt, Dies returned to his office, telephoned Hull, and repeated the substance of his conversation with the President. The secretary agreed that the outlook in the Pacific was dark, but he feared that such an investigation would upset the diplomatic talks then under way between Tokyo and Washington. He also knew that the United States was woefully unprepared for war in the Pacific. According to Dies, he told Hull, as he had Roosevelt, that his committee would comply with the administration's wishes.[40]

And so the story appeared in the American press on Sunday, September 21, that the plans of the Dies Committee "for exhaustive investigation of Japanese subversive activities" had been called off. The previous day, however, Dies told newspapermen that "the potential Japanese spy system in this country is greater than the Germans ever dreamed of having in the Low Countries." And he added, "It would be a tremendous force to reckon with in the event of war."[41]

In less than two weeks Senator Gillette took action. On October 2, in conjunction with Senator Edwin C. Johnson of Colorado, he introduced a Senate resolution calling for an investigation of Japanese subversion. He specifically cited "the activities of Japanese consular officials in Hawaii and in the Western States."[42]

No one except the Japanese knew how close to home Gillette's remarks struck. On October 3 Kita "referred to Senator Gillette's allegations as 'uninformed rumors.'" And he insisted, "I do not know of any subversive activities that Senator Gillette mentions." That included his own bailiwick. "The Japanese consulate here was not engaged in any such activities. . . . Therefore, I see no reason why this consulate should be investigated."[43]

Kita need not have worried. Gillette's proposed investigation swiftly ran afoul of the State Department. On October 11—even as the "bomb plot" message bounced around Washington—Hull told Gillette that he strongly opposed congressional investigation of Japan's consular officials lest such action interfere with the sensitive American-Japanese diplomatic conversations. In view of the tension between the two countries and the critical international situation, he could not approve measures that would offend Japan or might even provoke her to action. So he implored Gillette to drop the matter. "Please, Senator," he begged, "I appeal to you—don't rock the boat!" Like Dies, Gillette deferred to the secretary of state's wishes.[44]

Hull confirmed to the press that he and Gillette had "exchanged information," but being, as Stimson called him, "such a cagey old bird," he declined to reveal "whether he had indorsed the Senator's proposal." Nevertheless, reporters sensed that Hull "did not wish to do anything at the moment which would stir up further ill feelings between Japan and this country."[45]

By now, fairly certain that no investigation would topple his espionage apple cart, Kita put in a good word for the local Japanese. He informed reporters on October 16 "that an investigation of alleged 'anti-American activities' here will prove Hawaii's Japanese to be loyal residents of the territory."[46] So once again, as in the case of Tachibana in June and the Dies Committee in September, the White House and the State Department went far out of their way to avoid offending Japan. In a speech in Congress in January 1942, Dies asserted that if his committee had been "permitted to reveal the facts . . . on Japanese espionage and sabotage" in September, "the tragedy of

Pearl Harbor might have been averted."[47] Gillette, too, tells us that "if the investigation had been made, the chances are the Japanese would not have had the nerve to strike us on December 7, 1941."[48]

Both men could have been wrong—or of course, they could have been right. Kusaka wrote that obtaining continuous information about the enemy was one of the four major problems to be solved in executing the attack.[49] The cutting off of its primary source of intelligence in Hawaii might well have stiffened backbones in the Naval General Staff to the point of refusing Yamamoto permission to go through with it. Indeed, Yamamoto himself might have paused if he had had to rely on chance and not current intelligence in order to find Kimmel's Fleet in Pearl Harbor.

CHAPTER 32

"NO

MATTER

WHAT

THE COST"

One day in late September[1] Fuchida had just stretched in the unaccustomed luxury of a few minutes' rest at the Kagoshima command post when a sailor came to him with the report "Commander Genda has just arrived and would like to see you, sir." Fuchida jumped up, surprised and gratified, and hastened to greet his friend.

Genda got right down to business. "In case war comes between Japan and the United States, Yamamoto plans to attack Pearl Harbor," he told Fuchida. His classmate's eyes widened with astonishment, but Genda gave him no time to digest this chunk of raw meat. "If the plan is approved," he continued, "you are to be flight leader of the attack force."

With this, many pieces of the puzzle fell into place for Fuchida. Almost overwhelmed by the unexpected honor as well as the daring concept, he stammered his proud acceptance.

Having broken the news, Genda whisked Fuchida off to *Akagi* for a staff conference. On the way he explained that while the general outline had been completed, many details remained to be worked out, and he wanted Fuchida to have a hand in perfecting the operational plan.

The afternoon sun sparkled on Ariake Bay as the two airmen boarded *Akagi*. When they entered Kusaka's cabin, the tension in the air struck Fuchida with almost physical impact. He saw Nagumo and a sprinkling of his staff crowded around two tables. All the officers looked at Fuchida as if sizing him up, and under this barrage of appraising eyes he grew warm with embarrassment.[2]

Some of those present already knew Fuchida favorably. Kusaka, who had been skipper of *Akagi* when Fuchida served his first tour of duty aboard the flagship, considered him "a good airman and a brilliant leader of men."[3]

Genda's fine assistant, Yoshioka, characterized him as "a remarkable character and the best man I ever knew for his ability to get along with other people, his composure and coolness under pressure and fire."[4]

Fuchida knew Nagumo, but he had never served under him before. Although fully aware of the admiral's excellent record and general popularity in the Navy, Fuchida wondered if Nagumo was indeed the ideal leader for the revolutionary First Air Fleet. He knew Nagumo was not an air admiral, and he struck Fuchida as a conservative type.

The flight leader and Kusaka exchanged bows and smiles of mutual esteem. Then the chief of staff motioned Fuchida to approach the tables, one of which held a model of Oahu, the other a mock-up of Pearl Harbor on a larger scale. Kusaka briefed Fuchida on the plan's background. "We want you to begin the special training for this purpose," he emphasized.[5]

Next, Genda launched into a discussion of the torpedo program. He explained that the battleships moored in double rows beside Ford Island, only about 500 meters from the harbor shore. Moreover, on that shore stood high cranes and all the usual paraphernalia of a dockyard area. So far Japan had no torpedo which did not sink into the mud at a greater depth than the forty-foot waters of Pearl Harbor; however, while the technicians worked out a suitable missile, Fuchida could be supervising the flight training.

Privately Fuchida thought that his friend wanted plenty. Who but Genda, he reflected, would evolve a scheme to attack the U.S. Pacific Fleet in a citadel widely touted as impregnable, using a weapon not yet perfected! But he had the utmost respect for his classmate's farsightedness and daring spirit. Moreover, he had a streak of fatalism in his nature. As he wrote later, he felt "some affinity of destiny that I always found myself taking on the job of putting Genda's ideas into practice."[6]

Nagumo and his staff seemed to want Fuchida's opinion of the Pearl Harbor plan on the spot, but this was too big a project for a newcomer to express a snap judgment. Nor could Fuchida accept the torpedo scheme without a closer look at all the factors involved, so he asked to see a chart of Pearl Harbor to supplement the model. Yoshioka produced one, and with the actual water-level figures in front of him, Fuchida declared, "This is too shallow for a torpedo attack against the American warships. I suggest that no such strike be planned, for this is not an efficient attack method." All present thrashed out the matter for some time. Kusaka decided that they must leave the torpedo problem unsettled for the moment. Let Fuchida train his pilots along this line, but with no hint that anything special hung upon it.[7]

Fuchida next turned his attention to horizontal bombing, his own home ground. "We cannot rely only on torpedoes," he remarked. "Nor can we expect too much from dive bombing because the missiles are too light to penetrate the heavy armor of a United States battleship. We must work on high-level bombing and train incessantly until our bombardiers are good enough."

Fuchida knew all too well the difficulties which had almost ruled horizontal bombing out of the picture, but he believed that the torpedo program presented obstacles no less daunting. Even if the Japanese could solve the knotty problems of a workable torpedo and effective bombing technique, he could not imagine that the Americans would neglect the elementary precaution of installing antitorpedo nets around their ships. Genda based his assumption that the harbor would be free of such devices upon an intelligence report dated March 1941. Since then the United States had had ample time to place the nets. Moreover, Fuchida stressed that the American habit of double mooring meant that only the outboard ship would be vulnerable to torpedoes.[8] The entire inboard group would escape almost scot-free because the dive bombers could inflict but relatively light damage.

This suggestion was right in line with Genda's own thinking. He proposed that the high-level bombers fly no lower than 5,000 meters (16,404 feet) to avoid antiaircraft fire. Fuchida believed that 3,000 meters (9,843 feet) would be the minimum altitude from which they could pierce the armor plating on battleships yet permit a high percentage of hits. "The risk is worth running to ensure maximum destruction," he stated. The dive bombers could take care of the American carriers.[9] This argument also meshed with Genda's plans, and either by happy accident or design—for he knew his Genda—Fuchida had used the phrase "maximum destruction," the key to his friend's heart.

From the moment Genda explained his assignment, Fuchida brought a new dimension to the Pearl Harbor picture. Henceforth he and Genda formed a unique team—Genda the creative genius supplying the original ideas, Fuchida the aggressive activist hammering them into reality. Genda's mind was the rapier—flashing, pointed, flexible, deadly—Fuchida's, the broadsword—blunt-pointed but sharp-edged, solid, durable.

As the briefing drew to a close, Kusaka turned to Fuchida and charged him solemnly, "Let me repeat—this is the most secret thing of all secrets. I want to take every possible step to keep it even from your flying crews when they train for this mission."[10]

Nagumo had said little throughout the discussion, but he never took his eyes off Genda and Fuchida. More than once he broke into the conversation to ask the flight leader, "Is everything going to be OK?" Now he repeated his query. Fuchida answered honestly, "I can't tell you at this time, sir, because everything depends on our training from now on."

Fuchida turned back to Kusaka and pondered the chief of staff's words for a moment. Then he asked, "May I tell the group commanders our mission? They will not be able to do their best if they don't know what they are doing and what their objective is." After thinking this over seriously, Kusaka replied, "Very well, but not just yet. We will tell them a little bit later."[11] Kusaka still hoped that the Navy would not have to embark upon this reckless venture. Until the day of decision the fewer who knew of the scheme, the better.

The whole question of how best to use Japan's naval air power deeply concerned Nagumo as well as Kusaka. It also preyed on the minds of Tsukahara and Onishi of the Eleventh Air Fleet.[12] Nagumo and Tsukahara were old friends, having been classmates at both Eta Jima and the Naval Staff College.

They shared many opinions on the strategy and tactics of sea warfare and now agreed that they and representatives of their staffs should get together to discuss their mutual problems. So in late September Nagumo, Kusaka, Oishi, Genda, Yoshioka, and Ono traveled to Kanoya to represent the First Air Fleet. There Tsukahara, Onishi, Takahashi, and one or two others joined them to present the case of the Eleventh Air Fleet.[13]

At this place Tsukahara and most of his staff learned about the projected Pearl Harbor attack for the first time. Tsukahara reacted in a markedly negative way to what he considered a wild gamble which would devour ships, planes, and men urgently required for the Southern Operation. But he did not go deeply into the project except as it affected his own air operations.[14]

In case of war the immediate objective of the Eleventh Air Fleet, operating from Formosan land bases, would be to wipe out the growing air capability of the United States in the Philippines at the earliest possible moment. This was imperative if Japanese landings were to succeed. Tsukahara worried particularly over the lack of adequate fighter cover for his bombers. The Zero could not make the entire run to the target and back because the principal United States airfields lay in the Manila area, which added up to a radius of more than 500 miles.[15] What is more, some of these air bases lay out of reach of the bombers on Formosa. Destruction of such bases might have to wait until the invasion got under way, and what might happen in the meantime no man could foresee. The enemy could well launch a hard-hitting counter-offensive or even beat the Japanese to the punch. And Tsukahara had still another mission—a similar operation over Malaya from southern French Indochina.[16]

Under the circumstances, the Eleventh Air Fleet wanted strong carrier-based support—and the only source would be the First Air Fleet. So Tsukahara put the bite on Nagumo. Would he part with some of his planes to beef up the Eleventh Air Fleet? After some discussion both Nagumo and Kusaka agreed.[17]

Onishi, who chaired the meeting, had a good deal to say. By this time he had changed course 180 degrees about the Pearl Harbor venture, largely thanks to Kusaka's persuasion. The latter talked with Onishi many times during September. Onishi first came to listen to Kusaka's views, then to share them.[18] Naturally other considerations entered into Onishi's altered attitude. As chief of staff of the Eleventh Air Fleet he owed his primary loyalty to the mission of his own organization. To help Yamamoto lay the groundwork for a Pearl Harbor attack—an isolated chore—was one thing; to sponsor the project at the expense of his assigned duties was quite another.

Listening to Onishi, Yoshioka gained the impression that he believed Japan could not win a Pacific war with the United States no matter how it went about it. If Japan confined its push to the southern regions, even including the Philippines, the Americans would be angry, would even fight, but would remain open to negotiations. However, if it attacked Pearl Harbor, that would make the United States "so insanely mad" that any hope for a compromise peace would go up in flames.[19]

Genda did not think Onishi quite that pessimistic. He recalled Onishi's saying that the war would certainly be very difficult for Japan. Therefore, if it took the plunge, it must do so with a steely determination; otherwise, the dangers would overcome it.[20] Tsukahara likewise entertained grave doubts about the ultimate outcome of the conflict. He did not see how a long war "could terminate successfully for Japan."[21]

During the Kanoya meeting Genda held his peace. Obviously all the top brass had ranged itself solidly against the Pearl Harbor project, and Genda had better sense than to waste his strength butting against a brick wall. But behind his mask of silent courtesy he writhed at the prospect of stripping the First Air Fleet to clothe the Eleventh. Such a course, he believed, would gravely jeopardize the Hawaiian operation.[22]

The conference at Kanoya reinforced the Eleventh Air Fleet's conviction that it should have substantial carrier-based fighter support in its strikes against the Philippines. The discussions also pointed up sharply the lack of solid endorsement of the Pearl Harbor plan. Largely as a result of this parley, Kusaka and Onishi made up their minds to face Yamamoto directly with their opposition to his hazardous scheme.[23] Kusaka therefore requested Nagumo's permission to speak with Yamamoto. Nagumo gave it readily, for he feared that the plan would turn out to be a costly blunder. During the war games he had suggested that "appropriate recommendations should be made to Yamamoto."[24] Tsukahara authorized Onishi to join Kusaka in this mission.

If the two men felt some inner trepidation as they set forth, who could fault them? Yamamoto towered at the head of the Combined Fleet, an awesome Neptune to be propitiated rather than baited. But Kusaka would have fought the devil with his own pitchfork if necessary for the good of Japan. On this early autumn day[25] he needed every ounce of his moral courage. He knew that for months Yamamoto had been dead set on attacking Pearl Harbor.

Kusaka also knew that Yamamoto did not feel the same personal warmth toward him that he did toward Onishi. "Yamamoto liked Onishi very much because he was so frank," Kusaka explained after the war. "Yamamoto also liked me, but not in the same way. It would be more accurate to say that he admired me—that is, my puritanism, my morality. As for Onishi, Yamamoto liked him rather than admired him. He trusted Onishi implicitly however, and without reservations. But in my case there were certain limitations which Yamamoto imposed."[26]

Nevertheless, in this instance Kusaka could pull more weight than Onishi. The latter had only a personal connection with the Pearl Harbor plan, whereas Kusaka had an important official relationship to the operation. It was not the first time he had gone to the flagship "to discuss the inadvisability of the Pearl Harbor attack with Yamamoto."[27] But this occasion bore a special stamp of finality. The war games lay in the past, the political situation was reaching a climax, and the air training had entered a more active phase.

Yamamoto knew about the opposition to his plan, and naturally it displeased and disturbed him. Nonetheless, he received Kusaka and Onishi graciously. Along with Ugaki and several of his staff, Yamamoto listened "almost in silence" as the visitors argued against the terrible gamble.[28] Onishi, the last man in the world to look straight into Yamamoto's sardonic eye and argue against the Pearl Harbor project on the basis of its risks and operational difficulties, dwelt instead on the overriding importance of the southern strategy and the urgent need for carrier support against the Philippines. He also urged consideration of time. The longer the diplomatic crisis dragged out, the more alert the U.S. Navy would become to any possible Japanese move. He feared the time for exploiting the surprise factor to the full had already passed. Moreover, the weather in early winter would be unfavorable.[29]

Thereupon Yamamoto requested the opinion of his staff officer for air. Sasaki outlined the condition of the enemy's air force in the Philippines on the basis of information received from the Naval General Staff; from this he deduced that the Eleventh Air Fleet had just about enough tools to do the job.[30]

Onishi's manner was mild, more in the nature of one making recommendations than objections, but the atmosphere heated up when Kusaka spoke. In fact, he attacked Yamamoto's premise "very severely" and in his earnestness overstepped the bounds of Japanese politeness. "You are an amateur naval strategist, and your ideas are not good for Japan," he told Yamamoto roundly. "This operation is a gamble."[31]

"I like games of chance," Yamamoto retorted angrily. "You have told me that the operation is a gamble, so I shall carry it out!" Then his ready sense of humor came to the rescue, and he continued half in jest, "You always attack me for everything I do and think because my mind runs in speculative channels.[32] Don't talk so much of gambling, though I am very fond of playing cards and *shogi*."[33]

Then he called upon Kuroshima to rebut Kusaka's and Onishi's arguments. This the former did with irrepressible gusto.[34] Not only did invisible chains of loyalty blind him to Yamamoto, but he also believed almost devoutly in the Pearl Harbor plan. Yamamoto closed the discussion by declaring, "I understand your viewpoint very well, but this operation has my immovable confidence. Without this operation I cannot carry out the overall plan of war in the Pacific."[35]

Onishi accepted defeat with good grace, yet Kusaka remained unconvinced.[36] That night Onishi stayed aboard to play chess with Yamamoto, but Kusaka preferred to return to *Akagi*. Being a clever psychologist who knew how best to enlist the loyalty of his subordinates, Yamamoto accompanied Kusaka to the gangplank. Patting him gently on the shoulder, he said, "What you recommended was understandable, but as Commander-in-Chief I have resolved to carry out the Pearl Harbor attack no matter what the cost. So please do your best to develop the plan from now on." In a shrewd gesture of faith and confidence, he added, "I will place all the details of the project in your hands." He also specifically asked Kusaka to relate his wishes to Nagumo.

In the face of such stark sincerity, the trust in Yamamoto's eyes, and the veiled command in his voice, Kusaka vowed deep within himself to do his best. "Admiral, from now on, I won't say anything against this plan. I swear to exert my utmost efforts to develop your idea." With that shining promise in his heart Kusaka returned to *Akagi*.[37]

CHAPTER 33

"NOW

THE CLOUDS

WERE

RAISED"

K*aga* hummed with activity on October 2 as groups of officers from the other carriers of the First Air Fleet boarded the temporary flagship at anchor in Ariake Bay in response to Nagumo's summons. *Akagi* was under repair at Yokosuka Naval Base.[1] This gathering included Nagumo and most of his staff, the commanders in chief of the Second and Fifth Carrier Divisions and members of their staffs, the skippers of all six carriers, the air officers of each flattop, and a number of key flight officers, including Fuchida and Murata.[2]

Fuchida was beginning to worry about reconciling the need for secrecy with getting the most out of his fliers. They were brave, capable, and hardworking but lacked the special zing that a sense of direction would give them. Fuchida believed that the principal flight leaders should be informed so that they might infect their men with their own enthusiasm. He particularly wanted Murata to know the score in order to tap that little daredevil's reservoir of experience.[3]

Of the six carrier skippers, all captains, three had studied aviation at Kasumigaura: Kiichi Hasegawa of *Akagi*, Jisaku Okada of *Kaga*, and Tomeo Kaku of *Hiryu*. Ryusaku Yanagimoto of *Soryu* was something of a Navy legend. He neither smoke nor drank, enough to label a man as eccentric in the Japanese Navy. Although not a flier, he developed a sincere interest in naval aviation after he came to *Soryu*. For this reason, his officers and in particularly all his pilots admired him.[4] The other carrier captains present were Takatsugu Jojima from *Shokaku* and Ichibei Yokokawa from *Zuikaku*. It was said that Jojima could navigate a warship even on dry land.[5]

The air officers of Nagumo's flattops were responsible for such matters as launching, recovery, loading, fueling, and general handling of aircraft. In combat they controlled the flight deck. These officers were experienced pilots.

After October 15, 1941, they all held the rank of commander. At the time of the meeting aboard *Kaga*, each air officer was busily engaged in pilot training. Four of them also commanded air bases in Kyushu: Shogo Masuda of *Akagi*, at Kagoshima; Naohiro Sata of *Kaga*, at Tomitaka; Takahisa Amagai of *Hiryu*, at Izumi; and Ikuto Kusumoto of *Soryu*, at Kasanohara. The two remaining air officers, Tetsujiro Wada and Hisao Shimoda, served aboard *Shokaku* and *Zuikaku* respectively.

At this time the First Air Fleet was not a cohesive unit in one harbor. *Akagi* had anchored in Ariake Bay on September 16 to be near the center of flight training activities and spent most of the autumn in that location. Occasionally the flagship sailed to Saeki so that Nagumo could confer with Yamamoto aboard *Nagato*. On September 16 *Soryu* dropped anchor off Hosojima near the Tomitaka training field about halfway down the eastern coast of Kyushu. The carrier also acted as a floating supply depot, Tomitaka being only a temporary base and not well equipped. Her sister ship, *Hiryu*, arrived that same day near Izumi on the opposite side of Kyushu. Of the two new flattops, *Zuikaku* underwent finishing touches at Kure, the large naval base in the Inland Sea, while her pilots trained from *Shokaku*, which would anchor off Beppu Bay in northeastern Kyushu on October 10.[6]

"I asked you here because we are going to attack Hawaii in case Japan and the United States go to war." Nagumo spaced his words carefully. ". . . We must make every effort to be successful. The problem is to keep secret, for if there should be a leak it would mean certain defeat. But we cannot devote ourselves to training if we keep everything under a veil of secrecy. Neither could we plan and train effectively. . . ."[7] Here for the first time many officers learned their true mission.

"I keenly felt that my officers and men had not yet been sufficiently trained," stated Jojima. "What troubled me most was how to organize our training so that the new carrier could display her combined fighting strength to the fullest extent."[8]

Many of the air officers heartily endorsed Yamamoto's scheme. Shimoda thought the plan "wonderful," although it entailed a hair-raising risk. "But this . . . made the operation all the more potential," he explained, "because the greater the risk, the less chance the U.S. Navy would expect such a blow." At this conference Shimoda talked at length with Shimazaki, who would lead the second attack wave. "Shimazaki also thought it would be a success because the United States would never expect such a bold stroke."[9]

Sata believed that if Japan went to war, the Pearl Harbor plan was sound and necessary. He "never heard of anyone who objected to it," and he added that "the young officers had very good morale at the time and were enthusiastic about the plan."[10]

Amagai considered that the Japanese Navy would attack the U.S. Fleet at the outbreak of war, although he had not thought precisely in terms of Pearl Harbor. He was more pleased than surprised, however, when he heard of the plan. "Now the clouds were raised and everyone knew the score," he said, "an honest resolution to do his very best in the forthcoming attack was the daily oath of every officer present." Some of the carrier skippers were equally enthusiastic. Kaku considered the plan the greatest operation of its type in history and thought everyone should go all out to make it a resounding success.[11]

Kusaka followed Nagumo with a few remarks. "The success of this operation will depend upon the torpedo attack," he emphasized. Then Genda explained the plan. Using the models of Oahu and Pearl Harbor, he pointed out the bases marked for attack and the position of the ships. He assigned targets to the various air groups. Above all, he stressed specialization; for example, an air group assigned to dive-bomb warships would concentrate all of its training on that specific task. Time was too short to waste on any other objective.[12]

When this two-hour session ended, the First Air Fleet had passed another milestone on the road to Pearl Harbor. Not only did this important conference appreciably widen the circle of those in the know, but it also gave a sense of direction, purpose, and urgency to key officers in Nagumo's fleet.

No doubt Yamamoto would have been pleased had he witnessed the zeal and positive planning taking place aboard *Kaga*. By this time he had become very much concerned about the opposition to his plan. He knew that Nagumo and Kusaka had not changed their inner convictions; they had merely bowed to his own superior will and authority. "There are admirals in the Combined Fleet who are against the Pearl Harbor attack," he said to Watanabe shortly after his conference with Kusaka and Onishi. He added thoughtfully, "Perhaps it would be better to rely on young officers who can be trusted."[13]

Coincidentally or not, during the autumn Genda and Fuchida took an increasingly active role. Yamamoto had a sincere affection for both these aggressive officers. Fuchida he respected for his skill as a pilot and his ability to handle men; Genda he valued as a veritable quarry of "unique and remarkable" ideas.[14] The Commander in Chief took a deep personal interest in the First Air Fleet's training and from time to time dropped in to inspect it at Kagoshima, Kasanohara, and Ariake Bay. Also, Nagumo, Kusaka, and Oishi visited *Nagato* many times to meet with Yamamoto, Ugaki, and Kuroshima. On these occasions the First Air Fleet's top brass had been such wet blankets that Yamamoto became worried about the morale of the airmen.

Knowing that a commander's attitude can stamp itself on his men, Yamamoto occasionally dispatched Sasaki directly to Genda to inquire about the fliers' state of mind. In many respects he was more concerned about his eagles than about Nagumo, who, if necessary, could be replaced; not even Yamamoto could boot out all the flying officers in the First Air Fleet. Genda always reassured Sasaki and developed the habit of following up any Nagumo visit to *Nagato* by a discreet one of his own. On these occasions he would emphasize to Kuroshima and Sasaki that the airmen's morale was high and that those who knew the mission had great confidence in its ultimate success.[15]

Genda and Fuchida had free access to Kusaka's cabin with its models of Oahu and Pearl Harbor. Because Kusaka respected both men and lacked the technical knowledge to evaluate their suggestions properly, he wanted "to have both Genda and Fuchida freely display their ability as they wished." So he accepted their recommendations as far as possible and quietly kept an eye on their activities.[16] His policy tacitly acknowledged Genda and to a lesser degree Fuchida as personally responsible in the First Air Fleet for the Pearl Harbor operation. This placed Nagumo in an awkward situation, surrounded by men who moved with brisk assurance in a world to which he was a stranger. Yoshioka stated that the admiral's "position in the First Air Fleet was something like that of an adopted son. . . . He was lost in the atmosphere of aircraft, felt insecure, and had to ease his way around."[17]

Of course, Genda and Fuchida had their problems, too. By this time they had decided on two attack waves because it would be physically impossible to launch all of Nagumo's planes at the same time. Fuchida would lead the first assault, and Shimazaki would follow with the second about an hour later. Genda had chosen Shimazaki because he was senior among the second-wave pilots, knew his job, and was a forceful leader.[18]

One of Fuchida's headaches concerned the development of a high-level bomb capable of piercing the deck of an American battleship. The Navy held experiments beginning around the end of September to test a special missile converted from 16-inch shells. The Yokosuka Naval Air Corps under Rear Admiral Keizo Ueno conducted these trial runs at Kashima Field, southeast of Kasumigaura. The tests had been going on for about ten days, with no hits achieved, when Ueno requested Nagumo to send some of his best pilots with their own aircraft to Kashima to see if they could brighten the picture.

Nagumo immediately grasped the implications of these tests. He sent for Fuchida posthaste and explained the situation. "This experiment is vital," he said in effect, "and upon it depends the success or failure of the Pearl Harbor attack. You will proceed at once to Kashima with your most skillful pilots. If the target is not big enough, it must be enlarged regardless of expense. It should simulate *West Virginia*." He further charged Fuchida with the strictest secrecy. "You will not say a single word about Pearl Harbor or even hint at it."[19]

When Fuchida and his five falcons arrived at Kashima, he was the only person there who knew about Operation Hawaii and hence could understand the immediate application of the experiments. For the first two days his pilots had no better luck than the fliers from Yokosuka. The observers took a pessimistic view, and indeed, Fuchida had already suggested that the target be enlarged when success crowned their efforts. On the afternoon of the third day Furukawa registered a direct hit which smashed through the plate. Fuchida hastened back to the flagship with an oral report. Nagumo fretted lest the target not be an exact replica of *West Virginia*, but Fuchida could assure him that the greatest care and skill had gone into the preparation of the target.[20]

Nevertheless, he kept an ace up his sleeve. Furukawa's successful drop had been from 3,000 meters (9,843 feet). This reconciled a discrepancy which had been worrying the Pearl Harbor planners—how to secure maximum accuracy and at the same time sufficient impetus to penetrate the heavy deck armor of a United States battleship. Up to this time 4,000 meters (13,123 feet) had been considered the minimum to yield enough impetus, with 5,000 meters (18,404 feet) preferred to escape possible antiaircraft fire. When satisfied that 3,000 meters would be the most effective height, as he had suggested at his initial briefing, Fuchida so reported to Nagumo. He had some difficulty in convincing the admiral, who kept bringing up the matter of antiaircraft fire. After all, had not his trusted air officer, Genda, preferred that higher altitude? But Fuchida brushed aside Nagumo's scruples with an offhand "Don't worry about that."[21]

Fuchida also disapproved of the conventional nine-plane arrowhead formation and recommended that it be changed to a five-plane unit looking something like this:

X

XX

X　X

This formation provided more, though smaller, attack units, which could concentrate heavily on any given target. As a final factor, the First Air Fleet had ninety Type 97 bombers at its disposal. Of these, forty had been earmarked for torpedo use. By dividing the remaining fifty into groups of five, Fuchida could play ten individual chessmen on the vast board.[22]

But these breakthroughs would be of little use unless marksmanship in high-level bombing improved appreciably. This program had been well under way when Fuchida reported for duty and took it under his wing. He also put Yoshioka to work on it. At about the same time, Amagai reported to *Hiryu* as air officer, bringing to his job an excellent record. After the early October briefing he received two major tasks: to help with the horizontal bombing and with the torpedo problems. On October 10, when the last batch of fliers destined for the Fifth Carrier Division swelled the strength of the First Air Fleet, they joined in high-level training at Usa under Shimazaki.[23]

Fuchida devoted all his considerable energy to this program. Indeed, immediately after the briefing aboard *Kaga* all training stepped up sharply. Hitherto there had been no particular separation of the horizontal and torpedo bombers, the aircraft being the same—the Type 97—and the airmen training for both. Now Fuchida split them up.[24] Of the original nine units, he selected the best four for torpedo training, keeping the remaining five for his high-level program. Some anger and disappointment ensued because many airmen wanted to become torpedo pilots but could not qualify. Those selected had to be able to make quick, accurate decisions, had to be fearless, and had to be gifted with split-second timing.

Genda and Fuchida also determined that none of the Fifth Carrier Division's airmen should participate in the torpedo attack because they lacked know-how and experience. Moreover, Hara's dive and high-level bombers would attack only air bases because these offered much larger targets than warships.

Fuchida decided that the four torpedo units should attack in single file rather than in a tight formation, the long, thin line being especially well adapted to Pearl Harbor with its narrow channel and many obstacles. So, on a pleasant autumn day, Fuchida, with Murata hovering nearby, lined up his flying crews at Kagoshima. "You have finished your preliminary training which has simulated a fleet engagement," he told them, "and from today will train in shallow-water torpedoing against anchored ships as an advanced course." He tossed this off so casually that the pilots perceived nothing strange.[25]

"As training torpedoes are not yet ready," he continued, "you are only going through the motions. You will climb to two thousand meters under the flight commander's lead and charge over the eastern tip of Sakurajima [the extinct volcano jutting into Kagoshima Bay]. Then circle down the valley of the Kotsuki River at five-hundred-meter intervals. Maintaining an altitude of fifty meters, go down the valley from Iwasakidani toward Kagoshima, flying over the city at forty meters."[26]

These instructions came as a real shock. Fuchida, that stickler for flight discipline, was ordering them to overfly a city at a whisker's breadth over 100 feet! And worse was yet to come. "As you pass over the Yamagataya Department Store, to port you will see a large water tank on the shore. As you pass over it, come down to twenty meters and release a torpedo." They would find a target buoy about 500 meters from shore. As they released, they must keep on an even keel at 160 knots, then climb to starboard and return to base. By this time Fuchida's men were almost beyond surprise. At this level any serious mistake could crash the plane into Kagoshima Bay.

"This," Fuchida added somewhat redundantly, "is a difficult task." Cautioning them to be bold but careful, he ended: "Lieutenant Murata will demonstrate."[27] Walking with Murata toward the torpedo ace's plane, Fuchida remarked, "I hope you can do it." Highly entertained by Fuchida's offhand and deadpan manner of issuing these fantastic instructions, Murata grinned and said, "You could be a fine actor!" Thereupon he scrambled into his plane, took off, and performed the maneuver with beautiful precision.[28]

The people of Kagoshima were greatly surprised that day to see plane after plane streak out of the valley toward the bay, barely clearing the city roofs. Fuchida beamed with satisfaction. No one bungled as one after another the planes zigzagged down the narrow valley, straightening out almost on the surface of the water as if propelled by giant cannon.[29] Henceforth this practice took place daily. The good citizens of Kagoshima began to despair of the Navy's discipline, for the fliers seemed to buzz the city at will. Even the prostitutes in the red-light district told each other that those Navy pilots were becoming unusually fresh.[30]

Murata stressed to his torpedomen that in future operations they probably would have to fly over land areas first, then swoop down to water level to launch their torpedoes. He also emphasized that this launching would be in shallow waters and areas where maneuvering might be limited. Lieutenant Jinichi Goto, squadron commander of *Akagi*'s torpedo pilots, found both Fuchida's and Murata's instructions excellent. They never so much as hinted at their exact objective, so that neither Goto nor any of his companions suspected that their target would be the ships in Pearl Harbor.[31] Most of them conjectured that they might be training for an attack on Singapore, and Fuchida rather encouraged this convenient red herring.[32]

The Izumi neighborhood fared no better than Kagoshima. There the torpedomen from *Soryu* and *Hiryu,* under their squadron commanders, Lieutenants Tsuyoshi Nagai and Heita Matsumura respectively, trained strenuously day and night. Nagai was another dashing, fighting type like Murata, a heavy drinker and somewhat fat. A handsome young man, Matsumura worked hard. "Sometimes we trained twelve hours a day. It was very severe," he said.[33]

In August and throughout September Matsumura and Nagai received a number of young, green fliers to be assimilated into the trained crews. But the program moved along better than expected. Within a month to six weeks even the new arrivals could take part in a carrier-borne operation. They made some progress in night training, especially carrier launches and recoveries. The program featured night flights by large groups because at this time the plan called for the aircraft to take off and fly most of their approach in the dark, reaching Pearl Harbor by sunrise.[34] But the First and Second Carrier Divisions also worked on the difficult task of launching torpedoes at night in the face of enemy searchlights. Matsumora's units practiced against a rock off Akune in the southwest part of Kyushu.[35] His men kept in high spirits, but the local farmers complained that the continuous din of engines caused their chickens to stop laying.[36]

At the time Fuchida took over as flight leader, the proper release altitude for dive bombers posed a question. Originally the pilot started his dive at 4,000 meters (about 13,123 feet), releasing his bomb at 600 meters (1,969 feet). But after a short time Egusa, who was to lead the dive bombers in the second attack wave, suggested waiting until 450 meters (1,476 feet) before releasing the bomb, thus increasing the chance of a direct hit.

This was a dangerous step because the pilot might not be able to pull out. Fuchida was certain that his superiors would forbid such a hazardous scheme. But determined to squeeze the last ounce of efficiency out of the dive bombers, he took it upon himself to approve the change. That almost plunged him into hot water because shortly after this decision one of the dive bombers crashed, resulting in serious discussions at the upper level. In the meantime, however, the change in release point proved so effective that Nagumo agreed to go along with it.[37]

Egusa established his Second Carrier Division men at Kasanohara, a small training field near the large supply base at Kanoya. *Settsu,* an antique battleship moored in Ariake Bay, served as target for the dive bombers. They used dud bombs so constructed as to emit white smoke when they made a direct hit. They tried three types of missiles, usually settling for a 10-kilogram (22-lb.) model because anything larger ran the risk of sinking the old relic.[38] The bomb eventually selected was the Type 99 250 kg. (550 lb.), but the conventional bomb-releasing equipment required modification to accommodate this type. Work continued on this project throughout the autumn and was not completed until just before departure for the rendezvous in mid-November.[39]

Somewhere along the line the First Air Fleet faced the unwelcome possibility that something might prevent Fuchida from leading the attack. Therefore, he and Genda tabbed Lieutenant Commander Takashi Hashiguchi of *Kaga* as his replacement. Hashiguchi was one of the Imperial Navy's foremost authorities on horizontal bombing, with combat experience in the Shanghai area.[40] He had little of Fuchida's buoyant aggressiveness, being of a gentle disposition and calm demeanor.[41]

On October 10, when the last group from the Fifth Carrier Division arrived, certain personnel changes took place. Lieutenant Commander Kakuichi Takahashi of *Shokaku* outranked Egusa, so he formally became leader of the dive bombers and eventually led them in the first attack wave. Like Shimazaki, his brother-in-law and particular crony, Takahashi was a man of solid practicality with an interest in judo. He had a ruddy complexion and was large by Japanese standards, honest, good-natured, and slow to anger. He might not be the quickest person in any gathering, but what his deliberate mind absorbed it retained, and he was an anchor of dependability.[42]

Takehashi not only took over the general dive-bombing program but also personally supervised that of the Fifth Carrier Division at Oita in northeastern Kyushu. With this program a new element entered the Pearl Harbor formula because it aimed at dive bombing the naval air base on Ford Island and all the other airfields in the Pearl Harbor area.[43]

Fuchida did not have too much to do with the fighter training. Genda took a particular interest in it, and Itaya was among the top fighter pilots in the Navy. Both Genda and Fuchida, however, made every effort to secure young pilots full of fresh energy. Many of the pilots assigned to the First Air Fleet had had combat experience in China, but the two leading spirits of the flight program did not especially want to attack Pearl Harbor only with "old China hands," who would be set in their ways. While by no means despising the seasoning which comes with combat experience, Genda and Fuchida looked for eager, gingery youngsters to handle the fighter program.[44]

It appeared for a while that any warm body in the cockpit of a Zero would be welcome, for skilled fighter pilots were in short supply. After a discussion on September 24 between Combined Fleet and Naval General Staff representatives, they decided to divert skilled crews from the Third and Fourth Carrier Divisions to the First and Second. In particular, the number of Zeros should be increased. This left the Third and Fourth almost bare of fighter planes, but it could not be helped. Next, they plucked most of the best men from the Yokosuka Air Group, forcing a reduction in the number of instructors while increasing the trainees. Even though the operational forces would take over some of the training of these fledglings, such a cutting into Yokosuka's vital mission of experiment and study aroused bitter opposition in the Navy Ministry's Aeronautical Department and Personnel Bureau.

Top priority for Zeros went to the First, Second, and Fifth Carrier Divisions, with the Eleventh Air Fleet a poor fourth. The goal called for a full complement of Zeros to the First Air Fleet by early November.[45]

Thus, by early October Kyushu had exploded into new life as Nagumo's training machinery shifted into high gear. Those in the First Air Fleet now privy to Yamamoto's plan proceeded with a new sense of mission, grimly determined to succeed. If Nagumo's officers felt the weight of heavy responsibility, they also experienced a tremendous surge of pride to be part of an operation so vital that the destiny of their homeland depended on it. But Nagumo's nerves continued to scratch at him. Nor were any of his senior officers insensible to the enormous challenge and the inherent danger involved in the scheme. With so much left to do and so few weeks in which to do it, time was the worst devil of them all.

CHAPTER 34

"THE POWER,

THE PURPOSE

AND

THE PLAN"

Admiral Nakahara, chief of the Navy Ministry's Personnel Bureau, confided gloomily to his diary on October 2: "People say that the only alternative left for us is to choose war . . . that irresolution . . . cannot be borne any longer."

At the War College near beautiful Meiji Park, those who were "slated to become staff officers of each Corps of the Southern Army conducted further war games" from October 1 through 4. Uchida and Commander Yuji Yamamoto represented the Naval General Staff and presented the Navy's point of view to their Army colleagues.[1] Uchida formed the impression that the Army officially knew nothing about the Pearl Harbor plan, but that several Army officers privately did.[2]

Nor did Japan's embassy in Washington lack food for thought. On October 1 Terasaki of the American desk in Tokyo sent a long, ominous message to Counselor Iguchi. After expressing formal regrets that "the United States does not reciprocate our statesmanship," Terasaki continued with a few further remarks about "the exceedingly critical situation at home . . ." and added, "Time is now the utmost important element. Whether this matter materializes or not has a direct and important bearing on peace on the Pacific and even of the world. . . ."[3]

One American voice always ringingly confident spoke out to the American Bar Association in Indianapolis on October 1. Declared Knox:

> The best defense has always been a swift offense, and a navy is inherently an instrument of offensive action because of its mobility. Our purpose in having a navy is defensive, but when it comes to fighting the navy must always act offensively. . . .
>
> Always, an autocratic aggressor has the time factor in his favor. He can

determine when to act and he can keep secret his purpose until the hour of action arrives. . . . [4]

Thus the sun of October 3 (Japanese time)—October 2 in the United States—rose on a world far from serene. Peering over the horizon at Washington, it heralded Hull's seventieth birthday. One might have thought that he deserved a day's leisurely celebration with his family and friends. Instead, he summoned Nomura to give the ambassador an "oral statement" in reply to Japan's proposals of September 6, 23, and 27.[5]

As soon as Tokyo translated the American reply, a liaison conference met. Only Konoye, Toyoda, Tojo, Oikawa, and the two chiefs of staff attended, together with Terasaki, who read and explained the telegrams. He then summarized the reply: "Since it appears that although Japan agrees with the United States regarding principles, she differs on their application, the United States is doubtful about holding a meeting of the two heads of state."

Tojo suggested that the conference study this "extremely critical" matter further and not attempt to reply that same day. But Nagano cut through the fog ruthlessly. "There is no longer time for discussion. We want quick action." After Tojo had explained "the Empire's exceptions to the 'Four Principles,'" the meeting decided in favor of further study, with another conference to be held as promptly as possible.[6] It is therefore not surprising that Toyoda dispatched a message that day which backed down from Konoye's formerly agreeable stand, pulling back from the semblance of a concrete agreement with Hull's Four Principles.[7]

The Army High Command also met on October 6. It summarized its policy as follows:

> 1. The Army concludes that there is no hope in conciliatory settlement of the Japanese-American negotiations. Therefore, war is inevitable.
> 2. With regard to the question of the stationing and withdrawal of Japanese forces, there will be no change in the decided terms, including the wording.
> 3. If the Foreign Office believes there is a hope for conciliatory settlement, it may continue the negotiation with the deadline set at 15 October.

The next day Sugiyama got together with Nagano and reached "complete accord." But Oikawa, more conservative and cautious than Nagano, still harbored certain reservations.[8]

While the heat was figuratively on in Tokyo, it was literally so in Washington. The city sizzled under unseasonable temperatures in the nineties, much to Stimson's physical distress. Yet he was well pleased with a conversation he had with Hull following a "War Council" meeting on the sixth. The secretary of state asked Stimson for his "views of what a possible settlement would be in case the Japanese should throw down their hands and resolve to be good." Predictably Stimson replied that "no promises of the Japs based on words would be worth anything . . . there must be action"—specifically an evacuation of China and a commitment not to strike Siberia. He opposed the President's attending any meeting with Konoye without settlement of these points. What is more, "no actual promise of ours should be effective until the evacuation had taken place." These were heavy demands under the circumstances, but Hull agreed.[9]

The Japanese Army General Staff having just decided (1) that war was inevitable, (2) not to yield an inch in the matter of withdrawing troops from China, and (3) to give the Foreign Office only until October 15 to settle with Washington, this conversation between Hull and Stimson has its ironic aspects. The time line especially had never been more finely drawn. In a grim reversal of traditional roles, the leisurely, discussion-loving Orientals pressed for speed while the brisk, action-loving Americans dragged their heels.

Anyone reading the Magic intercepts could be forgiven for deciding that Japan's Foreign Office was suffering from fraying nerves. Toyoda dispatched another ominous and particularly disagreeable message to Nomura on October 10:

> Slowly but surely the question of these negotiations has reached the decisive stage . . . and the situation does not permit of this senseless procrastination. . . . Yes, I know you have told me your opinions quite sufficiently in a number of messages, but what I want is the opinions of the American officials and none other. . . . Hereafter, when you interview Hull or the President of the United States, please take Wakasugi or Iguchi with you and please send me without any delay the complete minutes of what transpires.[10]

To instruct an ambassador to take along a keeper whenever he contacted the host government was an unparalleled insult, particularly between Japanese. The same day Nomura shot back an answer unusually blunt even for him, tinged with understandable asperity:

> . . . I have repeatedly asked them to clarify what I do not understand, but they won't answer. . . .
>
> In other words, they are not budging an inch from the attitude they have always taken; however, they act is if they were ready to consider at any time any plans of ours which would meet the specifications of their answer of the 2nd.[11]

In the meantime, Toyoda informed Grew that on the third and again on the sixth he had instructed Nomura to talk to Hull on certain points. He added that he had heard from him only on October 9. Therefore, "a week of very valuable time had been wasted in an endeavor to elicit through the Japanese Ambassador information which, had it been received, would have measurably accelerated the present conversations. . . ." Toyoda knew better, but he needed to blame someone, and why not Nomura? Why couldn't he handle the Americans or at least make clear what they wanted? Toyoda added, however, "that since he had the impression that the Japanese Ambassador in Washington was apparently very fatigued, serious consideration was being given to the question of sending to Washington a diplomat of wide experience to assist the Ambassador. . . ."[12]

Evidently it did not dawn on Toyoda that the American secretary of state was not at Nomura's beck and call every minute and that when they did get together, Nomura did not have complete control of the conversation. If Roosevelt erred in assuming that the United States held the military initiative, the Japanese erred no less in assuming that the Americans would follow predictably Tokyo's diplomatic lead.

Actually, by this time the Japanese-American discussions had lost all relevance to the factual situation. The real issue was time. The Japanese wanted results in a hurry—a quick and satisfactory settlement with the United States—or, failing that, time enough to embark on the Southern Operation and solidify their position rapidly so they could resist the onslaught of the United States when it came and also be prepared to strike at the Soviets in Siberia in the spring of 1942 should that prove desirable. Thus, from the strictly military point of view, the Japanese High Command was justified in insisting that a decision for war or peace be made by October 15. On the other hand, the United States hoarded every minute to improve its armed forces and strengthen its position in the Pacific. From Magic intercepts addressed not to Nomura, but to Japan's diplomats in Asia and to a certain extent in Germany, selected members of the United States government knew that Japan was planning the conquest of Southeast Asia in the near future. If the Americans would stand aside and permit this, so much the better for Japan. If not, Japan would go ahead anyway.

That was the situation when at 1400 on Sunday, October 12, four members of the Japanese government met with Konoye at his private residence in Ogikubo: Foreign Minister Toyoda, War Minister Tojo, Navy Minister Oikawa, and President of the Cabinet Planning Board Suzuki. It was Konoye's fiftieth birthday; however, they had come not to celebrate, but to discuss the critical subject of peace or war. Accounts of this meeting differ somewhat, but three points are beyond cavil: Japan would continue its operational preparations, Oikawa was not willing to saddle the Navy with the sole responsibility for the war, and if Konoye were not prepared to lead the nation in the conflict, he would have to make way for someone who would.[13]

Perhaps Toyoda still hoped against hope for a miracle before the torrent of events swept him out of office, for he dispatched a significant message to Nomura covering projected talks with Welles. "The situation at home is fast approaching a crisis and it is becoming absolutely essential that the two leaders meet if any adjustment of Japanese-U.S. relations is to be accomplished. I cannot go into details now, but please bear this fact in mind. . . ."[14]

It is clear why Toyoda could not "go into details." If at this last minute Roosevelt agreed to meet with Konoye and set a definite date, the dramatic breakthrough would give the Cabinet a new lease on life. But if Washington realized how very tenuous a grasp Konoye retained on his office, neither the President nor any of his advisers would consider it further.

At 1600 on October 16 Konoye phoned Kido that he had collected letters of resignation from his Cabinet members. This came as a "great surprise" to Kido, who immediately informed the Emperor. At 1700 Hirohito received Konoye to accept his resignation. Half an hour later His Majesty conferred with Kido briefly about a new Cabinet.[15]

After this audience Kido had a long talk with Konoye. In Kido's opinion, only Oikawa or Tojo offered a realistic choice as the new premier. The two statesmen agreed that the Emperor must command the man selected "to disregard the imperial conference decision of September 6 and reexamine the entire situation." All things considered, Kido believed it better to place the responsibility squarely on the Army, which had precipitated the crisis. Possibly, too, if a Tojo government continued the talks in Washington, this might reassure the United States and bring about good results. This reasoning made sense to Konoye, who opted for Tojo, suggesting that the Emperor say a few words in favor of peace when he gave Tojo instructions to form a Cabinet. Tojo was famous for his passionate devotion to the throne, so neither Kido nor Konoye believed he would fail to respect the Emperor's wishes.[16]

On Friday, the seventeenth, Hirohito summoned Tojo and ordered him to form a Cabinet.[17] Although the general had precipitated the Cabinet crisis, there is no reason to believe that he brought down the Konoye government from any personal desire for the top job. The Japanese Army had always been well content to be the power behind the throne, sidestepping the ultimate responsibility. Kido had been clever when he recommended that Tojo as premier remain a general on active duty. For once, the Army would have to face the political consequences of its actions.

Tojo was not the stuff of which dictators or great leaders are made. He had none of Churchill's magnificence, Roosevelt's political acumen, Hitler's evil genius, Mussolini's extroverted dash, or Stalin's peasant shrewdness. But he was rigidly disciplined, honest, and a team of draft horses for work. He had a sharp but narrow mind and was quite simply a successful general in an organization which discouraged flair and personality, the perfect instrument of Japan's collective dictator—the Army.

The next day at mess aboard the flagship with his staff, Yamamoto, who had scant liking for Tojo, sounded off: "In this critical period Tojo has become premier. This is unsatisfactory. Even though he is bold, he doesn't know the background of the situation and he will be unable to improve matters."[18]

Of more direct interest to the Combined Fleet was the identity of the new navy minister. The finger of authority beckoned to Admiral Shigetaro Shimada, commander of the Yokosuka Naval Station. He had been in that post for only seven weeks, having just returned from the Asian mainland, where he had been in command of the China Area Fleet since May 1, 1940. So Shimada was quite out of touch with domestic politics.

On the credit side of the ledger, Shimada was sincerely devout, drank very little, smoked not at all, and was famed throughout the Navy for his devotion to his mother. He treated his subordinates with unusual kindness and consideration and spent Sunday mornings in visiting the families of those who had died in action. He had little temper and was good-natured and agreeable. These pleasing characteristics sprang spontaneously from a warmhearted, affectionate nature.[19]

To check over the debits, Shimada possessed a mind which, although alert, never plunged beneath the surface. Incorrigibly optimistic, he usually followed the line of least resistance and, despite his enormous self-confidence, seldom stood firmly on any subject. Behind his back many in the Navy called him *Yurufun. Yuru* means "loose"; *fun* is the light underwear Japanese wrestlers wear. The nearest American equivalent of this nickname might be Droopy Drawers. It implied, correctly, that Shimada sagged where he should support.[20]

Thus, at the very time when Japan needed a strong navy minister as never before, the Navy replaced a comparatively pliant one with a man even less qualified to stand up to Tojo.[21] Although he was the Navy's voice in the Cabinet, the navy minister by no means compared with Knox in his capacity as secretary of the navy. The navy minister was a full admiral on active duty, very much a part of the Navy itself, instead of a civilian holding both whip and checkrein. Thus, the Japanese Navy, like the Army, did not consider itself answerable to the civil government. This gave the Navy a large slice of uncontrolled power and helped build up the psychology, prevalent in both armed services, that the country existed to support the military, rather than vice versa.

In the wake of the Cabinet crisis the Japanese press made it unmistakably clear that Japan stood firm in its foreign policy. The official *Japan Times and Advertiser* blustered: "Japan is master of its own fate, has a free hand to proceed as it wills for the safeguarding of its own State. If it is necessary to fight America for that purpose, awful though even the thought of such a holocaust, Japan will not hesitate to defend its people and its interests. It has the power, the purpose and the plan. . . ."[22] Unfortunately Japan also had the bad judgment to employ them in a reckless war it could not possibly win.

CHAPTER 35

"PEARL

HARBOR

WILL BE

ATTACKED"

One day in early October the door to Nagumo's cabin aboard *Akagi* flew open and Yamaguchi burst in. He had just discovered that his Second Carrier Division was scheduled to participate in the Southern Operation instead of the Pearl Harbor attack, and he seethed with fury. Of all of Yamamoto's junior admirals, Yamaguchi most ardently supported the Hawaiian venture. That he, the Commander in Chief's confidant and cheerleader, should have to take his carriers to Southeast Asia instead of helping knock off the U.S. Pacific Fleet seared into his very soul.[1]

Kusaka happened to be present, and as usual, when a question arose concerning tactical air power, he summoned Genda, who had been just as dismayed as Yamaguchi to learn of this plan, which meant not only a mere three carriers for the attack but the breakup of aerial teams which had been practicing together. Genda came prepared to back up the fulminating admiral.

"Why won't they take the Second Carrier Division?" demanded Yamaguchi.

Kusaka replied rather flatly, "Because higher headquarters doesn't want to."[2]

"Why don't we enter a strong objection and have them change their plan? . . . If you really want to attack Hawaii, it has to be done with six carriers," countered Yamaguchi. "If the pilots of the Second Carrier Division are going to be transferred to the Fifth Carrier Division, there is nothing for me to do but resign," he roared at Nagumo. "And again you say that the cruising range of the Second Carrier Division is not sufficient. If we can reach Hawaii, that is good enough. When we run out of fuel we will just drift. The rest of the units can return to Japan without bothering about us."[3]

Turning to Genda, he appealed, "Genda, what do you think?" And

Nagumo's air officer, as angry as Yamaguchi but in better control of himself, replied, "I agree with you. How dare they develop such a silly plan?⁴"

Yamaguchi's blast astounded Nagumo and Kusaka. In reply Nagumo could only say, "Well, if that is an order from the Naval General Staff, there is nothing we can do about it." With that answer ringing in his ears, Yamaguchi shot out of Nagumo's cabin as unceremoniously as he had entered it.⁵

Hence we may assume that Yamaguchi was in a somewhat sullen mood when he clambered aboard *Nagato* along with numerous other officers on October 12 to participate in a special rehearsal of Operation Hawaii.⁶ Not entirely satisfied with the results of the September war games, Yamamoto had summoned key naval brass for a second round of table maneuvers aboard his flagship. He hoped to iron out certain difficulties and misconceptions before issuing Combined Fleet Operation Order No. 1, the master plan of the Imperial Navy. He also expected to clear the air of the irritating opposition within the fleet toward his own strategical concepts.

Anchored in Hiroshima Bay a short distance from the small port of Murozumi, *Nagato* had swarmed like a disturbed ant heap since the first light of dawn on October 9. Beginning that day and through the eleventh, Yamamoto held table exercises covering the Southern Operation. During these games the representatives of the First Air Fleet stayed overnight aboard *Mutsu*. Both Nagumo and Yamaguchi drank not wisely but too well. Yamaguchi, not entirely playfully, tried to choke Nagumo judo style to express his displeasure at being left out of the Pearl Harbor attack. The match swiftly threatened to get out of hand, and Kusaka stepped between the two just in time. Then he hustled Yamaguchi into an adjoining room to let him simmer down.⁷

By 0930 on October 13 *Nagato* was again awash with gold braid, this time those concerned with the Pearl Harbor attack plan.⁸ These included Nagumo with Kusaka, Genda, and other members of his staff. Yamaguchi and Hara attended, as did commanders of the support units—Mikawa of the Third Battleship Division and Omori of the First Destroyer Squadron, Shimizu and Mito from the Sixth Fleet with several of their submarine staff officers. Two representatives of the Operations Section of the Naval General Staff observed the exercise—Miyo, Tomioka's adviser on naval aviation, and Uchida.⁹

Although the Pearl Harbor exercise followed in general the successful second attempt at the Naval War College, an observer would have noted immediately certain important differences. For one thing, Yamamoto had decided that in addition to the Sixth Fleet's advance mission, as practiced in Tokyo, several undersea craft would accompany Nagumo's task force to act as scouts. Before, during, and directly after the actual attack, all the submarines in the Hawaiian area would operate under Nagumo to preserve unity of command.

Nagumo worried greatly lest a careless submarine skipper inadvertently foul up the operation by taking premature action or by letting the American defenders spot him before Fuchida's pilots launched their aerial attack. His airmen shared his concern to the fullest. Accordingly the participants in the table maneuvers drew a huge circle covering a 600-mile area around Oahu. They estimated the circumference of this circle as the outside limit American patrol planes could fly in any direction from their Hawaiian bases. This area they designated as the "danger zone," within which all submarines must operate with extreme caution. In the period before the air strike those inside the circle would remain submerged during daylight, surfacing only at night.[10]

Between the September war games and the October table maneuvers Nagumo's staff had agreed upon a rendezvous point. The inspiration came from Kusaka. When a lieutenant commander, he had made a thorough study of the Kuriles, during which time his ship had anchored in Hitokappu Bay on the island of Etorofu. Big enough to swallow the task force with room to spare, the bay had few communications with the outside world and was far removed from the main Japanese islands and the principal arteries of traffic. Draped in gray curtains of fog, the island offered excellent concealment and a perfect place from which to sortie.[11]

But the main difference between the September and October mock strikes was this: In conformity with the compromise plan worked out after the Naval Staff College exercise, only three flattops participated—*Kaga, Shokaku,* and *Zuikaku.* These were selected because of their long radius of action, while *Akagi, Soryi,* and *Hiryu* were earmarked for the Southern Operation.

With this emasculated force, once more Nagumo set forth on his paper journey. The First Air Fleet theoretically sailed from the Inland Sea, rendez-voused in Hitokappu Bay, and took the northern route to Hawaii. There, approximately 200 miles north of Oahu, the carriers launched two attack waves at dawn. The umpires ruled the air strike a success, with "moderate damage" inflicted on the United States ships and the task force escaping without serious losses.[12]

The task force setup used at the *Nagato* table maneuvers pleased no one except those responsible for the Southern Operation. And as intended, this practice session brought to the surface a number of problems, including the urgent question of how to synchronize the Pearl Harbor venture with the southern campaign. The vast invasion fleet with its convoys transporting thousands of troops and tons of supplies to Malaya would be under way long before X-Day, impossible to conceal on those well-traveled sea-lanes. If British reconnaissance planes or surface craft spotted and shadowed Kondo's ships, should the Japanese ignore the scouts or shoot them down?

Naturally Kondo would prefer to knock out any Allied scouts before they could relay his position to their headquarters, but on this point Nagumo was adamant. He insisted that there be no hostilities whatsoever until he had begun his Pearl Harbor strike. Yamamoto agreed and cautioned Kondo: "Do not begin your operation anywhere in the southern regions until it is clear that the air strike against Hawaii has been launched."[13] If anyone discovered the Southern Fleet prematurely, Kondo must change course and "head back to Japan in a deceptive gesture to throw the British off-balance."

Kondo was highly skeptical of the value of the Pearl Harbor operation and intent on the success of the southern campaign. So, when Yamamoto sketched out the Pearl Harbor picture for him, he immediately asked, "Where will we get all the ships for such extensive operations? How can Japan afford to divide her strength over such wide areas?" And he voiced vigorous objections to the Hawaiian venture because "it extends beyond the capabilities of the Japanese Navy and depends too much on innumerable factors beyond Japan's control." But Yamamoto shushed his complaints. "Don't worry," he said. "I will furnish you with more solid carrier strength as soon as the strike against Pearl Harbor is over."[15]

Mikawa, too, was dissatisfied. He had been training his Third Battleship Division (*Hiei, Kirishima, Kongo, Haruna*) in Bungo Channel between Kyushu and Shikoku. He fully expected that at some time during the Pearl Harbor operation his ships would tangle with the U.S. Pacific Fleet. Therefore, he clung tenaciously to his demand that his entire division should accompany the task force to Hawaii. The two battlewagons allotted to him seemed pitifully inadequate when measured against Kimmel's eight big bruisers. Mikawa had no quarrel with his cruiser strength (two heavies, *Tone* and *Chikuma*, and one light, *Abukuma*), but the possibility of finding the U.S. Pacific Fleet alert and on the prowl in the open seas rather than dozing around Ford Island called for far greater firepower than two battleships could muster.

But Yamamoto refused Mikawa's request. "The overall operational picture will not permit further diversion of battleship strength to the First Air Fleet," he told him firmly. "England is almost sure to send heavy naval strength into the South China Sea to protect Malaya and Singapore. We need the speed and guns of *Kongo* and *Haruna* to counter the British threat." The decision gave Mikawa many an anxious moment then and later; however, as a dutiful officer he determined to do his best with what Yamamoto allotted him.[16]

The maneuvers left a number of loose ends concerning submarines. Neither the exact number to participate nor the details of the operation had been determined. Whether the midget submarines would join the Pearl Harbor team depended upon technical problems, for Yamamoto gave them his theoretical approval either during or shortly before the table maneuvers.[17] From that moment the minisubs became an integral part of the Pearl Harbor plan. They were assigned to the Sixth Fleet, which began to prepare the afterdecks of the large submarines to transport them to and—everyone hoped—from Pearl Harbor like Japanese babies strapped to their mothers' backs.[18]

Some problems no amount of planning or training could solve. Upon the success or failure of the conversations in Washington depended the nature of the military operations Japan would launch. Yet no matter what the results of Nomura's efforts, the Combined Fleet had to be fully prepared for any eventuality. If the answer from Washington was acceptable, the Pearl Harbor strike would be withheld. But if it was negative, Yamamoto wanted to be in a position to strike as soon thereafter as possible.

Thus matters stood when the table maneuvers ended on October 12. That evening the fleet commanders and high-ranking members of their staff remained aboard *Nagato* for dinner. As usual, Yamamoto was a generous, kindly host. He good-naturedly vetoed shoptalk so that his guests might enjoy a pleasant meal with plenty of laughter, *sake,* and fellowship.[19]

The next day, beginning at 0900, a review of the general table tactics took place. Then, at 1600, began a special meeting of top admirals and senior members of the staffs. Yamamoto made it clear at the outset that all comments would be off the record, and no official minutes transcribed. However, he "diligently wrote down the gist of each man's ideas and plans."[20]

Ugaki opened the discussion with an urgent plea for unity. In essence he spoke as follows: "Every officer present no doubt has good ideas, but once Japan decides to go to war, the individual officer must forget his own particular concepts and follow those laid down by the Combined Fleet. As yet Operation Order Number One has not been finished; in fact, it is only in the preparatory stage. So now is the time and place for each commander to express his ideas. Once Admiral Yamamoto has established fleet policy, only one thing will remain—to execute that policy faithfully and loyally." To drive home his point, Ugaki quoted a proverb: "Too many steersmen will send the ship climbing the mountain."[21]

One by one the admirals accepted Ugaki's invitation to speak. Mikawa came first. He declared that from the navigational point of view alone, the attack on Pearl Harbor would be virtually impossible if carried out late in the year. High seas and bad weather would present insuperable difficulties in refueling.[22] Onishi declared that it was too late to strike Pearl Harbor. Once more he insisted that the Eleventh Air Fleet would need carrier-borne reinforcements against the Philippines.[23] Kondo suggested that Japan leave the United States alone. He preferred to take Malaya first, thus fighting against only the British and Dutch.[24] Nagumo took this opportunity to rumble like a newly activated volcano about the inherent risks of the Hawaiian venture, and so did Kusaka.[25]

The only admiral to speak out boldly in favor of Yamamoto's scheme was Yamaguchi, now dealt out of the game despite a fierce last-ditch stand at the table maneuvers. No dog in the manger, he believed in the Pearl Harbor plan whether he himself took part in it or not. He insisted that the Japanese must attack Hawaii at the outbreak of war. Nevertheless, he cautioned against overextending Japan's perimeter of expansion. Specifically he warned that any attempt to seize Rabaul, the advance Australian air base on the northern tip of New Britain Island in the Bismarcks, would stretch the nation's naval resources far too thin.[26]

"The general feeling on the part of the higher-ranking officers was that it was too late to execute the attack," said Genda. "They felt that it was too late for the surprise factor to play in important role. They thought, too, that the political scene had deteriorated so far that the American Navy would already be making preparations to meet an eventuality like a surprise attack."[27]

As the final speaker resumed his seat, the last flush of sunset was dying on the horizon. A hush of anticipation tinged with chilly awe swept the group as Yamamoto rose. He spoke slowly but with unmistakable determination. "I have been studying the entire strategical situation for some time," he told his audience, "and I have noted all the points various officers have made today. These ideas will be considered carefully and any constructive suggestions incorporated into the forthcoming fleet order. I realize that some do not think well of my plan, but the operation against Hawaii is a vital part of Japan's grand strategy." Then he slashed away any vestige of misunderstanding in a voice that cut like a knife: "So long as I am Commander in Chief of the Combined Fleet, Pearl Harbor will be attacked. I ask you to give me your fullest support. Return to your stations, and work hard for the success of Japan's war plan. Good luck!"[28]

Yamamoto's declaration cleared the atmosphere once and for all. Henceforth there would be no more bickering in the Combined Fleet, no more protests against the project, no more complaints from Nagumo or anyone else. Very well! Yamamoto could lead his horses to water, he could even make them drink, but he could not make all of them enjoy it. Nor could he erase from all minds the sobering picture of Japan's warships steaming off in virtually every direction at once and the hair-raising logistical problems such a vast, unprecedented campaign would mean. "What concerned us most was the magnitude of the problem facing the Combined Fleet," recalled Tsukahara. "When we went back to our stations, it was not with a tremendous surge of hope, but with the stark realization of gigantic tasks ahead."[29]

Similar considerations troubled Nakahara in the Navy Ministry's Personnel Bureau. "The Fleet is now under training aiming at December 8," he noted in his diary on October 11. ". . . The most important thing is this: In relation to the diplomatic situation, the right time to start a war is most difficult to decide—one may be too late in taking the initiative and the other may be too early. This has a close relation with the war preparations. . . ." Thus, as early as October 11 the Combined Fleet aimed at a target date of December 8— Sunday, December 7, in Hawaii.

While Yamamoto's firm pronouncement silenced opposition to the Pearl Harbor attack plan, it did not end discussions about ways and means, nor did Yamamoto intend that it should. Outstanding among these difficulties loomed the nagging question of the number of carriers that should participate. Naturally Genda had been sorely displeased with the "moderate damage" attained in the *Nagato* table maneuvers. Logically he attributed to insufficient carrier strength the meager results theoretically scored against the American ships. Allowing every possible margin for good luck and skill, the strike power represented by a mere three flattops could not inflict sufficiently grievous wounds to pay for the anticipated losses to the task force. While Genda was prepared to spend Japanese lives, he was not prepared to waste them. Kusaka heartily agreed, and from that day the two men joined forces in a firm stand against the compromise plan.[30]

Yamaguchi, too, was far from reconciled to a three-carrier attack force. In fact, he unblushingly backed up his air staff officer, Suzuki, when the latter averred during the table maneuvers that the cruising radius of *Soryu* and *Hiryu* was sufficient to make the trip without refueling. "You were wrong, and I know that you knew you were wrong," he told Suzuki.[31] But he could not reprimand his air staff officer for having the nerve to try.

Nor could he swallow his own bitter medicine without protest. A number of threads bound Yamaguchi's fighting heart to Operation Hawaii. It was Yamamoto's scheme, enough in itself to ensure Yamaguchi's loyal cooperation. He also believed, like Genda, that a massive air attack was the only means of assuring maximum damage to the enemy.

Illogically but understandably, Yamaguchi did not blame Yamamoto, the decision maker, for his plight. Instead, his wrath fell on Nagumo because he had opposed the plan from the beginning and was now ready to settle for a hit-and-run raid of only three carriers. His resentment came to a climax shortly after the *Nagato* table maneuvers. Once more Yamaguchi stormed into Nagumo's cabin. This time he waxed so insubordinate that Nagumo ordered him out. As he bolted through the door, Yamaguchi fired this parting shot: "If you have made a mistake, I will kill you!"[32]

CHAPTER 36

"WE

SHOULD BE

ON GUARD"

As soon as Roosevelt heard about the fall of the Konoye government, he canceled a scheduled meeting with his own Cabinet. Instead, he conferred for two hours, beginning at 1400 on October 16, with Hull, Stimson, Knox, Marshall, Stark, and the inevitable Harry Hopkins. They all feared that the incoming Japanese Cabinet would be "much more anti-American" than the outgoing. "The Japanese Navy is beginning to talk almost as radically as the Japanese Army, and so we face the delicate question of the diplomatic fencing to be done so as to make sure that Japan was put into the wrong and made the first bad move—overt move," wrote Stimson in his diary.[1]

In years to come the revisionist school of historians eagerly seized upon such unfortunate phraseology as evidence that Roosevelt deliberately maneuvered the Japanese into starting the Pacific war and specifically into attacking Pearl Harbor.[2] Actually the secretary of war had merely expressed one of those basic truths which everyone knows but seldom—at least at executive branch level—says out loud: that no government wishes to appear before its people and posterity in a bad light.

Later Stimson set forth his view ably: "If war did come, it was important . . . that we should not be placed in the position of firing the first shot, if this could be done without sacrificing our safety, but that Japan should appear in her true role as the real aggressor."[3] The evidence of history clearly indicates that the Roosevelt administration would have preferred to avoid war with Japan so that it might concentrate all of America's strength against Hitler.

The crisis in Tokyo "created very much of a stir" in the Navy Department. According to Stark's aide, "Everyone sensed the war was not far off."[4] Turner drafted a dispatch for Stark to send to Kimmel, King, and Hart, which the CNO "tempered . . . considerably" before speeding it on its way.[5] Even so, it contained a strong warning that Japan might go on the war path:

> The resignation of the Japanese cabinet has created a grave situation. If a new cabinet is formed it will probably be strongly nationalistic and anti-American. If the Konoye cabinet remains . . . it will operate under a new mandate which will not include rapprochement with the US. In either case hostilities between Japan and Russia are a strong possibility. Since the US and Britain are held responsible by Japan for her present desperate situation there is also a possibility that Japan may attack these two powers. In view of these possibilities you will take due precautions, including such preparatory deployments as will not disclose strategic intention nor constitute provocative actions against Japan. . . .

The message also asked that Kimmel notify the appropriate Army authorities and his naval district.[6]

By Japan's "desperate situation," Turner meant principally "her economic condition." He believed that there would be no possibility of war "for at least a month" between Japan and the Americans, British, and Dutch. Yet the situation differed "with respect to the Russians" because the Japanese "already had an army in Manchuria, deployed or not, we did not know." Japan also had "a great part of the Navy in her home waters, so that action against Russia could have been taken at an earlier date possibly."[7]

Turner was far from alone in estimating Japanese action in terms of the titanic battles thundering across the Soviet Union. Indeed, America had Russia on the brain—another red herring to confuse the trail of Japanese intentions. Miles thought it highly probable that the next Japanese Cabinet would be pro-Axis with the Army in the saddle. And it would quickly "take advantage of any weakening of the Siberian Army brought about by Russian reverses in Europe." This he pointed out to Marshall in a memorandum dated October 16.[8]

Bicknell of Short's G-2 also had the Soviet Union on his mind when his office prepared an estimate of the Japanese situation as of 1200 on October 17: ". . . it is fairly certain that Japan's basic policy . . . will remain unchanged; and it is expected that Japan will shortly announce her decision to challenge militarily any nation or combination of nations which might oppose the execution of said policies. . . ."[9] Bicknell listed as Japan's most likely moves:

> 1. Attack Russia from the east.
> 2. Pressure French Indo-China and Thailand for concessions in the way of military, naval, and air bases, and guarantees of economic cooperation.
> 3. Attack British possessions in the Far East.
> 4. Defend against an American attack in support of the British.
> 5. Attack simultaneously the ABCD block at whichever points might promise her greatest tactical, strategic, and economic advantages.[10]

He believed the last possibility—Japan's actual intention—to be the least likely because it would violate the Axis principle of "defeating one opponent at a time." Yet he could not rule it out because if Japan considered "war with the United States to be inevitable as a result of her actions against Russia, it is reasonable to believe that she may decide to strike before our naval program is completed." The obvious corollary followed: "An attack on the United States could not be undertaken without almost certain involvement of the entire ABCD block, hence there remains the possibility that Japan may strike at the most opportune time, and at whatever points might gain for her the most strategic, tactical, or economic advantages over her opponents."[11] Bicknell's estimate did not speculate, however, on what or where such points might be.

Stark, too, had in mind that the Japanese might play "the same game that Hitler did, that is, one at a time."[12] But to be on the safe side, he warned all merchant ships of "a possibility of hostile action by Japan against U.S. shipping."[13]

No one in Washington hit the panic button. Those in authority had long realized that Konoye's "moderation" was highly relative. Captain Pinky Schuirmann, Navy liaison officer with the State Department, sent Stark on October 17 a sensible, realistic summation:

> Present reports are that the new cabinet to be formed will be no better and no worse than the one which has just fallen. Japan may attack Russia, or may move southward, but in the final analysis this will be determined by the military on the basis of opportunity, and what they can get away with, not by what cabinet is in power.

Stark saw "very much eye to eye" with Schuirmann,[14] but he continued to take precautions. On October 17 he sent a directive to Hart, with an information copy to Kimmel, among others. Stark ordered Hart to route "all trans-Pacific U.S. flag shipping" to and from Far Eastern areas "plus Shanghai and India and East India area as defined in WPL 46 thru [sic] Torres Straits keeping to the southward and well clear of Orange mandates. . . ." Torres Strait lies between southern New Guinea and Cape York in northern Australia. Stark sent instructions to Kimmel the same day: "Because of the great importance of continuing to reenforce the Philippines with long range Army bombers you are requested to take all practicable precautions for the safety of the airfields at Wake and Midway."[15]

Kimmel acted promptly on Stark's directives. He alerted six submarines "to depart for Japan at short notice,"[16] directed the two undersea craft at Midway to assume a war patrol at a 10-mile radius, and dispatched two submarines to Wake for a 15-mile scouting circle. He ordered Bellinger to dispatch a squadron of twelve reconnaissance planes to Midway for daily patrol within 100 miles of the island. He further instructed Bellinger to prepare to send six of these aircraft to Wake and replace them from Pearl Harbor. And he directed both air and submarine commanders to "take offensive action only if attacked or if ordered to do so by CinCPAC."[17]

Kimmel also reinforced Johnston and Wake with "additional marines, ammunition and stores"; ordered more marines to Palmyra; placed Pye, who was with a contingent of ships on a routine training cruise to the Pacific coast, on twelve-hour notice to become effective October 20; and stepped up "security measures in effect in the operating areas outside Pearl Harbor." He also delayed until November 17 the sailing of *West Virginia*, the mock-up of which at that very moment was the target of Japanese bombing practice. The battleship was due for overhaul at Puget Sound. Moreover, Kimmel directed Bloch to alert the outlying islands.[18] Bloch immediately passed the order to Midway, Johnston, Palmyra, and the Marine detachment at Wake.[19]

Thus, within a few days of receipt of Stark's messages, Kimmel had his forces on the alert to spot any Japanese ship, submarine, or aircraft which might venture into the central Pacific. But they would not and could not shoot on sight. As the Navy Court of Inquiry's report observed, "Having in mind Japan's traditional tendency to distort legitimate actions of a powerful nation into deliberate threats to her own security and prestige, the War and Navy Departments were compelled to take every precaution to avoid offending her supersensitive sensibilities."[20]

As happened rather frequently, after sending quite a sharp alert, the Navy promptly smoothed it over. Apparently Stark did not swallow whole all of Turner's estimates. In addition to toning down the dispatch of October 16, he followed it with a personal letter to Kimmel dated October 17 which "very much astonished" Turner when he saw it later:[21]

> Personally I do not believe the Japs are going to sail into us and the message I sent you merely stated the "possibility." . . . In any case after long pow-wows in the White House it was felt we should be on guard, at least until something indicates the trend. . . .
>
> I think we could settle with Nomura in five minutes but the Japanese Army is the stumbling block. Incidentally, the Chinese also think that they will lick Japan before they get through and are all for keeping going rather than giving way anywhere. . . .

Then Stark added his usual postscript:

> Marshall just called up and was anxious that we make some sort of a reconnaissance so that he could feel assured that on arrival at Wake, a Japanese raider attack may not be in order on his bombers. I told him that we could not assure against any such contingency, but that I felt it extremely improbable and that, while we kept track of Japanese ships so far as we can, a carefully planned raid on any of these Island carriers in the Pacific might be difficult to detect. . . .

Stark could not know how wisely he wrote. But he obviously regarded the letter as at least semiofficial, for he sent a copy to Hart and asked Kimmel to show it to Bloch, as was his custom.[22]

Coincidentally, on October 17, Bloch reminded Washington of previous correspondence concerning local defense and security. All he had received worth mentioning was the old gunboat *Sacramento*, which had "no batteries, to speak of, with which the vessel can fight, and no speed with which she can run." The only aircraft available for antisubmarine patrol were Army planes not suitable for that purpose. He had only four destroyers—one of them without listening gear—and three Coast Guard cutters for submarine tracking. These would be needed also "for escort and security patrol in a very extensive front." He urged the assignment of "a number of small, fast craft . . . equipped with listening gear and depth charges," plus at least two squadrons of reconnaissance planes. He ended acidly: "Nearly all of the failures of the British have been caused by what may be expressed in the cliché 'Too little and too late.' It is hoped that we may profit from their errors."[23]

Kimmel endorsed Bloch's memorandum on the same date, October 17, proclaiming yet again his gospel of the tactical offensive:

> . . . There is a possibility that the reluctance or inability of the Department to furnish the Commandant, 14th Naval District, with forces adequate to his needs may be predicated upon a conception that, in an emergency, vessels of the United States Pacific Fleet may always be diverted for these purposes. If such be the case, the premise is so false as to hardly warrant refutation. A fleet, tied to its base by diversion to other purpose, of light forces necessary for the security at sea, is, in a real sense no fleet at all. Moreover, this fleet has been assigned, in the event of war, certain definite tasks, the vigorous prosecution of which requires not only all the units now assigned, but as many more as can possibly be made available.[24]

At Kimmel's headquarters many discussions took place on "General Tojo, what sort of a policy he would follow, and also regarding the character, general background, of the leading Japanese naval officers. . . ."[25] With this subject Layton came into his own when he briefed Kimmel daily at 0815.[26]

Layton knew Yamamoto personally. He considered Kimmel's opposite number a "very capable, a very thoroughly grounded and trained officer . . . he possessed more brains than any other Japanese in the High Command." He illustrated Yamamoto's character to Kimmel by saying that "he could win at poker among good poker players, and could play better bridge than most good bridge players, and . . . was a champion . . . of the Japanese chess game, 'Go.' " Layton cited these abilities to demonstrate that Yamamoto's mind was "keen, alert, and that also from my personal observation and from general Japanese service reputation, he was an outstanding officer."[27]

Naturally the subject of Japanese carriers also came up in the general discussion. Layton declared that Japan could not afford "to gamble too much wherein she might lose the war in the first battle when she had larger stakes, more vital stakes, at hand."[28] He sounded much like the opponents of Yamamoto's plan in the Naval General Staff and Combined Fleet.

By October 20 the first flush of excitement had begun to die down, and the War Department could inform Short: "Tension between United States and Japan remains strained but no repeat no abrupt change in Japanese foreign policy appears imminent."[29]

On October 22 Kimmel reported to Stark the dispositions he had made in accordance with instructions. Predictably he seized the opportunity to plead for more patrol craft and "at least two more squadrons of destroyers." He put in another pitch for *North Carolina* and *Washington*. "We have indications that one new battleship has been commissioned by the Japanese and rumors that an additional one will soon be placed in commission," he advised Stark. "Such a contingency will further disturb the balance of power in the Pacific."[30] Had he known the exact size of *Yamato* and *Musashi*, the new Japanese battleships— over 60,000 tons with nine 18.2-inch guns apiece—he would have been appalled. They were larger, faster, and more powerful by far than anything the United States had afloat.

Kimmel next begged for "all the long-range submarines that you can send us. They can be most effective in keeping destroyers and other patrol craft occupied near the Japanese bases, homeland and trade routes."[31] Far from giving Kimmel more submarines, Washington would soon transfer some of his best undersea craft to Hart's Asiatic Fleet as a further buildup against the Japanese threat in Southeast Asia.*

Kimmel wanted cruisers, too, to counteract anticipated "Jap raider activities. . . . Then, too, our own planned offensive operations require cruisers and more cruisers. The least you can do for us is to leave us with the cruisers we have. . . ." Next, the CinCUS turned his attention to his air arm. "The type of operations we have planned in the early stages of the war puts a premium on aircraft operations from carriers." Because the Pacific Fleet had only three— *Enterprise, Lexington,* and *Saratoga*—he asked that a merchant ship be "converted to a carrier for training purposes at San Diego."

Kimmel reported favorably on training, although gunnery radar on *Honolulu*-class cruisers had proved "a bitter disappointment" inasmuch as it was "apparently useless for the detection of aircraft." He also had prepared and forwarded to Stark "an exhaustive study on the installations and defenses of Wake, Midway, Johnston and Palmyra." He approved "investigation of an alternative land plane route" east of the Marshalls to Australia for the B-17s but pointed out that "there are not enough ships now available to handle our own island developments. Without greatly augmented shipping facilities we cannot possibly assume the additional burden for the Army."[32]

No one was more concerned with those Flying Fortresses than Stimson, who on October 21 dispatched an eloquent letter to Roosevelt in an attempt to convince him of the error of his ways in asking for these planes for the British:

> . . . A strategic opportunity of the utmost importance has suddenly arisen in the southwestern Pacific. . . . From being impotent to influence events in that area, we suddenly find ourselves vested with the possibility of great effective power. . . . We are rushing planes and other preparations to the Philippines from a base in the United States which has not yet in existence the number of planes necessary for our immediate minimum requirements in that

*See Chapter 42.

southwestern Pacific theatre. This is the result of our deferments to the British of last year. . . . Yet even this imperfect threat, if not promptly called by the Japanese, bids fair to stop Japan's march to the south and secure the safety of Singapore. . . . As you well know, however, the final success of the operation lies on the knees of the gods and we cannot tell what explosion may momentarily come from Japan. . . . [33]

Stimson was optimistic about the capability of the B-17. And by sending every available Flying Fortress to the Philippines to build up MacArthur's forces, Washington reduced Oahu to the level of a way station. This vitiated Marshall's original concept of protecting Hawaii by means of the B-17.

Stimson replied with a resounding "NO"—his own capitals—when Hull asked him on October 28 whether he favored "immediate declaration of war against Japan." He explained that he wanted to take advantage of "this wonderful opportunity of strengthening our position in the Philippines by air and to use it as a means of strengthening his diplomatic arm in forcing the Japanese to keep away from Singapore and perhaps, if we are in good luck, to shake the Japanese out of the Axis. . . ."[34]

At this crucial time the War and Navy departments fumbled an opportunity for the sort of integrated effort which might have helped immeasurably in evaluating information. A joint intelligence committee had been in the making since July 1 within the Joint Army-Navy Board. Stimson had approved its establishment on September 29; Knox, on October 1. But the committee did not meet until October 11 and did not get together again until after the war started. According to Miles, "there were still discussions and difficulties going on between the War and Navy Departments as to just what the functions of that committee would be, where it would sit, what rooms it would have, what secretary it would be allowed, et cetera."[35]

Left to themselves, G-2 and ONI might have worked out matters to their satisfaction, for Miles was a very old friend of both Wilkinson and his predecessor, Kirk.[36] At secretarial level, too, cooperation was the order of the day. Stimson's interest in Intelligence is obvious from his diary, and Knox "took a very strong personal interest" in his Intelligence division.[37]

But a controversy arose between Gerow of War Plans and his opposite, Turner, on the scope of the committee's functions. It was the old story. Gerow "wished the committee to collate, analyze and interpret information with its implications, to estimate hostile capabilities and probably [sic] intentions. Admiral Turner wished to limit it to presentation of such factual evidence as might be available, but to make no estimate or other form of prediction . . . Admiral Turner won."[38] Miles later testified that "Admiral Turner was practically Naval Operations through a large part of that time. Neither Gerow nor . . . myself [sic] could get very far with him."[39]

Washington kept an eye on the explosive possibilities in the Pacific, however. On October 23 Stark advised Kimmel and Hart, among others: "Until further orders all army and navy transpacific troop transports, ammunition ships and such others with sufficiently important military cargo will be escorted both ways between Honolulu and Manila. . . ."[40]

Little wonder that Kimmel seized the opportunity to have luncheon on October 29 with Hallet Abend. The correspondent had just completed a tour through Singapore, Manila, the Dutch East Indies, Australia, and New Zealand for the *Reader's Digest*. He gave Kimmel some interesting data, the "most vital" being that if the Japanese attacked the Soviets, the British Empire would declare war on Japan. Abend also stated that the Netherlands East Indies would follow suit. Kimmel gathered from the journalist that "the most probable direction for Japanese adventures is to the Northward"—that is, into Soviet territory. Naturally enough, after his talk with Abend, Kimmel asked Stark, "If they do embark on such an adventure and Britain and the Dutch East Indies declare war on Japan, what will we do?"[41]

It is most unlikely that Stark or his superiors, for that matter, were prepared to give Kimmel a definitive answer to this question. What is certain is that the State Department, in the person of Sumner Welles, knew "that both the Army and Navy were doing their utmost to persuade the President and the State Department that any break should be avoided, if possible; that negotiations should be continued for as long as possible."[42]

CHAPTER 37

"AS ONE

WITH THE

COMBINED

FLEET"

The thoughts and prayers of every loyal Japanese turned to Tokyo, where the "grand festival" of Yasukuni Shrine began on October 16. The Combined Fleet had been so busy that "the Harvest Thanksgiving Day was almost forgotten by all of the staff officers though I have no words to apologize," as Ugaki wrote in his diary. They had been test-firing with real shells, and Ugaki reflected that "it will not be so far off before they are fired in succession to destroy the enemy. . . ."[1]

Aboard *Akagi* off southern Kyushu events began to boil. Kusaka and Genda had returned from the *Nagato* table maneuvers just as distressed as Yamaguchi over the prospect of using only three—possibly four—carriers against Pearl Harbor. But they were far more constructive in their reactions. They had haunting visions of going off to war unable to fulfill their mission and of running into more trouble than they could handle.

Genda had always favored an all-out attack. Now that Kusaka had promised Yamamoto his support, he, too, believed that if they must attack the U.S. Pacific Fleet at Pearl Harbor, they should use maximum aerial striking power. That meant six carriers. Urged on by Genda, Kusaka cornered Nagumo and forced him to be realistic. Although still averse to the entire scheme, Nagumo had everything to gain by securing as much offensive strength as possible. So he authorized Kusaka to go to Tokyo and hammer out the carrier problem with the Naval General Staff.

Before his departure Kusaka conferred alone with Genda. "If we are forced to accept their plan, what shall we do?" he asked. Genda replied that they could not possibly carry out the operation successfully with fewer than six carriers and that the First Air Fleet must absolutely insist on this point. To himself he reflected that if the Navy's bigwigs would not budge, they might as well call off the Pearl Harbor attack.[2]

Kusaka left *Akagi* on October 17, prepared to give up his post if he did not succeed. Arriving in Tokyo the same day, he went straight to the offices of the Naval General Staff, where he presented his case to Tomioka and other members of the Operations Section. He insisted forcefully that six carriers must participate in the Pearl Harbor attack. "So long as the First Air Fleet is going to do the fighting," he maintained, "it should have the tools for the job."[3]

But Tomioka "took a very firm stand against six carriers." Again he stressed that the top-priority Southern Operation required at least two of the First Air Fleet's flattops. Moreover, the Naval General Staff believed that sending six carriers to Pearl Harbor would be too dangerous a concentration of Japan's irreplaceable naval air power. If anything went wrong—and who could deny that possibility?—the Navy would lose most of its long-range scoring punch. The gamble was simply too great.[4]

Realizing that he was wasting his time, Kusaka soon left. But convinced that he was right, he neither resigned nor flew back to *Akagi* defeated and discouraged. He fired off a telegram to Yamamoto explaining briefly what had happened. Then he flew directly to *Nagato* for a conference.[5]

Yamamoto listened attentively as Kusaka emphasized that not only did the Naval General Staff deny the First Air Fleet the extra carriers, but its opposition to the Pearl Harbor attack remained widespread and stubborn. He even asserted that he thought Yamamoto's own Combined Fleet officers had not backed him up strongly enough in his struggle with the top brass in Tokyo.

Then he reminded Yamamoto that at the end of September he had agreed to cease opposing the plan. At that time Yamamoto had given him every assurance of the combined Fleet's support in his efforts to develop the project. "Commander-in-Chief, did you not assure me that the details of this plan would be placed under my supervision and every possible effort would be made to meet my requirements for the operation?" Kusaka asked courteously but firmly.[6] The implication was clear. Now was the time for Yamamoto to make good his promise.

Yamamoto needed no urging. For some time he had been increasingly restive and worried. When Kusaka recounted the tale of his fruitless mission to Tokyo, Yamamoto realized that this was his chance to force the issue before the sands of time trickled to the bottom of the hourglass. "I will send someone to the Naval General Staff at once," he told Kusaka.[7]

The very next morning, October 18, Kuroshima flew to Tokyo. His task was twofold: first, to secure the consent of the Naval General Staff to Operation Hawaii; secondly, to induce its members to allot the First Air Fleet's six carriers to the mission. Yamamoto armed his personal emissary with a secret weapon and instructed him to use it if he had to.

Kuroshima found Tomioka in conference with Miyo, recently returned from the *Nagato* table maneuvers. Kuroshima announced at once that Yamamoto had sent him to Tokyo for the express purpose of "achieving immediately clarification" on the Pearl Harbor attack. Would it be approved in principle or not? he asked. If so, the First Air Fleet had to have six carriers for the mission. Time was running short, and Yamamoto needed an answer without delay.

Tomioka was not to be easily stampeded. He outlined the main reasons why he personally opposed Yamamoto's plan: It posed a terrible risk, no one could be certain that the U.S. Fleet would be in Pearl Harbor, technical difficulties such as torpedo bombing and refueling at sea remained to be solved, the Navy lacked sufficient air strength for so many operations, and the scheme would jeopardize Japan's all-important southern campaign by dividing its striking power.[8] This was virtually a repetition of the points he had made to Kuroshima in July.

And just as in July, Kuroshima scarcely waited for Tomioka to finish before he excitedly countered with a barrage of Yamamoto's best arguments. The U.S. Navy had enough strength concentrated at Pearl Harbor to strike the Japanese flank and endanger the success of the Southern Operation. In that invasion the Combined Fleet must divide into numerous units because it would have to execute simultaneous assaults over widespread areas. If the U.S. Fleet came out, the Japanese Navy could not reassemble its farflung forces in time to do battle successfully with the enemy in the western Pacific. What is more, no doubt the United States planned to seize the Marshall Islands. If this happened, Japan's defensive perimeter would be pierced, and the strategical position of its Navy greatly weakened. One sure way existed to block this threat: Smash the striking power of the U.S. Navy at its source. Like Cato thundering against Carthage, Kuroshima insisted, "Pearl Harbor must be attacked!"[9]

But Tomioka stood his ground. Realizing that logic had availed him nothing, Kuroshima exploded the bomb his chief had given him. "Admiral Yamamoto insists that his plan be adopted. I am authorized to state that if it is not, then the Commander in Chief of the Combined Fleet can no longer be held responsible for the security of the Empire. In that case he will have no alternative but to resign, and with him his entire staff."[10]

Tomioka could scarcely believe his ears. Miyo, too, was amazed. Yet they could not doubt that Kuroshima spoke the literal truth. The threat of Yamamoto's resignation introduced an entirely new dimension into the picture. Now Tomioka realized the full depth of Yamamoto's determination to execute the attack, and he permitted his professional judgment to crumble before the onslaught of Yamamoto's armored will.

Accordingly Tomioka told Kuroshima that he personally would agree to Yamamoto's plan, but he imposed the following conditions: (1) Six and only six carriers would be used in the attack; (2) the Combined Fleet would make no further demands on Japan's naval air strength; and (3) the First Air Fleet carriers would engage in the Southern Operation as soon as feasible after the Pearl Harbor attack.[11]

Kuroshima readily gave his word. But Tomioka wanted it in black and white, so Kuroshima brushed out his written promise. With this in hand and the threat of Yamamoto's resignation still ringing in his ears, Tomioka took Kuroshima to see his immediate superior, Fukudome.[12]

Here, too, Kuroshima tried reasoning first. "The entire staff of the Combined Fleet," he told Fukudome, "is confident of the practicability and the ultimate success of the Pearl Harbor attack."[13] As Fukudome described it, Kuroshima took a "very strong and positive" attitude and "virtually demanded that the Pearl Harbor operation be carried out."[14]

Kuroshima had no better luck with Fukudome than he had had with Tomioka, for Fukudome by no means shared Yamamoto's opinion on the subject of Operation Hawaii. And now, of course, he owed his first loyalty to Nagano. Therefore, Fukudome repeated the usual arguments against Yamamoto's madcap scheme. He added, too, that failure would upset Japan's entire war plan and react most unfavorably on all future operations[15]—a masterpiece of understatement.

Not to be denied, Kuroshima fired back that Yamamoto firmly believed that the all-important Southern Operation would not succeed unless the Japanese Navy first removed the threat posed by the U.S. Pacific Fleet at Hawaii. The Marshalls, which lay athwart the American path of advance, were not fortified strongly enough to offer a sufficiently protective barrier.[16]

Fukudome knew all these arguments by heart, and they impressed him no more now than they ever had. So, for the second time within an hour, Kuroshima hurled Yamamoto's thunderbolt. Fukudome recognized raw, crackling power when he heard it. The Naval General Staff could not keep Yamamoto unless it accepted his plan. Fukudome took Kuroshima next door to Ito, vice chief of the Naval General Staff, who had just been promoted to vice admiral on October 15. Having been Yamamoto's chief of staff from April 10 to September 1, he had a solid background in the Pearl Harbor planning. The enthusiasm of the Combined Fleet's staff for Yamamoto's grand design, however, had not rubbed off on him. Yet the urgency of the hour and Yamamoto's undisguised threat called for a prompt judgment one way or the other. Therefore, he immediately ushered Fukudome and Tomioka to the top of the hierarchy. Kuroshima waited in Ito's office until the other officers completed their session with Nagano.

In Nagano's office Fukudome spoke first. He reviewed the basic discussions which had taken place so far on the Pearl Harbor plan between the Combined Fleet and the Naval General Staff, their essential points of disagreement, the major problems involved in such an operation, and Yamamoto's stubborn insistence on its acceptance. Ito spoke next. He stressed the gravity of the hour and reminded Nagano that this question had been hanging fire for weeks. Now they had to reach a decision. He also emphasized Yamamoto's threat to resign.[17]

Nagano's colleagues tell us that he was a tired old man in October 1941. "When I could deliver a report without Nagano going to sleep, I considered it a very successful operation," said Tomioka.[18] To Nagano's credit, however, he realized his limitations. He had remarked more than once to his colleagues that perhaps his job needed younger blood. Yet, according to Tomioka, "About the end or middle of October, he noticeably and conspicuously changed his attitude and position toward the crisis."[19] This is not surprising, for Nagano had been no dove of peace at the liaison conferences. He could expect that Shimada would give him even less trouble than had Oikawa, and the new premier, Tojo, was a convinced expansionist. No wonder Nagano felt a tingle of new energy. But it did not animate him to the extent of trying conclusions with Yamamoto.

Now Nagano listened without comment or question until Ito and Fukudome had presented their case. "I was for the plan of the Naval Affairs Department," he testified, "as that seemed to be more logical but not to have the Commander of the Fleets resign, as he would have, if the plan did not go through. I thought the best thing to do was to approve."[20]

So Nagano merely stated that Yamamoto had studied the problem more thoroughly than anyone else. Since he was so determined and had so much confidence in the ability of the Combined Fleet to carry out the attack, it was probably best to let him execute the operation.[21] Nagano based his consent on two conditions: (1) The Pearl Harbor attack would not interfere in any way with the Southern Operation, and (2) nothing would be done to weaken the air strength of the Navy in its attack on the south.[22]

The officers then returned to Ito's office, where Ito informed Kuroshima that Nagano had sanctioned the Pearl Harbor attack. Kuroshima's heart pounded with joy. "Now Yamamoto and the staff of the Combined Fleet have been spared the embarrassment of resigning their positions," he told Fukudome happily.[23]

Nagano's authorization was not the final approval of the Naval General Staff. That came in early November, when Yamamoto's plan was incorporated into Combined Fleet Operation Order No. 1. Even then, no one could be absolutely certain that Japan would actually go to war with the United States since the decision rested ultimately with the government. Nevertheless, with Nagano's approval, the Japanese Navy had taken a very significant step. The long, bitter disputes, the ceaseless counterproposals, the agonizing hesitations came to an end. All concerned felt a new kinship and enthusiasm. "For the first time the members of the Naval General Staff began to feel as one with the Combined Fleet," said Fukudome. "They now were free to exert every possible effort in helping Yamamoto and his officers work out the details of the operation."[24]

The question inevitably arises: Did Yamamoto really mean to resign? Or was the threat that dedicated poker player's supreme bluff? Indeed, it is difficult to picture Yamamoto, a patriot who loved his Emperor and homeland above all else, abandoning his post in his nation's hour of need just because the Naval General Staff would not play the game by his rules.

Nagano might have turned Yamamoto down, ended the Pearl Harbor discussions once and for all, and—granted Yamamoto's threat was sincere— have gotten rid of him and his whole school of thought at one stroke. Why did he not do so? Apparently the answer is that he never considered going to war against the United States without Yamamoto at the helm of the Combined Fleet. "The idea was inconceivable," said Fukudome. "Although we in Tokyo were against the Pearl Harbor plan, Nagano had the utmost confidence in Yamamoto's abilities and judgment. He finally agreed because he knew Yamamoto was not bluffing. If this seems strange, it must be remembered that Yamamoto's position and influence in the Japanese Navy were unique. He was in truth a leviathan among men."[25]

Shortly before 1300 on October 20 *Nagato* arrived in Saeki Bay from Morozumi Anchorage. Kusaka and his opposite number from the submarines, Mito, visited the flagship with the skipper of the new superbattleship *Yamato*. Kusaka reported on his recent trip to Tokyo, impressing Ugaki not at all. He recorded rather acidly in his diary: "Had he been so enthusiastic as this time in the previous conference with the General Staff, the issue would have easily been settled, but he was rather a troublemaker as he reversed his previous opinion. I think the Senior Staff Officer [Kuroshima] must have had a hard time. . . ."[26]

The next day, October 21, the Operations Section of the Naval General Staff discussed "orders and directives to be sent out prior to the outbreak of war," which Uchida drafted. They also wound up the contingency combat plan for naval operations against the United States, Great Britain, and Holland. "It is expected that we are going to war on 8 December," Uchida noted.[27]

Kuroshima returned from Tokyo on October 22 crowned with the victor's laurels. When he told of the results, joy reigned aboard *Nagato*. Ugaki, no particular fan of Kuroshima's under normal circumstances, recorded in his diary: "It was a great success that he could conclude an agreement for the 'Amo' operation [the Pearl Harbor project] as the Fleet wanted. It seemed that the Commander-in-Chief had made up his mind to resign from his post if this agreement could not be made."[28]

But Yamamoto's triumph would ring hollow unless the First Air Fleet could be ready before the fast-narrowing gap between the diplomatic situation and the war preparations closed altogether. Ugaki felt a bit sour toward that organization:

> I judge that Yamamoto's resolution was made clear to Nagumo the other day when the latter pressed Yamamoto for an answer concerning the operation. But Nagumo's request was a bit too hasty, was it not? What the hell is the attitude of the First Air Fleet? In view of the fact that it has evaded Yamamoto's plan from the beginning, it should have suggested others for the job since it could not control its subordinates.
>
> That man Nagumo—not only does he have words with others but he is given to bluffing when drunk. Even now Nagumo is not fully prepared to send himself and his men into the jaws of death and achieve results two or three times greater than the sacrifices entailed. . . . If Nagumo and his Chief of Staff strongly oppose this operation, and feel they cannot carry it out, they should resign their posts.

Ugaki "expressed this idea to Yamamoto," who agreed. But after thinking it over, he and his chief of staff decided "that such a step should be avoided as long as the situation permits. . . ." Yamamoto also indicated that with Ozawa just appointed to command the Southern Expeditionary Fleet on October 18, the Navy had "no other adequate candidate for that post. . . ."[29]

The idea of replacing Nagumo was not new to Yamamoto. Several days after Kusaka and Onishi visited Yamamoto to express their opposition to the Pearl Harbor project, Yamamoto had said to Watanabe, "If there are any admirals who oppose the Pearl Harbor plan, I will get rid of them and we will proceed with admirals who are agreeable to the plan."[30]

The truth is, Yamamoto had no concrete reason to dismiss Nagumo. He had been a loyal and expert leader of the First Air Fleet. He never made any secret of his misgivings, but he had worked for his new fleet's success with all his considerable ability and could show an excellent record of taut ships, high morale, solid training accomplishments. It would be a shocking injustice to fire him out of hand because he opposed an operation which any sensible man—Yamamoto included—had to admit offered many serious hazards.

No one could deny that Nagano's permission to adopt the Pearl Harbor plan "in principle" left the strategic and tactical picture virtually unchanged. Approval did not guarantee success. What had been dangerous before remained dangerous. Despite Nagano's final word, a widespread belief still existed that the plan should not and could not be executed.

Curiously enough, no one saw the problems inherent in the Pearl Harbor project more clearly than did Yamamoto himself. And nowhere did he open his heart and mind more completely than in a letter dated October 24 written to Navy Minister Shimada.[31] First, Yamamoto frankly commiserated with Shimada on his appointment, declaring that he counted himself in such a crisis "extremely fortunate in being able to devote myself exclusively to affairs of the fleet." Then he confided in Shimada his fears of the heavy losses Japan would sustain and his consequent determination to open the war with "a powerful air force strike deep at the enemy's heart at the very beginning of the war and thus to deal a blow, material and moral, from which it will not be able to recover for some time."

Obviously Yamamoto had studied his opposite number at Pearl Harbor and respected him, for he went on: "Judging from Admiral Kimmel's character and the recent trend of thought in the American Navy, it does not appear to me likely that the American Navy will necessarily confine itself to the strategy of a steady frontal offensive." In other words, he doubted that the enemy would obligingly plunge into the massed strength of the Combined Fleet as visualized in the Great All-Out Battle concept.

Yamamoto turned his attention to a possible American offensive, with all the grim results this might entail for his beloved country. Then he returned to the subject closest to his heart:

> I have recently heard that there are some elements in the General Staff who argue that since the air operation to be carried out immediately upon outbreak of war was after all nothing more than a secondary operation in

which the chance of success was about fifty-fifty, the use of the entire air force in such a venture was too risky to merit consideration.

But even more risky and illogical, it seems to me, is the idea of going to war against America, Britain, and China following four years of exhausting operations in China and with the possibility of fighting Russia also to be kept in mind and having, moreover, to sustain ourselves unassisted for ten years or more in a protracted war over an area several times more vast than the European war theater. If, in the face of such odds, we decide to go to war—or rather, are forced to do so by the trend of events—I, as the authority responsible for the fleet, can see little hope of success in any ordinary strategy. . . .

One can almost feel Shimada's scalp begin to crawl. "These matters the senior staff officer of my fleet explained to the responsible authorities in Tokyo when he was there recently and obtained their approval," Yamamoto continued. "But there seem to be some who have misgivings as to my character and ability as supreme commander."

One wonders where Yamamoto got that idea. Naturally no such positive a personality ever moves through life without acquiring some enemies, yet the entire Naval General Staff had just collapsed at his threat of resignation. "The fact is," he went on, "that I do not think myself qualified for the post of Commander in Chief of the Combined Fleet, and besides, there is no time to think of one's own interests in a time of such national emergency as the present."

The first part of that sentence was Japanese politeness; the second part, pure Yamamoto. He therefore charged Shimada: "Please dispose of the various problems from the broad point of view and having regard to what I have set forth above." Thus obliquely, Yamamoto told his classmate that if Shimada had to toss him overboard to win consent to the overall strategy, so be it.

When, at the time of the revision of operational plans for the Combined Fleet, I caused air operations in the initial stage of the war to be included therein, the state of my mind was that this operation was so difficult and so dangerous that we must be prepared to risk complete annihilation. . . .

War with America and Britain should still be avoidable when the overall situation is taken into consideration, and every effort should of course be made to that end. But I wonder whether Japan, having been driven into the present situation, has the courage and strength necessary to make such a change of attitude now. I fear with trepidation that the only thing that can save the situation now is the imperial decision.

Yamamoto had never studied psychology, but he knew his countrymen, knew how agonizing it was for a Japanese to admit a mistake. Unfortunately, as the Japanese Cabinet was even then discovering, the imperial wishes did not suffice to turn the tide.

Considering Yamamoto's very real fears for the outcome of a Japanese-American-British war, one can only regret that he did not see and act upon the alternative available to him. If he had enough weight to force-feed the Pearl

Harbor scheme to the Naval General Staff, he might have carried sufficient influence to persuade the Navy to refuse to sanction hostilities that offered so little prospect of victory. In that case diplomacy might have saved the day.

Instead, Yamamoto devoted his skill and energy to selling a plan which, although it seemed an improvement on the one it supplanted, never inspired wholehearted confidence, being at best a calculated risk, as Yamamoto himself admitted. Worse still, Yamamoto's venture absolutely guaranteed that the United States would turn its full fury against Japan, destroying all possibility of a negotiated peace.

Exactly when Shimada learned about Pearl Harbor is not clear. While Yamamoto did not mention the subject by name in his letter of October 24, it is obvious from the phraseology that he knew Shimada would understand what he was talking about.

Yamamoto may have been testing Shimada's reaction in case he did indeed decide to relieve Nagumo. He still had a lurking desire to lead the attack himself, as he confided briefly to Fuchida one day about this time.[32] On the other hand, if he intended to put some starch into *Yurufun* and clear the decks for forceful naval action at Cabinet level, he failed lamentably. For Shimada was not the type to oppose Nagano, not to mention Tojo and Sugiyama. He would swim with the tide.

PART II

ACTION

CHAPTER 38

"OTHER

KIND OF

PEOPLE"

Uneasy and with a deep sense of futility, on October 20 Nomura sent his congratulations to Shimada, scrupulously routing the message through Shigenori Togo, the new foreign minister. He castigated the Navy for its failure to cooperate with him, then added, "I cannot tell you how much in the dark I am. I have talked along my own lines with the Secretary of State so often that, if we now explored the situation from a new angle, all my presence would do would be to confuse the situation. . . ."[1]

Nomura had not yet received a policy statement from the new government and obviously believed that, if he carried the Tojo ball, he would have to reverse his field. The foreign minister hastened to reassure him:

> . . . The new cabinet differs in no way from the former one in its sincere desire to adjust Japanese-United States relations on a fair basis. . . .
> We urge, therefore, that choosing an opportune moment, either you or Wakasugi let it be known to the United States by indirection, that our country is not in a position to spend much more time discussing this matter. Please continue the talks, emphasizing our desire for a formal United States counterproposal. . . . [2]

Evidently Togo's message with its all-too-familiar refrain and its whiff of chicanery struck Nomura as the last straw. He countered with one so moving that in reading it, even after all these years, one has the sensation of having inadvertently violated a friend's privacy:

> . . . I am firmly convinced that I should retire from office along with the resignation of the previous Cabinet.
> From the first, the Secretary of State has recognized my sincerity, but it

has been his judgment that I have no influence in Tokyo. So is the President's opinion, I hear. . . .

I am now, so to speak, the skeleton of a dead horse. It is too much for me to lead a sham existence, cheating others as well as myself. I do not mean to run away from the battlefield, but I believe that this is the course I should take as a public man.[3]

But Tokyo still had a use for Nomura. Togo fairly purred across the miles his "hope that you will see fit to sacrifice all of your own personal wishes and remain at your post."[4] Having put his hand to the plow, Nomura would not look back as long as his Emperor needed him. Many Japanese were glad to die for their country; Nomura was willing to do something perhaps more difficult: suffer humiliation on behalf of Japan.

On October 23 the liaison conference met in Tokyo to convene every day until the end of the month, except for October 26, when Premier Tojo and Shimada went to Ise to worship at the Grand Shrine. These conferences, all lengthy and some stormy, took up a series of eleven questions pertaining to national policy, and for historical purposes they may be considered as a unit.

A number of things rapidly became evident at these meetings. In the first place, despite the Emperor's calling for a clean slate when he appointed Tojo premier, the conferees could not lure the moving finger of time back to cancel the imperial conference of September 6. In fact, no one tried very hard to do so.

In the second place, Tojo quickly discovered that it was one thing to be war minister and chivvy the premier, quite another to be the head of government himself. He seemed to develop a mild political schizophrenia which both puzzled and disturbed his Army and Navy colleagues.

Thirdly, the rift between the Supreme Command and the War and Navy ministries had never been wider. Tojo insisted that the government take the time to study the situation, and Shimada was characteristically vague in his statements; but Sugiyama and Nagano clamored for a quick decision one way or the other.[5]

On October 30 the conference approved a program later known as Proposal A, which may be summarized as follows: There would be no change in regard to the Tripartite Pact and withdrawal of troops from either French Indochina or China; however, Japan would negotiate over China on the understanding that troops would remain there for twenty-five years. As for the Hull Four Principles, "to accept on principle with conditions attached" was impossible. The Japanese were willing to apply the concept of nondiscrimination of international trade in China if this also applied to the rest of the world.[6]

Meanwhile, the Navy forged full speed ahead. Once the Naval General Staff capitulated to Yamamoto, it incorporated his daring design into Japan's overall war plan. And because the Navy and Army must cooperate in this endeavor, the Army had to share the secret. So in late October and early November the Navy, through various channels, officially informed a group of key Army officers about the Pearl Harbor attack.[7] Of course, some of them had known what was in the wind since early September. But now at last the word was official.

The number of Army officers who found out about Operation Hawaii before the fact is too long and involved to examine here. When they heard about the operation, they had little to say. Tojo and his generals realized that much depended upon the Navy's ability to carry the war to the enemy and to sustain the offensive against the U.S. Pacific Fleet. So the Army would cooperate to the fullest extent possible.

Yet another governmental level remained to be told—the highest in the land. As soon as Nagano had accepted Yamamoto's Pearl Harbor operation in principle, the Operations Section under Tomioka prepared an outline of the overall war plan for Nagano to present to the Emperor. With this document, which carried the personal stamp of himself, Shimada, Ito, Fukudome, and Tomioka, in hand, Nagano arranged an audience with the Emperor in the Imperial Palace sometime between October 20 and 25.[8]

We do not know how Hirohito reacted to the news of Yamamoto's bold plan. But he must have realized that military preparations had gone much farther than he had anticipated and that his government had chosen to ignore his specific instructions to approach the Japanese-American negotiations with a clean slate. Versed in naval strategy, Hirohito could not have failed to note that this war plan reversed the traditional image of the fleet as Japan's floating Great Wall. The Emperor's shield had become the Emperor's sword.

Helping polish that sword was one of the least conspicuous of His Imperial Majesty's subjects, Yoshikawa. He wondered whether the "Big Island" of Hawaii might not hide something Japan should know about. So, at 0815 on October 13, he scrambled into a commercial aircraft and soared away to inspect Hawaii.

His main purpose was to discover any possible alternative anchorage to Pearl Harbor which the U.S. Pacific Fleet might use. He also made a special effort to check the number of Army personnel and installations. He told Kotoshirodo, who accompanied him at Okuda's request, that he was particularly interested in four sites: (1) Hilo Harbor; (2) Kilauea, which had a National Guard camp; in addition, there had been some talk of a new airport's being built in the lava flats; (3) South Point, where a new airfield was already under construction; and (4) Kohala with its Inter-Island Airways landing at Upholu.[9] By the time the two men left Hilo at 1000 on October 17,[10] Yoshikawa's sharp eyes had discovered a naval radio station and a military airfield. More important, he had come to the definite conclusion that no special hideaway for the U.S. Pacific Fleet existed in the outlying islands. The Americans were concentrating all their eggs in one basket.[11]

During a conversation at the consulate about Japanese espionage Yoshikawa held forth on the subject of "other kind of people," meaning nonnationals of the country which employed them. All nations, including Japan, engaged in this practice, but Yoshikawa doubted that such agents were worth their salt. They started off by submitting a large volume of information, but soon "the law

of diminishing returns began to operate." The employer found himself paying
the same amount for less and less information.[12]

On October 25 Yoshikawa's path crossed that of a man whose case is
tailor-made to prove the validity of the consular spy's strictures on "other kind of
people." This individual was Herr Doktor Bernard Julius Otto Kuehn. Suffice it
to say of Kuehn's background that he had joined the Nazi party in 1930. Since
April 1936 he and his wife, Friedel, and their family had been established in
Honolulu, ostensibly to enable him to study Japanese at the University of
Hawaii. He also attempted a career in real estate and in the furniture business,
without success. He spent some time in Japan in 1935 and again in 1936. The
general picture which Kuehn's career presents is that of a well-bred, fairly
well-educated drifter.[13]

The Nazi party could have decided quite early that this man had the
temperament for espionage. In his original statement to the FBI of January
1942, Kuehn made no mention of the interesting fact that during the period
1928 through 1930 he belonged to the German Navy's secret police, although
this came out later. Nor did he confide the still more interesting detail that he
had been under contract to the Japanese Navy since 1935. In that year he
contacted Captain Tadao Yokoi, the Japanese naval attaché in Berlin, and signed
an initial contract for two years at a salary of $2,000 a month plus $6,000 bonus
at the end of each year, with the contract renewable at the close of each period
if all went well.[14]

Kuehn also remained discreetly silent about an interview with Kanji
Ogawa in Japan that same year, at which time Kuehn discussed intelligence
plans with other officers of the Naval General Staff. Ogawa accepted Kuehn,
although with some misgivings. He worried about Kuehn's ability to do the job,
not so much because he mistrusted his recruit as because the man appeared too
nervous and jumpy for such an assignment.

Duly approved, the Kuehns settled in Honolulu and made themselves
agreeable. The Japanese renewed Kuehn's contract in 1938, although he had
earned the reputation at headquarters in Tokyo of being a "money eater."[15]

In March 1939 Ogawa stopped off in Honolulu en route to Washington to
give Kuehn a portable radio transmitter of special design with a "quickly
devised" aerial. The entire transmitter fitted into a suitcase and had a range of
100 miles. Ogawa also gave Kuehn instructions to lie low. If war came between
Japan and the United States, he was to use the equipment to send messages to
Japanese submarines waiting off Oahu. These submarines would relay the
messages to Japan.[16]

Naturally all these goings-on did not pass unnoted. The Kuehns had
incurred the suspicions of the District Intelligence Office, and by 1938 or early
1939 the DIO had spotted Kuehn as a probable agent for either Germany or
Japan, or both.[17]

After the freezing of Japanese assets in July 1941 Kuehn contacted Okuda
to request that he send a private code message to a friend in Tokyo concerning
some funds due Mrs. Kuehn; moreover, he hinted that the money was payment

for services rendered. Okuda then agreed to send the message.[18] No doubt he would have agreed to anything within reason to get Kuehn out of the consulate compound, where his presence must have caused him some uneasy moments.

When Tachibana returned to Tokyo to Naval Intelligence, he, too, took a good hard look at Kuehn and did not like what he saw. As he explained in his fluent but flavorful English:

> Kuehn was not only considered doubtful as to whether he would be loyal to his work, but his ability as a spy was so poor and primitive that it was feared he would not be able to get sufficient information for our intention of launching an air strike upon Pearl Harbor. He was not bold enough, too, to commit espionage activity in the face of danger. Moreover, there was a fear that our relation to him would be suspected by the U.S. with a result that he would play false to Japan and our secrecy might be leaked out through him. Therefore, it was decided to use him only when other means were of no avail, and preparations were made for that end.[19]

On the morning of October 25 Yoshikawa told Kotoshirodo that Okuda wished him to drive the two of them somewhere that afternoon, but he did not say where. Kotoshirodo asked Seki, "Where do you think we are going?" Seki had not the slightest idea.[20] At 1530 that afternoon Okuda and Yoshikawa left the consulate with Kotoshirodo at the wheel of his Ford. Holding something that resembled a money bag, Okuda sat in the back with Yoshikawa. At the intersection of Kuulei and Mauluni roads Kotoshirodo stopped the car, and Yoshikawa got out. Okuda directed Kotoshirodo to drive on a little further, park, and wait for Yoshikawa to return.[21]

Yoshikawa had to walk some distance before he reached the Kuehns' house. There he turned over to Kuehn a package and a letter. Kuehn stated that this contained a note typewritten in English, asking if he had a shortwave transmitter and if he "would be willing to make a test at a certain stated time which was on a night several nights later, on a certain wavelength."

This was not the sort of message Kuehn liked to receive from his employers. Yoshikawa handed him an envelope and a sheet of paper on which Kuehn scrawled his answer: He "was unable to make the test." He was "quite nervous" as he stuffed the reply into the envelope and gave it back to Yoshikawa. Declining a receipt, Yoshikawa departed. Kuehn promptly opened the packet and counted out $14,000, "mostly in new $100 bills, some $20 bills." Then he hastily shredded the note about the radio test and burned the scraps.[22]

Yoshikawa claimed that he did not know much about the relations between Kuehn and the Japanese Navy or Kita, although the consul general briefed him a bit about Kuehn before sending him on this errand. Any clerk could have delivered this money and the envelope with the message; however, Kita had told Yoshikawa that this was "a very important mission."[23] Probably he wanted Yoshikawa to have the opportunity of sizing up his successor because the Japanese Navy was keeping Kuehn on ice to take over Yoshikawa's duties once war started. In that event the Japanese would need "other kind of people" to keep the information flowing to Tokyo.

The information and funds which Yoshikawa passed to Kuehn had arrived by ship from Tokyo in the keeping of a "certain naval officer," concerning whose identity there is a conflict of evidence. He had a fivefold mission in relation to Kuehn: (1) to formulate an objective for the information to be procured and to revise Kuehn's code; (2) to establish a method of communication and outline of a test; (3) to prepare a radio transmitter and establish a reserve communications channel; (4) to expand the Kuehn spy ring; and (5) to deliver the necessary funds.[24]

Yoshikawa recalled Kuehn as being "very upset,"[25] and Kuehn himself admitted to nervousness. Did he suddenly realize that his pleasant path might soon end in an abrupt precipice—that matters were mounting to a climax when his employers would expect him to take up the real burden of responsibility and risk? Did this dilettante recognize that he might have to step into shoes much too large for him? Did this European who had dabbled in Oriental lore look into the flat dark eyes and see the soul of Asia, fathomless and ages old? We cannot know what troubled Kuehn's heart at that dramatic moment. We only know that the Nazi met the samurai—and the Nazi was afraid.

CHAPTER 39

"BASED ON

DECEPTION"

All warfare is based on deception," wrote Sun-tzu around 500 B.C., in that Chinese military classic *The Art of War.* He had further words of wisdom: "If the enemy leaves a door open, you must rush in."[1] At the psychological moment the United States had left a door ajar, and Tokyo hastened to thrust a foot over the threshold.

The economic midsummer freeze had immobilized Japanese commercial shipping between Japan and the United States. Tokyo opened negotiations with Washington in early August to release these ships. The Naval General Staff urged the Foreign Office to reach an agreement as soon as possible because it planned to use any renewed passenger service for espionage purposes. After several weeks of discussions Hull and Nomura agreed that three Japanese passenger vessels could make one voyage apiece from Japan to the United States, provided they carried no commercial cargo.

Accordingly the American and Japanese press announced on October 12 that three NYK (*Nippon Yusen Kaisha*) liners would depart from Japan for the United States with the following schedules: the *Tatuta Maru* to leave Yokohama on October 15 and arrive in San Francisco via Honolulu on October 30; the *Nitta Maru* to leave Yokohama on October 20 and arrive in Seattle on November 1; and the *Taiyo Maru* to leave Yokohama on October 22 and arrive in Honolulu on November 1.[2]

Bicknell thought there might be more than met the eye in the shipping agreement. "It will be recalled that the Japanese were careful to remove Japanese nationals from the interior of south China before spreading military operations to that section," he pointed out in his "Intelligence Estimate of the Japanese Situation" issued as of 1200 on October 25.[3]

The United States entered into the agreement in the hope that it would help alleviate the tension existing between the two countries. Whatever Tokyo's original purpose, the Third Bureau seized the chance to ship its own top secret spy mission to Hawaii. Japan's naval leaders had little reason to complain about the reports which Kita had been sending them via the Foreign Office, but Naval Intelligence wanted to double-check Kita's information. The Third Bureau also wished to have "experienced naval officers in their respective fields personally observe the actual conditions of Pearl Harbor."[4] It feared that the reports from Honolulu "lacked technical details"; moreover, "telegrams could not fully convey what was obtained there."[5]

The Naval General Staff selected for the task officers with excellent records and specialized knowledge. Commander Toshihide Maejima, the senior member of the team, was an expert on submarines. Confident, of sound judgment, and with a trained observer's knack for detail, Maejima would bring back a useful and realistic report. He had known about Yamamoto's plan for several months.[6] His partner, Sublieutenant Keiu Matsuo, whom the Sixth Fleet chose for the mission, had been working with the midget submarines.[7] He was to explore the possibilities of minisubs' penetrating Pearl Harbor.

The third member, Lieutenant Commander Suguru Suzuki, an aviation officer and a good friend of Genda's, was to play a more significant role in this vital espionage assignment than his submariner colleagues. Tall and thin, with an intelligent face and a sharp, nimble mind, Suzuki had served thirteen months in the Intelligence Section of the Naval General Staff with the specific duty of studying U.S. air power, and particular emphasis on carrier warfare.

Although not officially informed of the Pearl Harbor plan until early September, Suzuki attended the war games held in Tokyo that month, including the closely guarded discussions in the Secret Room.[8]

Tachibana informed Suzuki of his mission, and they set to work on the strategy to be followed during his assignment. Suzuki began a thorough, though necessarily hurried, study of Hawaii and Pearl Harbor, memorizing facts and figures so he would not have to keep notes, which might fall into unauthorized hands.[9]

When the *Tatuta Maru* sailed from Yokohama on October 15, she carried an entirely new crew under her captain, Sakao Kimura, a reserve naval officer. She also had on board a naval officer known only as "Lt. Cmdr. F," who was to confer with Kita in Honolulu, then continue to San Francisco, where he would collect information concerning Soviet, American, and other merchant ships bound for the Far East via the northern Pacific route, as well as all the intelligence he could pick up about the U.S. Navy on the West Coast.[10] Two other somewhat mysterious figures, one "Inspector Kuniaki Maeda" and a representative of the Department of Communications, Kenichi Tsuchiya, were also aboard. They have been identified respectively as Lieutenant Commander Minato Nakajima of the American Section of the Third Bureau and a Foreign Ministry courier.[11] The *Tatuta Maru* agents had another mission—"To establish a reserve communication channel" with Hawaii in case the United States should suspend normal communications to Japan or prohibit the use of code messages.[12]

The ship made the entire voyage to Hawaii with her radio transmitter silent. But that was not all. Shortly before she left Yokohama, Captain Bunjiro Yamaguchi gave her skipper a sealed envelope with instructions to guard it carefully and deliver it to the Japanese consul general in Honolulu, who was to board the vessel as soon as it docked. This envelope contained a high-priority request for information about the U.S. Navy in Pearl Harbor. It specifically asked Kita to prepare immediately a detailed map showing the exact size, strength, and location of every military installation on Oahu. A special mission would arrive shortly in Honolulu to pick it up and to confer with him on other matters of urgent importance.[13]

The *Tatuta Maru* docked in Honolulu Harbor at 1000 on Thursday, October 23. Shortly thereafter Kita went aboard, and Kimura handed him the sealed envelope. There is every reason to believe that either Kimura or a member of the special mission gave Kita another package containing the money which Yoshikawa delivered to Kuehn on October 25, together with instructions "to prepare radio transmitters and also to establish a reserve channel by use of amateur radio men."[14] The liner remained in Honolulu Harbor only one day and sailed for San Francisco on Friday afternoon, the twenty-fourth.

Back in Tokyo, Suzuki, Maejima, and Matsuo completed preparations for their secret mission. On October 21 at a final briefing in the Naval General Staff, Suzuki received an extensive questionnaire with orders to guard it with his life. Otherwise, all orders to both men were oral. First and foremost, they were to keep a sharp lookout for all ship movements in the northern Pacific sea-lanes, for the *Taiyo Maru* was to make a trial run of Nagumo's future course.[15]

Suzuki and Maejima had to double their vigilance in the critical area north of Midway. If U.S. patrol planes winged far enough out from there to spot the *Taiyo Maru*, the First Air Fleet would have to pursue a more distant course. Another vital span was the sea north and west of Oahu. There they must keep razor-sharp vigil for any plane or vessel that could possibly report the task force's approach.

The Naval General Staff also wanted a daily record of the weather and the condition of the sea. As they neared Honolulu, the special agents must note all ship movements of any kind in the waters surrounding Oahu. And while in port, they would seek answers to a host of searching questions.[16]

Neither Suzuki nor Maejima appeared on the passenger list. Suzuki assumed the occupation of assistant purser while Maejima took the role of a doctor, having studied some of the ABCs of medical science just in case.[17] Maejima sailed under the alias of Tsukada; Suzuki saw no reason to change his own name.[18] Matsuo blended among the passengers.[19]

The *Taiyo Maru* sailed from Yokohama on October 22. Like the *Tatuta Maru*, the liner observed strict radio silence and operated directly under the Japanese government for this trip. Throughout the voyage Suzuki, Maejima, and Matsuo paced the deck, scanning the tumbling waves, and swept the far horizon with their high-powered binoculars. Several times each day they checked weather and distance traveled. Suzuki daily prepared a report on visibility, direction and velocity of the wind, pitch and roll of the ship, and sea conditions. At night the special agents alternated their weary watch, each in turn concentrating on ship lights. It was a tiring, monotonous business, but with so much riding on the success of the Pearl Harbor attack, they could not overlook the slightest detail.[20]

When the *Taiyo Maru* changed course to approach Oahu from the north, the sea became calmer, the weather warmer, and Suzuki tenser. Before dawn on the morning of November 1 the ship reached the critical area 200 miles north of Oahu. Here for the first time throughout the voyage a U.S. patrol plane spotted the *Taiyo Maru*. Suzuki made a note: "Reconnaissance line—200 miles."

Proceeding at fourteen knots, the ship arrived at a point about 100 miles north of Oahu. Here Suzuki saw a formation of U.S. planes. Unlikely as it appears, according to Suzuki they began a simulated attack against the ship. So he jotted down another note: "Attack line 100 miles."[21]

Soon the port loomed ahead with its magnificent background of green mountains wreathed in white fog and early morning mist. Now Suzuki and his colleagues could tabulate the results. They were beyond expectation. The weather had been fine except for one brief storm. Sea conditions could be tricky but not impossible. They had sighted no patrol craft north of Midway, and reconnaissance north of Oahu seemed to extend not much farther than 200 miles. Above all, Suzuki and his fellow officers had not sighted a single vessel throughout the voyage. This discovery gave Suzuki hope and confidence.[22]

The *Taiyo Maru* nudged into Honolulu Harbor at 0830 on Saturday, November 1. The timing was perfect. As the liner slowly sought her moorings, Suzuki and Maejima stationed on the bridge with binoculars had an excellent opportunity to observe early-morning conditions around Oahu at the approximate time of the forthcoming attack. Moving into port over the weekend so that they could survey the scene on a Sunday, the day of the future assault, was no accidental stroke of good fortune. The Naval General Staff had planned it just that way.[23]

Suzuki claimed that he could see Pearl Harbor from the bridge. This may have been true, yet it was quite a feat, even if he used binoculars, because Pearl Harbor is six to seven miles from Honolulu Harbor. And during this period Suzuki missed several capital ships moored in the great naval anchorage.

Suzuki and Maejima decided not to take notes of anything aboard ship so that they would be safe if U.S. authorities suddenly inspected the *Taiyo Maru*. They elected not to go ashore. They set up a direct telephone line between the captain's cabin and the gangway. Thus, as they conferred with Kita or other members of the consulate, the Japanese posted at the gangway could alert them if any stranger or suspicious-looking person boarded ship.[24]

Kita came aboard the first day. He visited the ship three or four times, generally bringing along two members of the consulate to carry materials on or off ship. Suzuki revealed his true identity to Kita but to no one else from the consulate. That organization delivered newspapers to the ship every day. Tucked away in each bundle were memorandums and scratch slips of paper containing items of military information. Of course, these newspapers had to pass an American security guard. But that was easy. The particular member of the consulate carrying the papers would voluntarily flip through the pages; the inspector would nod his head and let him pass. Suzuki, Maejima, and Matsuo then searched through the bundle, extracted the pertinent memorandums, and proceeded with their work. Sometimes Suzuki climbed to the bridge to try to double-check information he had just received.[25]

Kita did not permit Yoshikawa near the vessel, although he was the logical person to brief Suzuki, Maejima, and Matsuo. Why subject him to a possible security inspection? Exposure of Yoshikawa might blow wide open the whole Japanese espionage net on Oahu. So Kita himself briefed the agents. As far as we know, no one actually mentioned the plan to attack Pearl Harbor during the conferences aboard the liner.[26]

At their first meeting the special agents told Kita they wanted every scrap of military information available on U.S. forces at Pearl Harbor, on Oahu, or elsewhere in the Islands. Suzuki took a particular interest in the exact strength and disposition of the U.S. Fleet, its training maneuvers and weekend habits. He also wanted to pin down the size of the air forces and the precise location of all military installations. Maejima and Matsuo were to ascertain the capacity of the U.S. Pacific Fleet for resisting submarine attacks in the waters adjacent to Pearl Harbor and to discover the most effective means of employing both large and midget submarines in the operation.[27]

During this first conference Suzuki gave Kita the questionnaire of some 100 items which the Third Bureau had prepared. As soon as he returned to the consulate, Kita turned it over to Yoshikawa for completion. It covered every possible subject of interest to the Naval General Staff.

"When I saw all those items and all those questions, a number of things popped into my mind," said a former member of the consulate. "Would it be possible for the Japanese to come all the way out here and launch a successful attack?" He added, "I do not recall any statement by consulate personnel that Pearl Harbor might be attacked. But after the episode of the ships and the important questionnaire, the implications were there. The consulate personnel who were in the know considered an attack possible. It all depended upon Japanese-U.S. negotiations."[28]

Yoshikawa also recognized that with the coming of the *Taiyo Maru*, following the *Tatuta Maru*, Japan had crossed an important threshold. "I thought the hour of crisis was approaching," he said.

Kita gave Yoshikawa strict instructions to write his answers as small as possible. Someone had to smuggle the report back aboard the *Taiyo Maru*, and Kita did not want it to be large or bulky enough to attract the attention of U.S. authorities.

Yoshikawa worked day and night on his report. He drew upon the wealth of material he had already collected, and he had Mikami drive him around the Pearl Harbor area for a current check on the U.S. Pacific Fleet and its anchorage. He also prepared a number of large maps. One of these showed Fleet dispositions at Pearl Harbor; another, U.S. air power on Oahu. He focused on all the airports and reserve fields, even golf courses, for the Americans might utilize these as emergency landing fields.[29]

The Naval General Staff also wanted to know whether the Americans could be caught napping. Yoshikawa's answers suggested they probably could. Suzuki agreed. For the day after the ship entered port, he jumped out of his bunk early and sped up to the bridge to survey the relaxed Sunday scene. He saw no training or bomber flights in the air, as he had seen on other days. He spotted only transport planes in the afternoon and a few vessels entering Honolulu Harbor.[30]

Air patrols in the Hawaiian area plagued the high brass in Tokyo as much as any other problem. Yoshikawa had turned a sharp eye on them since he arrived in Honolulu, and of late he had redoubled his scrutiny. He drew up observation records to cover every hour from dawn to dark: when patrol planes started their flights, how long they stayed out, the type and number of aircraft used, and their general arc of search. To the south aerial reconnaissance was fairly good, but to the north it was "at a minimum," "poorly organized," in fact, "downright bad." Of course, Yoshikawa could never be sure how far out the planes flew and whether they changed direction once beyond sight of Oahu. He had to make some educated guesses.[31]

Suzuki, too, watched the flights from bases on Oahu between dawn and dark every day the *Taiyo Maru* was in port. He always noted the number of aircraft, the type, color, height, speed, direction of flight, time of takeoff and return. If they were bombers from Hickam Field, he checked on their size (two-engine or four-engine), numbers, formation, and training area.[32]

Yoshikawa's report also gave Suzuki and Maejima an excellent analysis of weather conditions over Hawaii. This was no trick, for detailed weather coverage of the islands and a broad stretch of the surrounding Pacific appeared almost daily in the Honolulu press.[33]

How could a representative of the Honolulu consulate carry up the gangplank of the *Taiyo Maru* Yoshikawa's long report and its accompanying maps without being caught? But he did. Yoshikawa claimed that Kita took the information aboard, but Suzuki recalled that someone else did the job.[34]

Naturally, the special agents did not find answers to all their questions. Suzuki claimed he observed no carriers. He knew, however, that there were a substantial number of carrier planes on Oahu, from which he estimated the number of flattops in Hawaiian waters to be one or two. Yet during his stay in Honolulu Harbor both *Enterprise* and *Lexington* moored near Ford Island. Nor did Suzuki manage to obtain sufficient accurate information about the air bases on Oahu. Hickam proved something of an exception, but even there the facts were not entirely reliable. As for the big fighter base at Wheeler, Suzuki reported, "We were not able to investigate the facility."[35]

While Suzuki worked on the U.S. Fleet and American air power, Maejima and Matsuo concentrated mainly on submarine problems. One of the most important questions which they tried to answer was: What islands in the Hawaiian chain could provide relatively safe havens where the Japanese submarines could launch and receive their aircraft or pick up midget submarine crews or aviators following the attack? One of the most useful, they discovered, was Niihau.[36] Privately owned and sparsely populated, it lay just a few miles to the southwest of Kauai. Oddly enough, Fuchida, working independently on the basis of material available to him in Japan, made the same selection.[37]

A second topic for study was the problem facing Japanese submariners outside the entrance to Pearl Harbor and within the anchorage itself. On this score Maejima and Matsuo could not come up with positive answers, for much depended on U.S. patrols at the time of the attack and on the ability of the submarine skipper. Nor could one ignore the element of sheer chance.

Even so, they reached several conclusions. For one, a submarine captain operating outside Pearl Harbor could not possibly see Kimmel's ships within. Secondly, in the daytime a submarine skipper could recognize the narrow channel entrance to the anchorage from seven to eight miles out, provided he stood on the bridge. Thirdly, if he used only his periscope for sighting, he would have to approach within two or three miles of Pearl Harbor for a decent view of the entrance. Fourthly, recognition of the harbor mouth at night would require a navigational fix on landmarks around or near the channel entrance.[38]

In view of the tension of the times and the fact that the FBI, DIO, Army G-2, and Customs all had their eyes on the *Taiyo Maru*, it appears mystifying that the comings and goings between the Honolulu consulate and the special agents aboard the liner went off without a hitch. The answer was that American counterintelligence organizations were quite preoccupied with the returning and outgoing passengers. The customs officials thoroughly examined all the baggage of these returning travelers but found nothing of interest from either the naval or military standpoint. The outgoing passengers received an even closer screening.[39]

The vessel slid out of Pier 8 on the evening of November 5. Usually NYK liners headed out in an atmosphere of gay festivity, but this trip no colorful streamers floated down from the vessel, no throngs of laughing people waved good-bye. Still Suzuki, Maejima, and Matsuo had no complaints. They were sailing home with valuable foreknowledge of the enemy. A vigilant Coast Guard cutter trailed the liner out to sea. With the departure of the *Taiyo Maru*, the "last direct communication with Japan" had been cut.[40]

CHAPTER 40

"IN

THE HANDS

OF GOD"

$\mathbf{A}$gainst a background of autumnal beauty Nagumo's men continued their training for the Pearl Harbor attack. On the afternoon of October 23 two officers who had been to Germany on an inspection tour from February through August lectured Yamamoto's staff on their findings. One of these briefing officers, Lieutenant Commander Takeshi Naito, was a good friend of Fuchida's. Naito delivered a lecture in Kagoshima which Fuchida attended chiefly to pump him about the British torpedo raid on the Italian ships at Taranto.* Naito had been assistant naval attaché in Berlin at the time and had flown to Taranto to investigate the attack and estimate the damage. Naito stayed at Kagoshima overnight, and Fuchida interrogated him extensively all the next day.

What Naito told him about the British strike encouraged Fuchida greatly. Of course, conditions at Pearl Harbor would be different and far more difficult, with limited maneuvering space and many dockyard obstructions. Fuchida carefully kept Naito from suspecting that he had more than an academic interest in a remarkable episode of sea-air warfare.[1]

By this time Fuchida had a personal reason for encouragement, having been promoted to commander on October 15. Murata achieved on that date a well-merited move up to lieutenant commander. His men had been making steady progress. The depth recorders indicated a torpedo sinkage of twenty meters (approximately sixty-six feet), but beyond this they could not go, try as they might. The pilots could not understand the apparently unreasonable demand for a maximum depth of ten meters. What fleet would anchor in such

---

*See Chapter 5.

shallow water? They wondered darkly if Fuchida might not be feeling the strain.[2]

Fuchida knew that if his men realized the object of their training, they would redouble their efforts and grumble no more. Genda, too, thought it "a little too much" to work the men so hard when they did not know why.[3] He also feared possible security leaks in the First Air Fleet—not deliberate, of course, but through innocent chatter of the fliers who did not know the score.[4] But the upper echelon had not yet flashed the green light, so Fuchida "continued to demand more vigorous training," despite his sympathy for his men. Twenty meters might just as well be sixty; he could not concede one meter beyond ten.[5]

No blame could justly rest on the pilots or torpedomen, every one of whom labored unceasingly. They had done all that human beings could do with the existing tools. Even the ebullient Murata teetered on the verge of admitting defeat.[6] Operations and training had gone as far as they could; now it was up to the technicians.

Research testing had proceeded apace at Yokosuka in quest of a practical torpedo fin. From around early September for approximately a month, the Yokosuka Air Group experimented with one previously considered only as an aerial stablizer. Employing the Model II torpedo, they managed successful runs in twelve meters of water. Moreover, the fin so steadied the torpedo that it could run successfully in a narrow space. Torpedoes thus equipped, with the benefit of actual practice in their use, might answer the needs of the Pearl Harbor operation.

But no sooner had one problem been solved than another emerged: how to obtain enough modified torpedoes for practice. And here thoroughly frustrating news reached Fuchida and his men. Only 30 could be ready by October 15; the second batch of 50 would arrive by October 31; the final 100 would not be available until November 30.[7]

A related question also worried Fuchida exceedingly: the possibility of torpedo nets around the ships in Pearl Harbor. If the Americans had placed the nets, the attack would be almost useless in spite of the skill developed in Murata's painstaking training and the revolutionary breakthrough in the torpedo design.[8]

About late September experiments began at Yokosuka, seeking ways and means of cutting torpedo nets. Yet despite hard work, constant testing, and no dearth of ideas, the net problem remained unsolved. Fukudome tells us that in the event the Japanese discovered that nets protected the American ships, "it was decided to make bombings only against them, giving up torpedo attacks."[9]

When Fuchida and Murata realized that the Yokosuka experiments would not succeed, they discussed another possible solution. The basic reason why these projects failed, the two airmen agreed, was that the escort charge, whether an independent entity or a part of the initial torpedo itself, could not blast a hole large enough for the succeeding aviators to find and exploit. But if they could hit the net hard enough and high enough, almost level with the waterline of the target ship, it would open. So these two flight leaders, with Genda's sanction, decided that if necessary, some of the torpedo planes should dive into the net to break it open—a suicide attack foreshadowing the grim *kamikaze* technique used later in the war. The three did not discuss this idea with their airmen until arrival at the rendezvous in Hitokappu Bay.[10]

Meanwhile, Fuchida's horizontal bombers labored furiously in their own quest for improvement, with results which exceeded even Fuchida's expectations. To the five who would not give up on horizontal bombing—Genda, Furukawa, Fuchida, the test team of Watanabe and Aso—the Japanese Navy owed an immense debt of gratitude. Since the inception of the program in the spring they had increased their accuracy 70 percent and in effect had added a new operational weapon to Japan's naval air strength.[11]

Fuchida continued to give careful consideration to the inexperienced airmen of the Fifth Carrier Division. Because they had not attained skill in night flying, and could not do so in the limited time remaining, he suggested to Genda that the scheduled hour of attack be changed from 0630 to 0800 Hawaiian time. Since sunrise would be at 0606, takeoff at 0600 would enable them to be launched under cover of darkness, reach Oahu in time to achieve early-morning surprise, and still reap the benefits of daylight to and over the targets. This made sense to Genda, so he took it up with Nagumo, who altered the master plan accordingly.[12]

One more major problem faced the First Air Fleet. Of all the task force, only seven ships could make the long northern voyage from Hitokappu Bay to Oahu without refueling—the big carriers *Kaga*, *Shokaku*, and *Zuikaku;* the battleships *Hiei* and *Kirishima;* and the heavy cruisers *Tone* and *Chikuma*.[13] Because of Japan's traditional strategy of fighting in home waters and luring the United States Navy to the western Pacific, the Japanese had not built long-range ships or paid special attention to the techniques of refueling at sea. By mid-1941 they had practiced underway refueling of light cruisers and destroyers. The tanker preceded the ship it was replenishing, with a towline connecting the two. Both kept in motion for fear of submarines. This worked well enough for small vessels because these could follow astern the tankers without too much difficulty. Now, however, a new problem arose: how to service such big ships as *Akagi*, which had too much power and inertia to maneuver easily in case of necessity. A tanker could turn sharply, but a carrier or battleship with its much greater tactical diameter might snap the hose.[14]

Thus, the task force had a problem which no airman, however brilliant, could solve. But fortunately for the Japanese, they had on hand a sound, practical seaman. This project was right in Kusaka's line, and he went to work on it with a will. First, he determined that when the task force set out for Hawaii, every tank would be loaded to capacity and fuel containers would appear where never seen before. This would increase the individual oil supply of *Akagi*, *Soryu*, and *Hiryu*. The carriers had to be fully fueled at all times, because of the high-speed run necessary to whip up a stiff breeze of some thirty knots required for takeoff if nature did not oblige.

Kusaka therefore badgered the Military Affairs Bureau for a waiver of the Navy Ministry's safety directive against loading in certain vacant spaces. At first the Military Affairs people were far from cooperative. But with the help of an unnamed officer in the section who "could see something in the air," Kusaka got his way.[15] Both the Naval General Staff and the Navy Ministry agreed that in case of emergency a fleet commander in chief could lift this restriction. Careful checks then revealed that by using various drums, trim tanks, and the like, *Akagi, Soryu* and *Hiryu*, as well as the two battleships, could carry a good amount of extra oil. But this method was not practicable on *Abukuma* and the destroyers because their hull strength and stability did not permit it.[16]

In essence, the system which Kusaka and his colleagues worked out reversed the traditional refueling position. Henceforth carriers and battleships would precede their tankers. A simple idea? Yes, but someone had to think of it and test it. Destroyers could fuel three at a time—one on each side and one astern the tanker. But refuel they must every day of the cruise to Hawaii. Experiments made in mid-October proved Kusaka's system practicable. By the time the task force started for Hawaii crews of tankers and warships alike were confident they could handle the situation during the voyage.[17]

Toward the end of October Fuchida took another step forward. He divided the pilots into two sections for group training—all the fighters in one, all the bombers in another. These two groups locked in practice aerial combat four times, and the torpedo bombers used the fleet as a target ten times in one two-week period.[18]

After receiving the unwelcome news that the final batch of modified torpedoes would not be available until November 30, the Naval General Staff and the Combined Fleet urgently requested a speedup of the program. Nagumo's airmen would need the entire lot by the end of October. Of course, they could not so inform the ordnancemen, but the task force schedule called for departure to the rendezvous around mid-November. The modified torpedoes must be received and adjusted aboard each carrier before that date. Although more than willing to cooperate, the Naval Ship Administration could promise delivery of the last torpedo no earlier than November 20. Accordingly, all concerned arranged to load the last consignment aboard *Akagi* and *Kaga* when they put in at Sasebo for final war preparations.[19] According to Genda, Yukiro Fukuda of the Mitsubishi firm in Nagasaki had sensed that important matters were afoot—perhaps something would happen in the shallow waters of Vladivostok Bay. So, overcoming Mitsubishi's rules and regulations by hard driving and overtime, he completed the order by November 17.[20]

Genda traveled to Tokyo to hasten delivery and arranged to have some of the Yokosuka trainees help adjust the new fins in case they arrived too late for the First Air Fleet's crews to handle alone. Fuchida was in a gentle sweat of suspense when he received five to ten of the "Torpedoes, Improved II, with

Stability Equipment" at Kagoshima between October 30 and November 4. This number was insufficient for proper training.

The first tests proved the new modified torpedoes "effective but irregular." Then, one crisp autumn day, three real, not dummy, torpedoes equipped with the fins plunged into twelve meters of water. One hit bottom, but the others skimmed triumphantly to the target. Flying above Kagoshima Bay, Fuchida saw the two torpedoes running straight and true, their white trails cutting the blue surface. Two out of three successful torpedo runs, he calculated, meant an expectancy of twenty-seven hits out of forty launchings.[21]

Thus, by the end of October the Japanese had tied up many a loose operational end of the Pearl Harbor plan. The individual actors from Nagumo to the rawest recruit on *Zuikaku* knew their parts. Much remained to be done, but the preparations had reached the point of dress rehearsal.

On October 29 Tomioka and Commander Yugi Yamamoto came to *Nagato* to inform the Combined Fleet of the Naval General Staff's "operational principles, orders, directives, and the central agreement between the Army and Navy."[22] Commander Yamamoto was one of the promising young men with whom Tomioka's organization abounded. The son-in-law of ex-Foreign Minister Toyoda, he had charge of liaison with the Army and overall operations, specifically those concerning China.[23]

After Nagano approved the Pearl Harbor project, the Naval General Staff revised its war plan to include the outline of that operation. Then Nagano presented this "modified national defense plan of the Japanese Fleet" to the Emperor for approval.[24] Tomioka, who had conscientiously and stubbornly opposed the Pearl Harbor project, was now in the very thick of it. Once the Naval General Staff accepted Yamamoto's scheme, it moved full speed ahead and cooperated with the Combined Fleet in every possible way.[25]

Tomioka conferred with Admiral Yamamoto and various members of his staff for several hours.[26] Yamamoto was very pleased to see his bold design incorporated into the blueprint of the Naval General Staff. Hitherto he had authorized the planning, preparation, and training for the proposed attack exclusively on his own initiative. Now that he had the sanction not only of the top brass in Tokyo but of the Emperor himself, he stood on much firmer ground and no longer carried the entire load of responsibility on his own shoulders.[27]

The two emissaries also brought a letter from Fukudome explaining that when the Tojo Cabinet was formed, the Emperor had called for a reconsideration of national policy, "cleaning the slate." To that end, liaison conferences had met since the twenty-third. Because the premier had not disclosed his intentions, the Naval General Staff could not "figure out what conclusion would be reached." Therefore, it desired combat units "to exert further efforts in preparing for the worst contingency. . . ." Ugaki took a dim view of these political goings-on:

> Who could dare reduce our demands? There would be no alternative but to decide on war. If we dilly-dally doing nothing, we would only fall into the

enemy's trap. If we launch negotiations with a firm determination after having made up our minds to go to war and carrying out things to that end, he might unexpectedly give in. That will be the only way left for us facing today's crisis. Unless the enemy changes his mind, there will be no other way but to go to war. . . . [28]

Ugaki's sense of grievance spilled over into the entry for the next day, when Nagumo, along with a few Army officers soon to join the staff of the Southern Army, visited *Nagato.* Evidently Nagumo prodded the Combined Fleet for a definite deadline because Ugaki recorded: "They urge us to fix X-Day immediately but I wonder how the atmosphere in Tokyo is? I suppose they would not be able to reach a decision."[29]

Actually the Naval General Staff had already decided upon December 8, Japanese time, as X-Day. A number of factors went into the choice: (1) The United States was growing stronger day by day in the Pacific, especially in the Philippines; (2) in the dead of winter, weather conditions in the northern Pacific would virtually close that route to the task force, particularly if the Japanese waited until January or February; (3) stocks of war matériel, principally oil, were dwindling; (4) the phase of the moon had to be such as to give the task force maximum moonlight for night operations; (5) the Army wanted to make its move as soon as possible to avoid the worst of the monsoon season; and, last but decidedly not least, (6) intelligence indicated that the bulk of the U.S. Pacific Fleet could be found in harbor on a Sunday.[30]

During this visit to *Nagato* Nagumo could not hide his uneasiness. It is possible that others, too, had their misgivings about the Pearl Harbor venture but were more skilled at concealing their feelings. Ugaki, no admirer of the First Air Fleet's leader, could not resist a dig at him in the privacy of his diary: "Nagumo . . . appears to be extremely anxious about his special mission. I think it natural, but I hope he will not have nervous prostration before the operation takes place." Then he continued with conscious virtue:

> Life and death are in the hands of God. If Nagumo could inflict several times as much damage as he might receive, wouldn't that be enough to satisfy him? If I were to be assigned that mission right now—the appointment to be made by the Emperor—I would do my best, regarding the assigned mission as the greatest honor for a warrior and leave the rest to the grace of God. Nothing would worry me. No one can fight when he fears this and that. If there is more than 60% prospect of success, one should go ahead bravely and resolutely after making preparations to meet the worst.[31]

Apparently Ugaki would have done wonders. Perhaps if Nagumo actually swapped jobs with him, the scenery would have looked different from the other side of the fence, as Tojo had discovered on the political front.

CHAPTER 41

"COMPLETE

WAR

PREPARATIONS"

November 1, a day of strong winds and rough seas, found Yamamoto and his staff aboard *Nagato* in Tosa Bay off the coast of southern Shikoku, where they observed training maneuvers. At 1630 Yamamoto received an urgent confidential telegram from the Navy Ministry requesting him to come to Shimada's offical residence at noon on the third and to avoid anyone's notice.

Curiosity nibbled at Ugaki's mind all day. Would the Naval General Staff ask how long the Combined Fleet could postpone going to war in case of further negotiations? On that score Ugaki had no doubts. "We, as the Combined Fleet, have reached the following conclusion: 8 December is most preferable in view of completion of preparations, moon age and the day of the week." Could the summons mean that Yamamoto would become premier and concurrently navy minister? "This would be against his will."[1]

Actually a Cabinet crisis was narrowly averted that day. The last of the current liaison conferences had begun at 0900 and continued for about seventeen hours in an atmosphere of angry tension. The upshot of the conference was agreement on war, to begin "in early December," with negotiations to continue "until 0000 hours, 1 December." Before that date any clash that erupted as a result of Japan's air, submarine, and surface movements could be settled as a local incident.[2] The meeting also decided that if Proposal A failed, they would offer Washington an alternative, Proposal B:

1. Both Japan and the United States will pledge not to make an armed advance into Southeast Asia and the South Pacific area, except French Indochina.

2. The Japanese and American Governments will cooperate with each

other so that the procurement of necessary materials from the Netherlands East Indies will be assured.

3. The Japanese and American Governments will restore trade relations to what they were prior to the freezing of assets. The United States will promise to supply Japan with the petroleum Japan needs.

4. The Government of the United States will not take such actions as may hinder efforts for peace by both Japan and China.[3]

Rear Admiral Zenshiro Hoshina, chief of the Navy Ministry's War Mobilization Bureau, tells us that he learned of the Pearl Harbor attack plan at this time and that all members "present at this meeting understood that an attack against the U.S. Fleet would be made as the first step in the coming war with the U.S."[4] On November 5 an imperial conference confirmed the decisions of the liaison conference, already approved at a Cabinet meeting on November 4.[5] By now the war-horses had the bits between their teeth and approval was a foregone conclusion.

On board *Nagato* as she glided into Saeki Bay at 0500 on November 2, Ugaki watched the moon as it "hung on the edge of a mountain . . . as if it had just finished its job." At 1020 Yamamoto left for Tokyo, leaving his chief of staff in charge. That evening Ugaki received an urgent message from the First Bureau, asking the Combined Fleet's blessing on a gathering to be held in Tokyo from the eighth to the tenth to reach an "Army and Navy Central Agreement." Ugaki immediately replied, "No objection." He entered in his diary: "With this telegram we can see that they have made up their minds at last."[6]

He was substantially right. Uchida noted: "In the conference between the Cabinet and the Military General Staffs the decision was reached to fight the war."[7] Nakahara, too, recorded: "it was recently decided that the Government will . . . take positive steps. . . . It came to this: a change in political policy is absolutely necessary from the standpoint of war preparations."[8] No one seemed to note the incongruity of such an idea—like overeating to fit into an outsized shirt. These diarists recorded the decision for war as final, with no diplomatic embellishment and without awaiting imperial sanction.

At 1330 on November 3, Nagumo summoned to *Akagi* his commanders at each level together with their staffs. He could assemble them rapidly because the previous day, for the first time, all the ships scheduled to be a part of the task force had congregated in Ariake Bay.[9] Nagumo had decided that the time had come to inform them of the purpose of their long training.

To the best of his hearers' recollection, Nagumo said something like this: "Judging from the diplomatic situation, war with the United States seems unavoidable. In that event we plan to attack the American Fleet in Hawaii. Although final details have not been firmed up, Commanders Genda and Fuchida have mapped out a general plan. They will explain it to you. If, after hearing the explanation, you have any questions, feel free to ask them."[10]

Oishi explained the overall outline; then Genda presented the air attack plan, Fuchida helping with the details. Some of the airmen almost fell out of their seats in their astonishment. Most of them had realized for some time that their training was aimed at a particular objective and had speculated avidly about Singapore or Manila. "Surely, it's not Hawaii," many decided. Now they exulted, "I was born a boy at the right time!"[11]

A change of pace ensued the next day—a dress rehearsal for Operation Hawaii. Fuchida had scheduled many dry runs during October, originating from land bases instead of carriers to save precious fuel. But this time conditions would be as much like the actual attack as Fuchida could make them. So the task force sailed with most of the aircraft aboard their home carriers to a spot about 200 miles from Saeki. The first wave took off at 0700; the second at 0830 followed the general pattern of a defending force, but the Fifth Carrier Division did not participate.[12]

About twenty miles from Saeki, Fuchida ordered deployment. At his signal the dive bombers soared to attack level and the torpedo planes sought lower altitude. Below the attacking force the battlewagons of the Japanese Fleet lay in majestic array, just as the planners hoped their counterparts would rest in Pearl Harbor. Aboard ship, officers of the Combined Fleet watched with keen interest, Genda among them. Later he would collect reports from the other staff officers to pass to Fuchida.

After the first wave hit the "enemy," the second group of level and dive bombers swooped in. No torpedo planes would participate in the second wave because by that time the element of surprise would be lost. This time the high-level planes tore into Saeki Field while the dive bombers concentrated on the ships, particularly *Akagi* and *Soryu*.[13]

By 0930 the maneuver was over. The task force arrived back at Ariake Bay at dark, and Nagumo held a critique aboard *Akagi* next morning.[14] In comparing notes with Genda, Fuchida pointed out that it had taken much too long to rendezvous. Genda was dissatisfied with the approach to the target and general deployment; he handed Fuchida a sheaf of notes to mull over and pass on to the flight leaders. Both Genda and Fuchida, as well as the other knowledgeable observers, worried because only 40 percent of the torpedoes had leveled off at the correct depth. The others had dropped to fifteen or even twenty meters. However, the latter case was rare, and the prospects looked hopeful. Still, the perfectionist Genda was far from satisfied.[15]

Meanwhile, Commander Joseph Rochefort, at his Combat Intelligence Unit at Pearl Harbor, observed a certain amount of progress. A Japanese-language student and one of the best intelligence experts in the business, Rochefort was hot on the trail of Japan's carriers. Although unable to decode a good 90 percent of the Japanese naval material channeling through this unit, he and his group could winnow out a considerable amount of information without reading the actual text of the messages.[16]

Over the years American Combat Intelligence "had developed a pretty fair knowledge of the Japanese naval communication system which involved, among other things, a rather detailed knowledge of the radio circuits. . . ." At

Pearl Harbor they covered the circuits which seemed to promise the best results, lacking the manpower to cover all of them.[17] Even certain personality factors began to emerge. The radio operator on *Akagi*, for example, "played that key as if he were sitting on it," recalled Layton.[18]

Naval Intelligence on Oahu had been aware for some time that Japan's carriers were up to something. "The Japanese naval organization was so set up that originally the carriers or carrier divisions had been assigned to both First and Second Fleets," Layton explained. "Sometime in the middle of 1941 this organization was apparently dissolved. It took us some time to find out for sure. The carriers were lumped in one organization."[19] By coincidence, on November 3 local time, the day of the first full-scale practice for Operation Hawaii, Rochefort's unit noted a new address which "broke down as 'ITKOUKUU KANTAI'" of which the literal reading would be First Air Fleet. If this were correct, it would suggest "an entirely new organization of the Naval Air Forces. There are other points which indicate that this may be the case."[20] Although Layton, Rochefort, and their men were on the right track, they never imagined that they had spotted the organization which eventually would attack Pearl Harbor.

Yamamoto returned to *Akagi* at 2145 November 4, Japanese time. He told Ugaki that a decision had been reached: "'While negotiations will be continued, modifying our demands as much as possible, the Army and Navy will continue war preparations. The final decision will be made by noon [*sic*] of 1 December. In case we go to war, it will be some day in early December (the Navy intends to have the 8th as X-Day).'"

Shimada had asked Yamamoto's opinion on the need for personnel changes in the Combined Fleet. Predictably Yamamoto replied, "Since even one or two reshuffles in the high ranking posts would influence the morale of the whole Fleet, I do not want to see any change at all at this moment."[21] Thus, Yamamoto declined a golden opportunity to replace Nagumo under the guise of a routine personnel reassignment program, had he really desired to do so.

While in Tokyo, Yamamoto had conferred with Nagano. The latter wanted Yamamoto's reassurance that he would call back Nagumo's task force if (1) it were spotted; (2) the secret somehow leaked out; or (3) the negotiations succeeded at the last minute. Yamamoto agreed that the Combined Fleet would accept full responsibility for calling back forces deploying before December 1. After that, as he told Nagano, "the situation would be in the lap of the gods."[22]

November 5 began auspiciously with the second dress rehearsal for Operation Hawaii. It followed very much the lines of its predecessor, but this time a variation occurred. About eighty miles north of the target area the attackers ran into a group of fighter interceptors, and an air battle took place at about 0900. If Fuchida and his airmen did not achieve surprise in Hawaii, this was what they could expect. The rehearsal ended successfully at 1140. Genda was still not satisfied with the accuracy of the horizontal bombers. He considered that the men had hit a slump, probably caused by overtraining, but this did not concern him nearly so much as the exasperating torpedoes, which still sounded too deeply.[23]

Fuchida worried about overconcentration on certain ships. A few vessels had been struck again and again with others almost neglected. Poring over his chart, Fuchida found that the outboard ships—that is, those nearest the attackers—received the brunt of the onslaught.[24] This would have to be corrected so that they could bomb the inboard vessels as well.

Ugaki had nothing to say about this rehearsal if, indeed, he paid much attention to it. On November 5 the Combined Fleet staff worked hard preparing the Army-Navy agreement and Combined Fleet Operational Order No. 1. The Naval General Staff would issue Navy Order No. 1, with implementing Navy Directive No. 1, the same day. Although the Combined Fleet would not officially receive the latter two for another day or so, Yamamoto knew exactly what they would contain and wanted his own orders issued simultaneously. Navy Order No. 1 was brief and to the point:

> By Imperial Order, the Chief of the Naval General Staff orders Yamamoto Commander-in-Chief of the Combined Fleet as follows:
>
> 1. Expecting to go to war with the United States, Britain and The Netherlands early in December for self-preservation and self-defense, the Empire has decided to complete war preparations.
>
> 2. The Commander-in-Chief of the Combined Fleet will carry out the necessary operational preparations.
>
> 3. Its details will be directed by the Chief of the Naval General Staff.

Navy Directive No. 1 from the Naval General Staff was more detailed and ordered Yamamoto to take various measures preparatory to combat.[25]

Aboard *Nagato* Kuroshima had been working for months on the Combined Fleet's Operational Order No. 1. Ever since he had seen the Naval General Staff's original war plan, he thought Yamamoto's staff should develop an alternative one. Characteristically he brooded over his ideas for weeks before he began to set the order on paper and he started actual work on the project immediately after the September war games in Tokyo. At that point he put his juniors to work on various subsections of the scheme.

Around mid- or late October Kuroshima called in those reports. Then he worked virtually day and night preparing a draft which he showed to Ugaki. The chief of staff asked Kuroshima why he had gone so far in his planning. Indeed, the draft was less an operational order than a full-scale plan of war. Kuroshima explained that he had done this because he believed "an order should be written which would include all potential operations." He also thought that with time going by so rapidly it was wise to prepare not only an order but a general plan.[26]

Weather reports indicated that conditions on November 7 might not favor flying, so Yamamoto decided to start early on the sixth for the Army-Navy discussions in Tokyo. He took off with some of his staff officers, who were to confer with the Operations Section of the Naval General Staff on Combined

Fleet Operational Order No. 1. He left Ugaki to follow him later. Thus, Yamamoto missed the final dry run of the Pearl Harbor attack.

Because of a dense fog, the force concentrated on Saeki rather than on the ships in harbor. Ugaki wrote approvingly in his diary: "They have made great progress, which promises well for their big success in the near future."[27] As the task force steamed homeward from the launching point, *Nagato* blinked in Morse code: "The attack was splendid."[28] Genda did not agree. He considered the bombing tests "very poor," except for those which bombed the ships. "This result was really disheartening," he recalled.[29]

While Fuchida put his airmen through their paces, Yamamoto and his staff emplaned at Iwakuni for Tokyo. Kuroshima reread his draft order for the *n*th time, changing a word here, fixing a phrase there, always seeking perfection. Yamamoto and Watanabe passed the entire three-hour trip bent over the chessboard.[30]

On November 7, having followed Yamamoto to Tokyo, Ugaki visited the Navy Ministry, where he observed "every branch working hard and aggressively but cheerfully." Next, Ugaki met with a number of bigwigs of the Naval General Staff. Then he summoned his attendant staff officers to the First Council Room to work on "the final revision to the operational order of the Combined Fleet."

Combined Fleet Operational Order No. 1 was more than a directive for the tactical employment of Japan's naval forces; it presented a long-range strategic plan. Phase One called for the conquest and occupation of Japan's military objectives; Phase Two, for consolidation and defense against counterattack. The 100-page order also covered thousands of details. In brief, Japan's territorial ambitions demanded simultaneous action in virtually every corner of the Pacific, including the USSR's Maritime Provinces. Never had any nation envisaged such widespread operations.[31]

The Combined Fleet document astonished the Operations Section in Tokyo. It went far beyond anything that group had anticipated in case Japan went to war in the spring of 1942. The Combined Fleet staff had virtually completed the order before the First Bureau found out how greatly it differed in scope from the Naval General Staff's initial instructions. To Miyo the document "was the culmination of Japan's spirit of the offensive."

As air officer he took a particular interest in the plan, going over it carefully with Sasaki, Yamamoto's aviation expert. Miyo had a number of personal objections, the principal one being that it overextended the Japanese Navy to a fearsome extent. Nevertheless, the Operations Section did not object strenuously to Yamamoto's Combined Fleet order. It did not expect it would ever be implemented in its entirety. In the first place, it far exceeded the capacity of the Combined Fleet; in the second, when it came to launching these grandiose schemes, the Naval General Staff would have the power of veto. Of course, Fukudome and his men should have known that stopping Yamamoto once he was in motion was like trying to hold back the tide.

The conference between the Operations Section and Yamamoto's staff officers lasted only one day, and publication of the order began immediately thereafter. The Naval General Staff printed it, running off 700 copies—an astounding number for a top secret document—with yeomen from the Combined Fleet doing the job.[32] The order originally included the Pearl Harbor project, but this was deleted from the copies and appeared only in the original.[33] Fortunately Kusaka recorded for posterity a brief portion in the order pertaining to Operation Hawaii:

> 1. The Task Force will launch a surprise attack at the outset of war upon the U.S. Pacific Fleet supposed to be in Hawaiian waters, and destroy it.
> 2. The Task Force will reach the designated stand-by point for the operation in advance.
> 3. The date of starting the operation is tentatively set forth as December 8, 1941.[34]

Here in unmistakable terms is the task force's stated mission: to destroy the U.S. Pacific Fleet. All the thinking, planning, and training in terms of Pearl Harbor were for one reason only: Kimmel's ships were more likely to be found there than anywhere else.

The Navy Ministry top brass—chiefs of each bureau and department—also met that day, November 7. The Finance Bureau reported a supplementary budget demand, and the conferees agreed that reports on ship locations and the weather should be stopped.[35] It was just in time. Rochefort's Combat Intelligence group had excellent fixes on a number of Japanese units and was moving close to identifying the First Air Fleet. The intelligence summary for November 6 (November 7, Japanese time) noted a sharp tightening of Japanese communications security.[36]

While the last-minute planning shaped up in Tokyo, operational preparations continued in the First Air Fleet. Shortly after the final rehearsal—on either November 7 or 8—Genda flew from *Akagi* to Kagoshima to consult with the torpedo pilots in an attempt to solve the remaining difficulties: depth of the torpedo's initial plunge and percentage of hits.

These men were very discouraged. "All we can do is rely on the bravery of the other bombers," Murata said glumly. But they plucked up heart and worked out two methods of operation. In the first, at Murata's suggestion, the plane dropped the missile from twenty meters at 100 knots in level flight. This test used the modified torpedo with the new fin. The second technique, the brainchild of Lieutenant Asao Negishi, called for launch at 100 knots, altitude ten meters, nosing down 1½ degrees. It employed the Model 91-1 weapon because of the shortage of the modified type.

Genda instructed Murata and his men to try out these techniques within the next few days. Then he left for Omura and Sasebo to make further attack preparations. Murata did exactly as Genda directed, and to everyone's surprise, both methods succeeded beyond hope. Commander Shogo Masuda, commanding officer of Kagoshima Naval Air Base, who was also *Akagi*'s flight officer, quickly dispatched a triumphant telegram to Nagumo: "Achieved 82 percent hits."[37] This breakthrough occurred on November 11, 12, or 13 because Nagumo received the message at Iwakuni, where he attended a conference on those days.

Jubilation exploded aboard *Akagi* when those in the know received the results of the torpedo tests. Genda experienced a great surge of relief. He "thanked God" on the spot, emphasizing his belief that "help will come to those who keep up their efforts and devotion to their work." While the fine record of the horizontal and dive bombers had almost eliminated any possibility of canceling the strike if the torpedo attack failed, this last-minute triumph tied up the remaining operational loose ends.

Although both tests resulted in 82 percent hits, Genda and his fellow planners decided to stay with the first method, the easier to execute. Moreover, its greater speed and altitude would not expose the planes quite so mercilessly to antiaircraft fire. Genda now had no doubt that the venture could be a resounding success if the task force could achieve surprise.[38]

CHAPTER 42

"RINGING

BELLS

AND

BANGING

DRUMS"

The first of November found political and military leaders in Washington exceedingly apprehensive about a rumored Japanese drive against Kunming, with the objective of cutting China's lifeline, the Burma Road. The Joint Army-Navy Board considered this problem, among other issues, at an important meeting held on November 3. According to Marshall's information, Japan had not yet determined its course of action but "might be expected to decide upon the national policy by November 5." This was excellent intelligence because the imperial conference scheduled for November 5 did exactly that.

Ingersoll summarized naval reinforcements to the Asiatic Fleet. These included a "stated number of submarine units en route to the Philippines."[1] Naturally these submarines came out of Kimmel's hide. But the loss of twelve fine undersea craft did not bring an irate protest from him. With his innate honesty, he believed they could be of more use to the Asiatic Fleet "because they were closer to the Japanese homeland."[2]

In Tokyo Grew had allowed two weeks to size up the situation since Tojo took over.[3] Now, on November 3, he was ready to send the State Department his opinions. In spite of the inconveniences the economic freeze had caused, Japan had neither collapsed nor changed course. He warned that Japan might adopt "an all out, do or die attempt to render Japan impervious to foreign embargoes, even risking national hara kiri rather than cede to foreign pressure." He and his staff believed "that such a contingency is not only possible but probable."[4]

However, Grew advocated neither appeasement nor surrender of principles. His purpose was to ensure that the United States understood that "Japanese sanity cannot be measured by our own standards of logic." And he predicted: "Japan's resort to measures which might make war with the United States inevitable may come with dramatic and dangerous suddenness."[5]

The political events of early November coincided with a virulent anti-American outburst in the Japanese press. Ugaki noted these manifestations with approval, entering in his diary on November 4:

> By ringing bells and banging drums public ipinion should be aroused and the people prepared while we seek reflection and reaction on the part of the United States. If there is still no sign of reflection, our attitude will be modified a great deal so as to pretend that we are ready to give in. Nothing is more important than our political and strategical activities during this coming one week.

That same day the Foreign Ministry sent some most revealing messages to Nomura. Togo certainly did not give the ambassador a true picture of the situation; in fact, he could not afford to do so. After rambling on about Japanese good intentions and American iniquities, the message continued:

> . . . This time we are showing the limit of our friendship; this time we are making our last possible bargain, and I hope that we can thus settle all our troubles with the United States peaceably.
> . . . lest anything go awry, I want you to follow my instructions to the letter . . . there will be no room for personal interpretation.[6]

Nomura barely had time to reflect on this ominous communiqué when Togo shot off a four-part message transmitting Proposal A. After outlining its provisions, he went on:

> I think . . . the question of evacuation [of China] will be the hardest. . . . Our purpose is to shift the regions of occupation and our officials, thus attempting to dispel their suspicions. . . . I want you in as indecisive yet as pleasant language as possible to euphemize and try to impart to them the effect that unlimited occupation does not mean perpetual occupation. . . . [7]

As the impact of this remarkable message strikes home, one appreciates why at this particular time Togo sent for experienced diplomat Saburo Kurusu, whom he talked into going to the United States as a special envoy. The Tojo government still needed Nomura as front man in Washington, but it also needed someone a little better at palming aces. One can also understand why the American authorities, reading such messages with their evidence of outright deceit, placed no credence in the Japanese government's sincerity.

Tokyo followed Proposal A with Proposal B. Nomura was to put forth the latter if there appeared "to be a remarkable difference between the Japanese and American views." If necessary, he might add stipulations concerning evacuation, the Tripartite Pact, and nondiscrimination, as mentioned in Proposal A.[8]

The Navy noted on the same day—November 4—a significant phenomenon which it reported to Kimmel, Hart, and certain naval district commandants, including Bloch: Japan appeared to be withdrawing all its merchant vessels from the Western Hemisphere.[9] Intelligence expert Captain Ellis M. Zacharias considered the removal of commercial shipping back to Japan one of the "earliest indications of hostilities." Naval Intelligence "had long realized that. . . ."[10]

More and more Togo bore down on the harassed Nomura. On November 5 he sent the ambassador an actual deadline: "Because of various circumstances, it is absolutely necessary that all arrangements for the signing of this agreement be completed by the 25th of this month. I realize that this is a difficult order, but under the circumstances it is an unavoidable one. . . ."[11] Why the twenty-fifth? On that date (November 26, Japanese time) the task force would sortie from Hitokappu Bay.* To reach an agreement before the First Air Fleet got under way would save the Japanese a considerable investment in time, fuel, and manpower.

No one in authority in Washington was spoiling for a fight with Japan. On the contrary, Marshall and Stark sent Roosevelt on November 5 a joint estimate in which they affirmed bluntly: "At the present time the United States Fleet in the Pacific is inferior to the Japanese Fleet and cannot undertake an unlimited strategic offensive in the Western Pacific." Stark and Marshall pointed out: "If Japan be defeated and Germany remain undefeated, decision will still have not been reached. . . ." Therefore, "War between the United States and Japan should be avoided while building up defensive forces in the Far East, until such time as Japan attacks or directly threatens territories whose security to the United States is of very great importance." They recommended "military action against Japan" only in certain contingencies, the first being "A direct act of war by Japanese armed forces against the territory or mandated territory of the United States, the British Commonwealth, or the Netherlands East Indies. . . ."[12]

Little more than a month of peace remained when Nomura and Wakasugi called on Hull and his assistant Joseph W. Ballantine at 0900 on November 7. Nomura relayed his government's expressed wish to resume the conversations and handed Hull a document embodying Proposal A. He also asked for an interview with the President, which was later arranged for the tenth.[13] As always, the meeting was personally cordial, but Hull could not see that Proposal A contained anything "fundamentally new or offering any real recessions from the position consistently maintained by the Japanese Government."[14]

That afternoon Roosevelt summoned his Cabinet. The President started the session by asking Hull if he had anything in mind. Hull had plenty and spoke for some fifteen minutes on "the dangers of the international situation." He went over the conversations with Japan, emphasizing that in his opinion "relations were extremely critical and that we should be on the lookout for a

*See Chapter 48.

military attack anywhere by Japan at any time."[15] This was an uncanny prognostication, considering that the Naval General Staff and the Combined Fleet had just issued their operational orders.

This awareness that Japan might break out anywhere at any time did not help Kimmel. That very day, November 7, Stark wrote once more, regretfully turning down Kimmel's request for more destroyers and the two new battleships *North Carolina* and *Washington.* He ended on a worried note: "Things seem to be moving steadily toward a crisis in the Pacific. . . . A month may see, literally, most anything. . . ."[16] One month exactly! Few prophecies have ever hit more precisely on the nose.

That deadline pulsed like one of Ugaki's "banging drums" through the bloodstream of more than one Japanese. It imposed precious little time to integrate the submarines into the Pearl Harbor plan. Around the middle of October Captain Kaku Harada, skipper of the former seaplane tender *Chiyoda,* which was the home ship of the midget submariners, reduced the trainees' range of concentration to Singapore and Pearl Harbor. This gave them the first real clue to their mission. "When Captain Harada told us to pay particular attention to Pearl Harbor and Singapore," recalled Ensign Kazuo Sakamaki, an intelligent young trainee with a pleasant, round face, "we thought that one group would probably be used eventually against Pearl Harbor and another group against Singapore."

At the end of October they were graduated and received a ten-day leave. According to Sakamaki's recollection, shortly thereafter and before they transferred to their mother craft, Yamamoto received them all aboard *Nagato,* then moored at Hashirajima. He told the students that their work was highly important and meant much to the Navy. Dangerous operations such as those they were about to embark upon could have far greater success than regular surface action. They could outshine the older officers. So he urged them to be diligent, courageous, and dutiful.[17]

About the same time the young men scattered over Japan for their leave, Captain Hanku Sasaki, commander of the First Submarine Division, received orders which puzzled him considerably.[18] These instructions directed him to proceed to Kure to receive his submarines, which had been undergoing emergency modifications with a target date of November 10. Not even the Kure Naval Station knew what was in the wind, let alone Sasaki himself. The modifications included air-purifying equipment, protection against antisubmarine nets, and a telephone system. Most puzzling of all to Sasaki were certain changes being built on the stern of the hulls.[19]

His curiosity finally got the better of him, and he asked Matsumura for an explanation. "This equipment is to enable you to haul midget submarines close enough to Pearl Harbor to attack the U.S. Pacific Fleet," replied Matsumura. Thus, almost casually, Sasaki learned of his mission. The information nearly dismasted him. The idea of such a strike was enough to disconcert any man, but this waiting until virtually the last minute to give him the word seemed downright irresponsible. Moreover, Sasaki wondered whether the hulls could take the special equipment and weight of the midgets. His big submarines were themselves new and relatively untried. The whole submarine portion of the Pearl Harbor scheme had about it an impromptu air which troubled Sasaki's orderly mind. "There was too much hurry, hurry, hurry," he recalled disapprovingly.[20]

If Sasaki worried about the submarine participation, Fuchida hit the overhead. He heard the story early in November from his Eta Jima classmate Lieutenant Commander Tatsuwaka Shibuya, a submarine expert. The flight commander questioned what possible good the submarines could do. If the air attack succeeded, they would be useless. At best they represented an additional risk in a scheme already fraught with danger.

Fuchida could not help feeling slight disappointment in Yamamoto. It looked as if the Commander in Chief might be risking the entire Pearl Harbor plan to give the conventional forces a share in the glory. Fuchida did not doubt for an instant the bravery and ability for self-sacrifice of the midget submariners, but every one of his airmen, too, faced a more than fifty-fifty chance of dying for the Emperor. Fuchida never became reconciled to the idea of submarine participation and made no secret of his views.[21]

Shibuya, a stout, flush-faced man with a sunny disposition, had been assigned to the First Air Fleet on November 5. If he wondered what a carrier fleet wanted with a submarine officer, he kept it to himself. Arriving aboard *Akagi* on November 9, he met Nagumo and other key members of his staff. On that date Oishi informed him of the Pearl Harbor plan. Now his assignment made sense; in such a closely coordinated operation Nagumo needed a staff officer for submarines.[22]

On November 7 *Soryu* and *Hiryo* sailed respectively to Kure and Sasebo, their assigned naval stations. Each vessel had a home port for repairs, maintenance, and supplies, and the men of these stations took great pride in the ships under their care.[23] The Japanese were already weaving a cloak of secrecy around Nagumo's task force. Every day false communications emanated from Kyushu at the same time and on the same wavelength as during the training period. This would give eavesdroppers such as Rochefort's Combat Intelligence Unit the impression that the First Air Fleet remained in that area for routine training. Moreover, the Navy broadcast daily messages to Nagumo as intended during the cruise to Hawaii. To begin precisely on November 26, the scheduled day of sortie, might tip off the Americans that something unusual had started on that date.[24]

On November 9 *Shokaku* and *Zuikaku* put in at Kure, while on that day and the seventh respectively, *Akagi* and *Kaga* proceeded to Sasebo.[25] During their stay Rochefort's listeners identified *Akagi* correctly as the carrier flagship and located her in the Sasebo area. They also accurately spotted several carriers at Kure and Sasebo on November 10, Hawaii time.[26]

At these locations workers unloaded all unnecessary items from the carriers. Everything not required for efficiency or safety was ruthlessly pruned away to strip the carriers for action and make room for extra fuel. Oil drums filled every vacant or extra room, any gangway which need not be clear, even all decks except the flight deck. During the next four days Nagumo permitted his sailors to go ashore. Thus, the officers and crewmen not yet in the know believed themselves to be embarking on a routine training cruise.[27] Those who did know had become so acutely security-conscious by this time that they literally worried lest they talk in their sleep.[28]

At Genda's behest all aircraft had been winterized. Among other measures, the propellers received a thin coating of oil to prevent icing. There was an outside possibility that the task force might encounter an American scouting fleet in the Aleutians area, in which case his airmen had to be prepared to fight in freezing weather. Nagumo issued Striking Force Operations Order No. 1, directing his forces to complete battle preparations by the twentieth and to assemble at Hitokappu Bay. A number of personnel orders also came out, including one designating Murata as a flight commander aboard *Akagi*, while Goto officially left *Ryujo* for *Akagi*.[29]

No one kept busier than Shimizu. He, too, completed, an operational plan on November 10, covering his far-flung missions. His submarines had to reconnoiter Lahaina Roads, the Aleutians, and strategic points in the South Pacific. While his midgets slipped into Pearl Harbor, his large craft would surround Oahu. After the air strike they would pounce on any vessel that tried to sortie. His outpost submarines would attempt to destroy any United States ships located between the west coast and Hawaii.[30]

In one respect Shimizu had the advantage over Nagumo. Even the most barnacle-encrusted of battleship admirals agreed that the submarine had come to stay. Shimizu therefore experienced no such shortages or official reluctance to part with matériel as had plagued the airmen. The best was none too good for the submariners, and he had twenty-five first-class large undersea craft at his disposal besides the five midgets—thirty in all.

Thus, on November 10 Shimizu had a rather full house when he summoned all division, squadron, and individual submarine commanders aboard *Katori* in Saeki Bay for a conference. They heard Matsumura deliver the first official briefing, informing them that their objective was Pearl Harbor.[31] The next day, November 11, the Third Submarine Squadron under Rear Admiral Shigeyoshi Miwa slipped out of Saeki Bay bound for Pearl Harbor via Kwajalein. It sailed at 1111—the eleventh minute after the eleventh hour of the eleventh day of the eleventh month. This squadron of nine submarines left at such an early date because these craft, constructed for a relatively short radius of action, would have to refuel in the Marshalls.[32]

On the second leg of Miwa's journey he would leave Kwajalein for Oahu, following a route between Johnston and Palmyra islands. Once in the target area, his *I-72* and *I-73* had a most important mission. No later than December 6 (Japanese time) they were to reconnoiter Lahaina Roads, reporting all information on the anchorage, the west coast of Maui, and the east coast of Lanai Island, a short distance to the west. This information must be transmitted to the task force at least by December 7, Japanese time (December 6, local time). This would give Nagumo time to shift his attack plan to Lahaina if substantial U.S. forces were at anchor there.

Miwa's *I-74* also had a special mission. On X-Day it would crawl close to Niihau to rescue any fliers who might have been shot down or forced to land at sea. His other subs would attempt to sink any U.S. ship within range after the air strike.[33]

As Yamamoto moved his Combined Fleet toward the war he dreaded, he presented his usual picture of pleasantly resolute composure. But he let some of his unhappiness spill over in a letter to his friend Rear Admiral Teikichi Hori, written on November 11 as his first submarines moved out: "What a strange position I find myself in—having to pursue with full determination a course of action which is diametrically opposed to my best judgment and firmest conviction. That, too, perhaps, is fate."[34]

That morning Yamamoto and his entourage, including Ugaki, left Tokyo by train for Yokosuka, whence they flew to the Iwakuni Air Group, landing shortly after 1330. They immediately repaired to *Nagato*, which had sailed there to meet them. That day and the next, various ships converged on Iwakuni. The commanders in chief of all fleets except the Southern Expeditionary Fleet, with their chiefs of staff and senior staff officers, arrived by sea and land to participate in a Combined Fleet operational conference. These included Nagumo, Kusaka, and Oishi as well as Shimizu.[35]

At 0900 on the thirteenth, Yamamoto and Ugaki left *Nagato* to begin the meetings. After an "especially wonderful" opening message from Yamamoto, Ugaki briefed the conferees on Combined Fleet Operational Order No. 1.[36] Some time during this conference Nagumo received the news from the First Air Fleet of the torpedo training breakthrough. Both Yamamoto and Nagumo agreed with Genda's opinion that this would go far toward ensuring the success of the Pearl Harbor attack.[37]

At 0930 on November 15 all returned to work out Army-Navy agreements. Once more Yamamoto, representing both services, gave the opening address.[38] During this conference Yamamoto reaffirmed that he would call back the forces in case Japanese-American negotiations succeeded before the attack. He warned strictly that in the case of Operation Hawaii, the task force would be recalled even if the planes had already taken off from the carriers.[39]

Sometime before Yamamoto's departure for his flagship (about 1300), Shimizu arranged a private, personal discussion with the commander in chief, who was still concerned over the difficulties in rescuing the midget submariners from Pearl Harbor. Yamamoto insisted that Shimizu must feel free to cancel that portion of the operation if he considered it really suicidal. But Shimizu decided to reserve his final decision until he had talked to the midget submarine men themselves.[40]

On November 14 he went to Kure to see the "tubes" for the first time and to meet their crews. He gave each officer individually a copy of the orders. As they accepted their papers personally from the hand of their admiral, the submariners glowed with pride and exaltation.[41]

Next, Shimizu explained the role the midget submarines would play. The plan called for their release from the mother submarines on the night of X−1 Day, as close as possible to the main buoy just outside Pearl Harbor. The five "tubes" would enter the channel that night, secure their possition, then settle on the bottom. They must enter the harbor well before the air attack and, regardless of what opportunities presented themselves, absolutely must not start anything until the night of X-Day.[42]

But Lieutenant Naoji Iwasa, leader of the midget submariners, asked permission to launch his attack immediately after the air strike instead of waiting until dark. To remain submerged for such a long time might prove dangerous. More important, his men might achieve much more effective results during the period of enemy confusion. Shimizu demurred because he believed their chances of survival to be practically nil in the daytime, particularly inasmuch as the air attack would have stirred the Americans to savage retaliation. But Iwasa persisted, and the other minisub pilots enthusiastically backed his argument. Maximum damage to the enemy was what counted—not their own survival.

Heartened by this example of fighting spirit, Shimizu agreed to the change. Looking into these firm young faces, he was sure that their attack would be highly successful and Yamamoto would be very proud of them.[43]

The Navy now really began to move. On the thirteenth *Akagi* hoisted anchor and sailed off the coast of Kagoshima, where she picked up her planes and the rest of the flying officers, including Fuchida, Murata, and Masuda. On the afternoon of the fourteenth she slipped into Saeki Bay, there taking on board Nagumo, Kusaka, and Oishi. *Zuikaku* and *Shokaku* sailed from Kure to Beppu on November 16 and 17 respectively to collect their planes and men, while *Soryu* and *Hiryu* also gathered in their crews.[44]

The Japanese realized that such a mass evacuation of planes from their bases would attract considerable attention. Inasmuch as secrecy demanded that even the Japanese people remain in ignorance of the task force's movements, the Navy arranged a cover. Almost before Fuchida's bombers and fighters left the runways, aircraft of the Twelfth Combined Naval Air Corps landed at the training bases in Kyushu to continue the flight pattern. Throughout Japan shore units granted leaves to as many men as possible, so that the usual thread of blue wove through the tapestry of Japanese life.[45]

To mask the exodus from sharp enemy ears, the replacement aircraft exchanged dummy messages with the task force ships. They made no attempt to send fake messages for American consumption; this would have been an overelaboration and might defeat its own purpose.[46]

These precautions worked perfectly. "Carriers remain relatively inactive," estimated U.S. Combat Intelligence—later more correctly termed Communications Intelligence—on November 13. "The *Settsu* is still with them and a few may be engaged in target practice near Kure. . . .[47] So near and yet so far! Once again American intelligence analysts had walked up to the very gate of truth, only to have it slammed in their faces.

CHAPTER 43

"I SWEAR

TO BE

SUCCESSFUL"

"In spite of the world nearing the center of a great storm, what a fine day it is today!" Ugaki recorded in his diary for November 15, in the heady loveliness of Japan's Indian summer. Something about the nature of that storm the Emperor discovered later that same day. By 1300 an impressive array of Army and Navy leaders had gathered in the headquarters room of the Imperial Palace to explain to His Majesty the operational plans for Phase One of the projected war.

Some of those present had just come from a liaison conference which had met that morning. This meeting had approved a "Draft Proposal for Hastening the End of the War Against the United States, Great Britain, the Netherlands, and Chiang." To do this, the conference established a formidable program which contained some of the most deluded thinking on record for 1941, including the Great All-Out Battle, defeat of Great Britain and China, attempts to bring the Soviet Union "within the Axis camp," and endeavoring "to destroy the will of the United States."[1]

Although carefully prearranged, the operational briefing of the Emperor was thorough. From such high brass as Sugiyama, Nagano, and others, Hirohito gained a good idea of the broad scope of Japan's war plans and how his generals and admirals intended to implement them. Apparently His Majesty posed a few questions about the Southern Operation. Whether he asked any about the Pearl Harbor attack we do not know. In fact, the official Japanese study, *Hawai Sakusen*, states that this important conference did not include the Pearl Harbor project. But several officers who attended assure us that the Navy did indeed present an outline to the Emperor, however brief it might have been.[2]

This was only logical. In the first place, Hirohito had known of the plan since the end of October. Secondly, he had every right to such a briefing by virtue of his position as Commander in Chief. Thirdly, he had an excellent grasp of naval affairs, and it would have been an insult to his intelligence to believe he could overlook the absence from the planning board of six carriers, two battleships, three cruisers, and a whole squadron of destroyers, to say nothing of submarines and tankers.

The whole ominous atmosphere building up in Japan worried members of the American Embassy. Grew sent Hull a plain warning on November 17, referring to his disturbing message of the third:

> In emphasizing the need for guarding against sudden military or naval actions by Japan in areas not at present involved in the China conflict, I am taking into account as a possibility that the Japanese would exploit all available tactical advantages, including that of initiative and surprise. It is important, however, that our Government not (repeat not) place upon us, including the military and naval attaches, major responsibility for giving prior warning. . . .
>
> . . . our field of military and naval observation is almost literally restricted to what can be seen with our own eyes, which is negligible. . . . [3]

Certainly neither Grew nor his naval attaché, Smith-Hutton, knew that the Second Submarine Squadron had slipped out of the big base at Yokosuka on November 16, headed for Pearl Harbor. Its commander, Rear Admiral Shigeki Yamasaki, had been in the silent service since 1917. But his submarines dated back to the 1920s and needed modernization. The Yokosuka Naval Station had barely managed to make them operational in time. They would sail in a northeasterly direction far beyond Midway to scout for the enemy and would approach Oahu from the north.

Once in the target area, Yamasaki would deploy his seven submarines between Oahu and Kauai and between Oahu and Molokai. They were to keep an eye out for the U.S. Pacific Fleet and torpedo any ships in sight after the air attack. Thus, ten days before Nagumo was to plunge his task force into the gray waters of the northern Pacific, another unit of Shimizu's Sixth Fleet hissed eastward as part of Yamamoto's complex Hawaiian venture. [4]

The same day Commander Yasuchika Kayahara carefully nosed his submarine, *I-10*, out of Yokosuka. He was to proceed on a long sweep southeast to the Fiji Islands, where he would observe Suva Harbor, then sail northeast to Samoa, Christmas Island, and east of the Hawaiian chain to about 900 nautical miles southwest of San Francisco. His task was to check on possible U.S. Fleet movements in that enormous expanse of southern ocean. If he saw an American warship, his orders instructed him to track it, but not to fire a torpedo until after the air raid on Pearl Harbor. Once that first shot had crashed over Oahu, he would lurk between Hawaii and the West Coast to finish off any crippled ship which might try to limp back to San Diego or other ports in that area. [5]

At 0800 on November 17 *Nagato*, without escort, sailed from Iwakuni, and she anchored in Saeki Bay at 1340. At 1500 Yamamoto with Ugaki and other staff officers set out for *Akagi* to address key members of the First Air Fleet for what might be the last time. [6]

On the flight deck about 100 officers assembled: Nagumo and his staff, all commanders, their staffs, and the flight officers. As Yamamoto spoke, it became evident that he had not come to *Akagi* to deliver a stereotyped pep talk. His sincerity was all the more evident because he spoke off the cuff, whereas Kuroshima and Watanabe usually drafted his speeches.[7] His exact words are not available. But they made a deep impression on his hearers, a number of whom remembered the gist and some of his actual expressions.[8] Clearly he wanted to rescue the task force leaders from the snare of overconfidence and to make sure that they appreciated the quality of their opponents. For all the underestimation in 1941 was not on the American side. Many Japanese believed the United States to be a hollow shell, its people divided politically, softened by luxurious living and decadent morals, no match for the tough, disciplined men of Japan. But Yamamoto knew that the good-natured giant could be pushed just so far and that Pearl Harbor would be the end of the line.

"Although we hope to achieve surprise, everyone should be prepared for terrific American resistance in this operation," he told his listeners. "Japan has faced many worthy opponents in her glorious history—Mongols, Chinese, Russians—but in this operation we will meet the strongest and most resourceful opponent of all."

Yamamoto next spoke of his opposite number, Kimmel: "The American commander is no ordinary or average man. Such a relatively junior admiral would not have been given the important position of CinCPAC unless he were able, gallant and brave. We can expect him to put up a courageous fight. Moreover, he is said to be farsighted and cautious, so it is quite possible that he has instituted very close measures to cope with any emergency. Therefore, you must take into careful consideration the possibility that the attack may not be a surprise after all. You may have to fight your way in to the target." This sentence struck with the impact of an arrow into two men at least—Genda and Fuchida.

"It is the custom of *Bushido* to select an equal or stronger opponent," Yamamoto reminded his listeners in closing. "On this score you have nothing to complain about—the American Navy is a good match for the Japanese Navy."

After his address Yamamoto strode over to Fuchida and silently grasped his hand. The admiral's direct gaze reflected his confidence, and Fuchida felt his own eyes light up with an answering assurance of victory.[9]

All present then adjourned to the wardroom for a farewell party. The atmosphere was serious, full of dignity, even a little heavy. They ate the symbolic *surume* (dried cuttlefish) for happiness and *kachiguri* (walnuts) for victory, then drank a toast to the coming battle in the name of the Emperor— "*Banzai! Banzai! Banzai!*"

During this interlude Yamamoto remarked, "I expect this operation to be a success." Because a Japanese admiral customarily expressed "hope" for success at the outset of a mission, Yamamoto's use of the word "expect" impressed his hearers, heartening them by its implication of confidence.[10]

Shortly after Yamamoto's party returned to *Nagato*, Nagumo and his staff paid the flagship a return courtesy visit, and all lifted another glass to toast the success of the venture. "Perhaps I may be dull," Kusaka observed to Ugaki. "But I don't feel anything serious, though people say we are going to do an extraordinarily important job." To this Ugaki replied, "That's enough, isn't it?" Later he philosophized in his diary: "If we do our best, we can surely have the blessing of God. Even if we die, we need not blame anyone. Whichever way we take, we will reach the same goal. Thus we can find calm resignation."[11] Not that Kusaka, of all people, needed any lessons from the dramatic-minded Ugaki about "calm resignation."

At about 1600 *Soryu* and *Hiryu* with a four-destroyer escort left Saeki Bay for the rendezvous in the Kuriles. Then one by one the remaining ships glided out of the harbor, some close to the coastline, others as far out as 100 miles.[12] As *Hiryu* rounded Okinoshima, near the eastern entrance of Bungo Channel, a sailor casting trash overboard fell into the sea. This made the usually cheerful Lieutenant Heita Matsumura, the unfortunate man's chief, "feel dark about the future." When the carrier sailed off Ise Shrine, Matsumura tidied up his room and bowed toward the shrine in memory of his sailor.[13]

Near sunset *Soryu* passed the southern tip of Shikoku. Northward the carrier sped out of sight of land; then once more her men saw Japanese soil as they sailed through the Izu Islands, and turned east of Chiba with the Boso Peninsula in view. Now they had glimpsed the last of the Japanese mainland. But Yamaguchi was not the man to waste time gazing sentimentally at his native shores. On the cruise to Hitokappu Bay he put the Second Carrier Division through its paces in antiaircraft practice, refueling and navigating in the fog. The crew also maintained a sharp lookout because radio intelligence had warned them that an American submarine was moving north from the Philippines.[14]

At last fully equipped and ready to go, *Zuikaku* moved majestically from the Beppu area with her sister ship, *Shokaku. Zuikaku*'s crew still believed that the carrier had set course for a pilgrimage to Ise Shrine for a routine morale-building and recreational treat. Not until a day or so out to sea did they discover their true destination—Hitokappu Bay.[15]

As darkness settled over Saeki Bay, *Akagi* blacked out, weighed anchor, and slipped ghostlike out to sea in the silent company of two destroyers. That night Genda stood duty on the bridge. Eyeing him sympathetically, Nagumo said, "Air Staff Officer, you must be awfully tired. Thank you for what you have done. I will stay on the bridge so you can go below and take a rest." This was the first time Nagumo had openly acknowledged his air expert's efforts, and Genda was more touched than he cared to show. He replied gratefully, "I'm all right, sir. Heaven will punish me if I say I am tired from such worthwhile work."[16]

Akagi plunged along 100 miles off the coast, far down the Nanpo Islands, then swung straight north. As she approached the area of Yokosuka, Yokohama, and Tokyo, she hove to until nightfall because in that heavily congested shipping region she ran the most risk of being seen. She glided past unnoticed. Nor did she encounter any other ships on her way north.[17]

As the imposing array of ships moved out of Saeki Bay, *Nagato*'s seamen crowded the fore part of the main deck, waving farewell to their comrades of the task force. Yamamoto stood in company with his loyal staff officers. All were tense with excitement and with the awed realization of what this meant for them and for all Japan. They could not help wondering how many of these magnificent vessels would return, how many good companions they had seen for the last time. Yamamoto stood there for several hours, until finally not even his binoculars afforded him a glimpse of the last ship.[18]

It so happened that on the same day the task force sailed off, the *Taiyo Maru* reached Japan with the three special agents. Her skipper had steered the approximate route homeward that Nagumo's armada planned to take on its return trip from Pearl Harbor. Once more observations favored Yamamoto's design: air patrols weak north and west of Oahu; no planes visible in the Midway area; no ships sighted; the weather good; the condition of the sea satisfactory.[19] To avoid the delay of routine disembarkation, the Navy Ministry provided a motor launch to bring Maejima, Suzuki, and Matsuo ashore. Tachibana met them, informing Suzuki and Maejima that they were to make their reports that same afternoon to the Naval General Staff. Dressed as prosperous businessmen, these two immediately left for Tokyo.[20]

At 1400 they walked into a special room on the second floor of the Navy Ministry building, where many prominent members of the Naval General Staff had gathered: Nagano, Ito, Fukudome, Tomioka, Sanagi, Miyo, and several others from the Operations Section. A select group from Naval Intelligence also waited impatiently: Maeda, Ogawa, Yamaguchi, Tachibana, and one or two others.[21]

Suzuki reported first. He immediately struck an encouraging note: not a single vessel of any type seen during the round trip. Although the words rested easily on the ears, the possibility remained that the task force might be detected en route to Hawaii. The size of the expedition in itself presented an ever-present danger to a safe voyage. A single passenger vessel like the *Taiyo Maru* was one thing, but a task force of thirty ships spread across miles of ocean was quite another.

Suzuki's disclosures about the weather and the condition of the sea received unmixed satisfaction. But here again no one could be sure that the outward passage of the First Air Fleet would be as smooth as that of the *Taiyo Maru*. The members of the Naval General Staff, never enthusiastic about the Pearl Harbor attack, had to face the fact that the only certainty about the northern Pacific in late November and early December would be its uncertainty.

Although Naval Intelligence already possessed a mine of information on the U.S. Pacific Fleet at Pearl Harbor, everyone listened with rapt attention as Suzuki reported on the great base, stressing that many ships of all shapes and sizes had been in port on Sunday, November 2. Suzuki also explained that he had not seen an aircraft carrier while he was in Honolulu.[22] He had observed, however, a substantial number of carrier planes in the area.

The Naval General Staff representatives received Suzuki's disclosures on American air patrols with visible relief. Faulty air patrols could be the one chink in the armor of the American giant.

Suzuki next analyzed the enemy's military and naval installations on Oahu. He estimated the strength of both the American Army and naval air arms. He reviewed his conversations with Kita, presenting the group with the detailed military maps of Oahu and the other islands which Yoshikawa had prepared. Suzuki also discussed in part the extensive questionnaire which Yoshikawa had answered so thoroughly.

In conclusion Suzuki spoke of U.S. defense capabilities. The enemy could put up stiff resistance over Oahu, even if the task force were able to reach the target area undetected. Should the U.S. military be alert and ready, the Japanese would encounter serious difficulties. If Nagumo's airmen caught the enemy napping, however, they would have a good chance of a successful attack.

As soon as Suzuki finished his report, questions arose on every side. Ito wished to know whether they could be sure that the U.S. Pacific Fleet would be in Pearl Harbor on X-Day. Could that be the one Sunday morning when Kimmel's ships varied the routine?[23] Suzuki could not give Ito an unequivocal yes or no. He emphasized, however, that each weekend without fail found the bulk of the enemy's capital ships in Pearl Harbor. They had been in port the weekend he passed in Honolulu, and Kita assured him that the same pattern had been followed without variation for months.

Someone raised the question of Lahaina. Here, too, Suzuki stated that Kimmel's big ships no longer used that anchorage. Kita had told him that only destroyers and smaller craft anchored there now.[24]

Tomioka inquired about the U.S. carriers. Was it their habit to go off on special missions, and if so, what might these be? When the flattops left Pearl Harbor, did they proceed singly or as a group, and did sizable support forces always accompany them?[25] Suzuki could not throw much light on these practical questions.

Fukudome asked whether the enemy seemed ready for an outbreak of hostilities. Suzuki replied that on weekdays Oahu hummed with work groups and training maneuvers were in evidence. But on Sunday, November 2, the island had presented the opposite picture. Pearl Harbor awoke late from its morning slumbers; few planes darted through the skies; officers and men received the usual weekend liberties; activity on Oahu calmed down to a slow walk. And Kita had assured him that the weekend letdown had been standing operating procedure all summer and autumn.[26]

According to Suzuki, Nagano did not pose a single query. Instead, he looked and acted like a tired old man, dozing off repeatedly. Only in the first part of Suzuki's discussion and again during the question period did he seem to perk up and take a little notice.[27]

After Suzuki had finished, Maejima gave his report. He concentrated on problems involved in executing the submarine attack. He concluded that the submarine operation would have more than its share of difficulties, the midgets in particular. Maejima thought it exceedingly risky to launch them so close to Pearl Harbor and to try to enter the narrow bottleneck channel which antisubmarine nets could seal off quickly. The Japanese would have to exercise the utmost care to prevent the submarines from alerting the Americans and jeopardizing the entire aerial attack plan.[28]

Listening carefully to everything Suzuki and Maejima had to say, Tomioka concluded that however gratifying the intelligence they had brought back, they had far from guaranteed the success of Yamamoto's hazardous venture. "In spite of all the information in our hands on the United States Navy and the general military situation on Oahu, the Pearl Harbor attack remained at best a gambler's move," he said in retrospect.[29]

After the meeting Suzuki returned to his home in Tokyo. The next day he went to the Naval General Staff, where he worked with various members of the Intelligence Section, collating and organizing all the information available on Pearl Harbor, for he had still another vital mission to perform. That evening he boarded Mikawa's flagship, *Hiei*, at Yokosuka and sailed with him to the secret rendezvous in the Kuriles.[30] There he was to brief Nagumo and his staff before the task force sailed to Hawaii.

Immediately after the conference in Tokyo, Maejima went to Yokosuka to tell his story to the submariners there. Then he sped with Matsuo to Kure to lecture to the Special Attack Force. The two agents divulged their findings at Honolulu concerning the U.S. Pacific Fleet, how to locate and enter the Pearl Harbor channel, the transparency of the water, American antisubmarine protective measures, and the like.[31]

To Matsuo's keen disappointment, he discovered that he could not participate in the Pearl Harbor attack as a midget submariner because the Special Attack Force was scheduled to leave Kure the next day.* But upon Shimizu's recommendation, Sasaki took him along on board the flagship *I-22* because Matsuo had the most recent information available about the situation on Oahu.[32]

Early on the morning of November 18 the mother submarines left Kure for Kamekakubi, where they loaded the midgets aboard. These rested directly behind the conning towers. Two steel belts, controlled from inside the mother craft, held them in place. A telephone line connected the two so that the skipper of the midget submarine could talk to those aboard the mother boat.[33]

The special attack submarines took off one by one on a moonless night, gliding into the water like humpbacked ghosts. As soon as they passed through Bungo Channel and reached the open sea, they would sail twenty miles apart

---

*Matsuo was killed in action on May 31, 1942, when he participated with two other midget submariners in an attack on Sydney Harbor, Australia.

for security. They would also maintain radio silence, but keep fairly well lined up so that if necessary, they could close for blinker signals. However, this did not become necessary.

I-22 was the last to leave. About midnight she set out to sea.[34] Early on the morning of November 19 she passed the main body of the Combined Fleet. "On our way north out of Saeki Bay," Ugaki recorded, "we saw a queerly shaped submarine with no marks, heading south. It proved to be *I-22*, flagship of the Third Submarine Division, which had a midget sub aboard. . . ." When *I-22* identified herself in response to *Nagato's* challenge, Yamamoto's flagship blinked in reply: "Congratulations in advance on your success." And from his low-slung craft Sasaki flashed back: "I swear to be successful." Much impressed, Ugaki continued:

> A surprise attack on X-Day will be an entirely unexpected storm. How much damage they will be able to inflict is not the point. The firm determination not to return alive on the part of those young lieutenants and ensigns who smilingly embarked on their ships cannot be praised too much. The spirit of *kesshitai* [self-sacrifice] has not changed at all. We can fully rely upon them.[35]

The entire mood and atmosphere of the midget submarine operation had been sacrificial from the beginning. While the airmen worked with cool logic and a tough determination to shed buckets of blood for results but not one drop for gestures, there seemed to be an almost ghoulish insistence upon immolating the midget submariners for nothing. One cannot help wondering, if the amount of damage they could inflict was "not the point," what indeed was the purpose of training, arming, equipping them, and sending them forth?

The same day, November 19, another patrol submarine, *I-26*, left Yokosuka to scout in northern waters. Her skipper, Commander Minoru Yokota, had spent most of his adult life in the submarine service and had experienced almost every type of undersea mission imaginable. This was one of the hastiest, for *I-26* had not been completed at Kure until November 6, and Yokota did not learn about the Pearl Harbor project until shortly thereafter. His officers and crew, therefore, barely had time to become acquainted with their boat, let alone engage in any specialized training.

Mito had briefed Yokota along with the other submarine skippers at Yokosuka, but he told them very little about the projected air attack. Moreover, he stated that war was not yet a certainty, so the submariners must be extremely careful to pick up all radio messages from the homeland after they had left their bases. Yokota's personal instructions were to check on American naval activity in the Aleutians, then proceed to the west coast of the United States. He would report any enemy ship sighted but fire no torpedoes until after the air raid on Pearl Harbor.[36]

In the small hours of November 18 a number of Nagumo's destroyers churned out of Saeki Bay. Last to leave, at 0200, was *Akigumo*. "Full of anticipation. Something big awaits us," wrote the ship's executive officer, Lieutenant Commander Sadao Chigusa, in his diary. Exactly what, he did not know. A conference of commanders and executive and gunnery officers aboard the flagship—the light cruiser *Abukuma*—the previous day had covered "the outline of the campaign and how the gunnery officers should be prepared for war," but did not mention the Pearl Harbor attack.

Akigumo's formation consisted of seven destroyers and the tanker *Nippon Maru*. Refueling took place later that day, and Chigusa felt much displeased. "Details have not been sufficient and refueling takes too long," he recorded severely. Then he gave a brief picture: "Gymnastics with officers and crew; sang military songs. I did my best to raise morale but I lost my voice."[37]

While the midget submarines and destroyers were moving out, workmen at Sasebo labored frantically loading aboard *Kaga* the final batch of modified torpedoes. These had just arrived from Nagasaki, delaying the departure of that carrier a full day behind her sisters of the First Air Fleet. Just in case of any last-minute trouble with the new missiles, Commander Hisao Tsuchita, chief of the Water Torpedo Department at Yokosuka, sailed with her.[38] Most of the carriers carried with them certain noncrew members. This was because the high-level bombs, unusually long and thin, did not fit the conventional release equipment on the bombers. Because time did not permit the manufacture and installation of new bomb releases, workers boarded the flattops and modified this equipment during the voyage to Hitokappu Bay. Similar modifications of the dive bombers had been completed just before they left the home bases for Saeki Bay.[39] These workmen had no idea of their destination. When the task force left for Hawaii, they transferred aboard a tanker and remained at Hitokappu Bay until after the attack.[40]

Her suspense mercifully ended, *Kaga* sped directly to the rendezvous to distribute the precious torpedoes and join the fleet. As she rounded southern Kyushu with her two-destroyer escort, she recovered her complement of planes from their land bases. Her course lay about fifty miles offshore, and like *Akagi*, she saw no other ships en route.[41]

Ahead of the task force raced the gunboat *Kunajiri* to instruct the Yona post office on Etorofu to suspend all communications. Telephone, telegraph, postal service, and private travel to and from the island came to an abrupt halt, along with all normal sea traffic. The area's inhabitants became virtual prisoners until after the Pearl Harbor attack. The task force ships, too, took extraordinary precautions against communications leaks. Some even sealed the key points on their radio transmitters lest someone inadvertently touch them off. And to baffle the ships' crews, who as yet did not know the final destination, the men received issues of both summer and winter uniforms.[42]

On the voyage to Hitokappu Bay the ships kept busy with seamanlike drills. Aboard *Akagi* Nagumo drafted instructions for the flying personnel, both officers and men, for distribution at Hitokappu Bay after he had briefed them about the mission. He gave the document to Genda for completion. It contained nothing of a technical nature; in fact, it did not comprise instructions in the usual sense. Rather it might be called an exhortation explaining the purpose of the long training in naval air tactics and asserting that in this crisis Japan expected every man to do his utmost. Genda consulted with Fuchida, who had literary gifts, and the flight leader finished the document.[43]

Much more important, Yamamoto's farewell speech had given Genda and Fuchida unpalatable food for thought. They had based all their training on the assumption of surprise. Now at the eleventh hour Yamamoto warned them not to count on this. Therefore, Genda and Fuchida got together with Murata for some hard thinking.

They decided that if the attacking aircraft flew into a blast of antiaircraft fire, Murata's slow-moving torpedo planes must not approach the target first, as they had been practicing. The other bombers must precede them to cause as much confusion as possible and draw fire upward and away from the torpedo aircraft. In this way Murata's men might still be able to do considerable damage. Murata objected, not relishing the idea of following a trail which others had blazed for him, but Genda and Fuchida stood firm. More was at stake than Murata's amour-propre.

The three men worked out a system of signals. If the attackers did indeed catch the Americans napping, Fuchida would fire his flare pistol once. In that case, Murata and his torpedomen would thunder in to take full advantage of surprise and ensure maximum damage before the air filled with smoke. Then the dive and horizontal bombers would take their turn. But if Fuchida found the Americans on guard, he would fire twice, whereupon the dive bombers would charge in first, the horizontal bombers following. Only when these had drawn fire upward would Murata's vulnerable torpedo planes enter the scene.[44]

Three reconnaissance submarines, *I-19, I-21,* and *I-23,* under Captain Kijiro Imaizumi, formed the next group to swell the exodus of Japan's warships from the homeland. Being in a special category, not under Shimizu's direct command, Imaizumi had not attended the Sixth Fleet commanders' briefing held on November 10. Three days before his departure date of November 20 an officer of the Naval General Staff (probably Commander Ryunosuke Ariizumi) instructed him to sail in secret to Hitokappu Bay, where he would receive further instructions. Actually the Navy spirited him away without so much as a copy of formal orders. Naturally Imaizumi thought something unusual must be going on, but he never anticipated an attack on Pearl Harbor.[45]

In contrast, Rear Admiral Tsutomu Sato knew exactly where he was bound as he watched the rain-spattered hills of Yokosuka recede into the distance on November 21. Badly needed repairs had delayed his First Submarine Squadron, so that it left the homeland last of all. Now his four craft were finally on their way to the northeast on a course virtually the same as that of the Second Submarine Division, between the Aleutians and Midway, and with the same mission.[46]

Satisfied that his undersea fleet was under way, Shimizu returned to

Katori. The flagship weighed anchor for Truk in the Caroline Islands, where it would remain until December 2. On that date Shimizu and his staff would proceed to Kwajalein until after the attack.[47] Last to be seriously considered in Yamamoto's audacious plan, Shimizu's submarines became the first Navy units to depart in strength for the target area.

CHAPTER 44

"A

SITUATION

FULL OF

DYNAMITE"

By mid-November the false messages which the Japanese Navy was sending out to hide the location of its carriers confounded the intelligence picture for the Americans. Rochefort's Combat Intelligence Unit continued to have a fairly good grip on the submarines, although not by individual craft. His reports showed a move eastward, and he correctly tracked Shimizu to the Marshalls. And no one could miss the picture of a big Japanese buildup to the south. The signs made Rochefort exceedingly uneasy. "Beginning about the first of November," he testified, "it became apparent to us . . . that there was something afoot." He could not put his finger on it, although the pattern was similar to that which had appeared when the Japanese moved against Hainan and later against Indochina.[1]

But Oahu lost track of the carriers completely and became confused about the support ships. For instance, on November 15 Rochefort associated Battleship Division Three (*Hiei* and *Kirishima*) and Destroyer Squadron One with the "South Expeditionary Force." And the next day Rochefort's men placed *Zuikaku*, albeit with heavy reservations, in Jaluit in the Marshalls.[2]

Kimmel commented on the nonappearnce of Japan's carriers. Layton replied that "that happens frequently and it is a normal assumption that they were then in port."[3] As he explained later, "When carriers are not heard from . . . they are most likely in port, because there they are on low-frequency low-power circuits that cannot be heard. . . . It is only when they originate traffic themselves at sea that direction-finder bearings can be taken. . . ."[4]

Thus, Naval Intelligence on Oahu had a nagging feeling that something peculiar was going on in the Japanese Navy. The interceptor operators noted that Japanese communications became "very involved. They would send the same message time and time again. . . ."⁵ All this was part of the deliberate Japanese pattern of deception.

On the other hand, the Army on Oahu thought it had control of the situation. A test held on November 14 enabled Hawaii to detect carrier planes launching about eighty miles at sea. Within six minutes pursuit aircraft took off and intercepted the incoming bombers some thirty miles from Pearl Harbor. Lieutenant Colonel Carroll A. Powell, Short's signal officer, wrote: "All the general officers present were highly pleased. . . ."⁶

One official who did not sing the customary hosannas over conditions in Hawaii was Assistant Attorney General Norman M. Littell. Writing on November 14 to Marvin O. McIntyre, secretary to Roosevelt, he expressed considerable doubt about the effectiveness of the leadership in Hawaii:

> Appointments in peace time to the "Paradise of the Pacific" are one thing, but . . . in the increasing tensions of the Pacific, there must be able and fearless men in command, capable of making decisions and getting things done. I gained the impression of weakness on all sides. . . . The admiral in command at Naval Headquarters [Bloch] was a fine and widely experienced old gentleman past sixty, who, in command of one of the most exciting naval posts under the American flag, goes to bed at 9:30 P.M., because, as he told me, he "could not stay awake after that." The General in command for the Army [Short] was also past sixty, an estimable man of great experience . . . ⁷

Kimmel resented Washington's failure to act on his recommendations or to keep him posted. Later he insisted that these "repeated rebuffs . . . and constant insistence of the Navy Department that the major emphasis was to be placed upon operations in the Atlantic strongly contributed" to his own "estimate that an air attack of the nature and force of that delivered on 7 December was not to be expected." On November 16 he once more wrote to Stark, obviously in an irascible mood: "In repeated correspondence I have set forth to you the needs of the Pacific Fleet. These needs are real and immediate. I have seen the material and personnel diverted to the Atlantic. No doubt they are needed there. But I must insist that more consideration be given to the needs of the Pacific Fleet."⁸

At this very time someone missed another timely signal, this one from Captain Ellis M. Zacharias. Now in command of the cruiser *Salt Lake City,* he still took a keen interest in intelligence. Around this date a Curtis B. Munson came to Hawaii with instructions from Naval Operations (OPNAV) to "open everything to him." He sought out Zacharias about what to do in case of an armed uprising by the local Japanese in Hawaii or on the West Coast in the event of hostilities. He also wanted to know whether such a contingency was likely. Zacharias categorically discounted the possibility because war with Japan "would begin with an air attack on our fleet, and for that reason it would have to be conducted with the greatest secrecy, and therefore no Japanese . . . in the United States or in Hawaii, would be aware of the fact that such an attack was coming." Sometime after the Pearl Harbor strike Zacharias requested and obtained Munson's confirmation of this conversation. Munson added that Zacharias had also suggested that "the attack would conform to their [the Japanese] historical procedure, that of hitting before war was declared."

Zacharias tried several times to talk to Soc McMorris of War Plans about his views, but receiving the "brush off," the intelligence expert did not persist. He reasoned that if the higher-ups wanted his opinion, they would ask for it.[9]

Nomura, too, marshaled his thoughts on November 14 and composed what may well be the most straightforward and penetrating of his summaries. He ended: "I feel that should the situation in Japan permit, I would like to caution patience for one or two months in order to get a clear view of the world situation. . . ."[10] If, on November 14, Nomura could counsel patience for another month or two, obviously he had no idea that his country planned to initiate war on December 7 (Washington time), especially by a strike on Pearl Harbor. By this time Nomura's continual harping on the United States' long-range staying power, distaste for the Tripartite Pact, support of China and Britain, and the basic unity of its people must have made him the "Abominable No-man" to the Foreign Ministry.

The end of a session with Hull on November 15 found Nomura in such despair that he sent Togo suggestions for handling "the closing of the consulates and recalling of the Ambassador" should the talks break down and Japan "pursue an unrestricted course." His message makes clear, however, that he did not expect a Japanese-American war to break out, certainly not immediately. Rather, he anticipated "the same situation as now exists between Germany and the United States . . ."[11]—that is, virtual severance of diplomatic relations without a formal state of war.

But Tokyo wanted no part of the American attitude and so informed Nomura emphatically on the fifteenth, adding: "Whatever the case may be, the fact remains that the date set forth in my message #738 [November 25, Washington time] is an absolutely immovable one. Please, therefore, make the United States see the light, so as to make possible the signing of the agreement by that date."[12] Asking Nomura to break the deadlock and persuade the United States to sign a blank check for the Japanese in ten days was a manifest absurdity.

While those in on Magic paid fascinated attention to the diplomatic messages, one of the most significant tip-offs of the year slipped by unnoticed. On November 15 Tokyo enjoined its Honolulu consulate: "As relations between Japan and the United States are most critical, make your 'ships in harbor report' irregular, but at a rate of twice a week. Although you are no doubt aware, please take extra care to maintain secrecy."[13]

Unfortunately the Navy did not translate this highly important message until December 3. Yet time still afforded Washington the opportunity to alert Hawaii's defenders. Seldom has so much significance been crammed into so few phrases. Here for the first and only time Tokyo in so many words equated the consular reports with the relations between Japan and the United States. That in itself distinguished this particular dispatch and the Honolulu consulate from the stream of intercepts inundating Army and Naval Intelligence. Tokyo's asking for information on a twice-a-week basis indicated current, continuing interest. And the request to report at irregular intervals was an obvious precaution against establishing a habit pattern. Finally, Tokyo charged the consulate to "take extra care to maintain secrecy." What more evidence could one ask of a fox in the chicken coop? Yet we have no record that this message caused the smallest stir in Washington, let alone inspired anyone to tip off either Kimmel or Short.

But Washington was far from asleep at the switch. McCollum put his office on a twenty-four-hour-a-day basis early in November. He "felt that the situation between us and Japan was extremely explosive and would erupt at any time. . . ." He believed that if Japan went to war with the United States, it would begin with an attack on the Fleet.[14]

ONI's fortnightly summary for the period ending November 15 reflected some of McCollum's views: "The approaching crisis in United States-Japanese relations overshadowed all other developments in the Far East during the period." No one apparently expected Kurusu's mission to succeed, "the envoy himself reportedly expressing extreme pessimism. . . ."[15] Nevertheless, if the rest of Naval Intelligence agreed with McCullum's conjecture that Japan would strike the American Fleet, this long summary did not show it. On the contrary, it indicated that Japan was not yet "strong enough in Indo-China to attack Yunnan or even Thailand." And the Combined Fleet remained "in home waters, nearly in full force in the Inland Sea."[16]

If Tokyo's message of November 15 to Kita passed over Washington's head, Yoshikawa did not miss its full implications. Thenceforth he scouted the Fleet almost every day and made a special daily graph of the location and movements of all ships in harbor. Sometime in October he began destroying many reports from his secret file in Kita's office and thereafter kept the file weeded. Later he claimed that he did so only because he needed the space. Of course, he acknowledged that a certain danger existed in having too much material lying around.[17] Either way the massive destruction ensured that one month later he had the minimum of burning to do on short notice.

He gained the impression that the Pacific Fleet still operated on a peacetime basis. The ships did not appear to be particularly on the alert, and they paid almost no attention to camouflage. The Fleet returned to Pearl Harbor on weekends and granted shore leave to many officers and men. This was all to the good for the Japanese, although as a sailor Yoshikawa deplored the habit. He thought the U.S. Navy had no business adhering to a regular schedule with the political situation obviously so critical.[18]

Strangely enough, the worse the international situation, the safer Yoshikawa may have been. Sometime after December 7, Shivers told Fielder that he knew "the entire espionage ring centered around [sic] the Japanese Consulate, but diplomatic immunity prevented his investigation, and that anything he did might start the overt act which would create war."[19]

Yet at this very time Mayfield of the DIO initiated an action which could have blown Yoshikawa's mission and indeed the success of Yamamoto's Pearl Harbor project sky-high. David Sarnoff, president of the Radio Corporation of America (RCA), visited Honolulu in mid-November. Mayfield, who had been trying unsuccessfully to procure copies of the Japanese consulate's messages, arranged through Sarnoff "to obtain in a roundabout way certain information from the files of his company." Just how difficult a tussle, if any, Sarnoff had with his conscience we cannot say. But he held a reserve commission as an Army colonel, so presumably his patriotism overcame his legalistic scruples, as it had in Mayfield's case long since.[20] Thus, at last American counterintelligence had access to the files at which it had gazed so hungrily for so long. But luck still favored the Japanese. Their consulate, with fine impartiality, spread its business by month among the Honolulu radio companies, and it so happened that MacKay Radio, not RCA, handled the traffic for November.

The Japanese consulate used the J-19, not the Purple, diplomatic code. Rochefort was, in McCollum's words, "the only officer in our Navy who is a top-flight cryptographer and radio man, and who also has a thorough knowledge of the Japanese language."[21] Since he received the J-19 keys within twelve hours of their solution in Washington, he and his unit would have had little difficulty in decoding and translating the messages between Tokyo and Honolulu.[22]

The situation was like some cosmic practical joke set up by an unusually mordant-minded demon. While the Japanese Navy took the most elaborate precautions for communications security, the Foreign Ministry chattily gave itself away. In spite of the Japanese radio smoke screen, Hawaii's Combat Intelligence still picked up significant patterns. Had Layton and Rochefort been able to sit down with the consular intercepts spread out before them, along with Rochefort's communications gleanings, they might have cracked Yamamoto's secret. If Rochefort had received the messages from MacKay Radio as well as RCA, by the latter part of November he would have been breaking down the latest in the "bomb plot" sequence. More were to come in early December, culminating in a single message which was a virtual giveaway.

Meanwhile, the State Department gave Kurusu, Japan's special envoy, every cooperation, arranging to delay until November 7 the China clipper due to leave Hong Kong on the fifth so that Kurusu might embark. Kurusu looked like the complete American stereotype of a Japanese—short, slim, with reticent eyes behind the inevitable glasses, a mustache, and slanted brushstroke eyebrows imparting a perpetually surprised expression. What, if anything except camouflage, Japan hoped to gain by his mission, and how much—again, if anything—he knew about his country's plans for the near future, who can say with complete authority?

When his clipper reached Midway, it laid over for a day or two because of engine trouble, then went on to Honolulu, where it arrived at 1635 on November 12. Bicknell met Kurusu at the plane. "Oh, you are Colonel Bicknell!" exclaimed Kurusu as he looked up at the towering figure. And he conveyed greetings from a mutual friend. They drove to the Royal Hawaiian

Hotel by a back road which avoided Pearl Harbor, a fact which did not escape Kurusu's notice. During the drive he asked, "If we should be so unfortunate as to have war between our two countries, what do you think would be the attitude of the Japanese here in Hawaii?"

Looming over Kurusu like an amiable Saint Bernard set to guard a Pekingese, Bicknell replied rather quizzically, "Mr. Ambassador, I was just going to ask you the same thing!" After a brief silence in which the envoy appeared to be considering the implications of this remark, Bicknell spoke seriously: "Mr. Ambassador, do you think you are going to be able to do anything in Washington to avoid further trouble between our countries?" Kurusu answered with equal solemnity, "Frankly, I don't know, but I sincerely hope I can."[23]

Kurusu reached Washington at 1330 on November 15. That very day (November 16 in Tokyo) the Foreign Ministry sent Nomura a most disquieting reply to his excellent summary of the fourteenth:

> . . . you may be sure that you have all my gratitude for the efforts you have put forth, but the fate of our Empire hangs by the slender thread of a few days, so please fight harder than you ever did before. . . . In your opinion we ought to wait and see what turn the war takes and remain patient. However . . . the situation renders this out of the question. I set the deadline for the solution of these negotiations in my #736, and there will be no change. . . .

Thus, once more Tokyo insisted upon November 25 as the cutoff date. And on the fifteenth the Foreign Ministry had sent instructions to Washington, as well as several other Japanese diplomatic missions, for destroying code machines in the event of emergency.[24]

On the seventeenth, at 1030, Nomura presented Kurusu to Hull. The secretary of state took an immediate dislike to the new envoy.[25] Nevertheless, whatever his personal bias, Hull complimented Kurusu on the way he had "handled his relations with the public since coming to this country. He also spoke highly of the respect and confidence in which the Secretary and his associates hold the Japanese Ambassador."[26] The three diplomats adjourned to the White House for an appointment with the President at 1100. Although they talked together for an hour and a quarter, nothing new developed. Nomura took a certain comfort from Roosevelt's quoting William Jennings Bryan: "There is no last word between friends."[27]

When Hull, Nomura, and Kurusu met on the eighteenth, they faced the difficulty of working out a Japanese-American rapprochement while Japan was still tied to Germany. Hull even suggested "that Hitler would eventually, if he was successful, get around to the Far East and double-cross Japan." Kurusu protested that his country could not "abrogate the Tripartite Pact but that Japan might do something which would 'outshine' the Tripartite Pact." Eventually Nomura offered the possibility of restoring the situation to its status before the Japanese had moved into southern Indochina and the subsequent economic freeze. Hull was somewhat discouraging, pointing out that the troops withdrawn from French Indochina could be "diverted to some equally objectionable movement elsewhere." But he promised to take up the proposal with the British and Dutch.[28] Although Hull retained his poker face with the two Japanese, obviously he saw in this *modus vivendi* the bare possibility of an interlude in which Japan could edge away from all-out militarism toward a more reasonable approach.

If the Japanese Foreign Ministry wanted to keep peace with the United States, why did it not snap up Nomura's alternative? On the face of it the suggestion offered an acceptable breather. Each side gave up something tangible enough to provide evidence of good faith and in so doing removed two thorny obstacles: The Japanese pullout from southern French Indochina would take away the most immediate threat against the Allies in Southeast Asia, while the American financial thaw would cancel Japan's prime grievance.

Unfortunately, however, Togo's government wanted peace with the United States strictly on terms of full and simultaneous acceptance of all Japanese terms. What is more, Togo disliked Nomura's excursions into the forbidden field of creative diplomacy. Even before Nomura and Kurusu had shot off several messages on the eighteenth explaining the *modus vivendi* in enthusiastic detail, the Foreign Ministry had dispatched to Nomura instructions concerning the repatriation of those Japanese who had not boarded the special ships.[29] What Tokyo did not confide to Nomura and Kurusu was the fact that this entire mission, purportedly a second evacuation voyage by the *Tatuta Maru,* was a blind. The vessel would leave Japan in early December, sail eastward for a few days, then turn back to Yokohama—a hoax equally cruel to the Americans aboard and to the Japanese eagerly awaiting the chance to go home. In any case, this message was enough to make any ambassador nervous and to alert any good intelligence officer.

The same was true of the message which Tokyo dispatched to Kita in Honolulu that same day, November 18: "Please report on the following areas as to vessels anchored therein: Area 'N,' Pearl Harbor, Manila Bay *Honolulu* [italics in original], and the Areas Adjacent thereto. (Make your investigation with great secrecy.)" "Manila Bay" had been crossed out; presumably Naval Intelligence meant "Mamala Bay."[30]

Receipt and processing of these vital consular messages did not permit the Army to translate this one until December 5. The fact that the Americans had broken the J-19 code did not mean that they could read the messages automatically. The keys changed daily, and in order to break them, the decrypters had to have a fair volume of traffic to work on. It was, in Mr. X's words, "plenty tough."[31] Even so, the main delays resulted from transmitting the messages to Washington by mail. Here, then, was another valuable, if belated, hint to Washington that the Japanese were still interested in the exact location of Kimmel's ships in Pearl Harbor. Nor could anyone miss the emphasis on "great secrecy."

The Japanese would have been amazed to learn just how well United States counterintelligence knew "Morimura." Said Bicknell many years later: "He and his taxi driver were all over the goddamn place." But so long as he behaved like a tourist and stayed off government property, he was safe.

Bicknell attended most of the parties Kita threw at the consulate. These were always stag, "with a bottle of scotch at each place and a geisha girl pouring it out." All Bicknell got from these forays into enemy territory was a lot of free scotch and a respect for Okuda, whom he considered "the smart cookie, the mastermind."[32]

Kita promptly answered Tokyo with one of Yoshikawa's meticulous reports on November 18. It was detailed, precise, and suggestive.[33] But the Japanese messages which really raised a fuss in ONI and G-2 were two which the Foreign Ministry dispatched to Nomura on November 29:

> . . . In case of emergency (danger of cutting off our diplomatic relations), and the cutting off of international communications, the following warning will be added in the middle of the daily Japanese language short wave news broadcast.
>
> (1) In case of a Japan-U.S. relations in danger: HIGASHI NO KAZEAME [sic] ["East wind rain"].
>
> (2) Japan-U.S.S.R. relations: KITANOKAZE [sic] KUMORI ["North wind cloudy"].
>
> (3) Japan-British relations: NISHI NO KAZE HARE ["West wind clear"].
>
> This signal will be given in the middle and at the end as a weather forecast and each sentence will be repeated twice. When this is heard please destroy all code papers, etc. This is as yet to be a completely secret arrangement.
>
> Forward as urgent intelligence.[34]

Tokyo promptly followed this up with an amplification:

> When our diplomatic relations are becoming dangerous, we will add the following at the beginning and end of our general intelligence broadcasts:
>
> (1) If it is Japan-U.S. relations, "HIGASHI."
>
> (2) Japan-Russia relations, "KITA."
>
> (3) Japan-British relations, (including Thai, Malaya and N.E.I.): "NISHI."
>
> The above will be repeated five times and included at the beginning and end.
>
> Relay to Rio de Janeiro, Buenos Aires, Mexico City, San Francisco.[35]

Tokyo's "winds" dispatches went through the mill on November 28 and 26 respectively. From then on both services knocked themselves out to intercept the implementing messages. Washington directed Rochefort to establish "a listening watch on the most likely frequencies." So he sent four language officers to Aiea, "where they covered on a twenty-four hour basis one or more frequencies in addition to all the known broadcasts from Tokyo. Results were nil."[36] McCollum testified, "We were all looking for it. . . ." And so far as he knew, "we were continuing to look for that after the bombs had started falling on the fleet. . . ."[37]

Why the "winds" message caused such a stir when the much more significant "bomb plot" series did not is another of the Pearl Harbor mysteries. Certainly no one in Washington needed the Japanese Foreign Ministry to tell him that diplomatic relations with Japan were "becoming dangerous."

Kimmel and Bloch learned of the "winds" message as information addresses of a dispatch dated November 28 from the Asiatic Fleet, which also advised: "British and Comsixteen monitoring above broadcasts."[38] The senior United States Army representative in Java also scooped it in and on December 3 forwarded the information to Miles. This was the only version to use the word "war," his message including the sentence: "Japan will notify her consuls of war decision in her foreign broadcasts as weather report at end. . . ."[39] Either Java placed the worst possible interpretation on the Japanese wording, or the Foreign Ministry had alerted its Far Eastern diplomatic missions in much more forceful language than they had used to Nomura. Tokyo had done exactly that in connection with the imperial conference of July 2.

Consul General Walter Foote at Batavia advised State on December 4 in slightly less inflammatory phraseology—"When crisis leading to worst arises . . ." and "When threat of crisis exists . . ."—then threw cold water on the whole affair by adding prosaically, "I attach little or no importance to it and view it with some suspicion. Such have been common since 1936."[40]

No other aspect of the Pearl Harbor story has generated more heat and less light than the "winds" code. Was the implementing message received or not? It appears unlikely that Japan ever used the code. Normal channels of communication remained open between Tokyo and Washington until after the Pearl Harbor attack, so the need to broadcast "East wind rain" never arose.

Not that it really mattered. Looking backward down the corridor of time, one can appreciate that the joint congressional committee judged correctly when it reported: "Granting for purposes of discussion that a genuine execute message applying to the winds code was intercepted before December 7, we believe that such fact would have added nothing to what was already known concerning the critical character of our relations with the Empire of Japan."[41]

American authorities would have been much better advised to pay attention to such dispatches as the one which Tokyo sent to the Honolulu consulate on November 20: "Strictly secret. Please investigate comprehensively the fleet —— bases in the neighborhood of the Hawaiian military reservation." A garble left one word unintelligible; however, we may safely assume that the missing link is "air."[42] The Japanese took a particular interest in U.S. air power in Hawaii and the absolute necessity of pinning it down if the assault on the Fleet was to succeed. Even granted the garble, this message again deserved more attention than it evidently received, for nothing in it could be stretched to cover interest in Fleet movements.

Rochefort and his dedicated group meanwhile continued working frantically trying to trace the Japanese Fleet. Yet they missed the exodus of Nagumo's task force from assorted Japanese home bases for Hitokappu Bay. "Battleship Division Three, the Carrier Divisions and two destroyer squadrons have been associated in traffic. . . . No movement from home waters has been noted," read the summary of November 18. The signs indicated that the Commander in Chief of the Second Fleet would be "in command of a large Task Force comprising the Third Fleet, Combined Air Force, some carrier divisions, and Battleship Division Three."[43]

The summary from McCollum's office in Washington for the same date placed *Hiei* and *Kirishima* in the Kure-Saeki area: *Akagi, Kaga, Soryu*, and *Hiryu* in South Kyushu; *Zuikaku* in the Kure-Sasebo locality, with her sister, *Shokaku*, at Takao in Formosa, albeit with a question mark. Japan was winning the game of hide-and-seek.[44]

Rochefort looked for a particular pattern. He believed that a major Japanese operation would reveal itself in "three definite stages": first, "a large flurry of traffic"; then "a stage of apparent confusion . . ." caused by "the regrouping of the ships and the units"; third, radio silence would descend, "and when radio silence started then you knew something was up. . . ."[45]

The Japanese placed surprisingly little communications security around the forces to move south, just as they had never made any secret of their expansionist designs on that part of the world. Therefore, as Rochefort later pointed out, the estimates made at the Pearl Harbor and Cavite Combat Intelligence units were correct in every respect but one—Pearl Harbor.

There is no indication that anyone else on Oahu equated the Japanese movements with peril to Pearl Harbor. Kimmel frequently dropped in on Rochefort to discuss matters, but nothing in their testimony hints that these talks touched on a possible attack on the Fleet in its anchorage. As Rochefort said later, "No one thought in terms of Pearl Harbor at the time." Indeed, it was not Rochefort's business to evaluate. He picked up the data, summarized them, and passed them to Fleet Headquarters to interpret; he had "no other information available" aside from that which he "gathered by radio."[46]

Kimmel had added Soc McMorris to the very restricted list of those in the know concerning Rochefort's Combat Intelligence.[47] But the war plans officer, too, believed that "the Japanese interests lay in the Asiatic area and that they could more effectively utilize their full power in that area." He did not believe an attack on the Pearl Harbor region would result in sufficient damage to make it worthwhile. And he thought the Japanese would reason as he did. What is more, he regarded an attack "by saboteurs or by submarines as extremely probable." At no time, however, did he "envisage such an attack as actually occurred."[48]

Similar views prevailed among the Army personnel. Wooch Fielder had been trapped in the same snare which snapped shut over men with higher rank and much more experience than he. Fielder testified that he had "great confidence in the presence of our Navy here, and . . . just didn't know enough to visualize the approach of an enemy task force as long as our Navy was present. . . ." Moreover, he knew the Navy was responsible for long-range aerial reconnaissance and thought it was engaged in just that.[49] Doubt oozed all the way up to Marshall. The Chief of Staff believed that rather than risk an attack on Hawaii, the Japanese would "proceed on a more conservative basis of actual operations to the southward. . . ."[50]

But the Japanese planned to strike with terrifying power in both directions at once. In pursuit of this policy Togo gave short shrift to Nomura and Kurusu's suggestion of a temporary solution to the diplomatic problems. He advised Kurusu directly on November 19: "The Ambassador . . . having received our revised instructions . . . will please present our B proposal of the Imperial Government, and no further concessions can be made.

"If the U.S. consent to this cannot be secured, the negotiations will have to be broken off. . . ."[51]

Here Nomura seems to have come perilously close to losing his temper. He suggested, among other things, that maintenance of the status quo or initiating military action would "bring about a situation full of dynamite and finally lead us to an armed clash."[52] He also begged Tokyo to hold up at least four or five days in announcing the evacuation ships: " . . . At a time when we are thus pressing for an early reply, I feel that it would do us great harm were we to announce that we are having ships, with all the accompanying dark implications, leave on or about the 25th or 26th. . . ."[53]

Need we add that the Foreign Ministry declined these suggestions,[54] so indicative of Nomura's good faith and good sense?

The next day, Thursday, November 20, might not have been the most tactful occasion for presenting Proposal B. As Nomura explained to Tokyo, this was "America's biggest holiday. They call it 'Thanksgiving.' In spite of that, however, Mr. Hull not only agreed to talk with, but seemed glad to see both me and Ambassador Kurusu when we went to call on him."[55]

No longer able to stall off the evil hour in the face of Togo's direct order, Nomura and Kurusu handed Hull the fateful document. Hull promised to give it "sympathetic study,"[56] but he knew from Magic "that this proposal was the final Japanese proposition—an ultimatum. . . ."[57]

In exchange for providing Japan with all the oil it required, lifting the freeze, and discontinuing aid to China, the United States received only the promise of Japanese removal of troops from southern Indochina to the northern part of the country—the very thing Togo had just assured Nomura could not be done. In any case, such a move would have kept a dagger at the jugular vein of all Southeast Asia and the East Indies. True, the proposal agreed to no further Japanese moves into southeastern Asia and the southern Pacific, but that left a lot of Asia unaccounted for—notably Siberia and unoccupied China. Furthermore, the Japanese maintained utter silence about the Tripartite Pact. They offered no assurance that they would not supply Hitler through such a newly opened American trade channel. As Hull saw it, agreement would have meant condonement by the United States of Japan's past aggressions, assent by the United States to unlimited courses of conquest by Japan in the future, abandonment by the United States of its whole past position in regard to the most essential principles of its foreign policy in general, betrayal by the United States of China, and acceptance by the United States of a position as a silent partner aiding and abetting Japan in her effort to create a Japanese hegemony in and over the western Pacific and Eastern Asia.

In brief, "The Japanese proposal of November 20 . . . was of so preposterous a character that no responsible American official could ever have dreamed of accepting it."[58] Yet the secretary of state did not immediately thunder forth a flat no. In the first place, U.S. armed forces still needed time to prepare their defenses. In the second, Hull had an idea in mind for a last-minute means of deflecting the avalanche.

CHAPTER 45

"THINGS

ARE

AUTOMATICALLY

GOING TO

HAPPEN"

Lying about midway down the island of Etorofu, desolate Hitokappu Bay was an ideal hideout such as pirates might have used in an earlier day. About six miles wide and extending approximately the same distance inland, it provided ample anchorage and perfect concealment. The western shore was low, while the eastern consisted of high, steep bluffs with a narrow boulder beach. Except for a small cluster of shabby houses at Toshimoi—a dismal fishing village on the northern edge of the bay—and Uembetsu on the south, no buildings stood in the area. Heavy mists shrouded the waters when the task force arrived. Snow fell intermittently from black, wintry skies. A thick white blanket covered the beaches and the hills leading to Mount Onnenobori brooding in the distance.

For several days Nagumo's task force had been slipping into the rendezvous. "At 1515 we anchored," Chigusa recorded in his diary on November 22. "I shaved my long beard. Hitokappu Bay is occupied by powerful naval forces. Seeing these ships, I had a feeling of great confidence." Chigusa did not yet know about Operation Hawaii.

Imaizumi knew that some big operation was afloat when he sailed into Hitokappu Bay with his three submarines. So many ships? What was going on? He found out when he and his three submarine skippers reported aboard *Akagi*. "You are to accompany the task force to Hawaii as an advance patrol," Kusaka told him, handing over the necessary documents and instructions.[1] This plan was later changed because of poor visibility and the difficulty of communicating between the main body of the task force and the submarines.

Last to enter was *Kaga* on November 22 with her treasure of modified torpedoes, greeted with double joy not only for her cargo but for her auspicious presence. Superstitious as seamen all over the world, Japanese sailors considered *Kaga*, which had seen successful action off the China coast in 1932 and 1937, a "victorious" ship.

On November 22 Nagumo summoned his staff, plus Fuchida, to an intelligence briefing by Suzuki, to be held at 2000 in a carefully guarded room aboard *Akagi*. There Nagumo kept the scale models of Pearl Harbor and Oahu, plus the collected data on the prospective targets. Besides the information in his fact-crammed brain, Suzuki brought with him the map which Kita had given him aboard the *Taiyo Maru,* a detailed sketch of Pearl Harbor and naval installations, a record of the number and kind of planes on Oahu with airfield and hanger capacities. According to Suzuki, these reports described Pearl Harbor and Oahu down to such details as the thickness of the hangar roofs.[2]

Suzuki repeated in substance what he had told the Naval General Staff. He outlined the general disposition of the U.S. Pacific Fleet at Pearl Harbor, emphasizing in particular its habit of returning to base every weekend. He reported five groups of PBY flying boats—about sixty aircraft—at the Ford Island base, which provided hangar space as well as training and repair facilities for carrier-borne planes while their mother ships moored in Pearl Harbor. "There are additional PBY's at Kaneohe," he added, "possibly fifty planes, also a hangar and mooring buoys, and a land base under construction for fighter planes. Barber's Point does not have a hangar, but it is used as an operational base for carrier-borne planes. About eighty aircraft are in training there." He emphasized that Hickam Field bristled with air power, estimating the striking force at about 40 four-engine bombers and approximately 100 twin-engine bombers.[3]

Actually Suzuki's estimate, based on materials which Kita gave him in Honolulu, badly overshot the mark. Hickam Field housed only 12 heavy bombers (B-17Ds), and the Hawaiian Air Force had only 50 medium and light bombers (3 B-12s, 32 B-18s, 2 A-12s, and 12 A-20s), exactly half the number with which Suzuki credited it. All but the B-17s and A-20s were obsolescent types.[4]

Suzuki went on to describe the fighters, reporting some 200 P-40s, P-38s, and P-36s, with an additional 70 or so of other types. Obviously such an interceptor force could spoil the attack and inflict untold damage on the Japanese aircraft; the attackers would have to demolish the American pursuit planes on the spot. In fact, Suzuki's estimate of U.S. fighter craft was inaccurate. Martin had a total of 152 fighters (99 P-40s, 39 P-36s, and 14 P-26s). All but the P-40s were obsolescent. In all, Suzuki reported 455 Army planes on Oahu, whereas in the whole territory the Hawaiian Air Force had only 227 military aircraft, including 13 observation planes.[5]

Suzuki next moved to American utilization of their aircraft. "United States planes are not in the habit of engaging in mass flights over Oahu," he told the group. To Genda and Fuchida this indicated two important possibilities: The Japanese probably would not accidentally run into any large enemy training flights, and if they did, this no doubt would signify that the Americans had spotted the attackers and had risen to repel them. Therefore, every pilot must keep an eagle eye out for any sign of massive enemy air activity.

"United States air patrols are very good in the area south and southwest of Oahu, but generally inadequate to the north of the island," Suzuki explained. This agreed with other intelligence reports and, of course, was most welcome news to Nagumo, who planned to approach Pearl Harbor from the north. "The Navy's PBYs usually start their patrols around breakfast time and return before lunch," Suzuki concluded. "Then they take off again and come back before sunset. On the basis of my own observations and the reports I collected in Honolulu, I feel reasonably sure that United States scouting planes do not begin their patrols before sunrise, nor do they continue such activity after sunset."

This was top-priority intelligence—crucial for the potential success of Yamamoto's plan. During the September war games the same information emanating from the Honolulu consulate had guided Yamamoto and his colleagues. Apparently the Americans had made little if any change in the patrol pattern since late summer. If everything went according to plan, Nagumo's first attack wave would leave the carriers before the enemy began to patrol, giving the attackers an excellent chance of achieving success.

All during Suzuki's report Nagumo sat motionless as an idol, his eyes transfixing the special agent. When Suzuki finished, Nagumo expressed deep concern about four problems: (1) the possibility of being discovered en route or in the target area; (2) the state of enemy alertness on Oahu; (3) the chances of finding the U.S. Fleet in Pearl Harbor; and (4) the probability of enemy retaliation. Suzuki could not hope to dispel all of Nagumo's anxieties; he could only repeat what he had already told the Naval General Staff: The facts seemed to favor the task force.

The one sour note in Suzuki's report was his lack of precise information about the United States carriers. Genda and Fuchida hurled eager questions at him: "How many carriers are at Pearl Harbor? What are their movements, routines, dispositions?" Suzuki had but sparse answers. "I personally did not see a single carrier," he said, "but according to the latest reports, three are stationed at Pearl Harbor and move in and out of the area like the other ships of Kimmel's command."

This was correct as to number but inaccurate as to utilization. The unpredictable movements of the flattops were a constant headache to Yoshikawa.[6] The unwelcome prospect of not finding the American flattops conjured up a whole series of questions: If they proved to be out of harbor, would the attack go forward as planned or should the task force first scour the area in search of the missing vessels? If the First Air Fleet encountered one or more American carriers en route, should it attack on sight or wait for the green light from Tokyo?

Predictably Genda and Fuchida agreed to attack as planned, carriers or no carriers. If they crossed the task force's path on the way, existing circumstances must decide the issue, although both airmen inclined toward striking them whenever and wherever found. As they saw it, after Nagumo's ships left Hitokappu Bay, hostilities could break out at any time. The prospect of American carriers on the loose pleased Nagumo not at all. Throughout the ensuing days these ships haunted his mind, conditioning his thinking and actions as no other single problem.

Suzuki could offer no reassurance one way or the other, and his report might well be the last direct information they received. "We realized," as Kusaka put it, "that the flow of military intelligence from Honolulu to Tokyo could be cut off any moment while we were en route to Hawaii. We were also aware that even though the Naval General Staff might receive new information on Pearl Harbor, there was always the possibility that it could not reach us in the northern Pacific in time to be useful on the morning of the attack."[7]

Nagumo might have been grimly satisfied had he known that his own flattops were just as worrisome to the United States Navy as theirs to him. Combat Intelligence had completely lost track of the First, Second, and Fifth Carrier Divisions and never found them until after the attack.[8]

Despite its gaps, Suzuki's report had immense value, confirming the factors upon which the Japanese had prepared their planning. Nevertheless, it left Nagumo still bedeviled by all his original misgivings. Kusaka, who by no stretch of the imagination "tingled with optimism," admitted that it had a sobering effect on him, too. Fear of American air power on Oahu was the most important reason why Nagumo and his chief of staff agreed between them that the Pearl Harbor strike must be a one-shot attack.[9]

"I suppose those who are sailing in the north feel a sudden cold," Ugaki entered in his diary the next day, November 23, Japanese time, as a chill windstorm raged outside *Nagato*.

> . . . Should the U.S. know anything about our present resolution, she could not keep herself from taking measures against us. We have no time to lose. . . .
> Since we haven't the slightest idea of changing our mind, all things depend upon the U.S. attitude. Should the U.S. abandon the idea that she, being the watchdog of the world, can have everything go on as she wants, she can be saved. If she cannot realize this, it can't be helped. . . .

The same day Yamamoto addressed a final meeting of Army and Navy leaders at Tokuyama. "If the negotiations with the United States turn out to be successful," he stressed, "I will order the forces back before 0100 December 7. Upon this order each ship must withdraw immediately." This cut the margin very fine, and some of the commanders braved the lightning to complain that it was a "damned difficult order practically impossible to carry out." Thereupon Yamamoto thundered, "The purpose of establishing and training the Armed Forces for the past hundred years was only to maintain peace. If any officer here thinks he cannot obey, I order him here and now not to participate in this operation. And I demand that he resign at once."[10]

Few, if any, such scruples appeared to trouble Togo. With one foot he applied brakes to Nomura, halting every constructive suggestion, and with the other he stepped on the gas, urging the ambassador to continuous action within the deadline. "There are reasons beyond your ability to guess why we want to settle Japanese-American relations by the 25th . . ." he informed Nomura on November 22. Still, he extended the cutoff date to November 29. "This time we mean it, that the deadline absolutely cannot be changed. After that, things are automatically going to happen."[11]

In this emergency the State Department's policy was "to grab at every straw in sight" to gain time and keep the conversations alive. From November 21 through 25 Hull and his associates "made a desperate effort to get something worked out that might stay the hand of the Japanese armies and navies for a few days, or a few weeks. . . ."[12] One of the suggestions from which Hull worked originated with Harry Dexter White, a Treasury Department expert in international money matters. Morgenthau found it of sufficient merit to forward to Roosevelt and Hull. Neither Morgenthau nor White had access to Magic, so they could not know how far the Japanese had already committed themselves.[13]

While the Army and Navy had reservations about specific portions of Hull's *modus vivendi,* both Stark and Gerow, speaking for Marshall, who was taking a few days' rest in Florida, agreed that "the document was satisfactory from a military viewpoint."[14] In his memorandum to Stimson of November 21, Gerow explained that "adoption of its provisions would attain one of our present major objectives—the avoidance of war with Japan. Even a temporary peace in the Pacific, would permit us to complete defensive preparations in the Philippines and at the same time insure continuance of material assistance to the British. . . ." He added forcefully, "War Plans Division wishes to emphasize it is of grave importance to the success of our war effort in Europe that we reach a modus vivendi with Japan."[15]

But others did not agree, and the plan came to nothing because of the frantic protests of the Chinese, which Churchill seconded.[16] Between the very remote chance of purchasing a few weeks' time from Japan and the certainty of losing China, the choice was not difficult.

These frustrating events in Washington coincided with redoubled interest in Combat Intelligence at Pearl Harbor. Kimmel commented on the movements which Rochefort's summary "specifically notes . . . as the forerunner of operations, judging from past experience. . . ." At Kimmel's direction Rochefort initiated a message to Naval Operations and Cavite,[17] stressing that the Japanese "were engaged in a major operation, which would start in the immediate future, and that it was composed generally of two task forces. . . ." He gave the location, composition, and general heading, advising that there appeared to be "a very strong concentration in the Marshalls . . . at least one third of the submarines, and at least one carrier division unit. . . ." The Cavite unit agreed with most of Rochefort's findings, except for the location of the carrier division, because it had insufficient evidence to indicate that there were carriers in the Marshalls.[18]

While U.S. Combat Intelligence tried to track down Hirohito's fleet units, the Japanese were equally interested in American forces. Ugaki had ordered an operations map colored and pinned to his wall. He sat staring at it this cloudy November 24. Wherever his eyes rested, he saw "enemy forces in red marked everywhere. The Pacific is so vast!" Now that Japan's ships were actually deploying, Ugaki suffered a qualm or two. "Should things go on as planned, there will be nothing left to be hoped for, but . . . our plan from its beginning . . . inclined somewhat to wishful thinking," he admitted to his diary. As usual, however, Ugaki slapped away the importunate fingers of doubt. "Anyway, since this war is planned against heavy odds, we can scarcely go to war if we take each of them too seriously. What we need are a strong drive to push through, a readiness to meet any change, and to do our best to the last."[19]

On November 24 Stark addressed a top secret estimate to Kimmel and Hart:

> Chances of favorable outcome of negotiations with Japan very doubtful. This situation coupled with statements of Japanese Government and movements their naval and military forces indicate in our opinion that a surprise aggressive movement in any direction including attack on Philippines or Guam is a possibility. Chief of Staff has seen this dispatch concurs and requests addressees to inform senior Army officers their areas. Utmost secrecy necessary in order not to complicate an already tense situation or precipitate Japanese action.[20]

Despite its classification, this message contained little that Kimmel and Hart did not already know. For their own Combat Intelligence units were providing Washington with information on precisely the Japanese movements cited in this dispatch, although, of course, Washington had other authoritative sources.

Undoubtedly Kimmel would have reacted vigorously could he have followed all the Magic intercepts between Tokyo and the Honolulu consulate, particularly the "bomb plot" message of September 24 and those which followed, such as the professional summation of fleet activities by type which Yoshikawa prepared and which Kita dispatched on November 24.

This report confirmed that the U.S. Navy had virtually abandoned Lahaina as a capital ship anchorage, advised that Kimmel's submarines would probably be in harbor on Saturday and Sunday, and gave the Japanese an excellent idea of just where the American ships most likely trained at sea—the battleships "to the south of Maui or to the southwest," the heavy cruisers "doubtless going to Samoa," and the light cruisers seemingly to Panama. But not a word concerning the training area of Kimmel's elusive carriers.[21]

It is unfortunate that Kimmel, Layton, and Bicknell, as well as Short and his intelligence advisers, did not have the opportunity to read such messages. No one who knew Kimmel well could doubt that he would have done his best to spike Kita's guns despite Washington's disinclination to rock the boat, even if only by raising such a storm that no member of the consulate would have dared look at anything larger than a rowboat. For at this stage Japan, too, wanted no overt trouble on Oahu lest the Americans raise their guard. As usual, the message went to Washington by mail, so the Army could not translate it until December 16.

Roosevelt and his advisers wanted peace with Japan as long as possible, but every thoughtful newspaper reader in the United States knew that matters had reached a critical stage. As Stimson later wrote indignantly:

> . . . one would get the impression that the imminent threat of war in October and November 1941 was a deep secret, known only to the authorities in Washington who kept it mysteriously to themselves. Nothing could be further from the truth . . . the imminence of war with Japan was a matter of public knowledge and the people were being warned time and time again of the danger which was approaching.[22]

But they were not warned of the danger approaching Hawaii for the simple reason that nobody in Washington knew or suspected it. That included the President, who expected almost anything from the Japanese, although he was uncertain what they actually would do.

Japanese-American relations dominated a meeting of Roosevelt and his War Council held at noon on November 25. As Stimson described it, the President "brought up the event that we were likely to be attacked perhaps next Monday, for the Japs are notorious for making an attack without warning, and the question was what we should do. The question was how we should maneuver them into the position of firing the first shot without allowing too much danger to ourselves."[23]

Hull could offer no hope of a peaceful solution. "The Japanese are heavily armed, and they have been on this movement of conquest for a number of years, yoked hard and fast with Hitler most of the time. The Japanese are in control of the whole situation, we are not. . . ." Thus, Hull pinpointed the crux of the matter, something which Roosevelt never understood or, if he did, never admitted.

"The Japanese are likely to break out at any time with new acts of conquest by force," the secretary of state continued. "The question of safeguarding our national security lies in the hands of the Army and the Navy." This was a simple statement of fact; Hull did not intend to imply that the State Department "had relinquished its constitutional functions of continuing through diplomacy to try to preserve peace."

Hull ended by stating that in his judgment, "any plan for our military defense should include an assumption that the Japanese might make the element of surprise a central point in their strategy. They might attack at various points simultaneously with a view to demoralizing efforts of defense and of coordination for defense."[24] Hull had described Japanese strategy to perfection. But he did not anticipate that one of the "various points" which Japan would strike would be Pearl Harbor. On this score he had loads of company.

Stimson's well-known statement about "firing the first shot" forms the keystone of the so-called revisionist school of thought. Lifted out of context, it gives an entirely erroneous impression. No one who has examined the great mass of historical evidence on Pearl Harbor can doubt that the United States wanted to maintain peace with Japan for as long as possible. The government wished to remain free to assist Britain and defeat Hitler, even if this put the country in the position of bolstering Stalin.

Make no mistake about it, Japan was going to war, and those with access to Magic knew it. The problem, therefore, was not to maintain peace or war—that was already out of American hands. Not even all of Roosevelt's Cabinet, let alone Congress and the American people, knew the picture shaping up through Magic, and they could not be told the whole inside story without jeopardizing that infinitely precious source of information. So, as Stimson later wrote, "it was desirable to make sure that the Japanese be the ones to do this [fire the first shot] so that there should remain no doubt in anyone's mind as to who were the aggressors."[25]

Certainly the Japanese needed no encouragement from Washington to open hostilities. They had no intention of doing otherwise, unless, of course, they could achieve their expansionist goals through an American diplomatic surrender—within four days. But by this time that was manifestly impossible. For in exactly four hours from the commencement of this War Council meeting, Nagumo's task force was to sortie from Hitokappu Bay on its way to fire that first shot.*

---

*From the sortie of the task force through the attack, the interplay of events becomes increasingly complex and dramatic. Tokyo time was nineteen and a half hours ahead of the special U.S. military time zone for Hawaii, and fourteen hours ahead of Washington, D.C. Eastern Standard Time. For example, the War Council meeting began at 1200 in Washington; this was 0630 in Hawaii and 0200 on November 26, Japanese time. Keeping this time variation in mind will assist in following events, while the use of the military twenty-four-hour time scheme avoids the confusion of A.M. and P.M. See *Hearings Before the Joint Committee on the Investigation of the Pearl Harbor Attack* . . . , Part 12, pp. 341–44 for comparative time charts.

CHAPTER 46

"WHEREVER

IT MIGHT

BE FOUND"

Akagi hummed with activity as key personnel from every ship crowded her wardroom at Nagumo's call to attend a special conference on the morning of November 23. Here assembled the captains and staffs of the carriers, battleships, cruisers, and destroyers, Imaizumi and the skippers of his three submarines, and the commanding officer of *Kyokuto Maru*, flagship of the tankers.[1]

Nagumo opened the meeting with an electrifying announcement: "Our mission is to attack Pearl Harbor." A wave of excitement ran through the assembly. This was the first time Nagumo had openly revealed the objective to all his commanding officers and staffs, although many present had been privy to the plot for months.

Nagumo explained that the attack was not yet an absolute certainty. If negotiations between the United States and Japan proved successful, the task force would be ordered back; otherwise, there would be no alternative but to carry out the strike.[2] He appealed to each individual to do everything in his power to ensure the mission's success.[3]

Next, Kusaka outlined the action they would take in case the enemy spotted the task force en route. If the enemy sighted the entire task force any time before X−1 Day, Nagumo would turn his ships back to Japan. But if he and his staff believed the Americans had discovered only a portion of the Japanese ships, the task force would change course as conditions directed and proceed. However, if the enemy found them on X-Day or fired on them prior to that date, the Japanese must perforce fight it out.[4]

Having made these remarks, Kusaka introduced each succeeding speaker. Oishi discussed the task force organization, the route across the Pacific, precautions to be observed, and the duty of each unit during the dangerous voyage. Then he explained the main points of Task Force Order No. 1, which Nagumo had signed that very day.[5] It contained basic instructions for the task force covering passage to and from Hawaii and the overall aerial strike plan. Every officer present received a copy of this order and supplementary charts so that he could follow the ensuing discussions carefully. The order included this statement: "When the attacks have been completed the force will quickly withdraw. Upon returning to Japan the force will be re-equipped and supplied and then assigned a task in the Second Phase Operations."[6]

So Nagumo, it would seem, officially set the pattern of the operation: a hit-and-run raid. But this requires an explanation. Nagumo and Kusaka thought that a powerful two-wave attack of more than 350 planes would be enough to deal the U.S. Pacific Fleet an "all-out fatal blow." They could not conceive of the necessity for a second major strike. And they had reached this decision before the task force arrived in Hitokappu Bay.[7]

Even so, Nagumo issued another, seemingly contradictory task force directive on November 23—Operation Order No. 3. When the planes returned from their strikes against Oahu, this order stated, "preparations will be made immediately for the next attack. Carrier attack planes will be armed with torpedoes.

"If the land based air power has been completely knocked out, repeated attacks will be made immediately in order to achieve maximum results. However, if a powerful enemy force is in route to attack, subsequent attacks will be directed against it."[8] The idea of "repeated attacks" represented a concession to Genda and Fuchida.

Genda took the floor next, his exposition lasting about half an hour. "The primary objective of the attack is to destroy all U.S. carriers and at least four battleships," he began. "A closely related objective is the annihilation of U.S. air power on Oahu." He explained that the planes would concentrate initially on major fleet units. If they attempted to attack every vessel in Pearl Harbor, they would inflict only medium damage on any. And because of the shallow waters, the enemy could salvage moderately damaged ships within a reasonable time. That would nullify the main purpose of the operation: to immobilize the U.S. Pacific Fleet for at least six months.

Then Genda went into operational details. There would be two waves. The first, under Fuchida's immediate leadership, would consist of fighters and all types of bombing planes. This would launch about 230 miles north of Oahu in time to attack at about 0800. The second wave under Shimazaki would consist of horizontal and dive bombers plus fighters. Launching 200 miles north of Oahu, it would administer the *coup de grâce* to ships damaged by the first wave and complete the destruction of U.S. air power beyond the ability to retaliate.[9]

After completing its mission, each wave would rendezvous about twenty miles northwest of the westernmost tip of Oahu. Thence the planes would return to their carriers, and the task force would begin immediate preparations to meet a possible counterattack. In case such a battle developed, all horizontal bombers would convert to torpedoes; if such a sea battle did not materialize,

ORGANIZATION OF AIR ATTACK FORCE ON PEARL HARBOR

CLASSIFICATION	UNIFIED-COMMANDER	AIR ATTACK UNIT	UNIT COMMANDER	FLIGHT AND FLIGHT COMMANDER	ATTACHED CARRIER	TYPE OF PLANE	NUMBER OF PLANES	ARMAMENT	TARGET
AIR ATTACK FORCE ON PEARL HARBOR	COMDR. MITSUO FUCHIDA	FIRST ATTACK FORCE	COMDR. MITSUO FUCHIDA	1st FLIGHT HORIZONTAL BOMBING FORCE COMDR. MITSUO FUCHIDA	AKAGI	97 TYPE	15	ONE 800 KILOGRAM ARMOR PIERCING BOMB	BATTLESHIP
					KAGA		14		
					SORYU		10		
					HIRYU		10 (49)		
				1st FLIGHT SPECIAL GROUP TORPEDO FORCE LT. COMDR. SHIGEMARU MURATA	AKAGI		12	ONE 800 KILOGRAM AIR TORPEDO	BATTLESHIP CRUISER
					KAGA		12		
					SORYU		8		
					HIRYU		8 (40) — 185		
				2nd FLIGHT DIVE BOMBER FORCE LT. COMDR. KAKUICHI TAKAHASHI	SHOKAKU	98 TYPE	26	ONE 250 KILOGRAM LAND TARGET BOMB	17 PLANES FORD AIR BASE / 9 PLANES HICKAM AIR BASE / WHEELER AIR BASE
					ZUIKAKU		25 (51)		
				3rd FLIGHT AIR CONTROL FORCE LT. COMDR. SHIGERU ITAYA	AKAGI	ZERO TYPE	10	TWO 20 MILLIMETRE MACHINE GUNS	FORD & HICKAM AIR BASE
					KAGA		10		
					SORYU		8	TWO 7.7 MILLIMETRE MACHINE GUNS	WHEELER & BARBERS POINT AIR BASE
					HIRYU		6		
					SHOKAKU		5		KANEOHE AIR BASE
					ZUIKAKU		6 (45)* — 355		
		SECOND ATTACK FORCE	LT. COMDR. SHIGEKAZU SHIMAZAKI	1st FLIGHT HORIZONTAL BOMBING FORCE LT. COMDR. SHIGEKAZU SHIMAZAKI	ZUIKAKU	97 TYPE	27	8 PLANES—TWO 250 KG. LAND TARGET BOMBS / 16 PLANES—ONE 250 KG. LAND TARGET BOMB SIX 60 KG. ORDINARY BOMBS	HICKAM AIR BASE
					SHOKAKU		27 (54)		
				2nd FLIGHT DIVE BOMBER FORCE LT. COMDR. TAKASHIGE EGUSA	SORYU	98 TYPE	18	18 PLANES—TWO 250 KG. LAND TARGET BOMBS / 9 PLANES—ONE 250 KG. LAND TARGET BOMB SIX 60 KG. ORDINARY BOMBS	18 PLANES FORD AIR BASE / 9 PLANES KANEOHE AIR BASE
					HIRYU		18		
					AKAGI	ZERO TYPE	18	ONE 250 KILOGRAM ORDINARY BOMB	CRUISER BATTLESHIP DESTROYER
					KAGA		26 (80) — 170		
				3RD FLIGHT AIR CONTROL FORCE LT. SABURO SHINDO	AKAGI	ZERO TYPE	9	TWO 20 MILLIMETRE MACHINE GUNS	FORD & HICKAM AIR BASE
					KAGA		9		
					SORYU		9	TWO 7.7 MILLIMETRE MACHINE GUNS	WHEELER & KANEOHE AIR BASE
					HIRYU		9 (36)		

AN EXACT TRANSLATION OF COMMANDER FUCHIDA'S ORIGINAL CHART

*TWO FIGHTERS ABORTED IN TAKE-OFF

they might possibly launch a second major strike against Pearl Harbor. In that event they would convert the torpedo planes to horizontal bombers.

Next, Genda stressed the necessity for reaching Hawaiian waters undetected. No plane would launch until the morning of the attack; however, six fighters and three dive bombers must stand by on each carrier from sunrise to sunset to take care of any sudden contingency.[10]

Genda reiterated what Kusaka had already explained: If the enemy discovered the whole task force at any time before X−1 Day, the fleet would return to Japan. If U.S. aircraft challenged them before that day, they would shoot them down. But if such planes took no offensive action, the Japanese would let them alone. However, if enemy aircraft sighted the task force during X-Day, Nagumo's men would attack without question.[11]

At this point Genda explained that according to plan, the Naval General Staff would keep the task force informed about the U.S. Pacific Fleet on the basis of reports from the consulate. Nagumo would receive word on the morning of the attack from scout submarines searching Hawaiian waters. Nevertheless, the task force had to have its own source of information in case the other two failed. It also needed a final report just before the attack so that Genda and Fuchida might make any last-minute changes in tactics.

Genda unveiled two tentative plans to accomplish these ends, both involving exceedingly grave risks. We need consider only the second, the one actually put into effect. The heavy cruisers *Tone* and *Chikuma* would each launch a seaplane exactly one hour before the first-wave takeoff. These scouts would reconnoiter Pearl Harbor and Lahaina Roads. Each pilot would determine whether U.S. ships were located in his reconnaissance area, ascertain the exact number of major units and their dispositions, check on weather and wind, and advise the task force accordingly.[12] Nagumo and his staff recognized the dangers implicit in this arrangement. The scout planes took the chance of being sighted, and they would have to break radio silence to report. But Nagumo had to accept the calculated risk to reap the benefits of up-to-the-minute information.

Genda ended his discussion by describing the role of the fifty-four fighter-interceptors which would remain behind as a scouting and protective force. Each carrier would supply nine, and the total would be divided into three groups of eighteen planes each. One group would fly over the task force at all times, while the other two remained ready on the flight deck to take their turn or to act instantly in case of emergency. The first group would launch immediately after the departure of the second wave and would remain airborne for two hours. The second, then the third would follow in turn. Of each group, one flight of nine would patrol at 4,000 meters; the other, at half that altitude. These three interceptor groups would continue their mission until sunset of X-Day.[13]

Ono followed Genda to discuss communications during the coming voyage. He explained that radio transmission keys must be sealed and in some cases the fuses removed. Ships would receive messages but send none.

Communications would be by flag in the daytime and by specially focused narrowbeamed blinkers at night, when strict blackout prevailed.[14]

Sasabe, Nagumo's navigation and weather officer, then spoke briefly about the route to Hawaii and task force formations, of which the staff had worked out at least a dozen, depending upon the situation.[15] At the end of the conference all in attendance drank to the success of the operation and toasted the Emperor.[16]

Immediately after lunch Nagumo held another meeting in *Akagi*'s wardroom. His own staff attended, as did Yamaguchi and Hara, with their staffs, and all the flying officers, headed by Fuchida. Nagumo opened this meeting by reading the instructions which Genda and Fuchida had prepared for him en route to Hitokappu Bay.[17] When the young flying officers discovered that they would attack Pearl Harbor, "their joy was beyond description."[18]

Then the airmen took over. Genda spoke for almost an hour. For the benefit of those who had not attended the first session, he repeated what he had said that morning.[19] Then he analyzed the five major attack plans which he and Fuchida had prepared. They had worked out the plans with their flight commanders in Kyushu during September and October, so they were not pulling any major surprise. But they took full advantage of this last chance to rehearse, to coordinate group thinking, and to improve upon the design. Hitokappu Bay also provided the final opportunity to apprize Nagumo and his staffs of the manifold technical features involved in the forthcoming strike. Genda and Fuchida based their plans on five warrantable assumptions:

1. The U.S. Pacific Fleet would be in Pearl Harbor.
2. The U.S. Pacific Fleet would be in Lahaina Roads.
3. Part of the U.S. Pacific Fleet would be in Pearl Harbor and part in Lahaina Roads.
4. The U.S. Pacific Fleet would be at sea, and the task force would find it.
5. The U.S. Pacific Fleet would be at sea, but the task force would not find it.[20]

One need only discuss Plan No. 1, for that proved to cover the situation. The first wave, timed to strike Hawaii at approximately 0800, would consist of 189 aircraft: fifty horizontal bombers under Fuchida's personal direction; forty torpedo bombers under Murata; fifty-four dive bombers under Takahashi; and forty-five Zero fighters under Itaya.

While Murata's bombers sneaked in at low altitude to torpedo the capital ships, Fuchida's high-level bombers would plaster their decks. Itaya's fighters would dash in ahead of the main flight to seize control of the air, then in treetop-level assaults strafe the air installations. The dive bombers would concentrate on Hickam, Wheeler, and Ford Island, thus pinning down the U.S. fighters and bombers to prevent retaliation.[21]

The second wave would follow directly after the first, speed of execution being vital to the operation. This second wave would consist of fifty-four horizontal bombers under Shimazaki's personal direction, eighty-one dive bombers under Egusa, and thirty-six fighters under Lieutenant Saburo Shindo. Torpedo planes would not participate because they should have fulfilled their mission in the first wave, and with the surprise factor gone, another torpedo attack would risk an unacceptable rate of loss from the now-aroused and outraged enemy.

All of Shimazaki's horizontal bombers would attack Hickam, Kaneohe, and Ford Island, while Shindo's swarm of Zeros stafed the same targets along with Wheeler, thus completing the destruction of enemy air power. At this time Genda entertained high hopes that Murata's torpedomen would have capsized Kimmel's lightly armored flattops. As they floundered helplessly, Egusa's dive bombers would rip them so full of holes that salvage would be out of the question. [22]

After explaining all the alternate plans, Genda discussed preattack aerial reconnaissance: one patrol plane each from *Tone* and *Chikuma* to take off one hour before the first wave to scout Pearl Harbor and Lahaina respectively. He had scarcely finished when Murata jumped up with a strenuous objection. One hour between takeoff of the patrol craft and launching the first wave was too long, he insisted. The scouting flight was dangerous at best, and the period it covered in many respects the most critical of the entire operation. One hour, he maintained, might give the U.S. forces just enough time to discover the attack and prepare to repel it. Because so much depended upon surprise, he strongly urged that the time interval be cut in half. [23]

Murata's recommendation touched off a spirited round of discussion. Although a few thought the full hour satisfactory, the majority sided with Murata. Genda appealed to Ono for his expert opinion as communications officer. Ono doubted that half an hour would suffice to put the message through. But Murata declared that surprise was the most important single feature of the entire attack plan. If they achieved it, they need not worry about the success of the operation. If they did not, who knew what fate might await them?

Genda wanted to consider all the possibilities before making his final proposals to Nagumo. He therefore asked the patrol flight officers if they thought the reconnaissance aircraft could overfly Pearl Harbor and Lahaina the morning of the attack without being discovered. They answered with an emphatic negative. Moreover, they agreed that the Americans would shoot down the patrol planes, an unpleasant prospect for the reconnaissance pilots of *Chikuma* and *Tone*, both of whom were in the assembly. [24]

Next, he asked Fuchida how late in his flight to Pearl Harbor he could receive the patrol plane's report and still give his final attack orders to the first wave. Ever the realist, Fuchida replied that this would depend on the situation. But all things being equal, he would have to receive the report before his deployment order. This he would probably give a trifle before his lead plane reached the northern tip of Oahu, some twenty minutes before the actual attack. He emphasized that if his pilots did not know what was in the patrol report before they deployed, their bombing missions would probably suffer reduced effectiveness.

Despite the strong agreement among the flight officers that the time interval should be cut down, Genda temporarily shelved the problem so that the briefing might continue. To anticipate, the next morning he and Fuchida discussed the matter further, then recommended to Nagumo that the spacing be reduced to thirty minutes. After some deliberation Nagumo agreed.[25]

Once more Ono discussed communications. Again he stressed the urgency of radio silence, to be broken only in the sternest emergency. Not until Fuchida gave the final order for the attack could it be lifted, and then only for the flight leaders. His plan provided that if surprise were achieved, Fuchida would signal *"Tora! Tora! Tora!"* ("Tiger! Tiger! Tiger!")[26] Since any false move before that time could easily spoil the kill, each commander had his orders to refrain from any hostile act until Fuchida's message from Hawaii flashed across the airwaves, for if anyone jumped the gun and tipped off enemy forces, he could easily ruin Japan's overall plan. Japanese grand strategy everywhere had been based on the key factor of surprise, and all other operations carefully synchronized with the Pearl Harbor attack. Ono had arranged for one exception to the rule of radio silence: If a plane developed engine trouble, the pilot could send in his location.

Even after the assault was under way, Ono emphasized, radio messages must be kept to a minimum, both to avoid unnecessary confusion and, above all, to protect the location of the task force. However, in case any pilot lost his way on his return to his carrier, he could transmit a request for instructions. Ono was working on a special code for use in such an emergency.[27]

No sooner had he finished than Lieutenant Takehiko Chihaya, leader of the Eleventh Dive Bombing Group in the second wave, bounced to his feet. "I object to this plan of breaking radio silence no matter what the reasons might be at the moment of such a decisive battle which is do or die for Japan," he protested. Turning to the pilots, he challenged them: "What about this? Why don't we die in silence if our engines conk out?" He also insisted that the carriers should not reply to any appeal for help even after the attack. Such action would only aid the enemy in locating the task force, thus risking the success of the mission and the lives of everyone aboard the ships. The others agreed to a man that they would rather perish than break radio silence.[28]

That important point settled, Suzuki followed Ono as speaker. He gave a brief synopsis of the report he had delivered to Nagumo and his staff the previous evening. A short discussion then ensued on intelligence matters.[29]

One theme ran through the afternoon briefing and formed the framework of all five plans: Destroy the U.S. Pacific Fleet "wherever it might be found." In particular, smash Kimmel's carriers beyond all possibility of reclamation. From Yamamoto on down, the Pearl Harbor planners knew there would be no security for Japan's widespread forces as long as American naval aviation was on the prowl in the Pacific. They saw Pearl Harbor as merely the scabbard for the shining, deadly sword of United States sea power which Nagumo's task force must shatter before it flashed out to sunder irreparably Japan's dreams of Empire.

CHAPTER 47

"CLEAVE

THE ENEMY

IN TWO!"

The time had come to instruct each of the twenty-six groups of pilots on exactly how they fitted into the scheme of attack. Thus, Fuchida took over. He did not have to analyze every feature of the five attack plans because all flying personnel had practiced them from A to Z before the rendezvous and would review them once again before Nagumo turned prows eastward. Yet the strike leader would leave nothing to chance.

"We will launch the first attack wave about two hundred thirty miles north of Oahu," he announced. "At that time all pilots will face several immediate problems: takeoff, rendezvous, and heading for the target."

As each aircraft cleared the flight deck, it would turn outboard, circle over the task force, and assume a temporary altitude, thus avoiding confusion and collision. The planes from *Shokaku* and *Zuikaku*, aft in the carrier formation, would climb to 400 meters; those from *Kaga* and *Hiryu*, in the middle, would remain at 200 meters; *Akagi* and *Soryu*, to the fore, would also send their aircraft to 400 meters. Fuchida would lead his own group of fifteen planes to 500 meters so that he could best direct the assembly of the first wave.

With all planes airborne, his group would pass over *Akagi* as a signal to begin the flight to Pearl Harbor. The minute he headed south, all aircraft would assume flight formation: horizontal bombers directly behind the lead group at 3,000 meters; torpedo bombers to starboard at 2,800 meters; dive bombers to port at 3,500 meters. The Zeros at 3,800 meters would zigzag over the entire formation, keeping close watch for enemy planes. Shimazaki would follow the same procedure in leading the second wave, scheduled to launch about 200 miles north of Oahu.[1]

Fuchida next turned to the technical features of Attack Plan No. 1, by far the most likely. One of his main problems had been deployment just before the actual air strike. He now explained the signal system he had worked out so carefully. About the time his lead plane reached the northern tip of Oahu, he would fire a rocket pistol. At this signal the horizontal bombers would continue flight at 3,000 meters, the dive bombers climb to 4,000 meters, and the torpedo bombers gradually lose altitude to approach their targets as low as possible. The fighters would split into two groups: Itaya's twenty-seven to continue at 3,800 meters, while Lieutenant Kiyoguma Okajima's eighteen descended to 2,000 meters. All fighters would dash ahead of the bombers to seize control of the air.

On this point Fuchida cautioned his airmen to be most alert. If the information from the reconnaissance patrols and his own last-second observation led him to believe that they had caught the enemy unawares, he would fire his pistol once. In this case the torpedo planes would press in to take full advantage of surprise and assure the greatest number of hits on clear targets. But if he believed the enemy to be on guard, he would fire twice. At this signal the dive bombers would strike first, then the horizontal bombers, and Murata's men last. In this way the former would create so much confusion and draw such heavy fire upward that the torpedo bombers could sneak in virtually unseen, securing a high percentage of direct hits and suffering little damage in exchange.

Fuchida also instructed his pilots to take full advantage of every weather feature. The horizontal bombers would approach their targets against the wind to ensure the greatest possible accuracy in bombing. In contrast, the dive bombers would roar downwind to maintain a sharp angle of approach, plunge in steep, and pull out low. The torpedo planes would press in close according to the disposition of the enemy ships no matter what the weather. At this point Fuchida distributed a number of charts illustrating techniques designed to inflict maximum damage.

Likewise, he stressed the importance of mass concentration against a single target. Each high-level bomber carried only one bomb—an 800-kilogram projectile especially constructed from the 16-inch shells of the battleships *Nagato* and *Mutsu*, designed to penetrate the thick deck armor of *Maryland*-class battleships. Thus, each bomber had only one chance, and Fuchida was not too optimistic about the potential results. In fact, he would have settled for one hit out of five tries. So he instructed all bombardiers to make sure they had the best possible sighting before releasing their bombs, even if this meant two, three, or four runs over the target.

Fuchida had devised a chart to cover horizontal bombing attacks on ships berthed in pairs around Ford Island. He instructed his high-level bombardiers to strike ships doubly berthed, rather than a ship berthed singly, because the former presented a larger target. He also urged his airmen to exercise independent judgment. If they considered an enemy warship already destroyed, they should then move on to another target. Fuchida emphasized repeatedly that minor damage, even to every enemy ship in sight, would add up to an unsuccessful mission.

He urged all flight personnel: "Do your best to sink any ship in or near the

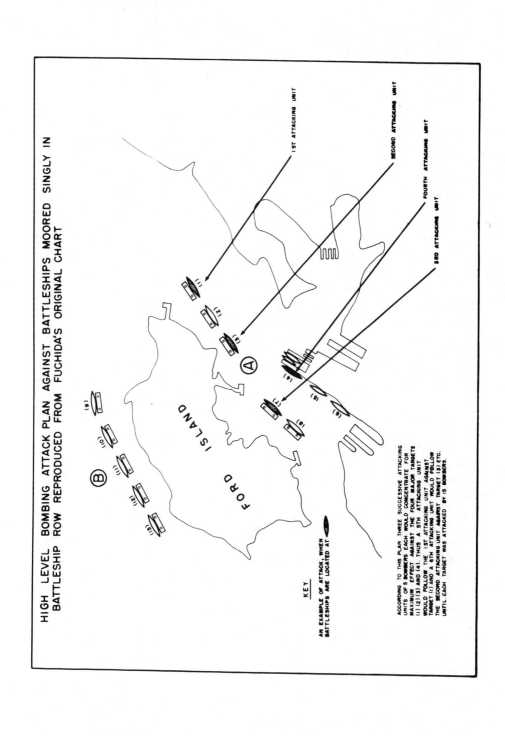

HIGH LEVEL BOMBING ATTACK PLAN AGAINST BATTLESHIPS MOORED SINGLY IN BATTLESHIP ROW REPRODUCED FROM FUCHIDA'S ORIGINAL CHART

1ST ATTACKING UNIT

SECOND ATTACKING UNIT

FOURTH ATTACKING UNIT

3RD ATTACKING UNIT

FORD ISLAND

(A)

(B)

KEY

AN EXAMPLE OF ATTACK, WHEN BATTLESHIPS ARE LOCATED AT

ACCORDING TO THIS PLAN THREE SUCCESSIVE ATTACKING UNITS OF 5 BOMBERS EACH WOULD CONCENTRATE FOR MAXIMUM EFFECT AGAINST THE FOUR MAJOR TARGETS (1)(2)(3) AND (4). THUS A 5TH ATTACKING UNIT WOULD FOLLOW THE 1ST ATTACKING UNIT AGAINST TARGET (1) AND A 6TH ATTACKING UNIT WOULD FOLLOW THE SECOND ATTACKING UNIT AGAINST TARGET (3) ETC. UNTIL EACH TARGET WAS ATTACKED BY 15 BOMBERS.

channel." One or more sunk in this vulnerable area might well incapacitate the entire base, in which case the results of the attack could far exceed expectations. Not only would the vessels in port then be relatively helpless, but those at sea would be denied use of Pearl Harbor. They would have to return to their Pacific coast bases or wallow at their enemy's mercy, out of fuel. The Japanese fervently hoped that some ships would try to escape, thus giving them the opportunity to cork up the channel.

Fuchida had worked out a plan whereby all of Murata's forty aircraft could attack at almost the same instant. According to this scheme, on receiving Fuchida's deployment order, Murata would lead his planes in a sweep over the western side of Oahu. Just as they reached a point almost due west of Pearl Harbor, they would divide into two sections and strike the target from two directions at once.

Murata would lead the main section, composed of two groups of twelve planes each. These would continue on a southeasterly course to a point slightly south of the outer channel entrance, then swing sharply northward, fly over Hickam Field, and attack Battleship Row, punching their deadly missiles into the most vulnerable target in relays of three to five planes each. Lieutenant Tsuyoshi Nagai would lead the smaller torpedo section—two groups of eight aircraft each—from the northwest and west to strike vessels at other strategic locations around Ford Island. Several bombers would also swing south to attack fleet units moored on the eastern side of the main channel. Thus, most of the capital ships in Pearl Harbor would come under simultaneous torpedo assault.

The Japanese worried constantly over the problem of antitorpedo nets, and at Hitokappu Bay they still lacked any firm intelligence on whether the enemy had or had not installed them. Anticipating that the Americans might well have taken this precaution as the crisis in the Pacific had become increasingly acute, Murata, Fuchida and Genda had devised a method of suicide tactics to break the nets. How to present this plan at the briefing posed a problem, for neither of the three had spoken to either Nagumo or Kusaka about their desperate scheme. For one thing, the top brass might veto the idea because Yamamoto had stressed that the Pearl Harbor attack should not be considered a suicide mission. They also wanted to protect these two leaders, already so heavily laden, from the responsibility of ordering their men to certain death. So Fuchida hurriedly read out the order as follows: "The first plane will make a charge route for the following planes by bombing the nets. If this plane should fail, each succeeding plane will try to bomb from inside or among the network by every effort."

This jumble of words mystified Nagumo, and he asked for clarification. A quick answer rolled smoothly off Fuchida's tongue: "It is a highly technical and special form of attack which the pilots understand." Apparently satisfied, Nagumo said no more. Thus, those torpedo pilots who knew of the plot kept their secret and would act on their own initiative if the situation warranted.

Fuchida carefully briefed his audience on the four alternative plans. When the flight leader had finished his two-hour exposition, Genda returned for a few

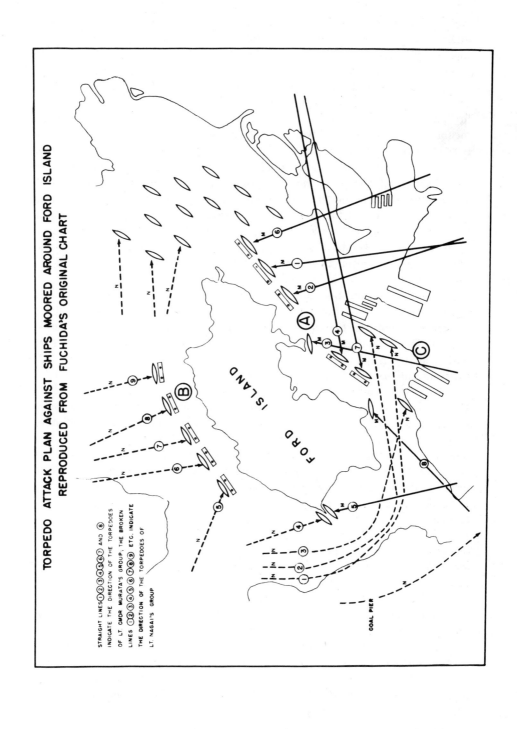

TORPEDO ATTACK PLAN AGAINST SHIPS MOORED AROUND FORD ISLAND
REPRODUCED FROM FUCHIDA'S ORIGINAL CHART

STRAIGHT LINES ①②③④⑤⑥⑦ AND ⑧
INDICATE THE DIRECTION OF THE TORPEDOES
OF LT CMDR MURATA'S GROUP, THE BROKEN
LINES ①②③④⑤⑥⑦⑧⑨ ETC. INDICATE
THE DIRECTION OF THE TORPEDOES OF
LT. NAGAI'S GROUP

FORD ISLAND

COAL PIER

supplementary remarks. He explained that if the task force could not locate the enemy's ships, it would move about fifty miles south of Oahu to receive the planes returning from their attack on the island. Nagumo's ships would probably continue to prowl the seas, seeking the enemy, because Naval Intelligence reported that the enemy frequently maneuvered in that area. If the quarry escaped them, Nagumo would retire to the Marshall Islands to await further orders. Even if the U.S. Pacific Fleet came back to base in the meantime, Genda doubted whether the task force would return to the attack because with the bombing of Oahu it would have lost the element of surprise.

After the briefing session broke up, the operational discussions aboard *Akagi* continued. This time, however, only the flight officers of the two attack waves attended. In the first stages Genda and Fuchida divided them into groups under their flight commanders according to type. Thus, Fuchida took over the four groups of horizontal-bombing personnel to examine their special problems, while Murata, Takahashi, Itaya, Shimazaki, Egusa, and Shindo did likewise for their respective airmen. Each leader painstakingly analyzed the function and objectives of his flight.

Intent on honing perfectly each fine edge of preparedness, Genda and Fuchida next divided the men into still smaller units under their group commanders until all twenty-six held a sort of seminar with their respective airmen. They examined every possible phase of the attack as it affected their particular group. Genda and Fuchida walked among them, making sure that everyone understood every point, leaving nothing to chance.

They also studied the same models of Oahu and Pearl Harbor which Fuchida had examined at his initial briefing. By now the relief map of Oahu looked considerably more lifelike because as Naval Intelligence acquired more precise information, tiny mock-ups of ground installations had been added. The model of Pearl Harbor, which the chief carpenter's mate aboard *Nagato* had constructed, had begun as a rather sparse outline of the anchorage's physical features. But as Japanese clandestine operations progressed, miniatures of each U.S. Fleet unit, carved to scale, took their places in the last-known locations of their originals.

The deeper one probes into the technical methods of the attack, the more one realizes how much depended upon surprise, exquisite timing, teamwork, fortitude, and a whole combination of refined skills. Genda and Fuchida's strategical and technical brainwork reveals a close attention to detail as well as flexibility. Like a well-designed skyscraper, the plan could sway a little with the prevailing winds. Yet one cannot help noting the swampy ground of assumptions on which it rested.

No one saw this weakness more clearly than Genda. "It was impossible to predetermine the course of action which any of our planned attack patterns would take," he said in retrospect. "We could only estimate the military possibilities as accurately as possible and leave the rest in the hands of fate. For so much depended on time and circumstances and other factors entirely beyond our control." [2]

That night a howling gale lashed Hitokappu Bay, and the weather turned bitterly cold, so many airmen remained aboard *Akagi* to end the day by splicing the mainbrace with *sake*, food, and merrymaking. Those who attended Nagumo's morning session had already returned to their vessels. There they informed their respective staff of Operation Hawaii.[3] Chigusa received the word on *Akigumo* after dinner, while the wind skirled around the destroyer like a a host of banshees. "I determined strongly to engage in battle," he wrote in his diary. But he could not help adding, "I am very sorry that I should take part in the attack against Hawaii where my brother now lives."[4]

The next morning the pinpoint study of the operation continued. Flight officers returned to the wardroom of *Akagi* in relays, bringing their enlisted personnel with them. Once more they analyzed the entire attack plan. This would be the last time that Genda and Fuchida with all the air crews would be together to iron out any last-minute problems or misunderstandings.

Fuchida stood before the models from morning until evening, briefing each group in turn, until he had explained the operation and their particular part in it more than twenty times. By the end of the session his customarily strong voice had faded to a hoarse croak.[5] Genda, too, worked tirelessly, coordinating the various attack patterns, plumbing every angle for hidden defects. In addition to the long conferences aboard *Akagi,* each carrier division held daily rehearsals aboard its own flagship.

Sometime that day Nagumo addressed the flying crews. "This Empire is now going to war with an arrogant and predestined enemy . . . and this Task Force . . . is going to launch a surprise attack on the enemy Fleet at Hawaii . . . hoping to destroy the United States Fleet once and for all." They were greatly honored to participate in "this glorious operation." He warned of many difficulties ahead, but he exhorted his men, "However difficult the situation you may face, don't lose your confidence in victory. Cope with it with calmness and composure. . . . Is there anything, no matter how difficult it may be, that cannot be done by an intrepid spirit and a burning loyalty?"[6]

All that day officers and men prepared their ships for the ordeal to come. Some refueled; others placed mantelets (protective mats) on the bridges and in radio rooms, checked communications security, equipment, ammunition, and guns. Some destroyers engaged in test firing. Aboard *Akagi, Kaga, Soryu,* and *Hiryu* experts brought along from Japan proper made the necessary adjustments on the new aerial torpedoes. On this day Yamamoto dispatched to Nagumo his orders to sortie: "The Task Force will move out of Hitokappu-Wan on 26 November and proceed without being detected to the evening rendezvous point (Lat 40°N, Long 170°W), set for 3 December. . . ."[7] So on the morrow Nagumo must set forth on the mission he had so strongly opposed.

True, Nagumo's mission orders which Yamamoto issued on November 22 had contained the qualification "In the event an agreement is reached in the negotiations with the United States, the Task Force will immediately return to Japan."[8] The new directions did not rescind this, but despite Yamamoto's good intentions, no realist aboard Nagumo's ships doubted that, with Japanese forces deploying for war, diplomacy had failed. Nor, despite Kusaka's and Genda's briefing, did any clear-thinking officer of the First Air Fleet believe for a minute that they would turn back if a U.S. naval unit discovered them beyond, for example, the international date line. How could the Japanese justify the presence of an enormous task force in those waters? They might repudiate the action of a single ship or explain it away, but not the major portion of Japan's naval air strength. Therefore, rational-minded men of the task force were convinced that once they embarked on the cruise, it would be virtually impossible to reverse the tide.

Certainly there was no thought of returning to peace, nothing ambivalent about the shipboard atmosphere that afternoon, when some of the skippers gathered their crews to inform them of their mission. "An air attack on HAWAII! A dream come true," wrote Seaman Iki Kuramoto in a delirium of satisfaction. "What will the people at home think when they hear the news? Won't they be excited! I can see them clapping their hands and shouting for joy. These were our feelings. We would teach the arrogant Anglo-Saxon scoundrels a lesson!"[9]

Yamaguchi broke the news to his officers and men on the flight deck of *Soryu.* He told them the story of his sword, made of the finest steel and expertly tempered. By long and hard training Yamaguchi had acquired complete confidence in his ability to use it flawlessly. In one blow, he boasted, it had cut a samurai helmet in half. Just as his exquisite sword severed the *kabuto,* so should the Second Carrier Division carry out the Pearl Harbor attack. Yamaguchi's final words rolled from his lips like drumbeats: "Cleave the enemy in two!" Then he led the assembly in singing the Navy's popular special attack hymn, "The Song of the Self-Sacrificing Warrior." Based on the blockade of Port Arthur in 1904 during the Russo-Japanese War, it told the story of another do-or-die mission, of great heroism and almost certain death. When they finished their song, they joined in three resounding cheers.[10]

That night the men of Nagumo's task force beseeched their ancestral gods for aid and protection in the dangerous operation ahead. As they prayed, the most they could possibly have asked for was safe and undetected passage to Hawaii, the U.S. Pacific Fleet in Pearl Harbor or Lahaina Roads, the enemy caught off guard, the attack a spectacular success, losses at an absolute minimum, and return of the task force undamaged to Japan. Under the best of circumstances, this was far more than they could reasonably have expected from even the kindest Providence.

CHAPTER 48

"A MATCH

FOR

ANYTHING

AFLOAT"

Following the briefing, a number of vexing problems troubled Nagumo. Among them, he dreaded the idea of sailing so far only to find that the U.S. Pacific Fleet was not at Pearl Harbor. He feared, too, that the enemy might discover the plot, sneak his warships off to some strategic spot, and spring his own surprise attack against the task force. All very well for Yamamoto to quote proverbs about going into the tiger's lair if you wanted the tiger's cubs, but what about the tiger? And had not Yamamoto cautioned the First Air Fleet only a few days ago at Saeki that it might have to fight its way into the target?

Having pledged his life to the sea, Nagumo knew that he served a temperamental queen who could turn on her most loyal courtiers with unpredictable hostility. A sudden, savage gale such as had churned Hitokappu Bay the previous night could render the imperative refueling absolutely impossible. Or a thick fog might sweep over his ships, socking in the carriers just when the planes, returning from their attacks, were nursing their last drops of precious fuel. On the other hand, the sea could kill him with kindness. Suppose it lay calm under sunny skies, the horizon unlimited in all directions? The task force would plunge forward as clearly visible as a herd of black cattle crossing a snowbound field.

The Commander in Chief also knew the weaknesses and limitations inherent in deploying a carrier task force so far from home. His flattops were vulnerable to submarines and aircraft; damage which a battleship could take in stride would leave a carrier a real sitting duck. At the September war games, even with the umpires bending over backward in favor of the home team, all had agreed that they must anticipate the sinking of several carriers. A single twist of fate, and Nagumo could go down in history as the man who lost the bulk of Japan's naval air strength within an hour. Oahu was a hornet's nest of naval and army aviation. Yet the plan called for Nagumo to close within 200 miles and knock out all of this air power simultaneously with the backbone of the enemy Fleet. Even granting that he achieved surprise, suppose his airmen did not destroy the long-range bombers on the ground? Did not the B-17s have a far greater combat radius than anything aboard Nagumo's carriers? The farther he peered into the dark pool of worry, the more threatening the reflections that frowned back at him.

At about midnight Nagumo gave up the attempt to sleep and sent for Suzuki. The special agent had just put on his nightgown when a messenger rapped on his door—Nagumo wished to see him. He quickly slipped into his kimono and hurried to the admiral's cabin. There he listened sympathetically as Nagumo poured out a flood of questions.

Of course, Suzuki could no more command the sea than could King Canute, nor could he guarantee against the accidental foul-ups and inevitable snafus of war. But he did his best to repair the frayed edges of Nagumo's nerves, assuring the admiral that he honestly believed the U.S. Pacific Fleet would be concentrated in Pearl Harbor on X-Day. He reminded him of the numerous intelligence reports which emphasized the enemy's habit of returning the ships to base every weekend without fail. Japanese agents had carefully observed this unbroken routine over a long period.

Thus reassured against his worst fear, Nagumo relaxed a trifle, and the two officers shared a drink of *sake*. Suzuki then returned to his cabin, feeling sorry for Nagumo and rather touched to discover that a vice admiral was subject to midnight blues just like any junior officer.[1]

A cold, sullen dawn stole over Hitokappu Bay on Wednesday, November 26. Low clouds hung from a leaden sky. Snow spilled to earth and swirled over the surface of the water, so that each ship saw her neighbor only as a gray, indistinct shape in the semidarkness.[2]

Blinker signals stabbed through the eerie half-light. Then at the stroke of 0600—which was 1030 November 25 in Hawaii and 1600 November 25 in Washington—decks and ladders thudded with the hurried steps of officers and men speeding to stations. Shouted orders pierced the air; the pull of giant chains sent cries of tortured steel across the bay. Huge turbines droned in the engine rooms as powerful propellers slashed the water. *Akagi*'s anchor chain stuck, delaying the sailing half an hour and sending a ripple of consternation through the superstitious. Then, one by one, the vessels of the task force glided like ghost ships from their secluded rendezvous and plunged into the Pacific.

Intelligence agent Suzuki watched the departure from the Coast Guard cutter *Kunashiri*. From a folding chair on the flight deck control post of *Akagi*, Fuchida looked out upon the receding coastline and the steadily widening stretch of gunmetal water separating him, it might be forever, from his devoted wife, Haruko, and their son and daughter.[3] Lieutenant Tomatsu Ema, a dive bomber pilot aboard *Zuikaku*, was the proud father of a month-old girl whom he had seen but once. Although not afraid to die for his country, he wanted to live, to come back to his wife and the joy of their only child.[4] His destroyer under way, Chigusa had little time for sentimental reflections. He had already written his wife and parents "a long, last good-bye forever letter," thanking his wife for the good years they had shared.[5]

But these were not the only emotions stirring in the hearts and minds of Nagumo's officers and men. Few had regrets or fears. For most members of the task force, the whole problem boiled down to what the grim business of war had been for all men in all ages: Kill or be killed. Amagai tells us that once they left the Kuriles, "the young officers simply did not give a damn what happened."[6]

Fuchida's eyes twinkled in amusement as he caught sight of *Akagi's* navigator, Commander Gishiro Miura. A charming officer, "always talking, laughing, and joking," Miura generally dressed casually aboard ship and slopped around in carpet slippers. But in honor of the sortie he had decked himself out in a bright new uniform and a new pair of glossy shoes. Observed Fuchida: "On the second day out, Miura was back in his slippers."[7]

As Nagumo stood on *Akagi's* bridge in the raw November air watching his magnificent fleet set sail, he would have been less than human had he not felt a flash of pride and a thrill of power. Across his vision moved the dark gray ships—carriers with their deadly punch, plodding battlewagons, sleek cruisers, tough little destroyers, submarines, and the smelly but vital tankers: a total of thirty vessels. They were his to lead to victory or defeat; his to guide, to direct, to command.

But if Nagumo had much to justify pride, he had much to make him uneasy. In only one field could he be sure of superiority in case he had to fight his way in to the target: He enjoyed a three-to-one advantage in carriers over Kimmel, who at this time had only *Lexington* and *Enterprise* in the central Pacific. *Akagi* and *Kaga* each carried eighteen fighters, eighteen dive bombers, and twenty-seven high-level or torpedo bombers.[8] Despite their excellent qualities, the two ships did not measure up to their counterparts, *Saratoga* and *Lexington*, which bested their Japanese rivals in everything except armament and tonnage. Although the Japanese Navy traditionally insisted on speed, its two veteran carriers were several knots slower than Kimmel's prize ships.

Soryu and *Hiryu* were relatively new, having been completed in 1937 and 1939 respectively. A serious handicap plagued both vessels—limited radius of action. Their combined oil capacity of 7,000 tons was far less than *Kaga's* alone. As *Soryu* and *Hiryo* got under way, Yamaguchi knew that each of his carriers labored under a fuel overload of 700 tons—a highly dangerous situation which he would never have tolerated under normal conditions. But this was not enough fuel to take him to Pearl Harbor for the action his soul craved, let alone home again.

Soryu and *Hiryu* could reach a maximum speed comparable to that of their opposite, the slightly larger *Enterprise*. More important, the latter could send aloft eighty-one to eighty-five aircraft, whereas Yamaguchi's flattops carried fifty-four apiece, divided equally among fighters, dive bombers, and horizontal-torpedo bombers.

The splendid *Shokaku* and *Zuikaku* enormously strengthened Nagumo's hand with their 29,800-ton displacement and 34.2-knot speed. Commissioned only in August and September 1941 respectively, they actually sailed on their shakedown cruise. Each carried seventy-two aircraft—eighteen fighters, twenty-seven dive bombers, and twenty-seven horizontal bombers. Both could make the voyage to Hawaii and back without refueling. But their crews were still as green as spring leaves. They would strike only land targets in the coming operation—"Mere secondary objectives," as King Kong Hara snorted acidly.[9]

More than once in sea warfare a great sailor has snatched victory from a superior foe; therefore, much depended upon the experience and personality of the admirals who commanded the carrier divisions. Nagumo would fight valiantly; but he had never served aboard a carrier until he took command of the First Air Fleet, and he had only textbook awareness of the techniques of naval air warfare. In these matters he had to rely on Genda and Fuchida. It speaks well for the fineness of Nagumo's character that he accepted this fact without jealousy or sulkiness, respected his assistants' gifts, and loved them as sons. Yamaguchi, reputed to be "the bravest officer in the Japanese Navy," felt very much at home because the atmosphere of aerial warfare was congenial to his aggressive character. Yet he had little more actual experience in that field than Nagumo. Hara, too, had never set foot on a carrier until given command of his division of flattops on September 15.

When the task force sailed from Hitokappu Bay, Nagumo did not know for certain the exact number of carriers Kimmel had in the area. But just to play it safe, the Naval General Staff estimated a total of four.[10] Actually only two carriers were operating out of Pearl Harbor when the First Air Fleet sortied. *Saratoga* was in Puget Sound for repairs. *Lexington* was just entering the Pearl Harbor channel when Nagumo lifted anchor in the Kuriles and by 1115 had come to rest in Berth F-9 after an eight-day cruise. *Enterprise* had been at anchor in Berth B-3 since 1057 on November 17, having just completed a week of maneuvers.[11]

Nagumo could rely upon a fine screening and escorting group under Omori, with his clear sailor's mind housed in a body somewhat like one of Snow White's seven dwarfs. His flagship *Abukuma's* 32.5 knots did not match Kimmel's light cruiser *Raleigh*, which could split the seas at 35; however, *Abukuma* carried eight torpedo tubes and could maneuver on the crest of a wave.

This splendid cruiser led nine of the newest and best destroyers under the Rising Sun flag. Proud of their "first-class" designation, Nagumo's trouble-shooters all bore the names of natural phenomena: *Akigumo, Hamakaze, Isokaze, Kagero, Shiranuhi, Tanikaze, Urakaze, Arare*, and *Kasumi*. But these poetic appellations were deceptive. Nagumo's destroyers could spring to battle at a moment's notice with their six 5-inch guns, tubes for the most deadly torpedoes in existence, and depth charges. They could also send up a destructive barrage from their antiaircraft batteries and lay a heavy smoke screen. Most were much larger and stronger than their opposite numbers at Pearl Harbor. Seven were of the new 2,100-ton *Kagero* class; the other two had a standard displacement of 1,500 tons—the same as that of the biggest destroyer at Hawaii, *Maury* of the *McCall* class.

In a good sea, Omori's gray terriers were supposedly capable of thirty-five knots, but the smaller American destroyers were designed for high speeds, too. And Kimmel could muster twenty-nine to Nagumo's nine—odds to dampen the most exuberant optimist. The very names of the U.S. tin cans, bestowed to honor sea heroes, reminded Nagumo that for the first time in modern history Japan was challenging a first-class naval power. He knew, too, that his savage little warships devoured huge quantities of oil and needed constant replenishment. If they could not refuel as planned, he would have to send them home, considerably weakening the First Air Fleet and leaving the carriers more vulnerable. Nagumo's problem was not just the cruise to Hawaii; he had to bring his ships back again.

Mikawa, commander of the supporting group, had an abiding faith in battleships and fretted because he did not have enough of them:

> Frankly I was apprehensive. With just two battleships and two cruisers under my command, I was operating with no margin of security at all. Our carriers were for the most part still untested, but I knew what fourteen- and sixteen-inch shells could do. I feared interception at sea and possible surface action—perhaps a running fight in to the target—and I was convinced that my four ships would be inadequate to protect our carriers in case the U.S. Fleet closed in. I have always thought, too, that if we had had four battleships in the task force, Nagumo's mind would have been more at ease concerning the operation.[12]

Nevertheless, he had two of Japan's finest ships with him. When the Emperor went to sea on maneuvers, as he often did, invariably he chose to board *Hiei*. The officers and crew of that handsome vessel fairly swaggered in their pride at serving aboard His Majesty's favorite. They were proud, too, that she led her sister ship, *Kirishima*, and the two heavy cruisers *Tone* and *Chikuma* as the flagship of Nagumo's supporting group. Longer and much more slender than their American counterparts, *Hiei* and *Kirishima* could race through the sea at almost thirty knots, eight to nine knots faster than Kimmel's old battlewagons, and their great cruising range could bring them to and from Hawaii without refueling. They carried 8- and 9-inch belt armor, far less than Kimmel's bruisers, which boasted 14- and 16-inch protection. Mikawa's big ships could muster eight 14-inch guns, compared to the eight 16-inchers of the *Maryland* class.

Furthermore, Kimmel outnumbered Nagumo four to one in battlewagons. So, if it came to an old-fashioned slugging match at sea, the Japanese might get the worst of it. Nagumo's strength lay in his speed and his superior aerial striking power. The whole concept of hit-and-run was not only embedded in Nagumo's philosophy but built into the ships themselves as well.

The two heavy cruisers *Tone* and *Chikuma* could run the waves at almost 36 knots, in contrast, for example, with the 32.7 knots of *San Francisco*, which was in the Hawaiian area. Thus, *Tone* and *Chikuma* could hit fast and get away quickly. Their eight 8-inch guns represented one gun per ship less than Kimmel's heavy cruisers, but they each had another weapon which the American heavy cruisers did not—six torpedo tubes to port and starboard. Japan's 24-inch oxygen-fueled torpedo had great range, speed, and explosive power. In most characteristics it more than doubled the performance of American models.[13] "Ship for ship we considered them a match for anything afloat in 1941," said Captain Keizo Komura, skipper of *Chikuma*. "In fact, we thought them superior to any heavy cruiser Kimmel had in the Pacific."[14]

With air patrols en route ruled out, Nagumo would rely heavily upon his scouting group of three submarines—the largest the Imperial Navy had ever built. *I-19*, *I-21*, and *I-23* each displaced about 2,581 tons (much larger than Kimmel's submarines), had a high surface speed of almost twenty-four knots, and a cruising range of 14,000 miles. They each carried a small one-man seaplane, capable of ninety knots and a flight time of about three hours. The submarines also had a formidable armament—those deadly torpedoes.

Drab and homely, the tankers of the two supply groups brought up the rear of the task force. But their importance far outweighed their lack of glamour because in their grubby holds they carried the lifeblood of Empire. Without them the proud First Air Fleet could never carry out its mission. Captain Masanao Oto commanded Supply Group No. 1 from his flagship *Kyokuto Maru*, with *Kenyo Maru*, *Kokuyo Maru*, and *Shinkoku Maru* also under his command. Supply Group No. 2, under Captain Kazutaka Niimi, consisted of his flagship, *Toho Maru*, and *Nihon Maru* and *Toei Maru*.

A graduate of the Naval Academy at Eta Jima commanded every one of Nagumo's tankers. Five of the officers had been long on the active list, while the other three had been called out of retirement when relations with the United States became critical. Although most of the tankers could steam at nineteen knots, *Toei Maru* could reach only sixteen, so the task force had to keep within her maximum speed.[15] Actually Nagumo's ships maintained a cruising speed of twelve to fourteen knots, slowing to nine knots while refueling.[16]

The trial runs on refueling had developed a reasonable skill, but anything could happen in the heavy seas of the northern Pacific. If planned refueling proved impossible, Nagumo would have to settle for filling up his biggest ships and proceeding on his mission with only three carriers (*Kaga*, *Shokaku*, and *Zuikaku*), the two battleships, the two heavy cruisers, and a few tankers—a force incapable of inflicting the amount of damage which would make the raid worth its anticipated losses. With such factors to consider, and in view of the odds he would have to face if he found the full might of the U.S. Pacific Fleet plowing toward him, one cannot blame Nagumo for his anxieties. None but a criminal fool would rush into such a situation with a light heart and a carefree mind.

Nagumo was no longer just any vice admiral. From this day forth he would be part of his nation's history for better or worse. If success crowned the task force, he would skyrocket to the heights, the visible sign and symbol of victory. Even if he died in the doing, his spirit would be invoked at Yasukuni Shrine by generations yet unborn whenever a Japanese sailor embarked on a dangerous course. As long as men went down to the sea in ships, they would study this operation and marvel at it. But if he failed, if he led his fleet to disaster, who could dig a hole deep enough to bury his shame? Would the Pacific itself contain water enough to wash his name clean? The promise of the mountaintop inevitably carried its alternative—the threat of the crevasse.

On Nagumo's shoulders rested a responsibility and a burden such as few commanders had ever borne in the history of naval warfare. The venture ripped out all the pages of Japanese naval tradition, violated their basic rules of strategy, and tossed into the classified waste the plans which Japan had long formulated to fight the U.S. Navy. It also heaved over the side the teachings of Sun-tzu, who wrote: "Military tactics are like unto water, for water in its natural course runs away from high places and hastens downward. So in war, the way to avoid what is strong is to strike what is weak."[17] Nagumo would attempt the exact opposite. He would steam straight into the jaws of the strongest naval base on earth. With his precious ships precisely in the most vulnerable position a superior enemy could ask, he would strike that selfsame foe at the very center of his vaunted power.

But no matter how Nagumo thought the fates had woven the threads of destiny, one thing stood supremely in his favor: He was standing out to sea undiscovered.

CHAPTER 49

"THAT

WAS THE

MONKEY

WRENCH"

On the morning of November 26 Stimson called the President to make sure he had received a copy of a G-2 report which he had sent to the White House the previous afternoon. This concerned a Japanese expedition of five divisions embarked in a group of between thirty and fifty ships which had been sighted southward-bound off Formosa. Roosevelt had not and, upon hearing the message, "fairly blew up. . . ." He said "that that changed the whole situation because it was evidence of bad faith on the part of the Japanese that while they were negotiating for an entire truce—an entire withdrawal—they would be sending this expedition down there to Indo-China."[1]

What is more, abandonment of the proposed *modus vivendi* necessitated a clarification of the issues. So Hull and several of his advisers set about preparing a note for submission to Nomura and Kurusu which the secretary took to Roosevelt that same morning for approval. The contents later became famous as the Hull Note or the Ten Points. We cannot deal with these points in detail here. Suffice it to say that, while firm, "there was nothing in there that any peaceful nation pursuing a peaceful course would not have been delighted to accept," as Hull testified later.[2]

Unfortunately at this time Japan was not a "peaceful nation pursuing a peaceful course." Hull never understood, for example, why the Japanese persisted in trying to build a house on Chinese quicksand when he offered them solid ground. To Tokyo the answer was simple: As the Asian master race they had the right—nay, the duty—to take over China. In Japanese eyes, Chungking deserved censure for obstinately refusing to bow to the manifest will of heaven. Moreover, the Japanese Army would never willingly allow the nation to follow a path on which peaceful trade and international amity took precedence over the warrior virtues. This would remove the military from the driver's seat.

The Hull Note was not an ultimatum. It restated the American position, which had not varied for months. True, Japan did not like it. But in view of Tokyo's note of November 20 and of the knowledge of Japanese intentions and movements which Washington possessed, Hull could have handed Japan a much stiffer document.

Grew was highly pleased with the Hull Note but soon found that Tojo's government fostered the impression that it was an ultimatum. "It suited the military to do so."³ The Ten Points did not appear in the Japanese press until after the war began, and then the government promptly confiscated the newspaper which printed them.⁴

So, in hot pursuit of the whole hog, Tokyo continued to press Nomura and Kurusu, stressing the urgency of time. On November 26 the Foreign Ministry authorized telephonic communications between the two ambassadors and Kumaichi Yamamoto, chief of the American Bureau. This dispatch gave the code for use in these talks, a rather cozy domesticated series of phrases which could create an innocuous conversation if deftly used. Roosevelt and Hull became respectively Miss Kimiko and Miss Fumeko. "To sell the mountain" meant "To yield," and of course, "Not to sell the mountain" meant "Not to yield." The words "The child is born" signified "Situation taking critical turn." The Navy became "Marriage Proposal," and the Army "Tokugawa."⁵

Even before receiving Hull's Ten Points, Nomura and Kurusu had just about decided that they were spinning their wheels. They sent off a joint message to Togo, advising him that "if we let the situation remain tense as it now is . . . the negotiations will inevitably be ruptured, if indeed they may not already be called so. Our failure and humiliation are complete. . . ." Nomura then offered a daring proposal:

> I believe it advisable at this junction to have the President wire to His Majesty the Emperor his desire for Japanese-American cooperation—and in reply to it have His Majesty send a telegram to the President, thereby clearing the present atmosphere and providing sufficient time for Japan to propose the establishment of a neutral zone comprising French Indo-China and Thailand.

Nomura and Kurusu also warned that Hitler would probably weasel out of his obligations and Japan would have to mark time in China because it could not fight two major wars at once.⁶

Togo had no use for the joint Nomura-Kurusu message.⁷ He wanted his representatives following the Tokyo line with no original arabesques. The idea was not that bad. Had Togo been quite the dove he would have posterity believe, he would have been willing to try anything once.

At about 1645 on this busy November 26 Nomura and Kurusu called on Hull for a talk lasting some two hours. Hull advised that the United States could not agree to Proposal B. With that, he handed over the two documents comprising the Ten Point program. The ambassadors protested that they could not report this program to Tokyo. After much fruitless discussion Nomura reminded Hull that Roosevelt had once remarked, "There are no last words between friends." He therefore asked him to arrange an interview with the President; Hull agreed to do it.[8]

Togo seized Hull's Ten Points as a precision-made escape hatch,[9] but his crocodile tears carry little conviction. At the very time Nomura and Kurusu were talking with Hull, Nagumo's task force had been at sea for twenty-four and a half hours and was engaged in the first of its refuelings en route to Pearl Harbor. As pointed out, Japan's submarines began deploying on November 11—a full fortnight before Hull presented his Ten Points. And this was only the Pearl Harbor chapter of the story.

The Japanese had already begun to activate their main war plan: seizure of the southern regions. In fact, the Malay invasion force had departed Hashiraji-ma November 24, two days before Nagumo's sortie from Hitokappu Bay. And the southern Philippine invasion force left Sasebo on the same date that the Pearl Harbor task force ventured into the Pacific.

Full of curiosity, Stimson telephoned Hull early on November 27 to find out "what his finale had been with the Japanese." According to Stimson, Hull replied, "I have washed my hands of it and it is now in the hands of you and Knox—the Army and the Navy."[10] Hull later denied ever expressing himself thus, and it certainly does not sound like him. As secretary of state he could not "wash his hands" of the sticky situation, and well he knew it.[11] Stimson may have confused Hull's remarks on this occasion with his statement of November 25 that "our national security lies in the hands of the Army and the Navy."

All agog, Stimson next called the President, who gave him "a little different view." The secretary of war suggested to Roosevelt that they alert MacArthur to be "on the qui vive for any attack and telling him how the situation was." Then Hap Arnold dropped in to show Stimson orders sending two "of our biggest planes" from San Francisco across the Mandates to photograph the area and get some idea of what the Japanese were doing there.[12] Incidentally, this mission of two B-24s never took place. The first was in a hangar on Oahu on December 7, and the Japanese destroyed it in the attack. The second did not reach the islands.[13]

Next, Knox and Stark came over to confer with Stimson and Gerow, the latter substituting for Marshall, on maneuvers in North Carolina. The four men devoted their main attention to the alert for MacArthur. Stimson again phoned Hull for an "exact statement . . . of what the situation was." Armed with his analysis, they carefully reviewed the proposed message to go out over Marshall's name.[14]

On November 27 Tokyo sent to its Washington embassy a circular containing yet another code. This became known as the "hidden word" code. Certain words to cover countries and happenings would be buried in an innocent-looking message. *Minami* would refer to the United States. To alert the recipients of these cables, they would end with the English word "Stop" rather than the Japanese *Owari*. [15]

That evening Kurusu put through a call to Yamamoto of the Foreign Ministry's American desk, completing the connection at 2327. After a brief exchange of civilities Yamamoto inquired, using the prearranged code, "How did the matrimonial question get along today?"

"Oh, haven't you got our telegram yet?" asked Kurusu. "There wasn't much that was different from what Miss Umeko said yesterday." This was a slip of either the tongue or the translator—the prearranged code for Hull was "Miss Fumeko." Kurusu continued. ". . . As before that southern matter—that south, SOUTH—southward matter, is having considerable effect. . . ." Obviously Kurusu was at a loss to weave the vital subject of Japan's overt moves in that direction, not included in the code, into the domestic pattern of marriage and childbirth which Tokyo had arranged.

"Oh, the south matter?" exclaimed Yamamoto, enlightened. "It's effective?"

"Yes," replied Kurusu, "and at one time, the matrimonial question seemed as if it would be settled. But—well, of course, there are other matters involved, too, but—that was it—that was the monkey wrench. . . ." Here we have a most significant acknowledgment from Kurusu that the "monkey wrench" tossed into the diplomatic machinery had been not the Hull Note, but Japan's aggressive preparations to move south.

"How do things look there?" he next inquired. "Does it seem as if a child might be born?"

"Yes," Yamamoto answered definitely, "the birth of a child seems imminent." No doubt he knew exactly whereof he spoke, having learned about the Pearl Harbor operation in the latter part of November.

Kurusu repeated Yamamoto's statement in a somewhat surprised tone, then started to ask, "In which direction . . ." but stopped abruptly at this slip. He picked up the broken thread neatly. "Is it to be a boy or a girl?"

Yamamoto hesitated, then with a little laugh followed Kurusu's lead back into the domestic code. "It appears as if it will be a strong healthy boy. . . . * Did you make any statement . . . regarding your talk with Miss Kimiko [Roosevelt] today?"

Kurusu disclaimed having given the press any information beyond the fact that he and Nomura had met with Roosevelt.

"The matrimonial question," Yamamoto continued, "that is, the matter pertaining to arranging a marriage—don't break them off."

"Not break them?" asked Kurusu blankly. "You mean talks." He added in

---

*American Intelligence believed that the "boy or girl" exchange meant nothing because it did not appear in the code, being merely Kurusu's way of guiding the conversation back into the pattern. However, Kurusu may have been subtly asking whether the "critical turn" meant war—i.e., a boy (warrior)—or some other development. This would tie in with his later mention of the Army's impatience.

helpless accents, "Oh, my." Then he gave a resigned laugh. "Well, I'll do what I can." After a brief exchange about the day's talk with the President, Yamamoto returned to "the matrimonial question," advising Kurusu, "I shall send you another message. However, please bear in mind that the matter of the other day is a very difficult one."

Kurusu assured Yamamoto that "they want to keep carrying on the matrimonial question. They do." Thus, after receiving Hull's note, Kurusu acknowledged that the United States wanted to keep the talks alive. He went on. "In the meantime we're faced with the excitement of having a child born. On top of that Tokugawa is really champing at the bit, isn't he?" Both diplomats laughed at this disrespectful reference to the Japanese Army. "That's why I doubt if anything can be done," Kurusu added realistically.

"I don't think it's as bad as that," Yamamoto countered. But he went on. "Well, we can't sell a mountain." This meant "We can't yield."

"Oh, sure, I know that," Kurusu agreed. "That isn't even a debatable question any more." After a few further exchanges the men broke the connection.[16]

At roughly the same time that Roosevelt and Hull were meeting with Nomura and Kurusu, an important conference was taking place in Kimmel's headquarters. Along with Kimmel and key members of his staff, Admirals Bloch, Halsey, Brown, and Bellinger were present. Short also attended, bringing with him Martin and Mollison. They discussed principally a proposal to send P-40s to Wake and Midway islands and to reinforce these outlying bases with Army troops. These moves had been under consideration in Hawaii and Washington for about a month.[17]

Although willing to send his aircraft and men if necessary, Short hesitated to release them from his control. "If I man these islands, I must command them," he declared.

"Only over my dead body," retorted Kimmel vigorously. "The Army should exercise no command over Navy bases."

"Mind you, I do not want these islands," replied Short amiably. "I think they are better manned by Marines. But if I must put troops and planes on them, then I must command them."[18]

This little passage at arms was perfectly good-natured, as each considered the awkwardness of divided command.

Far more important, any Army aircraft ferried to these outlying bases would have to be written off for use in the Hawaiian Islands. The distance was beyond the P-40's range of independent flight. Martin therefore proposed sending some of his obsolescent fighters "because those were the ones we could afford best to lose." Short disagreed. He believed that "if we are going up against the Japanese we wanted the best we had instead of the worst. . . ."[19]

Mollison registered his disapproval of the scheme. "Our mission is to protect Oahu," he pointed out, "and shipping out these Army planes will lessen our capability to do so."

"Why are you so worried about this?" asked Kimmel. "Do you think we are in danger of attack?"

"The Japanese have such a capability," answered Mollison cautiously.

"Capability, yes," conceded Kimmel, "but possibility?" With that he swung abruptly on Soc McMorris. "What do you think about the prospects of a Japanese air attack?"

"None, absolutely none," replied the Fleet war plans officer firmly.[20] More than McMorris's off-the-cuff evaluation influenced Kimmel's thinking on the morning of this critical day. The very fact that the War and Navy departments had authorized sending about 50 percent of Hawaii's P-40s to Wake and Midway indicated to him that responsible authorities in Washington "did not consider hostile action on Pearl Harbor imminent or probable."[21] Nevertheless, he decided to exercise his option and keep the Army fighter craft on Oahu, sending instead a squadron of Marine F-4Fs.[22]

Halsey remained with Kimmel until 1800, with only a break for lunch. "Do you want to take the battleships with you?" asked Kimmel.

"Hell, no!" Halsey retorted. "If I have to run I don't want anything to interfere with my running!" These two old friends and Naval Academy classmates agreed, however, that the battleships had to sortie with the *Enterprise* task force to keep up the pretense of a routine mission. Halsey could shed them as soon as possible. Fully appreciating that he might be standing into big trouble, he asked, "How far do you want me to go?"

"Goddammit, use your common sense!" replied Kimmel briefly.[23] The two men's eyes met with perfect understanding. Halsey believed he had just received "the finest orders that were ever given to a man." He "was very serious about it and probably shaking a little bit" because he "felt that we were going to be in a fight" before he returned to Pearl Harbor.[24]

CHAPTER 50

"TO BE

CONSIDERED

A WAR

WARNING"

$\mathbf{N}$ow it so happened that at 1430 on November 27, after Short
had left Kimmel's conference, his chief of staff, Colonel Tige Phillips, brought
him War Department Message No. 472,[1] signed "Marshall," which read:

> Negotiations with Japan appear to be terminated to all practical purposes with
> only the barest possibilities that the Japanese Government might come back
> and offer to continue. Japanese future action unpredictable but hostile action
> possible at any moment. If hostilities cannot, repeat cannot be avoided the
> United States desires that Japan commit the first overt act. This policy should
> not, repeat not, be construed as restricting you to a course of action that
> might jeopardize your defense. Prior to hostile Japanese action you are
> directed to undertake such reconnaissance and other measures as you deem
> necessary but these measures should be carried out so as not, repeat not, to
> alarm civil population or disclose intent. Report measures taken. Should
> hostilities occur you will carry out the tasks assigned in Rainbow Five [the
> Army's basic war plan] so far as they pertain to Japan. Limit dissemination of
> this highly secret information to minimum essential officers.[2]

Short went over the message with Phillips almost word for word. He received the impression "that the avoidance of war was paramount and the greatest
fear of the War Department was that some international incident might occur in
Hawaii and be regarded by Japan as an overt act."[3] It therefore behooved him
to be circumspect because the Japanese "were apparently looking for excuses."[4]

The instruction to undertake reconnaissance convinced Short that Marshall had not written the message. The Chief of Staff, having personally
approved Short's long-range aerial reconnaissance arrangement with Bloch,
knew that the Navy had that function in Hawaii.[5] It appeared obvious to Short

that "this message was written basically for General MacArthur in the Philippines," where the services had no such agreement.[6]

Short "knew from repeated conversations with the Navy that the Japanese naval vessels were supposed to be either in their home ports or proceeding to the south." Nor, to the best of his knowledge, did the Japanese have a land-based bomber capable of striking Oahu from their nearest base some 2,100 miles away, then returning home. Kimmel's carrier task forces at sea, plus the Navy's outlying bases, added up in Short's mind to the conclusion "that the chance of an attack by air was very slight, or that it was highly improbable." McMorris's positive statement in the P-40 conference and the fact that no one took exception to it reinforced this conviction.[7]

His own aircraft were already, as Phillips expressed it, "conducting . . . the only reconnaissance we were required to conduct, and that is inshore patrol from Bellows Field. . . ."[8] Short and Phillips also believed that Kimmel's task forces were engaged in whatever long-range scouting the Navy considered necessary and possible. "The Navy was not worried," Phillips testified, "and we had only six planes which they could have borrowed to make their distant reconnaissance more effective. Six planes could cover an arc of only 8°. . . ."[9]

Although the Hawaiian Air Force's inventory showed twelve B-17s, half of them were out of commission, having been cannibalized of necessary parts for bombers destined for the Philippines. Therefore, Short decided to go along with the joint plan drawn up in March. Just because he "had received this radio," he "did not believe that the War Department wanted us to abrogate the agreement with the Navy and start out on our own. . . ."[10]

In pondering Washington's instructions, Short seized upon all the things he must not do: Alarm the local population; offend the Japanese; confide in more than the essential officers. The rest sailed smoothly over his head. By what, for Short, was a logical, even inevitable mental progression—reconnaissance equals B-17s equals ferrying equals crews—he and Phillips arrived at training. "Since General MacArthur might expect to be attacked . . . it became even more important that we continue our training of ferry crews."[11] An all-out alert would seriously interfere with the Army's various programs.

Short had three alerts. Of these, No. 1 was "a defense against sabotage, espionage and subversive activities without any threat from the outside." No. 2 included all the measures contained in No. 1 and, in addition, defense against air, surface, and submarine attack. No. 3 was "a defense against an all-out attack, where everybody moved to their [sic] battle stations and carried out their [sic] duties as if there was a possible attempt at landing in sight."[12]

Short and Phillips agreed that while Alert No. 2 or No. 3 might "help to disorganize an air raid," such a Japanese attack was most unlikely. They thought that "preparation to defend against a bare possibility should be weighed against the urgent need to continue training."[13] Short "knew from 40 years' experience that if the Chief of Staff believed there was going to be an air attack or an all-out attack on Hawaii he would have said so."[14]

Thus, Short's sabotage psychosis came into full play. Not only was this hazard "paramount" to him, but he also believed it to be "the chief danger which the War Department feared. Sabotage had long been considered our primary danger in Hawaii. . . ."[15] He had yet other reasons for going to Alert No. 1. So many antisabotage exercises had taken place that they did not alarm the community. Then, too, he could not set up Alerts No. 2 or 3 without violating the direction to confine knowledge to the "minimum essential officers." If he sent up pilots with orders to shoot or dispatched soldiers to their battle stations, he would have to tell them why.[16]

So he decided to order Alert No. 1. That afternoon he conferred with Martin, and they agreed to do nothing that would interfere with training or ferrying B-17s to the Philippines.[17] He also talked with Major General Henry T. Burgin, the coast artillery commander. Short then sent the contents of the War Department message to the two division commanders, the Infantry Division, and the liaison officers. In line with the instructions to "limit dissemination," he informed no one else at this time.[18]

In addition, Short ordered the aircraft control and warning (ACW) system to operate from 0400 until 0700 daily as well as during regular hours. The six mobile stations had been operating daily except Sundays from 0700 to 1100 for routine training, and daily except Saturday and Sunday from noon to 1600 for training and maintenance. The three stationary sets were not in operation because their towers still lay on the pier at Oakland, California. Meanwhile, Short's people had been robbing the stationary apparatus of parts to keep the mobile sets going; indeed, his radarmen were most conscientious, having been working Sundays on their own.[19]

Nevertheless, Short obviously did not expect too much from his ACW net. As he later stated, "At that time we had just gotten in the machines and set up. I thought this was fine training for them. I was trying to get training and was doing it for training more than any idea that it would be real. . . ."[20] This ingenuous statement reveals an essentially sterile concept—a series of motions undertaken with no basic faith in their usefulness. Within an hour of receiving the War Department message, Short dispatched a brisk reply: "Report department alerted to prevent sabotage. Liaison with Navy reurad [an abbreviation for "reference your radio"] four seven two twenty-seventh."[21]

The same day Fielder received this message from Miles in Washington: "Japanese negotiations have come to practical stalemate. Hostilities may ensue. Subversive activities may be expected. Inform commanding general and Chief of Staff only."[22] This dispatch reassured Short because Miles "was responsible for giving us information not only about sabotage but information of any probable hostile action. The fact that the information he gave us related only to sabotage indicated that he did not expect other hostile action or he would have pointed it out. . . ."[23]

In some of his evaluations Short had been quite right. The War Department also sent Marshall's message, with minor alterations in phraseology, to the Caribbean Defense Command, to the Western Defense Command at the Presidio in San Francisco, and to MacArthur. The message to the latter did not contain the warning about disturbing the population.[24] According to Gerow, this was because Hawaii "had a big Japanese population" and the military "installations there were very close to the population; . . . if the civilian population happened to be alarmed, there would probably be headlines in the press. Those headlines would be quickly transmitted to Japan and would probably precipitate the very thing we were trying to avoid."[25]

If Gerow's thinking was not exactly crystalline, it fell in with Short's interpretation. Miles, however, was much more logical when he pointed out that the United States Army had "always attempted to do our job without unnecessarily disturbing or alarming or alerting the civilian population." He therefore thought that this stipulation "had practically no effect in that very important war-warning message."[26] But it certainly had on Short.

Short was correct also in his assumption that Marshall, having been on maneuvers on November 27, had not prepared the message. His name was signed "so that it would not go as a routine Adjutant General Message."[27] In one vital respect Marshall and Short were totally at cross-purposes. Far from assuming that sabotage represented the greatest danger to Hawaii, Marshall "was completely imbued with the idea that the great hazard that they were worried about out there was air attack."[28] Yet he himself, as we have seen, did not consider such an aerial strike probable. What is more, the warning message as originally drafted contained the words "needed measures for protection against subversive activities should be taken immediately." After checking with the deputy chief of staff, Miles and Colonel Charles W. Bundy, chief of the War Plans Group, Gerow deleted this sentence, believing such a warning should go as a G-2 dispatch "rather than confuse the two issues in one message."[29] One of the reasons Miles drafted the "subversive activities may be expected" message was to alert his G-2s in that regard.[30]

Moreover, the instruction in Marshall's message to undertake reconnaissance had been carefully phrased. Short was to conduct scouting, "but the character and nature of the reconnaissance was [*sic*] to be as he deemed necessary." In fact, those who drafted the message thought patrolling already under way; they included the instruction in case "the seriousness of the situation hadn't been brought sufficiently to their [the Hawaiian Department's] attention to increase the reconnaissance to the extent necessary."[31]

No one, in either Washington or Hawaii, attempted to clarify these misunderstandings because no one realized that a misunderstanding existed. Miles believed that from November 27, Hawaii had been alerted that "hostilities might occur at any time on the initiative of the Japanese." The steps which followed, such as the Japanese burning their codes, Roosevelt's appeal to Hirohito, and other actions, merely added emphasis. "That Fortress, like a sentinel on post, had been warned of the danger which was its sole reason for being. Anything else was considered to be redundant."[32]

That afternoon or early evening Lieutenant Harold S. Burr, Bloch's liaison officer with Short's headquarters, took the message to Captain John B. Earle, Bloch's chief of staff. Earle promptly escorted Burr to Kimmel's office.[33] The dispatch arrived at an opportune moment. Kimmel had just received a similar, even stronger message from the Navy Department:

> This despatch is to be considered a war warning. Negotiations with Japan looking toward stabilization of conditions in the Pacific have ceased and an aggressive move by Japan is expected within the next few days. The number and equipment of Japanese troops and the organization of the naval task forces indicates [*sic*] an amphibious expedition against either the Philippines Thai or Kra Peninsula or possibly Borneo. Execute an appropriate defensive deployment preparatory to carrying out the tasks assigned in WPL 46 [the Navy's basic war plan]. Inform district and army authorities. A similar warning is being sent by War Department. . . . [34]

Kimmel sent for Layton with instructions to paraphrase the dispatch and take it to Short. The words "a war warning" came as a shock to Layton, who "never saw anything like it before, and . . . was impressed by it." The contents appeared to fit the pattern which had already shown up in Combat Intelligence. Intent upon conveying the correct picture to Short, Layton worked up three paraphrases before he was satisfied with his product. [35] But to Kimmel's retrospective fury, Layton did not give the message personally to Short as directed. [36] Lieutenant Burr received it for delivery after hours. He drove directly to Fort Shafter, but finding neither Short nor Phillips, he left it with Colonel Donegan, the G-3. Donegan informed Burr the next day that Short had received it. [37]

Despite Kimmel's anger, there seems no reason to believe that who delivered the message would have made any difference. The Navy dispatch, so similar to the one Short had just received, had little, if any, further effect on him. He considered the expression "a war warning" as meaning "no more than saying that Japan was going to attack some place." Indeed, it appeared a pullback from the message of November 24 because that one "had stated that they expected Japanese action in any direction," including Guam, and now Washington had dropped Guam. [38]

Nor did Poco Smith believe that "a war warning" necessarily meant war. Although this message was the only one containing those specific words, the preceding dispatches could also have been considered "war warnings." [39] Kimmel regarded the phrase as being "a characterization of specific intelligence which the message contained." [40]

Admiral Turner, who drafted the dispatch, would have gone up in smoke had he known how comparatively little impact the key phrase made on Oahu. The term "war warning" was his own, "to express the strong conviction on the part of the Department that war was surely coming. . . ." He did not see how "there was any possibility of misinterpreting that sentence." [41]

Stark, Ingersoll, Turner, perhaps one or two others discussed the message on November 26 and 27. [42] Ingersoll made certain insertions in pencil on the document. He recalled particularly the "war warning" phrase. "Words of that kind had never been used in any dispatch before." [43] Hovering in the background, Stark's aide, Captain John L. McCrea, listened to the "discussion . . . as to whether or not the opening sentence . . . should be included. . . ." Turner pressed for it firmly, and Stark agreed. It "left a strong impression" on McCrea because "it went the whole way. . . ."[44]

The dispatch contained "some of the thoughts of the Army" in the hope that the two services would "take exactly the same action." The planners worked over the message at a Joint Board meeting held on November 26; they hoped and intended to make it "sharp and clear so there was no possibility of misunderstanding."[45]

Few naval dispatches have received such careful high-level attention. A number of important considerations went into its preparation. One of these was the Magic intercept of the Foreign Ministry's message to Nomura postponing the Japanese cutoff date to November 29. Although the Navy Department could not tell whether this would be "the date that the attack was to take place, or whether it was to be the day when the expeditions would start from their ports," it gave the United States two days for "proper deployments," which the Navy considered sufficient. Turner also learned from Pinky Schuirmann that Hull "had decided, or felt, that negotiations were of no further use." Hull's Ten Point note, however, had no effect on the preparation of the "war warning" message.[46]

The drafters took particular pains with the phraseology. By "deployment," Turner meant "a spreading out of forces . . . into the best positions from which to execute the operating plans against the enemy." He believed that the key phrase "appropriate defensive deployment" should immediately fix attention on Tasks G and H,[47] which were:

> Task G: Protect the sea communications of the Associated Powers by escorting, covering and patroling as required by circumstances and by destroying enemy raiding forces.
> Task H: Protect the territory of the Associated Powers in the Pacific area and prevent the expansion of enemy military powers into the Western Hemisphere by destroying hostile expeditions and by supporting land and air forces in denying the use of land positions in that hemisphere.[48]

As an example of the sort of action expected, Turner testified:

> Since . . . the danger position of Hawaii was to the north, because there were no little outlying islands there from which observation would have been made . . . an appropriate deployment would have sent some fast ships, possibly with small seaplanes, up to the north to assist and possibly to cover certain sectors against approach. . . . Of course, these ships would naturally have been in considerable danger, but that was what they were there for, because fighting ships are of no use unless they are in a dangerous position so that they can engage the enemy. . . .

Navy planners discussed whether or not to issue orders to attack if a Japanese fleet "came within a certain distance of Hawaii. . . ." Should a strong Japanese force come "even within 500 or 600 miles of Hawaii, their intention would be very apparent. . . ." This "most assuredly would have been an overt act," and the Navy "could not afford . . . to let the attack come in and be made without taking action. . . ." But the Navy Department decided this would be in Kimmel's province; therefore, they should avoid giving him detailed instructions.[49]

Turner left the dispatch with Stark, who went to see Knox about it "because it was an all-out." Indeed, he feared that he might be going a little too far, but "time was creeping up. . . ." Stark did not recall whether he informed the President before or after sending the message, but "within 24 hours, if not before, . . . it had his full approval."[50] Stark testified that the words "war warning" were "put at the beginning of the message to accentuate the extreme gravity of the situation . . . we felt that there was grave danger of Japan striking anywhere. . . .

"We went to what we thought was an all-out on this dispatch. . . . We considered it an unequivocal war warning . . . we gave most careful consideration before making this a war warning, for we had no definite information or evidence indicating an attack on the United States." Nevertheless, the southern situation appeared "so grave that we should warn our forces to be prepared for the worst."[51]

Stark did not anticipate an air attack on Hawaii, although he "knew it to be a possibility." He did not specifically list Hawaii with the Philippines, Thailand, Kra, or Borneo in the body of the message because he did not consider that territory as likely a target as the other areas. But if he could have eliminated the possibility entirely, he would not have instructed the Pacific Fleet to make a defensive deployment—"which directive was intended to have them take up a position or to take action against surprise."[52] Much less truculent than Turner, Stark defined "defensive deployment" in Kimmel's case as "taking a position as best he could with what he had for the defense of his fleet, whatever he had either at sea or in port, to the best of his ability and to guard against being caught unawares."[53]

Ingersoll testified that deployment measures for the Hawaiian area "were those regarding observation, the establishment of patrols, and the reinforcement of outlying positions in our own islands." Thus, considerable variation in interpretation of the term "defensive deployment" existed among the top three admirals in the Navy Department before the message ever left Washington.[54]

The Navy anticipated certain actions from Hawaii's defenders. According to Turner:

> We expected all war scouting measures to be undertaken, submarines to be sent out to protect our Fleet and territory . . . the carriers with their protective vessels to put to sea and stand in readiness for war . . . a high degree of readiness on board ships against attack of any form; and on shore . . . a high degree of readiness of defensive troops, including antiaircraft. The dispatch was prepared jointly with the Army. We expected a deployment of the Army on shore appropriate with a defensive state of

readiness, such as manning the coastal guns, and moving troops out to their deployment positions for defense of territory.[55]

To Kimmel, the message seemed to bring "the war with Japan closer than it had been," but it nevertheless directed his attention to localities other than Hawaii. Moreover, the War Department message with its "more cautious phrasing" and its "precaution against taking measures which might alarm the civilian population" led him to conclude that anything but a surprise submarine attack on ships in his operating area was "most improbable."[56]

He thought that if the Japanese struck the Philippines, they might well combine it with mass undersea raids against his ships. There had been several incidents during 1941 of unidentified propeller noises near Hawaii, but thus far Stark had directed him not to bomb such contacts. With the receipt of the "war warning" message, Kimmel decided to go ahead on his own. He "issued an order that any submarine contacts in the operating areas around the Island of Oahu should be depth bombed," and he so informed Stark.[57] This time Stark, although not personally "worried about an overt act . . . in the Hawaiian area so far as the Navy is concerned," took no exception to Kimmel's announced intention.[58]

The phrase "appropriate defensive deployment" was "a new term" to Kimmel. He decided that it meant "something similar to the disposition" he had made on October 16. But most of those measures, such as full security of ships at sea, were still in effect. While he considered stepping up the condition of readiness for the vessels in Pearl Harbor, he decided against it.[59]

Had Kimmel been defense-minded, he might have read into this directive the meaning which seemed so clear to Washington. But as Smith testified, "You must remember that what we were thinking about in the Pacific Fleet was not the defense of Pearl Harbor. We were thinking about the fleet and the readiness of the fleet . . . how soon they [the ships] could get out . . . and go into battle."[60] Thus, Kimmel decided: "It was absolutely essential that we maintain training in the Pacific Fleet up to the last minute."[61]

Kimmel made a serious and puzzling error when he failed to institute long-range aerial scouting. He saw the Army message directing reconnaissance and knew long-distance air patrol was the Navy's responsibility.[62] The action was in Bloch's bailiwick, but Kimmel should have instructed Bloch to put it into effect. Actually he did not even discuss the matter with Bellinger, nor did he show his air commander the "war warning" message. In fact, Bellinger saw none of the alerting messages from either the War or the Navy departments during October, November, and December until after the attack. He read in the Honolulu newspapers of "a tense situation," but as he said, "this had not been the first time during the year that such situations were indicated between the United States and Japan. Also, there were Japanese envoys in Washington . . . endeavoring to bring about a peaceful settlement." On the basis of this information, Bellinger did not believe himself justified in recommending to

Kimmel "that distant patrol search for the security of Pearl Harbor be undertaken at that time."[63]

Bellinger had a total of eighty-one patrol aircraft in the Hawaiian area, including twelve on Midway. Of these, twenty-seven were old PBY-3 types, and fifty-four the latest model PBY-5s. These arrived in increments of eighteen on October 28, twelve on November 8, and twenty-four on November 23. Therefore, they "were experiencing the usual shakedown difficulties of new planes and their maintenance was hampered by an almost complete absence of spare parts."[64] Halsey recalled "many discussions between Admiral Bellinger and Admiral Kimmel whether they would use a plane continually and keep a full coverage and have them all go to pieces at once, or put out the best partial covering they could and keep the planes in shape so that they could be used in case of emergency."[65]

Still, Kimmel did institute patrol measures at the outlying bases. He ordered one squadron from Midway to Wake, which departed on December 1 and reconnoitered en route. He replaced the Midway squadron with one from Pearl Harbor, which left on November 30 by way of Johnston Island, also patrolling the entire way and searching from Midway on December 2 through 6. *Enterprise* aircraft also conducted daily reconnaissance, as did those of *Lexington,* which left for Midway on December 5.[66] That took excellent care of the southwest approaches. But Kimmel initiated no action to cover the northwest sector, although in the frequent drills against a possible air raid this area "was considered the most vital . . . because the prevailing winds were from the northeast, and enemy carriers could thus recover their planes while retiring from the Oahu area," as Bellinger explained.[67]

Both Kimmel and Short exercised poor judgment in this crisis. Granted that the Navy did not have sufficient in-commission aircraft for a full 360-degree sweep, it had enough to cover the critical northern sector. The Navy Court of Inquiry absolved Kimmel of blame in this matter; nevertheless, the decision to keep the Fleet patrol planes available for sea operations necessitated a choice of priorities. Obviously, whatever the lip service various defensive plans for Oahu gave to the concept, Kimmel did not in the least anticipate an air attack at the initiation of hostilities. Otherwise, he would not have skimped on reconnaissance in favor of training, especially after he received the warning of November 27.

The Army investigating board chided Short for assuming, with "a large group of ranking subordinates," that the Navy was conducting this scouting from the task forces.[68] These assumptions and failures to communicate were not justifiable in view of the grave international situation. Short had only to ask Kimmel or Bloch, "Can I lend you my B-17s to help with your patrol?" to discover that the Navy was not carrying out its assigned mission of long-range reconnaissance. And a quick check with Washington would have revealed that the War Department meant exactly what it said in directing that Short institute reconnaissance. Stimson called it "a direct order."[69]

Yet the Navy must accept the lion's share of blame for the long-range scouting portion of this tragedy of errors. The responsibility ultimately was Kimmel's, but specifically it belonged to Bloch, who was responsible for the Navy's portion of the defense of Pearl Harbor, in particular for long-range air patrols.

Bloch was visiting a patient in the hospital on the afternoon of November 27, so Kimmel gave a paraphrase of the "war warning" to Earle. Bloch saw it the next morning. A day or so later he "directed the commander of the coast guard at Honolulu to put vessels outside to run up and down and listen for submarines. . . ." And the commander of inshore destroyers used Bloch's office to give his destroyer captains a pep talk in connection with the submarine alert. That was all.[70] By that time or shortly thereafter Bloch saw in the newspapers that conversations in Washington had been resumed, and that "had a very definite effect" on his mind.[71]

Yet during the summer he had recommended sending patrol planes on a 300-mile arc toward Jaluit, and Kimmel accepted the recommendation. Bloch did not recall the exact occasion,[72] but it may have been connected with Stark's top secret message to Kimmel about the imperial conference of July 2.* In late July, when the War Department gave Hawaii a "6-hour advance notice" of the economic freeze, Short promptly went to Alert No. 3, calling it off after a few days.[73] Obviously Kimmel and Short could go all out when they believed the situation justified; therefore, it is difficult to understand why they did not take similar action upon receipt of the "war warning."

Short's error was no less devastating then Kimmel's and Bloch's. His sabotage alert provided for disarming and massing the aircraft for ready protection against fifth-column dangers instead of leaving them armed and dispersed. He believed that thirty to thirty-five minutes' warning would give him "plenty of time to disperse the planes." But it would not "have been time to get them in the air,"[74] and that, after all, was their main reason for being on Oahu. Thus, the morning of December 7 found American aircraft huddled together with no ammunition available, a perfect target for Nagumo's bombers and fighters.

After the event Kimmel, Short, and the whole army of revisionist historians complained bitterly that Washington's warnings were ambiguous and insufficient. The plain fact is that the War and Navy departments could not warn of Japanese action they themselves did not anticipate. As the congressional committee cogently summarized:

> It was Washington's responsibility to give Admiral Kimmel its best estimate of where the major strategic enemy effort would come. It was Admiral Kimmel's responsibility as commander in chief of the Pacific Fleet to be prepared for the worst contingency, and when he was warned of war and ordered to execute a defensive deployment it was necessarily in contemplation that such action would be against all possible dangers with which the Hawaiian situation was fraught.[75]

---

*See Chapter 17.

The same goes in spades for Short, who had the responsibility for protecting the Fleet in harbor. Stimson later fumed:

> Under these circumstances . . . to cluster his airplanes in such groups and positions that in an emergency they could not take the air for several hours, and to keep his antiaircraft ammunition so stored that it could not be promptly and immediately available, and to use his best reconnaissance system, the radar, only for a very small fraction of the day and night, in my opinion betrayed a misconception of his real duty which was almost beyond belief.[76]

Nevertheless, one cannot absolve Washington of all blame. Too many assumptions existed there as well as on Oahu. Inasmuch as the War and Navy departments expected and intended Short and Kimmel to act in concert, they should have sent a joint CofS-CNO message, or at least made sure they used identical wording. The drafters could also have spelled out exactly what they meant. For example, if Turner wanted Kimmel to activate or prepare to activate Tasks G and H of WPL 46, he should have said so.

The War Department was particularly culpable in not checking up on Short's reply to Number 472, comparing the two messages and immediately advising Short that "precautions against sabotage" did not fill the bill. Short's reply went through Gerow to Marshall, along with MacArthur's reply to the warning message. Marshall initialed the latter but not the former. To the congressional committee he stated that he could not definitely recall having seen Short's reply, and he honestly acknowledged, "That was my opportunity to intervene and I did not do it."[77]

Short's answer went all the way up to Stimson, who described it as "susceptible of being taken, and was taken, as a general compliance with the main warning from Washington . . . it certainly gave me no intimation that the alert order against an enemy attack was not being carried out. . . ." He continued:

> I had no idea that being "alerted to prevent sabotage" was in any way an express or implied denial of being alert against an attack by Japan's armed forces. The very purpose of a fortress such as Hawaii is to repel such an attack, and Short was the commander of that fortress. Furthermore, Short's statement . . . that "liaison" was being carried out with the Navy, coupled with the fact that our message of November 27 had specifically directed reconnaissance, naturally gave the impression that the various reconnaissance and other defensive measures in which the cooperation of the Army and the Navy is necessary were under way and a proper alert was in effect.[78]

But that is not quite good enough. The message directed Short to "report measures taken." Surely his reply should have evoked a question in someone's mind in Washington. The actions taken and not taken on Oahu virtually guaranteed a successful Japanese attack. Kimmel and Bloch's sin was that of omission—failure to institute long-range aerial scouting. This almost ensured that the Japanese would come in undetected.

Short and Phillips's was a sin of commission—placing Hawaii's defenders on a sabotage alert. This not only distracted attention and energy from the real danger coming Hawaii's way but huddled the unarmed fighter planes together so that the Japanese would encounter pathetically little interceptor resistance once they reached Oahu. It also provided Nagumo's planes with easy targets. Thus, Short's measures were to help the Japanese achieve one of their important objectives—nailing the Hawaiian Air Force to the ground and preventing it from effectively interfering with the attack or retaliating against the task force.

These measures were in contradiction of the Martin-Bellinger and Farthing reports and all major war games held in the Hawaiian area since 1933. With the best of intentions all along the line, the "war warning" messages of November 27 left Hawaii less ready to meet a Japanese attack than it had been before the dispatches arrived.

CHAPTER 51

"OUR

DIPLOMATS

WILL HAVE

TO BE

SACRIFICED"

Poco Smith and Commander Arthur Davis, Kimmel's air officer, drove home the evening of November 27 in Davis's "beat-up Cadillac roadster."[1] Davis "had great difficulty in getting to Honolulu because of the caravans of trucks and troops."[2] In fact, "the streets were full of them, going in all directions, manning the bridges, public utilities. . . ." Smith believed this to be an all-out Army alert because he "thought they only had one kind" and so informed Kimmel the next day.[3]

Davis had not seen the "war warning" message and could not recall that Kimmel ever consulted with him about attack possibilities. However, the problem had come up at staff meetings, and he formed the opinion that Kimmel believed it "vitally necessary to continue as long as possible with training and other Fleet improvements and that going into a defensive status would interfere with this work."

But Davis believed "comprehensive and extensive air searches were practicable" and told Kimmel so when the admiral asked for his opinion. However, he stated that "this would very definitely interfere with . . . aviation training in the Fleet." And it could not have been maintained for long because of crew fatigue and matériel attrition, unless reinforcements arrived soon.[4] In retrospect, Davis believed that had Kimmel "sent out long searches, there is always the possibility that his patrols might have spotted the Japanese, and if they had discovered them at sea, the story could have been vastly different, especially for Kimmel personally."[5] Of course, certain precautions had been taken. These included air coverage for all seas in the Hawaiian area in which fleet units might operate and occasional long-distance searches. "The idea of these was to give the impression of a comprehensive search and at the same time to avoid really extensive interference with other forms of training."[6]

414

Nagumo's task force plunged ever eastward. Throughout the voyage the crews rose and retired with the sun, working under thorough security measures. Sharp-eyed lookouts scanned the sea, keeping an especially strict alert against U.S. submarines. During the first half of the trip one-fourth of the crews manned battle stations at all times. For the last half the proportion would be doubled. Six fighters stood constantly ready for flight aboard each carrier.[7]

By day training continued with unflagging zeal. Aboard *Akagi* Fuchida and all flight personnel studied the scale models of Oahu and Pearl Harbor until they knew them "backward, forward, and sideways." They also drilled incessantly in the recognition of enemy warships. Because the approach to the target was the main problem in torpedo attacking, Fuchida and Murata instructed such pilots to study the course of their approach inside out.[8]

Genda immersed himself in work lest he fall prey to profitless emotional strain. He felt the weight of his heavy responsibilities, which tried his nerves by day and robbed him of sleep at night. So he labored over the tactical plan, polishing and repolishing. Still, he could not help fretting lest his very closeness to the problem blur his mental vision. *Am I missing something very important?* he asked himself. He thanked his stars that the ships sailed closely together because the skippers and flight leaders could thus pour into Nagumo suggestions and opinions for modifications. Not a day went by without some change or adjustment to the attack plan.

Ever fighter-conscious, Genda asked Itaya "about his confidence" concerning the Zeros. Their leader replied immediately, "On the basis of our experience on the continent and our estimated capability of the American fighter planes, we can handle three of their planes with one, I think."[9]

For the horizontal bombers Genda had a seemingly impossible dream. One night he discussed it with Furukawa when the latter expressed confidence about results. Genda pointed out the flaw in their plan: "But the depth of the water in Pearl Harbor is only twelve meters and even though we achieve much damage the enemy can refloat the ships." That, Furukawa observed, could not be helped. Hungry for maximum damage, Genda declared, "If your bomb hits directly beside the turret and if it explodes in the powder magazine the ship will be reduced to fragments." Furukawa doubted they could bomb that skillfully. "Do it with spiritual strength," urged Genda, disciple of Onishi, who believed nothing impossible if propelled by sufficient willpower. "Genda, don't ask such unreasonable things!" protested Furukawa.[10]

In their own way, others strove for perfection as strongly as Genda. Aboard *Soryu* the dedication of Petty Officer Noboru Kanai, the Navy's crack bombardier, excited admiration. He never doffed his flying jacket. Every morning and afternoon he climbed into his plane in the hangar to run through bombing procedures. Apparently his persistence paid off, for he would be credited with a direct hit on *Arizona*.[11] The senior officers, with their heavy burden of responsibility, geared themselves for action even more grimly. They all slept in their uniforms and seldom, if ever, left the bridge.[12]

Task force formation varied according to weather and visibility. Nagumo

RADIUS OF ACTION OF THE PEARL HARBOR TASK FORCE AND MIDWAY NEUTRALIZATION UNITS (DECEMBER 1941)

CLASS	NAME OF SHIPS	NORMAL OR TRIAL DISPLACEMENT	TOP SPEED	ACTUAL RANGE	RANGE DURING TRIAL RUN	FUEL CAPACITY
AIRCRAFT CARRIERS	KAGA	42,500 TONS	28 KNOTS	6,500 NAUT. MILES 18 KNOTS	10,000 NAUT. MILES 16 KNOTS	8,200 TONS
	AKAGI	41,300 "	31 "	" MILES "	8,000 MILES "	6,000 "
	SHOKAKU	29,800 "	34 "	6,800 18 "	9,700 " 18 "	5,000 "
	ZUIKAKU	"	"	" "	" "	"
	HIRYU	20,250 "	34 "	5,400 18 "	7,600 18 "	3,500 "
	SORYU	"	"	" "	" "	"
BATTLESHIPS	KIRISHIMA	36,700 "	29.8 "	6,800 18 "	9,800 18 "	6,300 "
	HIEI	37,000 "	"	" "	" "	"
HEAVY CRUISERS	TONE	14,000 "	35.6 "	5,600 18 "	8,000 18 "	2,600 "
	CHIKUMA	"	"	" "	" "	"
LIGHT CRUISER	ABUKUMA	5,500 "	35 "	5,000 14 "	4,000 14 "	1,600 "
DESTROYERS	URAKAZE	2,500 "	35 "	4,000 18 "	6,000 18 "	600 "
	ISOKAZE	"	"	" "	" "	"
	TANIKAZE	"	"	" "	" "	"
	HAMAKAZE	"	"	" "	" "	"
	AKIGUMO	"	"	" "	" "	"
	KASUMI	"	"	3,500 18 "	5,000 18 "	"
	ARARE	"	"	" "	" "	"
	KAGERO	"	"	" "	" "	"
	SHIRANUHI	"	"	" "	" "	"
	SAZANAMI	"	"	" "	" "	"
	USHIO	"	"	" "	" "	"
SUBMARINES	19 IGO 19	2,600 "	23 "	14,000 16 "		800 "
	21 " 21	"	"	"		"
	23 " 23	"	"	"		"
SUPPLY SHIPS	KENYO-MARU	ABOUT 20,000 "	ABOUT 18 "	9,000 ABOUT 16 "		ABOUT 2,000 "
	KYOKUTO-MARU					
	KOKUYO-MARU					
	SHINKOKU-MARU					
	TOHO-MARU	8,000 "	16 "	7,000 14 "		450
	NIHON-MARU					
	TOEJ-MARU					
	SHIRIYA					

NOTE: PREPARED BY REAR ADMIRAL TOMIOKA, FORMERLY CHIEF OF THE OPERATION SECTION OF THE JAPANESE NAVY GENERAL STAFF.

FORMER CHIEF OF OPERATIONS

used a so-called protective formation during the day. In the vanguard four destroyers scouted ten kilometers apart. Behind this shield the six carriers advanced in two parallel columns. Destroyers guarded the flanks of the column, while tankers followed astern. Directly behind all the other vessels Mikawa's two fast battleships crashed through the heavy swells.

Nagumo had planned to use his three submarines as the eyes of the task force. But in view of the low visibility and communications difficulties, he feared the submarines might lose contact with the rest of the fleet if they sailed ahead. So Imaizumi placed his submarines about a kilometer to starboard of *Akagi*, maintaining that position throughout the voyage.[13]

At night and during heavy overcast Nagumo brought his ships closer together for easier communications. In strict blackout and radio silence, shepherding this large task force across the northern Pacific was no easy feat, for the ships had no course guide but the creamy wake of the vessels to the fore and an occasional blinker. Some mornings Nagumo awoke to find that one of his ships had virtually disappeared over the horizon. The sea was unusually calm for those latitudes at that season, so the ships could refuel whenever necessary, despite occasional unseasonable fog.[14] Thus, one by one the First Air Fleet's anticipated difficulties seemed to melt away.

But another worry began to oppress Nagumo. The diplomatic negotiations might succeed and Japan call off the war. Suppose he failed to receive the canceling message and crashed down on Pearl Harbor after his country had decided on peace! Kusaka admitted the seriousness of the problem, but because all vessels had instructions to tune in to a special wavelength to receive the awaited "Stop" or "Go" signal, he did not agonize over it as Nagumo did. Kusaka had his own fret: Suppose the Naval General Staff could not provide the task force with current intelligence?[15]

Genda feared that Nagumo's long face would cast a pall over his staffs and his airmen and eventually demoralize the fleet. Both he and Oishi, therefore, urged Kusaka to calm the admiral's nerves. Kusaka knew him to be a brave man, but he agreed that Nagumo worried about detection, refueling, keeping formation, black smoke emitting from the tankers, enemy submarines, and missing signals from Tokyo.[16] "Yes, the operation is a big risk," Kusaka told him, "but now that we are under way there is no use to worry. The only logical thing to do is to carry on fearlessly." However, Nagumo shook his head and replied, "You are too optimistic."

Kusaka wrapped himself in his usual kimono of ascetic calm, believing that at certain times the individual becomes caught up in problems he cannot solve by his own efforts. He thought that by concentrating on the immediate task to the exclusion of fruitless worries and speculations, the human being could tap a pure stream of spiritual strength to carry him through. So he practiced the mental disciplines of Zen Buddhism.[17]

He also continued his setting-up exercises. The amused young airmen who gathered every morning to watch him did not disconcert Kusaka in the least. "By such means I expect to live to be a hundred years old," he told them, an

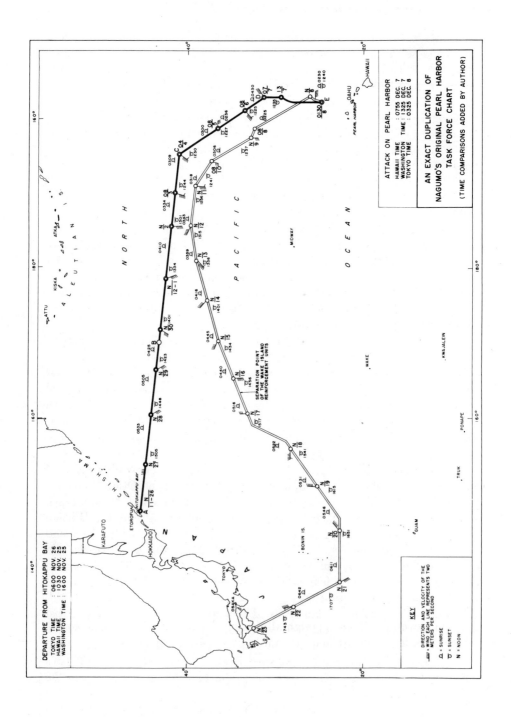

announcement greeted with shouts of laughter. In all the arrogant joy of youth, they could not see why anyone would want to live to be so old. And what soldier or sailor could count on surviving his current assignment, let alone reaching the century mark?[18]

Nothing could dampen the spirits of the pilots and air crews. Released from the tremendous pressure of intense training and the daily risks of a hazardous profession, they relaxed at night over such games as *go* and *shogi*. Fuchida circulated among them with smiling encouragement, while Murata, in top form, kept everyone laughing.[19] Aboard *Zuikaku*, Shimazaki plied himself with too much *sake* now and then and engaged in all types of peculiar antics.[20]

Despite their gaiety, most of the flying officers thought they would never come back alive. "They did not fear death," said Fuchida. "Their only fear was that the attack might not be successful and that they would have to return to Japan with their mission unfulfilled."[21]

In Washington Roosevelt looked old beyond his years when he convened his War Council at noon on the twenty-eighth. As he faced Hull, Knox, Stimson, Marshall, and Stark, in his hand he held a summary of Japanese military and naval movements dated November 27, signed by Marshall and Stark. Once more they begged for breathing space and recommended "no action which might lead to immediate hostilities" unless the Japanese attacked or directly threatened American, British, or Dutch territory.[22]

According to Stimson, everyone agreed that if the Japanese force headed southward "was allowed to get around the southern point of Indo-China and to . . . land in the Gulf of Siam, either at Bangkok or further west, it would be a terrific blow to all these Powers . . . this must not be allowed." The conferees believed "that if the Japanese get into the Isthmus of Kra, the British would fight." In that case the United States "would have to fight" also. Obviously, "if this expedition was allowed to round the southern point of Indo-China, this whole chain of disastrous events would be set on foot. . . ."[23]

At this meeting Hull reviewed his Ten Points. He also recommended "that any plans for our military defense should include an assumption that the Japanese might make the element of surprise a central point in their strategy and also might attack at various points simultaneously with a view to demoralizing efforts of defense and of coordination."[24] The conferees agreed that rather than do nothing or go to war, they should issue a warning to Japan "that if it reached a certain place, or a certain line, or a certain point, we should have to fight. . . ."[25]

On November 28 the Foreign Ministry issued espionage directions to Kita which included: "Report upon the entrance or departure of capital ships and the length of time they remain at anchor, from the time of entry into port until the departure."[26] Yoshikawa required no such reminder. On either the twenty-seventh or twenty-eighth he dispatched Kotoshirodo with Mikami to Pearl Harbor with instructions to "go all the way around." The two drove to the very end of the Pearl City peninsula. Kotoshirodo could see a carrier moored on the west side of Ford Island and wanted to find out the exact type. This was the last time Kotoshirodo scouted on his own, and later that same week he made his final excursion with Yoshikawa. After that the latter took over entirely.[27]

If the carrier was *Enterprise*, Kotoshirodo must have made this trip on November 27 because Halsey sortied at precisely 0800 on the twenty-eighth. As soon as he cleared the channel, he split his forces, taking for himself the flattop, three heavy cruisers, and nine destroyers. He designated this group Task Force Eight. He placed the three battleships and the remainder of the vessels under Rear Admiral Milo F. Draemel as Task Force Two, with instructions to sail to the usual exercise area. Then Halsey headed west.

As soon as he had moved outside signaling distance of Task Force Two and Pearl Harbor, Halsey directed *Enterprise*'s skipper, Captain George D. Murray, to issue Battle Order No. 1: "The *Enterprise* is now operating under war conditions. . . ."[28] He directed his ships "to put war heads in all torpedoes; to regard any submarine seen as hostile and sink it . . ." and to arm their aircraft with bombs and "shoot down any plane seen in the air that was not known to be one of our own." Task Force Eight maintained "full preparations for combat," ammunition at the ready, while aerial patrols swept the sky for 200 miles as it proceeded to Wake. Halsey believed "that the Japs would strike without declaration of war," but he did not expect an air strike on Pearl Harbor. Like Kimmel, he "thought it would be a submarine attack."[29] Thus, one of the carriers the Japanese hoped to destroy escaped the trap.

In Washington reverberations of the previous day's excitement still echoed in the War Department. Hap Arnold told Miles that "he was extremely worried about sabotage of planes." He therefore proposed "to send out drastic orders to all Air Forces at home and abroad to take all precautions against sabotage." Miles informed him that he had already sent out a general sabotage warning to his G-2s. This did not satisfy Arnold, who insisted upon specific directions "to all Air Corps Commands."[30]

So that morning Brigadier General Martin F. Scanlon, Miles's opposite on the Air Staff, appeared with the draft of such a message. Miles thought it too strong, whereas Scanlon meant it to carry a heavy punch because aircraft and their engines are particularly vulnerable to sabotage. Bearing in mind the Chief of Staff's policy against upsetting the civilian population, Miles wanted to add precautions. He also suggested that the message contain a direction against "illegal measures." Scanlon took this to mean that the Army should not "get over-excited and start throwing a lot of civilians in jail."[31] As the upshot of this long discussion, which eventually involved several other high-ranking officers, including Gerow, not one but two sabotage warnings went out that evening. Short's headquarters received the following:

> 482 28th Critical situation demands that all precautions be taken immediately against subversive activities. . . . Also desired that you initiate forthwith all additional measures necessary to provide for protection of your establishments, property, and equipment against sabotage, protection of your personnel against subversive propaganda and protection of all activities against espionage. This does not repeat not mean that any illegal measures are

authorized. Protective measures should be confined to those essential to security, avoiding unnecessary publicity and alarm. To insure speed of transmission identical telegrams are being sent to all air stations but this does not repeat not affect your responsibility under existing instructions. ADAMS

By the time the staff got through tinkering with Scanlon's message, it came out virtually identical with No. 482, although numbered 484 and marked for Martin's attention. It was signed first by Arnold, then by Major General Emory S. Adams, The Adjutant General. Fort Shafter thus received two almost identical sabotage warnings hard on the heels of the one already dispatched from Miles on the twenty-seventh.[32] Yet it never entered Miles's mind that these three messages so close together might "unduly emphasize" sabotage.[33]

This barrage of antisubversive messages did not cause Short to return to his original warning of November 27 (No. 472) for another hard look at it. The new dispatches merely reinforced his previous conviction because he believed Washington had his reply to No. 472 at hand when it prepared these latest instructions.[34]

Nevertheless, a decided difference existed between No. 472 and No. 482 which should have struck an alert military man immediately. The first, which contained not a single reference to subversion or sabotage, went out over Marshall's signature. The second bore the name of Adams, The Adjutant General. Therefore, No. 472 conveyed a military order from the Chief of Staff, and that order "directed" Short to "undertake such reconnaissance and other measures" as necessary to prepare for "hostile action." The Adjutant General had no command authority, and documents so signed did not carry the same force as those signed by Marshall. The War Department had this fact clearly in mind when it sent out 472.[35] Thus, it should have been readily apparent to Short that in Washington's eyes "hostile action" and "sabotage" were horses of very different colors.

This was a big day for meetings. From 1600 to 1800 the liaison conference met in Tokyo. There, apparently for the first time, Togo asked Nagano, "Tell me what the zero hour is. Otherwise I can't carry on diplomacy." Nagano replied, "Well, then, I will tell you." Lowering his voice, he said, "The zero hour is December 8 [December 7, Washington time]. There is still time, so you had better resort to the kind of diplomacy that will be helpful in winning the war."

Then Togo asked, "We can't continue to keep our diplomats in the dark, can we?" To this an unnamed person answered, "Our diplomats will have to be sacrificed. What we want is to carry on diplomacy in such a way that until the very last minute the United States will continue to think about the problem, we will ask questions, and our plans will be kept secret."[36]

The day moved inexorably to its close. Scanning his weather chart aboard *Nagato* in the Inland Sea, Ugaki wondered "how the task force up north heading east was getting on. I suppose they are having a hard time. Pray to God to let them have two days' good weather so they can refuel."[37]

CHAPTER 52

"THE

VACANT

SEA"

On November 29 Hull was the only one of the top four in the U.S. government who remained in Washington. Roosevelt had gone to Warm Springs, Georgia; Stimson and Knox had flown to Philadelphia that morning to attend the Army-Navy football game. In the late afternoon Hull received some inflammatory extracts of a speech Tojo was supposed to have delivered on November 30 (Japan time). After consulting with his Far Eastern experts and the "military authorities," Hull telephoned the President. He stressed "the imminent danger of a Japanese attack and advised him to advance the date of his return to Washington." Roosevelt agreed to come back on December 1.[1]

Rather more to the point were two significant espionage messages which the Foreign Ministry sent out on November 29. The San Francisco consulate received directions to make full reports beginning December 1 of the name, nationality, port of departure, port of destination, departure date, and so forth "in detail, of all foreign commercial and war ships now in the Pacific, Indian Ocean, and South China Sea."[2] This was certainly a comprehensive order, but quite understandable, for, among other things, Tokyo urgently wished to know whether any foreign vessels leaving San Francisco might sail within sight of Nagumo's task force. The Japanese were also interested in ships which might get in the way of the Southern Operation.

Of even more direct import was the dispatch sent to Kita: "We have been receiving reports from you on ship movements, but in future will you also report even when there are no movements."[3] Here was another telltale signpost on the road of Japanese naval espionage. The mice need not leave their hole to interest the cat. The U.S. Navy translated this on December 5, so it had two days to make something of it. As in the "bomb plot" message of September 24, this gave another clear indication that at Honolulu the Japanese concern centered in the ships in harbor no less—if indeed not more—than in their comings and goings.

Since his brief visit with Yoshikawa in the backyard of his home in late October, Kuehn, the sleeper spy,* had not been idle on Oahu. Although not supposed to take an active part in Japanese prewar espionage in Hawaii, sometime in either late October or November Kuehn prepared "a plan for transmittal of information relative to the United States Fleet." On or about November 28 he made a trip to the navy yard, obviously to check on Kimmel's ships. And around the thirtieth, he went to the Japanese consulate to deliver his plan (or code) to Okuda "relative to the movements and position of the several units of the United States Fleet."[4]

Such activity at this time directly violated Kuehn's contract with the Japanese Navy. It also ignored the instructions which a member of the *Tatuta Maru* mission brought to Kita from Ogawa and Yamaguchi of Naval Intelligence, charging Kita that he must (1) have Kuehn stop contacting the consulate; (2) tell Kuehn that his code was too complicated and must be simplified; and (3) instruct Kuehn not to engage in any intelligence activities before the outbreak of war.[5] Kuehn's bumbling into the delicate machinery of prewar espionage must have annoyed and worried the consulate. Why Kuehn, a person fairly well known in Honolulu and a property holder on Oahu, should jump the gun on his spying is strange indeed. He testified that either he or Kita suggested that Kuehn scout the U.S. Pacific Fleet.[6] It is difficult to believe that Kita did so because it directly contravened Tokyo's orders concerning Kuehn's utilization and does not align with the caution the consulate had insisted upon.

Some disagreement exists about the genesis of Kuehn's code. Kuehn testified that he prepared it in late November,[7] while Yoshikawa stated that Kita showed it to him soon after his visit to Kuehn in October.[8] The latter is probably correct because the order to simplify the code seems to have come with the *Tatuta Maru*.[9] It is unlikely that Kita, Okuda, or Yoshikawa had any hand in it because the code was typically Teutonic in its overelaboration, superabundance of detail, organization refined to chaos, and disregard of the human element. Yoshikawa considered it primitive and dangerous.[10]

As one might expect, the consulate told Kuehn that his system was too complicated. He therefore went home and reworked his plan for three days. Then he returned (probably on December 2) and gave Okuda an envelope containing the code, together with $500 for transmittal to his stepson in Germany. He also arranged for various other means of clandestine communications, such as radio station KGMB want ads and use of a boat with a star on its sail. This envelope included the information that seven battleships, six cruisers, two aircraft carriers, forty destroyers and twenty-seven submarines, "or some similar figure," lay in Hawaiian waters. As he later admitted, "those figures were purely fictitious, as far as I knew."[11]

---

*See Chapter 38.

The consulate must have wondered whom Kuehn thought he was fooling, for Kita and Okuda knew from Yoshikawa's and Kotoshirodo's reports how many ships lay in Pearl Harbor in late November. Certainly not forty destroyers and twenty-seven submarines—more than Kimmel had in the entire central Pacific—with an extra carrier tossed in for good measure, *Enterprise* having left harbor early on the twenty-eighth.[12]

In Washington on November 29, G-2 prepared its "Periodic Estimate of the Situation," projecting from December 1, 1941, to March 31, 1942. The report contained not the faintest hint that Japan might strike the U.S. Pacific Fleet in Pearl Harbor.[13] Nevertheless, Colonel Bratton recalled:

> . . . those of us in the Army who were studying this situation always listed, mentally at least, an attack on Hawaii as a capability, but in our discussions of the situation with our counterparts in the Navy it was always emphasized by the latter that their forces in the Pacific were alert and so stationed as to make such a Japanese attack impracticable or suicidal, and we therefore relegated such an attack to the realm of remote possibility.[14]

Miles, too, observed, "We had spent several hundred million in defense of Hawaii, we had our greatest fleet out there. That Hawaii could be attacked if Japan went to war was obvious to everyone."[15] He also testified:

> Of course we had had information for a great many years which had been considered in all our war plans in Hawaii that there was a certain part of the Pacific Ocean that we called the "Vacant Sea" in which there are practically no ships and in which large movements of ships could occur without anybody seeing them. It was that part of the ocean between the great southern routes that go from Hawaii to the coast of Japan and China, and the northern great circle routes that go near the Aleutians.[16]

That was exactly the area through which Nagumo's ships were sailing on the very day Miles's office prepared the report. What is more, G-2 had no illusions that Grew and his attachés in Tokyo could tip them off if a Japanese fleet left Japan. Said Miles: ". . . we never dreamed that we could rely on getting that information. It would have been almost a military intelligence miracle had we been able to spot a task force in forming and have known before it sailed where it was going."[17]

So Rochefort and his devoted workers in Combat Intelligence strained every nerve to keep track of Japanese ship movements. On November 27 his summary indicated: "No further information on the presence of Carrier Division Five in the Mandates." The same report advised: "Carriers are still located in home waters. . . ," so Japanese deception tactics continued to work effectively. The next day Rochefort had a disturbing development to note: "As has been previously reported the suspected [Japanese] Radio Intelligence net is very active and is becoming more so. . . . This activity is interpreted to indicate that the R.I. net is operating at full strength upon U.S. Naval Communications and IS GETTING RESULTS [Rochefort's capitals]."[18]

Rochefort's report was entirely accurate. From many interceptor stations the Fourth Department of the Naval General Staff monitored American naval radio traffic. It could tell, for instance, when Pearl Harbor signaled a battleship or when Kimmel's ships flashed Pearl Harbor. Sometimes it could estimate approximate locations, but not often. Japanese radio Intelligence was in much the same situation as Rochefort; that is, it could not decipher the contents of the messages it monitored and had to work from call signals alone. The two radio interception nets were like two warriors playing a deadly game of blindman's buff, groping for each other by sounds in the vast darkness of the Pacific. The Japanese divided American naval messages into three categories: Urgent, Ordinary, and Meteorological. The Naval General Staff kept a statistical record of all these messages, grouping them according to their importance and number. In this way it attempted to judge the scope of American fleet activity. The United States changed call signals from time to time. For several days thereafter the Japanese would be confused, but by hard work they solved the new patterns. However, after Pearl Harbor the U.S. Navy devised systems which made it extremely difficult for the Japanese even to break the call signals.[19]

Rochefort advised on November 29: "The HIYEI [*sic*] [Rochefort's capitals] sent one message to the Chief of Staff Third Fleet."[20] Obviously this was part of the Japanese smoke screen to conceal the movements of Nagumo's ships because at that very moment *Hiei* was en route to Pearl Harbor.

Communications Intelligence reported on November 30:

> Todays [*sic*] traffic consisted largely of despatches bearing old dates, some as far back as 28 November. No reason can be given for the retransmission of these messages unless the high volume of traffic for past few days has prevented the repetition of despatches. . . . The only tactical circuit heard today was one with AKAGI and several MARUS [Rochefort's capitals]. . . .

The Japanese repeated old messages to confuse the Americans. In this day's batch Rochefort's men identified *Kongo* and *Hiei* as being with the Second Fleet—the first correctly, the latter off the beam by many a mile.[21]

When Layton brought Kimmel this particular summary, the admiral noted the *Akagi*-Marus exchange and asked what Layton thought about it. Layton replied that *Akagi* was perhaps talking to some tankers "and probably going to get oil."[22] Of course, any talking *Akagi* did to her Marus was by signal flag or short-range blinker.

As Nagumo's First Air Fleet ended its fourth day sailing through the "vacant sea," the diarist Chigusa glanced at the calendar and wrote:

> At last today is the final day of November. Through the night we operated searchlights and deck lights because of the heavy fog to guard against collision. . . . This afternoon I navigated the ship and we refueled astern very slowly. The towing line broke. Very dangerous but fortunately no injuries. We tried again to refuel but it became dark and we gave up refueling. Our task force proceeds on course at 14 knots.

The nearer they came to Hawaii, the more uneasy Yoshioka became. Genda's assistant believed this same opportunity would never occur again. But he worried about being sighted by an American submarine or possibly a Soviet ship, and there was the possibility of the massive Southern Expeditionary Force's being spotted with the United States consequently increasing its patrols around Oahu.[23]

Genda was considerably less placid than his surface air would indicate. At times he was unusually silent and thoughtful. He noted that at his temples there had begun to appear a sprinkling of white hairs, which he attributed to his intensive work and worry.[24] Basically he had great confidence in the power and destructive ability of Japan's naval air arm. And he retained an abiding faith in himself, in Fuchida, in their airmen, and in their plans. Still, the realization of what lay ahead sometimes jerked him up sharply. At such moments he would stare out across the trackless Pacific and think: *Now we are advancing toward Pearl Harbor, not in a dream but in reality. May God help us!*[25]

Genda knew that Nagumo and Kusaka had already decided on one attack. So at every chance he urged Nagumo to keep his mind open, to remain flexible in his approach to the operation, and, above all, to launch repeated attacks. Hit the enemy again and again until he lay utterly helpless, no longer a naval threat to Japan. Time and again Genda beseeched Nagumo: Perform the unexpected, and go all out in the performance. But his words fell on stony ground. Nagumo consistently replied, "One attack only! One attack only!"[26]

Yet hoping and praying that the situation on Oahu would prove ripe for repeated attacks after completion of the two-wave assault, Genda prepared plans to help convince Nagumo to take any tide of good fortune at the flood and ride it to total victory. It would not be easy to open the door of the admiral's closed mind, but he could at least drive in a wedge in the hope that it would swing wide with the wind of success. His fertile mind devised four plans, any one of which he hoped Nagumo would put in operation if the airmen succeeded in their initial two-wave attack:

Plan I. Remain in the area about 200 miles north of Oahu for several days after the attack and exploit whatever situation arose. This might call for aerial searches to find and destroy U.S. fleet units not at Pearl Harbor. Or deliver repeated attacks against the remaining ships in Pearl Harbor as well as its installations. Then, satisfied that they had completed all possible damage, return to Japan via the far northern route that Nagumo had already chosen for his homeward voyage.

Plan II. In general the same plan as No. I, but return to Japan on a route not as far north as the one Nagumo had selected.

Plan III. The same as Nos. I and II, but return to Japan along the Hawaiian chain, passing only a short distance north of Midway. This would enable the task force to attack whatever U.S. Fleet units might be sailing in or near that area.

Plan IV. The same as the others, but return to Japan by sailing southward, passing Oahu on the west en route to the Marshalls. Genda considered this his best plan, for it would enable Nagumo to launch a second two-wave assault against Pearl Harbor or Kimmel's ships at sea on Sunday, December 7 (local time). Then, too, such a plan would allow Nagumo to launch repeated attacks against Oahu as the task force moved southward within easy striking distance of U.S. targets on Monday, Tuesday, or Wednesday of that week. Genda hoped that if Nagumo operated according to this plan—all else being equal—the Japanese could destroy the U.S. Pacific Fleet and put themselves in a position to take the Hawaiian Islands.[27]

"The most difficult and most agonizing period for every officer in the Naval General Staff who knew about Pearl Harbor." Thus Tomioka characterized the span of time as the task force sailed the "vacant sea" from November 26 to December 8. He and his colleagues had never been enthusiastic about Yamamoto's risky venture, and they did not change their minds now. Many still cherished a faint hope that diplomacy might succeed even at the last minute. But they could do nothing about that.

From the day Nagumo's task force left Hitokappu Bay, Tomioka's Operations Section stayed open all night. He arose early every morning and worked late. Convinced that the task force would be discovered the day of the attack, if not before, he worried constantly about those precious carriers. He prayed fervently to the gods to grant Nagumo's ships a safe voyage. But if anything unusual developed, the Naval General Staff intended to order the task force to return at once.[28] "The general attitude was to take no more chances than absolutely necessary," said Fukudome. "If there were any element of doubt or if things did not develop according to plan, the main objective was to get the task force home."[29] Tomioka and his officers kept a chart of Nagumo's estimated progress. Thus, on November 30 they could see that the task force had traveled more than one-third the distance to Hawaii. So far so good!

Although he and his colleagues could not intervene with Providence on Nagumo's behalf, they carried out their duties with their usual brisk efficiency. Every morning someone from the Meteorological Section of the Navy Ministry's Hydrographic Department briefed the Operations Section of the Naval General Staff on the weather in the Pacific. On the basis of these reports Tomioka and Miyo prepared daily forecasts, which were radioed to the task force. For obvious reasons these began two weeks before Nagumo's ships left Japan.[30]

To make the communications system more precise, the Naval General Staff gave every coded message a special number after the task force left Hitokappu Bay. And they repeated each of these messages several times to make sure that Nagumo received them, for it was absolutely imperative that he miss none of these dispatches, particularly one that might call his ships back or alert him to potential danger.

As double insurance, the Naval General Staff sent Nagumo a coded message every odd-numbered hour day and night during the voyage. For example, Message No. 13 would be sent at 0900 on December 1. Tokyo would repeat this at 1100, 1300, 1500, and so on through the day, unless newer information made it necessary to send a different dispatch.[31] All ships in the task force were required to receive messages from Japan, but *Hiei* and *Kirishima* had the most powerful receiving gear. So *Hiei* was responsible for monitoring all messages to the task force, relaying them to *Akagi*.[32]

Another system of conveying information to the First Air Fleet was by regular government broadcasts over Radio Tokyo. These were the routine transmissions which Japan sent several times daily to Japanese residents abroad. For the benefit of the task force, the Naval General Staff arranged to add an extra statement or two at the end of every broadcast, and in this way Nagumo received some of his weather reports. As noted, the task force maintained strict radio silence. Nagumo had authority to communicate with Tokyo in case of an accident, using a special call signal to disguise his sending vessel as a merchantman. As soon as Tokyo received this message, it would repeat it back to the task force so that Nagumo need not signal again. On the return voyage Nagumo could begin communicating with Tokyo once he passed beyond 800 miles from Oahu.[33]

Across the globe, on November 30 that eager Germanophile Ambassador Oshima met with Ribbentrop at the latter's request. Ribbentrop urged that now was the time for Japan to fight Britain and the United States. He made a definite commitment: "Should Japan become engaged in a war against the United States Germany, of course, would join the war immediately. There is absolutely no possibility of Germany's entering into a separate peace with the United States under such circumstances. The Fuehrer is determined on that point."[34]

The Americans translated their interception of Oshima's report to Tokyo on December 1. Kramer of ONI, on loan to Naval Communications, noted that it was the first time during 1941 that the Japanese "had opened up on the subject and progress of these negotiations to the Germans, their allies."[35]

The same day Togo advised Oshima that the conversations with the United States "in spite of the sincere efforts of the Imperial Government, now stand ruptured—broken. . . . In the face of this, our Empire faces a grave situation and must act with determination. . . ." Togo therefore instructed Oshima to interview Hitler and Ribbentrop:

> . . . Say very secretly to them that there is extreme danger that war may suddenly break out between the Anglo-Saxon nations and Japan through some clash of arms and add that the time of the breaking out of this war may come quicker than anyone dreams. . . .
>
> Say that by our present moves southward we do not mean to relax our pressure against the Soviet and that if Russia joins hands tighter with England and the United States and resists us with hostilities, we are ready to turn upon her with all our might; however, right now, it is to our advantage to stress the south. . . . [36]

When McCollum read this dispatch, it impressed him "as being a Japanese excuse to the Germans not to jump on the Russians"; nevertheless, he was convinced that the situation between the United States and Japan was "intensely acute."[37]

In London, Churchill had not yet seen these ominous messages because of the usual two- or three-day time lag between London and Washington on Magic. On November 30 he suggested to Roosevelt that they make another effort to avert war between their two countries and Japan by means of "a plain declaration . . . that any further act of aggression by Japan will lead immediately to the gravest consequences." He promised that Britain would either "make a similar declaration or share in a joint declaration." He closed: "Forgive me, my dear friend, for presuming to press such a course upon you, but I am convinced that it might make all the difference and prevent a melancholy extension of the war."[38]

The Imperial Palace experienced a brief detour on the road to war on November 30. Fate seemed to be offering Hirohito an opportunity to prove that his reign deserved the name of Enlightened Peace. At 1530 the Emperor sent for Kido. "His Imperial Highness the Prince Takamatsu came up to see me this morning," His Majesty informed his devoted chamberlain, "and told me that as the navy had been fully occupied after all and it appeared to have been disposed to avoid war with America if possible what on earth was the real intention in this regard?"[39]

From the phraseology it appears that the Emperor was either angry or perplexed, or both. The Navy had been giving the impression that it was opposed to war with the United States. Now, within a week after having been appointed to the Operations Section of the Naval General Staff, Prince Takamatsu had informed his august brother that the Navy had been preparing for war all along. Some of his fellow officers believe that His Highness, knowing that the Navy had no real confidence in victory, advised the Emperor on this occasion not to go to war.[40] By this time every member of the Operations Section knew about Pearl Harbor, and to function effectively as a member of that elite organization, His Highness would have to have known also.

In any case, Kido respectfully recommended that Hirohito send for Tojo, Shimada, and Nagano to clarify the matter. Immediately after this talk Tojo arrived, and after him Shimada and Nagano. According to Shimada, "The Navy was never confident of achieving victory over the United States but we were confident that we were better prepared at that time to fight than we would have been at any later date. . . . Admiral Nagano and I on November 30 told the Emperor that the Navy had made adequate preparations." Indeed it had! At 1835 the Emperor summoned Kido again, to inform him that Shimada and Nagano had answered his question "with considerable confidence, so instruct Tojo to proceed as prearranged." Kido telephoned this order to the premier at once.[41] The green light flashed on once again.

CHAPTER 53

"GLORY

OR

OBLIVION"

Palace politics never reached the ears of Nagumo and his staff. The time was drawing close to the deadline when they would be informed whether or not diplomacy had succeeded. In that event the task force would be recalled to Japan. Thus, everyone aboard ship paid close attention to reports on the talks in Washington.

One group of men found the voyage anything but exhilarating—the pilots selected as air cover over the carriers. They would be engaged in what promised to be a tame chore while their fellow airmen flew into the thick of battle; they had little to look forward to and considered the trip rather dull. A number of them whiled away their time playing cards or drinking *sake*, which was served after dinner.[1]

Shimoda, air officer aboard *Zuikaku*, had no quarrel with the drinking because one of his tasks was to keep morale high among the flight personnel. He and his group worried about the prospect of meeting a Soviet ship which might be returning to one of the Siberian ports from the United States, but fog shrouded the task force during the time when Shimoda thought its path might cross that of a homebound Soviet vessel.[2]

Mikawa fully expected his battleships and heavy cruisers to engage in surface action. It seemed to him highly improbable that the task force could reach Pearl Harbor undetected, and he still lamented the absence of *Kongo* and *Haruna*. In fact, he was not at all happy about Japan's grand strategy. In his opinion, the Japanese should first hit the U.S. Pacific Fleet with everything they had, then turn full attention to the Southern Operation.[3]

At this time another element of the Pearl Harbor forces was far in advance of the First Air Fleet. Commander Minoru Yokota was reconnoitering Alaskan waters in his submarine, *I-26*. After leaving Japan on November 19, he steered a direct course, running surfaced until he was within 600 miles of the Aleutians. From there he proceeded submerged during the daytime, surfacing at night. At a point about fifteen miles west of Attu he moved around to the east, approaching Kiska from the northeast. There he submerged and slipped boldly into the very harbor itself. To the best of his recollection, this was November 26.

As soon as he finished his check of Kiska, he continued eastward amid a violent snowstorm and reached Adak Strait from the north the next day. He found Adak Harbor too narrow to enter, so his observation could be only superficial. However, as he proceeded through these regions, he received the impression that American preparations were "very inadequate."

From Adak he followed the Aleutian chain westward and reached Dutch Harbor on November 29. He edged in close enough to see people onshore but did not risk sailing into the harbor. If the Americans sighted him, they might alert the U.S. Pacific Fleet and thereby jeopardize the entire Pearl Harbor operation.

Yokota reconnoitered Dutch Harbor on the morning of the twenty-ninth, then left that afternoon. Fearing possible detection, he doubled back north and followed the Aleutians on the west in a southward direction until he reached Amukta Passage. Then he proceeded eastward, transiting the passage on November 30, heading for a point on the great circle midway between Hawaii and San Francisco. *I-26* received every message which Tokyo sent to the task force, so Yokota kept right up-to-date on events, but he never dispatched a single message back. He saw nothing important enough to report, and the Naval General Staff and the Sixth Fleet had agreed: "No news is good news."[4]

A document captured much later gives an intriguing hint of the activities of the other lone scout, *I-10*, in the South Sea region. According to a listing of submarine-borne aircraft actions covering the period November 30, 1941, to November 11, 1942, and extending from Zanzibar to Oregon, *I-10* sent up a night air sortie on November 30 over Suva Bay in the Fiji Islands. "The document states succinctly that the plane 'did not return.' "[5] Even so, it managed to report sighting no enemy in the harbor. *I-10* searched three days for the missing scout, but in vain.

Did the aircraft fall victim to alert British defenses? Was the first blood shed in the Pacific war Japanese blood at British hands, eight days before the Pearl Harbor attack? Or did the aircraft perish in an accident, to join the untold thousands of disappearances at sea? *I-10* next headed for Samoa, where on December 4 she sighted an *Astoria*-class cruiser off Pago Pago Bay. Seeing no other large ships, she headed north, as scheduled, to arrive at a point some 1,300 miles south of Hawaii on the first day of the war.[6]

Daily refueling of Nagumo's destroyers demanded expert seamanship, precise timing, steady nerves, and constant precautions. The task seemed endless as one dreary day crawled into the next. Sakagami, Nagumo's refueling expert, had not expected much success, but a relatively tranquil sea permitted them to refuel every day. On occasion one of the big cables snapped. When it did, the end piece cracked and swung like a striking snake. Sometimes it struck a sailor and swept him overboard.[7]

To conserve fuel, the ships permitted no heating and the minimum use of electric lights. So everyone dressed warmly during the northern Pacific passage. Aboard most of the ships, officers and men washed in cold water, although *Shokaku* and *Zuikaku,* with their large fuel capacity, afforded the luxury of warm water. The good condition of the sea and the foggy weather so favored the task force that Yamaguchi and his officers "considered it a blessing from the gods and a good omen for the coming operation."[8] Nagumo, too, began to feel that the hand of Providence had spread protectingly over his fleet. When he heard Kusaka's devout thanks for the fine weather and sea conditions, he found himself echoing, "Truly, it is with God's help."[9]

Aboard *Nagato* in the Inland Sea on December 1 a certain fatalistic tranquillity prevailed. Yamamoto's staff had done everything it could to make the Pearl Harbor venture a success. Now the men must wait, hope, and pray like the Naval General Staff and everyone else.[10] Impatient for a crack at the enemy, Ugaki recorded in his diary: "At last the zero hour of the first of December came—the time to make decision has come. Is there still any room for consideration?"[11]

Yamamoto had received word that the Emperor would grant him an audience at 1045 on December 2, so he was "silent and thoughtful" this Monday. He knew that by custom the Emperor bestowed his personal good wishes upon the Commander in Chief on the eve of war. Before leaving for Tokyo, he met with some of his staff, instructing them to send a previously coded message to the task force with the fateful announcement after he met with the Emperor. The communications officer of the Combined Fleet had devised this code early in November.[12]

Yamamoto and his adjutant left *Nagato* in time to catch a 1600 train from Iwakuni.[13] He wore civilian clothes, taking his uniform along in a suitcase. In the current tense atmosphere, if he had traveled to Tokyo in uniform, he might as well carry a placard announcing, "Japan is going to war very soon." He was so bent upon keeping his presence in the capital a secret that he did not even inform his wife that he would be there, nor did he visit his family when he arrived.[14]

At 1400 the same day in Room East of the Imperial Palace, the last Imperial conference of 1941 met in an atmosphere of crisis, doubt, desperation, and ritualistic formality. All recognized the deadly seriousness of the hour; all knew that the fate of the Empire was at stake. They sat grimly in their assigned places, their faces weary, drawn. Tojo spoke last. "We are fully prepared for a long war," he emphasized, but ". . . would also like to do everything we can in the future to bring the war to an early conclusion." He ended in a burst of rhetoric:

> At the moment our Empire stands at the threshold of glory or oblivion. . . .
> Once His Majesty reaches a decision to commence hostilities, we will all
> strive to repay our obligations to him, bring the Government and the military

ever closer together, resolve that the nation united will go on to victory, make an all-out effort to achieve our war aims, and set His Majesty's mind at ease.

Everyone arose and bowed as the Emperor left the scene. The unnamed chronicler observed: "During today's conference, His Majesty nodded in agreement with the statements being made, and displayed no signs of uneasiness. He seemed to be in an excellent mood, and we were filled with awe."[15]

Of course, the real power of decision rested in the hands of the oligarchs who were using the Emperor to help achieve their objectives. Yet it is difficult to appraise Hirohito's position at this conference. Perhaps he thought he had done all he could and had resigned himself to the inevitable. Or perhaps he had decided to ride out the storm in the hope that he would be around afterward to salvage some of the wreckage. Be that as it may, his attitude at the imperial conference of December 1 had changed perceptibly from that of September 6, when he urged that diplomacy take precedence over war preparations. On December 1 he said nothing about peace, or diplomacy, or the vastness of China; nothing about the limitless Pacific; nothing about universal brotherhood; nothing about "cleaning the slate." Neither approval nor disapproval. Only silence.

Although officially this conference decided on war, a brief look at the major Japanese naval forces in motion on that date suggests that the conflict had already begun in everything but name.

Japan's Pearl Harbor submarine forces were on their way to Hawaii, beginning with Miwa's Third Squadron, which left home on November 11. Shimizu arrived at Truk aboard his flagship *Katori* on November 30. He would leave there on December 2 and on the fifth reach Kwajalein, whence he would direct the operation of his Sixth Fleet.[16] And by December 1 Nagumo's task force had covered about half the distance to Oahu.

Japan had already begun to deploy the ships of its immense Southern Operation when the imperial conference met in Tokyo.[17] The Guam Invasion Force of Vice Admiral Shigeyoshi Inoue's Fourth Fleet had left the Inland Sea on November 29 bound for the Bonin Islands, whence it would head for Guam on December 4. One of the Fourth Fleet's missions was to serve as a relay station between the Marshall Islands, Nagumo's task force, and Japan. It was also to assist Shimizu in his submarine operations from Kwajalein and to help the First Air Fleet in case of danger or battle.

The main body of the Second Fleet under Vice Admiral Nobutake Kondo sailed from the Inland Sea on November 29 for Mako in the Pescadores to arrive there on December 2 and depart for the south on December 4. Kondo's mission snapped with challenge: Destroy enemy fleet and air strength in the Philippines, Malaya, and the Netherlands East Indies; act as surface escort and support landings of Army forces in the Philippines, Malaya, the Netherlands East Indies, and Thailand; prepare for the invasion of Timor and Burma; and destroy enemy surface traffic in Southeast Asia.[18]

The Southern Expeditionary Fleet (Malaya Force) was well under way,

Admiral Husband E. Kimmel and staff aboard flagship *Pennsylvania*.

Admiral Isoroku Yamamoto and staff of Combined Fleet.

commanded by that forceful Vice Admiral Jisaburo Ozawa,* who had helped organize the First Air Fleet, backed the Pearl Harbor plan, and once nourished hopes of leading the attack. His ships began hoisting anchors in Japan as early as November 20, in small units to avoid attention.[19]

Largest numerically of all the southern armadas was the Philippine Invasion Force under Vice Admiral Ibo Takahashi. His fleet of almost 100 vessels had the mission of taking over the Philippines quickly and effectively, thus securing that vital flank to the Indies. His was another operation that ensured war with Japan's big rival across the Pacific. Takahashi led his main force out of the Inland Sea on November 22. On November 25, one day before Nagumo sortied from the Kuriles, aboard his flagship, the heavy cruiser *Ashigara,* Takahashi arrived in the Pescadores. There he remained until December 8, when he launched the big move against the Philippines—the occupation of Luzon.[20]

Rear Admiral Takeo Takagi moved Takahashi's Southern Philippine Support Force from the Inland Sea on November 24. Taking his own air power with him, Takagi headed directly for Palau, about 500 miles east of the southern Philippines. Thence he would sail on December 6 for Davao to begin the invasion, shut the back door to the Philippines, and open the east gate to the Indies.[21]

Like Kondo, Takahashi depended on Tsukahara's Eleventh Air Fleet for support in the northern Philippines. As X-Day approached, Tsukahara and his staff waited in suspense for news of Nagumo's task force. For Nagumo had to hit the U.S. Pacific Fleet hard enough so that it could not move against the flank of the huge Southern Operation already under way. Tsukahara had little faith in the Hawaiian venture, but he never criticized the strategy because Yamamoto had ordered it. He considered Operation Hawaii one of those campaigns which, if successful, would be cited as brilliant but, if unsuccessful, would be called stupid and foolhardy. He and his key staff members had strict instructions, like everyone else in the Southern Operation, to wait for the go-ahead signal from Nagumo.[22]

U.S. officials watches these ships and these forces moving south day by day, almost hour by hour, until virtual hypnosis set in. Thus it was that Japan's sweeping offensive southward misdirected American political and military attention and served as camouflage for Nagumo's task force.

Japan's Northern Force (Fifth Fleet) under Vice Admiral Hoshiro Hosogaya had been in position since the First Air Fleet sailed from Hitokappu Bay. Its main mission was to patrol and defend the waters east of Japan, including the Bonin Islands, and to guard the route of the Pearl Harbor attack force.[23]

A small naval unit designed as an auxiliary to the Pearl Harbor task force left Tateyama, a short distance southeast of Yokosuka, on November 28. This

---

*See Chapters 3,11.

was the Midway Neutralization Force under the command of Captain Kanamo Konishi. It consisted of the destroyers *Ushio* and *Sazanami,* with the tanker *Shiriya.* The object of this expedition was to bombard and neutralize the air base at Midway, thus ensuring a safe return for the Nagumo force, and to divert American attention by decoying reconnaissance flights.[24]

The skipper of *Shiriya* was Captain Minoru Togo, son of the great Admiral Heihachiro Togo. Captain Togo had served in this unspectacular but necessary command only since October 28, 1941, and learned about his mission in the latter part of November. Actually he grasped only a part of the story since he was not aware of his unit's purpose. It was not necessary to inform Togo about the Pearl Harbor attack; his job was only to keep two destroyers filled with oil. Togo had no ambition but to fulfill his task as best he could, yet he "feared that Japan would face the same destiny as Germany: no future prospects and eventual defeat." The trip to Midway was uneventful; the Japanese ships sighted no other vessels, and Togo had no reason to believe anyone had spotted the Midway Neutralization Force.[25]

In addition to these various far-flung forces, Japan possessed the Main Body of the Combined Fleet under Yamamoto, which would remain in the Inland Sea until after the Pearl Harbor attack. A formidable assortment embodying the heavy surface ship doctrine of sea power, the Main Body consisted of six battleships, two light carriers, two light cruisers, and thirteen destroyers. Yamamoto kept all these ships in home waters so that he could protect the homeland and any one of the Japanese flanks. From *Nagato* he followed the progress of Japan's widespread naval activities.

A mere handful of ships formed the China Area Fleet under Vice Admiral Mineichi Koga at Shanghai. This relatively weak organization would continue operations in China, destroy local enemy units, cooperate with the Army in capturing Hong Kong, and protect surface traffic in Chinese coastal waters.[26] Koga and his staff knew about Operation Hawaii and would withhold action until after the attack.[27]

Thus, except for the Main Body, Koga's force, and assorted minor units attached to the various naval districts, the great bulk of the Japanese Navy was at sea as of December 1, ready for war. This deployment in November—in some cases several weeks before the actual outbreak of hostilities—was one of the largest (if not the largest) of preconflict movements of warships the world had ever seen. So, before the imperial conference of December 1, Japan was acting as if its leaders had already agreed that diplomacy had failed. If actions speak louder than words, Japan had gone to war before the conference formalized the decision.

At 1700 on the evening of December 2 a telegram arrived aboard *Nagato* from Ito, directing the opening of a certain sealed top secret envelope. As his eager fingers tore upon the seals, Ugaki sensed that he had in his hands the orders he had awaited impatiently. His instinct was correct. Down the page ran the words "Our Empire has decided to go to war against the United States, England, and Holland early December." Ugaki immediately sent a message to the commanders in chief of each fleet: "Decision made, but date and time will be ordered later."[28]

Nagumo had been even more than usually concerned with security that day. At 0730 he signaled his ships:

> This force is already in the anticipated scouting areas from Kiska and Midway Islands. Tonight we will pass the 180 degree line and near the enemy zone. More strict air alert and strict lookout against enemy ships suspected of tracking us will be maintained. Particular attention will be paid not to reveal any light at night and to limit blinker signals as much as possible.[29]

Now, upon receipt of the "Go" signal, Nagumo knew that he would have to push forward on this gambler's venture he had so dreaded.

With each mile that his task force covered, his margin of time narrowed. So it was in Washington, too. Nomura and Kurusu arrived at the State Department for an appointment with Hull at 1015 on December 1. Among other things Hull stated, "The United States would be glad to give Japan all she wants in the way of materials if Japan's military leaders will only show that Japan intends to pursue a peaceful course." Then he added, "But we don't propose to go into partnership with these military leaders."[30]

The same day the Foreign Ministry gave Nomura and Kurusu a clear indication that the negotiations were entering the home stretch: "The four offices in London, Hongkong, Singapore and Manila have been instructed to abandon the use of the code machines and to dispose of them. . . ." By another circular of December 1, Togo instructed Nomura to get in touch with his naval attaché's office when "faced with the necessity of destroying codes"; the attaché had certain chemicals "on hand for this purpose."[31]

Hull saw the President at noon and went over the situation with him. Both agreed that a Japanese attack seemed in the making. They talked over the proposed message to the Emperor, to which Hull objected except as a last resort. But because both were snatching at any possible means to stretch out time, Hull showed Roosevelt two drafts "to get his reaction." They also decided to hold up acting upon Churchill's suggestion of a joint warning to Japan, at least until they had seen the result of the President's appeal to Hirohito, if he decided to send one.[32]

In the Naval General Staff Tomioka continued to live through a hell of anxiety and apprehension. His brilliant but conservative mind permitted no self-deception. He had a clear, realistic awareness of the dire possibilities in this incomparably dangerous mission. He had devoted the true energy of his keen intelligence to the Southern Operation; now, as he went about his duties, he fell prey to nightmare worries about the task force. Anything could happen, including a counterattack by Kimmel's carriers. In that case Tomioka had determined to send a message to Nagumo at once, urging him to break contact and get his ships home at all costs. Even before the task force left Hitokappu Bay, he had told Nagumo and Kusaka to exert every effort to save the force if events turned against them.

Tomioka would never forgive himself if disaster struck the First Air Fleet. He had strongly opposed Yamamoto's plan, yet under pressure he, along with the other members of the Naval General Staff, had succumbed to the steamroller power of Yamamoto's will and agreed to his foolhardy scheme. Bitterly he chided himself for having abandoned his convictions.

So much did Tomioka's thoughts dwell on the prospect of potential catastrophe at Hawaii that he, a samurai in mind and spirit, had prepared his own plan of atonement: He would take his life—but not in the time-honored Japanese tradition of *hara-kiri*. Only one way appealed to Tomioka's fastidious, logical, almost Gallic sense of fitness. On the day of Nagumo's sortie from Hitokappu Bay, he placed a .38 caliber revolver in the drawer of his desk. There it kept silent vigil as the task force devoured the miles to Hawaii. There it lay loaded and ready—ready to blow out the brain that had rejected its own reasoning power and accepted Yamamoto's daring plan.[33]

CHAPTER 54

"GREAT

UNEASE

IN ALL

OF OUR

MINDS"

For Kimmel, that weekend brought a certain letdown. "The 'few days' stated by the Navy Department on November 27 to be the time for an aggressive move by Japan went by without event." The discussions which Washington had "stated to be terminated . . . with the barest possibility of resumption, were in fact resumed. . . ." His superiors did not advise him what the State, War, and Navy departments knew through Magic—"that the resumption of negotiations was a Japanese trick. . . ." Therefore, the press and radio reports of developments on the diplomatic front suggested to Kimmel "a mitigation of the emergency which prompted the so-called 'warning.' "[1] Either Kimmel was reading the newspapers very superficially or, like so many American leaders in the autumn of 1941, he was clutching at straws.

Layton "couldn't understand why Washington didn't give us more information, but presumed that perhaps they didn't have it." This "was a source of considerable concern" to both him and Rochefort. The two officers remained glued to their telephones over the weekend, although Layton returned to his office on Sunday to confer with Kimmel.[2]

The night of November 30–December 1 brought a highly significant development. The Fourteenth Naval District's "Communications Intelligence Summary" for December 1 told the story:

All service radio calls of [Japanese] forces afloat changed promptly at 0000, 1 December. Previously, service calls changed after a period of six months or more. Calls were last changed on 1 November, 1941. The fact that service calls lasted only one month indicate [sic] an additional progressive step in preparing for active operations on a large scale. . . . It appears that the Japanese Navy is adopting more and more security provisions . . . prior to 0000, 1 December . . . an effort was made to deliver all dispatches using old

calls so that promptly with the change of calls, there would be a minimum of
undelivered dispatches and consequent confusion and compromises. Either
that or the large number of old messages may have been used to pad the total
volume and make it appear as if nothing unusual was pending. . . . [3]

In all of Rochefort's experience, this was the first time the Japanese had
changed call signs twice in a thirty-day period.[4] The event had its impact in
Washington, too. Turner regarded the change, along with the marked drop in
radio traffic, as "extremely significant that very important operations were
contemplated, and it was probable that nearly the entire Japanese Fleet had put
to sea. . . ."[5] In contrast, Wilkinson seems to have regarded the event as just
one more indication that "there was an emergency situation arising."[6]

Layton considered the call sign change "rather ominous" and anticipated
the inevitable "lack of identifiable traffic." He knew that a drop in volume did
not necessarily "indicate an immediate move but it fitted very well with the
picture of the southern movement. . . ."[7] According to Rochefort, "There was
great unease in all of our minds because of the lack of traffic."[8] That included
Kimmel, who underlined that portion of the "Communications Intelligence
Summary" when he received it. The admiral asked Layton to prepare a paper
showing the approximate locations of Japanese fleet units. Layton immediately
did so, depending principally upon Communications Intelligence. He delivered it to Kimmel on December 2.[9]

Layton listed neither Carrier Division One nor Two "because neither one
of those commands had appeared in traffic for fully 15 and possibly 25
days. . . ."[10] Kimmel promptly pounced upon this omission. "What! You don't
know where Carrier Division 1 and Carrier Division 2 are?"

"No, sir, I do not," replied Layton. "I think they are in home waters but I
do not know where they are. The rest of these units, I feel pretty confident of
their locations."

Thereupon Kimmel turned his ice blue gaze upon Layton. With "somewhat a stern countenance and yet partially with a twinkle in his eye," he
demanded, "Do you mean to say that they could be rounding Diamond Head
and you wouldn't know it?" To this Layton could only answer lamely, "I hope
they would be sighted before now."[11]

That "twinkle in his eye" haunted Kimmel for years because various Pearl
Harbor investigators apparently regarded it as a sign of undue levity in a serious
situation. This was certainly not the case. Kimmel had a picturesque way of
expressing himself to emphasize a point. Layton was uncomfortably aware that
far from joking, his chief was impressing upon him the fact that he did not know
the location of four Japanese flattops.[12]

The admiral was "very much interested" in the whereabouts of these ships.
He believed that if the Americans could locate them, he "would be able to
determine pretty closely where the main Japanese effort was going to be." But
he thought that postattack references to the "lost carriers" did not quite fit the

situation. "As far as we were concerned the carriers were never lost. . . . We did not even know we had lost them. We could not identify them."[13]

They might not even be on radio silence. They might simply be part of the unidentified traffic, which included the major part of the Combined Fleet. The change had involved at least 15,000 call signs. As of December 2, when Layton made his presentation to Kimmel, somewhat over 200 had been partially identified, but the carriers did not fall in that 1⅓ percent.[14] Moreover, the Japanese flattops had frequently disappeared into a void. Kimmel testified that in the six months before the attack "there existed a total of 134 days—in 12 separate periods—each ranging from 9 to 22 days, when the location of the Japanese carriers from radio traffic analysis was uncertain."[15]

Yet no one took the situation complacently. In Layton's graphic description, the Japanese "were showing all the symptoms of taking increased radio security . . . they were using multiple addresses and blanket coverage and what we call addressed to nobody from nobody, which everybody copied, and when they do that nobody is being talked to that you can identify. . . ."[16] He felt extremely apprehensive because the Japanese Navy seemed to be lining up for a major offensive and he, the intelligence officer with the duty "to keep track of the Japanese naval forces," had found no trace of the carriers except Division Three and sometimes Four.[17] Carrier Division Three (*Hosho* and *Zuiho*) was with Yamamoto's Main Body in the Inland Sea, Carrier Division Four (*Ryujo*) with Takagi's Southern Philippine Support Force then en route to Palau.

In Washington McCollum's office took due note of the change in call signs. His estimate for December 1, as usual, attempted to locate major Japanese fleet units. This day's report placed *Hiei* near Sasebo and *Kirishima* near Kure, with *Akagi* and *Kaga* in southern Kyushu and the remaining four of Nagumo's carriers at Kure.[18]

This was but a part of a very long memorandum which McCollum drafted the preceding Friday and Saturday, covering the full sweep of the worldwide intelligence picture.[19] Early on Monday, December 1, he "polished it up in some aspects" and took the memo to Wilkinson. Later that morning McCollum accompanied his chief to Stark's office, where Ingersoll, Turner, and "one or two other flag officers" had also gathered. Copies were distributed to everyone present; then McCollum read the memorandum aloud. In the discussion which followed, he expressed his opinion that "war or rupture of diplomatic relations was imminent" and asked "whether or not the fleets in the Pacific had been adequately alerted." Both Stark and Turner gave him "categorical assurance . . . that dispatches fully alerting the fleets and putting them on a war basis had been sent."[20]

The DIO's telephone tap on the Japanese consulate picked up on December 1 a conversation between Lawrence K. Nakatsuka of the Honolulu *Star-Bulletin* and an individual DIO termed "XX." From all indications "XX" was Okuda. Nakatsuka called to ask if the consulate had any information about an *Asahi* newspaper item which he had received through an Associated Press dispatch concerning the closing of Japanese consulates. But "XX" was "his usual blank self."[21]

Kita and Okuda may have known—indeed, almost certainly knew—much more than they could tip off to any reporter. The desk pad entry for the day contained the cryptic words "Within the predictable future."[22] Someone frequently jotted down on the pad odd little phrases which seem to reflect nothing more sinister than Kita or Okuda adding to their English vocabularies, but this remark was much too pat for coincidence. Whether they had in mind the date they could expect the "winds" broadcast, or whether they actually meant that the attack on Pearl Harbor would come shortly, only they could tell.[23]

Like the rest of the Japanese connected with Operation Hawaii, the consulate fulfilled its duty to the cause. On December 1 Kita dispatched an extensive report on ship maneuvers, an example of excellent reporting, careful observation, and calculation as well as logical conclusion.[24] This information would be of priceless value to the task force if it failed to discover Kimmel's ships in either Pearl Harbor or Lahaina and hence had to activate one of Genda's alternate plans to cover these eventualities.

Rochefort's airwave detectives continued to zero in on Japan's southward movements in spite of maddening difficulties. Code change or no, had Nagumo broken radio silence during this time there seems little doubt that Rochefort would have locked in on him. But Japan's strict security paid off, as indicated by Rochefort's summary for December 2:

> Almost a complete blank of information on the Carriers today. Lack of identifications has somewhat promoted this lack of information. However, since over two hundred service calls have been partially identified since the change on the first of December and not one carrier call has been recovered, it is evident that carrier traffic is at a low ebb.[25]

Other intelligence organizations also had their own problems on this day. The FBI had been listening in on a suspect in its own office building. Some telephone company employees accidentally discovered the tap and reported it to their superiors. The District Intelligence Office contact at the company passed this on to his own unit; then someone in DIO tipped off the FBI that its tap had been uncovered.

Shivers descended upon the telephone company and read the riot act about this violation of confidence. When Mayfield learned about this, he was angry with the FBI for failing to consult with him, and he worried about the breach of security. Immediately his thoughts turned to his taps on the Japanese consulate telephones. He knew about the Navy Department's instructions against rocking the international boat. If his surveillance at the consulate came to light, this could really blow up a storm.

Although few people in DIO knew it, the office had been covering five or six lines in the consulate, with an average traffic of fifty to sixty calls a day during 1941.[26] This traffic had produced nothing of sensational importance, but it had given valuable insights into the personalities of consulate members and those who dealt with them. And December 2, 1941, was precisely the wrong moment to sacrifice intelligence upon the altar of international amity. But that is just what Mayfield did. "At 4 P.M. Honolulu time in the 1941st year of Our Lord, December 2nd inst. I bade my adieu to you my friend of 22 months standing. Darn if I won't miss you!!

"Requiescat in Peace." Thus Chief Ship's Clerk Theodore Emmanuel signed off from his long watch.[27]

But it so happened that DIO had overlooked one telephone line—that to the cook's quarters—and this one the FBI had been covering ever since they found the omission. Mayfield had been upset because Shivers had not confided in him; now he turned the tables and failed to advise the FBI that he had withdrawn the Navy's taps. Had Shivers known, he would have acted promptly to replace the Navy's coverage with his own.[28] Here again we find a sad lack of coordination in a vital area when so much depended upon cooperation between U.S. agencies.

Kimmel's primary problem on December 2 continued to be the proposed moving of Marine Corps aircraft to outlying islands and the contemplated transfer of these bases to Army jurisdiction. He met with Short to discuss the matter[29] and wrote a long letter to Stark explaining it fully. Almost casually, in a postscript, he advised: "You will note that I have issued orders to the Pacific Fleet to depth bomb all submarine contacts in the Oahu operating area." In another PS he expressed his fear that "we may become so much concerned with defensive roles that we may become unable to take the offensive. . . ."[30] This characteristic missive proved the last in the extensive Stark–Kimmel correspondence of 1941 before the attack.

On December 2 the Foreign Ministry dispatched to Kita an important espionage message:

> In view of the present situation, the presence in port of warships, airplane carriers, and cruisers is of utmost importance. Hereafter, to the utmost of your ability, let me know day by day. Wire me in each case whether or not there are any observation [possibly a garble for "obstruction"] balloons above Pearl Harbor or if there are any indications that they will be sent up. Also advice [*sic*] me whether or not the warships are provided with antimine nets.[31]

Here was another indication that Japanese interest centered on Kimmel's ships "in port" as well as on their operational movements. This message contained more tip-offs than the simple phrase "in port." Tokyo also wanted to know about barrage balloons and nets—protective measures against attack from above and below. These queries resulted from Genda's and Fuchida's proddings, for they had to be sure on these two points before sending their planes to Oahu. It would be difficult to find a clearer expression of intent. But, although intercepted at 0707 on December 2, this message was not mailed until December 11. It reached Washington on December 26 and was translated on the thirtieth.[32]

Kita received instructions from Togo on December 2 to burn all his codes except one each of Types O and L. He was also to burn all secret documents, taking precautions against "outside suspicion." The Foreign Ministry added, "Since the foregoing measures are in preparation for and in consideration of an emergency, keep this matter to your Consulate alone, and we hope that you will hereafter carry out your duties with calmness and care."[33]

Tokyo sent similar messages to all of Japan's diplomatic officials in "North America (including Manila), Canada, Panama, Cuba, the South Seas (including Timor), Singora, Chienmai," as well as to all officials in British and Dutch territory. The message to Washington also ordered Nomura: "Stop at once using one code machine unit and destroy it completely. . . . At the time and in the manner you deem most proper dispose of all files of messages coming or going and all other secret documents."[34]

For the Honolulu consulate this meant that it would no longer use the high-grade J-19 system; it would have to rely upon the PA-K2. Thus, in the remaining days before the attack, information shuttled between Tokyo and Honolulu in a code which would prove much simpler for Rochefort and his men to break. And these dispatches would include some of the most revealing in the entire chain. Unfortunately for the Americans, DIO received the copies from RCA just too late to break before the attack.

Japan had a sleight-of-hand trick up its sleeve. This was the dispatch of the liner *Tatuta Maru* from Yokohama on December 2, ostensibly bound for San Francisco via Honolulu. The ship's announced purpose was to evacuate from Japan such foreigners as desired to depart and to bring back Japanese from the United States. In essence, all would leave American soil except staff members of the diplomatic missions and a scattering of financial interests. From San Francisco the liner was supposed to call at the Mexican port of Manzanillo on December 19, at Balboa on December 27, thence proceed back home. The press in both Japan and the United States publicized the sailing extensively.[35]

The scheduled voyage was in reality a planned hoax. *Tatuta Maru* would reverse course for home after the first few days en route. Her captain did not know about the Pearl Harbor attack. He merely had instructions that on or about December 8 he would receive important orders and must act accordingly. Commander Toshikazu Ohmae of the Navy Ministry, who knew the entire story, feared that when the ship began to turn back, the American passengers might hijack it and force the captain at gunpoint to continue straight to the United States. So Ohmae asked the commanding officer of the Tokyo Communication Corps for twenty pistols "for a special mission." He packed them in a box and took them to the skipper of the liner, with instructions to open the box at 0000 hours on December 8.[36]

In Tokyo Yamamoto awaited his summons to the palace to receive the imperial rescript wishing him success in the forthcoming conflict. In the northern Pacific on December 2 Nagumo rode herd on his armada, here pulling a ship back into the formation, there dispatching a destroyer on guard. He made a few changes in course and at 0722 ordered: "While the air raid force heads south with high speed . . . the submarine division will guard the rear of the main force following it with appropriate distance. After the main force reverses its course take the ordered position."[37]

Ugaki had seldom been busier. He drafted a message for Yamamoto to send to the fleet before going to war and came up with: "The rise and fall of our Empire depends upon this war. Each of you will exert your best effort to accomplish your mission." He showed this to Watanabe, asking him to consult with the other staff officers. Later Watanabe returned and suggested a minor change which Ugaki promised to consider. Obviously Ugaki felt a genuine concern that Yamamoto's exhortation should find a worthy place in Japan's naval annals. He remembered the famous signal which Togo had given his fleet at the Battle of Tsushima: "On this one battle rests the fate of our nation. Let every man do his utmost."[38] He decided:

> The draft must be by no means inferior to this. Because, although any war decides the fate of a country, it seems to us who are confronting the present situation that the very war we are going to have will really decide the fate of our country. . . . Our posterity may not regard this as an unusual case, but I myself regard this war as tantamount to Japan's going to war with the whole world.

At 1700 a telegram from Ito authorized the opening of Imperial General Staff Naval Order No. 12. "By this we are ordered to appeal to arms effective 0000 on 8 December and thereafter. The China Area Fleet and each Naval Station was ordered to appeal to arms after the receipt of word of the first attack by the Combined Fleet. Thank goodness!" With this pious reflection, at 0730 Ugaki dispatched to the Combined Fleet one of the briefest but most historical messages in the annals of naval warfare: *"Niitaka yama nobore ichi-ni-rei-ya."* ("Climb Mount Niitaka, 1208.")[39] This signified that X-Day had been established at 0000 December 8 (Japan time). Nagumo's task force received this information at 2000;[40] at this hour the First Air Fleet was about 940 miles almost directly north of Midway, well beyond the arc of U.S. reconnaissance flights.

Although many Japanese naval officers believe the exact wording of this dispatch had no particular meaning, being a more or less random code selection, one cannot but note that Mount Niitaka in Formosa was the highest peak in the Japanese Empire. And "Climb Mount Niitaka" signified that Japan was about to scale the most formidable symbolic mountain in its history.

CHAPTER 55

"SURE

INDICATION

OF WAR"

The dawn of Wednesday, December 3, crept over the Inland Sea. "The sea area in which our Task Force is sailing is covered with a high pressure zone and little change is expected for the time being . . ." wrote Ugaki, whose thoughts never strayed far from the First Air Fleet in those days. "What a providential help it is!" Then he burst into exultant belligerence:

> Don't they know that, while President Roosevelt had conferences with the Secretaries of the Army and the Navy together with both Chiefs of the armed forces, and at the same time Nomura and Kurusu explained our Empire's present and future stands in their talks with Welles on the 2nd, that the biggest hand will be at their throat in four days to come? I pray to God nothing will happen until then. It entirely depends upon Providential help.[1]

In Tokyo Yamamoto donned his uniform just before his audience with the Emperor at 1045 to receive the signal honor of an imperial rescript. After Yamamoto replied in the stiff, stilted phraseology which Ugaki had prepared, the little scene, as stylized as a *No* play, ran its predictable course. The Emperor seemed "serene after fully realizing the inevitability of going to war."[2] Yamamoto bowed himself out of the imperial presence, clutching in his hand the order to lead his Combined Fleet into the war he dreaded.

The task force had crossed the international date line but kept clocks and records on Tokyo time. But it was on December 3 local dating that it reached a point approximately 1,000 miles south and slightly east of Amukta Passage. At 0400 a message came in from the Naval General Staff transmitting word from the Honolulu consulate: "Six battleships, seven heavy cruisers (of which two were not certain), four light cruisers, eighteen destroyers, four submarines, the Lexington, twenty-six other vessels were in Pearl Harbor on the afternoon of the 29th."[3] Yoshikawa was somewhat off the beam concerning the cruisers and destroyers. But except for evidently including *Utah* in his count of battleships, he correctly reported the capital ships.[4] And they were the ones of deepest interest to the task force.

Hara instructed his two carriers: "From 0300 on the 4th on, be ready for immediate use of 16 knots and also for 20 knots with 20 minutes notice." And at 1256 Nagumo established an air alert for the next day to run from fifteen minutes before sunrise to fifteen minutes after sunset.[5]

As the earth's spin brought the morning of December 3 to Hawaii, its citizens could open the Honolulu *Advertiser* to read an astounding editorial which declared that Japan "is the most vulnerable nation in the world to attack and blockade. She is without natural resources. Four years of war already have left deep scars. She has a navy, but no air arm to support it." In precisely four days Honolulu would have firsthand information about that allegedly nonexistent air arm.

As the Navy on Oahu began its workday, the need to recover call signs still hampered Rochefort's eavesdroppers on the Japanese Navy. "No information on submarines or Carriers" came through.[6]

The principal interest and activity centered on the Japanese burning of codes and classified material. Mayfield telephoned Shivers, asking if he could verify that the consulate was actually carrying this out. About two hours later his tap on the cook's telephone struck oil. Chatting with "a Japanese person in Honolulu," the cook let slip that "the Consul General was burning and destroying all his important papers."[7] Shivers gave this information to Mayfield and Bicknell.

Bicknell considered this intelligence, added to other bits he had "from proved reliable sources," an indication of "very serious intent and that something warlike by Japan was about to happen somewhere." He also informed his FBI colleague that he had learned from the Navy that the Japanese had been ordered to destroy codes in Washington and elsewhere.[8] This information came in the form of a message from OPNAV to CinCAF, CinCPAC, the Fourteenth and Sixteenth Naval Districts:

> Highly reliable information has been received that categoric and urgent instructions were sent yesterday to Japanese diplomatic and consular posts at Hongkong, Singapore, Batavia, Manila, Washington and London to destroy most of their codes and ciphers at once and to burn all other important confidential and secret documents.[9]

McCollum originated this dispatch with the approval of Wilkinson.[10] Turner knew about it, for it was the subject of discussion at high naval level. As Turner later testified:

> . . . we all considered that that was an exceedingly important piece of information to send to Admiral Kimmel and to Admiral Hart, because the destruction of codes in that manner and in those places in my mind and

experience is a definite and sure indication of war with the nations in whose capitals or other places those codes are destroyed. . . . It indicates war within 2 or 3 days.[11]

Ingersoll considered this message and the "war warning" of November 27 "the two most important messages that were sent out. . . ."[12] The Navy Department knew the Japanese "were on the move and it would only be a question of a very short time when they would land somewhere. There wasn't any question about it. It was only the exact spot and when."[13] He and his colleagues believed that war "was a matter of possibly a very few days or maybe hours . . . that the first aggressive Japanese move would include us and this was only to emphasize all of the previous dispatches that war with Japan was imminent. The inclusion of Washington in the dispatch is conclusive evidence that such was the case."[14] Moreover, he believed inclusion of the consulates "clinched it . . . and it was war and not a rupture of diplomatic negotiations or diplomatic relations."[15]

Stark agreed that this action of Japan's was "one of the most telling items of information we had received, and our despatch . . . one of the most important despatches we ever sent. We felt that war was just a matter of time."[16]

Miles inferred from this information that the Japanese either "planned to initiate a war . . . or feared war coming suddenly. . . ." However, he did not send a similar message to Short, as he had done on the occasion of the "war warning," because he assumed that "a Navy message to Hawaii would be promptly transmitted to the Army authorities there." But he did order Creswell, the Army attaché in Tokyo, to destroy certain codes because "early rupture of diplomatic relations with Japan has been indicated."[17]

Another message, which went out from OPNAV to Hart, Kimmel, and the Fourteenth and Sixteenth Naval Districts, contained an unexpected bombshell:

> Circular twenty four forty four from Tokyo one December ordered London, Hongkong, Singapore and Manila to destroy Purple machine. Batavia machine already sent to Tokyo. December second Washington also directed destroy Purple, all but one copy of other systems, and all secret documents. British Admiralty London today reports embassy London has complied.[18]

Astoundingly, it was Safford who prepared this message. He had telephoned McCollum earlier that day and asked, "Are you people in Naval Intelligence doing *anything* to get a warning out to the Pacific Fleet?"

McCollum replied, "*We* are doing everything *we* can to get the news out to the Fleet." Safford interpreted McCollum's emphasis upon the pronouns as a hint that he might be running into difficulties in putting through a message. So Safford grasped the nettle, although he knew he "was overstepping the bounds as established by approved war plans and joint agreement between Naval Communications and Naval Intelligence." He described the message as being "written in highly technical language and only one officer present at Pearl Harbor, the late Lieutenant H. M. Coleman, U.S.N., on CinCPac's staff, could have explained its significance."[19] In this Safford proved correct.

It is almost incredible that this message slipped out. Not only did it give the number of the Japanese circular, a clear indication that Washington was reading over Tokyo's shoulder, but it mentioned Purple by name. On Oahu a special security officer signed for this message and delivered it to Kimmel, Smith, McMorris, DeLany, Layton, and Curts. Immediately fastening upon the unfamiliar word, Kimmel sent for Layton to ask "what a purple machine was." Layton had no idea but promised to find out.[20] He queried Lieutenant Coleman, the Fleet security officer, who had recently come from Washington. Coleman explained that "it was an electrical coding machine . . . that was used in the passing of messages between Japanese consuls and diplomats and the home office. The word 'purple' was to designate the type of the machine as an improvement over the old one called the 'red.'" At the time this information had "no special significance" for Layton. He knew "the Japanese Navy had an electrical coding machine"; evidently this was a diplomatic one being destroyed.[21]

He duly informed Kimmel. This helped to give the admiral "the impression that intelligence from important intercepted Japanese messages was being furnished" to him. In the past he had requested "all vital information" and had received assurance that he would get it; he based his estimates of the situation upon the assumption that he was getting it[22]—but he was not.

Most strangely, Kimmel did not consider the Japanese code destruction "of any vital importance. . . ."[23] It seemed to tie in with the rest of his intelligence about Japanese moves in Southeast Asia. "Japan would naturally take precautions to prevent the compromise of her communication system in the event that her action in southeast Asia caused Britain and the United States to declare war, and take over her diplomatic residences."[24]

There is a certain logic in his attitude. From his own Combat Intelligence he had a clear picture of gigantic forces moving southward from Japan, obviously headed for Southeast Asia. The Japanese had never concealed the fact that they considered these regions a predestined part of the Greater East Asia Co-Prosperity Sphere. Add to this Kimmel's sincere belief that resumption of the conversations in Washington had eased Japanese–American relations, and one can just possibly see why he regarded the code destruction programs as merely one more piece of the mosaic.

Kimmel knew that codes were burned periodically, "and in a time of tension like this we receive a great many scary reports." He thought that the Navy Department "might very well have enlarged somewhat on what they believed it meant." An evaluation would certainly have been helpful, but Kimmel and Bloch seem to have been the only officers concerned who missed the significance. Kimmel admitted that he "didn't draw the proper answer" from it.[25] But Safford's message should have removed any doubt of the urgency of the information. Routine burning of coded material was one thing; destruction of cipher machines was quite another.

Bloch's reaction was that the Japanese "might be doing it and they might not be doing it," and he did not know "what they were burning and whether it was something that was really filled with meaning, or not."[26] Therefore, he took no increased security measures beyond directing the DIO to arrange with the Army and the FBI for a close watch on the Japanese consulate.[27] He did not pass the message to Short, nor did he know whether or not Kimmel had done so.[28]

Actually Kimmel had not because he presumed the general received the information also[29]—another instance of assumptions in Washington working at cross-purposes with assumptions on Oahu. Short met with Kimmel, Bloch, possibly others that day but testified later that no one mentioned these code destruction messages to him.[30] However, Bicknell knew from Navy sources about the Japanese code burning, although he said he did not recall seeing the actual message of December 3. He was sure that if he had, he would have pointed out to Short "that when an Embassy or legation starts destroying its codes it is a sign that we are coming to a very rapid end of peaceful relations."[31]

With the dispatch of these messages Turner decided against further warnings to the Pacific and Asiatic Fleets. "The fact that this was going out in this manner was considered all that was necessary to insure that the Command-ers-in-Chief and the Commandants of the Fourteenth and Sixteenth Naval Districts thoroughly understood the urgency of the situation." Furthermore, "The enemy codes at Washington and Manila were to be destroyed, which definitely indicates war against the United States." Once the two nations were at war or on the verge of it, belligerent acts could occur anywhere.[32]

Kita, too, had his instructions that day from the Foreign Ministry: "Strictly secret. Would like you to hold your list of code words (also those used in connection with radio broadcast) right up until last minute. When break comes burn immediately and wire us to that effect."[33]

Kita's consulate had more to do on December 3 than destroy classified material. Kuehn had produced the "simplified" version of his code, which Yoshikawa prepared for dispatch to Tokyo. It was still fearsomely complicated, and the message contained some tip-offs which were amazingly indiscreet, especially because the consulate now had to rely upon the PA-K2 code. In the first place, after the usual address to the foreign minister, it included the heading:

> To: Chief of Third Section, Naval General Staff
> From: Fujii

This directly tied the consulate to Japanese Naval Intelligence. Not that anyone ever doubted the connection, but this clinched the matter. After the message was translated, American counterintelligence agents spent quite a bit of time tracking down Fujiis, with variant spellings, to no avail. Actually "Ichiro Fujii" was Kuehn's Japanese code name. The message contained references to locations where Kuehn owned property and even his post office box.[34]

Several versions of this message reached Washington from various sources. On the morning of Saturday, December 6, one picked up at Fort Hunt, Virginia, reached the desk of Dorothy Edgers, a research analyst in Kramer's office. McCollum, who had been instrumental in employing her, considered

Mrs. Edgers "an extremely able translator" with "a magnificent Japanese and a magnificent English education." A quick glance sufficed to convince Mrs. Edgers that this particular message was the most interesting in her basket. With the approval of a co-worker, she began to translate.[35] Although officially work stopped at noon, Mrs. Edgers worked overtime, finishing about 1400. She left her translation with Chief Ship's Clerk Harold L. Bryant, whose duty it was "to edit messages and write them up." She believed Kramer knew she was working on the message but could not recall whether or not she personally showed it to him.[36]

Kramer was a bit vague about this incident. He claimed that he did not see the message on that particular afternoon and, if he had seen it, would certainly have considered it important. He did not work on it until December 8, 9, and 10, "clearing garbles."[37] As we shall see, on Saturday afternoon Kramer had urgent Magic intercepts on his mind.

Yet important and suggestive as this message was, it did not provide a direct clue to the attack, such as certain revisionists have asserted. The late Lieutenant Commander Charles C. Hiles, a retired naval officer and student of Pearl Harbor, claimed that it gave "advance warning of the Pearl Harbor attack" and that it testified to "the extreme care that the Japanese devoted to the attack plan and their flair for the unusual."[38] Actually it originated with a muddleheaded German and had nothing to do with the attack. It simply suggested to Japanese Naval Intelligence certain signals which, if approved, Kuehn would use to report on the U.S. Pacific Fleet after war had begun.

Revisionist historian Dr. Harry Elmer Barnes declared that this message "left nothing to guesswork." He interpreted certain numbers in its text as being specific dates in December 1941—which they were not. These happened to end with the word "6th." On this slender basis Barnes deduced that "Kita's complex system of signals to be passed back to the approaching task force was to end on the night of the 6th, clearly implying that the task force was expected to be arriving at Hawaii by the night of the 6th, organizing off Oahu and put in readiness for the attack the next morning."[39] Had Barnes and others— including Shivers of the FBI—who fell into this same misinterpretation consulted Kuehn's testimony, they would have found that the numbers which they took to be definte dates referred instead to a number of days.[40] The word "6th" meant "six days" and had nothing to do with the night of December 6, 1941.

The earth's turn brought the sun's rays to the east coast of the United States. Dr. E. Stanley Jones, a minister and friend of the President who had been working hard in his own way to avert war between the United States and Japan, slipped through the East Gate into the White House bearing a message from Hidenari Terasaki, second secretary at the Japanese Embassy.

A few days earlier Kurusu had asked Terasaki to "approach the President through an intermediary . . . and suggest that he send a cable directly to the Emperor appealing for peace." The special envoy confided that he had already asked the government for permission to do this and had been refused. So the cablegram "must be sent over Tojo's head. . . ." Terasaki immediately agreed, although he fully realized the danger to himself, his American wife, and his little daughter if his part should be discovered. He met with Dr. Jones and arranged that as much of the appeal as could be put in writing reach Roosevelt in the utmost secrecy. But Terasaki insisted that a vital part could never be written down, hence Jones's call at the White House.

Roosevelt told Jones that he had been thinking of sending such a cable to the Emperor but hesitated to do so because he did not want "to hurt the Japanese here at Washington by going over their heads to the Emperor." Jones reassured him that the suggestion came from the embassy but that Nomura's personnel could not make their recommendation a matter of record since they were bypassing the government. To this Roosevelt answered with evident relief, "Oh, then, that wipes my slate clean; I can send the cable."

He could send the message through Grew, who as ambassador had the right to audience. They could only hope that Japanese telegraphers would not hold up its delivery to Grew. As their meeting drew to a close, Jones cautioned Roosevelt that he must "never refer to Mr. Terasaki in connection with the message." The President answered sympathetically, "You tell that young Japanese he is a brave man. No one will ever learn of his part in this from me. His secret is safe."[41]

CHAPTER 56

"ANOTHER

STRAW

IN THE

WIND"

Overall, the picture from Hawaii pleased Ugaki. "It is not fair to attack one asleep," he wrote in his diary on December 4. "This is the way to achieve an easy victory. . . . Public opinion does not appear to be making much noise. This is keeping pace with the slippery negotiations taken on our side. . . ."

In pursuit of those "slippery negotiations," the liaison conference met at 1400 that day to discuss, among other items, the "Final Communication to the United States." The conferees decided that Togo should prepare the text and coordinate the time of delivery with the Supreme Command. As a result, the next day Togo discussed the problem with Ito and Lieutenant General Shin'ichi Tanaka, chief of the First Bureau of the Army General Staff. They agreed upon 1300 December 7, Washington time, as the moment for delivery of the note to Hull.[1]

Since 1300 in Washington would be 0730 in Honolulu and the attack was scheduled for 0800, obviously the diplomatic niceties would not be allowed to interfere with the strategic necessities. In evident preparation for delivery of the note Tokyo instructed its embassy in Washington to retain their key to the remaining code in its custody until the last minute.[2]

On this day Nagumo's task force hit rough seas. "Maximum rolling sometimes 45 degrees to one side, therefore, refueling was cancelled today," Chigusa observed in his diary on December 4. In such circumstances lookouts had to be doubly perceptive now that the task force had entered the most hazardous leg of the cruise. Lady Luck still held her hand on Nagumo's shoulder, but she was a capricious mistress.

"The news of the position of enemy ships in Pearl Harbor comes again and again," Chigusa wrote. This included information which Yoshikawa had gathered concerning the pattern of movement of the U.S. capital ships—departure Tuesday, return on Fridays, or leaving harbor on Friday to return on Saturday of the following week. This occasioned worry that "the U.S. vessels anchoring in the harbor on 5th (Friday) might leave the harbor, thereby making their locations unknown to us. Everyone prays God to have the U.S. Fleet now in the Harbor stay a little longer."[3]

At 0925 on December 3 Nagumo signaled his force, expressing clearly his anxiety and sense of lurking danger:

> 1. It has already been ordered to go to war on 8 December, but so critical has become the situation in the Far East that one can hardly predict war would not explode by that time. So far no new information on Hawaii area received and also no indications of our Task Force being detected. But since the enemy intention is naturally far beyond prediction, strict attention will be directed to meet any unexpected encounter with an enemy.
> 2. It is intended that this force will operate as scheduled even if war breaks out before 8 December. . . . [4]

At 1040 on December 4, local time—henceforth all times pertaining to the task force are local—Nagumo further instructed: "When an enemy or Third Power's warship or merchant ship is sighted, her communication equipment will be destroyed if and when necessary to protect secrecy of our intention, and, in case of an emergency, she will be sunk."[5] Nagumo's signal should dispose of any idea that if his task force were spotted, he would have abandoned Operation Hawaii, despite Kusaka's and Genda's remarks at Hitokappu Bay. At X−3 Day the moment to recall the First Air Fleet for any reason short of a sudden diplomatic victory in Washington had passed.

As Nagumo's armada battled the sea, official Washington rocked before a gale blowing from the McCormick newspaper chain. This had published the estimate for Victory Parade—the official nickname for the "General Staff strategic plan of national action in case of war in Europe."[6] As Stimson exploded in his diary, "Nothing more unpatriotic or damaging to our plans for defense could very well be conceived of." Both he and the President had press conferences lined up for the fifth, and Roosevelt wisely decided to leave this ugly development for Stimson to handle, as he did very competently.[7] All in all, a thoroughly nasty political confrontation between the government and the isolationists seemed to be in the making, but within two days it had sunk into oblivion along with some of Kimmel's ships.

Obviously Congress expected no pressing business to develop over Friday, Saturday, and Sunday because on December 4 the lawmakers adjourned for the long weekend. Whether the President was equally sanguine is questionable. Among the Magic dispatches he saw the one concerning the burning of Japanese codes. His naval aide, Captain John R. Beardall, directed his attention to it: "Mr. President, this is a very significant dispatch." Roosevelt read the document carefully, then asked, "When do you think it will happen?" By this, Beardall supposed he meant when "war is going to break out, when we are going to be attacked, or something." He answered, "Most any time."[8]

McCollum took a grim view of the situation. He prepared a message based on a condensed version of the information contained in his summary of December 1 and also stated that "we felt everything pointed to an immediate outbreak of hostilities between Japan and the United States." He took this to his chief, Captain W. A. Heard, and together they brought it to Wilkinson, who directed McCollum to take the dispatch to Turner for consideration.[9]

Turner read it and made a number of corrections, "striking out all except the information parts of it, more or less. . . ." Then he showed McCollum the messages of November 24 and 27 respectively. This was the first time McCollum had seen these, and the "war warning" especially made a deep impression on him. Turner asked McCollum if he did not think that was enough. The intelligence expert replied tactfully, "Well, good gosh, you put in the words 'war warning.' I do not know what could be plainer than that, but, nevertheless, I would like to see mine go too."

One can see Turner's beetle brows join over his nose as he growled back, "Well, if you want to send it, you either send it the way I corrected it, or take it back to Wilkinson and we will argue about it." So back to Wilkinson McCollum trotted and talked it over. Finally, Wilkinson said, "Leave it here with me for a while." As far as McCollum knew, that was the end of the matter. He never found out what, if anything, Wilkinson did with it, and it never went out.[9] However, Turner told a somewhat different story of this incident. He claimed that McCollum "tore up his proposed dispatch" on the spot, saying, "That is enough," in reference to the messages of November 24 and 27.[10]

McCollum's proposed message did not warn of a Japanese attack in Hawaiian waters, nor could it do so because its author had no idea of such an eventuality. We cannot know exactly what it contained or how McCollum phrased his warning. It was still in draft form; hence no copies were on file. No one can say just what effect such a dispatch would have had upon Kimmel and Short had it ever reached them. A cynic might observe, "On the basis of their past performance, we can assume that one more warning would have made no more impression than its predecessors." However, better one message too many than one too few. The very accumulation might have had an effect. Sometimes, too, a certain turn of phrase can ring an alarm bell. But when about this date Stark, Ingersoll, and Turner reviewed the information sent to the commanders thus far, they "were all of the opinion that everything we could do had been done to get them ready for war, and that we had sent them sufficient information and directives."[11]

Although balked in his effort to alert the naval Commander in Chief, McCollum did arrange for the destruction of certain codes and classified documents held in various Far Eastern naval stations, including the naval attaché's office in Tokyo. Up to this time the "exact intentions" of the Japanese naval forces moving out had been "presumed," but now they had more or less crystallized.[12] McCollum suggested that Safford draw up these messages to the

naval attachés because they involved codes—a communications responsibility
—"so there would be no misunderstanding about which ones they were to
destroy." Accordingly Safford drafted the dispatch and released it directly.[13]

The naval station at Guam received an alert which Noyes had rewritten
from a much stronger original which Safford prepared. The latter was not trying
to use the dispatch as a war warning. He just wanted to make sure that Guam
"stripped ship" before a Japanese raid captured all the codes and ciphers—for
which Safford was "officially responsible." When Safford took the message to
Ingersoll for release, the deputy CNO noted that Turner's initials were missing.
So he instructed Safford to show it to Turner. The chief of War Plans "glanced at
it, snorted, and added his initials."[14]

However disdainful he was at the time, Turner later testified: "The fact
that we considered it necessary to burn codes was considered by the Department as an additional advisory warning to the Commanders-in-Chief."[15] But the
Far Eastern stations were not in CinCPAC territory, so neither Kimmel nor
Bloch received information copies. They did, however, receive copies of the
Guam dispatch. But Guam was a long way from Hawaii, and no one had ever
seriously considered it defensible. Under the circumstances the destruction of
its codes and classified material could scarcely have appeared more than a
logical and necessary precaution.

Kimmel busily made plans for the reinforcement of Midway. He ordered
Task Force Twelve, consisting of *Lexington,* the heavy cruisers *Chicago,*
Astoria, and *Portland,* and five destroyers, to move by direct route until 400
miles 130 degrees from Midway, a point they should reach by late morning on
December 7. Thence they would fly off the Marine planes destined to reinforce
the Midway garrison. Then the task force would return and resume normal
operations.[16]

At this critical juncture Nomura faced the loss of one of his best
aides—Terasaki. He had asked Tokyo on December 3 to postpone his popular
assistant's departure until "the sailing on the 19th" because he was in the midst
of "intelligence work."[17] But his superiors came back curtly on the fifth: "Will
you please have Terasaki . . . and others leave by plane within the next couple
of days."[18]

When the U.S. Navy translated this on December 6, Kramer placed a
double asterisk beside the name of Terasaki and added a pencil note: "Terasaki,
Second Secretary, is head of Japanese espionage in Western Hemisphere. He
and his assistants are being sent to South America." It was "rather rare" for
Kramer to add such footnotes; however, he thought Terasaki's being transferred at this time "a very significant point."[19]

U.S. Naval Intelligence knew that Terasaki "was an especially trained
espionage man and he had a number of especially trained men with him. His
chief concern during the summer was in setting up an espionage establishment
in Latin America. The fact that he was directed to leave was a further straw in
the wind."[20] G-2 agreed wholeheartedly. In fact, Bratton used the same
expression as Kramer, calling Terasaki's transfer order "another straw in the

wind. It meant that the time was running out, that the crisis was approaching."[21]

Of course, Nomura and Kurusu had another reason for wanting to keep Terasaki on tap—that delicate matter of the President's telegram to the Emperor. As soon as Tokyo's message of December 5 arrived, Kurusu sent off an urgent dispatch:

> . . . I feel confident that you are fully aware of the importance of the intelligence set-up in view of the present conditions of the Japanese–U.S. negotiations. I would like very much to have Terasaki, who would be extremely difficult to suddenly replace because of certain circumstances, remain here until we are definitely enlightened as to the end of the negotiations. I beg of you as a personal favor to me to make an effort along these lines. I shall have him assume his post as soon as his work here is disposed of.[22]

Counselor Iguchi also wanted a reprieve. He asked the Foreign Ministry's chief of the Communications Service for approval "to delay for a while yet the destruction of one of the code machines" because the U.S.–Japanese talks were still continuing.[23] He could not imagine what a workout that machine would soon give him and his colleagues.

In the War Department's G-2 an acute sense of impending trouble preoccupied Bratton. On Tuesday, December 2, he had told the members of his office that "something was going to blow in the Far East soon" and that his section would "henceforth remain open on a 24-hour basis."[24] Now he conferred with McCollum, asking, among other things, about the status of Kimmel's Fleet. "Are you sure these people are properly alerted? Are they on the job? Have they been properly warned?" he persisted.

Fresh from his own tussle to arrange for just such a warning and from his reading of the messages which Turner had shown him, McCollum replied confidently, "Oh, yes, the fleet has gone . . . to sea." On the basis of this conversation, Bratton assumed that all major Fleet units were out of Pearl Harbor. He recalled this conversation as "several days before the attack" and could not place it more definitely, but the sequence of events makes it likely that it took place on December 5. He did not remember McCollum's exact words.[25]

On December 5 the "winds" blew through the War and Navy departments. Noyes called Turner to tell him that the first "weather message" had come in. "What did it say?" Turner asked.

"North wind clear," answered Noyes. This phraseology did not fit in with the "winds" code established on November 19,* so Turner said firmly, "Well, there is something wrong about that."

"I think so, too," Noyes agreed. His call may have been based upon a Federal Communications Commission (FCC) intercept at 2200 Greenwich

---

*See Chapter 44.

Mean Time (GMT) December 4: "Tokyo today north wind, slightly stronger; may become cloudy tonight; tomorrow slightly cloudy and fine weather."[26] Probably this was one of the weather reports Tokyo broadcast throughout the cruise for the benefit of Nagumo's task force.

At about 0900 Noyes informed Sadtler that the message which "implied a break in relations between Japan and Great Britain" had come in. Sadtler thought this "the most important message I ever received." But he never saw an actual dispatch, and so far as he knew, "no such execute message was received in the War Department." He hurried to Miles's office with Noyes's information.[27] Miles sent for Bratton and instructed Sadtler, "Tell Bratton what you have just told me." Sadtler informed him that "the word had been received from Admiral Noyes to the effect that diplomatic relations between Japan and Great Britain were in danger." When Bratton returned to his office, he talked with either McCollum or Kramer—he could not recall which one—but his Navy friend knew no more about a "winds" message than did Bratton. He promised to let Bratton know if one came in. Then the colonel tried SIS, equally without results.

Bratton was not too convinced of the urgency of this message, if any. To him, the "winds" code was simply a means for Tokyo to contact its overseas diplomats if the usual channels failed. Furthermore, to Bratton the real indication of imminent severance of diplomatic relations was the "direct order given to the Japanese Ambassador to start burning his codes. That was the purpose of the whole thing. That was it.

"Any winds execute message received after that would simply just be another straw in the wind confirming what we already knew."[28]

Of the key personnel in a position to see a "winds execute," only Safford maintained, "There was a Winds Message. It meant War—and we knew it meant War." He pointed out that whereas the Japanese Embassy in Washington still retained a code machine, the ambassador in London had destroyed his. So "the winds message was intended for London." He further claimed that it read "England and the United States."[29]

Ingersoll thought he saw such a message but could not recall whether this was before or after December 7.[30] Certain officers came to his office with "a piece of paper . . . which purported to be a message sent in the wind code." Ingersoll "paid no further attention to it because of the fact that it simply confirmed, if it was a genuine message, . . . what we had already sent out regarding the destruction of codes, which was absolutely positive."[31] He later stated that since his earlier testimony he had learned that this was not a valid "winds execute."[32]

Bratton had had "a number of false alarms on this thing" in late November and the first week in December. He had been "waked at all hours of the night on several occasions by the FCC who repeated what they had picked up, believing it to be a part of the implementing message."[33]

In the course of his frequent conversations with ONI, Bratton learned that Kimmel had received a warning about the much more significant code burning and that "it would be repeated to the Army." Therefore, Bratton "felt that it was not necessary for us to send the same message in a different code, because that jeopardized the security of the code."[34] But "everybody was making such a hullaballoo about this winds business" that Bratton thought, "to be on the safe side," he should alert Hawaii "to let them listen in and get it, just as soon, if not sooner than we did."[35]

This put Bratton in a quandary. G-2 had no authority to send out intelligence based upon Magic. Moreover, for security reasons the Navy objected to highly classified material going out over the Army net. Not the man to let technicalities divert him, Bratton prepared and secured Miles's consent to a message in "rather innocuous form" to Short's G-2: "Contact Commander Rochefort immediately thru Commandant Fourteen Naval District regarding broadcasts from Tokyo reference weather."

On the basis of information from McCollum, Bratton believed that Rochefort "knew everything that we did in Washington at that time." He thought that if he "could get Fielder to go and talk to this Naval officer under any pretext whatsoever," this would accomplish the purpose—"to bring them closer together for an exchange of intelligence." Bratton had no reason to doubt that Fielder and Rochefort cooperated, but they could not be too close to suit him. "I wanted them to sit in each other's laps, if necessary." He thought war was coming, and he wanted them alerted.[36]

Bratton could have saved his time and trouble. In the first place, Fielder could not recall having seen this message, and if he had done so, he probably would have turned it over to Bicknell, who knew Rochefort and worked closely with Mayfield; in the second place, "the way the radio was worded it would not have seemed urgent or particularly important."[37] Bicknell testified to seeing this dispatch on Fielder's desk and to checking with Rochefort, who was monitoring for the "winds execute" message.[38] Rochefort never received any such implementation.[39] So the whole incident fizzled out and Bratton's well-intentioned efforts failed signally to alert anyone on Oahu to anything.

Rochefort had another interesting development on his mind. In accordance with Sarnoff's arrangement, RCA turned over to Mayfield a batch of messages from the Japanese consulate. Most were in code and dated December 3 and 4. Mayfield immediately gave them to Rochefort's office for decrypting and translation. Rochefort put his best men on the task, making it "a matter of paramount importance." Within twelve hours they had translated all but two or three and, by dint of working twelve to sixteen hours daily, had broken the remainder on the night of December 10.[40] By the slender margin of a few days, the United States missed its best chance of a preattack warning on the basis of Kita's traffic with Tokyo.

In his testimony Kimmel put his finger on one key spot: The significance of these messages was not so much the consulate's collecting and reporting the information but "Tokyo's anxiety to have it . . . there is no reason why they would have wanted that information unless they were going to use it on the ships while they were in the harbor."[41]

Tokyo did indeed want that information badly, with the Nagumo force rapidly closing in on the target. That morning it reached another significant point in its long journey. At 1130, after refueling the entire task force, Supply Group Two, consisting of the tankers *Toho Maru, Toei Maru,* and *Nihon Maru* and their escort destroyer, *Arare,* headed northwest for its rendezvous point, where it would pick up the rest of the fleet on its return voyage. As they pulled away, their officers and crewmen lined up on deck and saluted the task force in farewell. *Toho Maru* signaled "Good-bye" and "We hope your brave mission will be honored with success." Everyone felt "deeply moved by this signal," Chigusa recorded.[42]

This cutting down of Nagumo's oil reserves reduced his margin of safety, so he had to think and act accordingly. It was one of the factors which kept him to a stringent schedule, with little or no room for evasive actions or unplanned high-speed runs in the event of unexpected encounters with the enemy.

In quest of current information, Yoshikawa took Mikami's taxi to the Pearl Harbor vicinity by way of the old road which ran through Fort Shafter and past Red Hill. Kita passed along Yoshikawa's findings to Tokyo at 1904 that day. In some respects his information was incorrect, but he hit almost on the nose in reporting that on December 5 "*Lexington* and five heavy cruisers departed."

Lexington did indeed clear port at 0810, accompanied by the heavy cruisers *Chicago, Portland,* and *Astoria* with escort destroyers. Two other heavy cruisers also went out that day—*Indianapolis* and *Minneapolis.*[43] Evidently Lady Luck, who up to this point had beamed affectionately upon the Japanese, had decided to give the Americans a break. All three of Kimmel's carriers were safe—*Saratoga* on the West Coast, *Enterprise* near Wake, and now *Lexington* steaming off toward Midway.

The *Lexington* task force sailed with Rear Admiral John H. Newton, commander, Cruisers, Scouting Force, flying his flag from *Chicago.* Unlike Halsey, Newton had no indication that his mission might run into a war. His orders being to reinforce Midway, then "return to operating area and resume normal operations," there appeared to him "no special significance attached to it other than reenforcement." He thought there might be some danger from submarines, so he kept to a speed of seventeen knots by day, zigzagged, and sent out scout flights to cover his advance. These were "normal operations in connection with training." Again unlike Halsey, he "gave no special orders regarding arming of planes or making preparations for war other than had been routine."[44]

Newton had seen none of the later warning messages. But he had no complaints. He thought that he probably had received as much information as he needed, and he was by no means ignorant of the general situation. He had good radar, which he kept "manned at night, usually for exercise in the early hours of evening . . . but made frequent sweeps to make sure that our area was clear." He believed that the majority of his fellow officers "felt that the submarine menace was our greatest menace."[45]

Newton's immediate superior, Vice Admiral Wilson Brown, commander,

Scouting Force, also left Pearl Harbor on December 5 with Task Force Three, headed for Johnston Island. This group consisted of *Indianapolis* and five old destroyers converted into minesweepers. Brown did not anticipate an air strike on the U.S. Pacific Fleet at Pearl Harbor. The subject came up once that autumn, at which time he expressed the opinion that "Japanese fliers were not capable of executing such a mission successfully, and that if they did, we should certainly be able to follow their planes back to their carriers and destroy the carriers so that it would be a very expensive experiment."

Brown based his assessment of Japan's airmen as "distinctly inferior to American fliers" on the testimony of "an American who had spent twenty years in Japan as head of the Singer Sewing Machine." Of course, this businessman had never had occasion to observe Japan's Army and Navy fliers at work; however, "civilian aviation in Japan was so badly kept up that the Singer Sewing Machine Company had issued instructions to all their employees forbidding them to ever ride in Japanese commercial aviation, and that the general belief was that the Army and the Navy were not very much better."[46] Nothing could be more indicative of the difficulties in obtaining reliable intelligence upon the Japanese military establishment—a three-star admiral basing his estimate of Japanese Army and Navy air power upon the observations of the head of a sewing machine firm who had firsthand experience only of Japan's civil aviation!

While the two U.S. task forces moved out, a lone B-24 bomber touched down at Hickam Field from the mainland with the mission of photographing Truk and Jaluit in accordance with Washington's instructions to Short of November 27.* If attacked, the crew should "use all means in their power for self-preservation." From the Mandates they were to proceed to the Philippines. The War Department instructed Short to ensure that both their aircraft and any following would be "fully equipped with gun ammunition upon departure from Honolulu."[47]

Kimmel recalled this Army mission. It was the only time during his term as CinCPAC that Washington authorized reconnaissance of the Mandates, which Kimmel itched to scout. He had orders from the Navy Department "not to go anywhere near them . . . because the Japs might find out that we were interested."[48]

Washington's gingerly approach to scouting the area was probably another case of bending over backward to avoid an untoward incident with Japan. Thus, this B-24 mission represented a reversal of policy. Washington had decided that the information the scout might obtain justified the risk. But this aspect of the matter apparently did not occur to either Kimmel or Short. The latter immediately noted that the B-24 had only three guns—one .30 caliber and two .50 caliber in the tail—and no ammunition. Hence it was manifestly not prepared for combat in its flight from the West Coast to Oahu.

---

*See Chapter 48, The situation was explained there.

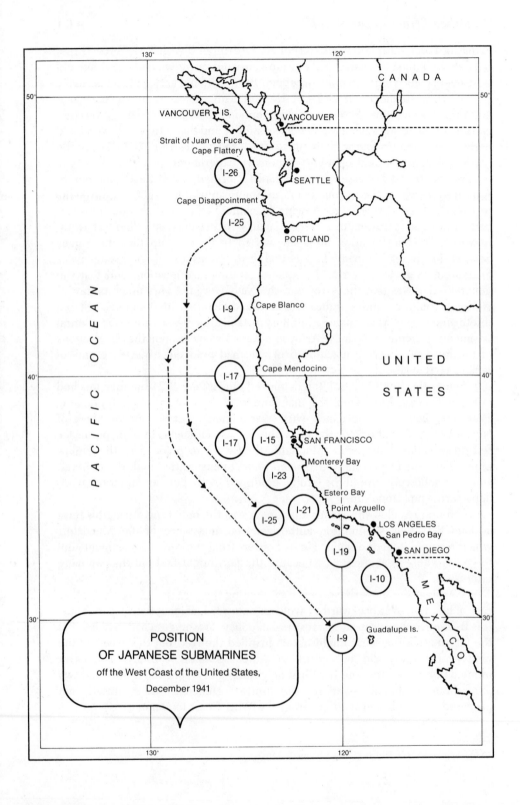

POSITION
OF JAPANESE SUBMARINES
off the West Coast of the United States,
December 1941

The arrival of this plane in such a condition, plus his instructions to arm it for the rest of its journey, indicated to Short "that the War Department considered Honolulu not the subject of a probably [*sic*] attack, and that flying from the mainland to Honolulu the hazard of carrying the extra weight of ammunition was greater than the possibility of being attacked by the Japanese."[49] This was not one of Short's brightest conclusions. Of course, no one in Washington anticipated hostile fighters engaging the bomber east of Hawaii. The arrival of such a reconnaissance aircraft at all, from whatever direction, should have sounded an alarm bell instead of a lullaby in Short's ears. At long last, the War Department was willing to risk annoying the Japanese in the Mandates to secure vital military information.

Near Wake Island, Halsey's task force received word from CinCUS on the morning of the fifth that an unidentified submarine had been reported in the operating area south of the Hawaiian Islands the previous night.[50] Some sharp-eyed American may well have spotted a Japanese submarine near the Islands. By December 3 the First, Second, and Third Submarine Fleets and the special attack units were within the 300-nautical-mile radius, and by the sixth they had completely encircled Hawaii. And certain submarines were considerably closer. On December 5, *I-71* was hiding in Alalakeiki Channel between Maui and Kahoolawe islands; *I-72* prowled in Kalohi Channel, which separates Molokai and Lanai, while *I-73* lurked in Kealaikahiki Channel, the deep waters between Maui, Kahoolawe, and Lanai. They were scouting the area of Lahaina Roads and Lanai Island.[51]

Somewhere between 1430 and 1530 on December 5 the destroyer *Selfridge* made an underwater contact but lost it. Another destroyer, *Ralph Talbot*, picked it up about five miles off Pearl Harbor, reported it as a submarine, and asked permission to depth-charge. But *Selfridge,* the squadron leader, refused, informing *Talbot* the intruder was a blackfish. Sniffed *Talbot's* skipper: "If this is a blackfish, it has a motorboat up its stern!"[52]

More than 3,000 miles away, Ugaki aboard *Nagato* knew that the clock would soon take over from the calendar to strike off first the hours, then the minutes. "So far operations appear to be going smoothly," he gloated. "Hawaii seems to be just like a rat in a trap. Let it have a dream of peace one more day."[53]

CHAPTER 57

"ON

A KEG

OF

DYNAMITE"

Saturday, December 6, 1941, was one of those days when the weather in Washington seemed colder than it actually was. A westerly wind whistled down Pennsylvania Avenue and rattled the bare branches of trees. Stimson had hoped to make a quick trip to his Long Island home to spend the night with his wife, Mabel. But "as the morning wore on, the news got worse and worse and the atmosphere indicated that something was going to happen." He conferred frequently with Marshall, Miles, and Gerow. Finally, he telephoned Mrs. Stimson that he could not leave the city, so she decided to return to the capital immediately.[1]

One subject of prime concern was a "triple priority and most urgent" telegram from Ambassador John G. Winant in London, received at 1040, conveying a report from the Admiralty. It told of "two parties seen off Cambodia Point, sailing slowly westward toward Kra 14 hours distant in time. First party 25 transports, 6 cruisers, 10 destroyers. Second party 10 transports, 2 cruisers, 10 destroyers."[2] No doubt these were Kondo's and Ozawa's units moving in on Malaya. OPNAV dispatched this to CinCPAC and to the commandants of the Fourteenth and Sixteenth Naval Districts.[3]

Obviously Japan's long-expected move south was under way in force. Stimson and Marshall discussed whether the thirteen B-17s scheduled to leave Hamilton Field in California might be attacked over the Pacific. After weighing the pros and cons, Marshall authorized them to leave that evening. He had sent Hap Arnold to the West Coast to make sure the planes had everything they required and would be able to take off.[4]

In Safford's unit, Op-20-G, tension was "at an all-time high." The "First Team" of experts sweated over the Japanese fleet JN-25 code. "The J-19 watch were batting their brains out trying to achieve solutions with minimum volume in any one key." Those on Purple duty "had to code and decode messages exchanged with London and Corregidor, plot direction-finder bearings of German submarines operating in the Atlantic, and 'process' messages coming in from other parts of the world, as well as handle Purple exchanges between Tokyo and Washington."

Safford had not left the office before 2200 for the past two weeks. Exhausted and fearing a breakdown, he planned to leave at 1630 for the rest of the weekend. At 1600 Lieutenant Commander George W. Linn, "the most experienced and most proficient cryptanalyst on the Purple watch list," was to come on duty.[5]

A special problem fretted Safford. Around closing time on the fifth the Registered Publications Section discovered that the Wake reinforcement had taken along many registered documents. Safford asked for an inventory. By working until after midnight, the section produced a list which almost raised Safford's scalp. "Every Pacific Fleet system that had been printed was 'up for grabs' by the Japanese." Safford prepared an "Urgent" warning to CinCPAC with information to Wake, which said in substance: "In view of imminence of war destroy all registered publications on Wake Island except this system and current editions of aircraft code and direction finder code."

Safford hurried the message to Captain Joseph R. Redman, the assistant director of Naval Communications, who approved it but hesitated to release it. Noyes was not available, being in conference. Several hours later Safford saw Noyes, who shouted, "What do you mean by using such language as that?" Safford answered, "Admiral, the war is just a matter of days, if not hours." Noyes retorted, "You may think there is going to be a war, but I think they are bluffing." Safford replied, "Well, Admiral, if all these publications on Wake are captured we will never be able to explain it." Noyes could not deny this, but he watered down the text, omitted Wake as an information addressee, and changed the precedence to "deferred."[6] The emasculated version for CinCPAC with information to CinCAF read:

> In view of the international situation and the exposed position of our outlying Pacific islands you may authorize the destruction by them of secret and confidential documents now or under later conditions of greater emergency. Means of communication to support our current operations and special intelligence should of course be maintained until the last moment.[7]

So another "war warning" bit the dust.

At 1100 Ferdinand L. Mayer called at the Japanese Embassy to see Kurusu. These friends of long standing had not met for eleven years but easily picked up the threads of their interrupted association. Soon Kurusu burst out, "Fred, we are in an awful mess." In order "to canalize the military effervescence," the civil government "had decided that the least harmful alternative was to allow the military to move into Indo-China since that neither directly threatened Siberia and the United States nor Singapore and Britain." Naturally Kurusu could not confide this to Hull. He begged Mayer to explain the situation to the secretary of state; he promised to do so. Despite his worry, Kurusu said that "the militarists were so much on the run and in such a difficult position that, unless hot-heads among them upset the applecart—which might be done at any time—he felt that the better element in Japan was really on its way to control the situation."[8]

In view of the realities of the moment, it is difficult to account for this pathetic flicker of optimism. At 2056 Tokyo time (0656 in Washington), Togo had advised Nomura that the ministry was sending a fourteen-part message in reply to the American proposals of November 26. "I imagine you will receive it tomorrow. However, I am not sure. The situation is extremely delicate, and when you receive it I want you to please keep it secret for the time being." He would tell Nomura later when to present it. "However, I want you in the meantime to put it in nicely drafted form and make every preparation to present it to the Americans just as soon as you receive instructions."[9] This dispatch became known as the pilot message. To complicate matters further, Tokyo added in another dispatch, "There is really no need to tell you this, but in the preparation of the aide memoire be absolutely sure not to use a typist or any other person.

"Be most extremely cautious in preserving secrecy."[10] Nomura was thus supposed to prepare an *aide-mémoire* suitable for presentation to Hull without a typist! Katsuzo Okumura, secretary of the embassy, was the only person among the officials who could type at all—"after a fashion."

At 0800 the anticipated fourteen-part message began to feed through the cables. Before midnight the first thirteen parts had been decoded, and Iguchi released the men, leaving a duty officer in charge.[11]

Japan, too, has its Pearl Harbor myths. Not the least is the placing of blame upon the embassy in Washington for so handling the fourteen-part message that it did not reach Hull's hands precisely at 1300 on December 7. In the first place, Tokyo set entirely too fine-cut a time schedule between dispatch and the hour for presentation. It made no provision for human error or mechanical snafus. In the second, the pilot message revealed no urgency beyond that inherent in the international situation—and that had been hanging fire for months. If Tokyo expected the lengthy document to be in a form suitable to present to the secretary of state by 1300 the next day, Togo should have set his deadline in the pilot message. But he established no such time limit.

Moreover, neither Nomura nor Kurusu nor, so far as we know, anyone else in the embassy staff knew that their hours of freedom were numbered. Nor did Tokyo transmit the message in numerical order. For example, Parts 4 and 9 went off simultaneously, as did 5 and 10, while 6 and 11 trailed after, and 7 and 8 did not leave until later still.[12] And the Foreign Ministry had specifically forbidden the embassy to use a typist. All in all, one is sorely tempted to believe that Tokyo was not averse to delay at the Washington end of the line.

The U.S. Navy Station 8 at Bainbridge Island, Washington, intercepted these messages within a few minutes of their dispatch and relayed them to Washington, D.C. The first of the batch to reach the Navy Department was

Part 4 at 1145, followed within four minutes by Parts 1, 2, and 3. Next, Army SIS received the pilot message at 1205, in the form of a teletype sheet from the Navy. A break of more than two hours ensued, until at 1451 Parts 5,6,7,8,11,12, and 13 arrived simultaneously.[13]

At this time many in the War and Navy departments kept hours which would have made a union organizer gibber. The personnel of G-2's Far Eastern Section concerned with Magic, as well as a division duty officer, were on duty all that afternoon and evening. Miles remained until late in the afternoon.[14] Bratton, too, was right on hand. He recalled seeing the pilot message around 1400, when it reached him from SIS. His office distributed it to Hull, Stimson, Marshall, Gerow, Miles, and within his own section. Bratton did not remember whether he or one of his assistants made the full rounds, but he did recall discussing it with Miles and Gerow. To them he remarked that a reply to the State Department note to Japan was on the way. He did not know just when; but it would be "in the near future," and he would keep them posted.[15]

There is some question about when the Navy circulated this message. Kramer, who made the distribution within the Navy and to the White House, believed on the basis of Navy records that he carried it around the next morning sometime after 1000 with "a number of other short messages."[16] However, Wilkinson recalled seeing it before he left his office.[17] Then, too, Beardall at the White House instructed Lieutenant Lester R. Schulz to remain on duty that afternoon because he, Beardall, had been informed that "there would be an important dispatch for delivery to the President." Because Beardall left the White House at 1730 or 1800,[18] we may safely assume that the government and the War and Navy departments knew that soon they would have a reply from Tokyo to Hull's note of November 26.

On the afternoon of the sixth Roosevelt decided upon the long-considered message to Hirohito. He sent his approved draft to Hull with a note in his forceful, nervous hand: "Shoot this to Grew. I think can go in gray code—saves time—I don't mind if it gets picked up."[19]

The President's letter was very much that of one gentleman to another, beginning with a reminder of "the long period of unbroken peace and friendship" during which Japan and the United States, "through the virtues of their peoples and the wisdom of their rulers," had prospered and "substantially helped humanity." After a brief review of the current situation he urged, "None of the peoples whom I have spoken of above [the Filipinos, East Indians, Malaysians, and Thais] can sit either indefinitely or permanently on a keg of dynamite." He assured Hirohito that the United States had no thought of "invading Indo-China if every Japanese soldier or sailor were to be withdrawn therefrom." He thought he could secure the same assurance from the other countries concerned, even China. And he concluded with solemn grace:

> I address myself to Your Majesty . . . so that Your Majesty may, as I am doing, give thought in this definite emergency to ways of dispelling the dark clouds. I am confident that both of us, for the sake of the peoples not only of

our own great countries but for the sake of humanity in neighboring
territories, have a sacred duty to restore traditional amity and prevent further
death and destruction in the world.[20]

For complicated reasons this letter did not reach Hirohito until after the
war had begun, and even if it had, one fears that attempting to stop Operation
Hawaii at this point would have been rather like commanding Niagara Falls to
flow uphill.

Kurusu heard the news that the letter had been sent while he was at the
home of F. Lammot Belin, former ambassador to Poland, with whom he and
Mayer were dining. Kurusu stated that "this was a very clever move on the part
of the Government"; the Emperor "could hardly say 'no,' nor could he say 'yes,'
and that this would cause many headaches in Tokyo and give much food for
thought."[21]

In Japan the clock had reached 0800 on December 7 (1800 December 6,
Washington time). Yamamoto's Main Body completed preparations to sortie at
fourteen knots on four hours' notice. Four hundred 40 cm. replacement rounds
had been loaded aboard each ship, and connections with shore cut off. "Now I
can see that all forces are going on their schedule silently and without a hitch,"
wrote Ugaki with satisfaction. "It is now certain that our first attack will be
successful."[22]

Nagumo's ships had reached a point about 600 miles north and slightly
west of Oahu. The skies were cloudy, with a wind of about twenty knots. At
0530 the task force received a message from Yamamoto conveying the gist of his
reply to the Emperor's rescript. Shortly thereafter he "respectfully related" the
rescript itself. Thereupon all officers and men "firmly determined to fulfill the
responsibility entrusted them by the Emperor, by destroying the U.S. Pacific
Fleet with utmost efforts."[23]

One hour later the entire armada engaged in its final refueling. These were
among the most sensitive moments of the whole voyage. The underway
refueling on this particular morning was a period when each ship commander
had to pay close attention to the business at hand and when the First Air Fleet
was the least combat-ready. Nagumo's ships lay within range of Martin's B-17s
and yet too far away from Pearl Harbor to launch an air strike against the U.S.
Pacific Fleet moored there. But the final refueling went off without difficulties.
The sea remained fairly calm, facilitating the operation considerably. By 0830
Supply Group One (*Kenyo Maru, Kyokuto Maru, Shinkoku Maru,* and *Kokuyo
Maru*), with the destroyer *Kanami* as escort, broke away and headed north-
ward.[24]

While the First Air Fleet moved closer to its target, Hawaii prepared for
another pleasant Saturday. But it was no holiday for the Fleet. The dawn air
patrol soared off south of Oahu toward its 300-mile limit.[25] At 0712 Lieutenant
Commander William P. Burford secured his destroyer *Monaghan* alongside
Dale at Buoy X-14 in Pearl Harbor. This placed his ship in a nest of four
destroyers north of the light cruiser *Detroit*. At 0830—precisely as the Nagumo

force finished refueling—he "assumed Ready Duty in readiness to get underway on an hour's notice. . . ." Burford had this duty aboard ship the entire day and had arranged for his wife, "Soldier," to pick him up at 0800 on Sunday.[26]

Commander Herald F. Stout, skipper of the destroyer-minelayer *Breese,* kept his crew on the jump almost all morning with emergency battle drills. A good 20 percent of his complement of almost 150 were raw recruits, and he wanted to bring them up to snuff as quickly as possible.[27]

The battleship *Oklahoma* hummed with activity as crewmen prepared for an inspection scheduled Monday. *"Okie"* was "a clean, happy ship, with a lot of spirit and rated high in athletics and gunnery. . . . The ship had a high quota of advancements among enlisted personnel," so she was a popular billet.[28]

At about 1000 Commander Cassin B. "Ted" Young edged his repair ship *Vestal* alongside *Arizona* in Battleship Row. Primarily designed for cruiser repairs, *Vestal* could do practically anything for any ship except build one from scratch. She had a peacetime complement of a little more than 600. Her short, well-built skipper came aboard *Arizona* to pay his respects to Rear Admiral Isaac Campbell Kidd, the First Battleship Division commander, and Captain Franklin Van Valkenburg, *Arizona's* skipper, while *Vestal's* Ensign B. C. Hesser conferred with the battleship's chief engineer about the work to be done.[29]

Aboard the light cruiser *St. Louis* Rear Admiral H. Fairfax Leary, who had succeeded Kimmel on February 1, 1941, as commander, Cruisers, Battle Force, held a critique of the maneuvers just completed. *St. Louis's* skipper, Captain George A. Rood, considered that the cruisers were "in a good state of readiness." Having refused an invitation to attend a picnic for members of the USNA class of 1911, Rood stayed aboard ship all day.[30]

One of the few people who expected trouble was Rear Admiral Milo F. Draemel, commanding Destroyers, Battle Fleet. Only one day back in port from Fleet exercises, he was highly sensitized to the possibility of some kind of Japanese move. He rather expected they might start something in the area that day, so he stayed aboard his flagship *Detroit* just in case.[31]

Kimmel arrived in his office bright and early. According to well-established routine, he listened to an intelligence report from Layton at 0815. At this time there had been "no positive indications of the location of the Japanese carriers with the exception of carrier division 3, which was associated with the Southern movement for some time."[32]

About 0800 that morning Layton had received the report from Washington concerning the Asiatic Fleet's sighting of Japanese movements. He told Kimmel that the situation was serious. Wishing a further opinion on the subject, Kimmel instructed Layton to take the wire to Pye and solicit his reaction. Accordingly Layton hurried to *California,* moored in Battleship Row on the eastern side of Ford Island, where he found Pye and his chief of staff, the efficient, imperturbable Captain Harold C. Train. After both officers had read the message, Pye asked Layton, "What do you think of the Japanese move south?"

"The problem is whether the Japanese will leave their flank open or whether they will take out the Philippines on their way south," the latter replied judiciously.

"Do you think they will leave their flank open?" questioned Pye.

"They never have," answered Layton simply.

After a little more deliberation Pye decided: "The Japanese will not go to war with the United States. We are too big, too powerful, and too strong." He turned to Train. "Harold, do you agree?"

"Emphatically!" Train rejoined.[33]

While this talk was under way, Kimmel reviewed dispatches and discussed the general situation with Smith, McMorris, and DeLany. They brought up to date his memorandum entitled "Steps to be Taken in Case of American-Japanese War Within the Next Twenty-four Hours." In no sense a detailed plan of action, this was a sort of checklist to remind the admiral of items necessary in such an event.[34]

The main subject on their minds, however, was whether or not to keep the remainder of the ships in Pearl Harbor. They agreed that as long as the U.S. Pacific Fleet remained in port, the Japanese would know exactly where to find it. On the other hand, with the carriers gone, would not the rest of the ships be even more vulnerable on the high seas without air cover? Moreover, the Army's "war warning" message had specifically directed Short not to alarm the civilian population. The sudden departure of the bulk of the Fleet at a weekend could scarcely fail to do so. The admiral therefore decided to keep his ships in harbor.[35]

Of course, other factors entered into Kimmel's decision. For one thing, he could not keep more vessels at sea without seriously depleting his fuel supply. He could not replenish more than one-eighth of the Fleet in any one twelve-hour period.[36]

Kimmel doubted the ability of the Japanese to carry out a carrier-borne air attack because, among other factors, of the short range of Yamamoto's flattops. While he believed the Japanese capable of sending submarines into the area, he considered the danger from undersea craft in Pearl Harbor itself "nil—nothing." For this reason the net at the entrance was not a true antisubmarine net; it was an antitorpedo net designed to prevent an enemy from sending a torpedo up the channel like a bowling ball barreling down an alley. Kimmel and his advisers knew of no type of submarine which could submerge completely in the shallow waters of the anchorage.[37]

Moreover, Kimmel had good reason to believe that in an emergency he could get his fleet to sea in short order. To facilitate a quick sortie, he had arranged that all ships entering turn so that they headed out before mooring. No longer did a massive capital ship block the passage for long periods while it turned.[38]

Above all, "the primary thing" Kimmel and his staff thought of constantly was "to be ready for offensive action." He fully expected that when and if war came, he would be "far from Pearl Harbor." Thus, many of his efforts centered on establishing "a permanent Army-Navy local defense coordination" to operate in his own and the Fleet's absence.[39] And as we have seen, he and his staff believed that Short's Hawaiian Department had gone on a full alert.

Sometime during Kimmel's conference Layton returned to give the admiral a brief summary of his discussion with Pye and Train. Either then or on another occasion during the morning he informed Kimmel that the Japanese consulate had been burning papers outdoors. This did not strike Kimmel as world-shaking news. The consulate had done so several times during the year. The first time it came to his attention Kimmel was "considerably concerned" and tried to find out all he could about it, but now it seemed more or less a routine matter.[40] At 1300 Kimmel's group went to lunch, then sat around the table, talking "for some time about the possibilities of this and that in connection with the situation." About 1400 or 1500 the admiral let them off the hook and repaired to his quarters.[41]

In the meantime, Layton joined a group of staff officers awaiting him for lunch. As he did so, the fleet readiness officer quipped, "Well, here comes Layton with his Saturday crisis!"

"What's up?" several officers inquired at once.

"There is a sighting message on the Japanese for the Gulf of Siam," explained Layton. "I have just delivered it to Pye and returned it to Kimmel."

"What do you think of the situation?" asked Curts.

Layton replied somberly, "The situation is extremely serious. I don't know about you gentlemen, but I expect to be in my office tomorrow."

"Come off it, Layton!" one of his friends scoffed. "You said that last Saturday!"

"The situation this week is far more serious than last Saturday," countered Layton grimly. With this dampening remark the group began lunch.[42]

The Hawaiian Department, too, held a staff meeting that morning at 0800, with Phillips presiding. Bicknell informed his colleagues that the Japanese consulate was burning its papers, an act which he considered "very significant, in view of the present situation."[43] There was no discussion about this, and those present did not appear to regard the development with any particular interest.[44]

Short later recalled with some difficulty that Fielder had given him this information but "apparently did not consider it a matter of importance." No one told him that "in that staff meeting there was a feeling that war was imminent on the part of at least one person there. . . ." Short admitted that Bicknell "was right in that respect." But he added, "He was a much less experienced man than the G-2,"[45] neither true nor relevant to the matter at hand. Certainly no one intimated that disaster was about to thunder down on them from the north. Perhaps Phillips spoke truly when he testified: "We felt secure against a raid, particularly with the Fleet here. . . ." The ships' presence "would increase the armament, the antiaircraft guns and all of that."[46]

Nor did Short and his staff realize that the Japanese consulate had been burning not merely papers—a routine procedure—but codes, a very different matter. Bloch that day advised OPNAV: "Believe local Consul has destroyed all but one system. . . ."[47] But Bloch, whose duty it was to keep the Army informed, did not so advise the Hawaiian Department.[48] Thus, each service had a piece of undisclosed information which could have been highly important to the other—that the Army was on antisabotage alert only and that the Japanese consulate had destroyed all but one code system.

At least one high-ranking Army officer thought that some concrete measures of self-help might be in order. Several days before, Major General Maxwell Murray, commanding the Twenty-fifth Infantry Division, had decided that the magazine area at Schofield, while adequate for peacetime, would be dangerously congested under combat conditions. He thought that "it would be just like a slaughter with the Japanese bombs dropping into that area while they were all drawing ammunition." So on this peaceful Saturday, company barracks and barrack rooms at Schofield bulged with "all infantry ammunition except high explosives. . . ." Although Murray knew he "violated the usual regulations," he counted the risk well taken to permit most of his men to have "as much as 30 rounds of ammunition in the belts; so they were ready for immediate action." Nevertheless, Murray thought only in terms of "a surprise raid" by "boat"—not of carriers or aerial bombs.[49]

At precisely 1130 Nagumo's task force swung due south to 180 degrees toward Hawaii and increased its speed to twenty knots. Ten minutes later *Akagi* broke out the historic "Z" flag which Togo had hoisted at Tsushima. Then she signaled the message from Yamamoto over which Ugaki had labored so conscientiously: "The rise and fall of the Empire depends upon this battle. Every man will do his duty." An American sailor would have noted instantly that this inspiring signal bore Combined Fleet Operational Order No. 13. But no such thought darkened the spirits of Nagumo's men, and they made the sea and sky ring with their cheers.[50]

Now more than ever, with the force bearing down on Oahu, the Japanese required last-minute information concerning conditions on the island. Early in the day Tokyo prodded the consulate: "Please wire immediately . . . the movements of the fleet subsequent to the fourth."[51] Yoshikawa had arisen around 0700. First he checked the weather, then breakfasted and carefully read the local papers. After a few routine chores at his office, at about 1000 he set off for Pearl Harbor to fulfill this newest request. Around 1300 he returned to the consulate to prepare a report for Kita. The consul skimmed a practiced eye over the contents of Yoshikawa's draft,[52] which read in part:

> At the present time there are no signs of barrage balloon equipment. In addition, it is difficult to imagine that they have actually any. However, even though they have made prepartions, because they must control the air over the water and land runways of the airports in the vicinity of Pearl Harbor, Hickam, Ford and Ewa, there are limits to the balloon defense of Pearl Harbor. I imagine that in all probability there is considerable opportunity left to take advantage for a surprise attack against these places.

      2. In my opinion the battleships do not have torpedo nets. The details are not known. I will report the results of my investigation.[53]

Kida nodded approval and directed Yoshikawa to encode and send the message immediately; he did.

It is certainly astonishing that Kita should have authorized that amazing reference to a surprise attack. There have been many small indications throughout our story that the consulate knew more than it ever cared to admit. Yoshikawa stated that in this case he "wanted to get the point across to Tokyo that if Japan attacked at that time, the chances for success would be good." He assured us that Kita agreed and, further, that Okuda may have read the dispatch before it went off; Okuda did not recall whether he had done so.[54] Probably he had not, for one can scarcely picture the shrewd vice consul permitting such an incendiary sentence to go to Tokyo, especially since the consulate now used only the PA-K2 code.

"If we had gotten that message on the 6th, I assure you the whole picture would have been different," said Bratton.[55] But a question has arisen on this point because a Navy translation by one Joseph Finnegan does not contain Yoshikawa's key words. Asked later which version he thought right, Finnegan replied, "Without hesitation, I believe the Army translation is correct." Although a Japanese-language officer, Finnegan had been away from the work for a little more than three years when, on December 9 or 10, Kimmel ordered him to Rochefort's unit.[56] And of course, Yoshikawa stated that he included the telltale sentence.

Had circumstances permitted immediate action on Yoshikawa's dispatch, there would have been time to warn Hawaii, time for Short to move to full alert, time for Kimmel to deploy for battle. But the Army could not translate this intercept until December 8. PA-K2 was not a top priority code and no snap to solve, being a checkerboard system with complicated spelling tables involving a shuttle transposition.[57] And the cryptanalysts could not know until they dug well into it that Yoshikawa's message held anything out of the ordinary.

CHAPTER 58

"THIS

MEANS

WAR"

As the cold dusk of December 6 closed over Washington, the men of Safford's shop were duly thankful that Togo's long opus arrived in English, so they did not have to translate it or worry about phraseology, but correcting a mistake in the key took some time. At around 1630 Safford said, "There is nothing I can do but get in your way and make you nervous. I am going home." By about 1900 they had finished decoding the thirteen parts so far received. Then they spent some two hours making the requisite copies, with help from their Army opposites.[1]

Kramer telephoned Wilkinson at about 2100 and received authority to make the necessary rounds. He also called the usual recipients to see if they would be in. He had no luck in raising Stark, who had gone to the National Theater to see *The Student Prince*. After finishing his calls, Kramer telephoned his wife, Mary, to commandeer her as chauffeur.[2]

When he scrambled into the car, his wife sensed "an air of tenseness about him."[3] They first stopped at the White House office building, where Kramer left Roosevelt's copy in the customary locked pouch with Lieutenant Schulz in the latter's cubbyhole in the mailroom.[4] Schulz carried the locked pouch to the main White House. "Someone from the usher's office" accompanied him to the President's study and announced him. He saw Roosevelt seated at his desk, with Harry Hopkins "pacing back and forth slowly, not more than 10 feet away."

Roosevelt's big hand grasped the sheaf of about fifteen typewritten pages, and he read carefully for about ten minutes. Then he passed the material to Hopkins, who also read it and handed it back, whereupon the President turned to him and said, "This means war." Schulz was "not sure of the exact words" but had no doubt about the meaning.

Hopkins agreed, and for about five minutes they discussed the deployment of the Japanese forces. Hopkins volunteered "that since war was undoubtedly going to come at the convenience of the Japanese, it was too bad that we could not strike the first blow and prevent any sort of surprise." Roosevelt nodded and answered, so far as Schulz could recall, "No, we can't do that. We are a democracy and a peaceful people." Then the President "raised his voice," and Schulz remembered his words definitely: "But we have a good record." No one mentioned Pearl Harbor, and nothing in the discussion indicated that "tomorrow was necessarily the day."

Roosevelt thought he should talk with Stark but, learning that he was at the theater, decided to wait until later. If the President paged the admiral or if Stark "left suddenly . . . undue alarm might be caused." He gave the papers back to Schulz, who left the study.[5]

The President appears to have reached Stark at his home by phone about 2330. The admiral later assumed that Roosevelt mentioned the Japanese note, but if so, it did not impress Stark as "anything that required action." Stark's attitude and his failure to recall the conversation suggest that Roosevelt had said nothing to indicate that war had drawn nearer. Indeed, Stark testified that they had already concluded that Japan was "likely to attack at any time in any direction," so the message was "a confirmation, if anything."[6]

Meanwhile, the Kramers proceeded from the White House to the Hotel Wardman Park to deliver the thirteen-part message to Knox. Kramer was rather silent, but his wife kept up a soothing murmur "about the children" and her hope that next day he "could sleep round the clock."[7] Knox took some twenty minutes to read the document. Because his wife and a friend were present, Knox, who was "very security-minded," had nothing to say about the contents. However, he instructed Kramer to be at 1000 the next morning at the State Department, where he—and presumably Stimson—would meet with Hull.[8]

It was now a few minutes before 2200, and Mrs. Kramer drove her husband to Wilkinson's home in Arlington. She had waited a few minutes when Wilkinson came out and brought her into the drawing room. He was having a small dinner party, his guests including Miles, Beardall, and two French officers. Feeling somewhat ludicrous in her old sweater and skirt, Mrs. Kramer sipped coffee and drinks with the others, while Wilkinson, Miles, Beardall, and Kramer went into the library.[9] There they read the message but made only general comments "to the effect that it certainly looked as though the Japanese were terminating negotiations."[10]

Whether Ingersoll and Turner received the thirteen parts that night is unclear. Both recalled reading the dispatch late on December 6, but Kramer declared that he did not call that night upon either of these admirals and knew of no other possible delivery. The clocks had reached half past midnight when

Kramer clambered back into his car and his wife drove him to his office, where he returned the copies in his possession to the safe. Upon learning from the watch officer that the anticipated fourteenth part had not come in, he called it a day, and the Kramers drove home.[11]

The Army picture is more difficult to piece together because of conflicting testimony. Bratton's evidence before the joint congressional committee seems to place events in context. He remembered the thirteen parts as ready between 2100 and 2200. He called SIS and found there was "very little likelihood" of the fourteenth installment's reaching them that night.

Bratton locked the material in a pouch and delivered it personally to the State Department duty officer sometime after 2200 with instructions that this was "a highly important message as far as the Secretary of State was concerned" and should be sent to his quarters. The duty officer assured him that he would do so, and after securing a receipt, Bratton returned to his quarters at around 2300. He called Miles's home, leaving a request that his chief return the call. Coincidentally, Miles phoned Bratton from Wilkinson's home. Having determined that the thirteen parts "had little military significance," he wanted only to assure himself that the full reply would be disseminated in the morning and that both officers would be in their offices at that time.

In Bratton's view, so far the message was not a declaration of war, nor was it a severance of diplomatic relations. And the fourteenth part "might have contained another proposal from the Japanese Government."[12] Thus, the Army took the sensible attitude that the message was primarily State's business and would keep overnight without spoiling. So the Marshalls enjoyed an undisturbed evening at their home in Arlington, where the Chief of Staff and his wife were "leading a rather monastic life."[13]

About the time Kramer completed his deliveries, Hap Arnold addressed the crews of the Thirty-eighth and Eighty-eighth Reconnaissance Squadrons, about to fly in B-17s to Clark Field in the Philippines, with their first stop at Hickam Field. "War is imminent," he told them. "You may run into a war during your flight."

"If we are going into a war, why don't we have machine guns?" asked Major Truman H. Landon.[14] A good question! But these bombers would fly unarmed because the Air Force was "trying to get every gallon of gas they could in the plane and they did not anticipate fighting . . . on that long hop from California to Hawaii."[15] Even so, the bombers would be perilously low on gas by the time they reached Hickam Field. Not only did the planes lack ammunition, but their machine guns were in Cosmoline and had not been boresighted. A skeleton crew of pilot, copilot, navigator, engineer, and radio operator manned each bomber, so they could scarcely have operated the guns even if they had been loaded and ready to shoot.[16]

Grew received Roosevelt's message for the Emperor at 2230 December 7, Japan time. Inasmuch as the dispatch had left Washington around 2100 (Eastern Standard Time) on the sixth and it showed that the Japanese post office had received it at noon Tokyo time on the seventh, this meant that the Japanese had held it up ten and a half hours[17]—another incident revealing that Japanese officialdom was not exactly eager for prompt communication with Washington on this particular day.

It so happened that on November 29 Lieutenant Colonel Morio Tomura of the Communications Section of the Army General Staff had asked Tateki Shirao, chief of the Censorship Office of the Ministry of Communications, to delay by five hours the delivery of all incoming and outgoing cables except those of the Japanese government. Then, on December 6, the holdup schedule was changed to five hours one day, ten the next. Thus, December 7 was a ten-hour day, which is why the Japanese sat on the President's message to the Emperor such a long time.[18]

Granted that high-handedness at relatively low levels characterized Japanese official life in this period, it is still quite incredible that these two individuals—a lieutenant colonel and a civilian—should have dared take such drastic action without at least tacit approval from above.

Grew took the decoded message to Togo at about a quarter past midnight and asked for an audience with the Emperor so that he might present it in person since he "did not want any doubt as to getting it in his hands." After some quibbling Togo agreed to present Grew's request to Hirohito. With that Grew left the Foreign Ministry. It was then about 0030 on December 8, Japan time (1030 December 7 in Washington, 0500 in Hawaii)—less than three hours before Fuchida's first wave would strike.[19]

At approximately 1400 on Saturday the FBI's Japanese translator in Honolulu completed the English transcript of a lengthy telephone conversation which had taken place on December 3 between a Japanese newspaperman in Tokyo and Mrs. Motokazu Mori, wife of a Honolulu dentist. The initiator of the call in Japan remarked, "I received your telegram and was able to grasp the essential points. I would like to have your impressions on the conditions you are observing at present. Are airplanes flying daily?"

"Yes," answered Mrs. Mori, "lots of them fly around." After some chitchat about the number of sailors in the Islands—not so many as at the beginning of the year—and Japanese-American relations on the Island—they were "getting along harmoniously"—the inquirer turned to the subject of the U.S. Pacific Fleet. But Mrs. Mori had little to say in that regard because "we try to avoid talking about such matters. . . ." Next, the voice from Tokyo asked, "What kind of flowers are in bloom in Hawaii at present?"

"Presently, the flowers in bloom are fewest out of the whole year. However, the hibiscus and the poinsettia are in bloom now," replied Mrs. Mori.[20]

The closer Shivers examined the transcript, the stronger aroma of fish it wafted to his experienced nostrils.[21] Dr. Mori was already on the FBI's list of suspects and had been ever since such a list existed.[22] Convinced that the conversation had some "military significance," Shivers telephoned Mayfield and Bicknell. This time he stood on firm legal ground because the attorney general had authorized him to tap overseas telephones.[23]

Mayfield was not in his office, so Shivers gave the gist of the message to Lieutenant Denzel Carr, a Japanese expert in ONI, asking him to get in touch with Mayfield. When Mayfield received the word, "he was sure there was some hidden message which would be of value if they could only decode it, but that there was nothing in the message in line with previous information indicating Japanese movements."[24] At about 1800 Mayfield telephoned Layton to stop by his office the next morning. That was the last Layton heard on the subject until the Navy Court of Inquiry in 1944.[25]

Shivers reached Bicknell at his home at about 1700 and told him that "he had something of high importance" which he should see immediately. Bicknell rushed downtown and within twenty minutes was poring over the transcript with his colleague. Shivers remarked that "this thing looked very significant to him, that something was going to happen."[26] Bicknell's "G-2 sense" told him "there was something very significant about this."[27] He immediately telephoned Fielder that he had some "extremely important" information that should be given immediately to the department commander. Fielder replied that he and Short were going out to dinner but for Bicknell "to be at Fort Shafter within the next ten minutes" and they would wait for him.[28]

Once more Bicknell jumped into his car and at about 1900 pulled up at Fielder's residence. The G-2 looked the document over, then said that they had better see Short, who lived next door. The three men sat down on Short's porch and mulled over the transcript. They considered it "very suspicious, very fishy," but "couldn't make heads nor [sic] tails of it."[29]

Short pointed out "that the message was a very true picture of what was going on in Hawaii at that time," That, Bicknell thought to himself, "was just the trouble with it; it was too accurate a picture." He had a frustrating feeling that the very things he "considered most suspicious seemed to be everyday affairs in their minds."[30] By this time the men had talked a good forty-five minutes and gotten nowhere. Short and Fielder gave Bicknell the impression that he was "rather perhaps too 'intelligence conscious,' and that this message was quite, quite in order, that it did describe the situation in Hawaii as it was, and that possibly there was nothing very much to get excited about. . . ."[31]

Disgruntled, Bicknell took back the document and examined it for about an hour at his office. Then he locked it in the safe and returned home.[32] Short and Fielder, already an hour late for their dinner engagement, joined their wives, who had been waiting for them in the car. Bicknell might have felt better had he known that his superiors discussed the Mori call all the way to Schofield Barracks and all the way home again. But they still "were unable to attach any military significance to it."[33]

No direct evidence has come to light thus far to indicate whether or not the Mori call actually contained coded information of military significance. However, Japanese Naval Intelligence had checked the international telephone system between Tokyo and Honolulu consistently since the September war games. It believed that this service would be discontinued if the United States established a state of emergency in Honolulu. So it is possible that the conversation which so upset Shivers and Bicknell was one of these trial balloons. Ironically, Ogawa tells us that such a check was made around 1500 on December 7, Tokyo time. This would be roughly 1900 December 6 in Oahu—just about the time Bicknell drove up to Fielder's home. Ogawa personally advised Nagano and Ito within the hour that everything was normal in Honolulu. "Both Nagano and Ito were pleased and greatly relieved," said Ogawa. He understood that a message would go to Nagumo's task force on the basis of this information.[34]

Tachibana also stated that Tokyo utilized the radiotelephone system between Honolulu and Tokyo:

> The conversations through this channel were exchanged completely in a commercial business form; key word conversations were only seldom used. By use of this channel we learned on 5 December the condition of U.S. warships in Pearl Harbor and on 7 December that Hawaii was quiet as usual with usual shore leave of sailors and no blackout at all.[35]

A message from Tomioka's Operation Section, which the task force received at 0150 Sunday, December 7, contained, among other items of interest, these words: "Telephone contacts made with Japanese and civilian indicate Oahu Island was very calm with no blackout."[36] Mrs. Mori had stressed this calm in her conversation, and of course, the message does tie in with the testimony of Ogawa and Tachibana.

About 1500 Yoshikawa set out for his last check on the Fleet. His taxi took him to Aiea, then swung off the highway to the Pearl City pier. Then he returned to his office to prepare his report. Once more Kita looked over his draft and pronounced it good. After processing it, Yoshikawa went to the commercial telegraph office to dispatch this, his last message,[37] at 1801. Its final sentence read: "It appears that no air reconnaissance is being conducted by the fleet air arm."[38]

As each of Kita's last messages reached the Foreign Office in Tokyo, they were passed to the Naval General Staff, where they wound up a few hours apart in Tomioka's Operations Section. He and his associates studied them briefly but carefully. The news from Hawaii was good: no barrage balloons over Pearl Harbor; no torpedo nets around the ships; no long-range air patrol; the bulk of the Fleet snugly in the great base. Of course, the carriers and a number of heavy cruisers had slipped through Japan's fingers and might spell trouble, but one could not expect to have everything one's own way. Tomioka set his encoders to work on each dispatch and sent off the first one at 1700 Japanese time, followed by the second an hour later. "As we sent these final, crucial messages," Tomioka recalled, "I prayed fervently to our ancestral gods that all would go well."[39]

The task force received a disappointing report at 1903 from the submarine *I-72*: "The enemy is not in Lahaina anchorage."[40] With that message went almost all of Genda and Fuchida's hopes of sinking the U.S. Pacific Fleet in Lahaina's depths. Although the last-minute check by aerial reconnaissance remained scheduled for the next morning, Genda decided to forget about Lahaina. "I made up my mind to strike nowhere but Pearl Harbor and concentrated all my attention on it," he recalled. He knew, too, that the time was rapidly approaching for the five midget submarines to enter Pearl Harbor. "The account of this most risking enterprise of the midget subs gave an enormous impression to the crews of the planes, encouraging them to the fullest extent."[41]

Genda napped in the Operations Room between 2000 and 2200. Then he arose and went on deck. There mechanics were tuning up the first-wave aircraft. Genda paused, listening to the engines roar and watching blue-white flames shooting from the exhaust pipes. His eyes still on the planes, he mounted the ladder to the bridge. Suddenly he "felt very refreshed, as if all the uncertainties were cleared away." Whatever lay ahead was in the laps of the gods. Worries about possible mistakes and doubts of success vanished like mist at dawn. In that transcendent moment he experienced "a sort of self-renunciation." His mind seemed "as bright and clean as a stainless mirror." He was ready for whatever might come, and he was not afraid.[42]

Neither was Fuchida, who paused at last to shed his flying suit and went to the wardroom for a final chat with Murata, Itaya, and a number of his fellow fliers. He advised them to retire early and get a good night's rest. "Hurry to bed," he charged them with a smile as he left the room. He himself retired at about 2200. "I slept soundly," he recalled. "I had set up the whole machinery of attack, and it was ready to go. There was no use to worry now."[43]

It would not be long before the mother submarines began to release their midgets. Aboard *I-24* Sakamaki peered through the periscope at the green and red lights blinking from Pearl Harbor and turned to confer with the submarine's skipper, Lieutenant Commander Hiroshi Hanabusa. His midget's one gyro-compass had been out of order and defied all efforts to fix it. "What are you going to do?" asked Hanabusa anxiously.

Sakamaki knew that it would be practically impossible to navigate his tiny craft thus handicapped, but he was much too excited and determined to think of pulling out. So was his crewman, Kiyoshi Inagaki. "We will go," Sakamaki declared firmly, whereupon Hanabusa, fired by the young man's enthusiasm, shouted with him, "On to Pearl Harbor!"[44]

After dinner that evening Bicknell still felt "pretty well frustrated." A telephone call around 2000 from Lieutenant Colonel Clay Hoppaugh, the signal officer of the Hawaiian Air Force, did nothing to improve his temper. "We have a flight of B-17s coming in from the mainland," Hoppaugh announced. "Will you put Station KGMB on the air all night so planes can home in on the signal?"

Bicknell exploded, "Why don't you have KGMB on the air every night and not just on the night we have airplanes flying? You folks have the money to do it."

"We'll talk that over some other time," Hoppaugh replied. For the time being, they had not much choice. So Bicknell called KGMB and asked it to stay on all night. The station did not know why, but the Air Force paid when it asked for this service. Actually it was a matter of common knowledge that whenever KGMB played music all night, aircraft flew in the next morning.[45]

Bloch spent his evening at home. He had played golf in the afternoon, read for a while, and then, very tired, went to bed about 2030.[46] Bellinger had an even less eventful evening. He had been laid up with the flu since Tuesday, and Sunday would be his first day up.[47]

When Young and Hesser left their morning conference aboard *Arizona*, they secured *Vestal* for the day and granted the crew 50 percent liberty. That night Young dined in his cabin, while Hesser joined the other officers in the wardroom. They talked about the current international situation and danger of war with Japan. Ensign Fred Hall, the assistant communications officer, prophesied that the Japanese would hit Pearl Harbor. "They will attack right here," he declared. Hall did not say when and why the Japanese would attack, and nobody asked him. It was just one of those statements that pop up in a friendly bull session. But Hesser never forgot it. And since Hall happened to be officer of the deck for the 0400–0800 watch Sunday morning, no doubt he never forgot it either.[48]

Short, Fielder, Phillips, and Major General Durward S. Wilson of the Twenty-fourth Infantry Division were among those who attended "Ann Etzler's Cabaret"—an annual charity dinner-dance which "one of the very talented young ladies had worked up" at the Schofield Barracks Officers' Club. Before going to the club, a large group, including General and Mrs. Short, gathered at the home of Lieutenant Colonel and Mrs. Emil Leard for cocktails. After the party at the club some of the guests returned to the Leard residence for nightcaps. But the Shorts left the club with the Fielders somewhere between 2230 and 2300 and went straight home.[49] They drove past Pearl Harbor, a magnificent sight with all its lights blazing. Short remarked to his G-2, "What a target that would make!"[50] He had no idea that his words would come true the next morning. He was looking forward to his usual fortnightly golf game with Kimmel.

Some of the Air Force officers, including Martin, attended a dinner party at the Hickam Field Officers' Club.[51] Mollison was at a similar function in the home of Lieutenant Colonel William C. "Cush" Farnum. While there, he received notice, at about 2230, of a long-distance call from San Francisco, saying that twelve B-17s would arrive in Oahu from the mainland at 0800 the next morning. Mollison called the duty officer to give him the estimated time of arrival. Because Mollison wanted to be sure he would be at the tower when they came in, he left the party immediately and went straight home.[52]

Colonel Robert H. Dunlop, Short's adjutant general, heard about the incoming B-17s when he dropped in on the officer of the day on his way to a movie with his wife and son. Dunlop tried to reach Phillips but could not until about 2300, when Phillips had returned from the party at Schofield. After Dunlop gave him the word, Phillips asked, "Bob, is there anything else you want to tell me?" Dunlop replied, "Tige, there isn't another thing." Everything was so normal, so calm. As Dunlop said, "There was absolutely no indication that anything was going to break the next day."[53]

Kimmel, Pye, and Draemel were among those who attended a small dinner party of about a dozen close friends given by Admiral and Mrs. Leary at the Halekulani Hotel. Kimmel mentioned to Draemel that he had an invitation to drop by the Japanese consulate—without an aide—to drink champagne. Distrusting the Japanese, Draemel urged the admiral not to go, and Kimmel assured him that he would not.[54] Kimmel was to be spared little enough in the days to come; at least the fates did not deal him this particular joker—sipping champagne with Kita on the eve of "Bloody Sunday."

This little gathering of a few old friends was much more to his liking, and he enjoyed himself in his rather stately fashion, chatting and nursing his usual single drink. True to form, he left early. At about 2130 he took his leave, reached his quarters around 2200, and turned in immediately.[55]

At midnight dancing stopped at the Royal Hawaiian Hotel, and the orchestra struck up "The Star-Spangled Banner." As Layton snapped to attention beside his wife, a wild urge seized him to shout, "Wake up, America!" and to grab his big, easygoing country by the scuff of the neck and shake it out of its enchanted sleep.[56]

CHAPTER 59

"THE JAPS

ARE

PLANNING

SOME

DEVILTRY"

N agumo's task force bore down on Oahu at twenty-four knots, the light cruiser *Abukuma* in the lead. Spread behind her in a fan-shaped wake sped four destroyers of the First Destroyer Squadron, on double alert for the slightest hint of interception. Gray and indistinct across the waves, the ships heralded the attack fleet thundering behind them.

About three miles astern *Abukuma*, *Hiei* and *Kirishima* crashed in column through the heavy swells. Flanking the battleships almost four miles to starboard and port roared the heavy cruisers *Chikuma* and *Tone*. This group of ships provided a strong protective shield against any sudden thrust of the enemy's main fleet from its mid-ocean bastion.

Approximately three miles behind this wedgelike phalanx, the carriers advanced in two parallel columns. To starboard, proudly in the lead, the flagship *Akagi* breasted the waves in grim majesty, followed in less than a mile by her sister, *Kaga*. To port *Soryu* and *Hiryu* plunged recklessly along. Last, as befitted their junior status, rushed *Shokaku* and *Zukaku*.

Modern destroyers sped along the flanks of the flattops, while two of these nautical watchdogs guarded their rear. Still farther astern, Imaizumi's three submarines glided through the black ocean like sea serpents.[1]

Navigator Miura bent over his chart to check course, speed, and distance, for he had to bring the task force to a position about 200 miles due north of Oahu somewhat before dawn. As he worked at his task, wireless operators strained for a last-minute report from the Naval General Staff or for any hint that the enemy might be on the *qui vive*. Genda spent the last hours before launching in assembling and checking all the latest radio information on U.S. Fleet dispositions at Pearl Harbor. Among them was a data-crammed telegram received at 0150:

> . . . In the evening of the 5th (local time), *Utah* and a seaplane tender
> entered the harbor. Ships in port on 6th are: nine battleships, three light
> cruisers, three seaplane tenders and seventeen destroyers, in addition to four
> light cruisers and two destroyers in the docks. . . . All heavy cruisers and
> carriers were out of the harbor. . . . No unusual condition was observed
> concerning the fleet. . . . [2]

The consulate had reported *Wyoming* as entering port, but the Naval General
Staff relayed it correctly as *Utah*.

At 0200 another message from Tomioka's Operations Section passed along
Yoshikawa's information that neither barrage balloons nor antitorpedo nets were
in use at Pearl Harbor. Needless to say, Tomioka did not include Yoshikawa's
indiscreet remark about time to make a surprise attack. [3]

The night was black, and the carriers tossed in heavy seas. On each flight
deck the maintenance men had lined up the aircraft in order of takeoff for the
first wave, with the second-wave planes in the same order below in the
hangars. Three principal duties occupied the minds of the air officers: to make
sure that all planes were operational; to provide pilots and flying crews with the
latest information on the enemy; and to send all aircraft aloft as smoothly as
possible. Immediately upon arising and dressing, each air officer picked up the
latest intelligence concerning Oahu. Then he went on deck to check the planes.
Maintenance crews stood by, both proud and anxious, as the air officers
inspected their handiwork. [4]

A waning moon peeked through the broken overcast to glimmer on the
waters off Pearl Harbor. About "1-¾ miles south of entrance buoys," the
minesweepers *Condor* and *Crossbill* plied their mechanical brooms. At 0342
something in the darkness "about fifty yards ahead off the port bow" attracted
the attention of Ensign R. C. McCloy, *Condor*'s officer of the deck. He called to
Quartermaster Second Class R. C. Uttrick and asked him what he thought.
Uttrick peered through the binoculars and said, "That's a periscope, sir, and
there aren't supposed to be any subs in this area." [5] This was clearly a problem
for the Channel Entrance Patrol. So at 0357 McCloy sent a message by yardarm
blinker to the destroyer *Ward*: "Sighted submerged submarine on westerly
course, speed 9 knots."

Thirty-five-year-old Lieutenant William W. Outerbridge had just received
command of *Ward* on December 5 and was mighty proud of it. At that moment
she was cruising at fifteen knots, patrolling a two-mile square just off the
entrance of Pearl Harbor. Alive to the critical relations between Japan and the
United States, Outerbridge considered it likely that *Condor* had spotted a
submarine. So he ordered General Quarters and asked *Condor* for its approximate course and distance. The minesweeper answered that she had last sighted
the submarine at about 1350, heading for the harbor entrance.

Outerbridge continued his sonar search, but unrewarded by any contact,
he secured from General Quarters at 0435. At precisely 0458 the protective net
to Pearl Harbor swung open to admit the two minesweepers. It would not close

until 0840. *Condor, Ward,* and the nearby radio station which picked up these signals did not report the contact.[6] The evidence was slim enough, and mistaken sightings were far from rarities in Hawaiian waters. Nevertheless, from that moment events began to go irretrievably wrong for the U.S. forces on Oahu. *Condor* had probably sighted a midget submarine sneaking up on the minesweeper with the intention of trailing her into the harbor when the net opened, and it may well have entered the harbor under the unwitting escort of *Condor* and *Crossbill.*

While Nagumo's task force bore steadily southward and Hawaii slept its last fear-free night for months to come, the teletypes clattered between the U.S. Navy's Bainbridge Island Station and the Navy Department in Washington. At 0238 Eastern Standard Time, Tokyo had sent off Part 14 of its reply to the American proposals. By the time Kramer reached his office in Washington at about 0730 the document was awaiting him.[7] It ended: "The Japanese Government regrets to have to notify hereby the American Government that in view of the attitude of the American Government it cannot but consider that it is impossible to reach an agreement through further negotiations."[8] This fourteenth part was not a formal declaration of war; it did not even rupture diplomatic relations. It merely broke off the discussions.

While Kramer prepared packets of the entire message for delivery, McCollum was "trying to digest the 13 parts of this thing" when Wilkinson sent for him. The two men went to Stark's office and talked briefly with him. Shortly after they left the CNO, Kramer delivered the fourteenth part to McCollum, who took it up with Wilkinson. They immediately returned to Stark's office and "pointed out to him the virulence and tenor of the language. . . ." Someone made the remark that "it looked right there that that was enough to indicate that we could expect war." Wilkinson suggested that an additional warning be sent to Pearl Harbor. Some discussion ensued, but "nothing was done at that time."

Kramer delivered the President's copies of the morning's harvest to the White House around 0940.[9] At about 1000 Beardall gave Roosevelt the material. As he remembered, Roosevelt read the fourteenth part, shook his head, and said "that it looked as though the Japs are going to sever negotiations, break off negotiations."[10] Just as the fourteenth part seemed to back away from the final break, so the President's reaction was milder than on the previous day.

Next, Kramer walked over to State; he reached Hull's office at 0950. He delivered his folder personally to Knox, who arrived five minutes later. From State, Kramer returned to his office, which he reached at 1020. No wonder his "most vivid impressions of that morning" were of "urgency and perspiration" from chasing about the Navy Department, to the White House and State, back to his office "as quickly as possible to see if anything new had come in," put it through the mill, "and then to dash out with it again."[11]

On the War Department side, Lieutenant John Schindel prepared to deliver the State Department's copies. He telephoned John F. Stone, a Foreign

Service officer serving as Hull's assistant, at 0730, asking him to get the secretary out of bed to receive the famous message. Schindel hand-carried it shortly thereafter.[12]

Bratton received the fourteenth part at his office between 0830 and 0900. He assembled the entire message and read it through "to see just exactly what it meant." While he was thus occupied, an intercept of a much shorter message from Togo to Nomura crossed his desk:[13] "Will the Ambassador please submit to the United States Government (if possible to the Secretary of State) our reply to the United States at 1:00 P.M. on the 7th, your time."[14]

This "immediately stunned" Bratton "into frenzied activity. . . ." The document "was peculiarly worded and the implication was inescapable that it was of vital importance."[15] One can readily see why. For one thing, it activated the fourteen-part message. For another, Sunday was not a normal working day for the diplomatic corps. And no other directive from Tokyo to its embassy in Washington had ever specified a precise hour for a meeting. Convinced that "the Japanese were going to attack some American installation in the Pacific area," Bratton "just wiped everything else" out of his mind and turned his office over to his assistant, Lieutenant Colonel C. Clyde Dusenbury.[16] Yet Bratton never imagined that the United States installation in danger might be Pearl Harbor. As he later explained, "Nobody in ONI, nobody in G-2, knew that any major element of the fleet was in Pearl Harbor on Sunday morning the 7th of December. We all thought they had gone to sea . . . because that was part of the war plan, and they had been given a war warning."[17]

He believed that a warning should go to the field commanders in all Pacific areas, but he had no authority to send one. So he hurried off, trying to find someone who could take action. But Marshall, Gerow, and Miles were not in their offices. In any case, Miles "could not issue a command message." With time slipping by, Bratton decided at about 0900 to telephone Marshall's quarters. An orderly informed him that the general had gone horseback riding. Bratton requested that he find the general and give him an urgent message to phone, that it was "vitally important" that Bratton "communicate with him at the earliest practicable moment." This request, made on a Sunday in a time of crisis and in such terms as Bratton used, clearly indicated that an emergency had arisen, but evidently no one delivered the message.[18]

Unfortunately no one was on duty in the War Department at that hour who could or would act promptly in Marshall's absence. Clocks in the War Department showed nearly 1030 when the general returned Bratton's call. The colonel explained that he had "a most important message" that Marshall "must see at once. . . ." He offered to bring it out, but Marshall answered, "No, don't bother to do that. I am coming down to my office. You can give it to me then."[19] Bratton clearly recalled having spoken with Marshall, but the Chief of Staff did not recollect talking directly with him.[20]

At about the same moment, Stimson and Knox began their meeting with the secretary of state. As Stimson recorded in his diary, "Hull is very certain that the Japs are planning some deviltry and we are all wondering when the blow will strike. . . ."[21]

This was just about the time Nagumo's pilots began preparing for their devastating blow. Some had awakened as early as 0330, having passed the night in writing farewell letters home, then tossing and turning restlessly in their bunks. Lieutenant Ema rose unrefreshed aboard *Zuikaku*. His dive-bombing mission was to strike Wheeler Field, and he had heard that it boasted strong antiaircraft batteries. If they shot him down, he would die for the Emperor and homeland. But he did not want to perish; he wanted to live, to watch his baby daughter grow into a beautiful woman like her mother.[22]

This would be the first combat mission for Sublieutenant Iyozo Fujita, a pleasant-faced young fighter pilot aboard *Soryu*, and he expected it to be his last. Before going to bed, he had invited sleep with several bottles of beer, then taken a bath. Now he donned clean clothing so that he would go into battle spotless, like the samurai of old. Then he pocketed a picture of his deceased parents. He felt completely in the hands of fate.[23]

Commander Ohashi, Hara's senior staff officer, had spent most of the night in *Shokaku*'s operations room, listening to KGMB for any clues to the situation on Oahu. He heard no hint of anything unusual and began to breathe more easily. Evidently the Americans had not yet discovered the task force. So he thought they stood a good chance of achieving surprise.[24]

Fuchida awoke at about 0500. He dressed with particular care, donning red underwear and a red shirt. He and Murata had purchased identical garments, reasoning that if either of them should be wounded in the forthcoming battle blood would not show up against the red material. Thus, the sight of their gore would not demoralize the other flying officers.

In the officers' mess he found Murata in flying togs, polishing off a hearty breakfast. Murata's eyes glinted, and he grinned impishly. "Good morning, Commander," he sang out. "Honolulu sleeps."

"How do you know?" asked Fuchida, sliding into his seat.

"The Honolulu radio plays soft music. Everything is fine," replied Murata, vigorously wielding his chopsticks.[25]

When the pilots finished breakfast, they collected in the ready room of each carrier for a final summing-up and pep talk. Just before the formal session on *Akagi*, Fuchida reported to Nagumo in the operations room. He saluted and said, "I am ready for the mission." Nagumo stood up, grasped Fuchida's hand, and replied, "I have confidence in you." Then he followed Fuchida to the dimly lit room where Hasegawa and the pilots waited.[26]

On the way, Fuchida encountered Genda. The two had formed a unique team; now Fuchida must carry on alone. For a second the two men poised in wordless sharing of the moment. Quickly Fuchida's brown face broke into his friendly grin, Genda cuffed him encouragingly on the shoulder, and Fuchida moved on to the ready room.[27]

Masuda reviewed the attack plan with emphasis on morale, takeoff, and return. Fuchida then spoke about strike methods, stressing in particular high-level bombing tactics. A blackboard showed the position of the U.S. Pacific Fleet in Pearl Harbor as of that morning. The airmen who would attack the ships studied the board carefully. Murata briefed the torpedomen, and Itaya emphasized control of the air to his fighters. Lastly, Nagumo gave the airmen his best wishes and assured them of his prayers and expectations of their success. Then Fuchida called the men to attention. He saluted Captain Hasegawa, who gave the order: "Take off according to plan."[28]

Hiryu's small ready room could not accommodate everyone. The overflow spilled into the narrow gangway, where many strained to hear Air Officer Amagai review the target objectives. He tried to keep his flying officers and crews relaxed, as though this attack were just another training mission. But Captain Kaku exhorted the airmen: "This is war between Japan and the United States. Every man must do his duty with a strong heart." Into this tense atmosphere torpedo pilot Matsumura brought a welcome note of humor. All the way from Hitokappu Bay to Hawaii he had worn a *masuku*—a gauze mask covering the mouth and nose to filter out germs, a common health measure in Japan. He pushed his food underneath it rather than take it off even at meals, claiming he did not want to catch cold and miss the attack. This morning he appeared without his mask, triumphantly revealing a brand-new mustache he had been sprouting in secret. "You looked better with the mask on," one of his comrades jeered.[29]

Dawn was still an hour away as the First Air Fleet approached the rim of the launching sector. Realizing that events would now move outside his field of competence, Nagumo said to Genda with simple dignity, "I have brought the task force successfully to the point of attack. From now on the burden is on your shoulders and the rest of the flying group." Genda replied, "Admiral, I am sure the airmen will succeed."[30]

Back in Washington, Kramer found the 1300 message awaiting him when he returned to his office from the State Department. Although he did not react as vigorously as Bratton, he realized that this was something out of the ordinary. So he instructed his chief yeoman to prepare another set of folders for immediate delivery. This took about five minutes.[31] While he waited, Kramer did some calculating. When any dispatch "of which time was an element" came in, ONI converted that time to the zones for Washington, the West Coast, Honolulu, Manila, and Tokyo. They included the last because the Japanese Navy ran all its business by Tokyo time. The primary object was to determine "whether it was sunset or sunrise, or moonset. . . ."[32]

As Kramer made a hobby of navigation, he worked out the problem on a navigator's time circle "to get a picture of how this 1 o'clock Washington tied up with the movement of the big Japanese convoy moving down on the coast of French Indochina. . . ." To Kramer 0730 at Hawaii meant that this "was probably the quietest time of the week aboard ship at Pearl Harbor. . . ." For Kota Bharu it came to two or three hours before dawn, "the normal time to institute amphibious operations."[33]

Just as Kramer was about to set off, the watch officer brought in "a plain language Japanese message." From the word "Stop" at its end, Kramer recognized this as belonging to the "hidden word" setup established on November 27.* He quickly dictated the sense of the dispatch to his yeoman and inserted the document in the folders. His translation read: "Relations between Japan and England are not in accordance with expectation."[34] In his haste he failed to note the word *Minami*, meaning the United States. By the time he discovered the error it was too late to matter, if indeed it ever did.[35]

Kramer stopped at Stark's office, where McCollum answered the door. Kramer showed him the 1300 message, pointing out the "tie-up of the time . . . with the scheme that had been developing for the past week or so in the Southwest Pacific. . . ." He also mentioned that the time would be 0730 in Hawaii. But that fact rang no alarm bell in either of their minds. The two officers agreed that although normally the Army covered the State Department, Kramer should take the message there on his way to the White House.[36]

McCollum carried the message to Stark. He too emphasized that 1300 in Washington would be 0730 in Honolulu, and "very early in the morning in the Far East . . . and that we didn't know what this signified, but that if an attack were coming, it looked like . . . it was timed for operations out in the Far East and possibly on Hawaii."[37] Nevertheless, McCollum later explained, "Pearl Harbor as such was never mentioned. The feeling that I had, and I think the feeling that most officers there had, was that at or near the outbreak of war with Japan, we could expect a surprise attack on the fleet."[38] But they also thought that with the onset of hostilities the Fleet would steam out of Pearl Harbor.

Meanwhile, Kramer walked to the State Department "almost on the double" and "at least trotted part of the way," covering the distance in about ten minutes. He delivered the folder to Stone. Once more he called attention to the time element. "The principal point of that was the conviction . . . that the Japanese intended to carry out their plans against Kota Bharu. . . ." There was no discussion that the timing had any significance in connection with an attack on Pearl Harbor. Kramer mentioned the 0730 hour in Hawaii "purely in passing and . . . primarily for the benefit" of those "who might not be familiar with the ships' routine or Fleet routine on a Sunday morning." He made only a general remark to the effect that 0730 on Sunday was probably the quietest time of the week. He especially wanted to get across to Knox, who was still with Hull, that this would be "a few hours before sunrise at Kota Bharu." From State, Kramer moved on to the White House, then back to the Navy Department.[39]

The morning's batch of messages had been giving the Japanese Embassy much more administrative trouble than it did the Americans. When Shiroji Yuki, Kurusu's first secretary, arrived at about 0900, he found Okumura "typing like mad" on the first thirteen parts of the Japanese reply. The final installment had arrived at least an hour or so before, but the duty officer had

---

*See Chapter 49.

experienced difficulty in rounding up the members of the cable office. They did not begin to work on it until roughly 1000. An hour later the 1300 message arrived at the Embassy. Okumura had finished the first thirteen parts, but his manuscript was messy. He began to retype it with the help of an interpreter. Inevitably feeling the rising tension, both men made a number of errors. They also received a few correcting cables, just enough to necessitate retyping the clean copy.[40]

At the approximate moment this trigger message arrived at the embassy— 0530 local time in the Hawaiian area—*Chikuma* and *Tone* each catapulted into the murky sky a single-engine Zero type of reconnaissance seaplane to reconnoiter Pearl Harbor and Lahaina Anchorage respectively. Both planes would survey their areas for a quarter of an hour and make sure their reports—which would break radio silence—were correct.

These two sinister doves flew from their arks unescorted into the very teeth of American defenses. Just one American eye looking into the sky at the right time could give Hawaii's defenders the key tip-off. But the Japanese accepted this calculated risk of discovery because the urgent need for last-minute, accurate information overrode the otherwise-paramount consideration of secrecy.[41]

Launching the fighters and bombers did not await the report from the scout planes. At 0550 the six carriers, now some 220 miles north of Oahu, turned with their escort vessels to port, headed almost due east into a brisk wind, and increased speed again to twenty-four knots. The flattops pitched violently as the foam-tipped waves rolled in long, high swells, sending spray over the flight decks. Takeoff would be exceedingly difficult with the carriers listing between eleven and fifteen degrees, but it had to be risked; the finely meshed gears of Japan's military machine were timed to this operation. So combat pennants sped up the mast to wave beside the "Z" flag.

As the airmen prepared to enter the cockpits, each tied around his head a *hachimaki* marked with the word *Hissho* (Certain Victory). When Fuchida approached his bomber, the senior maintenance officer walked up to him holding a specially made white *hachimaki*. "This is from *Akagi*'s crew," he said. "We would like you to carry this to Pearl Harbor on our behalf." Touched and pleased, Fuchida bowed his thanks and bound the scarf around his helmet.[42]

The weather delayed takeoff twenty minutes.[43] In this interval plane crews and maintenance men exchanged shouts of encouragement. Attention centered on the attack crews. Inasmuch as the Zeros would rise skyward first, all eyes on *Akagi* riveted on Itaya. Because the flight deck was crammed with planes, he had only a short run for his takeoff, and he dipped dangerously low coming off the bow. For a brief eternity watchers held their breaths. Then Itaya's Zero lifted triumphantly over the searching waves. He leveled off, turned, and "soared upward like a great bird."[44]

The rest of the fighters on all six carriers sped off one by one as quickly as possible. Fighter patrols also launched but not until all planes of the first wave had left the carriers. They would remain in position throughout the attack.[45]

After the fighters came the high-level bombers, Fuchida in the lead. These aircraft carried a crew of three: a pilot, a bombardier-observer, and a radio operator. Next, the dive bombers launched without incident. If Takahashi, their leader in the first wave, lacked the diamond worth of Fuchida, the burnished finish of Itaya, or the quicksilver dash of Murata, he more than pulled his weight as the fourth horseman of an apocalyptical hour by his strong, aggressive spirit. Like the other pilots, he carried a map of Oahu, a pistol, and some survival gear in case he had to ditch at sea.

Next came the torpedo bombers. These also carried a three-man crew of pilot, bombardier-observer, and radio operator. After Murata arrowed his bomber down the flight deck, his overloaded craft soared aloft as smoothly as a sea gull.[46]

Within fifteen minutes from Itaya's launch, of 185 planes scheduled for the first wave, 183 had taken off—43 fighters, 49 high-level bombers, 51 dive bombers, and 40 torpedo planes. It was the fastest launching on record, marred only by the loss of 2 fighters. One crashed on takeoff, but a destroyer quickly rescued the pilot. The second, from *Kaga*, developed engine trouble and had to be left behind. For almost fifteen minutes the aircraft circled the carriers in a huge arc. Those watching below could easily distinguish Fuchida's orange light from the flight commanders' yellow ones, flickering like fireflies in the darkness. At about 0620, at Fuchida's signal, made by taking his own group of high-level bombers across *Akagi*'s bow, the first attack wave set course for Oahu.[47]

As soon as the last torpedo plane took off, Nagumo ordered the First Air Fleet to turn south again at twenty knots. Crews worked frantically to raise the aircraft of the second wave to the flight deck. *Kaga*'s plane handlers cursed the old-style elevators which ran somewhat behind those of the other carriers. This delay, in addition to the roughening sea, stretched the planned launching time beyond schedule. Dawn was well advanced when the task force prepared to send off its second flight.[48]

While the decks were being readied, the second-wave leaders gave their charges some last-minute instructions. On *Soryu*, Fujita listened with his comrades to fighter pilot Lieutenant Fusata Iida's grim counsel. "What are you going to do in case you have engine trouble in flight?" he demanded. Then without pause he answered for himself: "In case of trouble I will fly straight to my objective and make a crash dive into an enemy target rather than make an emergency landing."[49]

Lieutenant Chihaya, the steady, introspective observer who commanded the Eleventh Dive Bomber Group from *Akagi*, gathered his crew members about him for a final briefing. Chihaya had an additional duty of leading back the fighters after the attack. Just before he climbed into his plane, Genda gave him strict orders to report as soon as possible on the strength of the enemy's antiaircraft fire. If this proved too destructive, Genda would rule out use of torpedo planes in case of another strike.[50]

At 0705 the carriers again turned eastward into the wind at increased speed. The sky was still quite cloudy, with visibility about twelve miles and ceiling around one mile. Ten minutes later the second attack wave began to rise skyward. Once more the fighters flew off first. Lieutenant Saburo Shindo from *Akagi*, commander of the second-wave control force, would lead thirty-six Zeros. Thirty-year-old Shindo "did not have any particular feelings" this morning—to him, it was just another operation.[51]

Next came Shimazaki, versatile and practical leader of the second wave. His 54 horizontal bombers from *Shokaku* and *Zuikaku* would blast Hickam, Ford Island, and Kaneohe, thus continuing the first wave's destruction of U.S. air power. Egusa led the second wave's 78 dive bombers—the largest single force in the entire attack. His objectives were battleships, cruisers, and destroyers. All went well for the second wave except for one dive bomber aboard *Hiryu* which developed engine trouble and had to be scratched. Within ninety minutes of the first wave's initial takeoff, the last dive bomber from the second was airborne. A formidable striking force of 350 planes now winged its way toward the targets.[52]

Meanwhile, at 0630, the battleships *Hiei* and *Kirishima* and the heavy cruisers *Tone* and *Chikuma* sent up patrol planes to search the area south of the task force and warn Nagumo of the possible approach of American ships and planes.

Nagumo turned the First Air Fleet south to a position about 180 miles from Oahu's northern tip. He watched apprehensively as the second attack wave faded into the sky. Kusaka stood beside him, "filled with deep emotion." Genda remained with them a little while, experiencing a tremendous welling of pride at the smoothness of takeoff. He was now convinced that they had captured the vital element of surprise. Then he went to the control room to await Fuchida's signal, which would send the rest of Japan's war machine crashing into action. On deck, the cheering hands, some with tears running down their sweat-stained faces, continued to wave their caps in farewell until the speeding planes shrank to pinpoints in the sky.[53]

CHAPTER 60

"AN

AWFUL

URGENCY"

Checking through his periscope, Sakamaki found to his horror that his midget submarine was moving away from Pearl Harbor. The defective gyroscope had swung it 90 degrees off course. According to plan, all five of Japan's small undersea craft should be on the bottom of the harbor by dawn, but his was still well outside. Since leaving *I-24*, Sakamaki and Inagaki had all they could do to ensure that the "tube" did not bob up to the surface. With the aid of his telescope and by keeping speed to a minimum, Sakamaki struggled to hold the submarine on course. Despite his best efforts, the malfunctioning craft floundered around in awkward circles.[1]

Sakamaki was not the only officer maddeningly frustrated that morning. In Washington Bratton grew more restive with each passing moment. Time ticked away, and still the Chief of Staff did not show up at the War Department. Miles arrived shortly after Bratton's call. Both the fourteenth section and the 1300 message struck Miles forcibly. To him they meant two things: "(1) That war is very likely because of the language used by the Japanese, and (2) something is going to happen coincident with 1 o'clock Washington time."[2]

Not until about 1125—just as Nagumo's carriers were turning into the wind preparing for takeoff—did Marshall appear. Miles and Bratton promptly descended upon him. When they walked in, Marshall was reading the entire Japanese reply while Bratton inwardly squirmed with impatience. Both he and Miles tried to interrupt Marshall and persuade him to read the other message which Bratton clutched in his hand. They might as well have tried to deflect a glacier.

After a seeming eternity Marshall finished and accepted the trigger dispatch.[3] He had no doubt that the time designated therein "had some very definite significance. . . ." He asked Miles and Bratton what they thought this

493

portended. Both replied that they "were convinced it meant Japanese hostile action against some American installation in the Pacific at or shortly after 1 o'clock that afternoon." About this time Gerow came in with Bundy, in charge of Pacific Affairs in War Plans. They concurred in this judgment.[4]

But exactly what American installation? Miles urged an immediate warning to the Philippines, Panama, the West Coast, and Hawaii.[5] Yet no one mentioned the timing of the 1300 message as it related to Hawaii. After some discussion everyone concurred "in urging that our outlying possessions be given an additional alert at once by the fastest possible means." So Marshall pulled up "a piece of scratch paper" and wrote out a longhand message. Then he picked up the White House phone and called Stark, probably at 1140. He informed the CNO "in a guarded way" what he proposed to do.[6]

When Stark answered this call, he had been discussing this identical Japanese message with Schuirmann. Stark told Marshall that "we had sent them so much already" that he "hesitated to send more." That ended the conversation for the moment.[7]

Nevertheless, Miles and Bratton continued to urge Marshall to send the warnings.[8] Within a minute or so Stark called Marshall back. He "would go along with" him and offered the use of his naval communications, which "were quite rapid when the occasion demanded it." Marshall replied that he believed "he could get it through very quickly." Stark then asked him to include in the dispatch "instructions to his people to inform their naval opposites."[9] Marshall did so and instructed Bratton to take the draft to the message center for dispatch "at once by the fastest safe means." As Bratton went out the door, Gerow called after him, "If there is any question of priority, give the Philippines first priority."[10]

It lacked but a few minutes of noon in Washington. There was "an awful urgency" about the deadline. Yet no one seems to have seriously considered telephoning. The Navy seldom used the scrambler for secret information because Noyes had warned not to depend on it for security. Marshall later testified that even if he had used the phone, he would have called first MacArthur, then Panama.[11]

Very shortly Lieutenant Colonel Edward F. French, officer in charge of the War Department Signal Center, "heard some commotion over in the code room" and left his office to investigate. He found Bratton, message in hand, "very much exercised." French had "never seen him more excited."[12]

Bratton handed French the draft. "The Chief of Staff wants this sent at once by the fastest safe means," he emphasized. French looked over Marshall's hasty scrawl and replied, "Well, will you help me get this into readable script? Neither I nor my clerk here can read General Marshall's handwriting." So Bratton read it to one of French's clerks, who typed it out from Bratton's reading. This took a few minutes.[13]

The message now read: "Japanese are presenting at one pm eastern standard time today what amounts to an ultimatum also they are under orders to destroy their code machine immediately. Just what significance the hour set may have we do not know but be on alert accordingly. Inform naval authorities of this communication. Marshall."[14]

Bratton glanced at his watch. The time was about 1158.[15] On Nagumo's task force the clocks read 0158 Tokyo time December 8—0628 December 7, local time. Fuchida's first wave was circling the carriers preparatory to its flight of destruction.

Leaving French to process his precious message, Bratton returned to Marshall's office. "Go back and find out how long it is going to take for this message to be delivered to the addressees," the Chief of Staff directed him. So Bratton hurried back to French and asked Marshall's question. After "a little figuring mentally," French informed him, "It will take about 30 or 40 minutes for it to be delivered to the person to whom it is addressed." This did not mean that Short would have it in his hands in that time. It would have to be deciphered, decoded, and delivered. Bratton assumed that the Army had direct communication with Hawaii and did not find out to the contrary until several days after the attack.[16]

The first message went to the Caribbean Defense Command promptly at 1200. Six minutes later the word went out to MacArthur, that for the Presidio following at 1211.[17] But the warning for Hawaii hit a snag. When French checked with his Signal Center, he discovered that atmospheric conditions had blocked off the channel to Honolulu since about 1030. The heavy static interfered even with San Francisco. French considered going to the Navy but decided that commercial service would provide quicker and safer transmission. He had a direct teletype to Western Union in Washington, which could handle the message straight to San Francisco, transfer it there to RCA, and thence to Honolulu. He had learned the previous day that RCA was installing a teletype circuit to Hawaiian Department Headquarters. So he sent the dispatch to Western Union at 1217.[18] Thus, the very atmosphere itself conspired to further Japanese luck.

Nevertheless, as the warning message got under way, the fates granted Oahu another alarm. *Antares*, a stores and supply ship with a lighter in tow, moved slowly toward Pearl Harbor. Her skipper, Commander Lawrence C. Grannis, awaited rendezvous with a tug which would bring *Antares* a harbor pilot to guide her home.

At precisely 0630 Grannis spotted a suspicious-looking object "about 1500 yards on starboard quarter." This thing did not resemble any submarine he had ever seen, but its conning tower was showing just out of the water. It seemed to be "obviously having depth control trouble and . . . trying to go down." So Grannis informed *Ward* of the sighting.[19]

Lieutenant (j.g.) O. W. Goepner had *Ward*'s deck, for Outerbridge had turned in. The destroyer's helmsman was the first to see the strange object. He and Goepner decided that it was probably the conning tower of a submarine. However, "they had never seen anything like it" in the U.S. Navy. "Captain, come on the bridge,"Goepner called to Outerbridge, who dressed and bounced out to have a look. *She is going to follow the* Antares *in, whatever it is,* he said to himself. *It couldn't be anything else but a sub. But whose?*

Outerbridge ordered General Quarters at 0640. Quickly his men brought up the ammunition and loaded the guns. All engines trembled as *Ward* lunged ahead full speed toward the sub. When the destroyer pulled up about fifty yards abeam the intruder, Outerbridge's men commenced firing. The first round "missed, passing directly over the conning tower." The second struck the submarine "at the waterline. . . . the junction of the hull and conning tower." The craft heeled "over to starboard" and "appeared to slow and sink." Then it apparently passed under *Ward's* stern and ran into "a full pattern of depth charges," set for about 100 feet. "The submarine sank in 1200 feet of water. . . ."[20]

So, strangely enough, the first shot of the Battle of Oahu came from an American ship instead of a Japanese aircraft, and the first blood shed was Japanese. Just as Genda and Fuchida feared, a submarine had triggered premature action. But Japanese luck held together, pinned by misunderstanding and tied with red tape.

Outerbridge immediately reported his action to the Fourteenth Naval District watch officer: "We have dropped depth charges upon sub operating in defensive sea area." Almost instantly he thought he should be more definite. So he reported a second time: "We have attacked fired upon and dropped depth charges upon submarine operating in defensive sea area." Thus, whoever saw the report "would feel, well, he shot at something." The Bishop Point Radio Station logged this in at 0653,[21] one hour and two minutes before Fuchida and his airmen struck.

The watch officer in Bloch's headquarters that morning was Lieutenant Commander Harold Kaminski, a World War I "retread" back on active duty a little more than a year. He took notes of the events and promptly tried to reach Bloch's aide. Failing that, he called the Fleet duty officer and gave the report to his assistant, Lieutenant Commander R. B. Black. Then he called Captain Earle, Bloch's chief of staff.[22]

Kimmel's duty officer happened to be bright young Commander Vincent Murphy, assistant war plans officer. He had come on duty the previous night armed with a memorandum from McMorris containing instructions on disposition of the ships in case war was declared or an attack took place. This involved getting Halsey's, Newton's, and Brown's units back to Pearl Harbor, then putting the war plans into effect.

Murphy was in his quarters dressing when Black phoned Kaminski's report to him. He instructed Black, "While I'm finishing dressing, call him and see what he's doing about it and whether or not he's called Admiral Bloch." Thereupon Black "dialed and dialed," but Kaminski's line was busy. When Black informed Murphy accordingly, the latter said, "All right, you go to the office and start breaking out the charts and position of the various ships; I'll dial one more time and then I'll be over." Murphy phoned, but the line was still busy. He then dialed the operator and instructed him to tell Kaminski to call him immediately and to break in on any conversation the district duty officer might be holding "unless it was of supreme importance."

As Murphy walked into his office, the phone was ringing. It proved to be Lieutenant Commander Logan Ramsey of Patrol Wing Two.[23] He passed along a report he had just received from the duty officer on Ford Island, Lieutenant Dick Ballinger. The latter advised that one of their planes "on intertype tactics" had "sunk a submerged submarine one mile off the entrance to Pearl Harbor." Murphy replied, "That's funny, we got the same sort of message from one of the DD's on the inshore patrol."

"Well," answered Ramsey, "you had better get going and I'll be down at my Operations Center soon." Hanging up, Ramsey donned slacks and aloha shirt and drove to the administration building on Ford Island which housed the Operations Center. He did not consider the morning's reports "definite information of an enemy attack." But he drew up a search plan for the PBYs postulated upon the Naval Base Air Defense Operating Plan, which called for a search to the northeast sector as first priority because this was believed to be the most likely approach direction for a Japanese attack.[24]

Ramsey had scarcely hung up when Kaminski called Murphy to report *Ward's* action. Murphy then telephoned Kimmel. The admiral had arisen at about 0700 to prepare for his golf game with Short. He had not yet dressed, shaved, or breakfasted when Murphy reached him, but he promptly replied, "I will be right down."[25] Like Earle, Kimmel was "not at all certain that this was a real attack." He later explained, ". . . we had so many . . . false reports of submarines in the outlying area, I thought, well, I would wait for verification of the report. . . ."[26] And so the previous cries of "Wolf!" threw Kimmel off stride at the very hour when the predators were heading for the fold.

Earle's first impression on hearing Kaminski's story was that this might be "just another of those false reports," so he requested Kaminski to send him confirmation. He also told him "to get in touch with the ready-duty destroyer and send her out at once and get ahold of the operations officer."[27] At 0712 he called Bloch. The two officers discussed the report for about "five or ten minutes to try to decide what was the reliability of this word and what steps should be taken. As the matter had been referred to the Commander-in-Chief," they decided to "wait further developments."[28]

Despite Earle's not unnatural skepticism, we have here a picture of alert professionals at work, neither going off half-cocked nor taking the reports lightly. Yet it is clear that the best intentions of all concerned strangled in telephone cord. By the time everyone had talked to everyone else a good half hour had passed. If the duty officer, either at CinCPAC Headquarters or at Ford Island, had possessed the authority to send out patrols and seek confirmation later, such action might have mitigated the damage soon to be suffered.

The Navy's most serious error in this preattack submarine chapter of the Pearl Harbor story was its failure to advise the Army that a destroyer had sunk an obviously hostile submarine in the Defensive Sea Area.[29] The incident might

have provided just the added weight needed to move the Hawaiian Department from the No. 1 alert to No. 2 or 3 because a submarine snooping near
Pearl Harbor could scarcely have been charged up to local saboteurs.

So enemy submarines, which Kimmel had always thought might one day
attack his ships, had tipped the Japanese hand in exactly the way Nagumo, his
staff, and his airmen had feared. U.S. forces had received several opportunities
to uncover Yamamoto's secret but had failed. They would be granted a few
more chances before black tragedy struck.

CHAPTER 61

"TORA!

TORA!

TORA!"

High over the Pacific, Nagumo's airmen winged their way toward the target. Lining the center of the formation, at about 9,800 feet, streaked ten triangles of high level bombers under Fuchida's personal command. Flanking to port, at some 11,000 feet, sped Takahashi's two groups of dive bombers. To starboard, Murata's four groups of torpedo planes roared at around 9,200 feet. Covering the entire force, fore and aft at 14,100 feet, snarled Itaya's fighters.

As daylight broke, the sun with its rays bore an almost theatrical semblance to the naval flag of Empire. Fuchida was so thrilled that he half stood up, as if to honor the beloved symbol. He looked behind him and saw his huge air armada following him in perfect formation, the sun flashing silver from its wings. For a full two or three minutes he watched the magnificent scene. *O glorious dawn for Japan!* he thought, in a surge of pride in his country, his men, and his mission.

His moment of drama over, Fuchida returned to business. It was now after 0700, and he tuned in to KGMB, directing his pilot to home in on this beam. As he sped through the slowly brightening sky, a thick mat of fleecy clouds, spread below at about 5,000 feet, screened his flight. In fact, the covering was a little too good. He might overfly Pearl Harbor, alerting all defenses without spotting his target, or even miss Oahu altogether.[1]

Had Fuchida been omniscient, he could have added another king-sized worry to the rest of his problems. As though reluctant to abandon the Americans without one more chance, even while the Navy fumbled the submarine contact, fate now gave the ball to the U.S. Army.

Located near Kahuku Point on the northern tip of Oahu at 230 feet above sea level, Opana Mobile Radar Station was generally conceded to be the best of

499

these sites. At 0400 Privates Joseph L. Lockard and George E. Elliott went on duty. The more experienced of the two in the radar field, Lockard instructed Elliott in use of the oscilloscope. At 0700 Lockard began to shut down the unit because that hour spelled the end of their morning's work.

Suddenly the oscilloscope picked up an image so peculiar that Lockard thought something must be wrong with the set, but a quick check proved otherwise. He took over from Elliott, deciding that "it must be a flight of some sort."[2] Elliott went to the plotting board. As of 0702, the flight appeared at 5 degrees northeast of azimuth at 132 miles. It was enormous, "probably more than 50" planes. Elliott suggested that they phone the reading to the Information Center. At first Lockard demurred because the normal operating hours had ended. But Elliott persisted. This would be a good test for the Information Center, being a nonscheduled exercise. Lockhard then told him to go ahead and send it in.[3] This conversation covered seven or eight minutes, and the scope showed the blip about 20 to 25 miles nearer Oahu.

Elliott called the Information Center and reached Private Joseph McDonald, the switchboard operator. Thinking that he was alone, the Information Center personnel having gone off duty, McDonald took the message. As he glanced around to check the time, he spotted Lieutenant Kermit Tyler, the pursuit officer and assistant to the controller on duty that morning.[4]

Tyler had pulled his first tour of duty as a pursuit officer on Wednesday, December 3—his only on-the-job experience before December 7. The duties of a pursuit officer were "to assist the Controller in ordering planes to intercept enemy planes or supposed enemy planes, after the planes got in the air."[5]

Located at Fort Shafter, the Information Center lay several miles east of Pearl Harbor and about thirty miles south of the Opana Station. During duty hours a group of plotters stood around a large table, marking on the map information telephoned from the various radar stations. But they recorded only the position of the plane or planes picked up on the radarscope. They had no way of distinguishing friend from foe. The controller and pursuit officer on duty could look down upon these activities from a large balcony at second-floor level.[6]

On this fateful morning, however, neither the controller nor the aircraft identification officer was on hand. Tyler began duty at 0400 with "seven or eight enlisted men." But at 0700 on the dot, the plotters "folded up their equipment and left." Thus, when Elliott's call came in, the only individuals still present in the Information Center were Tyler and McDonald.[7]

Impressed by Elliott's report, McDonald suggested that Tyler take the phone. This time Lockard spoke with him. He gave Tyler "all the information that we had—the direction, the mileage, and the apparent size of whatever it was. . . ." Tyler remembered that Lockard called the blips "the biggest sightings he had ever seen."[8]

It never crossed Tyler's mind that this incoming flight could be enemy aircraft. It could have been planes from a Navy carrier. But almost immediately the report rang a bell in his memory. On the way to the Information Center that morning he had listened to some Hawaiian music. Tyler recalled that according to a bomber pilot friend, the station played this music all night whenever B-17s flew from the mainland to Hawaii, acting as a beam for the navigators.

So Tyler felt sure that Opana had picked up a flight of the big bombers. His first reaction was one of relief that the Flying Fortresses were coming from the right direction. In one respect Tyler was perfectly correct: Landon's flight from California was approaching rapidly about 5 degrees off the Opana sighting. Of course, for security reasons Tyler could not explain his belief to Lockard and Elliott, so he merely replied, "Well, don't worry about it."[9]

This was about 0720. At this point the Opana scope showed Fuchida's first wave bearing 3 degrees, 74 miles away. Once more Lockard wanted to shut down, but Elliott insisted that they continue. So they kept on observing, posting their findings to an overlay chart and keeping a running log, until they lost the blips "due to distortion from a back wave from the mountains. . . ." At 0739 they made the last report of this particular sighting as 41 degrees, 20 miles.[10]

Lockard made one big mistake: He did not tell Tyler that the sighting contained more than fifty planes.[11] If he had, Tyler could scarcely have mistaken it for a flight of B-17s. Such a number would represent a good slice of the entire American inventory of this type of bomber.

Technically speaking, Tyler erred in not telephoning Major Kenneth P. Bergquist, operations officer of the Fourteenth Pursuit Wing. But from the practical standpoint, it made little real difference. Because of Short's Alert No. 1, an alarm at this stage would have meant exactly the chance given by *Ward*'s submarine contact and no more—an opportunity to disperse planes, to break out ammunition, and move up to No. 2 or 3 alerts. Neither at the time nor later in the day did anyone in the Army notify the Navy of the Opana sighting. This was a serious error because this clear track would at least have revealed the direction of the Japanese carriers and saved the Navy's later searchers a long, weary wild goose chase.[12]

While these events took place on land, destiny continued to play cat-and-mouse with the United States at sea. At 0703—exactly one minute after Fuchida's air flotilla appeared on the Opana screen—*Ward* "established sound contact on enemy submarine." The destroyer dropped more of her "ash cans" and at 0706 "sighted black oil bubble 300 yards astern."[13] Outerbridge was certainly proving his right to the proud title of destroyer captain.

At this moment Fuchida's pilot was actually homing in on the same continuous stream of languorous Hawaiian tunes which guided Landon's B-17s. Meanwhile, the reconnaissance plane from *Chikuma* hovered over Pearl Harbor, and the pilot sized up the terrain below. Oahu could not have presented a more peaceful, harmless appearance. At precisely 0735, satisfied that he had absorbed all he could, he relayed his information: "Enemy formation at anchor; nine battleships, one heavy cruiser, six light cruisers are in the harbor." Three minutes later he sent off to Nagumo an on-the-spot description of the meteorological conditions over Pearl Harbor: "Wind direction from 80 degrees, speed 14 meters, clearance over enemy fleet 1700 meters, cloud density 7." His mission fulfilled, he banked his aircraft gracefully and set out to rejoin the First Air Fleet.

Immediately following this message came less palatable news from the *Tone* patrol. The pilot confirmed the previous day's observations. "The enemy Fleet is not in Lahaina Anchorage," he reported. This disposed once and for all of the Japanese hope of trapping the American warships in Lahaina's deep waters. The alternative plans Genda and Fuchida had so painstakingly worked up and reviewed at Hitokappu Bay could be ruled out. Fuchida and his airmen could concentrate exclusively on Pearl Harbor. His mission over Lahaina completed, the scout combed a wide stretch of sea south of Pearl Harbor in a venturesome effort to gain some news of the undiscovered American flattops.[14] But the search did not go far enough to discover *Enterprise* some 200 miles at sea to the west.

At precisely 0733 RCA in Honolulu received Marshall's warning message from Washington. It was already three minutes past the deadline hour of 1300 Eastern Standard Time. Fuchida's first wave had reached a point exactly 15 degrees, 35 miles from the Opana Radar Station. The message found its way into a pigeonhole marked for Kahili, the district which included Fort Shafter. RCA messenger boy Tadao Fuchikami picked it up along with the rest of the cables in the Kahili slot. It was not marked priority, nor did anything in its appearance indicate it to be out of the ordinary. Messages in hand, Fuchikami mounted his motorcycle and roared on his way.[15]

By this time 1300 in Washington had come and gone, and the Japanese Embassy still struggled valiantly with the fourteen-part message. By 1230 it had decoded Part 14, but Okumura had not yet finished his clean copy of the remainder. Ready to leave for his appointment, Nomura "impatiently peeked into the office where the typing was being done, hurrying the men at work." Perhaps no one but a hunt-and-peck typist with an ambassador breathing down his neck could fully appreciate Okumura's sensations. It soon became evident that the deadline would overtake the typing, so Nomura requested and received an extension from Hull.[16]

Over the Pacific, Fuchida peered intently through his high-powered binoculars.[17] By now he should be within sighting distance of Oahu. As his eyes followed a pointing sunbeam through a chink in the clouds, he ejected a sharp "Ha!" of gratification. There it was—foam-fringed, lushly green, its gray-purple mountains wreathed in ghostly mists: a breathtaking sight in the morning sun. "This is the north point of Oahu," Fuchida told his pilot. As they sped onward, Fuchida gave the order *Tenkai* ("Take attack position") and instructed Mutsuzaki to watch out for enemy interceptors. So suddenly had they reached the island that each group barely had time to deploy. Fuchida picked up his rocket pistol. Until this moment matters had gone almost uncannily well for the Japanese. By the law of averages it was long past time for something to go wrong. Oddly enough, none other than the careful Takahashi, leader of the dive bombers, "goofed."

According to plan, one flare from Fuchida's rocket pistol would signal that surprise had been achieved, while two flares at two- or three-second intervals would indicate that the enemy was alert. At a single flare Murata's torpedomen would start their downward glide, while Itaya's fighters dashed ahead to seize control of the air. The slow torpedo bombers thus would have a clear path to their targets. The dive and high-level bombers would follow quickly. But if the Japanese faced an alert enemy, the torpedomen would wait until the dive and high-level bombers had diverted the attention of American gunners to the skies above the battleships, Then with the help of the fighters, the torpedomen would launch their deadly fish.

At 0740, assured of surprise, Fuchida fired a single shot. Then he noted that Lieutenant Masaharu Suganami, one of the fighter group leaders, must have failed to observe the signal because his planes did not take their proper formation. Therefore, after waiting for about ten seconds, Fuchida fired another rocket to alert Suganami. Takahashi saw this second shot. Misjudging the time interval between flares, he took it for the double signal and swooped down immediately with his dive bombers for the attack run on Ford Island and Hickam Field. Murata saw what had happened. Although he knew that Takahashi had erred, he had no choice but to lead his torpedomen to the target as quickly as possible. However, Takahashi was well on his way. Thus, it happened that bombs instead of torpedoes struck the initial blow.

Fuchida fairly ground his teeth in angry frustration as the precise tactical plan he, Genda, and Murata had so painstakingly worked out shattered against that unpredictable element—the human equation. But he soon saw that the order in which they attacked mattered little. The fact of success was assured; the only remaining consideration was its degree. At that moment Fuchida could look down the valley toward Pearl Harbor as if sighting along a gun barrel. As he did so, the fluffy morning clouds parted like stage curtains. Fuchida adjusted his binoculars. Caught in the circle of his vision lay the full power and glory of the U.S. Pacific Fleet.

What a majestic sight! he thought. *Almost unbelievable!* He counted seven battleships at their moorings. The scout plane, as well as the consulate, had reported nine. Where were the other two? Actually eight battlewagons were in Pearl Harbor. Fuchida did not see *Pennsylvania* in drydock, and the *Chikuma* scout, like Yoshikawa, had counted the target ship *Utah* as a battleship. Fuchida experienced one pang of disappointment. He had been hoping against hope that the early-morning report might be mistaken, that Kimmel's carriers would be in Pearl Harbor. But they were not.

At a point somewhat off Lahilahi Point, at 0749 Fuchida arrived at zero hour. With chills chasing each other up and down his spine, he gave Mutsuzaki the attack signal, *To, to, to,* the first syllable of *totsugekiseyo* (charge). Then he ordered the radioman to rap out the order for all pilots. Aboard *Nagato* in

the Inland Sea, a staff officer burst into Ugaki's cabin with the news, and
Yamamoto's chief of staff bounded for the Operations Room.[18]

Fuchida's radio was still clicking when the first wave broke into its
component parts. Fuchida swung around Barber's Point, and sure beyond all
possible doubt that they had indeed achieved maximum strategic surprise, at
0753 he sang out, *"Tora! Tora! Tora!"* ("Tiger! Tiger! Tiger!")—the code words
which told the entire Japanese Navy that they had caught the Pacific Fleet
unawares.[19]

Aboard *Akagi*, Kusaka was not in the least ashamed of the tears which
coursed down his wind-burned cheeks, impassive Zen Buddhist though he was.
Nagumo could not have uttered a word had life and honor depended on it.
Incredibly, miraculously, they had brought off Yamamoto's madcap venture!
With silent instinct, each man stretched out his hand to the other, and in their
eyes were all the words they could not speak.[20]

The U.S.S. *Arizona.*

The U.S.S. *Arizona* at Pearl Harbor after the Japanese attack
on December 7, 1941 (*Official U.S. Navy Photo*).

(Top) Capt. Kanji Ogawa, Asst. Chief, 3rd Bureau, Naval General Staff. (Center) RADM Minoru Maeda, Chief, 3rd Bureau, Naval General Staff. (Bottom) Lt. Cmdr. Itaru Tachibana, Intelligence Officer, 3rd Bureau, Naval General Staff.

(Above) Takeo Yoshikawa, Chancellor, Honolulu consulate. (At right) Nagao Kita, Consul General at Honolulu.

(Above) Lt. Cmdr. Alwin D. Kramer, Translation Section, Communications Division, Navy Department. (At right) Robert L. Shivers, Special Agent in Charge, FBI, Honolulu.

(At left) Cmdr. Laurence F. Safford, Chief, Security Section, Communications Division, Navy Department. (Below) Lt. Col. George W. Bicknell, Asst. G-2, Hawaiian Department, and Special Envoy Saburo Kurusu (left).

(Above) Members and staff of the Navy Court of Inquiry, July 24 to October 19, 1944. (*Slinkman Studio*). (Below) Members and staff of the Army Pearl Harbor Board, July 20 to October 20, 1944.

(Above) His Imperial Majesty Hirohito, Emperor of Japan, March 30, 1936, in coronation robes (*Wide World Photos*). (At right) General Hideki Tojo, War Minister, Konoye Cabinet; Premier, October 18, 1941.

Kichisaburo Nomura, Japanese Ambassador to the U.S. (left), with Secretary of State Cordell Hull (center) and Saburo Kurusu, Japan's special envoy for a "final attempt at peace," arriving at the White House on November 17, 1941 (United Press International Photo).

CHAPTER 62

"SOUND

GENERAL

QUARTERS"

Kimmel was still in his quarters dressing and awaiting confirmation of *Ward*'s report of the submarine sinking when Fuchida's first wave deployed a few miles north of Opana Station. At a point roughly opposite Haleiwa Field, Fuchida signaled for the general attack at 0750. Precisely one minute thereafter Murata called on his torpedomen for their strike. Northwest of Ewa the torpedo bombers split into two groups of eight planes each under Nagai and Matsumura and raced for the west side of Pearl Harbor. Another flight under Murata and Lieutenant Ichiro Kitajima, composed also of two groups but with twelve planes each, flew southeastward, then swung north and northwestward in a large arc over Hickam Field and headed directly for Battleship Row.

Each torpedo group attacked in formations of twos and threes. Every torpedo pilot had explicit instructions to close in on his target, even at the risk of his life. If his observer-bombardier thought he might miss, the pilot would make additional runs until quite sure of a hit. If, after several passes, the observer still could not get a good sighting, he was to use his judgment and choose another target.

Kimmel's telephone rang again. Murphy had called him back, this time to report that *Ward* had stopped a sampan hovering near the submarine action. Even as the duty officer spoke, Fuchida, now opposite Barber's Point, flashed to his horizontal bombers *Tsu, tsu, tsu*—much the same signal as his earlier *To, to, to,* but applicable only to his own group.[1]

Takahashi's dive bombers had already swung into action. The sound of airplanes attracted the attention of Rear Admiral William Rhea Furlong, in command of Battle Forces Pacific, a formidable fleet of service vessels. Furlong was strolling along the quarterdeck of his flagship, the minelayer *Oglala*, awaiting his call to breakfast. *Oglala* was so ancient she seldom left dock, and the reaction of a seasoned sailor newly assigned to her was likely to be a half-incredulous, half-affectionate "What a tub!" This particular morning she happened to be in *Pennsylvania*'s normal berth at Dock 1010, outboard the cruiser *Helena*. Furlong, who lived aboard the ship, was senior officer present afloat (SOPA) that morning.

Furlong paid little attention to the roar of engines until he saw a bomb drop. *What a stupid, careless pilot,* he said to himself, *not to have secured his releasing gear.* The missile exploded harmlessly in a shower of earth near the water's edge at the southwest end of Ford Island. As the pilot cut hard to port and sped up the channel, Furlong saw the red ball of the Rising Sun and reacted instantly. "Japanese! Man your stations!" he shouted. At his command *Oglala* flashed the alarm: "All ships in harbor sortie."[2]

On *West Virginia* Ensign Roland S. Brooks saw what he thought to be an internal explosion on *California* and ordered Away Fire and Rescue Party! Actually the flame and smoke came from a burning hangar on Ford Island. His order brought hundreds of officers and men swarming topside, giving his ship a few precious seconds' grace and undoubtedly saving hundreds of lives.[3]

At that instant, about 0775, Matsumura and Nagai led the third and fourth torpedo groups from *Hiryu* and *Soryu* respectively straight to the west side of Ford Island. In Matsumura's eagerness to confirm the vessels he dipped so low that his plane rustled the sugarcane and he felt "the warm air of an unending summer land." Within seconds a pair of torpedoes cut swift paths through the shallow water to the light cruiser *Raleigh* and the target ship *Utah*. This waste of priceless torpedoes infuriated Matsumura, who had specifically instructed his men to avoid *Utah*. But Lieutenant Tamotsu Nakajima, young and inexperienced, thought he saw one missile slam into her and followed suit. And very disgruntled he was later because he had not profited by his drill in the recognition of American ships. Listing heavily to port, *Utah* began to capsize.[4]

Raleigh's officer of the deck called the antiaircraft men to their guns, assuming the air action to be "part of a routine air-raid drill." But just then, about 0755, a torpedo struck the cruiser at Frame 58, flooding the forward engine room and Nos. 1 and 2 firerooms. At once Seaman First Class Frank M. Berry ran for the ship's alarm, but it did not go off because "the electricity went the first thing."

The concussion awakened Ensign John R. Beardall, Jr., twenty-two year-old son of the President's naval aide. He hurried to the quarterdeck in his red pajamas, and one of the first things he saw was "those big red balls . . . and it didn't take long to figure out what was going on." His antiaircraft battery went into action within five minutes because all of *Raleigh*'s 3-inch guns had their ammunition in the ready boxes. By 0805 *Raleigh* listed hard to port. In spite of counterflooding, the list continued. Captain R. Bentham Simons immediately directed efforts to save his ship from capsizing. Meantime, at 0800 another torpedo had hurtled between *Raleigh* and *Detroit* about twenty-five yards from the latter's stern, to bury itself harmlessly in the mud [5]

In these crucial early moments Nagai flew across Ford Island, intent on hitting *Pennsylvania* in dry dock. But seeing that the mooring slip would check the torpedo, he loosed his missile at *Oglala*. As if to compensate the Japanese for having missed *Detroit*, the torpedo slid under *Oglala* and burst against the light cruiser *Helena*, crippling both ships in one blow. *Oglala's* log described the result: "The force of the explosion lifted up fireroom floor plates and ruptured hull on port side." *Helena's* log recorded: "At about 0757½, a series of three heavy explosions felt nearby. At about 0758, ship rocked by violent explosion on starboard side."[6]

Incredibly, all this action took place while Murphy delivered his brief message to Kimmel. The duty officer was still speaking when a yeoman rushed into his office, shouting, "There's a message from the signal tower saying the Japanese are attacking Pearl Harbor and this is no drill." Murphy passed the shocking news to Kimmel. The admiral slammed down the receiver and dashed outside, buttoning his white uniform jacket as he ran.[7]

Next door to Kimmel, the lawn of the Earles' new home commanded a clear view of Battleship Row across the harbor. Kimmel and Mrs. Earle stood transfixed as the planes flew over "circling in figure 8's, then bombing the ships, turning and dropping more bombs." They "could plainly see the rising suns on the wings and would have seen the pilot's faces had they leaned out." Mrs. Earle's sympathetic heart spilled over in grief and pity for the admiral as he watched "in utter disbelief and completely stunned," his stricken face "as white as the uniform he wore."

"I knew right away that something terrible was going on, that this was not a casual raid by just a few stray planes. The sky was full of the enemy," he said later. Gazing toward his beloved ships with bombers and fighters swooping over them like vampire bats, they saw "*Arizona* lift out of the water, then sink back down—way down." In those terrible moments neither uttered a word; the ghastly picture before them said everything.[8]

History had already swept past Kimmel with the speed of a movie out of control, beyond human capability to see or comprehend. Any number of Americans saw Murata's flight as it lumbered in and peeled off to strike but assumed that local planes were practicing. Even when the first torpedoes began to fall, many observers reacted as did Lieutenant Lawrence Ruff, waiting for mass to begin aboard the hospital ship *Solace*: "Oh, oh, some fool pilot has gone wild."[9]

One individual who grasped the situation quickly was Bicknell, who had a panoramic view from the lanai of his home above and behind Pearl Harbor. From the viewpoint of Japanese strategy, the attack made sense to him; nevertheless, the reality astounded him. "Well, naturally, when you are looking out of your window on a peaceful Sunday morning and see a battleship blow up under your eyes, you are pretty apt to be surprised." Suddenly he began "mumbling about these 'poinsettias and hibiscus'" much to his wife's perplexity. It had suddenly occurred to Bicknell that the Mori telephone call might have contained a code for certain types of ships.[10] *

If so, the code words merely confirmed what the Japanese already had learned. As they dropped their torpedoes that morning, Murata's men knew exactly what types of ship they would find in position. Murata waited eagerly for his observer's report. Would the new fins, perfected so late and adjusted so hurriedly, really work? "*Atarimashita!* ["It struck!"]" cried the observer. The triumphant cry echoed and reechoed as one after another the planes sent off their lone but mortal missiles. Elatedly Murata radioed his report: "Torpedoed enemy battleships. Serious damage inflicted."[11]

This was the news that Japan's naval leaders awaited—the outcome of the all-important torpedo attack on Battleship Row. On that crucial mission hung the results of the entire operation. Genda's heart pounded with joy. *Now the attack will be a success,* he thought. Whatever fierce satisfaction Nagumo and Kusaka may have felt, they remained outwardly calm. They and their staff officers present on the bridge exchanged glances. A faint smile played over Nagumo's lips—the first time Genda had seen Nagumo smile since the task force left Hitokappu Bay.[12]

One of the first torpedoes to strike *West Virginia* came from Matsumura on his second swipe at Battleship Row. "A huge waterspout splashed over the stack of the ship and then tumbled down like an exhausted geyser . . . immediately followed by another one. What a magnificent sight!" So impressed was Matsumura that he told his observer to photograph the scene. But the man misinterpreted the order and blazed away with his machine gun, wrecking the antenna of his own plane.

"By this time enemy aircraft fire had begun to come up very fiercely. Black bursts were spoiling the once beautiful sky," Matsumura recalled. "Even white bursts were seen mixed up among them." The white smoke came from harmless training shells as the Americans hurled everything imaginable at the Japanese while seamen smashed the locks of the ships' magazines. Now those magazines began to yield their deadly harvest, and Matsumura soared away, picked up a fighter escort, and headed for the rendezvous point.[13]

Ensign Nathan F. Asher, on the bridge of the destroyer *Blue*, never understood how his men "got their ammunition from the magazines to the guns in the fast and swift manner that they did." A few of the crew had awakened with Sunday morning hangovers but later said "they had never sobered up so fast in their lives."[14]

As luck would have it, *Vestal*'s officer of the deck was CWO Fred Hall, who the previous night had predicted a Japanese attack on Pearl Harbor. Hall immediately recognized the red disk under the bombers' wings and ordered Sound General Quarters! But the quartermaster, jaw at half-mast, stared at Hall

---

*See Chapter 58.

as if he had lost his mind. "Goddamn it," howled the officer, "I said 'Sound General Quarters!' Those are Jap planes up there." And he himself pulled the signal at 0755. *Vestal* opened fire at 0805. A bomb struck her "at frame 110 port side." and "a second hit at frame 44 starboard side." Each bomb killed one man and wounded several others.[15]

Oklahoma was moored port side at Berth F-5, outboard of *Maryland* in an exposed position. Goto closed in on his target. Suddenly the big ship loomed directly before him. "I was about twenty meters above the water," Goto said later, "when I released my torpedo. As my plane climbed up after the torpedo was off, I saw that I was even lower than the crow's nest of the great battleship. My observer reported a huge waterspout springing up from the ship's location. *'Atarimashita!'* he cried. The other two planes in my group . . . also attacked *Oklahoma*."[16]

Electrician's Mate First Class Irvin H. Thesman was ironing a pair of dungarees in the power shop when the public address system blared out: "Man your battle stations! This is no shit!" Although startled by such uninhibited language over the ship's PA, Thesman thought it just another drill. So he grabbed a bag of tools and a flashlight and dogtrotted to his station in the steering gear compartment.[17]

Two hits in rapid succession had already torn into *Oklahoma*'s vitals. Boatswain Adolph M. Bothne found both the aircraft ammunition ready boxes and the fire and rescue chest locked. He picked up a hammer and a cold chisel from a gear locker. At that moment "a third torpedo hit in the middle of the ship, and the ship started to list noticeably. . . ." Bothne "had to walk uphill to go to the starboard side, and after they had the ready boxes open there and the ammunition out they had no air to load the guns, and one of the men said there was no fire locks on the guns."[18]

Hastening toward his battle station in Turret No. 4 amidships, Gunner's Mate Second Class Edgar B. Beck decided there was no point in continuing on his way because "it was clear that we were going over." So he decided to concentrate on helping his buddies through the shell hoist, their only means of escape. He knew that when the ship capsized, the 14-inch shells, which weighed about 1,400 pounds, would break loose and crush to death anyone in their path.[19]

Oklahoma's executive officer, Commander J. L. Kenworthy, was the senior officer aboard. He and the ship's first lieutenant, Lieutenant Commander W. H. Hobby, concluded "that the ship was fast becoming untenable and that an effort should be made to save as many men as possible." So Kenworthy ordered Abandon Ship and directed the men "to leave over the starboard side and to work and climb over the ship's side out onto the bottom as it rolled over."[20]

Murata's strike on *West Virginia* and Goto's on *Oklahoma* came practically together. Now a torpedo swept right under *Vestal* and, in the words of Chief Boilermaker John Crawford, "blew the bottom out of *Arizona*."[21] Major Alan Shapley, the tall, handsome commander of *Arizona*'s Marine detachment, was enjoying his breakfast when he felt "a terrific jar." Thinking one of the forty-foot boats must have dropped off the crane to the fantail, he ran topside to investigate. He vividly recalled some sailors standing at *Arizona*'s rail watching a flight of planes flash across the harbor. He heard one of the men remark, "This is the best goddamn drill the Army Air Force has ever put on!"[22]

Captain Van Valkenburg and Damage Control Officer Lieutenant Commander Samuel G. Fuqua reached the deck about the same time, and the captain proceeded to the bridge. Fuqua directed Ensign H. D. Davidson to sound General Quarters. About that time the ship "took a bomb hit on the starboard side of the quarterdeck, just about abreast of No. 4 turret."[23]

It was the torpedo strike which Kimmel and Mrs. Earle saw from Makalapa Heights. "I knew the ship had been hit hard," Kimmel said later, "because even then I could see it begin to list." He did not recall having summoned his car, but suddenly it appeared, braking to a screaming halt. His longtime driver, Machinist Mate First Class Edgar C. Nebel, was at the wheel. Kimmel dived into his car. As it roared off, Captain Freeland A. Daubin, commander of Submarine Squadron Four, jumped on the running board. The admiral and his hitchhiker reached headquarters at about 0805, just as *California* shuddered with her first torpedo, rapidly followed by another "port side at frame 110."[24]

California, flagship of Pye's battle force, was moored singly in Berth F-3. This put her below the tanker *Neosho* to the southward on the edge of Ford Island in the direction of Pearl Harbor's outer channel and the sea. Train felt two distinct but rather dull thuds against the ship. These were the torpedoes crashing home. Immediately she began to list to port. By now guns blazed aboard *California*.[25] But of all the battleships in Pearl Harbor that morning, she was least capable of absorbing punishment. In preparation for Monday's inspection several manhole covers had been removed and others loosened. When the two torpedoes struck, water poured into the fuel system, cutting off light and power. An alert ensign, Edgar M. Fain, directed prompt counterflooding measures which saved the vessel from capsizing.[26]

Up to this time the inboard battleships had escaped with little damage. Now Fuchida's horizontal bombers roared on the scene to strike them as well as the outboard craft. After giving his attack signal, Fuchida had dropped back from the lead position, the better to observe the action, yielding pride of place to his number two plane. The honor was well deserved, for this aircraft held Aso and Watanabe, the tireless bombing team which had made the initial breakthrough in high-level practice.*

On the first run over the target, air turbulence prevented proper sighting, and only the number three plane released its missile. Throughout training this bombardier had experienced difficulty in timing. When Fuchida saw the bomb plunge ineffectually into the water, he assumed that the culprit had blundered

---

*See Chapter 19.

and shook his fist at number three in a rage. The disappointed bombardier indicated by gestures that enemy fire had jarred his bomb loose. Fuchida felt remorseful for having jumped to conclusions but had no time to brood. His own plane now rocked as if hit by a giant club.

"Is everything all right?" he cried out.

"A few holes in the fuselage," his pilot replied reassuringly.[27]

Two shocks thudded against *West Virginia*. By the time Commander R. H. Hillenkoetter, her executive officer, reached the quarterdeck, the ship had begun to list rapidly to port. Then came a "third heavy shock to port." Soon the top of Turret No. 3 caught fire. Another stunning explosion threw Hillenkoetter to the deck.

When the attack began, Captain Mervyn Bennion, *West Virginia*'s skipper, and her navigator, Lieutenant Commander T. T. Beattie, soon found communications disrupted, so they "went out on the starboard side of the bridge discussing what to do." Lieutenant Claude V. Rickets asked and received permission to counterflood, which he did with the able assistance of a boatswain's mate named Billingsley. This helped correct her list and kept her from capsizing.[28]

As Kimmel dashed out of his car at headquarters, the explosion of bombs, the whine of bullets, the roar of planes, the belching guns of aroused defenders, the acrid smell of fire and smoke—all blended into a nerve-racking cacophony of chaos. Murata's bombardiers still dropped their torpedoes, while dive bombers pounced like hawks on nearby Hickam Field and Ford Island. Far above, high-level bombers rained their deadly missiles as fighters shuttled in and out, weaving together the fearful tapestry of destruction. Numb and stricken, Kimmel rushed into his office, his face a mask of bleak incomprehension as he tried to pull himself together amid the tumbling ruins of his world. He had neither time nor inclination for self-pity. "My main thought was the fate of my ships," he said, ". . . to see what had taken place and then strike back at the Japs."[29]

Now his staff began to rally to his side. Smith found Kimmel, shocked but composed, watching the attack from the War Plans Office with Pye. He reminded them that they should not be together; a single blast could kill them both and leave the Fleet without a commander in chief. Pye moved to the other end of the building.[30]

As Davis jumped out of his car, he observed a group of officers, enlisted men, and civilians standing around the headquarters, gaping into the sky. Conditions inside, in Davis's opinion, were not much better. The air officer immediately manned his telephone, trying to reach anyone, anywhere on Oahu, who could get the Navy's planes into the air to seek the source of the attacking aircraft.[31]

Hurrying down the hall to his office, Layton ran into Captain Willard A. Kitts, Jr., Kimmel's gunnery officer. The captain proved his bigness of character by greeting Layton generously: "Here is the young man we should have listened to." Grimly just, McMorris said to Layton, "If it's any satisfaction to you, you were right and we were wrong." Layton could have done without

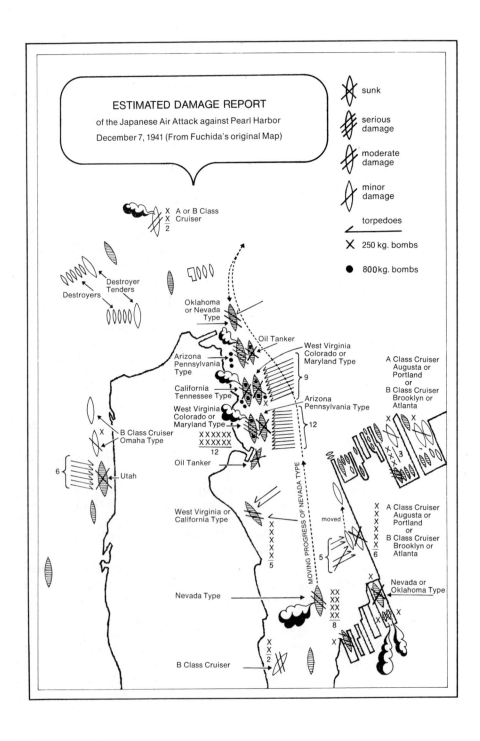

such concrete vindication as the Japanese were providing. He plunged into a sea of intelligence reports, which constantly grew more and more complex and confusing. Like Davis, he tried to find the nest of these Japanese sea hawks shooting up the Pacific Fleet.[32]

Murphy had already dispatched a message to CinCAF, CinCLANT, and CNO: "Enemy air raid, Pearl Harbor. This is not a drill." A few others followed. At 0812 Kimmel advised the entire Pacific Fleet and Stark: "Hostilities with Japan commenced with air raid on Pearl Harbor." Then at 0817 he instructed Patrol Wing Two: "Locate enemy force"—a succinct order easier to give than to accomplish.[33]

The atmosphere in Kimmel's headquarters struck Curts as one of "no hysteria, but ordered dismay." The communications officer joined Kimmel and Smith as they, too, tried to determine from what direction the attacking planes had come. The three officers could not see the actual strikes, but speedy reports kept them abreast of the situation. The effectiveness of the Japanese operation astounded them. But even Davis assumed that the enemy had but one carrier or two at the most.[34] At this time no one apparently recalled the Martin-Bellinger or Farthing reports, both of which had called the shots with almost uncanny accuracy.

Aboard the stricken *Oklahoma* about 150 men "perched along the blister ledge" at Bosun Bothne's direction. "Then the ship seemed to hesitate. . . ." At that moment the fourth torpedo struck. *Oklahoma* "bounced up, and when she settled down she turned over." Some of the men slid down the side into the water.[35] Mrs. Earle still watched the grisly scene from in front of her home. "Then slowly, sickeningly, the *Oklahoma* began to roll over on her side, until, finally, only her bottom could be seen. It was awful, for great ships were dying before my eyes! Strangely enough, at first I didn't realize that men were dying too."[36]

Thesman and his group in the steering gear compartment dodged to avoid being knocked senseless as lockers and spare parts tumbled down. At twenty-five, Thesman was the oldest in the group and felt responsible for his shipmates. Water began to trickle in through the ventilation system, and the sailors stuffed the ducts with mattresses, blankets, and anything else they could find.[37]

At this time the entire Japanese force seemed to concentrate their particular fury on the hapless *Arizona* and *West Virginia*. Just after *Oklahoma* heeled over, *Arizona* trembled with an indescribably fearful explosion and concussion which seemed to suck the very life out of the air. It may have been the dedicated, crack bombardier Kanai who sent down the missile that hit beside the No. 2 turret and detonated in the forward magazine.[38]

Almost 1,000 men perished in that frightful moment, including Admiral Kidd and Captain Van Valkenburgh. An ensign later told how the quartermaster had just reported to the captain a bomb hit "either by or on No. 2 turret." The next thing he knew, "the ship was sinking like an earthquake had struck it, and the bridge was in flames." Hastening forward after the first hit in a fruitless attempt to fight the fires, Fuqua met someone who informed him "that he observed a bomb go down the stack."[39] This story has persisted; however, some survivors believe it incorrect, pointing out that the angle of the stack would have prevented it and that such a strike would have exploded in the boiler room, not the magazine.[40] Fuqua, too, thought it improbable, but he did not intend to argue the point at that moment. Pausing only to order the forward magazine flooded, and finding that "all guns on the boat deck had ceased firing," he realized that "the ship was no longer in a fighting condition." He ordered Abandon Ship and set about rescuing the wounded.[41]

Strangely enough, the explosion that destroyed *Arizona* saved *Vestal*. The concussion put out her fires as though a giant candlesnuffer had been clapped over her. It also sent tons of debris down on her decks—"Parts of the ship, legs, arms and heads of men—all sorts of bodies," even living men. The explosion flung overboard about 100 men from *Vestal*, among them her skipper, Commander Young. *Vestal's* crew began to fish out of the water hideously burned refugees from *Arizona*. Aboard the repair ship each survivor received a shot of morphine, and shipmates hurried them to a hospital or to *Solace* as fast as possible.

About this time someone ordered Abandon Ship. Just as the first of the crew started to leave, a figure like some strange sea creature climbed out of the harbor and stood athwart the gangway. It was Young, oil dripping from his face and body, but none the worse for his dunking. "Where the hell do you think you're going?" he demanded of the officer of the deck.

"We're abandoning ship," the man replied.

"Get back aboard ship!" Young roared. "You don't abandon ship on me!" With that he and his remaining crewmen returned to their stations.[42]

Debris from *Arizona* also covered *Tennessee* and accounted for more of her damage than the two Japanese bombs which hit her. The attackers continued to pound *Arizona*, which took a total of eight bombs in addition to the torpedoes. The ship became totally untenable at approximately 1032. Of her complement of 1,400, fewer than 200 survived the attack.[43]

As though enraged because *West Virginia* seemingly refused to sink or capsize, Murata's torpedomen slammed more missiles into her. After she had taken six steel fish, Abe's flight of horizontal bombers dropped two bombs on her at 0808. A "large piece of shrapnel" struck Bennion in the stomach and mortally wounded him. Beattie sent for a pharmacist's mate, and Lieutenant Commander Doir C. Johnson hurried up with a big, well-built black mess attendant, Doris Miller. He had been the ship's heavyweight boxing champion, and Johnson thought he was just the man to help lift the captain out of danger.

The chief pharmacist's mate dressed Bennion's wound as best as he could. As smoke and flames engulfed the ship, Bennion ordered his subordinates to leave him where he was, the only order of his they ever disobeyed. He remained conscious, asking alert questions about the progress of the fight almost to the last. After he died, Johnson saw Miller, who was not supposed to handle anything deadlier than a swab, manning a machine gun, "blazing away as though he had fired one all his life." As he did so, his usually impassive face bore the deadly smile of a berserk Viking.[44]

Thus far *Nevada* had escaped the fate of the other battleships, being in a less vulnerable position. At 0802 her machine guns "opened fire on torpedo planes approaching at port beam." This was Kitajima's group from *Kaga*. One of his planes fell to the battleship's fire "100 yards on port quarter. . . ." A second dropped shortly thereafter, but not before releasing his missile, which at 0803 tore a huge hole in the ship's port bow about frame 40 and flooded a number of compartments. This was the ship's "greatest structural casualty."

Nevada's skipper, Captain F. W. Scanland, was not on board, but Lieutenant Commander J. F. Thomas, USNR, senior officer present, took over promptly and efficiently. At 0805—just as Fuchida's high-level bombers appeared "on both bows"—*Nevada* began to list "slightly to port." The battleship's 5-inch and .50 caliber guns opened immediate fire. Within a minute "several bombs fell close aboard to port. . . ." Counterflooding began two minutes later. Because burning fuel oil on the surface, ignited when *Arizona* received her first major strike, now threatened *Nevada*, "it was considered necessary to get under way to avoid further danger. . . ."[45]

Tales of heroism far beyond the call of duty abounded on *Nevada*, as on every ship in Pearl Harbor. Twenty-one-year-old Ensign Joseph K. Taussig, Jr., whose admiral father had weaned him on the subject of a war with Japan, was officer of the deck. When General Quarters sounded at 0801, he acted as air defense officer and went at once to his battle station on the starboard antiaircraft director. Being the senior officer present in the AA battery, he "took charge and directed its fire" even after a missile passed completely through his thigh. Refusing all efforts to take him to a battle dressing station, he "insisted in continuing his control of the AA battery and the continuation of fire on enemy aircraft. . . ."[46]

Although severely damaged, *Nevada* was still very much afloat and full of fight when Lieutenant Ruff scrambled up her side from *Solace*'s motor launch. He knew that, with the captain and other senior officers ashore, unusually heavy responsibilities would fall to him and to Thomas, who was belowdecks at his battle station. When Ruff got close enough to communicate, he suggested that Thomas run the ship's activities below while he, Ruff, would manage topside.[47]

One by one Murata's torpedo bombers, having discharged their missiles, roared away, picked up a fighter escort and winged northward. They had lost five torpedo planes, all from *Kaga*.[48] As always in dealing with contemporary battle reports, it is virtually impossible to determine exactly whom to credit with what specific kill. Indeed, American accounts were wildly at variance, as was only to be expected in view of the stunning surprise, the excitement of battle, and the billows of smoke rolling up from the burning ships. Moreover, the Americans were fighting, blind mad, and each man was eager to claim for his own outfit any aircraft he saw go down in flames.

When word reached Kimmel about the fate of his battleships, it wrung a groan of anguish from his lips. But much as the loss of his ships grieved him, what really tore his brave heart was the death and suffering of his men.[49] These were not neat rows of statistics to Kimmel. In that day the United States Navy was a small, neighborly community where almost everyone knew everyone else. A man might enlist on one ship and stay with her until he retired twenty or thirty years later. Comradeship at Annapolis, service together, and family intermarriage bound the officers with ties none the less binding for being intangible. Kimmel knew thousands of men at Pearl Harbor by sight, hundreds by name, and scores as personal friends. All of them, from seasoned skippers to the greenest sailors, were his men, his responsibility.

Curts was standing beside Kimmel at the window when a spent bullet crashed through the glass. It struck the admiral on the chest, left a dark splotch on his white uniform, then dropped to the floor. Kimmel picked it up. It was a .50 caliber machine-gun bullet. Somehow the slug seemed symbolic. Much as Kimmel craved the chance to avenge this terrible day, in his heart he knew that the debacle spelled the end of his career as CinCUS. Kimmel was not given to dramatics. But such was the depth of his sorrow and despair that he murmured, more to himself than to Curts, "It would have been merciful had it killed me."[50]

CHAPTER 63

"THEY

CAUGHT

THEM

ASLEEP,

BY GOD!"

Awaiting authentication of the submarine sinking report, Ramsey stood near a window of the Ford Island command center, watching the color guard prepare to hoist the flag. At about 0755 he heard the scream of a plane diving over the station, turned to Ballinger, and said, "Dick, get that fellow's number, for I want to report him for about sixteen violations of the course and safety regulations." As the plane went into its dive, each man looked out separate windows to follow its course. "Dick, did you get his number?" Ramsey asked. "No, but I think it was a squadron commander's plane because I saw a band of red on it," replied Ballinger.

"Check with the squadrons and find out which squadron commanders' planes are in the air," Ramsey ordered. That very instant Ballinger reported, "I saw something black fall out of that plane when it completed its dive."

At precisely 0757 an explosion reverberated from the hangar area. Ramsey's face changed in swift comprehension. "Never mind the squadron commander, Dick," he exclaimed. "That was a Jap plane and a delayed action bomb."[1] The words scarcely out of his mouth, Ramsey raced across the corridor to the radio room and ordered all radiomen on duty to send out in plain English: "AIR RAID, PEARL HARBOR. THIS IS NOT DRILL!"[2]

Thus, at exactly 0758 one of the most famous radio messages ever dispatched clicked over the airwaves. As we have seen, Kimmel's headquarters followed with a similar one, but it was Commander Logan Ramsey who first sent forth the word that woke the United States from its long sleep.

As the dive bombers whistled down, Ramsey dispatched a second message ordering all patrol planes to assigned sectors, with the object of locating the

517

Japanese Fleet. He had no idea how futile this effort was, how completely the attackers were clipping Hawaii's wings. Then he telephoned Bellinger: "The Japanese are attacking!" But his chief replied skeptically, "You wouldn't kid about a thing like that," and Ramsey had quite a time convincing him that he was not joking.[3]

This would be Bellinger's first day out of bed since his bout with flu, but he was not the man to stay behind when a war was beginning. "Come on, Charlie! Let's get down to headquarters," he called to Commander Coe, his war plans officer, who had just brought his wife and two children to the Bellinger home, where the basement provided shelter from the bombs.

"Admiral, at least let me get my pants on," protested Coe. So Bellinger drove off "like a bat out of hell," and Coe tore back to his quarters for suitable clothing. Driving "hell's bells" for headquarters, Coe passed officers and enlisted men making a beeline for their battle stations, while women and children plunged toward air-raid shelters. The sky swarmed with Japanese planes.[4] Within a few minutes Takahashi's dive bombers had destroyed about half of Ford Island's complement of carrier-based planes and made a shambles of the hangars.

Jumping out of his car on the seaplane parking apron, Ford's commanding officer, Captain Shoemaker, gazed at the appalling spectacle of flaming aircraft and the hangar "burning like a forest fire." Scarcely a plane remained undamaged on the apron. Seeing a petty officer and some sailors ducking behind what protection they could find, Shoemaker set them to pulling the untouched aircraft away from the fires. This was about all they could do, for when the Ford Island fire brigade clanged on the scene at that moment, they found no water pressure—*Arizona* had sunk on the water mains. Shoemaker's particular nightmare was the chance of a titanic holocaust from the tank farm and the possible explosion of the tanker *Neosho*, moored starboard side to Berth F-4, Ford Island. *Neosho* had finished discharging aviation gasoline to the dock only five minutes before the Japanese struck.[5]

At the tank farm Shoemaker found matters in better shape than he had dared hope. An alert ensign had turned on the water sprinklers above the giant tanks. Shoemaker looked out to *Neosho* with anxious eyes. She was berthed near the fuel supply. These tanks held gasoline, not oil. If they had been hit or if the Japanese struck *Neosho* and the ship blew up, the nearby battleships—*Maryland, Tennessee, West Virginia*—would have turned into infernos. But *Neosho*'s skipper, Captain John S. Phillips, had everything under control. Her AA battery was firing by 0810, and soon Phillips had his ship under way. By 0842 she was on course to Berth M-3 at Merry's Point.[6]

Meanwhile, Ramsey tried frantically to reach Patrol Wing One at Kaneohe by telephone. He hoped to get the PBYs off the ground to search for the enemy because the Japanese had complete command of the air over Ford Island.[7] But Kaneohe was in no position to help either Ford Island or itself.

Aviation Machinist Mate Third Class Guy C. Avery was lazing on his bunk in the sun porch of a bungalow on Kaneohe when he heard "the sound of a lone plane quite near our house. It passed and returned. 'To hell with the Army,' I thought. 'Every day is the same to them.' " But something in the sound of the engine roused his curiosity. He reached the window in time to see "Zeroes just beginning to fan out over the heart of the station and opening fire promiscuously." He shouted to his sleeping comrades, "The Japs are here! It's war!" To which one man replied comfortably, "Well, don't worry about it, Avery. It'll last only two weeks."

Avery checked his watch. It was 0748. "We were struck first of all and about seven minutes before Pearl Harbor," he wrote. "Our OD called nearby Bellows Field to warn them and to ask for help, but his call was regarded as a practical joke—but only for a few minutes, then it was too late."[8] In fact, a Kaneohe contractor, Sam Aweau, had phoned Hickam and Bellows fields that the Japanese had attacked, but no one believed him.[9]

Commander Harold M. "Beauty" Martin, Kaneohe's popular CO, had little to fight with. He had 303 sailors and 31 officers, as well as 93 Marines plus 2 officers. Even Martin's mobile antiaircraft had rolled back to an Army installation on December 5. He had only thirty-six PBYs and a few miscellaneous planes.

Of Kaneohe's aircraft, four were moored in the bay "at about a thousand yards apart." The remainder "were parked on the ramp except for four which were in No. 1 hangar." By the time Martin reached the administration building from his home "the first plane on the water had begun to burn. . . ." Zeros launched the attack, and dive bombers followed within a few minutes. The first bomb demolished Martin's only fire truck. Many of his personnel were so new that he wondered how they would perform in combat. He need not have worried. "It was remarkable," he said. "There was no panic. Everyone went right to work battling back and doing his job."[10] Even so, in a brief eight minutes the Japanese had struck Kaneohe a devastating initial blow, and they were not through yet. So when Ramsey completed his call, Kaneohe was in even worse shape proportionally than Ford Island.

By this time the waters lapping at Ford Island swarmed with rescue activity. Amid explosions, strafing, and blazing oil, able-bodied survivors helped their buddies off the burning battleships and into waiting launches, barges, or anything they could muster. These plied back and forth to Ford Island with wounded, burned, and shocked officers and men. The smart gigs of Admirals Pye and Leary darted about like water bugs, hauling aboard survivors from the ships and ferrying them ashore. Countless others dived from their ships, swam ashore, and scrambled onto the island, soaked with oil, barely clothed, many with varying degrees of burns and wounds.

The wounded arrived so fast that Lieutenant Cecil D. Riggs, staff medical officer of Patrol Wing Two, and his assistants could do no more than administer morphine, then mark foreheads with Mercurochrome to indicate they had injected the drug. Within the next hour and a half almost 300 casualties of all types arrived. The medics converted the Marine barracks and the main mess into temporary hospitals. Several other doctors and about fourteen or fifteen corpsmen arrived.[11]

Soon patients overflowed onto the patio, where Mary Ann Ramsey, Logan Ramsey's sixteen-year-old daughter, recorded their names and tried to do for them the little any untrained person could. She knelt beside one man after another, cradling him in her arms like a sick child, easing his last moments from the deep well of compassion the Japanese bombs uncapped. As each one died, she gently laid him down, covered him reverently, and moved on to the next shattered patient.[12]

Into Ford Island's "royal rat race," as Coe characterized the situation, flew a Navy SBD from *Enterprise*, with Commander H. L. "Brig" Young at the controls. He had with him Halsey's flag secretary, Lieutenant Commander Brum Nichol. Nichol's first impression was: "My God, the Army has gone crazy, having antiaircraft drill on Sunday morning." A little nearer, he recognized the red ball and tried unsuccessfully to limber his gun. "Then they went through the damndest amount of antiaircraft fire and bullets fire that he had ever seen, before or since, and finally got in to the field at Ford Island."[13] When the SBD rolled to a halt, Shoemaker greeted two exceedingly indignant and confused fliers as they climbed out, demanding, "What the hell goes on here?"[14]

Close on Young's wings came eighteen more aircraft from *Enterprise*. In fact, when Halsey received CinCPAC's message that an air raid was in progress he leaped to his feet, shouting, "My God, they're shooting at my own boys! Tell Kimmel!"[15] American antiaircraft did indeed shoot down one of Halsey's planes, which fell into the sea, but both pilot and observer were rescued. Itaya's Zeros shot down four, with only two American pilots living to tell the tale. Lieutenant (j.g.) Clarence Dickinson bailed out just west of Ewa Field. Eventually he reached Ford Island in a series of hitchhikes. Another SBD crash-landed at Burns Field, Kauai. The remainder, by hook or crook, got into either Ford or Ewa. Shoemaker gratefully scooped them in, and after the attack they went out to hunt the Japanese.[16]

At the control tower at Hickam Field, Colonel Farthing, the wiry Texan who commanded that installation, chatted with Lieutenant Colonel Cheney Bertholf, adjutant general of the Hawaiian Air Force. Captain Gordon Blake, base operations officer, stood by to guide in the expected B-17s—the same flight for which Tyler mistook Fuchida's blip on the Opana radar screen. Mollison phoned that he would arrive shortly.

Suddenly a cloud of planes screamed down from the north. Quickly the oncoming aircraft divided up and zoomed off in various directions, one section of nine bombers speeding toward Hickam. Farthing saw a plane flying slowly over Pearl Harbor—"just waddling like a duck." Sick horror gripped him when he spotted the Rising Sun of Japan and watched a torpedo splash into the water and streak for a battleship. Simultaneously a series of explosions thundered across Hickam Field.[17]

Mollison had halfway finished shaving when he heard two detonations. He threw a bathrobe over his pajamas and hurried outside to see what was going on. Just as he emerged, a Zero came flying down the street with death winking from each machine gun. At the same moment Captain Brooke E. Allen, an acting squadron commander of Hickam's bombers, burst out of his home opposite, bathrobe flapping, "exposing his nudity." Frantically waving his arms in the air and shaking his fist at the Zero, he shouted in a sort of desperate triumph, "I *knew* the little sons of bitches would do it on a Sunday! I *knew* it!"

"Brooke, this is no place for us to be," Mollison called to him. "Let's get into our clothes and get going." Suiting action to the word, the two officers hastened to their respective posts.[18]

Lieutenant Vernon H. Reeves saw what looked like an aircraft sprinkling toothpicks on the roof of Hangar No. 9. Actually a Japanese bomber had just made splinters of the roof. A plane sped by Reeves's window, its wingtip a scant yard from the ground. It appeared to be pouring lead into the door of the Officers' Club. Reeves's astonished admiration of the pilot's skill drove clear out of his mind any realization that the man was shooting up Hickam Field. Turning to some of his companions, he said, "He must be a German." Then he did a mental doubletake. He and his buddies hastened outside and started to fire their sidearms at the planes. Reeves had no conviction that he could hit one. "If we have to win the war with this damn thing," he said disgustedly, "we'll never make it."[19]

At headquarters Mollison called Phillips to break the news that Oahu was under Japanese attack. Phillips had already heard the bombs, and the thought went through his mind: *This is Sunday. What can this be? We planned nothing.* Now he met Mollison's information with an incredulous "You're out of your mind, Jimmy. What's the matter, are you drunk? Wake up! Wake up!"

The sorely tried Mollison gritted his teeth and held out the receiver so that Phillips could hear the crash of the bombs. Finally, Short's chief of staff took in the situation. "I can hear it," he said. "I can hear it. What do you want me to do?" Then, inspired: "I'll tell you what, I'll send over a liaison officer immediately." Mollison's jaw fell. So did the ceiling of his office, as if it shared the colonel's amazed frustration.[20]

Martin arrived at headquarters about ten minutes after Mollison and at Mollison's suggestion established himself on the ground floor instead of his upstairs office so that he would have two ceilings between him and the enemy. Mollison felt deep pity and concern for his chief. Not in good health, Martin was obviously a very sick man that morning. His old ulcer had broken open, and he was hemorrhaging internally.[21] But suffering in body and spirit, he was still an airman, and his "ambition at the time was to try to get the carriers if we possibly could."[22]

Out on the flight line, Allen had only one thought: *Get the bombers into the air and strike the enemy.* At the operations area he found Takahashi's planes "knocking the hell out of everything." The first bomb scored a direct hit on a repair hangar.[23] Another exploded in a supply building, hurtling myriads of nuts, bolts, and wheels through the air. A missile crashed through the roof of the enlisted men's hall, located in the center of the huge main barracks, killing thirty-five men instantly. Others poured out in anguished bewilderment, dragging with them their bleeding and moaning wounded.[24]

The base chapel took a direct hit. The "Snake Ranch," the enlisted men's new beer hall, was shattered. Another bomb opened the base guardhouse and released the prisoners, who immediately manned the gun a nearby sergeant was trying to mount alone. Still another missile struck the firehouse and tore into the water mains, lifting geysers ten to fifteen feet high, making it virtually impossible for the defenders to stem the inferno.[25]

Allen hurled himself into his B-17 and started three engines rolling; although he could not turn the fourth, he taxied the Flying Fortress away from its neighbors to safety. At that moment Zeros of the Second Carrier Division joined the dive bombers in strafing runs. Temporarily Allen had to abandon hope of taking off, as streams of incendiary bullets turned bomber after bomber into sheets of crackling flames.[26]

The Japanese concentrated on the formidable B-17s. Lieutenant Yoshio Shiga strafed them three or four times, pulling out of his run at a mere 120 feet or so. He observed that this type of bomber was extremely difficult to set afire, even when helpless on the ground.[27] In fact, at the end of the attack Martin could still get four B-17s into the air for a search.[28]

Straight into this inferno sped Landon's B-17s, a fourteen-hour flight behind them, unarmed, low on gas, and manned by skeleton crews. From Pearl Harbor, Chief Petty Officer Harry Rafsky, enlisted aide to Rear Admiral William L. Calhoun, commander, Base Force, saw the big bombers approaching and thought they belonged to the enemy. He said to himself: *Jesus Christ, the Japanese are really coming in now!*[29]

Landon was pleased to see a group of planes flying toward them from the south. *Here comes the Air Force out to greet us,* he thought. At that instant he saw the planes dive in with machines guns blazing, the sun glaring from the red disk of the Rising Sun. A voice over Landon's intercom barked, "Damn it, those are Japs!"

By skillful evasion Landon lost them. As he banked to land at Hickam, Blake warned from the control tower, "You have three Japs on your tail." Landon looked back; sure enough, three Zeros were hanging onto his plane like bats to a cliff, pouring in slugs right and left. To make matters worse, the United States forces on the ground also slammed shot and shell at him. It speaks well for the skill and nerve of the B-17 pilots that they managed to land under such conditions, but they did so, scattered all over the island.[30]

By this time Martin had called Bellinger, both because the Navy was responsible for the search and because he was supposed to turn control of his bombers over to the Navy in case of attack. Bellinger informed Martin that "he had no information whatever . . . as to which direction to go to find the carriers. . . ."[31] Not that it mattered. Neither Martin nor Bellinger had enough planes left airworthy to challenge Nagumo's armada successfully. When the first-wave attackers sped off to greener pastures, they had destroyed or seriously damaged about half of Hickam's aircraft and left behind them a hideous caricature of the smart, well-tended base it had been half an hour before.

As the Japanese swung down on their next target—Wheeler Field—First Petty Officer Kazuo Muranaka could see "through the breaks of clouds flashes of fire caused by hits on hangars. Looking at my comrades in their planes, I could see them grinning, with sharp eyes, hungry for good games. Making a single row formation, we went down through breaks in the clouds. Wheeler air base was already a sea of fire."[32] Lieutenant Akira Sakamoto's group of twenty-five dive bombers from *Zuikaku* had ignited the flames. Among his pilots was Ema, who had expected to run into a hotbed of flak and could hardly believe it when no U.S. interceptors or AA fire greeted them. He could see planes "the color of gold dust" lined up in tidy rows on the ground. Although some of the dive bombers returned to strafe four or five times, none was shot down over Wheeler. "It was more like a practice run than actual combat," said Ema.[33]

Colonel William J. Flood, the down-to-earth midwesterner who commanded Wheeler, had rushed the building of more than 100 U-shaped dirt bunkers, about ten feet high, in which to disperse his planes. But this morning, despite Flood's uneasy protests, Wheeler's fighters, in accordance with Short's directions, stood lined up under armed guard on the concrete mat in front of the hangars. As at Hickam, the aircraft were not as lethal as they looked. Of the eighty-two in commission, a mere fifty-two were modern types—P-40Bs and P-40Cs. All thirty-nine P-36As, twenty of which were ready to fly, were obsolescent. And all the fighters had their teeth drawn, for the ammunition belts were removed at night and placed in the hangars.

Flood had settled down to enjoy his morning newspaper when he heard "this awful *whang.*" After rushing outside, he saw Sakamoto's airmen "bombing and strafing the base, the planes, the officers' quarters and even the golf course. I could see some of the Japanese pilots lean out of their planes and smile as they zoomed by. . . . Hell, I could even see the gold in their teeth."[34]

As each bomber delivered its deadly load, it circled and swung into the target again to strafe. Zeros joined the bombers, and together they tore the base to shreds, sometimes flying so low that the pilots later found scraps of installation wires wrapped around their landing gear.[35] As soon as they hit one of the parked fighters, it became a fountain of flame. Then the craft next to it ignited until the whole area in front of the hangars was a flowing river of fire. Shouting orders, Major General Howard C. Davidson, in command of the Fourteenth Pursuit Wing, worked feverishly with his men, disengaging undamaged planes and hand pushing them to safety. Even this proved a challenging task because the Japanese had shot the tires off many of them.[36] "We did not have the guns loaded," Davidson testified later. "That was our biggest difficulty . . . especially since one of the hangars where we had a lot of our ammunition stored was afire, and the ammunition was afire too."[37]

Actually Wheeler had remarkably little protection against such an attack. When asked at the Army board what was Wheeler's scheme of antiaircraft protection, Flood replied, "Well, there wasn't any scheme. We didn't have any antiaircraft other than machine guns." He presumed his field was "covered by antiaircraft fire of the Department." What is more, Wheeler had no "place for immediate protection," no air-raid shelters.[38]

Lieutenants George S. Welch and Kenneth Taylor from Haleiwa Field had spent the night in a way after Yamamoto's heart—a poker game following a dance at the Wheeler Officers' Club. It was almost 0800 when the winners picked up the last chips. At the first crackle of firing Taylor "thought a Navy man had probably gone off the main route." But realizing the meaning of the scarlet disks, they finally reached Haleiwa by telephone and ordered their P-40s loaded. Then they scrambled into Taylor's car and headed for Haleiwa, urged along by Japanese "machine-gunning all around. . . ."[39]

Okajima found the air over Wheeler so full of Japanese planes that he decided to head elsewhere for better hunting. He led his men to Ewa Field, the Marine air base at Barber's Point.[40] The dive bombers stayed at Wheeler long enough to rip open hangars, completely demolish the post exchange, and slam into an enlisted men's barracks, killing several hundred on the spot and badly wounding others. "It was a pitiful, unholy mess," said Flood.[41]

By the time the bombers and fighters winged away they had knocked out at least one-half of Davidson's aircraft, including thirty of the new P-40s. Strangely enough, they had destroyed only four of the "obsolescent" P-36s.[42] Takahashi radioed the task force jubilantly: "Bombed Ford Island, Hickam and Wheeler. Terrible damage inflicted."[43]

Ewa Field had already received a baptism of fire before Sakamoto and his dive bombers followed Okajima. Indeed, the officer of the day, Captain Leonard Ashwell, sighted the Japanese bombers off Barber's Point at 0753— before they hit Pearl Harbor. Streaking in over the Waianae Mountains, twenty-one Zeros made repeated passes at Ewa's parked aircraft, firing one after the other until a good half had been destroyed or seriously damaged. Men erupted from their tents and ran through the fire for their planes. Gas spilled from the tanks and soon the area flamed with blazing puddles.

Corporal Duane W. Shaw, Ewa's fire truck driver, knew the planes already burning at the end of the runway could not be saved, but he hoped to rescue valuable equipment such as guns and spare parts. He pushed the pedal to its limit and urged his vehicle down the runway. It was like trying to run a steeplechase on an army mule, for the truck dated back to 1930 and refused to go over 42 mph. A strafer shot off the rear tires, and Shaw's valiant try ended in a screech of tortured rubber.

Ten or fifteen minutes after this initial strike, the dive bombers and fighters that had cleaned up at Hickam and Wheeler swooped in. They concentrated on buildings and personnel, not even sparing hospital tents.[44] As Shiga screamed down, he found himself facing a lone marine, firing at Shiga's 7.7 mm. guns with a pistol. Sidearms against a Zero! Shiga mentally "paid him a good respect. . . ."[45]

A group of marines improvised a gun mount from a scout plane, shot down one Zero, and winged a number of others. Against this, the attackers had destroyed or temporarily knocked out nine of Ewa's eleven Wildcat fighters, eighteen of the thirty-two scout bombers, and six out of eight utility planes. The dive bombers and fighters assigned the mission of achieving command of the skies over Oahu had fulfilled their task at a total cost of one dive bomber and three Zeros—an amazing record.[46]

Where were the Army's defenses that morning? How was such a thing possible? The testimony of Charles J. Utterback, head foreman for the district engineers, put the painful truth of that dreadful day in a nutshell: "The only thing I heard that morning, sir, was 'They caught them asleep, by God' . . . I think I heard that comment 50 times that day."[47]

When Short heard bombs exploding, his "first idea was that the Navy was having some battle practice. . . ." About "three minutes after eight" Phillips ran over with the message "that it was the real thing."

"I immediately told him to put into effect Alert No. 3," Short testified. "That's all the order we needed. And by 8:10 that had been given." For as Short explained, "I didn't know how serious the attack might develop. If they would take a chance like that, they might even take a chance on a landing of troops, and so I sent everybody to his battle position."[48] Thus, Short swung from one extreme to another—from defense only against sabotage to defense against a full-scale invasion.

Short's G-1, Colonel Throckmorton, rushed his wife to safety in the basement, then hastened to his office only some 400 feet away. Soon Major Swede Henderson, the headquarters commandant, charged in. "Where are the keys to the forward echelon?" he panted. The keys to the advance headquarters at Aliamanu Crater were in Donegan's safe, but Short's G-3 had not yet reached his office from early mass. No one knew the combination, but Throckmorton hopefully twirled the dial, and the door swung open. Throckmorton considered the feat providential, and everyone drew a breath of relief. Now Short and his staff could go to the crater and immediately set to work. For it was from this command post, several miles from Fort Shafter and under fifteen feet of rock, that Short expected to direct the defense of Oahu against a Japanese landing.[49]

While Colonel Dunlop, the department adjutant general, worked away, an officer's radio nearby played church music. The favorite old hymns struck Dunlop as positively macabre under the circumstances. But the music did not last long. Soon the radio cracked out urgent messages: "Get off the roads and stay off." "Don't block traffic!" "Stay at home!"[50]

As soon as Bicknell realized what was happening, he called first his OD in downtown Honolulu, then the OD at Fort Shafter: "There is an air attack on Pearl Harbor." Bicknell did not know who answered the phone. "But whoever the dimwit was said this: 'Go back to sleep, you're having a bad dream.'"

Bicknell was looking for Fielder when he bumped into Short, who seemed "in a state of animated confusion." He knew that Pearl Harbor was under attack but nothing concerning the progress of events. "What's going on out there?" the general asked.

"I'm not sure, General, but I just saw two battleships sunk," Bicknell replied.

Short stared at him incredulously and snapped, "That's ridiculous!" With that he walked away.[51]

Actually the Japanese paid much less attention to the Hawaiian Department's ground forces than to the Navy or the Hawaiian Air Force. They made no attempt to knock out Army installations except those connected with air power. Anyone in an analytical mood might have reflected that this neglect quite clearly indicated that the Japanese did not have immediate invasion on their minds.

At Camp Malakole at Barber's Point, Lieutenant Willis T. Lyman was preparing to go to church when the Japanese struck. "The first plane that we fired at . . . was approximately a hundred yards. The second plane was 75 feet at the lowest point . . . it was almost pointblank fire both ways," he testified. ". . . That plane . . . made a climbing turn to the left and wheeled out and kept dipping down . . . and struck the water some distance out."[52]

It was fitting that Fort Kamehameha, named for Hawaii's national hero, should account for another of Itaya's Zeros. Captain Frank W. Ebey of the Fifty-fifth Coast Artillery was reading Stephen Vincent Benét's *John Brown's Body* and had just reached "the surprise at Shiloh Church when the attack occurred." He had a full complement of men on hand, his supply sergeant hurried up with ammunition, and Ebey set up the machine guns on the tennis court at the rear of his quarters. These started to chatter at 0813.[53]

Just as Ebey's chief, Colonel William J. McCarthy, reached the battery at the lower end of Oahu Point, he saw a gruesome sight:

> . . . a Japanese plane had just struck a tree and caromed off the first tree and struck into a wall at my right at the ordnance machine gun shed. . . . The pilot was dead . . . stuffed in the tree, but the plane was on the ground, and the engine went around the ordnance shop. In caroming off he [*sic*] struck several men who were in the road. One man was completely decapitated. Another man apparently had been hit by the props, because his legs and arms and head were off, lying right on the grass.[54]

Lieutenant Stephen G. Saltzman, communications officer of the Ninety-eighth Coast Artillery Regiment at Schofield, heard "what sounded like two planes pulling out of a dive over Kam Highway" at about 0825. Grabbing a Browning automatic rifle from one of the men nearby and "a couple of clips of ammunition," he ran outside and dropped to his knees. Slightly behind him knelt Sergeant Lowell V. Klatt, in charge of wire communications, who also had snatched a BAR. Just at that moment the Japanese plane "opened up with his four machine guns." Saltzman was "too mad to be scared." The enemy pulled out of his dive to avoid high-tension wires, and after Saltzman and Klatt emptied their clips, he crashed on the other side of their building. Both men ran around the corner to check damage. The plane was burning so fiercely they could not get close. Klatt believed that the two Japanese must have been killed instantly, for they had made no effort to get out: ". . . they were just all crashed down in the cockpit. . . ."[55]

In Short's testimony about his defenses, he sounded quite complacent concerning the speed with which they reacted. For example, in speaking of the Sixty-Fourth Infantry's batteries, he said, ". . . there was no lost motion. There wasn't any confusion as to what should be done."[56]

No lost motion, but much lost time. Short had been so obsessed with guarding against a theoretical danger from within that he had made quick defense against an attack from without virtually impossible. By the time his antiaircraft guns were ready for action it was too late for them to have any significant effect. Of the four aircraft which fell to Army guns during Fuchida's first wave, all succumbed to machine-gun or BAR fire when they screamed down to strafe within range of these relatively limited weapons.

In Washington Knox had returned to his office at approximately 1300, following his conference with Hull and Stimson. Sometime later Stark and Turner joined him in a discussion which lasted about an hour. Presently they broke off and walked out of Knox's office into that of his confidential assistant, John H. Dillon. They were standing by Dillon's desk when a naval commander appeared at the door with a dispatch. Dillon recalled that the message went "something like 'We are being attacked. This is no drill.'"

Knox read it incredulously. Obviously confused, he blurted out, "My God, this can't be true, this must mean the Philippines." But the office of origin—CinCPAC—made the truth immediately evident. And Stark replied, "No, sir; this is Pearl."[57]

CHAPTER 64

"OH,

HOW POWERFUL

IS THE

IMPERIAL

NAVY!"

From the bridge of *Antares*, Grannis gazed in angry dismay toward the "confusion, blackness and disaster" of Pearl Harbor. Suddenly "one of the most beautiful sights" he had ever seen met his eyes—a destroyer breaking through the curtain of smoke and heading for the sea. The sun-spangled waters piled high on each side in impressive bow waves.[1] This was probably *Helm*, the first of several destroyers to clear Pearl Harbor. She had already been under way when the attack started. At 0817, as she emerged from the channel, she spotted a midget submarine struggling to free itself from the coral reef. *Helm* "increased speed to 25 knots, turned hard right toward enemy submarine," and fired, but none of her shots went home. The intruder broke loose and submerged at 0821.[2]

The craft held the unfortunate Sakamaki, who had managed to struggle this far. There he stuck three times on the coral in his attempts to penetrate the harbor. He might have fired on and perhaps hit *Helm*, but he decided to save his torpedoes. He had his instructions to aim at a battleship or a carrier, and he had his heart set on torpedoing *Pennsylvania*, unaware that the flagship was in dry dock. He should have settled for the destroyer. Either a shot from *Helm* or the crashing of his minisub into the reef knocked him temporarily unconscious and destroyed one of his torpedo firing mechanisms.[3]

Another destroyer to escape was *Aylwin*. She received orders to get under way at 0828, and a bomb dropping fifty yards off her starboard bow emphasized the directive. Another bomb explosion thrust the fantail against the anchor buoy. The destroyer's vibrations told her officers that one of her screws had been damaged.

Aylwin put to sea with an all-ensign officer complement. The four, of whom Ensign Stanley Caplan was senior, were naval reservists, and their combined sea experience totaled slightly more than one year. They were almost certain they could never get the ship out of harbor through the rain of bombs, but after much difficulty and maneuvering, *Aylwin* broke into the open sea at 0932. Her skipper, Lieutenant Commander R. H. Rodgers, pursued his ship out of harbor about an hour later, but Caplan did not stop because he had orders to rendezvous with *Enterprise* and because he feared that the numerous submarine contacts being reported made it too risky to heave to.[4]

Lieutenant Commander Harold F. Pullen and his gunnery officer of the destroyer *Reid* parked their car in the first available opening near the officers' landing. As Pullen looked toward Battleship Row, for the first time the real impact of the attack hit home. "My God, it looks like a movie set," he said to his companion. Suddenly he saw his little twenty-four-foot gig, and there at its controls was *Reid*'s cook. Since everyone else was manning the guns, the cook had decided to bring the gig to the dock in case some of the destroyer's officers showed up. Pullen was a proud man when he climbed over *Reid*'s side and one of his officers met him with: "Skipper, everything is under control." Because the destroyer had come in only a week before for a complete overhaul, Pullen worried that she might not be able to get out of this hideously dangerous situation for a long time, so he could not believe his ears when his chief engineer told him, "Captain, we can get going in half an hour."[5]

At Dock 1010 Captain Allen G. Quynn, chief of staff to Admiral Calhoun, waited for the launch to take him to the base force flagship *Argonne*. "Dock 1010 was a tragic and pathetic sight," he remembered. Rescue operations centered there. Wounded men dragged themselves ashore, some badly burned, some bleeding, many suffering excruciating pain. Others came by the ubiquitous small craft. Cars and ambulances, engines roaring, sirens screaming, raced on and off the dock. Officers and men trying to reach their duty stations congested the area. Many in their haste did not even wait for the launches but dived right off Dock 1010 and swam.[6] The Base Force Band, accustomed to working as a unit, organized itself into a stretcher-bearer team, carrying load after load of wounded to *Argonne*'s crowded sick bay.[7]

At 0830 Private Raymond F. McBriarty, an aerial gunner and armorer of the Forty-fifth Pursuit Squadron at Bellows Field, saw a single plane come in from the sea and open fire on the tent area. But "the bullets sounded just like blanks . . . and the ship looked like the AT-6 trainer." Quite unconcerned, McBriarty went to church.[8]

That lone strafer did Bellows a favor, for the warning gave Colonel Leonard D. Weddington, commander of the Sixth Air Service Area, about an hour's grace to disperse the planes. A small base a few miles south of Kaneohe, Bellows was permanent home of the Eighty-sixth Observation Squadron, which at the time had only six 0-47s and two 0-49s on hand. One squadron of P-40s was there also for "a month's gunnery practice."[9]

Almost from the moment of action Americans referred to the period between the first and second attack waves as the lull. But it was merely a high plateau between mountain peaks of action and on any other day would have seemed the most crowded minutes of their lives. Every installation on Oahu burst into activity as the defenders prepared for the next blow they were sure would come. Grimly determined and angry men cleared debris from runways, dispersed aircraft, set up machine guns and AA emplacements, patched up damaged but still airworthy planes. When the Japanese returned, they would find an alert enemy with many more guns blazing.

When Fuchida cried out, *"Tora! Tora! Tora!"* Shimazaki's second wave of 167 planes was about halfway to Oahu. Like the first wave, the second flew at staggered altitudes for greater maneuverability and better interception of enemy aircraft. Fifty-four high-level bombers ripped through cloud tops on the starboard wing of the flight at about 11,500 feet. They were divided into two groups of twenty-seven planes each. Shimazaki's own Sixth Group from *Zuikaku* was to complete the destruction at Hickam Field. The Seventh Group from *Shokaku* was under the immediate command of Lieutenant Tatsuo Ichihara. Eighteen of his planes would pound Ford Island, while the other nine knocked out Kaneohe.

At about 10,000 feet, slightly to port and somewhat below Shimazaki's planes, roared Egusa's seventy-eight dive bombers. Organized into four groups, they were to concentrate on the ships and wreck as many as possible beyond repair. Seventeen planes from *Soryu* flew under Egusa's immediate direction. Another eighteen were supposed to fly under Lieutenant Michio Kobayashi, but engine trouble kept him aboard *Soryu*. Chihaya commanded the Eleventh Group of eighteen dive bombers from *Akagi*, while *Kaga* provided twenty-six under Lieutenant Shigeo Makino.[10]

Lieutenant Shindo led thirty-five sleek Zeros on the prowl above the bombers. Actually his task would be more difficult than Itaya's. Shindo could not count on surprise, and the time lag of approximately thirty minutes between the end of the first attack and the beginning of the second would be just enough to enable U.S. forces to man their defenses in greater strength. Shindo's fighters were divided into three groups of nine planes, one of eight. Shindo led the First Air Control Group from *Akagi*, and Lieutenant Yasushi Nikaido the Second from *Kaga*. Iida headed the Third Air Control Group from *Soryu*; Lieutenant Sumio Nono, the Fourth from *Hiryu*. Besides cutting the enemy out of the skies over Oahu, Nono's and Iida's fighters would drench Wheeler Field and Kaneohe with hot lead.[11]

Shindo had confidence in the poised strength of the second wave, as well as in the shattering firepower of his Zero. But he cocked an eye for potential trouble ahead. He knew from experience in China about the unpredictable factors of aerial combat.[12]

Ofuchi, too, kept his eyes peeled for enemy planes. In due time Oahu emerged in the distance, rising over the edge of the sea. What was that hovering just above the clouds? Barrage balloons? No, they were puffs of brownish smoke, ack-ack exploding like subdued fireworks.[13]

Fujita flew a Zero from *Soryu* in Shindo's swarm of hornets. A leader of the second fighter unit in Iida's group, Fujita worried whether he could reach his objective. He also speculated about the first wave's success. Over Pearl Harbor he saw Shimazaki's high-level bombers floating like hawks in a single file high above their targets. "My one thought was to do as good a job as I could and hope to God I would get through it all alive," he said in retrospect.[14]

Just a moment before Shimazaki deployed the second wave, Bill Burford had his destroyer *Monaghan* on a southwesterly course between Pearl City and Ford Island. As ready-duty destroyer, *Monaghan* had been ordered to sea to support *Ward*. Now, with Pearl Harbor under attack, Burford wanted "to get out of that damn harbor as fast as possible." At exactly 0839 his signalman drew his attention to *Curtiss*. The seaplane tender had signaled a submarine sighting. An enemy submarine in Pearl Harbor's shallow waters? "Well, *Curtiss* must be crazy," said Burford flatly.

"That may be, Captain," the crewman conceded, "but what is that down there?" Burford followed his gesture off the starboard bow and saw "an over and under shotgun barrel looking up" at him at about 1,200 yards. "I don't know what the hell it is," he announced to those with him on the bridge, "but it shouldn't be there." With that he ordered flank speed and headed for the intruder to ram. Ships all around fired at the object, churning the waters with bullets. "It was a hectic few minutes," Burford recalled. "There was that sub coming directly at me, and I at him, and all that speed, and the firing by others, and a number of ships out ahead of me in restricted maneuvering space, and all that Japanese air attack behind us and our antiaircraft fire, their planes—God, a lot was going on in just a few minutes of time."

Soon the submarine "commenced surfacing in damaged condition and was hit directly with both 5″ and .50 caliber shells" from *Curtiss* at 0840—just ten minutes before Shimazaki ordered deployment. The submarine had a "5-inch shell hole through the conning tower, which killed the captain. He was blown into a mass of crumpled steel. . . ."

Monaghan hit the submarine a hard glancing blow which sucked it under the destroyer. As it swirled astern, the destroyer dropped two depth charges, risking that the "ash cans" might very well tear off her own stern. Indeed, the charges lifted *Monaghan* right out of the water. Even before the crash those aboard *Monaghan* observed "one torpedo track passing about 50 yards on starboard beam." But the midget's torpedoes did no damage, and *Monaghan's* depth charge "just tore the hell out of the bow." Burford's full-speed run carried the destroyer safely beyond the explosions, but into collision with a dredge, sustaining light damage. This was not enough to stop Burford in his seaward drive, and he cleared the entrance at 0908.[15]

Just when the submarine had entered Pearl Harbor one would hesitate to guess. The net had been open since 0458, when it admitted *Condor* and *Crossbill*. It did not close until 0840—exactly as Burford attacked the midget.[16] This allowed ample time for any or all of Japan's midget submarines to enter and, for that matter, get out again, except of course, for the one which *Ward* sank and that of the misfortune-plagued Sakamaki.

Shimazaki's second-attack wave crashed down on Oahu about ten miles east of Kahuku Point. When he ordered his airmen to deploy at 0850, the defenders had AA and other guns warmed up, and by the time he ordered "Attack!" five minutes later, the defense was something to reckon with. As Shimazaki's airmen swarmed in, Fuchida, who had been flying over Oahu to assess the damage, thought he might take over the second wave and direct its attack. But Shimazaki had the situation so well in hand that Fuchida let him go ahead while he continued to observe results.[17]

Shindo's Zeros swooped in first. Swinging slightly to the west, they divided into two groups. Half of the planes reversed to pass over Kaneohe from the northwest; the other half sped straight for Hickam and Ford Island. Over Kaneohe the first eighteen-plane group again split in two. Nine Zeros strafed the floatplane installation, then turned west and machine-gunned Wheeler Field; the other nine flew on southward, past Kaneohe to Bellows.

Iida's group hit Bellows at about 0900, in three units of three-plane V formations. McBriarty and another man mounted a gun in an aircraft and hit a plane flying "right down the runway" with no apparent objective. He "could see holes going in the fuselage behind the pilot," but he did not believe he scored a kill.

Iida's men did considerable damage. They wounded one man, set fire to a gasoline tank truck, damaged one 0-49 and one 0-47, and shot down one officer of the Forty-fourth Squadron trying to take off. Two others got airborne, only to fall victim to the Japanese immediately behind them. One "crashed into the beach and burned there"; the other landed in the water about three-quarters of a mile up the beach, and the pilot swam ashore.

Iida discovered unexpectedly big game at this little field. One of the incoming B-17s "landed about midrunway and went off the end of the ramp" with three men wounded. All nine Japanese machine-gunned the Flying Fortress repeatedly, but evidently the plane had already been wrecked in landing. The men of Bellows removed its guns and "placed them up for ground defense."[18]

Soon Iida and his group streaked back to Kaneohe, where nine of Shimazaki's high-level bombers had the base under attack. Most of the bombs fell "on the southern side of the hangars and on the southeastern corner of No. 1 hangar. This destroyed the planes in the hangars. The fire engine ignited the hangar itself."[19]

The Zeros "cruised around over us, firing sporadically at any likely target," recalled Avery. They strafed homes, cars, pedestrians. "Particularly did they harass the firemen who were fighting the blazes among the squadron planes standing on the ramp."[20]

Among Iida's group was Fujita. He had butterflies in his stomach as he sprayed machine-gun bullets at rooftop level and took a hit in his wing.[21] Iida drilled the station armory and swooped down just as an aviation ordnanceman named Sands stepped out the side door and got off a burst with a BAR. A sailor of the old school, he called to his mates in the armory, "Hand me another BAR! Hurry up! I swear I hit that yellow bastard!"[22]

As Iida moved in for the kill, the defiant sailor "emptied another clip" and escaped Iida's bullets, which "pockmarked the wall of the building." Iida appeared to break off the unequal duel and hastened to overtake his buddies, who had reformed and headed toward a mountain gap. But as he did so, a spray of gasoline began to flow from his plane, and he "headed directly back to the armory."[23] No doubt this was the moment when Iida, faithful to his preachings, pointed first to himself, then to the ground, thus indicating that he was going to plunge into the enemy.[24]

A sailor saw him returning and, evidently considering Iida Sands's particular pigeon, shouted, "Hey, Sands! That sonofabitch is coming back!" Sands grabbed a rifle; Iida roared straight at him. Ignoring the bullets splattering around him, Sands "emptied the rifle at the roaring Zero. . . . Iida ceased his fire a moment before passing over Sands' head. . . ."

The Zero crashed into a road winding up a round, flat-topped hill and struck the pavement about five feet below one of the married officers' quarters, "skidded across and piled up against the embankment at the opposite side." The impact ripped out the engine, turned the plane upside down, and shattered Iida's body to pieces. Avery was convinced that mercifully the pilot died before the crash because he took Sands's fire head-on and seemed to lose control of the plane at that instant.[25]

Horror-stricken, Fujita watched Iida's plunge to death. He mistakenly credited his friend with "crashing straight downward in the midst of a flaming hangar on Kaneohe Air Base."[26]

One other Japanese aircraft fell at Kaneohe, but the defenders could not identify the pilot, for the plane crashed into Kailua Bay. Iida and his unknown comrade probably would have counted their lives well lost. Kaneohe was about as wrecked as wrecked can be. Of Kaneohe's thirty-six PBYs, three on patrol flights escaped, six were damaged, the rest destroyed.[27]

Fujita re-formed Iida's group and led it toward Wheeler, determined to exact a savage vengeance. Suddenly sharp bursts of machine-gun fire flashed from the wings of U.S. fighters—Fujita was not sure of the exact number.[28]

When Lieutenants Taylor and Welch sped out of Wheeler to Haleiwa, they hoped to join battle immediately but received instructions to patrol Barber's Point. Finding no enemy in that sector, they returned to Wheeler for additional .50 caliber ammunition. "We had to argue with some of the ground crew," said Welch. "They wanted us to disperse the airplanes and we wanted to fight." As they were loading ammunition, the Japanese came back. The crew ran for cover, but the lieutenants took off.[29]

Fujita's guns poured bullets into an enemy fighter below him, and the American plane disappeared in a trail of black smoke. Another American—a P-40 or a P-36—came at him, all guns blazing. Fujita took his adversary's fire straight on, but although winged by AA fire and now with a shot-up engine, he fired at another plane. All around him his comrades engaged in a slashing dogfight with other American fighters. The Zeros handled beautifully and consistently outmaneuvered U.S. interceptors, yet the Japanese had as much as they bargained for.[30]

More than likely this was part of the air battle in which Taylor and Welch wound up. Here is Taylor's description: "I made a nice turn out into them and got in a string of six or eight planes. I don't know how many there were. . . . I was on one's tail as we went over Waialua, firing at the one next to me, and there was one following firing at me, and I pulled out. I don't know what happened to the other plane. Lieutenant Welch, I think, shot the other man down."[31] Welch added to the story: "We took off directly into them and shot some down. I shot down one right on Lieutenant Taylor's tail."[32]

After a spell Fujita decided enough was enough. He rocked his wings to signal the other pilots, and they tore off for the rendezvous. As a result, they did not stop to "attack any combat planes at Haleiwa," as Genda had planned.[33] Thus, Haleiwa became the only field of any consequence on Oahu which escaped Japanese attention, not because they did not know of its existence, as some Americans later assumed, but because two men from Haleiwa and their comrades chased off the attackers.

In the meantime, Shindo's and Nikaido's sixteen fighters sped to Hickam and Ford Island to prepare a clear field for Shimazaki's and Ichihara's fifty-four horizontal bombers, which were to complete the destruction of the two bases. Shindo approached Hickam Field at high altitude, but fierce AA fire drove him even higher. Then, as Shimazaki's horizontal bombers began their deadly work, Shindo dropped to treetop level to strafe. By now shell blasts filled the air, so he limited his strafing to one quick pass. He fought equally without fear and without pleasure. This was his job, and he worked with stolid thoroughness. His fighters "attacked with machine-gun fire the technical buildings behind the hangar lines and certain planes which by then were dispersed."

Before Shindo took off from *Akagi*, Genda had instructed him to assess the damage wrought by the second wave. So, after his single strafing operation, Shindo left his formation and "flew over Pearl Harbor at an altitude of 300 meters to make observation of the battle result." He wrapped up his report to Genda in just three words: "Inflicted much damage."[34]

The pilots of the second wave's high-level bombers, all of whom came from *Shokaku* and *Zuikaku*, were, for the most part, a jittery bunch as they flew on their maiden combat mission. Even a few like Lieutenant Takemi Iwami, who had had four or five years of flight experience and had tasted combat in China, knew they were in a scrap: "Identification of the targets was also not easy. The enemy's AA fire proved accurate and it came close to us even when flying over clouds." Nevertheless, luck stayed with the Japanese. Although several bombers of both waves returned to the carriers liberally peppered, none of the hits proved fatal.[35]

These inexperienced airmen scored direct hits on Hangars 13 and 15. The mess hall, already severely damaged in the first attack, took another bull's-eye, the concussion killing all the Chinese cooks, who had sought protection in the freezer room. "The hangars looked as if they were being lifted right off the ground."[36]

Lacking the all-important element of surprise which had brought the first wave through almost unscathed, Egusa's dive bombers met an aroused enemy striking back with all the ferocity and power at his command. Lieutenant Zenji Abe noted that as soon as they flew beyond northern Oahu, "fierce AA barrages began gradually to close in. . . . This gave me the cold shivers," he added candidly.[37] And Chihaya flashed back to *Akagi*, "Enemy defensive fire strong." That settled one question for Genda: If the task force launched a third major strike, the torpedo bombers would remain on the carriers.[38]

Egusa had orders to finish off any ships damaged in the first attack, preferably the battleships. Each plane carried one 250-kilogram bomb, so each bombardier had but one crack at the enemy. But when Egusa's bombers reached Pearl Harbor, they had little choice of targets. The heavy rolls of black smoke obscured the vessels, and the exploding ack-ack made accurate sighting almost impossible. The Japanese would have to hit what they saw when they saw it.

Ofuchi swooped down on a battleship moored along the south end of Ford Island. "When we went into our attack dive, my feelings were numbed and, truthfully, I didn't give a damn what happened. I just gave myself over to Fate," Ofuchi said. "But when the bomb was dropped, and we pulled up to level off, I really got scared."[39]

As the second wave broke over Pearl Harbor, doctors, nurses, corpsmen, and patients at the naval hospital scrambled for cover. Some vivid images would never leave Lieutenant Ruth Erickson's memory: doctors, inured by profession and experience to human suffering, shaken to the core; a physician holding a needle to insert into a patient's vein, his fingers quivering like reeds in the wind; the stench of burning flesh ripping up one's nostrils. "I can still smell it . . . and I think I always will," she said.[40]

By now Pearl Harbor was a hellpit of smoke—gray, brown, white, lemon yellow, black, and again black—acrid, foul, mushrooming billows erupting skyward, folding in and opening out like a mass of storm clouds. Out of this pall came a sight so incredible that its viewers could not have been more dumbfounded had it been the legendary Flying Dutchman—*Nevada*, heading into the channel, a hole the size of a house in her bow, her torn flag rippling defiance.

Nevada had been under partial steam when the first wave struck, and at 0850 the battleship got under way, Thomas at the conn, Ruff acting as navigator. Chief Quartermaster Robert Sedberry ably assisted.[41] When *Nevada* limped past the blazing *Arizona*, someone saw three survivors swimming nearby and tossed them a line. They climbed up and helped man *Nevada*'s starboard 5-inch gun. Heat from the burning battleship was so intense that the gunners had to cover their shells with their bodies lest they explode.

The capsized *Oklahoma* was "another terrifying and shocking sight." To some witnesses the fate of *Oklahoma* was the crowning horror of the day, worse even than the volcanic eruption aboard *Arizona*. The explosion of a battleship, although an awesome thing, was comprehensible. It even had a certain tragic grandeur. But for a battlewagon to overturn was unthinkable; it affronted human dignity. Something of this horrified incredulity held Ruff in its grip as *Nevada* moved abreast of the overturned vessel.[42]

When Egusa's men saw *Nevada* plowing along below them, they recognized a golden double opportunity to sink a battleship and at the same time bottle up Pearl Harbor. High above the scene, Fuchida had his pilot bank deeply for a better look. *Ah, good!* he thought. *Now just sink that ship right there!*[43] No wonder that, at 0850, "the Japanese bombers swarmed down on us like bees," as Ruff remarked. One even ignored *Neosho* backing up Battleship Row, and every American on Ford Island who saw the narrow escape gasped in relief.

In spite of the severity of the attack, which sent five bombs crashing into the fore part of the ship and the superstructure, Ruff was confident that *Nevada* would weather the storm. But her chances looked slim when at precisely 0907 she came under another hail of bombs, many of which were "near misses." One, however, struck the forecastle, killing "an unknown number of men." After "some real twisting and maneuvering," Thomas grounded the bow of the ship in the mud of Hospital Point at 0910. Five minutes later Captain Scanland came aboard, and by 1045 tugs had moved the battleship to the western side of Pearl Harbor's entrance channel, her "starboard quarter aground, bow south." Only then could Thomas and Ruff see the real extent of *Nevada*'s punishment.[44] The fore part of the ship had been virtually destroyed, and the superstructure badly damaged. She had lost 3 officers and 47 men killed, 5 officers and 104 men wounded.[45]

By 0930 *Oglala* listed about twenty degrees and her crew "couldn't stick to the decks any longer." So Furlong ordered Abandon Ship. At 1000 *Oglala* "finally turned over and came to rest on the bottom of her port side." Crawford, who had been blown off *Vestal* when *Arizona* exploded but made his way safely ashore, and Rafsky, hard at work aboard *Argonne*, later agreed that neither torpedo nor bomb damage really capsized *Oglala*. Both men insisted that the old girl "had a nervous breakdown and died of fright."[46]

Vestal, too, had to be moved out of danger. It was typical of Fuqua that in the midst of heartbreaking toil aboard *Arizona* he could spare a thought for the repair ship alongside. At 0845 he ordered her forward lines cut. Her after lines already parted, she got under way "on both engines, no steering gear." A tug pulled her bow away from the blazing battleship. The repair ship began to list to starboard and take water aft, both the shipfitter and blacksmith shops flooding. At 0945 Young remarked to Hesser, "The ship is getting into bad shape. We had better beach her." This they managed to do at Aiea, where she settled on a bed of coral.[47]

Admiral Calhoun reached *Argonne* "just at the beginning of the second wave. . . ." Shortly thereafter his Mine Force rescued most of the crew of

Utah. Two destroyers requested augmentation of their crews to put to sea. When Calhoun's people asked the *Utah* men for volunteers, "force was necessary to restrain the 200 of them from going where only 55 were wanted. The men were so anxious that they could not wait for the boat; they jumped overboard and swam over there, the 55 of them."[48]

The destroyer *Blue* got under way at 0847 with Ensign Asher commanding. "Two planes that dove over the ship were fired on by the .50 cal. machine guns. It is claimed that one of these planes, seen to crash near Pan American Airways Landing at Pearl City, was shot down by this vessel." When the plane went down, the crew "stopped shooting and proceeded to pat each other on the back." During the action Asher threw his field glasses at one of the diving planes. Later he was a bit apologetic about his irrational act; he guessed he "just was kind of mad."

Safely out of the harbor, Asher reduced speed to a sedate ten knots and commenced patrolling. At 0950 *Blue* dropped depth charges on a sound contact. Investigation revealed a large oil slick and "air bubbles rising to the survace, over a length of about 200 feet." So Asher believed that he had sunk this submarine.[49]

At 0902 Egusa's dive bombers made a direct hit on *Pennsylvania* in dry dock. Then, at approximately 0907, a high-altitude bomber scored a strike at "frame 83, starboard side of boat deck." However, *Pennsylvania* suffered remarkably little damage, considering her helpless position. Far worse than the material damage, the attack killed two officers and sixteen men and wounded thirty others from the enlisted ranks.[50]

Several of Kimmel's destroyers took a terrific mauling. A direct hit exploded in the forward magazine of *Shaw* as she lay in floating dry dock not far from *Pennsylvania,* ripping her whole bow off. Soon raging fires from Egusa's dive bombers engulfed *Cassin* and *Downes* so thoroughly that they had to be abandoned. Shortly thereafter magazine and torpedo explosions within each vessel shook them from bow to stern. *Cassin* rolled over against the stricken *Downes,* an almost unrecognizable ruin in the same dry dock as *Pennsylvania.*[51]

A large patch of burning fuel oil drifted toward *California.* His flagship gradually sinking and believing his proper place to be at sea, Pye told Train to get the staff together so that they could "shift over to any other ship of the force that could get out." A boat had already drawn alongside to take them off when he received a signal from Kimmel that no more ships should sortie.[52]

Of all the battlewagons, *Maryland* escaped with the least damage. Her position inboard of *Oklahoma* protected her from the torpedoes. Seaman Second Class Harlan E. Eisnangle lost all track of time. He had no idea whether his gun crew hit anything or not, "for when you are loading the gun under those conditions, you are acting from instinct. For you are scared and you do your job from the drills you have been doing"[53]—an unconscious tribute to Kimmel and Kitts with their unremitting gunnery program.

At 0908 dive bombers dropped two missiles on *Raleigh,* still quivering from the first-wave torpedo attack. One "struck *Raleigh* aft at frame 112. . . ."

Simons recorded its progress, adding, "In its path through the ship, this bomb missed our aviation gasoline tanks, containing three thousand gallons of high test gasoline, by about ten feet." The second bomb dropped "less than 100 yards to port." Then the pilot strafed the cruiser. To keep her from capsizing, Simons had his men jettison topside weights, about sixty tons in all.[54]

At 0920 more of Egusa's bombers swarmed down on *Honolulu*, flagship of Kimmel's Cruiser Force, moored at Berth 21. One bomb "struck the pier about 15 feet from the ship's side at frame 40. It penetrated dock and exploded under water." The concussion, however, caused a certain amount of damage and considerable flooding.[55]

Captain Rood felt *St. Louis* bounce in Berth B-17 when the bomb struck near *Honolulu*, moored beside her. The blast knocked down Commander Carl K. Fink, Rood's executive officer. *St. Louis*'s gunners thought they hit the attacking plane after it pulled out. All Rood wanted was to go after the Japanese. So he ordered the engine room, "Make preparations for getting under way. Full power, emergency." *St. Louis* was to have been in port for about a week for boiler repair. "Yet the men did jig time in getting those boilers ready so we could get steam up," said Rood. What is more, repairmen had cut a hole about four feet in diameter in the side of the ship in order to pass gear in and out. Before *St. Louis* could get under way, the men had to close this hole and weld it securely. This efficiency paid off as Rood backed the cruiser out in the direction of *Oklahoma* at 0931.

Edging his cruiser toward the open sea, he did not pause to maneuver around a dredge with its steel cable extending to Dry Dock No. 1. Instead, he ordered emergency full speed and "hit that cable a smashing blow and snapped it like a violin string." At 1004 *St. Louis*, making twenty-two knots in an eight-knot zone, cleared the channel. That very moment, looking off the starboard bow, Rood saw two torpedoes streaking for his ship, one just a short distance behind the other. *St. Louis* changed course and suddenly the steel fish exploded, sending geysers of water skyward. They had struck the coral near the channel entrance.

No doubt lightened by the release of its torpedoes, a midget submarine popped up near the surface. The cruiser commenced firing, and her men believed she hit the submarine's conning tower.[56]

The sortie of *St. Louis* was the last major ship action in Pearl Harbor. Egusa's bombers, racks empty, flew off to strafe Ewa, Hickam, and Ford Island. As Ofuchi raked Ewa Field, he saw several Japanese shot down.[57] They had run afoul of the indestructible Taylor and Welch, newly refueled and freshly armed. The two Americans had flown to Barber's Point to give the marines a hand. "We went down and got in the traffic pattern and shot down several planes there," Taylor testified. "I know for certain I shot down two planes or perhaps more; I don't know." These two men between them accounted for seven attacking aircraft. Records credited them with four planes in their first action, three in the second.[58]

At Hickam Field, Shimazaki's men had scarcely finished their task when a group of dive bombers, evidently having used up their bombs on Pearl Harbor, struck along the hangar line, strafing the aircraft. Allen was loading a B-17 when the strafers hit. His Flying Fortress had one engine "completely shot up and one wheel . . . shot from under it." So he searched until he found another airworthy B-17 and once more started to load.[59]

Elsewhere on Hickam a middle-aged colonel shouted at Reeves, "Do something, Lieutenant! Do something!" Reeves asked, not unreasonably, "What shall I do?" To this the colonel snorted, "I don't know, but do something!" As a pilot Reeves could not but respect the precision and tactics of the Japanese bombers. He and his friends noted that the American AA almost always shot behind the planes.[60]

Except for random strikes, the attack was over. The second wave cost the Japanese six fighter planes and fourteen dive bombers. Many others had been hit but escaped. Fuchida hovered over the fearful scene, assessing the damage and rounding up stragglers. His badly shot-up plane had circled for about two hours. As befitted a leader, he waited until the last of the rearguard fighters winged out of sight before he headed for *Akagi*.[61] He could not secure a definitive picture because the heavy smoke obscured his vision. Even so, he reported to the rejoicing Nagumo success beyond his wildest dreams. With a perfect view, this is what he could have tabulated:

Eight battleships, three light cruisers, three destroyers, and four auxiliary craft either sunk, capsized, heavily damaged, or damaged generally—eighteen vessels. Naval aviation, too, had suffered heavy losses: thirteen fighters, twenty-one scout bombers, forty-six patrol bombers, three utility craft, two transports, and one each observation/scouts and training craft. To this one must add the *Enterprise* craft shot down that morning and others later felled by American guns.

General Martin's Hawaiian Air Force took a terrific beating, with ultimate losses totaling four B-17s, twelve B-18s, two A-20s, thirty-two P-40s, twenty P-36s, four P-26s, two OA-9s, and one 0-49. In addition, eighty-eight pursuit planes, six reconnaissance aircraft, and thirty-four bombers had been damaged. At first it looked as though all these had been wrecked, but 80 percent were later salvaged. And the Japanese harvested an unexpected bonus with the destruction of Landon's B-17s. Hickam, Wheeler, Ford Island, Kaneohe, and Ewa suffered extensive damage to installations as well as to planes.

One turns now to the most grievous losses of all—the dead, the missing, the wounded. Casualties for the day totaled:

	KILLED, MISSING, AND DIED OF WOUNDS	WOUNDED [62]
Navy	2,008	710
Marine Corps	109	69
Army	218	364
Civilians	68	35
Total	2,403	1,178

By comparison Japanese losses were relatively insignificant—only twenty-nine planes. One large submarine and five midgets went down with all hands except for Sakamaki. No wonder Commander Sanagi of the Naval General Staff's Operations Section waxed lyrical in his diary entry for December 8:

> Our air force, together with the submarine force, achieved a great success unprecedented in history by the Pearl Harbor attack . . . which could only be done by the Imperial Navy. This success is owing to the Imperial Navy's hard training for more than twenty years. Our navy had made this hard training only for this one day.
>
> Nothing could hold back our Imperial Navy, which kept silent for a long time. But once it arose, it never hesitated to dare to do the most difficult thing on this earth. Oh, how powerful is the Imperial Navy!

CHAPTER 65

"THE

CHANCE

OF A

LIFETIME"

Nagumo and Kusaka stood on *Akagi*'s bridge peering into the sky. At last, at about 1010, "black points appeared far to the south one after another"—the first wave's aircraft were returning, some in formation, some singly. Soon the flight docks of all six carriers burst into life as each prepared to land its planes.[1]

Throughout the morning the weather had steadily worsened. Now high seas and tricky winds made landings difficult. Deck crews had to push a few badly damaged craft into the sea to clear the landing area for fuel-short planes circling impatiently overhead.[2]

Ema landed his dive bomber aboard *Zuikaku*, where his colleagues "went wild with joy when the first reports came in." Ema was "relieved and glad that he had survived the attack." But he did not think that all was over, for he believed that the enemy might launch a counterattack. Yet with the morning strike a success, Ema and the rest of the airmen thought the war would go well for Japan. Now at least they had a chance.[3]

Fuchida's mind raced with thoughts of a second assault that same afternoon. As his pilot ticked off the miles, Fuchida mentally earmarked for destruction the fuel-tank farms, the vast repair and maintenance facilities, and perhaps a ship or two bypassed that morning for priority targets.[4]

Meanwhile, all flying officers who recovered aboard *Akagi* reported at once to Air Officer Masuda. On the flight deck near the bridge, with Murata's aid, Masuda tabulated the results of the attack on a large blackboard. Genda hurried down from the bridge once or twice, then relayed the word to Nagumo and Kusaka, both of whom impatiently awaited a final tabulation. During one of Genda's visits to the blackboard the assembled pilots urged a second attack. Genda listened but offered no opinion.

Excitement rose to a high pitch around *Akagi's* blackboard. The immediate concern of the pilots and observers was an accurate assessment of results. But they also discussed American resistance to the first wave, all agreeing that the reaction, "considering all the facts on that morning, was surprisingly quick." The consensus was that without surprise such a great success would have been impossible.[5]

At about noon Fuchida's pilot swooped down on *Akagi's* rolling deck.[6] An elated smile lit Genda's thin face, and he wrung Fuchida's hand exultantly. Then Genda rushed back to the bridge. At that moment a sailor ran up with a message that Nagumo wanted to see Fuchida immediately. But he decided to wait until he had correlated his observations with those of the flight leaders. So he carefully looked over the large blackboard chart and listened to the reports of about fifteen flying officers as he sipped a cup of tea. Their observations tallied closely with Fuchida's, and he was satisfied that he could give his superiors a fairly accurate assessment. At this point another messenger informed Fuchida that he was to report to Nagumo and hurry.

He found Kusaka, Hasegawa, Oishi, Genda, and a few other staff officers gathered with Nagumo. Fuchida planned to give a formal briefing, listing events in order, but Nagumo broke in impatiently: "The results—what are they?"

"Four battleships sunk," replied Fuchida. "I know this from my own personal observation. Four battleships damaged," he added. Then he listed by berth and type the other ships his airmen had struck.

Again Nagumo interrupted. "Do you think that the U.S. Fleet could not come out from Pearl Harbor within six months?"

Uneasiness stirred Fuchida's mind, but he owed the admiral the truth. "The main force of the U.S. Pacific Fleet will not be able to come out within six months," he answered. Nagumo beamed and nodded.

Then Kusaka took up the questioning. "What do you think the next targets should be?" Fuchida drew a quick breath. The wording seemed to indicate an aggressive intent. He came back swiftly, "The next targets should be the dockyards, the fuel tanks, and an occasional ship." He saw no need to attack the battleships again.

Kusaka also took up the possibility of an American counterattack. Genda and Fuchida assured him that the Japanese controlled the air over both Oahu and the sea. Oishi interjected: "Is the enemy in a position to counterattack the task force?" This direct question again put Fuchida on the spot, and again he called the shots as he saw them. "I believe we have destroyed many enemy planes, but I do not know whether we have destroyed them all. The enemy most probably could still attack the Fleet." To this Oishi answered not a word, but his silence was eloquent.

Nagumo now returned to the discussion. "Where do you think the missing U.S. carriers are?" Fuchida explained that although he could not be sure, he thought most probably they were training somewhere at sea. Duty compelled him to add that no doubt by this time the carriers had received word of the attack and would be looking for the task force. Obviously this unpleasant suggestion made a deep impression on Nagumo. Oishi, too, fretted over a possible counterattack and asked Genda for his opinion. Not at all perturbed, Genda replied easily, "Let the enemy come! If he does, we will shoot his planes down."

Nagumo dismissed Fuchida with a few words of praise; then Genda took over. Despite Fuchida's impressive damage report, Genda was not satisfied. He knew his airmen had given Japan the golden chance that would never come again, so he wanted to finish the job. But he did not advocate another major strike that same afternoon. The planes had been refitted to attack ships at sea in case of an American counterattack. To hit Pearl Harbor again would require changing armament. Just such a move was destined to contribute heavily to the Japanese defeat at Midway. This process would hold up the takeoff until dark. Moeover, sea and air conditions had degenerated to the point where launching and recovering a group large enough to make the attack worthwhile "would have created confusion beyond the imagination" and resulted in many casualties.

Then, too, *Lexington* and *Enterprise* were still at large. Genda considered that "Nagumo would have been a standing joke for generations if he had attacked Pearl Harbor again" without first ascertaining their location. So Genda urged Nagumo: "Stay in the area for several days and run down the enemy carriers."

But the admiral felt like a gambler who has staked his life's savings on the turn of a card and won. His only idea was to cash in and go home as quickly as possible. He had risked Japan's First Air Fleet, and his ships had come through without a scratch. He could not bring himself to tempt fate again or undergo once more the harrowing strain of a second shuffle.[7]

Yet Nagumo held more than his share of high cards. His airmen had put most of Kimmel's battleships out of commission, badly damaged Short's air bases, and singed the wings of U.S. air power in the central Pacific. Oahu's defenders had fought back bravely, but for the most part they were stunned, confused, and demoralized, giving Nagumo a rich psychological advantage. U.S. military leaders on Oahu expected the Japanese to renew their attacks that same day and any time thereafter. Bellinger "thought that they probably would . . . refuel and come back" and could not understand why they did not.[8] Short feared that enemy might attempt a major landing.[9]

The Japanese firmly believed in surprise attack and were thoroughly convinced of the advantages inherent in the initiative. Yet they failed to exhibit that decisiveness of action which alone would have exploited their extensive gains in the early, crucial hours of the conflict. Why?

During the cruise, as we have pointed out, Genda had worked on several alternate plans to achieve maximum damage.* What he hoped Nagumo would

---

*See Chapter 52.

do now was send out patrols to find the American carriers and call the tankers down from the north to provide the necessary fuel for sustained operations. If they found the enemy's flattops, they should attack them as soon as possible. If they did not locate them, the task force should remain in the area and continue the search. Eventually they would discover their quarry. Then, after attacking and presumably destroying the carriers, they should go home by way of the Marshall Islands and attack Pearl Harbor repeatedly as the task force sailed past Oahu on the west.[10]

But sadly lacking in the Pearl Harbor picture was a contingency plan to cover such a circumstance as Nagumo now faced: how to exploit the situation in case the first- and second-wave attacks succeeded beyond expectation. So Nagumo did not send out patrols to find the missing carriers. As far as we know, he did not even ask his numerous submarines to make on-the-spot checks around Oahu and report the results. Genda's and Fuchida's efforts for a total victory at Pearl Harbor broke against a Maginot Line of closed minds. "Without hesitation" Kusaka "recommended to Admiral Nagumo to make a withdrawal," and Nagumo promptly concurred.

"The objective of this operation was to protect the flank and rear of the Southern Force," explained Kusaka. "Inasmuch as its objective was almost accomplished, I concluded that we should not remain . . . on the scene and also should not be distracted into lengthening the game indefinitely. . . ." Within his own frame of reference and in the context of the time, Nagumo thought his greatest contribution to Japan's future war effort would be to bring his task force back intact to fight another day. This had been one of the conditions under which the Naval General Staff had approved giving Nagumo six carriers.*

Nagumo and Kusaka appreciated Genda and Fuchida's ardent desire to hit the enemy again and again, but as Kusaka pointed out, "We had to strike a reasonable balance between fighting spirit and resources. With Japan's limited means and America's potential, Japan just could not afford to gamble her ships recklessly nor run risks where the possible dividends were unclear."[11]

The very ease of his victory threw Nagumo off-balance, as if he had rushed forward to break down a door just as someone opened it. Finding himself against all expectation without a scratch on his ships instead of having lost a third of his task force, he forgot about maximum damage to the enemy and began to think in terms of minimum damage to his task force. He and Kusaka agreed that the operation was 80 percent successful, the other 20 percent not worth the risk.

With the full advantage of surprise, the first attack wave had inflicted massive damage with a loss of only five torpedo bombers, one dive bomber, and three Zeros. When the second wave struck, despite the appalling punishment the Americans had taken, they extracted a price of fourteen dive bombers and six Zeros—still cheap, admittedly, but more than three times the cost of the initial

---

*See Chapter 37.

assault and with much less impressive results to show for it. Furthermore, in addition to the twenty-nine aircraft missing, seventy-four had been damaged. These twenty-three fighters, forty-one bombers, and ten torpedo planes owed their escape more to good luck than good management.

Yet these factors were not decisive. Yamamoto or Yamaguchi might have weighed them in the balance against the fruits of total victory and struck again without hesitation. But Nagumo did not have that type of mind. Nor was he flexible enough to meet new and unexpected situations with confidence and decision. Both traditional naval strategy and economics, reinforced by the thought processes of a lifetime, urged Nagumo homeward.

Moreover, Nagumo placed great reliance upon Kusaka. He, too, had opposed the Pearl Harbor operation, less out of concern for its risks than from a commonsense doubt of its necessity. In accordance with the military principle of "mass," he believed that the Japanese should have thrown everything in the the main theater. But after having said his say to Yamamoto and being overruled, Kusaka had given his word to do everything possible to further the scheme.* No man ever kept a promise better. Now he had fulfilled his obligation, and he wanted to move his ships and men as quickly as possible to the main area of operations, where in his opinion they should have been all along.

Nagumo's decision to turn back came as a disappointment to many of his airmen, who wanted to exploit their opportunity. "Most of the young flying officers were eager to attack Pearl Harbor again because they wished to inflict as much damage as possible," said Goto. "It was the chance of a lifetime, and many of the pilots felt the chance should not be passed up."[12]

Some of Shindo's fellow fliers "urged another attack," but he had the impression that many "felt much relieved after inflicting much damage to the enemy and wanted to go back to the homeland quickly." Shindo himself "thought another attack should be launched" but, true to his phlegmatic nature, "did not feel a strong impulse for urging it." In retrospect he believed plans for repeated attacks should have been incorporated into Operation Hawaii from the beginning.[13]

Most of the survivors agreed that another attack was practicable from the standpoint of aircraft condition and morale of the personnel. As a result, the pilots aboard *Akagi* asked Genda for an explanation of Nagumo's decision. He gave them three reasons: (1) The strike had already achieved its expected results; (2) a second attack would risk considerable damage to the task force; and (3) they did not know the position of the U.S. carriers. But his rationalizations did not prevent Genda from tagging Nagumo "a miscast misfit." He believed that a different situation would have prevailed had Yamaguchi or Onishi been at the helm. However, he blamed Nagumo less than he did the Personnel Section of the Navy Ministry.[14]

---

*See Chapter 32.

In contrast, Commander Hashiguchi, Fuchida's understudy, thought that a second all-out attack should not have been launched because the "damage inflicted upon enemy battleships by our forces was considered satisfactory." He saw no point in a second attack with the first-priority targets, Kimmel's carriers, not in port. Therefore, he agreed with Nagumo that the task force should not expend "crack air forces" to strike Oahu's military installations but save them "to wage the decisive battle someday with enemy carriers."[15]

As one might expect, Yamaguchi's Second Carrier Division was ready for more action. He had always wanted the Pearl Harbor strike to be decisive. At Hitokappu Bay he had urged Nagumo to make a second and, if necessary, a third major effort to crush the enemy and had been dismayed to find Nagumo already committed to a one-shot attack. According to his air staff officer, Suzuki, Yamaguchi now eagerly awaited orders for further action.[16] Not all his airmen blindly supported Yamaguchi. Lieutenant Heijiro Abe, for example, declared, "Since the enemy carriers, the top priority target, could not be located and the attack on Pearl Harbor had been more successful than expected, I was in favor of preserving our carrier strength intact in order to prepare for the next operation."[17]

Although the Fifth Carrier Division suffered only one casualty—a dive bomber—Hara and his senior staff officer, Commander Ohashi, rather doubted that Nagumo would order another full-scale strike. Nor were the airmen aboard Hara's flagship *Shokaku* particularly enthusiastic. Only the older, more experienced fliers discussed the possibility at all. Hara and Ohashi feared a land-based more than a carrier-based reprisal. They agreed that if the American flattops were near enough to hit the task force, they would already have done so. But they were not so sure about the situation on Oahu. Even now enemy bombers might be bearing down on the First Air Fleet. They believed that the Japanese should plan no further strikes until they had some solid facts to work on.[18] Aboard *Zuikaku*, Air Officer Shimoda ordered all planes prepared for another attack. "Such a step was only common sense," he said. Personally, he opposed such a venture because the enemy carriers remained unlocated and because he thought that by this time the Americans surely knew where to find Nagumo's fleet.[19]

Fuchida was sitting in the command post on the upper flight deck, wolfing his first food since a predawn breakfast, when the order came: "Preparations for attack canceled." *Akagi* broke out her signal flags to advise the rest of the task force that they would retire to the northwest. Fuchida rushed to the bridge to protest. He saluted Nagumo upon entering and asked, "Why are we not attacking again?" Nagumo opened his mouth to answer, but Kusaka forstalled him. "The objective of the Pearl Harbor operation has been achieved. Now we must prepare for other operations ahead."

So definite was Kusaka's tone that Fuchida had no opening for a rebuttal. Still, it took a firm act of will for him to swallow his disappointment and outrage. Not trusting himself to speak, he saluted, turned on his heel, and stalked out, "a bitter and angry man."

He chided himself for not having hedged on Nagumo's questions, miserably convinced that his assessment had tipped the balance for caution.[20] He need not have blamed himself. Nagumo had already committed his forces to a one-shot operation. The missing American carriers; the possibility of enemy retaliation from land-based aircraft; above all, the probability that U.S. submarines might be searching out the task force—these factors merely reinforced a decision previously reached. Kusaka, too, had long since made up his mind that the attack "should be carried out as swiftly as a demon flashing by and also it should be withdrawn as fast as the passing wind." He knew that only a few American bombers need strike the lightly armored carriers to reverse the entire tactical picture.[21]

Too large-minded to bear a grudge, Genda took the decision in good part. Nevertheless, he remained convinced that Nagumo should have completed the job. A brilliant tactician, he hated to see Japan fall this early in the war into the fatal error military textbooks call failure to pursue, which has turned so many victories to ashes. But in the final analysis Nagumo was the Commander in Chief, with the duty and responsibility of decision, and that was the end of it. Fuchida, more emotional than Genda and still keyed up with the nervous tension of combat, was so incensed that for the rest of the voyage home he spoke to Nagumo only when duty and courtesy demanded it.[22]

In Japan aboard *Nagato*, Ugaki confided his displeasure to his trusty diary. "Last night a telegram came in that the task force was withdrawing . . . not without being criticized as the quick pace of a fleeing thief and also as being contented with a humble lot," he wrote. "In a situation where we lost only thirty planes, the most essential thing is to exploit the achieved results of the attack. . . ."[23]

Kuroshima called together some of the junior members of the Combined Fleet staff that evening to discuss a second attack against Pearl Harbor. Most of them agreed that this should be done, provided the enemy carriers could be located. Aside from the American flattops, two other obstacles loomed. First, Nagumo's orders to his task force at Hitokappu Bay included a clause concerning "repeated attacks" but did not postulate another major assault. Kuroshima and his colleagues reasoned that Nagumo would have to issue new orders and re-form the task force. In radioing these orders to his tankers, which had moved farther northward, he might reveal his position and intentions to the enemy. Secondly, knowing Nagumo's negative attitude, they presumed that the admiral would consider his mission accomplished, that his staff would support him, and that to order him back toward Hawaii would create a morale problem.

The next morning at about 1000 Kuroshima summarized these points for Yamamoto and Ugaki at another staff meeting.[24] Of course, the final decision rested with Yamamoto, but his senior staff officer urged that he order a second assault. He pointed out that the radio reports of the action had been fragmentary, and the task force should strike again to remove any reasonable doubt that it had immobilized the U.S. Pacific Fleet.

Yamamoto listened to the discussion thoughtfully. The arguments contained certain inconsistencies which could not have escaped his notice. At this time the Combined Fleet was under the impression that a submarine had sunk an American carrier, so only one remained to menace the task force. Then, too, while his advisers worried lest in radioing orders to his tankers Nagumo reveal his position, they also assumed that the enemy knew where the First Air Fleet was and would be seeking it out. Furthermore, Nagumo had already broken radio silence to let Yamamoto know he was retiring.

However, Yamamoto knew that Nagumo would not attack again unless conditions were perfect, in which case, paradoxically, there would be no need for another assault. With his usual smiling irony he remarked that Nagumo no doubt felt like a thief who is desperately brave on his way to the scene of the crime and while actually committing it, but who then thinks only of escaping with the loot.

The Commander in Chief had the responsibility for a vast war plan for which the Pearl Harbor scheme, however close to his heart, was only a part. Had he been on the spot, he might have attacked again; still, he was astonished and delighted to get all his ships back intact. He made it a firm policy to leave decisions to the commander in the field, who could see the local situation and make up his mind on the basis of details necessarily hidden from the Combined Fleet staff. And to order Nagumo to reverse himself would be a stinging loss of face before his whole command. So Yamamoto vetoed the proposal to override the man on the spot.

In a significant diary item for December 9 (Japan time), Ugaki summarized what in his opinion constituted the reasons for Yamamoto's decision:

> 1. This time an approach could not be made without being detected. In consequence . . . our losses would be great although we could expect good results. There would be some chance, too, of our forces being flank attacked by enemy carrier planes; this might result in a pretty heavy blow to us. . . .
> 2. We haven't yet had a plan like that. It is not an easy task to draft a new plan and enforce it.
> 3. The most essential thing we have to consider right now is the mental factor involved. Who of those knowing the details of this operation from the beginning would dare to advocate strongly that we force another attack? What they [Nagumo's officers and men] did nearly reached the limit of their ability. To demand much more of them would only make them angry.

The list is illuminating, and nothing could sound less like Isoroku Yamamoto. Defense-mindedness, inflexibility, and misunderstanding of the airmen stand clearly revealed. Certainly Nagumo's fliers would have protested vigorously against the third assumption.

In Tokyo the Naval General Staff presented a picture of relative unanimity.[25] The night before the attack Nagano, Ito, Fukudome, and Tomioka remained in the Navy Club in downtown Tokyo. At about 0330 they heard that almost unbelievable *"Tora! Tora! Tora!"* Despite their intense joy and relief, they were still much concerned about the task force and expended more thought on the possibility of a U.S. counterattack than on the chance of another successful assault. After breakfast at the club they returned to headquarters, where further discussions took place. According to Fukudome, one of the members advocated a second all-out attack but decided against so ordering Nagumo for the same reasons that influenced Yamamoto.

While the success of the Pearl Harbor attack greatly exceeded its most optimistic expectations, the Naval General Staff interpreted the results in terms of Japan's master plan of conquest. The impetus of this propitious beginning provided further momentum for the grand push southward. Any steps to expand the results at Oahu should wait until Japan could exploit the vast resources it was now in a position to take over. Thus, temporarily turning its back on Hawaii, the Naval General Staff redoubled its efforts for the task it had always considered the number one priority.

The Navy Ministry never raised the question of a second attack on Pearl Harbor.[26] This is not surprising. Except for administrative details on personnel and supply, operations were outside its jurisdiction. And Shimada lacked the forceful personality necessary to invade the bailiwicks of Nagano or Yamamoto.

Was Nagumo's decision sound? The question raises a historical controversy which has never been settled and may never be. Both sides remained convinced of their own wisdom. Kusaka insisted that in the context of the hour and with the knowledge available to them, the decision to retire was correct, and if he had it to do all over again, he would recommend exactly the same course.[27] In contrast, the failure to follow through at Pearl Harbor haunted Genda. "Hawaii provided the key to all future operations in the Pacific," he declared. "Whoever controls Pearl Harbor holds the central Pacific firmly in his grasp. Unless Japan could take it and hold it, she could not defeat the U.S. Navy."[28]

Both Genda and Fuchida had been so personally involved in the attack that they rather lost sight of Yamamoto's original objective—to knock the Pacific Fleet *hors de combat* for about six months so that Japan could carry out its seizure of Southeast Asia without the U.S. Navy's striking its flank. Seen in this light, Nagumo and Kusaka fulfilled their mission.

Nevertheless, a number of American admirals agree that the Japanese made the wrong decision. Fleet Admiral Chester W. Nimitz remarked, "The fact that the Japanese did not return to Pearl Harbor and complete the job was the greatest help to us, for they left their principal enemy with the time to catch his breath, restore his morale, and rebuild his forces."[29]

Kimmel considered the base at Pearl Harbor would have been an even more lucrative target than the warships: ". . . if they had destroyed the oil which was all above ground at that time . . . it would have forced the withdrawal of the fleet to the coast because there wasn't any oil anywhere else out there to keep the fleet operating."[30]

On the other hand, Furlong pointed out that Nagumo followed classic naval doctrine in staying within the established boundaries of his task and refusing to be tempted into alluring side paths. "Their mission may have been wrong," said Furlong, "but they stuck with it." The fault as he saw it lay not in the execution, but in the original assignment of targets.[31]

Admiral Raymond A. Spruance, hero of Midway, had somewhat the same idea. "The Japanese attacked only military objectives," he said. "This was their mission, and they stuck to it." He, too, believed the Japanese could have done much more damage had they struck the submarine base, the tank farm, and the like. He thought that they worked over the ships effectively, but he added, "So long as anything was left, they had not completed the job."[32]

Despite his decision, Yamamoto "was still not satisfied with Nagumo," according to Tomioka. He never forgot Nagumo's original opposition to his plan. And at Pearl Harbor Nagumo carried out his orders but did not go one bit beyond them to exploit the situation fully. Yamamoto thought that he should have made a second major attack even though not so ordered.

Tomioka believed that Nagumo was not entirely at fault because carrying out orders according to the book was a general weakness in the Japanese Navy. Its officers lacked a sufficiently flexible outlook to adapt themselves to new situations which might permit them to go beyond their instructions. Tomioka further believed that the root of the problem lay in the Japanese educational system, which placed a high premium on cramming facts into students' minds rather than on individual thinking.[33]

When Ugaki recorded the discussion in Combined Fleet headquarters and the reasons for the verdict, he tried to be philosophical: "There is a saying, 'It is good tactics to conclude a game without committing too much.'" Then his true opinion burst forth: "Had I been the C-in-C of the task force, however, I would have firmly resolved to continue to attack strongly . . . until Pearl Harbor was completely destroyed."[34] But had Ugaki been aboard *Akagi* on that fateful morning, he might have reached the same conclusions as Nagumo and Kusaka.

Yet from the Japanese point of view, one is inclined to agree with Yamamoto's observation to Ozawa at Truk in late 1942: "Events have shown that it was a great mistake not to have launched a second attack against Pearl Harbor."[35] By failing to exploit the shock, bewilderment, and confusion on Oahu, by failing to take full advantage of its savage attack against Kimmel's ships, by failing to pulverize the Pearl Harbor base, by failing to destroy Oahu's vast fuel stores, and by failing to seek out and sink America's carriers, Japan committed its first and probably its greatest strategical error of the entire Pacific conflict.

PART III

AFTERMATH

CHAPTER 66

"AN

EXCITEMENT

INDEED"

The White House had passed a quiet morning on this crisp, cold Sunday, December 7. At about 1000 Beardall delivered the fourteenth part of Japan's famous message breaking off the Hull-Nomura talks. Having done so, he went to his office in the Navy Department because he wanted to be available for courier duty to the White House if necessary. He also had a natural curiosity about the situation and wanted to see what was going on.[1]

Following Beardall's departure, Rear Admiral Ross T. McIntire, the President's personal physician, sat with him from 1000 to 1200. Roosevelt was "deeply concerned over the unsatisfactory nature of Nomura and Kurusu's conversations with Secretary Hull." But he was firmly convinced that "Japan's military masters would not risk a war with the United States." They might "take advantage of Great Britain's extremity and strike at Singapore or some other point in the Far East, but an attack on any American possession did not enter his thought."[2]

After meeting with Chinese Ambassador Dr. Hu Shih for about forty minutes, the President lunched in his Oval Room study with Harry Hopkins, talking "about things far removed from war. . . ." Then at about 1340, Knox phoned to inform Roosevelt of the attack on Pearl Harbor. Hopkins thought "there must be some mistake . . . that surely Japan would not attack in Honolulu." But Roosevelt believed "the report was probably true." This was "just the kind of unexpected thing the Japanese would do and that at the very time they were discussing peace in the Pacific they were plotting to overthrow it."

At about 1405 Roosevelt called Hull and told him about the message from Hawaii. He also "advised Hull to receive Nomura and Kurusu" but to mention nothing about Pearl Harbor. He was merely "to receive their reply formally and coolly and bow them out."[3]

Hull's first thought was to refuse to see the envoys, who had reached the State Department at 1405 and scarcely seated themselves in the diplomatic waiting room. But on the "one chance out of a hundred" that the report was not true, Hull decided to observe the amenities. At 1420, in the company of Joseph W. Ballantine, a State Department expert on the Far East who had sat in on many of the conversations, he "received them coldly and did not ask them to sit down."

Handing Hull the note, Nomura explained "that he had been instructed to deliver at 1:00 P.M." and apologized for the delay. Hull asked "why he had specified one o'clock." Nomura replied "that he did not know but that that was his instruction." To this Hull remarked "that anyway he was receiving the message at two o'clock." Obviously he wanted to drill the time into the minds of the two envoys.

The secretary of state went through the motions of examining the document. Then he transfixed Nomura with a chilly eye. The cold contempt in his words cut more painfully than any blast of fury:

> I must say that in all my conversations with you during the last nine months, I have never uttered one word of untruth. This is borne out absolutely by the record. In all my fifty years of public service I have never seen a document that was more crowded with infamous falsehoods and distortions—infamous falsehoods and distortions on a scale so huge that I never imagined until today that any Government on this planet was capable of uttering them.

Lifting his hand to cut off any protest Nomura might have made, Hull nodded toward his door. When the envoys walked out, heads down, Nomura, at least, was obviously "under great emotional strain."[4]

Always reticent in his diary, Nomura wrote nothing about the hurt bewilderment which filled his kindly heart. The very brevity of his entry for December 7 was significant:

> The day on which diplomatic relations between Japan and America were severed. . . .
> 　　The report of our surprise attack against Hawaii reached my ears when I returned home from the state department; *this might have reached Hull's ears during our conversation* [Nomura's italics].

Indeed it had, as Nomura learned sometime later. He had not expected war to break out so suddenly, and the attack both surprised and stunned him.[5]

Stimson was having a late lunch at Woodley when the President phoned him the news. Stimson recorded his reaction in low key: "Well, that was an excitement indeed." Later in the day he sorted out his major thoughts:

> When the news first came that Japan had attacked us, my first feeling was of relief that the indecision was over and that a crisis had come in a way which would unite all our people. This continued to be my dominant feeling in spite

of the news of catastrophes which quickly developed. For I feel that this country united has practically nothing to fear while the apathy and divisions stirred up by unpatriotic men have been hitherto very discouraging.[6]

Shortly after noon Marshall summoned Colonel John R. Deane, secretary of the General Staff, and informed him that he expected to see the President at about 1500. He instructed Deane "to keep the office open and have some of the commissioned and civilian personnel report for duty." Thereupon Marshall drove to his quarters for lunch. About 1330 a Navy enlisted man rushed into Deane's office with the searing message that Pearl Harbor was under attack. Deane immediately phoned Marshall, who directed him "to contact Hawaii if possible and verify the message." Before Deane would do so, a confirming dispatch came in. Within ten minutes Marshall reached his office, where he remained until his appointment at the White House.[7]

Of all the men in Washington whom one might expect to make a beeline for the office that afternoon, Safford was noteworthy by his absence. Being "completely exhausted after two months of worry and almost sleepless nights," he had "slept the clock around—with 4 extra hours to boot. . . ." He was eating a belated breakfast when a Navy wife telephoned him "that the Japs were bombing Pearl Harbor and was her husband in danger?"

Convinced that a "winds execute" message had been received and almost maddened with frustration over the warning messages which had died aborning in Washington, Safford decided to stay home. He kept "a detective-model .38 and shoulder holster" in his desk and feared that with his weapon in reach he "would have murdered Noyes and tried to murder Stark also."[8]

Hull had left the State Department shortly after 1500.[9] He and Marshall arrived at the White House soon thereafter. Roosevelt's advisers gathered with strained intensity, aware that any additional reports from Oahu would be bad. Most of the information concerning Hawaii came by telephone from Stark in the Navy Department. His voice revealed his "shocked unbelief." It was the unhappy task of Grace Tully, Roosevelt's devoted secretary, "to take these fragmentary and shocking reports from him by shorthand, type them up and relay them to the Boss." The confusion and noise proved so distracting that she had to use the phone in the President's bedroom.

McIntire, Beardall, and others anxiously read over her shoulder as she transcribed. Reaction among them moved from initial incredulity to "angry acceptance as new messages supported and amplified the previous ones. The Boss maintained greater outward calm than anybody else but there was rage in his very calmness," Miss Tully wrote. "With each new message he shook his head grimly and tightened the expression of his mouth." Of course, Beardall had a particular cause for worry and distress—his son aboard the light cruiser *Raleigh* in Pearl Harbor.

During the afternoon Roosevelt telephoned Governor Poindexter on Oahu. While they were talking, suddenly the governor "almost shrieked into the phone." Roosevelt relayed the message to the men clustered around him.

"My God, there's another wave of Jap planes over Hawaii right this minute."

When Hull arrived at the White House, his face was "as white as his hair." In the bitter knowledge that he and his country had been thoroughly tricked, he told the President about his encounter with the Japanese envoys. Stimson and Knox "were cross-examined closely on what had happened, on why they believed it could have happened. . . . It was easy to speculate that a Jap invasion force might be following their air strike at Hawaii—or that the West Coast itself might be marked for similar assault."[10]

The incoming reports distressed Stimson exceedingly. "The news coming from Hawaii is very bad. . . . It has been staggering to see [that] our people there, who have been warned long ago and were standing on the alert, should have been so caught by surprise," he noted in his diary that day.

The President discussed troop and air force dispositions with Marshall, who assured him that he had ordered MacArthur to execute "all the necessary movement required in event of an outbreak of hostilities with Japan." Roosevelt also urged Hull to keep the South American republics informed and to maintain rapport with them. He directed Stimson and Knox to place guards around arsenals, munition factories, and bridges. But he did not want a military guard around the White House.

Marshall obviously wished to get on with his duties, and so did Stimson. Accordingly the latter did not remain long at the White House. He returned to the War Department, where he "started matters going in all directions to warn against sabotage and to get punch into the defense move."[11]

At 1600 Hull presided over a conference at State during which a press report came in announcing that Japan had declared war on the United States. Hull was "calm and maintained his characteristic poise in the face of this new and great emergency." But that did not prevent him from expressing "with great emphasis his disappointment that the armed forces in Hawaii had been taken so completely by surprise." The recorder of this meeting recalled that "time after time during recent months" Hull "had warned our military and naval men with all the vigor at his command that there was constant danger of a treacherous attack by Japan. He deeply regretted that these warnings had not been taken more seriously." The initial reaction of the State Department men at this conference was this:

> . . . that the Japanese, in their own interest, were exceedingly stupid in attacking Hawaii and thereby instantaneously and completely uniting the American people. However, after it became evident that our armed forces had suffered tremendous damage in Hawaii, there was less feeling that the Japanese had been stupid.[12]

At about 1600 several hundred men, women, and children—"mostly men with angry faces"—had gathered outside the executive offices. Some held children perched on their shoulders. Like most Americans, these people had believed deeply in the power and greatness of their country. How could a horrible thing like this happen to the United States?

Within the hour Stephen T. Early, Roosevelt's Press secretary, informed waiting newsmen that the President had begun dictating the first draft of his message to Congress asking for a declaration of war. With a few minor alterations this was the historic speech he made the next afternoon. Early next "released to the hushed reporters the most dread news of the day. . . ." Admiral Bloch had reported "heavy damage" and "heavy loss of life."

Slowly the sun sank behind the White House. Squirrels frisked through the bare branches of the trees dotting the lawn. Lights winked on in the windows of the executive offices. Passing cars slowed to a crawl as drivers and passengers craned their necks toward this combined home and powerhouse of government uniquely their own. Periodically White House police urged the spectators to move on, but some were always there, staring in almost total silence toward the lighted windows as if to penetrate the minds of those laboring inside.[13]

That evening the President dined in his study with his son James, Hopkins, and Miss Tully. "Harry looked just like a walking cadaver, just skin and bones." During the meal the President "did not talk about Pearl Harbor and he did not complain. It was an hour when he wanted to relax a bit," said his faithful secretary.[14]

Roosevelt's official family gathered at 2030 in the Oval Room, Hopkins being the only nonmember present. The President opened by stating that "this was the most serious meeting of the Cabinet that had taken place since 1861."[15] He continued, "You all know what's happened. . . . We don't know very much yet." Someone asked, "Mr. President, several of us have just arrived by plane. We don't know anything except a scare headline 'Japs Attack Pearl Harbor.' Could you tell us?"[16] The President then related the story as he knew it:

> And finally while we were on the alert—at eight o'clock . . . a great fleet of Japanese bombers bombed our ships in Pearl Harbor, and bombed all of our airfields. . . . The casualties, I am sorry to say, were extremely heavy. . . . It looks as if out of eight battleships, three have been sunk, and possibly a fourth. Two destroyers were blown up while they were in drydock. Two of the battleships are badly damaged. Several other smaller vessels have been sunk or destroyed. The drydock itself has been damaged. Other portions of the fleet are at sea, moving towards what is believed to be two plane carriers, with adequate naval escort.[17]

Aware of the awesome historic forces the attack had unleashed, Roosevelt was concerned about the address he wished to deliver to Congress the next day. So he slowly read the draft he had recently dictated. Stimson thought it superficial, being "based wholly upon the treachery of the present attack. . . . For that line of thought it was very effective but it did not attempt to cover the long standing indictment of Japan's lawless conduct in the past. Neither did it connect here in any way with Germany . . . ," as Stimson and Hull believed it should. The latter in particular wanted the President to make a long presentation covering the course of the negotiations, but the rest preferred the shorter message.

Stimson urged in addition that the President "ask for a declaration of war against Germany also," pointing out that "we know from the interceptions and other evidence that Germany had pushed Japan into this. . . ."[18] But the others preferred to wait. Those with access to Magic knew that Ribbentrop had given Hitler's word—for whatever that might be worth—that if war broke out between Japan and the United States, Germany would declare war.[19]

One seeks in vain for anything in Magic which could have given Stimson the notion that Berlin called the tune for Tokyo. Yet his reasoning grew from fertile soil and was consistent with the national propensity to underestimate Japan. It was difficult for these men in Washington to accept the fact that a military operation so swift, so ruthless, so painfully successful—in a word, so blitzkrieg—in nature did not originate with Hitler. During the day, when Bloch telephoned Stark, the CNO asked, "The submarine sunk in the harbor, is it German?"[20]

After the Cabinet meeting the leaders of the Senate entered: Majority Leader Alben W. Barkley, and Charles L. McNary, his Republican opposite; Thomas T. Connally, chairman of the Foreign Relations Committee, and his colleague Hiram W. Johnson; Warren R. Austin of the Military Affairs Committee. From the House came Speaker Sam Rayburn and Acting Majority Leader Jere Cooper; Minority Leader Joseph W. Martin; Sol Bloom, chairman of the Foreign Affairs Committee, and committee member Charles A. Eaton.[21]

To the assembled lawmakers the President landed his punches straight from the shoulder. "The effect on the Congressmen was tremendous. They sat in dead silence and even after the recital was over they had very few words."[22] Someone asked about Japanese casualties. "It's a little difficult," answered the President. "We think we got some of their submarines, but we don't know. . . . We know some Japanese planes were shot down." But, he pointed out, he had seen that sort of thing in the last war. "One fellow says he got fifteen of their planes and . . . somebody else says five. . . . I should say that by far the greater loss has been sustained by us, although we have accounted for some of the Japanese." A rumor had cropped up of a Japanese carrier sunk off the Panama Canal. Roosevelt did not credit it, although he wished he could. The Canal Zone had reported being "on the alert, but very quiet."

The President had received unconfirmed reports that Japan had either declared war on the United States or proclaimed that a state of hostilities existed. Actually, at 1600 EST on December 7, 1941, Japanese Imperial Headquarters proclaimed that a state of war existed between Japan and the United States and the British Empire.

Roosevelt added, ". . . the principal defense of the whole west coast of this country and the whole west coast of the Americas has been very seriously damaged today." He asked for and received authority for a concurrent resolution requesting him to address Congress at 1230 the next day. "Well, it is an awfully serious situation," he continued. "There is a rumor that two of the planes . . . were seen with swastikas on them. Now whether that is true or not, I don't know." So he did not automatically discount German participation in the air strike. He then proceeded to give a quite accurate outline of how the Japanese began the attack. He pointed out: "In other words, at dark, last night, they might very well have been four hundred or five hundred miles away from the Island, and therefore out of what might be called a good patrol distance. . . ."[23]

But Senator Connally was in no mood for anything that smacked of excuses. He had been slowly coming to a boil during the briefing. Now he burst out: "Hell's fire, didn't we do anything!"

"That's about it," answered Roosevelt.

Then Connally swung on Knox. "Well, what did we *do?*" he demanded.

Knox had started to answer when the irate senator interrupted him. "Didn't you say last month that we could lick the Japs in two weeks? Didn't you say that our navy was so well prepared and located that the Japanese couldn't hope to hurt us at all? When you made those public statements, weren't you just trying to tell the country what an efficient secretary of the navy you were?"

The unhappy Knox, "the most disturbed man present," fumbled for an adequate reply. Roosevelt said not a word; he simply sat with "a blank expression on his face." But Connally had by no means finished with the secretary of the navy.

"Why did you have all the ships at Pearl Harbor crowded in the way you did?" he prodded. "And why did you have a log chain across the mouth of the entrance to Pearl Harbor, so that our ships could not get out?" Possibly Connally had some idea of the antisubmarine net. Of course, no mechanical device hindered the sortie of any ship from Pearl Harbor.

"To protect us against Japanese submarines," Knox answered in a shaky voice.

"Then you weren't thinking of an air attack?" Connally asked.

"No," Knox admitted.[24]

"Well, they were supposed to be on the alert," Connally said, "and if they had been on the alert . . . * I am amazed by the attack by Japan, but I am still more astounded at what happened to our Navy. They were all asleep. Where were our patrols? They knew these negotiations were going on." This was the question everyone wanted answered. Knox did not attempt a rebuttal. As yet he had no facts upon which to base a reply.[25]

Not until almost 2300 did the congressional delegation and many of the Cabinet leave the White House. Some of the dignitaries had a word for the waiting reporters as they emerged. Everyone agreed that the country could anticipate, in Austin's phrase, "a vacation from politics." "Republicans will go along with whatever is done, in my opinion," promised McNary. And Martin stated, "Where the integrity and honor of the Nation is involved there is only one party."[26]

Back at the Treasury, Morgenthau foregathered with key members of his Department. Toward the end of the meeting Harry Dexter White, director of

---

*This break occurs in the transcript, indicating inaudibility.

monetary research, asked, "Has there been negligence or is it just the fortunes of war?"

"Harry, how the thing could happen—to me it is just unexplainable," answered Morgenthau. "They walked in just as easily as they did in Norway. And they didn't do it in the Philippines. Let Stimson take credit for that. . . . But I just—the Navy is supposed to be on the alert, and how this thing could have happened—all the explanations I have heard just don't make sense. . . ."

The secretary could not get over what had happened. "We have always been led to believe that the Navy was our first line of defense and Hawaii was impregnable. I mean that has been sold to us." Throughout the conference he harked back to the blow.

"They haven't learned anything here. They have the whole Fleet in one place—the whole Fleet was in this little Pearl Harbor base." He repeated like a record with the needle stuck: "The whole Fleet was there." He expressed his wonder how the Japanese could sneak in there because U.S. forces formerly "patrolled for 5 to 600 miles." And he proclaimed, "They never can explain this. They will never be able to explain it."[27] But all the lamentations and puzzlement could not turn back the clock.

CHAPTER 67

"OUR

FLAG

WAS

STILL

THERE"

Strangely enough, many citizens of Honolulu remained unaware of the true state of affairs for at least an hour after the attack began. Accustomed to the roar of aircraft and explosions from Army and Navy exercises, they accepted the fearful racket as no more than unusually realistic maneuvers. The radio warnings were not specific enough to spell out the situation for the average civilian. Then, on the 0900 broadcast from KGMB, Webley Edwards had a flash of inspiration. He added to his formal announcement, "This is the real McCoy," and the simple phrase carried conviction.[1]

Almost immediately a whole folklore centering on Hawaii's Japanese sprang up like a crop of toadstools from the fertile soil of suspicion and hysteria. Even Kimmel succumbed to the atmosphere. "The Fifth Column activities added great confusion and it was most difficult to evaluate reports received . . . ," he wrote to Stark on December 12.[2] The fact is, the Navy, the Army, and civilian Oahu did not need any fifth-column help to generate a state of confusion.

According to one tale, Japanese plantation laborers cut arrows in the cane fields, directing the attacking force to Pearl Harbor—a singularly illogical rumor. Missing Pearl Harbor from the air over Oahu would be like overlooking a bass drum in a telephone booth. The most troublesome fable—that the Japanese had poisoned the drinking water—may have originated on Ford Island. The pipeline there being out of commission, a resourceful supply officer took over the installation's three swimming pools as emergency reservoirs. Of course, this water had to be boiled. "All such rumors and reports were checked as expeditiously as possible. None of the cases investigated proved to be authentic."[3]

One of the *Star-Bulletin*'s reporters of Japanese ancestry "begged . . . to be allowed to go out on the street and cover the news." Riley H. Allen, the editor, feared that the young man "might be shot or locked up." Then Allen "finally decided that we would send him out to the Japanese consul and bring back what news he might find there."[4] This reporter probably was Lawrence Nakatsuka, who dropped by the consulate that morning in search of a story.

Like so many others on Oahu, the consulate's members had anticipated a leisurely Sunday. Kita and Okuda had an engagement to play golf with a friend. At about 0900 Kotoshirodo, hearing the distant thundering, walked the short distance from his abode to the consulate "to find out what all the commotion was about." He discovered Kita, Okuda, and others of the staff already assembled, looking worried. Yoshikawa appeared shortly, in shirt sleeves, hair mussed and clothes wrinkled. He remarked that it was a "noisy morning." He wanted to go up to the heights to see what was happening, but Kita forbade him to leave.[5]

Kita refused to admit to Nakatsuka that a Japanese attack was in progress, let alone make a statement about it. The reporter hurried back to his office for a copy of the day's extra and brought it to Kita as evidence. The blazing headline WAR! OAHU BOMBED BY JAPANESE PLANES was Yoshikawa's signal for action. He and Tsukikawa dashed for the code room, where they began to burn material furiously.[6]

After leaving Short's headquarters, Bicknell arrived at his office downtown, where he found his people issuing ammunition and small arms. Shivers was there, astonished and "scared all the way through," like almost everyone else. He and Bicknell wanted to pick up Japanese suspects immediately but were unable to do so because the provost marshal could not provide the necessary trucks and MP guards. This delayed the plan for several hours. "Bob Shivers and I were running around like two wild Indian dogs," Bicknell recalled.[7]

At about 1000 or 1100 Shivers asked Police Chief Gabrielson to put a guard around the consulate "for the protection of the consul general and the members of his staff and the consular property."[8] Gabrielson turned the assignment over to Captain of Detectives Benjamin Van Kuren and Lieutenant Yoshio Hasegawa. When they and a few colleagues arrived at the consulate, they found uniformed police officers with sawed-off shotguns already on guard. Kita stood in the driveway at the rear of the building, holding the *Star-Bulletin* extra.[9]

Van Kuren and his men trooped in through the back entrance. In the code room the police "found a wash tub on the floor" in which the Japanese were burning documents. The police also salvaged a brown "bellows type envelope" full of undestroyed papers. They brought their find to the FBI, which in turn gave it to Naval Intelligence for Rochefort to work on. Sometime that morning Bicknell went to RCA and commandeered the file of messages which the consulate had sent to and received from Japan.[10]

In the midst of all the drama at the consulate Mikami drove up in his taxi as arranged to take Kita and Okuda to the golf course—a supreme example of the business-as-usual mentality. He asked the guard to tell Okuda he had arrived.

Gentleman to the last, the vice consul sent word not to wait; he "probably would be unable to play golf that day."[11]

In the anchorage, oil oozing out of damaged vessels had caught fire, and the whole area around Battleship Row was aflame. "One of the most terrifying sights that day," said Train, "was to see those burning waters move down the channel and go out with the tide. It was ghostly, eerie, threatening and dangerous. And worst of all, there was nothing to put it out with."[12] So menacing did the burning oil become around *California* that at 1015 her skipper, Captain J. W. Bunkley, with Pye's approval, ordered Abandon Ship. But shortly afterward, when the fires cleared the vessel, Bunkley canceled the order.[13] Nevertheless, *California* had become unsuitable as a headquarters, so Pye removed himself and his staff and reported to Kimmel's office. The CinCUS reassured both them and himself: "I need you men." Though badly shaken by his terrible ordeal, Kimmel thought only of striking back against the Japanese.[14]

On and off ship survivors fought the fires valiantly. *Tennessee*'s crew tried to move her away from *Arizona,* but the ship did not budge. Apparently *West Virginia* had wedged her close to the quays. For the rest of the day and night *Tennessee* kept her engines turning "in order that the screw current could wash the burning oil from the stern. . . ."[15]

Fire engulfed *West Virginia* except for a small area forward. Some survivors of the battleship crossed to *Tennessee,* using a 5-inch gun as a bridge. Alongside, the garbage scow *YG-17* played her powerful hoses on *West Virginia* until the fires came under control[16]—a lowly scullery maid protecting a beleaguered queen.

Rescue crews swarmed over *Utah* and *Oklahoma,* cutting through the hulls, following the faint taps from inside as trapped crewmen pounded against the bulkheads. Not until Monday afternoon did Thesman and his men scramble out of *Oklahoma.* "It was a deep, powerful feeling . . ." he said, "like being dug up out of your own grave."[17]

A burning passion consumed the Americans to ferret out the enemy's flattops and exact a grim payment for the blood spilled this Sunday morning. But the hand of fate seemed to hover protectingly over Nagumo's task force. At first the defenders had no idea whatever whence the attack came. Soon, however, Kimmel's instinct told him that the enemy ships lay northward. At 1018 he advised his forces at sea: "Search from Pearl very limited account maximum twelve VP searching from Pearl. Some indication enemy force northwest Oahu. Addressees operate as directed Comtaskforce Eight to intercept enemy. Composition enemy force unknown."[18]

A Japanese submarine intercepted this message and sent it to the task force. Aboard *Akigumo* Chigusa noted in his diary, "Looks like enemy might catch us." But the Americans did not pursue this potentially profitable line of thought. From a direction finder at Heeia, Rochefort learned that the Japanese commander "bore either 357 or 178." This indicated the attackers lay north or south—the readings would be the same for either direction—and "through a limitation of aircraft operations he could be expected to be within 200 miles."[19]

McMorris's War Plans Division was "inclined strongly to believe that the attack had come from both the northward and the southward. . . ." Because the American carriers at sea were "already in the southward area," War Plans "felt that the chance of intercepting the northern route was probably quite remote, while the chance of intercepting the southern route looked, at least, to hold some promise. . . ."[20] A mental flip of the coin landed on the wrong side. At 1046 Kimmel notified Halsey's Task Force Eight, "D/F [direction finder] bearings indicate enemy carrier bearing 178 from Barbers Point."[21]

When Coe reached his office on Ford Island, Ramsey told him "to get on the operational telephone, call Army Air, and find out where the hell the Japanese planes were coming from and try to get any other information" he could. Coe did his best, but everything was chaos, confusion, and demoralization at the time. "Lines were not manned," he said, "and I could not get through to anybody." Even had they found Nagumo's carriers, they could not have done much about it. "We were simply not in a position to retaliate," said Coe.[22]

Other arrows pointed northward. When Landon was bringing in his B-17 that morning, he noticed some of the Japanese planes winging away in that direction. After he reported to Hawaiian Air Force Headquarters, he tried to interest someone in his information, but it seemed to him that nearly everyone was more preoccupied with fitting liners into their helmets in anticipation of another attack than in locating the task force and hitting it before it could launch further strikes.[23]

The Opana Station plotted a clear northbound track, which the radar control center at Fort Shafter recorded at 1027 and 1029. But according to Martin, "there was no indication of that course being an important one at that time." In fact, no one brought it to his attention "until they analyzed the history of the control chart" sometime later.[24] Kimmel testified that because of the Army's failure to inform the Navy of this intelligence, "the surface naval operations which ensued took a westerly direction with their aircraft scouting largely to the southwest. . . ."[25]

By 1127 Martin had four of Hickam's A-20 bombers ready for takeoff. The Navy had no instructions for them, so Martin gave them the "mission of trying to find the carrier that was south of Barbers Point."[26] There was indeed a large vessel in that location, but it was the heavy cruiser *Minneapolis*, on her way home from the Fleet operating area.[27] Her skipper instructed his radio room to advise Kimmel, "No carriers in sight," but somehow it came out "Two carriers in sight." Luckily the pilots heading toward her recognized *Minneapolis*.[28]

Another United States cruiser had a narrow escape that afternoon. The commander of "a squadron of seaplanes returned from Midway" reported a Japanese carrier and destroyer "well south of Pearl Harbor." Examined by virtually every member of Kimmel's staff, the pilot insisted that "he knew it was a Japanese carrier because he saw the Rising Sun painted on her deck." What is more, she "had the plan of a heavy cruiser painted on her deck as camouflage." The location being almost exactly that of Brown's task force, CinCPAC immediately directed Brown "to get the carrier." Brown replied that he believed his own cruiser *Portland* had been bombed. Scarcely able to credit this, headquarters radioed *Portland:* "Were you bombed this afternoon?" Back came the reply: "Yes, a plane dropped two bombs narrowly missing me astern."[29]

When Allen finally lifted his B-17 off the runway at Hickam, he, too, followed official intelligence and headed south, despite his private conviction that his prey lay northward. In due course he sighted "this beautiful carrier," which fired on him. So he went into a bomb run. But suddenly, in Allen's words, "God had a hand on me because I knew this was not a Jap carrier." He had spotted *Enterprise*. Allen pulled out of range and decided to try the northern direction; however, he had no luck. Then be turned back southward. Once more he saw *Enterprise*, now much nearer to Oahu, and two Navy Wildcat fighters looked him over suspiciously as he started back to Hickam.[30] From the timing it appears that Allen's initial swing south had been just long enough for Nagumo's carriers to voyage beyond his reach.

Sometime after the first aerial hunting parties took off, the Hawaiian Air Force received a map recovered from the Japanese pilot shot down near Fort Kamehameha. "This map had approximately ten courses laid out on it to a point northwest of the Island of Oahu, which indicated that they either had left carriers there or expected to return to carriers in that direction. . . ." Accordingly Martin dispatched other planes northward in the afternoon. They, too, found nothing.[31]

The principal American effort for the remainder of the day was preparation to fend off another attack, particularly a follow-through amphibious landing. Oahu's defenders could not imagine an aerial strike for its own sake and in effect were waiting for the enemy to drop the other shoe. Furthermore, in their eyes Fuchida's fliers had left behind an amazing amount of unfinished business. Both Kimmel and Smith expected that all ships in the harbor would be destroyed and that "the naval base would go too." But many of the ships were unscathed, the yards and docks relatively undamaged, and, above all, the tank farms intact.

Full of "fight and guts," Kimmel began to pick up the pieces and prepare for all-out defense. He and his chief of staff feared that the Japanese might be landing on Oahu at the very time Fuchida's planes blasted Pearl Harbor. Both officers, as well as other members of the staff, expected the Japanese to renew their attack and try to land into the bargain.[32]

One of the busiest men on Oahu was Mollison, working frantically to establish the Hawaiian Department's emergency headquarters in Aliamanu Crater. Mollison called the job "a real backbreaker," for the facility was rudimentary, being actually a series of old ammunition tunnels with neither housekeeping arrangements nor communications. Its condition stood as a silent witness to just how seriously the Army on Oahu took the necessity for an alternate headquarters. Mollison had to put his clutch into high gear to meet a 1430 deadline for occupancy.

He also felt responsible for Martin. The general lacked neither personal courage nor good sense; but his ulcer drained him of resistance, and the attack had shattered his morale. At about 1500 Martin turned to his chief of staff and stammered, "What am I going to do? I believe I am losing the power of decision." Mollison then realized that his good chief had reached the end of his rope. Immediately he arranged for Martin's admission to the Hickam Field hospital with orders that no one was to disturb him. But he had a private phone placed at Martin's bedside so he could communicate with the general when conditions demanded.[33]

Curts soon recognized that one of the principal postattack problems was keeping down civilian hysteria in Honolulu. The city had been damaged by about forty hits from American guns which overshot their marks. Although only one Japanese bomb fell on the city, naturally the citizens believed themselves to be under direct enemy bombardment. Curts was seriously annoyed with the Honolulu radio stations. With the best of intentions, they were broadcasting a series of messages designed to instruct and calm the population but which had the opposite effect. Therefore, he phoned the stations to stop disrupting the populace and to "knock off the damned foolishness."[34]

Shortly thereafter both KGU and KGMB went off the air, principally as a precaution against Japanese planes' using their beams as homing devices. But the silence was almost worse than the news flashes. Now the noncombatants had no information at all. This was particularly tormenting for the service wives clinging to their radios as a connecting link, however thin, with their loved ones caught in the Pearl Harbor inferno.

Naval and military radios also helped spread alarm and dismay. False reports came in thick and fast: At 1133 the destroyer *Sicard* "observed another horizontal bombing raid." The Japanese had long gone, so possibly the destroyer mistook Martin's bombers heading out to scout as more enemy planes. Some chilling invasion reports began to pour in: "Enemy troops landing on north shore. Blue overalls with red emblems." Later it developed that this rumor originated when the Japanese shot down a small training seaplane and the dungaree-clad mechanic aboard "dropped to safety." Other frightening reports raced through message centers: "Parachutists are landing at Barber's Point," "Enemy transports reported four miles off Barbers Point," "Parachute troops landing on North shore," "Enemy sampan about to land at Naval ammunition Depot," "Enemy landing party off shore Nanakuli. Friendly planes firing on them."[35]

At Kaneohe, Beauty Martin, "anticipating a Jap landing party," instructed each man "to bring two suits of whites to the mess hall to be dyed. There was no dye available but the uniforms were dipped in very strong, boiling hot coffee. They came out a dark brown." Avery, for one, did not regret the loss of the coffee. The attack had a peculiar physiological effect on him. From Sunday morning until Thursday morning he neither slept nor took "a morsel of food, nor a drop of liquid of any kind," yet he remained "alert and energetic."[36]

On Ford Island white-faced wives and children of officers filled the Bellinger's air-raid shelter, an abandoned gun emplacement. The thought nagged at Mrs. Bellinger: *What if this caves in and we're covered up? Will I be able to stand it?*[37]

As soon as Colonel Dunlop could snatch a moment, he returned home to satisfy himself about the safety of his wife and his eighty-one-year-old mother-in-law, Mrs. Lucy Ord Mason, who resided with them. A living link with America's past, she had lost her husband as a result of the Battle of Wounded Knee in 1890. She refused point-blank to seek shelter in the basement. These young Japanese whippersnappers did not scare her, and she would not abandon her twelve canaries, which she loved dearly.

The inevitable touch of comedy which lurks around the corner from tragedy arose in the Dunlop household that morning. Mary Lee Henderson, attractive wife of Major Swede Henderson, slept through the entire attack. At about 1030 she dashed over to the Dunlops' home and dumbfounded her neighbors by asking, "What has happened?"[38]

In a way, women such as Navy nurse Ruth Erickson who had specific duties cut out for them were better situated than the wives. The chief nurse worked out a schedule of rounds which sent Ruth off duty at 1600. Neither she nor many of her associates felt tired. "We were riding on nervous energy and wanted to keep right on going," she emphasized.[39]

In his report for the Navy's surgeon general, Admiral McIntire, Fleet Surgeon Captain Elphege A. M. Gendreau paid tribute to the men and women of his command: "I can only say: 'a hard job damned well done.' As for morale: 'God help the enemy!' " Then Gendreau expressed the eerie sense of unreality which so many had experienced that day: "I still expect to awaken from a bad dream or see the end of a war 'movie.' "[40]

From the bridge of *Argonne*, flagship of the Service Force, moored at the edge of 1010 Dock, Quynn looked across the harbor, watching *California* sink steadily into the shallow waters. Thick black smoke engulfed the battleship like a shroud. Several tugs, puffing and blowing, pushed at her sides to keep her from capsizing. As the fitful wind blew the angry clouds of smoke, Quynn caught a glimpse of the Stars and Stripes still fluttering gallantly from *California*'s stern. Quynn did not leave his post for seventy-two hours. Throughout that time he took courage and resolution from the sight of his country's banner—"proof through the night that our flag was still there."[41]

Caught in the grandfather of all traffic jams and held up by roadblocks, RCA messenger Fuchikami could not deliver until 1145 Marshall's warning to Short concerning Japan's "one o'clock" message. Duly decoded, it finally reached Dunlop at 1458.[42] As he read it, an ironic, macabre amusement welled up in him, and he could not suppress a bark of laughter. *The damn thing won't do any good now,* he said to himself. He handed it to an officer nearby. "Get this to General Short at once. Take it right to him."[43]

According to Major General Robert J. Fleming, Short received a copy of this message directly from the Signal Center prior to its transmission through adjutant general channels. Fleming, then a major, was assigned to the department G-4 and functioned as Short's personal troubleshooter. He was in the emergency headquarters when Lieutenant Colonel Carroll A. "Cappy" Powell, the signal officer, asked Fleming to hand the message to Short. Powell explained that having had "a couple of run-ins with the general," he did not want to be the one to give Short this dispatch because "General Short would probably go through the roof and land all over him." He thought that Fleming "would probably be safer from the flak. . . ." Fleming delivered it, and as Powell anticipated, "Short about went through the roof."[44]

Marshall's message came too late to be of any use to the Hawaiian Department. Yet Short later admitted that even if he had received the information by scrambler telephone, the fact that the Japanese were destroying their code machines, as indicated in the text, would have meant more to him than the mention of a specific time. But at least he could have asked Marshall what it meant to him. While scramblers were "not considered as safe as code," they were "reasonably safe."[45]

When Kimmel read a copy of Marshall's message thereafter, he flung it into the wastebasket in baffled fury. The Army's messenger, Captain William B. Cobb, talked it over with Davis, the Fleet air officer, and they tried "to account for the delay in transmittal." Kimmel considered the incident a prime example of fumbling vital intelligence.[46]

That afternoon painters coated the windows of Kimmel's headquarters black, so that the admiral and his staff could work late without showing a light. Unfortunately they painted on the inside of the panes. With the windows closed against the cooling breeze, the choking fumes and heat almost blinded and sickened these tormented men, already exhausted and heartsore.[47]

During the attack everyone had been so busy he had scarcely had time to think. Yet a cataclysmic fury gripped most of those who experienced the awful ordeal or witnessed it close to hand. "If I could have gotten my hands on any one of these Japanese," gritted Chief Crawford, "I would have crushed him like an insect."[48] Gunner's Mate Beck recalled, "There was a deep, powerful thirst for revenge on the part of every enlisted man. I wouldn't have given any Japanese a second of mercy after Pearl Harbor."[49]

Nightfall added the primal fear of darkness to the horrors and confusion of the day. "It fell suddenly like a heavy veil and with all its mysteries forced a dangerous intimacy, a threat from any direction at once," reminisced Quynn.[50] Brigadier General George P. Sampson, who was Short's assistant communications officer in 1941, remembered: "The night of December 7 was worse than the day because by then the people had had time to think. Their thoughts rubbed shoulders with their friends' and neighbors', and their fears were multiplied in the thinking and speaking about the attack."[51]

With pride smarting and nerves scraped raw, the defenders of Oahu lived through that night as a man might move through a haunted house—half-fearful, half-defiant, jumping at shadows, lashing out savagely at everything that crossed his path. "Things were so bad a dog wasn't safe on the streets," Guzak recalled. "The word was: 'Don't move at night! Anything that moves will be shot."[52] As bone-weary Curts groped his way through the blackout from Kimmel's headquarters to his room in the BOQ, various guards challenged him six or seven times with the order "Halt and be recognized!" Fortunately for him, he did and was.[53]

A report came to Fielder's office about midnight that someone was signaling with a blue light just back of Fort Shafter. Investigation revealed "an elderly Japanese dairyman milking cows." He had put blue cellophane around an old lantern because the blackout regulations permitted only blue light. As the palm fronds swayed back and forth, "it made the light seem to go on and off as if a flashlight was being flashed in rhythm."

The whispering campaign grew so bad that in a few days Short directed Fielder to go on the radio to refute the rumors. Fielder's particular favorite came from a man who asserted that "a dog down on Ewa Beach was barking in code to a submarine off shore." Added Short's G-2: "The guy that reported it was perfectly serious and actually believed it."[54]

Kaneohe was a nightmare. One of the two AA batteries was set up next to Avery's bungalow. Manning the guns were young "reservists with less than 90 days of Regular Army experience." The ordeal began when Avery heard a sentry's "fear frenzied voice screech, 'Halt!' " Then the man pulled the trigger.

> That touched off a crazy spree of firing by both batteries. . . . At what, neither they nor anyone else knew. Every soldier who had a rifle was firing furiously. The Air Station siren sounded General Quarters but no one had a battle station to man so it didn't matter. . . . Our phone rang; the Administration Bldg. wanted to know if we were under attack by landing parties. Nobody knew. . . . After a full ten minutes of this reckless, pell-mell firing their officers finally regained control and got the firing stopped—momentarily. . . . The alarm on our base aroused the curiosity of many civilians who drove their cars along that road to see what was happening . . . the two AA batteries now brought their guns to bear on those autos and riflemen sniped at them until all were driven from the road. No casualties! Sometime around midnight . . . a searchlight battery on the hill overlooking the town of Kaneohe began sweeping the skies. The AA batteries now found it expedient to shell the searchlight batteries.[55]

The hotel where Navy wife Kathleen Bruns Cooper stayed with a friend was blacked out, and someone wisely organized a first-aid group, which kept the women constructively occupied. At about 2200 a tremendous noise threw the whole hotel into an uproar. An antiaircraft shell had fallen about fifty yards across the street on the campus of Punahau High School. By good fortune, no one was hurt, but it formed a huge crater. Kathleen and her friends thought the enemy had returned. She and other Catholic women gathered in a room to say the rosary. At the end of each decade the non-Catholics chimed in, "Me, too, O Lord!"[56]

Colonel Dunlop helped organize the removal of about 400 women to a large cave then under construction outside Fort Shafter as headquarters for the

Coast Defense Forces. Although no creature comforts had been installed and the ground was covered with rubble, about ten feet of rock overhead provided protection from bombs.

Faced with evacuation and realizing that she and her daughter, Ruth Dunlop, might not return home for some time, Mrs. Mason gave her canaries enough food to last them for four days. Then she moved into the cave with Ruth and others.[57] Among them was Mrs. Short, who had been unable to leave Honolulu the preceding Friday as planned. She had anticipated sailing aboard an Army transport to the mainland for a holiday visit to Oklahoma City with their son, a West Point cadet. But the sailing had been postponed.[58] Now she and Mrs. Dunlop with other wives worked like galley slaves to clean up the forbidding cave and improvise sanitary facilities.[59]

That afternoon the women at Schofield received notification to gather at a certain barracks. After about three hours several buses pulled up, and the women hustled aboard. Among them was the wife of Major General Durward S. Wilson, commanding the Twenty-fourth Infantry Division. The drivers had no more idea of what went on than their passengers. The buses bumped at a snail's pace over unlighted roads. Tracer bullets laced through the night and contributed to the general hysteria, for naturally enough the women thought this to be enemy fire from the many landing parties reported. The bus in which Mrs. Wilson found herself became lost and, once back on the road again, stalled in a traffic jam for a full hour. By this time most of the women had abandoned all pretense of self-control and cried and screamed like the terrified children. Some knelt on the bus floor, moaning disconnected prayers. Mrs. Wilson wondered ruefully if the driver, between the traffic and the passengers, did not want to blow his brains out.[60]

Not all the stories of that night were those of terror and confusion. Calhoun testified:

> . . . there were between 300 and 400 bed patients in the Naval Hospital. That night at supper when they got ready to change them, practically every patient who was able to walk was absent. He had returned to his ship or any ship he could catch and had gone to sea. They did not return to the hospital for several days.[61]

Unhappily more than one American survived the attack only to fall to their own trigger-happy comrades. Even rescue boats still trying to fish men out of the oily waters were harassed and endangered by nervous marines, who constantly challenged them and blazed away if they were slow in answering. One of the most tragic incidents of the night occurred when six of the *Enterprise* pilots returned from searching for the Japanese carriers. "And once over Hickam," said Shoemaker, "all hell broke loose." He added:

> For by this time guns of every kind were spotted all over Hickam and the gunners, trigger-happy to begin with, were told to shoot to kill. So the planes ran into a blizzard of antiaircraft fire over Hickam. And by the time they got to

the Navy Yard and the battleship *Pennsylvania* they were baptized again. The planes came in with their running lights on and made a perfect target.[62]

Bosun's Mate French saw these planes approach Ford Island. "Everything in Pearl Harbor opened up on them," he said. "They didn't have a ghost of a chance and they flew in at only twelve hundred feet or a thousand feet. They had their running lights on, and the gunners should have known that they were our planes."[63]

One crashed, but the pilot parachuted to safety. Ensign James G. Daniels saved his life over Ford Island by flying straight for the gunners and dazzling them with his landing lights long enough to swoop out of range. Then he tried again, this time without lights, and touched down safely.[64] Shoemaker saw three go down in flames.

Throughout the night Ford Island continued to be plagued by false information from the Hawaiian Department's radar. "They were intermittent reports," Shoemaker recalled, "just enough to shake one up good. And there wasn't a goddamn thing we could do about it."[65]

Offshore, Commander Stout stood near the bridge rail on the starboard side of his destroyer *Breese,* watching the flakes of phosphorescence as porpoises played near the ship. "It was as black as the inside of a hat," he said, "and we were running on dead reckoning. The whole area was blacked out. We would look ashore and not see a damn thing except the waves washing in." At a short distance Stout observed what he thought was another porpoise. Then he noticed that there were two of them, and instead of swerving, they came straight for *Breese.* "It was a fish, all right," remarked Stout, "but not the type of fish I thought it was." He increased speed and turned seaward, escaping the torpedoes. But he never picked up the submarine which launched them, so he did not try to attack it. "There was no use dropping depth charges just for the hell of it," he explained, "because people were jittery enough as it was."[66]

A number of enemy submarines were lurking in Hawaiian waters, particularly *I-69* under Commander Katsuji Watanabe. He was the youngest standard submarine skipper in the Pearl Harbor operation and "most brave." At 1830 he received orders, apparently from Shimizu, to shift from his area some 17 miles southwest of Pearl Harbor and survey the central sector—a radius of about 8.5 nautical miles with Pearl Harbor at its center.

At 2000 Watanabe reported sighting four destroyers, which attacked him with depth charges at close range, apparently doing no damage. In fact, Watanabe had a hair-raising few days ahead of him. On December 8 *I-69* became caught in an antisubmarine net and remained underwater for thirty-eight hours before Watanabe managed to break her loose.

He helped start a legend when at 2101 on December 7 he "saw a very large flame heaving heavenward—a flame like a ship exploding in Pearl Harbor. After this very heavy antiaircraft followed." The time of this incident makes it virtually certain that he saw one of the *Enterprise* aircraft shot down and heard the AA fire which preceded and followed the tragic accident. Watanabe's account of his sighting, together with a report "from one of the midget submarines on the success of the attack" received at 0041 December 8, convinced the Japanese that not only had the midget attack been a huge success, but one of them had sunk *Arizona*. This story was widely touted in the Japanese press during the spring of 1942. No minisub inflicted any damage whatsoever upon any ship in or out of Pearl Harbor. The report is interesting, however, as showing that at least one midget was still on the prowl as late as 0041 December 8.[67]

Sakamaki and Inagaki had spent a thoroughly frustrating, exhausting day. Time after time they tried to penetrate Pearl Harbor, but at every attempt their uncontrollable minisub ran into the coral reef, finally destroying the second torpedo's mechanism. At last both men fell into a stupor from the foul air and from being knocked around in the collisions. Toward midnight Sakamaki awakened and opened the hatch to breathe deeply of the clean sea air. With the coming of dawn, the engine sputtered into silence. Sakamaki saw what he optimistically thought was Lanai Island near the rescue point. Actually he had drifted to a position off the Kaneohe-Bellows Field area.

After a final, futile effort to get the submarine moving, he and Inagaki set the fuse to scuttle the craft and dived overboard. The water was colder and rougher than Sakamaki anticipated; moreover, he was weakened from exhaustion, poisoned air, and almost unendurable nervous tension. He caught sight of Inagaki's head bobbing nearby, then lost it forever. He listened in vain for the charge to explode. Sick disappointment gripped him as he realized that he had failed even to destroy the submarine. Then a breaker seized him, and consciousness fled in a swirl of darkness. He came to lying on a beach. Raising his tired eyes, he saw an American soldier gazing down at him. Sergeant David M. Akui had just bagged the United States' Prisoner of War No. 1.[68]

Throughout the night Quynn kept his sleepless vigil on the bridge of *Argonne*. Pearl Harbor was still a mass of smoke and flame. Men were trigger-happy, overcharged with imagination and fears. In the distance, a sentry barked. Later a few shots rang out here and there—at whom scarcely anyone knew. The muffled boom of exploding depth charges reverberated through the darkness, set off against any midget submarine that might be in the harbor.

The next morning, when dawn spilled over the horizon, Quynn looked hopefully toward *California*. As the early mists cleared and the billows of smoke died down, he saw that she had not capsized; she had not sunk beyond recall. Though slowly settling, she stood on a fairly even keel. And from her stern the Stars and Stripes caught the breeze and proudly rippled into life.[69]

CHAPTER 68

"CLOUDS

OVER

MOUNTAINS"

The afternoon sun of December 7 receded into the fast-darkening sky of an equally fast-darkening world. At 1300 Nagumo had sent off to the Combined Fleet a hasty estimate of damage inflicted.[1] Shortly thereafter "all forces turned to the north at 26 knots."[2] But the task force was by no means safe yet, and Nagumo knew it. For better or worse, he had decided to retire, but would the enemy let him do so? What about the elusive American carriers and heavy cruisers? So once again he clamped radio silence over his ships. At 1715 he put the task force on all-out alert, ordering an aircraft patrol of the full 360-degree circle to a distance of 300 miles, to take off at dawn the next day. He added, "Make level bombers ready for torpedoing and dive bombing, and stand by for further orders."[3]

As one might expect, Genda viewed this patrol as a potential measure of the offensive. If, after all, Nagumo decided to launch a second attack, it would take place early the next morning. However, a major strike was impossible without confirming the location of the American carriers.[4]

As the First Air Fleet moved northward, Fuchida instructed all officers to develop their attack photographs at once for study in preparing a final assessment of damage inflicted. Courier planes from the other five carriers landed aboard *Akagi*, bringing data from their attack units. By late afternoon he had all the prints. The flight leaders studied them most of the night, and the next morning Fuchida turned in his battle report.[5]

Nagumo signaled to his command a few words of mingled praise and caution: "Brilliant success was achieved for our country through the splendid efforts of you men. But we still have a great way to go. After this victory we must tighten the straps of our helmets and go onward, determined to continue our fight until the final goal has been won."[6]

The morning of December 8 Nagumo dispatched the light cruiser

Abukuma and the destroyer *Tanikaze* to Supply Group One at the rendezvous point following final refueling before the attack. The two ships reached the tankers at about 2100, quickly refueled, and returned with them to the First Air Fleet.

Two or three of Nagumo's dawn patrol planes lost their bearings, ran out of fuel, and had to ditch, but destroyers picked up most of the airmen. A tanker fished out one reconnaissance pilot from *Soryu* and kept him aboard for the remainder of the homeward voyage. Those scouts who returned safely brought negative reports. So at 1530 Nagumo flashed to his command: "As a result of the air scouting, no enemy sighted within 300-mile circle. Be ready for the immediate use of 26 knots."[7]

Henceforth the narrative of the voyage returns to Japanese time unless otherwise indicated. Not until Wednesday, the eleventh, did Omori feel sufficiently assured to call his screening force staff together aboard his flagship *Abukuma* for a formal toast to celebrate their success.[8] By then news of the landings in Malaya and the unexpectedly good results of the air raids on Clark Field in the Philippines had poured more wine into the brimming cup of victory. They all relaxed in high spirits as they "celebrated with wild rejoicing" Japan's string of initial triumphs.[9]

One day on the homeward voyage Lieutenant Zenji Abe remarked to Nagumo, "It was said according to the radio that Admiral Kimmel had his head cut off." Nagumo's face fell, and he answered with a deep sigh, "I feel I have done a very sorry thing to him." Abe hastened to assure the admiral that he had spoken figuratively—Kimmel would be dismissed from his post, not executed. Abe had always respected Nagumo "for his noble character"; now, when he saw him "paying his sympathy to the enemy commander," Abe's admiration doubled.[10]

Soon a cloud of another nature appeared on Nagumo's horizon. At 2100 on December 9 he received Combined Fleet Order No. 14: "If the situation permits, the task force will launch an air raid upon Midway Island on its return trip and destroy it completely so as to make further use of it impossible."[11]

The Marine garrison at Midway had received word of the attack on Pearl Harbor. Consequently, the officers and men there were on the alert and had beaten off Konishi's Midway Neutralization Unit. His shells inflicted a certain amount of damage; they also killed four men and wounded ten.[12]

When the Combined Fleet received the radioed report of the Midway Neutralization Unit, Ugaki proposed that Yamamoto's staff reassess the possibility of attacking the atoll again. Two methods presented themselves: (1) Send back the two destroyers, or (2) order Nagumo's task force to strike Midway on its return voyage.[13] Because the destroyers had already proved ineffectual, the second course was the obvious choice.

The situation had its peculiar aspects. The principal reason for the Midway operation had been to protect the task force's route homeward. Now, in effect, Combined Fleet Headquarters was asking the First Air Fleet to turn aside from its retirement course and protect itself. This order irritated Kusaka, who considered it "like requesting a *sumo* wrestler who beat down a *sumo* champion to get a radish on his way back from his victorious ring."[14] Genda likewise opposed this move because he believed that the risks inherent in betraying the task force's position outweighed any possible benefits. Nagumo liked the Midway project no more than did his chief of staff and air officer, and to complicate matters, the weather was giving his ships a fearful beating.[15]

Genda had Midway very much on his mind, but not in connection with an isolated, somewhat pointless sideswipe on the way home. While the First Air Fleet cruised some 700 miles north of Midway, he offered Nagumo his newest plan: Sail to Truk for necessary overhaul, draw additional supplies, take on board several regiments of Army and Navy troops from the Marshalls and Carolines, and head back eastward. These forces could take Wake, Midway, and Johnston, thus forming a bridge across the Pacific for eventual seizure of the Hawaiian Islands and the ultimate destruction of the U.S. Pacific Fleet.

Genda believed that now was the time to put this daring scheme into operation, while the U.S. forces on Oahu still reeled from the shock of Pearl Harbor and American defenses of these outposts were at their weakest. To his thinking, occupation of Hawaii was necessary to control the central Pacific and achieve final victory. He also wanted to deny use of these islands to the United States as submarine bases. And he was sure that such a move against Midway and Johnston would smoke out the missing American carriers, which he was determined to find and destroy. With this strategy in mind, he did not favor turning aside to strike Midway.

At first Nagumo bent a receptive ear to Genda's ambitious plan. His self-confidence seemed to grow in proportion to the number of nautical miles between him and Pearl Harbor.[16] In Tokyo, too, a few days after the Pearl Harbor attack, several officers, including Maeda and Captain Yamaguchi, discussed the possibility of returning to Hawaii. These men believed that Japan should push its immediate advantage to the hilt. So they, with Ogawa, took up the matter with Fukudome and Tomioka.

The intelligence officers argued their case eloquently, along much the same lines that Genda presented to Nagumo. The Americans would have to mount and supply any defense of Hawaii all the way from the West Coast. Not only would quick occupation deprive Japan's major enemy of its most powerful military springboard in the Pacific, but it would also prevent repair of the ships damaged but not completely destroyed in the Pearl Harbor raid. The United States would also experience extreme difficulty in reinforcing Australia without the Hawaiian Islands as an intermediate base. And Japan could use to advantage the magnificent yards and depots on Oahu. Once more the intelligence experts urged that this operation be undertaken immediately, before the United States could gear its immense potential to military retaliation.

Although not unsympathetic to the aims of the proposal, Fukudome replied that the operation was not feasible. It would require a good 500,000 tons of shipping and a huge tanker fleet, which could not be spared from operations already in progress. Both he and Tomioka pointed out that they had no plan prepared for the occupation of Oahu, and makeshift, improvised measures held too many dangers. Suppose they did succeed in landing and even setting up a substantial garrison? The island would be highly vulnerable to American submarine and air attack. Moreover, Hawaii was not self-sufficient; Japan would have to feed the native population along with its own occupation forces. No one could deny the strategic value of the Islands, but at the moment obtaining the rich resources of Southeast Asia took priority. Later Japan might consider the plan, but for the time being the Operations Section of the Naval General Staff emphatically vetoed it.[17]

In the northern Pacific the wind increased steadily throughout December 12 and 13. Heavy seas and the worst swells experienced during the entire operation buffeted the carriers, washing overboard several of *Hiryu's* crew. *Akagi* pitched and rolled so steeply that planes could not possibly take off or land. The relentless pounding sprang numerous leaks in Nagumo's ships. Under the circumstances the admiral seized upon the quaifying pbrase "as far as the situation permits" in his attack orders and called off the Midway strike.[18]

Although Nagumo's decision disappointed Ugaki, the Combined Fleet made no objection. It had another and more pressing need for Nagumo's airmen—Wake Island. So far the skill and daring of the combined air and ground defenses had proved too much for the would-be invaders, and Captain Yano, chief of staff of the Fourth Fleet, asked Combined Fleet Headquarters for a carrier to provide direct air cover. So Yamamoto ordered Nagumo to send the Second Carrier Division to Kajioka's aid.[19] In view of these new instructions, Nagumo abandoned any idea he may have entertained of fully backing Genda's plan to sail to Truk and then return via the island chain to Oahu.

Accordingly on December 16 Nagumo ordered his heavy cruisers *Tone* and *Chikuma*, the carriers *Soryu* and *Hiryu*, and the destroyers *Tanikaze* and *Urakaze* to break off from the task force to attack Wake. Nagumo's radio to the Fourth Fleet at Truk clearly indicates that this detachment would not be able to make an all-out effort: "The task force cannot afford full cooperation because of the fuel problem. . . . As those forces cannot stay in the area for a long time, it must be understood that the force will retire from the area after making a single air raid on the enemy force and installation."[20]

The deadeye horizontal bombardier Kanai, credited with the amazing strike that exploded *Arizona*, was among those who attacked Wake. As if in vengeance for his deed at Pearl Harbor, the American defenders shot him down. His death was a serious blow to the Japanese Navy, which needed every one of its combat-tested airmen. Some of the pilots disapproved of the Wake operation or at least the First Air Fleet's part in it.[21] Abe pointed out after the war that the Japanese could not inflict a decisive blow against the United States at such an isolated outpost. At that early date they could only give a valuable preview of Japanese strategy and tactics to the Americans, who could thus learn how to cope with them.[22]

Meanwhile, Nagumo had been holding off sending his final damage report to the Combined Fleet until he considered his ships safely out of Hawaiian waters. Then, on December 17, he dispatched Battle Report No. 1. Considering the visual difficulties over the target area, Fuchida and the other observers had done a surprisingly good job of assessing results of the attack. The Japanese mistakenly credited themselves with an oil tanker destroyed and five more cruisers damaged than they actually hit, and they overlooked *Pennsylvania, Oglala, Vestal,* and *Curtiss.* Estimates of aircraft destruction fell much wider of the mark. Nagumo reported approximately 450 set afire and many others damaged in strafings and bombings or shot down in combat.

He added to his report, ". . . it is certain that, in addition to this, the Special Attack Unit of the Advance Force inflicted much damage by its bravest attack. . . ."[23] He had no shred of evidence to substantiate this statement, which was entirely false, but no doubt it pleased Yamamoto and Ugaki, both firm supporters of those gallant but ineffectual young submariners.

Watanabe wrote of the mixed feelings Nagumo's battle report engendered aboard *Nagato* upon its receipt on December 17:

> When this report first reached the Combined Fleet, the staff was very pleased and felt that the damage against Pearl Harbor and the lack of damage to the task force exceeded our expectations. Upon reexamination of the damage report, it was not so favorable as had been at first supposed. This was largely because Nagumo's force had not located the U.S. carriers. It was believed, nevertheless, that the Southern Operation could be carried out successfully during the period when the United States would be repairing its Pearl Harbor damage.[24]

And that had been the object of the attack in the first place. Reactions could be boiled down to the phrase "mission accomplished."

Nagumo's task force continued to make good time homeward. From the eighteenth on, the weather improved. On that day Chigusa recorded in his diary: "Patrol planes fly all day but get no information about submarines. . . . In the evening had a signal from the flagship that an enemy submarine was coming from the north and we might have a chance to meet it. . . ." But the chance did not materialize, for the excellent reason that no American submarines lurked in the area. Even so, such suspected sightings kept Kusaka, in charge of evasive movement, on the jump.

The same day Ugaki wrote a brief diary item concerning two Japanese submarines which collided "at night while patroling near Wake Island, both sinking instantly. That island is almost bewitched. . . ." Bewitched or not, it was doomed. Rear Admiral Koki Abe's detachment from the First Air Fleet made its initial strike on the atoll on December 21, assisting heavy reinforcements from the Fourth Fleet. When they pulled out on the afternoon of the twenty-third, Kajioka had claimed Wake for Japan, rechristening it Otori Shima (Bird Island).[25]

Meanwhile, the main body of the First Air Fleet continued westward. "A sea patrol plane flew over our forces," noted Chigusa on December 19. "It seems we are nearing Japan." Two days later Supply Group Two met the task force as directed and emptied the remainder of its fuel supply into the warships. On December 21 seven ships of the Twenty-first and Twenty-seventh Destroyer Squadrons from Tokuyama joined the First Air Fleet as additional protection against undersea danger. The next day half of Nagumo's serviceable planes whipped off their carrier decks and winged ahead to their home bases. The rest followed a day later.[26]

At 0600 on December 23 General Quarters sounded with Condition Two prevailing. "At last comes the day when we arrive back at the homeland," Chigusa wrote happily in his diary. At 0930 the task force went to Condition One readiness. "In the air above our forces many airplanes flew like birds," Chigusa continued. "Patrol ships belonging to the coast defense force patrolled on both sides of our forces." Even Kusaka with his marble calm thrilled as each passing vessel hoisted its flag in respect and sent congratulations to *Akagi.*[27]

The First Air Fleet dropped anchor in Hiroshima Bay at 1830. Ugaki immediately went to *Akagi* to welcome Nagumo and Kusaka and to chat briefly about the operation. Nagumo told him that everything had gone so favorably they could not help believing in the grace of God, and he especially commended the personnel of the supply train for their devoted skill. He pointed out, however, that the strict radio silence had made it difficult for him to keep the ships together.

Apparently Kusaka got a few sharp words off his chest, for Ugaki noted, "The order to make an air raid upon Midway Island on the way back, although it was sugar-coated by the condition of 'as far as the situation permits,' made the Chief of Staff angry as an individual."[28]

Early the next morning Nagumo and a party of his officers visited *Nagato* to pay their respects to Yamamoto. Nagano himself appeared at about 0930, beaming like a harvest moon. In response to eager requests, Nagumo amplified his radioed battle report. Around 1100 the party adjourned to *Akagi,* where praises showered upon the men of the First Air Fleet. Photographers' bulbs flashed as various groups posed for the inevitable pictures.

Although obviously in good spirits, Yamamoto stood slightly apart from the exuberant conviviality and mutual backslapping. "You men trained hard and patiently, and your operation against Pearl Harbor was a great success," he told the celebrating victors. "You must remember, however, that in spite of this important victory, we have only entered upon the first stage of this war and we have only completed one operation. You must guard scrupulously against a smug self-satisfaction with this initial success. There are many more battles ahead. I hope that you will continue in the same way to give your best to all coming tasks."

In less formal staff room festivities following Yamamoto's speech, *sake* flowed freely, and the stay-at-homes plied the returning conquerors with questions. Fuchida was the lion of the hour. Before he could fully satisfy one interrogator, another snatched him away. Nagano bestowed hearty congratulations upon him and exchanged his brimful *sake* cup with the flight leader as a sign of honor and camaraderie. Yamamoto presented Fuchida with a beautiful *kakemono* about four feet long inscribed in his own masterful calligraphy with this tribute: "The message of attack reaches my ears from more than 3,000 miles away—a message from Hawaii. Thinking of Flight Leader Fuchida's brilliant action on the early morning of December 8, so writes Isoroku Yamamoto."[29]

Most signal honor of all, the Pearl Harbor raiders learned that the Emperor wished to hear the account of the operation directly from those who had led the attack.[30] Nagano therefore arranged a strictly off-the-record audience with the Emperor for himself, Nagumo, Fuchida, and Shimazaki.

Fuchida and Shimazaki worked together on their reports. Fuchida would relate to His Majesty the story of the strike on the United States ships; then Shimazaki would brief Hirohito about the attack on the air bases. Because Shimazaki was far handier with the controls of an aircraft than with brush and paper, Fuchida had to write both reports.

Shortly after 1000 on December 26 Fuchida stood face-to-face with the man to whom he had dedicated his life. Later he admitted that leading the Pearl Harbor attack was much easier than telling the Emperor about it. With trembling fingers he spread out the large map of Oahu which he had prepared for the occasion. As protocol demanded, he addressed his remarks to the Emperor's aide, Major General Shigeru Hasunume, who relayed the story to Hirohito, translating it into the highly stylized court phraseology which was virtually a different language from standard Japanese. Despite this handicap, Fuchida noted with satisfaction that he held the imperial attention.

His Majesty examined closely the pictures and damage charts with which Fuchida illustrated his briefing. The Emperor asked a number of pertinent questions: On what basis were the damage estimates compiled? How accurate did Fuchida consider them? Were any civilian planes shot down? Were any hospital ships in the harbor? What was the initial reaction of the Americans? Were any Japanese planes shot down because they could not make it back to the carriers?

Fuchida's replies were equally crisp and to the point. Both Emperor and airman became so interested that time slipped by until Fuchida's allotted fifteen minutes had more than doubled. Shimazaki next took his turn, stammering out a brief description of the damage done to Oahu's airfields, only too happy to take no more than his scheduled ten minutes.

After a few questions from the Emperor a heavy silence fell for so long that Nagano started to rise. Suddenly Hirohito inquired, "Was any damage inflicted other than on ships, planes, and airfields?" Nagano asked Fuchida to answer. In his earnestness addressing His Majesty directly—a lapse of etiquette that was graciously overlooked—Fuchida replied in the negative. The airmen had been specifically instructed to bomb only military targets. As the Emperor prepared to rise, terminating the briefing, he said, "We would like to have the pictures remain in the palace as we wish to show them to Her Imperial Majesty the Empress." After this he retired from the room, to the deep bows of those who remained.

Fuchida knew he would never forget this day when he had been under the same roof with his Emperor, heard him speak, and spoken to him—the highest honor to which any Japanese could aspire. Yet a certain strain had hung over the interview. His Majesty had displayed the interest of a naval man in a great naval operation, the concern of a decent man for noncombatants, the instinct of a family man to share an experience with his wife. But he had shown no signs of exultation.

The frenzy of sudden fame engulfed Nagumo and Kusaka. Henceforth in Japanese history and in Japanese hearts these two officers would be linked forever—the admirals who had attacked Pearl Harbor. Yamamoto, too, had earned a place in Japan's naval Valhalla. He could take personal pride in the thought that he had pushed through his operation in the face of all opposition. Yet he knew only too well that one victory, no matter how spectacular, would not win the Pacific war.

Moreover, a special worry nagged at him. An honorable man, he had insisted that Japan's final diplomatic note be delivered before the strike on Pearl Harbor began. He delineated sharply between "a strategic surprise attack" and "a political sneak attack." After the event, when United States broadcasts castigating Japan for the "sneak attack" began to come in, Yamamoto is said to have called for an inquiry. A subsequent probe revealed that the note transmitted by the fourteen-part message of December 6–7 had been delivered to the State Department, but not exactly when. This worried Yamamoto, and he seemed "to have an unpleasant feeling about it."[31] Apparently no one told him that fifty-five minutes had elapsed between the commencement of hostilities and official submission of the final note to Hull.

It is scarcely likely that the Foreign Ministry would have cooperated wholeheartedly in Yamamoto's investigation. And it is questionable that full knowledge would have troubled him overmuch beyond one of his sudden explosions of anger because his expressed wishes had been ignored. He was not the man to chew the cud of the irreversible past.

Furthermore, the Japanese government never intended that the timing make any material difference; it was strictly a formalistic bow toward the conventions. Tokyo had left no margin for error. Irrespective of its legality, Japan's lightning thrust against Hawaii gave it control of the entire central and western Pacific. Now it could invade the El Dorado of the South without fear of the U.S. Navy's piercing it on the flank. The Rising Sun had never vaulted so high into the heavens. As surprised and amazed as the rest of the world, the Japanese stood in awe of their own achievements.

Ushering in the seventeenth year of his reign in accordance with age-old tradition, the Emperor proclaimed to his people the topic for the annually solicited New Year Welcome Poem: "Clouds over Mountains." The *Japan Times and Advertiser* commented lyrically upon the imperial choice: "Clouds over mountains are symbolic of a new day beginning."[32] Indeed, Japan soared high above the clouds that day, but from its position at the pinnacle of achievement, all mountains sloped downward.

CHAPTER 69

"NOT

ON THE

ALERT"

Japan's devastating air strike against Pearl Harbor aroused the people of the United States as no other event in their history ever had. From coast to coast, from north to south, the tragic words rasped over American tongues, burned into American minds. For most Pearl Harbor was a deep emotional experience, indeed, a traumatic shock.

Yet emotions churned deeper than shock. The American people reeled with a mind-staggering mixture of surprise, awe, mystification, grief, humiliation, and, above all, cataclysmic fury. The ingredients of this bone-deep anger and hatred were so emotional, so varied, and so tightly interwoven that it is difficult to sort them out in coherent and logical pattern. For one thing, Americans fairly gnashed their teeth at having been played for suckers. Certain observers, especially on the Pacific coast, watching cargoes of iron and other strategically valuable materials bound for Japan, had predicted that one day these items would make a round trip in the shape of Japanese bombs.[1] Now the whole country tacitly acknowledged that they had prophesied truly. The Arkansas *Gazette* summed up this aspect of America's wrath in a single, laconic comment: "It now turns out that Japan was one of our customers who wasn't right."[2]

Another fishbone that stuck in the national throat was Japan's initiating the air strike without formally declaring war. But nothing infuriated the American people more than the attack's having occurred while Japan was carrying on conversations with the United States, ostensibly in good faith, for a peaceful settlement of their mutual problems. All across the land editorial upon editorial denounced "the sly, cowardly attack executed at the very hour Japan's Machiavellian envoys were conducting 'peace' negotiations with our government. . . ."[3] Words failed the Atlanta *Constitution* "to express the utter

duplicity of the Japanese. . . ." And the Augusta (Georgia) *Chronicle* figuratively wrung its hands and clasped its brow: "Oh, the dishonesty and trickery of it
all!"[4]

Through all the conflicting emotions ran a thread of relief—relief that
Japan had taken the United States off the hook and made the decision for it;
relief that the onus of aggression rested upon the Axis; relief that the Americans
could stop the talk and half measures and get on with the real job; relief that the
isolationist-interventionist cleavage had fused into unity. "Since the clash now
appears to have been inevitable, its occurrence brings with it a sense of relief,"
philosophized the New York *Herald Tribune*. "The air is clearer. Americans can
get down to their task with old controversies forgotten."[5]

A thunderbolt of such unbelievable magnitude as Pearl Harbor generated
a dense fog of confusion as to the purpose and nature of the attack. Just what did
Japan hope to gain by its action? At first it appeared to bewildered Americans
that "Japan's powers of self-deception now rise to a state of sublime insanity."[6]
And how could one make sense of the motives of madmen? But some experts
made a valiant try.

Attempts to interpret the strike without knowing the full extent of the
punishment it had inflicted produced some peculiar guesswork. "The Hawaiian
attack was obviously a demonstration designed more for psychological effect
than for military damage," asserted newsman Paul Mallon.[7]

Some suggested that the operation may have been another "Manchurian
Incident" with the Japanese armed forces acting independently of the Tokyo
High Command.[8] This was a reasonable guess. Yamamoto, however, was a cat
of a very different breed from the warlords who had led Japan into the
Manchurian adventure. This time around the civil government could not hold
itself technically guiltless.

Many responsible newsmen assumed that Japan could never have pulled
off such an astounding feat on its own; the Germans must have been back of it.
Of this the Chicago *Times* had no doubts at all: "Had it not been for Adolf
Hitler, Japan would never have ventured upon such a suicidal course." The
New York *P.M.* declared, "The Nazi Government is master minding the
Japanese policy."[9]

Not only did the press credit Hitler with presenting to Japan a readymade
foreign policy, but it also saw his guiding hand in the strategy of the attack
itself. The Tulsa *Daily World* pointed out that the surprise and daring of the
strike indicated that "Japan had been carefully coached in such proceedings by
the Germans."[10] A surprising number of newspapers shared that view. One
receives the impression that to the gentlemen of the fourth estate, a thorough
shellacking at the hands of the demon genius of Berlin would be less
humiliating than one administered unaided by the hitherto-underrated Japanese. Some of these newshawks thought that Hitler might even have contributed planes and pilots to the attack.[11]

To be sure, many American newspapers did not fall victim to the myth of
German responsibility. They emphasized that the Japanese were "perfectly

capable of doing what they have done without any coaching from the Nazi Fuehrer."[12]

But these analyses and speculations could not satisfy the American citizenry. They were less interested in why the Japanese had attacked Pearl Harbor than in how they had got away with it. Obviously, as in the Charge of the Light Brigade, "someone had blundered." Equally obviously, that someone or those someones had to be American. So the people of the United States did not shoot all their flaming arrows at the Japanese; they aimed some at themselves and their leaders for having been caught short.[13] There thus began a frantic, years-long search to find a villain—some American or Americans who had failed or some dastardly conspirator who had deliberately engineered the attack.

Even before the verbal volcanoes erupted in the press and on the floor of Congress, Knox decided during the night of December 7 "to ask the President for permission to make a personal visit to Oahu," to determine the extent of the damage and if possible to find out why the Japanese had caught U.S. forces unprepared.[14] "That trip of mine to Hawaii was an inspiration that came to me just as I heard the President read his message," he wrote to Paul Scott Mowrer of the Chicago *Daily News* on December 18. "Immediately, the air was filled with rumors. There was a prospect ahead of a nasty congressional investigation, and I made up my mind in a flash to go out there and get the actual facts, and if the facts warranted it, to initiate the investigation myself."[15]

Knox had the reporter's instinct to go directly to the scene of the crime. No doubt, too, when Senator Connally raked him over the coals in the White House, he realized that the Congress and perhaps some of the press soon would be throwing dead cats at him. For Knox had indulged in some fatuous boasting concerning the Navy of which he was so proud. A sense of responsibility toward the Navy's officers, men, and ships also prompted him to make the dangerous trip to Oahu.

Thus, on Tuesday morning, December 9, Knox and a small party, including his aide, Captain Frank E. Beatty, departed Anacostia Naval Air Station. Two days later the plane landed safely at Kaneohe Bay. Beauty Martin met Knox at the seaplane ramp. He found the secretary friendly but intensely serious, eager to get to the bottom of the ugly business. Martin showed Knox and his party the devastated air station, the wrecked PBYs, the fire-blackened hangars, and the officers and men "trying to salvage something out of the wreckage."[16]

In Honolulu Kimmel met Knox at the Royal Hawaiian Hotel, whence they proceeded to the admiral's quarters. Kimmel invited Knox to stay with him, but the secretary politely declined. In view "of the investigative nature of his visit," he had given orders "that he would not be the guest of any senior officer on Oahu."

The group from Washington found an atmosphere of apprehension on Oahu. Beatty described the Hawaiian command as "definitely security minded" with conversations "carried on in whispers" and "much glancing around lest their words be overheard."[17] Many still suffered from post attack shock, and everyone recognized the danger inherent in the island's exposed position. Short deployed everything in the Hawaiian Department to stop a possible invasion. "We shot the works," reminisced Donegan.[18] But Fleming thought the attack had been a hit-and-run strike. In contrast, a certain top officer of the department engineers "became almost paranoid about the Japs' return." He "was really quite obnoxious with his prophecies of doom. This went on for several weeks, drove his subordinates to distraction and one into a nervous breakdown."[19]

The Islands were far from alone with their anxieties. In Washington fear for Hawaii scrambled like frightened mice up and down the spines of Navy leaders. On December 9 OPNAV informed Kimmel:

> . . . Because of the great success of the Japanese raid on the seventh it is expected to be promptly followed up by additional attacks in order [to] render Hawaii untenable as naval and air base in which eventuality it is believed Japanese have forces suitable for initial occupation of islands other than Oahu including Midway Maui and Hawaii. . . .
>
> Until defenses are increased it is doubtful if Pearl should be used as a base for any except patrol craft naval aircraft submarines or for short periods when it is reasonably certain Japanese attacks will not be made. . . .

Safford tells us that he informed Noyes that Turner was "all wet" in this evaluation. Safford "insisted that the PH attack was a hit-and-run affair and surely would not be repeated for several months at the earliest; that the Japanese had accomplished their objective by immobilizing our Pacific fleet; and that they would now proceed with the conquest of the Southeast area. . . ." Rather tactlessly Safford "also emphasized to Noyes that it was necessary at a time like this for somebody to keep his head."[20]

There was something to be said for both attitudes. Safford's estimate of the situation was absolutely correct. But Washington had just received the most graphic possible illustration that the so-called impossible could happen. The Navy's top brass would have been irresponsible had it not accepted the fact that as long as the Japanese possessed an air fleet capable of such feats, a return engagement could not be ruled out. Genda was urging that very thing upon Nagumo even as the task force steamed homeward.

To Stimson's disgust, the Navy's new obsession with Hawaii interfered with his attempts to work out a means to aid the Philippines:

> We have met with many obstacles, particularly because the Navy has been rather shaken and panic-stricken after the catastrophe at Hawaii and the complete upset of their naval strategy which depended upon that fortress. They have been willing to think of nothing except Hawaii and the restoration of the defense of that Island. They have opposed all our efforts for a counter-attack, taking the defeatest attitude that it was impossible before we even tried.[21]

To Knox and his group Pearl Harbor presented a grisly picture—"the shambles of the Battle Line of the world's mightiest fleet." Foremost in their minds, however, "was the human loss and suffering." Even as they watched, men removed bodies from the oil-covered waters while others worked briskly, "clearing up wreckage and preparing for another attack."[22]

Later Short appeared at Kimmel's quarters and talked with Knox "for probably an hour and a half to two hours." He briefed the secretary concerning the status on Oahu before the attack and on the air strike itself. He harped heavily upon the fifth-column string. Knox needed no great persuading to cast a bleak eye upon Hawaii's Japanese. At the end of his trip he reported to Roosevelt: "The activities of Japanese fifth columnists immediately following the attack, took the form of spreading on the air by radio dozens of confusing and contradictory rumors concerning the direction in which the attacking planes had departed, as well as the presence in every direction of enemy ships."[23] In fact, the Army and Navy on Oahu required no Japanese assistance in generating confusing messages on December 7.

In contrast with the misapprehension about the local Japanese, Oahu already had a good idea of the composition of the attacking force. "Papers discovered on a Japanese plane which crashed indicate a striking force of six carriers, three heavy cruisers, and numerous auxiliary craft including destroyers and other vessels."[24]

During Knox's visit there arose a question concerning a message which the secretary thought the Navy had sent to Kimmel and Hart and which they never received.[25] Certain revisionists insinuate that this means a warning must have been prepared on the sixth but was suppressed in Washington.[26] Of all people, Kimmel had the most to gain by sowing seeds of doubt on Washington's bona fides on the eve of Pearl Harbor. But like the sensible, honorable man he was, he gave the congressional committee a clear account of his conversation with Knox, with no "whodunit" embellishments:

> "Did you get Saturday night [December 6, 1941] the dispatch the Navy Department sent out?" I said, "No, I received no such dispatch." "Well," he said, "we sent you one." "Well," I said, "I am quite certain I did not receive it. However, there is always a possibility that my communication outfit might slip up and I will check."

Thereupon Kimmel did investigate and upon negative results, dropped the matter.[27] But the clearest testimony, the one which enables us to stand on solid historical ground, is that of Poco Smith, who was present at this conversation and, as he told the congressional committee, remembered it almost "word for word" because it impressed him at the time. This is how he recalled the phrasing of Knox's question to Kimmel: "But did you not receive on the Saturday preceding Pearl Harbor a warning message that we had learned surreptitiously that Kurusu and Nomura had been directed by their home government to deliver their final message to Mr. Hull at one o'clock on Sunday, December 7th?" When everyone answered no, Knox added, "That is strange. I know that such a message was sent to Hart and I thought it was sent to you."[28]

Obviously these men were discussing no previously unknown dispatch which satanic forces withheld from its addressees. They were talking about the famous warning which Marshall sent in association with Stark not on the night of December 6, but shortly after noon on December 7. Such a warning could not have been prepared on December 6 for one very good reason: The message from Tokyo upon which it was based was not received, decoded, and translated by the U.S. Army until the morning of December 7.

Kimmel was equally honest with Knox in other departments, and so was Short. Both admitted that they had not expected an air attack and that the Japanese had caught them unprepared and unawares. Kimmel had regarded a submarine attack as "the principal danger from a Japanese stroke without warning. . . ."[29]

Knox's findings in this regard seriously disturbed him. "It is simply incredible that both the Army and Navy could have been caught so far off first base," he told Mowrer in his letter of December 18. "They evidently had convinced themselves that an air attack by carrier born [sic] planes was beyond the realm of possibility, because they made no preparation whatever for such an attack." Believing implicitly in an American repulse of a nonexistent third wave at "about eleven o'clock" on December 7, Knox was sure that had the defenders been ready, they would have beaten off the initial assault.[30]

Kimmel was still Commander in Chief and still concerned with the war situation. He could see some positive aspects to his situation. His precious oil tanks had escaped destruction; so had his machine shops, his "Navy behind the Navy," and, above all, his invaluable carriers. On December 10 he had sent to Stark's office a message evidently in reply to OPNAV's of the previous day. He emphasized that he and his command were ready for action:

> Since the appearance of the enemy in this area all tactical efforts with all available forces have been vigorously prosecuted toward locating and destroy-ing enemy forces primarily carriers. Our heavy losses have not seriously depleted our fast striking forces nor [sic] reduced morale and determination. Pearl must be used for essential supply and overhaul facilities and must be provided with additional aircraft both army and navy also relief pilots and maintenance personnel. Pearl channels clear. Industrial establishment intact and doing excellent work. . . . [31]

But a gargantuan cleanup and repair task remained. At Ford Island Knox and his party saw further devastation. Most painful sight of all were the hundreds of wounded at Hospital Point, some "so terribly burned and charred as to be beyond recognition." That evening, Thursday, December 11, Governor Poin-dexter joined the group at dinner in the blacked-out hotel. They sat up most of the night discussing what they had seen and "planning for the morrow."[32] The next morning Knox visited the Hawaiian Department's command post for an extensive briefing. On this occasion the secretary did not "indicate in any way that he was not satisfied" with what Short had done. All told, he spent about two hours at the command post.[33] After picking up casualty lists, photographs of the damage, and various Japanese souvenirs, Knox and his colleagues left for Kaneohe that afternoon and shortly thereafter took off for the mainland.

As soon as his plane touched down at Washington, Knox hurried to the White House. The original copy of his report carries the notation in Roosevelt's handwriting, "1941—given me by F. K. 10 P.M. Dec. 14 when he landed here from Hawaii. FDR."[34]

How long the two men conferred and what passed between them we do not know. But the next day Roosevelt was so low in spirit that Pa Watson could not persuade him to leave the White House "for a drive or something." An aristocrat by birth and education, an actor by instinct, and a politician by choice, Roosevelt usually had a firm grip on his public image. Knox's briefing must have disturbed him very much indeed. Watson told Morgenthau that afternoon that Knox had been with the President "all night and day . . ." and he considered that "enough to make anybody feel bad" under the circumstances. No doubt Watson exaggerated the time, but Knox had given Roosevelt a large helping of unpalatable material to chew which had put him "off his feed."[35]

That morning, December 15, Knox met at the White House with the President, Hull, Stimson, and several others. Roosevelt gave Knox penciled notes covering all the information about the attack which he thought "could then, with the security of the nation at stake, be released to the public." Shortly after returning to the Navy Department from this meeting, Knox set up a press conference, stating that he and Stimson had been ordered to do so immediately "and that the services were to assume equal responsibility and blame for the damage caused by the Japanese attack—and for the failure to be prepared for such an attack."[36]

The secretary released his report on December 15. Despite Roosevelt's abridgments, Knox had a dramatic, graphic story to tell, and he told it well. He submitted a highly readable and surprisingly accurate account, considering the times, the data available, and the demands of security. He announced the loss of *Arizona*, *Utah*, *Cassin*, *Downes*, *Shaw*, and *Oglala* and the damaging of several other ships, including *Oklahoma*. This was not entirely candid but, in view of later salvage operations, not too far off the mark. He also listed casualty totals which exceeded the number of dead but underestimated the wounded.

In reply to questions, Knox expressed his belief that "between 150 and 300 planes took part in the attack, too many to have come from a single aircraft carrier"; that "apparently none was land-based"; and that so far as known, "none was flown by Germans." He also declared that "a rumor that the Navy had been forewarned" was untrue. Above all, he stressed the record of personal heroism. "In the Navy's gravest hour of peril, the officers and men of the fleet exhibited magnificent courage and resourcefulness. . . ." But Knox had to acknowledge the dominant, brutal truth:

> The United States services were not on the alert against the surprise air at-
> tack on Hawaii. This fact calls for a formal investigation which will be initi-

ated immediately by the President. Further action is, of course, dependent on the facts and recommendations made by this investigating board. We are all entitled to know it if (A) there was any error of judgment which contributed to the surprise, (B) if there was any dereliction of duty prior to the attack.

Along with his truthful contributions, Knox's report helped foster and perpetuate some of the Pearl Harbor legends. He seems to have either started or boosted the yarn that a bomb had "literally passed down through the smokestack" of *Arizona*. He also contributed heavily to Pearl Harbor mythology and added unfairly to the woes of all Japanese-Americans by remarking, "I think the most effective 'fifth column' work of the entire war was done in Hawaii, with the possible exception of Norway."[37]

The nation's press gave Knox's report heavy coverage. Naturally enough under the circumstances, many newspapers dwelt upon the aspects which were either directly or obliquely favorable to the United States.[38] But no amount of sugarcoating could disguise the bitter taste of the pill the Japanese had administered on December 7. The stark phrase "not on the alert" stood like an angel with a flaming sword between the United States and self-congratulations.

No one showed any tendency to disbelieve the more unpleasant of the secretary's findings. Coming from Knox, they struck with the impact of a battle-ax. Ever since he took office, his love for and pride in the Navy had colored virtually his every word and action. If any man would have bent over backward to excuse the Navy and let those concerned down softly, that man was Knox. A report derogatory to the Navy signed "Frank Knox" carried much more conviction than one signed by a detached observer. It was like Romeo taking Juliet to task. General agreement prevailed that an official inquiry was desirable, the sooner the better.[39] Knox's effort was magnificent journalism, but not a satisfactory investigation.

In one respect the Knox report did the Navy a disservice. It focused the spotlight of popular attention upon the Navy. To this day, discussion of the Pearl Harbor attack is likely to center on naval action and inaction, responsibilities, and failures, notwithstanding the fact that the Army had the prime mission of protecting the Fleet in harbor and also of guarding the Islands.

No Army report similar to Knox's emerged. Marshall had dispatched to Oahu Colonel Bundy of the War Plans Division to report on conditions and requirements, but unfortunately the colonel lost his life in an air crash en route. So the War Department relied upon Knox's information. [40]

Stimson knew that the Army no less than the Navy would have to take its medicine. "Knox agrees with me that there had been remissness in both branches of the service . . ." he confided to his diary on December 15. The two secretaries were "very anxious not to get into any inter-department scrap, but to keep the thing on a basis of no recrimination but inflexible responsibility and punishment."[41]

The Army and Navy relieved Short, Martin, and Kimmel of their commands on December 16. Stimson made the Army announcement the next day, taking his position "side by side with Knox as to the absence of preparedness on December 7th." He explained that this action "avoids a situation where officials charged with the responsibility for the future security of the vital naval base would otherwise in this critical hour also be involved in the searching investigation ordered yesterday by the President."[42]

The War Department had planned to send to Hawaii as Short's replacement Major General Herbert A. Dargue, a pioneer in aviation who commanded the First Air Force. But Dargue was killed in the same crash in California which took the life of Colonel Bundy.[43] Marshall wanted an airman to replace Short, so in Dargue's stead he selected Air Corps Lieutenant General Delos C. Emmons, who was in San Francisco at the time, and recommended Colonel J. Lawton Collins as Emmons's chief of staff. Emmons relieved Short on December 17. The change of command was quiet, unpublicized, without ceremony and without hard feelings between the two officers.[44]

A number of Short's staff officers believe the dismissal came as a most unpleasant surprise. "Short never thought that he was responsible or had been negligent," explained Donegan, "so he did not think he would be relieved."[45] On the other hand, Fleming thought that Short's dismissal hurt the general but did not genuinely shock him. On the afternoon of the attack Short told him "he was going to get relieved, he knew that." Nevertheless, Fleming emphasized: "I don't think Short ever expected that the United States Government and the United States Army would turn on him the way it did."[46]

Whether the fact of his relief or the manner of it most distressed Short, there is little doubt that the official ax delivered a punishing blow to his self-esteem. "Short took his relief extremely hard," said Fielder. "In fact, it crushed him and contributed to his ill health."[47]

Soon after the attack Mrs. Short returned to the mainland. Members of the general's former staff felt sorry for him but generally left him to himself. He had to come to terms with his painful situation in his own way, they reasoned. Meanwhile, the less said about his predicament, the better.[48]

On December 17 at about 1500 Kimmel officially turned over his command to Pye, his temporary successor. Facing each other straight and correct, the two men read their respective orders and shook hands, and Kimmel walked out of his office.[49] His relief left Kimmel downhearted and alone. Usually a fluent talker, thenceforth he said little, and his morale sank accordingly.[50] He understood the reason for his dismissal, but he fully expected to be reassigned.[51] Apparently Stark shared his belief, for he wrote to Kimmel on December 29: "Don't worry about our finding duty for you. I value your services just as much as I ever did and more and I say this straight from the heart as well as the head."[52]

At that stage a number of officers then in Hawaii agreed that under the circumstances Kimmel and Short had to go.[53] To Kimmel's loyal intelligence officer, Layton, the admiral's dismissal came as less of a shock than the appointment to succeed him of Pye—the same officer who on December 6 had assured Layton that the Japanese would not attack the United States.[54] Of course, Pye served as CinCPAC only in the fourteen-day interval between Kimmel's relief and Nimitz's assumption of command.

Kimmel remained in Hawaii pending the forthcoming investigation. In the evenings he often talked with Captain and Mrs. Earle. "We loved having him," Mrs. Earle wrote, "and I remember him saying, 'You know, not for three days after the attack did I realize what this would mean to me personally.' "[55]

What it meant was increasingly clear as Kimmel and Short became the lightning rods of public attention and censure. In general, the stateside press responded favorably when the Navy and War departments relieved them. Newsmen saw the step as logical and necessary. The Chicago *Tribune*, destined to carry many a figurative torch for Kimmel and Short, wasted little sympathy on them, observing on December 18, 1941:

> It is a military maxim that there is no excuse for surprise. The service regulations of both the army and navy require every officer to take adequate precautions for the security of his own forces, regardless of orders or lack of orders from his superiors. The officers who have been removed evidently failed to obey the first military commandment. . . .
>
> If commanders prove themselves unequal to their tasks they must be replaced at once lest greater harm befall the nation. . . .

The fate of Martin and Bellinger was much less harsh than that of their superiors. Bellinger remained in position on Oahu. Although relieved from command of the Hawaiian Air Force and replaced by Brigadier General Clarence L. Tinker, Martin received command of the Second Air Force, which defended "the vital northwest sector of the United States."[56]

At this point one must ask: What had happened to the principle of consistency? Shoemaker observed: "It was very strange that Kimmel and Short were investigated and then kicked out, but General MacArthur with his preattack information also got clobbered by the Japanese and yet remained free from investigation and ultimate dismissal."[57] MacArthur knew that Pearl Harbor had been attacked, knew the enemy was coming in his direction, and still, the first Japanese bombings and strafings found his planes parked helplessly on the ground and left his air force badly shattered.

Despite the undeniable irony of the circumstances which made a hero of one surprised and defeated commander and drove two others off active duty, few Americans with the interests of their country at heart can regret that MacArthur remained on the job or that Nimitz took early command in the Pacific. In the latter instance it was not a case of a good commander replacing a bad one, but of a good commander yielding place to a great one. The conditions were rough on Kimmel and Short, but life is seldom gentle, and war never.

CHAPTER 70

"DERELICTION

OF DUTY"

Soon after Knox returned to Washington, the President informed him that he wanted "to appoint a commission consisting of two Army and two Navy officers and a third civilian to investigate the responsibility for the losses at Hawaii and to make recommendations."

Late in the afternoon of December 15 Knox phoned Stimson accordingly. He also asked Stimson's opinion of a certain "Federal judge in Chicago" as the civilian member. Deciding that this man was not "an outstanding judge," Stimson preferred Supreme Court Associate Justice Owen J. Roberts.

Before 0900 the next morning Stimson phoned Marshall, informing him that he had decided upon Major General Frank B. McCoy as one Army member of the projected board. He asked Marshall to pick an air officer because he believed that the commission "should have an airman in view of the fact that the problem was really one of air and the problem of delinquency connected with it was also connected with air." The Chief of Staff agreed, later reporting that he considered Brigadier General Joseph T. McNarney "the best man." So Stimson relayed his suggestions for the Army members to Knox, who accepted Justice Roberts instead of his own nominee.[1]

At Stimson's suggestion and with Knox's concurrence, Roosevelt selected Roberts. He was a good choice to direct the investigation. Congressman Roy O. Woodruff of Michigan placed great faith in Roberts. "His presence and position on the Board alone would be sufficient to assure the Nation of a thorough, searching, and honest investigation of conditions and causes of the disaster of December 7."[2] Roberts had come to national attention when President Calvin Coolidge appointed him the special government prosecutor in the Teapot Dome and Elk Hill trial.

On December 17 the Roberts Commission met informally with Stimson and Knox in the former's office at his request. Knox "told them in considerable detail and with great effect what he saw on his recent visit to Hawaii." Stimson informed the commission that "the Army and Navy wanted to cooperate fully" and offered Roberts every possible assistance.[3] It is indicative of the psychological frenzy and fuzzy thinking of those December days that Stimson, so much the lawyer, met with and instructed a commission to investigate a case in which he was involved and that he permitted them to hear from Knox, also involved, what amounted to unsworn testimony which might be highly prejudicial.

To be just, the situation was enough to make a lawyer tear his hair. One literally could not find qualified commission members genuinely without prejudice. Only little green men from Mars could have reviewed this problem with coldly impersonal, judicial eyes. Every thinking man and woman in the country had read about the Pearl Harbor attack, and few indeed could hear testimony concerning the case with complete objectivity. What is more, in the closely knit armed services of 1941 almost any officer was bound to have dozens of friends stationed in Hawaii and so could not fail to be emotionally involved. No wonder Stimson and Knox paid particular attention to their recommendations for membership on the commission. On the basis of their previous records, those selected appeared highly qualified.

First in seniority stood sixty-nine-year-old Admiral William H. Standley, USN (Retired). He had been "a very outstanding Chief of Naval Operations" from 1933 to 1937. Roberts described him as "one of the keenest and ablest men I have ever known and one of the fairest." This assessment speaks well for Roberts's own fairness because Standley gave the chairman some difficult moments.

Next came Rear Admiral Joseph M. Reeves, USN (Retired). After years of service as an engineering officer, in 1925, at the age of fifty-three, he went to flying school, where he gained his pilot's and observer's wings. Roberts called Reeves "the outstanding original airman in the Navy." He told the congressional committee that Reeves "was Admiral of the United States Fleet more years than any other man in your life or mine" and that "wherever he appeared in Honolulu or anywhere else Navy men just flocked to him, as if to a father. . . ." When World War II broke out, Reeves "was called back to take care of the Navy's end of the lend-lease with Britain. . . ."[4] In Safford's judgment, "If F.D.R. had been looking for a whitewash, he never would have appointed men like Admiral Standley and Admiral Reeves to the Roberts Commission."[5]

But opinions concerning Reeves were not all sweetness and light. Standley informed Harry E. Barnes that Reeves had been "incompetent and disobedient" when he served under Standley and during the investigation had appeared "very antagonistic to Kimmel and Short."[6]

It is unfortunate that we do not have opinions from Kimmel concerning the personnel of the commission written before they published their conclusions, because his *post facto* comments may well—and understandably—be tainted with hindsight. He observed later: "Reeves was a fast talker and worshipped Roosevelt who had put Reeves in charge of disbursing aid to Russia under lend-lease and continued him in the job after we entered the war." Kimmel ended his comments about Reeves on a sour note: "He was a Roosevelt man body and soul if indeed he had a soul."[7]

The ranking Army member of the Roberts Commission was sixty-six-year-old Major General Frank B. McCoy. He had served on the Lytton Commission to evaluate the controversial Manchurian situation in the early 1930s, winning "a very high reputation among all nations involved for his balance and tact." Stimson considered that he had "the most outstanding record of any man in the Army" for appointment to the Roberts Commission, a position requiring "breadth of view, superlative character, and wide similar experience."[8] Standley agreed that McCoy truly wanted to get the facts about Pearl Harbor.[9] Kimmel later claimed that he did not "share Standley's opinion of McCoy. He was a Stimson man completely. He was smoother than Reeves, McNarney or Roberts but his interest was to clear Washington and condemn Short and me."[10]

The Army Air Corps representative, Brigadier General Joseph T. McNarney, was on active duty, but Stimson recommended him to the President as "the best air man we have for that purpose. . . . We have no retired officers in the Air Corps fit for this assignment, but McNarney has a reputation which commands the respect of everybody. . . . Marshall and I think he is the most competent man we have at the present time on air and ground joint requirements."[11]

At forty-eight McNarney was considerably younger than his service colleagues on the commission. During his career he earned a reputation as a real twenty-minute egg who would not give his best friend a break. In later days Stimson praised him as "clear-headed in his judgments, . . . highminded and loyal in everything. . . ." In April 1941, in which month he pinned on his first temporary star, McNarney went to London as an observer. In late autumn of that year Marshall sent for him to head a board to reorganize the War Department.

McNarney was on his way to Washington to take up this herculean task when he learned about the Pearl Harbor attack. It was "a very inconvenient thing" for Marshall to have McNarney tied up on the Roberts Commission when the reorganization was so urgent. But he recommended him because "he was an air man and a very able individual. . . ."[12] Kimmel had his own ideas about McNarney, most of which would melt type. "McNarney was a lying s.o.b. who had no more morals than a crawling snake," the admiral snarled.[13] Short, too, formed an unfavorable impression of McNarney. The general confided to Fleming that "McNarney seemed to be the s.o.b. of the Commission."[14]

Washington disclosed the appointments almost concurrently with the removal of Kimmel, Short, and Martin from their commands. Considerable satisfaction greeted the announcement. The San Francisco *Chronicle* declared on December 18: "From such a board we shall learn the truth, the whole truth, and nothing but the truth, and whatever action it recommends will be just to the men concerned and fair and constructive for the efficiency and morale of the army and the navy." Possibly the most widespread idea which the press conveyed to the public was that this commission would be a party to no whitewashing.[15]

Chairman Carl Vinson of the House Naval Affairs Committee decided "that his naval committee would not make an investigation 'since the president has announced such an outstanding board in the immediate future.' "[16] The press agreed that a congressional inquiry was neither necessary nor desirable because it would be a waste of time and money; it would be impossible to maintain secrecy; headline-hunting congressmen might capture the investigation; the inevitable controversy should be avoided in wartime—and the whole matter lay in the executive area anyway. Congress might have its innings in the future, but it should hold off until the Roberts Commission made its report.[17]

For all its top-notch personnel, the commission started out firmly on the wrong foot. On December 18 and 19 it heard two days of nonverbatim, unsworn testimony from a number of key officers, among them Marshall, Stark, Turner, Gerow, Wilkinson, Miles, and Bratton.[18] This was a most unfortunate arrangement, wasting important source material and leaving the door just enough ajar for someone to claim possible dirty work at the crossroads.

Roberts spent "an entire day" in Hull's office. But he emphasized that the commission "did not pass on" State Department or presidential policy—"that was not within our function at all." Roberts's sole concern regarding the State Department was whether or not Stark and Marshall had been warned of the situation which existed. Both of them, as well as Stimson and Knox, told the commission "that every time Hull gave them a warning they would go and repeat it to the Chief of Staff and to the Admiral. . . . That is all I was interested in," Roberts emphasized.

Surprisingly the commission knew about Magic. But, as Roberts said, "the Navy was rather chary about even telling us about the thing for fear there might be some leak from our commission." Roberts did not ask to see any of the messages. "The magic was not shown to us. I would not have bothered to read it if it had been shown to us," he explained. "All I wanted to know was whether the commanders had been advised of the criticalness of this situation . . . the commission found that they had had ample warning and that they had orders from headquarters."[19]

So here we have the stupefying picture of a Supreme Court justice and his colleagues accepting the unsupported word of interested parties that they had given Kimmel and Short sufficient warning, reaching findings and conclusions upon the basis of unsworn testimony of key witnesses, and expressing sublime indifference to the "best evidence"—Magic.

The commission commenced its hearings in Hawaii on December 22. Its members stayed at the Royal Hawaiian Hotel. Sporting new major's leaves, Brooke Allen served the commission by such chores as arranging for witnesses to be ready when needed. He recalled that Short always arrived alone except for his aide, while Kimmel generally brought with him several assistants. Once the admiral seized Allen by the shoulders, shook him, and shouted, "What are they trying to do, crucify me?"[20]

Quite a few people retrospectively thought Roberts and his colleagues were trying to do just that. Rear Admiral T. L. Gatch, the Navy's Judge Advocate General, remarked to Captain Robert A. Lavender, one of Kimmel's counsels, that evidently the Army had put men like McNarney on the commission "with the hopes that the blame could be shifted to the Navy."[21] Safford wrote to Hiles: "The jury . . . was not exactly 'fixed,' but it had 2 stooges plus 1 stool-pigeon so the Navy was outvoted from the start."[22]

In decided contrast, Fleming thought Kimmel "more or less got what was coming" because the Navy was responsible for long-range reconnaissance and certain high-ranking Navy officers—notably McMorris—had " 'pooh-poohed' the idea of any attack on Pearl."* But Fleming did have "some very, very strong thoughts, almost explosive thoughts, on the Roberts Commission's treatment of General Short."[23]

But for all the *post facto* recriminations, Allen, who worked closely with its members during its actual deliberations, thought the commission did a good job.[24] And Bloch, although "very sorry for both Kimmel and Short," could "pick no flaws with the logic of the Roberts Commision."[25] Any inquiry implies that something has gone wrong. And no realist could deny that Kimmel and Short were on the spot. Both were willing, cooperative witnesses because they, too, wished to get to the bottom of this ugly business and hoped to vindicate themselves.

Two days before Christmas the commission, then operating from Headquarters, Hawaiian Department, Fort Shafter, called Short as the first major witness. He brought no legal assistant and did not ask for counsel. Believing himself "absolutely not guilty in any sense," he was confident that he could take care of his own case. He did not even have anyone with him to handle documents.[26]

Nonetheless, Short had done a formidable amount of homework. As he had become accustomed to doing, he turned to Fleming, who "prepared General Short's defense before the Roberts Commission." Short selected the documents he considered pertinent, and Fleming dug them up. He "had a team of about 20 to 25 typists working around the clock" copying the papers. Then Fleming put the package together.[27]

After preliminary queries on name, rank, service record, and Short's command, the investigators drilled right into the warnings from Washington that led to alerts on Oahu. "In the period of the emergency, General, how many times were there warnings which caused alerts to be ordered here?" asked Roberts. "Give us your best memory."[28]

This was a logical follow-up of Roberts's concern with that very point in his

---

*See Chapter 49.

preliminary inquiries in Washington. Of course, this was a basic question. If Short could prove to the commission's satisfaction that he had not received an adequate warning that Japanese-American relations had seriously deteriorated, he would be in a much stronger position. The lack of such a warning, although not enough in itself to exonerate the Hawaiian command completely for its failure to carry out its prime mission successfully, certainly would have placed Short in a much better light.

Some of Short's testimony was devastating in its implications. His twin obsessions—sabotage and training—weave through it like patterns in a Persian rug. The general was honest in his replies. When he did not know the answer to a question, he said so. And he admitted to blunders. "I think that we made a very serious mistake when we didn't go to an alert against an all out attack."[29]

Short's testimony presents the image of a man with a large fund of information at his fingertips, who cooperated fully, gave the best answers he could under very trying conditions, stood by his convictions, and did not seek refuge in alibis—withal a fine human being. But we also see a man who became confused now and then and who did not understand his true mission. We likewise see one who lacked imagination and the ability to read between the lines, who did not seem to realize how strongly the tide had set against him.

Out of his deep conviction that he had done a good job on Oahu, Short made every effort to step out on the right foot. Proud of his efforts to awaken Hawaii to its responsibilities, he presented in evidence letters from community leaders attesting to their regard for him,[30] all of which was very understandable, for Short was not in the business of cutting his own throat.

Neither was Kimmel. The admiral sailed in with all guns loaded and decks cleared for action. Later he told the congressional committee, ". . . I was called before this commission and questioned at length, I had no time to prepare myself, I had been without sleep for some time, I was, to a considerable extent, strained. . . ."[31] Tired and strained he may well have been; however, he had spent considerable time and thought upon his preparations to meet the commission.

He asked Rear Admiral Robert A. "Fuzzy" Theobald, commander, Destroyers, Pacific Fleet, "to act as his counsel." Although glad to help, Theobald suggested that because he had no legal training, "it might be at least desirable to have an assistant counsel with legal knowledge." Kimmel answered "that he did not desire this, that all he wanted was a straightforward presentation of his conduct of Fleet affairs prior to and during the attack. . . ." Thereupon Theobald agreed.[32]

It is well that Kimmel acted to establish his position before he testified because the commission went far more deeply into the naval aspects of the attack than into the Army's side.[33] This was natural because the Navy's losses had been so spectacular, the very name "Pearl Harbor" exemplified American sea power, and of course, Knox had briefed the members about his own investigation before they left Washington.

Kimmel first appeared before the commission on December 27. His

testimony demonstrated that he was on the defensive. At times he appeared
the very pattern of the bluff, blustery old salt of legend. The fierce pride which
formed such a fundamental element of his character smarted under the
necessity of justifying himself, especially to a mixed commission headed by a
landlubber who admitted he was beyond his métier when speaking of naval
affairs.[34]

A strong, aggressive witness, Kimmel seized the initiative at the outset
and from time to time actually lectured the commission. The habit of command
was so ingrained in him that on occasion he virtually took charge of the
investigation. Like Short, he admitted to some errors. For example, he had not
believed on December 6 that war would break out at once. And he conceded
that he had missed the boat on the subject of the code burning. On the question
of immunity from torpedo attack in Pearl Harbor, he said, "Of course, I was
entirely wrong."[35]

Despite certain similarities—their honesty, loyalty, and genuine desire to
tell their stories so that the commission could understand them—Kimmel and
Short differed as much in their manner of testifying as in their respective
personalities. The general seemed far less sophisticated than the admiral. He
still did not fully appreciate how deep and rough were the waters he had to
breast. So he faced the commission with the self-assurance of naïveté. For this
reason he does not come across as a forceful witness. Kimmel had a stronger
sense of survival and was far more realistic than the general. He knew he was in
trouble and fought to keep his head above water. In a way, Short reminds one
of a well-trained bird dog eager to please. Kimmel said he had "every
confidence in the judgment of this Commission" and "absolutely no complaint"
about his treatment.[36] But one can see him bristle from time to time like a
vexed porcupine. Despite his disclaimer, he resented the commission's
handling of his case, and his resentment gathered momentum with the years.

After three or four days of waiting for the chance "to revise and correct" his
testimony, Kimmel asked for this opportunity. He received permission to come
to the Royal Hawaiian Hotel alone to do so. He claimed to have found many
omissions and inaccuracies. So he spent "the better part of two days" with
Theobald and his former stenographer, a chief yeoman, endeavoring "to
reconstruct an accurate version" of his testimony. On January 5 he wrote to the
commission asking that the record be revised accordingly.[37]

But it refused to alter the record. Roberts was not unsympathetic.
Nevertheless, the commission told the admiral, "The stenographic transcript to
our mind is correct as to what you said, Admiral, and we can't let you interlard
things that you did not say." However, they permitted Kimmel's corrections to
appear at the appropriate place. So the record shows both the original text and
Kimmel's adjustments. The commission also refused to substitute Kimmel's
revised testimony but, "so there would be no question of unfairness to him,"
agreed to include his document in the transcript as a supplement.[38]

At 1255 on January 9 the Roberts Commission dismissed Pye, its last
witness on Oahu, and the next day emplaned for the mainland. Upon arrival in

San Francisco on the eleventh the members exchanged plane for Pullman. In their drawing room they began to prepare findings on the basis of facts concerning which "there was no doubt." But when they arrived in Washington on the fifteenth, certain matters remained in doubt. So after various executive sessions they took further testimony from some of the top brass on Monday, January 19. From the questioning it is obvious that this final inquiry served two purposes: It filled in the commission members on those items which had not been entirely clear to them during their cross-country train journey, and it placed on record some testimony which they had taken "informally" before leaving for Hawaii. The main thrust of these sessions was the warning messages sent from the War and Navy departments to the Hawaiian commanders.[39]

The commission finished its work about 1430 on Friday, January 23. In the presence of his colleagues Roberts telephoned the White House, informing Miss Tully that the report "would be ready within an hour or so. . . ." The President relayed instructions through Miss Tully to bring the report to him at 1100 the next day.

At the appointed hour, seated behind his desk in his second-floor study, Roosevelt read the document "line by line." He devoted meticulous care to his task, following the words with his finger. "Two or three times he would shake his head and say 'Tsk, tsk,' or something of that sort." Occasionally he made a comment, apparently as much to himself as to Roberts.

Having finished his perusal, he asked in effect, "Is there anything in this report that might give our enemies information they ought not to have?" Upon Roberts's assurance that Stimson and Knox had cleared it, the President summoned his secretary Marvin O. McIntyre and directed him: "Mac, give that to the Sunday papers in full."[40]

The report falls into three main parts—an introduction explaining in general terms the work of the commission, its findings of fact, and its conclusions. Its first conclusions boil down to this: Hull, Stimson, and Knox had "fulfilled their obligations" in conferring with one another and with Marshall and Stark about pertinent events; the Chief of Staff and the CNO had fulfilled their "command responsibility" by issuing warnings and direct orders to Oahu. But it did not let the Washington authorities off scot-free. Among the contributory causes the report listed:

> Emphasis in the warning messages on the probability of aggressive Japanese action in the Far East, and on antisabotage measures.
> Failure of the War Department to reply to the message relating to the antisabotage measures instituted by the commanding general, Hawaiian Department.

The report did not criticize Martin, Bellinger, or the other generals and admirals at Hawaii. It merely stated: "Subordinate commanders executed their superiors' orders without question. They were not responsible for the state of readiness prescribed." The brunt of the report fell upon Kimmel and Short:

. . . In the light of the warnings and direction to take appropriate action, transmitted to both commanders between November 27 and December 7, and the obligation under the system of coordination then in effect for joint cooperative action on their part, it was a dereliction of duty on the part of each of them not to consult and confer with each other respecting the meaning and intent of the warnings and the appropriate means of defense required by the imminence of hostilities. The attitude of each, that he was not required to inform himself of, and his lack of interest in, the measures undertaken by the other to carry out the responsibility assigned to each other under the provisions of the plans then in effect, demonstrated on the part of each a lack of appreciation of the responsibilities vested in them and inherent in their positions as commander in chief, Pacific Fleet, and commanding general, Hawaiian Department.

. . . The Japanese attack was a complete surprise to the commanders, and they failed to make suitable dispositions to meet such an attack. Each failed properly to evaluate the seriousness of the situation. These errors of judgment were the effective causes for the success of the attack.[41]

So now Kimmel and Short had to endure—along with the bitterness of defeat, their sorrow at the death and suffering of their men, and the humiliation of removal from command—the charge of "dereliction of duty." Possibly only an individual who, like these two officers, had given decades of stainless service to his country could understand just what that scalding verdict meant to them. Duty was the cornerstone of their lives. The armed forces did not expect every man to be brilliant or victorious, but they did expect every man to be dutiful. The blow was doubly hard to bear because of the long, efficient careers which had preceded it. Kimmel in particular had always possessed the knack of impressing his superiors and hated to admit being in the wrong. So this charge landed a vicious right cross to his ego.

Nor was Short the man to turn the other cheek to such a stinging slap. Fleming had found the general a dynamic officer who "had a temper. He didn't show it very often but when somebody goofed Short could be very, very brutal." Now the Roberts Commission had told the entire world in "very, very brutal" terms that he himself had "goofed." Short would have been less than human had he not writhed under this humiliation.

Fleming considered that the Roberts Commission made the general "the goat" for the Navy. Fleming stressed that the Army was not responsible "for the long range defense of the Hawaiian Islands. . . . But then the Roberts Commission turned around and pointed much more of a finger of guilt at General Short than it did at Admiral Kimmel."[42]

Actually Kimmel and Short suffered equally from the Roberts Commission's findings unless one accepts Fleming's premise that the Navy's long-distance reconnaissance responsibility lifted all blame from Short's shoulders. This is somewhat difficult to do in view of the fact, which Short never denied, that the Hawaiian Department's primary responsibility was to defend the Fleet at its moorings.

Those who castigate the Roberts Commission as a cover-up and who adopt the conspiracy thesis apparently assume that because Kimmel and Short were not solely guilty, they must be entirely innocent. This is not the case. Roberts and his colleagues could not overlook their mistakes. Yet the verdict of "dereliction of duty" was unduly harsh. Far more just was the assessment that the failures of the two commanders were due to "errors of judgment."

The executive order of December 18, 1941, establishing the Roberts Commission had given it the mandate of determining whether "derelictions of duty" or "errors of judgment" had influenced the Japanese success at Pearl Harbor and, if so, who was responsible therefor.[43] It is possible that the commission may have interpreted these instructions literally, thus leaving it no choice but to use those specific phrases, just as a jury must choose between "guilty" or "not guilty."

To a certain extent the aftermath of the Roberts Commission demonstrated the problems inherent in releasing the report of an investigative body without at the same time releasing the evidence upon which it was based. Of course, the government could not have published the full testimony because much of it dealt with defense matters legitimately classified. But, however justifiable, the net result was that the public of the day had no way of judging the validity of the Roberts Commission's findings and conclusions because the full testimony was not released until February 17, 1946.[44] The people had to rely upon the press for comment and analysis. Yet the press knew no more than its readers.

Although the document humbled American pride, many commentators rejoiced that it had been published, thus demonstrating that the government had leveled with the people.[45] But these sentiments could not soften the unpleasant revelations. In some respects the press overreacted. The commission had cited—correctly—the failure of the two commanders to confer about the various warnings. But by the time the newspapers got through with the subject the average American could well believe that Kimmel and Short barely spoke. "Judging from the Roberts Report there was practically no cooperation" between the two, reported Gould Lincoln in a typical comment.[46]

A large segment of the press, as exemplified by the Wheeling (West Virginia) *News-Register,* wanted "to see those directly responsible, shorn of their rank and drummed out of the service" because "those entrusted with the defense of Hawaii were the enemy's best ally in making the attack successful."[47] Congress added its bit to the clamor. "It's high time we were getting rid of these incompetents . . ." exclaimed Representative Dewey Short of Missouri. "We've got a lot of gold braiders around here who haven't had a new idea in 20 years. They should be court-martialed."[48]

A number of lawmakers praised the Roberts Commission and agreed with its findings. Congress, however, was accustomed to surveying problems from the political angle, and many lawmakers distrusted a strictly military interpretation. Even Representative William J. Ditter of Pennsylvania, who voiced his state's pride in its native son, Justice Roberts, did not believe the report had gone far enough: "The Commission is the creature of the executive branch of the Government. I believe this Congress owes it to the country to initiate its own inquiry. . . ."[49] Already the seeds of revisionism began to shoot up like bean sprouts. Representative Fred L. Crawford of Michigan suggested that "the ineptitude of the men in charge at Pearl Harbor, was simply a reflection of what was taking place in Washington. . . ."[50]

At this stage of the Pearl Harbor investigations not even confirmed antiadministration newspapers adopted the idea that Washington was guilty instead of Kimmel and Short; the thesis went no further than that Washington shared their guilt.[51] Some, such as Knox's own paper, the Chicago *Daily News*, entered a plea for mercy: ". . . many people are thinking that the officers directly accused have already been punished enough by the knowledge that the responsibility for what happened was theirs."[52] This may well have expressed Knox's personal opinion. No doubt he much preferred to drop the whole subject of Pearl Harbor and get on with prosecuting the war. Then, too, he knew very well that valid courts-martial for Kimmel and Short were out of the question during the war because Magic and other highly classified material in all probability would be seriously compromised.

Other papers also pleaded against throwing the two commanders to the lions. Those who spoke for mercy, however, acted upon the good old American principle of not kicking a man when he is down, not from any doubt that Kimmel and Short were guilty as charged.[53] Almost no journalists questioned the logic of the commission's findings.

Many newspapers agreed that the warnings to Hawaii absolved Washington of blame. This was one of the areas in which headlines, column headings, and editorials blew up certain findings out of all proportion. If the reader scrutinized the entire report, which most major newspapers printed in full, he could follow the course of events and keep the whole matter on an even keel. But if he hastily skimmed the headlines, he could easily receive the impression that Washington had bombarded Kimmel and Short with repeated and explicit warnings of a Japanese attack against Hawaii which the two commanders had deliberately disregarded: WASHINGTON WARNINGS THAT JAPS MIGHT RAID HAWAII WAS IGNORED;[54] REPEATED WARNING OF JAP RAID IGNORED BY TWO COMMANDERS.[55]

Stimson had been pleased in general with the commission's efforts. "It is an admirable report, candid and fair, and thorough in its study of the facts." Then his sharp mind cut through to a major weakness: ". . . the printed report does not and could not go into what is the real underlying basis of the trouble, namely that both services had not fully learned the lessons of the development of air power in respect to the defense of a navy and of a naval base."[56] A number of journalists agreed that the lack of air-mindedness lay at the root of the tragedy, and the cause of unification of the armed forces received a stiff shot in the arm.[57]

In some ways the Roberts Commission was the most controversial of the Pearl Harbor investigations. In the first place, it began its work too near the stunning events of December 7, 1941, to have a proper historical perspective.

The American people wanted a quick, definitive answer to how the Japanese had been able to inflict upon the United States the most incredible, disgraceful defeat in its history. The Roberts Commission uncovered no deep, dark secrets, dredged up no astonishing revelations. As the Bismarck *Tribune* affirmed, the report verified only what the American people already knew. "This nation understood that someone had been asleep at the switch as soon as the first incomplete reports came in. . . ."[58]

In the second place, the appointment of the commission had received such nationwide acclaim that no five men could have lived up to the expectations engendered. And with publication of the report came such a flood of comments that to a certain extent the actual report became engulfed in a whirlpool of verbosity. The overreaction in some newspapers made it appear that Kimmel and Short had been far more culpable than they actually were or than the Roberts report had charged.

Thirdly, the commission received much unfavorable publicity during the congressional investigation and subsequently from certain revisionists.[59] It earned the latter's hostility by dumping the major load of blame on Kimmel and Short and failing to indict Roosevelt and his administration.

There is no valid reason to doubt the integrity of Roberts and his colleagues. These men were not headhunters or political hacks, dependent upon the goodwill of the "organization." Each had served long and well under both Democratic and Republican administrations. Nor need one necessarily challenge the good faith of the Washington authorities. Obviously something had gone wildly askew with the defenses of Oahu, and every dictate of common sense urged that the trouble spot be located and corrected as soon as possible, if only to preclude a recurrence there or elsewhere.

The transcript of the proceedings reveals that the commissioners conducted their inquiry searchingly but courteously. They let witnesses have their say, asked intelligent questions, and stayed on the main track of the investigation. Manifestly they could not have found that everyone in the Army and Navy on Oahu had done exactly as he should have. The evidence to the contrary confronted them in the shape of sunken and damaged warships, blasted planes, burned-out hangars, wounded men, and new graves.

Later investigations, concerned primarily with matters of policy and with the whys and wherefores of Pearl Harbor, as a general rule called their witnesses from the civilian "big shots" and military top brass. Roberts and his colleagues likewise interviewed generals, admirals, staff officers, and key civilian leaders on Oahu. But they also questioned junior officers, enlisted personnel, and civilians who manned the ships and installations which the Japanese struck. These men had no positions to protect, no policies and decisions to explain and defend. So they told their stories in simple, direct English. This testimony is absolutely basic for anyone who wants to know how it was on Oahu on December 7, 1941. For this reason the Roberts transcript is one of the most human, most fascinating, and most important of all United States source documents on Pearl Harbor.

Roberts was the pioneer investigator. His commission had at its disposal no such bountiful harvest as today is available to the most casual student of the Pacific war. So the only honest way to evaluate the Roberts report is to forget all the information which came out at subsequent hearings and consider only the testimony and documentation which the commissioners had at their disposal. But far from being the last word on the subject, as some newspapers believed, the Roberts report had barely scratched the surface. In the very nature of things other investigations had to follow.

CHAPTER 71

"THE

ASHES

OF A

BITTER

PAST"

When Kimmel finished his testimony before the Roberts Commission, he bade farewell to his devoted staff. His friend Admiral Train accompanied him to the plane which would carry him to the mainland and a new phase of his life. He recalled Kimmel's remarking in essence, "Train, we are at war now, and I do not intend to do anything about this at present." There spoke a man loyal to his Navy and his country, but a man who reserved to himself the right to act later. As his plane climbed into the clouds, he swore an oath to himself: He would do everything in his power to cleanse from his good name the stain of imputed failure.[1]

Time blurred Fleming's memory somewhat, but he believed he and perhaps a few others accompanied Short and the general's aide, Captain Louis W. Truman, to the airport to see them off by clipper on January 11. To Fleming Short seemed the same as ever.[2] Yet Short's departure from Honolulu marked the beginning of the hard winter of his life. At the Presidio in San Francisco he received a telegram directing him to proceed to Oklahoma City "on temporary duty to carry out instructions of Secretary of War and upon completion and receipt of advice this office proceed to Washington DC and report to The Adjutant General for further temporary duty in Office Chief of Staff."[3]

This message certainly gives the impression that Marshall intended Short to come to Washington and talk with him or at least with someone in his office. Yet a scribbled note, in itself unidentifiable, is listed in the Pearl Harbor documentation under date of January 13, 1942, as "handwritten note (Gen. Marshall) on wording of the acceptance of Gen. Short's retirement." This note reads: ". . . accepted, effective ———, without prejudice to future action in the interests of the government."[4]

As best we know, up to this time Short had not considered retirement.

Certainly he had not requested it, yet obviously Marshall was thinking in terms of Short's removal from active duty before the Roberts Commission had even submitted its findings. In fact, Marshall's note was dated two days before Roberts and his colleagues returned to Washington.

When Kimmel and Short arrived on the West Coast, they still held some hopes for their future careers. With the publication of the Roberts report that terrible, damning charge "dereliction of duty" exploded another landmine in the battlefield of their lives. "Errors of judgment"—yes. They could live with that. But "dereliction of duty"! Neither officer could possibly accept that awful indictment. Years later Kimmel said in bitter remembrance, "The Roberts Commission had one aim, to wreck Short and me."[5]

General and Mrs. Short were visiting the latter's parents in Oklahoma City when the story broke. The general had declined any comment since arriving on the mainland. When local newsmen asked "if he had any statement to make," he replied crisply, "Not a word."[6] He could have said plenty had he wished. He was proud of his testimony before the Roberts Commission and thought he had done well.[7] So its conclusion "completely dumbfounded" him. As he later testified, "To be accused of dereliction of duty after almost forty years of loyal and competent service was beyond my comprehension."

Shaken to his foundations, he immediately telephoned Marshall and asked if he should retire. He recalled Marshall's replying, "Stand pat but if it becomes necessary I will use this conversation as authority." Short answered that he would place himself entirely in Marshall's hands, "having faith in his judgment and loyalty." To the best of Short's recollection, this conversation took place about 1300 on Sunday, January 25. Although Short would have much preferred to stay on active duty, he decided after hanging up that in fairness to Marshall he should write a formal application for retirement for the Chief of Staff to use if he considered this advisable in the future. This he did, forwarding it in a personal letter to the Chief of Staff. Marshall never replied to this letter.[8]

On the morning of January 26 Stimson and Marshall talked over "what we shall do in respect to General Short. The President has virtually left it in our hands," Stimson noted in his diary. Marshall told his chief that Short had phoned him to apply for retirement. Marshall also informed Stimson "that Stark in the Navy was hoping that Kimmel would do the same thing." Wanting to make sure that no one went off half-cocked and that justice would be done, Stimson pointed out that "these men must be protected against being visited with punishment in the heat of the excitement which would not be given to them in cool blood. . . . "[9]

Later that day Marshall wrote a memorandum to Stimson confirming that he had talked with Short and had told him "to take no action at the present time, that we had not yet had an opportunity to read the proceedings, let alone arrive at any conclusions." Marshall continued:

> I am now of the opinion that we should accept General Short's application for retirement today and do this quietly without any publicity at the moment.

Admiral Stark has requested me to advise him if we do this, as he proposes to communicate this fact to Admiral Kimmel in the hope that Kimmel will likewise apply for retirement.[10]

Yet no hint that the Navy planned to force Kimmel into retirement appears in the cordial letter which the chief of the Bureau of Navigation, Rear Admiral Randall Jacobs, wrote to Kimmel on January 24: "I have just discusssed with Admiral Stark, the question of your next duty. . . . Stark wants you for the General Board and I, too, feel that that is the place for you."[11] The General Board, traditional Happy Hunting Ground of senior admirals, would have been a logical spot for Kimmel, where he could have performed useful work in the company of his peers. Consider, too, Stark's friendly note to Kimmel of January 27:

Marshall informed me yesterday while we were talking over the situation, that Short had submitted a request for retirement. We all thought that this information would be of interest to you. . . . I do not want you in any sense to consider the transmission of this information as request on you by the Department to follow suit. . . . If and when we have any definite recommendations—suggestions—we will definitely say so.[12]

The same day the Roberts report appeared in the press—January 25—the commandant of the Twelfth Naval District at San Francisco told Kimmel that the chief of the Bureau of Navigation had telephoned him that he "had been directed by the Acting Secretary of the Navy" to inform Kimmel "that General Short had submitted a request for retirement." Kimmel later learned that the direction came from Knox. Naturally the admiral took this message and the quasi-official manner of its delivery as a none-too-gentle hint that he follow Short's example. Until then the thought of retiring had never crossed his mind, but he duly submitted the request on January 26.[13]

The next day reporters tracked down Admiral and Mrs. Kimmel at the Fairmont Hotel in San Francisco. The admiral was scarcely more communicative than Short. "I don't want to see anyone and I can't see anyone," he told representatives of the San Francisco *Examiner* brusquely.[14] The San Francisco *Chronicle* quoted him further: "I am waiting for the Navy Department to tell me what to do next."[15]

On January 28 the commandant informed Kimmel that Stark had telephoned that the notification had not been meant to influence him. But he wrote to the Bureau of Navigation: "I desire my request for retirement to stand, subject only to determination by the Department as to what course of action will best serve the interests of the country and the good of the service."[16] Stark greatly admired his old friend's attitude. "I never knew of a man to put up a manlier, straighter, finer front than did Admiral Kimmel in this entire picture at that time," he testified. "His whole bearing was exemplary and what I would have expected of him."[17]

Evidently Stark wasted no time in passing the word from Kimmel up the line. On the afternoon of the twenty-eighth Roosevelt informed Stimson of

Kimmel's application for retirement. Stimson countered that Short had done the same. He also told the President that in his view "the objections to an immediate court martial were (1) that at present it would inevitably make public matters which are military secrets; (2) that it would be impossible to give the defendants a fair trial." The President agreed and proposed three courses of action: First, the Army and Navy should act "on parallel lines"; secondly, they should wait "about a week and then announce that both officers have applied for this immediate retirement and that this is under consideration"; and thirdly, approximately one week later they should "announce that the applications have been accepted but with the distinct condition . . . that this does not in any way bar a subsequent court martial; that the reason for this is the impossibility of a court martial without the disclosure of military secrets and also that at present it would be impossible to give them a fair trial."[18]

On February 7 the Navy and War departments announced that Kimmel and Short had applied for retirement. The story indicated that the decision to accept or not rested "exclusively with the President" through the secretaries of war and the navy. The retirements would not preclude courts-martial because, regardless of duty status, an officer remained an officer.[19]

The requests for retirement aroused considerable interest in Washington. In the State Department Hornbeck suggested to Sumner Welles that "the interests of the United States might conceivably be better served" by assigning Kimmel and Short to nonoperational jobs rather than "by taking them out of harness and 'turning them out to graze'—and draw their pensions." He added thoughtfully:

> The United States has put a lot of money into the training of those officers; the officers themselves have accumulated education and experience; a bad mistake, especially one of omission, does not wipe out and nullify inherent capacity to serve; and these officers if assigned to some new tasks, would probably work harder at them than at anything they have ever done before. . . . [20]

Hornbeck's suggestion contained much merit, and in a less sensitive matter this reasoning might have prevailed. But in wartime a general and an admiral need the absolute confidence of their men and the nation. At the time several courses were possible: First, exonerate Kimmel and Short and send them into command positions; secondly, follow Hornbeck's suggestion and retain them on active duty in staff or advisory capacities; thirdly, get them out of the way as gracefully as possible.

On February 16 Knox formally approved Kimmel's request for retirement, effective March 1, 1942, "without condonation of any offense or prejudice to future disciplinary action." Five days later Stark still appeared to have no idea of the decision reached at Cabinet level. On February 21 he wrote to Kimmel:

> A few days ago I thought that you would have something definite before long. I am inclined to think now that this is not the case, and that for the time being at least you will just be continued on leave. . . .

Pending something definite, there is no reason why you should not settle yourself in a quiet nook somewhere and let Old Father Time help this entire situation, which I feel he will—if for no other reason than that he always has. . . . [21]

Like the memorandum from Marshall to Stimson about Short's retirement, this letter raises questions. It seems incredible that after five days Stark should still be unaware that Knox had formally accepted Kimmel's retirement. Perhaps somewhere along the line communications had slipped a gear. Perhaps, too, Stark still hoped that at the last minute Roosevelt, so devoted to the Navy, might yet order Kimmel reassigned rather than permit him to retire. During the congressional investigation Stark told his counsel and good friend David W. Richmond that he had begged the President to keep Kimmel on active duty. "You can be absolutely sure that here is an officer who would never be caught again, and who would work his heart out in a new command. He is a valuable officer and the Navy needs him." This was the burden of Stark's plea. But Roosevelt was adamant that Kimmel must go.[22]

It was typical of Stark that at a time when his own star was setting he should have gone to the White House to urge not his own cause, but that of his friend. The CNO had a better mind than many have given him credit for; however, it was not a subtle mind. He may not have understood that by retaining Kimmel in a position commensurate with his rank, the government tacitly would have excused the Navy from all the blame for Pearl Harbor, leaving the Army, in the person of Short, dangling alone from the hook. One can visualize the interservice bitterness this would have engendered. Roosevelt could not retain one officer without the other, and to keep both would be to negate the Roberts report. There again one can imagine the howls of outrage from one end of the country to the other. With a major double-barreled war on his hands, Roosevelt had little choice in the interests of national harmony. Only an unequivocal conviction of Kimmel's total blamelessness could have allowed Roosevelt to act as Stark wished.

Stark's suggestion that Kimmel trust himself to "Old Father Time" was in keeping with the CNO's philosophic, rather slow-paced nature. But it was not the advice to commend itself to Kimmel, an impatient man full of drive. Moreover, in the meantime, Kimmel had received Knox's approval of his retirement, and the wording "without condonation of any offense or prejudice to future disciplinary action" cut him to the heart. "I do not understand this paragraph . . ." he wrote Stark on February 22. He continued:

I stand ready at any time to accept the consequences of my acts. I do not wish to embarrass the government in the conduct of the war. I do feel, however, that my crucifixion before the public has about reached the limit. . . .

I feel that the publication of paragraph two of the Secretary's letter of February 16 will further inflame the public and do me a great injustice. . . .

You must appreciate that the beating I have taken leaves very little that can be added to my burden. . . . [23]

Kimmel suffered greatly in this period from insults and threats. He felt a furious contempt for those spineless cowards who called him on the telephone, wrote him unsigned letters, or slid anonymous notes under the door of his hotel room in San Francisco and fled before he had the chance to confront them.[24]

At this particular time Stark had every reason to be preoccupied with his own affairs. In March 1942 the President decided to remove him as CNO and send him to London as commander, U.S. Naval Forces in Europe—quite a comedown at the time. Stimson's diary indicates that Stark's reassignment was part of the overall shakeup of the Navy. Roosevelt was far from happy with that organization at the time in spite of his usual bias toward the sea service. On March 6, following a Cabinet meeting, Knox told Stimson "that he had practically settled his troubles in the Navy. Stark is going to London and Turner is going to sea." Stimson congratulated Knox "on these steps forward. . . ."[25]

Meanwhile, Short suffered his own ordeal at the hands of the War Department. A letter of February 17 from the acting Chief of Staff to The Adjutant General containing Stimson's instructions for handling Short's case is highly revealing. It ordered that "a letter be prepared for the signature of The Adjutant General [TAG] . . . stating in effect that his [Short's] application for retirement for over 30 years' service is accepted effective February 28, 1942, without condonation of any offense, or prejudice to any future disciplinary action." The orders were to contain that specific statement. An officer would deliver the letter to Short in person, obtain a receipt, then immediately telephone TAG to report whether or not he had accomplished his mission. As soon as TAG had this report, he would advise the Bureau of Press Relations and the assistant chief of staff, Personnel (ACS G-1). In turn they would inform Stimson and make no press release until he had so directed. Then came the knockout punch:

> That in the event a reply is received by the War Department from General Short within 24 hours from the time of delivery of the letter in question, which would indicate that he does not desire to retire under the conditions stated, The Adjutant General will then take the necessary action to accomplish the retirement of General Short under the orders referred to above.

The War Department was making very sure indeed that Short received his orders, and if he did not accept them, it would retire him anyhow. But Short submitted the official papers on February 18.[26]

The President wished to consult Stimson and Knox before the retirements were made public. Being confined to his bed with bronchitis, Roosevelt wanted the matter kept "in cold storage" until he was able to see the two secretaries. The delay worried Stimson somewhat because he feared "it may leak out in garbled form from someone near the defendants. . . ."

Not until the twenty-fifth did Stimson and Knox have their talk with the President. By that time Roosevelt had reversed his field, having reached the conclusion "that the temper of the people requires the court martial on the issue which has been raised by the Roberts Board having found that there was a dereliction of duty on their part. He would prefer to have it raised by the men requesting court martial themselves, in which case the trial could be delayed until a time when it could be held without injury to the public interest." Stimson pointed out to the President "the fact that the two men had merely reflected the general attitude of the whole country at that time. . . ." Roosevelt replied "he realized that and they should not be severely punished—a matter which he would have in his control." Stimson gained the impression that his chief was "evidently thinking of a stern reprimand."[27]

The War Department was on the job early the next morning. At 0815 Bridadier General Myron C. Cramer, The Judge Advocate General, personally hand-carried to Marshall a memorandum which explained that the retirement arrangement left the door open to court-martial in the future. But he thought nothing could be gained by a public commitment to court-martial the officers "at any specific future time." The document added:

> The defense would certainly attempt to pass part of the blame to the War Department. Such evidence or argument, if publicly aired, would tend to discredit the War Department and cause a lack of confidence by the people in the men in charge of the war operations. This would certainly be so if the trial should result in acquittal or a mild sentence.[28]

This assessment tacitly admitted that Short's conviction was far from assured. Of course, even in peacetime the War Department would think long and hard before it court-martialed a general. The last such occasion had taken place in 1926—the notorious Billy Mitchell case.[29] And that had resulted in wounds to the Army's prestige which still ached in damp weather.

But more than image was involved. When Stimson reached his office, he found Marshall, Cramer, and a representative of G-1 pondering the matter. He explained the problem in his diary:

> . . . a defendant officer . . . could not ask for a court martial as a matter of right. They pointed out also that, if the President himself ordered the court martial, it might open him as a reviewing officer to the charge of bias when it came to his passing upon the sentence of the court. This would not apply to the case of the Secretary of War ordering the charges to be preferred.

This appeared to place the monkey squarely on Stimson's back. So they came up with a statement which Cramer "seemed to think was all right."

Knox objected that the format "didn't conform to what the President wanted; the President wanted us to get the officers themselves to ask for the proceeding." Stimson countered that such action by Roosevelt "would necessarily lead to the suspicion that there was a bargain on the subject or, at the other extreme, it could be charged that he had dragooned them into doing it." Finally, they phoned Roosevelt, who agreed to the proposed format. Stimson instructed Marshall to have Short "notified by telegram or telephone in the language of this paper which I was going to do and to give him the reason for it; that I wanted him to know from me personally rather than from the press."[30]

On February 28 the War and Navy departments announced that Short's
and Kimmel's requests for retirement had been accepted effective February 28
and March 1 respectively. They were to be tried by courts-martial "at such time
'as the public interest and safety' permits" on the charge of "dereliction of
duty." The Los Angeles *Times* very properly pointed out that the Articles of
War contained no specific charge of "dereliction of duty."[31]

Short was in San Antonio and "not available for comment. . . ."[32] In this
instance Short had the advantage over Kimmel. Stimson had insisted that the
general receive a personal notification prior to the press release. The Navy
accorded the admiral no such courtesy; he learned of his prospective court-
martial "through the public press. . . ."[33]

Like a wounded fox, Kimmel had gone to his native earth. He disappeared
into his boyhood home in Henderson, Kentucky, while his wife went to
Princeton to visit their son Ned. During Kimmel's stay with two of his brothers
in Henderson he did not leave the house or even permit himself to be seen at a
window. When the news of the court-martial came through the United Press,
Ed Klinger, a reporter for the Evanston (Indiana) *Press*, received the assignment to inform Kimmel. For some minutes Klinger's phone call could not
penetrate beyond Hubbard, a determined and efficient buffer between his
brother and the outside world. But at last he persuaded Hubbard to permit him
to speak with the admiral. The reporter read the news bulletin. "There was no
answer, but there was sound—the sound of deep, steady breathing." After
about five minutes Klinger asked, "Admiral, are you all right?" Kimmel
answered, "Yes. Was there anything else?" Klinger encouraged him to comment in justice to himself. After another long silence the admiral spoke. "No,
not even to the extent of saying 'no comment.' I thank you for your courtesy."
Then he broke the connection.[34]

Needless to say, the press was not equally taciturn. Many newspapers
were still out for the hides of Kimmel and Short.[35] The Honolulu *Star-Bulletin*
proclaimed that the ordering of courts-martial for the two officers was "in
accordance with the basic principle of justice in our American democracy. . . .

"A sentry found asleep at his post, a pilot who drowses at the wheel, are
certain of exemplary punishment. In wartime they are not allowed merely to
retire. . . ." More in sorrow than in anger the *Star-Bulletin* assured its readers:
"This is not to rake over the ashes of a bitter past but to point to the reason why
now it is the considered judgment of the war and navy departments (which
undoubtedly means the judgment of the president, too) that Short and Kimmel
should stand courtmartial. . . ."[36]

The talents of Kimmel and Short did not go entirely to waste. Fortunately
industry found a place for them. In September 1942 Short joined the Ford
Motor Company in Dallas, Texas, as head of its traffic department. At the time
the plant was "engaged solely in the manufacture of war materials."[37] Thus,
Short continued to serve his country on the civilian front. Kimmel augmented
his retirement checks of $6,000 a year by joining the shipbuilding firm of
Frederic R. Harris Company in July 1942. The firm's chief, himself a retired

rear admiral, put Kimmel to work in New York City "on drydock blueprints for the Pacific campaigns." Kimmel resented being deprived of the opportunity to serve on the battle line; nevertheless, he flung himself into his new arena with might and main. Harris later claimed that "if it had not been for Kimmel's knowledge of battleships and their needs, the Pacific campaigns would have been delayed a considerable time. Drydocks served a very important part in the stationing of ships in areas where docks had been unheard of."[38]

As 1942 drew toward its close, the Pearl Harbor picture presented an image of blurred lines and misty colors. Kimmel and Short hovered in a psychological limbo, neither acquitted nor condemned. Not only was this highly unsatisfactory for the two officers, their families and friends, but it also placed the individual American in a position where he or she could not help wondering why, if the commanders were guilty, they had not been punished. And if they were innocent, why were they not on active duty? The government was in an equally amorphous state, in which it could not explain its stand to the public for security reasons and in which the possibility of compromising Magic was an ever-present danger. Every day might see the loss, through enemy action, accident, or illness, of key witnesses essential to valid courts-martial. Sooner or later some action would be necessary if the ship of truth were not to be permanently beached.

CHAPTER 72

"SOMETHING

OUGHT

TO BE

DONE"

Not even the progress of the war stifled the insatiable interest throughout the United States in the intriguing question of responsibility for the failures at Pearl Harbor. One factor which kept the memory green was the two-year statute of limitations in courts-martial. In an undated letter hand-carried to Kimmel on August 27, 1943, Knox reminded him that the cutoff date in his case would be December 7, 1943. In view of the war he appealed to Kimmel "in the best interests of all concerned . . . not to plead the statute of limitations. . . ." The secretary assured the admiral of trial "at the earliest practicable date." On September 7 Kimmel replied that he desired court-martial "at the earliest practicable date" but forwarded a waiver after changing the form submitted to him to assure that his trial "would be in open court."[1]

On September 11 Stimson told The Judge Advocate General, Cramer, "that inasmuch as the Navy had gotten a waiver of the statute of limitations out of Admiral Kimmel, we would be justified in asking General Short for the same thing." He expressed the opinion that Short "will not be harmed; on the contrary he will probably be benefited by the delay." Conforming with War Department wishes, Short submitted a formal waiver on September 20.[2]

Preparing for his own future defense with the same vigor he had devoted to readying the Fleet for war, Kimmel wrote to Knox on November 26, 1943. He requested copies of correspondence between CinCPAC and the Navy Department from January 1, 1941, to December 17, 1941. This included all communications "which could be construed as warnings of hostilities" as well as those "directing dispositions of fleet detachments or units, including aircraft and marines," and all reports from CinCPAC of disposition of such units. Furthermore, he wanted all recommendations which he and Bloch had submitted "for the supply of personnel and equipment to the fleet, the 14th

Naval District, the outlying islands, and the Army establishment in the Hawaiian Area." In addition to this formidable list, Kimmel wanted copies of the Navy Department, Pacific Fleet, and Fourteenth Naval District war and operating plans "in effect on December 7, 1941." He also asked for a copy of the publication entitled *Joint Action of the Army and Navy* and a complete transcript of the proceedings of the Roberts Commission.

Knox forwarded this request to Navy Judge Advocate General Gatch on November 30, 1943, asking him to assemble the material and prepare it for transmittal to Kimmel. Gatch in turn passed the task to CNO, asking that his office collect the material, except, of course, for the Roberts report.

Kimmel's request staggered the CNO's office, and Vice Chief of Naval Operations F. J. Horne wrote Knox a long letter on December 16, pointing out the horrendous problems of personnel, time, and security that were sure to arise. On December 23 Admiral Ernest J. King, who since March 18, 1942, had held the combined offices of CNO and Commander in Chief, United States Fleet (Cominch), appended a sensible indorsement to Horne's letter. "Since it is obvious that the material requested by Admiral Kimmel will be required sooner or later, I recommend that it be assembled now." However, in view of the intelligence angle, he recommended "that a reply be made to Admiral Kimmel to the effect that while security considerations will not at this time permit delivery of the material requested, he is assured that it is being collected and preserved so as to be available at the appropriate time."[3]

Congress was keeping an eye on the statute of limitations. On the morning of December 7, 1943, Senator Barkley phoned Stimson that a bill had passed the House and was pending in the Senate to waive the statute of limitations in the court-martial cases of delinquency "occurring in the defense of Pearl Harbor." He asked whether Stimson had any objection. The secretary replied that Short had already waived this statute, but Stimson "had no objection to the action of Congress if they wanted to take it."[4]

Three days later Stimson met with Cramer and the latter's assistant, as well as Colonel Otto Nelson, assistant secretary of the General Staff. They discussed "the hasty statute" which Congress had passed. Once more Congress wanted to know if the War Department objected. On Cramer's advice, Stimson wrote to the director of the budget that he did not. In fact, Cramer thought the statute null "because it was not signed until a day or two after the two years' Statute of Limitations had expired." Stimson had "a little doubt on this point. . . ." He considered the legislation useless because they already had Short's waiver. "In case he should change his mind and plead it," Stimson wrote in his diary, "if the court held the plea still valid, we could still punish him for conduct unbecoming a gentleman and dismiss him from the Army on that score."[5] That would certainly be stretching the catchall Article of War to its limit, if not well beyond.

Kimmel continued to collect material for a confrontation. On January 18, 1944, be called upon his classmate Bill Halsey, on leave in Wilmington, Delaware. Evidently the ebullient Halsey was cocked and primed for battle in his friend's behalf. "Admiral Halsey is outraged at the treatment I have received," Kimmel recorded. "He will make it his mission after the war is over to see that I am vindicated. He has two officers on his staff preparing the data and opinions which I requested . . . in August 1943. He will make an affidavit and forward it to me."

However, Halsey advised Kimmel "to wait until after the war" before taking any steps to clear himself, because such action prior to that time would have "repercussions that will adversely affect the war." Kimmel then stated his "present policy": ". . . to get ready in every way by taking depositions and preparing my case in detail; to take no steps to force the issue but if the issue be forced I would be glad of it."[6]

Nevertheless, the Pearl Harbor problem could not stand indefinitely on one leg waiting for the conflict to end. At a press conference on February 25, 1944, Knox announced the assignment of Admiral Tommy Hart "to collect testimony from Navy officers concerning the Japanese attack on Pearl Harbor for use at the court martial of Admiral Kimmel and General Short. . . ." He wanted the job done at once "because many of the officers were scattered throughout the world and many were engaged in hazardous duties." Knox described this inquiry as "an attempt to be absolutely square with Admiral Kimmel," pointing out that "a high ranking officer in whom both the accused and the Navy Department had confidence" would take the testimony. He explained that "there was no change in the decision to postpone the court martial until after the 'war situation had subsided and the trial can be held safely.' "[7]

Already, on February 22, Hart had held his first official session, a very brief one devoted to formalities.[8] A dedicated, efficient officer, Hart had commanded the Asiatic Fleet in 1941. His orders did not require "findings of fact or opinion. . . ." He told the congressional committee, "It would have been going out of my field to have volunteered any." His precept was "recording testimony that was being forgotten, or worse yet, was being lost on account of men dying." He had neither instructions from nor discussion with Knox. He dealt entirely with Gatch, who told Hart "that Admiral Kimmel himself had pointed out . . . that testimony was being forgotten and lost and that something ought to be done."[9]

Those such as Knox and Kimmel who were worrying about testimony's being lost naturally had in mind the hazards of war. By a strange twist of the Norns' thread, Knox himself died of a heart attack on April 28, 1944,[10] while the Hart inquiry was in progress, an event which not only denied future Pearl Harbor investigations important testimony but deprived the nation of one of its most popular and effective public servants.

In May another flurry of congressional interest arose over the statute of limitations, due to expire early in June 1944. On May 30 Republican Senator Homer Ferguson of Michigan released a letter from Kimmel and said he "had a communication from Short which he did not feel at liberty to disclose."[11] Probably this "communication" was less than sensational. On June 12, 1944,

Short informed Kimmel in a brief note that he had received a wire from Ferguson "but decided to continue my policy of giving out no publicity." Short added, "I suppose we shall continue to be a political football until the election is over but do not anticipate any real action by the War and Navy Departments."[12]

Despite Kimmel's having advised Halsey that he did not intend to force the issue, actually he kept the pot boiling to ensure that his case remained in the public eye. His letter to Ferguson urgently called for "a free, open and public trial at the earliest practicable date," asserting "that he had retired from the Navy against his wishes."[13]

The Army's explanation that Short had waived the statute of limitations for the duration of the war or six months thereafter did not satisfy Ferguson. He wrote to The Judge Advocate General on June 3, 1944, making the very cogent point that "the army has not seen fit to take a waiver from anyone other than General Short. They have assumed on their part, at least up to two days ago, to hold to the theory that there could be only one person guilty for what happened" at Pearl Harbor.[14] Ferguson continued to bird-dog this waiver through various extensions until at last Congress extended the statute expiration date to six months after the defeat of Japan.[15]

The spate of publicity in late May and early June by no means mollified Kimmel. Full of bile, he wrote his attorney Charles Rugg on June 2 with this somewhat sinister suggestion: "I suppose there is no such thing as instituting a libel suit against the United States Government, but I think we might think over this phase of the procedure. At any rate, the press should get a lead along this line." The admiral believed he should avoid testifying before any investigation. "If I am subpeonaed [sic] and forced to attend, I should confine my remarks to a statement that I am ready, willing and anxious to appear before a general court martial, but that I am not interested in an investigation conducted and directed by interested parties who themselves should be defendants." By the summer of 1944 Kimmel had convinced himself that virtually every man's hand was against him. In a letter to Rugg on July 17 he even expressed fear that his and Rugg's telephones might be tapped.[16]

Meanwhile, Hart continued his work. As might be expected from one so capable, he did an excellent job of obtaining an authoritative record of recollections and views. Later Hart explained his procedure to the congressional committee:

> . . . my first idea was to get on paper the evidence of those people whom we might lose, and after a few days of taking testimony of men in Washington I went out into the field, out into the Pacific, to get that testimony, and the general sequence was that I first examined those who were outside of Washington when the war began rather than those who were there.

Hart interviewed forty witnesses, nineteen of whom appeared before no other inquiry. He urged Kimmel to participate. In fact, Hart's orders from Knox directed him to notify Kimmel "that he has a right to be present, to have counsel, to introduce, examine, and crossexamine witnesses, to introduce matter pertinent to the examination and to testify or declare in his own behalf at his own request."[17] Kimmel always complained about the absence of these opportunities before the Roberts Commission; now Knox offered them all. But Kimmel decided not to accept.

He later wrote that he did not participate in Hart's investigation on advice of counsel "because the stipulation demanded of me would have placed my fate completely in the hands of the Secretary of the Navy. This I did regretfully because it was through my efforts that this investigation was initiated."[18] Kimmel told the author that he did not take part because he "did not want his hands tied."[19] In any case, Kimmel was dead set on a court-martial and exceedingly suspicious of any action that might interfere with or prejudice his position in such a trial.

Of all the admirals the Navy could have assigned to this task, Hart was possibly the one best qualified to give Kimmel a knowledgeable hearing. He too had commanded a fleet in the Pacific in December 1941 and had suffered at Japanese hands. Yet Kimmel denied himself what was perhaps the most auspicious opportunity he ever had to present his case, marshal his chosen witnesses, and cross-examine others.

Hart wrote to Stark on May 20, 1944, giving him a brief account of his inquiry and explaining that he had decided against coming to London to take Stark's testimony. Stark wrote back one of his long, pleasant letters on June 2. Knox had informed him of Hart's mission, and Stark "was delighted that it was in such eminently fair and capable hands." He was not at all surprised that Hart's inquiry had led "into the Department. It couldn't help it." He added, "Feeling as I do about Kimmel, my one thought about a court martial has been that it would put him in a much better light. Were it not for this, and if he did not desire it, I would doubt the wisdom of a court." Stark assured Hart: "I should be more than glad to have a talk over the whole thing with you as I have often wracked my brain as to wherein I may 'have done those things which I ought not to have done, and left undone those things which I should have done,' but as a rule I get not very far."[20]

Hart ended his inquiry on June 15, 1944. Despite the valuable material produced, Congress was not satisfied. Senator Ferguson, who felt "very keenly about Pearl Harbor," introduced a resolution establishing an Army Board and a Navy Court of Inquiry.[21]

The initiative for this action seems to have come from Kimmel and two of his attorneys, Rugg and Lieutenant Edward F. Hanify, USNR. The two lawyers went to Washington, where Rugg discussed the proposed legislation "with certain key figures in the House and the Senate." At the end of a day's discussion "the proposed draft of legislation was pretty well worked out. . . ." Hanify polished the draft in the Supreme Court's law library, then took it to the office of Senator David I. Walsh of Massachusetts, whose secretary typed it.[22] Eventually Ferguson, destined to be an important member of the Pearl Harbor congressional committee, set the ball rolling for the Army as well as the Navy inquiries. These investigations were held concurrently, the Army's from July 20 to October 20, the Navy's from July 24 to October 19, 1944.

The Army Pearl Harbor Board represented the three mainstreams of the officer corps—the ranks, the National Guard, and West Point. Its president, Lieutenant General George Grunert, had enlisted as a private in 1898. He was no stranger to the military problems of the Far East, having commanded the Philippine Department in 1940 and 1941. Since 1942 he had been deputy chief of staff for Army Service Forces. His steady eye and decisive mouth under a small, clipped mustache hinted that he was not to be trifled with.

The next ranking member was moon-faced Major General Henry D. Russell. Behind his glasses his alert gaze bespoke undoubted intelligence. A Phi Beta Kappa graduate of the University of Georgia, he also held a law degree from that institution. In 1916 he had entered the service through the National Guard. Since September 16, 1940, he had been a two-star general on active duty.

The board's junior member, Major General Walter H. Frank, was its airman and West Pointer. He knew Hawaii well, having commanded the Eighteenth Wing there from September 1938 to November 1940. Although Frank looked as if he would have been at home lecturing peacefully in a college classroom, according to Mollison, he had "kept the air literally blue with the Navy" during his duty on Oahu. Since his Hawaiian assignment Frank had held several top posts, including that of the VII Air Force Service Command in England. His latest position was heading the Air Service Command at Patterson Field, Ohio.[23]

In later years Marshall informed his biographer, Forrest C. Pogue, "I gave no instructions about the Army inquiry except that there must be no friend of mine on the board."[24] Evidently he got his wish. The board's assistant recorder, Major Henry C. Clausen, gained the impression that "the Chief of Staff was not these three men's most admired person." MacArthur had replaced Grunert in the Philippines at Marshall's orders, and Clausen believed that Grunert "had no love for Marshall." Clausen further claimed that Marshall had prevented Frank from receiving his third star, so Frank was not fond of the Chief of Staff either. Clausen also pointed out that Russell had trained a regiment and wanted to accompany it overseas, but Marshall had relieved him and kept him in the United States.[25] Later, when both the Army board and a follow-up inquiry which Clausen conducted had been completed, Clausen asked Marshall why these particular generals, who had reason to dislike him, had been selected. Marshall replied simply, "The only reason for their assignment was their availability."[26]

If the suspicion lurks that the Army board might not be averse to taking Marshall down a peg or two, there is rather more solid cause to believe that the Navy entered the arena armed with a few preconceptions of its own. Much sympathy and support for Kimmel existed at all levels of the Navy. Writing to Kimmel on June 10, 1944, Poco Smith assured his former chief: "The reaction of Naval officers is all in your favor. They feel, as I do, that you will never be brought to trial and that there are a great many things unsaid about Pearl Harbor." Almost without exception, the former naval personnel interviewed for this study lined up in Kimmel's corner. During the formation of the Navy Court of Inquiry, Gatch made no secret of his pro-Kimmel bias. Captain Robert A. Lavender, USN, one of Kimmel's counsels, on July 1 relayed to his client this information from Gatch:

> . . . he [Gatch] told the Senate Committee that he could not possibly draw up any specifications that could be proved based upon investigation of the Roberts Report. He also said that he told the Committee in the very first sentence that he uttered that he had known you personally throughout all of his official life, that he had before Pearl Harbor the greatest admiration and respect for your ability and it had not changed in any particular since.

Apparently Gatch expected the situation "to develop into a general controversy between the Army and the Navy, as to the ultimate responsibility." He also told Lavender "that all the Officers in the Department were behind" Kimmel. He assured Lavender that he hoped Kimmel would participate "and bring out everything" that he had "and pull no punches."[27]

With the Navy's top legal light taking such an attitude—that the investigation of Pearl Harbor was predestined to become a cat-and-dog fight between the Army and the Navy to see whose tail would drag the tin can and that the Navy Department's officers were solidly behind Kimmel—one scarcely needed a crystal ball or tarot deck to predict the course of events.

In distinct contrast with Kimmel, Stark, who with Kimmel and Bloch had been designated "interested parties," had precious little help from the organization which he had formerly headed. Sometime in the summer of 1944 he received a dispatch ordering him home to testify before the Navy court, but his orders gave Stark no idea what was in store for him. He would face the court "colder than a mackerel," as his legal assistant, Lieutenant (j.g.) David W. Richmond, said.

Stark persuaded Hart to serve as his counsel. Hart's testimony before the congressional committee indicates that he was by no means eager to take on this task, and if a war had not been in progress, he "certainly would not have done it." One can understand that Hart might have had qualms about serving as counsel to an officer he had decided not to interview during his own investigation. His decision not to question Stark told its own story of just how important he considered Stark's potential evidence to be. And now here was Stark in the position of an "interested party" before an official court of inquiry! No wonder Hart wanted legal assistance, and they agreed upon Richmond.

Admiral Royal E. Ingersoll, who had been Stark's assistant CNO, also served as one of his counsels before the Navy court but was not very active in that capacity.[28]

The Navy fielded an impressive court of inquiry. The members were senior to Stark and Kimmel. Wiry, pinch-featured Admiral Orin G. Murfin was its president. He had been a classmate of Hart's in the Annapolis class of 1897. He knew the Pacific well from experience as commander, Asiatic Fleet; commandant, Fourteenth Naval District, and commander of the navy yard at

Pearl Harbor. He had retired on May 1, 1940.[29] Richmond believed that Murfin had passed his prime and showed it during the sessions of the court.[30]

Next came Admiral Edward C. Kalbfus. Nicknamed Old Dutch, this large, fleshy man with a jutting nose and thick hands looked as if he could well have served under Holland's banner in its great seafaring days. His post-World War I assignments included director of War Plans; command of Destroyers, Battle Force; and president of the War College. Although he reached statutory retirement age on December 1, 1941, he continued to serve as president of the War College. From 1942 to 1943 he was a member of the Navy General Board. In July 1944, the same month he joined the Navy court, he assumed additional duty as director of naval history.[31] Richmond found him a man of good judgment and common sense.[32] Vice Admiral Charles Wellborn, Jr., who had served as Stark's aide, agreed that Kalbfus "was commonly regarded as a good solid Naval Officer—not brilliant, but sound."[33]

Vice Admiral Adolphus Andrews completed this seagoing triumvirate. Columnists Drew Pearson and Robert Allen once referred to this handsome, rather theatrical-looking officer somewhat nastily as "famous in Washington for his beautifully tailored clothes and for having been aide to Presidents of the United States." But he had also served as chief of the Bureau of Navigation and had enjoyed various sea commands, including that of the Hawaiian Detachment. In 1942–1943 he commanded the Eastern Sea Frontier, as such being in charge of the Navy's antisubmarine operation. In that capacity he struck Stimson as "perfectly useless. . . ."

Although placed on the retired list on November 1, 1943, Andrews continued on active duty as chairman of the Navy Manpower Survey Board, which post he held when he joined the Navy court.[34] He may have brought with him a personal prejudice against Stark. Wellborn suspected that Andrews "may have considered Admiral Stark at least partially responsible for his not getting his fourth star, so he had a reason for an unfriendly feeling for Admiral Stark."[35]

Kimmel was more than satisfied with this court, and with good reason. "Murfin stated that Andrews was a most loyal friend of mine, and that he was positive, intelligent and most earnest in his efforts to make sure that I was completely cleared," Kimmel recorded later. Murfin also told Lavender "that he expected Kimmel to explode on several occasions on the stand, that as a matter of fact he hoped Kimmel would explode. . . ." What is more, he had "deliberately" asked questions to that end. The fact that Kimmel kept his temper and confined himself to answering questions "fully, frankly and forcefully" made Murfin "all the more angry" on Kimmel's behalf.[36]

Kimmel looked forward to placing on record some information which had recently come to his attention. In February 1944 Safford had visited Kimmel. In a three-hour conference he told the admiral that he, Kimmel, might soon be court-martialed and that he, Safford, would be a witness. So he had been collecting data and refreshing his memory. He had found that certain vital information had not been sent to Kimmel. His "sense of justice" offended,

Safford sought out Kimmel to give him its essence orally.[37] "This information made me almost sick," said Kimmel.[38]

In the summer of 1944 King authorized Lavender to inspect the files containing the intercepts. Lavender had forty-three of these messages copied and authenticated. General McNarney, formerly of the Roberts Commission, who in 1942 had become deputy Chief of Staff, objected to the director of Naval Communications. As a result, the latter did not deliver the messages to Lavender.

Not the man to suffer rebuffs patiently, especially at the hands of McNarney, whom he despised, Kimmel officially requested the Navy court to place Lavender's collection of intercepts in evidence. But the Navy Department refused. Follow-up brought the answer that his letter of request "had been misplaced." Undaunted, the admiral personally delivered another to the deputy Commander in Chief. "Tell those bastards in the Navy Department that it will do no good to lose my letters," he said vigorously. If they did so, he "would write the same letter daily to the Secretary of the Navy" until he got action. During this discussion a clerk brought in his original letter.[39] Perhaps it really had been mislaid; perhaps someone realized that Kimmel was perfectly capable of bombarding them with daily missives for years on end until he obtained results.

CHAPTER 73

"FULL

AND FAIR

DISCLOSURE"

Stark appeared before the Navy court as its first witness on July 31, calm but completely unprepared and in an understandable state of confusion. He had had no time to prepare for the Court of Inquiry, and the files and records of his service as CNO were not available to him during his brief time in Washington before the court convened. So he asked for time to check up and prepare himself.[1] The court granted an extension until 1000 on Monday, August 7. Typically the feisty Kimmel had the last word: "I have been branded throughout this country as the one responsible for the Pearl Harbor disaster," he declared. He urged that the court summon witnesses from the Army, the State Department, and "any other federal department" to establish all the necessary facts. He revealed the sense of urgency that drove him: "People may die who can make statements before this court sufficient to establish the facts and to refute the utterly false and misleading statements made throughout the Roberts Commission."[2]

It must bave been maddening for such a conscientious commander as Stark to be forced to devote his prime energies to defending past actions when the present cried for his full attention. Kimmel had no such official problems to distract his mind, but he was increasingly involved in the upcoming presidential election, not as a campaigner but as a symbol. If the Republicans could prove—or even plant a convincing suspicion—that Roosevelt and his administration had dragged the United States into the war, had had preknowledge of the Japanese attack which they failed to convey to Kimmel and Short, or were suppressing pertinent facts about Pearl Harbor, they would have found the perfect campaign issue.

As early as July 3, 1944, George H. E. Smith, secretary of the Senate Minority Steering Committee, sounded out Herbert Brownell, chairman of the

Republican National Committee, about charging the New Deal with responsibility for the American entry into World War II. At this point Smith toyed with a "you-scratch-my-back-and-I'll-scratch-yours" arrangement with the Democratic National Committee: If the Democrats would cease harping on the Depression, the Republicans would lay off the war.

Four days later Smith reported to Senator Robert A. Taft, chairman of the Minority Steering Committee, that he was preparing to visit Rugg in Boston to obtain some materials. Kimmel had expressed to Rugg his willingness "to take Mr. Taft into our confidence, trusting to his integrity and his judgment." On August 4 Smith wrote to Taft that Pearl Harbor material which "would show that the Administration must share in the responsibility for that disaster" could be worked into a magazine article.[3]

Thus assured of powerful support for his cause, Kimmel opened the session on August 7 loaded for bear. He understood "that the judge advocate had requested access to certain secret files in the Navy Department, to which he also would like to have access, and that as yet the matter had not been acted upon." The court's judge advocate, Commander Harold Biesemeier, replied that he had written to the secretary of the navy setting forth Kimmel's request. He added that "he did not consider the said documents immediately necessary to the proceedings of the court."[4]

Following this exchange, Stark resumed the stand. His most interesting remarks concerned the critical warning message of November 27.* Mincing no words, he emphasized what he had expected from Kimmel and the Army in consequence. While Stark could not overlook Kimmel's responsibilities, he made sure that the court remembered that the defense of Pearl Harbor and the ships at moorings was the Army's mission.[5]

The next day, August 8, Kimmel again called for the documents from the Navy Department. One can appreciate why he and his counsels were most eager to place the Magic messages and other data in evidence before Stark returned to London. Stark was still bound to secrecy in that respect, both by oath and by his own strong security-consciousness. Unless the Navy released him by giving the documents to the court, of necessity his testimony would be incomplete.

Kimmel had another string to his bow. In the record of the Hart inquiry he learned that Ingersoll "knew of a special Japanese code by means of which, on or about December 4, 1941, he learned the Japanese were about to attack both Britain and the United States." Obviously Kimmel meant the "winds" code. He explained that he made this statement "to show the reason why he had been endeavoring to obtain access to the secret messages in the Navy Department, and to appeal to the court for assistance in obtaining such access."[6]

Back on the stand, although asked some questions about his sources, Stark never mentioned Magic. "I was relying primarily on information which I had from sources available to me, and which I considered responsible information."[7] Such security-inspired evasions probably are the main reason why Kimmel later

---

*See Chapter 50.

accused Stark of perjury to the court.[8] Stark's oath to protect Magic constantly crossed his oath as a witness and left him, like other witnesses, in a most uncomfortable position.

The session of August 9 opened with Stark's counsel examining him,* mostly about war plans. Asked what action he expected the Hawaiian Department to take upon receipt of Marshall's warning of November 27, Stark went for the Army foot, horse, and artillery:

> I expected the Army to utilize its warning system to the utmost. . . . I expected them to make ready a maximum number of planes possible. I expected them . . . to man their batteries, both fixed and mobile. I expected them to implement arrangements which they had with the Navy in joint agreements. I expected them to take some sabotage measures. In other words, I expected them to assume a maximum state of readiness in defense of Pearl Harbor. . . . In particular, I would have expected the Army to have ready their pursuit planes, some of them certainly in instant readiness, and full alertedness with regard to others. . . . These were the principal or certainly the primary weapon of defense against the air attack coming in from the sea.[9]

Following the noon break another development roused Kimmel to further efforts. He had learned that day that "certain vital, pertinent data" would be denied the court on orders of the acting secretary of the navy, although the secretary had approved their availability. Kimmel continued passionately: "Without a full and fair disclosure of all known and available evidence, this inquiry is futile. Against such evasion of the clear mandate of Congress and the demands of simple justice, I most solemnly protest."[10]

The denial of data which Kimmel had anticipated came through the next day, August 11.[11] He would not take this without a scrap. At the outset of the afternoon his counsel submitted a long statement again calling for the material and suggested that the proceedings of the court be classified "in the same degree of secrecy as that of the documents." Sooner or later they would become public property. When that time came, the entire Navy would "feel the effects of the public disapprobation" which would arise if it developed that the Navy had not furnished the court with all available evidence.[12]

The court temporarily wound up its questioning of Stark in a brief session on Saturday, August 12. According to Lavender, "Murfin indicated that all the members of the Court were thoroughly disgusted with Stark."[13] Richmond doubted this applied to Kalbfus but stated that Murfin and Andrews were unfriendly toward Stark from the start of the proceedings.[14] Wellborn, who was devoted to Stark, nevertheless could picture what might lay behind the harsh

---

*It is virtually impossible to determine who is interrogating before the Navy court. The transcript does not identify individuals and indicates the "interested party" as questioning even when the individual concerned was not present. But according to Richmond, Hart took on the task the first day; thereafter Richmond did most of the questioning on Stark's behalf. (Interview with Richmond, November 1, 1977.)

judgment: "Admiral Stark . . . liked to check documents rather than rely on memory alone. Nor was he able, as was General Marshall, to express himself extemporaneously in invariably clear concise grammatical sentences. He was more of the type of General Eisenhower, in this respect."[15]

Yet the written record of Stark's testimony shows little of Eisenhower's fractured syntax. By the same token, the transcript of Marshall's comments is not that much better than Stark's. From the record of the Navy court one receives the impression that Stark was a solid, direct, cooperative witness, a man of quiet sincerity, doing his best under the severe handicap of protecting Magic. Of course, he stood up for himself and his staff officers, and that defense might have antagonized those who may have hoped for a solid pro-Kimmel front.

If the court wanted to absolve the Navy of all responsibility for Pearl Harbor, Short unwittingly helped the cause along. The transcript of his testimony of August 14 is not impressive. He was garrulous and obscure, and he provided damaging glimpses into his own mind. Realizing that he had a problem, he requested and received "interested party" status so that his counsel, Brigadier General T. H. Green, could be present.[16]

In a long statement Short complained about his shortages of guns, men, and equipment, especially in the Coast Artillery and the Hawaiian Air Force. He explained that in addition to radar, he had 100 lookout stations scattered "pretty much on the high ground around the whole island." Their purpose was to spot ships or planes. They had a good communications tie-in. But they were not on station on the morning of December 7 "because they were not alerted for aircraft attack or for attack by a landing force, or an all-out attack."

Here was a touch of sheer *Alice in Wonderland*—the stations supposed to warn of approaching ships or planes were not on duty because nobody expected the attack of which they were supposed to warn! Short did not improve matters by stating that while the Army had "some sound detectors" for use instead of radar in some places, they, too, were not in use on the morning of December 7 "because the command was not alerted that way."

The general did not totally lack a sense of self-preservation. Asked if the commanding general of the Hawaiian Department was responsible for the defense of Pearl Harbor, he shot back: "Supported by the naval forces."[17]

Short had not been at his best before the court. For one thing, he constantly invoked the vocabulary of complaint. For another, his testimony makes abundantly clear that he had little conception of the true crisis he faced in December 1941. Perhaps he felt ill at ease testifying to a group of Navy officers unfamiliar with the technical aspects of his job and with no particular reason to sympathize with him. He must have realized that this body had no authority either to condemn or to absolve him; however, his case was inextricably linked with that of Kimmel, and inevitably the fallout of the court's findings would affect him for better or worse.

Kimmel came to bat the next day, August 15. Like Short, he suffered from misdirection. He did not seem to understand that in Japanese eyes his ships, a mobile and potentially dangerous force, would constitute the prime target. "I thought it was much more probable that the Japs would attempt a raid on Pearl Harbor if the Fleet were away than if it were there. However, at no time did I consider it more than a possibility, and one which ordinary prudence would make us guard against."[18] But on December 7, 1941, "ordinary prudence" had been lacking.

When Kimmel returned to the stand on August 16, Stark's counsel asked about his decision to bomb any submarine found in the operating area. Kimmel replied revealingly, "I would say that the war warning dispatch gave me an excuse to do something that I had wanted to do for several months."[19] This answer makes clear that although the admiral scorned the message of November 27 in retrospect, at the time he seized upon its warning aspects when it suited his inclination and preoccupation to do so.

Under his counsel's skillful guidance, Kimmel had considerable to say about the projects for reinforcing Wake and Midway. Counsel asked if this project did not "modify the war warning as connoting no prospect of an immediate attack on Pearl Harbor. . . ." Kimmel replied, "It tended to and did reduce, in my mind, the chances of an attack on Pearl Harbor insofar as the Navy Department had any idea that there was imminence of an attack on Pearl Harbor."[20] Yet the Wake-Midway message had been received and thrashed out before receipt of the "war warning." So the latter should have "modified" the former, not vice versa.*

When Bloch's counsel asked about responsibility for distant patrols, Kimmel came as close as he ever did to putting the finger on Bloch: "And when the Commandant of the 14th Naval District was charged with this duty by the Naval Frontier Coast Defense plan, it was his duty to keep himself informed, and in my opinion when he considered it necessary to request planes for the purpose of performing the duties" for which he was responsible.[21]

For some time the Republicans had been fairly quiescent in their plan to use Pearl Harbor as a campaign issue, but on August 24 Senator Sinclair Weeks of Massachusetts began to roll up the big guns. He placed in the *Congressional Record* an article by Bill Cunningham which had appeared in the Boston *Herald* on August 22. Cunningham called for the opportunity for Kimmel "to clear his name." So far, he wrote, "writers and commentators tiptoe as delicately around the subject as if it were a nest of sleeping rattlesnakes. . . ." He urged action to prevent "an American Dreyfus case" before it was too late.[22]

One can understand why the loyal opposition was eager for an early start in the presidential race. Lawmakers on Capital Hill could read in their morning papers headlines that pealed forth like golden trumpets: JAP HOMELAND—BOMBED; PATTON'S TANKS 165 MILES FROM GERMAN BORDER; FRENCH, YANKS OCCUPY PARIS. . . ."[23] Useless to oppose this sort of thing with coolly reasoned

*See Chapters 49 and 50.

argument, with economics or traditional ideology! The man associated in the public mind with such an outpouring of good news could be elected if he had two heads. The GOP badly needed an emotional issue, something to create an instinctive revulsion.

But while the Republicans warmed up in the bull pen, the Navy Court of Inquiry continued its unreported efforts on the diamond—Navy Department Headquarters. Monday, August 28, was a memorable day for Kimmel. The court received the documents Kimmel had fought to obtain. Stark objected not to the contents, "but because their use here may compromise many years of hard work the results of which are most important to the Nation's future interests." The court, however, did not sustain his objections, and into the record went a large bloc of Magic and a few consular messages. This represented a tribute to Kimmel's iron will and tenacity of purpose and to his legal team, especially Rugg, who directed the effort.[24]

According to Lavender, the dispatches which triggered the most response were some of the "bomb plot" series.[25] Yet we have a peculiar twist at this point in the Pearl Harbor story. The original "bomb plot" message of September 24, 1941, does not appear in the Navy court's exhibits. This was the dispatch which divided Pearl Harbor into areas for use in espionage reporting and which set forth specifics Tokyo wanted from the Honolulu consulate.* Whatever the reason for its omission, the fact that this key dispatch did not appear in the exhibits may help explain why a number of witnesses discounted the importance of the few "bomb plot" series messages under consideration.

Nevertheless, Kimmel had won his point. At considerable risk to the security of Magic, the Navy Department had given the court all the documents for which Kimmel through Lavender had asked, excepting the ever-elusive "winds execute."† Revelation of the Magic and consular documents clarified a number of ambiguities in the preceding testimony. Now the court faced what amounted to another investigation. The principal questions had become these: Was information available in Washington which one could reasonably argue had tipped off Japanese intentions? And if so, had someone in Washington deliberately withheld information from Kimmel?

If both questions could not be answered in the affirmative, then the admiral was no better off than before. Indeed, his situation would have worsened, for as long as he could claim the Navy Department was refusing to release pertinent evidence, doubts about the Navy's motives must always remain. At this point that evidence was open to the scrutiny of the court. If Kimmel and his able counsel could not convince the court that the documents proved him the victim of at best stupidity and at worse conspiracy in Washington, the admiral might find that he had won the battle and lost the war.

On August 29 one of the most controversial of all the Pearl Harbor witnesses took the stand. In his usual confident manner, Safford told of the "winds" code

---

*See Chapter 31.
†See Chapter 56.

and its alleged "execute." Safford recounted a number of secondhand stories, some of which were stricken as hearsay.[26] But he set wheels turning which would grind the gears of the Pearl Harbor machinery for years to come. To Richmond he seemed "sincere but a man with a mission—to prove the existence of a non-existent 'winds execute.' "[27]

The court held no session on Friday, September 1, probably to accommodate the schedule of the next witness, General Marshall. The Army could use a witness of stature before the Navy court, and Marshall certainly filled the bill. At the same time, as he explained to the court on September 2, after Pearl Harbor his "whole attention was turned to other things from that instant, and I didn't see a record or look at a thing until, as a matter of fact, the last day or two, trying to get something for this board—so I haven't probed into the matter. I was busy with something else. That was water over the dam."

Asked how he rated Short, Marshall replied laconically, "Very superior officer." He considered Hawaii "far and away the most heavily provided installation of ours in or out of the country, for defense. It had had first priority in the Army for years. . . ."[28]

Marshall did not claim perfect memory. His testimony is laced with such replies as "I do not recall," "I have no recollection," "I don't know about that." He did not remember his whereabouts on the night of Saturday, December 6, and evidently considered the point of little interest. "I don't know where I was. I never thought of it until this instant." He had no memory one way or the other about seeing Short's answer to the warning message of November 27.[29] Such replies can be frustrating to a court or board trying to pin down specifics. But witnesses like Stark and Marshall who frankly admit that they do not know or remember everything can be more credible than those who testify in assured detail to matters of which they have no direct knowledge.

Following Marshall's appearance, the court temporarily moved from Washington to the Pearl Harbor Navy Yard to take the testimony of several witnesses who could not come to Washington. While the court moved toward Honolulu, Republicans in Congress mounted an increasingly heavy offensive. Congressman Noble J. Johnson of Indiana declared on September 5 that in his opinion, Kimmel and Short had not been court-martialed "because the administration is afraid to let the facts be known." He asserted: "If action is not had now, there is no reason to believe that the facts will ever become known as long as President Roosevelt remains Commander in Chief."

On September 6 Congressman Hugh D. Scott, Jr., of Pennsylvania posed some questions which he claimed were "being freely discussed in Washington and elsewhere." After a long, highly colored summary of the diplomatic highlights of 1941, Scott demanded, "Let us have the truth, the whole truth, and nothing but the truth. Only thus can the innocent be absolved, the guilty judged, the dead ultimately vindicated, and the public interest served."[30]

Scott's remarks and their attendant publicity worried George Smith of the Minority Steering Committee. He feared lest "piecemeal" leaking of "the facts" be in the administration's interest. "This lets the steam out of the issue. . . ."

So Smith urged haste upon Senator Taft: "Each day's delay at this critical time decreases our chances of using the best methods of action. The leaks that are daily occurring and the rapid passage of time are frittering away the best issue we have."[31]

Smith obviously believed his thesis that the Roosevelt administration was responsible for the United States' entry into the war. On September 12 he wrote to Rugg, urging strongly that Kimmel take the initiative *"with his story, written in the right way* [Smith's italics]." In fact, the story was already written and ready. "But it will need the help, advice and information that Admiral Kimmel alone can give."

In pressing his case, Smith revealed his belief that, militarily speaking, Kimmel was on the spot. ". . . the Administration will put strong emphasis on the fact that enough warnings should have put the Pearl Harbor Army and Navy on the extreme alert despite the failure of Washington to keep them informed," he wrote. "It will play up the technical situation to the utmost; and it will be very, very difficult for Admiral Kimmel to explain away that case." Smith was absolutely correct. Then he added, "The diplomacy leading up to Pearl Harbor is the bulwark of Admiral Kimmel's defense—not the technical situation at Pearl Harbor."[32]

At this time the fortunes of war had plunged Kimmel and his family to the depths of personal tragedy. The very day, September 6, that Scott addressed the House, evening papers announced the loss of the submarine *Robalo*, under command of the admiral's thirty-one-year-old son, Lieutenant Commander Manning M. Kimmel. The submarine had failed to return from patrol duty. All hands had been "officially listed as missing," and the next of kin notified.[33]

Small wonder that Kimmel did not accompany the court to Oahu. Even if he could have steeled himself to look upon Pearl Harbor once more, something had happened to push self-vindication into second place, for perhaps the first time since December 7, 1941. He had to share his sorrow with his wife, Dorothy, in the dignity of privacy.

But Bloch made the trip to Hawaii. Acutely conscious of the implications of being an "interested party," he attended all the sessions, which began on September 9. The first witness was Rear Admiral Soc McMorris, now Nimitz's chief of staff. Homely as a meat cleaver and just as sharp, McMorris demonstrated in some ways a broader gauge of thinking than Kimmel and his counsels could have wished. Like Stark and Ingersoll, he considered the Fleet to have been "on a war footing." Unlike Kimmel, he had recognized the seriousness of Japan's ordering the destruction of codes. He "felt that that message, more definitely than anything that had gone before, indicated the probability of a war with Japan that would involve the United States."[34]

Richmond believed McMorris's testimony damaged Kimmel's cause. Certainly McMorris did not agree with his former chief in all respects. In particular, the fact that McMorris grasped the significance of the code destruction message, which Kimmel did not, reflected unfavorably upon the latter. Even so, Richmond had come to believe Kimmel's shortcomings far less than those of the Army.[35]

The court held no session on Tuesday, September 12. The next day it heard the testimony of one destined to become a center of controversy—Commander Kramer. He both helped and hindered Kimmel's cause. Seemingly he confirmed receipt of some sort of "winds execute" message. On the other hand, he pooh-poohed the "bomb plot" series.[36] Safford had claimed that when Kramer showed Knox the "one o'clock" message,* he had pointed out the time, saying that "it undoubtedly meant a surprise air raid on Pearl Harbor in a few hours."[37] This story Kramer contradicted. That session ended the court's visit to Oahu, and it soon returned to the West Coast.[38]

On Friday, September 15, the day hearings began in San Francisco, the Washington *Post* called for an end to the secrecy shrouding Pearl Harbor, over which a "first-class political row" seemed to be brewing. "Wholly apart from the guilt or innocence of Kimmel and Short, the American people have a right to know the background of the Pearl Harbor catastrophe. And there is no reason that we know of for keeping them in the dark." That was the problem. The press and public did not know the government's reason—Magic—for keeping the entire background under wraps.

September 16 saw the entrance of a new actor on the Pearl Harbor stage. Representative Bertrand W. Gearhart, Republican from California, called for total publication of the Roberts report and its related material. He claimed to believe that the report "was doctored in the White House." He stressed: "The election is less than two months away. Clever maneuvering has made it impossible to tell the truth of Pearl Harbor by courts-martial or congressional investigation before the balloting."[39]

Representative Forest A. Harness of Indiana offered a resolution calling for a special five-man committee to investigate Pearl Harbor, declaring, "The public is demanding and should be told before the November election, all the facts connected with the Japanese attack." If Roosevelt were not responsible, "he should be cleared promptly. . . ." But if the President had been culpable "in directing our military activities in Hawaii, the American people should have the true facts before they are called upon to pass judgment on his fitness for reelection. . . ."[40]

Undeterred by this tacit vote of no confidence, the Navy court convened in Washington on September 21, when Admiral Richardson made a brief appearance. Exuding confidence as he usually did, he discussed mainly the air patrol system he had employed as CinCUS. Strangely enough, the witness, the court, the judge advocate, and the counsel did not so much as mention Richardson's conference with Roosevelt in 1940. Richardson further stated that he "unofficially, orally, and in writing" had made specific recommendations about basing the Fleet, and he summarized his objections to Pearl Harbor as a base.[41]

---

*See Chapter 59.

The session of Friday, September 22, occupied only two hours, but it made up in interest what it lacked in length. Rear Admiral Thomas Withers, who had been Kimmel's commander of submarines in 1941, proved a thought-provoking witness. He knew of the "war warning," having been present at the conference held in consequence:

> Admiral Kimmel handed me this dispatch to read. I read it, and he said, "What do you think that means?" I said, "I think it means war." Then I think Admiral Bloch, who was present, sort of made fun of me; I had that impression—asked me what I would do, would I sink ships? And I said I would sink ships if they came within 500 miles of Hawaii and didn't turn back.[42]

Actually Bloch did not attend the conference on November 27. But it speaks ill for the atmosphere in that gathering that at least one senior officer present sneered at a colleague who believed that a "war warning" was precisely that.

With the court entering the home stretch, Senator Ferguson called for the findings of the Army and Navy boards to be "made public as soon as their reports were completed." This could be in "about two weeks." There was nothing political about these investigations, and the boards should release their reports "well ahead of the election."[43]

Monday, September 25, saw the final questioning of the two present "interested parties." Typically Kimmel had much to say; Bloch, little. After the introduction of a number of letters from Stark, Kimmel described the reorganization of the Fleet which he made upon becoming CinCPAC.

"I felt that before hostilities came that there would be additional information, that we would get something more definite, and when the attack came without this information, of course I was inclined to blame myself for not having been much smarter than I was," he testified. But when he later found "that information was, in fact, available in the Navy Department" which would have changed his attitude, "I ceased to blame myself so much." He proclaimed, "without looking into the exact wording," that the Hull Note "was a veritable ultimatum . . . and they [the Japanese] were forced to do something."[44]

He was equally sure the "bomb plot" series indicated an air attack on Pearl Harbor. He also insisted upon the significance of the "winds execute." However, he conceded that it was difficult to say what he would have done had he received it.[45] At times the transcript gives the impression that the court was coaxing Kimmel into a favorable position, in effect leading the witness, as in this exchange:

> Q. Had you sighted that force at the outer rim of a distant patrol and, in accordance with your directive, let them make the first war move, could you have done anything other than to alert your command?
>
> A. Admiral, I could not have done anything under the orders which I had at the time, and had I attacked the Japanese naval force 700 miles from Oahu, I would have violated my orders. . . .

Possiby Kimmel's attorneys had suggested a strategy of presenting the admiral as the helpless pawn of the Navy Department, but such a position was foreign to his nature. No one who knew Kimmel could picture him standing by immobile while a Japanese armada bore down upon him. Evidently his honest heart rebelled, for a little later he continued: ". . . if we had sighted anything 700 miles from Oahu, I think I would have found some means to handle the situation, insofar as the forces I had available would have permitted me."[46] That sounds much more like Kimmel. After all, he had had no inhibitions about ordering his Fleet to sink any unidentified submarine in the operating area—orders which might well have placed him in the technical position of having fired the first shot.

Wednesday, September 27, wrapped up the inquiry except for preparing the report. To clarify their positions, the three "interested parties" submitted final statements. Stark's was brief and forceful, written in the third person, the work of Hart and Richmond. Stark having returned to London, one of his counsels must have read it for him.* His statement bore down heavily upon the Army's responsibility. "The Naval Base was and still is the seat of our power over the Pacific and in the last analysis the Army forces, Oahu, were stationed there for its defense—and for that alone." The Navy's sole responsibility in that respect was "to support the Army's effort. . . ." But the Navy "had no authority over the main defensive agency—the aircraft warning system, the fighter planes and their direction in combat." The document closed with a real sock to the jaws of Short and Martin: ". . . whatever may have been Navy failures, on or before 7 December 1941, failures in judgment, of commission, or of omission, all of these failures combined constitute something quite minor as compared with the failure of the Army Interceptor Command on Oahu."[47]

Kimmel's statement is much longer and in the first person. No doubt the admiral played a large part in its preparation. Richmond thought that Kimmel read it to the court himself, although the record does not show one way or the other. He began by denying the rumor that he had been given command of the Fleet because he was a crony of Roosevelt's, and he went into the circumstances of his retirement. He summarized the weaknesses of Pearl Harbor, local plans for defense, his manpower problem, and other aspects of command.

He conceded "deficiencies in the equipment which the Army needed to exercise its proper function" to defend Pearl Harbor. But he declared forcefully: ". . . the Army was charged with and made responsible for the defense of the fleet base at Pearl Harbor." For emphasis he added, "No orders or instructions issued at any time lessened or mitigated the Army's responsibility for such defense."

He tore into the Roberts report with its accusation of dereliction of duty. "I solemnly deny the truth of these charges," declared Kimmel. "I am satisfied

---

*Richmond did not recall precisely but thought Hart probably read it in Stark's stead. (Interview with Richmond, November 1, 1977.)

that the evidence before this Court establishes beyond doubt the inaccuracy of these charges." The substance of his plea was this: "In brief, in the light of the information I had, and the means at hand, I adopted the measures I did, not lightly, but in the exercise of my most considered judgment, supported and sustained by a group of distinguished and experienced officers who represented a cross-section of the best naval brains in the world."[48]

In many respects Bloch's statement is the most remarkable of the three. His attorneys had done their homework well. The statement is formidably footnoted, giving the source of each point made, either from the testimony or the appropriate document. Bloch was present but, his statement being couched in the third person, one cannot be sure whether he or one of his counsels read it.

Bloch's statement was a public relations masterpiece of self-justification and self-presentation. His attitude toward the admirals on the court blended flattery and a subtle assumption of fellowship with a delicate stressing of their responsibilities. "Hindsight . . . cannot be permitted to influence the factual reconstruction. Speculation . . . as to what any one believes he would have done at the time, should not distort our perspective." His next words reminded his hearers that they were all old sailors together: "It is quite certain that there is not a man in this room who, granted the choice, would not have cheerfully traded his life to have prevented—indeed, even to have minimized—the tragic events of that forenoon." Again he reminded the court of its awesome responsibilities:

> It goes without saying that the findings must be supported by clear and convincing evidence, which leads exclusively to and is consistent with but one single conclusion. . . . Your report will be public opinion; public opinion can strip an individual of his reputation and honor.
>
> Hence, the preparation of your report is a serious duty and when completed and approved the Service, and ultimately the public, will recognize that "the moving finger writes, and having writ, moves on; nor all our piety nor wit shall lure it back to cancel half a line, nor all our tears wash out a word of it."

Just what the admirals made of being lectured on their duties by an officer who as an "interested party" was more or less in the dock, they kept to themselves.

Like Stark and Kimmel, Bloch stressed "the undiluted primary responsibility of the Army to defend and protect Pearl Harbor. . . . It was never more than a limited responsibility of the Navy to support the Army with what it happened to have present at the base in case of attack." Having no information independent of that of Kimmel, "he had no basis from dissenting from the decisions of the Commander-in-Chief in regard to distant reconnaissance." His statement ended:

> During the period in question Rear Admiral Bloch did not seek to avoid responsibilities which were his. He does not do so now. With what he had at

the time, Rear Admiral Bloch did all that anyone could do. Of the courses of action open to him, he took those prompted by good judgment—and he fully and conscientiously performed his every duty.[49]

In short, Bloch's position was a sort of hurt surprise that anyone could blame him for anything or even consider him an "interested party."

The court's judge advocate, Biesemeier, did not believe "it would serve any useful purpose for him, at this time, to make any argument" based on the "very voluminous" evidence.[50] Inasmuch as none of the "interested parties" wanted any argument either—in any sense of the word—the investigation ended on this, its thirty-third day.

CHAPTER 74

"WE

HAVE

A JOB

TO DO"

The Army Pearl Harbor Board had somewhat different problems from Admiral Murfin and his group. For one thing, the Hawaiian Department had been responsible for the defense of the U.S. Pacific Fleet in Pearl Harbor. The members of the board knew this before they met and during the investigation made no attempt to prove or even hint otherwise. But no one could say, in effect, "The Hawaiian Department failed to perform its mission; therefore, the Hawaiian Department is solely responsible for the disaster at Pearl Harbor." The case was not that simple. Modifying factors such as the Navy's responsibility for long-range aerial reconnaissance complicated the problem. The relationships between the Hawaiian Department and the War Department as well as the international situation in 1941 offered potentially fertile fields for investigation. Above all, the board had to try to determine why and how the Japanese could have caught such a competent, conscientious general as Short so far off base.

A fundamental difference obtained in the conduct of the Army board and the Navy court because of dissimilar regulations. At the Navy court the "interested parties" were authorized to attend all hearings, listen to all testimony, have counsel, and cross-examine. In marked contrast, Short could not hear the proceedings of the Army board, had no cross-examining privilege, and was permitted counsel only when testifying. His counsel, Brigadier General T. H. Green, could not sit in during the testimony of other witnesses or cross-examine them.[1] This was not because anyone wished to be less than just to Short. As the names of the bodies imply, the Navy held a court, the Army convened a board. For this reason the Navy inquiry clung rather closely to its own bailiwick and allowed relatively little hearsay or profitless and irrelevant speculation.

One cannot say as much for the Army board. It did not rebuke hearsay, and it encouraged speculation. Investigative mirages lured the members into deserts of arid inquiry. Still, if the Army board took a broad-gauge approach in its hearings, its actual record is in pleasing contrast with the Navy court's. One knows exactly who is speaking. Corrections in the text are entered in the proper place. Each day's session begins with a cover sheet listing the witnesses of the day and the documents placed in evidence.

Not being a court of inquiry, the board members were "not bound by the ordinary rules of evidence." At the same time, as Russell remarked, "What we may do may be a precedent for a long time or may have an influence on things for a long while, and we have got to go about it cautiously and not make any mistakes." They feared the extension of the statute of limitations might be illegal, waiver or no waiver.

The generals realized that in any case time had them in a nutcracker. "I think probably if a bunch of lawyers got together they could laugh this all off and call it a bunch of poppycock," said Grunert. "But we have a job to do and if you won't do it before the act expires, what will the charge of the press be? 'Whitewash, and by direction.' " Grunert added, "We could swear ourselves blue in the face that we never received any directive or influence of any kind but they would say it was dragged out until the thing was over."

Colonel Charles W. West was the board's recorder. He and his staff corresponded to the counsel and staff of a comparable civilian group, such as the later joint congressional committee. He pointed out another pitfall: "I think we can easily spend two or three months until November 8th . . . and yet I know you would be accused of putting the thing off until after the election. If you rush in and do the job in sixty days you will be accused of not doing a thorough job, as the Roberts Commission."[2] So in all likelihood no illusion of emerging as folk heroes animated these officers as they commenced the hearings on Monday, August 7, 1944, in Marshall's office in the Pentagon.

Grunert explained to the Chief of Staff that in view of the limited time to cover a large field, individual members had been assigned certain "objectives or phases of inquiry," although the entire board would pass upon them. Russell had been assigned to the War Department aspects. With this introduction Russell took over the questioning.[3]

Presently Marshall asked for "about 10 minutes of a closed session." His estimate fell far short; they remained closeted for fifty-seven minutes. During that time Marshall briefed the three generals on Magic, cautioning them that its compromise would seriously limit "military success and the saving of American lives. . . ." Marshall's later testimony makes it clear that during this closed session of August 7 he went into specifics. In this off-the-record briefing he spoke only to the three actual members of the board.[4] So here was an incongruous situation—West and his associates were supposed to assist the board in assessing the whys and wherefores of Pearl Harbor, yet they were denied knowledge of a vital category of information.

On Tuesday, August 8, the board met in the Munitions Building, where it had established its base of operations. The first witness was Brigadier General John L. McKee, who in the latter part of 1941 had handled matters in the War Plans Division concerning Hawaii. At that time the defense of the Hawaiian Coastal Frontier was assigned Category D, which "did not visualize a major attack . . . which would result in the occupation of the area by a hostile force." Category D did include "raids, air attacks, and blocking of channels" with reconnaissance "by surface craft, submarine, or carrier-based aviation."

McKee did not believe that placing long-distance reconnaissance under the Navy relieved Short of all responsibility for aerial scouting. If the Navy commander did not act, McKee saw "no reason why the Army Commander could not inaugurate reconnaissance on his own responsibility. . . . He had the means." Frank inquired, "If he conducts distant air reconnaissance, his carrying capacity is taken up with gasoline instead of bombs, and he finds something, what is he going to do about it?" McKee remarked, "He could certainly have alerted his antiaircraft artillery, and the troops could have assumed their defense positions. . . ."[5]

After the noon break General Hap Arnold, Chief of the Army Air Corps, took the stand. He explained that the Army Air Corps had never considered the joint plans for defending Hawaii sound. Its staff feared that the Hawaiian Air Force would waste B-17s on reconnaissance, and when the time came to use them as a striking force, they would not be available. Thus, Arnold echoed Kimmel's save-the-planes-for-combat rationale. Arnold had no use for Hawaii's command-by-cooperation arrangement. "In our opinion, there never was any clear-cut line there as to the duties of the Army and the Navy as far as the air was concerned, because the air overlaps both."

He quoted Rainbow 5, the basic war plan, which instructed Short: "Hold Oahu against attacks by land, sea, and air forces, and against hostile sympathizers." Arnold added, "No strings attached. So Rainbow 5, as I understand, was in conflict with the joint agreement." In his opinion, "under Rainbow 5, and with the instructions received from General Marshall, the Commanding General, Hawaiian Department, had sufficient authority to extend his reconnaissance anywhere he wanted to."[6]

After Arnold came General Herron, who had preceded Short in command of the Hawaiian Department. A discussion of his alert held in the summer of 1940 brought out that he had only one type: "a total alert."* Still, he thought that in any event the Japanese could have done considerable damage, although the Army would have "knocked down a lot of their planes. . . . That was what we were there for, to . . . defend the ships and the harbor. Whether or not we saved our own planes was not important relatively."[7] Herron seems to have been one of the few witnesses before any Pearl Harbor investigation who understood that weapons of war exist primarily for use when needed, not to be kept safe for their intrinsic value.

---

*See Chapter 5.

Another excellent witness followed Herron—his former chief of staff, Major General Philip Hayes. He related that when notified of the economic freeze against Japan in the summer of 1941, Short "decided to go into maneuver positions which were battle positions, had press releases made out so that they could be given to the evening paper, to the effect that the Hawaiian Department was taking the field for a 10-day maneuver period." Thus, he had initiated an all-out alert upon the pretext of maneuvers.[8] This was positive thinking and makes all the more puzzling his failure to do the same thing in the much more acute crisis of November 1941. His actions in the summer of that year demonstrate that he could have gone on full alert without unduly alarming the population.

Altogether Short had a tough two-man act to follow when he came center stage before the Army board. His testimony occupied all of Friday and Saturday, August 11 and 12. Much of it concerns facts already dealt with in this study. To his fellow generals he stressed the extent of his reliance upon the Navy, revealing an exaggerated idea of the Navy's scouting. He seems to have been sure the Navy conducted reconnaissance for about 300 miles in each direction as "part of the task force exercise" whenever Kimmel had a task force out. "I knew that they were doing that kind of work constantly." Of course, he realized that full coverage was impossible.

He had the impression that Navy reconnaissance under the agreement was from the task forces, Midway, Johnston, Wake, and probably Panama. "But none was going out from Oahu?" Russell asked. Short answered, "No; I don't think so, because it would have been a big waste of planes."[9] The statement demonstrates that Short misunderstood the type of reconnaissance that Kimmel's task forces were undertaking. Moreover, he was so sure of himself in this respect that he did not realize he was confused and therefore did not seek clarification from Kimmel or Bloch.

In spite of the urgency of the hour, he and Kimmel had held no formal conferences about the warning messages of November 27. However, they exchanged dispatches and "talked the thing over. . . ." That prompted Grunert to ask, "Did you discuss with the Navy whether they considered your Army Alert No. 1 was sufficient?" Short retorted arrogantly, "I didn't ask them whether they considered it. I told them that was what we were on."[10]

He declared that if he had taken measures "to meet any eventuality," he would have acted counter to the instructions not to alarm the public, disclose intent, or provoke Japan. In evident perplexity and exasperation, Grunert remarked, "They [the people of Oahu] knew that the Army was kept over there to defend the island. Are they [the Army] supposed to be impotent and not to be trusted to take ammunition out? I cannot understand the psychology." Short insisted that with the newspapers "writing scare headlines," for the Army to have taken out live ammunition would have been exactly what the War Department told it not to do.[11] This demonstrates again that Short seized upon the negative aspects of his instructions rather than take positive action to protect the Fleet.

In a brief windup session on August 12 Short displayed distrust or ignorance about the functions of fighter aircraft. He admitted that if he had been on Alert No. 3, the damage might have been less. But he did not believe that it "would have kept those low-flying planes from getting in, because the antiaircraft was almost helpless against them. . . ." Short did not say what might have happened to "those low-flying planes" had his aircraft been able to pounce on them as they flew over Oahu. A little later Short took his leave, thanking the board "for very courteous treatment."[12]

Short's testimony does not display him in a favorable light. Certainly one could expect him to make the best possible case for himself, but his defenses leave a poor impression. One sees the picture of an energetic, capable officer very much at home with the technical side of his job but lacking in imagination and the qualities of leadership. What is more, he was surprisingly dependent upon others—the War Department to spell out exactly what he should do, the Navy to warn him of approaching danger. Yet he did not try to determine upon how firm a foundation that trust rested, evidently fearing that he might upset the delicate balance of Army-Navy cooperation.

Short had plenty of company in his reliance upon the Navy for advance warning. For one, General Mollison, who testified on Tuesday, August 15, had "every confidence" that the Navy would inform him if any enemy came near Hawaii. And Mollison agreed with Short's decision to go to Alert No. 1.* He did not think a more stringent alert would have put them in a better position to meet the attack. The only exception would have been that the Japanese "disabled a good many planes on the ground that perhaps might have been unhurt or undamaged if we had had them in dispersed positions."[13] Of course, that was quite an exception.

A refreshing witness took the stand on Thursday, August 17. In 1941 Lieutenant Colonel H. E. Brooks, then a captain, had commanded a field artillery battery at Schofield Barracks. When Grunert asked if his family knew "what to do in case of an attack," Brooks replied disconcertingly, "My wife knew she had to go to the hospital and have a baby right away." He and his family did not fear an attack on Oahu. "We were too dumb to realize that they might hit the Island. . . ." He gave the board valuable insights into the thinking of the junior officers on Oahu. General Frank asked him whether "there must have been some sort of an apprehension among the high command of an attack on the Island?" Brooks declared, ". . . If there was apprehension it was not evident to us. As a matter of fact, it was just the other way."

This prompted Frank to probe deeper. "There was nothing said or done to develop a warmindedness in the command?" he asked. "That is right, sir," said Brooks. And he added, " . . . In fact, because it was in the tropics we did very little work in the afternoon. It was just the opposite of a warlike attitude."[14] His

---

*See Chapter 50.

comment provides one clue to the Pearl Harbor riddle—psychological unpreparedness.

When Admiral Pye appeared that day, August 17, he seemed to realize that the Army board might have some very different ideas about Pearl Harbor from those of the Navy court. In particular he approached the subject of long-distance air patrols with the wariness of a cat weaving along a shelf of bric-a-brac. He insisted that even after he assumed command of the Fleet, he "had nothing whatsoever to do with it." Russell could not quite accept that: "When you put your ships into the Port at Pearl Harbor, you did not lose interest in the possibility of their being destroyed, I am sure." Pye countered, "I didn't lose interest in that. I lost confidence in the people whose job it was." The CinCPAC had overall responsibility, the commandant of the 14th Naval District had charge of the planes, and Bellinger was under him. "Those are the three who had direct responsibility for reconnaissance."[15] One wonders if Pye realized how damning his testimony really was.

Once more Lieutenant Colonel Kermit Tyler had to prod his unpleasant memories of December 7. His story brought out the absence of anyone in the Information Center to evaluate sightings. "Well, why were you there at all?" asked Russell. Tyler replied ingenuously, "Sir, I really don't know." Grunert recapitulated the situation:

> . . . there seemed to be a lack of organization and common sense and reason on this. You went up there to do duty as a pursuit officer in the information center. There was nobody to do the work with, because the controller was not there, and the Navy liaison man wasn't there . . . and then, at the end of the tour, at 7 o'clock, everybody disappeared except the telephone operator and you. . . .

In apparent disgust, he asked Tyler, "You had no particular duty, did you?" Tyler answered, "No, sir; we hadn't." Thereupon Grunert announced to the world at large, "It seems all 'cock-eyed,' to me—and that, on the record, too."[16] This appears to be as accurate a summation of the Hawaiian Department's Information Center on December 7 as one could hope for.

Thus far the board's record reveals a pattern of courteous, if close, give-and-take. But henceforth little flames of temper and frustration flicker through the transcript. The next witness virtually asked for trouble at the hands of an increasingly unhappy board. When Phillips took the stand on Friday, August 18, Grunert drilled at once into essentials. "Can you tell me the primary mission of the Army in Hawaii?"

This most rudimentary of questions seems to have struck Phillips broadside, for he immediately assumed a defensive posture. Queries about the alerts also sent him off into the protective underbrush.[17] Frank mentioned that Army dogma was to "consider the worst thing that the enemy can do to you, and make your decision to meet it." He queried, "Do you feel that that was done in this case?" This initiated a verbal folk dance with Frank and Phillips skipping in and out of the circle. "You just will not answer that question, will you?" asked the exasperated Frank.[18]

Grunert tried hard to discover why, in the face of warnings of attack, the Army dwelt only on sabotage. Phillips took refuge in statistics: "We had 165,000 Japanese there." That was not good enough for Grunert: "Were they not sort of a bugaboo?" he queried. But Phillips clung to his position like a bat to a cliff.[19]

Throughout the investigation Grunert would return again and again to the vexing question of the Hawaiian Department's obsession with sabotage. He seemed to feel instinctively that if he could resolve this problem, he would have fitted into position a large piece of the Pearl Harbor puzzle. Unfortunately his quest was doomed because he was trying to dissect an emotion under the microscope of logic. And of all emotions, fear is one of the least susceptible to such analysis.

When Colonel Throckmorton took the stand on August 21, he shed an almost embarrassingly vivid light on the spadework for the Joint Coastal Defense agreement. ". . . considerable pressure had to be brought to get the Navy to sit down at a table with us and actually put the framework of the joint agreement into writing and then get Admiral Bloch to sign it," he told Grunert. This was during Herron's tenure, when Throckmorton was G-3. Eventually he suggested that the Army write the agreement and submit it to the Navy. The Navy liaison officer was "delighted" with this. "So the Army wrote the agreement without the aid of the Navy." Throckmorton took it to Pearl Harbor, "and, with just a few minor changes, Admiral Bloch signed it. . . ."[20] This example of the let-George-do-it mentality leaves one wondering just how well Bloch understood what he signed.

The board had its chance to evaluate Bloch on Tuesday, August 22. He added no new points to his testimony before the Navy court and proved as elusive as the Loch Ness monster. He was even obscure about the phrase "This is a war warning." He had never heard it used to begin a dispatch. "The obvious conclusion is that that is naval phraseology, and it is not naval phraseology insofar as I know." That was not all. According to Bloch, "the term 'defensive deployment' has never been used in any textbooks, tactical books, or tactical instructions and orders that I know of, in the Navy."[21] One receives the impression that any instructions not couched in "naval phraseology" or included in standard naval textbooks ranked with Babylonian cuneiform as something no bluff old salt could be expected to master.

The board secured a more detailed picture when Bellinger took the stand on Thursday, August 24. He described the "normal procedure for vitalizing" the Naval Base Defense Air Force: Bloch would send out a dispatch, which included the word "drill," of an air raid on Pearl Harbor. "This placed the search-and-attack groups in a functioning status." Bellinger in turn ordered all aircraft placed "in the highest degree of readiness. At this point . . . searches were immediately started. . . ."[22] If Bloch was the individual to activate the Naval Base Defense Air Force for a drill, he certainly was the one responsible for doing so in a genuine crisis situation such as that signaled by the "war warning" of November 27 or the presence of an enemy submarine in the Pearl Harbor operating area early in the morning of December 7, 1941.

Kimmel was the last witness the board heard before it left for the West Coast. He appeared on Friday, August 25, accompanied by Hanify. The board plunged into the relationship between Kimmel and Bloch in the important area of long-distance reconnaissance. Kimmel explained that when Bloch "agreed to this plan he had been informed that he would eventually have 109 patrol planes assigned to him and that the Army would have something on the order of 200 flying fortresses. . . ." This attitude of pie-in-the-sky does not gibe with Kimmel's statement that the joint defense plan "was a realistic plan based on what was available. . . ."[23]

As the questioning drew to a close, Grunert offered Kimmel the opportunity to make any further statement of say "anything that you want to bring to the Board's attention." That was all Kimmel needed. Out popped the cork: "Since Pearl Harbor information has come to my knowledge that vital information in the hands of the War and Navy Departments was not supplied to responsible officers . . ." on Oahu. "I am further certain that several days prior to 7 December, 1941, there was information in the War Department and the Navy Department that Japan would attack the United States and, very probably, that the attack would be directed against the fleet at Pearl Harbor, among other places. . . ." Kimmel further declared "that there was information in the War and Navy Departments on 6 December, 1941, that the hour of the attack was momentarily imminent, and that early on 7 December, 1941, the precise time of the attack was known. . . ." Kimmel added bitterly, "All this information was denied to General Short and to me."[24]

Of course, the board knew about the Magic items from Marshall's briefing. But they had never heard anyone say that Washington had information which indicated an attack on Pearl Harbor, much less "the precise time" of the strike. This was a quantum leap into a new dimension. The board was scheduled to leave for San Francisco to conduct hearings at the Presidio, but it immediately began laying groundwork to prepare for its invasion of this fresh territory. It asked for Marshall to reappear when the board returned to Washington and requested of the State Department that Grew be made available as a witness. It also sought from Hull information "as to the truth or falsity" of the statement that on November 26, 1941, the United States had delivered "an ultimatum" to Japan. This Hull firmly denied.[25]

Thus, approximately midway in its inquiry the Army board broadened its range considerably. It had to decide whether the Pearl Harbor attack had been the inevitable outcome of State Department diplomacy. It had to ponder the meaning or lack of meaning in the "winds" complications. And it had to determine whether the War Department really had definitive indications of a forthcoming attack on Pearl Harbor which Marshall and his staff withheld from Short, from either stupidity or malice. If all of Kimmel's allegations proved true, how would this affect Short's position? Would the extenuating circumstances outweigh the failed mission, or would the stain of disgrace spread without fading?

The board opened hearings at the Presidio in San Francisco on Tuesday, August 29, with General Martin. Grunert seemed almost overcome by the contrast between the solid, realistic Martin-Bellinger Report and the action Short's command took upon receipt of the warning of November 27. "Here you make an estimate and you seem to hit it right on the nose as to what actually did happen, and then when the time comes you pay no attention to that. You say, 'I am afraid of sabotage.' " Martin explained that from the information Short had, "he was not of the impression that they were alarmed about an attack on the Hawaiian Islands." Exasperated, Grunert repeated, "Then what are you out there for? You are out there as an outpost, aren't you?"[26]

The last major witness of the day was Colonel Donegan. As Short's G-3 in the latter part of 1941, he should have provided valuable insights, but he was both reluctant and belligerent. When asked about Phillips's competence as chief of staff, Donegan fluttered, "I would rather not answer. We have been warned on this thing. . . ." He was equally reluctant concerning Fielder: "I would rather not discuss personalities." Evidently annoyed, Grunert shot back, "Well, discuss officialities, then. Officially, was he considered O.K.?" Donegan's reply told plenty: "As far as I know, he was as good a G-2 as I was a G-3."[27]

Most of the hearings in the Presidio were a dead loss in solving the mystery of Pearl Harbor. But the pace picked up once the board reached Oahu. Questioning at Fort Shafter began on Friday, September 8, with Major General Henry T. Burgin, who had commanded the Coast Artillery under Short. Burgin spoke of the difficulty in obtaining ammunition from its custodians. Grunert retorted that guns were "no good without ammunition" and wanted to know what warning had been anticipated. This varied, said Burgin, "but six hours was considered to be the maximum." He explained further, "There were no instructions forbidding the antiaircraft or any other outfit from having the ammunition, but it was just impossible to pry the ammunition loose from the Ordnance, the G-4's, or from General Short himself."[28]

The next morning, Saturday, September 9, a real collector's item came before the board. Frank H. Locey, who in 1941 had been president of the Board of Forestry and Agriculture for Hawaii, had worked closely with Short and admired him greatly. ". . . I think that General Short was a savior to this country on December 7th," Locey said extravagantly. He distrusted the local Japanese so much that he called any talk of statehood for Hawaii "the most asinine thing I ever heard." Evidently his principal reason was the possibility that Hawaii might send a Japanese-American to Congress—an idea which obviously he rated a disaster second only to Moana Loa's blowing its top. "Now the Japs started to crawl into our House of Representatives. . . . Then one crawled into the Senate. . . . Why, Goddamit, if we got statehood, some day we would have a Japanese governor and a couple of Japanese delegates in Washington."[29] One would like to picture the board smiling after Locey departed, breathing figurative fire and brimstone. Unfortunately at least one of its findings revealed some contamination from the digs of Locey and a few others.

Shivers, formerly in charge of the FBI in Honolulu, took the stand on September 12. Surprisingly he established himself as one of the Pearl Harbor myth makers. In the first place, he thought the maps captured after the attack revealed that Japanese submarines had been in Pearl Harbor prior to the strike. He also believed that the Japanese had hit *Utah* in mistake for *Saratoga* because the maps showed the carrier in that position. And he asserted:

> If we had been able to get the messages that were sent to Japan by the Japanese consul, we would have known, or we could have reasonably assumed, that the attack would come, somewhere, on December 7; because, if you recall, this system of signals that was devised by . . . Otto Kuehn for the Japanese consul general simply included the period from December 1 to December 6.[30]

His comment proves that even an experienced FBI agent is not immune to misinterpretation of the material in hand.

For the next few days the board slogged through a morass of basically irrelevant material. Then it returned to San Francisco for two more days of hearings at the Presidio. It concluded its business there on Thursday, September 21, and headed east. Meanwhile, Stimson devoted considerable time and attention to preparing his testimony. His assistant, Robert Patterson, reported that Roosevelt "was worried for fear there would be an adverse report by the Grunert Committee just before election. . . . The President rather characteristically isn't worried at all about the Navy inquiry but is worried about the Army and was anxious to have the termination of the inquiry postponed until after Election."

Once more Roosevelt's keenly developed political instinct collided with the secretary's equally acute sense of justice and legality. Stimson thought that "any attempt to approach the Board would be sure to be fraught with great criticism, and justly."[31]

He devoted the morning of September 26 to his testimony. Typically he started off by stressing that after the investigation he would have "a quasi-judicial duty" to ascertain what procedures the facts might justify. Therefore, "by becoming a witness, I have to 'watch my step' very carefully that I do not get into a position of advocacy or bias toward any person who may afterwards be proceeded against or concerned with the action which your report may recommend." At first he had wondered whether he "could properly appear at all" but had decided that the board was entitled to the facts he could give it.[32]

Later Stimson wrote in his diary his impressions of the two-and-a-half-hour hearing. He "sensed a feeling of questioning, not to say criticism, in the attitude of the Board as we opened, although they did nothing that was at all unfair." Then, as the session proceeded and "the full impact" of notes covering the weeks preceding Pearl Harbor "got in their work," he thought "the attitude of the Board showed reassurement as to the situation. At any rate, I did my best to give them everything, although of course one always feels after such an engagement that he might have done better."[33]

As events moved rapidly forward, Marshall worried increasingly about the security of Magic. In September he learned "that it was the purpose of the Republican party, in the campaign that was then in progress, to launch a detailed attack on the Administration in connection with the Pearl Harbor incident."[34] This Republican ploy held explosive military possibilities. What particularly alarmed Marshall was a tip-off "that the question of cracking the Japanese codes might become involved in the campaign. . . ." Appalled at the prospect, Marshall decided on a bold move. Gambling upon the patriotism and good sense of Governor Thomas E. Dewey of New York, Republican candidate for President, Marshall determined to appeal to him to protect the all-important Magic secret.

In the utmost secrecy, without informing either Roosevelt or Stimson, he wrote to Dewey, laying the problem on the line in the frankest terms. He described the Magic machine and explained that "our main basis of information regarding Hitler's intentions in Europe is obtained from Baron Oshima's messages from Berlin reporting his interviews with Hitler and other officials to the Japanese Government. These are still in the codes involved in the Pearl Harbor events." He went on urgently: "You will understand from the foregoing the utterly tragic consequences if the present political debates regarding Pearl Harbor disclose to the enemy, German or Jap, any suspicion of the vital sources of information we possess. . . ." In view of the seriousness of the problem, Marshall added, "I am presenting this matter to you in the hope that you will see your way clear to avoid the tragic results with which we are now threatened in the present political campaign."[35]

Dewey decided to go along with Marshall. Later, when this story broke, some of Dewey's more ardent supporters hailed his action as "one of the most extraordinary examples of patriotism and self-restraint that's ever been exhibited, because it was tantamount to giving up his chance to become President of the United States."[36] This reaction was more partisan than logical, for one may hazard the guess that had Dewey blown Magic while the war was in progress, he could not have been elected dogcatcher of Point Barrow, let alone President of the United States.

Unaware of this dramatic development, the Army board settled back into its Munitions Building command post and plugged away at extracting pertinent information from its witnesses. On September 27 the board questioned former Ambassador Grew. By far the most important part of his testimony pertained to the Hull Note.* He expressed his view of that document in terms no one could possibly misunderstand: "It was in no sense an ultimatum, either in tone or substance."[37] If the board had dropped the subject there, much future controversy could have been avoided. However, Colonel Harry A. Toulmin,

---

*See Chapter 49.

Jr., the board's executive officer, asked, "What do you think, then, Mr. Grew, was the motivating cause and incident that brought about the decision of Japan to go to war? At what time do you think factually something occurred that committed them to this course of action?" Grew replied, ". . . it has always been my belief that it was about the time of the receipt of Mr. Hull's memorandum of November 26 that the button was touched."[38]

Meanwhile, Short had received a transcript of the Roberts Commission and what was available of the Army board's record. On September 29 he wrote to Stimson: "I fail to find a disclosure of certain vital information which high Washington officials appear to have had prior to December 7, 1941, of the imminence of an attack by the Japanese. . . ." Citing certain actions, he continued forcefully:

> The facts upon which these actions and statements were based clearly go to the very essence of the present inquiry. I believe, therefore, that you will readily agree that a full and complete disclosure of all the information which was in the hands of Washington officials prior to December 7, 1941, with regard to the imminence of an attack, should be obtained and made a matter of record in the proceedings of the current investigation. . . . [39]

Like Kimmel, Short was coming out of his corner slugging. In fact, the entire situation was boiling toward a climax. That afternoon, Friday, September 29, Short appeared for his second hearing, accompanied by his counsel, General Green. Evidently Short had sought this session. He referred to Kimmel's statement, which he was sure the admiral would not have made "unless he had factual data to corroborate it." Short also produced a copy of his letter to Stimson. After a bit of reviewing of previous evidence, the board dismissed Short.[40]

At Grunert's direction, West read into the record an interesting exchange. On August 11 Short had written to ask for a transcript of the testimony—his own and that of others taken to date. Grunert recommended that the first request be granted, the second denied, because of "the danger of publicity, the granting to one witness what is denied to others, and the possible jumping to conclusions as to the Board's report. . . ." Grunert was willing to allow Short or Green access to exhibits, but at the board's headquarters, with the understanding that the exhibits were to remain with the board. However, the War Department, through Green to Short, granted the latter's request.[41]

Obviously a trend was developing—a curious one which might be termed openness within security. Hence, when Marshall testified again on the same crammed-full September 29, the session was top secret but on the record. Marshall appeared more self-confident and at ease than before. This time he could work from the letter the board had sent him on August 31, concerning the items in Kimmel's statement. Marshall's precise mind seems to have been more at home with a clearly established plan of approach than in answering questions off the cuff. Grunert asked the key one of this session: "Do you consider that the Commanding General of the Hawaiian Department was furnished with sufficient information from the War Department on which he could reasonably and intelligently base a decision as to the defensive measures that he should take to meet any probable eventuality?" Marshall answered firmly, "I do."[42]

After leaving the Pentagon on October 2, the board held no more sessions until Friday, October 6, at which time it closed its hearings. But documents sizzled back and forth between the board and the War Department. On October 2 Stimson replied to Short's letter of 27, informing the general that he might "rest assured that the Board is exploring all sources bearing upon the subject. . . . I am directing General Grunert to permit your Military Counsel to examine its exhibits in the presence of a member of the Board. No copies of these exhibits, however, may be made." Deputy Chief of Staff McNarney forwarded this correspondence to the board on October 3. The same day Grunert wrote back to McNarney a letter exuding alarm for the security of the highly classified documents involved. After explaining the board's measures for protecting these items, Grunert requested "authority to withhold from General Short and his counsel the records referred to, both as to copies of transcripts of testimony and exhibits." The next day McNarney replied stiffly, ". . . the Secretary of War thoroughly considered this question prior to his reply to General Short and is not disposed to reverse his considered opinion."

Grunert impressed upon Green the significance of Magic and warned him "that General Short has not been granted the authority to know what has been disclosed to you in this warning to you nor to be informed of what you glean by an examination of the secret records and files."[43]

With this the Magic story reached the apex of absurdity. The imagination boggles at the picture of a counsel granted access to evidence he was not at liberty to discuss with his client. The almost neurotic concern for the security of Magic licked like a sullen tongue of flame through the pre-Pearl Harbor period and the postattack investigations. And in the nature of fire, it threw off smoke. By early autumn of 1944 Short knew that Washington was withholding something. Naturally he suspected that this was evidence damaging to the government, hence favorable to him.

The War Department would have been well advised at this time to take Short into its confidence, as the Navy Department had Kimmel in connection with the Navy court. Not even his harshest critic ever questioned Short's integrity and patriotism or considered him a security risk, and as a retired officer he was still subject to military justice. But fear is not conducive to cool reason.

CHAPTER 75

"ERRORS

OF

JUDGMENT"

The report of the Army board was of great concern to the War Department. Marshall recalled that it arrived at headquarters on the day Brigadier General Thomas T. Handy replaced McNarney as deputy chief of staff, and they "were both together at the time." Marshall asked Handy, "Have you a copy of that that I can read?" Instead of turning over the report, Handy explained its "general nature" and told Marshall of the "strictures" against him. Marshall informed the congressional committee that Handy "advised me not to read it because I was implicated in the statements of the board for various derelictions and therefore, as that would be a concern of mine and I was Chief of Staff, he thought the whole matter should be handled entirely on the Secretary of War side of the Department, the civil side, and therefore . . . I did not read it."[1]

In its report the Army board announced self-righteously that it had been "conscious of the deep spiritual and moral obligation, as well as its professional and patriotic duty, to present an impartial and judicial investigation and report." It claimed to have "set out with no thesis to prove, nor person to convict. Our approach has been, we hope, diligently and completely factual; and also equally impartial."[2] It did not quite achieve this laudable end. Its report reveals a deep bias against the War Department and against prewar government policy in general.

The second chapter dealt with background, drawing a sketch of events in 1940 and 1941 which leaves the impression that everyone in the United States was sticking straws in his or her hair:

> The winds of public opinion were blowing in all directions; isolationists and nationalists were struggling for predominance; public opinion was both against war and clamoring for reprisal against Japan; we were negotiating for

peace with Japan, and simultaneously applying economic sanctions that led only to war. . . .

Such was the confusion of men and events, largely unorganized for appropriate action and helpless before a strong course of events, that ran away with the situation and prematurely plunged us into war.[3]

The report was by no means devoid of sense; indeed, it contained much solid fare. Perhaps the board's most unfortunate error was the serious misinterpretation of Grew's testimony pertaining to the Hull Note. The report referred to this as "the document that touched the button that started the war, as Ambassador Grew so aptly expressed it."[4] As we have seen, Grew said nothing of the kind.

The board labored under another, related misapprehension. It believed that the Japanese had timed the Pearl Harbor attack

as an answer to our counter proposals of November 26, which the Japanese considered an ultimatum; because it was on or after the delivery of that document against which General Marshall and Admiral Stark warned too late, that the task force of Japan that attacked Hawaii moved out of its rendezvous at Tankan Bay on the 27th or 28th of November to launch the attack. . . . [5]

The reader knows that Nagumo's task force sortied on the morning of November 26, local time,* well before Hull presented his note to Nomura and Kurusu.

The board was equally mistaken about certain aspects of the situation on Oahu. The members gave far more credit to the German sleeper spy, Otto Kuehn, than he deserved:

. . . the Otto Kuehn trial revealed his complete disclosure of the fleet dispositions and locations in Pearl Harbor in the period December 1 to December 6. . . .

Undoubtedly the information of the alert, the placing of planes wing-to-wing, etc., as well as the disposition of the fleet was reported by Kuehn through the Japanese Consul. . . . [6]

On the basis of two maps salvaged from midget submarines, the board deduced erroneously that:

. . . the Japanese must have been in the harbor a few days before the attack and evidently were moving in and out of the harbor at will. . . . As the ships actually in the harbor on December 7th were somewhat different from those shown on the map, it is conclusive proof that this submarine was in the harbor and probably advising the fleet of Japan as to our dispositions prior to December 7th.

The report rambled on about very interesting but irrelevant material pertaining to construction in the Hawaiian Islands and took several unwarranted digs

---

*See Chapter 48.

at the local Japanese. While conceding that Short had erred in concentrating upon sabotage, the report offered a unique rationale:

> It is obvious that the reason why the Japanese aliens did not commit sabotage was that they did not want to stimulate American activity to stop their espionage and intern them. . . . Short appears to have completely misapprehended the situation, the psychology and intention of the enemy, by putting into effect his sabotage alert.[7]

Along with this complacent assurance of its ability to read the collective mind of the alien Japanese in Hawaii, the board expressed an equally astounding political opinion: ". . . we permitted the introduction into the population of the islands of Japanese, to the extent of 30% of the total population or 160,000." Inasmuch as the first generation of immigrants, the Issei, at that time totaled only about 37,500, one wonders how the United States could have screened out the remainder who had arrived in Hawaii via the maternity wards. The board also remarked, with an air of grievance, "This policy of encouraging the Japanese and permitting them to become dominant in the affairs of the island has even gone so far as to permit the Japanese to become important political factors with membership in both the Senate and House of Hawaii, and to dominate, by way of majority, the Island governing councils in some of the islands. . . ."[8] It is difficult to believe that the generals realized the implications of their words. Any Japanese-American in Hawaii had the right of every citizen to vote and to be elected to public office.

The board concluded, "The extent of the Pearl Harbor disaster was due primarily to two causes. . . ." The first was Short's failure "adequately to alert his command for war. . . ." The second was the War Department's failure to direct Short "to take an adequate alert, and the failure to keep him adequately informed as to the developments of the United States-Japanese negotiations, which in turn might have caused him to change from the inadequate alert to the adequate one." The report assigned tangential responsibility to Hull because his action "in delivering the counterproposals of November 26, 1941, was used by the Japanese as the signal to begin the war by the attack on Pearl Harbor."

Of the three officers blamed, Short came off best. Primarily the board decided that he had failed to

> place his command in a state of readiness for war in the face of a war warning. . . . The information which he had was incomplete and confusing but it was sufficient to warn him of the tense relations between our government and the Japanese Empire and that hostilities might be momentarily expected. This required that he guard against surprise to the extent possible and make ready his command so that it might be employed to the maximum and in time against the worst form of attack that the enemy might launch.

Short also failed to have reached an agreement with Kimmel and Bloch to implement the existing plan for joint action, to inform himself of the effectiveness of the Navy's long-distance reconnaissance, and to "replace inefficient staff officers."[9]

Marshall took a far heavier pounding. In brief, the board faulted him for his failure to have kept his three deputy chiefs of staff fully informed, to have kept Short abreast of the international situation "and the probable outbreak of war at any time," and to have acted on Short's reply to the warning message of November 27. They also held him blameworthy for delay in sending Short "important information" on December 6 and 7 and his "admitted lack of knowledge of the condition of readiness of the Hawaiian Command" during November and December 1941.[10]

Gerow fared even worse. The former chief of War Plans had been pulled out of his command of the Fifth Corps in Luxembourg to testify and was grilled mercilessly, especially by Russell, whose lengthy questioning was stringent to the point of hostility.[11] The board criticized Gerow "for drafting the confusing message of November 27," then failing to follow through on Short's unsatisfactory reply; for failing to determine the Hawaiian Department's "state of readiness" following the warning; and for assuming that this famous message gave Short "all the information he needed for full preparation for war" without determining "if that was a fact." In the board's opinion Gerow also should have corrected "Short's mistake in going to Alert Number 1 instead of to Alerts Number 2 and 3," and he should have directed immediate activation of the Joint Hawaiian Coastal Defense Plan.[12]

In a separate top secret memorandum for Stimson the board dealt with the highly classified matters it had considered. It reached the rather startling conclusion that the State, War, and Navy departments in November and December 1941

> had a reasonably complete disclosure of the Japanese plans and intentions, and were in a position to know what were the Japanese potential moves that were scheduled by them against the United States. . . .
>
> The messages actually sent to Hawaii by either the Army or Navy gave only a small fraction on this information. No direction was given the Hawaiian Department based upon this information except the "Do-Don't" message of November 27, 1941. . . . [13]

The board cited specifically the Japanese deadline date of November 29; the known concentration of Japanese fleet units; the establishment of the "winds" codes; the code destruction dispatch of December 3; and the fourteen-part and "one o'clock" messages.[14] It accepted Safford's account of the alleged "winds execute," saying, "This original message has now disappeared from the Navy files and cannot be found."[15]

Stimson's assistant Harvey Bundy telephoned a summary of the Army board's findings to Stimson on the weekend of October 21–22. And it was "a very poor report according to Bundy. . . ." It posed "a big problem" for the secretary. "While I am not criticized explicitly in the report, the report does criticize Marshall and Gerow for things that I knew about and participated in and I have got therefore to be very careful not to be biased in the action I take."[16]

The Navy court's report was definitely protective of the Hawaiian command. It declared that Kimmel and Short had been "personal friends" who conferred frequently. "Each was informed of measures being undertaken by the other in the defense of the Base to a degree sufficient for all useful purposes." The report dwelt upon extenuating circumstances, such as the demand for men and munitions exceeding the national supply. "Although shortages were inevitable, it is a further fact that they had direct bearing upon the effectiveness of the defense of Pearl Harbor."[17]

There had been no misunderstanding on the part of the Army and Navy that the "defense of a permanent naval base is the direct responsibility of the Army. The Navy is expected to assist with the means provided the naval district. . . ." In the case of naval districts outside the continental United States, the commandant was, in addition to the usual duties of that position, "an officer of the Fleet." This was "the circumstance that links the Commander-in-Chief, Pacific Fleet, with the duty of assisting the Army in defending the permanent naval base of Pearl Harbor."[18] This officially relieved Bloch of responsibility but left Kimmel dangling on the hook. The court hastened to repair the damage. Local defense plans were sound. But their effectiveness

> depended entirely upon advance knowledge that an attack was to be expected within narrow limits of time and the plans were drawn with this as a premise. It was not possible for the Commander-in-Chief of the Fleet to make Fleet planes permanently available to the Naval Base Defense Officer, because of his own lack of planes, pilots, and crews and because of the demands of the Fleet in connection with Fleet operations at sea.[19]

The court blessed and approved the conditions of readiness in effect aboard ship in Pearl Harbor on December 7 and stronly supported Kimmel's decision not to institute long-range reconnaissance. "Where planes are not available to cover all sectors," the report observed, "the selection of the sectors to be covered is left purely to chance. . . ."[20] This was an astounding assessment. There is such a thing as an informed, well-considered estimate of action to be taken.

The court would not go into details of "certain other important information" for security reasons. Stark's stand, it stated, was that the war warning "completely covered the situation. The fact remains, however, that this message, standing alone, could not convey to the commanders in the field the picture as it was seen in Washington."[21]

The court mildly scolded Stark for "having important information in his possession during this critical period, especially on the morning of 7 December," which he failed to transmit to Kimmel.[22] But a little later it declared that even if Stark had phoned the warning message of December 7 in plain language, "there was no action open to Admiral Kimmel which could have stopped the attack or which could have had other than negligible bearing upon its outcome."[23] Such fatalism was worthy of a Muslim bowing to the will of Allah or a Hindu untouchable resigned to his karma. It accorded ill with the bracing Occidental tenet that the Lord helps those who help themselves.

The document wended its way to the predestined conclusion: "Finally, . . . the Court is of the opinion that no offenses have been committed nor serious blame incurred on the part of any person or persons in the naval service." And it recommended "that no further proceedings be had in the matter." All told, the report gives the impression that the members of the court tried very hard to convince themselves and their readers that with minor exceptions, the entire U.S. Navy had been the helpless victim of circumstances. Over the report brood the gray ghosts of two sentences: "The attack of 7 December 1941, on Pearl Harbor, delivered under the circumstances then existing, was unpreventable. When it would take place was unpredictable."[24]

Naturally the fact that the War and Navy departments did not immediately release the results of their respective investigations aroused a storm of criticism. From Boston Rugg pronounced, "This inconsistent and dilatory procedure is unjust to Admiral Kimmel. He is entitled to hear the verdict of the court promptly." Robert R. Reynolds of North Carolina, chairman of the Senate Military Affairs Committee, saw no reason for the secret classification. "There are too damn many secrets," he declared vigorously. "It looks to me like it's time for the American people to know how Pearl Harbor happened. The Japanese certainly know and the only reason for keeping anything secret is to keep it from the enemy."[25]

Stimson would have to wait almost a month before receiving The Judge Advocate General's recommendations, but Gatch hastened to place his legal analysis of the Navy report on record in a first endorsement dated November 2. He had few quarrels with the court's findings. He noted the "apparent contradiction" between the findings against Stark and the final opinion that no serious blame attached to anyone in the Navy. But he thought that this was "not a real incongruity" because "the evidence adduced did not prove that Admiral Stark's failure to transmit the information in question to Admiral Kimmel was the proximate cause of the damage suffered by the Fleet on 7 December, 1941. . . ." So, subject to his comments, Gatch found the report "legal."[26]

King, too, wasted no time in forwarding the report to Secretary of the Navy James V. Forrestal. Obviously no one on the uniformed side of the Navy Department wanted to be responsible for delaying the report beyond election day. In a separate letter of November 3 King furnished his comments concerning the security problems involved. He stated unequivocally that the top secret volume of the proceedings "must not be made public." And he preferred to release none of the report. Publication of abridged findings could only have "undesirable results." In brief, King wanted the Navy Department to sit tight and reveal nothing, letting the political chips fall where they might.[27] His attitude made considerable sense. In the field and on the high seas American officers and men were laying their lives on the line. The least their superiors in Washington could do was keep faith with them and take all possible precautions to guard the precious Magic secret.

By second endorsement of November 6 King concurred in the findings, opinions, and recommendations of the court subject to Gatch's opinion and his own remarks. He agreed with some of the findings, disagreed with others. He concurred that there was "not adequate evidence to support general court martial proceedings, but this does not bar administrative action, if such action is found appropriate." Then came the big admission: "Despite the evidence that no naval officer was at fault to a degree likely to result in conviction if brought to trial, nevertheless the Navy cannot evade a share of responsibility for the Pearl Harbor incident. That disaster cannot be regarded as an 'act of God,' beyond human power to prevent or mitigate." King concluded sternly:

> The derelictions on the part of Admiral Stark and Admiral Kimmel were faults of omission rather than faults of commission. In the case in question, they indicate lack of the superior judgment necessary for exercising command commensurate with their rank and their assigned duties, rather than culpable inefficiency.
>
> . . . Since trial by general court martial is not warranted by the evidence adduced, appropriate administrative action would appear to be the relegation of both of these officers to positions in which lack of superior judgment may not result in future errors.[28]

On November 11 Stimson talked "a little bit" about the Army report with Marshall for the first time. Three days later the secretary found the Chief of Staff experiencing an uncharacteristic but natural letdown of morale. "As usual he was so modest that he admitted to me that he thought his usefulness to the Army had been destroyed by this Board's report. . . . I told him that was nonsense, to forget it. But he was very grateful for the work I had done on it and the fight that I was making for him."

Later that day Stimson and Forrestal had "a long talk" about the reports and rather optimistically concluded "that we were not very far apart and that there was to be no clash between the standards and views of the two Departments. . . ."[29]

A fundamental question plagued both departments—how much, if anything, to reveal concerning the findings and conclusions of these inquiries. On November 20 for the first time Stimson brought into the case his public relations officer, Major General Alexander Surles, who had been on leave. The principal problems were the swipes at Marshall and Gerow. Marshall presented a special case. Not only did Stimson consider the criticism of his Chief of Staff totally unjustified, but he also saw in Marshall "the strongest man there is in America . . . the one on whom the fate of the war depends. . . ." One can forgive Surles that "his first reaction was to try to keep back the findings." He feared lest the Navy "ride in behind our publicity and escape it themselves and leave us to bear the whole brunt of it." But Stimson convinced him "that if we do not take the initiative ourselves and publish the fact that Marshall has been criticized at the same time with the vindication of it, why it will leak out in a much more disadvantageous way. . . ."[30]

The day after Stimson's conference with Surles, Forrestal landed a haymaker on Stimson's hopes for parallel action. In a phone conversation Forrestal warned that his public statement would be short, and he would send it over. Stimson recorded indignantly: "After all the preliminaries, the preambles, and recitals, it consisted of just one sentence in which he said that . . . it was not in the public interest or something like that to take any proceedings against any naval officers." A sorely troubled man, Stimson took off for the White House.

After lunch the President brought up the subject. "I think the less said the better . . ." he remarked. Stimson explained that the Army "could not afford to go ahead and be frank when the Navy was not being frank." He showed the President the Army board's conclusion, which he read carefully. When he came to the names of those criticized, he exclaimed, "Why, this is wicked; this is wicked." However, "he still adhered to his view that the safer plan was to follow as nearly as possible the Forrestal method." Stimson expressed his fear "that Congress could get after us, get at the papers and get at the facts. . . ." To this Roosevelt replied "that we must take every step against that and that we must refuse to make the reports public. He said that they should be sealed up and our opinions put in with them and then a notice made that they should only be opened on a Joint Resolution of both Houses of Congress approved by the President after the war. . . ."

Back at the Pentagon Stimson set his assistants to work drafting a paper more in line with Roosevelt's desires. But it would "say at least that we believe there have been delinquencies in the War Department and also that Short was guilty of delinquency."[31]

The secretary of war flew to Highhold on the afternoon of Friday, November 24. On the way he dug into The Judge Advocate General's critique of the Army board report. Stimson called it "really a humdinger. . . ."[32]

Even Flaubert would have acknowledged that "humdinger" was *le mot juste*. Cramer had a gift of pithy expression. He made a very important point which seems to have been generally overlooked: "Short is in a dilemna [*sic*] in contending that distant reconnaissance was a Navy responsibility . . . because it only became a Navy responsibility if and when the Joint Army and Navy Agreement was put into effect. Yet Short made no effort to put it into effect, even in part."[33] Because the Navy never made this obvious defense for its own failure to institute long-distance air patrols, this particular responsibility appears to have changed hands by a sort of tacit agreement.

The top secret portion of the report did not impress Cramer from the standpoint of evidence. He called it "mainly a collection of conclusions by the Board" based upon transcripts and exhibits. "These references in turn indicate that the testimony given by the witnesses consists largely of their conclusions or evaluations of certain intercepts. . . . Moreover, the quantum of the information thus received by the War Department and not sent to Short has been magnified out of all proportion. . . ."[34] Cramer believed that "while there was more information in Washington than Short had, Short had enough information to indicate to any responsible commander that there was an outside threat against which he should make preparations." But he believed that Short's mistakes "were honest ones, not the result of any conscious fault, and having in mind all the circumstances, do not constitute a criminal neglect of duty."[35]

With the strictures against Marshall, Cramer disagreed totally. In the case of Gerow, he agreed with some, but not all, of the board's criticisms. He added, "The nature of the errors and the fact that he has since demonstrated his great qualifications for field command indicate that his case is now far removed from disciplinary action."[36] This may seem a non sequitur, but it made better sense than the ridiculous action the Navy took in Stark's case—proclaiming as unfit for high command an officer who had served with a large degree of competence in a top job throughout the war.

Cramer saw nothing to be gained by court-martialing Short even after circumstances permitted such a trial. So he suggested a statement by Stimson "pointing out that General Short was guilty of errors of judgment, for which he was properly removed from command, and that this constitutes sufficient disposition of the matter at this time."[37]

Thus, the Army and Navy investigations had not solved the Pearl Harbor puzzle. They had produced much valuable evidence, but their reports with the resulting legal opinions and suggestions had only dumped a large problem upon their respective departments. With the exception of its mild strictures against Stark, the Navy court blamed nobody. Of course, one was at liberty to read between the lines and decide that inasmuch as the naval establishment on Oahu was without spot or blemish, the fault must lie with the Army. At the opposite end of the scale, the Army board swung at Marshall, Gerow, and Short and even glancingly at Hull.

Nor had the upper-level evaluations helped matters much. King bracketed Kimmel with Stark as blameworthy but recommended that Forrestal maintain secrecy beyond a parallel statement with Stimson. Cramer exculpated Marshall, recommended no action against Gerow, and suggested that Stimson issue a statement to the effect that Short, while he had erred, had been punished enough. It would take all the considerable skill of Stimson, Forrestal, and their advisers to reconcile the apparently irreconcilable.

For Stimson November 30 "was a red letter successful day because at last after all these pullings and haulings we have got the first step of the Pearl Harbor report settled." Forrestal had reworked his draft while the War Department had made some changes in its own. That afternoon Forrestal and Stimson phoned Roosevelt at Warm Springs, Georgia, and received his authority to release the two statements simultaneously "within the next two or three days." Although relieved, Stimson feared that this was not "a final settlement. . . ." He thought "it was a great mistake not to go into a frank full statement of what had happened and what we have done. . . ."[38]

There is little doubt that Roosevelt mismanaged the release of the

Army-Navy statements. Stimson had been correct. Never famous for the common touch, he nevertheless had an abiding faith in the basic nobility of the American people, an assurance that they would act as they should once they had the facts. The Roosevelt who so overreacted in his conference with Stimson, urging security measures just short of locking up the reports in Fort Knox, was not the Roosevelt who had established such an understanding dialogue with the electorate for so many years. Today, knowing that death awaited him in fewer than five months, one can see that illness had already taken a toll of his sharp reflexes and political acumen. He should have dealt frankly with the public, as Stimson wished to do, and should have insisted that Forrestal do the same. Marshall, Gerow, and Stark needed no coddling, Kimmel and Short had nothing to lose, and Roosevelt would not have placed his administration in such an equivocal position.

Forrestal returned the Navy court's report to that body by third endorsement on December 1: ". . . I find that the evidence obtained to date indicates that there were errors of judgment on the part of Admiral Kimmel and Admiral Stark. I am not satisfied, however, that the investigation has gone to the point of exhaustion of all possible evidence." He directed further investigation, specifically to include the testimony of Wilkinson and McCollum. Forrestal added that he was withholding his decision on any proceedings against any naval officer pending completion of this additional investigation.[39]

The findings of the court gave the signal loud and clear to exonerate Kimmel, had Forrestal been so inclined. Indeed, had he accepted the legality of the findings—and Gatch had so certified—he would have had little choice. It was King who flung the monkey wrench into the machinery by linking Kimmel with Stark as blameworthy, a conclusion he could scarcely avoid in logic. The Pearl Harbor debacle had been far too serious to permit every American naval officer involved to escape judgment. If everyone had done just as he should, why had the Japanese won so signal a victory? Still, Forrestal's public statement was mild enough:

> The net result of the findings of fact and opinion of the Pearl Harbor court of inquiry, as reviewed . . . is that the evidence now available does not warrant and will not support the trial by general court martial of any person or persons in the naval service.
>
> The Secretary . . . has found that there were errors of judgment on the part of certain officers in the naval service, both at Pearl Harbor and at Washington.[40]

Stimson followed Cramer's advice and in his statement of December 1 took Short off the hook:

> So far as the Commanding General of the Hawaiian Department is concerned, I am of the opinion that his errors of judgment were of such a nature as to demand his relief from a Command status. This was done on January 11, 1942, and in itself is a serious result for any officer with a long record of excellent service, and conscientious as I believe General Short to be. In my judgment, on the evidence now recorded, it is sufficient action.[41]

These statements were all very well up to a point, but both left much territory untouched. Certain lawmakers took up the cudgels. Senator Ferguson, whose resolution had set the twin investigations in motion, clearly was dissatisfied with the fruit that ripened from the seed he had planted. "The question in the public mind is this: How could it happen that our fleet could be sunk and our boys would be killed at Pearl Harbor without any one's being to blame?" Thereupon he called for "a full dress senate investigation."[42]

The joint press releases represented an important breakthrough in the Pearl Harbor story. Newspapers picture Kimmel as "smiling and obviously in good spirits" while Short's "sparkling eyes expressed satisfaction. . . ."[43] Nevertheless, the action could not have entirely satisfied either these men or their ardent supporters. True, there was no mention of that hateful, rankling phrase "dereliction of duty." But a mere announcement that neither man had done anything to warrant court-martial was cold comfort at best. Kimmel and Short could only look hopefully toward exoneration at some future time. From his home in Dallas Short issued a statement to the effect that when the entire story was told, he was "certain of complete vindication in the eyes of the American people." Rugg spoke for Kimmel. He declared that Forrestal's statement had cleared the admiral of charges of dereliction of duty. "When the people have the full facts, they will agree."[44]

Actually, whatever mask of smiling "good spirits" Kimmel presented to the press, he was exceedingly angry over the turn events had taken. In Washington on December 6 and 7 he visited certain members of the court and of the Navy Department. He talked "at some length" with Andrews. The latter believed that Kimmel "would be pleased with every word of the findings," although he did not discuss details. He advised Kimmel "to 'blow the lid off' and publish everything." While Kalbfus gave Kimmel the impression that he thought the latter "was not to blame in this matter," he advised Kimmel "that in view of all the circumstances there was nothing that I could do at the present time, that the war effort came first and that unjust as the action may appear to me or to others, the only thing I could do was to stand and take it."[45]

In his interview with Gatch, Kimmel asked what would happen to him if he "published the story containing the secret matter." Gatch replied, "You would be brought to trial before General Court Martial on charges that you had divulged secret matter and you would be convicted, thereby confusing the whole issue and absolutely discredit [sic] you." If Kimmel published a statement containing no secret information, "the Navy Department would merely state that you are a liar and you would be unable to prove any of your contentions unless you reverted to the secret matter."

Kimmel asked Gatch what assurance he could give "that the record of this court, including the findings, would not be tampered with or destroyed." Gatch told Kimmel that as long as he, Gatch, was The Judge Advocate General, the copy in his safe "would not be tampered with." Kimmel trusted Gatch "but pointed out that he might be relieved at any time and that his successor might be picked with the view of doing away with all or part of this record."[46]

The Husband E. Kimmel who awoke to the dawn of December 7, 1941, would have died rather than knowingly betray any of the classified material entrusted to his care. Now, exactly three years later, he was considering publication of one of the nation's most precious top secrets, with the almost certain result of lengthening the war and costing thousands of lives—and for what? To try to cleanse his name of a charge of "errors of judgment"—a charge from which no human being can ever be entirely free. And this dark picture is made no brighter by the failure of the Navy's top lawyer to point out that in so doing, Kimmel would betray his country and his fellow fighting men, an action infinitely worse than "errors of judgment" at Pearl Harbor.

Earlier in the week King had been reviewing the records and reports of the Army board. He briefed Forrestal thereon by a memorandum dated December 3. All told, he found nothing in the record of the Army board to cause him to modify his opinions in connection with the Navy court

> except in relation to the cooperation between Admiral Kimmel and General Short. . . . I am no longer of the opinion that cooperation between these two officers was adequate in all respects. . . . However, . . . this fault was part and parcel of the general blindness to Japanese potentialities in the Central Pacific which was the basic cause of the Pearl Harbor disaster.

So King still believed that Stark and Kimmel "failed to display the superior judgment they should have brought to bear in analyzing and making use of the information that became available to them."[47]

When Kimmel visited King on the third anniversary of the attack, the Cominch appeared "friendly and sympathetic" toward Kimmel. He "strongly implied" that the court had "completely cleared" Kimmel. Nonetheless, King was sure that the proceedings and findings would not be published before the end of the war. Until that time Kimmel "had no redress. . . ." The Cominch waxed confidential concerning some of the background of the investigations. Roosevelt had "stated that Stark is performing highly valuable services and cannot be spared." Nor could Marshall. King, too, believed Marshall to be "irreplaceable." The Cominch explained that "while the findings were drawn to permit publication," he recommended against that action, believing "that the Japs might be able to deduce the source of the information which is still of great value to the Navy." Among other items of what was obviously a long session, King informed Kimmel that the "further inquiry" being contemplated "had no bearing whatsoever" on Kimmel's action.

Kimmel emerged from the Navy court and particularly its aftermath a confirmed revisionist. "Immediately after Pearl Harbor I felt that no matter how hard and how conscientiously I had tried that I had not been smart enough and to that extent must accept blame for Pearl Harbor. . . . I now refuse to accept any responsibility for the Pearl Harbor catastrophe."[48]

Displeasure with the War and Navy departments' handling of the reports was by no means limited to Kimmel, Short, and their personal supporters. Far from quieting the anti-Roosevelt furor of preelection days, the joint statements of Stimson and Forrestal added to the discord. While avoiding the venom and simplistic conclusions expressed in some newspapers, the Washington *Post* was also unhappy. Dissatisfaction breathed from a lengthy editorial. "The question that springs out from both reports is this: Who were the officers in Washington who failed in their duty?" The *Post* urged: "would it not be possible to eliminate that testimony that might be valuable to the enemy and then let the public have the story?"[49] This illustrated the public relations problem which plagued Washington. To excise from the evidence the information which might be of value to the enemy and still present "the story" to the public would be like Shylock's attempting to cut off his pound of flesh without spilling blood.

There is no question that the Army and Navy inquiries had been a serious burden on the War and Navy departments at a time when their every thought should have centered on winning the war promptly with the least possible cost in lives. Yet the whole exercise had not been without value. For all their faults, the investigations produced records of considerable worth.

In the case of the Roberts Commission, the chief value of its record was the preservation of on-the-spot descriptions of the attack written while memories of the event were still fresh. So, in the Army and Navy investigations, the reports are of secondary importance to the testimony. The former are the work of judgment with a spicing of prejudice. But in the words of the witnesses one begins to experience the atmosphere of preattack Washington and Oahu and to grasp how it all could have come about.

On the military side one finds a strange compartmentalism. The War and Navy departments could not imagine that State Department business could possibly be of direct interest to a field commander. On Oahu the Army and Navy were proud of their "command by cooperation" but quite unable to see the difference between friendly cooperation and the active official coordination necessary for a full team effort in a crisis.

The civilians who testified on Oahu were mostly of the territorial upper crust—intelligent, civil-minded, somewhat paternalistic, and in general tolerant by the standards of the day. Through their words one can visualize the comfortable sense of security engendered by a flower-crowned land blessed—or perhaps slightly cursed—by a climate so benign that it had bred out of its children the prickling awareness of danger. And over all hovers the simple belief of a primarily maritime society in the enveloping protection of the U.S. Pacific Fleet.

CHAPTER 76

"WE WANT

THE TRUTH"

Although unpublished temporarily, neither the Army nor the Navy report concurred in the Roberts Commission's finding of "dereliction of duty" on the part of Kimmel and Short, as the Stimson and Forrestal press releases tacitly indicated. But both reports had left a number of loose ends. Sometime in December 1944 Forrestal asked former CinCUS J. O. Richardson "if he considered himself available to pursue the investigation on Pearl Harbor." Richardson refused on the grounds that he was prejudiced against Roosevelt and Stark, hence had to disqualify himself "as an impartial investigator."[1]

So Forrestal turned to Vice Admiral H. Kent Hewitt, who conducted the supplemental inquiry from May 15 to July 11, 1945. Principally it delved into the everlasting "winds" hassle and considered fresh information concerning the Japanese side which had become available after the Navy Court of Inquiry disbanded. Hewitt was not one of the admirals, such as Halsey, who captured the public imagination, no doubt in part because of his serious, calm personality. During World War II he made a splendid record in amphibious operations. In 1945 he became the commander of the U.S. Eighth Fleet with the rank of full admiral. He knew something about the problems of the U.S. Pacific Fleet, for he had commanded Cruiser Division Eight at the time it transferred with other of Kimmel's ships to the Atlantic in May 1941.[2]* Obviously Forrestal had not dumped this amplifying inquiry into the lap of just any admiral who happened to be available.

---

*See Chapter 15.

Hewitt modestly assumed that he drew the assignment because he was "the first ranking flag officer released from the war zone who had no interest in it, who hadn't been out there at the time, who had no personal interest one way or the other." Normally Hewitt enjoyed a brainteaser, being "one of these double-crostic addicts." But he took no pleasure in this task, which he termed "very disagreeable duty." In fact, Hewitt's designation to conduct this inquiry points up the virtual impossibility of discovering a senior admiral who actually had "no personal interest" in what happened at Pearl Harbor on December 7, 1941. True, Hewitt had not been on the spot, literally or figuratively. But he had been stationed in the Pacific Fleet earlier in that year and inevitably had some preconceived ideas and emotional slants.

For one thing, he had seen "no efforts on the part of the army at that time to be ready to defend the base at Pearl Harbor with anti-aircraft guns." He contrasted the Hawaiian Department's activities, or lack of them, in this regard with those of the Coast Artillery in Panama in 1940. "A year later, in Hawaii, which was much more exposed than Panama to possible enemy attack, no such steps had been taken." More important, Hewitt had served directly under Kimmel and "was very fond of him and a great admirer of him."[3]

Kimmel kept a wary eye on this investigation before and during its progress. On May 8 he requested Forrestal's permission to be present at Hewitt's sessions; "to have counsel, to introduce, examine and cross-examine witnesses; to introduce matter pertaining to the examination; and to testify or declare" in his own behalf. The secretary replied in part on May 15:

> It was decided that the further investigation . . . could be more expeditiously performed if it were conducted without the assistance of those who were designated as interested parties by the Court of Inquiry, and that the best interests of all concerned would be served by the prompt completion of the investigation. . . . Accordingly, I believe that I must refuse your request. Of course, you may testify before Admiral Hewitt to any facts which you have not previously presented, whether it be at his request or on your own initiative.[4]

Thus, Forrestal left the door slightly ajar. His reasoning made considerable sense. If Kimmel did not take advantage of the opportunity to bring forward facts to which he had not previously testified, he tacitly admitted that he had none to present. And if Forrestal accorded Kimmel full rights as an "interested party," in justice he must include the other "interested parties," Stark and Bloch. This would result in a duplicatory rather than supplemental investigation.

During an interview on May 18 Kimmel advised King of Forrestal's action. King "seemed rather disturbed by this" and promised to take it up with the secretary. He also volunteered "that, in his opinion, there was no real need for any further investigation of the Pearl Harbor attack as the points raised were of no real importance and could not affect any decisions made as a result of the

Court of Inquiry." If Kimmel reported King's remarks correctly, one wonders why the Cominch had recommended that same "further investigation."

Kimmel told King "that an unchecked and unrestrained further investigation might be damaging to me; that I would not stand idly by and permit this to happen; and that I propose to take every means in my power to be sure that nothing would be brought out by Hewitt which I was not given an opportunity to refute and to question."

King "felt very keenly" for Kimmel, but the only advice he could give was that Kimmel bide his time and demand a court-martial "at the earliest practicable date."[5] Nowhere in Kimmel's record of his interviews with King following the Navy court is there a hint that King told the former CinCUS that he, King, had officially pointed out to Forrestal that Kimmel was not entirely blameless in connection with Pearl Harbor.

Hewitt "would have been happy to have him [Kimmel] appear, but Forrestal himself ruled against it." Hewitt did not consider himself "in a position to argue with the Secretary of the Navy about it." He would have done so had he believed the matter to be of sufficient importance. But he did not. He had read "very thoroughly" all the records of the previous investigations and did not see how Kimmel "could add anything" to this testimony.[6]

Hewitt had as his counsel John F. Sonnett, special assistant to the secretary of the navy. Later Forrestal described him as "painstaking, careful and *completely loyal* [Forrestal's italics]." The secretary informed President Truman that his report on the Navy court "was very largely based" on Sonnett's research.[7]

Hewitt interviewed thirty-seven witnesses and bore down heavily on Intelligence, questioning such key personnel as Wilkinson, McCollum, Kramer, Rochefort, Safford, Layton, and Mayfield as well as a number of small fish in the intelligence and communications ponds. Twenty-one of Hewitt's witnesses appeared before no other Pearl Harbor investigative body. These included Captain Outerbridge, former skipper of the destroyer *Ward*, and Dorothy Edgers, who translated the controversial "Kita" message of December 3 containing Kuehn's complicated code. In particular, Lieutenant Colonel William F. Friedman, who contributed so much to the breaking of the Japanese Purple code, testified only to Hewitt and the later Clarke inquiry. Thus, the Hewitt investigation brought to light some excellent material on intelligence and added to the growing volume of evidence about Pearl Harbor.

Hewitt opened his inquiry in the Office of the General Board of the Navy Department in Washington on Monday, May 15, 1945. The next day he heard McCollum, one of the two witnesses he had been specifically directed to interview. McCollum explained that by November 1941 the Navy was "almost wholly dependent upon radio intelligence" for the location of Japanese forces.[8] Therefore, when the Japanese Navy changed its call signals, this caused McCollum and his associates much concern, for they interpreted the change "as a possible indication of action to come." The Intelligence unit at Hawaii had the same information as it had in the Navy Department on this score.[9]

McCollum lent no support to the idea of receipt of a "winds execute" involving the United States. After the attack "a dispatch was translated which indicated war with England."[10]

Safford appeared before Hewitt with a persecution complex in full bloom. On Friday, May 11, Sonnett met with Safford, asked him "many questions," and discussed discrepancies between Safford's testimony and that of other witnesses. Safford seemed to distrust Sonnett from this initial encounter.[11]

Hewitt asked the questions when Safford first testified at his inquiry. Safford continued to insist there had been a "winds execute," and he gave the names of a number of people who he claimed had seen it. He remembered "that all hands had been very nervous about our ability to receive this 'winds' execute when it should come in, because we were not certain of the power or the frequency, of the time of anything. . . ." He was full of satisfaction that despite the difficulties, his people "hadn't missed it. We had done our part properly."[12] This rather touching pride of accomplishment may help explain why Safford clung tenaciously to his story. How could he concede that all that skill and dedication had been of little or no value?

The obvious witness to follow Safford was Kramer, whom Safford constantly quoted. Sure enough, Kramer appeared on Tuesday, May 22. But time had modified his memory: "I am now at least under the impression that the message referred to England and possibly the Dutch rather than the United States, although it may have referred to the United States, too."[13]

Hewitt finished his first inquiries in Washington on Friday, May 25, and moved with his assistants to Pearl Harbor. There he set up shop in the Visiting Flag Officers' Office at Pacific Fleet Headquarters. Whereas Hewitt had done the questioning in Washington, Sonnett picked up the ball at Pearl Harbor. The first witness, appearing on May 29 and 30, was Layton. As had McCollum, he stated that the change in Japan's call signs on November 1 and again on December 1 "indicated progressive steps in preparing for active operations on a large scale."[14] This was important because it proved beyond question that the Hawaiian commands had not existed in cloistered withdrawal from the world, helplessly dependent upon Washington for all information on developments in the Pacific. Instead, they had at their disposal vital intelligence pointing to a major Japanese armed venture in the near future.

Hewitt's second "must" witness, Admiral Wilkinson, former director, ONI, came up for questioning on Tuesday, June 5. His testimony made it quite clear that his office had been more or less shunted onto a siding when it came to high-level activities other than intelligence gathering. Responsibility for dissemination of information to the Pacific Fleet "was never fully determined. We issued the reports and the bi-weekly summary of the situation, but I was told that the deductions of future movements were the function of War Plans rather than of Intelligence . . ." explained Wilkinson. "My understanding at the time was, and still is, that I would report to War Plans and the Chief of Naval

Operations the latest operational information deduced from all sources and that they would forward to the fleet such items as they felt should be so forwarded."[15]

Wilkinson was very vague about the "winds" problem. He did not recall who had told him about December 7 that an "execute" came in. "I recall some mention of it, but not until after the attack, but I no longer attributed importance to it since the overt act had occurred."[16]

Hewitt and his colleagues wound up their questioning in Hawaii on June 8 and spent the next day interrogating at San Francisco's Federal Building. On Tuesday, June 19, the inquiry was back in the General Board Offices in Washington. There on Friday, June 22, Safford made his second appearance, with Sonnett doing the questioning. Little of fresh interest emerged.[17]

On Friday, July 6, Kramer was back again, with Sonnett questioning. Kramer left matters in a rather unsatisfactory state. He neither totally contradicted Safford's story nor unequivocally supported it. According to Kramer, some sort of message had come in, but he could not pinpoint its nature exactly.[18]

The last witness before Hewitt was Safford, returning for a third appearance on July 11. This day's questioning dealt primarily with the "hidden code" message received on the morning of December 7. Safford never muted his hostility toward Sonnett.[19] Later he told the congressional committee that Sonnett tried to make him change his testimony and to convince him that he was "suffering from hallucinations." Sonnett crisply labeled this charge "nonsense." He denied any effort on the part of himself or anyone else connected with the Hewitt inquiry to persuade Safford or any other witness to change his testimony.[20]

In later years Hewitt remarked, "Secretary Forrestal had some very set ideas . . . and he wanted me to find things which I couldn't find and didn't find. I think he was disappointed that I didn't make a report in accordance with some of his ideas." Regrettably Hewitt cited no specifics.[21] Actually, whenever Forrestal's long endorsement to the Navy court's and Hewitt's reports noted differences between the two, in general he agreed with Hewitt.[22]

Hewitt's report boils down to twenty-nine conclusions. The principal difference between them and those of the Navy court is that Hewitt could admit that Navy personnel had made mistakes. He paid just tribute to Kimmel as having been "energetic, indefatigable, resourceful, and positive in his efforts to prepare the Fleet for war."[23] But he could not completely exonerate his friend. Despite Stark's "unfortunate" failure to communicate to Kimmel "important information which would have aided him [Kimmel] materially in fully evaluating the seriousness of the situation," Hewitt believed Kimmel "did have sufficient information in his possession to indicate that the situation was unusually serious. . . ."[24]

Among Kimmel's options Hewitt listed establishment of "long distance air reconnaissance, covering the most probable approach sectors to the extent possible," and "a higher condition of anti-aircraft readiness. . . ." He also suggested installation of antitorpedo nets; maintenance of "a striking force at sea in readiness to intercept possible attack forces"; keeping "the maximum force of the Fleet at sea, with entry into port at irregular intervals"; and checking the Army "as to readiness of antiaircraft defenses and aircraft warning installations."[25]

Balancing Safford's testimony against that of other witnesses, Hewitt decided that "no message was intercepted prior to the attack which used the code words relating to the United States."[26]

After reading Hewitt's report, Gatch seems to have begun to back down a bit from his intensely pro-Kimmel attitude. In his second endorsement to King, dated August 10, 9145, he noted that "the responsible officers" had "failed to exercise the discernment and judgment to be expected from officers occupying their positions," in particular "their failure to appreciate, from the information available to them, that Pearl Harbor was a likely target for aerial attack and their failure to take the necessary steps to prevent or minimize such a surprise attack."[27]

He remarked that Kimmel and Short, having "entertained the same fallacious views," would only have reinforced these errors through more contacts. He did not believe there was "sufficient evidence to warrant conviction of any of the officers concerned of any offense known to naval law." It would be impossible to prove either neglect of duty or culpable inefficiency "as the acts of omission of these officers do not rise above the status of errors of judgment." Still, he believed the Navy "morally obligated to order Admiral Kimmel tried by court-martial" should Kimmel insist.[28] By third endorsement dated August 12, 1945, King concurred in general with Hewitt's findings and with Gatch's recommendations.[29]

Kimmel came to feel much animosity toward Hewitt; but many years later he decided that he had misjudged him, and he was big enough to admit it to Hewitt in writing. Nothing could exceed the cordiality with which Hewitt received Kimmel's "welcome letter."[30] Thus, in their twilight years these two admirals relaunched their friendship in sunny waters.

In evaluating the findings of the Navy court and Hewitt's investigation, Forrestal reached a stern decision: Stark and Kimmel, "particularly during the period from 27 November to 7 December, 1941, failed to demonstrate the superior judgment for exercising command commensurate with their rank and assigned duties." Accordingly he directed that neither should hold any position in the Navy requiring "the exercise of superior judgment."[31] Thus, Forrestal gave Stark no such support as Stimson had given Marshall.

Stimson was even less happy with the Army board than Forrestal was with the Navy court. He decided to continue his inquiry "until all the facts are made as clear as possible and until the testimony of every witness in possession of material facts can be obtained. . . ." Behind this cautiously worded statement was Safford's testimony. He had mentioned a number of officers who should be able to shed light on the "winds execute" message. Obviously someone from the Army should talk with the Army people involved.

Furthermore, "the whole subject of magic . . . being opened up in the final week of the board proceedings" meant that someone should question again all those who had testified before the Army board "at a time when they were under compulsion not to reveal the details of magic and ask them all about magic."[32]

Clearly, for the entire board to reconduct the hearings would be impractical. Yet someone would have to do the job. Stimson settled upon Major Henry C. Clausen, assistant recorder of the Army board. To the congressional committee, Clausen modestly stated that the Army had selected him from among those connected with the board "because I was the fellow they could spare the most."[33] It is unlikely this was the only reason Stimson tabbed him. The secretary had an excellent eye for a good man and could recognize efficiency when he saw it. Clausen had worked his way through high school and law school and practiced for a number of years in California. In June 1942 he volunteered for the Army, which sent him as a captain to The Judge Advocate General Department, where he remained for more than three years. Clausen's judicious gaze reflected the astute lawyer which he was. Something in his eyes also revealed a touch of the mystic, a quality which led him to become a deeply committed Freemason of the thirty-third Degree.[34]

In many ways Clausen's investigation paralleled Hewitt's: Clausen was to concern himself principally with the Army; Hewitt, with the Navy. They could interrogate each other's people if the lines crossed.[35] To be certain that his precept gave him all the authority he would need, Clausen himself wrote his enabling memorandum, which Stimson signed. This document could scarcely have been broader. Not only did it require witnesses to answer Clausen's questions, but it also directed them to volunteer any pertinent information they might have. Moreover, it specifically overrode any existing security directives so that Clausen could receive copies of any documents he might require.[36]

Clausen consulted in a general way with Harvey Bundy, Stimson's special assistant, about "the most feasible way of getting the facts in an accurate, objective and impartial method. . . ." Clausen had "always liked the way the FBI would get the statements from the witnesses," then examine them on the basis of their statements. So he and Bundy agreed that he should "receive the evidence in the form of affidavits."[37]

This mission aroused considerable subsequent suspicion. But regardless of retrospective likes and dislikes, Clausen traveled more than 55,000 miles by air from November 23, 1944, to September 12, 1945, interviewing ninety-two people, forty-three of whom testified before him. Seven more gave him signed statements. Of these, thirty are not on record before any other investigation. These range from MacArthur to Chief Ship's Clerk Theodore Emmanuel, who maintained the telephone tap on the Japanese consulate in Honolulu.[38]

Clausen recorded no verbatim oral testimony. His method was to type an affidavit based upon his conference with each witness. Having completed the affidavit, he would talk with the witness again and go over the affidavit point by point. One reason he used this procedure was to enable those interviewed to revise and correct their statements in their own handwriting. Thanks to his memorandum of authorization from Stimson and the backing of G-2, the witnesses cooperated fully.[39]

As a result, a veritable harvest of intelligence material poured out of the Clausen transcript like fruits from a cornucopia: Hawaiian Department G-2 "Estimates of the Situation"; military attaché reports; dozens of valuable intercepts; FBI reports; current documentation concerning the Japanese consulate at Honolulu, replete with information about the espionage activities therein; data about Kuehn and his spying for Japan.

Meanwhile, another Army inquiry was under way, "pursuant to oral instructions of the Chief of Staff, U.S. Army." From September 14 to 16, 1944, and again from July 13 to August 4, 1945, Colonel Carter W. Clarke checked up on matters "concerning handling of certain Top Secret documents." At the time Clarke was deputy chief of the Military Intelligence Service.[40] Marshall ordered this investigation at the recommendation of Major General Clayton Bissell, the G-2. There was "so much confusion over the handling of the records and what the records were with regard to the time of receipt, transmission and so forth, that he thought it was advisable to have an investigation to reduce this down to as exact a statement as they could get. . . ."[41]

Stimson's diary entry for May 18, 1944, indicates that certain rumors had reached the State Department and the Congress concerning handling of Army records:

> Senator Styles Bridges of New Hampshire came to ask about the destruction of records by our G-2. . . . The Senators have gotten worried for fear we are destroying records. It is a ridiculous thing. All that we were doing was to be cleaning up the old records of G-2, none of which were complete and which were very greatly encumbering the work of the Bureau.

Stimson called in McNarney, and they satisfied Bridges, who had come "in a friendly way" and would "help against the Senators who might otherwise have blatted about it to the press." Of course, such periodic weedings were absolutely necessary if the nation's defense forces were not to founder in a sea of paper. But this incident might have aroused suspicion in quarters ready and eager to be suspicious.

With the help of the inquiry's counsel, Lieutenant Colonel Ernest W. Gibson, Clarke conducted his sessions rather informally, some in round-table style. Nevertheless, "All the testimony taken was stenographically reported and transcribed." He interviewed twelve witnesses, including Miles and Bratton. The latter's testimony throws much light on his own position, his relationship to Magic, and the handling of the Magic material. Clarke's inquiry also contributes to an understanding of what went on in the War Department on the morning of December 7, 1941.

The Clarke material is essential to an evaluation of the thorny "winds" controversy. This inquiry pertained mainly to that debate and to the possibility that a "winds execute" had come in and later been destroyed. In his concise, intelligent summation, Clarke reported that he found "that no written message implementing the Winds Code message was ever received by G-2, and . . . that no records pertaining to Pearl Harbor had been destroyed by G-2 or by anybody connected with G-2."[42] That should have helped lay the myth to rest, but it did not. The revisionists kept the thesis of the "winds execute" and the Washington "cover-up" alive and kicking for years.

Kimmel watched all developments concerning Pearl Harbor with a jaundiced eye. Convinced of his own innocence, he lived, worked, and planned with unremitting, almost obsessed persistence for the day of complete vindication. Both he and Short regarded the prospect of eventual court-martial as much less a threat than a promise. They would have welcomed the opportunity to confront a clear-cut issue and put their case to a jury of their peers.[43] But Magic held both of them locked behind an invisible barrier. After the service investigations Kimmel and Short must have understood perfectly why courts-martial were out of the question until the conflict had ended. When they joined their country's service, they fully realized that they might be called upon to die for it. One might have expected them to shoulder the temporary burden of full blame as their silent contribution to victory.

But Kimmel was no willing sacrificial lamb. As keenly as a frontiersman scouting for game, he watched for any opportunity to state his case. On March 31, 1945, his searchlight eye discovered on page 5 of the New York *Herald Tribune* a small Associated Press dispatch headed "Military Secrets Bill Offered." Datelined the previous day from Washington, it read:

> A penalty of $10,000 or ten years in prison could be imposed for disclosure of state or military secrets under a bill introduced today by Senator Elbert D. Thomas, Democrat of Utah. The bill would apply to citizens of this or a foreign country who divulged, without permission of the department or agency head, any information regarding codes, coding methods, coded material, or the design or use of military equipment.

This seemingly innocuous proposal rang shrill alarm bells in Kimmel's alert mind.[44] It so happened that in Washington service scuttlebutt had reached Safford's ears that "this bill would block any court-martial of Kimmel and Short, and that was its purpose." Immediately following Pearl Harbor, Safford "had been very bitter against Admiral Kimmel." He thought that the proposed warning which McCollum had prepared on December 4, 1941, had gone to Kimmel. Safford "could not understand how anybody, with the receipt of that information could not have been completely ready for the attack on Pearl Harbor, in fact with his fleet at sea, and Pearl Harbor just an empty nest."

After learning that Kimmel had never received the message, Safford believed that he had done the admiral an injustice and wanted to do "something to make amends." With all the force of his intense nature, Safford swung to the other extreme. He became a fervent supporter of Kimmel's and almost obsessively suspicious of Washington, especially of Stimson and Marshall. So he tipped off Lavender to the gossip about this legislation,[45] officially designated Senate Bill 805, Seventy-ninth Congress, First Session.

Kimmel immediately mailed the *Herald Tribune* article to Rugg in Boston for investigation. A few days later, when Kimmel was in Washington, Rugg telephoned him that the Senate had passed the bill on April 9. "I was desperate," the admiral later wrote Harry E. Barnes, "because if this bill became a law we would have been able to get nothing about the Japanese intercepts in the public record."[46]

In anxious haste Kimmel communicated with a number of his supporters in Congress. He learned that the Senate had passed the bill while Ferguson was in the Caribbean area. Ferguson explained that "he required a unanimous consent for the Senate to reexamine and revote the bill. He was not prepared to offer the required amendments, either to render it innocuous or defeat it, and he therefore contented himself with delay until he could get additional ammunition."

Pending action upon Ferguson's application, the legislation would not go before the House. "Apparently most of the Military Affairs Committee of the House are out of Washington," Kimmel wrote Rugg, "so there will be a respite before the Bill is acted upon unless the agency which has so far succeeded in railroading this measure through is equally as active as it has been." In an attempt "to forestall this contingency," Kimmel met with the Washington *Post*'s publisher, Eugene Meyer; the chief editorial writer, whose name Kimmel could not recall; and the managing editor, Alexander F. Jones. The admiral

> pointed out to them that the press was very much interested in this Bill, that if it became a law the press, the radio commentators and columnists could not publish anything unless they determined that it had never been coded or until they got a clearance from the head of the department who had placed the matter in code. In other words, the government will establish a complete censorship over everything that the press did.

After examining the document, Jones remarked "that if this Bill becomes a law every columnist, including Drew Pearson, will be in jail." Kimmel rejoined rather acidly that he thought "that was the only good feature contained in the bill." Despite Kimmel's low opinion of columnists, Meyer and his associates were grateful to the admiral for calling the legislation to their attention. Kimmel informed Rugg, "This Bill had entirely escaped the notice of the press in Washington, or at least the implications and the provisions of the Bill had not been understood." The admiral credited the publicity which followed his tip-off to the press with the bill's delay and eventual defeat in the House.[47]

On April 12, 1945, General Green sent Short a copy of SB-805, explaining, "Under existing laws and regulations you would be prevented from improperly conveying or publishing secret information while it was secret. This bill would go further and would prevent disclosing any information transmitted or learned through a code whether or not it is still secret." Green had conferred with

Kimmel and Lavender on April 11, and he told Short, "Kimmel was all up in the air. They are undoubtedly responsible for this action." By this Green apparently meant the furor in the morning papers. He added, "In the event you are called upon to make a statement I recommend that you make no comment."

Green further mentioned the Clausen investigation, which was still under way. "The Navy has an Admiral doing the same thing," Green continued. "Obviously, the only purpose is to make good on the promise made by both Secretaries to continue the investigation. I see no danger in this."[48]

If Green intended to reassure Short, he did not succeed. At this time Short labored under a number of misapprehensions which contributed to his exceeding bitterness toward Washington. One of these was the nature of the alleged "winds execute." Short noted: "On December the 5th, 1941, Tokyo broadcast the message, 'East Winds Rain.' In terms of the code this meant an attack on Pearl Harbor." With such notions spooking about his head, it is not surprising that Short believed that the "missing evidence would have placed the responsibility on the White House, and the State, War and Navy Departments." So Short was not disposed to take SB-805 in stride. To his thinking, it "was intended to stifle the Press and hobble Congress. . . . This resolution would have prevented Admiral Kimmel or me or any official who had had access to code messages from testifying in regard to events leading up to the attack at Pearl Harbor."[49]

In Washington matters were working toward a climax of a very different nature. Summoned to the White House at 1746 on April 12, 1945, Stimson and the rest of the Cabinet received word of the death of their President at Warm Springs, Georgia.[50] Roosevelt's passing was a stunning shock for the country. This strong, elusive, debonair, maddening President had been in office for three full terms and part of a fourth term. Naturally his successor was the subject of much curious, rather dubious, even somewhat resentful speculation. Few could have predicted the special place Harry S Truman would enjoy in American hearts and history. Under his guidance the European conflict ended and the war against Japan thundered toward atomic climax. But the nation had by no means forgotten the unfinished business of Pearl Harbor.

Truman favored "complete and full disclosure" and at first Forrestal leaned toward that view. At his request Truman held a conference on the morning of August 29 with many representatives of the War and Navy departments. Apparently Forrestal had pulled back from full disclosure; now he feared that they were "being stampeded in taking action without due consideration." He worried that release of the Navy report, especially King's and his own endorsements, "would tend to prejudice public opinion against Kimmel and might accordingly make more difficult his vindication by general court martial." But Truman wanted the reports released.[51]

That afternoon the reports exploded in the nation's newspapers with a burst of headlines. Although they had to compete with banner stories about the first Allied landings on the Japanese home islands, they held their own on the front pages the next morning. Nothing could more clearly attest the enduring fascination which Pearl Harbor held for press and public.

At "a hurriedly called press conference," Truman issued a statement which included the following:

> You will notice in the Secretary's statement . . . that he takes sharp issue with the criticism of General Marshall, adding that the criticism "is entirely unjustified."
>
> The conclusion of the Secretary of War is that General Marshall acted throughout this matter with his usual "great skill, energy and efficiency." I associate myself whole-heartedly with this expression of the Secretary of War.

What is more, Truman declared, "the country as a whole is basically responsible in that the people were unwilling to take adequate measures to defense [*sic*] until it was too late to repair the consequences of their failure to do so."[52]

Initial reaction to the reports appears to have been virtually unanimous. Editors and officeholders of whatever political persuasion chorused that the full truth had eluded the investigators. It could be found—if at all—only by congressional inquiry or by courts-martial.[53] This time, however, a different spirit pervaded the cries for military trials than had animated those following the Roberts Commission's findings. The Congress and the press wanted justice rather than vengeance.

The Chicago *Tribune* took issue with Truman's judgment that "the country is as much to blame as any individual. . . ." An extremely critical editorial ended with this ominous promise: "TRIBUNE readers are going to know all about Pearl Harbor before we are thru [*sic*]. They will know even if readers of other newspapers don't."[54]

Demands mounted for an end to ambiguity. The documents published had not included the testimony which is available today in the Pearl Harbor documentation; they were only the summarizing reports. Having no way to determine for themselves the logic of the findings, readers naturally wondered how the two inquiries could have produced such different results. The Navy court censured no one except Stark, only mildly at that; the Army board blamed nearly everybody in sight. No wonder that Americans, like Goethe, called for more light. The Honolulu *Advertiser* expressed its dissatisfaction in an excellent editorial:

> The reader is struck by what seems an amazing number of contradictions and quick dismissal of points that appear to lend themselves to deeper and more searching scrutiny. The conclusions . . . are far from satisfactory. They are not clear-cut. They contain innuendos against men, yet they neither condemn nor exonerate them. . . .
>
> The thinking, except in a few places, was sloppy. . . . Such untidiness of national mind is what today prompts the call for a scapegoat. But we want no crucifixions. We want the truth, straight and clear and no double talk. Admiral Kimmel and General Short should have their day in court.[55]

It may seem strange that at this time, with widespread support for his long-held wish for court-martial, Kimmel declined one. On the day before publication of the reports Forrestal at last offered the admiral this opportunity. However, Kimmel thought the conditions unpropitious. He suspected Forrestal of "merely trying to muddy the waters." There seems to be no reason to question Forrestal's good faith. The Navy Department long since had promised the public that when the war ended, Kimmel would be court-martialed. In fact, the secretary had bent over backward by offering the admiral a choice. But Kimmel replied on September 8: "In view of the agitation for a Congressional Investigation before Congress reconvened and the action of the Senate in ordering a joint Congressional Investigation of Pearl Harbor, I wish to defer my reply to your letter of 28 August 1945 until that investigation is completed."[56]

That "agitation" had been inevitable. The investigations following the Roberts Commission shared one fundamental weakness: All were entirely military, hence open to charges of special pleading and of personal bias. Roosevelt had appointed the Roberts Commission; therefore, all these investigative bodies had been instruments of the executive branch. To balance the scales of justice, one thing remained—an all-out investigation by a joint committee of the Congress.

CHAPTER 77

"A

PARTISAN

MATTER"

By early September 1945 a number of anti-New Deal elements had begun to coalesce. On August 31, George H. E. Smith, secretary of the Senate Minority Steering Committee, wrote to the indefatigable Senator Ferguson, with copies to a number of Republican leaders, including Taft. In summary he concluded that "despite the sincerity of all the investigators" of the Army and Navy inquiries, "there is an effort (1) to fasten some blame on a few persons on the lower levels of responsibility; (2) to let all of them off lightly; and (3) to throw as much of the blame as possible on impersonal factors. . . ." Smith conceded, "Gross derelictions of duty are clearly evident all along the line. . . ." In his opinion, however, the political aspects outweighed the "technical."

Smith implored Republican leaders to rattle this "skeleton in the Roosevelt Administration's closet . . . with vigor and determination in season and out." He suggested that it was "not entirely coincidence" that the Army and Navy reports appeared "at the very moment that newspapers are announcing in large headlines that MacArthur lands in Tokyo."[1]

But if headlines may distract attention, as Smith implied, they can also rivet it. So perhaps it was "not entirely coincidence" that the Chicago *Tribune* chose September 2, 1945, to publish a long, acidly antiadministration article from the pen of John T. Flynn, longtime Roosevelt critic. The next day the *Tribune*'s editorial page fairly licked its chops:

> John T. Flynn's report on the Pearl Harbor disaster . . . is the blackest charge ever placed against an American President and his administration. . . . Never before in our history did a President maneuver this country into a war for which it was unprepared, and then, thru [*sic*] insouciant stupidity or worse, permit the enemy to execute a surprise attack costing the lives of 3,000

Americans, an attack of which he and his cabinet members had substantial forewarning 24 hours before.

Apparently the Democrats were quite willing to subject the Pearl Harbor problem to congressional scrutiny. On September 6 Majority Leader Alben W. Barkley of Kentucky announced that Congress should make "its own thorough, impartial, and fearless inquiry. . . ." He wanted a joint Senate-House effort because he feared that separate inquiries might result in disparate reports "which would contribute to further confusion in the minds of the public" and of the Congress. Senator Ferguson had prepared a similar resolution, which he decided not to offer in view of Barkley's action. After some procedural discussion the resolution was adopted in an atmosphere of high-minded nonpartisanship.[2]

The Henderson (Kentucky) *Gleaner and Journal* asserted that with the publication of Flynn's article, "The drift that things have taken was a foregone conclusion. . . ." Kimmel's hometown newspaper had valiantly championed the admiral and Short, but it viewed both Flynn and the upcoming investigation with an unhappy eye. This spunky small-town journal saw what many a high-powered newspaper either failed to see or did not comment upon: Flynn had done no good to Henderson's most famous son.

> The justification of Flynn's investigation was to clear the names of Admiral Kimmel and General Short, but his report is clearly an effort to smear Roosevelt, pushed to such an extreme that Kimmel and Short are totally eclipsed. In fact the overall effect is to harm rather than to help them for Flynn has made it a partisan matter in which a democrat doesn't want to be caught in bed with Flynn.

The *Gleaner and Journal* expected nothing constructive from the congressional inquiry, of which the end result could only be "agitation as eternal as it is useless."[3]

On September 11 Representative Adolph J. Sabath of Illinois presented to the House the Senate's Concurrent Resolution 27. He urged its passage so that "the blame if such there be" might rest "squarely on the blameworthy." In behalf of the other side of the House, Minority Leader Joseph W. Martin, Jr., of Massachusetts expressed gratification with "the almost unanimous support for this congressional investigation"—an inquiry into "too serious a subject to permit of partisanship." There ensued a long debate, in which member after member spoke in favor of the resolution. Controversy swirled not over the investigation, but over the composition of the committee. The Republicans wanted equal representation; the Democrats preferred the usual preponderance of majority members. The Democrats won the issue in a canter, enjoying as they did a comfortable control of the House.[4]

It would be fatuous to pretend that forces other than concern for truth and justice, or even partisan politics, were not at work. While the conflict lasted, power and glamour had centered almost exclusively in the executive branch. What better way to remind the American people of the authority of Congress than a full-scale investigation of a subject in which the public took an avid interest? More than one lawmaker—Harry S. Truman among them—had leaped into the national consciousness by means of such an inquiry. Millions of dollars' worth of free publicity, a national forum to sound off one's views—what politician could resist such a mouth-watering opportunity?

On September 15 the press announced the membership of the joint committee which was to submit its report by January 3, 1946. Speaker of the House Sam Rayburn told reporters that he had "simply picked the best men he could find for the job," selecting the Republican members on the advice of Minority Leader Martin. Rayburn's remarks to the press held a touch of gloom. "It is to be hoped and prayed that there will be no politics in this investigation," he declared, "but . . . and it's a big but."[5]

The ten-member committee consisted of three Democrats and two Republicans each from the Senate and House. Barkley chaired the body. As senator from Kentucky he could have called Kimmel and Bloch his constituents. Later Barkley served as Truman's Vice President, affectionately known as the Veep. Unusually likable and a gifted raconteur, he was to be one of the few Vice Presidents to impress their personalities upon the public without succeeding to the presidency. Barkley was less than delighted with his appointment to the Joint Committee on the Investigation of the Pearl Harbor Attack, for his position as majority floor leader gave him "all the work that any human being ought to be expected to do. . . ." Nevertheless, on the committee he went, and his colleagues unanimously—except for his own vote—elected him chairman.[6]

Senator Walter F. George was another Democratic party war-horse, although no friend of Roosevelt's domestic policies. He wielded enormous authority, being the fourth-ranking senator and the chairman of the powerful Finance Committee. When appointed to the Pearl Harbor committee, he had shown no special interest in the Japanese attack. He had, however, a keen personal interest in the war, for his son Marcus, a Navy flier, had lost his life in the Atlantic. George would not be a very energetic member of the committee. He would ask few questions, and many of these would be of a routine nature.[7]

By comparison with Barkley and George, Senator Scott W. Lucas of Illinois was almost a newcomer. He had been elected to the House in 1934 and moved to the Senate after the November election of 1938. He was a member of the Senate Farm Committee, and although he did not agree with Roosevelt on all matters, he was considered a New Dealer.[8]

Senator Owen Brewster had served two terms as governor of Maine. Then, in 1934, his constituents sent him to the House of Representatives, whence he moved to the Senate in 1941. Destined to be a colorful figure in the Pearl Harbor investigation, Brewster, an ardent Republican, "had pressed for a Pearl Harbor investigation from the beginning" and was to become one of the most energetic and resourceful of all the probers.[9]

Ferguson, the Republican who had pushed through the extensions of the statute of limitations so that Kimmel and Short might have courts-martial, was relatively new to the Senate. He won his first seat on November 3, 1942. His membership in the Institute of Pacific Relations and the Council on Foreign Relations attested to his interest in international affairs.[10] Senator Arthur H. Vandenberg, his colleague from Michigan, praised Ferguson, who as a circuit judge had earned an enviable reputation as a gangbuster in Detroit, "probably the most fearless and effective searcher after truth the Middle West has seen in all its jurisprudence."[11] According to *The New York Times*, "Senator Ferguson's appointment was in recognition of his insistent demands of years for a Pearl Harbor inquiry."[12]

The top selectee from the House, hence slated to be the committee's vice chairman, was Jere Cooper of Tennessee. A middle-of-the-road politician, he was the senior Democrat on the Ways and Means Committee. He had come to Congress in 1929 and been there ever since. His colleagues found him a hard worker and student of government as well as a logical, unemotional man of good faith.[13]

Democrat J. Bayard Clark of North Carolina, with service since 1929, was a member of the House Rules Committee and generally voted on the conservative side. Little known outside the Seventh District of his native state, he did not stand for renomination in 1945. Democrat John W. Murphy of Pennsylvania was in his second term in Congress, having come to the House in 1943. At forty-two, he was comparatively young as congressmen went, but he would prove to be a forceful, keen-minded interrogator.[14]

Gearhart of California stood staunchly on the Republican side. Possessor of an intriguing personality with peculiar quirks and a few zany ideas, he had caused no little controversy with a bill to make Iceland the Forty-ninth state. This interesting bachelor would prove to be one of the most eager of the Republicans during the investigation. No one had a dull moment when Gearhart went into his act.[15]

His colleague was Frank B. Keefe from Wisconsin, who had been in Congress since 1938. Although essentially a conservative, he had a good voting record on social legislation. Fifty-seven at the time of the investigation, he was a physical giant of a man whose sheer size and stentorian voice projected a high charge of energy.[16] Keefe and Gearhart were destined to be indefatigable, persistent questioners. All four congressmen were considered strong supporters of their parties.

Although no member of the committee was a military expert, the group was as well qualified as one might expect under the circumstances. All were experienced legislators; all were lawyers, half of them former prosecutors. Nor were they prejudiced against the military. Of the selectees who had been in Congress when the draft came up for vote in 1941, only one—Keefe—had voted against it. Three members—Lucas, Cooper, and Gearhart—had been department commanders of the American Legion for their respective states.[17] Each brought to the task his own strengths, weaknesses, and prejudices.

The committee selected its chief legal adviser carefully, "counting on its counsel to do the spadework." The first nominee was William D. Mitchell. He had impeccable credentials for such a position. This seventy-one-year-old lawyer had been solicitor general for Coolidge and attorney general in Hoover's Cabinet. Surprisingly, *Who's Who* listed him as a Democrat. This ambiguity did not worry the committee. "Nobody considered his party affiliations," said Ferguson. "We are determined not to have any politics in the investigation."

When Mitchell came from New York to Washington for a meeting, he informed the committee of his wish "to have one thing very definitely understood, that if he developed any facts, regardless of where they led or how they pointed, he was not . . . to have the carpet pulled out from under him when he was proceeding." The lawmakers assured Mitchell "that he would have that authority and that right," nor would the committee "put any brakes upon him. . . ." Moreover, he "had free rein in choosing his own men" for his staff.[18]

For his assistant Mitchell selected Gerhard A. Gesell, son of the famed child psychologist Arnold Gesell. Young Gesell was a bright, practical lawyer who went straight to the point and did not waste his own or anyone else's time. In 1945 he was well launched upon a career destined to culminate in a distinguished judgeship. So he had more profitable ways to spend his days than taking on a thankless job with the congressional committee. But because he knew and respected Mitchell, although only by reputation, he agreed to serve. Being a public-minded individual, he was pleased at the appointment and found the work interesting, if at times frustrating.[19]

To expect a congressional probe of an issue so highly controversial as Pearl Harbor without politics' raising its ugly head was simply not in the cards. One could not look for cordial unanimity to prevail indefinitely in the committee. On November 2 Brewster punctured the investigation's bubble of sweetness and light. It so happened that Truman had issued an executive order to prevent release to the public of information "regarding the past and present status, techniques or procedures, degree of success attained, or any specific results of any cryptanalytic unit activity under the authority of the United States Government or any Department thereof." Of course, this was to ensure the continued protection of the entire cryptanalytic system. But to assist the investigation, on October 23 Truman made "a specific exception" to this:

> The State, War and Navy Departments will make available to the Joint Committee on the investigation of the Pearl Harbor Attack, for such use as the committee may determine, any information in their possession material to the investigation, and will respectively authorize any employee or member of the armed services whose testimony is desired by the committee to testify publicly before the committee concerning any matter pertinent to the investigation.[20]

In effect, this opened all the relevant files to the committee and would bring Magic into the daylight during the hearings. This would seem to be enough to satisfy reasonable expectations. But Brewster claimed that Truman's directive "placed a complete ban on the discussion by any member of the armed services with anyone whatsoever in the field of this investigation. . . ." This interpretation was so farfetched that one can scarcely credit that Brewster reached it by honest misreading. Nor was he satisfied with Truman's exception permitting testimony to the full committee or counsel. The minority members wanted this further amended "so that any officer or other employee of the Government might be free to discuss any phase of the matter with any member of the committee. . . ." Brewster proposed to ask the chairman and counsel "whether an individual member of the committee might examine government records to ascertain their condition, the order in which they have been kept, why certain records are missing, and why certain files have been destroyed, as we have been reliably informed."[21]

In other words, if the minority members had their way, each individual on the committee could become a one-man investigation with the power to confer privately with prospective witnesses and to check any and all government records on his own, reporting or not reporting his findings to the full committee, depending upon his own judgment and the dictates of his conscience.

Ferguson took up the torch in support of Brewster's position. To his credit, he presented to the Senate the Truman order and its amendment verbatim. Considerable talk ensued. Then Barkley remarked, "I doubt whether we would ever be ready to proceed with public hearings, if every member of the committee were authorized separately . . . to bore around in all the departments of Washington. . . ." Senator George thought that Truman would authorize "any agent selected by the committee" to examine papers. And he emphasized, "That is exactly the point in this controversy. There is a great tempest in a teapot here. The committee has all the authority it needs."[22]

On November 6 the minority members presented to the House a virtuoso performance, each yielding to the other at the psychological moment with the smooth timing of a Nureyev-Fonteyn ballet routine. They took up the "winds execute," with the melodramatic charge that Kramer had been "badgered and beset" to change his testimony; the Clausen and Hewitt investigations; and a number of intercepts. Gearhart revealed quite a few misconceptions. "When I speak of Japanese messages, always bear in mind we cracked their codes long ago," he remarked. "We knew everything they were saying to each other." Before Pearl Harbor the United States had by no means broken all of Japan's codes. Then, too, Gearhart boldly declared, "Now every strategist who had been reading these messages, both the Army and Navy officers, immediately interpreted the 1 o'clock directive to mean only one thing—it meant that the first bomb would fall at about 7 o'clock in the morning at Hawaii."[23] This was totally false and gave the House as well as the country an entirely misleading impression. It is difficult to determine whether Gearhart was deliberately exaggerating to build up his case against the administration or whether he honestly misunderstood the situation.

The Republicans on the committee might not approve of Truman's memorandum of authorization, but they took advantage of it. On November 8 Gearhart and Keefe decided to call upon Kramer, who was under treatment at the Bethesda Naval Medical Center. When they reached Bethesda, however, they found that Kramer and his wife had left for the day.[24] KEY PEARL HARBOR WITNESS VANISHES, screamed a four-column heading on the front page of the New York *Journal-American*. In the best James Bond tradition, Keefe told reporters that "we intend to pick up the captain's trail."[25] Actually Kramer and his wife, Mary, had "disappeared" no farther than a brief shopping safari into darkest Washington and were available the next day for "a long interview" with the two congressmen.

Gearhart told reporters that they had found Kramer "very cooperative and gracious." Two days later he informed the press that Kramer was prepared "to tell a story which will prove the charge of the committee minority that intercepted and decoded messages on Dec. 3, 4 and 6, 1941, revealed that war was an immediate certainty, and that Hawaii was the only likely place for the initial blow."

Keefe's turn came again the next day. He alerted the press that he expected to take the floor of the House "to offer proof" that Kramer "was driven into a nervous breakdown and then isolated in detention because he stubbornly proposed to testify to Congress that he carried to the White House on the night of December 6, 1941, a warning that the Japanese would raid Pearl Harbor at sunrise the following morning."[26]

Perhaps Keefe and Gearhart honestly saw themselves as playing admirable roles in this strange drama. A tip-off from someone—unnamed but probably Safford—had delivered into their hands a man who could make it all come true. If Kramer had really told his superiors that Japanese messages pointed to an attack on Pearl Harbor early in the morning of December 7, if he could confirm the receipt and suppression of the "winds execute," if he had been "beset and beleaguered" to become part of a cover-up, the two congressmen would have found the keys to the kingdom. It would mean that the top brass in Washington, including Roosevelt, knew that Japan was going to strike, knew where and when the blow would fall, deliberately withheld the information from Kimmel and Short, then tried to bury the body.

The American people would never forgive nor forget such a sequence of guilt. The Roosevelt legend would be discredited for good and all, and the deluded nation would turn to the Republicans for leadership. No wonder Keefe and Gearhart wanted to nail Kramer into a figurative box and sit on the lid. Whatever their motives, they had done an efficient hatchet job on the captain. They had openly undermined in advance whatever testimony he might give not to their liking.

Sometime during this period Stark invited Kramer to his home, where Stark, Richmond, and Stark's other legal advisers talked with him. Their attitude was this: If Safford was correct in his testimony, they should spread it out in the open air and have done with it. But Kramer specifically stated that he could not share Safford's opinion about the "winds execute" message. So Stark's group let the matter rest there.[27]

Such antics as those of Gearhart, Keefe, and other members of the committee might well remain mercifully buried in the *Congressional Record,* except that they had an unfortunate effect upon the investigation. The high promise of the beginning had fallen, never to be quite recovered; partisan politics and acrimony had entered an inquiry crying for coolheaded, impersonal logic; sterile lines of questioning had opened, destined to waste days, even weeks of valuable time.

Shortly after 1000 on Thursday, November 15, Barkley arose in the high-ceilinged caucus room of the Senate Office Building and gaveled the committee to order.[28] The ornate room had a capacity of about 500, and every available place had been filled long since. The large marble-walled chamber had been hung with visual aids, and an eight-by-ten-foot relief map of Oahu stood near the table around which the committee grouped itself. Kimmel arrived early and secured a front seat, while Short took a strategic position at a table close to the witness chair. Flashbulbs popped; newsreel cameras spun; klieg lights glared; photographers dodged about, seeking the best shots.[29]

After some preliminary skirmishing between the chairman and Senators Brewster and Ferguson, Mitchell opened the official inquiry by offering some startling documentation. The title alone of "Exhibit No. 1" was enough to excite the imagination: "Intercepted Diplomatic Messages Sent by the Japanese Government Between July 1 and December 8, 1941." This material included many exchanges between Tokyo and its embassy at Washington. Now the entire country knew that the United States had been reading over the shoulder of Japan's Foreign Office throughout 1941.

Mitchell and Gesell, working closely together, had insisted upon bringing the coded material into the open as a sine qua non of the investigation. Thus, one of the highlights of the hearings shone brightly on the first day of the inquiry. Exhibit No. 2 was another powerhouse of revelation—messages concerning military installations, ship movements, assorted Japanese espionage reports, and the like. They included the controversial "bomb plot" series.[30]

Thus began the congressional investigation destined to hold public attention as perhaps none other between the Teapot Dome of the twenties and the Watergate of the seventies. Representatives of the War and Navy department staffs briefed the committee on the events of December 7 so that they would have at least the essentials of the case in hand when they called the first witness.[31] This was Admiral Richardson, who took the stand quite late in the afternoon of November 19. He provided the audience and the avid press with more than one sensation and proved "a hard-to-handle witness for both Republicans and Democrats."[32]

Hull appeared on November 23. The ex-secretary resembled a fine old etching come to life, his black pinstriped suit setting off his white hair and clear-cut features.[33] In his statement and direct testimony he vigorously defended the administration's policy toward Japan. He had no illusions about the powers of diplomacy in dealing with the Axis: ". . . when I would be talking with the representatives of these thugs at the head of governments abroad . . .

they would look at me in the face but I soon discovered that they were looking over my shoulder at our Navy and our Army. . . ."[34]

Hull's appearance drew the largest attendance at the hearings to that date, spilling out of the seats into the aisles. Hull walked slowly out of the room to enthusiastic applause, even the reporters joining in the cheers.[35]

To finish the day's session, former Assistant Secretary of State Sumner Welles took the stand and continued to testify all of Saturday, November 25. He was a dry witness compared to his former chief, but the lean precision of his language made any misunderstanding virtually impossible and helped clarify the diplomatic picture for 1940–1941.[36]

Hull really opened fire on November 27. Lucas asked him to comment upon the Army board's report which suggested that Hull had "issued the ultimatum that started the war." His irate eye traveling along the committee table, Hull snapped, "If I could express myself as I would like I would want all of you religious minded people to retire." This remark drew appreciative smiles from the packed house. Hull continued:

> I stood under that infamous charge for months, when every reasonable minded person knew that the Japs were on the march of invasion in the Pacific area to get supreme control over it. . . .
> They were off on this final attack and no one was going to stop them unless we yielded and laid down like cowards, and we would have been cowards to have lain down.[37]

Former Ambassador Grew followed Hull on the stand. Gearhart questioned him closely about Hull's Ten-Point Note. Obsessed with the idea that it was an ultimatum, he tried every trick he knew to induce witnesses to agree with him. In presenting his own view of the Hull Note as one of admiration, be artfully attempted to lure Grew into his web of thought: "I am trying to get you to admit that that document is what every American in his heart wanted it to be. I don't think you should dodge on this ultimatum word. That, in days to come, is going to be one of the most glorious incidents in American history."[38] Unless Gearhart had experienced a conversion as sudden and complete as that of Saul of Tarsus on the road to Damascus, that statement was the height of hypocrisy. But Grew was too wise and experienced to nibble on Gearhart's lump of sugar.

Ray Coll, Jr., editor of the Honolulu *Advertiser*, who attended these early sessions, shared the opinion, building up in many quarters of the press, that the committee should start seeking some military answers: "Men in uniform have constituted a fair percentage of the audience . . . but it has been noticed that they don't stay long. . . . These men would like to know why the Army and Navy were caught napping on Dec. 7, not why the United States and Japan could not reach a peaceful settlement of their differences."[39]

Possibly this trend penetrated the consciousness of the Republicans because from early in December their statements became less raucous. Partisan debate and sniping did not cease entirely, for the momentum had grown too strong for a sudden halt. And old habit patterns had worn deep grooves. The Pearl Harbor anti-Roosevelt campaign was no sudden aberration; it was the product of years of conditioning. In the soft afterglow of history it is easy to forget the venomous hatred that Roosevelt inspired in certain quarters. His hard-core opponents considered him a national disaster, an egomaniac bent upon destroying the American system and the American character. They held him personally responsible for every misfortune which befell the United States during his presidency. It was natural that they should see Pearl Harbor as the end product of some dark design by "That Man in the White House."

But the investigation had not proceeded as the minority members obviously hoped and expected. The revelations anticipated from Richardson had fizzled out like damp firecrackers. On the political side he had drawn the curtain from no sinister Pearl Harbor secrets because he knew no such secrets to reveal. He had disagreed with Roosevelt's policies toward the U.S. Pacific Fleet, but he had produced nothing to bolster the theory that the President had staked it out deliberately. Thus, the fond hope of relishing whatever beans Richardson might spill died upon the witness chair.

On the tactical side Richardson's testimony had been equally disappointing to sensation-mongers. His frankly expressed opinion that a Japanese task force which accomplished what it did at Pearl Harbor probably could have been equally successful at Puget Sound[40] pulled the rug from under one of the principal anti-Roosevelt theses—that the Fleet would have been secure from attack if stationed on the West Coast.

Nor had the minority scored significant victories on the diplomatic front. Hull had proved himself more than capable of defending his own and Roosevelt's foreign policy. In a magnificent *tour de force* of logic and controlled emotion, he had heaped scorn upon his hostile inquisitors. And the ovation Hull received from spectators and even the chronically cynical newsmen proved that he had the sympathy of the audience.

Welles had backed up Hull's position to the hilt. Every knowledgeable Washington watcher knew that Welles had been on terms of at best an armed neutrality with Hull; therefore, his testimony in behalf of Hull's regime and policies carried especial weight. Grew, too, had seriously weakened the isolationist-revisionist position. He demolished the impression left by the Army board's report that he considered that the Hull Note of November 26 had "touched the button" for war in the Pacific.

Increasingly the press reacted unfavorably toward the tactics of the minority members. A cartoon in the Atlanta *Constitution* portrayed the GOP elephant, a tin can tied to its tail, mired in a morass labeled "Pearl Harbor Smear."[41] Nor did the party stand solidly behind its lawmakers on the committee. A group of junior Republican congressmen stated publicly, "We emphatically reject any suggestion that our Government should have acquiesced in Japan's program of aggression."[42] All in all, the minority members would have been both stupid and politically insensitive—and that was far from the case—had they not concluded the time had arrived to retire the battle-ax in favor of the rapier. They could safely leave the rough stuff to the more rabid elements of the antiadministration press.

Yet the members of both parties continued to indulge in acrimonious exchanges which wasted time, clouded issues, and derailed valuable trains of thought, while up and down the nation demands increased that the committee pay more attention to essentials. The New York *Herald Tribune* reminded its readers of all the warnings that had gone out to Hawaii. Yet the attack had come as a surprise. "Why it did so is the essential mystery of Pearl Harbor, and the one imperative and constructive task of the present investigation is to clear up that mystery in all of its aspects."[43]

Those who expressed such views were correct. Indeed, the really disturbing thing about the political efforts of the minority members was their total irrelevance to the important question in hand: Why were the U.S. Pacific Fleet and the Hawaiian Department caught unprepared on December 7, 1941? Roosevelt could have turned into a werewolf every night of the full moon; he could have had secret agreements with the British, Chinese, or Eskimos; Hull could have ground out "ultimatums" wholesale. These things could have had no effect whatever upon the primary duty of the armed forces to be alert anywhere and everywhere under the American flag.

CHAPTER 78

"THE

EVIDENCE

PILES

UP"

On November 29 the investigation began to get down to the military essentials, with Miles following Grew on the stand. Miles comes across as an excellent witness. He could not be drawn into guesswork outside his own area of G-2, and he had a fine command of English. His keen disappointment at Short's failure to take adequate precautions following the warning of November 27 is the strongest overall impression that arises from his testimony. Miles stressed that an attack on Hawaii "was inherent in any war in which we might become involved with Japan. That is why we built the fortress." At this point Short, seated nearby, flushed, then smiled.[1]

Miles had not seen Short's brief response to the message of November 27 at the time it reached Washington. But when he read it, he considered it "a totally inadequate reply. . . ." This was all too true. A little later in the questioning, when Murphy asked why the War Department had not sent more warnings, Miles replied, "You do not have to tell a commanding general but once that a danger faces him." Up to that moment Short had remained quite impassive. But at Miles's remark he glared at him and restlessly fingered a piece of paper on the table.[2]

Gerow took the stand on December 5. The principal item under discussion was the Army's message of November 27. Gerow pointed out that he came into the matter because it required operations on Short's part. War Plans was responsible for operational messages; G-2, for informational ones. When Gerow saw Short's reply, he assumed that it answered the G-2 dispatch which Miles had sent. The message number cited in Short's brief response meant nothing to Gerow. He regretted that he had not tried to find out because "such an inquiry . . . would probably have developed the fact that the commanding general in Hawaii was not at that time carrying out the directive in the message signed 'Marshall.' " It never occurred to Gerow that Short, "an experienced commander," would not "take some reconnaissance and other defensive measures after receipt" of the principal warning. Nevertheless, Gerow declared courageously, ". . . if there was any responsibility to be attached to the War Department for any failure to send an inquiry to General Short, the responsibility must rest on the War Plans Division, and I accept that responsibility as Chief of War Plans Division."[3]

"It's almost unique, somewhat refreshing, to have someone stand up in the open and assume whatever blame may be in the offing . . ." remarked the Baton Rouge *State-Times*. And it praised Gerow for displaying "a soldier's courage. . . ."[4]

Apparently some dedicated Washington watchers thought something lay behind Gerow's acceptance of War Plans' responsibility. According to Coll of the Honolulu *Advertiser*, ". . . there was considerable speculation among correspondents and others present as to whether the general was making a big sacrifice of his otherwise estimable record in order to relieve Gen. Marshall, his superior, of any blame."

After that day's session Coll asked Short "if he cared to make a statement . . . on the message controversy." But Short preferred to maintain his silence. "As you know, I haven't been making any statements," he told Coll smilingly, "and will reserve my reply for delivery when called to testify."[5]

Coll anticipated that all would not be "milk and honey" when Marshall took the stand. ". . . Meanwhile the little group of do-gooders that sit every day behind the row of committeemen goes right ahead clicking knitting needles and you can see their woolen sox take form as the evidence piles up. . . ."[6]

To this day one can sense the electric tingle of excitement as the crowd in the hearing room awaited Marshall's first appearance. The war had ended a mere four months before, and these people still stood close to the pyramid of military victory—millions of GIs at its base, thousands of noncoms and officers, dozens of generals, tapering up to Eisenhower and MacArthur, and at the peak, holding it all together, George C. Marshall. He had no great battles to his credit; his duty station had been Washington, D.C. He projected neither the fatherly warmth of Eisenhower nor the austere glamour of MacArthur. What earned him the respect of a nation? Fundamentally the answer is quite simple: This man, not a West Pointer, personified the West Point motto—Duty, Honor, Country. Could the fetid breath of scandal reach him?

Marshall's entrance resembled an ancient Roman triumph in miniature. The audience, which included a large number of servicemen and women, filled every seat, overflowed onto the deep windowsills, and stood "3 abreast up in the aisle as far as the red velvet rope separating the committee" and its satellites from the rest of the room.[7] A row of generals and admirals occupied the front seats. Coll expressed the hope "that the chamber floor was well braced against this additional weight of gold braid and brass." Short "was a quiet but intent listener" to Marshall's testimony. Kimmel, too, "followed every word. . . ."[8]

An obvious line of strategy for the Democrats to follow in dealing with Marshall was this: After the counsels laid the foundations, the majority members should question the witness as briefly as possible consistent with the points they wished to make. They could depend upon the Republicans to turn the general inside out. Thus, the whole committee would profit from this minute testimony, while the minority members drew upon themselves whatever criticism might accrue from chivvying a popular figure. Whether by accident or design, that is precisely what happened.

Among the matters Marshall dealt with were British-American relations in pre-Pearl Harbor days; the Herron alert of 1940; the problems of furnishing the Hawaiian Department with aircraft; radar; various staff meetings; the "bomb plot" series; Marshall's activities and whereabouts on December 7, 1941; and, of course, the "winds" messages. Marshall recalled the dispatch establishing that code but no "winds execute."[9]

The committee decided to accept responsibility for placing in evidence the full text of Marshall's letters to Dewey, although they contained references to "the technical cryptoanalytical methods which we had adopted to break the Japanese code. . . ." Undeniably the committee had to consider the Magic material, but there was no real excuse for publicizing clues to the methodology involved in obtaining it. Murphy declared that the disclosure would "add immeasurably to the difficulty of our armed services and will contribute nothing to the actual inquiry."[10]

Each of the Democratic members polished off his portion of the questioning with dispatch. Under Barkley's inquiries Marshall, like Gerow, took a measure of blame for not acting when Short's reply to the warning of November 27 came through the War Department. Marshall did not recall whether or not he had seen it but presumed that he had. "In any event that was my opportunity to intervene which I did not do."[11]

In thus taking his medicine, Marshall had "enhanced, rather than damaged, his reputation . . ." declared the Hartford *Courant*. "General Marshall did not hide behind General Gerow's confession. . . . Here is no buck-passing, no evasion of responsibility for what did and did not take place in the War Department."[12] Here, too, was the unequivocal answer to the speculations that Gerow had set himself up or had been set up as a whipping boy for Marshall.

Beginning on December 8, the Republicans entered the ring. They did not treat Marshall gently. In this apocalyptic confrontation, Gearhart took first crack at Marshall. Ferguson followed and kept Marshall on the stand for an incredible nine and a half hours. His first session, for the balance of December 8, covered a potpourri of subjects which we need not examine. Back in full battle array on Monday, December 10, Ferguson pursued a rather erratic course, obviously aimed at demonstrating prewar belligerence on the part of the Roosevelt administration. He took the general exhaustively through messages, memorandums, and minutes virtually line by line.

The next day Ferguson plunged with unabated energy into such subjects as the war warnings, delivery of Japan's final message, the Army board, and the

Clausen investigation.[13] The afternoon was wearing on when Keefe took over from Ferguson, so he confined himself to laying some groundwork.

In an interesting exchange he guided Marshall down the years of building up Oahu as "an impregnable fortress"; Army and Navy war plans for possible conflict with Japan; maneuvers "to implement those plans . . ."; air and submarine defenses; the gradual deterioration of U.S.-Japanese relations.[14] One would have expected Keefe to explode with the corollary: Then why were both Washington and Oahu surprised when Japan attacked? He did not do so. Yet the passage demonstrated why the armed forces' psychological unpreparedness for Pearl Harbor was so incongruous and so puzzling.

Keefe and Marshall resumed on the morning of December 12. This session produced no new information. Keefe was quite courteous, and his line of inquiry is easy to follow, for he stayed closely to a chronological approach, in pleasing contrast with other members, who played verbal hopscotch all over the landscape.[15]

By this time Marshall appeared tired. And Frederick G. Othman of the United Press noted that Short and Kimmel were "getting fidgety from sitting so long in the senate's chairs. Whoever designed those chairs knew nothing about human anatomy." The difference in personality between the two protagonists was not lost upon Othman: "The general is not a clubby guy. He speaks only to his lawyer and then not much. The admiral, however, is beginning to feel at home. He stood in line . . . to get his lunch in the cafeteria . . .," confining himself to a modest 20-cent bowl of navy bean soup.[16]

December 13 saw the end of Marshall's testimony, and he hurried from the room to a round of applause.[17] In reviewing his testimony before the various investigations, one cannot but feel that the real man kept getting in the way of the legend, according to which Marshall was an unassuming gentleman of phenomenal memory. Be that as it may, in some respects he was not a good witness. He had a rather rambling style and did not express himself well. He knew that he was not at his best when testifying. During a conference in Stimson's office on July 21, 1941, the talk turned to various struggles with Congress. "They will insist on my going up there," Marshall remarked worriedly. ". . . I make a poor witness and I will ruin myself."[18]

Perhaps Marshall did not do himself justice when he spoke extemporaneously. He lacked the punch of Hull, the clarity of Stimson, the salt of Kimmel, the swift cut to the center that makes Ingersoll's testimony a pleasure to read. Marshall gave many monosyllabic answers and replies of the "I-do-not-recall" variety. These do not create trust and confidence, although they may well represent the exact truth.

Marshall might have resolved a number of problem areas and refreshed his memory by conferring with some of his former colleagues. But he had imposed upon himself a rigid discipline of silence in regard to Pearl Harbor. In a letter to Hull on December 14, 1945, explaining why he had not paid his respects before leaving for his new post as special envoy to China the next morning, Marshall wrote: "Since the Pearl Harbor issue was raised in Congress, I have thought it

wise not to discuss the matter with any of the individuals concerned. . . ." He
further explained that he desired that when he testified,

> there be no possibility of a claim or assertion being made that I had connived
> with other leading witnesses to present a story more favorable to me than the
> facts might justify. For the same reason I never read the report of the Pearl
> Harbor Board or even of the Roberts Board—I did not think it wise to divert
> my concentrated attention from the war effort to concerns regarding me
> personally, and I did not wish to be influenced, possibly subconsciously, in
> what I recalled regarding the occurrences at the time.[19]

Marshall had scarcely left the scene when the inquiry almost fell apart.
Mitchell and his staff resigned on December 14. Just one member, Assistant
Counsel John E. Masten, continued to serve with the new staff. Mitchell was not
politically minded. He was a beaver for work despite his age, often putting in
twelve hours a day at his task, as did Gesell. They believed that their mission
was to determine what had caused the tragic defeat at Pearl Harbor and that the
question of why Japan and the United States went to war was irrelevant to the
purpose of the investigation. So they found frustrating the preoccupation with
gathering political plums.

Mitchell reminded the committee that he and his assistants had taken the
assignment with the understanding "that they would not be held for any
considerable time after January 1st." And the inquiry had not worked out as
expected. "Since the start of the hearings it has become increasingly apparent
that some of the members of the committee have a different view than that
entertained by counsel, either as to the scope of the inquiry or as to what is
pertinent evidence," he told his colleagues. He offered to continue until the
new legal staff could "pick up the case and carry on."

One has to sympathize with Mitchell. Obviously the committee would not
finish anywhere near the deadline of January 3; in fact, it had barely begun to
tap the prospective witnesses. What is more, Mitchell and Gesell had served
without pay. Gesell rather regretted the necessity of resigning. He was not the
type of man who readily abandoned an unfinished job, and he had developed a
keen interest in this particular one. He would have liked to stay on to the end
and write the final report.[20] However, the two counsels had worked together so
closely that Mitchell's resignation inevitably entailed that of Gesell.

Barkley termed the legal staff's resignation "a tragedy." Obviously much
distressed, he feared for the effectiveness of the inquiry. He seriously
considered retiring from the committee and returning to his job as majority
floor leader. Senator George, too, cast a thoughtful eye toward his important,
temporarily abandoned tasks as chairman of the Finance Committee.[21]

On Monday, December 17, the committee called to the stand Admiral
Wilkinson, former director of Naval Intelligence. He proved an articulate,
intelligent witness. In "brisk, business-like tones" he explained many technical
details of the respective functions of Communications and Intelligence concerning Magic, the Intelligence setup on Oahu, and the "bomb plot" series. He

regretted that he had not attributed to these "the bombing target significance which now appears."[22]

"It never occurred" to him that "it would be appropriate or advisable" to warn Pearl Harbor specifically against a surprise air raid for these reasons: He thought Hawaii knew of the possibility, reaching conclusions about "enemy functions" was not his province, and he believed "that an approaching force would be detected before it could get into attack range."[23]

Wednesday, December 19, found Wilkinson back on the stand covering a variety of items, among them the Herron alert of 1940, a subject which particularly interested Keefe. Barkley finally dismissed Wilkinson that afternoon with a few gracious words of appreciation.[24]

The committee had recorded Wilkinson's important testimony with little time to spare. On February 21, 1946, he perished when a friend's car he was driving plunged off a ferry at Norfolk, Virginia. The Honolulu *Star-Bulletin* observed: "He was gallant and brave to the last. His final act on earth was to push his wife from the car that was doomed. . . ."[25]

As the inquiry proceeded, one thing was becoming more and more evident: The most recent witnesses had been damaging to Kimmel and Short. Not surprisingly Brewster suggested to reporters that the time was ripe to put them on the stand. "They ought to testify soon," he said. "Then, perhaps, we'll be looking elsewhere to place some of the blame."[26]

The order in which witnesses should appear had been the subject of a running battle between Mitchell and Gesell on one side and the minority members, particularly Ferguson, on the other. The Republicans had wanted to put Kimmel and Short on the stand at the outset of the hearings. These two men were key witnesses who had waited to tell their stories publicly while the months lengthened into years. Then, too, no doubt the minority members reasoned that to take the testimony of the two Hawaiian commanders at the beginning would place the Washington witnesses and the committee itself on the defensive. For their part, Mitchell and Gesell wanted to build up a substantial background of evidence before they called Kimmel and Short so that their stories would fit into the broadest possible perspective.[27]

Actually the position of Mitchell and Gesell was rather favorable to Kimmel and Short. The longer they waited to testify, the more they would know about the thinking of other witnesses; thus the better their opportunity to prepare a rebuttal. And they would have the psychological advantage of the last word.

As it happened, only two more Washington witnesses appeared before Kimmel and Short began their long-awaited public hearings. As soon as Wilkinson left the stand, Admiral Turner took over. "Took over" is correct, because whenever Kelly Turner joined a gathering, the spotlight followed him. The little time remaining on December 18 dealt with Turner's career and the functions of the War Plans Division, including the responsibility for strategic estimates. The next day Mitchell questioned him for the entire session, devoting considerable attention to the Navy's "war warning" of November 27, which Turner had prepared. Turner had seen Short's reply thereto and "wondered at it." But he did not call it to the attention of the Army authorities. He "felt that if anything was wrong it would be attended to." He saw no reason why he should have sent Kimmel "some further message" that "at least mentioned the possibility" of an air raid. "What was he going to take a defensive deployment against?" Turner asked. And he answered himself: "Just one thing. That is the meat of the dispatch. It is all in there."[28]

Kimmel did not attend the session of December 21.[29] This may have been just as well. He was not famous for concealing his feelings, and Turner came down very hard on him that day. He declared that in his opinion Kimmel did not comply with the order to take defensive deployment. If he had done so, he could have reduced "the disastrous effects" and perhaps inflicted "considerable damage on the Japanese Fleet." He could see no possibility of misinterpreting the sentence "This dispatch is to be considered a war warning."[30]

One of the highlights of Turner's testimony was his assertion that in 1941 he thought "the chances were about 50-50 that we would get a heavy raid in Hawaii." The obviously skeptical Murphy pounced on this expressed opinion. His forceful interrogation of the strong-minded Turner was a real battle of giants. They also dueled sharply over the apparent lack of cooperation between War Plans and ONI, especially Turner's failure to check with Wilkinson before assuring Stark that Kimmel was receiving Magic.[31]

In questioning Turner, Gearhart devoted most of his attention to political considerations. He took the same astounding position he had taken with Grew—fulsome praise of the very diplomatic instrument he had condemned as triggering the war. But Turner did not step into this booby trap.[32]

Turner's testimony clearly indicated that the Navy Department Headquarters had been no monolithic structure. There had been serious differences of opinion and some maneuvering for position. But in the essential point under the committee's consideration—how could Pearl Harbor have happened?—his opinions concerning the Navy and Kimmel had been substantially the same as those of the War Department's witnesses toward the Army and Short: The commanders on Oahu had received what their superiors deemed adequate warning to place their commands on the alert for whatever warlike action Japan might take.

On December 21 questioning came to a temporary halt for the holidays. The committee knew that a long road lay ahead. On December 20 in closed session it had voted to continue the inquiry until February 15. During the Christmas recess disaster struck a blow that could have robbed the investigation of much authenticity. On Saturday, December 22, Short entered Walter Reed Army Hospital, "threatened with pneumonia." Hospital authorities could offer no assurance when he would be able to testify. While his condition was serious, they did not "feel unduly alarmed about him." Still, the general was not robust, and pneumonia could have been deadly. But evidently Short had no intention of dying until he had spoken his piece in open session. He rallied over

Christmas, and on the twenty-sixth the hospital could report that Short was "resting considerably more comfortably."[33]

The investigation still pulsed with rumor, innuendo, myth, and controversy, but the trajectory had veered sharply downward. It had cruised too long in the stale air of politics, and people had become tired of investigators who smudged their arguments with political rhetoric. The bite of newspaper opinion was beginning to leave deep teethmarks. Something exceedingly dramatic would have to erupt to recapture the original widespread interest in the inquiry and to hold the front pages of the nation's press. Not that such considerations should be dominant. The imperative duty of each member of the congressional committee was to dig up the skeleton of truth, even if only a dozen people in the United States cared about it.

Stark took the stand on the last day of 1945. His appearance produced no such outpouring of interest and admiration as had that of his former opposite, Marshall. The interruption of the hearings had broken the public's attention span. No doubt many were not yet ready to cut into the holiday season to spend their precious time in a stuffy chamber on Capitol Hill when they could read all about it in the papers and hear the highlights on the radio. One suspects, however, that the primary reason why Stark roused less interest than Marshall was the man's personality. He was a most likable individual and a gentleman to his fingertips, but he lacked the characteristic called star quality, that indefinable something which would bring out a cheering crowd on the last day of a cold Washington December.

Stark had called upon his competent counsel before the Navy court, David W. Richmond, for legal assistance. Another bright young lawyer, James E. Webb, who "felt very strongly" that when Stark sent his "war warning" message, "he had discharged his responsibility," offered his services to the admiral. Stark could have found no more capable advocate. Webb would later become director of the Bureau of the Budget; undersecretary of state; and director of NASA, among other important positions. Webb recommended adding Hugh Obear, who could give the team prestige and clout. Obear was a prominent attorney who had been president of the District of Columbia Bar Association. From time to time Stark's son-in-law, a lawyer from Philadelphia, joined the group.

Richmond wanted Stark to take a strong stand, perhaps blame Marshall, as the Army board had done. But Stark refused. "No. I do not want to point the finger at anyone. I have to live with myself, and I want to live a long time." In any case, Stark thought the world of Marshall and would never have tried to spare himself at Marshall's expense.

Stark and his legal battery prepared an extensive statement for the admiral to read before the committee. Its substance was entirely his own. He decided to state the facts as he knew them as extensively documented as possible and leave the conclusions to the committee.[34]

His presentation of this statement, which took most of the day, was well organized. First, he offered a brief outline of his actions since becoming CNO on August 1, 1939, to persuade Congress to authorize the necessary men, matériel, and money to establish a potent two-ocean sea service.[35] Next, he gave a brief but meaty exposition concerning war plans. "I avoided, wherever I could, giving specific and categoric instructions to the commanders in chief," he explained. "War plans developed under my directions . . . were broad outlines of tasks and objectives, leaving the detailed operating plans to the commanders in chief, who were on the spot and familiar with the peculiar problems affecting their forces."

Stark asked the committee to keep in mind two things in connection with the Navy's basic war plan (WPL 46): "First, that the Atlantic and European area was considered to be the initial decisive theater. . . . Second, the plan was . . . predicated on the availability of forces actually in hand." Those were not sufficient "to wage all-out war in both oceans. . . . I considered, as did my principal advisers, that the forces allocated to the Pacific Fleet were adequate for the execution of the tasks assigned."[36]

Stark then tackled the thorny questions of basing the Pacific Fleet at Pearl Harbor and the later transfer of ships to the Atlantic.[37] By far the major portion of his statement dealt with his actions to keep his Fleet commanders informed. This was natural, because in this area lay the principal objections to Stark's performance as CNO. He liberally sprinkled his narrative with extracts from his correspondence with Kimmel and others, wisely endeavoring "to stick to the record of events as they happened. . . ."

Attorneys for both Stark and Kimmel agreed that these letters were "pertinent and material to the inquiry. . . ."[38] They were well advised to do so, because nowhere else in the Pearl Harbor records do the two admirals show to better advantage. This correspondence is untainted by hindsight or self-service. Stark's missives reveal him as having a sincere interest in keeping his Fleet commanders posted, a deep concern about future events and the Navy's role in them, his high regard for Kimmel, and—by no means least important—the dedication to duty which caused him to devote his Sundays to writing these long, detailed accounts to Kimmel and other key officers. Throughout 1941, in letter after letter, dispatch after dispatch, Stark had sounded the drumbeat of warning.

Thus, be believed the letters and dispatches he had sent to Kimmel and Hart "sufficient to keep them informed on the important military and political developments in the Pacific as we knew them, and that they had received adequate information and directives to be on guard."[39]

The year 1946 opened with a very special New Year's celebration. For the first time since December 7, 1941, a shrilling telephone or doorbell would mean a friend calling with the compliments of the season—at worst a wrong number or a salesman. No more of that half second of heart-stopping fear that this time it would be the dreaded telegram from the government. No wonder Americans staged the most joyous, noisy wingding since 1939. Columnist Jack Tarver of the Atlanta *Constitution* indulged in a little tongue-in-cheek prophecy: "The Pearl Harbor investigation will hear 3,649 witnesses, fill countless volumes with testimony, and ultimately reach the conclusion that the Japs caught us unprepared because we were unprepared."[40]

The committee held no hearings on New Year's Day but had a busy session reviewing Stark's statement and letters as well as Short's testimony at previous inquiries. The caucus room was sparsely populated when the committee reconvened on January 2.[41] In general, the majority members concerned themselves with naval matters, the minority with the political aspects, although of course, the lines frequently crossed.

Under Mitchell's questioning that day, Stark confirmed Turner's testimony about the misconception that Kimmel's command could decode and translate Magic. To his credit, Stark did not exploit this inviting escape hatch. ". . . I want to make it plain that that did not influence me in the slightest regarding what I sent," he stated. "I felt it my responsibility to keep the commanders in the field . . . informed of the main trends and of information which might be of high interest to them." Washington had the benefit of other sources along with Magic, all of which information the Navy Department "welded together" and sent out. So Stark considered that he was keeping Kimmel informed.[42]

Barkley asked probing questions about Kimmel's failure to institute long-distance reconnaissance. His persistence finally elicited Stark's admission that the Hawaiian commands "did not obey the instructions. . . ." Stark further conceded that while the attack surprised him, he was astonished, too, "that certain steps had not been taken to intercept it and be on the lookout for it."[43]

On January 3 Murphy questioned Stark on a wide variety of subjects. Then Gearhart took his turn. Immediately he mounted a pet hobbyhorse: Where were Stark and Marshall on the night of December 6, 1941? Stark's memory was a total blank on that point.[44] Indeed, the events of December 7 seem sufficient to have wiped the previous evening from his mind.

Thus far Stark's testimony had developed no such bonanza of editorials as had Marshall's. As in mid-December, interest centered more on the committee's executive sessions than on the open hearings. On January 3, the day the committee optimistically had planned to submit its report, it announced the unanimous selection of Washington attorney Seth W. Richardson to replace Mitchell as chief counsel. Its members had made their choice during the midday break on January 2. Ray Richards of the Milwaukee *Sentinel's* Washington office almost fell over himself rushing to bury the hatchet in Richardson's skull:

> It was cynically taken for granted in Washington tonight that the new chief counsel of the Pearl Harbor investigating committee . . . will try to be an even more ardent defender of the administration than was the retiring counsel. . . .
>
> Richardson's livelihood depends on his standing with the administration. He is a member of a Washington law firm headed by New Dealers from 'way back. The firm lives on government favor.[45]

Richards neglected to mention that Richardson was known as a convinced Republican and harsh critic of Roosevelt, who had crossed swords with the administration on many occasions.

Barkley had asked J. Edgar Hoover for an FBI man to fill one of the gaps left by the wholesale staff resignations. Hoover summoned one of his gingery young agents, Edward P. Morgan. "I am assigning you to a very complex and highly controversial investigation," Hoover told Morgan. He added with reckless disregard for metaphors, "You call the shots and let the chips fall where they may."

Morgan was an excellent selection. Despite his youth—thirty-three-years —he had an unusually broad background as an educator and auditor. After receiving his LL.M. degree from Georgetown University, he joined the FBI and became in succession a field agent, supervisor, instructor in the FBI Academy, and special agent in charge of field offices. In March 1947, when chief inspector, he would resign from the FBI to practice law. A striking-looking man, he resembled to no small degree television's all-time favorite lawyer, the early Perry Mason, portrayed by Raymond Burr. Somewhat appalled by "the monstrous scope of the thing," which was completely off the track of his FBI work, Morgan began reading "almost night and day" to catch up with the evidence and exhibits already presented so that he would be prepared for the transition of the staffs.[46]

By the time Stark came back to the witness chair on January 4 the minority members seemed almost frantic to prove a prewar American commitment to the British, although no one explained how such an agreement would have affected the ability of the Japanese to whale the tar out of the American defenses at Pearl Harbor. Ferguson, who followed Gearhart, was hot on this trail and questioned Stark long and closely on the subject. If Stark wanted to take postmortem revenge upon Roosevelt, he could have easily done so by a few judicious "I don't recalls." But in this area Stark's memory was clear, and he was not the type to curry favor by dishonest equivocation. So Ferguson got no help from him.[47]

Soon after the noon recess of January 5 Ferguson turned the admiral over to Keefe, who asked a number of questions about Stark's "war warning" and the Navy Department's expectations of Kimmel in consequence. Stark had not asked Kimmel to report measures taken. "That was not Navy custom. It was not my practice, it never has been, to tell the 'how to do,' but rather the 'what to do.'" Stark was obviously uncomfortable with this line of questioning, which compelled him to admit that had he been CinCPAC, he would have acted differently from Kimmel in certain areas. But prodded by Keefe, he asserted, "My feeling is that I certainly would have had my planes out. . . ."

However reluctant Stark may have been to hurt his old friend, his testimony had damaged Kimmel's case. It was all the more destructive for being sincere and in no way malicious. True to his character, Stark insisted that Kimmel "was within his rights to exercise his judgment. . . ." When the committee had heard Kimmel's testimony, they could weigh Stark's judgment against his. Keefe was by no means unsympathetic. He remarked, "Well, I realize the delicacy of these questions, Admiral Stark, because Admiral Kimmel is your friend. . . ." Stark replied warmly, "One of the closest and finest I ever had and one of the finest I ever knew."[48]

Indeed, Stark displayed firm loyalty to his former Fleet commanders and staff officers. He lost no opportunity to praise Kimmel, and when he had to disagree with him, he phrased his remarks impersonally. He tried hard to prove that there never had been "any real difficulty" between Wilkinson and Turner in regard to the evaluation of intelligence.[49]

In mop-up operations at the end of Stark's testimony, Gearhart leaned hard on the admiral concerning Halsey's orders to his ships as they set out on their mission to Wake Island.* Gearhart continued his inquisition until Barkley took a hand: "What you are being asked, Admiral, is, if . . . the orders were given, it constituted an overt act which justified an attack on Pearl Harbor." Shortly thereafter he dismissed Stark with praise as well as thanks.[50]

On the basis of the record, the committee treated Stark much more gently than it did Marshall. Perhaps some of the season's peace and goodwill animated the members; perhaps Stark's attractive personality defused some of the heavy artillery. Although the usual opinion of those consulted for this study was that Marshall had a keener mind than Stark, the transcript shows that in many instances Stark expressed himself more clearly than did his former opposite. Stark also appeared to be better prepared than Marshall, with a fresher grasp of the documentation. The two officers were as one in their firm denial of any prewar commitment to Britain or of any desire to fight Japan if it could be avoided. Their assessments of what they had expected of their Hawaiian commanders upon receipt of the warning messages of November 27 were virtually identical, allowing for the differences between the services.

The strength of Stark's testimony lay in the force of his documentation and in his thesis that the original sources should speak for themselves. He resisted speculation and made a conscientious effort to see the year 1941 without benefit of hindsight. And he refused to testify outside his own field of competence. Throughout the investigation Stark tried to put a favorable construction on matters and to be considerate of everyone. Yet he stood by his guns. His replies carried the ring of self-assurance, authority, and confidence in his own rightness.

With Stark's testimony the committee reached an important watershed. It had heard a matched set of top Washington military and naval witnesses—the AC/S G-2 and the director of Naval Intelligence, the directors of War Plans, and at the crown the Chief of Staff and the Chief of Naval Operations. These men had done well by themselves and their institutions. They had been intelligent,

---

*See Chapter 51.

courteous, and cooperative. They had admitted to human errors of judgment but had denied any malice aforethought on their part or that of the Roosevelt administration. In so doing, they had maintained their dignity in the face of intense provocation. In fact, as we have seen from the press reaction, the long-winded questioning and badgering to which the minority members had subjected them had ricocheted back upon the questioners.

CHAPTER 79

"A

FIGHTING

CHANCE"

The hearings resumed with the first of the two witnesses so many had waited agog to hear. Kimmel took the oath on January 15. Now for the first time the committee and the nation could hear the testimony of the man who had commanded the U.S. Pacific Fleet on that terrible day. His appearance generated so much interest that a pause of almost five minutes ensued to permit photographers to snap him. As they did so, Kimmel presented the image of a man self-assured and confident. He faced the committee with no hint of apology; he came to accuse, not to excuse. Slowly and clearly he began to read a prepared statement of 108 typed pages.[1]

Kimmel figuratively declared war with almost his first words: ". . . I shall describe how the Pacific Fleet was deprived of a fighting chance to avert the disaster of December 7, 1941, because the Navy Department withheld information which indicated the probability of an attack at Pearl Harbor at the time it came." After a review of his appointment as CinCUS and the basing of the Fleet in Hawaii, he launched upon his grievances. "The so-called 'war warning' dispatch of November 27 did not warn the Pacific Fleet of an attack in the Hawaiian area," he asserted. And he declared tartly, "The phrase 'war warning' cannot be made a catch-all for all the contingencies hindsight may suggest."[2]

Kimmel bore down hard upon the fact that Washington withheld from him much vital information concerning Japan. He was especially bitter, and with considerable justice, because he did not receive the "bomb plot" series. "Surely, I was entitled to know of the intercepted dispatches between Tokyo and Honolulu on and after September 24, 1941, which indicated that the Japanese move against Pearl Harbor was planned in Tokyo."[3] He was equally unhappy at being denied Japan's final note and in particular the "one o'clock" message. He was sure that had Washington kept him fully informed, the course of history would have been changed. If on December 5 he had had "all the important information then available in the Navy Department," he "would have gone to sea with the fleet, including the carrier *Lexington* and arranged a rendezvous at sea with Halsey's carrier force, and been in a good position to intercept the Japanese attack." As late as the morning of December 7, if the Navy had sent its information plus the 1300 deadline, Kimmel's "light forces could have moved out of Pearl Harbor, all ships in the harbor would have been at general quarters, and all resources of the fleet in instant readiness to repel an attack."[4] He added from the depths of a heart full of pain and anger:

> The Pacific Fleet deserved a fighting chance. It was entitled to receive from the Navy Department the best information available. Such information had been urgently requested. I had been assured that it would be furnished me. We faced our problems in the Pacific confident that such assurance would be faithfully carried out.

He ended his statement on an upbeat note: "History, with the perspective of the long tomorrow, will enter the final directive in my case. I am confident of that verdict." With that, the admiral rested his defense. Spectators applauded long and heartily.[5]

Kimmel's statement was something of a *tour de force* of research, organization, and persuasive argument, propelled by a dynamic personality. It held no deliberate deceit, which Kimmel would have scorned. And because he believed implicitly every word he spoke, he conveyed the unmistakable stamp of sincerity.

But his statement evoked mixed reactions. Those of the committee members "divided somewhat along party lines." To the press Gearhart declared that in his opinion Kimmel had made "a fine statement that ought to clear up a lot of things." But Lucas thought the admiral had left "many questions unanswered." Keefe demonstrated a burgeoning ambivalence. Apparently Kimmel had "made use of every opportunity to tell his story" in this, his first public appearance in his own defense. However, Keefe added, "The weakest part of his statement was where he attempted to prophesy what he would have done if he had been furnished all of the information that Washington had."[6]

The Honolulu *Star-Bulletin* expressed strong criticism in a stinging editorial:

> Three characteristics in the Kimmel statement stand out:
>
> His readiness to shift full and complete responsibility for what happened to his superior, Admiral Harold R. Stark, and the navy department.
>
> His meticulous, even slavish, resort to regulations to explain his own position. (Admiral Kimmel apparently does not believe in the saying that rules are for those who don't know when to break them!)
>
> His utter and amazing lack of imagination in estimating the possibility of a direct attack on Pearl Harbor when relations with Japan were so strained.

The *Star-Bulletin* conceded that the authorities in Washington had much more information than they sent to either Kimmel or Short. And it found Stark's "failure to pass along the contents of intercepted Japanese code messages . . . inexcusable." But no one would "explain away the fact that Kimmel was the man on the ground. The fact that others shared his responsibility does not mitigate his own responsibility. . . ."[7]

Following Kimmel's opening statement, counsel and committee members questioned him from the sixteenth through the twenty-first. Richardson started the ball rolling. He was impersonal, nonbelligerent, asking few, if any, judgmental questions. The admiral replied fluently, assertively, the very picture of someone who knew his business. He revealed himself as a man of iron with the rigid strength that can be weakness, never having learned how to bend. His very positiveness made his inconsistencies doubly noticeable.

He realized that the Navy's strategy in the Pacific was defensive and that he had only enough ships for raids on the Marshalls. But in his opinion even the defense partook of the nature of the offense: "The most important part of any defensive attitude is the offensive action you take to carry it out."[8] This theme of offensive-mindedness recurred throughout his testimony.

With obvious sincerity he stressed his cooperation with Short and the undoubted fact that defense of Pearl Harbor was the Army's business. And he was not obsessed with protecting only the ships; he wanted Pearl Harbor "to be able to defend itself even though the Pacific Fleet were wiped out." But he never looked over the Army's antiaircraft batteries, did not know that Short had three types of alert, and did not visit the Information Center to see for himself how the radar setup operated, although those were essential factors in the defense of his precious anchorage and of the Fleet at its moorings.[9]

Kimmel was aware of the vulnerability of the Fleet at Pearl Harbor. "We feared the worst, all right. We feared it all the time," he stated. And he added later, "We considered . . . the probabilities and possibilities of an air attack on Pearl Harbor." Yet he thought the danger of a Japanese aerial strike on December 7, 1941, "very slight." However, he refused to admit that this was an error of judgment. He had never seen the expression "a war warning" in a message in all his naval experience, but he "did not consider it an extraordinary term."[10]

Members of the committee took over the examination late in the morning of January 17. Having been absent until that day, Barkley deferred his turn until he could check over the testimony. Therefore, Cooper batted first. He delivered crisp questions and probed until he got satisfactory answers. The committee excused Kimmel at 1530 to admit some documents. Evidently nothing loath to cut short his ordeal, Kimmel urged his four-man counsel team, "Let's get the hell out of here."[11]

Friday, January 18, found Kimmel back on the stand under examination by Clark. He asked very few questions, centering on the type of attack which might have been anticipated and what Kimmel thought he would have done had he been "reasonably sure . . . that a surprise air attack was going to be made there."

Senator George had been perhaps the least vocal of all the members, and he did not spoil his record. "The wise old owl of the Senate," as Morgan labeled him, asked Kimmel only a few questions dealing principally with WPL 46, the Navy's basic war plan.[12]

Then Lucas took over. He went exhaustively into the circumstances of Kimmel's appointment and his relationship with Roosevelt, the basing of the Fleet at Pearl Harbor, the war warnings, and air reconnaissance. More than one reporter noted that Kimmel's temper was wearing thin.[13] Indeed, one cannot wonder at his irritation. By this time the very words "war warning" must have assumed nightmarish qualities, producing an automatic reaction of angry defensiveness.

Of all the areas under discussion, Kimmel reacted most vigorously to anything pertaining to long-distance aerial reconnaissance. And well he might, for this was the "soft underbelly" of his defense. He strove mightily to convince the committee of two rather contradictory theses: First, that he could not have established an effective patrol; secondly, that he did have patrols aloft. He told Lucas that "on Monday, Tuesday, Wednesday and Thursday of the week preceding the attack we did, in fact, send out patrol planes in the northwestern sector to a distance of about 400 miles."[14] Actually the patrols in effect on those days were related to the Halsey and Newton task forces to Wake and Midway respectively. By December 6 the only search in the Hawaiian area was limited to a segment with a 150-mile radius from *Enterprise,* headed home almost directly west of Oahu. And in the hours before the attack on December 7 aerial reconnaissance from Oahu consisted of a very short flight due south of Pearl Harbor—180 degrees off the sensitive area.[15]

In response to Lucas's questions Kimmel stressed the critical shortage of long-range reconnaissance planes and "spare patrol plane crews. . . ." He stated firmly, "Now the Navy Department should have known, and did know beyond doubt, that I had no means to conduct a search over a considerable period." Lucas interjected, "I agree with you." Kimmel continued, "Now I might have made a token search and I might have been able to come here and say I made a token search. . . . I did not do that. I have never done that kind of thing, and I will not do it."[16]

Perhaps unwittingly, Kimmel was laying a smoke screen. There was never any question of either a 360-degree search "over a considerable period" or of a "token search," if by that expression Kimmel meant a few planes sent aloft on a random pattern. What he should have done—and what he had planes and crews to have done—was cover the critical northern sector.

But Kimmel was absolutely fixed in his refusal to admit a fault. Lucas asked him, "Notwithstanding that humiliating and far-reaching sea disaster, you now contend that with the information you had available to you you did all that any prudent commander could do to prevent or to minimize the surprise attack on

Pearl Harbor on December 7?" Kimmel shot back, "I think that is a fair statement." With that exchange Lucas completed his interrogation.[17]

Murphy, who followed Lucas, was the most persistent of the majority members. His questioning lasted to the end of January 18 and into the afternoon of the next day. He prodded into a number of Kimmel's weak areas, such as his failure to consult with Bellinger upon receipt of the "war warning." Kimmel could not see why he should have done so. Bellinger "was not the only air man we had there. He was rear admiral in charge of this patrol wing. . . . I felt capable of giving him any orders that he required."

Murphy was not interested in orders. He was talking about "a staff consultation . . . to discuss with your airman the necessity for taking any measures appropriate to the occasion." But Kimmel did not appear to get the point. A little later he innocently underlined his failure to understand the importance of dealing with airmen in reaching a decision involving air operations. Murphy wanted to know if Kimmel had discussed "the question of a raid" with Soc McMorris in view of the "war warning." Kimmel replied:

> I discussed all phases of the situation with McMorris almost daily; not almost daily but daily, and we went over the whole situation and at no time did McMorris recommend to me that we put out these planes for reconnaissance purposes, and he would have done so had he considered it necessary. He is a very able, outspoken officer and a man in whom I had the highest confidence.[18]

Able, outspoken, and trustworthy McMorris undoubtedly was. But he was not an air officer, hence quite out of his element in the field of aerial reconnaissance.

Kimmel's plight since Pearl Harbor had been a prime talking point with the anti-Roosevelt faction, so naturally the minority members made the most of their opportunity. Brewster took him around the track in a canter, along lines bringing out the admiral's best qualities—his devotion to duty, his capacity for hard work, and his common sense. For example, Kimmel did not claim that he should have had a Purple machine. It seemed to him "that if all this was being done in Washington and they were supplying me with information, that that was a solution to the problem."[19]

The committee adjourned at 1635 on Saturday, to resume on Monday, January 21. John T. Flynn, in Washington to cover the hearings, took advantage of the weekend break to dash off a few conclusions based less upon Kimmel's testimony than upon his own invincible misconceptions. He claimed that the admiral had his ships in Pearl Harbor because "The very orders he received required them to be there."[20] This farfetched contention stubbed its toe upon Kimmel's own integrity. During the afternoon of January 21, when the members were asking Kimmel some final miscellaneous questions, Murphy spoke up: "Admiral, I just want to spike what I think is another rumor. It is a false one. Was there anyone in Washington in any authority whatsoever who issued any orders to you which obliged you to have the fleet in Pearl Harbor on December 7, 1941?" Kimmel answered with one word: "No."[21]

Gearhart took up when the session resumed on Monday. Then Ferguson had his innings. He went into a number of controversial topics obviously aimed at discrediting Roosevelt. Kimmel had no use for the late President, but he also had a native honesty which derailed some lines of inquiry. So Ferguson struck out when he suggested somewhat obliquely that the Japanese might have decided not to attack if Oahu had been alerted: "Suppose that they [the Japanese] had flashed to that fleet the fact that the Hawaiian Islands were fully alerted and knew that there was something going to happen and our ships would have gone out, how would that have interfered with the Japs other than probably to have stopped them coming in?" Here was an excellent opportunity for Kimmel to claim, or at least insinuate, that Washington had withheld information from him to ensure that the Japanese would strike. But once again he spoke with the voice of direct-minded honor: "I don't understand how it would have interfered in the slightest degree."[22]

As low man in seniority, Keefe was the last to tackle the witness. He told Kimmel, "So far as I am concerned, you have acquitted yourself magnificently." This evoked vigorous applause from the audience. Gearhart must have agreed, for he wrote Kimmel on January 21, "As I told you when you left the hearing room, your appearance must be taken as a complete triumph. You entered the room with the confidence of a champion and came out with the bout. If any one under trying circumstances ever vindicated himself more completely, I have yet to hear about it."[23]

Secure in his armor of self-assurance, Kimmel had not been in the least in awe of these high-powered lawmakers, either those trying to fence him in or those trying to lighten his path. When they made what he considered a mistake or showed misunderstanding, he contradicted them without fear or favor. With his strongly ingrained habit of command, he did not hesitate to take the conn or suggest a course of action if he believed his inquisitors needed straightening out. And he preferred to testify to nothing of which he did not have direct knowledge.

In many respects Kimmel was an impressive witness. He was articulate without being voluble and obviously had at his fingertips every detail of the operations of the Pacific Fleet. If he felt any qualms of embarrassment or discomfort at thus being on the public grill, he concealed them admirably. At times he seemed to consider himself less a witness being questioned then an instructor conducting a seminar.

He projected an innocent arrogance which could be both irritating and oddly touching. He did not seem to understand why, having dealt with a subject to his satisfaction, anyone should wish to replow the same ground. Then, too, he made damaging admissions without in the least realizing that they were damaging. The following comment provides an example in point: "Well, if anybody will define for me what a war warning message is I would be better able to tell you whether I construed it as such."[24] The obvious answer was that "a war warning message" might be defined as a message containing the words "This dispatch is to be considered a war warning." But Kimmel's absolute self-confidence acted as a mental and moral anesthesia against the tiny alerts which the nerve endings might signal to a man less sure of himself.

In presenting his case, Kimmel made two psychological errors. First he placed so much stress upon his belief that the Navy Department had shortchanged him that he laid himself open to the impression of being overly dependent upon his superiors and of lacking initiative and imagination. And his determined effort to pass the buck was curiously at variance with the service tradition of accepting responsibility.

Kimmel's second error was his obstinate refusal to concede that he might possibly have made a mistake, even one of judgment. Such self-righteousness is always irritating, whereas the American people usually react sympathetically to anyone who frankly admits to being less than divinely inspired. Marshall and Gerow had reaped a harvest of goodwill by publicly admitting they had erred and regretted doing so.

That Washington possessed data which it should have shared with Kimmel is undeniable. But his assurances that had this information been in his hands, he would have interpreted it correctly and been prepared to meet the Japanese assault are open to question. Such second-guessing, known to mystery story aficionados as the "had-I-but-known" syndrome, must always be speculative.

Certain facts, however, are matters of record. The military establishment in the Hawaiian Islands, of which Kimmel was an important part, existed to protect that territory against one possible enemy and only one—Japan. For years before 1940 Fleet exercises and war games in the area had concentrated upon one major problem—defense against a Japanese attack. During 1940 and 1941 the rapidly deteriorating relations between Washington and Tokyo were common knowledge. With this background in mind, one must wonder just how much effect any additional information from his superiors would have had upon Kimmel's thinking.

After Kimmel's 16-inch-gun attack on Washington, people eagerly awaited Short's testimony. On Tuesday, January 22, he arrived at the hearings with Mrs. Short in a car which the War Department had furnished him along with a WAC driver. Since his hospitalization Short had been able to walk around for some time, but he had not attended recent sessions and still appeared gaunt. His neat blue-striped suit hung loosely from his stooped shoulders. But he was just as forceful in his own defense as Kimmel and rejected Barkley's offer to have someone read his typed statement. This was his long-awaited opportunity, and he did not propose to sit by passively while the unemotional voice of a substitute spoke for him.

He had to rest frequently as he read his sixty-one-page statement, pausing often to sip a glass of water. This process took up most of the day.[25] In its salient features, Short's statement markedly resembled Kimmel's. He had scarcely begun to speak before he asserted, "There was in the War Department an abundance of information which was vital to me but which was not furnished to me. This information was absolutely essential to a correct estimate of the situation and correct decision. . . . Had this information been furnished to me, I am sure that I would have gone on an all-out alert."

Instead, he prepared for sabotage and reported to that effect. "The War Department had 9 days in which to tell me that my action was not what they wanted," he declared. "I accepted their silence as a full agreement with the action taken."[26]

Short stated that he had not known "that the Japanese were under orders to destroy their codes and code machines." Like Kimmel, he particularly stressed the "one o'clock" message. To him it "indicated a definite break of relations at 1 P.M. and pointed directly to an attack on Hawaii at dawn. Had this vital information been communicated to Hawaii by the fastest possible means, we would have had more than 4 hours to make preparations to meet the attack which was more than enough for completing Army preparations."[27]

Short obliquely criticized his naval colleagues for failing to advise the Army of the submarine action early on December 7, 1941. He also pointed out that from November 27 to December 6 the Navy "made no request for Army planes to participate in distant reconnaissance." He interpreted this to mean that the Navy "had definite information of the locations of the Japanese carriers or that the number unaccounted for was such that naval ships and planes could make the necessary reconnaissance" without the Army's help.[28]

Thus, Short's self-defense rested upon the assumption that he and his advisers would have accomplished what Marshall and a much larger staff of experts had failed to do—correctly interpret all the bits and pieces of information and fit them into a perfect pattern—and then the Hawaiian Department would have taken prompt, effective action against the Japanese.

As Short neared the end of his presentation, he summed up his frustrations: "I do not feel that I have been treated fairly or with justice by the War Department. I was singled out as an example, as the scapegoat for the disaster." He continued with this surprising statement: "My relatively small part in the transaction was not explained to the American people until this joint congressional committee forced the revelation of the facts."[29] It seems incredible that Short honestly believed he could sell the idea that the commanding general of the Hawaiian Department, directly responsible for the protection of the Pacific Fleet in harbor, had played only a "relatively small part" in the Pearl Harbor drama.

Spectators in the half-filled room applauded heartily as the general finished. Throughout his statement Mrs. Short listened carefully, apparently worried lest the heat and glare from the klieg lights prove harmful to her husband. The committee, too, was concerned about Short's health and excused him for the day without further questioning. Then the members went into executive session.[30]

The hearings resumed the next morning, January 23. Among the audience was Short's son, a fine-looking young man just returned from overseas.[31] Under brief, businesslike questioning by Assistant Counsel Samuel H. Kaufman,

Short outlined his previous service, the circumstances of his appointment to the Hawaiian Department, and some of his early problems on the job. The lack of information from Washington was his ark of refuge, and he ran up its gangplank at any hint of danger. One factor in Short's insistence upon Washington's culpability was his impression that his superiors knew more than they did. "I believe the War Department actually had the information 4 hours before the attack," he stated, "so they could have told me the exact place."[32]

Like Kimmel, Short patently believed every word he spoke, so not surprisingly his generalized blame of his superiors culminated in explicit hostility toward Marshall. Again Short stressed that if events necessitated "a general alert" of the Hawaiian Department, he expected Marshall "to do one of two things: Either to order the general alert or to give me sufficient information to justify me in ordering it."[33]

Short's 360-degree arc of animosity also took in his naval opposites. Kaufman wanted to know how Short accounted for Kimmel's testimony that he did not know the Hawaiian Department had been only on antisabotage alert and, in fact, did not know that the Army "had anything else but an all-out alert." Short answered, "The only way I can account for that would be poor staff work on the part of the staff of the Fourteenth Naval District. . . . We had furnished them with 10 copies of our staff operating procedure, which somebody in that naval staff certainly must have dug into and known what it meant."[34]

When Barkley took over, he mentioned that "all the high officers in Washington" who had appeared before the committee had testified that notwithstanding the "bomb plot" series, "they did not really expect an attack at Pearl Harbor and were surprised when it came." So if Short and Kimmel had received those messages, would they "have reached any different conclusion from that reached by everybody in Washington?" Short's reply made sense: "I think there was a possibility because Pearl Harbor meant a little more to us. We were a little closer to the situation, and I believe we would have been inclined to look at that Pearl Harbor information a little more closely."[35]

Much less rational was his reply when Barkley asked if anything outside of the "bomb plot" series pointed to an attack on Pearl Harbor. Short cited Japan's changing the diplomatic deadline from November 25 to November 29, 1941. He thought anyone familiar with weather conditions in Alaska and the Aleutians who "happened to think along that line . . . would have drawn a direct conclusion. . . . And to a Navy man that might well mean that the condition was getting to the point where the fueling of ships at sea would be hazardous." Barkley suggested that the weather in Alaska would not necessarily indicate where the Japanese intended to strike. But Short declared, "If they went by the northern route, they would be probably going to either Seattle or Hawaii."[36] All this demonstrated hindsight at its hindmost.

For the balance of January 23 and part of the next morning, Cooper had some searching questions about the Army's dispatch of November 27. He tried to determine "with this message of the Chief of Staff before you, without the word 'sabotage' mentioned in it at all, I am just wondering how you got the impression that your reply of 'an alert against sabotage' was responsive to this message." Short's answer gushed from the fountain of his conviction: "Because there was no information that indicated anything in Hawaii other than internal disorders."[37]

George had not been present during most of Short's testimony, so he asked only a few questions, all in the area of air reconnaissance. One of his queries was very penetrating: How could Short construe the warning of November 27 "to mean an alert against sabotage when the use of the word 'reconnaissance' here certainly would indicate something beyond an alert against sabotage . . . ?" Short's reply was less than pellucid: "Since I was not . . . since the Army was not taking any reconnaissance I did not report it because it was a naval function. . . ."[38]

Clark's questioning filled out the morning of January 24. Once more Short met a running fire of queries about his reaction to the message of November 27. Clark wanted specifics: "Could you give the committee an illustration of any internal disorder, you had had before that?" Short's answer was a masterpiece of its kind: "I had tried to state that we had tightened the ring so that there would not be any. We had succeeded; there never was."[39] As one reads Short's evidence, it becomes more and more clear that where sabotage is concerned, one is not dealing with a coolly considered estimate of the situation—one is dealing with obsession. Short's reply to Clark reminds one of a man terrified of drowning who builds a dam in the Sahara, then proudly claims that his dam was the reason the Sahara did not flood while he was in the vicinity.

During Lucas's questioning following the noon recess, Short came as close as he ever did to criticizing Kimmel personally: "I do not intend to give the impression that I am making an out and out statement of what defensive deployment meant, but I couldn't conceive of any defense not including reconnaissance."[40]

The formidable Murphy followed Lucas for the rest of January 24 and continued past the next day's noon recess. He queried Short closely concerning his utilization of his staff and subordinate commanders. Murphy told a representative of the Honolulu *Star-Bulletin* that the point "he was driving at" was that "nobody knew what anyone else was doing" on Short's staff.[41] One hesitates to go quite that far, but there seems little doubt that Short could have used his staff more efficiently.

The inquiry got under way again on January 26 with Ferguson at the conn. Short could scarcely have found a more sympathetic interrogator, nor Ferguson a more willing interrogee. Under the senator's deft guidance the general accepted a fanciful thesis already becoming popular with the burgeoning revisionist school. He thought that in the event of full mobilization, "if that had been reported to the Japanese, they would have turned back the attacking force . . . because they would have felt, or they would be sure that they would take heavy losses. Surprise was the only opportunity that they had to succeed."[42] Of course, Short had no way of knowing that Yamamoto had warned the First Air Fleet that it might have to fight its way into the target and that the Japanese fully anticipated "heavy losses."

Ferguson carefully made it clear that Short did not include the congressional committee in his litany of resentment. To his inquiry Short stated, "I consider that this hearing has been extremely fair, very thorough, and that I have been accorded very great courtesy by the chairman and by every member of the committee."[43]

In contrast Ferguson made every possible attempt to place Washington in a bad light. His efforts to establish Short as a put-upon victim of Washington's alleged stupidities and plottings had a few negative side effects. Short revealed himself as having been fully as much as Kimmel a prey to the "had-I-but-known" syndrome, and as having been overly dependent upon his superiors. He also gave the impression of indulging in that most unlovely quality, self-pity.

After one has threaded one's way carefully through the thickets of Short's testimony, an uneasy sense persists that he lacked breadth of vision and a grasp of reality. Nor does he appear to have understood that a military commander's duty is to prepare for the worst and be ready for it at a moment's notice. Granted that Short did not receive from Washington all the information he should have, the picture nevertheless emerges of a man with a narrow-gauge mind, a person lacking the flair for his mission.

Keefe followed Ferguson. His brief interrogation was sympathetic, but he did pin Short down with some "flat, plain, square" questions, among them this one in the form of a statement: "Well, you could have done a pretty good job with the stuff you had out there if you had been on the alert and had been expecting an attack." To which Short answered, "Yes, sir."

Keefe's questioning ended with a painful crack at G-2: "Now, your position in this case is that Intelligence, so far as Washington was concerned, failed?" Short agreed uncompromisingly, "A hundred percent." Keefe added, "And thus Pearl Harbor occurred. Is that your defense?" And Short answered, "Yes, sir."[44]

A final round of tying up loose ends followed. Soon thereafter Short's appearance ended on a civilized note with a final statement of thanks and appreciation from the witness and a few gracious words from Barkley thanking him for his "courtesy and patience" and the hope that he would soon recover his health. A patter of applause followed Short out of the room.[45]

Even across the years there is something appealing about this pale, slender figure in the suit too big for him, his voice periodically fading to a whisper, fighting for his reputation like the soldier he was. At times one glimpses the crisp, positive officer the War Department deemed worthy of three stars and one of the nation's most important commands.

One of the Pearl Harbor story's most bewildering puzzles is this: Why were the Pacific Fleet and the Hawaiian Department caught unawares when all concerned claimed to have been alive to danger? Nowhere does one sense this dichotomy more sharply than in the testimony of Kimmel and Short. We hear over and over of Fleet exercises and war games, SOPs, estimates, plans, studies, staff consultations—all aimed at protecting the Fleet and the territory from a potential Japanese attack. Yet the reality caught them napping.

As we have seen, Short insisted repeatedly, persistently, and waspishly that Washington had denied him essential information. In a way he had little choice of tactics. His only hope for public vindication lay in convincing the congressional committee that everything would have ended much differently on Oahu on December 7, 1941, had his superiors not deprived him of information essential to an accurate estimate of the situation. On the other hand, that weapon was a double-edged sword. By stressing his dependence upon the upper echelon, inevitably Short diminished his own stature. At times his testimony, like Kimmel's, leaves one with the uncomfortable feeling that if some natural disaster or enemy action had cut off Hawaii from Washington, he would have been at a total loss. In conveying this atmosphere, the two witnesses surely did themselves less than justice, for initiative is one of the principal components of command, and it is scarcely likely that each had reached his pre-Pearl Harbor eminence without displaying that quality.

Certainly as CinCPAC Kimmel had never demonstrated any hesitancy in running the Fleet the way he wished. He had reorganized the task force structure and chosen a top-notch staff, which he led in a masterly fashion. In his dealings with Washington he had not asked what his superiors wanted; he had told them what he wanted. And when the occasion demanded, he had gone to Washington in person, clear to the White House to present his views.

Short had handled his department less forcefully, but of course, he had operated at a lower command level than Kimmel. However, he, too, had been no Uriah Heep in his dealings with Washington. He knew what the Hawaiian Department needed, and he bombarded headquarters with stern, well-argued demands for materials to do the job.

Yet for all of Kimmel's and Short's efforts, the Japanese caught their commands by surprise. Perhaps it was only human that these two conscientious officers, secure in their belief that they had done their best with the means at hand, should seek someone else to blame.

For a good four years Kimmel and Short had hoped, waited, and fought for a public hearing. It would not be surprising if in that time they had come to regard such an open session as a sort of Promised Land where cheering crowds would proclaim their innocence, where their records would be restored to pre-Pearl Harbor stainlessness, where the miscreants in Washington would suffer just punishment for their sins. Now the two men had had their day in the limelight, had said everything they wanted to say before the congressional committee with all the publicity such a hearing entailed. Yet their evidence had not produced the definitive revelations many had hoped for, nor did it solve the Pearl Harbor mystery.

Of course, Kimmel and Short would have to wait for the final report before they could know the committee's verdict. Yet these two intelligent men must have read as many newspapers as they could lay their hands on to find out what impression they had made. The result could not have been completely reassuring. In the main, reaction had been reserved. The open hearing had not provided public apologies and restoration of honors. It looked very much as if that Promised Land had turned into a fata morgana which faded at the approach.

CHAPTER 80

"FIXING

THE BLAME"

With Stark, Kimmel, and Short off the agenda, newspapers could afford to relax their coverage of a story which they believed had lost the public attention. But the congressional committee could not truncate an important investigation out of boredom. It still had to examine a number of key witnesses. Each contributed something to an understanding of what had happened in relation to Pearl Harbor.

Justice Roberts testified on the afternoon of January 28. This feisty witness appeared "in a belligerent mood." An old hand at the inquiry game, he answered legitimate questions fully but pulled up short anyone who went over the line. Convinced of the absolute fairness of his Commission and proud of its members, he explained its procedures in detail and defended it vigorously.[1]

Controversy flared with Captain Ellis M. Zacharias, whose testimony had been interrupted to accommodate Roberts. Zacharias was a longtime expert on Japan who had served many years in Intelligence. His pride in his chosen field rang through every word he spoke. He asserted that failure to appreciate the importance of intelligence had been "one of the greatest contributing factors" to the tragedy at Pearl Harbor.[2]

He claimed that he had called upon Kimmel in his headquarters sometime between March 26 and 30, 1941, at which time he told the admiral, if Japan decided to go to war with the United States, "that it would begin with an air attack on our fleet on a week-end and probably a Sunday morning; that the attack would be for the purpose of disabling four battleships." In reply to a question from Kimmel, Zacharias emphasized

> that the most probable method of attack would be by aircraft carriers supported by appropriate ships; that such an attack would come in undoubt-
> edly from the northern [sic] because this was the prevailing winds in the

Hawaiian Islands; they would come in and launch their attack downwind . . . the ships and the force which brought the planes to launch them would retreat as quickly as possible directly upwind to escape any damage which they felt might come.

Kimmel asked how such an attack could be prevented. Zacharias said "that the only possible way of doing it would be to have a daily patrol out to cover the approach of the Japanese, and that this patrol must go out at least 500 miles." Kimmel answered, "Well, we have neither the personnel nor the matériel with which to carry out such a patrol." The captain replied confidently, "Well, Admiral, you better get them because that is what is coming." Zacharias told the committee that Poco Smith had been present and would probably remember the details of this conversation.[3]

Kimmel's testimony in this regard is ambivalent, and Smith flatly contradicted Zacharias. He called the story "the testimony of clairvoyance operating in reverse." And he added, "I am absolutely positive that at this meeting there was never mentioned the question of an air attack on Pearl Harbor. . . ."[4]

So here we have two honorable, intelligent, and experienced officers telling contrary stories. This situation is by no means unique in the Pearl Harbor problem, but this particular incident is one of the most nagging. And there it rests to this day.

The committee had planned to continue questioning Smith but moved him aside to permit first the appearance of Captain McCollum, then Admiral Bellinger, both of whom were "under very imperative orders." The former's testimony took up all of January 30. The only member to quiz McCollum at any length was Ferguson, who questioned him closely about the "winds" matter and took him almost line by line over his testimony before Admiral Hewitt.[5] The record of McCollum's interrogation leaves one with a pleasing impression that a firm, knowledgeable hand had been on the tiller on ONI's Far Eastern Section in 1941.

Bellinger's testimony, which filled the entire session of January 31, may have taken some wind out of the pro-Kimmel sails. Bellinger had been in charge of the Pacific Fleet's air reconnaissance in 1941. Yet Kimmel not only did not consult him about the "war warnings" but also did not speak with him from around November 26, 1941, until the attack. And Bellinger had no authority to activate distant air patrols under the Martin-Bellinger plan without orders from the CinCPAC.[6]

When Poco Smith returned to the witness chair on the morning of February 1, Murphy gave him a hard time about the failure to consult either Bellinger or Davis, the Fleet aviation officer. Smith protested that Halsey was "the No. 1 airman in the whole area. He had more planes than all of them."[7] No one could question Halsey's professional expertise, and he was a close friend of Kimmel's. But he was a task force commander, neither the Fleet aviation officer nor the patrol wing commander. In those capacities Davis and Bellinger should have been consulted in evaluating what to do in those critical days following receipt of the "war warning."

The Zacharias-Smith controversy and Bellinger's testimony had focused attention, by no means all of it favorable, upon Hawaii and in particular upon Kimmel. If anyone could reverse this trend, it would be the next witness, Captain Safford, an ardent champion of Kimmel, a firm believer in the villainy of the Navy Department, and high guru of the "winds execute" school of thought. With the grim determination of a spawning salmon, he had swum up the stream of evidence against receipt of such a message. As he was quite as brainy as Smith and as dogmatic as Zacharias, committee watchers could count upon a display of inquisitorial pyrotechnics.

Safford was obviously ill at ease. He bit his lips and doodled nervously as he read a prepared statement to what had become for him virtually an article of faith: "There was a Winds Message. It meant War—and we knew it meant War."[8] Both counsel and committee members delved *ad infinitum* into whether or not such a message had been received prior to December 7. Safford remained firmly convinced that it had.

Safford's undoubted genius in his own field and his total sincerity shine forth from his testimony. His personality and reputation were such as to compel respect and attention for any position he might take. Nevertheless, his demeanor before the committee was not likely to inspire total credence in his "winds execute" story except in those disposed to believe it. "Cross-examined for three days, Safford and his startling statement rapidly wilted. He flushed, hedged, and his voice quavered into long silences."[9] Of course, the captain's patent discomfort did not necessarily betoken a guilty conscience or discredit his testimony. To subject such a hard-shelled introvert as Safford to the ordeal of appearing before a congressional committee in a high noon of publicity verged upon "cruel and inhuman punishment." Moreover, for all his fluster he did not budge from his main premise.

On another score Safford was a maddening witness. It was very difficult to pry a straight "yes" or "no" out of him. He also had a bad habit of getting off the direct evidence and presenting his personal opinions as facts. Richardson cautioned him in this regard several times.[10] In spite, or perhaps because, of Richardson's determined efforts to keep Safford on the rails, the captain admired Richardson, whom he considered "far superior to Mitchell in every way."[11]

Safford had a recess on the afternoon of February 5, while the committee heard Rear Admiral Frank C. Beatty and Major John H. Dillon, USMC, both of whom had been aides to Knox in 1941. The committee questioned these officers briefly, principally in regard to the suggestion that the Navy Department had prepared a warning message to Hawaii on December 6, 1941. As we have seen, this line led nowhere.[12]*

The next morning Safford returned for further interrogations, which were in the nature of mopping-up operations. As he thankfully made his escape from

---

*See Chapter 69.

the caucus room, "a beautiful lady" stopped him. "I am Mrs. Richardson," she said. "Do you understand me? I am Mrs. *Seth* Richardson, Captain, you were simply wonderful! You did not let them bully you into changing your story." To the battered Safford she seemed "an angel from Heaven."[13]

If Barkley and his associates hoped for a breather after Safford, they were doomed to disappointment. Captain Kramer was nearly as difficult a witness as his predecessor on the stand, but for the opposite reason. In his almost painful eagerness to tell the precise truth and in his concern for detail, some of his statements were as obscure as Safford's had been through generalization.

Intent upon clearing up one particular legend, Murphy asked, "Now, were you ever beset or beleaguered by anybody in regard to this case? And, if so, I think the committee are entitled to every detail." Kramer replied, "At no time have I been what is termed beset and beleaguered, sir."[14]

Some of Safford's testimony had astonished Kramer, and he wanted to set the record straight. He agreed that there had been a "winds execute" message, but not for the United States. He had seen the item in question "not over 10 or 15 seconds," and he recalled it dealt only with England.[15] He had had "at least half a dozen conversations during the past year with Captain Safford going over a number of points connected with Pearl Harbor."

These intrigued Lucas. "Did you ever agree with him in these discussions that this particular message in controversy was a genuine implementing winds message?" he asked. Kramer answered, "No, sir; I did not. I tried to disillusion him of that idea since it was so diametrically contrary to the conception of it that I had."[16]

Dropping in for one of his periodic visits to the investigation, journalist Frederick C. Othman wrote appreciatively: "I hadn't been in the room more than five minutes before the white hair of Sen. Homer Ferguson . . . began to look like an unmade bed. He was shouting at . . . Kramer, who shouted back at him."[17] While sparring with Ferguson, Kramer demolished another Pearl Harbor myth. On November 9, 1945, the Chicago *Tribune* had contended that Kramer warned Knox at the State Department on the morning of December 7 that the "one o'clock" message meant an attack on Pearl Harbor. Kramer explained that he had mentioned "something about the time of day at Pearl Harbor . . . purely in passing. . . ." The idea that Pearl Harbor might be attacked never entered his mind.[18]

Lucas pursued the point tenaciously: "From all the information you received through magic, including the much-discussed purported winds execute message, was there ever received one single word, line, phrase, or sentence that would lead you to believe that Pearl Harbor was going to be struck by the Japs on December 7, 1941?" Kramer answered, "There never was, sir."[19]

After the complex examinations of Safford and Kramer, the committee had a treat in store. Admiral Royal E. Ingersoll was a dream witness, genial, crisp, and to the point. Armed with that most uncommon quality, common sense, the former assistant CNO dealt with a number of subjects, among them relations with Japan, the Atlantic orientation, shortages, the safety of the Fleet in Pearl Harbor, the fourteen-part message, and the alleged agreement with the British.[20]

Following Ingersoll's testimony, Colonel Clausen vigorously defended his own good faith and that of Stimson in carrying on his investigation. He denied any efforts to make witnesses change their previous stories and took up the cudgels in behalf of the truthfulness of those he had questioned.[21]

By logical progression Bratton, the intelligence officer who was one of the supposed victims of Clausen's alleged browbeating, followed him on the stand on the afternoon and evening of February 14. With his burly body and forthright manner, Bratton looked like an unlikely candidate for bullying. He gave the committee a dramatic account of events in Marshall's office late in the morning of December 7.[22] He told of the efforts to intercept a "winds execute" and that "a number of false alarms" had come in. Like Ingersoll, Bratton believed that the real tip-off of Japan's intention to fight the United States had been its code-burning order.* Bratton was "most positive" that he never saw a "winds execute" until after the attack, and he found it "hard to believe that any such execute message could get into the War Department" without crossing his desk.

"Nobody in ONI, nobody in G-2, knew that any major element of the fleet was in Pearl Harbor on Sunday morning the 7th of December," he emphasized. "We all thought they had gone to sea." Lucas asked, "Why did you think that?" Bratton replied, "Because that was part of the war plan, and they had been given a war warning."[23]

On February 14 light dawned upon Lucas in a very important matter: ". . . I cannot see how this committee can conclude this hearing without calling a couple of witnesses from Hawaii. We have been investigating Washington all this time." Inspiration came a little late. Deadline to finish the investigation was the next day. But even in so routine a matter as requesting an extension, politics reared its snaky head. The Democrats wanted another week of hearings "with an additional month or so to complete the report. . . ." The Republicans preferred "anywhere from two weeks to two months more hearings, and a still longer time to draft the report to Congress." Somehow they worked out their problems. On February 15 Congress extended the inquiry until June 1, "with the understanding that public hearings, so far as the present schedule of witnesses was concerned, would end" on the night of February 20.[24]

The irrepressible newsman Othman reported: "The wretches with the black pencils scribbling accounts of the proceedings for their newspapers are rooting for the lawmakers to finish by Friday, but admit that is wishful thinking. They have organized the East Wind Rain Survivors' Association. . . . They plan a binge on adjournment day."[25] More sedately Drew Pearson decided that "two major points" had arisen from the "confusing mass of data" thus far assembled: "Congress can pass no legislation which can keep Admirals and

---

*See Chapter 55.

Generals on the alert" and nothing had developed "which changes the basic responsibility of the commanders who were on the spot."[26]

Three witnesses followed Bratton on February 15. Colonel Sadtler, former chief of the Military Branch of the Signal Corps, testified mainly in the "winds" area.[27] Commander Lester R. Schulz told the story, stirring in its simplicity, of delivering the thirteen-part message to Roosevelt on the evening of December 6, 1941.[28] Captain Rochefort, who commanded the Navy's Communications Intelligence Unit on Oahu in 1941, took the stand for the balance of February 15 and part of the next day. He described attacking the Japanese naval systems and what his unit could and could not do in the diplomatic code area. His people had monitored the voice circuits which Washington listed for the "winds execute," but he had not attached much importance to that message.[29]

On February 15 Lynn Crost of the Honolulu *Star-Bulletin* dealt with that subject with a light touch:

> . . . even committee members chuckled recently as a privately prepared cartoon passed from hand to hand around the committee room.
>
> It showed a navy captain, flatly recumbent on his stomach, tongue hanging out limply and eyes glazed. A scrub woman standing over him was talking to her helpers:
>
> "I don't know what's wrong with the captain. I just came in and told him there was a paper here that said 'east wind rain.' "

Unfortunately the committee had not finished with that vexing problem, so voracious of time and energy. Rear Admiral Noyes, former head of Naval Communications, testified on February 16 that he had seen messages supposed to be the "execute," but none had checked out as authentic. He did not think the one about which Safford testified was genuine. Among other reasons, it had not followed the pattern the Japanese had prescribed.[30]

Noyes's testimony ended what promised to be the last full week of the inquiry. The committee still had a few loose ends to knot. On Monday, February 18, it heard from Admiral Hart, now a Republican senator from Connecticut, about his own record-taking investigation.[31]

The committee had a tiger by the tail when it turned from Hart to Captain Layton, who had been Kimmel's Fleet intelligence officer. Layton spoke clearly and pulled no punches, so Keefe acknowledged: ". . . you are one witness that we have had here who talks plainly and frankly and you know what you are talking about. . . ."[32] On at least one occasion Layton jarred whatever self-satisfaction the committee may have entertained. In reply to an inquiry from Lucas, Layton bluntly expressed his belief "that the investigation has hurt our national security to an incalculable degree by so much publicity being given to the decryption activities."[33] This was a sobering thought to carry with them as the committee members moved toward the close of the investigation.

The session of February 19 was something of an anticlimax. The first witness, Colonel Robert E. Schukraft, had been officer in charge of radio intercepts for the chief signal officer at the time of Pearl Harbor. He testified almost exclusively in the "winds" area. He had seen an alleged "execute" about December 4 or 5, 1941, but concluded that it was a false alarm.[34]

Colonel Phillips, Short's former chief of staff, followed Schukraft and provided a change from the eternal "east wind rain." He confirmed Short's testimony that upon receipt of the message of November 27 the general consulted only with his chief of staff. One also sees in Phillips's testimony the utter failure to understand the extent and nature of the Navy's task force reconnaissance, a fact which demonstrated the lack of any real substance to the Army-Navy liaison of which Kimmel and Short were so proud. Like Short, Phillips stressed the Navy's disbelief in an air raid on Oahu.[35] So once more a representative of the Hawaiian Department put the finger on Soc McMorris, although not by name. Yet his famous dictum that the chance of a Japanese air strike was nil was not a revelation from Mount Sinai—it was the estimate of an intelligent, experienced, but by no means omniscient U.S. Navy officer. His ideas certainly did not preclude Short and/or Phillips from making an independent estimate.

Much to Phillips's credit, he added to his exposition. ". . . I fully approved of General Short's decision to order alert No. 1. I feel also that I share any responsibility that he bears for that decision. That decision turned out to be wrong, but it was as right as we could make it at the time on the information we had."[36]

John F. Sonnett followed Phillips for the rest of that day and into the next morning. He testified concerning the Hewitt investigation and especially Safford's allegations.[37*] Following Sonnett, the hearings temporarily turned away from the brass as former Sergeant George E. Elliott explained the nature of the radar operation and the historic Opana sighting.[38] Only two witnesses remained, the first of whom, Captain John M. Creighton, dealt almost exclusively with matters in the Far East area.[39]

It seemed appropriate that the last man to testify should be Colonel George Bicknell, Short's assistant G-2 in 1941. He told his story clearly, forcefully and without equivocation. He gave some information which added to the impression that Army-Navy cooperation had left something to be desired. Bicknell had evaluated and transmitted to the Navy in Hawaii all intelligence he received. But he knew that the Navy had not reciprocated completely.

Not that communication between Bicknell and his own superiors had been perfect. He had been present when Phillips read the Marshall message of November 27 to the staff. But neither Short nor Fielder discussed it with Bicknell. He knew that an antisabotage alert had been instituted only after the troop movement commenced to implement it. Perhaps one reason why his superiors did not consult Bicknell was that they knew quite well what his opinion would be. "My feelings on that question have been expressed to practically every commanding general whom I have come in contact with, and

---

*See Chapter 76.

that was that we would never have any sabotage trouble with the local Japanese, and we did not."[40]

Following Bicknell came the last-minute introduction of various documents. Barkley thanked everyone concerned for his efforts. Finally, he officially adjourned the sessions at 1715, subject to the call of the chair.[41]

Throughout March the committee held no public sessions, but Stark and Marshall returned to the stand for an open hearing on Tuesday, April 9. Among other things, they testified to their whereabouts on the evening of December 6, 1941. Marshall had little to add beyond his previous testimony. His memory remained a blank on how he had spent the evening of December 6, 1941, but his own records contained nothing to show that he had not been at home. In any case someone was available in his quarters at all times to accept calls.[42]

Since Stark first testified, Commander Schulz had indicated that the admiral had attended the National Theater that evening.[43] Stark "very clearly" recalled having seen *The Student Prince,* which was playing at the National at the time, but he could not connect it with the night in question.[44] Gearhart had taken the peculiar attitude that "the greatest mystery of all these Pearl Harbor investigations" was the whereabouts of Marshall and Stark on the night of December 6.[45] He pitched into Stark on April 11 and seemed to think that the admiral had had nothing on his mind but Pearl Harbor in the weeks immediately following that event. "You were constantly interrogated in presenting evidence, were you not, and digging up evidence in connection with this affair, until you left for London?"

"No, I was not," Stark answered firmly. "I was busy fighting a war up until the time I left for London. . . . I was not going into post mortems."[46]

Rear Admiral Beardall, who had been Roosevelt's naval aide, also testified that day, primarily concerning the events of December 6 and 7. The rest of the session was devoted to placing in the record various documents and information previously requested.[47]

The members met again on May 23 for what promised to be the last formal session. The previous week, on Keefe's motion, they had voted to close the book that date. At last Richardson uttered the welcome words "That, I think, completes all of the records that we have." At the curtain close, Barkley thanked the staff, the FBI, and the liaison officers for their cooperation. He paid special tribute to the press. Brewster proved he could be a graceful loser by associating himself, on behalf of the minority, with Barkley's expression of appreciation. So with everyone in reasonable accord the committee adjourned at 1215 on May 23 subject to the call of the chair.[48]

No sooner had the package been neatly wrapped when it came untied. On the night of January 25 Captain and Mrs. H. D. Krick visited the Starks. Krick had been Stark's flag lieutenant when he commanded Cruisers, Battle Force, and the two families had remained in close touch. Krick reminded Stark that on the evening of December 6, 1941, they all had dined together, gone to see *The Student Prince,* then returned to Stark's home, where the CNO had returned a call from the White House. Stark still had no independent memory of these events, but deciding in his conscientious way to set the record straight, he "got up around 2 or 3 in the morning" and wrote a longhand draft of a letter which he gave to Barkley later that day.

Barkley hastily summoned the committee, not all of whom were available because of Memorial Day. Stark's testimony was brief. The whole evening of December 6, 1941, had left no impression on his mind probably because the pattern was quite routine. The two couples attended "many, many functions together. . . ." And telephone calls to and from Roosevelt were no novelty.[49]

Some question arose on the propriety of admitting this evidence. Richardson sensibly proposed that they take Krick's testimony, then decide whether or not to use it. That is what they did. Theoretically the action may be open to question because the inquiry had been officially closed, but in view of the fuss over Stark's whereabouts the night before the attack, it would have been most unwise not to attempt to settle the issue.

Krick's story was short but precise. When Lucas asked how he remembered the occasion so well, Krick's reply was so human that it carries conviction: "Because I was a very small fish, and great things were transpiring, and you don't forget that sort of thing." Pearl Harbor's happening the next day impressed the memory upon him.[50]

So there seems little doubt that half of Gearhart's "greatest mystery" was solved. But one can understand why Lucas begged Stark, "Don't find any more friends, please. When friends come in say nothing about Pearl Harbor." Those present broke into sympathetic laughter.[51]

Up to this time the staff had been so involved in the nuts and bolts of the investigation that no one had given much thought to preparing a draft report that would stand up. Now Richardson and Kaufman wrote drafts, both of which Morgan considered inadequate. He had come to like Richardson very much but recognized that he was something of a broad-brush artist. The chief counsel was not the type to prepare a solid report, every sentence of which must be researched and backed up by citation from the mountains of evidence. Then, too, Morgan feared that neither Richardson nor Kaufman might be able to escape the pull of their political biases. Richardson was a hard-boiled Republican; Kaufman, a convinced Democrat.

In contrast, Morgan had no personal or ideological ax to grind. He neither hoped for nor expected any political advantages from his work with the committee. He was on loan from the FBI, and to that organization he would return. Morgan's law degree, his experience as an accountant, investigator, and instructor had schooled him in deduction and attention to detail. In addition, he held an M.A. in English and genuinely enjoyed working with the language. With these thoughts in mind and with no one's knowledge, Morgan began to put a draft together. He worked on a crash basis and became so wrapped up in the project that he would awaken in the middle of the night and write a chapter. He submitted his manuscript to every member of the committee.[52]

Morgan had entered the picture when the committee had finished approximately half its hearings, and he had had to catch up on the previous testimony while at the same time performing his duties as assistant counsel. Even under the best of conditions, Morgan's draft would represent an admirable combination of research, logic, and writing. In the circumstances, it was truly a remarkable job. No wonder the majority decided to make it their point of departure. In fact, they accepted much of it without change. Morgan himself made a number of adjustments before the members signed the final document. Some of his original language was considerably more forceful than that which finally saw publication, and in a number of cases he deleted passages in order to keep the finished narrative free of judgments.[53]

All this drafting and discussion process took time, and at a closed session on July 2 the committee decided to ask Congress for another extension—the fifth—this time to July 16. Thereupon they recessed "amid indications of difficulties over fixing the blame for the success of the Japanese attack." Nevertheless, Barkley was optimistic that they could meet the new deadline and expressed hope for a unanimous report. This was somewhat unrealistic since Ferguson had been lining up his views, which he might sign as a minority report if he continued to disagree with the main one.

The full committee ended its discussions in two closed sessions on July 15—exactly eight months after its first meeting. It released on July 20 what Stimson called "a very fair report,"[54] which, all things considered, is true.

To all intents and purposes, a single set of investigators had conducted two separate investigations in the same room at the same time—one of the Japanese success at Pearl Harbor, the other of the United States' prewar foreign policy. Thanks to the persistence and stamina of the minority members, the committee had leaned heavily toward a probe of what had happened in Washington before and during December 7, 1941. As a result, the committee cut heavily into the proposed list of witnesses from the Oahu end, leaving some highly significant areas untouched. In particular one must question the decision not to call Bloch. Cogent reasons existed for placing him on the stand. In the first place, he had been commandant of the Fourteenth Naval District under both Richardson and Kimmel. As such he was Short's opposite number. The committee had maintained a judicious balance of Army-Navy testimony, and it is incredible that they should have cut off this sound principle at the Hawaiian sea frontier. Secondly, Bloch had been base defense officer, responsible for the Navy's share in protecting the ships in Pearl Harbor as well as the shore installations. This per se should have made him a key witness. His responsibility for helping defend his base was direct; Kimmel's was indirect. Thirdly, Bloch had been an "interested party" before the Navy court. In justice, he deserved the same opportunity to present his case in public as the committee had given the other two "interested parties." Fourthly, several times before the committee Kimmel had spoken of his expectation that Bloch would take the stand.[55] Such comments should have alerted the committee that Bloch could give valuable insights. Fifthly, Short had commented upon what he termed "faulty staff work" on the part of the Fourteenth Naval District. This was a serious charge because the entire pattern of military action on Oahu had been, in Short's phrase, "command by cooperation." Yet evidently the idea of how to conduct such a system had been to leave Army-Navy liaison in the hands of a young reserve officer, Lieutenant Harold D. Burr. Bloch lived in Washington and attended many of the sessions, so he was readily available to the committee.

Then, too, one wonders why the committee did not insist upon hearing from Soc McMorris's own lips what lay behind his assessment on November 27, 1941, that the prospects of a Japanese air attack on Oahu were "None, absolutely none." Nor should one forget Captain Davis, Kimmel's aviation officer, for Pearl Harbor was essentially an air problem. Another notable absentee was General Martin. Surely the testimony of the commanding general, Hawaiian Air Force, and cosigner of the Martin-Bellinger Report, was essential to a proper picture of what took place on Oahu.

Thus, it appears that the committee wearied of the investigative drudgery and quit before it finished the job. Of course, one could be cynical and reflect that further investigation into the military and naval picture on Oahu could neither enhance nor harm the memory of Franklin D. Roosevelt, hence neither increase nor decrease the prestige of the Democrats or Republicans. Still, the committee had to cut off somewhere or saddle the American people with the production costs of a run which might rival that of Agatha Christie's marathon hit *The Mousetrap.*

As anticipated, the committee could not reach a unanimous verdict. The majority report, based upon Morgan's draft, listed twelve conclusions. The first five of these affixed the Japanese strike in its political setting and placed "ultimate responsibility" upon Japan. The majority "found no evidence to support the charges" that Roosevelt, Hull, Stimson or Knox "tricked, provoked, incited, cajoled, or coerced Japan into attacking this Nation . . ." They divided the military responsibility into two parts—at Hawaii and in Washington. The Hawaiian commands had failed:

(a) To discharge their responsibilities in the light of the warnings received from Washington, other information possessed by them, and the principle of command by mutual cooperation.

(b) To integrate and coordinate their facilities for defense and to alert properly the Army and Navy establishments in Hawaii, particularly in the light of the warnings and intelligence available to them during the period November 27 to December 7, 1941.

(c) To effect liaison on a basis designed to acquaint each of them with the operations of the other, . . . and to exchange fully all significant intelligence.

(d) To maintain a more effective reconnaissance within the limits of their equipment.

(e) To effect a statement of readiness throughout the Army and Navy establishments designed to meet all possible attacks.

(f) To employ the facilities, matériel, and personnel at their command . . . in repelling the Japanese raiders.

(g) To appreciate the significance of intelligence and other information available to them.

One cannot fault the logic of these conclusions. The majority softened this devastating list of failures by deciding that they constituted "errors of judgment and not derelictions of duty."

The report pointed an accusing finger at the Army's War Plans Division for failing to advise Short "that he had not properly alerted the Hawaiian Department" when he replied to the warning of November 27. The report also hit War Plans and Intelligence of both the War and the Navy departments for not giving "careful and thoughtful consideration" to the "bomb plot" series and for not furnishing these messages to the Hawaiian commanders. The majority report likewise chided War Plans and Intelligence for failure to perceive the significance of the "one o'clock" message and sending the information to "all Pacific outpost commanders. . . ."[56]

All members except Ferguson and Brewster signed the report. Keefe qualified his signature with some "additional views." He went along with most of the conclusions and recommendations; however, he thought the facts had been marshaled, "perhaps unintentionally, with the idea of conferring blame upon Hawaii and minimizing the blame that should properly be assessed at Washington." He faulted the War and Navy departments for not keeping Kimmel and Short posted on diplomatic activities and for failing to send such vital intercepts as the "bomb plot" series, which he stated unequivocally "meant that the ships of the Pacific Fleet in Pearl Harbor were marked for a Japanese attack." So while Keefe concurred "in the findings of the committee with respect to responsibilities of our commanders in Hawaii," he believed their mistakes to be "directly related to the failures of the high command in Washington to have their organizations fully alerted and on a war footing. . . ." He likewise concluded "that secret diplomacy was at the root of the tragedy."[57] This was diametrically opposed to the conclusions of the report which he signed, and it pointed up his fixation on Washington.

Ferguson and Brewster submitted a minority report which has so many points in common with Keefe's comments that either one copied from the other or else worked from a common source. They may well have been the paper which, according to Percy L. Greaves, Jr., Keefe had used and which "Kimmel's able counsel" had prepared.[58]

Ferguson and Brewster reached a total of twenty-one conclusions, some of which are worth consideration. "Judging by the military and naval history of Japan, high authorities in Washington and the Commanders in Hawaii had good grounds for expecting that in starting war the Japanese Government would make a surprise attack on the United States." This was true enough and is an important part of the eternal enigma of Pearl Harbor.

In the opinion of the two senators, Roosevelt's decision to wait for a Japanese attack rather than ask Congress to declare war "increased the responsibility of high authorities in Washington to use the utmost care in

putting the commanders at Pearl Harbor on a full alert for defensive actions
. . . in language not open to misinterpretation. . . ." No reasonable person can
argue with that premise. But here one enters the area of language, which is an
art, not a science, so that all too often what is crystalline to the sender is opaque
to the recipient.

To nobody's surprise, Brewster and Ferguson dealt harshly with Roosevelt.
But they did not accuse him of baiting the Japanese into attacking Pearl Harbor.
In its final summation the minority report listed those specifically charged with
"failure to perform the responsibilities indispensably essential to the defense of
Pearl Harbor . . ."—Roosevelt, Stimson, Knox, Marshall, Stark, and Gerow.
Yet for all their strictures upon Washington for lack of clarity in its instructions
to Hawaii, Brewster and Ferguson did not name Turner, whose office had
prepared the controversial "war warning" message and who was quite as guilty
as Gerow of faults at War Plans Division level.

Ferguson and Brewster did not exculpate Kimmel and Short, citing them
for "failure to perform the responsibilities in Hawaii. . . ."[59]

With all its faults of omission and commission, with all its irrelevancies and
partisan bickering, the congressional committee conducted the most valuable
of all the Pearl Harbor investigations. An old saying goes "Truth is the daughter
of time." Several years had elapsed since the attack, the war had ended, and
Magic as well as some Japanese evidence had become available.

As so often seems to be the case with congressional inquiries, the
report—the document with which the general public is most familiar—is of
less historical value than the testimony and documentation upon which it is
based. For such reports represent opinions, and those opinions, however
honest, may be influenced by preconceptions, political expediencies, and the
pressures of public opinion. The report is the coda to the investigative
symphony, and for the symphony one must be grateful, even though it remains
forever unfinished.

CHAPTER 81

"THE

VERDICT

OF

HISTORY"

The congressional inquiry ended as it had begun—to a fanfare of headlines, a chorus of editorials, and indignant rolls of revisionist kettle-drums.[1] Such gifted, convinced revisionist writers as Greaves and Flynn, and such an able lawyer as Rugg who was very properly devoted to Kimmel's interests, had masterminded preparation of the minority report.[2] Who could blame them if they believed they had the situation firmly under control? But the American lawmaker is unpredictable. Just when the coaches believe they have their men set up for an off-tackle thrust, some senator or congressman may seize the ball and carry it on a wide sweep around end. That is precisely what happened. Gearhart and Keefe signed the majority report, much to the disgust of the coaching staff.

Flynn's venom knew no bounds. He could not credit Keefe and Gearhart with honesty. He was certain they had acted contrary to their convictions. For Gearhart's defection he had a ready explanation. His district in California had "an overwhelming majority of Democratic votes. . . ." Gearhart had "voted a whitewash of Hull and Roosevelt and to blacken the names of Kimmel and Short whom he believes innocent—in order to get himself enough Democratic votes to come back to Congress." But Keefe's straying from the fold apparently puzzled Flynn. "For days he was fulminating against the plans of the Democrats. . . . Why did he change his mind?"[3]

One hesitates to join in guessing what made Keefe tick. However, the transcript of the investigation indicates that he was by no means devoid of independent judgment, and presumably he had not reached national level without a certain amount of political acumen. It was one thing to make partisan hay before and during congressional hearings; it would have been quite another to support publicly a verdict for which no solid evidence had been presented at those hearings. No proof had been forthcoming of malicious wrongdoing in the administration; Kimmel and Short had failed to clear themselves of all shadow of blame; the "winds" lead had expired with a whimper. So it was not astonishing that Keefe joined the mainstream, albeit with serious reservations.

The Chicago *Tribune* cast Gearhart as one of the villains of the piece. "Colleagues of Gearhart speculated that he succumbed to Democratic pressure . . . because of fears for his political future." When a reporter asked Gearhart why he had signed the majority report, he "testily replied that 'the report speaks for itself.' " On the subject of his letter to Kimmel upon completion of the admiral's testimony,* Gearhart "asserted that 'views change as additional evidence is presented.' "[4] So one has the choice of seeing Gearhart as a traitor to his convictions who bowed to political pressure or as a man sufficiently open-minded to adjust his views to the weight of evidence. Morgan recalled that Gearhart became "progressively quite mellow" as the investigation proceeded.[5] The congressman was a long way from being a fool, and it would not be surprising if he had come to recognize that his preconceived notions needed revising.

Had the critics of Keefe and Gearhart been able to lift their eyes to a wider horizon than one limited on the north, east, south, and west by Franklin D. Roosevelt, they might have appreciated that the two congressmen had done the Republican party a favor. They had presented it to the public as an organization sufficiently broad-minded to encompass honest differences of opinion on important issues. What is more, they had enhanced the credibility of the investigation and its conclusions. For the congressional committee to hand the American people two reports with signatures following strictly party lines would have been little short of tragic. Who could have blamed John and Jane Q. Public if they had shrugged off such a result as just another ego trip for lawmakers at the taxpayers' expense, with every member of the committee voting exactly as he might have been expected to do before a word of testimony had been taken?

Kimmel had welcomed the congressional probe. But he did not comment upon the report at its release. He wanted to read it through before making a statement.[6] The fact is, he was exceedingly surprised. "The findings of the Republican Minority of the Commission [*sic*] was a terrific shock to Rugg, and likewise to me," he wrote his old friend and ardent supporter Admiral Harry E. Yarnell on September 13, 1946, "because Rugg had kept me informed of what they assured him would be the gist of the report." However, it was all "water under the dam," and Kimmel had "no regrets at having pursued the course of action" which he followed. He squeezed a few drops of comfort from the situation. "I was disappointed, of course, at the Minority findings, but a careful reading shows that the Minority did everything but clear me completely and did place the major part of the blame in Washington where it belongs." The majority report "was about what we expected, but they labored so much to keep

---

*See Chapter 79.

any blame away from Washington that I think it is quite apparent to any careful reader that was their object from the beginning."[7]

Interviewed in Dallas, Short expressed displeasure. "The majority members of the investigation committee are entitled to their point of view," he said, "but I am satisfied that the testimony presented at the hearings fully absolved me from any blame and I believe such will be the verdict of history. As I have stated before, my conscience is clear."[8]

Nevertheless, the committee had not "fully absolved" either Kimmel or Short. Thus, the two commanders did not reach their goal—complete exoneration of themselves and the placing of all blame upon their superiors in Washington. But at least the investigation had publicly cleared them of the cruelly wounding charge of "dereliction of duty."

Short's testimony before the congressional committee reveals that he was exceedingly bitter toward the War Department. But having said his say, he did not make self-justification a lifework. Instead, he and Mrs. Short retired to their Georgian-style residence in Dallas. No one could mistake their home for other than what it was—the retirement haven of a couple whose whole adult life had been involved in the Army. Pictures, maps, and reference books, a framed set of medals flanked by two certificates—all testified to where Short's heart would always be. In this congenial atmosphere Short, like so many sensitive spirits, turned to flowers, tending roses and zinnias behind protective hedges. He lived such a "quiet, even secluded life" that when he died, a neighbor could say, "I've been here more than a year, and I have never seen the general that I know of."

Perhaps Short realized that he had made enough mistakes to justify at least part of his punishment. Perhaps he disdained to explain his case or ask for sympathy any more than an eighteenth-century French aristocrat would have appealed to the knitting women around the guillotine. Perhaps he was simply tired. He passed from life quietly, keeping his secrets. "He never, as you might say, let down his hair—even to me," his son, Major Walter Dean Short, told reporters. "He laid all the facts about Pearl Harbor before the congressional committee. . . . There was no book for him to write, nothing more that he could say."[9]

Perhaps the general had nothing more to say, but what about the man? What of the Walter C. Short, independent of his uniform, who lived and moved, hoped and dreamed, who married a beautiful woman and fathered a fine son to carry on in his footsteps? What did he think, what did he feel, how did he react? Historians who wish to understand that Walter C. Short must work without the general's help. And who can deny that there is something admirable about his dignified silence?

Members of Short's command agree that his long ordeal, following the shock and grief of the attack, contributed to his untimely death at the age of sixty-nine.[10] The pneumonia he suffered in December 1945 permanently weakened him. The general had been ill with heart disease for several months, seriously so for more than two weeks, when death claimed him on September

3, 1949, at his home in Dallas. Four days later he was buried at Arlington National Cemetery with full military honors. Only his widow, son, daughter-in-law, a few close relatives, and former associates like his troubleshooter Fleming and his aide Truman attended the simple Episcopal rites. September is summer in Washington, but as the pallbearers carried Short's casket to his final resting place on a wooded hill below the Lee mansion, a few autumn leaves spangled the green grass, as if winter were coming to the year prematurely, as it had to the general.[11]

Kimmel was made of sterner stuff. When the storm passed, the admiral had been destroyed, but the man stood like a rock, sustained by his own conviction that he had done his best and by the steadfast loyalty of the many officers and sailors who could not believe ill of him. He severed his connection with the Frederic R. Harris Company in 1947, and with his wife, Dorothy, moved to Groton, Connecticut, to be near his son Thomas Kinkaid Kimmel, then instructing at the Submarine School.[12] Thus, the admiral kept in touch with the life of the service which had been Dorothy's only rival for his heart. The Navy was in his blood. He could not live without the sight and sound of the sea and the bustle of the docks.

There he could have dwelt in placid contentment had he chosen to do so. But he allowed the memory of Pearl Harbor to consume his life. As CinCPAC he had never taken the will for the deed, but he could not understand why current history did not accord him that leniency. Justifying himself before the American people became a fixation.

Yet one cannot wonder that Kimmel turned almost morbid. He had grown to eminence in an atmosphere of clear-cut quid pro quo. If one obeyed the laws of God and man, studied diligently, denied oneself, worked hard, took one's place in the community, discharged one's duties, dealt justly with one's fellowman, one would prosper and reach the end of the road full of years and honor.

Kimmel had done all these things. But after nine months, almost to the day, as CinCUS, fate had dealt him this crushing blow. It must have seemed to Kimmel that either the premise upon which he had built his life had been a delusion or he had done something wrong somewhere along the line. It is a question which of these choices would be the more intolerable to Kimmel's straightforward mind and proud spirit.

Then, too, the human psyche has its own self-sealing properties. For Kimmel to acknowledge even to himself that he shared to the slightest measure in the guilt of Pearl Harbor would be to leave himself open to a hell of remorse and memory. He experienced his moment of truth on December 7, 1941, when he held a spent bullet in his fingers and murmured, "It would have been merciful had it killed me."* Then the fire doors slammed shut. The fault must lie elsewhere.

---

*See Chapter 62.

Kimmel died of a heart attack on May 14, 1968, in his eighty-sixth year. No newspapers devoted more space to the story of his passing than the Honolulu *Star-Bulletin* and the *Advertiser.* What could be more fitting? With Hawaii, rather than with Kentucky, where he was born, or with Connecticut, where he died, his name would be forever linked—and no more so than in his own mind. The *Advertiser* and *Star-Bulletin,* which combined forces on Sundays, published an editorial on May 15, 1968, which contained neither vindictiveness nor sentimentality. It ended: "He [Kimmel] was caught in the net of the Navy dictum that the man on the bridge is responsible for his ship. It may not be fair but it is just. The buck stops there. . . ."[13]

Had U.S. forces discovered and beaten off Nagumo's task force or made the attackers suffer unacceptable losses over the target, Kimmel and Short would have received the credit. By the same token, they cannot escape the onus of surprise and defeat. Short in particular must carry a large portion of blame.

According to Fleming, ". . . Short's concept of defending the Hawaiian Islands was to defend them away from Hawaii" by means of "fleet action and also air action and bases which would not be subject to direct attack by the Japanese."[14] This theory has overtones of passing the buck. In the nature of geography, defending Hawaii from a distance would have to devolve upon the Navy. Short's principal task at hand was to guard the Navy's ships without which long-distance defense would be impossible.

As we have seen, Short took hold well, and those who served under him seem to have held him in considerable respect. But he became tremendously preoccupied with training for its own sake. "Short was a good scout," said Bicknell, "but he got so wrapped up in the training business that he could not see the other issues at stake."[15] As a result, in Hawaii, to quote Representative Hamilton Fish of New York, "We were in a state of preparedness instead of a state of alertness."[16] Short was so busy honing his blade that he forgot its sharpness mattered little unless it was ready to hand.

Whatever his previous attitudes and programs, Short's concentration upon training should not have survived receipt of the warning dispatch of November 27. The congressional majority report believed that message gave "ample notice to a general in the field that his training was now secondary—that his primary mission had become execution of the orders contained in the dispatch and the effecting of maximum defense security."[17]

Instead, his other fixation sprang into full flower. He was so certain that he had nothing to worry about except sabotage that he did not even consult his field commanders to seek their interpretation of the warning of November 27. His fear of the local Japanese was one of his considerations in upholding his Ordnance Department's refusal to issue ammunition to troops. General Burgin testified: "As long as the ammunition could be left locked up in the magazines, it was pretty safely guarded and could not be tampered with to any great extent."[18]

So when the Japanese hit unexpectedly, the fixed batteries had some ammunition nearby at Burgin's insistence, but it was boxed. The mobile guns and batteries had none. Their ammunition was stored in Aliamanu Crater, several miles away. And the mobile batteries were not in field position.[19] More eloquently than any human testimony the silent guns of Oahu bear witness to just how seriously Short took the possibility of attack from without.

Short compounded the initial mistake by not working closely with the Navy in this situation, which obviously called for mutual understanding and joint action. Short "was sure from all of our talk that everybody understood just what was being done."[20] But Poco Smith erroneously told Kimmel that a full Army alert was in effect.* Bloch, too, thought that the Army was under "a complete alert" and did not find out that it had been for sabotage only until Short so informed him after the attack.[21]

Two other factors—both negative—entered into Short's decision to initiate Alert No. 1. For one, to him the warning indicated that the War Department's paramount idea was "that no international incident must take place in Hawaii that would provoke the Japanese or give them an excuse."[22] The second was Short's concern lest total alert frighten the civilian population.

We cannot stress too strongly that all the American failures and shortcomings which contributed to the Japanese victory at Pearl Harbor stemmed from the root disbelief that the Japanese would undertake the risky venture. Had Short even halfway accepted the possibility, such intangibles as the attitude of the local populace and the Japanese government would have had to yield to the urgent necessity of preparing to perform the Hawaiian Department's prime mission.

In his testimony Short seemed confident that because long-range air patrols came under the Navy, he could safely ignore Washington's order to undertake reconnaissance. Yet he had a means of reconnaissance in hand which the War Department had expected him to utilize when it sent that directive. This was radar, a function which Short mishandled throughout 1941. As usual, he attempted to dump the blame on Washington because some stateside systems had been installed before Hawaii received any equipment.[23]

But that cannot excuse the chaotic conditions which existed in the Hawaiian Department in regard to the aircraft warning system (AWS). The testimony of radar expert Lieutenant Commander William E. Taylor was devastating. "At no time before December 7, 1941, did this Command furnish either the authority or impetus badly needed to get the work or organization properly started."[24]

No attitude on the part of Washington, no lack of equipment or funds can explain or excuse the failure to establish at least approach lanes or a reporting system to account for planes in Hawaiian skies. All that such procedures required was an appreciation of the value of incoming aircraft identification and fighter direction—abundantly demonstrated in the Battle of Britain—plus a

---

*See Chapter 51.

little initiative and cooperation. But unfortunately those qualities, equally costless and priceless, appear to have been missing.

Short did run his radar for a brief time daily as we have seen and, in so doing, displayed inconsistency. Radar was of no use against his bugaboo, sabotage, and if he admitted the possibility of an air attack, as his use of radar implied, why did he not institute Alert No. 2 or No. 3? Perhaps the key lies in Short's words about his radar operation—that he was "doing it for training more than any idea that it would be real."[25] All that goes far toward explaining the situation at the Opana Station and the Information Center on the morning of December 7.

Of all the mistakes, oversights, and blunders on the American side of the Pearl Harbor story, none contributed more to Japan's success than did Short's. Not only did he fail to perform his mission, but he also did not truly understand it. And in the crisis of November 27 he narrowed his vision to the point where the whole military power at his command—and it was considerable—stalked a mouse while the tiger jumped through the window.

Short's opposite number, Bloch, held what Captain Paul B. Ryan, USN, described to Fleming as "a retirement job . . . nice quarters, not too much work. . . ."[26] Yet Navy regulations and existing war plans assigned to the commandant, Fourteenth Naval District, important duties that called for an alert individual at the peak of physical and mental powers. In addition, as naval base defense officer Bloch was responsible for sharing with the Army "joint supervisory control over the defense against air attack," working with the Army "to have their anti-aircraft guns emplaced," exercising "supervisory control over Naval shore-based aircraft, arranging through Commander Patrol Wing Two for coordination of the joint air effort between the Army and Navy."[27]

Like Short, Bloch had his problems and shortages. But, again like Short, he was psychologically unprepared to use the means at his disposal. To have performed one of his primary functions required nothing but a telephone, a staff car, and a little get-up-and-go. Direct, professional liaison with Short was Bloch's, not Kimmel's, responsibility. Unfortunately some of Bloch's actions lead one to wonder how much thought he gave to his duty to cooperate with the Army. He sent the Hawaiian Department as liaison officer a young lieutenant who, although bright and willing, lacked the experience and the clout necessary to represent the Navy effectively. This Bloch did because Lieutenant Burr was the man he could spare, not because he was best qualified. As of December 1, Bloch "had no knowledge as to whether or not they were standing regular watches" on the AWS. Nor did he "make any inquiries about it."[28] Thus, Bloch took a cavalier attitude toward one of the best means of alerting Hawaii to the approach of a hostile force.

In matters not directly connected with the Army Bloch also showed lack of judgment. He was at least partially responsible for the Fleet's being placed on so rigid an operating program that its movements were readily predictable. Largely at Bloch's request, Richardson had established a fixed schedule. "The reason being that I desired to economize on the tug hire," Bloch explained.

". . . I desired to have as little interruption with the dredging operations in the channel as possible."[29] Bloch rated business as usual above security of ship movements.

Later one of the Fleet commanders wrote to Kimmel that surprise drills "were interfering with certain other exercises. . . ." So he asked that surprise drills "should be laid out ahead of time." Kimmel directed Bloch to comply. Short and Bloch arranged a schedule and "always let them know, ahead of time, when we would have a drill."[30] Apparently neither Bloch nor Short pointed out that this procedure was fine for practicing techniques, but an obvious washout in teaching how to cope with surprise.

Relations between the district and the naval air arm were little short of surrealistic. Take, for instance, the Joint Air Agreement of March 21, 1941, and its implementing operating plans. The aircraft had other tasks assigned them, "but when we sounded an air-raid alarm, they all got together" and became the Base Defense Air Force. Oahu's defenders "had drill after drill . . . in order that the acts and operations of this Air Force would be automatic. . . ." But this arrangement did not go into effect until M-Day had been declared. And while the plan called for "air search for enemy ships," this was "only in the event of an attack." No plan existed for a situation short of war. The command confusion was such that Bloch admitted he did not know whether Kimmel would hold him or Bellinger responsible if anything went wrong.[31]

At first Bloch denied to the Navy court that his duties as naval base defense officer included aerial reconnaissance. Yet the Joint Coastal Frontier Defense Plan (JCD-42) clearly so specified.[32] He finally admitted to the Army board that he had accepted that responsibility but stressed that his "obligations for distant reconnaissance would not become binding until that plan was operative." Asked if Short realized that Bloch lacked the facilities to fulfill his part of the agreement, Bloch demonstrated his talent for broken-field running: "I cannot say that I never told him and I cannot say that I did tell him."[33] Bloch tried hard to place upon Washington the blame for failing to activate JCD-42. This will not hold water. As the congressional majority report pointed out, ". . . the execution was essentially a responsibility resting in Hawaii."[34]

The status of Bellinger's patrol aircraft between November 27 and the attack was Condition B-5—50 percent of both matériel and personnel on four hours' notice. This status, which Bloch had directed, was, according to Bellinger, "the normal readiness prescribed for normal conditions."[35] Once again, this time in the face of a clear warning, alert measures bowed to routine.

To Bloch it seemed "obvious that the Commandant of the District couldn't use the patrol planes without permission of the Fleet because the planes were employed by the Fleet on other missions." But Bloch could have asked for that permission. Had he recommended instituting at least partial air reconnaissance, undoubtedly Kimmel would have given him the green light. That is precisely what happened in an alert during the summer of 1941.[36]

Bloch sailed through the Pearl Harbor investigative fires without being so much as singed, in no small measure thanks to his acumen in maintaining a low profile. But one cannot help agreeing with Captain Zacharias's belief that a contributing factor to the Japanese success at Pearl Harbor was Kimmel's reluctance to tell Bloch to get on the stick or he would find someone who would.[37]

Two of Kimmel's mistakes he inherited. The decision not to use antitorpedo nets around the battleships was Richardson's; still, Kimmel neither rescinded nor modified it. Ideal nets were never available to him.[38] Yet if Kimmel had taken the possibility of aerial torpedo strikes on his ships as seriously as the Japanese took the possibility of antitorpedo nets protecting the American vessels, we can imagine him hounding the Navy Department to speed up development and production of such nets.

When Kimmel took over, he changed the schedule which Richardson had instituted at Bloch's instigation, but he maintained some of the rigidity. The predictable movements of fleet units enabled Japanese agents to report to Tokyo that major vessels were invariably in port over the weekends. This information was a foundation stone of Japanese planning.

But we agree with Forrestal "that his [Kimmel's] most grievous failure was his failure to conduct long-range air reconnaissance in the more dangerous sectors from Oahu during the week preceding the attack."[39] Kimmel's lack of sufficient aircraft for 360-degree coverage is not an acceptable excuse for not using such planes as were on hand. Bloch's figures indicate that thirty-six aircraft were available. He observed that if these "could have maintained a 360-degree patrol as far as their radius of action would permit them to do, it would have been very thin on the outer circumference."[40]

But thirty-six planes, however inadequate, are thirty-six more than none. Moreover, the Army had twenty-one B-18s in commission. The Navy could have requested use of these medium bombers, which, if not ideal for the purpose, were usable.[41] A coverage of 360 degrees was not called for. Both the Navy and Army aircraft could and should have been utilized on the basis of such carefully reasoned estimates as the Martin-Bellinger and Farthing reports and of the experience gleaned from Fleet exercises.

One cannot be sure that long-range patrol planes winging northward on or before the morning of December 7 would have located Nagumo's task force. The odds were slim, to be sure, but by rejecting long-distance aerial reconnaissance, Kimmel reduced those odds to zero. If successful, such scouting might well have enabled the ships in harbor to be alert, Short's fighter planes armed and aloft, his ground defenses manned and ready. If unsuccessful, at least Kimmel would have done his manifest duty.

He reached his decision without consulting his most concerned subordinates. Bloch did not receive a copy of the "war warning" until the next day. Nor did Kimmel seek the advice and professional judgment of Davis, his Fleet aviation officer, or of Layton, his Fleet intelligence officer. Bellinger did not even know about the message. We cannot say definitely what the result would have been had Kimmel sought Bellinger's opinion. But this we know: Bellinger could have told Kimmel that he was "in agreement with Admiral Davis that the greatest possibility of a successful air attack lay in an attack coming in from the sector of the north because of the prevailing wind conditions" and that he had enough aircraft available to have covered that sector for "at least a week. . . ."[42]

Equally regrettable is the fact that Kimmel did not notify Short when he received word on December 3 that the Japanese had ordered certain consulates and embassies, including the one in Washington, to destroy their codes. His failure to appreciate the importance of this step may well have been as tragic in its consequences as was his decision of November 27 against long-range reconnaissance. With this later information he had the chance to reconsider his former assessment of the situation. But as blindly as any dark-starred hero of Greek or Elizabethan drama, Kimmel ignored the opportunity.

Kimmel and his advisers must share blame with the higher headquarters for failure to comprehend the implications when Japan's major carriers dropped out of radio traffic. They were not moving south; Rochefort had a very good line on that operation. To add a still more lurid hue to the picture, on December 1 the Japanese Navy changed its call signs for the second time within a month—an unheard-of action. Yet both Hawaii and Washington assumed, with deadly inaccuracy, that Japan's main carrier strength remained in home waters. In Ingersoll's words, Kimmel "was the man who was in charge of the methods of determining the location of the Japanese Fleet through radio intelligence. . . ."[43] Japanese blackout of the task force, the dummy message traffic, and American complacency effectively canceled out the possibility of locating Japan's First Air Fleet by this means. But such factors do not excuse the Army and Navy for not closing all mouseholes when the Japanese flattops disappeared.

For years Kimmel had worked, planned, and studied with one end in view: When and if war came, he would be on the bridge of his flagship speeding to engage the enemy. So he did not recognize the voice of opportunity when it murmured in his ear, "This is your hour," for that hour demanded of him that for the moment, he cease polishing the sword and pick up the shield. He lacked the perception to read the meaning of the warnings and events of those last ten days before disaster and the flexibility to adjust his orientation from training to defense.

Some of their more ardent sympathizers termed Kimmel and Short "scapegoats." This is one of those "loaded" words which one should use with the utmost care. It signifies a blameless creature punished for the sins of others. Kimmel and Short were no more blameless than they were solely blameworthy. The stain of error permeates the entire American fabric of Pearl Harbor from the President down to the Fourteenth Naval District and the Hawaiian Department. There are no Pearl Harbor scapegoats.

Mistakes at Washington level were many and varied, but it seems most unlikely that any one of them in itself was a decisive factor. Roosevelt's solicitude that the public not be alarmed during the mounting crisis in the autumn of 1941 had a baleful effect. The instruction not to upset the citizenry watered down the Army's warning to Short of November 27.

A related administration error was the length to which the executive branch went to handle the Japanese with kid gloves. In pursuance of this policy, the United States kept open the Japanese consulates although it closed the German and Italian; gave spies like Yoshikawa a free hand and squelched the efforts of Senator Gillette and Congressman Dies to dig into Japanese espionage. This attitude entered into Kimmel's hesitancy to activate the Short-Bloch defense plan. "It might have been considered by the Japanese an overt act," he explained to the Army board.[44] The Army, too, carried this reluctance to irritate Japan to absurd lengths. One reason why Marshall did not telephone Short on the morning of December 7 was that "it could be construed as an overt act involving an immediate act of war against Japan."[45]

War and Navy Department errors fell into two main areas. First was the failure to keep Kimmel and Short adequately posted. Even Kimmel conceded that Hawaii did not need a Magic machine, but more thorough information on the trends of U.S.-Japanese relations would have been helpful, especially in the late autumn. And more than once Stark followed up an official warning of dark developments by a personal letter downgrading the danger.

The prime error, however, lay in keeping from the Hawaiian commanders the contents of the consular messages, especially the "bomb plot" series. The fact that Washington did not evaluate this information at its real worth is inexcusable. No attempt to explain away or minimize these messages stands up before their content. Kimmel and Short had every right and the urgent need to receive the full text of the exchanges between Tokyo and Honolulu whenever these referred to ships of the Fleet or military installations in the Islands or in any fashion pointed to tactical espionage.

Both Washington and Oahu erred seriously in connection with the warnings of November 27. Turner placed himself on a hot spot when he testified that he "thought the chances were about 50-50 that we would get a heavy raid in Hawaii. . . ."[46] This estimate imposed upon him the clear duty of saying so plainly in his directive to Kimmel. Such a warning could have done no harm and might have done inexpressible good. Not only would it have alerted Kimmel in unmistakable terms, but it also would have cleared the Navy Department of blame for failing to do just that.

The War and Navy departments should have ridden herd on Kimmel and Short following dispatch of these warnings, despite the usually sound policy of not breathing down the necks of major field commanders. This was no ordinary situation. Stimson and Knox, Marshall and Stark should have insisted upon receiving daily or at least very frequent follow-ups on the situation from all addressees. Such reports would have revealed quickly the inconsistencies between what Washington had intended be done in the Hawaiian area and what Kimmel and Short actually did. Instead, when Gerow received Short's reply to the message of November 27, he assumed it answered the G-2 sabotage warning dispatched the same day. A quick check of the number which Short cited against the file copies of the two dispatches would have proved that this was not the case. One of Gerow's assistants should have performed this routine task before the general saw the incoming dispatch. The Navy did not even have a reply to interpret or misinterpret, having asked none of Kimmel. Hence a number of key officials in the Navy Department believed that he had sent his Fleet to sea. Unfortunately throughout the Pearl Harbor story we find a plethora of assumptions based upon too few facts.

Another communications problem arose on the morning of December 7. Despite Marshall's realization that the "one o'clock" message was very significant, he failed either to use the scrambler phone or to ensure that the message went to Hawaii on a priority basis. And that information could have been on its way much earlier had anyone on duty possessed the power or initiative to act before the Chief of Staff reached his office. But, as the Army board noted, "Complete authority to act in General Marshall's absence does not seem to have been given to any one subordinate. . . ."[47]

On that same occasion Stark should have sent a Navy message to duplicate and thereby stress Marshall's dispatch or, better yet, have phoned Kimmel personally. Stark movingly testified to the Navy court about his self-examination to determine where he might have been "derelict" or "might have omitted anything." The only such incident he could recall was his not having paralleled the Marshall message.[48]

All these failures at all levels have a common denominator—the gap between knowledge of possible danger and belief in its existence, as Forrestal noted in his fourth endorsement to the Navy and Hewitt reports:

> . . . although the imminence of hostile action by the Japanese was known, and the capabilities of the Japanese Fleet and Air Arm were recognized in war plans made to meet just such hostile action, these factors did not reach the state of conviction in the minds of the responsible officers . . . to an extent sufficient to impel them to bring about that implementation of the plans that was necessary if the initial hostile action was to be repelled or at least mitigated.[49]

This fundamental disbelief is the root of the whole tragedy. All other acts or failures to act are its stalks, branches, and fruit. Captain Gilven M. Slonim, USN, has put the matter in a nutshell of wisdom: "Possibilities and probabilities, capabilities and intentions become academic when one does not accept the credibility of his own estimates. Americans did not believe."[50]

Yet it would be a mistake of the first magnitude to credit the success of the Pearl Harbor operation solely to American errors. We have seen how meticulously the Japanese perfected their planning; how diligently they trained their pilots and bombardiers; how they modified weapons to achieve maximum damage; how persistently they dredged up and utilized information about the U.S. Pacific Fleet. They balked at no hazard, ready to risk a wild leap to achieve their immediate ends.

Yamamoto was primarily responsible for conceiving the plan, but literally hundreds ensured its success, from Nagumo to the lowliest grease monkey. We must acknowledge the special roles played by that remarkable combination

Genda and Fuchida. Genda with his originality and bold intelligence, Fuchida with his practical industry and contagious enthusiasm became the brain and heart behind the tactical plan. With few exceptions the Pearl Harbor planners were positive thinkers. Nevertheless, they did not let optimism degenerate into sloppiness. They understood that to a degree a man makes his own luck. He must reach out to pluck the fruit, not wait for it to fall into his mouth. Nevertheless, plain, unadulterated luck played a significant part in Japan's success.

As an example, the weather provided relatively smooth seas and an abundance of fog, thus permitting Nagumo to refuel and hide his ships at the same time. Moreover, at the perfect moment, just in time to permit accurate strikes, the clouds over Oahu parted in so propitious a manner that in briefing the Emperor, both Nagumo and Fuchida referred to the phenomenon as obviously caused by divine intervention. Such factors were totally beyond human power to arrange. The flight of B-17s approaching Oahu at almost the same time as Fuchida's first wave, thus disguising the incoming attack force, was another bit of good fortune completely out of Japanese hands. What is more, the whole series of American blunders and misunderstandings were so many unexpected bonuses for the Japanese.

The tremendous gamble paid off with Japan's greatest victory of World War II. It made its play and cashed in its winnings, but its triumph was only temporary. The Japanese fought the long, agonizing conflict which ensued with all the skill and bravery which were their glory and the senseless brutality which was their bane, but never again would Hirohito's Navy touch the heights of that first attack. For never again would it have the time to exploit fully the national gifts for painstaking craftsmanship, exquisite design, and ceaseless patience. And never again would the Japanese catch Uncle Sam so completely asleep at the switch.

As the initial shock and gloom wore off, the American public began to realize that the Pearl Harbor attack had been by no means an unmitigated disaster. Even Bloch, no wild-eyed progressive, said in retrospect, "The Japanese only destroyed a lot of old hardware. In a sense they did us a favor.[51] Far more quickly and thoroughly than the Americans could have done themselves, the Japanese had kicked the U.S. Navy upstairs into a swift, modern force with the carrier at its heart.

The shallow waters in the anchorage preserved most of the stricken ships to fight another day. The salvage and restoration of those ships are a saga of expertise, tenacity, hard work, and invincible optimism. Before the Pacific war ended, all but three of Japan's victims had been renovated and helped harass the Axis to final defeat. One of the three—the target ship *Utah*—would not have engaged in the conflict in any case. Just two combat battleships—*Arizona* and *Oklahoma*—were beyond salvage.[52]

Of infinitely more value than the repair of shattered ships was the welding together of the American people into a mighty spear and shield of determination. No more did Americans ask whose fight it was or question what they should do about it. Yet one must not exaggerate the type of unity the Japanese bestowed upon the Americans. The entire nation had not suddenly become of unanimous mind; the national energies had mobilized to achieve a single, readily identifiable goal.

The Japanese gave each American a personal stake in the titanic struggle for the minds and bodies of mankind which raged in Europe and Asia. After December 7, 1941, Americans no longer could look upon the war from a distance as an impersonal, ideological conflict. The sense of outrage triggered a feeling of direct involvement which resulted in an explosion of national energy. The Japanese gave the average American a cause he could understand and believe to be worth fighting for.

Thus, in a very special way Pearl Harbor became the turning point of the world struggle. The United States could—and undoubtedly would—have entered World War II eventually in some other way. No doubt in the long run the manpower, resources, and industrial might of the United States would have prevailed. But Pearl Harbor ensured that American strength would be concentrated into an arrow point of resolution, that the entire nation would stand as one man and woman behind the men at the front.

Military history is one of the most rapidly shifting of all studies. Strategy and tactics alter with fluctuating world conditions, technology, and leadership; alliances about-face so that the deadly enemy of yesterday may easily become the cherished friend of today; the daring revolutionary of one war suffers a sea change into the rigid dogmatist of the next; weapons and other matériel become obsolete almost before they leave the drawing board. But Pearl Harbor demonstrated one enduring lesson: The unexpected can happen and often does.

APPENDIX

NOTES

Chapter 1
"CANCER OF
THE PACIFIC"

1. *Japan Times and Advertiser* (Tokyo), January 1, 1941.
2. *Nichi Nichi,* January 1, 1941; quoted in the *Japan Chronicle* (Kobe), January 17, 1941. All newspaper dates are quoted for the country's local time.
3. United States Department of State, *Papers Relating to the Foreign Relations of the United States: Japan, 1931–1941,* Vol. II (Washington D.C., 1943), pp. 165-166 (cited hereafter as *Foreign Relations.*)
4. Joseph C. Grew, *Ten Years in Japan* (New York, 1944), p. 359 (cited hereafter as *Ten Years in Japan.*)
5. *Japan Times and Advertiser, January 24, 1941.*
6. September 3, 1940. Quoted in *Japan Advertiser.* On October 18, 1940, the *Japan Advertiser* was sold to the *Nippon Times,* which took the name *Japan Times and Advertiser.* This newspaper became the mouthpiece of the Japanese Foreign Office.
7. Proceedings of the International Military Tribunal sitting at Tokyo (cited hereafter as *Far East Mil. Trib.*), International Prosecution Section (IPS), Doc. No. 3125, October 20, 1947; Kichisaburo Nomura,

Beikoku ni Tsukai Shita (Tokyo, 1946), pp. 12–17; interview with Adm. Kichisaburo Nomura, May 7, 1949 (hereafter Nomura).
8. Interview with Nomura, May 7, 1949.
9. *Ten Years in Japan,* p. 367.
10. Ibid., p. 358.
11. *Hochi,* January 23, 1941, quoted in *Japan Times and Advertiser,* January 24, 1941.
12. February 8, 1941, quoted in *Japan Times and Advertiser,* February 9, 1941.
13. *Japan Times and Advertiser,* January 27, 1941.
14. *Japan Advertiser,* September 6, 1940.
15. Letter, Adm. Isoroku Yamamoto to VADM. Mineichi Koga, January 23, 1941. Courtesy of RADM. Teikichi Hori, close friend and confidant of Yamamoto (hereafter Hori).
16. *Japan Times and Advertiser,* January 27, 1941.

Chapter 2
"ON A MOONLIGHT NIGHT
OR AT DAWN"

1. Letter from Cmdr. Masataka Chihaya, February 4, 1970, who was aboard *Nagato* at the time (hereafter Chihaya).
2. Courtesy of Hori.
3. *Reports of General MacArthur: Japanese Operations in the Southwest Pacific Area,*

Vol. II, Part I (Washington, D.C., 1966), p. 33, n. l.

4. Courtesy of Hori.
5. Courtesy of Juji Enomoto, legal adviser to the Japanese Navy (hereafter Enomoto).
6. Courtesy of Hori.
7. Interview with Capt. Yasuji Watanabe, February 21, 1949 (hereafter Watanabe).
8. Kumao Harada, *Saionji Ko to Seikyoku* (Tokyo, 1950–1956), Vol. I, p. 36 (cited hereafter as *Saionji-Harada*). The translation here used is the one in the English-language edition, *Saionji-Harada Memoirs*, Part XXIV, pp. 2987–88.
9. Shigeru Fukudome, *Shikan: Shinjuwan Kogeki* (Tokyo, 1955), p. 150 (cited hereafter as *Shikan: Shinjuwan Kogeki*).
10. Interview with VADM. Shigeru Fukudome, April 27, 1950 (hereafter Fukudome).
11. *Shikan: Shinjuwan Kogeki*, p. 151; interview with Fukudome, May 4, 1950.
12. *Shiban: Shinjuwan Kogeki*, p. 152.
13. Interview with Fukudome, May 4, 1950.
14. Courtesy of Hori. This disposes of the long-standing myth that Pearl Harbor had been under active consideration for years.
15. Interview with Enomoto and Shuichi "George" Mizota, who often served as Yamamoto's interpreter and translator, May 15, 1950 (hereafter Mizota).
16. The following extracts are from a document discovered in 1964, which actually is a draft. It was Yamamoto's custom to write and sign both an original draft and a final letter in communicating with most of his colleagues; presumably Oikawa destroyed the letter as Yamamoto requested. The family of Capt. Shigeru Fujii, a member of Yamamoto's staff, found this draft among Fujii's effects and presented it to the Historical Department of the Japanese Self-Defense Force. A photostatic copy of this draft may be found in the Japanese-language edition of the book *Tora! Tora! Tora!*, by the author, published in Japan in 1966, p. 43. As far as we know, the first person to state that Oikawa knew of Yamamoto's plan in January 1941 was RADM. Sokichi Takagi. See his article, "Ningen Yamamoto Isoroku," *Bungei Shunju* (January 1950), p. 95.

Chapter 3
"DIFFICULT BUT NOT IMPOSSIBLE"

1. Minoru Genda, *Kaigun Kokutai Shimatsu Ki (Hasshin Hen)* (Tokyo, 1961), p. 131 (cited hereafter as *Hasshin Hen*).
2. Interview with Capt. Atsushi Oi, February 15, 1951 (hereafter Oi).
3. Interview with VADM. Ryunosuke Kusake, December 2, 1947 (hereafter Kusaka).
4. The facts concerning Yamamoto's letter to Onishi come from Genda, who read it and conferred at length with Onishi. Interviews with Captain Minoru Genda, March 24, 1947; March 15, 1948; November 4, 1950 (hereafter Genda). See also Minoru Genda, *Shinjuwan Sakusen Kaikoroku* (Tokyo 1972), pp. 10–12 (cited hereafter as *Shinjuwan Sakusen Kaikoroku*); and Minoru Genda, "Higeki Shinjuwan Kogeki," *Bungei Shunju* (December 1962), pp. 198–200 (cited hereafter as "Higeki Shinjuwan Kugeki").
5. Interviews with Oi, February 15, 1951, and Nomura, May 11, 1949.
6. Interview with RADM. Sadatoshi Tomioka, February 17, 1948 (hereafter Tomioka).
7. Interview with Capt. Kosei Maeda, September 15, 1955 (hereafter Maeda).
8. Letter, Yamamoto to Shimada, October 24, 1941. Courtesy of Hori.
9. Interview with Maeda, September 15, 1955.
10. Interview with Genda, March 15, 1948; *Hasshin Hen*, p. 128.
11. Interview with Genda, March 24, 1947.
12. Ibid., March 25, 1947.
13. Ibid., November 4, 1950.
14. Interview with Capt. Sadami Sanagi, August 11, 1949 (hereafter Sanagi).
15. Interview with Genda, November 4, 1950.
16. Ibid., March 25, 1947.
17. Ibid., November 4, 1950.
18. Ibid., March 25, 1947.
19. Ibid., March 15, 1948.
20. Genda affidavit, June 1947. See also *Shinjuwan Sakusen Kaikoroku*, pp. 10–17, and "Higeki Shinjuwan Kogeki," pp. 198–200. Hitoshi Tsunoda et al., *Hawai Sa-*

kusen (Tokyo, 1967), has little to say about these early discussions (cited hereafter as *Hawai Sakusen*).

21. Interview with Tomioka, September 1, 1955.
22. Interview with Capt. Mitsuo Fuchida, July 28, 1947 (hereafter Fuchida).
23. Interview with Genda, March 22, 1947; *Hasshin Hen*, p. 162.
24. *Far East Mil. Trib.*, Interrogation of Genda, March 28, 1945. Later Genda changed his mind about the order of importance. During World War II he insisted on speed first and maneuverability second.
25. Interview with Genda, March 15, 1948.
26. Ibid., March 22, 1947.
27. *Hasshin Hen*, p. 139.
28. Interview with Genda, March 23, 1947; *Hasshin Hen*, pp. 141–142. See also *Shinjuwan Sakusen Kaikoroku*, pp. 68–71, 74.
29. Minoru Genda, *Kaigun Kokutai Shimetsu Ki (Sento Hen)* (Tokyo, 1962), p. 23 (cited hereafter as *Sento Hen*); interviews with Genda, March 23 and 24, 1947. See also *Shinjuwan Sakusen Kaikoroku*, pp. 48–49.
30. *Far East Mil. Trib.*, Interrogation of Genda, November 28, 1945.
31. *Sento Hen*, pp. 31–32; *Shinjuwan Sakusen Kaikoroku*, pp. 55–58.
32. Interviews with Chihaya, March 19, 1947; Genda, March 22, 1947. Report of seventy-nine pages which Genda prepared for the author in Japanese on the subject of Pearl Harbor in May 1947 (cited hereafter as Genda's Analysis).
33. Signed statement by Genda, March 19, 1951.
34. Interview with Genda, August 31, 1955.
35. The main points in Genda's draft are based on interviews with him on March 25, 1947, March 15, 1948, and November 4, 1950, and on Genda's Analysis. See also *Shinjuwan Sakusen Kaikoroku*, pp. 18–20.
36. Cable from Genda through Chihaya, September 26, 1969.
37. Genda's thoughts on the three types of bombing in the days before 1941 can be found in *Sento Hen*, pp. 42–47.
38. Genda's Analysis.
39. Interview with Genda, March 25, 1947.
40. Genda's Analysis and interview with Genda, March 25, 1947.
41. Interview with Genda, March 15, 1948.
42. "Outline Developments of Tactics and Organization of the Japanese Carrier Air Force," prepared for the author by VADM. Jisaburo Ozawa (cited hereafter as Ozawa's Outline). In his first interview with the author on December 15, 1948, Ozawa stated that Yamamoto specifically discussed his Pearl Harbor plan with him in February 1941. Later, after much reflection, Ozawa changed his testimony to the story given in this chapter.

Chapter 4
"NO CREDENCE IN THESE RUMORS"

1. Interview with Capt. Shigeshi Uchida, April 20, 1951. Hereafter Uchida.
2. *Hearings before the Joint Committee on the Investigation of the Pearl Harbor Attack, Congress of the United States, Seventy-ninth Congress* (Washington, D.C., 1946), Part 29, pp. 2145–46 (cited hereafter as *PHA*).
3. Letter, Capt. Henri H. Smith-Hutton, USN (Ret.), to the author, July 20, 1973; *PHA*, Part 14, p. 1042.
4. *PHA*, Part 2, p. 572.
5. Ibid., p. 561.
6. Telephone conversation with RADM. Arthur H. McCollum, November 4, 1968. Hereafter McCollum.
7. *PHA*, Part 36, p. 14.
8. Letter, McCollum to the author, September 20, 1969.
9. Ibid.; *PHA*, Part 8, pp. 3381–82.
10. Telephone conversation with McCollum, November 4, 1968.
11. See the following reports: Hawaiian Department, "Joint Army and Navy Maneuvers, Raid Phase, Jan. 29–31, 1933," and Commandant, 14th Naval District, Commander, NOB, Pearl Harbor, undated, "Joint Exercise Report. Both are in the Classified Operational Archives Branch, Naval History Division, Washington Navy Yard, Washington, D.C.
12. Letter, McCollum to the author, September 20, 1969.
13. *PHA*, Part 14, p. 1044.

14. Letter, McCollum to the author, September 20, 1969.
15. *PHA*, Part 2, p. 778.
16. Ibid., p. 819.
17. Ibid., Part 26, pp. 450–51.
18. Letter, McCollum to the author, September 20, 1969.
19. *PHA*, Part 27, p. 56.
20. Ibid., Part 26, p. 207.
21. Ibid., Part 2, pp. 876–77, corrected by Part 5, p. 2488.
22. *Congressional Record*, Vol. 87, Part 2, February 19, 1941, p. 1198.

Chapter 5
"YOU HURT THE PRESIDENT'S FEELINGS"

1. *PHA*, Part 14, p. 943.
2. Ibid., Part 1, p. 304.
3. Ibid., Part 15, pp. 1594–97.
4. Ibid., Part 27, pp. 125, 121.
5. Ibid., Part 26, p. 22.
6. Ibid., Part 5, p. 2453.
7. Ibid., Part 27, pp. 119–120.
8. Ibid., Part 1, p. 272, 229–230.
9. Ibid., pp. 262–63.
10. Ibid., p. 297.
11. Ibid., Part 14, p. 963.
12. Ibid., Part 1, p. 282.
13. Ibid., pp. 264–66.
14. VADM. George C. Dyer, USN (Ret.), *On the Treadmill to Pearl Harbor: The Memoirs of Admiral James O. Richardson, USN (Retired)*, (Washington, 1972), pp. 435–36 (cited hereafter as *On the Treadmill*).
15. *PHA*, Part 1, pp. 305–06.
16. Ibid., Part 14, pp. 964–69.
17. For a detailed study see Don Newton and A. Cecil Hampshire, *Taranto* (London, 1959).
18. *PHA*, Part 14, p. 973.
19. Ibid., Part 4, pp. 1939, 1983.
20. Ibid., Part 14, pp. 973–74.
21. Ibid., p. 975.
22. Ibid., Part 1, p. 285.
23. Memorandum for the Secretary from Stark, November 12, 1940, papers of Franklin D. Roosevelt, the Franklin D. Roosevelt Library, Hyde Park, N.Y., President's Secretary's File, Box 63 (cited hereafter as PSF, Roosevelt Papers).
24. *PHA*, Part 5, p. 2172.
25. Telephone conversation with VADM. Charles Wellborn, Jr., April 19, 1969, and subsequent correspondence (hereafter Wellborn).
26. Unpublished diary of Henry L. Stimson, Yale University Library, New Haven, Conn., May 6 and November 30, 1941 (cited hereafter as Stimson Diary).
27. *PHA*, Part 14, p. 985.
28. Ibid., p. 986.
29. Ibid., pp. 986–87.
30. Ibid., pp. 988–89.
31. Ibid., p. 990.
32. Ibid., p. 991.
33. Ibid., pp. 991–92.
34. Ibid., Part 1, pp. 322–23.
35. Interview with VADM. William Ward Smith, November 29, 1962 (hereafter Smith).
36. Interviews with RADM. Dundas P. Tucker, August 21 and 22, 1964 (hereafter Tucker).
37. Interview with VADM. George C. Dyer, October 20, 1969 (hereafter Dyer).
38. Interview with VADM. Walter DeLany, November 2, 1962 (hereafter DeLany). *PHA*, Part 23, pp. 1227–28.
39. Interview with RADM. Husband E. Kimmel, November 29, 1963 (hereafter Kimmel).
40. Husband E. Kimmel, *Admiral Kimmel's Story* (Chicago, 1955), pp. 6–7 (cited hereafter as *Admiral Kimmel's Story*).
41. *PHA*, Part 4, pp. 1939–40: Part 23, p. 1114.
42. Ibid., Part 24, p. 1363.
43. Ibid., p. 1364.
44. Ibid.
45. Ibid., Part 14, pp. 993–94.
46. Ibid., p. 997.
47. Ibid., p. 998.
48. Ibid., Part 1, pp. 339–40.
49. Ibid., pp. 323–24.

Chapter 6
"THAT MUST HENCEFORTH BEAR RESPONSIBILITY"

1. Honolulu *Advertiser*, February 2, 1941.
2. *PHA*, Part 5, p. 2172.

3. The following summary of Kimmel's career is based in part upon his service record and "Officer's Record of Fitness," courtesy of Kimmel.
4. *PHA,* Part 23, p. 1227.
5. Interview with Capt. Allen G. Quynn, December 30, 1963 (hereafter Quynn).
6. Interview with Capt. Walter J. East, August 7, 1964 (hereafter East).
7. Honolulu *Star-Bulletin,* February 5, 1941.
8. Ibid., February 8, 1941.
9. This summary of Short's career is taken from *PHA,* Part 7, pp. 2966–77, and Part 22, pp. 31–32.
10. *PHA,* Part 22, p. 32.

Chapter 7
"OUR FIRST CONCERN IS TO PROTECT THE FLEET"

1. Stimson Diary, September 16, 1941.
2. *PHA,* Part 14, pp. 1003–04.
3. Ibid., Part 3, p. 1063.
4. Ibid., p. 1064.
5. Ibid., pp. 1064–65.
6. Stanley D. Porteus, *And Blow Not the Trumpet: A Prelude to Peril* (Palo Alto, Calif., 1947), p. 285 (cited hereafter as *And Blow Not the Trumpet*).
7. *PHA,* Part 3, p. 1065.
8. Ibid., Part 24, pp. 1835–37.
9. Ibid., p. 1838.
10. Ibid., Part 22, p. 85.
11. Interview with Adm. Claude C. Bloch, November 28, 1962 (hereafter Bloch).
12. *PHA,* Part 10, pp. 4933–34.
13. Ibid., Part 39, p. 60; Part 7, p. 3098.
14. Ibid., Part 22, p. 7; Part 29, p. 1627.
15. Ibid., Part 3, p. 1067.
16. Ibid., pp. 1068–70.
17. Ibid., p. 1069.
18. Ibid., p. 1071.
19. Ibid., p. 1073.
20. A.A. Hoehling, *The Week Before Pearl Harbor* (New York, 1963), p. 38 (cited hereafter as *The Week Before Pearl Harbor*).
21. *PHA,* Part 16, p. 2153.
22. Ibid., p. 2155.
23. Ibid., p. 2151.
24. Ibid., Part 22, p. 335.
25. Ibid., p. 336.
26. Ibid., p. 337.
27. Ibid., pp. 338–39.
28. Ibid., Part 23, p. 1137.
29. Ibid., Part 16, p. 2228.
30. Ibid., Part 32, p. 222.
31. Ibid., Part 39, pp. 302–3.
32. Ibid., Part 16, p. 2229.
33. Ibid., p. 2160.
34. Ibid., Part 23, p. 1220.
35. Ibid., Part 1, p. 29.
36. *Admiral Kimmel's Story,* p. 28.
37. *PHA,* Part 28, p. 911.
38. Interview with Bloch, November 28, 1962.
39. Interview with Adm. Maurice E. Curts, November 16, 1962 (hereafter Curts).
40. Interview with Smith, November 14, 1962.
41. Interviews with DeLany, November 2, 1962; Smith, November 14, 1962.

Chapter 8
"THE HOTBED OF ESPIONAGE"

1. Interview with Lt. Gen. Charles D. Herron, June 10, 1955 (hereafter Herron).
2. Interview with Otojiro Okuda, May 23, 1950 (hereafter Okuda).
3. *PHA,* Part 35, p. 555.
4. Interview with Okuda, May 23, 1950.
5. Letter, Hart to Bloch, December 15, 1940, Papers of Adm. Claude C. Bloch, Library of Congress, Washington, D.C., Box 2 (cited hereafter as Bloch Papers).
6. Interviews with Okuda, May 23, 1950, and August 27, 1955.
7. *PHA,* Part 35, p. 355.
8. Ibid., Part 12, pp. 311–12.
9. Honolulu *Star-Bulletin,* February 10 and 5, 1941; letter, Bloch to Riley H. Allen, March 4, 1941, Bloch Papers, Box 1.
10. PHA, Part 12, p. 259.
11. Honolulu *Star-Bulletin,* March 22, 1941; interviews with Okuda, May 23, 1950, and August 27, 1955.
12. Interview with Takeo Yoshikawa, July 13, 1950 (hereafter Yoshikawa).
13. Interview with Okuda, May 23, 1950, and with a former member of the Japanese consulate in Honolulu who prefers to remain anonymous.

14. Interview with Yoshikawa, September 14, 1955.
15. Ibid., July 13, 1950. See also Takeo Yoshikawa with Lt. Col. Norman Stanford, USMC, "Top Secret Assignment," *United States Naval Institute Proceedings* (December 1960), p. 33 (cited hereafter as "Top Secret Assignment").
16. Interview with Yoshikawa, July 15, 1950.
17. *PHA*, Part 35, p. 363.
18. Interview with Yoshikawa, July 13, 1950.
19. *PHA*, Part 35, pp. 356–57, 392, 367.
20. Ibid., p. 529.
21. Ibid., p. 327: interview with Yoshikawa, September 10, 1955.
22. Ibid., pp. 384, 362.
23. Ibid., pp. 355, 327.
24. Interview with Yoshikawa, July 16, 1950.
25. Ibid., July 15 and 16, 1950; September 10, 1955; *PHA*, Part 25, p. 356.
26. *PHA*, Part 35, p. 381; interviews with Yoshikawa, July 15, 1950, and September 10, 1955.
27. Interview with Yoshikawa, September 10, 1955.
28. Ibid., September 11, 1955.

Chapter 9
"IN RATHER A SPOT"

1. Honolulu *Advertiser*, August 24, 1939; Honolulu *Star-Bulletin*, August 23, 1939.
2. *PHA*, Part 23, pp. 857–58.
3. Ibid., Part 35, p. 567.
4. Ibid., Part 23, p. 1022.
5. Ibid., Part 26, p. 333.
6. Ibid., Part 23, p. 920.
7. Ibid., p. 652.
8. Ibid., Part 36, p. 331.
9. Ibid., Part 35, p. 84.
10. Ibid., p. 100.
11. Ibid., Part 10, pp. 5089–90.
12. Ibid., Part 35, p. 566.
13. Ibid., Part 23, p. 914.
14. Ibid., Part 35, p. 569.
15. Ibid., Part 36, p. 312. For a thorough study of the field of cryptanalysis, see David Kahn, *The Codebreakers* (New York, 1967).
16. *PHA*, Part 34, p. 34.
17. Chicago *Tribune*, Special Supplement, December 7, 1966, p. 10. An untitled, anonymous article appears in this supplement, its author identified only as "a former high official who bore heavy responsibilities at the time of the Pearl Harbor attack. . . ." The author has communicated often and at length with this individual, both orally and in writing. To respect his desire for anonymity, he is cited hereafter as Mr. X and his article as Mr. X's Article.
18. *PHA*, Part 36, pp. 61–62.
19. Mr. X's Article, pp. 5 and 10.
20. *PHA*, Part 33, p. 915.
21. Ibid., Part 10, p. 4751.
22. Ibid., p. 4773.
23. Ibid., Part 36, pp. 46–47, 61.
24. Mr. X's Article, p. 10. Mr. X tells us that the British later reneged on this agreement and did not furnish the United States the German Enigma code as agreed.
25. *PHA*, Part 36, p. 60.
26. Ibid., Part 35, p. 82; Part 8, pp. 3399, 3896.
27. Ibid., Part 10, p. 4725; Part 8, p. 3894.
28. Ibid., Part 8, p. 3926; Part 9, pp. 4168, 4171.
29. Ibid., Part 8, pp. 3400–01, 3895.
30. Ibid., Part 9, pp. 4508–09.
31. Ibid., Part 2, pp. 858, 865.
32. Ibid., Part 5, p. 2468.
33. Ibid., Part 35, p. 96; Part 36, p. 23; Part 4, p. 1734; Part 8, p. 3899.
34. Ibid., Part 2, pp. 447, 464; Part 9, p. 5035.
35. Ibid., Part 8, pp. 3681–82; Part 34, p. 95; Part 35, p. 96.
36. Ibid., Part 36, pp. 64–65.
37. Ibid., Part 33, pp. 851–52.
38. Ibid., Part 7, pp. 3374–75.
39. Ibid., Part 4, p. 1923.
40. Ibid., Part 10, pp. 4845–46.
41. Ibid., Report, p. 524.
42. Ibid., Part 4, pp. 1926–27.

Chapter 10
"THE MOST LIKELY AND
DANGEROUS FORM OF ATTACK"

1. Honolulu *Advertiser*, Honolulu *Star-Bulletin*, November 4, 1940.
2. *PHA*, Part 22, p. 200: interview with Brig. Gen. James E. Mollison, April 13, 1961 (hereafter Mollison).

3. Interviews with RADM. Logan C. Ramsey, December 6, 1962 (hereafter Ramsey); Smith, November 29, 1962; Mollison, April 13, 1961.
4. Unpublished papers of Gen. H. H. Arnold, Library of Congress, Washington, D.C. (cited hereafter as Arnold Papers).
5. *PHA*, Part 8, p. 3451; interviews with Ramsey, December 6, 1962: Adm. Arthur C. Davis, January 30, 1963 (hereafter Davis); RADM. James M. Shoemaker, January 31, 1963 (hereafter Shoemaker); VADM. Charles F. Coe, January 23, 1963 (hereafter Coe).
6. *PHA*, Part 24, pp. 1389–90.
7. Ibid., Part 8, p. 3452.
8. Ibid., Part 22, pp. 349–350.
9. Ibid., p. 350.
10. Ibid., pp. 350–51.
11. Ibid., p. 351.
12. Ibid. The entire Martin-Bellinger Report appears in *PHA*, Part 22, pp. 349–54.
13. Ibid., Part 4, p. 1941.
14. Ibid., Part 39, p. 304.
15. Ibid., p. 64.
16. Ibid., p. 304.
17. Ibid., p. 309.
18. Ibid., Part 4, p. 1896.
19. Honlulu *Star-Bulletin,* April 7, 1941.

Chapter 11
"HOW CAN AIR POWER BE USED MOST EFFECTIVELY?"

1. Interviews with Watanabe, August 16, 1969; RADM. Kameto Kuroshima, April 28, 1948 (hereafter Kuroshima). *Nagato* underwent overhaul from April 3 to June 3, 1941. During this period Yamamoto selected the battleship *Mutsu* as his temporary flagship. Interview with Watanabe, October 24, 1949.
2. *Hawai Sakusen,* pp. 92–93.
3. Interview with Capt. Akira Sasaki, July 18, 1949 (hereafter Sasaki).
4. Interview with Kuroshima, April 28, 1948; *Hawai Sakusen,* p. 92.
5. Interview with Chihaya and Fuchida, May 23, 1948.
6. Letter from Chihaya, August 1, 1969; interviews with Genda, August 31, 1955, and Sasaki, July 18, 1949.

7. Interview with Watanabe, October 27, 1947.
8. *Shikan: Shinjuwan Kogeki,* p. 146.
9. Interview with Kuroshima, April 28, 1948.
10. Interview with Capt. Takayasu Arima, November 21, 1948 (hereafter Arima).
11. Interview with Sasaki, July 19, 1949.
12. *Hawai Sakusen,* p. 93; interview with Watanabe, July 15, 1947.
13. Essay entitled "How the Japanese Task Force Idea Materialized," which Genda with the assistance of Chihaya prepared for the author and which is in the author's files (cited hereafter as Genda Essay on Task Force). *Shikan: Shinjuwan Kogeki,* pp. 193–94.
14. Interviews with Ozawa, December 15, 1948; Sanagi, August 11, 1949. See *Hawai Sakusen,* pp. 124–26.
15. *Shikan: Shinjuwan Kogeki,* p. 192.
16. Genda Essay on Task Force; interview with Ozawa, December 15, 1948.
17. Interview with RADM. Sadatoshi Tomioka, February 17, 1948 (hereafter Tomioka).
18. *Shikan: Shinjuwan Kogeki,* p. 152; interview with Fukudome, April 27, 1950.
19. Interview with Tomioka, February 17, 1948.
20. Interviews with Tomioka, July 9, 1947; Uchida, April 20, 1951; Kuroshima, May 3 and 5, 1948.
21. Interview with Capt. Tatsukichi Miyo, April 27, 1947 (hereafter Miyo).
22. Interviews with Capt. Fumio Aiko, December 21 and 28, 1964 (hereafter Aiko).

Chapter 12
"THE REAL POWER AND POTENTIALITIES"

1. Unpublished diary of Chuichi Nagumo. Courtesy of Mrs. Nagumo. The reader unfamiliar with Japanese names is cautioned against confusing Nagumo, Commander in Chief of the First Air Fleet, with Nagano, chief of the Naval General Staff.
2. Interview with RADM. Katsuhei Nakamura, May 29, 1951 (hereafter Nakamura).
3. Among those who attest to Nagumo's af-

fectionate concern for his men are Genda, *Sento Hen,* p. 37, and Capt. Tameichi Hara, IJN, with Fred Saito and Roger Pineau, *Japanese Destroyer Captain* (New York, 1961), pp. 34–35.

4. Interview with Adm. Nishizo Tsukahara, May 14, 1949 (hereafter Tsukahara).
5. Interview with Genda, August 31, 1955.
6. Interview with Cmdr. Goro Sakagami, September 22, 1955 (hereafter Sakagami).
7. Interview with Genda, August 31, 1955.
8. Interview with Sakagami, September 22, 1955.
9. The material on Adm. Yamaguchi in this chapter is based on his service record and numerous discussions with members of his staff and other officers of the First Air Fleet.
10. Interview with Watanabe, December 7, 1947.
11. Interview with Capt. Kyozo Ohashi, October 25, 1949 (hereafter Ohashi).
12. Interview with Cmdr. Susumu Ishiguro, April 6, 1948 (hereafter Ishiguro).
13. Ryunosuke Kusaka, *Rengo Kantai* (Tokyo, 1952), p. 2 (cited hereafter as *Rengo Kantai*).
14. Interviews with Kusaka, April 24, August 23, June 24, and December 2, 1947.
15. All members of the First Air Fleet consulted for this study agree that this was Nagumo's general reaction to the Pearl Harbor plan.
16. Interview with Kusaka, December 2, 1947; *Rengo Kantai*, p. 6; "Higeki Shinju-wan Kogeki," p. 202.
17. Interview with Sakagami, September 22, 1955.
18. Interviews with Capt. Eijiro Suzuki, May 2 and June 12, 1948 (hereafter Suzuki).
19. This was the opinion of virtually every Japanese officer consulted for this study.
20. Interview with Suzuki, May 29, 1948.
21. Interview with Ohashi, October 25, 1949.
22. Interview with Ishiguro, May 1, 1948.

Chapter 13
"WITH GUARDED APPROVAL"

1. State Department Memorandum of Conversation, February 14, 1941. Papers of Cordell Hull, Library of Congress, Washington, D.C., Box 60 (cited hereafter as Hull Papers). See also Cordell Hull, *The Memoirs of Cordell Hull* (New York, 1948), Vol. II, pp. 987–88 (cited hereafter as *Hull Memoirs*).
2. Interview with Nomura, May 7, 1949.
3. *Hull Memoirs,* Vol. II, p. 988.
4. *Current Biography,* 1940, p. 412.
5. State Department Memorandum of Conversation, March 8, 1941, Hull Papers Box 60; *Hull Memoirs,* Vol. II, pp. 986, 988–90.
6. *PHA,* Part 20, pp. 4298–4300.
7. Raymond James Sontag and James Stuart Beddie, eds., *Nazi-Soviet Relations 1939 –1941: Documents from the Archives of the German Foreign Office* (Washington, D.C., 1948), pp. 291–314.
8. Herbert Feis, *The Road to Pearl Harbor: The Coming of the War Between the United States and Japan* (Princeton, 1950), pp. 186–89 (cited hereafter as *The Road to Pearl Harbor*).
9. *Ten Years in Japan,* pp. 379–80.
10. *Hull Memoirs,* Vol. II, pp. 984–85. For excellent accounts of the Walsh Drought mission see the following: Robert J. C. Butow, *The John Doe Associates: Backdoor Diplomacy for Peace,* 1941 (Stanford, Calif., 1974) (cited hereafter as *John Doe Associates);* John H. Boyle, "The Walsh-Drought Mission to Japan," *Pacific Historical Review* (May 1965), pp. 141–60 (cited hereafter as "The Walsh-Drought Mission"); Robert J. C. Butow, "Backdoor Diplomacy in the Pacific: The Proposal for a Konoye-Roosevelt Meeting, 1941," *The Journal of American History* (June 1972), pp. 48–72 (cited hereafter as "Backdoor Diplomacy").
11. State Department Memorandum of Conversation, March 8, 1941, Hull Papers, Box 60.
12. *Hull Memoirs,* Vol. II, p. 991.
13. State Department Memorandum of Conversations, April 14 and 16, 1941, Hull Papers, Box 60; *Hull Memoirs,* Vol. II, pp. 995–96.
14. "Backdoor Diplomacy," pp. 55–57. For an excellent discussion of this mixup, see Butow's article "The Hull-Nomura Conversations: A Fundamental Misconception," *American Historical Review* (July 1960), pp. 822–36.

15. *PHA*, Part 4, p. 1861.
16. Ibid., p. 1862.
17. Ibid., Part 11, pp. 5475–76.
18. Ibid., Part 4, p. 1863.
19. Shigonori Togo, *The Cause of Japan* (New York, 1956), p. 61 (cited hereafter as *The Cause of Japan*).
20. *PHA*, Part 20, p. 3992. Portions of Konoye's Memoirs are reproduced in this volume.
21. Masuo Kato, *The Lost War* (New York, 1946), pp. 25–27 (cited hereafter as *The Lost War*).
22. Attachment to State Department Memorandum of Conversation, May 12, 1941, Hull Papers, Box 60. See also *Hull Memoirs*, Vol. II, pp. 1000–01.
23. "Backdoor Diplomacy," pp. 57–58. See also "The Hull-Nomura Conversations," pp. 832–34.

Chapter 14
"THE STRONGEST FORTRESS IN THE WORLD"

1. Stimson Diary, April 21, 1941.
2. Ibid., April 22, 1941.
3. Ibid., April 23, 1941.
4. Ibid., April 24, 1941.
5. *PHA*, Part 15, p. 1635. On the copy reproduced therein, the *aide-memoire* is undated but bears the remark "Came to file 5/3/41."
6. Ibid.
7. Ibid.
8. Ibid., Part 12, p. 323.
9. Ibid., Part 15, p. 1635.
10. Ibid., Part 3, p. 1092; Part 15, p. 1635.
11. Honolulu *Star-Bulletin*, May 12, 1941.
12. Honolulu *Advertiser*, May 13, 1941.
13. Ibid., May 14, 1941.
14. Honolulu *Star-Bulletin*, May 15, 1941.
15. Wesley Frank Craven and James Lea Cate, eds., *The Army Air Forces in World War II* (Chicago, 1948), Vol. I, p. 172 (cited hereafter as *AAF in WW II*).
16. Honolulu *Star-Bulletin*, May 24, 1941.
17. *PHA*, Part 15, pp. 1622–23.
18. Ibid., p. 1623.

Chapter 15
"CRITICAL IN THE ATLANTIC"

1. Memorandum, Smith to the author, October 23, 1963.
2. Stimson Diary, November 29, 1940.
3. Ibid., December 16, 1940.
4. Ibid., December 29, 1940.
5. Ibid., January 27, 1941.
6. Ibid., March 24, 1941.
7. Ibid., March 25, 1941.
8. Ibid., April 10, 1941.
9. *PHA*, Part 15, pp. 1485, 1487. The document in question bears on its cover sheet the penciled notation:
   "Approved by Sec Navy 28 May 41
   . . . Sec Army 2 June 41.
   Not approved by President."
   However, the policies set forth therein became those of the United States.
10. Ibid., pp. 1491–92.
11. Ibid., Part 16, pp. 2160–61.
12. Ibid., p. 2161.
13. Ibid., p. 2163.
14. Ibid., Part II, pp. 5503–4.
15. William L. Langer and S. Everett Gleason, *The Undeclared War, 1940–1941* (New York, 1953), pp. 445–46 (cited hereafter as *The Undeclared War*).
16. *PHA*, Part 16, p. 2164.
17. Ibid., p. 2230.
18. Stimson Diary, April 29, 1941.
19. *PHA*, Part 19, p. 3457.
20. Ibid., Part 16, p. 2165.
21. Ibid., pp. 3458–59.
22. Stimson Diary, May 5, 1941.
23. Ibid., May 6, 1941.
24. *PHA*, Part 19, pp. 3460–61.
25. Stimson Diary, May 13, 1941.
26. Ibid., May 15, 1941.
27. *PHA*, Part 16, pp. 2168–69.
28. Ibid., Part 33, p. 696.
29. Ibid., Report, pp. 149–50.
30. Ibid., Part 12, p. 260.

Chapter 16
"THE KISS OF DEATH"

1. *PHA*, Part 16, p. 2226.
2. Ibid., Part 23, p. 1231.

3. Memorandum, Smith to the author, October 23, 1963.
4. *PHA*, Part 23, p. 1231.
5. Ibid., Part 16, p. 2233–34.
6. Ibid., pp. 2234–35.
7. Ibid., p. 2236.
8. Ibid.
9. Ibid., p. 2237.
10. Ibid., pp. 2237–38.
11. Ibid., p. 2238.
12. Ibid.
13. Stimson Diary, May 23, 1941.
14. Ibid., May 24, 1941.
15. Ibid., May 25, 1941.
16. Washington *Post*, May 28, 1941.
17. Stimson Diary, May 27, 1941.
18. Interview with Kimmel, November 20, 1963.
19. Letter, Knox to Capt. Morton L. Deyo, USN, June 13, 1941. Unpublished papers of Frank Knox, Library of Congress, Washington, D.C., Box 1 (cited hereafter as Knox Papers).
20. Interview with Kimmel, November 30, 1963; *PHA*, Part 32, p. 99.
21. *PHA*, Part 33, p. 692.
22. This account of Kimmel's meeting with Roosevelt is based upon Memorandum, "Interview with the President, 1425 –1550, Monday June 9 1941," Navy Department Office Symbol Op-12D-2-McC, signed by Adm. H. E. Kimmel. (Originally Secret, now Unclassified), Classified Operational Archives Branch, Naval History Division, Washington Navy Yard, Washington, D.C.
23. *PHA*, Part 33, p. 693.
24. "Interview with the President," op, cit.
25. *PHA*, Part 33, p. 692.
26. Stimson Diary, June 18, 1941.
27. *PHA*, Part 36, p. 401.
28. Memorandum, Smith to the author, October 23, 1963.

Chapter 17
"JAPAN'S FOREIGN POLICY WILL NOT BE CHANGED"

1. Stimson Diary, June 23, 1941.
2. Stark described this interview in a letter, July 31, 1941, to Capt. Charles H. Cooke, Jr., copy to Kimmel. *PHA*, Part 16, p. 2175.
3. Honolulu *Star-Bulletin*, June 26, 1941.
4. *PHA*, Part 20, p. 3993.
5. Unpublished diary of Admiral Kichisaburo Nomura, June 29, 1941, in the author's files, courtesy of Nomura (cited hereafter as Nomura Diary).
6. A number of translations exist of this document, which is entitled "An Outline of the Policy of the Imperial Government in View of Present Developments." The author has used the version reproduced in *PHA*, Part 20, pp. 4018–19.
7. *PHA*, Part 12, p. 1.
8. Ibid., Part 14, p. 1396.
9. Ibid., Part 16, p. 2171.
10. Ibid., Part 7, p. 2932.
11. Nomura Diary, July 3, 1941.
12. Hull Papers, Box 72–73.
13. Stimson Diary, July 5, 1941.
14. Ibid.
15. Ibid., July 8, 1941.
16. Diary of Marquis Koichi Kido, July 17, 1941 (cited hereafter as Kido Diary).
17. *PHA*, Part 20, pp. 3997–98.
18. Ibid., Part 12, p. 3.
19. State Department Memorandum of Conversation, July 17, 1941, Hull Papers, Box 60.
20. *PHA*, Part 12, p. 2.
21. *The Undeclared War*, p. 642.

Chapter 18
"AS IF HE WERE BEYOND PENALTY"

1. For a detailed account of this journey, see *PHA*, Part 35, pp. 360–62; 378–79.
2. Interview with Yoshikawa, September 11, 1955. However, no messages from Tokyo to Honolulu to this effect appear in *PHA*.
3. Interview with Genda, December 25, 1947.
4. *PHA*, Part 35, p. 356.
5. Interview with Yoshikawa, July 14, 1950.
6. *PHA*, Part 35, p. 386; interview with Yoshikawa, July 14, 1950.
7. *PHA*, Part 12, p. 260.
8. Ibid., Part 35, p. 363.
9. Interview with Yoshikawa, July 15, 1950.
10. *PHA*, Part 35, p. 371.
11. *Hull Memoirs*, Vol. II, p. 1011.

12. Interview with Capt. Itaru Tachibana, August 19, 1950 (hereafter Tachibana).
13. Interview with RADM. Edwin T. Layton, May 20, 1958 (hereafter Layton).
14. *Hull Memoirs,* Vol. II, pp. 1011-12; Nomura Diary, June 18, 1941.
15. Interview with Tachibana, August 19, 1950.
16. Interviews with RADM. Kanji Ogawa, February 9 and March 30, 1949 (hereafter Ogawa).
17. Don Whitehead, *The FBI Story: A Report to the People* (New York, 1956) (cited hereafter as *The FBI Story).*
18. Interview with Tucker, August 22, 1964.
19. *PHA,* Part 23, p. 858.
20. Ibid., p. 869.
21. Ibid., Part 35, pp. 538-39.
22. Ibid., Part 23, pp. 860-61.
23. Ibid., p. 861.
24. Ibid., p. 862.
25. Ibid., p. 866.
26. Ibid., p. 880.
27. Ibid., p. 863.
28. Ibid., Part 10, pp. 5093-94.
29. Walter Davenport, "Impregnable Pearl Harbor," *Collier's* (June 14, 1941), p. 77.
30. *PHA,* Part 35, pp. 217-18.
31. Ibid., p. 218.
32. Ibid.
33. Ibid., p. 153.
34. Ibid., p. 531.
35. Interview with Yoshikawa, July 16, 1950.
36. *PHA,* Part 35, p. 531.
37. Ibid., p. 555.
38. Ibid., p. 531.

Chapter 19
"WE WANT HUSTLERS!"

1. *Hawai Sakusen,* p. 130.
2. *Japan Times and Advertiser,* May 28, 1941.
3. *Hawai Sakusen,* p. 130.
4. *Rengo Kantai,* p. 10.
5. *Sento Hen,* p. 35.
6. Interview with Genda, April 6, 1947.
7. *PHA,* Part 33, p. 1318. A fathom measures six feet.
8. Ibid., Part 32, p. 255.
9. *Shikan: Shinjuwan Kogeki,* p. 212.
10. Ibid., p. 213.

11. Ibid., p. 214; interviews with Aiko, December 21 and 28, 1964.
12. *Hawai Sakusen,* p. 143. See also *Shinjuwan Sakusen Keikoroku,* pp. 217-18.
13. Interview with Genda, April 6, 1947.
14. *Rengo Kantai,* p. 9.
15. *Sento Hen,* pp. 37, 43-44. See also *Shinjuwan Sakusen Kaikoroku,* p. 21.
16. *Shikan: Shinjuwan Kogeki,* p. 210. See also *Shinjuwan Sakusen Kaikoroku,* p. 232.
17. *Hawai Sakusen,* pp. 135-36.
18. *Sento Hen,* p. 44. See also *Shinjuwan Sakusen Kaikoroku,* p. 231.
19. Interview with Genda, December 28, 1947.
20. *Sento Hen,* p. 44.
21. Ibid., p. 45.
22. Interview with Genda, April 7, 1947. See also *Hawai Sakusen,* p. 136.
23. *Sento Hen,* p. 45.
24. Ibid., p. 47. See also *Shinjuwan Sakusen Kaikoroku,* pp. 231-32.
25. *Shikan: Shinjuwan Kogeki,* p. 203.
26. *Hawai Sakusen,* p. 137.
27. *Shikan: Shinjuwan Kogeki,* p. 203.
28. Interview with Genda, April 7, 1947.
29. *Sento Hen,* p. 46.
30. Interview with Genda, April 7, 1947. See also *Shinjuwan Sakusen Kaikoroku,* pp. 231, 238-39. CPO Akira Watanabe should not be confused with Capt. Yasuji Watanabe of Yamamoto's staff.
31. Interview with Ishiguro, May 1, 1948.
32. *Hawai Sakusen,* p. 96.
33. Unpublished notes of Cmdr. Shigeshi Uchida, April 10, 1941 (cited hereafter as Uchida Notes).
34. *Hawai Sakusen,* p. 96.
35. Interview with Genda, March 15, 1948. This historic report was probably lost with *Akagi* at Midway.
36. Ibid., April 7, 1947.
37. Interview with Kuroshima, May 5, 1948.
38. *Hawai Sakusen,* p. 121.
39. Interview with Kuroshima, May 5, 1948.
40. Ibid.
41. *Hawai Sakusen,* p. 121.

1953), pp. 9–30 (cited hereafter as *Fall of the Philippines*).

29. Interview with Tomioka, July 16, 1947.
30. Interview with Admiral Koshiro Oikawa, April 10, 1949 (hereafter Oikawa).

Chapter 20
"PLENTY OF POTENTIAL DYNAMITE"

1. *PHA*, Part 16, p. 2173.
2. Nomura Diary, July 24, 1941.
3. *PHA*, Part 5, p. 2383.
4. Ibid., Part 16, pp. 2173–74.
5. Ibid., Part 14, pp. 1344–45.
6. State Department Memorandum of Conversation, July 23, 1941, Hull Papers, Box 60. See also *Hull Memoirs*, Vol. II, pp. 1013–14, and Memorandum for the Files, July 24, 1941, of telephone conversation between Hull and Welles on July 23, Hull Papers, Box 72–73.
7. State Department Memorandum of Conversation, July 24, 1941, Hull Papers, Box 60.
8. *PHA*, Part 20, p. 4373.
9. Nomura Diary, July 24, 1941.
10. Interview with Capt. Sutegiro Onoda, October 13, 1949 (hereafter Onoda).
11. Interview with Miyo, May 10, 1949.
12. Interview with Ishiguro, May 1, 1948.
13. Interview with Suzuki, May 29, 1948.
14. *The Secret Diary of Harold L. Ickes*, Vol. III, *The Lowering Clouds 1939–1941* (New York, 1954), p. 588 (cited hereafter as *Ickes Secret Diary*).
15. *PHA*, Part 14, p. 1327.
16. Interview with Nomura, May 7, 1949.
17. *PHA*, Part 20, pp. 4038–40.
18. Quoted in *Japan Times and Advertiser*, July 29, 1941.
19. *Ten Years in Japan*, pp. 411–12.
20. *Ibid.*, pp. 413–14.
21. Interview with Tomioka, July 16, 1947.
22. Nomura Diary, July 30, 1941.
23. *PHA*, Part 12, p. 8.
24. Roosevelt Papers, PSF, Box 67.
25. Takushiro Hattori, *The Complete History of the Greater East Asia War*, (Tokyo, 1953), Vol. 1, p. 166. Translation by 500th Military Intelligence Service Group. Colonel Hattori was a member of the Operations Section of the Army General Staff (cited hereafter as *Complete History*).
26. Interview with Tomioka, July 16, 1947.
27. *PHA*, Part 20, p. 4034.
28. Louis Morton, *United States Army in World War II: The War in the Pacific: The Fall of the Philippines* (Washington, D.C.,

Chapter 21
"A CUNNING DRAGON SEEMINGLY ASLEEP"

1. *PHA*, Part 16, p. 2174.
2. Ibid., p. 2242.
3. Ibid., p. 2239.
4. Ibid., p. 2175.
5. Ibid., p. 2176.
6. Ibid., p. 2177.
7. Ibid., Part 14, p. 1346.
8. Ibid., Part 12, p. 9.
9. Ibid.
10. Ibid.
11. Ibid., p. 10.
12. Stimson Diary, August 8, 1941.
13. Nomura Diary, August 4, 1941.
14. *PHA*, Part 20, p. 4000.
15. Nomura Diary, August 6, 1941; State Department Memorandum of Conversation, August 6, 1941, with attached Proposal by the Japanese Government, Hull Papers, Box 60.
16. *PHA*, Part 12, pp. 12–13.
17. Ibid., pp. 13–14.
18. Ibid., Part 14, pp. 1254, 1273–74.
19. Ibid., p. 1279.
20. Interview with Nomura, May 7, 1949.
21. Stimson Diary, August 9, 1941.
22. *Complete History*, p. 154.
23. Interview with Tomioka, February 17, 1948.
24. Interview with Watanabe, November 25, 1947.
25. Honolulu *Star-Bulletin*, August 13; Honolulu *Advertiser*, August 14, 1941.
26. Honolulu *Star-Bulletin*, August 6, 1941.
27. Interview with Yoshikawa, September 10, 1955.
28. Stimson Diary, August 12, 1941.
29. *PHA*, Part 16, p. 2244.
30. Ibid., Part 14, p. 1401.
31. Uchida Notes, August 14 and 16, 1941.
32. *PHA*, Part 14, pp. 1346–47.
33. Ibid., Part 12, pp. 17–18.

Chapter 22
"PROPHETIC IN ITS ACCURACY"

1. Interview with Kuroshima, May 5, 1948.
2. Ibid., May 3, 1948.
3. Ibid., May 5, 1948.
4. Uchida Notes, August 7, 1941.
5. Interview with Kuroshima, May 5, 1948.
6. *Hawai Sakusen,* p. 97.
7. Ibid., pp. 97–98.
8. Ibid.
9. Ibid., p. 99. These arguments were much the same as those which Fukudome, Tomioka, Miyo, Sanagi, and Uchida gave the author in numerous interviews.
10. Ibid., interview with Kuroshima, May 5, 1948.
11. Interviews with Admiral Zengo Yoshida, March 18 and 20, 1950 (hereafter Yoshida).
12. The full title of this study is "Some Considerations Concerning the Basic Defense Doctrine of Oahu." It is filed at the Air Force Historical Section, Maxwell AFB, Montgomery, Ala. Courtesy of Dr. Frank Futrell.
13. *PHA,* Part 14, p. 1019.
14. Interview with Maj. Gen. William E. Farthing, August 17, 1955 (hereafter Farthing).
15. *PHA,* Part 14, p. 1021.
16. Ibid., p. 1022.
17. Ibid., pp. 1022–23.
18. Ibid., p. 1024.
19. Ibid.
20. Ibid.
21. Ibid., p. 1025.
22. Ibid., pp. 1025–26.
23. Ibid., p. 1026.
24. Ibid., p. 1027.
25. Ibid., p. 1028.
26. Ibid., p. 1030.
27. Ibid.
28. Ibid., p. 1031.
29. Ibid.
30. Ibid., Part 39, p. 75.
31. Ibid., Part 27, p. 88. In his testimony Marshall gave the figure of 148 B-17s. Ibid., Part 3, p. 1120. In all probability Arnold's figure is the more accurate.
32. Ibid., p. 438.

Chapter 23
"PRESENT ATTITUDE AND PLANS"

1. *PHA,* Part 15, p. 1626.
2. Arnold Papers.
3. Interviews with Mollison, April 13 and 15, 1961.
4. Interview with Maj. Gen. Howard C. Davidson, July 6, 1962 (hereafter Davidson).
5. *Ten Years in Japan,* pp. 416–17.
6. Ibid., pp. 417–21.
7. *Foreign Relations,* pp. 559–65.
8. State Department Memorandum of Conversation, August 17, 1941, Hull Papers, Box 60; *Foreign Relations,* p. 554 ff.; *Hull Memoirs,* Vol. II, pp. 1018–20. The original draft proposal is reproduced in *PHA,* Part 14, pp. 1255–68.
9. *PHA,* Part 16, pp. 2179, 2182–83.
10. State Department Memorandum of Conversation, Hull Papers, Box 60; Nomura Diary, August 28, 1941.
11. *Complete History,* pp. 170–71.
12. Uchida Notes. Unfortunately Uchida did not date this entry within the month.
13. Ibid., July 28–29, 1941.
14. *Complete History,* pp. 170–71.
15. Uchida Notes, August 19 and 20, 1941.
16. Ibid., August 23, 1941.
17. For an excellent explanation of the influential position of these officers, see Robert J. C. Butow, *Tojo and the Coming of the War* (Princeton, N.J., 1961), pp. 170–71; 243–44 n (cited hereafter as *Tojo and the Coming of the War*).
18. *Complete History,* pp. 171–72.

Chapter 24
"A VERY STRONG FIGHTING SPIRIT"

1. Mitsuo Fuchida, *Shinjuwan Sakusen No Shinso: Watakushi Wa Shinjuwan Joku Ni Ita* (Nara, Japan, 1949), pp. 36–37 (cited hereafter as *Shinjuwan Sakusen No Shinso*).
2. Interviews with Genda, December 28, 1947, and September 5, 1955.
3. The biographical and character sketch of Fuchida that follows is based upon many

interviews with him as well as the recollections of his former associates and his official career brief.

4. Interview with Genda, December 28, 1947.
5. Ibid. See also *Shinjuwan Sakusen Kaikoroku*, p. 224.
6. While Murata's former colleagues agree on his character and abilities, this sketch is based mainly on an interview with Fuchida, December 10, 1963.
7. Some Japanese naval officers believe Murata joined *Akagi* later in the autumn. But both Genda and Fuchida stated that Murata trained with the First Air Fleet in August.
8. Interview with Genda, December 28, 1947; *Shinjuwan Sakusen Kaikoroku*, pp. 187–202, 246, 248, 251.
9. Interview with Fuchida, December 10, 1963.
10. Interview with Genda, December 28, 1947.
11. *Sento Hen*, p. 42.
12. Interview with Genda, December 28, 1947.
13. Interview with Fuchida, December 10, 1963.
14. *Shikan: Shinjuwan Kogeki*, pp. 198, 207.
15. Ibid., p. 206.
16. *PHA*, Part 13, p. 644.
17. *Shikan: Shinjuwan Kogeki*, p. 195. For an interesting account of this unique plane, see Masatake Okumiya and Jiro Horikoshi with Martin Caidin, *Zero!* (New York, 1956).
18. Interview with Ishiguro, May 1, 1948.
19. Interview with Lt. Cmdr. Heita Matsumura, January 8, 1945 (hereafter Matsumura).
20. Interview with Ishiguro, May 1, 1948.
21. *Shikan: Shinjuwan Kogeki*, pp. 194–95.
22. *Rengo Kantai*, p. 15.
23. Interview with Genda, September 5, 1955.
24. Interview with Ohashi, October 25, 1949.
25. Interview with VADM. Chuichi Hara, September 6, 1955 (hereafter Hara); statement dated December 26, 1951, which Hara submitted to the author through Chihaya.

Chapter 25
"RESOLVED TO GO TO WAR"

1. Interview with Adm. Mitsumi Shimizu, November 5, 1948 (hereafter Shimizu); written statement of Shimizu to the author through Chihaya, July 21, 1969 (cited hereafter as Shimizu Statement).
2. Interview with Fuchida, August 27, 1967.
3. *PHA*, Part 32, p. 234; Part 39, p. 305.
4. Interview with RADM. Hisashi Mito, September 21, 1947 (hereafter Mito).
5. Kazuo Sakamaki, *I Attacked Pearl Harbor* (New York, 1949), p. 33 (cited hereafter as *I Attacked Pearl Harbor*); interview with Lt. Kazuo Sakamaki, October 17, 1947 (hereafter Sakamaki); Anthony J. Watts and Brian G. Gordon, *The Imperial Japanese Navy* (Garden City, N.Y., 1971), pp. 362–64 (cited hereafter as *Imperial Japanese Navy*).
6. *The New York Times*, September 2, 1941.
7. Quoted in *Japan Times and Advertiser*, September 3, 1941.
8. *PHA*, Part 12, p. 25.
9. The quotations from this document are taken from Nobutake Ike, ed. and trans., *Japan's Decision for War: Records of the 1941 Policy Conferences* (Stanford, Calif., 1967), pp. 135–36 (cited hereafter as *Japan's Decision.*) See also *PHA*, Part 20, p. 4022; *Complete History*, pp. 172–76; and *Far East Mil. Trib.*, Defence Document 1579. There are some differences in the various translations of this program.
10. Uchida Notes, September 3, 1941.
11. Boston *Sunday Globe*, September 7, 1941.
12. Honolulu *Star-Bulletin*, September 6, 1941.

Chapter 26
"WAVES AND WINDS SO UNSETTLED"

1. In his book *Journey to the Missouri* (New Haven, 1950), p. 43, Toshikazu Kase termed Konoye "a shy squirrel sheltered in the deep forests. . . ." (cited hereafter as *Journey to the Missouri*).
2. Kido Diary, September 5, 1941.

3. *PHA*, Part 20, p. 4004. See also *Tojo and the Coming of the War*, pp. 253–54.
4. Kido Diary, September 5, 1941. A number of accounts exist of the imperial conference of September 6 and this meeting which preceded it. The author has attempted to reconcile these discrepancies and present the events by fusing fact and probability.
5. *Complete History*, p. 176.
6. Ibid.
7. *PHA*, Part 20, p. 4004.
8. *Shikan: Shinjuwan Kogeki*, pp. 82–83, n. 7. See also *Tojo and the Coming of the War*, p. 255; *PHA*, Part 20, p. 4004.
9. *PHA*, Part 20, p. 4005.
10. *Complete History*, p. 176.
11. *Shikan: Shinjuwan Kogeki*, pp. 82–83, n. 7. Almost a year later, on August 23, 1942, Nagano gave Nomura a blow-by-blow account of this audience. Interview with Nomura, May 11, 1949.
12. Nomura Diary, September 4, 1941.
13. *Hull Memoirs*, Vol. II, p. 1023 ff. See also *PHA*, Part 2, pp. 424–26.
14. *Japan Times and Advertiser* (morning edition), September 6, 1941.
15. Kido Diary, September 6, 1941; *Complete History*, p. 177 ff.; *Japan's Decision*, p. 138 ff.
16. *Complete History*, p. 182.
17. *PHA*, Part 20, p. 4005.
18. *Complete History*, p. 182.
19. *PHA*, Part 20, p. 4005.
20. The title of this poem comes from the Kido Diary, September 6, 1941; the translation, from *Complete History*, p. 182. Several translations of the poem exist, but this version conveys most closely the form and spirit of the original as well as the atmosphere of the hour.
21. *PHA*, Part 20, p. 4005.
22. Ibid.
23. *Complete History*, p. 182.
24. *PHA*, Part 20, p. 4005.
25. *Ten Years in Japan*, p. 425. See also Joseph C. Grew, *Turbulent Era: A Diplomatic Record of Forty Years, 1904–1945*, Part II (Boston, 1952), pp. 1324–33 (cited hereafter as *Turbulent Era*); *Foreign Relations*, pp. 604, 645.
26. *PHA*, Part 2, p. 663.
27. *Ten Years in Japan*, p. 426.
28. Ibid.
29. Ibid., p. 427.
30. *Turbulent Era*, p. 1329.
31. Ibid., pp. 1332–33.
32. *PHA*, Part 2, p. 663, corrected by Part 5, p. 2482.
33. For an interesting exposition of this triumvirate, see Hugh Byas, *Government by Assassination* (New York, 1942), pp. 134–36. 134–36.
34. *PHA*, Part 12, p. 27.
35. Ibid., Part 20, p. 4214. Roosevelt sent Grew's letter to Hull for suggested reply under date of October 29, 1941.
36. Ibid., Part 2, p. 717.

Chapter 27
"A SERIOUS STUDY"

1. The exact date of this meeting is in question. *Hawai Sakusen*, p. 100, states that the First Air Fleet completed its draft of Operation Hawaii on August 28, but both Kusaka and Genda recall this meeting as taking place in early September.
2. Interview with Kusaka, December 2, 1947. The author has also depended on Genda and Sakagami for the mood and atmosphere of this meeting.
3. Interview with Kusaka, December 2, 1947.
4. Ibid., August 23, 1947.
5. Ibid., June 29, 1947; *Rengo Kantai*, pp. 8–9.
6. *Rengo Kantai*, p. 12.
7. Interview with Kusaka, December 2, 1947.
8. Interview with Genda, April 6, 1947. See also *Shinjuwan Sakusen Kaikoroku*, pp. 112–14.
9. Strangely enough, *Hawai Sakusen* has nothing to say about Genda's work on the prospective routes to Pearl Harbor.
10. The exposition of the southern route is based on interview with Genda, June 10, 1947.
11. Interview with Genda, September 3, 1955.
12. The exposition of the central route is based upon interview with Genda, June 6, 1947.
13. The exposition of the northern route is also based upon interview with Genda, June 6, 1947.
14. *Hawai Sakusen*, p. 174.

15. Interview with Watanabe, August 16, 1969.
16. Interview with Kusaka, June 29, 1947.
17. Interviews with Genda, April 6 and June 6, 1947; Kusaka, August 24, 1947, and March 7, 1949. See also *Shinjuwan Sakusen Kaikoroku*, p. 113.
18. Interviews with Genda, June 6 and 10, 1947.
19. Interviews with Genda, April 6, June 6 and 10, 1947; Kusaka, August 24, 1947, and March 7, 1949.
20. Interviews with Genda, November 4, 1950; Fuchida, December 10, 1963.
21. Interview with Cmdr. Chuichi Yoshioka, September 21, 1949 (hereafter Yoshioka).
22. Ibid.
23. Interview with Genda, December 28, 1947.
24. Interview with Fuchida, December 10, 1963.
25. Interview with Fukudome, May 2, 1950.
26. *Hawai Sakusen*, p. 100.
27. Interview with Genda, March 15, 1948.

Chapter 28
"THE WAR GAMES"

1. The material in this chapter is based on all the pertinent publications in English and Japanese, but the author's best source of information has been a series of intensive interviews with virtually every surviving ex-naval officer who attended the war games of September 1941.
2. Interview with Watanabe, April 12, 1948.
3. *Hawai Sakusen*, p. 101.
4. Interview with Fukudome, May 2, 1950.
5. Interviews with Miyo, May 10, 1948; Sanagi, August 23, 1949.
6. Interview with VADM. Nobutake Kondo, December 18, 1948 (hereafter Kondo).
7. Interview with Tsukahara, May 6, 1949.
8. Interview with Kondo, December 18, 1948.
9. Interview with RADM. Shikazo Yano, February 21, 1950 (hereafter Yano).
10. Interview with Kusaka and Genda, August 24, 1947.
11. *Hawai Sakusen*, p. 101.
12. Interviews with Kusaka and Genda, August 24, 1947; Tomioka, July 23, 1947.
13. Interview with VADM. Gunichi Mikawa,

January 12, 1949 (hereafter Mikawa).
14. Interview with RADM. Sentaro Omori, March 26, 1949 (hereafter Omori).
15. Interview with Watanabe, April 21, 1948.
16. Exactly when Nagano first heard about Yamamoto's plan remains something of a mystery. Several Japanese ex-naval officers interviewed thought he might have known by the end of July 1941. Fukudome tells us that he informed Nagano of the venture right after the September war games. (*Shikan: Shinjuwan Kogeki*, p. 154.) Certainly his invitation to the Secret Room strongly hints that he was in the know.
17. Interview with Fukudome, May 2, 1950.
18. Interview with Sasaki, July 19, 1949.
19. Interview with Kusaka and Genda, August 24, 1947, as well as testimony of those officers, Sasaki, and others over numerous interviews. See also *Shinjuwan Sakusen Kaikoroku*, p. 115.
20. Interview with Genda, March 11, 1948.
21. *Hawai Sakusen*, pp. 102–03.
22. Interview with Genda, March 11, 1948. The games followed tactical plans which Genda had prepared aboard *Akagi*. *Shinjuwan Sakusen Kaikoroku*, p. 161.
23. Interview with Genda, March 11, 1948.
24. *Hawai Sakusen*, p. 103.
25. Interview with Sanagi, August 16, 1949.
26. *Hawai Sakusen*, p. 103.
27. Interview with Genda, March 11, 1948.
28. *Hawai Sakusen*, p. 103.
29. Ibid., p. 103. This source states that the first wave consisted of 54 fighters, 63 torpedo planes, and 72 bombers—a total of 189 aircraft. These figures are open to question because they exceed the number used in the first wave against Pearl Harbor originating from six carriers.
30. Interview with Sasaki, July 19, 1949.
31. Interview with Watanabe, April 21, 1948.
32. Interview with Genda, March 11, 1948. See also *Hawai Sakusen*, p. 104. The latter lists a second practice wave of 36 fighters, 54 bombers and 81 torpedo planes—a total of 171. Again, these figures are questionable because they slightly exceed the number actually used in the second wave against Pearl Harbor originating from six carriers.
33. Testimony of Kusaka and Genda; *Hawai Sakusen*, p. 104.
34. Interview with Genda, March 11, 1948.

35. Interview with Tomioka, August 7, 1947.
36. Testimony of Kusaka and Genda.
37. Interview with Tomioka, August 7, 1947.
38. *Hawai Sakusen*, p. 104.
39. Interviews with Sasaki, July 19, 1941; Sanagi, August 16, 1949.
40. *Hawai Sakusen*, p. 104.
41. Interview with Kusaka and Genda, August 24, 1947.
42. Interview with Sasaki, July 19, 1949.
43. Testimony of Kusaka, Mikawa, Tomioka, and others.
44. Interview with Sasaki, July 19, 1949.
45. Interview with Kuroshima, May 10, 1949.
46. Interviews with Watanabe, July 15, 1947, and January 8, 1948.
47. Interview with Mikawa, January 12, 1949.
48. Interview with Sanagi, August 16, 1949.
49. *Hawai Sakusen*, pp. 101, 104.
50. Interviews with Genda, March 11, 1948; Sanagi, August 16, 1949; Ogawa, February 16, 1951.
51. Extract from Sanagi's diary. This entry is undated, but it covers the Pearl Harbor war games critique. See also *Hawai Sakusen*, p. 104.
52. *Hawai Sakusen*, p. 101.

Chapter 29
"TIME WAS RUNNING OUT"

1. Interview with Yoshioka, September 21, 1949.
2. Interview with Mikawa, January 12, 1949. See also *Shinjuwan Sakusen Kaikoroku*, pp. 115, 118, 122.
3. Interview with Ogawa, April 13, 1949.
4. Interview with Maeda, March 12, 1949.
5. Interview with Shimizu, November 5, 1948.
6. Interview with Fukudome, May 2, 1950.
7. Interview with Tomioka, December 8, 1947.
8. Interview with Miyo, May 24, 1949.
9. Interview with Tsukahara, May 6, 1949.
10. Interview with Kusaka, August 24, 1947.
11. Interview with Yoshioka, September 21, 1949.
12. Interview with Genda, September 3, 1955.
13. Interview with Miyo, May 24, 1949. See also *Japan's Decision*, p. 142, and *Complete History*, p. 180, for thoughts on a

potential war with the Soviet Union.
14. This account of the conference follows in general the Sanagi diary. Inasmuch as he did not record all the discussion, the diary has been supplemented by interviews with Fukudome, Tomioka, Miyo, Uchida, Sanagi, Kuroshima, Sasaki, Kusaka, and Genda. See also *Hawai Sakusen*, pp. 105–7, which relies heavily on the Sanagi diary, and *Shinjuwan Sakusen Kaikoroku*, pp. 151–54.
15. Interview with Genda, August 25, 1947.
16. Sanagi diary, September 24, 1941; *Hawai Sakusen*, p. 105.
17. Interview with Miyo, May 17, 1949.
18. Sanagi diary, September 24, 1941; interview with Genda, August 25, 1947; *Hawai Sakusen*, pp. 105–06.
19. Interview with Genda, August 25, 1947; *Hawai Sakusen*, p. 106; Sanagi diary, September 24, 1941.
20. Sanagi diary, September 24, 1941; *Hawai Sakusen*, p. 106.
21. Ibid.
22. Interview with Genda, August 25, 1947; Sanagi diary, September 24, 1941; *Hawai Sakusen*, p. 106.
23. Interview with Miyo, May 17, 1947.
24. Interviews with Genda, August 25, 1947, and March 11, 1948; Sanagi diary, September 24, 1941; *Hawai Sakusen*, pp. 106–07. See also "Higeki Shinjuwan Kogeki," p. 205.
25. Interviews with Kuroshima, May 10, 1948; Genda, August 25, 1947, and March 11, 1948. See also *Shinjuwan Sakusen Kaikoroku*, p. 154; "Higeki Shinjuwan Kogeki," p. 205.

Chapter 30
"BUT WHAT ABOUT THE PACIFIC?"

1. *The New York Times*, September 12, 1941.
2. See, for example, Washington *Post*, September 12, 1941; Miami *Herald*, September 14, 1941; Detroit *Free Press*, September 13, 1941.
3. Stimson Diary, September 12, 1941.
4. See, for example, the opinion expressed in the joint congressional committee's minority report, PHA, Report, pp. 546–47.
5. PHA, Part 3, pp. 1119–20.

6. Ibid., Part 16, p. 2248.
7. Ibid.
8. Ibid., p. 2249.
9. Honolulu *Star-Bulletin*, September 10, 1941.
10. Ibid., September 16, 1941.
11. September 20, 1941.
12. Honolulu *Star-Bulletin*, September 18, 1941.
13. *PHA*, Part 14, p. 1354.
14. For representative comments, see Seattle *Post-Intelligencer,* Los Angeles *Times,* Boston *Daily Globe,* September 12, 1941; Mobile *Register,* September 13, 1941.
15. September 18, 1941.
16. *PHA*, Part 18, pp. 3026–27.
17. Ibid., Part 17, p. 2705.
18. Ibid., Part 24, pp. 2010–11.
19. Ibid., Part 16, pp. 2209–10.
20. Stimson Diary, September 23, 1941.
21. *PHA*, Part 16, pp. 2212–13.
22. Ibid., p. 2213.
23. Ibid., pp. 2213–14.
24. Ibid., Part 12, pp. 32–33.
25. *Ten Years in Japan*, p. 433.
26. State Department Memorandum of Conversation, August 28, 1941, Hull Papers, Box 60.
27. *PHA*, Part 12, p. 39.
28. Ibid., p. 41.
29. Ibid., p. 40.

Chapter 31
"A SIGNIFICANT AND OMINOUS CHANGE"

1. Interview with Tachibana, August 9, 1950.
2. Statement by Tachibana, September 10, 1950.
3. *PHA*, Part 12, p. 261.
4. Ibid., Part 9, p. 4534.
5. Ibid., Part 2, pp. 886–88.
6. Ibid., p. 904.
7. Ibid., p. 817.
8. Ibid., Part 9, p. 4526.
9. Ibid., p. 4534.
10. Ibid., pp. 4563–64.
11. Ibid., pp. 4594–95.
12. Ibid., Part 29, p. 2454.
13. Ibid., Part 9, pp. 4177, 4194.
14. Ibid., pp. 4195–96.
15. Ibid., Part 4, p. 1725.
16. Ibid., Part 8, p. 3411.
17. Ibid., Part 4, pp. 1748–49.
18. Ibid., pp. 1840–41.
19. Ibid., Part 8, pp. 3390–91.
20. Ibid., p. 3391.
21. Ibid., p. 3405.
22. Ibid., Part 5, p. 2175.
23. Ibid., Part 4, p. 2019.
24. Ibid., Part 33, pp. 883–84.
25. Ibid., Part 33, p. 897.
26. Ibid., Part 5, p. 2177.
27. Ibid., pp. 2175–76.
28. Ibid., Part 4, p. 1922.
29. Ibid., Part 7, pp. 2956–57.
30. Ibid., Part 6, pp. 2542–43.
31. Ibid., Part 2, p. 795.
32. Interview with Yoshikawa, September 11, 1955.
33. *PHA*, Part 12, p. 262.
34. Interview with Yoshikawa, September 14, 1955.
35. *PHA*, Part 35, p. 357.
36. Ibid., p. 382.
37. Interview with Yoshikawa, September 10, 1955.
38. *PHA*, Part 4, p. 1841.
39. *Investigation of Un-American Propaganda Activities in the United States, Hearings Before a Special Committee on Un-American Activities, House of Representatitives, Seventy-Seventh Congress, First Session, on H. Res. 282, Appendix VI, Report on Japanese Activities,* Government Printing Office, Washington D.C., 1942., pp. 1725–26.
40. Interview with Congressman Martin Dies, March 1, 1955 (hereafter Dies).
41. Washington *Times-Herald,* September 21, 1941.
42. *Congressional Record,* Vol. 87, Part 7, October 2, 1941, p. 7592.
43. Honolulu *Star-Bulletin*, October 3, 1941.
44. Interview with Senator Guy M. Gillette, February 19, 1955 (hereafter Gillette).
45. Washington *Evening Star,* October 11, 1941; Stimson Diary, October 7, 1941.
46. Honolulu *Star-Bulletin,* October 16, 1941.
47. William Gellerman, *Martin Dies* (New York, 1944), p. 223.
48. Interviews with Dies, March 1, 1955, and Gillette, February 19, 1955.
49. *Rengo Kantai*, p. 6.

Chapter 32
"NO MATTER WHAT THE COST"

1. In numerous interviews with Genda and Fuchida, neither could pinpoint the date more precisely.
2. Interview with Fuchida, August 23, 1967. See also *Shinjuwan Sakusen No Shinso*, pp. 40–49.
3. Interview with Kusaka and Genda, August 23, 1947. See also *Shinjuwan Sakusen Kaikoroku*, p. 182.
4. Interview with Yoshioka, September 23, 1949.
5. Interview with Fuchida, August 23, 1967.
6. *Shinjuwan Sakusen No Shinso*, p. 45.
7. Interview with Fuchida, August 23, 1967.
8. Ibid.
9. Ibid.
10. *Shinjuwan Sakusen No Shinso*, p. 49.
11. Interview with Fuchida, August 23, 1967.
12. Interview with Kusaka and Genda, August 24, 1947.
13. Interview with Yoshioka, September 22, 1949. This account of the Kanoya meeting is based upon interviews with all those present who survived the war. *Hawai Sakusen*, p. 109, gives the date as September 29, 1941.
14. Interview with Tsukahara, May 6, 1949.
15. Interview with Genda, April 10, 1950.
16. Interview with Tsukahara, May 14, 1949.
17. Interview with Kusaka, August 27, 1949.
18. *Rengo Kantai*, p. 4; *Shinjuwan Sakusen Kaikoroku*, p. 165.
19. Interviews with Yoshioka, September 21 and 22, 1949.
20. Interview with Genda, April 10, 1950.
21. Interviews with Tsukahara, May 14, 1949; Kusaka, August 27, 1949.
22. Interview with Genda, September 10, 1950.
23. Interview with Kusaka, August 27, 1949.
24. Interview with Yoshioka, September 21, 1949.
25. The exact date of this meeting is difficult to determine. Kusaka recalled it as taking place almost immediately after the Kanoya conference. *Hawai Sakusen*, p. 109, gives the date as October 3. If the latter is correct, the meeting took place aboard *Mutsu* because *Nagato* was under repairs

October 2–8, 1941; but Kusaka always spoke to the author of the meeting as being aboard *Nagato*.
26. Interview with Kusaka, August 25, 1947.
27. Ibid., June 29, 1949.
28. *Rengo Kantai*, p. 5.
29. Interview with Kusaka, June 29, 1947. See also *Shinjuwan Sakusen Kaikoroku*, p. 166.
30. *Hawai Sakusen*, p. 109.
31. Interview with Kusaka, August 23, 1947.
32. Ibid., June 29, 1947.
33. *Rengo Kantai*, p. 5.
34. Interview with Kuroshima, May 10, 1948.
35. Interview with Kusaka, August 23, 1947.
36. Interview with Kuroshima, May 10, 1948.
37. *Rengo Kantai*, pp. 5–6.

Chapter 33
"NOW THE CLOUDS WERE RAISED"

1. Interview with Genda, April 6, 1947. Also *Shikan: Shinjuwan Kogeki*, p. 202; *Shinjuwan Sakusen Kaikoroku*, p. 192; "Higeki Shinjuwan Kogeki, p. 206. These accounts give conflicting dates. *Hawai Sakusen*, for example, gives the date as October 7. Genda's earlier testimony is probably correct.
2. Interviews with Genda, April 6, 1947; Capt. Naohira Sata, November 23, 1947 (hereafter Sata).
3. Interview with Fuchida, May 25, 1947.
4. Ibid.
5. Interview with Watanabe, August 16, 1969.
6. Interviews with Fuchida, May 25 and 27, 1947. Masuda received his appointment on March 25, 1941; all the others on September 1, 1941, except for Kusumoto, who received his on September 15, 1941, and Shimoda, who was not appointed to his post until September 25, 1941.
7. *Shinjuwan Sakusen Kaikoroku*, p. 195; interview with Cmdr. Takahisa Amagai, September 14, 1949 (hereafter Amagai).
8. Statement by RADM. Takatsugu Jojima, July 17, 1951 (hereafter Jojima).
9. Interview with Capt. Hisai Shimoda, November 21, 1949 (hereafter Shimoda).
10. Interview with Sata, November 23, 1949.

11. Interview with Amagai, September 14, 1949.
12. *Shinjuwan Sakusen Kaikoroku,* pp. 196–97; "Higeki Shinjuwan Kogeki,"p. 206; interviews with Shimoda, November 21, 1949; Genda, April 6, 1947.
13. Interview with Watanabe, April 12, 1948.
14. Interview with Fuchida, May 25, 1947.
15. Interview with Genda, August 24, 1947; *Shinjuwan Sakusen Kaikoroku,* pp. 111, 202, 261.
16. *Rengo Kantai,* pp. 13–14.
17. Interview with Yoshioka, September 23, 1949.
18. Interview with Genda, December 28, 1947.
19. Interview with Fuchida, May 28, 1947.
20. Ibid.
21. Ibid. See also *Shinjuwan Sakusen No Shinso,* pp. 63–64; *Shinjuwan Sakusen Kaikoroku,* pp. 213–14.
22. Interviews with Fuchida, May 24 and 27, 1947. See also *Shinjuwan Sekusen No Shinso,* p. 61.
23. Ibid., May 27, 1947.
24. Interview with Lt. Cmdr. Jinichi Goto, January 31, 1950 (hereafter Goto).
25. *Shinjuwan Sakusen No Shinso,* p. 53.
26. Ibid., p. 54.
27. Ibid., p. 55.
28. Ibid., pp. 55–56.
29. Ibid., pp. 56–57.
30. Interview with Fuchida, May 24, 1947.
31. Interview with Goto, January 31, 1950.
32. Interview with Fuchida, May 24, 1947.
33. Interview with Matsumura, January 8, 1965.
34. Interview with Fuchida, May 27, 1947.
35. Interview with Matsumura, January 8, 1965.
36. Interview with Amagai, September 14, 1949.
37. Interview with Fuchida, May 28, 1947.
38. Ibid., May 25, 1947.
39. *Shikan: Shinjuwan Kogeki,* p. 196.
40. Interview with Genda, December 28, 1947.
41. Interview with Fuchida, December 10, 1963.
42. Interview with Genda, December 28, 1947.
43. Interview with Fuchida, May 25, 1947.
44. Interview with Fuchida, July 23, 1948.
45. *Shikan: Shinjuwan Kogeki,* p. 196.

Chapter 34
"THE POWER, THE PURPOSE AND THE PLAN"

1. Uchida Notes, October 1 through 4, 1941.
2. Interview with Uchida, April 27, 1951.
3. *PHA,* Part 12, pp. 46–47.
4. *The New York Times,* October 2, 1941.
5. Oral Statement, October 2, 1941, Hull Papers, Box 72–73; State Department Memorandum of Conversation, October 2, 1941, Hull Papers, Box 60.
6. *Japan's Decision,* pp. 180–81; *Complete History,* p. 190.
7. *PHA,* Part 12, p. 54.
8. *Complete History,* p. 191.
9. Stimson Diary, October 6, 1941.
10. *PHA,* Part 12, pp. 62–63.
11. Ibid., p. 63.
12. *Ten Years in Japan,* pp. 455–56.
13. *Complete History,* pp. 192–93. See also *PHA,* Part 20, p. 4009: Kido Diary, October 12, 1941. For an excellent account of the Japanese Cabinet crisis, see *Tojo and the Coming of the War,* pp. 268–309.
14. *PHA,* Part 12, p. 64.
15. Kido Diary, October 16, 1941. A translation of Konoye's letter of resignation appears in *PHA,* Part 20, pp. 4025–26.
16. *PHA,* Part 20, p. 4011. See also Kido Diary, October 16, 1941; *Tojo and the Coming of the War,* pp. 291–93.
17. Kido Diary, October 17, 1941.
18. Interview with Watanabe, October 24, 1949.
19. Interview with VADM. Yorio Sawamoto, April 18, 1948 (hereafter Sawamoto). He was vice navy minister under both Oikawa and Shimada.
20. Interview with Tomioka, July 9, 1947.
21. Interviews with RADM. Sokichi Takagi, May 20, 1951 (hereafter Takagi); Sawamoto, April 12, 1949; VADM. Zenshiro Hoshina, June 24, 1951 (hereafter Hoshina).
22. October 23, 1941.

Chapter 35
"PEARL HARBOR WILL BE ATTACKED"

1. Genda's Analysis.
2. *Shinjuwan Sakusen Kaikoroku,* p. 162.

3. Ibid., pp. 162–63; Genda's Analysis.
4. *Shinjuwan Sakusen Kaikoroku,* p. 164.
5. Genda's Analysis.
6. This account is based primarily on interviews with virtually every surviving ex-naval officer who participated in this exercise. The schedule is based on *Hawai Sakusen,* p. 112. See also "Higeki Shinjuwan Kogeki," p. 207.
7. Interview with Kusaka, June 29, 1947; *Shinjuwan Sakusen Kaikoroku,* p. 165.
8. Watanabe, who with Kuroshima was primarily responsible for planning and organizing the table maneuvers, estimated that some fifty officers attended. In "Higeki Shinjuwan Kogeki," p. 207, Genda erroneously dated this event as October 22.
9. Uchida Notes, October 11, 1941.
10. Interview with Shimizu, November 12, 1949.
11. Interviews with Kusaka, December 12, 1947; Genda, June 6, 1947. See also *Rengo Kantai,* p. 12.
12. Interview with Genda, March 12, 1948; "Higeki Shinjuwan Kogeki," p. 207.
13. Interview with Shimizu, November 12, 1948.
14. Interview with Kondo, December 11, 1948.
15. Ibid.
16. Interview with Mikawa, January 19, 1949.
17. *Hawai Sakusen,* p. 113, says that the decision to use midget submarines in the Pearl Harbor operation was made at the *Nagato* table maneuvers. *Shikan: Shinjuwan Kogeki,* p. 224, dates the occasion as "early October."
18. Interview with Arima, November 21, 1948.
19. Interview with Watanabe, October 24, 1949.
20. Interview with Arima, November 21, 1948. Watanabe thought the conference so important that it should be recorded. So, shortly after the war began, he wrote down his recollections, and Yamamoto prepared for him a ten-page report from his own notes. This report was burned during one of the numerous air raids on Tokyo. After the war Watanabe reconstructed the story of the meeting for the author. We discussed the subject for the last time on August 16, 1969.

21. Interviews with Watanabe, October 24, 1949; Mikawa, January 19, 1949.
22. Interviews with Watanabe, October 24, 1949; Kuroshima, May 12, 1948.
23. Interviews with Watanabe, October 24, 1949; Genda, June 2, 1947; Kuroshima, May 12, 1948.
24. Interview with Watanabe, October 24, 1949.
25. Ibid. Also Arima, November 21, 1948.
26. Interviews with Kuroshima, May 12, 1948; Watanabe, October 24, 1949.
27. Interview with Genda, June 2, 1947.
28. Interview with Watanabe, October 24, 1949. See also *Shinjuwan Sakusen Kaikoroku,* p. 116.
29. Interview with Tsukahara, May 6, 1949.
30. Interview with Genda, March 12, 1948.
31. Interview with Suzuki, June 12, 1948.
32. Ibid., May 28, 1948.

Chapter 36
"WE SHOULD BE ON GUARD"

1. Stimson Diary, October 16, 1941.
2. The revisionist school ranges from the moderate—that the United States could and should have kept out of World War II—to the extreme—that Roosevelt deliberately incited the Japanese to attack at Pearl Harbor and withheld information from Kimmel and Short to ensure that the Japanese would strike. A few major revisionist works are: Harry Elmer Barnes, ed., *Perpetual War for Perpetual Peace* (Caldwell, Ida., 1953); Charles A. Beard, *President Roosevelt and the Coming of the War 1941* (New Haven, 1948); John T. Flynn, *The Roosevelt Myth* (New York, 1948); George Morgenstern, *Pearl Harbor: The Story of the Secret War* (New York, 1947); Charles C. Tansill, *Back Door to War* (Chicago, 1952); Robert A. Theobald, *The Final Secret of Pearl Harbor* (New York, 1954).
3. *PHA,* Part 11, p. 5419.
4. Ibid., Part 26, p. 295.
5. Ibid., Part 4, p. 1944; Part 16, p. 2214.
6. Ibid., Part 14, p. 1327.
7. Ibid., Part 4, pp. 1945–46.
8. Ibid., Part 14, p. 1359.
9. Ibid., Part 18, p. 3196.

10. Ibid., p. 3197.
11. Ibid., p. 3198.
12. Ibid., Part 5, p. 2147.
13. Ibid., Part 14, p. 1402.
14. Ibid., Part 16, pp. 2215–16.
15. Ibid., Part 14, p. 1403.
16. Ibid., Part 16, p. 2249.
17. Ibid., Part 17, pp. 2478–79.
18. Ibid., Part 16, p. 2249.
19. Ibid., Part 17, p. 2478.
20. Ibid., Part 39, p. 302.
21. Ibid., Part 4, p. 2006.
22. Ibid., Part 16, pp. 2214–15.
23. Ibid., Part 17, p. 2466.
24. Ibid., p. 2467.
25. Ibid., Part 26, p. 235.
26. Ibid., p. 227.
27. Ibid., p. 235.
28. Ibid.
29. Ibid., Part 14, p. 1327.
30. Ibid., Part 16, pp. 2249–50.
31. Ibid., p. 2250.
32. Ibid., pp. 2250–51.
33. Stimson attached a copy of this letter to his diary at the appropriate date.
34. Stimson Diary, September 28, 1941.
35. *PHA*, Part 2, p. 909.
36. Ibid., Part 34, p. 59.
37. Ibid., Part 5, p. 2358.
38. Ibid., Part 2, p. 911.
39. Ibid., Part 34, p. 59.
40. Ibid., Part 14, p. 1403. This is a paraphrase.
41. Ibid., Part 16, p. 2251.
42. Ibid., Part 2, p. 470.

Chapter 37
"AS ONE WITH THE COMBINED FLEET"

1. Unpublished diary of VADM. Matome Ugaki, October 17, 1941 (cited hereafter as Ugaki Diary).
2. Interviews with Genda, June 2, 1947, and March 12, 1948.
3. Interview with Kusaka, May 16, 1948; Uchida Notes, October 17, 1941.
4. Interview with Kusaka, May 16, 1948.
5. Ibid.; also Miyo, August 27, 1955; Kuroshima, May 10, 1948.
6. *Rengo Kantai*, p. 16.
7. Interview with Kusaka, May 16, 1948.
8. Interviews with Tomioka, August 7, 1947; Kuroshima, May 10, 1948; Miyo, May 30. 1949.
9. Interviews with Tomioka, August 5, 1947; Kuroshima, May 12, 1948; Miyo, May 30, 1949.
10. Interview with Kuroshima, May 12, 1948.
11. Interviews with Miyo, May 30, 1949; Tomioka, August 5, 1947.
12. Interviews with Kuroshima, May 12, 1948; Miyo, May 30, 1949.
13. Interview with Kuroshima, May 10, 1948.
14. Interview with Fukudome, May 4, 1950.
15. Interview with Kuroshima, May 12, 1948.
16. Ibid., May 10, 1948.
17. Interview with Fukudome, May 4, 1950.
18. Interview with Tomioka, July 9, 1947. This was also the general opinion of Fukudome, Miyo, Uchida, and others.
19. Interview with Tomioka, February 25, 1948.
20. Interrogation of Nagano, March 26, 1946, at Sugamo Prison, Tokyo, *Far East Mil. Trib.*, File No. 19.
21. Interview with Fukudome, May 4, 1950.
22. Interview with Kuroshima, August 7, 1947. There has been some discussion on the exact date when Nagano gave his consent. *Hawai Sakusen*, p. 107, implies that he did so in the latter part of September, following the war games in Tokyo, and ties the Naval General Staff's approval to the carrier *Zuikaku*, which became available on September 25. But the testimony of so many officers concerned plus a whole combination of events points to October 19 or 20 as the date of Nagano's consent.
23. Interviews with Fukudome, May 4, 1950; Kuroshima, May 10, 1948.
24. Interview with Fukudome, May 4, 1950.
25. Ibid., May 19, 1950.
26. Ugaki Diary, October 20, 1941.
27. Uchida Notes, October 21, 1941.
28. Ugaki Diary, October 22, 1941.
29. Ibid.
30. Interview with Watanabe, December 5, 1947.
31. Courtesy of Hori. The following extracts are all from Yamamoto's letter to Shimada of October 24, 1941.
32. Interview with Fuchida, May 25, 1947.

Chapter 38
"OTHER KIND OF PEOPLE"

1. *PHA*, Part 12, p. 80.
2. Ibid., p. 81.
3. Nomura Diary, October 22, 1941; see also *PHA*, Part 12, p. 81.
4. *PHA*, Part 12, p. 82.
5. For a detailed treatment of these important conferences, see *Complete History*, pp. 197–200; *Japan's Decision*, pp. 185–99.
6. *Complete History*, p. 200. See also *Japan's Decision*, pp. 197–98; *PHA*, Part 12, pp. 94–95.
7. Interview with Tomioka, August 12, 1947.
8. Ibid.
9. *PHA*, Part 35, p. 362.
10. Ibid., p. 380.
11. Interviews with Yoshikawa, July 14, 1950, and September 14, 1955.
12. *PHA*, Part 35, p. 365.
13. Record of Trial of Kuehn, Bernard Julius Otto, CN 226070, Clerk of Court, United States Army, Court of Military Records, Nassif Bldg., Falls Church, Va. pp. 41–57 (cited hereafter as Kuehn Trial). See also *PHA*, Part 35, pp. 328, 491; Affidavit of Otto Kuehn, January 1, 1942, Doc. No. 6256A (cited hereafter as Kuehn Affidavit).
14. Interviews with Ogawa, March 16, 1949; Capt. Tadao Yokoi, September 29, 1955 (hereafter Yokoi). See also *PHA*, Part 35, p. 491.
15. Interview with Ogawa, March 16, 1949.
16. Ibid.
17. *PHA*, Part 35, p. 332.
18. Kuehn Trial, p. 55.
19. Statement by Tachibana, August 9, 1950.
20. *PHA*, Part 35, p. 332; Kuehn Trial, pp. 112, 120. It seems certain that the following events took place on October 25, 1941, although the testimony is no more exact than a vague recollection of the latter part of October. Kuehn insisted that a Japanese ship was in port, and the only Japanese liner in Honolulu around that date was the *Tatuta Maru*, which arrived on October 23 and left for San Francisco on the twenty-fourth. Kuehn's son Eberhard definitely remembered that it was a Saturday, which would make it the twenty-fifth.
21. Kuehn Trial, pp. 112–13; *PHA*, Part 35, p. 331.
22. *PHA*, Part 35, p. 331. See also Kuehn Trial, p. 50.
23. Interviews with Yoshikawa, July 15, 1950, and September 11, 1955.
24. Statement by Tachibana, August 9, 1950.
25. Interview with Yoshikawa, September 11, 1955. See also *PHA*, Part 35, p. 328.

Chapter 39
"BASED ON DECEPTION"

1. Thomas R. Phillips, ed., *Roots of Strategy: A Collection of Military Classics* (Harrisburg, Pa., 1940), pp. 23, 57 (cited hereafter as *Roots of Strategy*).
2. Honolulu *Star-Bulletin*, August 9, 1941. The story of these three ships can be followed in the Japanese, Hawaiian, and U.S. mainland press.
3. *PHA*, Part 35, p. 198.
4. Interview with and statement by Tachibana, August 9, 1950.
5. *Shikan: Shinjuwan Kogeki*, pp. 187–88.
6. Interview with Cmdr. Suguru Suzuki, February 12, 1949 (hereafter S. Suzuki). See also *Shikan: Shinjuwan Kogeki*, p. 188.
7. Interview with Tachibana, August 9, 1950. See also *Shikan: Shinjuwan Kogeki*, p. 230.
8. Interview with S. Suzuki, February 12, 1949.
9. Suguru Suzuki, *Shinjuwan Gunko Kaimetsu* (an essay published in a biographical volume on Suzuki's uncle Admiral Kantaro Suzuki: *Doto No Nakano Taiyo*), pp. 200–01 (cited hereafter as *Suzuki Essay*). In an interview with the author on February 12, 1949, Suzuki recalled Capt. Bunjiro Yamaguchi as having conducted this briefing.
10. *Shikan: Shinjuwan Kogeki*, p. 188.
11. Ladislas Farago, *The Broken Seal* (New York, 1967), p. 242 (cited hereafter as *The Broken Seal*). See also *PHA*, Part 35, p. 400.
12. Interview with and statement by Tachibana, August 9, 1950.

13. Interviews with S. Suzuki, February 12, 1949; Okuda, September 4, 1955.
14. Statement by Tachibana, August 9, 1950.
15. Interview with S. Suzuki, February 12, 1949.
16. Ibid.
17. *Suzuki Essay*, p. 201.
18. Interview with S. Suzuki, February 12, 1949.
19. *Shikan: Shinjuwan Kogeki*, p. 230.
20. Interview with S. Suzuki, February 12, 1949.
21. *Suzuki Essay*, pp. 202–03.
22. Ibid., p. 203.
23. Ibid., p. 206 ff.
24. Ibid., pp. 206–07.
25. Ibid., p. 207.
26. Interview with S. Suzuki, February 12, 1949.
27. Ibid.
28. Interviews with Yoshikawa, July 15, 1950, and with a former member of the Honolulu consulate who wishes to remain anonymous, September 9, 1967.
29. Interviews with Yoshikawa, September 11, 14, 1955.
30. *Suzuki Essay*, pp. 209, 239.
31. Interview with Yoshikawa, July 15, 1950.
32. *Suzuki Essay*, p. 219.
33. See, for example, Honolulu *Star-Bulletin*, November 3, 1941.
34. Interviews with Yoshikawa, September 11, 1955; S. Suzuki, February 12, 1949.
35. *Suzuki Essay*, pp. 217, 223–24.
36. Ibid., p. 229.
37. Interview with Fuchida, February 27, 1964.
38. *Suzuki Essay*, pp. 230–31.
39. *PHA*, Part 35, pp. 342–43, 517, 569.
40. *Suzuki Essay*, p. 209.

Chapter 40
"IN THE HANDS OF GOD"

1. Interview with Fuchida, February 25, 1964.
2. *Shinjuwan Sakusen No Shinso*, p. 60.
3. Genda's Analysis.
4. *Shinjuwan Sakusen Kaikoroku*, pp. 186–87.
5. *Shinjuwan Sakusen No Shinso*, pp. 60–61.
6. *Shikan: Shinjuwan Kogeki*, p. 206.

7. Ibid., p. 214. See also *Hawai Sakusen*, pp. 144–45.
8. Interview with Fuchida, March 7, 1953.
9. *Shikan: Shinjuwan Kogeki*, pp. 215–16. See also *Hawai Sakusen*, p. 145.
10. Interviews with Fuchida, March 7, 1953; Goto, February 7, 1950. See also *Shinjuwan Sakusen Kaikoroku*, p. 221.
11. *Shikan: Shinjuwan Kogeki*, pp. 204–05; *Shinjuwan Sakusen No Shinso*, p. 64. See also *Hawai Sakusen*, p. 139.
12. Interview with Fuchida, May 27, 1947. See also *Shinjuwan Sakusen No Shinso*, p. 63; *Shikan: Shinjuwan Kogeki*, pp. 234–35.
13. *Rengo Kantai*, pp. 8–9.
14. Interview with Kusaka, June 29, 1947.
15. *Rengo Kantai*, pp. 11–12.
16. *Shikan: Shinjuwan Kogeki*, pp. 218–19.
17. Interview with Kusaka, June 29, 1947. See also *Shikan: Shinjuwan Kogeki*, p. 219; *Hawai Sakusen*, p. 197.
18. Genda's Analysis.
19. *Shikan: Shinjuwan Kogeki*, p. 215. See also *Hawai Sakusen*, p. 145.
20. *Shinjuwan Sakusen Kaikoroku*, pp. 219–20.
21. *Shinjuwan Sakusen No Shinso*, pp. 76–77, 61. See also *Hawai Sakusen*, p. 145.
22. Ugaki Diary, October 29, 1941; interviews with Fukudome, May 10, 1950; Tomioka, August 12, 1947, and February 25, 1948; Miyo, July 12, 1949; Uchida Notes, October 29, 1941; *Shikan: Shinjuwan Kogeki*, p. 243.
23. Interview with Miyo, June 21, 1949.
24. Interview with Tomioka, August 12, 1947.
25. Ibid., February 25, 1948.
26. Ugaki Diary, October 29, 1941.
27. Interview with Tomioka, August 12, 1947.
28. Ugaki Diary, October 29, 1941.
29. Ibid., October 30, 1941.
30. Interview with Tomioka, August 12, 1947.
31. Ugaki Diary, October 30, 1941.

Chapter 41
"COMPLETE WAR PREPARATIONS"

1. Ugaki Diary, November 1, 1941.
2. Interview with Hoshina, June 7, 1951; *Complete History*, p. 206.

3. *Japan's Decision*, p. 210.
4. Interview with Hoshina, June 7, 1951.
5. *Japan's Decision*, p. 237.
6. Ugaki Diary, November 2, 1941.
7. Uchida Notes, November 2, 1941.
8. Nakahara Diary, November 2, 1941.
9. *Hawai Sakusen*, p. 203, gives the cited date and place. Recollections of various participants range from November 1 to 5.
10. Interview with Fuchida, July 26, 1947.
11. Genda's Analysis.
12. *Hawai Sakusen*, p. 203, gives the date and times. Again, various sources disagree on the dates of the dress rehearsals.
13. Interviews with Fuchida, July 26, 1947; Suzuki, June 12, 1948.
14. *Hawai Sakusen*, p. 203.
15. Genda's Analysis; interview with Fuchida, July 26, 1947. See also *Shinjuwan Sakusen Kaikoroku*, p. 214.
16. *PHA*, Part 10, pp. 4674, 4682.
17. Ibid., p. 4687.
18. Interview with Layton, July 22, 1964.
19. *PHA*, Part 10, p. 4836.
20. Ibid., Part 35, p. 63.
21. Ugaki Diary, November 4, 1941.
22. Interview with Fukudome, May 10, 1950; Ugaki Diary, November 4, 1941.
23. Genda's Analysis. See also *Hawai Sakusen*, p. 203.
24. Interview with Fuchida, July 29, 1947.
25. Ugaki Diary, November 4 and 7, 1941.
26. Interview with Kuroshima, May 12, 1948.
27. Ugaki Diary, November 6, 1941.
28. Interview with Fuchida, July 24, 1947.
29. Genda's Analysis. See also *Hawai Sakusen*, p. 204.
30. Interview with Watanabe, October 31, 1949.
31. Ugaki Diary, November 7, 1941. The text of Combined Fleet Top Secret Operational Order No. 1 appears in *PHA*, Part 13, p. 431 ff. See also *Hawai Sakusen*, pp. 225–26.
32. Interviews with Miyo, July 12 and 28, 1949.
33. *Hawai Sakusen*, pp. 225–26.
34. *Rengo Kantai*, p. 20.
35. Ugaki Diary, November 7, 1941.
36. *PHA*, Part 35, p. 64.
37. Genda's Analysis. See also *Shinjuwan Sakusen Kaikoroku*, pp. 214–16, 221; "Higeki Shinjuwan Kogeki," pp. 208–09.
38. Ibid.

Chapter 42
"RINGING BELLS AND BANGING DRUMS"

1. *PHA*, Part 2, pp. 651–52.
2. Ibid., Part 6, p. 2626.
3. Ibid., Part 2, p. 719.
4. Ibid., Part 14, pp. 1051–52.
5. Ibid., pp. 1056–57.
6. Ibid., Part 12, pp. 92–94.
7. Ibid., pp. 95–96.
8. Ibid., pp. 96–97.
9. Ibid., Part 14, p. 1403.
10. Ibid., Part 7, p. 3245.
11. Ibid., Part 12, p. 100.
12. Ibid., Part 14, pp. 1061–62.
13. Ibid., Part 12, p. 104; State Department Memorandum of Conversation, November 7, 1941, Hull Papers, Box 60.
14. *PHA*, Part 2, p. 429.
15. Ibid.
16. Ibid., Part 16, pp. 2219–20.
17. Interview with Ens. Kazuo Sakamaki, October 18, 1947 (hereafter Sakamaki).
18. Interview with RADM. Hanku Sasaki, October 23, 1950 (hereafter H. Sasaki).
19. *Hawai Sakusen*, pp. 204–05; *Shikan: Shinjuwan Kogeki*, p. 226.
20. Interview with H. Sasaki, October 23, 1950.
21. Interview with Fuchida, August 27, 1967.
22. Interview with Capt. Tatsuwaka Shibuya, July 3, 1948 (hereafter Shibuya).
23. *Hawai Sakusen*, p. 198.
24. Interview with Ishiguro, April 6, 1948.
25. *Hawai Sakusen*, p. 198.
26. *PHA*, Part 35, p. 66.
27. Interviews with Genda, August 30, 1947; Fuchida, July 27, 1947. See also *Hawai Sakusen*, p. 198.
28. Interview with Lt. Yuzo Tsukamoto, at the time a fighter pilot aboard *Zuikaku*, February 15, 1950 (hereafter Tsukamoto).
29. Interview with Genda, June 11, 1947. Because of the date of this order, some Japanese believed that Murata did not work with the torpedomen until that time. However, interviews and documents clearly indicate that he led the torpedo program much earlier than November 10.
30. Interview with Shimizu, November 12, 1948. See also *Hawai Sakusen*, pp. 185–87.

31. Interviews with Mito, September 25, 1947; Shimizu, November 12, 1948. See also *Hawai Sakusen*, p. 250.
32. Interviews with Mito, September 25, 1947; Shibuya, August 7, 1949.
33. Interview with Shibuya, August 7, 1949. See also *Shikan: Shinjuwan Kogeki*, pp. 221–22, 254–57.
34. Courtesy of Hori.
35. Ugaki Diary, November 11–12, 1941.
36. Ibid., November 13, 1941.
37. Interview with Genda, August 29, 1947; *Hawai Sakusen*, p. 230.
38. Ugaki Diary, November 14, 1941.
39. *Hawai Sakusen*, p. 231.
40. Interview with Shimizu, November 5, 1948.
41. Ibid., November 12, 1948.
42. Ibid.; statement by H. Sasaki, October 30, 1950. See also *Hawai Sakusen*, pp. 250–51; *Shikan: Shinjuwan Kogeki*, pp. 229–30.
43. Ibid.
44. Interviews with Genda, August 30, 1947; Fuchida, July 27, 1947. See also *Hawai Sakusen*, p. 198.
45. Interview with Fuchida, July 27, 1947; statement by Fuchida, July 28, 1947. See also *Shinjuwan Sakusen No Shinso*, p. 81.
46. Interview with Fuchida, July 27, 1947.
47. *PHA*, Part 35, p. 67.

Chapter 43
"I SWEAR TO BE SUCCESSFUL"

1. *Japan's Decision*, pp. 247–49.
2. The material concerning this conference is based on interviews with Fukudome, Tomioka, Uchida, and others, as well as Uchida Notes and other materials.
3. *PHA*, Part 14, pp. 1058–60.
4. Interviews with Shibuya, July 24, 1948, and August 7, 1950. See also *Shikan: Shinjuwan Kogeki*, pp. 254, 256–57; *Hawai Sakusen*, p. 204.
5. Interviews with Shibuya, July 24, 1948, and August 7, 1950; Capt. Minoru Yokota, February 23, 1951 (hereafter Yokota). See also *Shikan: Shinjuwan Kogeki*, p. 257.
6. Ugaki Diary, November 17, 1941.
7. Interview with Watanabe, February 2, 1948.
8. In reconstructing Yamamoto's remarks

which follow, the author has relied principally upon interviews with Kusaka, Genda, Fuchida, Kuroshima, Watanabe, Sasaki, and Ishiguro, as well as Genda's Analysis. See also *Shinjuwan Sakusen No Shinso*, p. 83; *Shinjuwan Sakusen Kaikoroku*, p. 170.
9. *Shinjuwan Sakusen No Shinso*, p. 83.
10. Interview with Ishiguro, May 15, 1948.
11. Ugaki Diary, November 17, 1941.
12. Interviews with Ishiguro, May 15, 1958; Amagai, October 5, 1949.
13. Statement by Matsumura, January 19, 1951.
14. Interviews with Ishiguro, May 15, 1958; Amagai, October 5, 1949.
15. Interview with Shimoda, November 21, 1949.
16. *Sento Hen*, p. 37; *Shinjuwan Sakusen Kaikoroku*, p. 131; "Higeki Shinjuwan Kogeki," p. 210.
17. Interview with Genda, August 30, 1948, Genda's Analysis. See also *Shinjuwan Sakusen No Shinso*, pp. 82, 85.
18. Interview with Watanabe, February 2, 1948.
19. Interviews with S. Suzuki, February 19, 1949. See also *Suzuki Essay*, p. 236.
20. Interviews with S. Suzuki, February 19, 1949; Tachibana, August 9, 1950.
21. The following account of Suzuki's briefing is based upon interview with him of February 19, 1949, and *Suzuki Essay*.
22. Interview with S. Suzuki, February 19, 1949; *Suzuki Essay*, p. 217.
23. Interview with S. Suzuki, February 19, 1949.
24. *Suzuki Essay*, pp. 234–37.
25. Interview with Tomioka, September 6, 1955.
26. Interviews with Fukudome, May 19, 1950; S. Suzuki, February 19, 1949. See also *Suzuki Essay*, pp. 209–16.
27. Interview with S. Suzuki, February 19, 1949; *Suzuki Essay*, pp. 209, 216.
28. Interviews with Fukudome, May 19, 1950; Tomioka, September 6, 1955; S. Suzuki, February 19, 1949.
29. Statement by Tomioka, September 6, 1955.
30. *Suzuki Essay*, p. 198.
31. *Shikan: Shinjuwan Kogeki*, pp. 189, 230. See also *Hawai Sakusen*, p. 251.
32. Interview with H. Sasaki, October 24, 1950.

33. Ibid.; Sakamaki, October 19, 1947. Sakamaki's testimony concerning these last days in the homeland is virtually identical with Sasaki's, but he consistently recollected events as taking place one day ahead.
34. Interview with H. Sasaki, October 24, 1950.
35. Ugaki Diary, November 19, 1941; interview with H. Sasaki, October 24, 1950.
36. Interviews with Shibuya, July 24, 1948; Yokota, February 23, 1951.
37. Unpublished diary of RADM. Sadao Chigusa, November 17 and 18, 1941 (cited hereafter as Chigusa Diary).
38. *Hawai Sakusen*, p. 198; *Shinjuwan Sakusen Kaikoroku*, p. 220. *Shikan: Shinjuwan Kogeki*, p. 215.
39. *Shikan: Shinjuwan Kogeki*, p. 211.
40. Interview with Fuchida, March 3, 1948.
41. Interview with Cmdr. Naohiro Sata, November 23, 1949 (hereafter Sata). See also *Hawai Sakusen*, p. 198.
42. Interview with Genda, August 30, 1947; *Rengo Kantai*, p. 13. See also *Shinjuwan Sakusen No Shinso*, p. 82.
43. Interview with Genda, August 30, 1947.
44. Interview with Fuchida, February 29, 1948.
45. Interview with Capt. Kijiro Imaizumi, June 29, 1950 (hereafter Imaizumi).
46. Interview with Shibuya, July 24, 1948.
47. Interview with Shimizu, November 20, 1948.

Chapter 44
"A SITUATION FULL OF DYNAMITE"

1. PHA, Part 23, p. 679.
2. Ibid., Part 35, pp. 68–71.
3. Ibid., Part 23, p. 661.
4. Ibid., p. 659.
5. Ibid., p. 664.
6. Ibid., Part 18, p. 3187.
7. Ibid., Part 20, p. 4482.
8. Ibid., Part 22, p. 326; Part 16, pp. 2252–53.
9. Ibid., Part 7, pp. 3241–42. 3348–49; Part 18, pp. 3294, 3301.
10. Ibid., Part 12, pp. 127–29.
11. Ibid., p. 133.
12. Ibid., p. 130.
13. Ibid., p. 262.
14. Ibid., Part 8, pp. 3440–43.
15. Ibid., Part 15, p. 1796.
16. Ibid., p. 1805.
17. Interview with Yoshikawa, September 14, 1955.
18. Ibid., July 14 and 16, 1950.
19. PHA, Part 22, p. 177.
20. Ibid., Part 23, pp. 646–647, 653.
21. Ibid., Part 8, p. 3395.
22. Comments concerning this study which Mr. X prepared for the author (cited hereafter as Mr. X Comments).
23. Interviews with Bicknell, September 7 and 12, 1967.
24. PHA, Part 12, pp. 137–38.
25. Hull Memoirs, Vol. II, pp. 1062–63.
26. State Department Memorandum of Conversation, November 17, 1941, Hull Papers, Box 60.
27. Nomura Diary, November 17, 1941. See also PHA, Part 12, pp. 141–43.
28. State Department Memorandum of Conversation, November 18, 1941, Hull Papers, Box 60.
29. PHA, Part 12, p. 153.
30. Ibid., p. 263.
31. Mr. X Comments.
32. Interview with Bicknell, September 8, 1967.
33. PHA, Part 12, pp. 262–63.
34. Ibid., p. 154.
35. Ibid., p. 155.
36. Ibid., Part 36, p. 33.
37. Ibid., Part 8, p. 3411.
38. Ibid., Report, p. 470.
39. Ibid., p. 471.
40. Ibid., p. 470.
41. Ibid., p. 192.
42. Ibid., Part 12, p. 263.
43. Ibid., Part 35, pp. 70–71.
44. Ibid., Part 15, pp. 1878–79.
45. Ibid., Part 28, p. 870.
46. Ibid., pp. 870–71; interview with Rochefort, September 1, 1964.
47. Ibid., Part 10, p. 4832.
48. Ibid., Part 28, pp. 1496–97.
49. Ibid., p. 1556.
50. Ibid., Part 3, p. 1086.
51. Ibid., Part 12, p. 155.
52. Nomura Diary, November 19, 1941. See also PHA, Part 12, p. 158.
53. PHA, Part 12, p. 159.
54. Ibid., p. 160.
55. Ibid., p. 161.
56. State Department Memorandum of Con-

versation, November 20, 1941, Hull Papers, Box 60.
57. *PHA,* Part 2, p. 431.
58. Ibid., Part 11, pp. 5370–71.

Chapter 45
"THINGS ARE AUTOMATICALLY GOING TO HAPPEN"

1. Interview with Imaizumi, June 29, 1950.
2. Interview with S. Suzuki, February 19, 1949.
3. The material concerning Suzuki's report aboard *Akagi* is based upon interviews with him, Kusaka, Genda, and Fuchida; also *Suzuki Essay.*
4. *PHA,* Part 12, p. 323. These figures do not agree precisely with those given in the Arnold Papers.
5. Ibid. Again, discrepancies exist between these figures and those in the Arnold Papers.
6. Interview with Yoshikawa, September 14, 1955.
7. Interview with Kusaka, May 12, 1949.
8. See, for example, *PHA,* Part 35, p. 74.
9. Interview with Kusaka, May 12, 1949. See also *Shinjuwan Sakusen Kaikoroku,* p. 254.
10. Sekichi Takagi, *Yamamoto Isoroku To Yonai Mitsumasa* (Tokyo, 1950), p. 85.
11. *PHA,* Part 12, p. 165.
12. Ibid., Part 2, p. 554.
13. The entire *modus vivendi* is reprinted in *PHA,* Report, pp. 35–36. Drafts, correspondence, etc. are reproduced in Part 14, pp. 1084–1177.
14. *PHA,* Part 14, p. 1103.
15. Ibid., p. 1106.
16. For correspondence on this subject, see *PHA,* Part 14, pp. 1160–61, 1300.
17. *PHA,* Part 26, pp. 230–31.
18. Ibid., Part 28, pp. 866–67. A copy of the Fourteenth Naval District report is reproduced in Part 15, pp. 1889–91.
19. Ugaki Diary, November 24, 1941.
20. *PHA,* Part 14, p. 1405.
21. Ibid., Part 12, pp. 263–64.
22. Ibid., Part 11, p. 5418.
23. Stimson Diary, November 25, 1941.
24. *Hull Memoirs,* Vol. II, p. 1080.
25. *PHA,* Part 11, p. 5421.

Chapter 46
"WHEREVER IT MIGHT BE FOUND"

1. Interview with Genda, August 31, 1947. Most of the material contained in this chapter is based upon interviews with Genda and Fuchida. Others who contributed are Kusaka, Shibuya, Yoshioka, Sakagami, Ohashi, Suzuki, Ishiguro, Mikawa, Omori, Imaizumi, S. Suzuki, Amagai, Sata, Shimoda, and a number of the pilots. See also *Shinjuwan Sakusen Kaikoroku,* pp. 258, 261; "Higeki Shinjuwan Kogeki," p. 211.
2. Interview with Fuchida, February 29, 1948.
3. Interview with Genda, August 31, 1947.
4. Ibid. This concept of the task force's turning back if discovered before Decmeber 6 is highly controversial and will be discussed later.
5. Ibid.
6. *PHA,* Part 13, p. 418. *Hawai Sakusen,* pp. 233–35, differs somewhat from the interpretations given in *PHA.*
7. Interview with Kusaka, May 12, 1949.
8. *PHA,* Part 13, p. 421. See also *Hawai Sakusen,* pp. 233–35.
9. Interview with Genda, August 31, 1947.
10. Ibid.
11. Ibid.
12. Ibid.
13. Actually the number of interceptors varied with the situation. According to *Hawai Sakusen,* p. 239, this total may not have exceeded forty-six: twelve planes each from *Zuikaku* and *Shokaku;* six each from *Soryu* and *Hiryu;* five each from *Akagi* and *Kaga.*
14. Interview with Genda, August 31, 1947.
15. Interview with Ishiguro, April 6, 1948.
16. *Rengo Kantai,* p. 21.
17. Interview with Genda, August 31, 1947.
18. *Rengo Kantai,* p. 21; interview with Fuchida, February 29, 1948.
19. Interview with Genda, August 31, 1947.
20. Interview with Fuchida, February 29, 1948.
21. Ibid.
22. Ibid.
23. Ibid.
24. Ibid.

25. Ibid.
26. *Shinjuwan Sakusen Kaikoroku,* p. 262.
27. Interviews with Genda, June 11 and August 31, 1947; Fuchida, February 29, 1948.
28. Ibid. See also *Shinjuwan Sakusen Kaikoroku,* p. 263.
29. Interview with Fuchida, February 29, 1948.

Chapter 47
"CLEAVE THE ENEMY IN TWO!"

1. The following account of Fuchida's briefing is based on extensive interviews with him of February 28 and March 3, 1948; April 10, 1949: March 7, 1953; and follow-up interviews. See also *Shinjuwan Sakusen No Shinso,* pp. 95–114.
2. Interview with Genda, August 29, 1955.
3. *Shinjuwan Sakusen No Shinso, pp. 115–16.*
4. Chigusa Diary, November 23, 1941.
5. *Shinjuwan Sakusen No Shinso,* pp. 116–17.
6. *Shikan: Shinjuwan Kogeki,* pp. 265–66.
7. *PHA,* Part 13, p. 418.
8. Ibid. This gives the date for Nagumo's mission orders as November 22. According to Chihaya, Yamamoto issued Combined Fleet Operation Order No. 5 on November 21. Letter, Chihaya to the author, July 5, 1970.
9. Ibid., p. 516.
10. Interviews with Suzuki, June 12, 1948; Ishiguro, May 15, 1948; Cmdr. Seiroku Ito, October 27, 1950 (hereafter Ito).

Chapter 48
"A MATCH FOR ANYTHING AFLOAT"

1. Interview with S. Suzuki, February 19, 1949; *Suzuki Essay,* p. 210.
2. Chigusa Diary, November 26, 1941.
3. *Suzuki Essay,* p. 211; interview with Fuchida, August 23, 1967.
4. Interview with Lt. Tomatsu Ema, May 27, 1950 (hereafter Ema).
5. Interview with Chigusa, February 11, 1958.

6. Interview with Amagai, October 5, 1949.
7. Interview with Fuchida, August 23, 1967.
8. *Shikan: Shinjuwan Kogeki,* p. 197. Various accounts and authorities differ slightly as to the aircraft strength of the Japanese carriers. Chihaya's figures quoted in a series of reports which he prepared for the author (cited hereafter as Chihaya Reports) on aircraft aboard the task force carriers are: *Akagi* sixty-six, *Kaga* seventy-two, *Soryu* fifty-seven, *Hiryu* fifty, *Shokaku* and *Zuikaku* sixty-eight each. These figures are probably as nearly correct as possible. Characteristics of Japanese and American vessels compared in this chapter come from the above sources and from *Jane's Fighting Ships,* issue of 1942.
9. Interview with Hara, September 6, 1955.
10. Interview with Tomioka, September 6, 1955.
11. Logs of *Saratoga, Lexington,* and *Enterprise.* All U.S. ships' logs cited in this study are in the National Archives, Washington, D.C.
12. Interview with Mikawa, March 5, 1949.
13. For comparisons between Japanese and American torpedoes, see Samuel Eliot Morison, *The Rising Sun in the Pacific* (Boston, 1948), p. 23 (cited hereafter as *Rising Sun in the Pacific*); and Morison's *Coral Sea, Midway and Submarine Actions* (Boston, 1949), pp. 191–232 (cited hereafter as *Coral Sea*).
14. Statement by Capt. Keizo Komura, January 20, 1951 (hereafter Komura).
15. The material concerning Japanese tankers is taken from Chihaya Reports.
16. *Daigo Koku Sentai Senji Nisshi* (War Diary of the Fifth Carrier Division), December 1941, "Operations and General Matters," p. 1 (cited hereafter as Fifth Carrier Division Diary).
17. *Roots of Strategy,* p. 36.

Chapter 49
"THAT WAS THE MONKEY WRENCH"

1. Stimson Diary, November 26, 1941.
2. *PHA,* Part 2, p. 555.
3. Ibid., p. 685.
4. Ibid., pp. 569, 772.
5. Ibid., Part 12, p. 178.

6. Ibid., pp. 180–91; Nomura Diary, November 26, 1941. The Army translation renders the proposal for a personal presidential message as to be directed to Togo; however, Nomura's diary makes plain that he sent, and Togo's memoirs that he received, a suggestion that Roosevelt get in touch with the Emperor.
7. *The Cause of Japan*, p. 166.
8. State Department Memorandum of Conversation, November 26, 1941, Hull Papers, Box 60; *PHA*, Part 12, pp. 181–85. The complete oral statement Hull gave to Nomura and Kurusu is reproduced in *PHA*, Part 19, pp. 3652–55.
9. *The Cause of Japan*, pp. 176–77.
10. Stimson Diary, November 27, 1941.
11. *Hull Memoirs*, Vol. II, p. 1080.
12. Stimson Diary, November 27, 1941.
13. *PHA*, Part 27, p. 167.
14. Stimson Diary, November 27, 1941.
15. *PHA*, Part 12, pp. 186–88.
16. Ibid., pp. 188–91.
17. Ibid., Part 5, p. 2154; Part 7, p. 2042.
18. Ibid., Part 36, p. 207.
19. Ibid., Part 26, p. 322.
20. Interview with Mollison, April 11, 1961. See also *PHA*, Part 27, p. 412; Part 28, p. 1497.
21. *PHA*, Part 6, p. 2519.
22. Ibid., Part 17, p.2480.
23. Fleet Adm. William F. Halsey, USN, and Lt. Cmdr. J. Bryan III, USNR, *Admiral Halsey's Story* (New York, 1947), pp. 73–75 (cited hereafter as *Admiral Halsey's Story*); interviews with Smith, December 9, 1962; Davis, January 30, 1962; Ramsey, December 6, 1962.
24. *PHA*, Part 26, pp. 322–25.

Chapter 50
"TO BE CONSIDERED A WAR WARNING"

1. *PHA*, Part 7, p. 2980.
2. Ibid., Part 14, p. 1328.
3. Ibid., Part 7, p. 2935.
4. Ibid., p. 3167.
5. Ibid., p. 3048.
6. Ibid., p. 3016.
7. Ibid., Part 27, p. 157.
8. Ibid., Part 10, p. 4943.
9. Ibid., p. 4937.
10. Ibid., Part 27, pp. 155–56; Part 7, p. 3047.
11. Ibid., Part 10, p. 4937.
12. Ibid., Part 27, p. 156.
13. Ibid., Part 10, p. 4938.
14. Ibid., Part 7, p. 3029.
15. Ibid., p. 2943.
16. Ibid., pp. 2946, 3130.
17. Ibid., Part 27, p. 158.
18. Ibid., p. 156.
19. Ibid., Part 7, pp. 2941, 3033, 3035.
20. Ibid., Part 22, p. 35.
21. Ibid., Part 14, p. 1330.
22. Ibid., p. 1329.
23. Ibid., Part 7, p. 3032.
24. Ibid., Part 23, p. 1106; Part 14, pp. 1328–29.
25. Ibid., Part 4, p. 1605.
26. Ibid., Part 2, p. 917.
27. Ibid., Part 3, p. 1419.
28. Ibid., p. 1423.
29. Ibid., Part 23, p. 1106. Gerow did not indicate which of Marshall's three deputies he consulted, but it probably was Maj. Gen. William Bryden, who attended the 0930 meeting of November 27 with Stimson and Gerow. Bryden was "senior and acting" in Marshall's absence. Memorandum, Gerow to Chief of Staff, November 28, 1941, Hull Papers, Box 72–73; *PHA*, Part 27, p. 88; Part 23, p. 1106.
30. *PHA*, Part 2, pp. 828–31.
31. Ibid., Part 23, p. 1109.
32. Ibid., Part 2, p. 839.
33. Ibid., Part 10, p. 4856; Part 28, p. 1597.
34. Ibid., Part 14, p. 1406.
35. Ibid., Part 10, pp. 4835, 4856, 4866.
36. Interview with Kimmel, November 30, 1963.
37. *PHA*, Part 36, p. 221; Part 28, p. 1597. Burr told the Army board that Kimmel gave this message to him, but this appears to be in error.
38. Ibid., Part 7, pp. 3026–27.
39. Ibid., p. 3370.
40. Ibid., Part 32, p. 234.
41. Ibid., Part 4, pp. 1916, 2001; Part 26, p. 280.
42. Ibid., Part 4, p. 1947.
43. Ibid., Part 33, p. 814.
44. Ibid., Part 26, p. 295.
45. Ibid., Part 4, p. 1948.
46. Ibid., pp. 1947, 2039.
47. Ibid., pp. 1951, 1956–58.
48. Ibid., Part 18, pp. 2877–41. The Pacific

Fleet's tasks appear on pp. 2889–90.
49. Ibid., Part 4, pp. 1951–52.
50. Ibid., Part 5, p. 2151.
51. Ibid., p. 2125.
52. Ibid., pp. 2149–50.
53. Ibid., p. 2152.
54. Ibid., Part 26, p. 466.
55. Ibid., p. 280.
56. Ibid., Part 32, p. 234.
57. Ibid., pp. 232–33.
58. Ibid., Part 5, p. 2152.
59. Ibid., Part 32, pp. 235–36.
60. Ibid., p. 415.
61. Ibid., p. 220.
62. Ibid., p. 219.
63. Ibid., Part 8, p. 3455.
64. Ibid., p. 3454.
65. Ibid., Part 16, p. 329.
66. Ibid., Part 32, pp. 231–32.
67. Ibid., Part 8, p. 3453.
68. Ibid., Part 39, pp. 63–64.
69. Ibid., Part 29, p. 2075.
70. Ibid., Part 22, pp. 464–65.
71. Ibid., Part 26, p. 25.
72. Ibid., Part 22, p. 464.
73. Ibid., Part 27, pp. 138–40.
74. Ibid., Part 7, p. 2995.
75. Ibid., Report, p. 108.
76. Ibid., Part 11, p. 5429.
77. Ibid., Part 3, pp. 1421–22.
78. Ibid., Part 11, pp. 5429–30.

Chapter 51
"OUR DIPLOMATS WILL HAVE TO BE SACRIFICED"

1. Interview with Davis, January 30, 1963.
2. PHA, Part 8, p. 3535.
3. Ibid., Part 7, pp. 3371–72.
4. Ibid., Part 26, pp. 104–06.
5. Interview with Davis, January 30, 1963.
6. PHA, Part 26, p. 105.
7. Interview with Genda, June 11, 1947. See also Rengo Kantai, p. 22.
8. Interviews with Genda, December 25, 1947; Goto, February 7, 1950.
9. Sento Hen, pp. 50, 42; Shinjuwan Sakusen Kaikoroku, pp. 269–70; "Higeki Shinjuwan Kogeki," pp. 211, 246.
10. Shinjuwan Sakusen Kaikoroku, pp. 241–42.
11. Interviews with Genda, December 25, 1947; Suzuki, June 12, 1948.

12. Interview with Lt. Sadao Yamamoto, March 23, 1950 (hereafter S. Yamamoto); Rengo Kantai, pp. 23–24.
13. The formations discussed here are based on charts in Chigusa's Diary. See also Hawai Sakusen, p. 266.
14. Rengo Kantai, pp. 23–25. See also Shinjuwan Sakusen No Shinso, p. 128.
15. Ibid., p. 28.
16. Interviews with Kusaka, March 7, 1949; Genda, June 4, 1947.
17. Interview with Kusaka, March 7, 1949.
18. Interview with Fuchida and Chihaya, May 23, 1948.
19. Interview with Goto, February 7, 1950.
20. Interview with Shimoda, February 7, 1949.
21. Interview with Fuchida, March 3, 1948.
22. Stimson Diary, November 28, 1941; PHA, Part 14, p. 1083.
23. Stimson Diary, November 28, 1941.
24. PHA, Part 2, p. 440. See also Hull Memoirs, Vol. II, pp. 1080, 1087.
25. Stimson Diary, November 28, 1941.
26. PHA, Part 12, pp. 264–65.
27. Ibid., Part 35, pp. 383–84.
28. Admiral Halsey's Story, pp. 75–76.
29. PHA, Part 26, pp. 324, 319, 326.
30. Ibid., Part 2, pp. 834–35.
31. Ibid., Part 29, pp. 2127–34.
32. Ibid., Part 14, p. 1330.
33. Ibid., Part 2, p. 836.
34. Ibid., Part 7, pp. 2936–37.
35. Ibid., Part 2, pp. 877–78.
36. Japan's Decision, pp. 261–62.
37. Ugaki Diary, November 29, 1941.

Chapter 52
"THE VACANT SEA"

1. PHA, Part 2, p. 441. See also Hull Memoirs, Vol. II, pp. 1089–90.
2. Ibid., Part 12, p. 311.
3. Ibid., p. 263.
4. Kuehn Trial, pp. 3, 5.
5. Interview with Ogawa, April 13, 1949.
6. PHA, Part 35, p. 329.
7. Ibid.
8. Interview with Yoshikawa, September 11, 1955.
9. Interview with Ogawa, April 13, 1949.
10. Interview with Yoshikawa, September 11, 1955.

11. *PHA*, Part 35, pp. 329–30; Kuehn Trial, pp. 61–62. The former indicated that Kuehn reported twenty destroyers.
12. Ibid., p. 330.
13. Ibid., Part 34, pp. 176–81.
14. Ibid., p. 19.
15. Ibid., p. 57.
16. Ibid., Part 27, pp. 58–59.
17. Ibid., p. 62.
18. Ibid., Part 17, pp. 2631–32.
19. Interview with Tomioka, January 19, 1948.
20. *PHA*, Part 17, p. 2633.
21. Ibid., p. 2635.
22. Ibid., Part 10, p. 4836.
23. Interview with Yoshioka, September 23, 1949.
24. Interview with Genda, June 6, 1947.
25. Genda's Analysis, p. 9.
26. Interview with Genda, June 4, 1947.
27. Ibid., November 26, 1949; November 6, 1950.
28. Interviews with Tomioka, November 24 and December 8, 1947.
29. Interview with Fukudome, May 19, 1949.
30. Interviews with Sanagi, August 23 and 25, 1949.
31. Interview with Ishiguro, April 6, 1948.
32. Interviews with Mikawa, January 22, 1949; Genda, December 25, 1947.
33. Interview with Ishiguro, April 6, 1948.
34. *PHA*, Part 12, pp. 200–02.
35. Ibid., Part 33, p. 860.
36. Ibid., Part 12, p. 204.
37. Ibid., Part 8, p. 3440.
38. Telegram, Churchill to Roosevelt, November 30, 1941, Hull Papers, Box 49.
39. Kido Diary, November 30, 1941.
40. Interview with Watanabe, May 29, 1948.
41. Kido Diary, November 30, 1941; *Far East Mil. Trib.*, Ex. No. 3565.

Chapter 53
"GLORY OR OBLIVION"

1. Interview with Tsukamoto, February 15, 1950.
2. Interview with Shimoda, November 21, 1949.
3. Interviews with Mikawa, January 12 and 22, 1949.
4. Interview with Yokota, February 23, 1951.
5. *PHA*, Part 13, pp. 650–51.
6. *Hawai Sakusen*, p. 289.
7. Interview with Sakagami, September 22, 1955.
8. Interview with Ito, October 27, 1950.
9. Interview with Kusaka, March 9, 1949.
10. Interview with Sasaki, July 20, 1949.
11. Ugaki Diary, December 1, 1941.
12. Interview with Watanabe, March 29, 1948.
13. Ugaki Diary, December 1, 1941.
14. Interview with Watanabe, March 29, 1948.
15. *Japan's Decision*, p. 283. See also *Complete History*, pp. 231–34.
16. Interview with Shimizu, November 20, 1948. See also *Hawai Sakusen*, p. 290.
17. The sources for the Japanese ship movements described in this chapter are two studies which Capt. Toshikazu Ohmae prepared for the author: "Combined Fleet Task Organizations, 7 December 1941" and "The Battle Order of the Japanese Fleet Prior to December 1941, with Dates of Departure and Arrival of Major Units" (cited hereafter as Ohmae Studies). These are in the author's files.
18. Ohmae Studies; interview with Capt. Iwao Kawai, April 16, 1951 (hereafter Kawai).
19. Interview with Ozawa, December 22, 1948.
20. Ohmae Studies.
21. Ibid.
22. Interviews with Tsukahara, May 6 and 14, 1949.
23. Ohmae Studies.
24. Ohmae's Report on the Midway Neutralization Unit, in the author's files; statement by Cmdr. Hiroshi Uwai, skipper of *Sazanami*, June 15, 1950 (hereafter Uwai).
25. Interview with RADM. Minoru Togo, October 11, 1950 (hereafter Togo).
26. Ohmae Studies.
27. Interview with Cmdr. Inao Otani, June 23, 1950 (hereafter Otani). Otani, a former member of Naval Intelligence, was on Koga's staff in November 1941.
28. Ugaki Diary, December 1, 1941.
29. Fifth Carrier Division Diary.
30. State Department Memorandum of Conversation, December 1, 1941, Hull Papers, Box 60.
31. *PHA*, Part 12, pp. 208–09.
32. *Hull Memoirs*, Vol. II, pp. 1091–92.
33. Tomioka told the author this story several times in the course of some forty interviews during the period 1947–1965.

Chapter 54
"GREAT UNEASE IN ALL OF OUR MINDS"

1. *PHA*, Part 33, p. 703.
2. Ibid., Part 26, p. 234.
3. Ibid., Part 17, p. 2636.
4. Ibid., Part 10, p. 4680.
5. Ibid., Part 4, p. 1962.
6. Ibid., p. 1756.
7. Ibid., Part 26, p. 234.
8. Ibid., p. 221.
9. Ibid., Part 10, pp. 4837–38.
10. Ibid., p. 4839.
11. Ibid., Part 36, p. 128.
12. Ibid., Part 10, pp. 4839–40.
13. Ibid., Part 6, pp. 2597–98.
14. Ibid., Part 10, pp. 4841–42.
15. Ibid., Part 6, p. 2523.
16. Ibid., Part 10, p. 4893.
17. Ibid., p. 4838.
18. Ibid., Part 15, pp. 1895–96.
19. Ibid., pp. 1774–1842.
20. Ibid., Part 8, pp. 3384–85.
21. Ibid., Part 35, p. 205.
22. Ibid., p. 401.
23. Ibid., p. 120.
24. Ibid., Part 12, pp. 265–66.
25. Ibid., Part 17, p. 2638.
26. Ibid., Part 9, pp. 4367, 4376.
27. Ibid., Part 35, p. 206.
28. Ibid., p. 44.
29. Ibid., Part 7, p. 3101.
30. Ibid., Part 16, pp. 2253–56.
31. Ibid., Part 12, p. 266.
32. Ibid., Part 9, p. 4375.
33. Ibid., Part 35, p. 472.
34. Ibid., Part 12, pp. 215–16.
35. See, in particular, *Osaka Mainichi and Tokyo Nichi Nichi,* November 30, 1941; *Japan Times and Advertiser,* December 6, 1941; Honolulu *Advertiser* and Honolulu *Star-Bulletin,* November 24, 1941; Los Angeles *Times,* November 24 and 26, 1941.
36. Interview with Ohmae, July 3, 1947; *Complete History,* p. 235.
37. Fifth Carrier Division Diary, December 2, 1941; *Dai San Sentai Nisshi* (Diary of the Third Battleship Division), December 2, 1941 (cited hereafter as 3d BB Division Diary).
38. Of many translations, the author prefers this one, found in the Preface of Noel F. Busch's book *The Emperor's Sword: Japan vs. Russia in the Battle of Tsushima* (New York, 1969).
39. Ugaki Diary, December 2, 1941.
40. Fifth Carrier Division Diary, December 2, 1941.

Chapter 55
"SURE INDICATION OF WAR"

1. Ugaki Diary, December 3, 1941.
2. Ibid., December 5, 1941.
3. 3d BB Division Diary, December 3, 1941.
4. *PHA*, Part 4, p. 1676.
5. Fifth Carrier Division Diary.
6. *PHA*, Part 17, p. 2639.
7. Ibid., Part 35, p. 43.
8. Ibid., p. 30.
9. Ibid., Part 14, p. 1407.
10. Ibid., Part 4, p. 1753.
11. Ibid., p. 2002.
12. Ibid., Part 9, p. 4226.
13. Ibid., p. 4233.
14. Ibid., Part 26, p. 468.
15. Ibid., Part 9, p. 4233.
16. Ibid., Part 5, p. 2131.
17. Ibid., Part 2, pp. 840–41.
18. Ibid., Part 14, p. 1408.
19. Ibid., Part 26, p. 392. See also Part 8, p. 3668.
20. Ibid., Part 10, p. 4842.
21. Ibid., Part 33, p. 833.
22. Ibid., Part 6, pp. 2540–41.
23. Ibid., p. 2764.
24. Ibid., p. 2521.
25. Ibid., Part 22, p. 379.
26. Ibid., Part 26, p. 27.
27. Ibid., Part 32, p. 304.
28. Ibid., Part 27, p. 789.
29. Ibid., Part 6, pp. 2596–97, 2764.
30. Ibid., Part 7, pp. 2956, 2996, 3101, 3105.
31. Ibid., Part 10, p. 5112.
32. Ibid., Part 26, p. 283.
33. Ibid., Part 23, p. 875.
34. Ibid., Part 35, pp. 322–25, 330; Part 12, pp. 267–68; interview with Yoshikawa, September 11, 1955.
35. Ibid., Part 36. pp. 303–04; Part 8, p. 3446.
36. Ibid., Part 36, p. 304; Part 8, p. 3892; Part 9, p. 4171; Mr. X Comments.
37. Ibid., Part 9, p. 4171.

38. Chicago *Tribune*, December 7, 1966, Special Supplement, p. 6.
39. Harry Elmer Barnes, "Pearl Harbor After a Quarter of a Century," *Left and Right: A Journal of Libertarian Thought*, Vol. IV (1968), pp. 25, 42. Cited hereafter as "Pearl Harbor After a Quarter of a Century."
40. *PHA*, Part 12, p. 267; Part 29, p. 1673; Part 35, p. 330. The clearest version of the full text appears in Part 35, pp. 321–22.
41. Gwen Terasaki, *Bridge to the Sun* (Chapel Hill, N.C., 1957), pp. 66–69.

Chapter 56
"ANOTHER STRAW IN THE WIND"

1. *Japan's Decision*, pp. 284–95; *The Cause of Japan*, pp. 208–09.
2. *PHA*, Part 12, pp. 231–32.
3. 3d BB Division Diary, December 4, 1941.
4. Fifth Carrier Division Diary, December 4, 1941.
5. Ibid., December 5, 1941.
6. *PHA*, Part 11, p. 5433.
7. Stimson Diary, December 4 and 5, 1941.
8. *PHA*, Part 11, pp. 5284, 5513.
9. Ibid., Part 8, pp. 3388–90, 3412.
10. Ibid., Part 4, p. 1970.
11. Ibid., Part 5, p. 2132.
12. Ibid., Part 8, p. 3417.
13. Ibid., pp. 3413–14.
14. Ibid., p. 3588; Mr. X Comments.
15. *PHA*, Part 26, p. 283.
16. Ibid., Part 17, p. 2475.
17. Ibid., Part 12, p. 227.
18. Ibid., p. 234.
19. Ibid., Part 9, pp. 4201–02.
20. Ibid., Part 33, p. 860.
21. Ibid., Part 9, p. 4577.
22. Ibid., p. 4202.
23. Ibid., Part 12, p. 236.
24. Interview with Lt. Col. John B. Schindel, August 3, 1956 (hereafter Schindel).
25. *PHA*, Part 9, p. 5480.
26. Ibid., Part 4, p. 1968.
27 Ibid., Part 10, pp. 4629–30; Part 35, p. 99.
28. Ibid., Part 9, pp. 4521–22.
29. Ibid., Part 8, pp. 3579.
30. Ibid., Part 33, p. 807.
31. Ibid., Part 9, pp. 4225–26.
32. Ibid., p. 4268.

33. Ibid., p. 4520.
34. Ibid., p. 4541.
35. Ibid., p. 4543.
36. Ibid., pp. 4347, 4595–96.
37. Ibid., Part 35, pp. 88–89.
38. Ibid., Part 9, p. 4347.
39. Ibid., Part 35, p. 27.
40. Ibid., Part 16, pp. 2311–12; Part 26, p. 219.
41. Ibid., Part 6, p. 2610.
42. Chigusa Diary, December 6, 1941 (December 5, local time).
43. *PHA*, Part 35, pp. 383, 389.
44. Ibid., Part 26, pp. 342–44.
45. Ibid., pp. 346–48.
46. Ibid., pp. 148–49.
47. *PHA*, Part 24, p. 1780; Part 7, p. 2996.
48. Ibid., Part 28, pp. 944–45.
49. Ibid., Part 24, p. 1780.
50. Ibid., Part 18, p. 3255.
51. Study, "Submarine Activities in Pearl Harbor," which Shibuya prepared for the author and which is in the author's files (cited hereafter as Shibuya Study).
52. Interview with Cleveland Davis, August 8, 1964. On December 5, 1941, he was chief fire control technician aboard *Ralph Talbot*.
53. Ugaki Diary, December 6, 1941 (December 5, Hawaiian time).

Chapter 57
"ON A KEG OF DYNAMITE"

1. Stimson Diary, December 6, 1941.
2. *PHA*, Part 14, p. 1246.
3. Ibid., Part 15, pp. 1680–81.
4. Ibid., Part 3, p. 1121.
5. Mr. X Comments; *PHA*, Part 36, p. 86.
6. *PHA*, Part 29, pp. 2395–2400; Mr. X Comments.
7. *PHA*, Part 14, p. 1408.
8. Ibid., Part 20, pp. 4528–35.
9. Ibid., Part 12, pp. 238–39; Part 14, p. 1413.
10. Ibid., Part 12, p. 245.
11. Kiyoshi Murata, "'Treachery' of Pearl Harbor," *Nippon Times*, June 8, 1956, (cited hereafter as "'Treachery' of Pearl Harbor"); *PHA*, Part 14, pp. 1413–15.
12. *PHA*, Part 14, pp. 1414–15.
13. Ibid. The time of receipt of Parts 9 and 10

is not given in the documentation. The Army decoded them, and the Navy typed them.

14. Ibid., Part 2, p. 900.
15. Ibid., Part 9, pp. 4510, 4513.
16. Ibid., p. 4015.
17. Ibid., Part 4, p. 1761.
18. Ibid., Part 11, p. 5271.
19. Ibid., Part 14, p. 1238.
20. Ibid., pp. 1240–45.
21. Ibid., Part 20, p. 4535.
22. Ugaki Diary, December 7, 1941.
23. 3d BB Division Diary, December 7, 1941; *Dai Ichi Suirai Sentai Senji Niishi* (War Diary of the First Destroyer Division), December 7, 1941 (cited hereafter as 1st DD Division Diary).
24. Chigusa Diary, December 7, 1941.
25. *PHA*, Part 6, p. 2728.
26. Log of *Monaghan;* interview with RADM. William P. Burford, August 18, 1964 (hereafter Burford).
27. Interview with RADM. Herald F. Stout, August 8, 1964 (hereafter Stout).
28. Telephone conversation with Lt. Irvin H. Thesman, August 12, 1964. He was an electrician's mate first class aboard *Oklahoma* in December 1941; interview with CWO-4 Edgar B. Beck, August 6, 1964. He was a gunner's mate second class aboard *Oklahoma* in December 1941 (hereafter respectively Thesman and Beck).
29. Interview with Lt. Cmdr. B. C. Hesser, August 10, 1964 (hereafter Hesser).
30. Interview with Adm. George A. Rood, July 24, 1964 (hereafter Rood).
31. Interview with RADM. Milo F. Draemel, January 17, 1963 (hereafter Draemel).
32. *PHA*, Part 23, p. 658.
33. Interview with Layton, July 22, 1964. See also *PHA*, Part 26, pp. 236–37.
34. *PHA*, Part 22, pp. 380, 384.
35. Interview with Smith, November 29, 1962.
36. *PHA*, Part 6, pp. 2569–70.
37. Ibid., pp. 2596, 2579, 2828.
38. Ibid., Part 8, p. 3522.
39. Ibid., Part 6, pp. 2591, 2582–83.
40. Interview with Layton, July 22, 1964; *PHA*, Part 6, p. 2793.
41. *PHA*, Part 22, p. 384.
42. Interview with Layton, July 22, 1964.
43. *PHA*, Part 10, p. 4967; Part 22, p. 191.
44. Ibid., Part 22, p. 178.
45. Ibid., Part 7, p. 3104.
46. Ibid., Part 22, p. 146; Part 10, p. 4987.
47. Ibid., Part 14, p. 1409.
48. Ibid., Part 7, p. 3104.
49. Ibid., Part 22, pp. 160–61.
50. Chigusa Diary, 3d BB Division and 1st DD Division diaries, December 7, 1941.
51. *PHA*, Part 12, p. 269.
52. Interview with Yoshikawa, July 16, 1950.
53. *PHA*, Part 12, p. 269.
54. Interviews with Yoshikawa, September 11, 1955; Okuda, August 27, 1955.
55. *PHA*, Part 9, p. 4582.
56. Ibid., Part 36, pp. 251–52.
57. Mr. X Comments.

Chapter 58
"THIS MEANS WAR"

1. *PHA*, Part 29, p. 2382; Part 8, p. 3563; Mr. X Comments.
2. *PHA*, Part 8, pp. 3900–01; Part 33, p. 779; Part 4, p. 1762; Report, p. 219.
3. Letter, Mrs. Alwin Kramer to the author, December 3, 1970.
4. *PHA*, Part 8, pp. 3901–02.
5. Ibid., Part 10, pp. 4661–69.
6. *PHA*, Part II, pp. 5543–60.
7. Letter from Mrs. Kramer, op. cit.
8. *PHA*, Part 8, pp. 3902–03, 3907.
9. Letter from Mrs. Kramer, op. cit.
10. *PHA*, Part 8, p. 3903; Part 4, pp. 1762–63; Part 11, p. 5272.
11. Ibid., Part 4, p. 1970; Part 9, pp. 4230, 4026–30, 4045; postscript by Captain Kramer to letter from Mrs. Kramer, op. cit.
12. *PHA*, Part 9, pp. 4513–16.
13. Ibid., Part 2, pp. 925–26; Part 3, p. 1110.
14. Interview with Lt. Gen. Truman H. Landon, December 15, 1959 (hereafter Landon).
15. *PHA*, Part 3, p. 1121.
16. Ibid., Part 27, p. 96; Part 18, p. 2965; Part 22, p. 45.
17. Ibid., Part 2, pp. 569–70, 692–93.
18. IMTFEC Exhibit No. 1225, July 30, 1946, Affidavit of Tateki Shirao; IMTFEC Document No. 2669A, "Extracts from Diary of Shirao, Tateki"; *The Undeclared War*, pp. 396–97.
19. *PHA*, Part 2, pp. 693–94.
20. Ibid., Part 35, pp. 274–75.

21. Ibid., Part 31. pp. 3188–89; Part 10, p. 5106.
22. Ibid., Part 10, p. 5108.
23. Ibid., Part 29, p. 1666.
24. Ibid., Part 31, pp. 3188–89.
25. Ibid., Part 10, pp. 4870–71.
26. Ibid., pp. 5099–5100.
27. Ibid., Part 27, p. 738.
28. Ibid., Part 10, p. 5091.
29. Ibid., Part 28, pp. 1542, 1558.
30. Ibid., Part 10, pp. 5091, 5097.
31. Ibid., Part 28, p. 1558; Part 27, p. 738.
32. Ibid., Part 10, p. 5113; interview with Bicknell, September 8, 1967.
33. *PHA*, Part 28, p. 1542; Part 22, p. 175.
34. Interview with Ogawa, March 2, 1949.
35. Statement by Tachibana, August 9, 1950.
36. 1st DD Division Diary, December 8, 1941.
37. Interview with Yoshikawa, July 16, 1950.
38. *PHA*, Part 35, p. 390; Part 12, p. 270.
39. Interview with Tomioka, January 26, 1948.
40. 1st DD Division Diary, December 7, 1941.
41. Genda Statement, June 11, 1947.
42. Interview with Genda, June 6, 1947; *Shinjuwan Sakusen Kaikoroku*, pp. 271–72.
43. Interview with Fuchida, December 10, 1963.
44. *I Attacked Pearl Harbor*, pp. 19–21.
45. Interview with Bicknell, September 8, 1967; *PHA*, Part 18, p. 3015.
46. *PHA*, Part 22, p. 508.
47. Ibid., p. 565.
48. Interviews with Hosser, August 10, 1964; Lt. Cmdr. Harley F. Smart, August 21, 1964 (hereafter Smart). In 1941 Smart was a lieutenant aboard *Vestal*.
49. *PHA*, Part 22, pp. 87, 156; Part 10, p. 4983; interview with Col. and Mrs. Emil Leard, October 17, 1963 (hereafter Leard).
50. Honolulu *Star-Bulletin*, December 7, 1966.
51. *PHA*, Part 22, p. 200.
52. Interview with Mollison, January 30, 1963.
53. Interview with Col. Robert H. Dunlop, October 10, 1963 (hereafter Dunlop).
54. Interview with Draemel, January 17, 1963.
55. *PHA*, Part 6, p. 2826.
56. Interview with Layton, July 22, 1964.

Chapter 59
"THE JAPS ARE PLANNING SOME DEVILTRY"

1. The formation for the high-speed rum is taken from Chigusa Diary. See also *Hawai Sakusen*, p. 317.
2. 1st DD Division Diary, December 8, 1941.
3. Fifth Carrier Division Diary, December 8, 1941.
4. Interview with Shimoda, November 21, 1949.
5. *PHA*, Part 37, p. 1299; log of *Condor*, December 6, 1941; Cabell Phillips, "Ten Years Ago This Friday," *The New York Times Magazine* (December 2, 1951), p. 9.
6. Interview with RADM. William W. Outerbridge, September 8, 1970 (hereafter Outerbridge); *PHA*, Part 37, pp. 1296, 1299, 703; Part 36, pp. 55–56: Part 13, p. 494; log of *Ward*, December 7, 1941.
7. *PHA*, Part 8, pp. 3907–08; Part 14, p. 1415.
8. Ibid., Part 12, p. 245; Hull Papers, Box 60.
9. *PHA*, Part 8, pp. 3907, 3392–93; Part 33, p. 858.
10. Ibid., Part 11, pp. 5273–74.
11. Ibid., Part 8, pp. 3907–08; Part 9, p. 4109.
12. Interview with Schindel, July 14, 1956.
13. *PHA*, Part 9, pp. 4516, 4523–24; Part 35, p. 98.
14. Ibid., Part 12, p. 248.
15. Ibid., Part 9, pp. 4517, 4527.
16. Ibid., pp. 4571, 4548.
17. Ibid., p. 4534; Part 3, p. 1114.
18. Ibid., Part 9, pp. 4595, 4524.
19. Ibid., p. 4524.
20. Ibid., Part 3, pp. 1108, 1327; Part 11, pp. 5175–76.
21. Stimson Diary, December 7, 1941.
22. Interview with Ema, May 27, 1950.
23. Interview with Sublt. Iyozo Fujita, February 2, 1951 (hereafter Fujita).
24. Interview with Ohashi, November 18, 1949.
25. Interview with Fuchida, December 10, 1963.
26. Mitsuo Fuchida, "I Led the Air Attack Against Pearl Harbor," ed. Roger Pineau,

United States Naval Institute Proceedings (September 1952), p. 945 (cited hereafter as "I Led the Air Attack.")

27. Interview with Fuchida, December 10, 1963.
28. Ibid.; also Genda, January 26, 1950; "I Led the Air Attack," p. 956.
29. Interviews with Amagai, October 5, 1949; Matsumura, January 8, 1965; Goto, January 17, 1950.
30. Interview with Genda, December 26, 1947; *Shinjuwan Sakusen Kaikoroku*, pp. 272–73.
31. *PHA*, Part 8, p. 3908.
32. Ibid., pp. 3393–94.
33. Ibid., p. 3910; Part 9, p. 4048.
34. Ibid., Part 8, p. 3909; Part 12, p. 251.
35. Ibid., Part 8, p. 3920; Part 9, pp. 3970–71.
36. Ibid., Part 8, pp. 3909, 3430.
37. Ibid., Part 36, p. 26.
38. Ibid., Part 8, p. 3396.
39. Ibid., Part 9, pp. 4043, 4053; Part 8, pp. 3909, 3912; Part 5, p. 2095; Part 33, pp. 859–60.
40. "'Treachery' of Pearl Harbor."
41. Interview with Genda, November 3, 1950; *Shinjuwan Sakusen Kaikoroku*, p. 121.
42. Interviews with Genda, December 12, 1947; Fuchida, December 10, 1963: Amagai, October 5, 1949; *Shinjuwan Sakusen Kaikoroku*, p. 121.
43. Statement by Matsumura, January 19, 1951.
44. Interview with Lt. Keizo Ofuchi, January 19, 1950 (hereafter Ofuchi).
45. Interviews with Genda, December 28, 1947, and November 3, 1950; *Hawai Sakusen*, p. 332.
46. Interviews with Ofuchi, January 19, 1950; Fuchida, December 10, 1963; Ema, May 27, 1950.
47. Interviews with Genda, December 27, 1947; Amagai, October 4, 1949; Fuchida, December 10, 1963.
48. Interview with Genda, December 28, 1947.
49. Interview with Fujita, February 2, 1951.
50. Interviews with Ofuchi, January 19, 1950; Genda, December 29, 1947; *Shinjuwan Sakusen Kaikoroku*, p. 264.
51. Statement by Lt. Saburo Shindo, January 17, 1951 (hereafter Shindo).
52. Interviews with Genda, December 28,

1947; Fuchida, December 10, 1963; Amagai, October 12, 1949; *Shinjuwan Sakusen Kaikoroku*, p. 262. Some discrepancies exist concerning the number of planes which participated. The figures used in this study came from Genda, Fuchida, other airmen, Chihaya, and *Hawai Sakusen.*
53. Interview with Genda, December 28, 1947; *Rengo Kantai*, p. 34.

Chapter 60
"AN AWFUL URGENCY"

1. Interview with Sakamaki, October 19, 1947; *I Attacked Pearl Harbor*, pp. 36–38.
2. *PHA*, Part 2, p. 933.
3. Ibid., Part 9, pp. 4517–18, 4552–53: Part 14, p. 1410.
4. Ibid., Part 29, p. 2309; Part 9, p. 4518.
5. Ibid., Part 14, p. 1410.
6. Ibid., Part 9, p. 4518; Part 15, p. 1633.
7. Ibid., Part 5, p. 2132.
8. Ibid., Part 14, p. 1410.
9. Ibid., Part 5, p. 2133.
10. Ibid., Part 9, p. 4519.
11. Ibid., Part 2, p. 931; Part 33, p. 882; Part 29, p. 2313.
12. Ibid., Part 34, p. 32; Part 23, p. 1105.
13. Ibid., Part 9, p. 4519.
14. Ibid., Part 14, p. 1334.
15. Ibid., Part 9, p. 4519.
16. Ibid., p. 4555; Part 14, p. 1411.
17. Ibid., Part 15, p. 1640.
18. Ibid., Part 34, p. 33; Part 27, pp. 109, 114; Part 23, p. 1103.
19. Interview with Capt. Lawrence C. Grannis, July 24, 1963 (hereafter Grannis); log of *Antares*, December 7, 1941.
20. Interview with Outerbridge, September 8, 1970; *PHA*, Part 36, pp. 56–57; log of *Ward*, December 7, 1941; Report of W. W. Outerbridge, December 13, 1941, DD139/A16-3/(759), Classified Operational Archives Branch, Naval History Division, Washington Navy Yard, Washington, D.C.
21. *PHA*, Part 36, p. 57; Part 37, p. 704.
22. Ibid., Part 23, pp. 1035–37.
23. Ibid., Part 26, pp. 203–09.
24. Ibid., Part 32, p. 444; interview with Ramsey, December 6, 1962.

25. *PHA*, Part 26, pp. 209–10; interview with Kimmel, December 1, 1963.
26. *PHA*, Part 23, pp. 1125, 1193.
27. Ibid., Part 23, pp. 1051–52, 1038.
28. Ibid., Part 22, p. 499.
29. Ibid., Part 28, p. 1554.

Chapter 61
"TORA! TORA! TORA!"

1. Interviews with Fuchida, December 10, 1963; Genda, December 27, 1947.
2. *PHA*, Part 27, pp. 530–32; Part 10, p. 5064.
3. Ibid., Part 10, pp. 5029, 5046. See also Record of Readings opp. p. 5058.
4. Ibid., Part 29, p. 2122; Part 10, p. 5041.
5. Interview with Lt. Col. Kermit Tyler, August 21, 1964 (hereafter Tyler); *PHA*, Part 32, p. 342.
6. Interview with Tyler, August 21, 1964; *PHA*, Part 27, p. 568.
7. Interview with Tyler, August 21, 1964; *PHA*, Part 18, p. 3015; Part 32, p. 342.
8. Interview with Tyler, August 21, 1964; *PHA*, Part 27, p. 532; Part 29, p. 2122.
9. Interview with Tyler, August 21, 1964: *PHA*, Part 27, p. 569; Part 22, p. 223.
10. *PHA*, Part 10, Record of Readings opp. p. 5058, pp. 5028, 5033; Part 18, p. 3015.
11. Interview with Tyler, August 21, 1964.
12. *PHA*, Part 7, p. 3075: Part 23, p. 1162.
13. Log of *Ward*, December 7, 1941.
14. Interview with Genda, December 26, 1946; "I Led the Air Attack," p. 947.
15. *PHA*, Part 35, p. 211; Part 10, Record of Readings opp. p. 5058; Walter Lord, *Day of Infamy* (New York, 1957), p. 174 (cited hereafter as *Day of Infamy*); *Broken Seal*, pp. 380–81.
16. " 'Treachery' of Pearl Harbor."
17. This account of the initiation of the attack is based upon interview with Fuchida, December 10, 1963; "I Led the Air Attack," p. 947.
18. Ugaki Diary, December 8, 1941.
19. Interview with Fuchida, December 10, 1963.
20. *Rengo Kantai*, p. 35.

Chapter 62
"SOUND GENERAL QUARTERS"

1. *PHA*, Part 26, p. 210; interview with Fuchida, December 10, 1963.
2. Interview with RADM. William R. Furlong, November 16, 1962 (hereafter Furlong); log of *Oglala*, December 7, 1941; *PHA*, Part 16, p. 2257; Part 22, pp. 594–95.
3. *Rising Sun in the Pacific*, p. 104.
4. Interview with Matsumura, January 19, 1951; Statement by Lt. Tamotsu Nakajima, January 28, 1951. The logs of most of the nearby ships give the account of *Utah*'s fate. Her own log was lost.
5. Logs of *Raleigh* and *Detroit*, December 7, 1941; *PHA*, Part 23, pp. 746–50; interview with Capt. John R. Beardall, Jr., November 17, 1970 (hereafter Beardall); "Supplementary Battle Report, Captain R. B. Simons, USN, Commanding USS RALEIGH, 7 December, 1941" (cited hereafter as Simons Report).
6. Interview with Fuchida, March 4, 1948; logs of *Oglala* and *Helena*, December 7, 1941: *PHA*, Part 22, p. 596.
7. Interview with Kimmel, December 1, 1963; *PHA*, Part 26, p. 210; Part 23, p. 898.
8. Interviews with Mrs. John B. Earle, September 22, 1970 (hereafter Mrs. Earle); Kimmel, December 1, 1963; letter, Mrs. Earle to the author, October 16, 1964.
9. Interview with RADM. Lawrence A. Ruff, July 28, 1964 (hereafter Ruff).
10. *PHA*, Part 10, pp. 5098, 5118; Part 27, p. 741.
11. Interview with Goto, January 17, 1950; *Rengo Kantai*, p. 35.
12. Interview with Genda, November 30, 1950; *Shinjuwan Sakusen Kaikoroku*, p. 280.
13. Statement by Matsumura, January 19, 1951.
14. *PHA*, Part 23, pp. 696–97.
15. Interview with Hesser, August 10, 1964; log of *Vestal*, December 7, 1941.
16. Interviews with Goto, January 19 and 24, 1950.
17. Interview with Thesman, August 12, 1964.

18. *PHA*, Part 23, pp. 723–24.
19. Interview with Beck, August 6, 1964.
20. Statement by Cmdr. J. L. Kenworthy, December 16, 1941, contained in Action Report, Commander-in-Chief, United States Pacific Fleet, Serial 0479, 15 February 1942, Report of Japanese Raid on Pearl Harbor, 7 December 1941. (Vol. 3) Enclosure E, Classified Operational Archives Branch, Naval History Division, Washington Navy Yard, Washington, D.C. Cited hereafter as Action Report.
21. Interview with John Crawford, August 8, 1964 (hereafter Crawford).
22. Interview with Lt. Gen. Alan Shapley, October 11, 1967 (hereafter Shapley); William H. Ewing, "High Dive Off the Mainmast," Honolulu *Star-Bulletin*, December 7, 1961.
23. Statement by Ens. H. D. Davidson, Vol. 2, Encl. E, Part 1, Action Report.
24. Interview with Kimmel, December 1, 1963; log of *California*, December 7, 1941.
25. Interview with Adm. Harold C. Train, November 27, 1962 (hereafter Train).
26. *Rising Sun in the Pacific*, pp. 111–12.
27. Interview with Fuchida, March 4, 1948; "I Led the Air Attack," pp. 948–49.
28. Statements by Cmdr. H. R. Hillenkoetter and Lt. Cmdr. T. T. Beattie, Vol. 3, Encl. F, Action Report; *Rising Sun in the Pacific*, pp. 104–06.
29. Interview with Kimmel, December 1, 1963.
30. Interviews with Smith, November 14, 1962, and June 15, 1964.
31. Interview with Davis, January 30, 1963.
32. Interview with Layton, July 22, 1964.
33. *PHA*, Part 24, p. 1365; Part 26, p. 210.
34. Interview with Curts, November 16, 1962.
35. *PHA*, Part 23, p. 725.
36. Letter from Mrs. Earle, op. cit.
37. Interview with Thesman, August 12, 1964.
38. Log of *Nevada*, December 7, 1941. *Arizona*'s log was lost.
39. *PHA*, Part 23, pp. 634–36.
40. Interview with Shoemaker and Coe, January 31, 1963.
41. *PHA*, Part 23, pp. 634–36.
42. Interviews with Hesser, August 10, 1964; Smart, August 21, 1964.
43. *Rising Sun in the Pacific*, p. 109.
44. Statements by Beattie, op. cit.; Lt. (j.g.) C. V. Ricketts, Vol. 3, Encl. E, Action Report; interview with Johnson, July 25, 1964; statement by Abe, October 14, 1950.
45. Log of *Nevada*, December 7, 1941; statement by Lt. Ichiro Kitajima, October 18, 1950 (hereafter Kitajima); letter from Capt. Joseph K. Taussig, Jr., January 8, 1963.
46. Letter from Taussig, op. cit.; action report of *Nevada*, contained in Action Report, Vol. 3; Capt. Joseph K. Taussig, Jr., "I Remember Pearl Harbor," *United States Naval Institute Proceedings* (December 1972), p. 20.
47. Interview with Ruff, July 28, 1964.
48. *Shinjuwan Sakusen Kaikoroku*, p. 266.
49. Interview with Davis, January 30, 1963.
50. Interviews with Curts, November 16, 1962; Kimmel, December 1, 1963; *PHA*, Part 23, p. 899.

Chapter 63
"THEY CAUGHT THEM ASLEEP, BY GOD!"

1. Interview with Ramsey, December 6, 1962; *PHA*, Part 32, p. 444.
2. Report of Patrol Wing Two, Action Report, Vol. I.
3. Interview with Ramsey, December 6, 1962.
4. Interview with Coe, January 23, 1963; *PHA*, Part 22, p. 565.
5. Interview with Shoemaker, January 31, 1963; *PHA*, Part 37, p. 1270; log of *Neosho*, December 7, 1941.
6. Interview with Shoemaker, January 31, 1963; log of *Neosho*, December 7, 1941; Charles Rawlings and Isabel Leighton, "Fat Girl," *Saturday Evening Post* (February 6, 1943), p. 10.
7. Interview with Ramsey, December 6, 1962.
8. Letters to the author from Guy C. Avery, December 16, 1953, and November 4, 1963 (hereafter Avery).
9. Honolulu *Advertiser*, December 6, 1966. This newspaper printed highlights of Commander Martin's report to Bloch of

the activities at Kaneohe on December 7, 1941.

10. Interview with Adm. Harold M. Martin, November 10, 1970 (hereafter Martin); *PHA*, Part 23, pp. 738–39.

11. Interview with RADM. Cecil D. Riggs, January 14, 1964 (hereafter Riggs).

12. Interview with Ramsey, December 6, 1962.

13. *PHA*, Part 26, p. 330.

14. Interview with Shoemaker, January 31, 1963.

15. *Admiral Halsey's Story*, p. 77; *PHA*, Part 26, p. 330.

16. *PHA*, Part 23, p. 611; interview with Shoemaker, January 31, 1963: *Rising Sun in the Pacific*, p. 121.

17. Interview with Farthing, August 17, 1955.

18. Interview with Mollison, April 15, 1963; *PHA*, Part 22, p. 124.

19. Interview with Col. Vernon H. Reeves, October 27, 1969 (hereafter Reeves).

20. Interview with Mollison, April 15, 1961; *PHA*, Part 22, p. 134.

21. Interview with Mollison, April 15, 1961.

22. *PHA*, Part 22, p. 194.

23. Interview with Maj. Gen. Brooke E. Allen, July 17, 1962 (hereafter Allen).

24. Interview with Lt. Col. Francis Gutzak, October 19, 1953 (hereafter Gutzak).

25. *Day of Infamy*, pp. 80, 111, 113.

26. Interview with Allen, July 17, 1962.

27. Interview with Lt. Yoshio Shiga, December 21, 1964 (hereafter Shiga).

28. *PHA*, Part 12, p. 323.

29. Interview with CPO Harry Rafsky, August 11, 1964 (hereafter Rafsky).

30. Interview with Landon, December 15, 1969.

31. *PHA*, Part 22, p. 194.

32. Statement by 1st PO Kazuo Muranaka, December 17, 1941 (hereafter Muranaka).

33. Interview with Ema, May 27, 1950.

34. Interview with Brig. Gen. William J. Flood, July 11, 1962 (hereafter Flood); *PHA*, Part 12, p. 323.

35. Interview with Ema, May 27, 1950.

36. Interview with Davidson, July 6, 1962.

37. *PHA*, Part 22, pp. 117–18.

38. Ibid., Part 28, p. 1487.

39. Ibid., Part 22, pp. 249–50.

40. Statement by Muranaka, December 17, 1949.

41. Interview with Flood, July 11, 1962.

42. *PHA*, Part 12, p. 323.

43. Chigusa Diary, December 8, 1941; *Rengo Kantai*, p. 35.

44. Interview with Duane W. Shaw, November 19, 1970 (hereafter Shaw).

45. Interview with Shiga, December 21, 1964.

46. *PHA*, Part 12, pp. 351–52; Part 13, p. 410.

47. Ibid., Part 22, pp. 304–07.

48. Ibid., pp. 57, 25.

49. Interview with Col. Russell C. Throckmorton, September 11, 1967 (hereafter Throckmorton).

50. Interviews with Dunlop, October 11 and 23, 1963.

51. Interview with Bicknell, September 8, 1967.

52. *PHA*, Part 22, pp. 299–300.

53. Ibid., pp. 262–64.

54. Ibid., pp. 265–66.

55. Ibid., pp. 273–76, 279.

56. Ibid., p. 47.

57. Ibid., Part 8, pp. 3819, 3835–38.

Chapter 64
"OH, HOW POWERFUL IS THE IMPERIAL NAVY!"

1. Interview with Grannis, July 24, 1964.

2. Log of *Helm*; Theodore Roscoe, *United States Destroyer Operations in World War II* (Annapolis, 1953), p. 49 (cited hereafter as *Destroyer Operations*).

3. Interview with Sakamaki, October 19, 1947.

4. Capt. Burdick H. Brittin, USN (Ret.), "We Four Ensigns," *United States Naval Institute Proceedings* (December 1966), pp. 106–09: log of *Aylwin*, December 7, 1941.

5. Interview with RADM. Harold F. Pullen, September 12, 1964 (hereafter Pullen).

6. Interview with RADM. Allen G. Quynn, December 30, 1963 (hereafter Quynn).

7. Interview with Rafsky, August 11, 1964.

8. *PHA*, Part 1, p. 51; Part 22, pp. 293–94.

9. Ibid., Part 23, pp. 742–43; Part 28, p. 1570.

10. Interviews with Genda, December 27, 1947; Fuchida, December 10, 1963; interview with and statement from Chihaya, June 10, 1951; *Hawai Sakusen*, p. 339.

11. Interviews with Genda, December 28, 1947; Fuchida, December 10, 1963; *Hawai Sakusen*, p. 339.
12. Statement by Shindo, January 17, 1951.
13. Statement by Ofuchi, January 19, 1950.
14. Interview with Fujita, February 2, 1951.
15. Interview with Burford, August 18, 1964; Simons Report; *PHA*, Part 32, p. 309; logs of *Monaghan* and *Curtiss*, December 7, 1941.
16. *PHA*, Part 13, p. 494.
17. Interviews with Fuchida, March 4, 1948; January 6, 1949.
18. *PHA*, Part 1, p. 51; Part 22, pp. 293–96; Part 28, p. 1571.
19. Ibid., Part 23, p. 740.
20. Letters from Avery, November 4 and December 1, 1963.
21. Interview with Fujita, February 2, 1951.
22. Letter from Avery, November 4, 1963.
23. Ibid., November 4 and December 1, 1963.
24. Interview with Fujita, February 2, 1951.
25. Letter from Avery, November 4, 1963.
26. Interview with Fujita, February 2, 1951. Genda perpetuates this legend in his book *Shinjuwan Sakusen Kaikoroku*, p. 282.
27. *PHA*, Part 23, p. 740; *Rising Sun in the Pacific*, p. 122.
28. Interview with Fujita, February 2, 1951.
29. *PHA*, Part 22, pp. 249–51, 254.
30. Interview with Fujita, February 2, 1951.
31. *PHA*, Part 22, p. 250.
32. Ibid., p. 254.
33. Interview with Fujita, February 2, 1951.
34. Statement by Shindo, January 17, 1951.
35. Statement by Lt. Takemi Iwami, October 20, 1950 (hereafter Iwami).
36. *PHA*, Part 1, p. 50; interview with Allen, July 17, 1962.
37. Statement by Lt. Cmdr. Zenji Abe, October 19, 1950 (hereafter Z. Abe).
38. Interview with Genda, December 29, 1947.
39. Statement by Ofuchi, January 19, 1950.
40. Interview with Capt. Ruth Erickson, September 7, 1971. Hereafter Erickson.
41. Log of *Nevada*, December 7, 1941; *Rising Sun in the Pacific*, pp. 109–10; *Day of Infamy*, p. 133.
42. Interviews with Ruff, July 28, 1964; Coe, January 23, 1963.
43. Interview with Fuchida, December 10, 1963.
44. Interview with Ruff, July 28, 1964; log of *Nevada*, December 7, 1941.
45. *Rising Sun in the Pacific*, p. 110.
46. Log of *Oglala*, December 7, 1941; *PHA*, Part 22, p. 598; interviews with Crawford, August 8, 1964; Rafsky, August 11, 1964.
47. *PHA*, Part 23, p. 635; log of *Vestal*, December 7, 1941; interviews with Smart, August 21, 1963; Hesser, August 14, 1964.
48. *PHA*, Part 22, pp. 590–91.
49. Log of *Blue*, December 7, 1941; *PHA*, Part 23, pp. 693–94, 698.
50. Log of *Pennsylvania*, December 7, 1941; *Rising Sun in the Pacific*.
51. *PHA*, Part 22, p. 596; *Rising Sun in the Pacific*, p. 118.
52. Log of *California*, December 7, 1941; interview with Train, November 27, 1962; *PHA*, Part 22, pp. 533–34.
53. Letter from Harlan E. Eisnangle to the author, November 24, 1964 (hereafter Eisnangle).
54. Log of *Raleigh*, December 7, 1941; Simons Report.
55. Log of *Honolulu*, December 7, 1941.
56. Log of *St. Louis*, December 7, 1941; interviews with Rood, July 24, 1964; RADM. Carl K. Fink, November 17, 1970 (hereafter Fink).
57. Statement by Ofuchi, January 19, 1950.
58. *PHA*, Part 22, p. 250; Part 1, p. 55.
59. Ibid., Part 22, p. 125; interview with Allen, July 17, 1962.
60. Interview with Reeves, October 27, 1969.
61. "I Led the Air Attack," pp. 951–52.
62. *PHA*, Part 22, pp. 60–61; Part 7, pp. 3069–70; Part 12, pp. 357–58.

Chapter 65
"THE CHANCE OF A LIFETIME"

1. *Rengo Kantai*, p. 37; 3d BB Division Diary, December 8, 1941.
2. Interviews with Amagai, October 12, 1949; Genda, June 4, 1947.
3. Interview with Ema, May 27, 1950.
4. Interview with Fuchida, December 11, 1963.
5. Interview with Goto, January 24, 1950; *Shinjuwan Sakusen Kaikoroku*, pp. 280–81.
6. This account of Fuchida's briefing and

questioning is based upon interview with him, December 11, 1963.

7. Interview with Genda, November 28, 1949; *Shinjuwan Sakusen Kaikoroku,* pp. 304–05.

8. *PHA,* Part 22, p. 584.

9. Ibid., p. 57.

10. Interview with Genda, June 4, 1947.

11. *Rengo Kantai,* pp. 37–38; interview with Kusaka, May 16, 1948.

12. Interview with Goto, January 24, 1950.

13. Statement by Shindo, January 17, 1951.

14. Interview with Goto, January 24, 1950; Minoru Genda, "Shinjuwan Kishu to Sannin no Teitoku" (The Surprise Attack Against Pearl Harbor and Three Admirals), *Bungei Shunju* (May 1968), p. 187 (cited hereafter as "Shinjuwan Kishu").

15. Statement by Lt. Cmdr. Takashi Hashiguchi. The statement is undated, but it was obtained in 1950, when the author secured a number of such statements from Japanese participants in the attack (hereafter Hashiguchi).

16. Interview with Suzuki, June 12, 1948.

17. Statement by Lt. Cmdr. Heijiro Abe, October 14, 1950 (hereafter Abe).

18. Statement by Sublt. Iwakichi Mifuku, March 6, 1951 (hereafter Mifuku).

19. Interview with Shimoda, November 21, 1949.

20. Interview with Fuchida, December 11, 1963.

21. *Rengo Kantai,* p. 21; interview with Kusaka, May 16, 1948.

22. Interview with Fuchida, December 11, 1963.

23. Ugaki Diary, December 9, 1941.

24. This account of the discussion in the Combined Fleet staff is based upon interviews with Watanabe, November 7 and 14, 1949; Kuroshima, June 14, 1948.

25. This account of the discussions in the Naval General Staff is based upon Sanagi Diary and interviews with Fukudome, Tomioka, Ogawa, and Sanagi.

26. Interview with Sawamoto, April 10, 1949.

27. *Rengo Kantai,* p. 38.

28. Statement by Genda, November 16, 1961.

29. Interview with Fleet Adm. Chester W. Nimitz, September 4, 1964 (hereafter Nimitz).

30. *PHA,* Part 6, p. 2812.

31. Interview with Furlong, December 1, 1962.

32. Interview with Adm. Raymond A. Spruance, September 5, 1964 (hereafter Spruance).

33. Interview with Tomioka, December 8, 1947.

34. Ugaki Diary, December 9, 1941.

35. Statement by Ozawa, December 22, 1948.

Chapter 66
"AN EXCITEMENT INDEED"

1. *PHA,* Part 11, pp. 5272, 5275, 5286–88.

2. VADM. Ross T. McIntire, *White House Physician* (New York, 1946), pp. 136–37.

3. Robert E. Sherwood, *Roosevelt and Hopkins: An Intimate History* (New York, 1948), pp. 430–31 (cited hereafter as *Roosevelt and Hopkins*).

4. State Department Memorandum of Conversation, December 7, 1941, Hull Papers, Box 60; *Hull Memoirs,* Vol. II, pp. 1096–97.

5. Interviews with Nomura, May 7 and 9, 1949.

6. Stimson Diary, December 7, 1941.

7. *PHA,* Part 14, p. 1411.

8. Letter, Safford to Lt. Cmdr. Charles C. Hiles, March 29, 1967. Papers of Lt. Cmdr. Charles C. Hiles, University of Wyoming, Laramie, Wy., Box 14 (cited hereafter as Hiles Papers). In a telephone conversation on November 9, 1972, Mr. X told virtually the same story to the author.

9. *Hull Memoirs,* Vol. II, p. 1097.

10. Grace Tully, *F. D. R., My Boss* (New York, 1949), pp. 254–55 (cited hereafter as *F. D. R., My Boss*).

11. *Roosevelt and Hopkins,* p. 432; Stimson Diary, December 7, 1941.

12. "Conference in the Office of the Secretary of State, 4:00 to 6:00 P.M.," December 7, 1941, Hull Papers, Box 72–73.

13. Washington *Post* and Washington *Star,* December 8, 1941.

14. Interview with Grace Tully, December 15, 1970.

15. Stimson Diary, December 7, 1941.

16. Frances Perkins, *The Roosevelt I Knew* (New York, 1946), p. 379.

17. *PHA*, Part 19, pp. 3503–04.
18. Stimson Diary, December 7, 1941.
19. *Hull Memoirs*, Vol. II, pp. 1099–1100.
20. *PHA*, Part 20, p. 4523.
21. Ibid., pp. 4517–18.
22. Stimson Diary, December 7, 1941.
23. *PHA*, Part 19, pp. 3504–06. The transcript of Roosevelt's remarks at the Cabinet and congressional meetings of December 7 does not make a clear demarkation between the two.
24. Thomas T. Connally, *My Name is Tom Connally* (New York, 1954), p. 249.
25. *PHA*, Part 19, pp. 3506–07.
26. Washington *Times-Herald,* Washington *Post,* December 8, 1941.
27. Diaries of Henry Morgenthau, Jr., Franklin D. Roosevelt Library, Hyde Park, New York, December 7, 1941, Box 470 (cited hereafter as Morgenthau Diaries).

Chapter 67
"OUR FLAG WAS STILL THERE"

1. This is a well-remembered incident. See *Day of Infamy*, p. 160; Honolulu *Star-Bulletin,* December 7, 1966; Honolulu *Advertiser,* December 9, 1941.
2. *PHA*, Part 16, p. 2257.
3. Ibid., Part 35, p. 338; interview with Shoemaker, January 31, 1963; San Francisco *Chronicle*, December 31, 1941.
4. *PHA*, Part 28, pp. 1620–21.
5. Ibid., Part 35, p. 372.
6. Captain Benjamin Van Kuren, "Report of Police Activities in Connection with the Japanese Consulate Subsequent to December 7th, 1941 and Up to February 8th, 1942," February 13, 1943, courtesy of Fielder (cited hereafter as Van Kuren Report); interview with Yoshikawa, September 14, 1955; *Day of Infamy*, p. 170.
7. Interviews with Bicknell, September 8 and 12, 1967.
8. *PHA*, Part 23, pp. 873–74.
9. Van Kuren Report.
10. *PHA*, Part 23, p. 192; Part 27, p. 740; Van Kuren Report.
11. *PHA*, Part 35, pp. 371–72.
12. Interview with Train, November 26, 1962.
13. Log of *California*, December 7, 1941.
14. Interview with Train, November 26, 1962.
15. Log of *Tennessee*, December 7, 1941.
16. *Rising Sun in the Pacific*, pp. 106–07.
17. Interview with Thesman, August 12, 1964.
18. *PHA*, Part 24, p. 1371.
19. Ibid., Part 23, p. 683; interview with Capt. Thomas E. Dyer, December 9, 1970.
20. *PHA*, Part 22, p. 529.
21. Ibid., Part 24, p. 1371.
22. Interview with Coe, January 23, 1963.
23. Interview with Landon, December 15, 1959.
24. *PHA*, Part 22, p. 205.
25. Ibid., Part 23, p. 1162.
26. Ibid., Part 22, p. 194.
27. Ibid., Part 12, p. 345; Part 32, p. 426.
28. *Rising Sun in the Pacific*, p. 215.
29. *PHA*, Part 32, pp. 426–27.
30. Interview with Allen, July 17, 1962.
31. *PHA*, Part 22, p. 195.
32. Interviews with Smith, November 14, 1962; Kimmel, December 1, 1963.
33. Interview with Mollison, April 15, 1961.
34. Interview with Curts, November 16, 1962.
35. *PHA*, Part 37, pp. 1251–55; Part 32, p. 426; Simons Report.
36. Letter from Avery, December 1, 1963.
37. St. Louis *Post-Dispatch*, December 18, 1941.
38. Interview with Dunlop, October 10, 1963.
39. Interview with Erickson, September 7, 1971.
40. Roosevelt Papers, BF Box 64.
41. Interview with Quynn, December 30, 1963.
42. *PHA*, Part 22, p. 217; Part 35, pp. 211–12.
43. Interviews with Dunlop, October 10 and 23, 1963.
44. Taped reminiscences of Maj. Gen. Robert J. Fleming, Jr., March 7 and 31, 1975, Hoover Institution on War, Revolution and Peace, Stanford, Calif. 94305, (cited hereafter as Fleming Tapes); reply dated January 11, 1977, to questionnarie which the author submitted to Fleming (cited hereafter as Fleming Questionnaire).
45. *PHA*, Part 22, pp. 46–47; Part 23, p. 977.
46. Interview with Kimmel, December 1, 1963; *PHA*, Part 35, p. 212.

47. Interview with Davis, January 30, 1963.
48. Interview with Crawford, August 8, 1964.
49. Interview with Beck, August 8, 1964.
50. Interview with Quynn, December 30, 1963.
51. Interview with Brig. Gen. George P. Sampson, October 18, 1963 (hereafter Sampson).
52. Interview with Guzak, October 19, 1953.
53. Interview with Curts, November 16, 1962.
54. Notes by Fielder for a talk which he delivered before the Rotary Club in Honolulu on December 7, 1966. Courtesy of Fielder (cited hereafter as Fielder Notes).
55. Letter from Avery, December 1, 1963.
56. Interview with Mrs. Frank Cooper, March 6, 1966.
57. Interview with Dunlop, October 10, 1963.
58. St. Louis *Post-Dispatch*, December 8, 1941.
59. Interview with Dunlop, October 10, 1963.
60. Interview with Mrs. Durward S. Wilson, January 22, 1963.
61. *PHA*, Part 22, p. 591.
62. Interview with Shoemaker, January 31, 1963.
63. Interview with French, August 11, 1964.
64. *PHA*, Part 23, p. 612; *Day of Infamy*, pp. 206–07.
65. Interview with Shoemaker, January 11, 1963.
66. Interview with Stout, August 12, 1964; log of *Breese*, December 7, 1941.
67. Interviews with Shibuya, August 7 and 21, 1948; *PHA*, Part 13, pp. 495–96, 409. A report of *I-69*'s post-Pearl Harbor actions may be found in Part 13, pp. 505–11.
68. Interview with Sakamaki, October 19, 1947; *I Attacked Pearl Harbor*, pp. 44–46; *Day of Infamy*, p. 234.
69. Interview with Quynn, December 30, 1963.

Chapter 68
"CLOUDS OVER MOUNTAINS"

1. 1st DD Division Diary, December 8, 1941.
2. Chigusa Diary, December 8, 1941.
3. Fifth Carrier Division Diary, December 8, 1941.
4. *Shinjuwan Sakusen Kaikoroku,* pp. 305–06.
5. Interview with Fuchida, June 24, 1949.
6. 1st DD and Fifth Carrier Division diaries, December 9, 1941.
7. Ibid.; Chigusa Diary, December 9, 1941; interviews with Genda, December 30, 1947; S. Yamamoto, March 23, 1950; Cmdr. Toshio Hashimoto, April 20, 1950; *Rengo Kantai,* p. 41.
8. Interview with Omori, March 26, 1949.
9. Interviews with Amagai, October 19, 1949; Kitajima, October 18, 1950.
10. Statement by Z. Abe, October 19, 1950.
11. 1st DD and Fifth Carrier Division diaries, December 9, 1941; *Rengo Kantai,* p. 42.
12. *PHA*, Part 24, pp. 1559–61; Lt. Col. Robert D. Heinl, Jr., USMC, *Marines at Midway* (Washington, D.C., 1948), pp. 11–15.
13. Ugaki Diary, December 8, 1941.
14. *Rengo Kantai,* p. 42.
15. "Shinjuwan Kishu," p. 188; Chigusa Diary, December 11, 1941.
16. Interviews with Genda, August 26, 1947; March 10 and 26, 1948; February 3, 1950. See also "Shinjuwan Kishu," p. 188.
17. This account of the discussions in the Naval General Staff is based upon interviews with Maeda, March 12, 1948; Ogawa, March 30, 1949; Tomioka, April 2, 1949; Mikawa, March 5, 1949; Oikawa, April 1, 1949.
18. Chigusa Diary, December 12 and 13; *Shinjuwan Sakusen Kaikoroku,* p. 122.
19. Ugaki Diary, December 12 and 16, 1941; interview with Yano, February 3, 1950; Lt. Col. Robert D. Heinl, Jr., USMC, *The Defense of Wake* (Washington, D.C., 1947).
20. 1st DD Division Diary, December 16, 1941.
21. Interviews with Suzuki, June 12, 1948; S. Yamamoto, March 23, 1950.
22. Statement by Z. Abe, October 19, 1950.
23. 1st DD Division Diary, December 17, 1941.
24. Watanabe Private Papers, December 18, 1941. Courtesy of Watanabe.
25. *Rising Sun in the Pacific,* pp. 253–54.
26. Chigusa and Fifth Carrier Division diaries, December 21, 1941.

27. *Rengo Kantai,* p. 46.
28. Ugaki Diary, December 23, 1941.
29. The account of the receptions aboard *Nagato* and *Akagi* is based upon interviews with Kusaka, Mikawa, Genda, Fuchida, Kuroshima, and Watanabe; Ugaki Diary, December 24, 1941.
30. The story of the imperial briefing is based upon numerous interviews with Fuchida, especially that of July 29, 1947, which was devoted almost entirely to that subject.
31. *Shinjuwan Sakusen No Shinso,* pp. 209–11; interviews with Kusaka, June 29, 1947, and Kuroshima, May 17, 1948.
32. January 1, 1942.

Chapter 69
"NOT ON THE ALERT"

1. Tacoma (Wash.) *News Tribune,* December 8, 1941.
2. Little Rock, December 8, 1941.
3. Alexandria (Va.) *Gazette,* December 8, 1941.
4. Both December 8, 1941.
5. December 8, 1941.
6. *The New York Times,* December 8, 1941.
7. Sioux City *Journal,* December 9, 1941.
8. See, for example, Tacoma *News Tribune,* December 8, 1941.
9. Both December 8, 1941.
10. December 8, 1941.
11. See, for example, Richmond *Times-Dispatch,* December 11, 1941; San Antonio *Express,* December 12, 1941.
12. Bangor (Me.) *Daily Commercial,* December 8, 1941.
13. See, for example, Bismarck *Tribune;* Boise *Capital News,* both December 9, 1941.
14. VADM. Frank E. Beatty, USN (Ret.), unpublished essay, "Secretary Knox and Pearl Harbor," 21953, (cited hereafter as "Knox and Pearl Harbor.") In the author's files. Courtesy of Dr. Harry E. Barnes. Beatty's article appeared in *National Review* (December 13, 1966) under the title "The Background of the Secret Report." This version differs in several respects from the manuscript in the author's possession. All quotations from Beatty's essay used in this study are from the unpublished manuscript.

15. Knox Papers, Box 1.
16. "Knox and Pearl Harbor"; interview with Martin, September 14, 1971.
17. "Knox and Pearl Harbor"; interview with Smith, November 28, 1962.
18. Interview with Col. William E. Donegan, April 15, 1972 (hereafter Donegan).
19. Fleming Questionnaire.
20. Letter, Safford to Harry E. Barnes, with attached message, OPNAV to CinCPAC, 091812 December 1941, Papers of Harry Elmer Barnes, University of Wyoming, Laramie, Wyo., Box 61 (cited hereafter as Barnes Papers).
21. Stimson Diary, December 14, 1941.
22. "Knox and Pearl Harbor."
23. *PHA,* Part 22, p. 94; Part 5, pp. 2338, 2340.
24. Ibid., Part 5, p. 2341.
25. Ibid., Part 22, pp. 376–77; Part 5, p. 2344.
26. See, for example, Robert A. Theobald, *The Final Secret of Pearl Harbor* (New York, 1954), pp. 108–09; George Morgenstern, *Pearl Harbor: The Story of the Secret War* (New York, 1947), pp. 271–72.
27. *PHA,* Part 6, pp. 2835–37.
28. Ibid., Part 7, p. 3360.
29. Ibid., Part 5, p. 2338.
30. Knox Papers, Box 1.
31. Roosevelt Papers, Map File, Box 36.
32. "Knox and Pearl Harbor."
33. *PHA,* Part 22, p. 95; Part 7, p. 3165.
34. "Knox and Pearl Harbor." The original Knox Report is in the Roosevelt Papers, PSF, Box 64. It is reproduced in *PHA,* Part 5, pp. 2338–45, and Part 24, pp. 1749–56.
35. Morgenthau Diaries, Book 473.
36. "Knox and Pearl Harbor."
37. St. Louis *Post-Dispatch,* December 15–16, 1941. Every American newspaper examined for this study gave much coverage to this story.
38. See, for example, Atlanta *Constitution,* Washington *Post,* both December 17, 1941.
39. See, for example, Chicago *Tribune,* December 17, 1941.
40. *PHA,* Part 3, p. 1530; Part 7, p. 3260.
41. Stimson Diary, December 15, 1941.
42. Ibid., December 17, 1941; *Nevada State Journal* (Reno), December 18, 1941.
43. *PHA,* Part 7, p. 3260.
44. Interviews with Gen. J. Lawton Collins,

Setpember 22, 1976 (hereafter Collins);
Fielder, March 29, 1972.

45. Interview with Donegan, April 15, 1972.

46. Fleming Tapes, March 7 and 31, 1972;
Fleming Questionnaire.

47. Interview with Fielder, March 29, 1972.

48. Interview with Donegan, April 15, 1972.

49. Interview with Draemel, January 17,
1963.

50. Interviews with Smith, December 9,
1962; Ramsey, December 6, 1962; DeLany, November 2, 1962.

51. *The Accused*, p. 138.

52. *PHA*, Part 17, p. 2733.

53. Interviews with Sampson, October 18,
1963; Johnson, July 25, 1963; Collins,
September 22, 1976, among others.

54. Interview with Layton, July 22, 1964.

55. Letter, Mrs. Earle to the author, October
16, 1964.

56. Honolulu *Star-Bulletin*, January 29, 1942.

57. Interview with Shoemaker, January 31,
1963.

Chapter 70
"DERELICTION OF DUTY"

1. Stimson Diary, December 15–16, 1941.

2. *Congressional Record*, Vol. 87, Part 9,
December 19, 1941, p. 9992.

3. *PHA*, Part 7, p. 3283; Stimson Diary,
December 17, 1941.

4. *PHA*, Part 7, p. 3300.

5. Letter, Safford to Hiles, February 1, 1962,
Hiles Papers, Box 9.

6. Interview between Adm. William H.
Standley and Harry E. Barnes, June 1,
1962. Courtesy of Dr. Barnes (cited hereafter as Standley-Barnes interview).

7. Letter, Kimmel to Barnes, July 12, 1962,
Barnes Papers, Box 61.

8. Letter, Stimson to Roosevelt, December
16, 1941, Roosevelt Papers, PSF, Box 85,
quoted in *PHA*, Part 7, p. 3260.

9. Standley-Barnes interview.

10. Letter, Kimmel to Barnes, July 12, 1962,
op. cit.

11. Letter, Stimson to Roosevelt, December
16, 1941, op. cit.

12. Stimson Diary, October 20, 1944; *PHA*,
Part 3, pp. 1438, 1204.

13. Interview with Kimmel, November 30,
1963.

14. Fleming Questionnaire.

15. A number of press comments about the
Roberts Commission are quoted in *PHA*,
Part 24, pp. 1289–1300.

16. Honolulu *Star-Bulletin*, December 17,
1941.

17. For further opinions on this subject see
PHA, Part 24, pp. 1297–99.

18. *PHA*, Part 7, pp. 3261–62. 3269–80, 3272;
Part 22, pp. 1–3.

19. Ibid., pp. 3278–80, 3262. Roberts did not
know the full story of Magic when he
testified before the congressional committee. Ibid., p. 3274.

20. Interview with Allen, July 17, 1962.

21. Letter, Lavender to Kimmel, July 4,
1944, papers of RADM. Husband E. Kimmel, University of Wyoming, Laramie,
Wyo., Box 4 (cited hereafter as Kimmel
Papers).

22. Letter, Safford to Hiles, February 1, 1962,
Hiles Papers, Box 9.

23. Fleming Tape, March 31, 1975; Fleming
Questionnaire.

24. Interview with Allen, July 17, 1962.

25. Letter, Bloch to Richardson, March 3,
1942, Bloch Papers, Box 3.

26. *PHA*, Part 7, p. 3155.

27. Ibid., p. 3009; Fleming Tape, March 31,
1975; Fleming Questionnaire.

28. Ibid., Part 22, pp. 32–33. Short's full
testimony before the Roberts Commission
appears in *PHA*, Part 22, pp. 31–106; Part
23, pp. 975–92.

29. Ibid., Part 23, p. 987.

30. Ibid., Part 22, pp. 70–72.

31. Ibid., Part 6, p. 2602.

32. Comments by Theobald, March 20, 1944,
to a questionnaire which Kimmel submitted to him, Kimmel Papers, Box 31 (cited
hereafter as Theobald comments).

33. Kimmel submitted a prepared statement
of seventeen typed pages. *PHA*, Part 23,
p. 894. His full testimony is covered in
PHA, Part 22, pp. 317–459; Part 23, pp.
893–901, 931–47, 1049–51. His revised
testimony appears in Part 23, pp. 1123–
1244.

34. *PHA*, Part 22, p. 390.

35. Ibid., pp. 373, 379, 418.

36. Ibid., pp. 416, 424.

37. Ibid., Part 23, p. 897; Part 6, p. 2816;
letter, Kimmel to Barnes, op. cit.

38. Ibid., Part 7, p. 3268; Part 23, p. 1121.

39. Ibid., Part 23, pp. 1075–1114, 1271–74; Part 7, pp. 3262–63; Stimson Diary, January 15, 1942.
40. *PHA*, Part 7, pp. 3265–66, 3282.
41. Ibid., Part 39, pp. 1–21.
42. Fleming Tapes, March 7 and 31, 1974.
43. *PHA*, Part 23, pp. 1247–48.
44. Washington *Post*, February 17, 1946.
45. See, for example, Cleveland *Plain Dealer*, San Antonio *Express*, January 26, 1942; *Daily Worker*, January 27, 1946.
46. "The Political Mill," Washington *Star*, January 27, 1942.
47. January 26, 1942.
48. Washington *Post*, January 25, 1942.
49. *Congressional Record*, Vol. 88, Part 1, January 27, 1942, pp. 735, 744.
50. Ibid., p. 744.
51. See, for example, *The New York Times*, Washington *Post*, Chicago *Tribune*, all January 26, 1942.
52. January 28, 1942.
53. See, for example, Tucson *Daily Citizen*, January 31, 1942; Louisville *Courier-Journal*, January 26, 1942.
54. Denver *Post*, January 25, 1942.
55. *Arizona Republic* (Phoenix), January 25, 1942.
56. Stimson Diary, January 25, 1942.
57. See, for example, Denver *Post*, Washington *Times-Herald*, January 26, 1942.
58. January 26, 1942.
59. See, for example, article by Percy L. Greaves, Jr., "The Pearl Harbor Investigations," which appears in *Perpetual War for Perpetual Peace*, pp. 407–81. Greaves's discussion of the Roberts Commission appears on pp. 413–19.

Chapter 71
"THE ASHES OF A BITTER PAST"

1. Interviews with Train, November 27, 1962; Kimmel, December 1, 1963.
2. Fleming Questionnaire; *PHA*, Part 19, p. 3795.
3. *PHA*, Part 19, p. 3797.
4. Ibid., pp. 3799, 3789.
5. Interview with Kimmel, November 29, 1963.
6. Tulsa *Daily Oklahoman*, January 25, 1942.
7. Interview with Fielder, March 29, 1972.

8. *PHA*, Part 7, pp. 3133–36, 3139.
9. Stimson Diary, January 26, 1942.
10. *PHA*, Part 7, p. 3139.
11. Kimmel Papers, Box 3.
12. *PHA*, Part 17, p. 2732.
13. Ibid., pp. 2727–28.
14. January 27, 1942.
15. January 28, 1942.
16. *PHA*, Part 17, p. 2728.
17. Ibid., Part 5, p. 2431.
18. Stimson Diary, January 28, 1942.
19. *The New York Times*, February 8, 1942.
20. Memorandum, Hornbeck to Welles, February 12, 1942, Papers of Stanley K. Hornbeck, Hoover Institution on War, Revolution and Peace, Stanford, Calif., 94305, Box 309 (cited hereafter as Hornbeck Papers).
21. *PHA*, Part 17, pp. 2730–31.
22. Interview with David W. Richmond, May 27, 1977 (hereafter Richmond).
23. *PHA*, Part 17, pp. 2729–30.
24. Interview with Kimmel, December 1, 1963.
25. Stimson Diary, February 25 and March 6, 1942.
26. *PHA*, Part 19, pp. 3800–01, 3805, 3814.
27. Stimson Diary, February 18, 20, and 25, 1942.
28. *PHA*, Part 19, pp. 3809–10.
29. Baltimore *Sun*, January 26, 1942.
30. Stimson Diary, February 26, 1942.
31. *The New York Times*, Los Angeles *Times*, March 1, 1942.
32. Tulsa *Daily Oklahoman*, March 1, 1942.
33. *PHA*, Part 17, p. 2728.
34. San Francisco *Examiner*, March 1, 1942; Evansville (Ind.) *Press*, December 7, 1966.
35. See, for example, Los Angeles *Times*, March 2, 1942.
36. March 2, 1942.
37. *The New York Times*, September 20, 1942.
38. *The Accused*, p. 150; *The New York Times*, July 15 and August 11, 1942.

Chapter 72
"SOMETHING OUGHT TO BE DONE"

1. *PHA*, Part 19, p. 3822; Washington *Post*, May 30, 1944.

2. Ibid., pp. 3818, 3825; Stimson Diary, September 11, 1943.

3. Papers of Fleet Adm. Ernest J. King, Operational Archives, U.S. Naval History Division, Washington, D.C., Box 4 (cited hereafter as King Naval Papers).

4. Stimson Diary, December 7, 1943.

5. Ibid., December 10, 1943.

6. Memorandum, January 24, 1944, Kimmel Papers, Box 33.

7. *PHA*, Part 19, p. 3858; *The New York Times*, February 26, 1944.

8. *PHA*, Part 26, p. 9.

9. Ibid., Part 10, pp. 4824–25, 4801.

10. *The New York Times*, April 29, 1944.

11. Washington *Post*, *The New York Times*, May 30, 1944.

12. Kimmel Papers, Box 4.

13. Washington *Post*, *The New York Times*, May 30, 1944.

14. *PHA*, Part 19, p. 3917.

15. *The New York Times*, May 28, 1945.

16. Kimmel Papers, Box 4.

17. *PHA*, Part 10, pp. 4801–02; Part 26, pp. 2–4.

18. *Congressional Record*, Vol. 104, Appendix, August 5, 1958, p. A6997.

19. Interview with Kimmel, December 1, 1963.

20. Papers of Adm. Harold R. Stark, Operational Archives, U.S. Naval History Division, Washington, D.C., Box 2 (cited hereafter as Stark Papers).

21. *PHA*, Part 19, p. 3931; Part 29, pp. 2239, 2248.

22. Letter, Hanify to Kimmel, February 2, 1967, Kimmel Papers, Box 14.

23. *Who's Who in America, 1944–1945* (Chicago, 1944), pp. 843, 1936, 717; interview with Mollison, April 13, 1961.

24. Forrest C. Pogue, *George C. Marshall: Ordeal and Hope 1939–1942* (New York, 1966), p. 429 (cited hereafter as *Ordeal and Hope*).

25. Interview between Henry C. Clausen and Harry E. Barnes, January 3, 1964, courtesy of Barnes (cited hereafter as Clausen-Barnes interview).

26. Interview with Clausen, November 16, 1976.

27. Kimmel Papers, Box 4.

28. Interviews with Richmond, May 27 and November 1, 1977; *PHA*, Part 10, p. 4818.

29. Official Navy biography, courtesy of Navy

Department; *Who's Who in America, 1944–1945*, p. 1532.

30. Interview with Richmond, May 27, 1977.

31. Official Navy biography; *Who's Who in America, 1944–1945*, p. 1112; *On the Treadmill*, p. 7.

32. Interview with Richmond, May 27, 1977.

33. Written comments of VADM. Charles Wellborn, Jr., to the author, August 10, 1977 (cited hereafter as Wellborn Comments).

34. Official Navy biography; *Who's Who in America, 1944–1945*, p. 44; "Washington Merry-Go-Round," Louisville *Courier-Journal*, March 2, 1942; Stimson Diary, December 27, 1942.

35. Wellborn Comments.

36. Record of interview between Murfin and Lavender which took place "in the latter part of July 1945." Kimmel wrote it up on July 27, 1945, on the basis of a conversation with Lavender in New York City on July 26, 1945. Kimmel Papers, Box 33 (cited hereafter as Murfin-Lavender interview).

37. *Admiral Kimmel's Story*, p. 131.

38. Interview with Kimmel, December 1, 1963.

39. *Admiral Kimmel's Story*, pp. 123–24.

Chapter 73
"FULL AND FAIR DISCLOSURE"

1. Interview with Richmond, November 1, 1977; *PHA*, Part 32, p. 16.

2. *PHA*, Part 32, p. 19.

3. Papers of Robert A. Taft, Library of Congress, Washington, D.C., Box 657 (cited hereafter as Taft Papers); letter, Kimmel to Rugg, June 7, 1944, Kimmel Papers, Box 4.

4. *PHA*, Part 32, p. 21.

5. Ibid., pp. 50–52.

6. Ibid., Part 33, p. 727.

7. Ibid., Part 32, p. 56.

8. Memorandum, December 8, 1944, of Kimmel's interview with King, December 7, 1944, Kimmel Papers, Box 33.

9. *PHA*, Part 32, p. 73.

10. Ibid., p. 103.

11. Ibid., p. 119.

12. Ibid., pp. 130–31.
13. Murfin-Lavender interview.
14. Interview with Richmond, November 1, 1977.
15. Wellborn Comments.
16. *PHA*, Part 32, p. 169.
17. Ibid., pp. 172–75.
18. Ibid., p. 222.
19. Ibid., p. 259.
20. Ibid., p. 267.
21. Ibid., p. 272.
22. *Congressional Record*, Vol. 90, Part 10, Appendix, pp. A3711–12.
23. Washington *Post*, August 10, 23, 24, 1944.
24. *PHA*, Part 33, p. 735; interview with Richmond, November 1, 1977.
25. *The Accused*, p. 157.
26. *PHA*, Part 33, pp. 771, 780–81.
27. Interview with Richmond, November 1, 1977.
28. *PHA*, Part 32, pp. 557, 554–55.
29. Ibid., Part 33, pp. 820–21, 826, 828–29.
30. *Congressional Record*, Vol. 90, Part 10, Appendix, p. A3870; Part 6, pp. 7573–7676.
31. Letter, Smith to Taft, September 11, 1944, Taft Papers, Box 657; Washington *Post*, September 10, 1944.
32. Taft Papers, Box 657.
33. Honolulu *Star-Bulletin*, September 6, 1944; San Francisco *Examiner*, September 7, 1944.
34. *PHA*, Part 32, p. 574.
35. Interview with Richmond, May 27, 1977.
36. *PHA*, Part 33, pp. 853–54, 866.
37. Ibid., p. 781.
38. Ibid., pp. 859–60.
39. San Francisco *Examiner*, September 17, 1944.
40. Honolulu *Star-Bulletin*, September 18, 1944.
41. *PHA*, Part 32, p. 627.
42. Ibid., p. 649.
43. *The New York Times*, September 24, 1944.
44. *PHA*, Part 32, pp. 653–60.
45. Ibid., Part 33, pp. 921–22; Part 32, p. 670.
46. Ibid., Part 32, p. 663.
47. Ibid., Part 33, pp. 687–90.
48. Ibid., pp. 696–97, 707, 710.
49. Ibid., pp. 712, 715, 719, 726.
50. Ibid., Part 32, p. 685.

Chapter 74
"WE HAVE A JOB TO DO"

1. *PHA*, Part 7, pp. 3149–50.
2. Minutes of meeting, July 20, 1944, Record Group 107, Materials Pertaining to Army Pearl Harbor Board, National Archives, Washington D.C., Box 8 (cited hereafter as Army PHB Materials).
3. *PHA*, Part 27, pp. 11–12.
4. Ibid., p. 13; Part 35, p. 104; Part 3, p. 1330; Part 29, pp. 2308–09; Part 9, p. 4427.
5. Ibid., Part 27, pp. 37–41, 51–53.
6. Ibid., pp. 92–95.
7. Ibid., pp. 125, 130.
8. Ibid., p. 139.
9. Ibid., pp. 157, 200, 205–06.
10. Ibid., p. 210.
11. Ibid., p. 227.
12. Ibid., pp. 243–44, 287.
13. Ibid., pp. 414–15.
14. Ibid., pp. 509–11.
15. Ibid., p. 551.
16. Ibid., pp. 570–72.
17. Ibid., pp. 576–78.
18. Ibid., pp. 583–84.
19. Ibid., pp. 587–88.
20. Ibid., p. 734.
21. Ibid., pp. 784, 788.
22. Ibid., Part 28, p. 829.
23. Ibid., pp. 910–11.
24. Ibid., pp. 946–47.
25. Ibid., Part 29, pp. 2330, 2279–85; Record Group 165, Army PHB Materials, Box 4.
26. *PHA*, Part 28, pp. 960–61.
27. Ibid., pp. 1014, 1017.
28. Ibid., pp. 1356–61.
29. Ibid., pp. 1454–57.
30. Ibid., Part 29, pp. 1668–70, 1672.
31. Stimson Diary, September 21, 1944.
32. *PHA*, Part 29, p. 2064.
33. Stimson Diary, September 26, 1944.
34. Memorandum for the President, September 22, 1945, Papers of Gen. of the Army George C. Marshall, George C. Marshall Research Foundation, Lexington, Va., Box 42 (cited hereafter as Marshall Papers).
35. *PHA*, Part 3, pp. 1125, 1132–33.
36. Philadelphia *Record*, September 22, 1945.
37. *PHA*, Part 29, pp. 2148, 2151–53.

38. Ibid., pp. 2151–53.
39. Ibid., p. 2434.
40. Ibid., pp. 2251, 2258–59.
41. Ibid., pp. 2269–70.
42. Ibid., p. 2313.
43. Ibid., pp. 2435–37.

Chapter 75
"ERRORS OF JUDGMENT"

1. *PHA*, Part 3, pp. 1331–32, 1345.
2. Ibid., Part 39, pp. 25–27.
3. Ibid., p. 28.
4. Ibid., p. 137.
5. Ibid., p. 38.
6. Ibid., p. 100.
7. Ibid., p. 102.
8. Ibid., pp. 43–44.
9. Ibid., pp. 175–76.
10. Ibid., pp. 144–45.
11. Ibid., Part 29, pp. 2155–2214.
12. Ibid., Part 39, p. 143.
13. Ibid., pp. 221–22.
14. Ibid., pp. 228–29.
15. Ibid., p. 225.
16. Stimson Diary, October 21–22, 1944, a double entry for Saturday and Sunday.
17. *PHA*, Part 39, pp. 299, 301.
18. Ibid., p. 303.
19. Ibid., p. 304.
20. Ibid., pp. 306, 308.
21. Ibid., p. 317.
22. Ibid., p. 318.
23. Ibid., p. 330.
24. Ibid., pp. 321, 308.
25. *The New York Times*, October 22, 1944.
26. *PHA*, Part 39, pp. 331–32.
27. Ibid., pp. 332–34.
28. Ibid., pp. 343–45.
29. Stimson Diary, November 11, 14, 1944.
30. Ibid., November 20, 1944; May 25, 1943.
31. Ibid., November 21, 1944.
32. Ibid., November 24, 1944.
33. *PHA*, Part 39, p. 241.
34. Ibid., p. 244.
35. Ibid., pp. 253–54.
36. Ibid., pp. 264, 267.
37. Ibid., pp. 267–69.
38. Stimson Diary, November 30, 1944.
39. *PHA*, Part 39, p. 354.
40. New York *Herald Tribune*, December 2, 1944.

41. *PHA*, Part 35, p. 4.
42. Chicago *Tribune*, December 2, 1944.
43. Cleveland *Plain Dealer*, Dallas *Morning News*, December 2, 1944.
44. *The New York Times*, Dallas *Morning News*, December 2, 1944.
45. Memorandum, December 8, 1944, of Kimmel's interviews with Andrews and Kalbfus, December 6, 1944, Kimmel Papers, Box 33.
46. Gatch-Kimmel interview.
47. *PHA*, Part 39, pp. 385–96.
48. Memorandum, December 8, 1944, of Kimmel's interview with King, December 7, 1944, Kimmel Papers, Box 33.
49. December 3, 1944.

Chapter 76
"WE WANT THE TRUTH"

1. Letter, Kimmel to Rugg, March 14, 1945, Kimmel Papers, Box 5.
2. Official Navy biography, courtesy of Navy Department; *Who's Who in America, 1944–1945*, p. 950; *The New York Times*, May 9, 1945.
3. Reminiscences of Adm. H. Kent Hewitt, Oral History Research Office, Columbia University, New York, pp. 24–53, 24–33, 13–6, 13–7 of transcript in Operational Archives, U.S. Naval History Division, Washington, D.C. (cited hereafter as Hewitt Reminiscences).
4. Kimmel Papers, Box 5.
5. Memorandum, May 22, 1945, of Kimmel's interview with King, May 18, 1945, Kimmel Papers, Box 33.
6. Hewitt Reminiscences, pp. 24–57, 24–53, 24–55, 24–56.
7. Letter, Forrestal to Truman, September 26, 1944, Papers of James V. Forrestal, Princeton University Library, Princeton, N.J., Box 57 (cited hereafter as Forrestal Papers).
8. *PHA*, Part 36, p. 13.
9. Ibid., pp. 16–17.
10. Ibid., p. 24.
11. Ibid., Part 18, pp. 3345, 3349; Part 10, p. 5011.
12. Ibid., Part 36, pp. 71–74.
13. Ibid., p. 81.

14. Ibid., p. 128.
15. Ibid., pp. 230–31.
16. Ibid., p. 235.
17. Ibid., pp. 312–18.
18. Ibid., pp. 339–40.
19. Ibid., pp. 355–57.
20. Washington *Post,* February 3, 1946.
21. Hewitt Reminiscences, p. 24–5.
22. *PHA,* Part 39, pp. 355–83.
23. Ibid., p. 526.
24. Ibid., p. 524.
25. Ibid., p. 526.
26. Ibid., p. 523.
27. Ibid., p. 388.
28. Ibid., pp. 388–89.
29. Ibid., pp. 387–88.
30. Exchange of letters between Kimmel and Hewitt, March 12 and 17, 1967, Kimmel Papers, Box 15.
31. *PHA,* Part 39, pp. 382–83.
32. Ibid., Part 35, p. 5; Part 9, p. 4304.
33. Ibid., Part 9, p. 4421.
34. Biographical sketch contained in Clausen's book, *Clausen's Commentaries on Morals and Dogma* (Washington, D.C., 1974), pp. 213–16; interview with Clausen, November 16, 1976.
35. *PHA,* Part 9, pp. 4312–13.
36. Ibid., Part 35, p. 5; interview with Clausen, November 16, 1976.
37. *PHA,* Part 9, pp. 4307–08.
38. Ibid., Part 35, pp. 1–2; Part 9, p. 4309.
39. Ibid., Part 9, pp. 4425–26; interview with Clausen, November 16, 1976.
40. PHA, Part 34, pp. 1–2, 8.
41. Ibid., Part 3, pp. 1332–36.
42. Ibid., Part 34, pp. 3, 76.
43. Ibid., Part 19, p. 3815; Part 7, p. 3142; interview with Smith, November 29, 1962.
44. Letter, Kimmel to Barnes, September 2, 1963, Barnes Papers, Box 66. See also *Admiral Kimmel's Story,* pp. 127–28.
45. *PHA,* Part 8, pp. 3858–59; Mr. X Notes. Mr. X tells us that to protect Safford, Kimmel made no mention of him in his account of this incident.
46. Letter, Kimmel to Barnes, op. cit.
47. Letter, Kimmel to Rugg, April 12, 1945, Kimmel Papers, Box 5; *Admiral Kimmel's Story,* p. 127. Kimmel also discussed the SB-805 incident in an interview with the author, December 1, 1963.
48. Letter, Green to Short, April 12, 1945, Papers of Maj. Gen. Walter C. Short, Hoover Institution on War, Revolution and Peace, Stanford, Calif., 94305 (cited hereafter as Short Papers).
49. Undated memorandum, "STATEMENT REFERENCE SECRET DOCUMENTS PERTAINING TO PEARL HARBOR AND NOT KNOWN TO ME UNTIL THE SUMMER OF 1944," Short Papers.
50. Stimson Diary, April 12, 1945.
51. Forrestal Diaries, August 17, 18, 29, 1945.
52. *The New York Times,* August 30, 1945.
53. See, for example, *The New York Times;* Washington *Evening Star,* August 30, 1945.
54. September 1, 1945.
55. August 31, 1945.
56. Interview with Kimmel, November 30, 1963; *PHA,* Part 19, pp. 2943–44.

Chapter 77
"A PARTISAN MATTER"

1. Taft Papers, Box 657.
2. *Congressional Record,* Vol. 91, Part 6, pp. 8338–44.
3. September 7, 1945.
4. *Congressional Record,* Vol. 91, Part 7, pp. 8499–8507.
5. Washington *Post, The New York Times,* September 15, 1945.
6. *Who's Who in America, 1944–1945,* p. 103; *Congressional Directory, 79th Congress, First Session, August 1945* (Washington, 1945), p. 3 (cited hereafter as *Congressional Directory*); *Congressional Record,* Vol. 91, Part 7, September 27, 1945, p. 9069.
7. *Who's Who in America, 1944–1945,* p. 765; *Congressional Directory,* pp. 20, 162; *Current Biography,* June 1955, pp. 29–31.
8. *Who's Who in America, 1944–1945,* p. 1298; *Congressional Directory,* p. 24.
9. *Who's Who in America, 1944–1945,* p. 233; *Congressional Directory,* p. 43; *Current Biography,* May 1947, pp. 4–6.
10. *Who's Who in America, 1944–1945,* p. 644; *Congressional Directory,* p. 50.
11. *Congressional Record,* Vol. 91, Part 8, November 9, 1945, p. 10589.

12. September 15, 1945.
13. *Who's Who in America, 1944–1945*, p. 430; *Congressional Directory*, p. 116; *Current Biography*, March 1955, pp. 11, 14.
14. *Who's Who in America, 1944–1945*; pp. 378, 1535; *Congressional Directory*, pp. 89, 103; *The New York Times*, September 15, 1945.
15. *Who's Who in America, 1944–1945*, p. 760; *Congressional Directory*, pp. 10–11; Washington *Post*, October 13, 1955.
16. *Who's Who in America, 1944–1945*, p. 1121; *Congressional Directory*, p. 131; *The New York Times*, September 15, 1945.
17. *The New York Times*, Washington *Post*, September 15, 1945.
18. *The New York Times*, September 27, 1945; *PHA*, Part 4, p. 1587; *Congressional Record*, Vol. 91, Part 8, November 2, 1945, pp. 10355, 10347.
19. Interview with Judge Gerhard A. Gesell, October 1, 1976 (hereafter Gesell).
20. *Congressional Record*, Vol. 91, Part 8, November 2, 1945, pp. 10341–43.
21. Ibid., 10341–42; Washington *Post*, November 3, 1945.
22. *Congressional Record*, Vol. 91, Part 8, November 2, 1945, pp. 10343, 10346, 10348, 10355.
23. Ibid., pp. 10444–48.
24. Ibid., November 14, 1945, p. 10684.
25. November 9, 1945.
26. *Congressional Record*, Vol. 91, Part 8, November 14, 1945, p. 10684; New York *Daily News*, November 10, 1945; Milwaukee *Sentinel*, November 10 and 13, 1945.
27. Interview with Richmond, May 27, 1977.
28. *PHA*, Part 1, p. 1.
29. Milwaukee *Journal*, November 15, 1945; Lansing *State Journal*, November 16, 1945; *Time* (November 26, 1945), p. 23.
30. *PHA*, Part 1, p. 23; Topeka *Capital*, November 23, 1945; interview with Gesell, October 1, 1976.
31. *PHA*, Part 1, pp. 26–231.
32. Ibid., pp. 253–341; Philadelphia *Record*, November 21, 1945.
33. Milwaukee *Journal*, November 24, 1945; San Francisco *Chronicle*, December 2, 1945.
34. *PHA*, Part 2, pp. 452, 455.
35. *The New York Times*, Washington *Post*,

November 24, 1945.
36. *PHA*, Part 2, pp. 541 ff.
37. Ibid., pp. 614–15; Washington *Post*, Mobile *Register*, November 28, 1945; Washington *Star*, November 27, 1945.
38. *PHA*, p. 591.
39. Honolulu *Advertiser*, December 1, 1945.
40. *PHA*, Part 1, p. 300.
41. December 7, 1945.
42. *The New York Times*, December 1, 1945.
43. December 3, 1945.

Chapter 78
"THE EVIDENCE PILES UP"

1. *PHA*, Part 2, p. 819; Honolulu *Advertiser*, December 2, 1945.
2. *PHA*, pp. 879, 901; *The New York Times*, New York *Daily News*, New York *Herald Tribune*, December 4, 1945.
3. *PHA*, Part 3, pp. 1019, 1031, 1033, 1036.
4. December 7, 1945.
5. December 6, 1945.
6. December 7, 1945.
7. Washington *Post*, December 7, 1945.
8. Honolulu *Advertiser*, December 8, 1945; Des Moines *Register*, December 7, 1945.
9. *PHA*, Part 3, pp. 1052 ff.
10. Ibid., pp. 1124–25; Mobile *Register*, December 10, 1945.
11. *PHA*, p. 1141.
12. December 14, 1945.
13. *PHA*, Part 3, pp. 1183–1347.
14. Ibid., pp. 1347–49.
15. Ibid., pp. 1347 ff.
16. Milwaukee *Journal*, December 12, 1945.
17. *PHA*, Part 3, p. 1539; Des Moines *Register*, December 14, 1945.
18. Memorandum of Conference in the Office of the Secretary of War, 9:15 A.M., July 21, 1941, Marshall Papers, Box 29.
19. Marshall Papers, Box 51.
20. Interview with Gesell, October 1, 1976; *PHA*, Part 4, pp. 1585–87.
21. *PHA*, Part 4, pp. 1587–91; *The New York Times*, Washington *Post*, December 15, 1945.
22. *PHA*, pp. 1728–35, 1741–47; New York *Herald Tribune*, December 18, 1945.
23. Ibid., pp. 1756–57.
24. Ibid., pp. 1884–89, 1911.

25. February 22, 1946.
26. Albany (N.Y.) *Knickerbocker News*, December 17, 1945.
27. Interview with Gesell, October 1, 1976.
28. *PHA*, Part 4, pp. 1911–18, 1959–60, 1963.
29. Dallas *Morning News*, December 22, 1945.
30. *PHA*, Part 4, pp. 1991–2001.
31. Ibid., pp. 1962–63, 2006–09, 2016–32.
32. Ibid., pp. 2037–40.
33. Honolulu *Advertiser*, Washington *Post*, December 25, 1945; Washington *Star*, December 24 and 26, 1945.
34. Interviews with Richmond, May 27 and November 1, 1977; James E. Webb, June 27, 1977 (hereafter Webb); letter, Webb to the author, June 24, 1977.
35. *PHA*, Part 5, pp. 2097–2101.
36. Ibid., pp. 2101–05.
37. Ibid., pp. 2105–08.
38. Ibid., pp. 2134, 2097.
39. Ibid., p. 2133.
40. January 1, 1946.
41. Honolulu *Advertiser*, San Francisco *Chronicle*, January 2, 1946; "The News of the World in Review," *The New York Times*, January 6, 1946.
42. *PHA*, Part 5, pp. 2175–77.
43. Ibid., pp. 2203, 2222.
44. Ibid., pp. 2278–92.
45. San Francisco *Chronicle*, *The New York Times*, Milwaukee *Sentinel*, January 3, 1946.
46. Interview with Edward P. Morgan, October 26, 1976 (hereafter Morgan); *Congressional Record*, Vol. 98, Part 8, January 15, 1952, p. A140.
47. *PHA*, Part 5, pp. 2332–34, corrected by Part 6, p. 2673.
48. Ibid., pp. 2441–45, 2450, 2451.
49. Ibid., pp. 2460–61.
50. Ibid., pp. 2475–77.

Chapter 79
"A FIGHTING CHANCE"

1. Louisville *Courier-Journal*, January 16, 1946; Baltimore *Evening Sun*, January 15, 1946.
2. *PHA*, Part 6, pp. 2498, 2518.
3. Ibid., pp. 2541–43.
4. Ibid., pp. 2551–52.
5. Ibid., p. 2554; Washington *Post*, January 16, 1946.
6. *Christian Science Monitor*, January 16, 1946.
7. January 16, 1946.
8. *PHA*, Part 6, p. 2572.
9. Ibid., pp. 2579–80, 2583, 2587.
10. Ibid., pp. 2582, 2590–92, 2630.
11. Ibid., pp. 2634–40, 2647–49; Honolulu *Advertiser*, January 18, 1946.
12. *PHA*, pp. 2707, 2711–24.
13. Ibid., pp. 2729–30.
14. Ibid., p. 2729.
15. Ibid., Part 21, Exhibit 16 following p. 4780; interview with Morgan, October 26, 1976.
16. *PHA*, Part 6, pp. 2720, 2723.
17. Ibid., p. 2752.
18. Ibid., pp. 2752–56, 2802.
19. Ibid., p. 2834.
20. San Francisco *Examiner*, January 20, 1946.
21. *PHA*, Part 6, pp. 2844, 2906.
22. Ibid., p. 2876.
23. Ibid., p. 2893; Part 7, p. 2947; Dallas *Morning News*, San Francisco *Chronicle*, January 22, 1946; Kimmel Papers, Box 6. This letter also appeared in the Chicago *Tribune*, July 21, 1946.
24. *PHA*, Part 6, p. 2659.
25. Honolulu *Star-Bulletin*, January 15, 1946; *Newsweek* (February 4, 1946), p. 29; Washington *Star*, January 22, 1946; Louisville *Courier-Journal*, *Christian Science Monitor*, Washington *Post*, January 23, 1946; San Francisco *Chronicle*, January 23 and 27, 1946; *PHA*, Part 7, pp. 2921–22.
26. *PHA*, Part 7, p. 2922.
27. Ibid., pp. 2954–57.
28. Ibid., pp. 2951, 2959.
29. Ibid., p. 2964.
30. Washington *Post*, *The New York Times*, San Francisco *Chronicle*, January 23, 1946.
31. Des Moines *Register*, Miami *Herald*, January 24, 1946.
32. *PHA*, Part 7, p. 2978.
33. Ibid., p. 2972.
34. Ibid., p. 2984.
35. Ibid., p. 3012.
36. Ibid., pp. 3010–11.
37. Ibid., pp. 3026–29.
38. Ibid., p. 3049.

39. Ibid., p. 3053.
40. Ibid., p. 3070.
41. Ibid., pp. 3098–3105; Honolulu *Star-Bulletin,* January 25, 1946.
42. *PHA,* pp. 3168–69.
43. Ibid., p. 3173.
44. Ibid., pp. 3222–24.
45. Ibid., p. 3231; Dallas *Morning News,* Houston *Post,* January 27, 1946.

Chapter 80
"FIXING THE BLAME"

1. Dallas *Morning News,* January 29, 1946; *PHA,* Part 7, pp. 3278, 3261–63.
2. *PHA,* Part 7, p. 3317.
3. Ibid., pp. 3235, 3237–40, 3329.
4. Ibid., Part 6, pp. 2604, 2639, 2642; Part 7, p. 3356.
5. Ibid., Part 8, pp. 3380–81, 3416–42.
6. Ibid., p. 3488, 3504.
7. Ibid., pp. 3525–26.
8. Washington *Post,* February 2, 1946; San Francisco *Chronicle,* February 10, 1946; *PHA,* Part 8, p. 3579.
9. San Francisco *Chronicle,* February 10, 1946.
10. *PHA,* Part 8, pp. 3632–33, 3666, 3635, 3638, 3640.
11. Mr. X Notes.
12. *PHA,* Part 8, pp. 3814–38.
13. Mr. X Notes.
14. *PHA,* Part 9, p. 3965.
15. Ibid., pp. 3932–33, 3942.
16. Ibid., p. 3947.
17. Honolulu *Advertiser,* February 14, 1946.
18. *PHA,* Part 9, p. 4053.
19. Ibid., p.4148.
20. Ibid., pp. 4231, 4247, 4249, 4257, 4268.
21. Ibid., p. 4302.
22. Ibid., pp. 4517–20.
23. Ibid., pp. 4522, 4528, 4534, 4563.
24. Ibid., pp. 4464–65; Washington *Post,* February 15 and 16, 1946; *The New York Times,* February 16, 1946.
25. Honolulu *Advertiser,* February 14, 1946.
26. "Washington Merry-Go-Round." Dallas *Morning News,* February 15, 1946.
27. *PHA,* Part 10, pp. 4628–59.
28. Ibid., pp. 4659–72.
29. Ibid., pp. 4672–4710.

30. Ibid., pp. 4729, 4731–32. 4740–43.
31. Ibid., pp. 4793–4829.
32. Ibid., p. 4855.
33. Ibid., p. 4909.
34. Ibid., pp. 4916–20.
35. Ibid., pp. 4936–37.
36. Ibid., p. 4938.
37. Ibid., pp. 5009–27.
38. Ibid., pp. 5027–75.
39. Ibid., pp. 5080–89.
40. Ibid., pp. 5100–01, 5103.
41. Ibid., pp. 5150–51.
42. Ibid., Part 11, pp. 5175–5200.
43. Ibid., Part 10, p. 4664.
44. Ibid., p. 5154.
45. Ibid., Part 9, p. 4471.
46. Ibid., Part 11, p. 5238.
47. Ibid., pp. 5269–91.
48. Ibid., pp. 5365, 5535, 5541–42.
49. Ibid., pp. 5543–45, 5556, 5548, 5550.
50. Ibid., pp. 5552, 5560.
51. Ibid., p. 5555.
52. Interview with Morgan, October 26, 1976.
53. Letter, Morgan to the author, November 4, 1976.
54. *The New York Times,* July 7 and 16, 1946; Washington *Post,* Milwaukee Journal, July 21, 1946.
55. *PHA,* Part 6, pp. 2581–82.
56. Ibid., Report, pp. 251–52.
57. Ibid., pp. 266–66A, 266E–66F, 266H–66I, 266S–66T.
58. Letter, Greaves to Hiles, June 15, 1962, Hiles Papers, Box 9.
59. *PHA,* Report, pp. 497–502, 504–06, 573.

Chapter 81
"THE VERDICT OF HISTORY"

1. All newspapers reviewed for this study covered the congressional report. For representative sampling, see Washington *Evening Star,* New York *Herald Tribune,* Nashville *Tennesseean,* Chicago *Tribune,* July 21, 1946; Chicago *Times, Christian Science Monitor,* Milwaukee *Journal,* July 22, 1946.
2. Evidence that these individuals assisted in preparing the minority report is contained in letters, Flynn to Barnes, February 26,

1946, Greaves to Barnes, July 2, 1946, Barnes Papers, Box 32; and Greaves to Hiles, June 15, 1962, Hiles Papers, Box 9.

3. Milwaukee *Sentinel*, July 21, 1946.
4. July 21, 1946.
5. Interview with Morgan, October 26, 1976.
6. San Francisco *Chronicle*, July 21, 1946.
7. Kimmel Papers, Box 6.
8. Washington *Star*, Washington *Post*, San Francisco *Chronicle*, July 21, 1946.
9. Washington *Post*, September 4, 1949; Dallas *Morning News*, December 2, 1944; Honolulu *Advertiser*, September 5, 1949.
10. Interviews with Wilson, January 22, 1963; Mollison, November 8, 1963.
11. Honolulu *Advertiser*, September 4 and 5, 1949; Houston *Post*, Dallas *Morning News*, *The New York Times*, September 4, 1949; San Antonio *Express*, September 5, 1949; Dallas *Morning News*, September 8, 1949.
12. Honolulu *Star-Bulletin*, May 15, 1968 and December 6, 1966.
13. For other representative accounts, see Louisville *Courier-Journal*, Hartford *Times*, Washington *Post*, Washington *Evening Star*, May 15, 1968.
14. Fleming tape, March 31, 1975.
15. Interview with Bicknell, September 7, 1967.
16. *Congressional Record*, Vol. 87, Part 9, December 19, 1941, p. 10051.
17. *PHA*, Report, p. 126.
18. Ibid., Part 28, pp. 1359–60.
19. Ibid., Part 22, p. 168.
20. Ibid., p. 103.
21. Ibid., p. 474.
22. Ibid., Part 7, p. 3032.

23. Ibid., Part 11, p. 5425; Part 7, p. 3039.
24. Ibid., Part 26, pp. 375–82.
25. Ibid., Part 22, p. 35.
26. Fleming tape, March 31, 1975.
27. *PHA*, Part 6, pp. 2894–95; Part 22, pp. 461–62.
28. Ibid., Part 22, p. 468; Part 26, pp. 28, 20–21.
29. Ibid., Part 22, pp. 490–91.
30. Ibid., p. 473; Part 26, p. 19.
31. Ibid., Part 27, pp. 769–70, 793.
32. Ibid., Part 32, p. 307; Part 15, p. 1432.
33. Ibid., Part 27, pp. 774–76.
34. Ibid., Part 33, p. 715; Report, pp. 86–87.
35. Ibid., Part 32, p. 504.
36. Ibid., Part 26, pp. 18, 23; Part 22, p. 464.
37. Ibid., Part 18, p. 3296.
38. Ibid., Part 5, p. 2350; Part 23, p. 1092.
39. Ibid., Part 39, p. 368.
40. Ibid., Part 22, p. 487.
41. Ibid., Part 12, p. 323; Part 3, p. 1085; Part 27, p. 423.
42. Ibid., Part 8, pp. 3455, 3525–26, 3504.
43. Ibid., Part 9, p. 4241.
44. Ibid., Part 28, p. 919.
45. Ibid., Part 29, p. 2312.
46. Ibid., Part 4, p. 1962.
47. Ibid., Part 39, pp. 144–45.
48. Ibid., Part 32, p. 99.
49. Ibid., Part 39, p. 365.
50. Capt. Gilvin M. Slonim, USN, "Have We Learned the Lesson of Pearl Harbor?" *Navy* (December 1966), p. 15.
51. Interview with Bloch, November 28, 1962.
52. For an interesting account of the salvage and reclamation of the ships, see VADM. Homer N. Wallin, USN (ret.), *Pearl Harbor: Why, How, Fleet Salvage and Final Appraisal* (Washington, D.C., 1969).

SOURCE MATERIAL

Professor Gordon Prange died in May 1980. Only a few months earlier he wrote a long letter to McGraw-Hill that detailed the depth of his historical research, the significance of the interviews, and the newness of the material he had uncovered during his thirty-seven years of working on *At Dawn We Slept*.

McGraw-Hill believes Dr. Prange's letter to be so important that his comments are produced herewith:

Ask anyone who was alive and of the age of reason on December 7, 1941, where he was and what he was doing when he heard the news. I have never yet met anyone who could not do so, for the attack branded itself into the individual, national—yes, even world—consciousness. So I have not devoted more than thirty years of my life to something of limited appeal.

Here for the first time this endlessly fascinating subject is covered from beginning to end from both the U.S. and Japanese points of view. I do not think anyone can read my manuscript without agreeing that my scholarship and credibility are unimpeachable. I say this without apology and with no sense of false modesty. After all, if I do not believe in my own worth and honor as a writer and a scholar, why should a publisher?

Circumstances granted me a once-in-a-lifetime opportunity to gather material directly from the source. As you know, I spent about a year in Japan as a Navy officer in 1945–46. Then I returned to Tokyo for five years to work with General Willoughby in the G-2 Historical Section. My last two years (1949–51) in Japan I served as chief of the entire section. During this period I had the closest association with Japanese ex-Navy and Army officers who were connected with not only the Pearl Harbor story but Midway and other campaigns in the Pacific. I had learned about Pearl Harbor at the feet of those who planned and executed Operation Hawaii. I went back to Japan for most of the summer of 1955 and returned for six months in 1964–65 under the auspices of the *Reader's Digest* for more research and interviews. So I saw the Pearl Harbor problem

796

over a long period. This gave me a broad perspective and time to reflect carefully upon the many facets of this most complicated subject.

When I came to research the American side of Pearl Harbor, I found that once again my experience in the Navy and the occupation gave me a special advantage. The many U.S. ex-officers whom I interviewed could regard me as, if not a resident in, at least a knowledgeable and sympathetic visitor to their own world. So they talked with me freely about their experiences and shared their thoughts candidly. I made several trips over the years to Hawaii, talked at length with eyewitnesses there, and examined the scenes of the action.

Thanks to these unusual experiences, *I am the only individual who has come to grips with the entire Pearl Harbor problem and conducted extensive research and interviews on both sides of the Pacific.* Moreover, I know both the academic world and the armed forces from the inside. Those writing upon this subject with a knowledge of the military viewpoint, such as Kimmel and Theobald, were pleading a special case and had no idea whatsoever of scholarly research and presentation. By the same token those others dealing with Pearl Harbor, such as Harry Elmer Barnes, whether serious historians or popularizers, had no direct experience of the contemporary military picture, hence made many assumptions which do not hold water. Having served as both a professional historian and a U.S. naval officer, I can see both sides and present them from personal experience.

A number of subjects in my book break fresh ground. Most of the material concerning the Japanese military side of this volume has *never* been published in English.

Take, for instance, the story of the early planning for Pearl Harbor. I explode the idea that the Japanese had planned the attack for years. I can pinpoint virtually the exact day in the spring of 1940 when Yamamoto first mentioned the subject to his chief of staff, Fukudome. I can prove that Navy Minister Oikawa, contrary to his sworn testimony to the International Military Tribunal of the Far East, knew about Yamamoto's plan in early January 1941. I explain the important role played by Onishi as the catalyst between Yamamoto and Genda. While it is generally known that Genda was the tactical planner, this work gives a true picture of the man, gets behind his thinking, reveals exactly what his first plan consisted of and how the contributions of others gradually fell by the wayside until the plan actually adopted could be called with truth Genda's plan.

I follow Yoshikawa and others in the Japanese consulate. Although some of Yoshikawa's activities as Japan's "master spy" on Oahu have come to light, the real story of the Japanese consulate in Honolulu in Japan's scheme of espionage on Oahu has not. And here I score a bull's-eye with excellent material from my friend Otojiro Okuda, vice-consul in 1940–41; Richard Kotoshirodo, an employee in the consulate who often accompanied Yoshikawa on his espionage missions and went on some on his own hook; and, last but far from least, Yoshikawa himself, the rights to whose story I purchased and whom I interviewed in depth in Japan in 1950 and again in the summer of 1955.

I have explained the "bomb plot" message of September 24, 1941, from Tokyo to the consulate. This has been discussed many times, but never in such depth and with such authority. I reveal for the first time that this actually was a definite request for information about ship docking directly related to the Pearl Harbor attack. As late as the congressional investigation of 1945–46, considerable doubt existed on this point, many insisting that this message and later ones of the series indicated nothing more than

Japan's "nicety" of intelligence. Actually it was, in Kimmel's words, "a significant and ominous change" in the nature of the intelligence being gleaned on Oahu.

Then, too, the story of U.S. war games on Oahu in January 1932—a simulated attack against Pearl Harbor—is almost all new. So in my material on the formation, composition, and personnel of the First Air Fleet, which became a reality on April 10, 1941. Much of what I have to say about Kimmel and his staff breaks new ground. As you know, I spent four days interviewing Kimmel at his home; thus I have been able to include much material not available in the documentation. These interviews also gave me the opportunity to arrive at a firsthand assessment of the admiral's character and personality. My analysis of General Short, too—about whom almost nothing has been written—and the members of his staff represents a major contribution. So does my treatment of his war games of May 12, 1941.

The whole account of Japanese planning and training—air and submarine—adds a new dimension. Likewise, the material on the Japanese war games of September in the Naval Staff College and those aboard *Nagato* in October. So does the story of the resistance to Yamamoto's plan in his own First Air Fleet and the Naval General Staff and how Yamamoto finally beat down all opposition.

Another original feature is my weaving together of the Japanese and American sides of the story into a cohesive and intriguing whole. Just a few examples:

- Yamamoto's and Onishi's discussion about Pearl Harbor aboard *Nagato* at the end of January 1941 corresponded almost to the day with Grew's report to the State Department concerning a potential Japanese attack against Pearl Harbor.
- The Martin-Bellinger Report of March 31, 1941, coincided with the time when Yamamoto and his Combined Fleet staff began to work in earnest on the Pearl Harbor concept.
- "Plan for the Employment of Bombardment Aviation in the Defense of Oahu" went to Washington from Hawaii on August 20, 1941, at the time when the First Air Fleet was intensifying its training in Kyushu.

These are but three examples of many such instances, so many that one comes to have a sense of the eerie. It almost appears that a telepathic contact existed between the Japanese planners and their American counterparts. This in itself provides a special element of reader interest.

Another special feature is the story of who knew about Pearl Harbor, when, why, and under what circumstances. I was able to achieve this only by intensive interrogations. This had enabled me to give a new twist to the story and to refute the myth that Pearl Harbor was a supersecret in the Japanese Navy with only a few key people privy to the plot. In fact, as I show, about 100 Navy and Army officers, plus a few key civilians and, most important, Emperor Hirohito, knew about Operation Hawaii.

As the book moved to the actual attack, we have more of the same. Again, just a few examples:

- The sections dealing with the rendezvous at Hitokappu Bay contain absolutely new material. No other work on Pearl Harbor does more than mention that this was the gathering point for the ships before departing for Pearl Harbor. Actually, the Japanese did far more there—they reviewed the entire plan, conducted numerous important briefings, made some crucial decisions, and considered a number of alternate tactical plans. Knowledge of these events is essential to understanding just how thoroughly and efficiently the Japanese planned this attack.

- Another highlight relates to the period after the task force left Hitokappu Bay before it reached launch point on the morning of December 7. This portion of the story represents a painstaking and dramatic dovetailing of all the significant political, diplomatic, and military events taking place during that eleven-day period in Japan, on Oahu, and in Washington. On the basis of excellent source material I have been able to follow the task force's cruise day by day. No one has ever attempted this. I am especially indebted to Genda, Fuchida, Kusaka, and Commander Yokoto, skipper of the submarine, *1-26*, and to Rear Admiral Chigusa, whose diary I have exploited. I cited the invaluable diary of Rear Admiral Matome Ugaki. The entries pertaining to the period immediately before Pearl Harbor have *never* been published in any language.

- I also place much emphasis upon the intelligence picture. I continue to follow the activities in the consulate, especially in relation to the continuing flow of information to and from Tokyo as part of the significant "bomb plot" series. I have much new material concerning the special intelligence mission of Commander Suzuki and his colleagues to Hawaii to secure last-minute information. I also deal with the messages from Tokyo to the task force which the United States could not translate because it had not yet broken the naval codes involved. I have taken great pains to explode the myth that the message of December 3, 1941, sent by the German Otto Kuehn (in the pay of Japan) was a tip-off of Japan's intention to attack Pearl Harbor on December 7.

  December 6 was a crucial day. Thanks to the valuable new material, I am fairly well satisfied that no one has previously given a more valid account of the events of December 6. I am particularly indebted to a most interesting letter from Mrs. Alwin Kramer, wife of Commander Kramer of Naval Intelligence, and to Captain Safford of Naval Communications. His personal recollections helped straighten out some erroneous conclusions which Farago reached in his book *The Broken Seal*. I am much indebted to Safford, who was one of the most gifted cryptanalysts in the history of cryptography. He had something of a guilt complex about Kimmel and as a result became a rabid revisionist, so I had to be cautious in evaluating his material. But where he spoke from experience, he was superb. I wish I could credit him in my acknowledgments, but he insisted upon anonymity.

- Of course, the climax is the attack itself. These chapters contain much of human interest. Besides analyzing the air strike militarily, I let the reader see it through the eyes of more than twenty Japanese airmen and numerous U.S. personnel whom I interviewed. Pearl Harbor is a saga of swift action, stark tragedy, and great heroism. Witness the death of airman Fusata Iida at Kaneohe and the frightful scenes I have described aboard *Arizona*. I have also included some very interesting, touching, and at times amusing information from a number of women on Oahu during the attack.

  Most were service wives, but Captain Ruth Erickson, USN Nurse Corps, gave me a wonderful story. One of my most thought-provoking chapters is the one in which I analyze this question: Why did the Japanese hit and run; why did they not stay in the area as Genda wanted Nagumo to do and complete the job of destroying the U.S. Pacific Fleet? This is an original piece of work.

I believe that the natural human desire to know "what happened next?" should lead to considerable interest in the Pearl Harbor story after the actual attack.

Among the many items of new information in the book, I may cite that it contains the only authoritative account of which I know concerning the hectic events on Oahu on December 7 following the withdrawal of the task force. No one can appreciate the depth of the shock the Japanese administered to the U.S. forces on Oahu unless he sees this picture. One of my prime sources was Major General Robert Fleming, who was Short's troubleshooter. The book also contains what I consider to be the finest account extent of events in Washington, D.C., especially at the White House, on December 7 following the attack. In bringing this account to life, I am especially indebted to the diary of Secretary Morgenthau, to Grace Tully, who, as you know, was Roosevelt's secretary in 1941, and to Mrs. Stephen Early, widow of Roosevelt's press secretary.

Another original contribution is the story of the Nagumo force's voyage back to Japan set in the context of related events. These include the long briefing of Emperor Hirohito in the Imperial Palace on December 26 about the Pearl Harbor attack by Admiral Nagumo, Fuchida, and Shimazaki. Most of this narrative is based upon Japanese sources hitherto unavailable in English and primarily upon interviews with Japanese eyewitnesses available nowhere but in this manuscript.

I am particularly pleased with my study of U.S. reactions to the attack. This forms a real revelation of current public opinion which should be an eye-opener for the generation which does not remember World War II. This material has always been available, but no one else has seized upon its possibilities.

The account of Knox's trip to Oahu immediately following Pearl Harbor has never received the treatment it deserves in book form. Admiral Beatty, Knox's aide, published an account in a magazine, but I have used his original manuscript, which differs in some respects from the published version. I have included unpublished material from the Roosevelt Library at Hyde Park. I follow this gripping story with a discussion of the relief from their posts of Kimmel and Short and compare the treatment accorded them with what happened to MacArthur, who had been equally surprised with much less excuse.

I also deal with the Roberts Commission—the first and one of the most controversial of the official inquires into Pearl Harbor. The revisionists have damned this investigation out of hand, and no one has ever checked objectively into its personnel, proceedings, and findings. In fact mine is the only work to deal in depth with the various Pearl Harbor inquiries. This should be a definite plus for the study because at this particular time the American public is very investigation-conscious. The continuing preoccupation with Watergate, the refusal to let the Kennedy and King assassinations fade away, "Koreagate," and similar cases have created a climate which should generate especial interest in the most fascinating, controversial case in U.S. history.

I have also dealt closely with the service inquiries—one conducted by Admiral Hart, the Navy Court of Inquiry, and the Army Pearl Harbor Board, plus the follow-through investigations by Vice Admiral Hewitt, Colonel Clausen, and General Clarke. In addition to the rich lode of the congressional inquiry reports, I have wonderful material from David Richmond, a distinquished attorney who served as Stark's counsel before the Navy court and the Congressional inquiry. To the best of my knowledge, no one has interviewed him before about Pearl Harbor. I am also indebted to Colonel Clausen and General Clarke, although the latter insists upon anonymity. Throughout these proceedings I have woven the story of Kimmel's persistent fight to clear his name. Much of this comes from interviews with Kimmel and from hitherto-unexploited documents in his papers. This material is most intriguing, for Kimmel was not the type to mince words.

I report on the appointment and proceedings of the congressional committee plus a nationwide sampling of newspapers of the day. Of course, the prime source was the record of the committee, but various private papers and other unpublished sources revealed many touches of interest. Judge Gesell of Watergate fame gave me an interesting interview; Richmond added data which enabled me to give a real picture of Stark on the stand. Above all, Edward Morgan, a very successful Washington attorney, who wrote the draft of the majority report, proved a gold mine. He allowed me to reproduce and quote from his draft, which in a number of instances was much more forcefully expressed than the product which finally saw the light. He also presented me with valid insights on members of the committee.

I also have entirely new material from the Kimmel and Barnes papers. I deal with them on a personal note, telling of the last days of Kimmel and Short, including my reminiscences of the admiral as depicted in my long interviews with him.

I also assess responsibility for Pearl Harbor with special emphasis upon the American side. This has been a historical task of infinite difficulty which no one else has heretofore attempted in depth. Perhaps I should say "contributions" to the disaster rather than "responsibility" for it. "Responsibility" in the Occidental and particularly the military-naval sense would leave us with Yamamoto and Nagumo, Short and Kimmel. Yet that is much too simple. Just as many Japanese contributed to making Operation Hawaii an outstanding success, many Americans did the same toward the American defeat.

I come to grips with what I believe to be the root trouble—the stark disbelief that such an attack was possible. This is a complex matter, and I think that this is a real contribution. Then I take up how much, if at all, the American people as a whole were to blame from the standpoint of public opinion and public complacency. Moving up channels, I consider the role of the Congress, which I believe was an indirect one. Reviewing the *Congressional Record* for 1941 leads me to believe that the almost total preoccupation of Congress with the war in Europe contributed to the climate of the time which made the attack possible.

I deal with the charges of the revisionist historians against Roosevelt. It is time someone took an objective look and scotched some of these absurd theses, not because they are anti-Roosevelt but because they are illogical and in some cases border on the nonsensical. So I have taken pains to present the actual facts of the background and incidents involved. (See Appendix: Revisionists Revisited.)

I discuss Secretaries of War and Navy Stimson and Knox, then Secretary of State Hull. I point out that in some instances Stimson and Knox could have done more, but I cannot accept either of them as the villain of the piece. It is still fashionable to say Hull was not sufficiently flexible. This notion was propounded again on a recent program in Eric Sevareid's *Between the Wars* TV series. I think, on the contrary, that the commentators do not understand the nature of a totalitarian state—that to them bending means bowing.

I deal with what I consider to be Roosevelt's mistakes. I have devoted considerable thought and space to Roosevelt because he was so closely related to the Pearl Harbor problem and because he is one of the most challenging and complicated of all American Presidents. His character and his administration never fail to interest the reader, so I have gone after this subject tooth and nail.

No one before this book has dwelt in such detail upon the roles played by various officers in Washington below the level of the CNO and Chief of Staff. I have produced the first study ever made that really considers Stark's part in the whole Pearl Harbor business. Following Stark, I move to Marshall and, among other things, refute the unfounded revisionist canards about him, although I point out that he did make mistakes.

Whereas most Pearl Harbor studies have very little or nothing to say about General Short's role in the disaster, I have devoted much space to him and his responsibility as commanding general of the Hawaiian Department, charged with the protection of the Fleet at moorings. This really gets down to the nitty-gritty of the Oahu scene.

Another genuine scoop is the section concerned with Admiral Bloch. No one else has more than mentioned him in connection with Pearl Harbor, yet as commandant of the Fourteenth Naval District, he was Short's opposite and responsible for the Navy's share of protecting Pearl Harbor. As an example of the important material contained in the Short and Bloch chapters, may I cite the unbelievable radar situation existing on Oahu. It was no thanks to either Bloch or Short that two young privates picked up the incoming Japanese flight on the morning of December 7. But I fear it was largely thanks to them that the radar sighting did not trigger instant, effective action. Bloch especially is blameworthy in this connection. That the system worked at all is to the credit of a few field and company grade officers who more or less took the project into their own hands.

I have devoted much space to Kimmel. I analyze his personality as a contributing factor to the debacle, his reactions to the various warning messages from Washington and his overall performance as CinCPAC. Much of this material was never publicly considered before. My conclusion is that Kimmel cannot avoid a large share of the responsibility.

Source Material

As you well know, I have burrowed far more deeply into the published and unpublished materials on Pearl Harbor than anyone in the historical and writing professions. Exploitation of the record of the congressional inquiry into the disaster was in itself a major project. This consists of forty volumes and included not only the testimony before the congressional committee, but those of the other investigations as well—Roberts Commission, Hart inquiry, Army board, Navy court, Clausen, Hewitt, and Clarke follow-up investigations. These volumes were never indexed, and I do not believe that anyone who has not tackled them can visualize the problem involved in extracting the wheat from the chaff. No doubt this is one of the main reasons why no one has exploited this rich mine heretofore. I have two complete sets of these documents, and my research assistant and I have covered them at least five or six times. In fact, my old set is so dog-eared from use it looks as though it were ready to cry.

In addition, I have relied heavily upon a wide variety of other published and unpublished materials in both the United States and Japan. For your guidance and convenience I have prepared a list of all the "Major U.S. Documentation" I have used. This will give you the names of the papers plus their location. I think you will agree that forty-five (45) different sources is a most impressive list. Then, too, my enclosure gives no hint of the extent of some of these papers, such as President Roosevelt's, General Marshall's, and others, which are organized in a wide variety of categories. The same can be said for those documents of the International Military Tribunal of the Far East which I had in my personal custody as chief of the G-2 Historical Section in Japan after the Tribunal finished its work.

Also enclosed is my list of "Major Japanese Documentation" both published and unpublished. May I emphasize again that I purchased all foreign-language rights to the diary of Admiral Matome Ugaki, Yamamoto's chief of staff, and that his entries from mid-October until December 8, 1941, represent a historical treasure which to the very best of my knowledge has not been published in Japanese or exploited in any publication. The reason is that the Ugaki family has tried to hide the degree to which the admiral was involved in the Pearl Harbor attack. But I have all these pre-Pearl Harbor entries and have used them extensively.

I also paid Admiral Sadao Chigusa a good price for the exclusive use of his diary concerning the period when Nagumo's task force left the Inland Sea in mid-November 1941 until it returned to Japan after the attack. This has enabled me to give the reader daily on-the-spot reports on the First Air Fleet as it sailed across the Pacific to Hawaii. This in itself is a real scoop.

Newspapers, Magazines, and Books

In addition to documents, contemporary newspapers provided much valuable and interesting material for my study. In pursuit of the contemporary viewpoint, the mood and atmosphere of the hour, and to determine what information was and was not available to readers and to take the pulse of public opinion, I have cited more than 150 newspapers. This, of course, does not include many others which I examined but which for various reasons (mostly the question of space available) I decided not to use. In addition to the above-mentioned documentation I have read and cited 219 books, far too many to list here. Of course, I shall include them in my bibliography.

Interviews

Documentation is most essential to all historical writing. But it is always skeletal and by no means tells the whole story. This is especially true of the Japanese side of Pearl Harbor because Operation Hawaii was simply too hot to spell out line by line, reproduce, and distribute to the dozens of officers who would carry out the attack. If such procedure had resulted in leaks, the element of surprise—the most important ingredient in Yamamoto's plan—would have been lost. Thus much of the Pearl Harbor thinking, planning, development, and execution remained in the minds of the officers of the Naval General Staff, the Combined Fleet, the Navy Ministry, and the First Air Fleet which prepared and carried out the attack.

And right there is where I have made my ten-strike. So permit me to give you a general picture of the nature and extent of the interviews I have held with Japanese and U.S. officers in one way or another associated with Pearl Harbor. These interviews have provided me with excellent material. They enabled me not only to spice my narrative considerably and take the reader behind the scenes but also to give the story a really intimate and authentic stamp. These interviews *can never be duplicated because many of the individuals, both in Japan and the United States, have since died.*

I hope the above will permit you to see the depth to which I carried out this historical procedure. First a word about the Japanese.

I covered all three branches of the Japanese Navy—The Naval General Staff, the Navy Ministry, and the Combined Fleet. Because the latter carried out the attack, I put my major emphasis upon Yamamoto, his admirals, and the First Air Fleet under Admiral Nagumo. Many of my interviews lasted anywhere from three to five hours, some a half day, and others even longer.

The Combined Fleet

Take the staff of the Combined Fleet. It was my good fortune to have had eight long interviews during 1950, in 1951, and again in 1955 with Yamamoto's chief of staff, Admiral Fukudome. We also corresponded at some length. From him I learned the story of Yamamoto's early thinking in 1940.

Admiral Kameto Kuroshima, Yamamoto's senior staff officer, was the most unusual officer I met in Japan and one of the most helpful. Though somewhat of a recluse, he and I got along famously. He came to my home nine times during the occupation and, with his philosophical bent of mind, gave me an excellent picture of the Combined Fleet, Japanese naval strategy, and Yamamoto. He was exceedingly loyal to his chief, who sent him on key missions to Tokyo when the chips were down in 1941. I saw Kuroshima again when I went back to Japan in 1955 and in 1965 spent the entire day of Sunday, January 17 with him.

Another special case is Captain Yasuji Watanabe, a longtime member of Yamamoto's staff, a favorite of the admiral's and one of the best friends and helpers I had in Japan. He knew Yamamoto and the Combined Fleet thoroughly, worshiped the admiral, and went to Bougainville to find Yamamoto's body after he had been shot down. He was a big, friendly man, full of fun and good humor, who visited often in my home in Tokyo. I saw him frequently during the six months I was in Japan in 1964–65, and he spent two days with me in my home here in Maryland before his untimely death from cancer several years ago. I had forty interviews with him on Pearl Harbor, Yamamoto, and the Combined Fleet and another dozen or so on Midway. He always brought a large box of cards and notes to our conferences after we became good friends and invariably could date and pinpoint every subject we talked about. In fact, he and I were planning to coauthor a biography of Yamamoto, and we both had begun collecting material.

Other members of Yamamoto's staff with whom I talked at some length included Captain Akira Sasaki, air officer; Captain Tatsuwaka Shibuya (six interviews); and Captain Takayasu Arima. The last two were submarine experts. Captain Shigeru Fujii, who joined Yamamoto's staff on December 1, 1941, provided me with some useful fill-in information in spite of the fact that he was a very sick man during the occupation.

Naval General Staff

Over a period of thirty-one years I also interviewed some of the most prominent surviving members of the Naval General Staff. This included Admiral Fukudome, who transferred from Yamamoto's Combined Fleet on April 10, 1941, to become chief of the First Bureau of the Naval General Staff. Thus he was able to give me not only a firsthand picture of the Combined Fleet staff but a view of the highest naval echelon as well.

Admiral (Baron) Sadatoshi Tomioka, chief of the Operations Section of the Naval General Staff, was another unique person in the preparation of my Pearl Harbor story. He was a mine of information, for his section was the nerve center of the Naval General Staff, and as chief of operations, he knew every plan in the Navy, why it was formulated, and who executed it. He too visited often in my home in Tokyo, and talked with me at length when I went back for the summer of 1955 and again in 1964–65. *In toto*, I had more than forty interviews with him. Invariably polite and considerate, he gladly assisted me in every manner, and supplied me with notes, special documents, maps, charts, diagrams, some of which he specially prepared. Only with the close cooperation of such fine gentlemen as Admiral Tomioka have I been able to dig so deeply into the Japanese side of the Pearl Harbor story.

Other members of Tomioka's Operations Section who visited often in my home and with whom I talked at length were Captain Sadamu Sanagi (air), who permitted me to use his diary; Captain Tatsukichi Miyo (air), who worked with me on Midway as well, and who was reliably informed; and Captain Shigeshi Uchida, a planning specialist on the United States. He talked with me at some length when I was in Japan, permitted me to use his notes, and also visited me in my home in Maryland in the early 1950s, when we delved into the Pearl Harbor problem again in detail. I also had about a two-hour conference in 1951 with Prince Takamatsu, brother of Emperor Hirohito.

Other members of the Naval General Staff with whom I talked at some length included Admiral Nobutake Kondo, vice chief from October 21, 1939, to September 1, 1941; Admiral Minoru Maeda, chief of intelligence; and his knowledgeable assistant, Admiral Kanji Ogawa, whom I interviewed in depth and who paved the way for my purchase of the foreign-language rights to Admiral Ugaki's diary.

Additional members of the Naval General Staff with whom I had interviews (in several cases three or four) were: Admiral Kanji Kishimoto, a submarine expert; Admiral Ichiro Yokoyama, Japan's last naval attaché in Washington in 1941; Captain Ryunosuke Ariizumi, another sub expert; Captain Sutegiro Onodo, a political specialist; Captain Itaru Tachibana, intelligence, who was caught as a spy in the United States in 1941; his colleague Suguru Suzuki, who made a last-minute intelligence mission to Hawaii and then to the task force during its rendezvous in Hitokappu Bay; and Captain Iwaro Otani, who also worked in an intelligence capacity in 1941. Then there were Captain Tadao Yokoi, naval attaché in Berlin in 1941, and his assistant, Captain Katsuo Shibata.

The Navy Ministry

In this housekeeping department of the Japanese Navy I also had the good fortune to be able to talk with key personnel. Most important among these was Admiral Koshiro Oikawa, onetime aide to Emperor Hirohito and Navy minister before the advent of Tojo's Cabinet in mid-October 1941. I had six long conferences with him, and he gave me some excellent material on his ministry; but he shied away from Pearl Harbor because he had sworn under oath before the International Military Tribunal of the Far East that he knew nothing about Operation Hawaii. However, Yamamoto had written him a letter on January 7, 1941, explaining his plan to attack Pearl Harbor. I found out about this letter before I left Japan in 1951, and spoke to Oikawa about it. Although somewhat embarrassed, he finally said to me, "If Yamamoto says I knew something about Pearl Harbor, then it must be so."

The vice chief of the Navy Ministry under both Oikawa and his successor Shimada, Admiral Yorio Sawamoto, was most helpful and gave me an inside view of the Navy Ministry, an analysis of its principal officers and who knew about Pearl Harbor and when. Admiral Toshitane Takata, head of the First Section of the Military Affairs Bureau, gave me another look into the problems of the Japanese Navy, particularly its shipbuilding program. Admiral Zenshiro Hoshima of the War Mobilization Bureau provided me with solid material on the political aspects of the Pearl Harbor problem, as did Admiral Sokichi Takagi, who has written several books and articles on various aspects of the Japanese Navy and its leaders.

One of the best stories of all came from Captain Fumio Aiko, a torpedo expert in the Aeronautical Bureau. He gave me not only a clear picture of how the Japanese developed the fins which enabled torpedoes to run in the shallow waters of Pearl Harbor but also some behind-the-scenes tips on who knew about the operation at an early date.

Other officers who provided me with relevant material on the ministry and Pearl

Harbor were: Admiral Shigeyoshi Inoue; Admiral Katsuhei Nakamura, a liaison officer who knew much; Captain Toshikazu Ohmae; and Captain Atsushi Oi. The last three officers were members of the G-2 Historical Section whom I knew intimately. Captain Ohmae, one of the most knowledgeable officers on the Japanese Navy, was a guest in my home at least two dozen times during the occupation. I saw him again in Tokyo in 1955 and in 1964–65. The same can be said for Captain Oi, who has written a good deal and has been a true friend and adviser over the years.

The Japanese Consulate in Honolulu

Besides acquiring a good background knowledge concerning the Japanese consulate in Honolulu from U.S. documents and personnel, I was able to talk at length with Japanese members of that organization. Otojiro Okuda, the vice-consul during most of 1940 and all of 1941, gave me the best material on the operations within the consulate and the specifics of Japan's legal espionage on Oahu. I talked with him on all my tours in Japan and have corresponded with him from time to time. I bought the rights to the story of Takeo Yoshikawa, Japan's so-called master spy in Hawaii in the 1950s. I talked with him in 1950 and spent several days with him in 1955. But he proved to be an elusive character and an unreliable witness, for he wanted everyone to think that he was a genuine James Bond, whereas he was a clever observer who enjoyed diplomatic immunity so long as he stayed away from restricted U.S. areas on Oahu—which, contrary to some of his more recent testimony, he shunned like the plague. A windfall came to me from Richard Kotoshirodo when I visited Hawaii in the summer of 1967. He was a Japanese American, spoke excellent English, worked in the Japanese consulate in 1941, and engaged in espionage missions on his own. He knew Okuda, Yoshikawa, and other members of the consulate well. In a series of conferences and friendly chats over drinks and dinners, I acquired a new dimension concerning Japanese espionage in Hawaii in 1941, the consulate, and its various members.

International Military Tribunal of the Far East

When the International Military Tribunal of the Far East completed its work, all the documentation, which included numerous interrogations of key Japanese Navy and Army officers, was declassified. Then it was turned over to the G-2 Historical Section, of which I was chief at the time. This provided me with an opportunity of examining this material after work hours in the evening, or on weekends. As a result, I have in my files the full interrogations of a number of prominent Japanese Navy and Army officers before the Tribunal and partial notes on many others. Although these interrogations did not provide me with the excellent material on Pearl Harbor I collected in my private interviews, they gave me valuable background on the Japanese Navy and Army, their leaders, and Japan's road to war in the Pacific.

I have only enough space in this report to mention the chief interrogees: Admiral Osami Nagano, chief of the Naval General Staff; Admiral Shigetaru Shimado, Navy minister after Oikawa; Admiral Takazumi Oka, chief of the Bureau of Navy Affairs; and a number of others.

From the Japanese Army's side of the story I have the interrogations of General Hideki Tojo, prime minister and minister of war; General Akira Muto, chief of the Military Affairs Bureau of the Army General Staff; General Shinichi Tanaka, also of the General Staff; and several other members.

Then, too, I have most of the interrogation of Shigenori Togo, foreign minister in Tojo's Cabinet.

The Sixth Fleet

I was fortunate enough to interview some of the members of the Sixth Fleet (submarines) which launched the undersea attack against Pearl Harbor. One cannot understand Operation Hawaii unless he knows about this part of Japan's grand design against the U.S. Pacific Fleet. Admiral Mitsumi Shimizu, Commander in Chief of the Sixth Fleet and good friend of Yamamoto's, gave generously of his time and knowledge. I talked to him during the occupation and again in 1964–65, at which time he permitted me to quote from his voluminous diary. His chief of staff, Admiral Hisashi Mito, a real submariner, also contributed much to this part of the Pearl Harbor story. So did Captain Kaku Harada and Hanku Sasaki, who trained the midget submariners and launched them from their mother subs on their fatal cruise the night of December 6. Luckily enough, I was able to have six interviews with Lieutenant Kazuo Sakamaki, the only surviving member of the midget submarine attack.

The Fourth Fleet

This was the outfit that attacked Wake Island in 1941. The mission of the Fourth Fleet was to serve as a relay radio station between the Marshall Islands, the task force, Pearl Harbor, and the homeland. Conferences with some of the key officers of this fleet gave me another perspective on Japan's overall war plan and the absolute necessity of timing all operations in the central and southern Pacific to synchronize with Admiral Nagumo's air strike against Pearl Harbor. The officers who helped me most on this phase of Japan's grand strategy were Admiral Shigeyoshi Inoue, Commander in Chief of the Fourth Fleet; Captain Iwao Kawai, Inoue's senior staff officer in 1941; Admiral Masamichi Kajioka, who headed the Wake Island attacking force; and his chief of staff, Admiral Shikazo Yano.

The Eleventh (Land-Based) Air Fleet

This was the organization in the Japanese Navy, operating from Formosa and Indochina in December 1941, which struck the Philippines and sank *Prince of Wales* and *Repulse* off Malaya. This was the outfit of which Admiral Takijiro Onishi, Yamamoto's early confidant, was chief of staff. The Commander in Chief of the Eleventh Air Fleet, Admiral Nishizo Tsukahara, a most knowledgeable officer on all phases of the Japanese Navy, gave me much material on Admiral Onishi, the Japanese naval air force, and the relationship of the Pearl Harbor attack to the Southern Operation, Japan's major war plan. His senior staff officer, Captain Kosei Maeda, furnished me revealing glimpses of Onishi's character and his early work on Yamamoto's plan. I also received material from Admiral Sadaichi Matsunaga, commander of the Twenty-second Air Flotilla, which struck the British ships from Indochina in December 1941.

Attacking Fleets in the South

I mentioned in my discussion of the Naval General Staff that I talked with Admiral Nobutake Kondo, who served as its vice chief under Prince Fushimi and Admiral Osami

Nagano from October 21, 1939, to September 1, 1941. But Kondo became Commander in Chief of the Second Fleet, which attacked in the southern regions. In this capacity he had to know about Pearl Harbor and the major war plan in El Dorado of the South. As such he gave me valuable information concerning the coordination of Japan's grandiose plans and the officers who executed them, particularly Admiral Ibo Takahashi, Yamamoto's first chief of staff and Commander in Chief of the Third Fleet, based on Formosa.

Admiral Jisaburo Ozawa, a real sea dog, who was Commander in Chief of the Southern Expeidtionary Fleet in 1941, proved to be exceedingly helpful. He was a good friend of Yamamoto's, an original and courageous thinker, who knew the Japanese Navy from keel to mast. He was the catalyst behind the formation of the First Air Fleet on April 10, 1941, and he knew much concerning the early planning of Pearl Harbor and its coordination with the Southern Operation. I had many conferences with him in my home during the occupation and saw him again in 1955. He was one of my favorite Japanese admirals. In fact, I helped keep him alive in the winter of 1948 by paying him well for preparing various projects on the Japanese Navy in 1940–41.

Miscellaneous Interrogees

This list includes some of the most important people I met and talked to since I began my Pearl Harbor project. First a word about my loyal assistant, Commander Masataka Chihaya. He it was who paved the way for me to see and talk with Japanese Navy and Army officers and civilians. I have had countless private conversations with him on Pearl Harbor, for he knew much about it because his brother, Lieutenant Takehiko Chihaya, was an air observer in the first attack wave against Pearl Harbor. Commander Chihaya has done translations for me, checked on original sources, photocopied articles in Japanese magazines and newspapers, and double-checked facts and figures of every kind. He spent a week with me in my home last summer here in Maryland. I could not begin to estimate the number of times we talked together about Pearl Harbor.

In this category are several of the most prestigious admirals ever to serve in the Japanese Navy. For example, Admiral Zengo Yoshida, a classmate of Yamamoto's at the naval academy and former Commander in Chief of the Combined Fleet. He gave me fresh information of Yamamoto's student days, his concepts on the Imperial Fleet and Operation Hawaii. So did Admiral Soemu Toyoda, who talked with me a number of times and permitted me to see some of his private papers. He was the commander of the Kure Naval Base in 1941 and was a strong candidate to succeed Oikawa as Navy minister in October of that year. A superior officer of high intelligence and moral courage, he succeeded Admiral Koga as the Commander in Chief of the Combined Fleet on May 5, 1944 and became chief of the Naval General Staff on May 29, 1945. So he was in a position to know much and gave me quality information on the year 1941 and the Japanese Navy in general.

Admiral Kichisaburu Nomura occupies a special place on this list. He had a long, illustrious career in the Navy, then became Foreign minister on September 25, 1939, and finally ambassador to the United States in early 1941. Although he knew nothing about the planning and execution of the Pearl Harbor attack, he told me much about the Japanese Navy, its officers, and his work as ambassador in Washington. I talked with him in my home during the occupation and again when I returned to Japan in 1955.

Two other Japanese in this category were also kind and helpful. Admiral Teikichi Hori, Yamamoto's Eta Jima classmate and perhaps his closest friend in the Navy, increased my understanding of Yamamoto as a person and an officer. He also permitted me to use and to photograph many of Yamamoto's letters which he had collected. So did Mitsuari Takamura, a Hokkaido businessman who was also a close friend of Yamamoto's. I also had a long session with Mr. Takamura in Tokyo on his relationship to Yamamoto and his assessment of his friend as a person.

The venerable Admiral Katsunoshin Yamanashi, who enriched my knowledge of Yamamoto and the Japanse Navy, also belongs on this list. So do Juji Enomoto and George Mizota. The former, a lawyer, was one of the legal counsel for the Japanese Navy, knew Admirals Yamamoto and Nagano and other bigwigs, and enjoyed talking about them. Mr. Mitzota, a graduate of Stanford University who spoke impeccable English, served as Yamamoto's interpreter when he headed the Japanese delegation to the London Naval Conference in 1934–35. He too knew many Japanese naval officers intimately and had a solid grasp on the organization as well.

Several Japanese Army officers also deserve a high place on this list. Chief among them is Colonel Takushiro Hattori, chief of the Operations Section of the Army General Staff in 1941. A member of the G-2 Historical Section, Hattori was a treasure trove of information on the Japanese Army. A protégé of General Tojo's and a man of keen intelligence, he learned about Pearl Harbor in the summer of 1941 and knew when and under what circumstances the high-ranking generals in the Army became privy to Yamamoto's bold design. I talked to Hattori dozens of times during the occupation, saw him again in 1955, when I returned to Tokyo, and corresponded with him at length before his death a number of years ago. He is the author of a four-volume work on the war in the Pacific which I have in English translation. General T. Kawabe, General Seizo Arisue, Colonel S. Sugita, and Professor Mitsutaro Araki and his wife also gave me interesting material on the Japanese Army in 1941 and Japan's march to war in the Pacific.

Tadeo Wikawa also belongs here. I learned to know him in the early days of the occupation, had lunches and dinners with him. We talked primarily about the diplomatic problems of 1941. He had an American wife, spoke English well, and was a member of the unofficial peace mission to the United States in early 1941 led by Father Drought.

The First Air Fleet

I carried on my most important and most intensive interviews among the members of Nagumo's task force. There I worked in depth and struck pay dirt, for I spoke at length or communicated with more than fifty people who engaged in Operation Hawaii.

Let me begin with Admiral Nagumo's officers. His chief of staff, Admiral Ryunosuke Kusaka, was a willing collaborator who often stayed in my home in Tokyo when he came on a visit from Osaka. A venerable gentleman, Kusaka and I became good friends, went on trips together to Japanese shrines and the like, and talked about Pearl Harbor as though we had known each other all our lives. I had ten interviews with him, in which he gave me some of the best material I have on Nagumo, the reaction and thinking concerning Yamamoto's bold venture and the staff of the First Air Fleet, the voyage to Hawaii, and the attack. When I returned to Japan in 1964–65, I had dinner with Kusaka in Osaka in October, then spent the next day with him in his spacious home.

The person who knows more about Pearl Harbor than any living Japanese is Captain Minoru Genda, air staff officer of the First Air Fleet. Believe it or not, I had seventy-two interviews with him on Operation Hawaii. Some of these lasted as long as three or four hours. He lived in Kyushu when I was first in Japan, and when he came to Tokyo, he stayed in my home for a week or ten days at a time. Thus I became closely acquainted with him and was able to get the true story of Pearl Harbor from him and to learn as much as I could about his colleagues and the First Air Fleet. I talked to him at length again when I visited Japan for several months in 1955; I also spoke with him on several occasions when he visited my home here in the States and when I returned to Japan for a six-month stay in 1964–65. Thus I discussed the problems of Pearl Harbor with him over a period of more than twenty-five years. Genda also prepared special studies for me on Pearl Harbor, which he wrote in Japanese and which I had translated into English. I consider my materials on Genda a priceless source of information.

Captain Tatsuwaka Shibuya shifted from Yamamoto's staff to Nagumo's late in 1941. He gave me a clear picture of the role of the three submarines in the task force, the cruise to Hawaii, the attack, and the return voyage to Japan as seen from the decks of the task force flagship *Akagi*. Genda's assistant, Commander Chuichi Yoshioka, brought many interesting facts concerning Nagumo, Kusaka, Genda, and others to my attention and supplied much other interesting material in the six interviews I had with him. He knew English fairly well, was a Christian, and cooperated 100 percent. Commander Gore Saka-gami, Nagumo's engineering officer, gave me a picture of things from an engineers point of view—oil storage problems aboard the ships and the like. Captain Gishiro Miura, Nagumo's navigator, told me in correspondence the story of Pearl Harbor from the navigational side—speed during the cruise; arrival at the right spot north of Oahu at the correct time; and fascinating details one was not likely to get from other officers.

Admiral Gunichi Mikawa, leader of Nagumo's support force—battleships and cruisers—related in four long sessions all his problems and thoughts concerning Pearl Harbor from the time he heard of the plan in the summer of 1941 to the end of the attack and the cruise home. His material added a new dimension, for his views were those of a battleship admiral in an operation in which carriers, the new element in Japan's offensive sea power, carried the day.

My interviews with Admiral Sentaro Omori, who commanded the destroyers, gave me the story from the standpoint of the smaller vessels and from one who thought the whole business a terrible risk. In numerous interviews Admiral Sadao Chigusa, executive officer of the destroyer *Akigumo*, increases my knowledge of Pearl Harbor with many anecdotes about the cruise and gave it all a solid, authentic stamp by permitting me to quote in full from his diary.

Admiral Chuichi "King Kong" Hara, Commander in Chief of the Fifth Carrier Division—*Shokaku* and *Zuikaku*—in two long long interviews in 1955 told me a fascinating yarn from a Johnny Come Lately in the Pearl Harbor drama. Admiral Tatasugu Jyojima, skipper of *Shokaku*, answered a questionnaire that also added to my general knowledge of the operation. So did a number of sessions with Captain Kyogo Ohashi, Admiral Hara's senior staff officer.

From the Second Carrier Division's staff—*Soryu* and *Hiryu*—I was able to talk at length with three of Admiral Yamaguchi's officers. Captain Seiroku Ito, senior staff officer aboard *Soryu* from August 20, 1941, gave me three interviews; while Captain Eijiro Suzuki, air staff officer, Genda's classmate at Eta Jima and a strong backer of Yamamoto's plan, provided me with fascinating and enthusiastic accounts of Yamaguchi, the early planning, training, last-minute preparations, cruise, attack, and reactions aboard the carrier *Soryu*. Commander Susumu Ishiguro told me about a little-known subject, communications. This included the training period, the takeover of southern Indochina in July 1941, the mock attacks in the Inland Sea area in early November, the cruise to Hawaii, and the return voyage to Japan.

Through Captain Kijiro Imaizumi, who was commander of the three big submarines—*I-19*, *I-21* and *I-23*—that accompanied the task force across the Pacific and back to Japan, I became acquainted with aspects of the operation I would have missed had I not talked with him. The same can be said for Captain Minoru Yokota, skipper of the submarine *I-26*, which scouted the Aleutians and the northern Pacific for the First Air Fleet while it was en route to Hawaii.

I learned much about the Midway bombardment unit, a little-known subject, from Admiral Minoru Togo, son of the famous Togo who destroyed the Russian fleet at the Battle of Tsushima at the end of May 1905. The son, an honest and straightforward type, was skipper of the tanker *Shiriya* in this part of the Pearl Harbor operation. Captain Hiroshi Uwai, skipper of the destroyer *Akebono*, prepared a statement for me on his participation in this action.

A valuable source of information concerning all phases of air training, personalities of the pilots, problems of the attack, and reactions to the air strike came from the air officers of the carriers *Kaga* (First Carrier Division), *Hiryu* (Secnd Carrier Division), and *Zubkaku* (Fifth Carrier Division). Each carrier had an air officer whose main duties were to supervise and check on every phase of their pilots' work: training in Kyushu; maintenance of planes; health and physical condition of all airmen; briefings; supervision of table maneuvers en route to the target; takeoffs and landings of planes at the time of the attack; and interrogation of the pilots after they returned to their carriers. As such, these officers knew a tremendous amount about their airmen and the technical aspects of the air strike.

It was my very good fortune to have had four long interviews with Captain Takahisa Amagai from the carrier *Hiryu*. He was literally soaked in his subject and gave me the best information I have on this aspect of Operation Hawaii. Captain Naohiro Sata from the carrier *Kaga* and Captain Hisao Shimoda from *Zuikaku* also helped to widen my horizon.

The Airmen Who Participated in the Attack

Luck was with me on this phase of the Pearl Harbor venture, for I was able to interview or secure statements or answers to questionnaires from twenty-five airmen who participated in the air strike against Hawaii. I cannot explain the entire story of the airmen in this report, but let me give you a brief rundown. First of all, a word about Captain Mitsuo Fuchida, who led the air attacking forces. I had 50 long discussions with him concerning Operation Hawaii and another 100 or so on the Battle of Midway, his war career, his conversion to Christianity, and subsequent evangelism. He, too, stayed in my home in Tokyo for weeks at a time when I lived in Japan. He visited my home in the United States several times in the 1950s and 1960s. Then in 1964 he lived with me and my family for about four months when I began working on his biography, now under contract with McGraw-Hill. The *Reader's Digest* in the summer of 1964, sent us to Japan. There we were together virtually every day from September 1964 through January 1965. We traveled the length and breadth of Japan together during this period. So I learned all he could tell me about Pearl Harbor and the war in the Pacific. He also provided me with maps, charts, diagrams, pictures, and some of his private papers. He and Genda gave me the best material I have on Pearl Harbor.

But other airmen contributed much, too. For example, the torpedo bombing pilots in the first wave. Now these were a rare breed because their bombing was dangerous and not many survived the war. However, I had four long sessions with Jinichi Goto aboard *Akagi*, who gave me an excellent account of the whole torpedo bombing program and vivid scenes of the attack itself. So did Heita Matsumura from *Hiryu*, a brave but carefree type who added many human touches. I also received useful statements from torpedo crewmen Atsumi Nakajima from *Soryu* and Kazuyoshi Kitajima from *Kaga*.

I acquired a very good picture of the problems of high-level bombing and the participants in this phase of the attack from Fuchida, who specialized in this technique. I also had a long session on this type of air attack with Sadao Yamamoto and four statements from other horizontal bombing airmen, including Takashi Hashiguchi, who was to take over leadership of the first wave in case anything happened to Fuchida.

Two long interviews with Tomatsu Ema, a dive bombing pilot aboard *Zuikaku* in the first wave, gave me a real touch of the human element among pilots and an excellent picture of the attack over Wheeler Field. Sessions with Toshio Hashimoto, observer from *Hiryu* during the first wave, and Keizo Ofuchi from *Akagi*, second wave, did the same. In long statements other pilots gave me additional information on the dive bombing attack.

Some of the best combat action material I have came from the fighter pilots. Iyozo Fujita, who had a remarkable war record, told me the story of the dramatic death of his friend Fusata Iida over Kaneohe in the second wave. In an interview with Yoshio Shiga, which covers almost eight typewritten pages I received another excellent picture of the attack. He was the first pilot to fly off *Kaga*. Yuzo Tsukamoto provided me with the story of fighter cover over the task force during the two air strikes. Saburo Shindo from *Akagi* gave me a good statement concerning the second wave, and Masanobu Ibusuki, also from *Akagi* (second wave), who helped shoot down a U.S. B-17 over Oahu, added helpful material.

Last, but not least, a statement from Haruo Takeda, who piloted the patrol plane from the cruiser *Tone* and who scouted the target area before the attack, gave me some highly interesting pre-air-strike information.

Interviews with American Personnel

I interviewed and corresponded with numerous Americans who were directly or indirectly involved in the Pearl Harbor attack or in the investigations which followed Japan's devastating air strike. As with my Japanese interrogees, some of my interviews with U.S. personnel were in depth and covered three- and four-hour sessions, some even longer. I also attempted here to consult those people who knew the most about Pearl Harbor. I saw no reason to interview those who had only a marginal relationship to the event just for the sake of padding my list of interrogees. Time does not permit me to exhaust this story, but may I give you a brief account of what I have done.

Admiral Husband E. Kimmel and His Staff

I spent four consecutive days with Admiral Kimmel in his home in Groton, Connecticut, during late November and early December 1963. He gave me many of his private papers and permitted me to examine much of his correspondence, to make notes and copy it. In the course of these most pleasant and profitable interviews I came to know the man as he was. Members of his staff in 1941 whom I interviewed were:

1. Vice Admiral William Ward "Poco" Smith, chief of staff. Admiral Smith is a special case. He took me under his wing and treated me like a son. We enjoyed lunches, dinners, drinks, movies, and drives in the country together. He helped

smooth the way for my interviews with Kimmel and with other members of Kimmel's staff.

2. Admiral Walter S. DeLany, operations officer.
3. Admiral Maurice S. "Germany" Curts, communications officer.
4. Captain Walter J. East, assistant communications officer. This officer and his wife, Joan, were especially helpful when I was in San Diego during the summer of 1964. They also took me under their wing, paved my road to many interrogees, and helped me out in every possible way.
5. Rear Admiral Edwin T. Layton, intelligence officer.
6. Admiral Arthur C. Davis, air officer.
7. Commander Paul C. Crosley, flag secretary.

This was an excellent cross section of Kimmel's staff. Through them I learned much about the Pacific Fleet, its Commander in Chief, and how he operated.

Naval Installations on Oahu

1. Guy C. Avery, Kaneohe. He wrote me two long, excellent letters about this little-known base.
2. Admiral Claude C. Bloch, commandant, Fourteenth Naval District.
3. Admiral Charles Coe, Bellinger's operations officer on Ford Island.
4. CPO Thomas E. Forrow, Ford Island.
5. Victor Kamont, Ford Island.
6. Edward P. Lepinsky, Ford Island.
7. Admiral Harold M. Martin, commanding officer, Kaneohe.
8. Rear Admiral Logan Ramsey, Ford Island.
9. Bert Richmond, Kaneohe.
10. Rear Admiral Cecil D. Riggs, medical officer, Patrol Wing Two, Ford Island.
11. Duane W. Shaw, Ewa Field (marine).
12. Rear Admiral James Shoemaker, Ford Island.

Officers and Men Aboard Ships

1. Captain John R. Beardall, Jr., *Raleigh.*
2. CWO-4 Edgar B. Beck, *Oklahoma.*
3. Rear Admiral William P. Burford, CO of destroyer *Monaghan.*
4. John Crawford, enlisted man aboard *Vestal.*
5. Cleveland David, enlisted man aboard *Ralph Talbot.*
6. Rear Admiral Milo F. Draemel, commander, Destroyers, Battle Fleet.
7. Admiral George C. Dyer, *Indianapolis.*
8. Harlan E. Eisnagle, *Maryland.*
9. Rear Admiral Carl K. Fink, chief of staff aboard *St. Louis.*
10. Howard C. French, *Oklahoma.*
11. Admiral William R. Furlong, *Oglala.* Admiral Furlong deserves a special tribute. He received me in his home in Washington Saturday morning after Saturday morning at 9:30. We generally worked until 12:30, then walked about ten blocks to a restaurant for lunch, returned to his home, and worked until about 3:00 P.M. He was exceedingly cooperative, full of suggestions and ideas, and wrote letters in my behalf to Admiral Kimmel.
12. Captain Lawrence C. Grannis, *Antares.*

13. Lieutenant Commander B. C. Hesser, *Vestal.*
14. Commander Doir C. Johnson, *West Virginia.*
15. Emil Johnson, *Tern.*
16. Earl C. Nightingale, *Arizona.*
17. William D. Osborne, Jr., *Arizona.*
18. Rear Admiral William W. Outerbridge, *Ward.*
19. Rear Admiral Harold F. Pullen, *Reid.*
20. Rear Admiral G. Quynn, chief of staff, Base Force, aboard *Argonne.*
21. Harry Rafsky, Rear Admiral William L. Calhoun's enlisted aide aboard *Argonne.*
22. Admiral George A. Rood, captain of light cruiser *St. Louis.*
23. Rear Admiral Laurence A. Ruff, *Nevada.*
24. Lieutenant General Alan Shapley, USMC, *Arizona.*
25. Admiral R. Bentham Simons, captain of *Raleigh* (papers and pictures).
26. Lieutenant Commander Harley F. Smart, *Vestal.*
27. Admiral Raymond A. Spruance, *Northampton.*
28. Rear Admiral Herald F. Stout, *Bresse.*
29. Captain Joseph K. Taussig, Jr., *Nevada.*
30. Lieutenant Irvin H. Thesman, *Oklahoma.*
31. Chaplain (Lieutenant Commander) Walter L. Thompson, with a destroyer squadron.
32. Admiral Harold C. Train, chief of staff aboard *California.*

General Walter C. Short's Staff

Although General Short died before I could talk to him, I interviewed, talked to, or corresponded with virtually every member of his staff:

1. Colonel Russell C. Throckmorton, G-1.
2. Brigadier General Kendall J. "Wooch" Fielder, G-2. Fielder was especially helpful. After lunch and one long session he took me to his home and permitted me to make copies of materials which he had collected on Pearl Harbor.
3. Colonel George W. Bicknell, assistant G-2 (located in Honolulu). Bicknell and his wife, Dorothy, treated me like a member of the family. They answered question after question, and the colonel also let me use his private papers.
4. Colonel William E. Donegan, G-3.
5. Major General Morrill W. Marston, G-4.
6. Brigadier General Robert Dunlop, adjutant general.
7. Colonel Kenneth E. Thiebaud, assistant to Dunlop.
8. Brigadier General George P. Sampson, assistant signal officer.
9. Major General Robert J. Fleming, assistant G-4. Fleming was General Short's troubleshooter and is another special case. He acquired materials on General Short from the Hoover War Library for me which I photocopied *in toto.* He also answered a long questionnaire, his replies constituting sixty-one longhand pages. In addition, I spent almost an entire day with him last August in Washington and have corresponded with him at length.

Army Posts on Oahu

1. Major General Durward S. Wilson, CO, Twenty-fourth Infantry, Fort Shafter.
2. Colonel Charles W. Davis, Fort Shafter.

3. Colonel Emil Leard, Schofield Barracks.
4. Captain Robert Dunlop, Jr., Fort de Russy.
5. Philippe A. Michaud, enlisted man at Schofield Barracks.
6. George Sanger, enlisted man at Schofield Barracks.

The Hawaiian Air Force and Other Airmen

1. Lieutenant General Truman H. Landon, led the B-17s which arrived at Oahu during the attack.
2. Major General Brooke E. Allen, Hickam Field.
3. Major General Howard C. Davidson, Wheeler Field.
4. Brigadier General William J. Flood, Wheeler Field.
5. Brigadier General James Mollison, chief of staff, Hawaiian Air Force.
6. Colonel William C. Farnum, Hickam Field.
7. Colonel W. J. Paul, USA, on HAF staff as liaison with Hawaian Department.
8. Colonel Vernon H. Reeves, Hickam Field.
9. Lieutenant Colonel Francis Gutzak, Hickam Field.
10. Lieutenant Colonel Kermit Tyler, Wheeler Field.
11. Captain William H. Heydt, Hickam Field.
12. Chief Warrant Officer Alton W. Freeman, Hickam Field.
13. John R. Shark, a corporal at Wheeler Field.

All of the above-mentioned personnel were helpful. But I enjoyed a close relationship with a number of these officers. General Mollison, who was General Frederick L. Martin's chief of staff, was a man apart. Kind, knowledgeable, and generous with his time, he, too, took me under his wing and in a number of lengthy interviews helped me see the Air Force side of the Pearl Harbor story. So did Colonel "Cush" Farnum, with whom I enjoyed a warm friendship until his death several years ago. Then, too, Colonel Reeves was on the Air Force faculty at the University of Maryland, and Colonel Gutzak, an enlisted man at Hickam in 1941, was a student in one of my classes at the University of Maryland.

U.S. Intelligence Officers

In trying to solve the mystery that is Pearl Harbor, I made a special attempt to burrow deeply into the intelligence side of the American story. Here is a list of those who were especially helpful:

1. Colonel George C. Bicknell, assistant G-2, Hawaiian Department.
2. Colonel Rufus S. Bratton, chief, Far Eastern Section, G-2, War Department.
3. Brigadier General Carter W. Clarke, deputy chief, Military Intelligence, G-2, War Department.
4. Lieutenant Commander Thomas H. Dyer, member, Communications Intelligence Unit, Fourteenth Naval District.
5. Brigadier General Kendall J. Fiedler, G-2, Hawaiian Department.
6. Colonel Allen Haynes, G-2, Schofield Barracks, Hawaiian Department.
7. Captain Wilfred J. Holmes, member, Communications Intelligence Unit, Fourteenth Naval District.
8. Captain Alwin D. Kramer, assistant chief, Far Eastern Section, ONI, Navy Department.
9. Rear Admiral Edwin T. Layton, Fleet intelligence officer.

10. Rear Admiral Arthur N. McCollum, chief, Far Eastern Section, ONI, Navy Department.
11. Captain Joseph J. Rochefort, chief, Communications Intelligence Unit, Fourteenth Naval District.
12. Captain Laurence F. Safford, chief, Communications Security Unit, Navy Department.
13. Lieutenant Colonel John Bayard Schindel, member, Far Eastern Section, G-2, War Department.

May I add that Colonel Bratton was General Willoughby's deputy G-2 in Japan, where I came to know him well. Ditto for Lieutenant Colonel Schindel, who was in the G-2 Historical Section when I was head of that organization in the Far East Command, Tokyo.

Women on Oahu

The following Navy, Army, and civilian women either wrote to me or told me fascinating stories about their experiences during and after the Pearl Harbor attack. Some of these were outstanding, especially the one by Captain Ruth Erickson, Navy nurse at the hospital near Hospital Point.

1. Mrs. George Bicknell.
2. Mrs. William Burford.
3. Mrs. Frank Cooper.
4. Mrs. John B. Earle.
5. Mrs. Walter East.
6. Captain Ruth A. Erickson.
7. Mrs. Kendall J. "Wooch" Fielder.
8. Mrs. Allen Haynes.
9. Mrs. Wilfred J. Holmes.
10. Mrs. Charles Kengla.
11. Mrs. Emil Leard.
12. Mrs. Robert L. Shivers.
13. Mrs. William Ward Smith.
14. Mrs. Durward S. Wilson.
15. Mrs. Cassin B. Young.

Mainland United States

1. Admiral Thomas M. Dykers, at Pearl Harbor until April 1941, then at New London, Connecticut.
2. Mrs. Stephen T. Early, wife of Roosevelt's press secretary.
3. Commander Dermott Hickey, a former member member of Admiral Stark's staff.
4. Mrs. Alwin Kramer.
5. Fleet Admiral Chester W. Nimitz, director, Bureau of Navigation on December 7, 1941, and who replaced Admiral Pye as CinCPAC.
6. Vice Admiral W. R. Smedberg, Admiral Stark's aide.
7. Grace Tully, secretary to Roosevelt.
8. Vice Admiral Charles Wellborn, Admiral Stark's flag secretary.

In addition to the above, a number of officers included under the heading of "U.S. Intelligence Officers" were located in Washington, D.C.

Special Group

1. Dr. Harry E. Barnes.
2. Colonel Henry C. Clausen.
3. General J. Lawton Collins.
4. Representative Martin Dies, Texas.
5. Judge Gerhard A. Gesell.
6. Senator Guy Gillette, Iowa.
7. Ambassador Joseph C. Grew.
8. Kilsoo Haan, Korean intelligence gatherer on Oahu.
9. General Charles Herron, former commanding general, Hawaiian Department.
10. Edward P. Morgan, FBI agent who acted as assistant counsel for the congressional committee investigating Pearl Harbor. He has taken a special interest in this project and has been most helpful and cooperative.
11. Curtin B. Munson, special agent for Roosevelt.
12. David W. Richmond, Stark's attorney before the Navy Court of Inquiry and the congressional committee. He was and continues to be exceedingly helpful.
13. Admiral John Shafroth, with Cruisers, Southeast Pacific.
14. James E. Webb, one of Stark's counsel before the congressional committee.

LIST OF MAJOR PERSONNEL

Aiko, Cmdr. Fumio
Torpedo expert, Aeronautical Bureau, Navy Ministry

Allen, Capt. Brooke E.
Acting squadron commander of bombers, Hickam Field

Amagai, Cmdr. Takashisa
Air officer, *Hiryu*

Andrews, VADM. Adolphus
Member, Navy Court of Inquiry

Arnold, Maj. Gen. Henry H.
Commanding general, Army Air Forces

Barkley, Alben W.
Majority leader of Senate; chairman, joint congressional committee

Beardall, Capt. John R.
Naval aide to President Roosevelt

Bellinger, RADM. Patrick N. L.
Commander, Patrol Wing Two

Bicknell, Lt. Col. George W.
Assistant G-2, Hawaiian Department

Bloch, RADM. Claude C.
Commandant, Fourteenth Naval District

Bratton, Col. Rufus S.
Chief, Far Eastern Section, G-2

Brewster, Owen
Senator from Maine; member, joint congressional committee

Brown, VADM. Wilson
Commander, Scouting Force

Burford, Lt. Cmdr. William P.
Captain, *Monaghan*

Calhoun, RADM. William L.
Commander, Base Force

Chigusa, Lt. Cmdr. Sadao
Executive officer, *Akigumo*

Clark, J. Bayard
Congressman from North Carolina; member, joint congressional committee

Clarke, Col. Carter W.
Deputy Chief, Military Intelligence Service; conducts inquiry

Clausen, Maj. Henry C.
Assistant recorder, Army board; conducts follow-up inquiry.

Coe, Cmdr. Charles
Operations and plans officer under Bellinger

Cooper, Jere
Congressman from Tennessee; vice chairman, joint congressional committee

Cramer, Brig. Gen. Myron C.
The Judge Advocate General

Curts, Cmdr. Maurice E.
Communications officer, Pacific Fleet

Davis, Cmdr. Arthur C.
Aviation officer, Pacific Fleet

DeLany, Capt. Walter S.
Operations officer, Pacific Fleet

Donegan, Lt. Col. William E.
G-3, Hawaiian Department

Draemel, RADM. Milo F.
Commander, Destroyers, Battle Fleet

Dunlop, Col. Robert H.
Adjutant, Hawaiian Department

Earle, Capt. John B.
Chief of staff, Fourteenth Naval District

Egusa, Lt. Cmdr. Takashige

Dive-bombing leader, First Air Fleet

Farthing, Col. William E.
Commanding officer, Fifth Bomb Group

Ferguson, Homer
Senator from Michigan; member, joint congressional committee

Fielder, Lt. Col. Kendall J.
G-2, Hawaiian Department

Fleming, Maj. Robert J., Jr.
Assistant G-4, Hawaiian Department.

Flood, Col. William J.
Commanding officer, Wheeler Field

Forrestal, James V.
Secretary of the navy, May 1944–September 1947

Frank, Maj. Gen. Walter H.
Member, Army board

Fuchida, Cmdr. Mitsuo
Leader, air attack on Pearl Harbor

Fujita, Sublt. Iyozo
Fighter pilot, *Akagi*

Fukudome, VADM. Shigeru
Chief of staff, Combined Fleet, November 1939–April 10, 1941; then chief, First Bureau, Naval General Staff

Fuqua, Lt. Cmdr. Samuel G.
Damage control officer, *Arizona*

Furlong, RADM. William R.
Commander, Battle Forces, Pacific

Furukawa, Lt. Izumi
Aerial observer, *Akagi*

Gatch, RADM. T. L.
Judge advocate general, Navy Department

Gearhart, Bertrand W.
Congressman from California; member, joint congressional committee

Genda, Cmdr. Minoru
Air staff officer, First Air Fleet

George, Walter F.
Senator from Georgia; member, joint congressional committee

Gerow, Brig. Gen. Leonard T.
Chief, War Plans Division, War Department

Goto, Lt. Jinichi
Torpedo squadron commander, *Akagi*

Green, Brig. Gen. Thomas H.
General Short's counsel; deputy JAG

Grew, Joseph C.
U.S. ambassador to Japan

Grunert, Lt. Gen. George
Chairman, Army board

Halsey, VADM. William F.

Commander, Aircraft, Battle Force

Hara, RADM. Chuichi
Commander in Chief, Fifth Carrier Division

Hart, Adm. Thomas C.
CinC Asiatic Fleet; conducts inquiry

Hasegawa, Capt. Kiichi
Captain, *Akagi*

Herron, Lt. Gen. Charles D.
Commanding general, Hawaiian Department, 1940

Hewitt, VADM. H. Kent
Conducts inquiry

His Imperial Majesty Hirohito
Emperor of Japan

Hopkins, Harry
Adviser to President Roosevelt

Hull, Cordell
Secretary of state

Iida, Lt. Fusata
Fighter pilot

Imaizumi, Capt. Kijiro
Commanding reconnaissance submarines with task force

Ingersoll, RADM. Royal E.
Deputy Chief of Naval Operations

Itaya, Lt. Cmdr. Shigeru
Leader of fighter pilots, first wave

Ito, RADM. Seiichi
Chief of staff, Combined Fleet, April 10–August 10, 1941; then vice chief, Naval General Staff

Kalbfus, Adm. Edward C.
Member, Navy Court of Inquiry

Keefe, Frank B.
Congressman from Wisconsin; member, joint congressional committee

Kimmel, Adm. Husband E.
Commander in Chief, U.S. Pacific Fleet

King, Adm. Ernest J.
Commander in Chief, Atlantic Fleet; later Commander in Chief, United States Fleet

Kita, Nagao
Consul general at Honolulu

Knox, Frank
Secretary of the navy

Konoye, Prince Fumimaro
Premier, July 1940—October 1941

Kotoshirodo, Richard M.
Clerk in Honolulu consulate

Kramer, Lt. Cmdr. Alwin D.
On loan from Far Eastern Section, ONI, to Translation Section, Communications Division, Navy Department

Kuroshima, Capt. Kameto
Senior staff officer, Combined Fleet

Kurusu, Saburo
Special envoy to Washington

Kusaka, RADM. Ryunosuke
Chief of staff, First Air Fleet

Landon, Maj. Truman H.
Leader of B-17 flight, Thirty-eighth
Reconnaissance Squadron

Lavender, Capt. Robert A.
One of Admiral Kimmel's attorneys

Layton, Lt. Cmdr. Edwin T.
Intelligence officer, Pacific Fleet

Lucas, Scott W.
Senator from Illinois; member, joint
congressional committee

Maeda, RADM. Minoru
Chief, Third Bureau, Naval General staff

Maejima, Cmdr. Toshihide
Submarine expert, *Taiyo Maru* mission

Marshall, Gen. George C.
Chief of Staff, U.S. Army

Martin, Maj. Gen. Frederick L.
Commanding general, Hawaiian Air Force

Martin, Cmdr. Harold M.
Commanding officer, Kaneohe

Masuda, Cmdr. Shogo
Air officer, *Akagi*

Matsumura, Lt. Heita
Flight commander, *Hiryu* torpedomen

Matsuo, Lt. Keiu
Midget submariner, *Taiyo Maru* mission

Matsuoka, Yosuke
Foreign minister, July 1940–July 1941

Mayfield, Capt. Irving
Head, District Intelligence Office

McCollum, Cmdr. Arthur H.
Chief, Far Eastern Section, ONI

McCoy, Maj. Gen. Frank B.
Member, Roberts Commission

McMorris, Capt. Charles E.
War plans officer, Pacific Fleet

McNarney, Brig. Gen. Joseph T.
Member, Roberts Commission; later
deputy Chief of Staff, U.S. Army

Mikami, John Yoshige
Taxi driver for Honolulu consulate

Mikawa, VADM. Gunichi
Commander, Support Force (Third
Battleship Division and Eighth Cruiser
Division)

Miles, Brig. Gen. Sherman
Acting ACS/Intelligence, War Department

Mitchell, William D.

Counsel, joint congressional committee

Miyo, Cmdr. Tatsukichi
Member, Operations Section, First
Bureau, Naval General Staff

Mollison, Lt. Col. James A.
Chief of staff, Hawaiian Air Force

Morgan, Edward P.
Assistant to Seth Richardson, joint
congressional committee

Morgenthau, Henry, Jr.
Secretary of the treasury

Murata, Lt. Shigeharu
Torpedo bomber leader, First Air Fleet

Murfin, Adm. Orin G.
President, Navy Court of Inquiry

Murphy, John W.
Congressman from Pennsylvania;
member, joint congressional committee

Nagai, Lt. Tsuyoshi
Flight commander, *Soryu* torpedomen

Nagano. Adm. Osami
Chief, Naval General Staff

Nagumo, VADM. Chuichi
Commander in Chief, First Air Fleet

Nakahara, RADM. Giichi
Chief, Personnel Bureau, Naval General
Staff

Newton, RADM. John H.
Commander, Cruisers, Scouting Force

Nomura, Adm. Kichisaburo
Ambassador to the United States

Noyes, RADM. Leigh
Chief, Communications Division, Navy
Department

Ofuchi, Lt. Seizo
Dive bomber observer, *Akagi*

Ogawa, Capt. Kanji
Asst. chief, Third Bureau, Naval General
Staff

Ohashi, Cmdr. Kyozo
Senior staff officer, Second Carrier
Division until September 1, 1941; then
senior staff officer, Fifth Carrier Division

Oikawa, Adm. Koshiro
Navy minister in Konoye Cabinet

Oishi, Cmdr. Tamotsu
Senior staff officer, First Air Fleet

Okuda, Otojiro
Vice consul in Honolulu

Omori, RADM. Sentaro
Commander, First Destroyer Squadron

Onishi, RADM. Takijiro
Chief of Staff, Eleventh Air Fleet

Ono, Lt. Cmdr. Kenjiro

Communications officer, First Air Fleet
Outerbridge, Lt. William W.
  Captain, *Ward*
Ozawa, VADM. Jisaburo
  Commander, Third Battleship Division
Phillips, Lt. Col. Walter C.
  Chief of Staff, Hawaiian Department
Pye, VADM. William S.
  Commander, Battle Force
Quynn, Cmdr. Allen G.
  Chief of staff, Base Force
Ramsey, Lt. Cmdr. Logan C.
  Operations officer under Bellinger
Reeves, RADM. Joseph M.
  Member, Roberts Commission
Richardson, Adm. James O.
  Commander in Chief, U.S. Fleet, 1940
Richardson, Seth W.
  Counsel to joint congressional committee
Richmond, Lt. David
  Attorney for Admiral Stark
Roberts, Owen J.
  Chairman, Roberts Commission
Rochefort, Cmdr. Joseph J.
  Chief, Communications Intelligence Unit,
  Fourteenth Naval District
Roosevelt, Franklin D.
  President of the United States
Ruff, Lt. Lawrence A.
  Nevada
Rugg, Charles
  Attorney for Admiral Kimmel
Russell, Maj. Gen. Henry D.
  Member, Army board
Safford, Cmdr. Laurence F.
  Chief, Security Section, Communications
  Division, Navy Department
Sakagami, Cmdr. Goro
  Engineering officer, First Air Fleet
Sakamaki, Ens. Kazuo
  Midget submariner
Sanagi, Cmdr. Sadamu
  Member, Operations Section, First
  Bureau, Naval General Staff
Sasabe, Lt. Cmdr. Otojiro
  Navigation officer, First Air Fleet
Sasaki, Cmdr. Akira
  Staff officer for air, Combined Fleet
Sasaki, Capt. Hanku
  Commander, First Submarine Division
Schuirmann, Capt. Roscoe E.
  Navy liaison officer with State
  Department
Shibuya, Lt. Cmdr. Tatsuwaka

Submarine officer, First Air Fleet
Shiga, Lt. Yoshio
  Fighter pilot, *Kaga*
Shimada, VADM. Shigetaro
  Navy minister, Tojo Cabinet
Shimazaki, Lt. Cmdr. Shigekazu
  Squadron commander, *Zuikaku*, leader,
  second wave
Shimizu, VADM. Mitsumi
  Commander in Chief, Sixth Fleet
  (Submarines)
Shindo, Lt. Saburo
  Leader, second-wave fighters
Shivers, Robert L.
  Special agent in charge, FBI, Honolulu
Shoemaker, Capt. James H.
  Commander, Ford Island Naval Air
  Station
Short, Lt. Gen. Walter C.
  Commanding general, Hawaiian
  Department
Smith, George H. E.
  Secretary, Senate Minority Steering
  Committee
Smith, Capt. William Ward
  Chief of staff, Pacific Fleet
Sonnett, John F.
  Counsel, Hewitt inquiry
Standley, Adm. William H.
  Member, Roberts Commission
Stark, Adm. Harold R.
  Chief of Naval Operations (CNO)
Stimson, Henry L.
  Secretary of war
Suzuki, Lt. Cmdr. Eijiro
  Air officer, Second Carrier Division
Suzuki, Lt. Cmdr. Suguru
  Aviation expert, *Taiyo Maru* mission
Tachibana, Lt. Cmdr. Itaru
  Intelligence expert, Naval General Staff
Takahashi, Lt. Cmdr. Kakuichi
  Dive bomber leader
Taylor, Lt. Kenneth
  Fighter pilot, Haleiwa Field
Thomas, Lt. Cmdr. J. F.
  Nevada
Throckmorton, Lt. Col. Russell C.
  G-1, Hawaiian Department
Togo, Shigenori
  Foreign minister, Tojo Cabinet
Tojo, Gen. Hideki
  War minister, Konoye Cabinet; premier,
  October 18, 1941.
Tomioka, Capt. Sadatoshi

Chief, Operations Section, Naval General Staff.

Toyoda, VADM. Teijiro
Foreign minister, third Konoye Cabinet

Train, Capt. Harold C.
Chief of staff, Battle Force

Truman, Harry S.
President of the United States effective April 12, 1945

Tsukahara, Adm. Nishizo
Commander in Chief, Eleventh Air Fleet

Turner, RADM. Richmond Kelly
Chief, War Plans Division, Navy Department

Uchida, Cmdr. Shigeshi
Member, Operations Section, Naval General Staff

Ugaki, RADM. Matome
Chief of staff, Combined Fleet, from August 10, 1941

Watanabe, Capt. Yasuji
Staff officer, Combined Fleet

Watson, Maj. Gen. Edwin M.
Military aide to President Roosevelt

Welch, Lt. George S.
Fighter pilot, Haleiwa Field

Wilkinson, Capt. Theodore S.
Captain, *Mississippi*; director of Naval Intelligence, October 15, 1941

Yamaguchi, Capt. Bunjiro
Member, Third Bureau, Naval General Staff

Yamaguchi, RADM. Tamon
Commander in Chief, Second Carrier Division

Yamamoto, Adm. Isoroku
Commander in Chief, Combined Fleet

Yoshikawa, Takeo
Chancellor, Honolulu consulate

Yoshioka, Lt. Cmdr. Chuichi
Asst. air officer, First Air Fleet

Young, Cmdr. Cassin B.
Captain, *Vestal*

Zacharias, Capt. Ellis M.
Captain, *Salt Lake City*; intelligence expert

THE PEARL HARBOR INVESTIGATIONS

ROBERTS COMMISSION
December 22, 1941–January 23, 1942

Associate Justice Owen J. Roberts, U.S.
Supreme Court, chairman
Adm. William H. Standley, USN (Ret.)
[Member]
RADM. Joseph M. Reeves, USN (Ret.)
[Member]

Maj. Gen. Frank B. McCoy, USA (Ret.)
[Member]
Brig. Gen. Joseph T. McNarney, USA
[Member]
Walter Bruce Howe, recorder
Lt. Col. Lee Brown, USMC, legal adviser
Albert J. Schneider, secretary

THE HART INQUIRY
February 22, 1944–June 15, 1944

Adm. Thomas C. Hart, USN (Ret.)
Capt. Jesse R. Wallace, USN, counsel*

Lt. William M. Whittington, Jr., USNR,
assistant counsel

ARMY PEARL HARBOR BOARD
July 20–October 20, 1944

Lt. Gen. George Grunert, president
Maj. Gen. Henry D. Russell, [Member]
Maj. Gen. Walter H. Frank, [Member]

Col. Charles W. West, recorder
Maj. Henry C. Clausen, asst. recorder
Col. Harry A. Toulmin, Jr., executive officer

*Relieved on May 9, 1944, and Whittington became counsel.

NAVY COURT OF INQUIRY
July 24–October 19, 1944

Adm. Orin G. Murfin, USN (Ret.),
  president
Adm. Edward C. Kalbfus, USN (Ret.)
  [Member]

VADM. Adolphus Andrews, USN [Member]
Cmdr. Harold Biesemeier, USN, judge
  advocate

HEWITT INVESTIGATION
May 15–July 11, 1945

VADM. H. Kent Hewitt
Mr. John F. Sonnett, counsel
Lt. Cmdr. Benjamin H. Griswold, USNR,

aide to Admiral Hewitt
Lt. John Ford Baecher, USNR, assistant to
  Mr. Sonnett

CLAUSEN INVESTIGATION
November 23, 1944–September 12, 1945

Maj. Henry C. Clausen

CLARKE INVESTIGATION
September 14–16, 1944
July 13–August 4, 1945

Col. Carter W. Clarke, USA

Lt. Col. Ernest W. Gibson, USA

JOINT CONGRESSIONAL COMMITTEE INVESTIGATION
November 15, 1945–July 15, 1946

Alben W. Barkley, senator from Kentucky,
  chairman
Jere Cooper, representative from
  Tennessee, vice chairman
Walter F. George, senator from Georgia
Scott W. Lucas, senator from Illinois
Owen Brewster, senator from Maine
Homer Ferguson, senator from Michigan

J. Bayard Clark, representative from North
  Carolina
John W. Murphy, representative from
  Pennsylvania
Bertrand W. Gearhart, representative from
  California
Frank B. Keefe, representative from
  Wisconsin

Counsel (through January 14, 1946)

William D. Mitchell, general counsel
Gerhard A. Gesell, chief assistant counsel

Jule M. Hannaford, assistant counsel
John E. Masten, assistant counsel

(After January 14, 1946)

Seth W. Richardson, general counsel

Samuel H. Kaufman, associate general
counsel

John E. Masten, assistant counsel

Edward P. Morgan, assistant counsel

Logan J. Lane, assistant counsel

ABBREVIATIONS USED IN TEXT

AC/S	Assistant Chief of Staff
BB	Battleship
CinCAF	Commander in Chief, Asiatic Fleet
CinCLANT	Commander in Chief, Atlantic Fleet
CinCPAC	Commander in Chief, Pacific Fleet
CinCUS	Commander in Chief, United States Fleet
CNO	Chief of Naval Operations
Cominch	Commander in Chief, United States Fleet (after March 18, 1942)
DD	Destroyer
DIO	District Intelligence Office
FCC	Federal Communications Commission
G-2	Intelligence (Army)
GMT	Greenwich Mean Time
JAG	Judge Advocate General
NYK	Japanese steamship line Nippon Yusen Kaisha
ONI	Office of Naval Intelligence
OPNAV	Chief of Naval Operations
SIS	Signal Intelligence Service
SOP	Standing Operating Procedure
TAG	The Adjutant General
USAFFE	U.S. Armed Forces Far East

SELECTED BIBLIOGRAPHY

Unpublished Sources Located in the Author's Personal Files

Action Report, Commander-in-Chief, United States Pacific Fleet, Serial 0479, 15 February 1942, Report of Japanese Raid on Pearl Harbor, 7 December 1941. Classified Operational Archives Branch, Naval History Division, Washington Navy Yard, Washington, D.C.

Morgan, Edward P. An Approach to the Question of Responsibility for the Pearl Harbor Disaster. This is the draft report which became the basis for the majority report of the joint congressional committee. Author's files, courtesy Mr. Morgan.

Avery, Guy C. Letters to the author, November 4 and December 16, 1963.

Beatty, VADM. Frank E., USN (Ret.). "Secretary Knox and Pearl Harbor." This article in altered form was published in *National Review* (December 13, 1966) under the title "The Background of the Secret Report." Author's files, courtesy Dr. Barnes.

Interview between Lt. Col. Henry C. Clausen and Dr. Harry E. Barnes, January 3, 1964. Author's files, courtesy Dr. Barnes.

Earle, Mrs. John B. Letter to the author, October 16, 1964.

International Military Tribunal Sitting at Tokyo. Proceedings. Various interrogations and documents, author's files.

Fielder, Brig. Gen. Kendall J. Notes for talk delivered before the Rotary Club in Honolulu on December 7, 1966. Author's files, courtesy Fielder.

Fleming, Maj. Gen. Robert J., Jr. Reply, January 11, 1977, to questionnaire which the author submitted to General Fleming.

———. Letter to the author, March 23, 1977.

Genda, Minoru. Report on Pearl Harbor prepared for the author, May 1947. Author's files.

———. "How the Japanese Task Force Idea Materialized," essay prepared for the author. Author's files.

Memorandum, "Interview With the President, 1425–1550, Monday June 9, 1941," Navy Dept OP-12D-2-Mc, signed by Adm. H. E. Kimmel. Originally secret, since declassified., Navy History Division, Washington Navy Yard, Washington, D.C.

Kramer, Mrs. Alwin D. Letter to the author, undated, received March 23, 1976.

Affidavit of Otto Kuehn, 1 January 1942, Document No. 62562, Clerk of Court, US Army, Court of Military Records, Nassif Bldg., Falls Church, Va.

Record of Trial of Kuehn, Bernard Julius Otto, CM226070, Clerk of Court, US Army, Court of Military Records, Nassif Bldg., Falls Church, Va.

Materials Pertaining to Army Pearl Harbor Board, RG 107, National Archives, Washington, D.C.

Record Group 165 (WD General and Special Staff), Plans and Operations Division, Pearl Harbor Investigative Records 1941–1946, National Archives, Washington, D.C.

Ohmae, Capt. Toshukaze. Report on the Midway Neutralization Unit. Author's files.

———. Combined Fleet Task Force Organization, 7 December 1941; The Battle Order of the Japanese Fleet Prior to 7 December 1941, with Dates of Departure and Arrival of Major Units. Author's files.

Oi, Capt. Atsushi. "The Japanese Navy in 1941," essay prepared for the author.

Outerbridge, W. W. Report, DD139/A16-3/(759), Classified Operational Archives Branch, Naval Historical Division, Washington Navy Yard, Washington, D.C.

Ozawa, VADM. Jisaburo. Outline Development of Tactics and Organization of the Japanese Carrier Air Force, prepared for the author.

Memorandum, November 16, 1944, by Charles Rugg, of conversation between Rugg and Justice Roberts held November 14 and 15, 1944. Author's files, courtesy of Dr. Barnes.

Shibuya, Capt. Tatsuwaka. "Submarine Activities in Pearl Harbor," study prepared for the author.

Shimizu, VADM. Mitsumi. Statement of July 21, 1969, based upon his diary for 1941, prepared for the author.

Smith-Hutton, Capt. Henri H. USN (Ret.). Letter to the author, July 20, 1973.

Study, "Some Considerations Concerning the Basic Defense Doctrine of Oahu," Air Force Historical Section, Maxwell AFB, Ala.

Van Kuren, Benjamin. "Report of Police Activities in Connection with the Japanese Consulate Subsequent to December 7th, 1941 and up to February 8th, 1942," February 13, 1943. Author's files, courtesy General Fielder.

Interview between Adm. William H. Standley and Dr. Harry E. Barnes, June 1, 1962. Author's files, courtesy Dr. Barnes.

"Supplemental Battle Report, Capt R. B. Simons, USN, Commanding USS RALEIGH, 7 December, 1951." Author's files, courtesy Admiral Simons.

Smedberg, VADM. W. R., III. Comments to the author, July 27, 1977.

Taussig, Joseph K., Jr. Letter to the author, January 8, 1963.

Uchida, Cmdr. Shigeshi Uchida. Unpublished notes. Author's files, courtesy Capt. Uchida.

Wellborn, VADM. Charles, Jr. Comments to the author, August 10, 1977.

———. Letter, July 26, 1977 to the author.

"Mr. X". Comments on this study prepared for the author.

Diaries

(Some of these diaries have been published in whole or in part; however, the author worked exclusively from the unpublished versions)

RADM. Sadao Chigusa (courtesy Admiral Chigusa)

James V. Forrestal, Princeton University Library, Princeton, N.J.

Marquis Koichi Kido

Breckenridge Long, Library of Congress, Washington, D.C.

Henry Morgenthau, Jr., Franklin D. Roosevelt Library, Hyde Park, N.Y.

VADM. Chuichi Nagumo (courtesy Mrs. Nagumo)

RADM. Giichi Nakahara (courtesy Admiral Nakahara)

Adm. Kichisaburo Nomura (courtesy Admiral Nomura)

Capt. Sadamu Sanagi (courtesy Captain Sanagi)

Henry L. Stimson, Yale University Library, New Haven, Conn.

RADM. Matome Ugaki

War diaries of First Destroyer Division; Third Battleship Division; Fifth Carrier Division

Collected Papers

Gen. of the Air Force H. H. Arnold, Library of Congress, Washington, D.C.
Harry Elmer Barnes, University of Wyoming Library, Laramie, Wyo.
RADM. Claude C. Bloch, Library of Congress, Washington, D.C.
Stephen T. Early, Franklin D. Roosevelt Library, Hyde Part, N.Y.
James V. Forrestal, Princeton University Library, Princeton, N.J.
RADM. William R. Furlong, Operational Archives, U.S. Naval Historical Division, Washington
    Navy Yard, Washington, D.C.
Adm. Thomas C. Hart, Operational Archives, U.S. Naval Historical Division, Washington Navy
    Yard, Washington, D.C.
Cmdr. Charles C. Hiles, University of Wyoming Library, Laramie, Wyo.
Harry Hopkins, Franklin D. Roosevelt Library, Hyde Park, N.Y.
Stanley K. Hornbeck, Hoover Institution on War, Revolution and Peace, Stanford, Calif.
Cordell Hull, Library of Congress, Washington, D.C.
RADM. Husband E. Kimmel, University of Wyoming Library, Laramie, Wyo.
Fleet Adm. Ernest J. King, Library of Congress, Washington, D.C.
Fleet Adm. Ernest J. King, Operational Archives, U.S. Naval Historical Division, Washington
    Navy Yard, Washington, D.C.
Frank Knox, Library of Congress, Washington, D.C.
Gen. of the Army George C. Marshall, George C. Marshall Research Foundation, Lexington, Va.
    Xerox copies of official records in National Archives, WDCSA SGS (Secretariat) (1939–1941).
President Franklin D. Roosevelt, Franklin D. Roosevelt Library, Hyde Park, N.Y.
Maj. Gen. Walter C. Short, Hoover Institution on War, Revolution and Peace, Stanford, Calif.
Adm. William H. Standley, University of Southern California Library, Los Angeles, Calif.
Adm. Harold R. Stark, Operational Archives, U.S. Naval Historical Division, Washington Navy
    Yard, Washington, D.C.
Robert A. Taft, Library of Congress, Washington, D.C.
Adm. Richmond Kelly Turner, Operational Archives, U.S. Naval Historical Division, Washington
    Navy Yard, Washington, D.C.
RADM. Yasuji Watanabe, courtesy of Admiral Watanabi.

Taped Reminiscences

Maj. Gen. Robert J. Fleming, Jr., March 7 and 31, 1975, Hoover Institution on War, Revolution
    and Peace, Stanford, Calif.
Adm. Thomas C. Hart, Oral Research History Office, Columbia University, New York; transcript in
    Operational Archives, U.S. Naval Historical Division, Washington Navy Yard, Washington,
    D.C.
Adm. H. Kent Hewitt, Oral Research History Office, Columbia University, New York; transcript in
    Operational Archives, U.S. Naval Historical Division, Washington Navy Yard, Washington,
    D.C.

Official Primary Sources

Japanese Monograph No. 102, *Submarine Operations, December 1941–April 1942*, prepared by
    Military History Section, Headquarters, Army Forces Far East, Tokyo, Japan. Author's files.
Congressional Record, Volumes 87–104. Government Printing Office, Washington, D.C., 1941–58.
Hearings Before the Joint Committee on the Investigation of the Pearl Harbor Attack, Congress of

the United States, Seventy-ninth Congress, Government Printing Office, Washington, D.C., 1946.

Investigation of Un-American Propaganda Activities in the United States. Hearings Before a Special Committee on Un-American Activities, House of Representatives, Seventy-seventh Congress, First Session, on H. Res. 282, Appendix VI, Report on Japanese Activities, Government Printing Office, Washington, D.C., 1942.

Published Sources

Barnes, Harry E. "Pearl Harbor After a Quarter of a Century." *Left and Right: A Journal of Libertarian Thought,* Vol. IV. (1968).

Beatty, VADM. Frank E. "Another Version of What Started War with Japan." *U. S. News & World Report* (May 28, 1954).

Boyle, John H. "The Walsh-Drought Mission to Japan." *Pacific Historical Review* (May 1965).

Brittin, Capt. Burdick S. "We Four Ensigns." *United States Naval Institute Proceedings* (December 1966).

Burtness, Paul S., and Warren U. Ober "Secretary Stimson and the First Pearl Harbor Investigation." *Australian Journal of Politics and History* (April 1968).

Butow, R. J. C. "Backdoor Diplomacy in the Pacific: The Proposal for a Konoye-Roosevelt Meeting, 1941." *The Journal of American History* (June 1972).

———. "The Hull-Nomura Conversations: A Fundamental Misconception." *American Historical Review* (July 1960).

Chamberlain, John. "Pearl Harbor." *Life* (September 10, 1945).

Conroy, Hilitary. "The Strange Diplomacy of Admiral Nomura." *Proceedings of the American Philosophical Society* (June 18, 1970).

Current, Richard N. "How Stimson Meant to 'Maneuver' the Japanese." *The Mississippi Valley Historical Review* (June 1953).

Davenport, Walter. "Impregnable Pearl Harbor." *Collier's* (June 14, 1941).

Drake, Col. C. B. "A Day at Pearl Harbor." *Marine Corps Gazette* (November 1965).

Duncan, Col. R. L. "Without Warning." *The American Legion Magazine* (December 1957).

"Extracts from the Diary of VADM Shigetaro Shimada." *Bungei Shunju* (December 1976).

Feis, Herbert. "War Came at Pearl Harbor: Suspicions Considered." *Yale Review* (Spring 1956).

Ferrell, Robert H. "Pearl Harbor and the Revisionists." *The Historian* (Spring 1955).

Fuchida, Capt. Mitsuo. "I Led the Air Attack Against Pearl Harbor," Roger Pineau, ed. *United States Naval Institute Proceedings* (September 1952).

Fukudome, VADM. Shigeru. "Hawaii Operation." *United States Naval Institute Proceedings* (December 1955).

Genda, Minoru. "Higeki Shinjuwan Kogeki." *Bungei Shunju* (December 1962).

———. "Shinjuwan Kishu to Sannin no Teitoku." *Bungei Shunju* (May 1968).

Herzog, James H. "Influence of the United States Navy in the Embargo of Oil to Japan, 1940–1941." *Pacific Historical Review* (August 1966).

Hill, Norman. "Was There an Ultimatum Before Pearl Harbor?" *American Journal of International Law* (April 1948).

Hohjo, Sei-ichi. "The Nine Heroes of Pearl Harbor Attack." *Contemporary Japan: A Review of Far Eastern Affairs* (April 1942).

Hone, Thomas C. "The Destruction of the Battle Line at Pearl Harbor." *United States Naval Institute Proceedings* (December 1977).

Hosoya, Chihiro. "Miscalculations in Deterrent Policy: Japanese-U.S. Relations, 1938–1941." *Journal of Peace Research* (1968, No. 2). Oslo, Norway.

Hughey, A. Miles. "How We Got the News of Pearl Harbor." *The American Legion Magazine* (December 1970).

Kittredge, Capt. T. B. "The Muddle Before Pearl Harbor." *U. S. News & World Report* (December 3, 1954).

Kohase, Matsuji. "A Hidden Episode Concerning Niihau Island." *Suiko* (October 1973).

Morison, Samuel Eliot. "The Lessons of Pearl Harbor." *Saturday Evening Post* (October 26, 1961).

Morton, Louis. "Pearl Harbor in Perspective: A Bibliographical Survey." *United States Naval Institute Proceedings* (April 1955).

Murata, Kiyoaki. "'Treachery' of Pearl Harbor." *Nippon Times* (June 8, 1956).

Nomura, Adm. Kichisaburo. "Stepping-Stones to War." *United States Naval Institute Proceedings* (September 1951).

Perkins, Dexter. "Was Roosevelt Wrong?" *Virginia Quarterly Review* (Summer 1954).

Pierce, Philip N. "Twenty Years Ago." *The Leatherneck* (December 1961).

Rawlings, Charles, and Isabel Leighton. "Fat Girl." *Saturday Evening Post* (February 6, 1943).

Richardson, Seth W. "Why Were We Caught Napping at Pearl Harbor?" *Saturday Evening Post* (May 24, 1947).

Russell, Bruce M. "Pearl Harbor: Deterrence Theory and Decision Theory." *Journal of Peace Research* (1967, No. 2).

Russell, Maj. Gen. H. D. "More Light on Pearl Harbor." *U. S. News & World Report* (May 7, 1954).

Sabin, VADM. L. S. "Rising Suns over Pearl." *Shipmate* (December 1966).

Slonim, Capt. Gilvin M. "Have We Learned the Lesson of Pearl Harbor?" *Navy* (December 1966).

Standley, Admiral William H. "More About Pearl Harbor." *U. S. News & World Report* (April 16, 1954).

Strong, Mary Katherine. "Washington at Pearl Harbor." *Current History* (February 1946).

Sturm, Ted R. "Mission: War! (A B-17 on December 7, 1941)." *Airman* (December 1965).

Suzuki, Suguru. "Shinjuwan Gunio Kaimetsu," included in Suzuki Takeshi, *Doto No Nakano Taiyo*, privately printed, 1969.

Takagi, RADM. Sokichi. "Ningen Yamamoto Isoroku." *Bungei Shunju* (January 1950).

Takagi, Sokichi. "Shunjuwan Kogeki: No Hyoketsu Kudaru." *Bungei Shunju* (December 1956).

Wellings, RADM. Joseph H. "Pearl Harbor Lessons and Problems of Today." *Shipmate* (March 1974).

Wohlstetter, Roberta. "Sunday, December 7, 1941, and the Monday Morning Quarterbacks." *Air Force and Space Digest* (December 1966).

(Mr. X) Untitled, anonymous article in Chicago *Tribune* special supplement of December 7, 1966.

Yoshikawa, Takeo, with Lt. Col. Norman Stanford, USMC. "Top Secret Assignment." *United States Naval Institute Proceedings*, (December 1960).

Books

Agawa, Hiroyuki. *Yamamoto Isoroku.* Tokyo: Shincho Sha, 1966.

Baker, Leonard. *Roosevelt and Pearl Harbor.* New York: Macmillan Co., 1970.

Barkley, Alben W. *That Reminds Me.* New York: Doubleday, Garden City, 1954.

Barnes, Harry E., ed. *Perpetual War for Perpetual Peace.* Caldwell, Ida.: The Caxton Printers Ltd., 1953.

Beard, Charles A. *President Roosevelt and the Coming of the War.* Yale University Press, 1941.

Bergamini, David. *Japan's Imperial Conspiracy.* New York; William Morrow & Co., Inc., 1971.

Brownlow, Donald G. *The Accused: The Ordeal of Rear Admiral Husband Edward Kimmel, U. S. N.* New York; Vantage Press, 1968.

Burns, James MacGregor. *Roosevelt, The Soldier of Freedom.* New York; Harcourt Brace Jovanovich, Inc., 1970.

Busch, Noel F. *The Emperor's Sword: Japan vs. Russia in the Battle of Tsushima.* New York: Funk & Wagnalls, 1969.

Butow, Robert J. C. *The John Doe Associates: Backdoor Diplomacy for Peace, 1941.* Stanford Calif.: Stanford University Press, 1974.

———. *Tojo and the Coming of the War.* Princeton, N.J.: Princeton University Press, 1961.

Byas, Hugh. *Government by Assassination.* New York: Alfred A. Knopf, 1942.

Chihaya, Masataka. *Teikoku Rengo Kantai.* Tokyo: Kodansha, 1969.

Clark, Blake. *Remember Pearl Harbor!* New York: Modern Age Books, 1942.

Connally, Thomas T. *My Name Is Tom Connally.* New York: Crowell Publishing Co., 1954.

The Correspondents of *Time, Life,* and *Fortune. December 7, The First Thirty Hours.* New York: Alfred A. Knopf, 1942.

Craven, Wesley Frank, and James Lea Cate, ed., *The Army Air Forces in World War II,* Vol. I. Chicago: University of Chicago Press, 1948.

Current, Richard N. *Secretary Stimson: A Study in Statecraft.* New Brunswick, N.J.: University Press, 1954.

Drury, Allen. *A Senate Journal, 1943–1945.* New York: McGraw-Hill Book Co., 1961.

Dyer, VADM. George C. *On the Treadmill to Pearl Harbor: The Memoirs of Admiral James O. Richardson, USN (Retired).* Washington, D.C.: Naval Historical Division, Department of the Navy, 1973.

———. *The Amphibians Came to Conquer: The Story of Admiral Richmond Kelly Turner.* Washington, D.C.: Naval History Division, Department of the Navy, 1971.

Farago, Ladislas. *The Broken Seal.* New York; Random House, 1967.

Feis, Herbert. *The Road to Pearl Harbor.* Princeton, N.J.: Princeton University Press, 1950.

Flynn, John T. *The Truth About Pearl Harbor* (pamphlet privately printed in New York, 1944).

Fuchida, Mitsuo. *Shinjuwan Sakusen No Shinso; Watakushi Wa Shinjuwan Joku Ni Ita.* Nara, Japan: Yamato Taimusu Sha, 1949.

Fukudome, Shigeru. *Shikan: Shinjuwan Kogeki.* Tokyo: Jiyu Ajiya-sha, 1955.

Furer, RADM. Julius Augustus. *Administration of the Navy Department in World War II.* Washington, D.C.: Navy History Division, Department of the Navy, 1959.

Gellermann, William. *Martin Dies.* New York: The John Day Co., 1944.

Genda, Minoru. *Kaigun Kokutai Shimatsu Ki (Hasshin Hen).* Tokyo: Bundgei Shunju Shinsha, 1961.

———. *Kaigun Kokutai Shimatsu Ki (Sento Hen).* Tokyo: Bundgei Shunju Shinsha, 1962.

———. *Shinjuwan Sakusen Kaikoroku.* Tokyo: Yomiuri Shimbun, 1972.

Grew, Joseph C. *Ten Years in Japan.* New York: Simon & Schuster, 1944.

———. *Turbulent Era: A Diplomatic Record of Forty Years, 1904–1945,* Part II, Walter Johnson, ed. Boston: Houghton-Mifflin Co., 1952.

Halsey, Fleet Adm. William F., USN, and Lt. Cmdr. J. Bryan, III, USNR. *Admiral Halsey's Story.* New York: McGraw-Hill Book Co., 1947.

Hara, Capt. Tameichi, with Fred Saito and Roger Pineau. *Japanese Destroyer Captain.* New York: Ballantine Books, 1961.

Harada, Kumao. *Saionji Ko to Seiyoku.* Tokyo: Iwanami Shoten, 1950–56.

Hattori, Takushiro. *Daitoa senso zen-shi ("The Complete History of the Greater East Asia War").* Tokyo: Hara Shobo, 1953.

Heinl, Lt. Col. Robert D., Jr. *The Defense of Wake.* Washington, D.C.: Historical Section, Division of Public Information, Headquarters U.S. Marine Corps, 1945.

———. *Marines at Midway.* Washington, D.C.: Historical Section, Division of Public Information, Headquarters U.S. Marine Corps, 1948.

Hirose, Hikota. *Yamamoto—Gensui Zensen Yori no Shokanshu.* Tokyo: Tocho Shoin, 1943.

Hoehling, A. A. *The Week Before Pearl Harbor.* New York: W. W. Norton & Co., 1963.

Huie, William Bradford, *The Case Against the Admirals: Why We Must Have a Unified Command.* New York: E. P. Dutton & Co., 1946.

Hull, Cordell, *The Memoirs of Cordell Hull.* New York: Macmillan Co., 1948.

Ickes, Harold L., *The Secret Diary of Harold L. Ickes,* Vol. III, *The Lowering Clouds 1939–1941.* New York: Simon & Schuster, 1954.

Ike, Nobutake, ed. *Japan's Decision for War: Records of the 1941 Policy Conferences.* Stanford, Calif.: Stanford University Press, 1967.

Jablonski, Edward. *Flying Fortress.* Garden City, N.Y.: Doubleday, 1965.

Kahn, David. *The Codebreakers.* New York: Macmillan Co., 1967.

Kase, Toshikazu. *Journey to the "Missouri."* New Haven, Conn.: Yale University Press, 1950.

Kato, Masuo. *The Lost War.* New York: Alfred A. Knopf, 1946.

Kimmel, Husband E. *Admiral Kimmel's Story.* Chicago: Henry Regnery Co., 1955.

King, Fleet Adm. Ernest J. and Walter Muir Whitehead. *Fleet Admiral King: A Naval Record.* New York: W. W. Norton & Co., 1952.

Kondo, Ryoshin. *Umi-Washi No Chichi—Yamamoto Gensui* ("Yamamoto, Father of Sea Eagles"). Tokyo: Unedi Shobo, 1943.

Kusaka, Ryunosuke. *Rengo Kantai.* Tokyo: Mainichi Shimbun, 1952.

Langer, William L. and S. Everett Gleason. *The Undeclared War: 1940–1941.* New York: Harper & Brothers, 1953.

Lash, Joseph P. *Roosevelt and Churchill 1931–1941: The Partnership That Saved the West.* New York: W. W. Norton Company, New York: 1976.

Lord, Walter. *Day of Infamy.* New York: Holt, Rinehart & Co., 1957.

Marshall, Katherine T. *Together: Annals of an Army Wife.* New York: Tupper & Love, 1946.

McIntire, VADM. Ross T. *White House Physician.* New York: G. P. Putnam's Sons, 1946.

Millis, Walter. *This Is Pearl! The United States and Japan—1941.* New York: William Morrow & Co., 1947.

Morgenstern, George. *Pearl Harbor: The Story of the Secret War.* New York: Devin-Adair Co., 1947.

Morison, Elting E. *Turmoil and Tradition: A Study of the Life and Times of Henry L. Stimson.* Boston: Houghton-Mifflin Co., 1960.

Morison, Samuel Eliot. *Coral Sea, Midway and Submarine Actions, May 1942–August 1942.* Boston: Little, Brown & Co., 1949.

———. *The Rising Sun in the Pacific.* Boston: Little, Brown & Co., 1948.

Morton, Louis. *United States Army in World War II: The War in the Pacific: Strategy and Command: The First Two Years.* Washington, D.C.: Department of the Army, Office, Chief of Military History, 1962.

Nomura, Adm. Kichisaburo. *Beikoku ni Tsukaishite.* Tokyo: Dai-isshu, Saron Rinji Jokango, Tsuhan, 1946.

Okumiya, Masatake, and Jiro Horikoshi, with Martin Caidin. *Zero!* New York: E. P. Dutton, 1956.

Otaka, Seijiro. *Kishu-ka Boryaku-ka* ("Surprise Attack or Treachery"). Tokyo: Jiji Tsushin-sha, 1954.

Perkins, Frances. *The Roosevelt I Knew.* New York: Viking Press, 1946.

Phillips, Maj. Thomas R. *Roots of Strategy: A Collection of Military Classics.* Harrisburg, Pa: The Military Service Publishing Co., 1940.

Pogue, Forrest C. *George C. Marshall: Education of a General.* New York: Viking Press, 1963.

———. *George C. Marshall: Ordeal and Hope, 1939–1942.* New York: Viking Press, 1966.

———. *George C. Marshall, Organizer of Victory, 1943–1945.* New York: Viking Press, 1973.

Porteus, Stanley D. *And Blow Not the Trumpet: A Prelude to Peril.* Palo Alto, Calif.: Pacific Books, 1947.

Potter, John Deane. *Yamamoto, The Man Who Menaced America.* New York: Viking Press, 1965.

Prange, Gordon W. *Tora! Tora! Tora!* Tokyo: Reader's Digest, 1966.

Roosevelt, Eleanor. *This I Remember.* New York: Harper & Brothers, 1949.

Roscoe, Theodore. *United States Destroyer Operations in World War II.* Annapolis: United States Naval Institute, 1953.

———. *United States Submarine Operations in World War II.* Annapolis: United States Naval Institute, 1949.

Sakamaki, Kazuo. *I Attacked Pearl Harbor.* New York: Association Press, 1949.

Schlesinger, Arthur M., Jr., and Roger Bruns, eds. *Congress Investigates: A Documented History, 1792–1974,* Vol. 5. New York: Chelsea House, 1975.

Schroeder, Paul W. *The Axis Alliance and Japanese-American Relations 1941.* Ithaca: Cornell University Press, 1958.

Sherwood, Robert E. *Roosevelt and Hopkins: An Intimate History.* New York: Harper & Brothers, 1948.

Sontag, Raymond James, and James Stuart Beddie, eds. *Nazi-Soviet Relations 1939–1941: Documents from the Archives of the German Foreign Office.* Washington, D.C.: Department of State, 1948.

Standley, Adm. William H., and RADM Arthur A. Ageton. *Admiral Ambassador to Russia.* Chicago: Henry Regnery Co., 1955.

Stimson, Henry L., and McGeorge Bundy. *On Active Service in Peace and War.* New York: Harper & Row, 1947.

Takagi, Sokichi. *Yamamoto Isoroku To Yonai Mitsumasa.* Tokyo: Bungei Shunju Shinsha, 1950.

Takei, Daisuke. *Yamamoto—Gensui Iei Kaisetsu.* Tokyo: Unedi Shobo, 1943.

Tansill, Charles C. *Back Door to War.* Chicago: Henry Regnery Co., 1952.

Terasaki, Gwen. *Bridge to the Sun.* Chapel Hill, N.C.: University of North Carolina Press, 1957.

Theobald, RADM. Robert A. *The Final Secret of Pearl Harbor.* New York: Devin-Adair Co., 1954.

Togo, Shigenori. *The Cause of Japan.* New York: Simon & Schuster, 1956.

Toland, John. *The Rising Sun: The Decline and Fall of the Japanese Empire, 1936–1945.* New York: Random House, 1970.

Tsunoda, Hitoshi, et al. *Hawai Sakusen.* Tokyo: Boeicho. Boei Kenshujo Senshishitsu, 1967.

Tully, Grace. *F.D.R., My Boss.* New York: Charles Scribner's Sons, 1949.

United States Department of State. *Papers Relating to the Foreign Relations of the United States: Japan, 1931–1941,* Vol. II. Washington, D.C., 1943.

Wallin, VADM. Homer N., USN (Ret.). *Pearl Harbor: Why, How, Fleet Salvage and Final Appraisal.* Washington, D.C.: Naval History Division, Department of the Navy, 1968.

Watson, Mark S. *United States Army in World War II: The War Department: Chief of Staff: Prewar Plans and Preparations.* Washington, D.C.: History Division, Department of the Army, 1950.

Watts, A. J., and B. G. Gordon. *The Imperial Japanese Navy.* Garden City, N.Y.: Doubleday & Co., 1971.

Whitehead, Don. *The FBI Story: A Report to the People.* New York: Random House, 1956.

Wilson, Rose Page. *General Marshall Remembered.* Englewood Cliffs, N.J.: Prentice-Hall, 1968.

Wohlstetter, Roberta. *Pearl Harbor, Warning and Decision.* Stanford, Calif.: Stanford University Press, 1962.

Zacharias, RADM. Ellis M. *Secret Missions.* New York: G. P. Putnam's Sons, 1946.

Newspapers

Albany (N.Y.) *Knickerbocker News*

Albuquerque *Journal*

Alexandria (Va.) *Gazette*

Annapolis *Evening Capital*

Arizona Republic (Phoenix)

Arkansas Gazette (Little Rock)

Asahi

Asheville *Citizen*

Atlanta *Constitution*

Augusta *Chronicle*

Baltimore *News-Post*

Baltimore *Sun*

Bangor *Daily Commercial*

Baton Rouge *State Times*

Birmingham (Ala.) *News*

Bismarck *Tribune*

Boise *Capital News*

Boston *Daily Globe*

Boston *Herald*

Boston *Post*

Boston *Sunday Globe*

Brooklyn *Eagle*

Burlington *Free Press and Times*
Charleston *Gazette*
Charlotte *News and Courier*
Charlotte *Observer*
Chattanooga *Times*
Cheyenne *Tribune*
Chicago *Daily News*
Chicago *Herald-American*
Chicago *Sun*
Chicago *Times*
Chicago *Tribune*
Christian Science Monitor
Chugai Shogyo
Cincinnati *Enquirer*
Cleveland *Plain Dealer*
Columbus *Evening Dispatch*
Daily Kennebec Journal (Augusta, Me.)
Daily Mail (London)
Daily Real Estate Report and Abstract of Records (Fresno, Calif.)
Daily Telegraph (London)
Daily Worker (New York, N.Y.)
Dallas *Morning News*
Denver *Post*
Des Moines *Register*
Detroit *Free Press*
Detroit *News*
Deutsche Allgemeine Zeitung
El Paso *Times*
Emporia *Gazette*
Evansville (Ind.) *Press*
Greensboro *Daily News*
Hartford (Conn.) *Courant*
Hartford (Conn.) *Times*
Henderson (Ky.) *Gleaner and Journal*
Hochi
Hong Kong *Telegraph*
Honolulu *Advertiser*
Honolulu *Star-Bulletin*
Houston *Post*
Idaho Sunday Statesman (Boise)
Indianapolis *News*
Indianapolis *Star*
Jackson (Miss.) *Clarion-Ledger*
Japan Advertiser (Tokyo)
Japan Chronicle (Kobe)
Japan Times (Tokyo)
Japan Times and Advertiser (Tokyo)
Japan Times and Mail (Tokyo)
Jefferson City (Mo.) *Daily Capital News*
Kansas City *Star*
Knoxville *Journal*
Kokumin
Lansing *State Journal*

Lewiston (Me.) *Evening Journal*
London Gazette
London *Times*
Los Angeles *Times*
Louisville *Courier-Journal*
Lynchburg *News*
Mainichi Shimbun
Manchester *Guardian*
Manchester (N.H.) *Union*
Meridian (Miss.) *Star*
Miami *Herald*
Milwaukee *Journal*
Milwaukee *Sentinel*
Miyako
Mobile *Register*
Montgomery *Advertiser*
Montpelier (Vt.) *Evening Argus*
Mount Vernon (Ohio) *News*
Muskogee (Okla.) *Daily Phoenix*
Nashville *Banner*
Nashville *Tennesseean*
Nevada State Journal (Reno)
Newark (N.J.) *News*
New Orleans *Times-Picayune*
New York *Daily News*
New York *Herald Tribune*
New York *Journal-American*
New York *P.M.*
New York *Post*
New York *Sun*
The New York Times
New York *Tribune*
Nichi Nichi
Nippon Times
Nippu Jiji (Honolulu)
Norfolk *Virginia-Pilot*
Omaha *World-Herald*
The Oregonian (Portland)
Oregon Journal (Portland)
Osaka Mainichi and Tokyo Nichi Nichi
Paducah *Sun-Democrat*
People's Daily World (San Francisco)
Philadelphia *Inquirer*
Philadelphia *Record*
Philippines Herald (Manila)
Pittsburgh *Post-Gazette*
Pittsburgh *Press*
Pittsburgh *Sun-Telegraph*
Portland (Me.) *Press Herald*
Providence *Journal*
Richmond (Va.) *Times-Dispatch*
Rochester *Democrat and Chronicle*
Rockford (Ill.) *Star*
Sacramento *Union*

St. Louis *Post-Dispatch*
St. Louis *Star-Times*
St. Paul *Pioneer Press*
Salt Lake Tribune (Salt Lake City, Utah)
San Antonio *Express*
San Francisco *Chronicle*
San Francisco *Daily Commercial News*
San Francisco *Examiner*
Seattle *Post-Intelligencer*
Seattle *Times*
Sioux City *Journal*
South Side Journal (St. Louis, Mo.)
Springfield *Union*
Stars and Stripes
The State (Columbia, S.C.)
Stockton (Calif.) *Daily Evening Record*
The Straits Budget (Singapore)
Tacoma *News-Tribune*
Toledo *Blade*

Topeka *Capital*
Tucson *Daily Citizen*
Tulsa *Daily Oklahoman*
Tulsa *Daily World*
Tulsa *Tribune*
Wall Street Journal (New York, N.Y.)
Washington *Daily News*
Washington *Evening Star*
Washington *News Digest*
Washington *Post*
Washington *Times-Herald*
Wheeling *News-Register*
Wilmington (Del.) *Evening Journal*
Wilmington (Del.) *Morning News*
Wisconsin State Journal (Madison)
Women's Voice (Chicago)
Wyoming State Tribune—Cheyenne State Leader
Yomiuri

Interviews

Capt. Fumio Aiko
Maj. Gen. Brooke E. Allen
Capt. Takahisa Amagai
Mrs. Mitsutaro Araki
Capt. Takayasu Arima
Dr. Harry Elmer Barnes
Capt. John R. Beardall, Jr.
CWO-4 Edgar B. Beck
Col. George W. Bicknell
Adm. Claude C. Bloch
Col. Rufus S. Bratton
RADM. William P. Burford
Mrs. William P. Burford
Cmdr. Masataka Chihaya
Lt. Col. Henry C. Clausen
VADM. Charles F. Coe
Gen. J. Lawton Collins
Mrs. Frank Cooper
John Crawford
Capt. Paul C. Crosley
Adm. Maurice E. Curts
Maj. Gen. Howard C. Davidson
Adm. Arthur C. Davis
Col. Charles W. Davis
Mrs. Charles W. Davis
Cleveland Davis
VADM. Walter DeLany
Rep. Martin Dies
Col. William E. Donegan
RADM. Milo F. Draemel

Brig. Gen. Robert H. Dunlop
Capt. Robert H. Dunlop, Jr.
VADM. George C. Dyer
Mrs. John B. Earle
Mrs. Stephen T. Early
Capt. Walter J. East
Mrs. Walter J. East
Lt. Tomatsu Ema
Juju Enomoto
Capt. Ruth A. Erickson
Col. William C. Farnum
Maj. Gen. William E. Farthing
Brig. Gen. Kendall J. Fielder
RADM. Carl K. Fink
Maj. Gen. Robert J. Fleming, Jr.
Brig. Gen. William J. Flood
CPO Thomas E. Forrow
CWO Alton W. Freeman
Howard C. French
Capt. Mitsuo Fuchida
Lt. Iyozo Fujita
VADM. Shigeru Fukudome
RADM. William Rhea Furlong
Capt. Minoru Genda
Judge Gerhard A. Gesell
Sen. Guy M. Gillette
Lt. Cmdr. Jinichi Goto
Capt. Lawrence C. Grannis
Ambassador Joseph C. Grew
Lt. Col. Francis Gutzak

VADM. Chuichi Hara
Cmdr. Toshio Hashimoto
Col. Takushiro Hattori
Col. Allen Haynes
Mrs. Allen Haynes
Capt. William H. Heydt
Lt. Gen. Charles D. Herron
Cmdr. Dermott Hickey
Capt. Wilfred J. Holmes
RADM. Teikichi Hori
VADM. Zenshiro Hoshina
Capt. Kijiro Imaizumi
VADM. Shigeyoshi Inoue
Cmdr. Susumu Ishiguro
Capt. Seiroku Ito
Cmdr. Doir C. Johnson
RADM. Takatsugu Jojima
Capt. Iwao Kawai
Mrs. Charles A. Kengla
RADM. Husband E. Kimmel
RADM. Kaneji Kishimoto
Capt. Keizo Komura
Adm. Nobutake Kondo
RADM. Kameto Kuroshima
VADM. Ryunosuke Kusaka
Lt. Gen. Truman H. Landon
RADM. Edwin T. Layton
Col. Emil Leard
Mrs. Emil Leard
Capt. Kosei Maeda
Maj. Gen. Morrill W. Marston
Adm. Harold M. Martin
Shigeharu Matsumoto
Lt. Heita Matsumura
RADM. Arthur H. McCollum
VADM. Gunichi Mikawa
RADM. Hisashi Mito
Capt. Tatsukichi Miyo
Shuichi "George" Mizota
Brig. Gen. James E. Mollison
Edward P. Morgan
Curtis B. Munson
RADM. Katsuhei Nakamura
Earl C. Nightingale
Fleet Adm. Chester W. Nimitz
Adm. Kichisaburo Nomura
RADM. Kanji Ogawa
Capt. Kyozo Ohashi
Capt. Toshikazu Ohmae
Capt. Atsushi Oi
Otojiro Okuda
RADM. Sentaro Omori
Capt. Sutegiro Onoda
Cmdr. Inao Otani

RADM. William W. Outerbridge
VADM. Jisaburo Ozawa
RADM. Harold F. Pullen
RADM. Allen G. Quynn
CPO Harry Rafsky
RADM. Logan C. Ramsey
Col. Vernon H. Reeves
David Richmond
RADM. Cecil D. Riggs
Cmdr. Joseph J. Rochefort
Adm. George A. Rood
RADM. Laurence A. Ruff
Cmdr. Goro Sakagami
Lt. Kazuo Sakamaki
Brig. Gen. George P. Sampson
Capt. Sadamu Sanagi
Capt. Akira Sasaki
RADM. Hanku Sasaki
Capt. Naohira Sata
VADM. Yorio Sawamoto
Lt. Col. John B. Schindel
Lt. Gen. Alan Shapley
Duane W. Shaw
Capt. Tatsuwaka Shibuya
Lt. Yoshio Shiga
Adm. Mitsumi Shimizu
Capt. Hisao Shimoda
RADM. James M. Shoemaker
Lt. Cmdr. Harley F. Smart
VADM. William Ward Smith
Mrs. William Ward Smith
Capt. Henri H. Smith-Hutton
Adm. Raymond A. Spruance
Capt. Eijiro Suzuki
Capt. Suguru Suzuji
Capt. Itaru Tachibana
RADM. Sokichi Takagi
Adm. Sankichi Takahashi
H.I.H. RADM. Prince Takamatsu (through
    Cmdr. Chihaya)
Mitsuari Takamura
Lt. Irvin H. Thesman
Col. Kenneth E. Thiebaud
Col. Russell C. Throckmorton
RADM. Minoru Togo
Adm. Soemu Toyoda
Adm. Harold C. Train
Adm. Nishizo Tsukahara
Lt. Yuzo Tsukamoto
RADM. Dundas P. Tucker
Grace Tully
Lt. Col. Kermit Tyler
Capt. Shigeshi Uchida
Capt. Yasuji Watanabe

James E. Webb
VADM. Charles Wellborn, Jr.
Maj. Gen. Durward S. Wilson
Mrs. Durward S. Wilson
Lt. Sadao Yamamoto
Adm. Katsunoshin Yamanashi
RADM. Shikazo Yano

Capt. Tadao Yokoi
Capt. Minoru Yokota
RADM. Ichiro Yokoyama
Adm. Zengo Yoshida
Takeo Yoshikawa
Cmdr. Chuichi Yoshioka
Mrs. Cassin B. Young

In addition to the above, a number who granted Dr. Prange interviews requested anonymity.

Statements

The following submitted written statements in lieu of or in addition to personal interviews:

Lt. Cmdr. Heijiro Abe
Lt. Cmdr. Zenji Abe
Capt. Minoru Genda
VADM. Chuichi Hara
Lt. Takashi Hashiguchi
Col. Takushiro Hattori
Lt. Masanobu Ibusuki
Lt. Cmdr. Takemi Iwami
Lt. Ichiro Kitajima
Lt. Heita Matsumura
Lt. Cmdr. Iwakichi Mifuku
First Petty Officer Kazuo Muranaka

Lt. Tamotsu Nakajima
Lt. Keizo Ofuchi
Lt. Kiyokuma Okajima
Otojiro Okuda
Lt. Yoshikazu Sato
Lt. Yoshio Shiga
Adm. Mitsumi Shimizu
Lt. Saburo Shindo
Capt. Itaru Tachibana
Lt. Haruo Takeda
Cmdr. Hiroshi Uwai

REVISIONISTS REVISITED

In Chapters 139 through 143 of his original manuscript for Volume Four of his book, Gordon Prange discussed the revisionist school at great length. The following is a summary:

While the Pearl Harbor attack united the American people, it was too much to ask that unity in the war effort would also create political unity. The legend began that Pearl Harbor was Roosevelt's fault—a legend that flourished in the postwar revisionist school.[1]

The more reasonable revisionists confined themselves to criticism of Roosevelt's approach to foreign affairs. William L. Neumann believed that American foreign policy before World War II was unsound because the Soviet Union was the ultimate gainer.[2] The major thrust of William Henry Chamberlin's book *America's Second Crusade* was that if the United States had kept out of the war, communism would have been contained.

Neumann's and Chamberlin's conclusions were arguable for two reasons. First, a President and his State Department cannot be lords of the future. And in 1941 any menace to the United States from the Russians and the Chinese was problematical, while the threat from the Nazis and the Japanese militarists was immediate. Secondly, their theses tacitly implied that if the United States stood aside while Hitler swallowed the British Empire and the Soviet Union, *der Führer* thereupon would settle down with a contented sigh, and the Third Reich and the United States would coexist like the lion and the lamb. Even the most cursory look at Hitler's record makes this notion questionable.

Another brand of revisionists believed that Roosevelt deliberately dragged the United States into the war. This group stopped short of claiming that he schemed to have the Japanese attack Pearl Harbor. For example, Charles A. Beard, in *President Roosevelt and the Coming of the War 1941*, wrote a blistering indictment of Roosevelt, his administration, and in particular, his foreign policy. According to Beard, the President was a warmonger who deceived the American people, violated his antiwar campaign pledge of 1940, and maneuvered the Japanese into firing the first shot.

Nowhere in his book did Beard directly accuse Roosevelt of knowing that the Japanese were going to attack Pearl Harbor. But he made his points in a subtle and sophisticated way. Without actually misquoting, he judiciously pruned the evidence. For example, he wrote, "Secretary Stimson testified before the Army Pearl Harbor Board that he was not surprised by the Japanese attack—on Pearl Harbor."[3] Here is the actual exchange in question: Russell asked Stimson, "Then you were not surprised at the air attack on the 7th of December?" Stimson replied, "Well, I was not surprised, in one sense, in any attack that would be made; but I was watching with considerably more care, because I knew more about it, the attack that was framing up in the southwestern Pacific. . . ."[4] This conveys quite a different impression from Beard's selective extract.

Percy L. Greaves, Jr., too, conceded, "Washington did not know, or at least no evidence has been adduced that Washington knew, precisely, that the attack would fall on Pearl Harbor although they [sic] had good reason to expect that it might."[5]

John T. Flynn, in his pamphlet *The Truth About Pearl Harbor*, believed that the President "wanted to provoke Japan to attack. But he . . . certainly never looked for an attack that would kill 3,000 Americans and knock the American Navy and Army out of the war in a day. . . ."[6]

Harry Elmer Barnes was the leading spirit of the thesis that Roosevelt had planned the whole thing deliberately, knew about the attack on Pearl Harbor in advance, and wanted it to happen. He believed the President guilty of a triple conspiracy. First, Roosevelt needed an attack on this country because of his campaign promise that Americans would not be sent to war unless the United States was attacked. Secondly, to permit such an attack unobstructed, he arranged that Kimmel and Short should receive none of the information available in Washington from Japanese decoded material. Thirdly, he conspired to cover up the failure to warn the Hawaiian commanders.[7]

A surprising number of naval personnel interviewed for this study fell into the Roosevelt-planned-it category.[8] To such dedicated Navy men it seemed impossible that the U.S. Pacific Fleet could have been so appallingly surprised and defeated unless treachery had been involved, and they identified with Kimmel's interests. ". . . I am glad to learn you are going ahead on Kimmel," wrote Rear Admiral Dundas P. Tucker to Lieutenant Commander Charles C. Hiles on June 2, 1968, "because you will be clearing not only him, but the professional Navy as a whole. . . ."[9]

Some of the more vociferous revisionists were careless with facts. Although Chamberlin's book was published in 1950, by which time the composition of Nagumo's task force was known, Chamberlin stated that it was "under the command of Admiral Isoroku Yamamoto. . . ." Such a mistake is not evidence of bad faith, but it is the sort of factual error that casts doubt upon a historian's credibility. Chamberlin also wrote, "As early as November 28 it was known in Washington that a Japanese flotilla . . . was steaming down the China coast toward an unknown destination. Only the main objective of the impending offensive, Pearl Harbor . . . did not visibly figure in Japanese calculations." Of course, this fleet was not the one headed for Hawaii, as a glance at the map would show. Further, Chamberlin would have us believe that "The commanders on the spot were encouraged to maintain a normal, 'business as usual' attitude until the attack actually took place. . . ."[10] This was far from the case.

Rear Admiral Robert A. Theobald's book *The Final Secret of Pearl Harbor* was the quintessence of revisionism. It pictured the Navy as a collective Andromeda chained to the rock of Pearl Harbor while Roosevelt and subsidiary vultures Stimson, Marshall, *et al.* hovered around, waiting for the Japanese dragon to play its predestined part. In reviewing this book, Commander Masataka Chihaya, formerly of the Imperial Japanese Navy, put his finger on the key weakness of this position: "Even if one admits Adm. Theobald's assertion that President Roosevelt wanted to have Japan strike first, there would have been no need to have all the major ships of the U.S. Fleet sit idly in the harbor to be mercilessly destroyed and many killed."[11]

Such a blood sacrifice was by no means necessary to force the American people to accept entry into the war. The loss of men, ships, and planes grieved and shocked the nation; what angered it, as we have seen, was Japan's striking under cover of diplomacy before declaring war.

No such considerations disturbed Barnes. According to him, when Hitler did not oblige by attacking the United States:

> . . . it became essential for Roosevelt to do all possible to assure that Japan would provide the indispensable attack that was needed to unite the American people behind him in the war. To bring this about it appeared necessary to prevent Hawaiian commanders from taking any offensive action which would deter the Japanese from attacking Pearl Harbor which, of necessity had to be a surprise attack.[12]

This peculiar concept ignores two facts: The Japanese never expected Operation Hawaii to be a shoo-in, and the reason for the Hawaiian Department's existence was to protect the Fleet and the Islands against a Japanese attack.

Therefore, if the President planned to enter the war by the so-called back door, every dictate of common sense urged that he take Kimmel and Short into his confidence, at least to the extent of warning them that the Japanese were coming. In that case, the Pacific Fleet's carrier task forces would have been lying in wait, reinforced by the battleships; the radar systems would have been operating at full strength; reconnaissance aircraft, destroyers, and submarines would have been scouting the area; antiaircraft batteries would have been in position with ammunition at the ready; the Hawaiian Air Force's planes would have been fueled, armed, and poised for immediate takeoff. Under those circumstances Pearl Harbor could have been an entirely different story, as the Japanese acknowledge.[13]

Barnes assumed that if Nagumo knew his target had been alerted, he would have called off the strike.[14] Research shows that during Kusaka's briefing at Hitokappu Bay the admiral stated that if the enemy sighted the task force before X-Day minus one, Nagumo would return to Japan. But if the Americans spotted only part of the Japanese fleet, Nagumo would change course and proceed toward Oahu. Moreover—and this is most important—if fired on, the Japanese would fight it out. Genda echoed these instructions.[15]* But it is difficult to regard as realistic the suggestion that Operation Hawaii would or could have been aborted had the Americans discovered the task force before December 6. Nothing in the planning and training for the venture lends credence to the idea that Nagumo was to scratch the mission if sighted.

Barnes's theory assumes that Nagumo had complete control of the situation and could go ahead or turn homeward at will. But on December 6 Nagumo was well east of Midway, heading southeast. That night he turned due south. Even in the best of times a Japanese carrier task force would have difficulty explaining its presence in that location. It is absurd to suggest that in December 1941 a U.S. fleet encountering Nagumo's armada would figuratively say, "Anybody can get lost. Just go home and no harm done."

---

*See Chapter 46.

Then, too, the whole object of the attack was to destroy Kimmel's ships wherever they might be found, in port or at sea. In fact, the Japanese would have preferred to sink their prey in waters deep enough to swallow them forever. Therefore, it is probable that had Nagumo encountered a U.S. task force while he was en route to Pearl Harbor, he would have attacked at once, not turned tail.

Most important, a ready foe was precisely what Nagumo expected. Yamamoto had instructed him and his officers that they must be prepared to fight their way in to the target. When they actually did achieve complete surprise, the Japanese were as amazed as they were elated.

In brief, Barnes and some of his followers indulged in a prime example of reverse logic. With all the force at their command, these people wanted to prove Roosevelt guilty of Pearl Harbor. To do so, they had to convince the public that the President deliberately withheld information from Kimmel and Short. And the only way to make sense of that concept was to hypothesize that the Japanese would have turned back if detected.

Yet had Kimmel taken the actions which the Navy Department expected when it issued the war warning of November 27, he would have been alerted and scouting his sea area for possible intruders. Suppose he found them? Stark, no firebrand, testified that if the enemy were spotted within 800 miles north of Oahu, he would have fired. [16] No doubt the much more aggressive Kimmel would have done the same. Failure to do so would have, in Gerow's words, "jeopardized his defense" and constituted failure to obey the warning contained in the message of November 27. [17]

Neither Stark nor Gerow considered such a forceful meeting of an obvious peril to constitute an "overt act" within the meaning of the warning message. While Washington wanted the Japanese to bear the onus of aggression, it certainly did not intend Kimmel and Short to stand still to be attacked if they knew danger was approaching. Had the defenders of Hawaii discovered and tried to fight off the Japanese task force, there would have been the shooting war, without the element of surprise and with no help from Roosevelt.

If the revisionists claimed that the President lured the Japanese into sending the bulk of their carrier strength across the Pacific so that the U.S. Navy could destroy it, this would make sense strategically. It would be Japan's Great All-Out Battle concept in reverse. However, Prange thought it an absurdity to assert that Roosevelt risked the prime units of the U.S. Pacific Fleet—the very tactical tools the United States would need in a Pacific conflict—to justify a declaration of war.

Kimmel attempted to reconcile this incongruity with his own firm conviction of Roosevelt's and Marshall's guilt. In an interview with Neumann, Kimmel stated that he did not believe they "wanted to sacrifice the Pacific Fleet." He thought, as did Neumann, that ". . . they assumed that one American could deal with five Japanese and that even a surprise attack would be beaten off without great losses. . . ." [18]

Nevertheless, if by some quirk of logic one could accept tethering a few obsolescent battleships in Pearl Harbor to tempt the Japanese, one boggles at the idea of staking out the whole military establishment on Oahu for that purpose. The revisionist position implied that Roosevelt and his advisers knew that the Japanese would hit the ships rather than the much more strategically and logistically important shore installations and fuel supply. Washington had no way to determine this. In fact, sound strategy dictated the reverse and, as we have seen, all concerned could not believe that the attackers would sail away without striking these vital targets.

Furthermore, any "baiting" on Roosevelt's part presumably would be aimed at

Tokyo's foreign policy level, including the War and Navy ministries and indirectly the General Staffs. Yet those were the very elements that fought the Pearl Harbor plan tooth and nail. The President could not hypnotize Yamamoto into planning to attack Pearl Harbor and imbue him with the courage to buck the Naval General Staff. Certainly Roosevelt could not foresee that organization's folding up under Yamamoto's threat to resign.

Another consideration reduced the extreme revisionist thesis to its ultimate absurdity. How could the President ensure a successful Japanese surprise attack unless he confided in the Hawaiian commanders and persuaded them to allow the enemy to proceed unhindered? Kimmel's and Short's business was to be on the alert at all times. Roosevelt would have to assume that the Hawaiian outpost would be on its toes. To carry the revisionist theory to its logical conclusion, one would have to include as parties to the plot Kimmel, Short, their subordinate commanders, and key members of their staffs. In no other way could the alleged plotters have ensured that the Japanese would come in unopposed.

One of the principal, if unofficial, objectives of the congressional committee was to clarify Roosevelt's role in relation to Pearl Harbor. But a number of publications had already made up their minds. In September 1945 John Chamberlain asserted in *Life*, ". . . Roosevelt . . . knew in advance that the Japanese were going to attack us. There is even ground for suspicion that he elected to bring the crisis to a head when it came."[19]

For sheer scurrility, however, we could award the wreath of poison ivy to a small Chicago newspaper, *Women's Voice*, which editorialized on December 27, 1951, concerning alleged events on Oahu: "The order the night before, to go into town, to get drunk. . . . Those who returned to the ships in the night were kept from coming on board by officers with drawn revolvers. . . ." Planes had been defueled "to make absolutely sure that no plane could be gotten into the air. . . ." A staff sergeant, prudently unidentified, claimed that he did take off in his aircraft. And what did he find? ". . . planes manned by white men, men whom I knew—British and Americans. There seemed to be a few Japs, but the shooting was done by white men . . ." Three other young men contributed enthusiastically to this myth: "There were Jap planes mixed in, but a lot of them did not shoot, and we afterward found they were photo fellows. . . ."

A "civilian contractor" put on the capstone: "He said it was well known that Roosevelt with Churchill's help planned the whole thing, and called in the Japs to help, promising them the Philippine Islands." That remark really ties up the revisionist package with a neat bow. If one believes this article, Roosevelt did not merely bait the Japanese into attacking; he bribed them into partnership. And the Japanese did not truly attack at all; the Americans with a few British did it. The Japanese just trailed along to take pictures.

Another widely circulated myth claimed that Roosevelt knew about the Pearl Harbor attack well in advance thanks to the Soviet Union. This tale credits Richard Sorge, head of the famous communist spy ring in Tokyo, with learning about Japan's plan to strike Hawaii and passing the information to Moscow, which thereupon informed Washington. A host of correspondents and writers bought this yarn and from it wove a whole fabric of indictments and unverified conclusions.[20] However, a slight tug at the end of the yarn unravels the whole fabric. Research reveals that Sorge did not crack the Pearl Harbor secret, hence could not advise Moscow, which hence could not advise Washington, which hence could not sit on the information.

The Roosevelt-as-villain thesis tacitly assumed that if Pearl Harbor had not occurred, the United States would not have entered the war. Yet if the Naval General

Staff had vetoed Yamamoto's plan or if, once under way, Nagumo had aborted the air attack, the political situation between the two countries would not have changed. Precisely the same forces that launched the war would have remained—the same tensions between Tokyo and Washington, the same conflicts of interest, the same ideological antagonisms, the same determination on Japan's part to absorb Southeast Asia into its Co-Prosperity Sphere, the same American commitment to China; the same obligation on the part of Washington to protect American territory and citizens outside the continental United States.

Japan's massive Southern Operation for the conquest of Southeast Asia and command of the western Pacific was under way well before December 7, 1941. And that offensive included an attack on U.S. forces in the Philippines preparatory to taking over the islands. Can one seriously believe that Washington would have shrugged off such an attack on American lives and property as Japan delivered against the Philippines?

Nor were Japan's belligerent actions triggered by Hull's so-called ultimatum of November 26. The Pearl Harbor games of September 16, 1941, were predicated upon an X-Day of November 16.[21] Only when it became evident that the task force could not be ready by that date was the attack postponed until December 7.

Prange hesitated to deal in absolutes, for he believed that the human equation was always subject to change without notice, but in the context of the time, he felt that war between Japan and the United States was virtually inevitable by late 1941, Pearl Harbor or no Pearl Harbor.

He also believed that one must consider the situation in the Atlantic, which could scarcely have been more explosive. Both Washington and Berlin had ignored incidents that gave at least technical excuse for declaring war. Almost certainly, sooner or later something would have happened that the United States or Germany would have found impossible to brush aside. If Roosevelt wanted war, he had no reason to push for it in the Pacific, especially in such an insane manner as encouraging the Japanese to hit Pearl Harbor.

Roosevelt never pretended to be neutral in thought and paid only lip service to neutrality in deed. He sailed exceedingly close to the wind. Yet he knew that the United States was not ready militarily to take up the terrible burden to which history called it. Hence the apparent inconsistency of American actions in the late autumn of 1941. Perhaps no President ever faced a more cruel dilemma than Roosevelt at that time. One may well believe that he felt an enormous release from tension when the Japanese took him off the hook. The entire timing of Pearl Harbor argued against the revisionist position. Throughout 1940 and 1941 U.S. diplomacy vis-à-vis Japan reflected a determined, almost frantic desire to buy time while the armed forces built up to the point where the country could become the "arsenal of democracy" and at the same time be able to resist Axis aggression in both theaters. On December 7, 1941, they still had a long way to go. Deliberately to bring about the very eventuality against which both Army and Navy had pleaded would have been the sheerest madness.

What is more, Germany need not have invoked the Tripartite Pact when Japan struck the United States. The treaty called for Japan and Germany to come to each other's aid if attacked by a power not then in the war. Nothing was said about mutual aid if Germany, Japan, or Italy did the attacking. Japan used this loophole to escape joining its Axis partner in the Russo-German war, so why should Hitler feel any obligation toward the ally that had turned him down?

In his speech of December 8, 1941, asking Congress to declare "a state of war" with Japan, Roosevelt carefully avoided including Germany, although Stimson urged him to do so. The fact that Hitler decided upon war with the United States was probably less to honor the Tripartite Pact than a practical decision that the time was ripe. Otherwise, Hitler could have played a diplomatic masterstroke by disassociating himself from Japan's action. This would have given the United States and Great Britain precisely what they did not want—a war in Asia that would divide British strength and drain off American arms and supplies from the European front.

Basic to the argument that Roosevelt wanted to haul the United States into war by way of Japan is the assumption that during much of 1941 the President had a secret agreement with Churchill that if Japan struck British territory, the United States would enter the conflict. Revisionists hold to this theory tenaciously despite evidence to the contrary.

Of course, the beleaguered British desired the United States as an active ally. But—and this is what the revisionists did not appear to understand—the British believed that a firm commitment from the United States in regard to the Far East would be the surest way of guaranteeing Japan's good behavior. Churchill yearned to see full American might brought to bear in the Atlantic. But preattack documents make it quite clear that he wanted Japan reined in lest it cut the British lifeline in the Indian Ocean.[22] So he would have preferred American involvement in Europe without the British being plunged into a major war in the Far East. In a telegram to Roosevelt on May 15, 1940, he listed Britain's "immediate needs," which ended, "Sixthly, I am looking to you to keep that Japanese dog quiet in the Pacific. . . ."[23]

By October 1940 matters had simmered down sufficiently for Churchill to risk reopening the Burma Road. He asked Roosevelt if the President could send a large American squadron "to pay a friendly visit to Singapore. . . ." He explained, "I should be very grateful if you would consider action along these lines as it might play an important part in preventing the spreading of the war."[24]

Churchill realized that a formal British-American alliance against Japan would entail certain risks. Japan might lower its head and charge instead of pulling in its horns. Nor did Churchill minimize the problems war with Japan would pose. But in his view, ". . . the entry of the United States into the war would overwhelm all evils put together."[25] So Churchill, as positive a thinker as ever, looked for the silver lining, and was prepared to make the best of it regardless of which way the Japanese jumped.

There could be no question that most American hearts, as well as the national interests, pulled toward the white cliffs of Dover. And Roosevelt, backed by a majority of Congress, had bent neutrality far off center with the lend-lease arrangement. Therefore, the United States most urgently wanted to concentrate upon the Atlantic and avoid a confrontation with Japan. Stark's famous Plan DOG laid it on the line: "Any strength that we might send to the Far East would, by just so much, reduce the force of our blows against Germany and Italy."[26]*

Greaves asserted, "Early in 1941 administration officials reached a secret agreement with British and Dutch officials, which committed us to go to war against Japan if Japanese forces crossed a certain line."[27] It so happened that representatives of the U.S. and British Army and Navy staffs held discussions in Washington from January 29 to March 27, 1941. These discussions culminated in a secret military agreement (ABC-1 of March 1941).[28] Roosevelt did not approve ABC-1, but the United States later amended Rainbow Five (its major war plan) to fit this strategy. Attempts were made at Singapore in April 1941 to work out an American-British-Dutch operating plan for the Pacific which set forth certain Japanese actions, which failure to counteract would place the signatories

---

*See Chapter 5.

at a military disadvantage.[29] Doubtless this is the "secret agreement" to which Greaves referred. However, both Marshall and Stark withheld approval because, among other reasons, ABC contained "political matters" and the proposals set forth did not constitute "a practical operating plan."[30] These plans and discussions did not commit the United States politically to go to war with Japan, Germany, or both; they outlined the military strategy to be followed if the country joined the conflict.

The transferring of ships from the Pacific to the Atlantic and the institution of patrols in that ocean strained neutrality.* Still, all this de facto support fell short of a formal alliance. Never famous for consistency, Roosevelt could have called a halt should circumstances appear so to dictate.

The famous meeting between Roosevelt and Churchill in Argentia Bay is a favorite target of revisionists. Barnes entertained no doubt that at Argentia Roosevelt and Churchill "arranged the details of entering the second World War through the backdoor of a war with Japan."[31] Actually Churchill's prime consideration in the Pacific was not to spread the war but to contain it. He feared that the Japanese Navy might cut Britain's lifeline to the Commonwealth. And he believed that only a firm declaration of mutual commitment by the United States, the British Empire, the Netherlands, and perhaps the Soviet Union would restrain Japan.[32]

For all of Roosevelt's sympathy with the British, at Argentia he knew that the time was not ripe for a promise to threaten Japan with war for the sake of a third party. All moral considerations aside, he held a very poor hand. The United States was militarily unprepared to challenge Japan and in short order might be in even worse shape. In a few days the draft extension would come before the House of Representatives. If Congress scuttled the draft, the United States would not have enough of an army to defend itself, let alone help anyone else. What actually happened as a result of Argentia was that Roosevelt presented to Nomura a note promising to take "any and all steps which it may deem necessary" to safeguard the rights of American nationals and the security of the nation. It contained no word about American action in the event the Japanese attacked British or Dutch territory.[33]*

Matters took a sharp turn on December 1, when Roosevelt met with Harry Hopkins and British Ambassador Lord Halifax. He thought the time had come for London and Washington to "settle what they would do in the various situations which might arise." If Japan attacked the British or Dutch, they "should obviously be all together. . . ." But to clear up certain matters "which were less plain," he wanted Halifax to ask for his government's policies in various eventualities.

Halifax already had instructions to tell the United States government that the British expected the Japanese to hit Thailand. Such an attack probably would include "a seaborne expedition to seize strategic points in the Kra Isthmus." The British "proposed to counter this . . . by a rapid move by sea into the Isthmus" to hold a line just north of Singone. But because of the dangerous political disadvantages should the Japanese beat the British to the punch, London "wanted to know urgently what view the United States Government would take of this plan, since it was most important for us to be sure of American support in the event of war."

Roosevelt assured the ambassador that his country "could certainly count on American support, though it might take a few days before it was given."[34]

On December 2 Churchill informed Foreign Minister Anthony Eden by memorandum:

---

*See Chapters 15 and 16.
*See Chapter 23.

. . . If the United States declares war on Japan, we follow within the hour. If, after a reasonable interval, the United States is found to be incapable of taking any decisive action, even with our immediate support, we will, nevertheless, although alone, make common cause with the Dutch.[35]

Thus Churchill pledged support to the United States in much less equivocal terms than those Roosevelt used to Halifax.

Despite all these developments, Churchill and his government could not be certain that American "support" in Southeast Asia would mean that the United States would enter the European war. Hitler had only to keep his brown shirt on, and Great Britain might find itself with war on another front, assured of American "support" but not necessarily armed participation, and with the United States still out of the major conflict in Europe.

On the evening of December 3 Roosevelt informed Halifax that the British could count on "armed support." But the British understood that he still clung to a faint hope that he might work out a temporary truce with Japan through his personal approach to the Emperor.[36]

So, after dodging the issue all year, on December 1 Roosevelt promised the British support in the Far East, and on December 3 armed support. The reason was clear: The problem was no longer one of restraining the Japanese; they were on the move. The only question was exactly where they would strike first. Of course, Roosevelt could not commit the United States to war with Japan on behalf of the British, the Dutch, the Thais, or anyone else. For this he would need congressional authority. "Armed support" for the British did not automatically involve going to war on their behalf; the United States had been giving Britain "armed support" against Hitler for months while technically clinging to neutrality.

In any case, the President's somewhat equivocal commitment came much too late to have any relationship to the Pearl Harbor attack. Throughout 1941, while Roosevelt hesitated and the British fretted, the Japanese planned and trained for Operation Hawaii. By December 5 Nagumo had received orders to "Climb Mount Niitaka" and his ships' prows were irrevocably headed eastward. Shimizu's submarines were lurking in Hawaiian waters. Above all, neither Yamamoto nor the Naval General Staff was considering Roosevelt's preferences. The Japanese based their naval strategy upon the foreign policy of one country and one only—Japan.

Now let us consider a few incidents not previously mentioned in this study. These occurred in the week before Pearl Harbor, and all appeared highly suspicious, if not downright proof of Roosevelt's guilt in the eyes of certain revisionists. One of the best known of these incidents is that of the "three little ships."

Stark had been speculating with the President about the ultimate target area of the Japanese expedition headed south. To assist in reaching a conclusion, Roosevelt directed that a special mission of three small vessels be dispatched toward the Indochina coast as pickets.[37] Accordingly, on December 2, 1941, the Navy Department instructed Hart to comply "as soon as possible and within two days if possible. . . ." The little craft were to "establish identity as U.S. men-of-war." One was "to be stationed between Hainan and Hue, one vessel off the Indo-China Coast between Camranh Bay and Cape St. Jacques, and one vessel off Pointe de Camau."[38]

The Navy was not particularly thrilled with this mission because it was already receiving information about those areas from Hart's aerial reconnaissance.[39] And Hart did not seem to feel any sense of urgency: ". . . the *Isabel* was dispatched in consequence of this instruction and was nearing her station when the Japanese attack occurred. The second one to be made ready was on the point of sailing and third was not yet ready."[40] *Isabel* departed on December 3 and on the afternoon of the fifth sighted the coast of Indochina. Ten minutes later she received orders to return immediately to Manila.[41]

In a wild flight of imagination Barnes wrote, "If the *Isabel* episode had been handled in the manner that Roosevelt wished and provided the maximum provocation to trigger-happy Japanese pilots or gunners there might not have been any attack on Pearl Harbor and the fleet there could have been saved."[42] This is leaping to conclusions with a vengeance. As the reader knows, Nagumo had exacted from Yamamoto an ironclad promise that no Japanese shot would be fired in Southeast Asia until he had commenced his attack on Pearl Harbor. Moreover, the Japanese were not striking Pearl Harbor just to oblige Roosevelt. They were out to immobilize the U.S. Pacific Fleet for at least six months. A hunter looking for bear will not call off the chase because someone else in the party has bagged a field mouse.

What exactly did Roosevelt have in mind? So far no evidence has come to light beyond what is contained in the message initiating the mission. But anyone who had followed Roosevelt's career in relation to the Navy could have predicted that sooner or later he probably would engage in some such stunt. His track record shows that he had a well-nigh indestructible faith in small craft.[43] It was quite in character that he should want to use the "three little ships" for scouting even though Hart was already covering the job by aerial reconnaissance. The project was not one of Roosevelt's brighter ideas, but there is no concrete reason to cite it as an example of malice aforethought.

Three messages from widely separated sources provided the revisionists with more grist for their mill. One of these originated with the U.S. military attaché in Australia, Colonel Van S. Merle–Smith. He and his assistant, Lieutenant Robert H. O'Dell, attended a conference in Melbourne on December 4. This conference "principally concerned itself with the movement of a Jap Task Force in the South China Sea."

As a result of this meeting, Merle–Smith instructed O'Dell to prepare a cable concerning the convoy and the fact that "the Dutch had ordered the execution of the Rainbow Plan, A-2." This shook up O'Dell considerably. "That was to go into effect only in case of war and here the Dutch had ordered it." Air Chief Marshal Sir Charles Burnett, chief of staff of the Royal Australian Air Force, asked Merle–Smith to hold up the cable until he had reported the information at a meeting of the War Cabinet scheduled for that evening. Meanwhile, O'Dell coded the cable, preparing one for MacArthur and one for Short, with the request that the latter repeat the dispatch to Washington. The attachés did not notify G-2 in Washington because of the time factor.[44]

Another reason impelling Merle-Smith to contact Short directly was the understanding "that A-2 fell into the Rainbow Plan and that certain action was called for by the American Navy under Plan A-2" and Short "would naturally inform the Navy" that the Dutch had activated it.[45]

Why, if he believed this to be a matter involving the U.S. Navy, did not Merle–Smith turn the problem over to his naval colleague, Captain Charles A. Coursey? He was informed of the incident, but O'Dell did not believe Coursey sent a message. "I'm not qualified to say for certain," O'Dell testified, "but he was not in the same state that we were about it."[46]

Perhaps Coursey took the incident more calmly because the Navy was already in close touch with the Dutch and British about those Japanese ship movements. In any case, it is well-nigh impossible to picture Kimmel sending his Fleet off to war on the basis of fifth-hand information—Dutch to Australians to U.S. attachés to Short to

Kimmel. At the very least the admiral would have sought confirmation from Washington. As it happened, the Hawaiian Department did not decode the message but sent it to the War Department to be decoded and repeated. The record indicates that the message was received in the War Department Message Center at "7:58 P.M." on December 7.[47]

When Barnes discovered this message, he was sure that he had a great scoop. Morgenstern, Greaves, and later Ladislas Farago had mentioned the subject but "did not develop its full significance."[48] Either unable or unwilling to see the difference between a war plan and a duly ratified treaty or pact, Barnes declared that "the United States had been put into war with Japan by the action of the Dutch government, on December 3rd, Washington time. . . ." He decided that once more the authorities in Washington had deliberately withheld another warning from Short. "It certainly could have been sent to Short in time to produce an alert during the 5th, Washington time, and averted the Japanese attack on Pearl Harbor. . . ." The fact that the records indicate the War Department did not receive the message until about five hours after the attack had begun did not faze Barnes in the least. He concluded that the times of dispatch and receipt had been doctored.[49]

All of which was drawing a long bow because Rainbow Five was not an instrument to declare war; it was a plan for conducting the war once it started. Moreover, the Netherlands East Indies had no authority to commit the United States to war, regardless of what actions the Dutch took or recommended for their own protection.

Another message helped convince Theobald, for one, that war with Japan had already been arranged. This dispatch went from Budapest to Tokyo on December 7, 1941: "On the 6th, the American Minister presented to the Government of this country a British Government communiqué to the effect that a state of war would break out on the 7th."[50]

Obsessed with Roosevelt's alleged iniquities, Theobald jumped to this conclusion: "Everyone in Washington and London, acquainted with Magic, was convinced that Japan would initiate war with the Anglo-Saxon nations that day. The British Government had so informed the Hungarian Government the day before."[51]

Actually this message had nothing to do with Japan and the United States. On December 6 Great Britain had served notice on the Hungarians—and the Finns and Rumanians—that if they did not agree to cease fighting the Soviet Union, London would declare war on them. This action was meaningless to the British war effort but would place these satellite countries on the Axis side of the table in peace talks after the conflict ended. Anyone could have determined the meaning of the Budapest-Tokyo message by checking the newspapers for December 6, 1941, where the story generally merited the front page.[52]

The third of these messages went to Hart from Captain John M. Creighton, the U.S. naval observer at Singapore. This arrived in Manila on December 7 and quoted a dispatch that Air Chief Marshal Sir Robert Brooke-Popham, British Commander in Chief, Far East, had received from London outlining three circumstances under which the British had "received assurance of American armed support" and authorized him to activate if necessary his defense plans covering those eventualities without reference to London.[53]

The congressional committee tried unsuccessfully to pinpoint the exact source of Creighton's information, but Creighton had forgotten. He had advised Hart because he considered it his duty "to try to give him any current information or reports. . . ." He realized "that a policy involving whether we were going to assist Britain in a contingency had to come from Washington," not London.[54] So did Hart, apparently, for he radioed OPNAV with an information copy to CinCPAC at about 0645 GMT on December 7: "Learn from Singapore we have assured British armed support under three or four eventualities. Have received no corresponding instructions from you."[55]

Therein lay the problem. However Creighton received the word, it was accurate, and had Washington been as prompt to clue in its armed forces as London had been, much confusion at the time, and much postwar suspicion, could have been avoided. Gerow, for example, knew of "no such assurances" as Hart cited.[56] Noyes assumed Hart's message to be "somebody misinterpreting the ABC agreement," which of course was "purely a military agreement. . . ."[57]

Certainly the United States was not formally allied to Great Britain until Congress so declared. But revisionists continued to assert that, in Barnes's words, "Roosevelt knew by the forenoon of the 6th, if not on the 5th, that the United States was already at war with Japan due to our commitments to the British and Dutch under ABCD and Rainbow 5."[58]

Revisionists such as Barnes and Theobald believed their tissue of unsupported assumptions and assertions. By the same token, those who cannot swallow their thesis are not necessarily blind adulators of Roosevelt. The President made his mistakes in 1941, as did almost everyone else involved in Pearl Harbor. But in a thorough search of more than thirty years, including all publications released up to May 1, 1981, we have not discovered one document or one word of sworn testimony that substantiates the revisionist position on Roosevelt and Pearl Harbor.

Donald M. Goldstein
Katherine V. Dillon

Notes: Revisionists Revisited

1. Some major revisionist books include Charles A. Beard, *President Roosevelt and the Coming of the War 1941*; William Henry Chamberlin, *America's Second Crusade*; John T. Flynn, *The Roosevelt Myth*; George Morgenstern, *Pearl Harbor*; Frederic R. Sanborn, *Design For War*; Charles C. Tansill, *Back Door to War*; Robert A. Theobald, *The Final Secret of Pearl Harbor*; Harry E. Barnes, ed., *Perpetual War for Perpetual Peace* and *The Court Historians versus Revisionism*; Husband E. Kimmel, *Admiral Kimmel's Story*.
2. William S. Neumann, "How American Policy Toward Japan Contributed to War in the Pacific," *Perpetual War for Perpetual Peace*, p. 265.
3. Charles A. Beard, *President Roosevelt and the Coming of the War 1941* (New Haven, Conn., 1948), p. 373.
4. *PHA*, Part 29, p. 2080.
5. Percy L. Greaves, Jr., "The Pearl Harbor Investigations," *Perpetual War for Perpetual Peace*, p. 425.
6. John T. Flynn, *The Truth About Pearl Harbor* (pamphlet privately printed in New York City, 1944), pp. 3, 13, 28.
7. See, for example, Harry E. Barnes, "What Happened at Pearl Harbor?" *Peace News* (London), December 7, 1962.
8. Gordon W. Prange, interviews with Crawford and Rafsky, August 8, 1964; Johnson, August 8, 1964; Smart, August 21, 1964; Burford, August 18, 1964; Forrow, August 16, 1964.
9. Hiles Papers, Box 15.
10. William Henry Chamberlin, *America's Second Crusade* (Chicago, 1950), pp. 165, 120, 159.
11. *Nippon Times*, May 2, 1954.
12. "Pearl Harbor After a Quarter of a Century," p. 18.
13. *Nippon Times*, May 3, 1954.
14. "Pearl Harbor After a Quarter of a Century," p. 90.
15. Gordon W. Prange, interview with Genda, August 31, 1947.
16. *PHA*, Part 5, pp. 2475–76.
17. Ibid., Part 4, p. 1671.
18. Letter, Neumann to Barnes, June 21, 1961, Barnes Papers, Box 58.
19. John Chamberlain, "Pearl Harbor," *Life* (September 10, 1945), p. 110.
20. See, for example, John O'Donnell's column "Capitol Stuff," New York *Daily News*, May 17, 1954; Ralph de Toledano, *Spies, Dupes and Diplomats* (New York and Boston, 1952), p. 4; Hans-Otto Meissner, *The Man with Three Faces* (New York, 1956), p. 218. Dr. Prange made a special study of the Sorge case. A condensation of his manuscript book on the subject appeared in the *Reader's Digest* (January 1967) under the title "Master Spy."

21. *Hawaii Sakusen*, pp. 102–103.
22. See Sumner Welles's "Memorandum of Conversation" with Churchill on this subject, *PHA*, Part 14, pp. 1273–74.
23. Roosevelt Papers, Map Room File, Box 1.
24. Telegram, Churchill to Roosevelt. October 4, 1940, Roosevelt Papers, Map Room File, Box 1.
25. Winston S. Churchill, *The Grand Alliance* (Boston, 1950), pp. 587–88.
26. Roosevelt Papers, PSF, Box 63.
27. "The Pearl Harbor Investigations," *op cit.*, p. 410.
28. The text of ABC-1 is reproduced in *PHA*, Part 15, pp. 1485–1550.
29. *PHA*, Part 15, p. 1564. See pp. 1551–84 for full text of ABD.
30. Ibid., pp. 1678–79. For an excellent account of these prewar discussions and plans, see Mark S. Watson, *Chief of Staff: Prewar Plans and Preparations* (Washington, 1950), pp. 367–410. This volume is one of the series *United States in World War II*, subseries *The War Department*.
31. "Pearl Harbor After a Quarter of a Century," p. 19. For similar views, see Robert A. Theobald, *The Final Secret of Pearl Harbor* (New York, 1954), p. 4; the San Francisco *Examiner*, January 2, 1946.
32. State Department Memorandum of Conversation, August 10, 1941, *PHA*, Part 14, pp. 1269–74.
33. State Department Memorandum of Conversation, August 17, 1941, Hull Papers, Box 60.
34. Sir Llewellyn Woodward, *British Foreign Policy in the Second World War*, Vol. II (London, 1971), pp. 170–71.
35. *Grand Alliance*, pp. 600–01.
36. Woodward, *op. cit.*, p. 173; The Earl of Birkenhead, *Halifax* (Boston, 1966), p. 529.
37. *PHA*, Part 5, pp. 2190–91.
38. Ibid., Part 14, p. 1407.
39. Ibid., Part 9, pp. 4252–54.
40. Ibid., Part 10, p. 4807.
41. Log of *Isabel*, December 5, 1941, National Archives, Washington, D.C.
42. "Pearl Harbor After a Quarter of a Century," p. 110.
43. Rear Admiral Julius Augustus Furer, USN (Ret.), *Administration of the Navy Department in World War II*, p. 47.
44. *PHA*, Part 34, p. 60. The full text of this message appears in Part 34, p. 172.
45. Ibid., Part 29, p. 2303.
46. Ibid., Part 34, p. 63.
47. Ibid., p. 172.
48. "Pearl Harbor After a Quarter of a Century," p. 112. See George Morgenstern, *Pearl Harbor: The Story of the Secret War* (New York, 1947), pp. 306–07; "The Pearl Harbor Investigations," pp. 430–31; *Broken Seal*, pp. 347–49.
49. "Pearl Harbor After a Quarter of a Century," pp. 106–14.
50. *PHA*, Part 5, p. 252.
51. *Final Secret*, p. 117.
52. See, for example, the Washington *Post*, December 6, 1941.
53. *PHA*, Part 10, pp. 5082–83.
54. Ibid., pp. 5081–89.
55. Ibid., Part 14, p. 1412.
56. Ibid., Part 3, p. 1000.
57. Ibid., Part 10, pp. 4762–63.
58. "Pearl Harbor after a Quarter of a Century," p. 36.

INDEX

ABOUT THE AUTHOR

Gordon W. Prange was born in Pomeroy, Iowa, on July 16, 1910. He was educated at the University of Iowa and the University of Berlin. He taught at the University of Maryland as an instructor, assistant professor, associate professor, and full professor from 1937 until his death in May 1980. During World War II he served as an officer in the Naval Reserve, and during the occupation of Japan, from December 1945 until July 1951 he joined General Headquarters, Far East Command, Tokyo, as a civilian. From October 1946 to June 1951 he was chief of MacArthur's G-2 Historical Section, and from June through July 1951 was acting director of the Military History Section. Hence he brought to his research and writing about Pearl Harbor an unusual experience of background in the Army and Navy as well as in the academic field.